Get more out of your textbook with the FREE Book Companion Site.

Created to help you master key themes and concepts and build skills, the activities in this free resource help you test and broaden your knowledge.

bedfordstmartins.com/huntconcise

Online Study Guide. Get immediate feedback on your progress with Self-Tests and Defining Terms activities designed to check your understanding of chapter concepts and key terms. Other resources, such as map and visual activities, note-taking outlines, and more, help reinforce concepts and ideas presented in the textbook.

Make History. Access our online database with thousands of images, maps, Web links, and documents. Browse by topic, date, or resource type.

Online Research and Reference Aids. Research guides, models for documenting sources, plagiarism tutorials, and other resources provide you with the support you need to refine your research skills, effectively evaluate sources, and organize your findings.

THIRD EDITION

The Making of the West

Peoples and Cultures

A Concise History

Lynn Hunt
University of California, Los Angeles

Thomas R. Martin
College of the Holy Cross

Barbara H. Rosenwein
Loyola University Chicago

Bonnie G. Smith
Rutgers University

Bedford / St. Martin's
Boston ∎ *New York*

For Bedford / St. Martin's

Publisher for History: Mary Dougherty
Director of Development for History: Jane Knetzger
Developmental Editor: Danielle Slevens
Senior Production Editor: Rosemary R. Jaffe
Senior Production Supervisor: Dennis Conroy
Executive Marketing Manager: Jenna Bookin Barry
Editorial Assistant: Robin Soule
Production Assistants: Alexis Biasell, Samuel S. Jones, and Alexandra Leach
Senior Art Director: Anna Palchik
Text Designer: Lisa Buckley
Copyeditor: Barbara Jatkola
Proofreaders: Linda McLatchie and Stella Gelboin
Indexer: Leoni Z. McVey
Photo Researcher: Gillian Speeth
Cover Designer: Donna Lee Dennison
Cover and Title Page Art: The Wedding Dance, c. 1566 (oil on panel). Pieter Bruegel the Elder
   (c. 1525–1569). The Detroit Institute of Arts, U.S.A./City of Detroit Purchase/The Bridgeman
   Art Library International.
Cartography: Mapping Specialists, Ltd.
Composition: MPS Limited, A Macmillan Company
Printing and Binding: RR Donnelley and Sons

President: Joan E. Feinberg
Editorial Director: Denise B. Wydra
Director of Marketing: Karen R. Soeltz
Director of Editing, Design, and Production: Marcia Cohen
Assistant Director of Editing, Design, and Production: Elise S. Kaiser
Managing Editor: Elizabeth M. Schaaf

Library of Congress Control Number: 2009924677

Preface

THE DRAMATIC EVENTS OF THE LAST DECADE have pushed us to look at the history of the West in new ways. The terrorist attacks of September 11, 2001, the subsequent wars in Afghanistan and Iraq, and a global financial and economic crisis all have roots in the past. Digging down to those roots helps us make better sense of the present, and at the same time gives us a better appreciation of how the past differs from the present. We welcome the challenge of incorporating and explaining these momentous events and believe that our project's basic goal and approach are well suited to meeting the challenge presented by them. From the very beginning, we have insisted on an expanded vision of the West that includes the United States, fully incorporates eastern Europe, and emphasizes Europe's relationship with the rest of the world, whether through trade, colonization, migration, cultural exchange, or religious and ethnic conflict. This approach enables us to explain how globalization can seem both promising and problematic, now and in the past.

Textbooks, even very good ones, must constantly evolve. New developments, whether in the form of events or historical approaches, require new efforts at synthesis. This observation applies not just to the recent past, where change is evident at every level, but also to all the other epochs in history, right back to what has been called "prehistory." New archaeological discoveries and techniques for studying the remains of the past continually produce fresh evidence, even about peoples who lived before the invention of writing. Contrary to popular opinion, the past never stands still, and so authors of textbooks must constantly gather up the new evidence, consider the new approaches, and rewrite history accordingly. We relish the opportunity and take seriously the responsibility of providing a coherent narrative of the West that will enable students to understand the world they live in now.

Central Themes and Approach

Our title, *The Making of the West: Peoples and Cultures, A Concise History* makes three enduring points about our themes and approach: (1) that the history of the

West is the story of a process that is still ongoing, not a finished result with only one fixed meaning; (2) that "the West" includes many different peoples and cultures; that is, that there is no one Western people or culture that has existed from the beginning until now. To understand the historical development of the West and its position in the world today, it is essential to place the West's emergence in a larger, global context that reveals the cross-cultural interactions fundamental to the shaping of Western identity. Finally, (3) that a "concise" approach is ideally suited to meet the needs of instructors who wish to assign additional supplementary readings, who need to cover the entire introduction to Western civilization in a single semester, or who find a comprehensive textbook too detailed and daunting for their students. By reworking, condensing, and combining thematically related sections throughout the text ourselves, we've created a brief edition that preserves the narrative flow, balance, and power of our full-length work. We've also provided for maximum flexibility by publishing *A Concise History* in an electronic format (see below) and three print versions. Volume I extends from the beginning of civilization to 1740; Volume II picks up at 1340, for courses on Europe from the Renaissance to the present; and a one-volume softcover edition treats the whole of Western history.

We know from our own teaching that introductory students need a solid chronological framework, one with enough familiar benchmarks to make the material readily digestible, but also one with enough flexibility to incorporate the new varieties of historical research. That is one reason we present our account in a straightforward, chronological manner. Each chapter treats all the main events, people, and themes of a period in a common context; thus students are not required to learn about political events in one chapter, and then backtrack to concurrent social and cultural developments in the next. The chronological organization also accords with our belief that it is important, above all else, for students to see the interconnections among varieties of historical experience—between politics and cultures, between public events and private experiences, between wars or economic crisis and everyday life. Our integrated approach allows students to appreciate these relationships; it captures the spirit of each age and sparks students' historical imaginations. For teachers, our chronological approach ensures a balanced account, allows the flexibility to stress themes of one's own choosing, and perhaps best of all, provides a text that reveals history not as a settled matter but as a process that is constantly alive, subject to pressures, and able to surprise. Our task as authors, moreover, is to integrate the best of social and cultural history with the enduring developments of political, military, and economic history, offering a clear, compelling narrative that sets all the key events and stages of the West's evolution in a broad, meaningful context.

In writing *The Making of the West: Peoples and Cultures, A Concise History,* it has been our aim to communicate the vitality and excitement as well as the fundamental importance of history. If we have succeeded in conveying some of the vibrancy of the past and the thrill of historical investigation, we will be encouraged to start rethinking and revising—as historians always must—once again.

Textual Changes

Unlike most scholarly books, a textbook offers historians the rare chance to revise the original work, to keep it fresh, and to make it better. It has been a privilege to bring our own scholarship and teaching to bear on this rewriting. In this third edition, we have kept our emphasis on a strong central story line that incorporates the best of new research, but we have worked to make the narrative even more concise, focused, and accessible.

In this edition, we have further highlighted thematic coverage to help students discern major developments. Coverage of the Renaissance and Reformation has been revised thoroughly, with more on Renaissance art and architecture, the Ottomans' influence on the West, and a consolidated treatment of the European Reformation. We have worked to make key developments clearer in other chapters as well. Changes to this end include refocused sections on Pompey and Julius Caesar in Chapter 4 and Romanization in Chapter 5; a new section on the political transformation of the Roman Empire in Chapter 6; a reorganized treatment of Islam and Byzantium in Chapter 7; a consolidated discussion of the medieval papacy and lay piety in Chapter 10; newly consolidated coverage of the scientific revolution in Chapter 12; refocused sections on the execution of Louis XVI in Chapter 16 and nineteenth-century social reform in Chapter 17; and consolidated and strengthened coverage of Robespierre and Napoleon in Chapter 16, and of industrialization in Chapter 17.

We have also added new material and drawn on new scholarship on topics such as the emergence of civilization, in light of recent findings in Turkey (Chapter 1); the origins of the Black Death (Chapter 11); the Atlantic system and the creation of a new public sphere (Chapter 14); and the conflict in the Middle East, the effects of increasing globalization, and the global economic crisis (Chapter 24).

A final way we have chosen to help students identify and absorb major developments is by adding and refining "signposts" to guide students' reading. New chapter-opening focus questions, posed at the end of the opening vignettes, encapsulate the essence of the era covered in the chapter and guide students toward each chapter's core message. To help students as they read, we have worked hard to ensure that chapter and section overviews outline the central points of each section clearly, and that section headings are as clear and strong as possible. We have also condensed some material to better illuminate key ideas, resulting in a textbook that is a good deal shorter than the previous edition, and—we hope—a clearer, more accessible read for students.

Pedagogy and Features

More and more is required of students these days, and not just in Western Civilization courses. We know from our own teaching that students need all the help they can get in assimilating information, acquiring skills, and learning about historical debate.

With these goals in mind, we retained the class-tested learning and teaching aids that contributed to the previous edition, but we have also added more such features.

Each chapter begins with a *vivid anecdote* that draws readers into the atmosphere and issues of the period and raises the chapter's main themes, supplemented by a full-page illustration that echoes the anecdote and similarly reveals the temper of the times. A *new Chapter Focus Question* provides students with an overarching theme to help guide their reading. *Review questions* strategically placed at the end of each major section help students check their comprehension of main ideas. Bolded *key terms* in the text are defined in the *Glossary of Key Terms* at the end of the book. A list of author-selected *Suggested References*, now present in every chapter, directs students to print and online resources for further investigation. Each chapter closes with a *new graphical Timeline*, which enables students to see the sequence and overlap of important events in a given period, and two *Chapter Review Questions* that encourage their analysis of chapter material.

The map program of *A Concise History* has been widely praised as the most comprehensive of any brief survey text. In each chapter we offer a set of three types of maps, each with a distinct role in conveying information to students. On average, three to four *full-size maps* show major developments; one to three *"spot" maps*— small maps that emphasize a detailed area from the discussion—aid students' understanding of specific but crucial issues; and a *Mapping the West* summary map at the end of each chapter provides a snapshot of the West at the close of a transformative period and helps students visualize the West's changing contours over time. In addition to the *more than 160 maps*, numerous charts and graphs visually support the narrative, including innovative *Taking Measure* features, which highlight a chart, table, graph, or map of historical statistics that illuminates an important political, social, or cultural development.

It has been our intention to integrate art as fully as possible into the narrative and to show its value for teaching and learning. *Over 260 illustrations*, carefully chosen to reflect this edition's broad topical coverage and geographic inclusion, reinforce the text and show the varieties of visual sources from which historians build their narratives and interpretations. All artifacts, illustrations, paintings, and photographs are contemporaneous with the chapter; there are no anachronistic illustrations—no fifteenth-century peasants tilling fields in a chapter on the tenth century! We know that today's students are very attuned to visual sources of information, yet they do not always receive systematic instruction in how to "read" or think critically about such visual sources. Our substantive captions for the maps and art help them learn how to make the most of these informative materials, and we have frequently included specific questions or suggestions for comparisons that might be developed. Specially designed visual exercises in the *Online Study Guide* supplement this approach.

Supplements

We have taken great care in revising and augmenting the comprehensive and well-integrated set of print and electronic resources for students and instructors that support the third edition of *The Making of the West: A Concise History.*

FOR STUDENTS

Print Resources

Sources of THE MAKING OF THE WEST, **Third Edition**—Volumes I (to 1740) and II (since 1500)—by Katharine J. Lualdi, University of Southern Maine. This companion sourcebook provides written and visual sources to accompany *The Making of the West: A Concise History.* Political, social, and cultural documents offer a variety of perspectives that complement the textbook and encourage students to make connections between narrative history and primary sources. A correlation guide showing how the documents align with each textbook chapter appears in *Sources of THE MAKING OF THE WEST* and on the *Book Companion Site.* The reader is available free when packaged with the text.

The Bedford Series in History and Culture. Over one hundred titles in this highly praised series combine first-rate scholarship, historical narrative, and important primary documents for undergraduate courses. Each book is brief, inexpensive, and focused on a specific topic or period. Package discounts are available.

Rand McNally Atlas of Western Civilization. This collection of over fifty full-color maps highlights social, political, and cross-cultural change and interaction from classical Greece and Rome to the post-industrial Western world. Each map is thoroughly indexed for fast reference. The Atlas is available for $3.00 when packaged with the text.

The Bedford Glossary for European History. This handy supplement for the survey course gives students historically contextualized definitions for hundreds of terms—from Abbasids to Zionism—that students will encounter in lectures, reading, and exams. The Glossary is available free when packaged with the text.

Trade Books. Titles published by sister companies Farrar, Straus and Giroux; Henry Holt and Company; Hill and Wang; Picador; St. Martin's Press; and Palgrave Macmillan are available at a 50 percent discount when packaged with Bedford/St. Martin's textbooks. For more information, visit bedfordstmartins .com/tradeup.

New Media Resources

THE MAKING OF THE WEST: A CONCISE HISTORY e-Book. This electronic version of *The Making of the West: A Concise History* offers students unmatched value—the complete text of the print book, with easy-to-use highlighting, searching, and note-taking tools, at a significantly reduced price.

FREE *Online Study Guide* at bedfordstmartins.com/huntconcise. The popular *Online Study Guide for* THE MAKING OF THE WEST: A CONCISE HISTORY is a free learning tool to help students master the themes and information presented in the textbook and improve their historical skills. Assessment quizzes help students to evaluate their comprehension, a flashcard activity tests students' knowledge of key terms, and a wide range of further quizzing, map, and primary document analysis activities provides them with the opportunity for further study. Instructors can monitor students' progress through the online *Quiz Gradebook* or receive e-mail updates.

Jules R. Benjamin's A Student's Online Guide to History Reference Sources at bedfordstmartins.com/huntconcise. This Web site provides links to history-related databases, indexes, and journals, plus contact information for state, provincial, local, and professional history organizations.

Bedford Bibliographer at bedfordstmartins.com/huntconcise. This simple but powerful Web-based tool assists students with the process of collecting sources and generates bibliographies in four commonly used documentation styles.

Diana Hacker's Research and Documentation Online at bedfordstmartins.com/huntconcise. This Web site provides clear advice on how to integrate primary and secondary sources into research papers, how to cite sources correctly, and how to format in MLA, APA, *Chicago,* or CBE style.

The St. Martin's Tutorial on Avoiding Plagiarism at bedfordstmartins.com/huntconcise. This online tutorial reviews the consequences of plagiarism and explains what sources to acknowledge, how to keep good notes, how to organize research, and how to integrate sources appropriately. The tutorial includes exercises to help students practice integrating sources and recognizing acceptable summaries.

FOR INSTRUCTORS

Print Resources

Transparencies. This set of full-color acetate transparencies includes all maps and many images from the parent textbook to help instructors prepare lectures and teach students important map-reading skills. A correlation guide showing how the transparencies align with the brief text appears in the *Instructor's Resource Manual* and on the *Book Companion Site.*

New Media Resources

Instructor's Resource Manual at bedfordstmartins.com/huntconcise/catalog. This manual by Dakota Hamilton, Humboldt State University, offers both experienced and first-time instructors tools for presenting textbook material in exciting and engaging ways. It includes an outline of main chapter topics, annotated chapter outlines, lecture strategies, ways to start class discussions, answer guidelines for questions in the book, tips for discussing the documents and working with visual sources, mapping exercises, suggestions for in-class activities (including using film, video, and literature), and take-home essay questions. Each chapter concludes with a guide to all the chapter-specific supplements available with *The Making of the West: A Concise History*. The manual also features essays on approaches to the Western Civilization course.

Instructor's Resource CD-ROM. This disc provides instructors with ready-made and customizable PowerPoint multimedia presentations built around chapter outlines, maps, figures, and selected images from the textbook, plus jpeg versions of all maps, figures, and selected images. Outline maps are provided in PDF format for quizzing or handouts. Also included are chapter questions formatted in PowerPoint and MS Word for use with i>clicker, a classroom response system.

Computerized Test Bank. The test bank, by Joseph Coohill, Pennsylvania State University at New Kensington, and Frances Mitilineos, Loyola University Chicago, offers over eighty exercises per chapter, including multiple-choice, fill-in-the-blank, short-answer, primary-source analysis, and essay questions. The answer key includes textbook page numbers and correct answers for all questions except the essays. Instructors can customize quizzes, add or edit both questions and answers, and export questions to a variety of formats, including WebCT and Blackboard.

Book Companion Site at bedfordstmartins.com/huntconcise. The companion Web site gathers all the electronic resources for the text, including the *Online Study Guide* and *Quiz Gradebook,* at a single Web address, providing convenient links to lecture, assignment, and research materials such as PowerPoint chapter outlines and the digital libraries at *Make History.*

Make History at bedfordstmartins.com/huntconcise. Comprising the content of our five acclaimed online libraries—*MapCentral, The Bedford History Image Library, DocLinks, HistoryLinks,* and *PlaceLinks*—*Make History* provides one-stop access to relevant digital content including maps, images, documents, and Web links. Students and instructors can browse this free, easy-to-use database by course, topic, date, or resource type and can download the content they find. Instructors can also create entire collections of content and store them online for later use or post their collections to the Web to share with students.

Content for Course Management Systems. A variety of student and instructor resources developed for this textbook is ready for use in course management systems such as Blackboard, WebCT, and other platforms. This e-content includes nearly all of the offerings in the book's *Online Study Guide,* as well as the book's *Test Bank.*

Videos and Multimedia. A wide assortment of videos and multimedia CD-ROMs on various topics in European history is available to qualified adopters. Contact your Bedford/St. Martin's sales representative for more information.

Acknowledgments

In the vital process of revision, the authors have benefited from repeated critical readings by many talented scholars and teachers. Our sincere thanks go to the following instructors, as well as three anonymous reviewers, whose comments often challenged us to rethink or justify our interpretations and who always provided a check on accuracy down to the smallest detail.

Marjorie Berman, *Red Rocks Community College*
Scott G. Bruce, *University of Colorado at Boulder*
Tamara Chaplin, *University of Illinois at Urbana*
Stephanie Christelow, *Idaho State University*
Marcus Cox, *The Citadel*
Jason Coy, *College of Charleston*
Cara Delay, *College of Charleston*
Gillian Hendershot, *Grand Valley State University*
David Hudson, *Texas A&M University*
Geoffrey Jensen, *University of Arkansas*
Brian Nance, *Coastal Carolina University/American Academy in Rome*
Ian Petrie, *Saint Joseph's University*
Craig Pilant, *County College of Morris*
James Sack, *University of Illinois at Chicago*
Jim Slocombe, *Champlain Regional College*
Charles Steinwedel, *Northeastern Illinois University*
Matthew Stith, *University of Arkansas*
David Tengwall, *Anne Arundel Community College*
Victor Triay, *Middlesex Community College*
Kirk Tyvela, *Sinclair Community College*
Rachelle Wadsworth, *Florida Community College at Jacksonville*
Janet Walmsley, *George Mason University*

Many colleagues, friends, and family members have helped us develop this work as well. They know how grateful we are. We also wish to acknowledge and thank the publishing team at Bedford/St. Martin's who did so much to bring this revised edition to completion: president Joan Feinberg, editorial director Denise Wydra, publisher for history Mary Dougherty, director of development for history Jane Knetzger, editor Danielle Slevens, freelance editors Jim Strandberg and Debra Michals, editorial assistant Robin Soule, executive marketing manager Jenna Bookin Barry, managing editor Elizabeth Schaaf, senior production editor Rosemary Jaffe, art researcher Gillian Speeth, permissions manager Sandy Schechter, and senior art director Donna Dennison. Our students' questions and concerns have shaped much of this work, and we welcome all our readers' suggestions, queries, and criticisms. Please contact us at our respective institutions or via history@bedfordstmartins.com.

Brief Contents

Contents

Chapter 1

The Emergence of Western Civilization, to 500 B.C.E. *3*

Chapter 3
From the Classical to the Hellenistic World, 400–30 B.C.E. *85*

Chapter 4

The Rise of Rome, 753–44 B.C.E. *119*

Chapter 5
The Roman Empire, 44 B.C.E.–284 C.E.   *155*

Chapter 6

The Transformation of the Roman Empire, 284–600 C.E. *197*

Chapter 7
Islam, Byzantium, and the West, 600–750   *237*

Chapter 8

Emperors, Caliphs, and Local Lords, 750–1050 *271*

Chapter 9
The Flowering of the Middle Ages, 1050–1200 *311*

Chapter 10

The Medieval Search for Order, 1200–1340 353

Chapter 11
Crisis and Renaissance, 1340–1500 *393*

Chapter 12

Struggles over Beliefs, 1500–1648 435

Chapter 13
State Building and the Search for Order, 1648–1690 *481*

Chapter 14

The Atlantic System and Its Consequences, 1690–1740 *521*

Chapter 15

The Promise of Enlightenment, 1740–1789 *561*

Chapter 16
The French Revolution and Napoleon, 1789–1815 *599*

Chapter 17

Industrialization and Social Ferment, 1815–1850 *639*

Chapter 18

Constructing the Nation-State, c. 1850–1880 683

Chapter 19

Empire, Modernity, and the Road to War, c. 1880–1914 *729*

Chapter 20

War, Revolution, and Reconstruction, 1914–1929 *779*

Chapter 21

An Age of Catastrophes, 1929–1945 *825*

Chapter 23

Postindustrial Society and the End of the Cold War Order, 1965–1989 *909*

Chapter 24

The New Globalism, 1989 to the Present *947*

Maps and Figures

FIGURES

Authors' Note
The B.C.E./C.E. Dating System

WHEN WERE YOU BORN?" "What year is it?" We customarily answer questions like these with a number, such as "1991" or "2008." Our replies are usually automatic, taking for granted the numerous assumptions Westerners make about how dates indicate chronology. But to what do numbers such as 1991 and 2008 actually refer? In this book the numbers used to specify dates follow a recent revision of the system most common in the Western secular world. This system reckons the dates of solar years by counting backward and forward from the traditional date of the birth of Jesus Christ, over two thousand years ago.

Using this method, numbers followed by the abbreviation B.C.E., standing for "before the common era" (or, as some would say, "before the Christian era"), indicate the number of years counting backward from the assumed date of the birth of Jesus Christ. B.C.E. therefore indicates the same chronology marked by the traditional abbreviation B.C. ("before Christ"). The larger the number following B.C.E. (or B.C.), the earlier in history is the year to which it refers. The date 431 B.C.E., for example, refers to a year 431 years before the birth of Jesus and therefore comes earlier in time than the dates 430 B.C.E., 429 B.C.E., and so on. The same calculation applies to numbering other time intervals calculated on the decimal system: those of ten years (a decade), of one hundred years (a century), and of one thousand years (a millennium). For example, the decade of the 440s B.C.E. (449 B.C.E. to 440 B.C.E.) is earlier than the decade of the 430s B.C.E. (439 B.C.E. to 430 B.C.E.). "Fifth century B.C.E." refers to the fifth period of 100 years reckoning backward from the birth of Jesus and covers the years 500 B.C.E. to 401 B.C.E. It is earlier in history than the fourth century B.C.E. (400 B.C.E. to 301 B.C.E.), which followed the fifth century B.C.E. Because this system has no year "zero," the first century B.C.E. covers the years 100 B.C.E. to 1 B.C.E. Dating millennia works similarly: the second millennium B.C.E. refers to the years 2000 B.C.E. to 1001 B.C.E., the third millennium to the years 3000 B.C.E. to 2001 B.C.E., and so on.

To indicate years counted forward from the traditional date of Jesus's birth, numbers are followed by the abbreviation C.E., standing for "of the common era" (or "of the Christian era"). C.E. therefore indicates the same chronology marked by the traditional abbreviation A.D., which stands for the Latin phrase *anno Domini* ("in the year of the Lord"). A.D. properly comes before the date being marked. The date A.D. 1492, for example, translates as "in the year of the Lord 1492," meaning 1492 years after the birth of Jesus. Under the B.C.E./C.E. system, this date would be written as 1492 C.E. For dating centuries, the term "first century C.E." refers to the period from 1 C.E. to 100 C.E. (which is the same period as A.D. 1 to A.D. 100). For dates C.E, the smaller the number, the earlier the date in history. The fourth century C.E. (301 C.E. to 400 C.E.) comes before the fifth century C.E. (401 C.E. to 500 C.E.). The year

312 C.E. is a date in the early fourth century C.E., while 395 C.E. is a date late in the same century. When numbers are given without either B.C.E. or C.E., they are presumed to be dates C.E. For example, the term *eighteenth century* with no abbreviation accompanying it refers to the years 1701 C.E. to 1800 C.E.

No standard system of numbering years, such as B.C.E./C.E., existed in antiquity. Different people in different places identified years with varying names and numbers. Consequently, it was difficult to match up the years in any particular local system with those in a different system. Each city of ancient Greece, for example, had its own method for keeping track of the years. The ancient Greek historian Thucydides, therefore, faced a problem in presenting a chronology for the famous Peloponnesian War between Athens and Sparta, which began (by our reckoning) in 431 B.C.E. To try to explain to as many of his readers as possible the date the war had begun, he described its first year by three different local systems: "the year when Chrysis was in the forty-eighth year of her priesthood at Argos, and Aenesias was overseer at Sparta, and Pythodorus was magistrate at Athens."

A Catholic monk named Dionysius, who lived in Rome in the sixth century C.E., invented the system of reckoning dates forward from the birth of Jesus. Calling himself *Exiguus* (Latin for "the little" or "the small") as a mark of humility, he placed Jesus's birth 754 years after the foundation of ancient Rome. Others then and now believe his date for Jesus's birth was in fact several years too late. Many scholars today calculate that Jesus was born in what would be 4 B.C.E. according to Dionysius's system, although a date a year or so earlier also seems possible.

Counting backward from the supposed date of Jesus's birth to indicate dates earlier than that event represented a natural complement to reckoning forward for dates after it. The English historian and theologian Bede in the early eighth century was the first to use both forward and backward reckoning from the birth of Jesus in a historical work, and this system gradually gained wider acceptance because it provided a basis for standardizing the many local calendars used in the Western Christian world. Nevertheless, B.C. and A.D. were not used regularly until the end of the eighteenth century. B.C.E. and C.E. became common in the late twentieth century.

The system of numbering years from the birth of Jesus is far from the only one in use today. The Jewish calendar of years, for example, counts forward from the date given to the creation of the world, which would be calculated as 3761 B.C.E. under the B.C.E./C.E. system. Under this system, years are designated A.M., an abbreviation of the Latin *anno mundi*, "in the year of the world." The Islamic calendar counts forward from the date of the Prophet Muhammad's flight from Mecca, called the *Hijra*, in what is the year 622 C.E. The abbreviation A.H. (standing for the Latin phrase *anno Hegirae*, "in the year of the Hijra") indicates dates calculated by this system. Anthropology commonly reckons distant dates as "before the present" (abbreviated B.P.).

History is often defined as the study of change over time; hence the importance of dates for the historian. But just as historians argue over which dates are most significant, they disagree over which dating system to follow. Their debate reveals perhaps the most enduring fact about history—its vitality.

About the Authors

LYNN HUNT (Ph.D., Stanford University) is Eugen Weber Professor of Modern European History at University of California, Los Angeles. She is the author or editor of several books, including most recently *Inventing Human Rights* (2007) and *Measuring Time, Making History* (2008). She has in press a co-authored work on religious toleration in early eighteenth-century Europe.

THOMAS R. MARTIN (Ph.D., Harvard University) is Jeremiah O'Connor Professor in Classics at the College of the Holy Cross. He is the author of *Sovereignty and Coinage in Classical Greece* (1985) and *Ancient Greece* (1996, 2000) and is one of the originators of *Perseus: Interactive Sources and Studies on Ancient Greece* (www .perseus.tufts.edu). He is currently conducting research on the career of Pericles as a political leader in classical Athens as well as on the text of Josephus's *Jewish War*.

BARBARA H. ROSENWEIN (Ph.D., University of Chicago) is professor of history at Loyola University Chicago. She is the author or editor of several books, including *A Short History of the Middle Ages* (2001, 2004, 2009) and *Emotional Communities in the Early Middle Ages* (2006). She is currently working on a general history of the emotions in the West.

BONNIE G. SMITH (Ph.D., University of Rochester) is Board of Governors Professor of History at Rutgers University. She is the author or editor of several books, including *Ladies of the Leisure Class* (1981); *The Gender of History: Men, Women and Historical Practice* (1998); and *The Oxford Encyclopedia of Women in World History* (2007). Currently she is studying the globalization of European culture and society since the seventeenth century.

Additional Acknowledgments

Chapter 1, page 16: Figure 1.2: "Egyptian Hieroglyphs." Print of Egyptian hieroglyphs chart from *Detail of Book of the Dead—18th Dynasty Tomb of Thutmosis III, Valley of the Kings.* Reprinted by permission of Bridgeman/Art Resource, NY.

Chapter 5, page 189: Taking Measure: "The Falling Value of Roman Imperial Coinage, 27 B.C.E.–300 C.E." From *The Archeology of the Roman Economy* by Kevin Greene. Copyright © 1990. Reprinted by permission of The University of California Press via Rightslink.

Chapter 8, page 296: Taking Measure: "Sellers, Buyers, and Donors, 800–1000." Graph created by Lluís de Figueras, featured in *Dot et douaire dans le haut moyen âge* by F. Bougard, L. Feller, and R. Le Jan, eds. Copyright © 2002. (École française de Rome Service des publications, 2002, 193, Table 1.) Reprinted by permission of the French School of Rome.

Chapter 9, page 345: Figure 9.3: "Floor Plan of a Cistercian Monastery." Adaption of three figures (8a, 8b, and 8c) from page 75 in *Monasteries of Western Europe* by Wolfgang Braunfels, Thames & Hudson Ltd., London.

Chapter 10, page 360: Taking Measure: "Sentences Imposed by an Inquisitor, 1308–1323." From *Portraits of Medieval and Renaissance Living: Essays in Memory of Dave Herlihy* by Samuel K. Cohn Jr. and Steven A. Epstein. Copyright © 1996. Reprinted with permission from the University of Michigan Press. **Page 385:** Figure 10.1: "Elements of a Gothic Cathedral." After image in *Dictionnaire raisonné de l'architecture française du XIe au XVIe siècle* (Paris 1859–1868) by Eugène Emmanuel Viollet-le-Duc. Copyright © Calmann & King (London). Reprinted by permission of Laurence King Publishing, Ltd.

Chapter 12, page 463: Taking Measure: "The Rise and Fall of Silver Imports to Spain, 1550–1660." From Chart 1, "Total Imports of Treasure in Pesos (450 Maravedis) by Five-Year Intervals," page 35, in *American Revolution and the Price Revolution in Spain, 1501–1650,* edited by Earl J. Hamilton. Courtesy of Harvard University Press.

Chapter 13, page 491: Taking Measure: "The Seventeenth-Century Army." From *Armées et sociétés en Europe de 1494 à 1789* by André Corvisier. (1976, page 126). Courtesy Presses Universitaires de France.

Chapter 14, page 525: Figure 14.1: "African Slaves Imported into American Territories, 1701–1800." Adapted from *The Atlantic Slave Trade: A Census* by Philip D. Curtin. Copyright © 1969 by the Board of Regents of the University of Wisconsin System. Reprinted by permission of The University of Wisconsin Press. **Page 532:** Taking Measure: "Relationship of Crop Harvested to Seed Used, 1400–1800." Adapted from Figure 2.8, page 56, in *World Trade Since 1431: Geography, Technology, and Capitalism* by Peter J. Hugill. Copyright © 1993 The Johns Hopkins University Press. Reprinted with permission of The Johns Hopkins University Press.

Chapter 17, page 642: Taking Measure: "Railroad Lines, 1830–1850." From *European Historical Statistics 1750–1970,* edited by B. R. Mitchell. Copyright © 1975. Reprinted by permission of Macmillan Publishers, Ltd.

Chapter 18, page 710: Taking Measure: "Decline of Illiteracy, 1850–1900." From *The Birth of New Europe: State and Society in the Nineteenth Century* by Theodore S. Hamerow. Copyright © 1983 by the University of North Carolina Press. Used by permission of the publisher.

Chapter 19, page 743: Taking Measure: "Population Growth Worldwide, 1890–1910." From *International Historical Statistics: Africa, Asia, and Oceania, 1750–1993,* Third Edition, 3, 56, 57; *International Historical Statistics: The Americas, 1750–1993,* Fourth Edition, 6, 24; *International Historical Statistics: Europe, 1750–1993,* Fourth Edition, 4, 8, edited by B. R. Mitchell (London: Macmillan Reference). Copyright © 1998 Macmillan Publishers, Ltd. Reprinted by permission of the publisher.

Chapter 20, page 814: W. B. Yeats. "Sailing to Byzantium." (3 lines) From *The Collected Works of W. B. Yeats Volume I; The Poets,* revised, edited by Richard J. Finneran. Copyright © 1928 by The Macmillan Company. Copyright renewed © 1956 by George Yeats. Reprinted with the permission of Scribner, a Division of Simon and Schuster Adult Publishing Group. All rights reserved.

THIRD EDITION

The Making of the West

Peoples and Cultures

A Concise History

The Emergence of Western Civilization

To 500 B.C.E.

THE MESOPOTAMIAN *EPIC OF CREATION* explains that war between the gods created the universe. The goddess Tiamat, furious over her husband's destruction, threatened to destroy the other gods. Her enemies swore to make the male god Marduk their king if he protected them. Marduk—"four were his eyes, four were his ears; when his lips moved, fire blazed forth"—crushed Tiamat and her army of snaky monsters. He then created human beings from the blood of her fiercest monster to be the gods' servants.

Gold Bull's Head Decoration for a Musical Instrument from Ancient Iraq
This bull's head, made of gold leaf and lapis lazuli (a semiprecious stone prized for its vivid blue color), decorated a lyre—a stringed instrument similar to a harp. It was found in a tomb in the royal cemetery at Ur, in what is today southern Iraq, and was probably made in the period 2650–2550 B.C.E. The scenes below the beard, carved from mother of pearl, show animals walking upright like human beings and a mythological figure who appears to be a combination of a man and perhaps a scorpion. The donkey shown just above him is playing a lyre like this one. The meaning of the bull's head and the scenes remains a mystery. *(© University of Pennsylvania Museum [image #SR-142913].)*

This myth explained a belief—there is a divine world more powerful than the human—that goes back to the time before **civilization**, when people lived as hunter-gatherers to find food instead of farming. When a period of global warming that began about ten to twelve thousand years ago led to the invention of agriculture and then eventually to the emergence of civilization around 4000–3000 B.C.E. in the cities of Mesopotamia (the region between the Euphrates and Tigris rivers, today Iraq), religious beliefs remained strong. Historians define civilization as life based on agriculture and increased trade, with cities containing large buildings for political and religious purposes; the technology to produce metals, textiles, pottery, and other manufactured objects; and the knowledge of writing.

Civilization arose at different times in different places, but always with a religious core. In Mesopotamian civilization, rulers believed that the gods held them responsible for maintaining order on earth and honoring

3

the gods. Egyptian civilization, which began about 3100–3000 B.C.E., showed its religious dedication by building enormous temples and pyramids. Civilizations emerged starting about 2500 B.C.E. in India, China, and the Americas. By 2000 B.C.E., civilizations had appeared in Anatolia (today Turkey), on islands in the eastern Mediterranean Sea, and in Greece.

The peoples of Mesopotamia, Egypt, the eastern Mediterranean, and Greece created Western civilization by interacting with each other. Building on concepts from their Near Eastern neighbors, the Greeks originated the idea of the West as a region with its own type of civilization. They identified Europe as the West (where the sun sets) and considered it to be different from the East (where the sun rises). The peoples of Europe made Western civilization by exchanging ideas, technologies, and objects with other peoples through trade, travel, and war. The making of the West depended on cultural, political, and economic interaction among diverse groups. The West remains a constantly evolving concept, not a fixed region with unchanging borders and members.

The process of different peoples learning from one another and adapting the knowledge and the beliefs of others for their own purposes produced intended and unintended consequences. The spread of metallurgy (using high heat to extract metals from ores), for example, created better tools and weapons but also increased social differences among people. **Hierarchy** (status differences among people), like the ranking among the gods that myth described, became an enduring characteristic of human civilization.

CHAPTER FOCUS QUESTION   What changes did early Western civilization bring to human life?

From the Stone Age to Civilization and Empire in Mesopotamia, to 1200 B.C.E.

Important patterns of life that developed in the time before civilization have persisted ever since. About four hundred thousand years ago, people whose brains and bodies resembled ours appeared first in Africa. Called *Homo sapiens* ("wise human beings") by scientists, they were the immediate ancestors of modern human beings. Spreading out from Africa, they gradually populated the rest of the earth. Anthropologists call this time before civilization the Stone Age because people made tools and weapons from stone as well as bone and wood; they did not yet know how to work metals. The Stone Age is divided into two periods: the earlier part is the Paleolithic (Old Stone), and the more recent is the Neolithic (New Stone), beginning around 10,000 to 8000 B.C.E.

The most important change in the patterns of human life in ancient times occurred during the Stone Age. People originally lived as hunter-gatherers in the Paleolithic Age. They usually roamed to find food, hunting and gathering in the wild. The shift from Paleolithic to Neolithic patterns of life was supremely important because climate change that altered the patterns of plant growth allowed hunter-gatherers slowly to learn to farm, domesticate animals, and, in the end, establish permanent settlements that grew into cities. This change had such radical consequences for human life that historians call it the Neolithic Revolution.

Another great change took place when people learned to work metals by smelting copper ore. They then invented bronze, a metal alloyed from copper and tin that could be shaped into durable tools, sharp weapons, and lustrous jewelry. Archaeologists call the period from approximately 4000 to 1000 B.C.E. the Bronze Age. The rulers of Bronze Age Mesopotamian cities battled one another for glory, territory, and especially access to copper and tin. The drive to acquire metal ores pushed the Akkadians (named after Akkad, their capital city on the Tigris River) to create the first **empire**, a gigantic political state under a single ruler controlling formerly independent territories.

From Paleolithic Life to the Neolithic Revolution, 400,000–4000 B.C.E.

The most significant Stone Age developments were the evolution of hierarchy and the Neolithic Revolution. Paleolithic hunter-gatherers perhaps originally lived in egalitarian societies (meaning all adults enjoyed a rough equality in making decisions for the group). They roamed in groups of twenty to fifty, hunting animals, catching fish and shellfish, and gathering plants, fruits, and nuts. Women with young children mostly foraged to gather plants close to camp; they provided the group's most reliable supply of nourishment. Men did most of the hunting of dangerous wild animals far from camp, although recent archaeological evidence shows that women also participated, especially in hunting with nets. Objects from distant regions found in burials show that hunter-gatherer bands traded with one another. Trade spread knowledge—especially technology, such as techniques for improving tools, and art for creating beauty and expressing beliefs—that changed lives. Using fire for cooking was a major innovation because it allowed people to eat wild grains that they could not digest raw.

Evidence from graves shows that hierarchy, a persistent characteristic of human society, eventually emerged in Paleolithic times. Some Paleolithic burials contain weapons, tools, animal figurines, ivory beads, seashells, and bracelets alongside the corpses, which indicate that some dead persons had greater status and wealth than others. Hierarchy probably emerged as men acquired prestige from bringing back meat from long hunts and fighting in wars. (The many traumatic wounds seen in male skeletons show how frequent warfare was.) Older women and men also earned hierarchical status based on their experience and longevity at a time when illness and accidents killed most people before age thirty. The decoration of corpses with red paint and valuable objects suggests that Paleolithic people wondered about the mystery of death and perhaps believed in an afterlife. Paleolithic artists also sculpted statuettes of human figures, probably for religious purposes.

Climate and geography—the fundamental features of the natural environment—defined a new way of life for human beings some twelve thousand years ago. This very gradual process started when a climate change in the late Paleolithic period brought warmer temperatures and more rainfall. This change in the weather increased

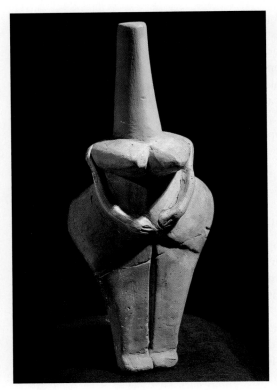

Prehistoric Venus Figurine
Archaeologists have discovered small female figures, like this one from Romania, at many late Paleolithic and Neolithic sites in Europe. They predate writing, so we cannot be sure of their significance, but many scholars assume that their hefty proportions are meant to signal a special concern for fertility. These female figures may represent prehistoric people's vision of rare good fortune: having enough food to become fat and produce healthy children. The statuettes are called Venus figurines after the Roman goddess of love. (Erich Lessing/Art Resource, NY.)

the amount of wild grains people could gather in the foothills of the Near East's Fertile Crescent, an arc of territory that curved up from what is today the Jordan valley in Israel, through eastern Turkey, and down into the foothills and plains of Iraq and Iran (Map 1.1).* This more plentiful food supply led Paleolithic hunter-gatherers to settle where wild grains grew most abundantly and animals such as gazelles grazed in large numbers. Recent archaeological excavation in Turkey suggests that around eleven thousand years ago, such groups organized to erect stone monuments to worship gods believed to help people find food. The more reliable supply of food allowed them to raise more children, and the increased social organization promoted larger settlements. The more hungry mouths that were born, however, the greater the need for food became.

---

*The meanings of the terms *Near East* and *Middle East* have changed over time. Both originally reflected a European geographic point of view. During the nineteenth century, *Middle East* usually meant the area from Iran to Burma, especially the Indian subcontinent (then part of the British Empire); *Near East* meant the Balkan peninsula (today the countries of Croatia, Slovenia, Bosnia-Herzegovina, Macedonia, Yugoslavia, Albania, Greece, Bulgaria, Romania, and the European portion of Turkey) and the eastern Mediterranean. The term *Far East* referred to the Asian lands that border the Pacific Ocean. Today, *Middle East* usually refers to the area encompassing the Arabic-speaking countries of the eastern Mediterranean region, Israel, Iran, Turkey, Cyprus, and much of North Africa. Ancient historians, by contrast, commonly use the term *ancient Near East* to designate Anatolia (also called Asia Minor), Cyprus, the lands around the eastern end of the Mediterranean, the Arabian peninsula, Mesopotamia (the lands north of the Persian Gulf, today Iraq and Iran), and Egypt. Some historians exclude Egypt from this group on strict geographic grounds because it is in Africa (the rest of the region lies in Asia). In this book, we observe the common usage of the term *Near East* to mean the lands of southwestern Asia and Egypt.

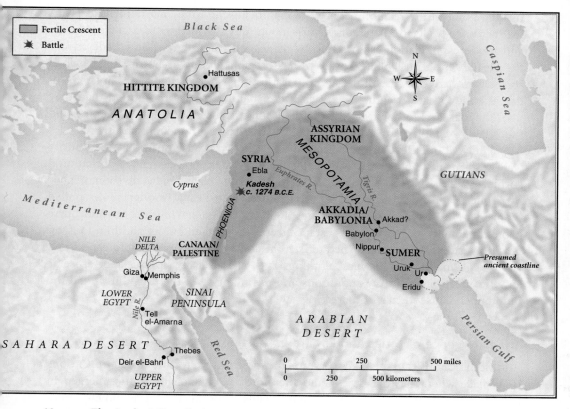

Map 1.1 The Ancient Near East, 4000–3000 B.C.E.
The large region we call the ancient Near East included a variety of landscapes, climates, peoples, and languages; monarchy was the usual form of government. Trade by land and sea for natural resources, especially metals, kept the peoples of the region in constant contact with one another, as did the wars of conquest that the region's kings regularly launched.

The Neolithic Revolution began when, after thousands of years of trial and error, people in the Fertile Crescent invented agriculture by sowing seeds from wild grains to produce regular harvests. Since women had more experience gathering plants than men, they probably played the major role in developing farming, while men continued to hunt. Recent research suggests that people also learned to domesticate animals about the same time that they began to farm. By some nine thousand years ago, keeping herds for food was widespread in the Near East, which was home to wild animals that could be domesticated, such as sheep, goats, pigs, and cattle.

Historians call agriculture and the domestication of animals the "farming package" that defines the Neolithic Revolution. The change in the way people got their food had revolutionary effects on human life because it produced many permanent settlements and surpluses of food. Some Neolithic people lived as pastoralists (herders moving around to find grazing land for their animals), but farmers had to reside in a settled location to raise crops year after year. Fixed settlements marked a turning point in the relation between human beings and the environment as farmers increasingly diverted streams for irrigation. DNA evidence from ancient bones and modern populations shows that by 4000 B.C.E., immigrants and traders from the Fertile Crescent, by interacting with local populations in Europe, had helped spread knowledge of agriculture and domestication as far as the European shores of the Atlantic Ocean. Eventually, farmers were able to produce more food than they needed. That farmers could produce agricultural surpluses meant other people could specialize in architecture, art, crafts, metalwork, textile production, and trade.

The Neolithic Revolution led to more hierarchy because positions of authority were needed to supervise the complex irrigation system that generated agricultural surpluses, and also because greater economic activity created a new division of labor by gender. Men began to dominate agriculture when heavy wooden plows pulled by oxen were invented, sometime after 4000 B.C.E. Not having to bear and nurse babies, men also took over long-distance trade. Women and older children took on new domestic tasks as they turned milk from domesticated animals into cheese and yogurt and made their families' clothing. This gendered division of labor arose as an efficient response to the conditions and technologies of the time, but it had the unintended consequence of increasing men's status.

The Emergence of Cities and Empire in Mesopotamia, 4000–1200 B.C.E.

Additional significant changes in human society and technological inventions took place when the first cities—and therefore the first civilization—emerged in Mesopotamia about 4000–3000 B.C.E. in the plains bordering the Tigris and Euphrates rivers (Map 1.1, page 7). Cities developed there because the climate and the land could support large populations. Mesopotamian farmers operated in a challenging environment: temperatures soared to 120 degrees Fahrenheit and little rain fell, yet the rivers flooded unpredictably. They maximized agricultural production by devising the technology and administrative arrangements necessary to irrigate the arid flatlands with water channeled from the rivers. A vast system of canals controlled flooding and turned the former desert green with food crops. The need to construct and maintain a system of irrigation canals in turn led to the centralization of authority in Mesopotamian cities, which controlled the farmland and irrigation canals lying outside their fortified walls. This political arrangement—an urban center exercising control over the nearby countryside—is called a **city-state**. Mesopotamian city-states were independent communities competing with each other for land and resources.

The people of Sumer (southern Mesopotamia) established the earliest city-states. Unlike other Mesopotamians, the Sumerians did not speak a Semitic language (the group of languages from which Hebrew and Arabic came); the origins of their language remain a mystery. By 3000 B.C.E., the Sumerians had created twelve independent city-states, such as Uruk, Eridu, and Ur, which repeatedly battled each other for territory. By 2500 B.C.E., these cities had expanded to twenty thousand residents or more. The rooms in Sumerians' mud-brick houses surrounded open courts. Large homes had a dozen rooms or more.

Agricultural surpluses and trade in commodities and manufactured goods made these cities prosperous. Sumerians bartered grain, vegetable oil, woolens, and leather with one another, and they acquired metals, timber, and precious stones from foreign trade. Traders traveled as far as India, where the cities of Indus civilization emerged about 2500 B.C.E. The invention of the wheel for use on transport wagons around 3000 B.C.E. strengthened the Mesopotamian economy. Temples and the rulers' families dominated the Sumerian economy because they controlled large farms and gangs of laborers, but some private households also became rich.

Increasingly rigid forms of hierarchy evolved in Sumerian society. Slaves, owned by temples and by individuals, had the lowest status. People became slaves by being captured in war, by being born to slaves, by voluntarily selling themselves or their children (usually to escape starvation), or by being sold by their creditors when they could not repay loans (debt slavery). Children whose parents dedicated them as slaves to the gods could rise to prominent positions in temple administration. In general, however, slaves existed in near-total dependence on other people and were excluded from normal social relations. They usually worked without pay and lacked almost all legal rights. They could be bought, sold, beaten, or even killed by their masters because they were considered property.

Slaves worked in domestic service, crafts production, and farming, but scholars dispute whether they or free laborers were more important to the economy. Free persons performed most government labor, paying their taxes with work rather than with money, which was measured in amounts of food or precious metal (coins were not invented until much later). Most slaves had little chance of becoming free, although owners sometimes liberated slaves in their wills, and slaves could purchase their freedom from earnings that some owners let them keep.

Hierarchy became so strong in Mesopotamian society that it led to the political system—monarchy—that became the most widespread form of government in the ancient world. In monarchies, the king was at the top of the hierarchy, like the ruler of the gods. His male descendants inherited his position. To display their exalted status, royal families lived in elaborate palaces that served as administrative centers and treasure-houses. Archaeologists excavating royal graves in Ur have revealed the rulers' dazzling riches—spectacular possessions crafted in gold, silver, and precious stones. These burials also have yielded grisly evidence of the top-ranking status of the king and queen: servants killed to look after their royal masters after death.

Patriarchy—domination by men in political, social, and economic life—already existed in Mesopotamian city-states, probably as an inheritance from the development of hierarchy in Paleolithic times. A Sumerian queen was respected because she was the king's wife and the mother of the royal children, but her husband held supreme power. The king formed a council of older men as his advisers, but he publicly acknowledged the gods as his rulers; this concept made the state a theocracy (government by gods) and gave priests and priestesses public influence. The king's greatest responsibility was to keep the gods happy and to defeat attacks from rival cities. The king demanded taxes from the working population to support his family, court, palace, army, and officials. The kings, along with the priests of the large temples, regulated most of the economy in their kingdoms by controlling the exchange of food and goods between farmers and crafts producers in a system known as a **redistributive economy**.

In religion, Mesopotamians continued earlier traditions by practicing **polytheism**: worshipping many gods who were thought to control different aspects of life, including the weather, fertility, and war. People believed that their safety depended on the goodwill of the gods, and each city-state honored one deity as its special protector. To please their gods, city dwellers offered sacrifices and built ziggurats (temple towers) soaring as high as ten stories. Mesopotamians believed that if human beings angered the gods, divinities such as the sky god Enlil and the goddess of love and war Inanna (also called Ishtar) would punish them by sending disease, floods, famine, and defeats in war.

Myths told in long poems such as the *Epic of Creation* and the *Epic of Gilgamesh* expressed Mesopotamian ideas about the challenges and violence that human beings faced in struggling with the natural environment and creating civilization. Gilgamesh was a legendary king of Uruk who longed to cheat death. He forced the young men of Uruk to labor like slaves and the young women to sleep with him. When his subjects begged the mother of the gods to grant them a protector, she created Enkidu, "hairy all over . . . dressed as cattle are." A week of sex with a prostitute tamed this brute, preparing him for civilization: "Enkidu was weaker; he ran slower than before. But he had gained judgment, was wiser." After wrestling Gilgamesh to a draw, Enkidu became his friend, and they defeated Humbaba, the ugly giant of the Pine Forest, and the Bull of Heaven. The gods doomed Enkidu to die soon after these triumphs. Depressed about the human condition, Gilgamesh sought the secret of immortality, but a thieving snake ruined his quest. He decided that the only immortality for mortals was winning fame for deeds. Only memory and gods could live forever.

Mesopotamian myths, living on in poetry, song, and art, greatly influenced other peoples. A late version of the Gilgamesh story recounted how the gods sent

The Ziggurat of Ur in Sumer
King Ur-Nammu and his son Shulgi built this huge temple to honor the gods in their city of Ur, in what is today southern Iraq, in the early twenty-first century B.C.E. It had three massive terraces, one above another, connected by stairways. The mud-brick core of the structure was covered with baked bricks held in place with tar. The walls were more than seven feet thick to support the enormous weight of the terraces. The total height is uncertain, but the first terrace alone soared some forty-five feet above ground level. (Hirmer Fotoarchiv, Munich, Germany.)

a huge flood over the earth. They warned one man, instructing him to build a boat. He loaded his vessel with his relatives, workers, possessions; domesticated and wild animals; and "everything there was." After a week of torrential rains, they left the boat to repopulate the earth and regenerate civilization. This story recalled the frequent floods of the Mesopotamian environment and looked ahead to the later biblical account of the great flood covering the globe and Noah's ark.

The invention of the technology of writing in Mesopotamia transformed the way people exchanged stories and ideas. Sumerians originally invented this new technology to do accounting. Before writing, people drew small pictures on clay tablets to keep count of objects or animals. Writing developed when people created symbols instead of pictures to represent the sounds of speech. Sumerian writing did not use an alphabet (a system in which each symbol represents the sound of a letter), but rather a system of wedge-shaped marks pressed into clay tablets to represent the sounds of syllables and entire words (Figure 1.1). Today this form of writing is called **cuneiform** (from *cuneus,* Latin for "wedge"). For a long time, writing was a professional skill for accounting mastered by only a few men and women known as scribes.

The possibilities for communication over time and space exploded when people began writing down nature lore, mathematics, foreign languages, and literature. In the twenty-third century B.C.E., Enheduanna, the daughter of King Sargon of the city of Akkad, composed the oldest written poetry whose author is known.

c. 3100 B.C.E.	c. 3000 B.C.E.	c. 2500 B.C.E.	c. 2100 B.C.E.	c. 700 B.C.E. (Neo-Assyrian)	Sumerian reading + meaning
					SAG Head
					NINDA bread
					GU$_7$ eat
					AB$_2$ cow
					APIN plough
					SUHUR carp

Figure 1.1 Cuneiform Writing
The earliest known form of writing developed in different locations in Mesopotamia in the late 3000s B.C.E., when meaning and sound were associated with signs such as these. The scribes who mastered the system used sticks or reeds to press dense rows of small wedge-shaped marks into damp clay tablets or chisels to engrave them on stone. Cuneiform was used for at least fifteen Near Eastern languages and continued to be written for three thousand years.

A Cuneiform Letter in Its Envelope
Written about 1900 B.C.E., this cuneiform text records a merchant's complaint that a shipment of copper contained less metal than he had expected. His letter, written on a clay tablet several inches long, was enclosed in an outer clay shell marked with the sender's private seal. This envelope protected the inner text from tampering or breakage. (© Copyright The Trustees of The British Museum.)

Written in Sumerian, her poetry praised the life-giving goddess of love, Inanna: "the great gods scattered from you like fluttering bats, unable to face your intimidating gaze . . . knowing and wise queen of all the lands, who makes all creatures and people multiply." Later princesses who wrote love songs, lullabies, dirges, and prayers continued the Mesopotamian tradition of royal women becoming authors.

Metallurgy was another technology that generated life-altering change in this period. Bronze, a new invention, could be sharpened into deadly swords and spearheads. Rich men found a new way to display their status by paying artisans to decorate their weapons with ornate engravings and inlays, as on costly guns today. Metal weapons also differentiated men's and women's roles in society by highlighting the masculine role of warrior.

The development of metallurgy helped lead to the world's first empire, in Akkadia (Map 1.1, page 7). Because Mesopotamian kings craved a reliable supply of metals to support their royal status, those who had no ore in their territory had to get it by trade or by conquest. The first empire arose about 2350 B.C.E., when King Sargon launched invasions seeking metals and glory. His violent campaigns conquered lands from Sumer all the way to the Mediterranean Sea, creating the world's first political superpower (a state able to dominate others). These conquests also spread Mesopotamian literature and art throughout the Near East. Although the Akkadians spoke a Semitic language, not Sumerian, after conquering Sumer they adopted much of the defeated land's religion, literature, and culture. Other peoples later conquered by the Akkadians were thus exposed to Sumerian beliefs and traditions, which they in turn adapted to their own purposes. In this way, war had the unintended consequence of promoting cultural interaction between peoples.

The Akkadian Empire's great size did not preserve it. Neighboring hill peoples, the Gutians, defeated it around 2200 B.C.E. A Mesopotamian poet offered a religious explanation for this defeat: King Naram-Sin, enraged at the god Enlil when his capital's prosperity waned, reduced Enlil's temple to "dust like a mountain mined for silver." Enlil then punished the Akkadians by sending the Gutians swooping down from their "land that rejects outside control, with the intelligence of human beings but with the form and stumbling words of a dog." This account reflects the Mesopotamians' deep-seated belief that the gods held ultimate power over human destiny.

Commerce, Law, and Learning in Mesopotamia, 2200–1200 B.C.E.

Mesopotamian innovations in private commerce, law, and learning influenced later Western civilization. These innovations took place in two kingdoms, Assyria and Babylonia, which emerged in the second millennium B.C.E. after the fall of the Akkadian Empire. The Assyrians, a Semitic people descended from the Akkadians, lived in northern Mesopotamia (Map 1.1, page 7). By becoming middlemen in the long-distance trade between Anatolia and southern Mesopotamia, the Assyrians became the Near East's leading merchants. They produced woolen textiles to exchange for Anatolian copper, silver, and gold, which they sold throughout Mesopotamia. In earlier Mesopotamian societies, the kings and priests had directed a largely state-run redistributive economy. This tradition never totally disappeared, but by 1900 B.C.E., the Assyrian kings were allowing private individuals to trade with other city-states and regions on their own. Assyrian investors sought profits by financing donkey caravans to travel hundreds of rocky and dangerous miles to Anatolia.

The expansion of private, profit-based commerce set an enduring precedent for later times, especially in the need to create binding contracts, which in turn required laws. It was the king's sacred duty to render justice in commercial disputes as well as for crimes. The record of the king's decisions is today called a law code. King Hammurabi (r. c. 1792–1750 B.C.E.) of Babylon, a great city on the Euphrates River, instituted the most famous set of early laws. Hammurabi proclaimed he was showing Shamash, the Babylonian sun god and god of justice, that he was fulfilling a king's responsibility: "So that the powerful may not oppress the powerless, to provide justice for the orphan and the widow . . . let the victim of injustice see the law which applies to him, let his heart be put at ease."

Hammurabi's code divided society into a three-part hierarchy: free persons, commoners, and slaves. We do not know what made the first two categories different, but free persons outranked commoners in the hierarchy of Babylonian society. An attacker who caused a pregnant woman of the free class to miscarry, for example, paid twice the fine levied for the same offense against a woman of the commoner class. A member of the free class who killed a commoner was fined instead of executed. For social equals, the code specified "an eye for an eye."

Widespread participation characterized the Babylonian justice system. People assembled as courts to determine most cases. The laws primarily concerned the king's interests as a property owner who leased innumerable tracts of land to tenants in return for rent or services. For offenses against property, the laws imposed severe penalties, including mutilation or a gruesome death for crimes as varied as theft, wrongful sales, and careless construction. In this patriarchal society, women had limited legal rights, but they could make business contracts and appear in court. A wife could divorce her husband for cruelty; a husband could divorce his wife for any reason. However, divorced wives were entitled to recover the property they had brought to the marriage.

Hammurabi's laws reveal much about urban life in Bronze Age Mesopotamia. Burglary and assault apparently plagued city dwellers. Marriages were arranged by the groom and the bride's father and sealed with a legal contract. Laws about surgery inform us about the work of doctors. Mesopotamian medicine included magic as well as potions and specific diets. Magicians treated illness by interpreting signs, such as the patient's dreams or hallucinations, and casting spells. Archaeological excavations and cuneiform records reveal that Mesopotamian cities had numerous wineshops, often run by women proprietors, offering drinks and a place to relax. Residents also found relief from the odors and crowding through open spaces set aside as parks. The world's oldest known map, an inscribed clay tablet showing the outlines of the Babylonian city of Nippur about 1500 B.C.E., indicates that a sizable section of the city was parkland.

Mesopotamians made especially influential achievements in mathematics and astronomy. Mathematicians used algebra to solve complex problems and knew how to derive the roots of numbers. They invented positional notation (the system of writing numbers in which each position is related to the next by a fixed multiple of value, as in our system based on a multiple of ten) and a system of reckoning based on sixty, still used in our division of a circle into hours, minutes, and degrees. Mesopotamians' skill in describing the paths of the stars and planets probably arose from a desire to make predictions about the future, based on the astrological belief that the movements of celestial objects affect human life. The charts and tables compiled by Mesopotamian stargazers laid the foundation for later advances in astronomical knowledge.

REVIEW   How did life change for people in Mesopotamia when they began to live in cities?

The Emergence of Egyptian and Hittite Civilization, 3100–1200 B.C.E.

Africa was home to the second great civilization to shape the West: Egypt. Egyptians created a wealthy, deeply religious, and strongly traditional civilization ruled by kings. Unlike Mesopotamia, Egypt was politically united under a strong central authority. The Egyptian kings' desire for immortality in the afterlife led them to build some of the largest tombs in history, the pyramids. Egyptian architecture and art inspired later Mediterranean peoples, especially the Greeks.

The height of Egyptian power came under the New Kingdom (c. 1569–1081 B.C.E.),* when the Hittite kingdom in Anatolia became Egypt's most aggressive rival (Map 1.1, page 7). The Hittites had become a powerful people by about 1750 B.C.E. They flourished because they inhabited the fertile upland region of Anatolia and controlled trade there and southward into the Levant** (today Syria, Lebanon, Israel, and Jordan), the commercial crossroads of the eastern Mediterranean and the persistent site of conflict among Near Eastern powers.

---

*Every date in Egyptian history is approximate and controversial, and different scholars use different dates because the evidence is often contradictory. Those used here are taken from the articles and "Egyptian King List" in *The Oxford Encyclopedia of Ancient Egypt,* edited by Donald B. Redford (2001).

**The name *Levant,* French for "rising (sun)"—that is, the East—reflects the European perspective on the area's location.

The Ancient Levant

Life in Old Kingdom Egypt, 3100–2190 B.C.E.

Geography propelled Egyptian history. Egypt's people lived mainly in farming villages in a narrow band of land along both sides of the Nile. Their irrigated farms extended several miles away from the river's banks. The Nile overflowed its banks once every year for several weeks, when melting snow from the mountains of central Africa gradually swelled its flow. This predictable and gentle flood enriched the soil near the river with nutrients from silt and diluted harmful deposits of mineral salts. Unlike the random deluges in Mesopotamia, the Nile's flood occurred at the same time every year and benefited the land. Trouble came only if dry weather in the mountains kept the river from overflowing. Deserts east and west of the Nile protected Egypt from invasion, except through the Nile delta in the north and on the southern frontier with Nubia. Deposits of metal ores, trade by sea, and lush agriculture made Egypt prosperous, but it had fewer and smaller cities than Mesopotamia. From their ample supplies of grain, the Egyptians made bread and beer, the most popular beverage.

Egypt's population included a diversity of people, whose skin color ranged from light to very dark. The modern controversy over whether Egyptians were people of color is anachronistic; ancient Egyptians presumably identified themselves by geography, language, religion, and social traditions and not by race. Later peoples, especially the Greeks, admired Egyptian civilization for its great antiquity and religious devotion. Some nineteenth-century historians minimized Egypt's contribution to Western civilization, but ancient peoples did not. Like everyone else in history, ancient Egyptians learned from other peoples. For example, they probably learned the technology of writing from the Sumerians, but they developed their own scripts rather than adopting cuneiform. To write formal and official texts, they used an ornate, picture-based script known as hieroglyphs (Figure 1.2).

The first large-scale Egyptian state emerged about 3100–3000 B.C.E., when King Menes united Upper (southern) Egypt and Lower (northern) Egypt.* By around 2687 B.C.E., the kings following Menes had forged a centralized state, known today as the Old Kingdom, which lasted until around 2190 B.C.E. (Map 1.2). By traveling and trading southward, Egyptians learned that the Nubians had already built extensive settlements and produced complex art by Menes' time. At places such as Afyeh, near the Nile's First Cataract, a Nubian social elite lived in dwellings much grander than the small huts housing most of the population. Egyptians constantly

---

*Upper and Lower refer to the direction in which the Nile River flows—from south of Egypt northward to the Mediterranean Sea.

Hieroglyph	Meaning	Sound value
	vulture	glottal stop
	flowering reed	consonantal I
	forearm and hand	ayin
	quail chick	W
	foot	B
	stool	P
	horned viper	F
	owl	M
	water	N
	mouth	R
	reed shelter	H
	twisted flax	slightly guttural
	placenta (?)	H as in "loch"
	animal's belly	slightly softer than h
	door bolt	S
	folded cloth	S
	pool	SH
	hill	Q
	basket with handle	K
	jar stand	G
	loaf	T

Figure 1.2 Egyptian Hieroglyphs
Ancient Egyptians developed their own system of writing about 3100 B.C.E., using pictures such as these. Because this formal script was used mainly for religious inscriptions on buildings and sacred objects, Greeks referred to it as *ta hieroglyphica* (the sacred carved letters), from which comes the modern term *hieroglyphs*. Egyptian hieroglyphs employ around seven hundred pictures in three categories: ideograms (signs indicating things or ideas), phonograms (signs indicating sounds), and determinatives (signs clarifying the meaning of the other signs). Eventually (the chronology is unsure), Egyptians also developed the handwritten cursive script called *demotic* (Greek for "of the people"), a much simpler and quicker form of writing.

interacted with Nubians while trading for raw materials such as gold, ivory, and animal skins, and Nubia's hierarchical organization perhaps influenced the development of centralized authority in Egypt's Old Kingdom. Eventually, however, Egypt's power overshadowed that of its southern neighbor.

The strength or weakness of the central authority determined Egyptian political history. When the kings were strong, as during the Old Kingdom, the country was

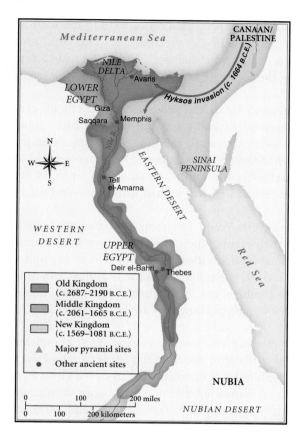

Map 1.2 Ancient Egypt
The Nile River, closely embraced by arid deserts, provided Egyptians with water to irrigate their fields and a highway for traveling north to the Mediterranean Sea and south to Nubia. The only easy land route into and out of Egypt lay through the Nile delta into the northern Sinai peninsula and on into the coastal area of the Levant. Egyptian kings therefore always fought to control these areas to secure the safety of their land.

stable, and trade flourished with the Levant and other Mediterranean areas. However, political instability resulted when regional governors or prominent priests, whose status was second only to that of the royal family, refused to support the king. The king's success depended on his properly fulfilling his religious duties. Egyptians worshipped many gods, often depicted as creatures with both human and animal features, such as the head of a jackal or a bird atop a human body. They did not worship animals; rather, they believed that each god had a particular animal to serve as the bearer of the god's divine soul. A picture or statue of a divinity had to include the animal so the image would include the soul. Egyptian religion told lively stories about the passion-filled lives of the gods to explain their powers. Deities were associated with powerful natural objects, emotions, qualities, and technologies. Examples include the sun god Re; Isis, goddess of love and fertility; and Thoth, god of wisdom and the inventor of writing.

Egyptians regarded their king as a god in human form, but they recognized that the man on the throne was mortal, seeing a difference between the individual king's human existence and the divine origin of his rule. As a system of government, monarchy was regarded as divine because it represented on earth the supernatural, eternal force that created harmony and stability in the universe. This force was called *maat* (meaning "truth," "justice," or "correct balance"). The king had to rule by promoting maat, thereby keeping the forces of nature in balance for the benefit of his people.

An Egyptian king ensured his people's safety and prosperity by strictly observing ritual. For example, he had to keep to a specific time for taking a bath, going for a walk, or having sex with his wife. Above all, the king was responsible for summoning the divine power that made the Nile overflow. If his prayers failed to make the flood occur, his political authority was gravely weakened. If he could not produce annual floods and keep the people well fed, he had lost maat—and might lose his kingdom.

Old Kingdom rulers used expensive building programs to demonstrate their devotion to the gods and proclaim their status. Their great buildings were mainly the temples or tombs constructed outside their cities. In the suburbs of Memphis, the first capital (south of modern Cairo), these kings erected the most stunning proofs of their piety and status: huge tombs in the form of pyramids. These monuments formed the centerpieces of groups of buildings for royal funerals and religious ceremonies.

The Old Kingdom rulers spent vast sums of money on these huge complexes because Egyptians had a strong belief in life after death. In the twenty-sixth century B.C.E., King Cheops commissioned the biggest of them all—the so-called Great Pyramid at Giza. At about 480 feet high, it stands taller than a forty-story skyscraper. Covering over thirteen acres and extending 760 feet on each side, it required more

The Pyramids at Giza in Egypt
The kings of Old Kingdom Egypt constructed enormous stone pyramids for their tombs. Pyramids were the centerpieces of large complexes of temples and courtyards stretching to the banks of the Nile or along a canal leading to the river. The burial chambers lay at the end of long, narrow tunnels snaking through the pyramids' interiors. The largest pyramid, shown here, is the nearly five-hundred-foot-high Great Pyramid of King Cheops, erected in the twenty-sixth century B.C.E. (© John Lawrence/SuperStock.)

than two million blocks of limestone, some of which weighed fifteen tons apiece. Quarried in the desert, the stone was floated to the site on river barges and dragged on rollers and sleds up earthen ramps into position. A prayer from about 2300 B.C.E. expresses the royal hopes for the pyramids: "O divine Atum, put your arms around King Neferkare Pepy II, around this construction work, around this pyramid. . . . May you guard lest anything evil happen to him throughout the course of eternity." So the royal family would be comfortable in their new existence, they packed their tombs with gilded furniture and luxury items. Archaeologists have uncovered two full-size cedar ships buried next to the Great Pyramid, meant to carry King Cheops on his voyage into eternity.

Their need to manage the labor and expenses for their mammoth projects led Old Kingdom rulers to centralize their administration and strengthen the social hierarchy. The king and queen topped the social order. Brothers and sisters in the royal family could marry each other, perhaps because such matches were believed necessary to preserve the purity of the royal line or to imitate the marriages of the gods. The priests, royal administrators, regional governors, and commanders of the army ranked next in the hierarchy. The common people, who did all the manual labor, made up the great majority of free people in Egypt. (Slaves became more common after the Old Kingdom.) Free workers had heavy obligations to the state. For example, although they were not slaves, they were required to work on the pyramids. On occasion they received wages, but mostly their labor was a way of paying taxes. Rates of taxation reached 20 percent on the produce of free farmers.

Women generally had the same legal rights as men. They could own land and slaves, inherit property, pursue lawsuits, transact business, and initiate divorces. Old Kingdom portrait statues display the equal status of wife and husband: each figure is the same size and sits on the same kind of chair. Men dominated public life, while women devoted themselves mainly to private life, managing their households and property. When their husbands went to war, however, women often took on men's work: some women held government posts, served as priestesses, managed farms, and practiced medicine.

The formal, even rigid appearance of Egypt's art illustrates how much its people valued religion, order, and predictability. Almost all sculptures and paintings were made for tombs or temples. Old Kingdom artists excelled in stonework, from carved ornamental jars to massive portrait statues of kings and queens. These statues represent the person either standing stiffly with the left leg advanced or sitting on a chair or throne, stable and poised. Concern for appropriate behavior also appears in the Old Kingdom literature the Egyptians called instructions, known today as wisdom literature. These texts told high officials how to act. In the *Instruction of Ptahhotep*, for example, the king advises his minister Ptahhotep to tell his son, who will follow him in office, not to be arrogant or overconfident just because he is well educated and to seek advice from ignorant people as well as from the wise.

Life in Middle Kingdom and New Kingdom Egypt, 2190–1200 B.C.E.

The Old Kingdom's stability disintegrated when temporary climate change shrank the annual Nile flood. This disaster caused starvation, which triggered civil unrest, which in turn discredited the kings. By 2190 B.C.E., regional governors seized and held on to power until a strong king finally restored central authority, initiating what historians call the Middle Kingdom (c. 2061–1665 B.C.E.). Judging from the period's abundant literature, this restoration of the monarchy gave Egyptians pride in their homeland. The Egyptian narrator of *The Story of Sinuhe*, for example, reports that he lived luxuriously during a forced stay in Syria but still dreamed of returning: "Whichever deity you are who ordered my exile, have mercy and bring me home! . . . Nothing is more important than that my body be buried in the country where I was born!" The Middle Kingdom fell apart, however, around 1665 B.C.E., when irregular Nile floods again undermined royal power.

The weakening of the king's authority led to a foreign takeover. A Semitic people from the Syria-Palestine region, whom the Egyptians called the Hyksos, gained control of Lower Egypt around 1664 B.C.E. (Map 1.2, page 17). As with the foreign wars of the Akkadians, the Hyksos' takeover of Egypt generated cultural interchange. The Hyksos transplanted elements of foreign culture to Egypt by introducing bronze-making technology, horses and war chariots, more powerful bows, new musical instruments, humpbacked cattle, and olive trees.

The New Kingdom of Egypt (c. 1569–1081 B.C.E.) formed when leaders of Thebes in southern Egypt defeated the Hyksos rulers. Its kings used diplomacy and war to advance Egypt's interests. Known as pharaohs (meaning "the Great House," that is, the royal palace and estate), New Kingdom rulers rebuilt central authority by restricting the power of regional governors. They earned the title "warrior-pharaohs" by invading Nubia and the Sudan to the south, in search of gold and other precious materials, and by fighting in Palestine and Syria to control trade routes. As before, religion remained the kings' most important activity. The principal festivals of the gods, for example, involved lavish public celebrations. A calendar based on the moon governed the dates of religious ceremonies. (The Egyptians also developed a calendar for administrative and fiscal purposes that had 365 days divided into twelve months of thirty days each, with the extra five days added before the start of the next year. Our modern calendar comes from it.)

The New Kingdom kings and queens built most of Egypt's magnificent temples, whose sculpted columns set a precedent for later Greek architecture. Queen Hatshepsut in the fifteenth century B.C.E., for example, erected a massive sanctuary at Deir el-Bahri near Thebes. After her husband (who was also her half brother) died, Hatshepsut proclaimed herself "female king" and co-ruler with her young stepson. To observe Egyptian political traditions, which did not include a queen ruling on her own, she had official artists portray her as a man sporting a king's beard and male clothing.

A dispute over religion threatened the stability of the New Kingdom in the fourteenth century B.C.E., when the pharaoh Akhenaten changed traditional practice. He made the cult of Aten, the shining disk of the sun, the centerpiece of royal worship and excluded

Queen Hatshepsut as Pharaoh Offering *Maat*
This eight-and-a-half-foot-tall granite statue shows the New Kingdom queen Hatshepsut dressed as a male pharaoh and wearing a ceremonial beard. She is performing her royal duty of offering *maat* (the divine principle of order and justice) to the gods. Egyptian religion taught that the gods "lived on maat" and that the land's rulers were responsible for providing it. Hatshepsut had this statue and many others placed in a huge temple she built outside Thebes in Upper Egypt. (The Metropolitan Museum of Art, Rogers Fund, 1929 [29.3.1]. Photography by Schechter Lee. Photograph © 1986 The Metropolitan Museum of Art.)

other deities and their supporters. Akhenaten's reforms did not aim at pure **monotheism** (belief in the existence of only one god, as in Judaism, Christianity, and Islam), as some scholars assert, because they did not change the divine status of the king. His wife, Queen Nefertiti, tried to restrain him when she realized the hostility that his changes had created in the priesthood and the general population, but he kept on, even neglecting the defense of Egypt to devote himself to religion. His religious reform died with him; during the reign of his successor, Tutankhamun (r. 1355–1346 B.C.E.), famous today as a result of the discovery of his unlooted tomb in 1922, the traditional solar cult of Amun-Re reclaimed its leading role.

Most Egyptians' daily lives focused on manual labor and religion. Working as farmers or crafts producers, ordinary people devoted much attention to deities outside the royal cults, especially to gods they believed protected them. They venerated Bes, for instance, a dwarf with the features of a lion, as a protector of the household. They carved his image on amulets, beds, headrests, and the handles of mirrors. Magic also played a large role in people's lives. They used spells and charms to ward off demons, smooth the course of love, take revenge on enemies, and find relief from disease and injury. Egyptian doctors made medicinal use of herbs, knowledge that was passed on to later civilizations, and they could perform surgeries, including opening the skull.

Like royalty, ordinary people prepared for the afterlife. Those who could afford it arranged to have their bodies mummified and their tombs outfitted with all the goods needed for the journey to their new existence. A mummy's essential equipment included a copy of the *Book of the Dead*—a collection of magic spells to ward off danger and gain a successful verdict from the divine jury that put every soul on trial. To avoid experiencing death a second time, the *Book* instructed, dead people had to convince the jury of gods by sworn statements such as "I have not committed crimes against people; I have not mistreated cattle; I have not robbed the poor; I have not caused pain." Souls who received positive judgments experienced a mystical union with the god Osiris, the head judge of the dead.

Life in the Hittite Kingdom, 1750–1200 B.C.E.

The greatest external threat to the safety of New Kingdom Egyptians came from the aggressive wars of the Hittite kingdom, which emerged about 1750 B.C.E. in Anatolia (Map 1.1, page 7). The Hittites spoke an Indo-European language from the family of languages that eventually spread over most of Europe. The original Indo-European speakers had migrated as separate groups into Anatolia and Europe from somewhere in western Asia. Recent archaeological discoveries there of women buried with weapons suggest that Indo-European women originally occupied positions of leadership alongside men; the prominence of Hittite queens in official documents perhaps sprang from that tradition.

Hittite kingship was based on religion—the worship of Indo-European gods and local Anatolian deities. The king served as high priest of the storm god and had to maintain strict purity. His drinking water, for example, was always strained, and his water carrier was executed if so much as a hair was found in a drink. Like other Near Eastern rulers, Hittite kings felt responsible for maintaining divine goodwill toward their subjects. One of them, King Mursili II (r. 1321–1295 B.C.E.), issued a set of prayers begging the gods to end a plague: "What is this, o gods, that you have done? Our land is dying. . . . O gods, whatever sin you behold, either let a prophet come forth to identify it . . . or let us see it in a dream!"

The Hittite rulers launched long-range military campaigns to acquire metals and control trade routes. The Hittites did not owe their success in war to a special knowledge of making weapons from iron, as was once thought, because iron weapons did not become common until after 1200 B.C.E. They did excel in the use of war chariots, however. Hittite kings particularly wanted to dominate the lucrative trade from Mesopotamia and Egypt. In 1595 B.C.E., therefore, their army raided as far as Babylon, overthrowing that kingdom.

They also invaded the Levant, the principal crossroads leading to Egypt. Previously, independent Canaanite city-states, such as the bustling ports of Ugarit, Byblos, and Tyre, had dominated the Levant. There, the interaction of traders and travelers from different cultures created about 1600 B.C.E. a supremely important innovation in writing technology: the alphabet. In this new system, a simplified picture—that is, a letter—stood for only one sound in the language. This offered a dramatic improvement in ease of writing over cuneiform and hieroglyphic scripts. The Canaanite alphabet later became the basis for the Greek and Roman alphabets, from which came modern Western alphabets.

REVIEW   How did religion guide the lives of people in Egyptian and Hittite civilization?

From the Sea Peoples to the Reemergence of Empires in the Near East, 1200–500 B.C.E.

Widespread attacks, generated by invasions of separate bands of shipborne raiders known as the Sea Peoples (their origins remain uncertain), wiped out or weakened many states in the eastern Mediterranean region from about 1200 to 1000 B.C.E. The depopulation and economic collapse that resulted in many areas, as well as our dim knowledge of what happened, has led historians to talk of the "Dark Age." Egypt lost its international power forever during this troubled period when the New Kingdom fell apart about 1081 B.C.E.

In the Near East, recent archaeological excavation suggests that this period lasted only about a century, with empire then once again emerging as the system of government. The constant striving for imperial wealth and territory kept the Near East on the same violent political and military path—monarchy and empire—as in the past. By 900 B.C.E., the Neo-Assyrian (New Assyrian) Empire ruled the region. First the Neo-Babylonian Empire and then the Persian Empire, the greatest the world had ever seen, followed.

Hebrew (or Israelite) civilization, centered in the southern Levant, lost its independence to these Near Eastern empires, but its religion—Judaism—became influential in Western civilization. The Hebrews' religion, originally reflecting influences from their polytheistic Canaanite neighbors, took a long time to develop into monotheism. Eventually, however, the Hebrew ideas of belief in one god and basing a religion on scripture became essential concepts for major religions that deeply influenced Western civilization.

From Neo-Assyrian to Babylonian to Persian Empire, 900–500 B.C.E.

The collapse of the Egyptian and Hittite kingdoms allowed the aggressive Neo-Assyrian rulers to build an empire by 900 B.C.E. by seizing supplies of metal and controlling trade routes. Their armies drove westward until they punched through to the Mediterranean coast (Map 1.3). Neo-Assyrian monarchs constantly pursued foreign expansion, and for the first time their armies made foot soldiers, instead of cavalry, the principal striking force. Trained infantrymen excelled in the use of military technology such as siege towers and battering rams; archers rode in chariots. Campaigns against foreign lands brought back plunder to supplement the kingdom's agriculture and long-distance trade. Conquered peoples had to pay annual tribute to the Assyrians, supplying raw materials and luxury goods such as incense, wine, dyed linens, glass, and ivory.

Neo-Assyrian kings treated conquered peoples brutally to keep order. They herded large numbers of people from their homelands to Assyria, forcing them to build temples and palaces. This merciless policy had an unintended cultural consequence: so many Aramaeans were deported from Canaan to Assyria that Aramaic largely replaced Assyrian as Assyria's native, everyday language. When not waging war, Neo-Assyrian men loved to hunt, and the more dangerous the animal, the better. The king hunted lions as proof of his vigor and power. Although the Neo-Assyrian imperial administration preserved countless documents in its archives, literacy apparently mattered less to the kingdom's males than war, hunting, and practical technology. Ashurbanipal (r. 680–626 B.C.E.) was the only king to proclaim his scholarly accomplishments: "I have read complicated texts, whose versions in Sumerian are obscure and in Akkadian hard to understand. I do research on the cuneiform texts on stone from before the Flood." Women of the social elite probably

Map 1.3 Expansion of the Neo-Assyrian Empire, c. 900–650 B.C.E. Like their Akkadian, Assyrian, and Babylonian predecessors, the Neo-Assyrian kings dominated a vast region of the Near East to secure a supply of metals, access to trade routes on land and sea, and imperial glory. They built the largest empire the world had yet seen. Also like their predecessors, they treated disobedient subjects harshly and intolerantly to try to prevent their diverse territories from rebelling.

learned to read, but they were excluded from the male dominions of hunting and war. Public religion, which included deities adopted from Babylonia, also reflected the prominence of war in Assyrian culture. Even the Assyrian cult of Ishtar (the Babylonian name for Inanna), the goddess of love and fertility, glorified warfare.

The Neo-Assyrian kings' harshness made their own people, especially the social elite, dislike their rule. Rebellions were common, and in the seventh century B.C.E. they crippled the kingdom. The Medes, an Iranian people, and the Chaldeans, a seminomadic Semitic people who had driven the Assyrians from Babylonia, combined forces to destroy the Neo-Assyrian capital at Nineveh in 612 B.C.E. and end the kings' imperial power.

The Chaldeans established the Neo-Babylonian Empire, which became the most powerful empire in Babylonian history. King Nebuchadnezzar II (r. 605–562 B.C.E.) spent lavishly to turn Babylon into an architectural showplace, rebuilding the great temple of its chief god, Marduk; creating the famous Hanging Gardens (so named because lush plants drooped over its terraced sides); and constructing a dazzling city gate dedicated to the goddess Ishtar. Blue-glazed bricks and lions molded in yellow, red, and white decorated the gate's walls, which soared thirty-six feet high.

The Chaldeans adopted traditional Babylonian culture and preserved much ancient Mesopotamian literature, such as the *Epic of Gilgamesh*. They also created many new works of prose and poetry, which educated people often read aloud publicly for the enjoyment of the many illiterate members of the population. Particularly popular were fables, proverbs, essays, and prophecies that taught morality and proper behavior. This wisdom literature, a Near Eastern tradition going back at least to the Egyptian Old Kingdom, greatly influenced the later religious writings of the Hebrews.

The Chaldeans' advances in astronomy became so influential in the ancient Mediterranean world that the word *Chaldean* became the Greeks' word for "astronomer." People's main reason for observing the stars was the belief that the gods communicated their will to humans through events in nature, such as eclipses and the movements of the stars and planets, abnormal births, smoke curling upward from a fire, and the trails of ants. The interpretation of these events as messages from the gods was characteristic of the mixture of science and religion in ancient Near Eastern thought, which so deeply influenced the Greeks.

The Persian Empire, the Near East's last and greatest empire, began when Cyrus (r. 559–530 B.C.E.) overthrew Median rule in Persia (today Iran) by conquering Babylon in 539 B.C.E. A rebellion there by Marduk's priests, provoked when the king had promoted a different deity, had weakened the Chaldean dynasty. Cyrus profited from this religious crisis by promising to restore traditional Babylonian religion, thereby winning local support. According to an ancient inscription, he proclaimed: "Marduk, the great lord, caused Babylon's generous residents to adore me."

Later Persian kings expanded their rule by following Cyrus's principles of military strength and cultural tolerance. Darius I (r. 522–486 B.C.E.) greatly extended Cyrus's conquests by pushing Persian power eastward to the Indus valley and westward to Thrace (Map 1.4). Organizing this vast territory into provinces, Darius assigned each region taxes payable in the form best suited to its local economy— precious metals, grain, horses, or slaves. He required each region to send soldiers to staff the royal army. A network of roads and a courier system for royal mail aided communication among the far-flung provincial centers. The Greek historian Herodotus reported that neither snow, rain, heat, nor darkness slowed the couriers from completing their routes as swiftly as possible (an achievement later transformed into the U.S. Postal Service motto). The kings' belief in their divine right to rule everyone, everywhere would provoke great conflicts—above all, the war between Persians and Greeks that would break out around 500 B.C.E.

The revenues flowing into the imperial treasury made the Persian king wealthy beyond imagination and supported the royal hierarchy. So special was the monarch that servants held their hands before their mouths in his presence so that he would not have to breathe the same air. In sculpture adorning the immense palace at Persepolis, artists carved royal figures larger than other people. The king's purple robes were more splendid than anyone else's, and no other person could walk on the red carpets spread before him. To show that he used his gargantuan resources to help his loyal subjects, the king often provided meals for fifteen thousand nobles, courtiers, and other followers at one sitting—although he himself ate hidden from his guests' view. The king punished lawbreakers and rebels harshly, mutilating their bodies and executing their families. Greeks, in awe of the Persian monarch's power and luxury, referred to him as "the Great King." So long as his subjects—numbering in the millions and of many different ethnicities—remained peaceful, the king let them live and worship as they pleased.

Map 1.4 Expansion of the Persian Empire, c. 550–490 B.C.E.
Cyrus (r. 559–530 B.C.E.) founded the Persian Empire, which his successors expanded to be even larger
than the Neo-Assyrian Empire, which it replaced. By the later years of Darius's reign (r. 522–486 B.C.E.), the
Persian Empire had expanded east as far as the western edge of India; to the west, it reached Thrace,
the eastern edge of Europe. Persian kings, unlike their imperial predecessors, won their subjects' loyalty
with tolerance and religious freedom, although they treated rebels harshly.

Ruling as absolute autocrats with the power to make the rules for everyone
else, the Persian kings believed they were superior to all humans. They regarded
themselves not as gods but as the agents of Ahura Mazda, the supreme god of Persia. As Darius said in his autobiography, which was carved into a mountainside in
three languages, "Ahura Mazda gave me kingship . . . by the will of Ahura Mazda
the provinces respected my laws."

Persian religion, based on the teachings of the legendary prophet Zarathus-
tra (and called Zoroastrianism from the Greek name for this holy man), made
the god Ahura Mazda the center of worship. It seems, however, not to have been
pure monotheism. Its most important doctrine was a moral dualism: perceiving the

The Great King of Persia
Like their Assyrian predecessors, the Persian kings decorated their palaces with large relief sculptures emphasizing royal dignity and success. This one from Persepolis shows officials and petitioners giving the king proper respect when entering his presence. To symbolize their elevated status, the king and his son, who stands behind the throne, are depicted as larger than everyone else. **For more help analyzing this image, see the visual activity for this chapter in the Online Study Guide at** bedfordstmartins.com/huntconcise. (Courtesy of the Oriental Institute of the University of Chicago.)

world as the arena for an ongoing battle between good and evil. Ahura Mazda's two children, according to Persian belief, made different moral choices: one chose the way of the truth, and the other chose the way of the lie. Humans were also free to choose: Zoroastrianism promised salvation to those following the way of the truth and damnation to those taking the way of the lie. The Persian religious emphasis on ethical behavior had a lasting influence on others, especially the Hebrews.

The Development of Hebrew Monotheism, to 539 B.C.E.

The Hebrews' enduring impact on Western civilization comes from the book that became their sacred Scriptures, the Hebrew Bible (known to Christians as the Old Testament), and their monotheistic religion. The Hebrew Scriptures deeply affected the formation of not only Judaism but also Christianity and, later, Islam. Unfortunately, no source provides clear information on the origins of the Hebrews or their religion. The Bible tells stories to explain God's moral plan for the universe, not the full history of the Hebrews, and archaeology has not yielded a clear picture.

The traditional version of the early history of the Hebrews places them in Mesopotamia. From there, Abraham, in about 1900 B.C.E., led his followers to ancient Palestine, at the southeast corner of the Mediterranean Sea, where the Canaanites ruled (Map 1.1, page 7). Supposedly divided into twelve tribes, the Hebrews never formed a political state in this period. The biblical story of Joseph bringing Hebrews to Egypt may belong between 1600 and 1400 B.C.E., during the time of Hyksos rule.

By the thirteenth century B.C.E., the pharaohs had conscripted the male Hebrews into labor gangs for farming and construction work.

The biblical narrative then relates the central event in Hebrew history: the sealing of a covenant between the Hebrews and their deity, Yahweh, at Mount Sinai after Yahweh instructed Moses to lead the Hebrews on an exodus out of bondage in Egypt about 1250 B.C.E. This agreement declared that if the Hebrews promised to worship Yahweh as their only God and to live by his laws, Yahweh would make them his chosen people and lead them into a promised land of safety and prosperity. This binding arrangement demanded human obedience to divine law and promised punishment for unrighteousness. As God described himself, he was "compassionate and gracious, patient, ever constant and true . . . forgiving wickedness, rebellion, and sin, and not sweeping the guilty clean away; but one who punishes sons and grandsons to the third and fourth generation for their fathers' iniquity" (Exodus 34:6–7). The religious and moral code that bound the Hebrews was written down in the Ten Commandments and the Pentateuch (the first five books of the Hebrew Bible), or Torah.

Many of the laws in the Pentateuch recalled earlier Mesopotamian rules, such as those of Hammurabi, but Hebrew law differed because it applied the same rules and punishments to everyone, regardless of their social position. Hebrew law also ruled out vicarious punishment—a Mesopotamian tradition ordering, for example, that a rapist's wife be raped. Hebrew women had less extensive legal rights than men, such as in seeking a divorce. Crimes against property never carried the death penalty, as they frequently did in other Near Eastern societies, and Hebrew law protected slaves against glaring mistreatment.

Many uncertainties cloud our understanding of how the Hebrews acquired their monotheism. It seems that it took much longer to develop monotheism than the biblical account suggests. In the time of Moses, Yahweh-religion was not yet monotheistic because it did not deny the existence of other gods, such as Baal of Canaan. Fully developed Hebrew monotheism did not emerge until well after 1000 B.C.E., by which time the first Hebrew kingdom had formed. Solomon (r. c. 961–922 B.C.E.) brought the united nation to the height of its prosperity, largely as a result of trade. He displayed his wealth by building in Jerusalem a temple to Yahweh that was richly decorated with gold leaf; it became the center of Hebrew religion.

After Solomon, the monarchy split into two kingdoms: Israel in the north and Judah in the south. The Neo-Assyrians conquered Israel in 722 B.C.E. and deported its population to Assyria. In 597 B.C.E., the Neo-Babylonians conquered Judah; ten years later, they destroyed Solomon's temple and sent most of the Hebrews into exile in Babylon. When the Persian king Cyrus overthrew the Babylonians in 539 B.C.E., he permitted the Hebrews to return to Palestine, which was called Yehud from the name of the southern Hebrew kingdom, Judah. From this geographical term came the name *Jews,* a designation for the Hebrews after their Babylonian exile. In keeping with the policy of cultural tolerance, Cyrus allowed them to rebuild their temple in Jerusalem and practice their religion. After returning from exile, the Jews in the ancient world remained a people subject to the political domination of various

Near Eastern powers, except for a period of independence during the second and first centuries b.c.e.

Jewish prophets, both men and women, preached that the Hebrews' defeats were divine punishment for neglecting the Sinai covenant and mistreating the poor. Some prophets also predicted the end of the present world following a great crisis, a judgment by Yahweh, and salvation leading to a new and better world. Yahweh would save the Hebrew nation, the prophets thundered, only if Jews learned to observe divine law strictly. This **apocalypticism** ("uncovering" of the future), which recalled Babylonian prophetic wisdom literature, would later influence Christianity.

Jewish religious leaders developed strict regulations requiring people to maintain ritual and ethical purity in all aspects of life. Ethics applied not only to obvious crimes but also to financial dealings. Jews had to pay taxes and offerings to support Yahweh's temple, and they had to forgive debts every seventh year. Jews therefore created laws based on ethics as the focus of the world's first monotheism. They retained their cultural identity by following their religious laws, regardless of where they lived. In this way, Jews who did not return to their homeland could maintain their identity while living among foreigners. Over time, the Diaspora (dispersion of population) came to characterize the history of the Jewish people.

Hebrew monotheism made the preservation and understanding of a sacred text, the Hebrew Bible, the key to a religious life. Making scripture central to religion became a crucial development in the history of Judaism, as well as in Christianity and Islam, because these later religions placed their own sacred texts, the Christian Bible and the Qur'an, respectively, at the center of their beliefs and practices. The Hebrews thus passed on ideas that have endured to this day, such as the belief in monotheism, the importance of scripture in religion, and a commitment to a covenant between God and a people who are promised salvation if they obey divine will.

> **REVIEW**   How did religion affect the history of the Near East from 1200 to 500 b.c.e.?

The First Greek Civilization, 8000–750 b.c.e.

Early Greek civilization developed through the interaction of peoples inhabiting islands and coastal areas in the middle Mediterranean region. By 8000 b.c.e., settlements of Indo-European speakers dotted the mountainous Greek mainland and the islands of the Aegean Sea. By 7000 b.c.e., Anatolian peoples had migrated to the large island of Crete, southeast of the Greek mainland (Map 1.5). The type of language spoken by these early Cretans, called Minoans, remains uncertain, but they created the first civilization in this part of the world in the late 2000s b.c.e. Eventually, they lost their preeminence and power to their warlike neighbors on the mainland, the Mycenaeans. When Mycenaean civilization was destroyed during the extended warfare that affected the eastern Mediterranean from about 1200 to 1000 b.c.e., the Dark Age of depopulation and poverty that followed almost ended Greek civilization.

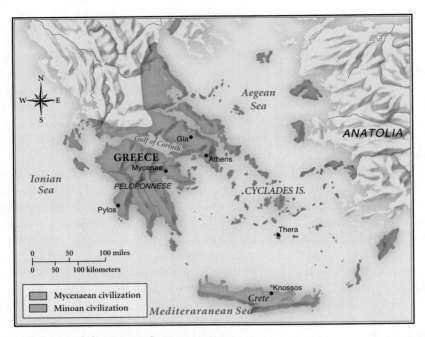

Map 1.5 Greece and the Aegean Sea, c. 1500 B.C.E.
Mountains, islands, and sea defined the geography of Greece. The rough terrain and seasonally stormy sailing made travel a chore. The distance from the mainland to the largest island in this region, Crete, where Minoan civilization arose, was sufficiently long to keep Cretans isolated from the turmoil of most of later Greek history. **For more help analyzing this map, see the map activity for this chapter in the Online Study Guide at** bedfordstmartins.com/huntconcise.

Minoan and Mycenaean Civilization, 2200–1000 B.C.E.

Crete offered a fine home for settlers because it had fertile plains, adequate rainfall, and sheltered ports for fishing and seaborne trade. By 2200 B.C.E., the inhabitants of Crete created what scholars call a palace society, referring to the many-chambered buildings that were both the residences of the rulers and the centers of political, economic, and religious administration. The palaces seem to have been independent; no one ruler controlled Crete. We call this civilization Minoan because a prominent archaeologist who excavated there believed that its greatest ruler was King Minos, famous in Greek myth because his wife gave birth to the half-man, half-bull Minotaur (Minos's bull).

Minoan farmers developed Mediterranean polyculture—growing olives, grapes, and grain on the same farm, which became the hallmark of agriculture in the region ever after. This innovation made the best use of agricultural labor because these crops' different growing cycles allowed the same laborers to take care of them all. Farmers could thus produce valuable and versatile products such as olive oil and wine. This combination of crops provided a healthy way of eating (today called the Mediterranean diet) that stimulated population growth. Minoans also developed deep-hulled sailing ships that promoted long-distance trade in commodities by sea.

Minoan Wall Painting from Knossos, Crete
Minoan artists painted with vivid colors on plaster to enliven the walls of buildings. This painting from the palace at Knossos depicts an acrobatic performance in which a youth leaped in an aerial somersault over the back of a charging bull. Some scholars speculate this dangerous jump was a religious ritual instead of just a circus act. Unfortunately, time and earthquakes have severely damaged most Minoan wall paintings, and the versions we see today are largely reconstructions, painted around surviving fragments of the originals. (© National Archaeological Museum, Athens, Greece/The Bridgeman Art Library.)

Minoan rulers enforced a redistributive economic system. The Knossos palace, for example, held hundreds of gigantic jars holding 240,000 gallons of olive oil and wine. The rulers evidently decided how much each farmer or crafts producer had to contribute to the palace storehouse and how much of those contributions would then be redistributed to each person in the community for basic subsistence or as an extra reward.

Independent rulers on the mainland also controlled redistributive economies. This civilization, called Mycenaean from the hilltop site of Mycenae in the Peloponnese (the large peninsula forming southern Greece), emerged in the centuries after 2000 B.C.E. By 1400 B.C.E., Mycenae had a fortified settlement with a palace and rich tombs. Because mountainous Greece had little fertile land but many useful ports, settlements tended to arise near the coast. Greeks always depended on the sea: for food, for trade with one another and with foreign lands, and for naval raids on rich targets.

Seaborne commerce strongly promoted cultural interaction, as underwater archaeology reveals. Off Uluburun in Turkey, for example, divers discovered a late-fourteenth-century B.C.E. ship carrying such a mixed cargo and varied personal possessions—from Greece, Egypt, Canaan, Cyprus, Babylon, and elsewhere in the Near East—that attaching a single "nationality" to this vessel makes no sense.

Connections by sea brought Minoans and Mycenaeans into close contact. Many objects found on the mainland display designs clearly inspired by Cretan traditions. At the same time, the two peoples remained different in important ways.

The Mycenaeans burned sacrifices to the gods; the Minoans did not use fire in this way. The Minoans distributed sanctuaries across the landscape in caves, on mountaintops, and in country villas; the Mycenaeans kept their sanctuaries inside their palaces. When the Mycenaeans started building palaces in the fourteenth century B.C.E., unlike the Minoans they designed them around rooms with prominent ceremonial hearths and thrones for the rulers.

Mycenaeans eventually achieved dominance over Crete, possibly in a war over international trade. Later Greeks recalled this conquest of Crete with the myth describing how Theseus of Athens defeated the Minotaur: when Minos forced the Athenians to send youths for the creature to devour in his labyrinth, Theseus slew the monster and found his way out of the maze by backtracking along the thread that the king's daughter Ariadne, who had fallen in love with the handsome hero, told him to leave to mark his path.

By the time Mycenaeans ruled Crete, war at home and abroad was the principal concern of well-off Mycenaean men. Contents of Bronze Age tombs in Greece reveal that no wealthy man went to his grave without his war equipment. Their warlike spirit, however, probably ruined the Mycenaeans during the Sea Peoples period (c. 1200–1000 B.C.E.). At this time, the palace settlements of eastern Greece constructed such massive defensive walls that later Greeks believed giants had built them. The fortifications of coastal sites would have protected coastal palaces against invading Sea Peoples, but the great wall around the palace at Gla, far inland where foreign sea raiders could not easily reach, suggests fear of a land-based threat, too. Archaeologists therefore speculate that local warfare among Mycenaeans, made worse by earthquakes, led to what is called "systems collapse," destroying the Mycenaean states by about 1000 B.C.E. The disappearance of the redistributive economic system devastated Mycenaeans who did not have farms, as they depended on their rulers' system for their subsistence. The catastrophic fall of Mycenaean civilization brought on the Greek Dark Age.

The Greek Dark Age, 1000–750 B.C.E.

Greek civilization almost ended in the Dark Age (1000–750 B.C.E.). Political systems collapsed, the economy contracted, and the population shrank. Conditions were so depressed that Greeks even lost the technologies of writing and of illustrating people and animals in art. They did preserve their traditional divisions into groups speaking different dialects of the same language, namely Ionians, Dorians, and Aeolians. They regarded themselves as sharing a Greek identity because they worshipped the same gods.

The conditions of the Dark Age eventually led to new social values. When the palace-based rulers of Mycenaean Greece fell, competition for leadership in society became wide open. The men and women who proved themselves excellent in action, words, and religious knowledge became the new social elite. Excellence became a competitive value: individuals earned high social status by outdoing others. The new emphasis on individualism shows up in burial practices, as cremation replaced inhumation and graves housing multiple corpses. Men displayed excellence through achievement in war and persuasiveness in speech, while women displayed excellence by managing a household of children, slaves, and the family's storerooms. Members of the elite accumulated wealth by controlling agricultural land, which people of lower status farmed for them as tenants or slaves.

The rebuilding of Greek life after the Dark Age required the establishment of social and political values that recognized both individual excellence and justice in a community. Tension between these two ideals was inevitable. The poems of Homer and Hesiod express these ideas so powerfully that later Greeks regarded them as the foundational literature of Greek identity.

Later Greeks believed that Homer was an eighth-century B.C.E. blind poet from Ionia (today Turkey's western coast) who composed the epic poems *The Iliad* and *The Odyssey*. The stories in these poems explore the consequences of making individual excellence the principal social value. *The Iliad* tells the story of the Greek army attacking the Anatolian city of Troy. (The Trojan War was one of the many wars of the Sea Peoples period.) The manliest Greek hero is Achilles, who displays his surpassing excellence in *The Iliad* by choosing to die gloriously in battle rather than return home safely but without glory. *The Odyssey* describes the hero Odysseus's ten-year adventure finding his way home to his family in Greece after the fall of Troy. It also describes the struggle of his wife, Penelope, to protect their household while her husband is missing. Penelope proves herself the best of women, showing her excellence by outwitting treacherous neighbors and preserving her family's prosperity.

The Iliad and *The Odyssey* reveal how the quest for individual excellence could produce both wondrous accomplishments and brutal inhumanity. In *The Iliad*, after Achilles kills Hector, the prince of Troy, he mutilates his body. When Hecuba, the queen of Troy and Hector's mother, sees this outrage, she bitterly shouts, "I wish I could sink my teeth into his liver in his guts to eat it raw." Homer's poems suggest that the gods could promote reconciliation, but they also reveal that the level of suffering in the human condition means excellence comes at a supremely high price.

Hesiod's poetry stresses the value of justice supported by a community. Like Homer a poet of the eighth century B.C.E., Hesiod tells stories influenced by Near Eastern myths, such as the Mesopotamian *Epic of Creation*. His poems explain that existence, even for deities, entails sorrow and violence. They also show that justice is part of the divine order of the universe. In *Works and Days*, Hesiod identifies Zeus, king of the gods, as the source of justice: "Zeus ordained that fishes and wild beasts and birds should eat each other, for they have no justice; but to human beings he has given justice, which is far the best." Hesiod emphasizes that men from the elite should demonstrate excellence in their relations to their social inferiors by promoting justice through persuasion instead of force: "When his people in their assembly get on the wrong track, [a good leader] gently sets matters right, persuading them with soft words." Hesiod proclaims that the divine origin of justice should be a warning to "bribe-devouring chiefs" who impose "crooked judgments." By the end of the Dark Age, the outrage that ordinary people felt at not receiving just treatment was producing pressure for a new form of social and political organization in Greece.

New technology as well as new values came to Dark Age Greece. Contacts with the Near East retaught Greeks how to write, this time learning the alphabet from Phoenician traders from Canaan. Eastern art inspired Greeks once more to include lively figures in their paintings. Trade also brought to Greece the new technology of iron metallurgy. Because iron ore was available in Greece, iron was cheaper than bronze. The relatively low cost of iron tools helped revive farming, which in turn rebuilt the population. By the eighth century B.C.E., Greece was emerging from its Dark Age.

REVIEW   What were the consequences of the Greek Dark Age?

Remaking Greek Civilization, 750–500 B.C.E.

Beginning in the eighth century B.C.E., Greeks gradually remade their civilization on new social and political principles, inventing citizenship based on freedom and the sharing of power in city-state government. The Greeks' contacts with Egypt and the Near East had helped them emerge from the Dark Age, but they now created their own version of the city-state, striking out in new directions in politics, art, literature, philosophy, and science.

The best evidence of a revival of a sense of Greek identity is the founding of the Olympic Games, traditionally dated to 776 B.C.E. Every four years, the games took place as part of a religious festival at Olympia, in the northwest Peloponnese, in a huge sanctuary dedicated to Zeus. There, male athletes from elite families from communities all over Greece competed in sports based on activities needed for war: running, wrestling, jumping, and throwing. Horse and chariot racing were added to the program later, but the main event remained a two-hundred-yard sprint. Women were barred on pain of death, but they had their own separate Olympic festival on a different date in honor of Hera, queen of the gods; only unmarried women could compete.

Historians date the end of the Greek Dark Age and the beginning of the Archaic Age (750–500 B.C.E.) near the time when the Olympics began. The Archaic Age gave birth to the Greek city-state (**polis**) as an independent community of citizens inhabiting a city and the countryside around it. Greece's geography, dominated by mountains and islands, promoted the creation of city-states that remained fiercely independent communities (Map 1.6). The ancient Greeks never constituted a united nation. During the Archaic Age, Greeks established settlements around the Mediterranean in a process traditionally called colonization. This modern term, however, is misleading because it implies that governments originated and administered colonies in foreign lands. In reality, individual entrepreneurs' desire for profit from trade,

Map 1.6 Archaic Greece, c. 750–500 B.C.E.

The Greek heartland lay in and around the Aegean Sea, in what is today the nation of Greece and the western edge of the nation of Turkey (ancient Anatolia). The "mainland," where Athens, Corinth, and Sparta are located, is the southernmost tip of the mountainous Balkan peninsula. The many islands of the Aegean area were home mainly to small city-states, with the exception of the large islands just off the western Anatolian coast, which were home to populous ones.

especially in raw materials such as metals, and from acquiring farmland on foreign shores drove the founding of most new settlements. By about 580 B.C.E., Greeks had settled in Spain, present-day southern France, southern Italy and Sicily, North Africa, and along the Black Sea. Greek settlements in the east were fewer, perhaps because the monarchies there restricted foreign immigration.

Citizenship and Freedom in the Greek City-State

The Greek city-state was a new form of political organization because all free inhabitants were considered citizens, and all male citizens could usually participate in governing. Some historians argue that the Greeks modeled their city-states on the older city-states on the island of Cyprus and in Phoenicia in the Levant, but this conclusion seems flawed because those city-states were ruled by kings and were not based on the concept of free citizens sharing power in governing. The most famous ancient analyst of Greek politics and society, the philosopher Aristotle (384–322 B.C.E.), insisted, "Humans are beings who by nature live in a city-state." Anyone who existed outside such a community, Aristotle concluded, must be either a simple fool or superhuman. Greeks founded more than a thousand separate city-states, most with populations ranging from several hundred to several thousand citizens.

Citizenship was a new concept because it assumed a basic level of political and legal equality—above all, the expectation of equal treatment under the law for citizens regardless of their social status or wealth. Women had the protection of the law, but they were barred from participation in politics on the assumption that female judgment was inferior to male. The most dramatic indication of political equality in a Greek city-state was the right of all adult male citizens to vote on laws and policies in a political assembly. Not all city-states reached this level of power sharing and participation, however. In some, the social elite kept a stranglehold on politics, with a small group or, more rarely, a single person or family dominating. Greeks called rule by a small elite group oligarchy, and rule by one person tyranny.

Although the Greeks' ideas of citizenship and equality before the law remained imperfect by modern Western standards, the fact that they developed these concepts at all is remarkable because legal inequality between rich and poor in the free population was the rule in the ancient Near East and in Greece itself before the polis came into existence. Given the lack of precedent, how and why the poor in Greece gained citizenship and equality before the law remains a mystery. The greatest population increase in the late Dark Age and in the Archaic Age occurred in the ranks of the poor. These families raised more children to help farm more land, which otherwise would have lain idle because of the depopulation brought on by the worst of the Dark Age. There was no precedent for extending even limited political and legal power to this growing segment of the population, but most Greek city-states did so.

For a long time, historians attributed the general widening of political and legal rights to a so-called hoplite revolution, but recent research undermines this theory. Hoplites were infantrymen who wore metal body armor, carrying a large shield in one hand and wielding a spear in the other. They constituted the main strike force of the volunteer militia that defended each city-state. In the eighth century B.C.E., a growing number of men could afford to buy hoplite equipment (the use of iron had cut its cost). It seems likely that the new hoplites believed they were entitled to a say in politics because they bought their own equipment and voluntarily trained hard to defend their communities. According to the hoplite revolution theory, the new hoplites forced the social elite to share political power by threatening to refuse to serve in the militia. The problem with that theory is that hoplites were not poor. How, then, did poor men, too, win political rights, especially the vote in the assembly? It is perhaps possible that modern historians underestimate the military importance of the poor men who fought in the army as unarmed fighters, disrupting the enemy's infantry by hurling barrages of rocks, and that the poor earned the vote for this service. Whatever the reason for the designation of poor men as citizens with roughly the same rights as the rich, this unprecedented decision constituted the most innovative feature of the transformation of Greek society in the Archaic Age.

A Hoplite's Breastplate
This bronze armor protected the chest of a sixth-century B.C.E. hoplite. It had to be fitted to his individual body; the design is meant to match the musculature of his chest and symbolize his manliness. The Greek soldier would have worn a cloth or leather shirt underneath to prevent the worst chafing, but such a heavy and hot device could never be comfortable, and soldiers often removed them despite the danger. A slave would have carried the soldier's armor for him until the moment of battle, when he would have donned his protective gear just before facing the enemy. (Olympia Museum © Archaeological Receipts Fund.)

As the notion of the citizen's freedom became stronger, the practice of slavery—the opposite of freedom—became ever more widespread in Archaic Age Greece. Individual Greeks and the city-states themselves owned slaves. Public slaves sometimes lived on their own, performing specialized tasks such as detecting counterfeit coins. Temple slaves "belonged" to the deity of the temple, for whom they worked as servants. Private slaves totaled perhaps a third of the population by the fifth century B.C.E. They did all sorts of jobs, from household chores to crafts production to farm labor. Their masters controlled their lives and could punish them or demand sexual favors at will. Most owners did not brutalize their slaves because that damaged their human property. Slaves lacked any right to family life and had no property or legal rights. As Aristotle put it, slaves were "living tools." Sometimes owners let slaves earn money to purchase their freedom, or promised freedom at a future date to encourage hard work. Slaves who gained their freedom did not become citizens but instead joined the population of noncitizens officially allowed to live in the city-state. Despite the bitter nature of their existence, Greek slaves rarely revolted on a large scale except in Sparta, perhaps because elsewhere they were of too many different origins and nationalities to organize. No Greek is known to have called for the abolition of slavery.

Women, like slaves, lacked the right of political participation in the city-state. Freeborn women, however, counted as citizens, enjoyed the protection of the laws, and—in a crucial role respected by everyone—performed numerous religious functions. Citizen women had recourse to the courts in disputes over property, although

A Greek Woman at an Altar
This vase painting from the center of a large drinking cup shows a woman in rich clothing pouring a libation to the gods onto a flaming altar. In her other arm, she carries some sort of religious object. This scene illustrates the most important and frequent role of women in Greek public life: participating in religious ceremonies, both at home and in community festivals. This painting style is called red figure because the picture's details are painted over the reddish color of the baked clay, which shows through to depict the surfaces of the figures, such as skin or clothing. (The Toledo Museum of Art, Toledo, Ohio. Purchased with funds from the Libbey Endowment, Gift of Edward Drummond Libbey [1972.55].)

they usually had to have a man speak for them. Before marriage, a woman's father served as her legal guardian; after marriage, her husband did. The paternalism of Greek society—men acting as "fathers" to regulate the lives of women and safeguard their interests as men defined them—demanded that all women have male guardians to protect them physically and legally.

The expansion of slavery in the Archaic Age added new responsibilities for women by increasing the size and complexity of households. While their husbands farmed, participated in politics, and met with their male friends, wives managed the household by raising children, supervising the cooking, keeping the family's financial accounts, making clothing, directing the slaves, and tending them and other family members when they were ill. Poor women also worked outside the home, tilling gardens and selling produce and small goods such as ribbons and trinkets in the market found at the center of every settlement. Women rich and poor attended funerals, state festivals, and public rituals, and they controlled cults reserved exclusively for female worshippers. Their religious functions gave them freedom of movement and prestige. At Athens, for example, by the fifth century B.C.E. elite women officiated as priestesses for more than forty different deities and enjoyed benefits such as salaries paid by the state.

Greek patriarchy allowed men to control human reproduction and therefore the inheritance of property. Families arranged marriages, and everyone was expected to marry and produce children. The bride brought to the marriage a dowry of property (land yielding an income, if she was wealthy) that her children would inherit. Her husband was legally obligated to preserve this dowry and to return it to his wife if they divorced. A husband could divorce his wife at will. Legally, a wife could leave her husband on her own initiative to return to the guardianship of her male relatives, but her husband could force her to stay if her family refused to help her. Except in certain cases in Sparta, monogamous marriage was the rule in Greece, as was a nuclear family (that is, husband, wife, and children living together without other relatives in the same house). Citizen men could have sexual relations without penalty with slaves, foreign concubines, female prostitutes, or willing preadult citizen males. Citizen women, single or married, had no such freedom. Sex between a married woman and anyone other than her husband carried harsh penalties for both parties.

Sparta was the Greek city-state that went the farthest in supporting community values. Spartans placed obedience and discipline above individual desires because Sparta's survival was threatened by rebellion from its economic foundation: the great mass of slaves called helots, who were owned by the community and did almost all the work. Helots were Greeks from neighboring towns and regions that the Spartans had conquered. The helots greatly outnumbered Sparta's citizens, so Spartans had to spend their lives training to defend against the helots as well as foreign enemies. Helots toiled as farmers and servants so that Spartan men and women would not have to stoop to manual labor. Spartan men wore their hair very long to show that they were "gentlemen" warriors, not laborers.

Sparta's helots faced constant violence and humiliation. Every year Spartan officials formally declared war on them so that a citizen could kill without penalty any helot thought to be disobedient or dangerous. Spartans devoted their lives to constant preparation for war. Boys left home at age seven to live in barracks, drilling and eating together to learn discipline. Any youth unable to complete the harsh training fell into disgrace and lost citizen rights. Adolescent boys in Sparta often were involved in homosexual relationships with older men. A boy would be chosen as a special favorite by a man to promote love for a fellow soldier at whose side he would one day march into battle; their relationship could include sex. The elder partner was supposed to help educate the young man in politics and community values and not just exploit him for physical pleasure. Both were expected to marry women. Homoerotic sex between adult males was considered disgraceful, as it was between women of all ages (at least according to the reports of men).

Sparta and the Peloponnese, c. 750–500 B.C.E.

Spartan women were known throughout the Greek world for their various freedoms, including property ownership and being able to exercise in public in short outfits. Citizen women were expected to use their liberty from manual labor to stay fit so they could bear healthy children to sustain the Spartan population. They could own property, including land. Women also were expected to teach their children Spartan values. One mother became legendary for handing her son his shield on the eve of battle and sternly telling him, "Come back with it—or on it!"

Athens exemplified a greater concern for the value and values of the individual. During the Archaic Age, it took the first steps toward democracy, a new system of government that gave equal political and legal rights to all male citizens, and toward an economy based on international trade by sea. In 594 B.C.E., an economic crisis that pitted rich against poor unexpectedly promoted change when Solon, appointed as a mediator, outlawed debt slavery and created a council to guide the legislative work of the assembly. The council's members were chosen by lottery and could serve only two annual terms (not in succession), ensuring wide participation. Equally important was Solon's decision to empower any citizen to bring charges in court on behalf of any victim and to appeal any magistrate's judgments to the assembly. These reforms gave ordinary citizens a real share in the administration of justice. Finally, Solon convinced the Athenians to improve the economy by exporting olive oil.

Some elite Athenians vehemently opposed Solon's political reforms because they wanted oligarchy. The unrest they caused opened the door temporarily to tyranny in Athens, and the family of Peisistratus held power from 546 to 510 B.C.E. by championing the interests of the poor. A rival elite family finally got the tyranny overthrown by denouncing it as unjust and inducing the Spartans, the self-proclaimed defenders of Greek freedom, to "liberate" Athens. Cleisthenes, an ambitious politician, found that he could win prominence only by promising greater democracy to the masses. Beginning in 508 B.C.E., he delivered on his promises and came to be remembered as "the father of Athenian democracy" for his reforms. His complex political reorganization achieved its goal of promoting participation in governance by as many male citizens as possible. It would take another fifty years of controversy before Athens's democracy reached its full form, but Cleisthenes' changes opened the way to an unprecedented way of life based on people persuading, not compelling, each other to achieve common goals. Athenian citizens believed in the rule of law, but they chose individual freedom and responsibility for themselves (though not for their slaves) over forced social regimentation like that in Sparta.

New Ways of Thought and Expression

A spirit of intellectual change spread across Greece in the late Archaic Age that corresponded to the political idea that persuasion, not force or social status, should motivate people's decisions. In city-states all over the Greek world, new ways of thought inspired artists, poets, and philosophers. Ongoing contacts with the Near East exposed the Greeks to traditions from which to learn and create something new. Artists became expert at rendering increasingly realistic three-dimensional figures. Sculptors made their statues less stiff and more varied, from gracefully clothed young women to muscular male nudes, and made them come alive with gleaming paint.

Poets expanded the Near Eastern tradition of expressing personal emotions in poetry by developing lyric poetry, a new type of verse similar to popular songs

**Archaic Age Sculpture
of a Dead Warrior**
This Athenian marble statue dating from
about 530–520 B.C.E. shows the stiff posture and smiling expression that Archaic
Age Greek sculptors used for "heroic
nudes" portraying dead young men. These
statues had a striding stance recalling the
style of Egyptian art and were painted
in bright colors. This one, standing six
feet four inches tall, retains traces of red
paint. An inscription on its base addressed people passing by: "Stand and
weep at this monument of Croesus, now
dead. Raging Ares [the Greek war god]
destroyed him battling in the front line."
(The Art Archive/National Archaeological Museum
Athens/Dagli Orti.)

and stressing individual feelings. Composed in diverse rhythms and performed to
the music of a lyre (a kind of harp that gives its name to the poetry), Greek lyric
poems could be short and for one singer, or long and for a chorus. Archilochus of
Paros, who lived in the early 600s B.C.E., became infamous for his unheroic lines
about throwing down his shield in battle so he could flee to save his life: "Oh, the
hell with it; I can get another one just as good." Sappho, a lyric poet from Lesbos
born about 630 B.C.E., became famous for her love poems, writing, "Some would say
the most beautiful thing on our dark earth is an army of cavalry, others of infantry,
others of ships, but I say it's whatever a person loves." In this poem Sappho was
expressing her longing for a woman she loved, who was far away.

Greek philosophers in the Archaic Age developed radically new explanations
of the nature of the universe and the role of the gods. Most of these thinkers came
from Ionia. This location placed them in close contact with Near Eastern knowledge, especially astronomy, mathematics, and myth. Because there were no formal
schools, pupils who studied privately with these philosophers helped spread the new
ideas. Inspired by Babylonian astronomy, Ionian Greek philosophers expressed the

bold idea that laws of nature, not the whims of individual gods, governed the universe. Pythagoras, who emigrated from the island of Samos to the Greek city-state Croton in southern Italy about 530 B.C.E., taught that patterns and relationships of numbers explained the entire world and promoted the systematic study of mathematics and its relation to music.

Ionia and the Aegean,
c. 750–500 B.C.E.

Ionian philosophers insisted that they could discover the workings of the universe because nature was not random but in fact determined by what we today call the laws of physics or laws of nature. They named the universe *cosmos*, meaning an orderly arrangement that is beautiful. The order of the cosmos encompassed not only the motions of stars and planets but also the weather, the growth of plants and animals, human health, and so on. Because the universe was ordered, it could be understood, and its events could be explained by thought and research. Early Greek philosophers, therefore, looked for the first or universal cause of things, a problem that scientists still pursue. The philosophers who taught these ideas about the cosmos believed they needed to give reasons for their conclusions and to persuade others by arguments based on evidence. That is, they used logic. This mode of thought, called **rationalism**, was a crucial first step toward science and philosophy as these disciplines exist today. The rule-based explanation of the causes of things developed by these philosophers contrasted sharply with the traditional mythological explanation that the gods' wishes controlled the universe. Naturally, many people had difficulty accepting such a startling change in their understanding of the world, and the older tradition explaining events as the will of different gods lived on alongside the new idea, which did not deny the existence of the divine but insisted that discoverable truths determined the course of events.

The Ionian philosophers' most important achievement was the idea that people must give reasons to justify their beliefs, rather than just make assertions that others must accept without evidence. This insistence on logic as the key to understanding the world gave people hope that they could improve their lives through their own efforts. As Xenophanes from Colophon (c. 580–480 B.C.E.) put it, "The gods have not revealed all things from the beginning to mortals, but, by seeking, human beings find out, in time, what is better." This saying well expressed the value Archaic Age Greek philosophers attached to intellectual freedom, a new idea corresponding to the value given to the new ideals of the individual citizen's freedom and legal equality as guaranteed in the community of the city-state.

REVIEW   How did Greek life change in the Archaic Age?

Conclusion

In a sense, civilization emerged as an accident of climate change. Stone Age people existed for a long time before the features of life that historians associate with civilization slowly developed when global warming made agriculture and domestication of animals possible (the so-called Neolithic Revolution). That, in turn, led to vastly growing populations and settled farming communities, which led to the formation of cities and political states. Eventually some of the states in the Near East became imperial giants, while others, especially the later Greek city-states, remained small. Most ancient states were ruled as monarchies, perhaps reflecting the religious belief that a king ruled the gods and that this was therefore the proper form for rule. Political diversity nevertheless developed when some Greeks decided to be governed as citizens in democracies, an unprecedented decision stressing individual values that created a kind of egalitarian society (at least for citizen men) not seen since early Paleolithic times. Intellectual diversity also emerged in Greece with the creation of rationalism to explain the world and its workings based on reason and persuasion rather than myth. Religious change

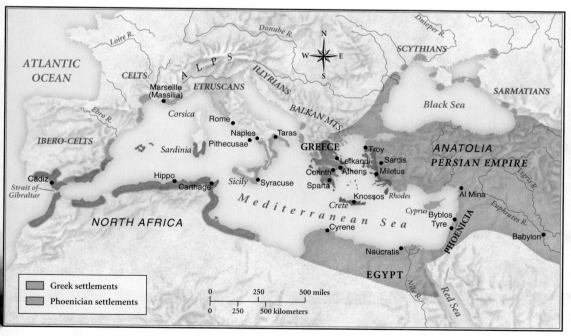

Mapping the West Mediterranean Civilizations, c. 500 B.C.E.
At the end of the sixth century B.C.E., the Persian Empire was far and away the most powerful civilization touching the Mediterranean. Its vast territory and riches gave it resources that no Phoenician or Greek city could match. The Phoenicians dominated economically in the western Mediterranean, while the Greek city-states in Sicily and southern Italy rivaled the power of those in the heartland. In Italy, the Etruscans were the most powerful civilization; the Romans were still a small community struggling to replace monarchy with a republic.

came with the creation of monotheism by the Hebrews (perhaps influenced by Persian Zoroastrianism). The Hebrews' development of a scripture-based monotheistic religion was a development second to none in its consequences for later history.

Some patterns of life that dated back to the Stone Age persisted after the emergence of civilization, especially the importance of social hierarchy, religion, trade, and war. Long-distance trade grew when private commerce developed, and commercial exchange was a powerful mechanism for cultural interchange. Both ideas and technologies, from writing to metallurgy, were spread among diverse peoples by trade and also by the unintended consequences of war. Although people may not have always intended to share their knowledge, their desires for the goods that trade and conquest could win and for the excitement that travel and foreign adventure could generate led to the depth and breadth of interchange and interaction that created the first stages of Western civilization.

CHAPTER REVIEW QUESTIONS
1. How did life in the Greek city-state differ from that in earlier Mesopotamian and Egyptian civilization?
2. How were the ideas of Ionian philosophers different from mythic traditions?

For practice quizzes and other study tools, see the Online Study Guide at bedfordstmartins.com/huntconcise.

For primary-source material from this period, see Chapters 1 and 2 of *Sources of THE MAKING OF THE WEST*, Third Edition.

TIMELINE

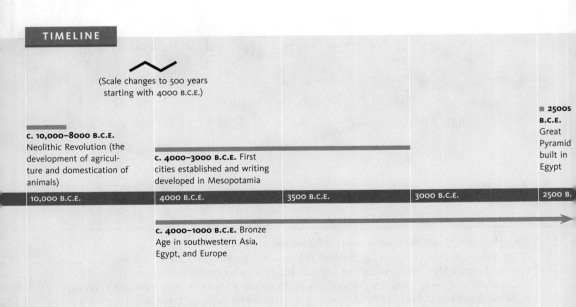

(Scale changes to 500 years starting with 4000 B.C.E.)

C. 10,000–8000 B.C.E. Neolithic Revolution (the development of agriculture and domestication of animals)

C. 4000–3000 B.C.E. First cities established and writing developed in Mesopotamia

■ **2500S B.C.E.** Great Pyramid built in Egypt

| 10,000 B.C.E. | 4000 B.C.E. | 3500 B.C.E. | 3000 B.C.E. | 2500 B. |

C. 4000–1000 B.C.E. Bronze Age in southwestern Asia, Egypt, and Europe

Suggested References

*Primary sources are indicated with an asterisk.

Archaeological excavation is our best resource for understanding the long period of history from the Stone Age to the rise of the Greek city-state.

Ancient Olympic Games: http://www.perseus.tufts.edu/Olympics/

*Barnes, Jonathan. *Early Greek Philosophy.* 1987.

Brosius, Maria. *Women in Ancient Persia (559–331 B.C.).* 1996.

Bryce, Trevor. *The Kingdom of the Hittites.* 1998.

*Dalley, Stephanie, trans. *Myths from Mesopotamia: Creation, the Flood, Gilgamesh, and Others.* 1991.

Ehrenberg, Margaret. *Women in Prehistory.* 1989.

Hodos, Tamar. *Local Responses to Colonization in the Iron Age Mediterranean.* 2006.

Moore, A. M. T. *Village on the Euphrates: From Foraging to Farming at Abu Hureyra.* 2000.

Nigosian, S. A. *The Zoroastrian Faith: Tradition and Modern Research.* 1993.

Osborne, Robin. *Greece in the Making, 1200–479 B.C.* 1996.

Szapakowska, Kasia. *Daily Life in Ancient Egypt: Recreating Lahun.* 2008.

Virtual Museum of Nautical Archaeology (including the Uluburun shipwreck): http://ina.tamu.edu/vm.htm

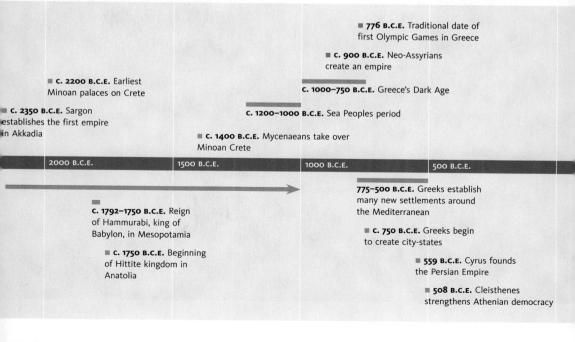

776 B.C.E. Traditional date of first Olympic Games in Greece

C. 900 B.C.E. Neo-Assyrians create an empire

C. 2200 B.C.E. Earliest Minoan palaces on Crete

C. 1000–750 B.C.E. Greece's Dark Age

C. 2350 B.C.E. Sargon establishes the first empire in Akkadia

C. 1200–1000 B.C.E. Sea Peoples period

C. 1400 B.C.E. Mycenaeans take over Minoan Crete

| 2000 B.C.E. | 1500 B.C.E. | 1000 B.C.E. | 500 B.C.E. |

775–500 B.C.E. Greeks establish many new settlements around the Mediterranean

C. 1792–1750 B.C.E. Reign of Hammurabi, king of Babylon, in Mesopotamia

C. 750 B.C.E. Greeks begin to create city-states

C. 1750 B.C.E. Beginning of Hittite kingdom in Anatolia

559 B.C.E. Cyrus founds the Persian Empire

508 B.C.E. Cleisthenes strengthens Athenian democracy

The Greek Golden Age

C. 500–400 B.C.E.

THE PROSPERITY AND INDEPENDENCE that Greece had achieved in the Archaic Age (750–500 B.C.E.) almost came to an abrupt end. In 507 B.C.E., the Athenians, fearing a Spartan invasion, sent ambassadors to the Persian king, Darius I (r. 522–486 B.C.E.), to request a protective alliance. The Persian Empire was then the greatest power in the ancient world. The diplomats met with one of the king's governors in the western region of the empire, an area in Anatolia (modern Turkey) inhabited by Greeks. After the royal administrator heard their plea, he replied, "But who in the world are you and where do you live?" This incident hints at the dangers that threatened Greece at the time. First, the two major powers of mainland Greece—Athens and Sparta—were hostile to each other. Second, the Persian kingdom was expanding westward and had already conquered the Ionian Greeks in Anatolia. Yet neither the Persians nor the mainland Greeks knew much about each other. This mutual ignorance sparked a bloody conflict between Persia and Greece that we call the Persian Wars (499–479 B.C.E.), which were then followed by decades of war between the Greek city-states throughout the rest of the fifth century B.C.E.

This century of almost continuous war became the period of Greece's most enduring cultural and artistic achievements, which raises the question of the direct and indirect effects of war on civilization. Athenian political, social, and cultural accomplishments in the fifth century B.C.E. had such a lasting impact that historians call this period the Golden Age. This Golden Age opens the Classical Age of Greek history, a modern title that covers the period from about 500 B.C.E. to the death of Alexander the Great in 323 B.C.E.

A Greek Warrior Leaves Home for Battle

This vase, made about 450 B.C.E. to hold wine, shows a well-armed Greek infantryman (hoplite) leaving for battle. The vase painter portrayed the warrior in full armor to make the scene more dramatic. In real life, a slave would have carried the nearly seventy pounds of metal armor to the battlefield, where the soldier would have put it on at the last minute. The warrior holds a thrusting spear, his main battle weapon, but also wears a sword from a strap over his shoulder for close-in fighting. The man on the left is probably the warrior's father, his age indicated by his cane. The woman is probably his wife, who is ready both to pour a libation to the gods for her husband's safety and to give him a last drink before he leaves home on his dangerous mission.

(© Copyright The Trustees of The British Museum.)

Athenians in the Golden Age created Greece's leading state, developing a "radical" democracy at home while establishing a regional empire. They achieved economic prosperity and produced artistic and cultural accomplishments that dazzled the Greek world. While other commercially oriented city-states also became prosperous in this period, it was Golden Age Athens that created innovations in drama, art, architecture, and thought that have deeply influenced Western civilization up to the present. Some of these changes angered Greeks at the time, however, because they conflicted with traditional ideas, especially people's religious fear that abandoning their ancestors' beliefs and practices would anger the gods and bring down divine punishment.

The Peloponnesian War, a bitter struggle between Athens and Sparta that dragged on from 431 to 404 B.C.E., ended the Golden Age. This period of cultural blossoming therefore both began and finished with destructive wars, with Greeks standing together in the first one and tearing each other apart in the concluding one.

CHAPTER FOCUS QUESTION What were the direct and indirect consequences of war on Athens in the fifth century B.C.E.?

The Persian Wars, 499–479 B.C.E.

Bad diplomacy sparked the Persian Wars. At their meeting with the Persian regional governor, the Athenian ambassadors accepted the Persian terms for an alliance: formally submitting to Persian authority by presenting symbolic tokens of earth and water. Although the Athenian assembly became angry when they discovered that their diplomats had submitted to a foreign power, they never informed the Persian king Darius that they were rejecting the alliance. He therefore continued to believe that Athens remained an obedient ally. This misunderstanding eventually led to two Persian invasions of Greece, the so-called Persian Wars.

Since the Persian Empire dwarfed the city-states of Greece in every resource, from gold to soldiers, war between this huge empire and these usually small communities was like a fight between an elephant and a pack of undersized dogs. Making the situation grimmer was the Greek city-states' tendency to fight one another instead of cooperating. Greek victory in such a mismatch seemed unthinkable.

The Ionian Revolt and the Battle of Marathon, 499–490 B.C.E.

The Persian Wars began in 499 B.C.E., when the Ionian Greek city-states tried to regain their independence by revolting against Persia. Athens sent troops to aid the rebels, but a Persian counterattack sent them fleeing and crushed the revolt by 494 B.C.E. (Map 2.1). King Darius erupted when he learned that the Athenians had aided the Ionian Revolt: not only had they dared attack his kingdom, but they had done it, as far as he knew, after submitting to his authority. To remind himself to punish these traitors, Darius ordered a slave to say to him three times at every meal, "Master, remember the Athenians."

Map 2.1 The Persian Wars, 499–479 B.C.E.

The Persian Wars originated in the failed revolt (499–494 B.C.E.) of the Greek city-states in Ionia against Persian control. To punish the Greeks, the Persian king Darius (r. 522–486 B.C.E.) first sent an expedition by sea, whose infantry the Athenians defeated on the Marathon plain in 490 B.C.E. Darius's son Xerxes (r. 486–465 B.C.E.) then led a mammoth invasion of Greece, starting from Sardis in Ionia. The Persians' unexpected naval defeat at Salamis (480 B.C.E.) and their defeats on land at Plataea and Mycale (479 B.C.E.) ended the Persians' attempt to extend their empire into Europe. Compare the relative sizes of Greece and the Persian Empire to get an idea of how bold it was for Greeks to attack Persians in Asia.

In 490 B.C.E., Darius sent a fleet to punish the Athenians; he expected them to surrender without a fight. The Athenians, however, confronted the imperial invaders at Marathon, on the northeastern coast of Athenian territory. The Athenian soldiers, who had never before encountered Persians, grew nervous just seeing their strange (to Greek eyes) outfits—pants instead of the short tunics and bare legs that Greeks regarded as manly dress. The Greek commanders sent their hoplites (heavily armed infantry) against the enemy at a dead run, to shorten the time that Persian archers could shoot at them. The Greeks stomped across the Marathon plain in their clanking metal armor (seventy pounds per man) under a hail of arrows to engage the Persians in hand-to-hand combat. The Greeks' heavier thrusting spears and swords gave them the edge, and they drove their opponents backward into a swamp and slaughtered the Persians who failed to splash their way to their ships.

The Athenian army then hurried the twenty-six miles from Marathon to Athens to guard the city against a Persian naval attack. (Today's marathons recall the legendary run of a messenger who raced ahead to announce the victory, after which he dropped dead from exhaustion.) The Persians then sailed home, leaving the Athenians to rejoice in disbelief at their victory. The greatest honor a family could claim was that one of its men had once been a "Marathon fighter."

The symbolic importance of the battle of Marathon outweighed its military significance. The expedition's defeat enraged Darius because it injured his prestige, but it did not threaten his empire. The Athenians' success demonstrated the depth of their commitment to preserve their freedom. The unexpected victory at Marathon boosted Athenian self-confidence, and the city-state's citizens ever after boasted that they had withstood the feared Persians on their own, without Sparta's help.

The Persian Invasion of 480–479 B.C.E.

The Greeks' dedication to freedom was never more evident than when Darius's son and successor, Xerxes (r. 486–465 B.C.E.), invaded Greece in 480 B.C.E. to avenge his father's defeat. So immense was Xerxes' army, the Greeks claimed, that it took seven days and nights to cross a pontoon bridge over the Hellespont, the narrow strait between Anatolia and mainland Greece. Xerxes expected the Greek city-states to surrender immediately once they learned the size of his forces. Some did, but thirty-one city-states united to fight the Persians. This alliance, known as the Hellenic League, accomplished the incredible: protecting their independence from the world's superpower.

The united Greeks chose Sparta as their leader because of its famous hoplite army. The Spartans demonstrated their courage when three hundred of their men held off Xerxes' huge army for several days at the narrow pass called Thermopylae (warm gates) in central Greece. A warrior summed up Spartan bravery with his response to a remark that the Persian archers were so numerous that their arrows darkened the sky in battle. "That's good news," he said. "We'll get to fight in the shade." The Spartans died holding their position.

Luck and courage characterized Athenian participation in the war. The fortunate discovery of rich silver ore in their territory a few years earlier gave the Athenians the money to build a fleet of two hundred warships. The state claimed mineral rights, and the commander, Themistocles, persuaded the democratic assembly to vote to spend the mining revenue for national defense instead of making payments to citizens. Courage and a dedication to freedom led the Athenians to evacuate their city instead of surrendering when the Persians marched on Athens. Themistocles then tricked the other, less aggressive Greek leaders into facing the larger Persian navy in a sea battle in the narrow channel between the island of Salamis and the west coast of Athenian territory. The narrowness of the channel prevented the Persians from using all their ships at once and let the heavier Greek ships, each rowed into battle by a crew of 170, win by ramming the flimsier Persian vessels. When Xerxes observed that his most aggressive naval commander appeared to be the one woman among the admirals, Artemisia, ruler of Caria in Anatolia, he shouted, "My men have become women, and my women, men." In 479 B.C.E., the Greek infantry, headed by the Spartans, defeated the remaining Persian land forces at Plataea (Map 2.1, page 49).

The victory in the Persian Wars produced social and political consequences

A Persian Royal Guard
This life-size panel formed part of the decoration of a courtyard in a palace built by the Persian king Darius I. The warrior shown here perhaps represents one of the elite royal guards known as "immortals." An inscription records that the craftsmen who made these panels came from Babylon in Mesopotamia, which was part of the far-flung Persian Empire. (The Granger Collection, NY.)

in Athens. The war effort had cut across social and economic divisions because the city-state's forces included not only the social elite and hoplites but also the thousands of poorer men who rowed Athens's warships. The pride and confidence

REVIEW   What factors led to and determined the outcome of the Persian Wars?

these men earned from their military service led them to expect greater influence in Athenian society and democracy.

Athenian Empire and Democracy in the Golden Age, 479–431 B.C.E.

Following the Persian Wars, Athens became the most famous Greek city-state by establishing the so-called Athenian Empire, a modern label for the regional alliance that Athens dominated, and by creating what modern scholars call **radical democracy**, meaning that male citizens participated actively in governing and voted not only to elect leaders but also to set policy and enforce justice. The growth of Athens's international power, along with its silver mines, brought in greatly increased revenues that the Athenian assembly voted to spend on public buildings, art, and festivals.

The Establishment of the Athenian Empire, 479–460 B.C.E.

The Athenian Empire arose following the Persian Wars when Sparta and Athens became enemies instead of allies. Sparta already headed an alliance of Greek city-states called the Peloponnesian League, and Athens needed similar support to rival the power of Sparta and also be ready to face the Persians if necessary. (The Persian Empire remained potent and could strike back at any time.)

In 477 b.c.e., therefore, Athens allied with city-states whose locations exposed them to possible Persian retaliation—in northern Greece, on the islands of the Aegean Sea, and along the western coast of Anatolia. Most of the allies started out with strong navies, and all solemnly swore never to desert the coalition. The alliance, called the **Delian League** because its treasury was originally located on the island of Delos, also had an assembly. At this point, every ally had an equal say in making decisions.

The special arrangements for financing the alliance's naval operations allowed the Athenians in time to dominate the alliance and thus establish an "empire." Each ally paid annual "dues" based on its size and prosperity. Because they were required, these dues were actually "tribute." Larger member states supplied triremes (the premier warships) with rowers and their pay (Figure 2.1); smaller states shared the cost of a ship and crew or contributed cash instead. Over time, more and more members paid cash because they found it too demanding to build warships and train crews. (The modern construction and launching in Greece of a full-size, operating trireme rowed by volunteers has demonstrated the enormous skill and

The Delian and Peloponnesian Leagues

Figure 2.1 Triremes, the Foremost Classical Greek Warships
Innovations in military technology and training fueled a naval arms race in the fifth century B.C.E., when Greek shipbuilders devised larger and faster ramming ships called triremes. The boats were powered by 170 rowers seated in three rows, one above the other as shown in the illustration of the rowers from behind (top). These ships' radical new design with triple banks of oars made them expensive to build and required extensive crew training. Only wealthy and populous city-states such as Athens could afford to maintain large fleets of triremes. No ancient trireme survives to show exactly how such a warship was built, but this relief sculpture (bottom) found on the Athenian acropolis and dating from about 400 B.C.E. gives a glimpse of what a trireme looked like from the side when being rowed into battle. Sails were used to power the ship only when not in combat. (The Art Archive/Acropolis Museum Athens/Dagli Orti.)

practice required.) Athens, far larger than most league members, possessed the necessary shipyards as well as many poorer men eager to earn pay as rowers.

The Delian League turned into the Athenian Empire because most Delian League allies stopped furnishing triremes and paid Athens to build ships for the alliance. With no navies of their own, they could not defend themselves against Athens if they disagreed with league policy or wanted to stop paying tribute. As the Athenian historian Thucydides observed, rebellious allies "lost their independence," and the Athenians became "no longer as popular as they used to be." This unpopularity was the price Athenians paid for making themselves the leading naval power in the eastern Mediterranean. They insisted that their dominance of the Delian League was justified because it kept the alliance strong enough to protect Greece from the Persians, and they were right about the alliance's effectiveness. By 460 B.C.E., their fleet had driven the enemy from the Aegean Sea region, quashing any Persian threat to Greece for the next fifty years.

The consequences of their surprising success in war led the Athenians to experience an inflation of their expectations. A sea-based empire proved irresistible. Crucially, it allowed Athens to defend the trade routes needed to import the food necessary to feed a growing population that could no longer be supported by local agriculture. In addition, Athenians acquired riches by plundering Persian outposts, exacting tribute from allies, and collecting taxes from the commerce in grain, olive oil, wine, pottery, sculpture, metals, and slaves that thrived across the Mediterranean Sea. Other city-states, such as Megara and Corinth, also flourished as a result of maritime trade in this period, but Athens grew richer than them all. The Athenian assembly, made up of male citizens over age eighteen, decided how to spend the city-state's increasing revenues. Poor and rich alike therefore had a stake in keeping the fleet active and the league members paying for it. The poor men who rowed the ships came to depend on the pay they earned on league expeditions. Members of the social elite enhanced their social status by commanding campaigns and spending their portion of the plunder on public festivals and buildings to win public recognition, which they craved more than wealth. Debates over policy in the assembly concerned how Athens should spend the money it was taking in, not whether it was just to compel formerly free allies to remain tribute-paying subjects of the empire.

Radical Democracy and Pericles' Leadership, 461–445 B.C.E.

The establishment of Athenian empire led to radical democracy because the poorer men who rowed the Athenian navy, recognizing their essential role in securing Athens's security and prosperity, gained more political power by voting for leaders who supported their demands. The first change they demanded was making the judicial system of Athens just as democratic as the process of passing laws in the assembly. Members of the elite led this initiative, whether because they believed it was the people's just reward or because they wanted the esteem bestowed on leaders—or perhaps for both these reasons. Pericles (c. 495–429 B.C.E.), one of Athens's most socially prominent citizens, became the leading Golden Age politician by supporting the popular desire for greater democracy.

Government in Golden Age Athens gradually became so thoroughly shared by male citizens that today it is called radical democracy. Its principles were clear: equal protection under the law for all citizens regardless of wealth; direct and widespread participation in the assembly to make laws and policy by majority rule; random selection and rotation of jurors, most officials, and the members of the Council of 500 (which prepared the agenda for the assembly); and punitive rules against corruption. There was no written constitution and no protection for minority rights; the assembly could make any decision it desired. The need for competence and excellence at the highest level of government was recognized in two ways: first, by filling the top public offices—the ten "generals," who managed the city-state's military and financial affairs—not by a lottery but by election to an annual term;

second, by not setting a limit on how many terms a man could serve. The generals' power, however, remained subject to constant democratic scrutiny: any citizen could demand a full investigation of a general's conduct in office.

Reforming the justice system was essential to creating radical democracy. Ever since Cleisthenes' reforms at the end of the sixth century B.C.E., certain officials and ex-officials had rendered most judicial verdicts. Although these officials were now chosen annually by lottery to make their selection democratic, they were still susceptible to bribery and pressure from the social elite. Since even democratically enacted laws meant little if applied unfairly, the masses demanded reforms to halt unfair or corrupt judgments.

The opportunity for change arose in 461 B.C.E., when a prominent member of the elite sought the people's political support by sponsoring a reformed court system based on randomly selected juries. His reforms made it nearly impossible to bribe or pressure jurors. They were chosen by lottery from male citizens over thirty years old, the selection was made only on the day of the trial, all trials were concluded in one day, and juries were large (from several hundred to several thousand). No judges presided; only one official was present—to stop fistfights. Jurors voted after hearing speeches from the accuser and the accused, who had to speak for themselves, although they could pay someone else to compose their speeches and ask others to speak in support. A majority vote of the jurors ruled, and no appeals were allowed.

Majority rule was the operative principle for enforcing accountability in Athenian radical democracy. The most striking example of this principle was the procedure called **ostracism** (from *ostracon*, meaning a "piece of broken pottery," the material used for casting ballots). Once a year, all male citizens could scratch on a ballot the name of one man they thought should be ostracized (exiled for ten years). If at least six thousand ballots were cast, the man who received the most "votes" was expelled from Athenian territory. He suffered no other penalty, and his family and property remained behind undisturbed. Ostracism was not a criminal penalty, and ostracized men recovered their citizen rights after their exile.

Ostracism was meant to protect radical democracy; a man could, therefore, be ostracized if the majority perceived his prominence as a threat to their interests. An anecdote about the famous politician Aristides illustrates this possibility. He was nicknamed "the Just" because he had proved himself so fair-minded in setting the tribute amounts for Delian League members. On the day of the ostracism, an illiterate farmer handed Aristides a pottery fragment and asked him to scratch the name of the man's choice on it.

"Certainly," said Aristides. "Which name shall I write?"
"Aristides," replied the countryman.
"All right," replied Aristides as he proceeded to inscribe his own name.
"But tell me, why do you want to ostracize Aristides? What has he done to you?"
"Oh, nothing," sputtered the man. "I don't even know him. I just can't stand hearing everybody refer to him as 'the Just.'"

True or not, this tale demonstrates that Athenians assumed that the right way to protect democracy was always to trust the majority vote of freeborn, adult male citizens, without any restrictions on a man's ability to decide what he thought was best for democracy. It also shows that men seeking political success in Athenian democracy had to be ready to pay the price that jealousy or spite could exact.

Pericles became the most influential politician of the Golden Age by devising innovations to strengthen the egalitarian tendencies of Athenian government. Brilliant at public speaking—the most important skill for a politician in radical democracy—Pericles repeatedly persuaded the assembly to pass laws increasing its political power. In return, he gained such popularity that he was regularly elected as a general, at one point fifteen years in a row. Pericles' most important democratic innovation was pay for service in public jobs filled by lottery. This allowed poorer men to leave their regular work to serve in government. Early in the 450s B.C.E., he convinced the assembly to use state revenues to pay a daily stipend to men who served on juries, in the Council of 500, and in numerous other posts. The amount was approximately what an unskilled worker could earn in a day. The generals received no pay because the prestige of their position was considered its own reward.

Another Periclean innovation strengthened citizen identity, which was a source of pride and profit under radical democracy. In 451 B.C.E., Pericles sponsored a law making citizenship more exclusive by mandating that it would be given only to children whose mother and father were both Athenian by birth. Thereafter, men less often married foreign women (previously common among the elite), which in turn raised the social status of citizen women.

Finally, Pericles supported the interests of poorer men by recommending frequent naval attacks against enemies in Greece and against Persian control of Cyprus, Egypt, and the eastern Mediterranean. The assembly's confidence reached such a fever pitch that they voted to wage war on three different fronts simultaneously. The Athenians' ambitions at last exceeded their resources, however, and by 450 B.C.E., they had to pull back from the eastern Mediterranean and stop fighting against the Peloponnesian League. In the winter of 446–445 B.C.E., Pericles engineered a peace treaty with Sparta designed to freeze the balance of power in Greece for thirty years and thus preserve Athenian control of the Delian League. Pericles dropped his aggressive foreign policy because he realized that preserving radical democracy at home depended on Athens not losing its power over its allies.

The Urban Landscape of Golden Age Athens

The empire strengthened Athens by promoting seaborne trade from all around the Mediterranean, and the profits helped finance glorious public architecture, art, and religious festivals in the city. This splendor contrasted with the simplicity of people's homes in both the city and the countryside. In town, houses were wedged tightly against one another along narrow, winding streets. Their bedrooms, storerooms, and dining rooms were arranged around an open-air courtyard. People only rarely decorated their rooms with paintings or art, and furniture was scarce. Toilets usually consisted of a pit dug outside the front door, which was emptied by collectors paid to dump the excrement outside the city at a distance set by law. Poorer people rented small apartments.

Wealthy citizens were expected to spend money to enrich everyone's life in the city-state. Generals who became rich by raiding Persian settlements in the eastern Mediterranean used this wealth to beautify the city, not to build themselves mansions. They paid for public landscaping that included shade trees, running tracks for exercise, and gathering places that included stoas (narrow buildings open along one side whose purpose was to provide shelter from sun or rain). One successful general's family built the Painted Stoa in the heart of the city, on the edge of the **agora**, the central market square. The crowds that came to the agora daily to shop and chat about politics would cluster inside this shelter. There they could gaze at its bright paintings, which depicted the glorious exploits of the general's family and thus publicized the family's dedication to the city-state. The rich also paid for other major public expenses, such as equipment for warships and entertainment at city festivals. This custom was essential because Athens, like most Greek city-states, had no regular direct taxes on income or property.

The most prominent new architectural monuments in Golden Age Athens were huge buildings, especially temples, paid for with public funds. These building projects made a statement about the Athenians' pride in their success and their expectations for the future. Pericles persuaded the assembly to build the city's most expensive project ever on the rocky hill at the center of the city called the *acropolis* (Map 2.2). The centerpieces were a new temple of Athena on the crest of

Map 2.2 Fifth-Century B.C.E. Athens

The urban center of Athens with the agora and acropolis at its heart measured about one square mile, surrounded by a stone wall with a perimeter of some four miles. Fifteen large gates flanked by towers and various smaller doors allowed traffic in and out of the city; much of the Athenian population lived in the many villages (demes) of the surrounding countryside. Most of the city's water supply came from wells and springs inside the walls, but, unusually for a Greek city, Athens also had water piped in from outside. The Long Walls provided a protected corridor connecting the city to its harbor at Piraeus, where the Athenian navy was anchored and grain was imported to feed the people.

The Acropolis of Athens
Like most Greek city-states, Athens grew up around a prominent hill (acropolis), whose summit served as a special sanctuary for the gods and as a fortress to which the population could retreat when an enemy attacked. The invading Persians burned the buildings on the Athenian acropolis in 480 B.C.E. The Athenians left the charred remains in place for thirty years to remind themselves of the sacrifice they had made for their freedom. In the 440s B.C.E., they began erecting the magnificent temples and other public buildings that have made the city famous for its monumental marble architecture. (© akg-images, London/ John Hios.)

the hill to house a giant statue of the goddess, and a mammoth entrance building with columns straddling the western entrance of the acropolis on the way to the temple. Comparing the value of a day's wages then and now, we can calculate that these buildings easily cost more than the modern equivalent of a billion dollars, a phenomenal sum for a Greek city-state. Pericles' political rivals denounced him for squandering public funds, an example of the bitter political competition for leadership in radical Athenian democracy.

The vast new temple built for Athena—the Parthenon (the house of the virgin goddess)—was started in 447 B.C.E. and became Greece's most famous building. The Parthenon honored Athena as the divine champion of Athenian military power. Inside the temple stood a gold and ivory statue nearly forty feet high depicting the goddess in battle armor, holding in her outstretched hand a six-foot statue of Victory (*Nike* in Greek). Like all Greek temples, the Parthenon was built to be a house for its divinity, not as a gathering place for worshippers. Only priests and priestesses could usually enter the temple; public religious ceremonies took place out front. Its design followed standard temple architecture: a rectangular box on a raised platform, a plan the Greeks probably derived from Egyptian temples. Columns on a raised porch surrounded the box on all sides. The Parthenon's columns were carved in the simple style called Doric, in contrast to the more elaborate Ionic and Corinthian styles, all of which are often imitated in modern buildings (Figure 2.2).

The Parthenon, highly visible and extremely expensive, proclaimed the self-confidence of Golden Age Athens. Constructed from twenty thousand tons of Attic marble, it stretched nearly 230 feet in length and 100 feet wide. Its massive size conveyed an impression of power. The temple's sophisticated architecture demonstrated the Athenians' ability to construct order that was both apparent and real: because perfectly rectangular shapes in large-scale architecture appear curved to the human eye, subtle curves and inclines were built into the Parthenon to produce an illusion of completely straight lines and to emphasize its massiveness.

The elaborate sculptural frieze of the Parthenon announced the temple's most innovative and confident message: Athens's citizens possessed the special goodwill

Figure 2.2 Styles of Greek Capitals
The Greeks decorated the capitals, or tops, of columns in these three styles to fit the different architectural "canons" (their word for precise mathematical systems of proportions) that they devised for designing buildings. The "pillow" atop Doric columns evolved into the Ionic style sporting "ears" (volutes). Corinthian capitals with their elaborately carved leaves were a later outgrowth of Ionic. These styles were widely imitated in later times, as on many U.S. state capitols and the U.S. Supreme Court Building in Washington, D.C.

of the gods. The frieze, a continuous band of figures, was carved in relief around the top of the walls inside the porch that ran along all four sides of the building. This sort of decoration usually appeared only on Ionic-style buildings. Adding it to a Doric-style temple was a striking departure meant to attract attention. The Parthenon's frieze portrayed Athenian men, women, and children in a parade in the presence of the gods. Depicting the procession in motion, like a filmstrip in stone, the frieze included youths riding spirited horses and women carrying sacred implements. As usual on Greek temples, brightly colored paint and shiny metal attachments enlivened the figures of people and animals.

The Parthenon frieze made a unique statement about how Athenians perceived their relationship to the gods. No other city-state had ever gone beyond the traditional function of temples—glorifying and honoring the community's protector gods—by adorning a temple with representations of its citizens. A temple adorned with pictures of citizens being viewed by the gods amounted to a claim of special closeness between the city-state and the gods. This assertion reflected the Athenians' interpretation of their success in helping turn back the Persians, in achieving leadership of a powerful naval alliance, and in amassing wealth that made Athens richer than all its neighbors in mainland Greece. Their success, the Athenians believed, proved that the gods were on their side.

Like the Parthenon frieze, the changes that Golden Age artists made in freestanding sculpture broke with tradition. Archaic male statues had only one pose: arms pressed to their sides and left leg striding forward, imitating the unchanging posture of Egyptian statuary. This style gave them an appearance of stability; even a hard shove seemed unlikely to budge them. By the time of the Persian Wars, Greek sculptors began to express motion in their art. Male statues could have bent arms and the body's weight on either leg. Female statues, too, had more relaxed poses and clothing that hung in a way that hinted at the shape of the curves underneath. The faces of Golden Age sculptures were self-assuredly calm rather than smiling like Archaic Age figures. This spirited new style suggested the confident energy of the times but also hinted at the possibility of instability: Golden Age sculptors took more chances with the balance of their statues.

REVIEW   What factors prompted political change in fifth-century B.C.E. Athens?

Traditional Ways of Life and New Ideas in Athens's Golden Age

Traditional beliefs about the importance of religion in public and personal life remained strong in Golden Age Athens, as did traditional expectations about the lives of women, slaves, and resident foreigners. New ideas, however, attracted great attention in education, philosophy, history, and medicine. The appearance of teachers called **Sophists** and the ethical views of the philosopher Socrates created special controversy and tension. The most visible reflection of the tension was the growing popularity of state-funded drama, tragedies and comedies whose plots explored the problems that pride, lack of vision, and unanticipated bad luck could bring to human beings.

Traditional Public and Personal Religion

Since Greeks believed that their well-being depended on divine goodwill, religion played a central role in public life. Each city-state honored a particular god or goddess, such as Athena at Athens, as its protector and patron, while also worshipping many other deities. The community showed its religious devotion by sacrificing animals and holding festivals paid for with public funds. Individuals could find a personal relationship with the gods in the rituals of **hero cults** and **mystery cults**. The twelve most important gods were envisioned assembling for banquets atop Mount Olympus, the highest peak in mainland Greece. Zeus headed this immortal pantheon; joining him were Hera, his wife; Aphrodite, goddess of love; Apollo, sun god; Ares, war god; Artemis, moon goddess; Athena, goddess of wisdom and war; Demeter, goddess of agriculture and fertility; Dionysus, god of pleasure, wine, and disorder; Hephaestus, god of fire and technology; Hermes, messenger god; and Poseidon, sea god.

Like the peoples of the ancient Near East, the Greeks believed that humans must honor the gods to thank them for blessings received and to receive blessings in return. This idea of reciprocity between gods and humans underlay the Greeks' understanding of the nature of the gods. Deities did not love humans, though in some mythological stories they took earthly lovers and produced half-divine children. Rather, they helped humans who paid them honor and did not anger them. Gods offended by humans could punish them by sending calamities such as famine, earthquakes, epidemic diseases, or defeat in war. Greeks did not expect to achieve paradise at some future time when evil would finally be vanquished forever.

Sacrifice was the most important religious activity. As an Athenian official remarked, "Our ancestors handed down to us the most powerful and prosperous community in Greece by performing the prescribed sacrifices. It is therefore fitting for us to offer the same sacrifices they did, for the sake of the success that those rites have brought us." Each god's cult—the set of prayers and rituals for worshipping a particular divinity—had its own traditions. Sacrificing large animals such as cattle and sheep provided occasions for the community to assemble and reaffirm its ties to the divine world, and for individual worshippers to benefit from the community's relationship with the gods by sharing the roasted meat from the sacrifice. People who were not rich—the great majority of the population—particularly loved the feasting that followed a large-animal sacrifice because meat was too costly for them to buy regularly. Sacrifices could also be bloodless offerings—fruits, vegetables, and small cakes.

Public religious festivals brought the community together for worship and entertainment. Some religious occasions were for women only, such as the three-day festival for wives held to honor Demeter. Other celebrations and rituals were for everyone, featuring sacrifices and festivals with parades, plays, musical performances, and athletic competitions. Athens boasted of having the most festivals, with nearly half the days of the year featuring one. Its great festival in honor of Dionysus, the god of wine, sex, and ecstatic joy, attracted an international audience to see tragedies and comedies performed in an outdoor theater seating fifteen thousand. People all over the Greek world worshipped Dionysus for his power to bring happiness and also the knowledge of the harsh consequences of going too far in drinking and sexual activity.

Greek religion also encouraged personal devotion. Greeks believed that people received divine protection as a reward for appropriate action in worship, not just for belief. They had to perform sacrifices, pray and sing hymns praising the gods, and undergo ritual purification. Preserving these religious traditions mattered deeply to most people because they offered a safeguard against the precarious conditions of human life in a world in which early death from disease, accident, or war was commonplace. Families marked significant moments such as birth, marriage, and death with prayers, rituals, and sacrifices. They honored their ancestors with offerings made at their tombs, consulted seers about the meanings of dreams and omens, and sought out magicians for spells to improve their love lives or curses to harm their enemies.

Hero cults and mystery cults were especially important for personal religion. Hero cults were rituals performed at the tomb of an extraordinarily famous local man or woman. People believed that dead heroes could reveal the future through oracles, heal illnesses and injuries, and provide protection in battle. The only hero to whom cults were established all over the Greek world was the strongman Heracles (or Hercules, as his name was later spelled by the Romans). His superhuman feats gave him an appeal as a protector in many city-states.

Mystery cults had a special appeal because they offered the hope of protection from dangers in this life and of a better fate in the afterlife. The Athenian mystery cult of Demeter and her daughter Kore (also called Persephone), headquartered in the village of Eleusis, attracted men and women from all over the Mediterranean world. Its central rite was the Mysteries, a series of initiation ceremonies into the secret knowledge of the cult. The proof of how seriously people took these Mysteries is that no one ever revealed their secret throughout the thousand years during which the rites were celebrated.

Women, Slaves, and Metics in Traditional Society

Traditional expectations of behavior governed women's lives. Women were not confined to their homes, as scholars used to claim, but they were expected to avoid close contact with men who were not family members or good friends. In the home, women dressed and slept in rooms set aside for them that men could not enter without permission. The rooms opened onto a walled courtyard where women could walk in the open air, talk, supervise the family's slaves, manage the family's supply of food and other essentials, and interact with other members of the household and visitors, male and female. Here in her "territory," a woman would spin wool for clothing, converse with women friends, play with her children, and give her opinions on various matters to the men of the house whenever she felt like it. Rich women maintained pale complexions because they stayed out of the sun. This paleness was much admired as a sign of a life free of hard work outdoors, and women regularly used cosmetics made of powdered white lead to give themselves the desirable paleness. (People believed that this level of exposure was not dangerous; even today, no one knows precisely how much contact with lead is toxic.) Poor women had little time for socializing because they, like their husbands, sons, and brothers, had to leave their homes—usually crowded rental apartments—to work. They often set up small stalls to sell bread, vegetables, simple clothing, or trinkets.

Athenian life offered many occasions for women to go out: religious festivals, funerals, births at the houses of relatives and friends, and trips to workshops to buy shoes or other domestic articles. Sometimes her husband escorted her, but more often a woman was accompanied only by a slave and could act independently. Many upper-class women most likely viewed their limited contact with men outside the household as a badge of superior social status. In a gender-segregated society such as that of upper-class Athens, a woman's primary personal relationships were probably with her children and other women.

Men restricted women's freedom of movement partly to reduce uncertainty about the paternity of their children and to protect their daughters' virginity from seducers and rapists. Since citizenship guaranteed the city-state's political structure and a man's personal freedom, Greeks felt it crucial to ensure that a boy truly was his father's son and not the child of a foreigner or a slave. Women who bore legitimate children earned higher status and greater freedom in the family, as an Athenian man explained in this excerpt from a court case:

> When I decided to marry and had brought a wife home, at first my attitude towards her was this: I did not wish to annoy her, but neither was she to have too much of her own way. . . . I kept an eye on her as was proper. But later, after my child had been born, I came to trust her, and I handed all my possessions over to her, believing that this was the greatest possible proof of affection.

Citizen women, like men, could own property, including land (the most valued possession in Greek society), and they were supposed to preserve it to hand down to their children. A daughter's share in her father's estate usually came to her as her dowry (the money and property a woman brought to her marriage). Husband and wife co-owned the household's common property. The husband was legally responsible for preserving the dowry and using it for the support and comfort of his wife and children. At her death, her children inherited the dowry. In a divorce, the wife got her property back.

Athenian laws concerning heiresses reveal the society's goal of enabling males to establish and maintain households. If a father died leaving only a daughter, his

Vase Painting of a Woman Buying Shoes
Greek vases were frequently decorated with scenes from daily life instead of mythological stories. Here, a woman is being fitted for a pair of custom-made shoes by a craftsman and his apprentice. Her husband has accompanied her on the expedition and, to judge from his gesture, is participating in the discussion of the purchase. This vase was painted in so-called black-figure technique, in which the figures are rendered as black outlines, with their details incised into a background of red clay. Painters later reversed this technique on red-figure vases so that they could draw pictures with greater precision and elegance of line. **For more help analyzing this image, see the visual activity for this chapter in the Online Study Guide at** bedfordstmartins.com/huntconcise. (Henry Lillie Pierce Fund. Photograph © 2011 Museum of Fine Arts, Boston [01.8035].)

property went to her, but she could not dispose of it as she pleased. Instead, the law required her father's closest male relative—her official guardian after her father's death—to marry her, with the aim of producing a son. This child inherited the property when he reached adulthood. This law applied regardless of whether the heiress was already married (without any sons) or whether the male relative already had a wife. The heiress and the male relative were both supposed to divorce their present spouses and marry each other to preserve the father's line and keep the property in his family. Bearing male children brought special honor to a woman because sons meant security for parents. Sons could appear in court in support of their parents in lawsuits and protect them in the streets of Athens, which for most of its history had no police force. By law, sons were required to support elderly parents. So intense was the pressure to produce sons that stories of women who smuggled in male babies born to slaves and passed them off as their own were common. Such tales, whose truth is hard to gauge, were credible because husbands customarily stayed away at childbirth.

Women remained barred from political participation, which meant that men might overlook women's contributions to the city-state. In his play *Medea* of 431 B.C.E., the Athenian dramatist Euripides had his heroine insist that women who bear children are owed at least as much respect as hoplites: "People say that we women lead a safe life at home, while men have to go to war. What fools they are! I would much rather fight in the army three times than give birth to a child even once." Medea's claim seems persuasive, given the high risks of childbirth under the medical conditions of antiquity. In any case, ancient sources confirm that many women remained engaged and interested in issues affecting the city-state as a whole. They often had strong opinions on politics and public policy, but they had to express their views privately to their husbands, children, and relatives.

A small number of Athenian women were able to ignore traditional restrictions on their public behavior because they gave up the usual expectations of marrying or were too rich to care what others thought. The most talked-about women of the former category were called companions. Often foreigners, they were physically attractive, witty in conversation, and educated to sing and play musical instruments. They often entertained at **symposia** (dinner parties for men only), and sometimes they sold sexual favors for a high price. Their independent lives set companions apart from citizen women, as did the freedom to control their own sexuality. Equally distinctive was their skill in conversing with men in public. Companions charmed men with their witty, joking conversation. Their characteristic skill at clever remarks and verbal jabs allowed companions a freedom of speech denied to "proper" women.

Some companions lived precarious lives subject to exploitation and even violence at the hands of their male customers, but the most skillful could attract lovers from the highest levels of society and live in luxury on their own. The most famous companion was Aspasia from Miletus, who became Pericles' lover and bore him a son. She dazzled Athens's upper-class males with her brilliant conversation and confidence. Ironically, Pericles' own law restricting citizenship to children of two Athenian parents meant that their own child was not a citizen.

Only the wealthiest citizen women could speak to men openly with the frankness of companions. One such was Elpinike, a member of a superrich Athenian family of great military distinction. She once publicly criticized Pericles for having boasted about the Athenian conquest of a rebellious ally. When some other Athenian women praised Pericles for his success, Elpinike sarcastically remarked so all could hear, "This really is wonderful, Pericles, . . . that you have caused the loss of many good citizens, not in battle against Phoenicians or Persians, like my brother Cimon, but in suppressing an allied city of fellow Greeks."

In contrast to citizen women, slaves and **metics** (immigrants who were granted permanent residency in Athens in exchange for paying taxes and serving in the military) were truly "outsiders" living inside city-state society. Individuals and the city-state alike owned slaves, who could be purchased from traders or bred in the household. Unwanted newborns abandoned by their parents (a practice

Vase Painting of a Symposium

Upper-class Greek men often spent their evenings at symposia—drinking parties that always included much conversation and usually featured music and entertainers. Wives were not included. The discussions could range widely, from literature to politics to philosophy. Here, a female musician, whose nudity shows she is a hired prostitute, entertains the guests, who recline on couches, as was customary. The man on the right is about to fling the dregs of his wine, playing a messy game called *kottabos*. (Reproduction by permission of the Syndics of the Fitzwilliam Museum, Cambridge. Master and Fellows of Corpus Christi College, Cambridge.)

called infant exposure) were often picked up by others and raised as slaves. Athens's commercial growth in this period increased the demand for slaves to provide manual labor. Slaves probably made up 100,000 or more of the city-state's estimated 250,000 residents in Pericles' time. (This population made Athens an extraordinarily large city-state.) Slaves worked in homes, on farms, in crafts shops, and, if they were truly unfortunate, in the cramped and dangerous silver mines, whose riches boosted Athens's prosperity. Unlike Sparta's helots, Athens's slaves never rebelled, probably because they originated from too many different places to be able to unite.

Golden Age Athens's wealth and cultural vitality attracted many metics, who worked in Athens as traders, crafts producers, entertainers, and laborers. By the start of the Peloponnesian War in 431 B.C.E., these immigrants made up perhaps half the free population. Metics had to pay for the privilege of working in Athens through a special foreigners' tax and military service. Citizens valued metics' contributions to the city's prosperity but only rarely offered them citizenship.

Metics sometimes found themselves forced into making a living outside the mainstream, especially as prostitutes. Men, unlike women, were not penalized for sexual activity outside marriage. "Certainly you don't think men beget children out of sexual desire?" wrote the upper-class author Xenophon. "The streets and the brothels are swarming with ways to take care of that." Men could have sex with female or male slaves, who could not refuse their masters, or they could have sex with various classes of prostitutes, depending on how much money they wanted to spend.

Traditional Education and the New Ideas of the Sophists

Tradition dictated the course of education in Golden Age Athens until the time of radical democracy in the mid-fifth century B.C.E., when the appearance of a new kind of teacher with disturbing ideas created high tensions. All education was private. Well-to-do families paid private tutors to teach their sons to read, write, and perhaps sing or play a musical instrument. They also hired trainers to instruct the boys in athletics. Physical fitness was considered vital for men because it was thought to be ugly and disgraceful to be out of shape, and because all male citizens and metics ages eighteen to sixty could be called up for military service. Men exercised daily in public, open-air facilities called gymnasia, paid for by wealthy families. The daughters of upper-class families usually learned to read, write, and do arithmetic; a woman with these skills would be better prepared to manage a household and help her future husband run their estate. Poorer girls and boys learned a trade and perhaps a bit of reading and arithmetic by assisting their parents in their daily work. If they were fortunate, they would become apprentices learning from skilled crafts producers. It is uncertain how many people could read and write; most people probably could not. The predominance of oral rather than written communication meant that people usually absorbed information by ear. Songs, speeches, narrated stories, and lively conversations were central to Greek life.

Young men from prosperous families traditionally acquired the skills to become successful participants in Athenian democracy by observing their fathers, uncles, and other older men as they debated in the Council of 500 and the assembly, served as public officials, and made speeches in court. In many cases, an older man would choose an adolescent male as his special favorite to educate. The younger man would learn about public life by spending his time in the company of the older man and his adult friends. During the day, the youth would observe his mentor talking politics in the agora, help him perform his duties in public office, and work out with him in a gymnasium. The evening would be spent at a symposium, where the entertainment ranged from serious political and philosophical discussion to riotous partying fueled by endless cups of wine.

This type of relationship could lead to sexual relations between the youth and the older male, who would normally be married. Although both male homosexuality between adults and female homosexuality in general were regarded as wrong throughout the Greek world, sexual relations between older mentors and younger favorites were considered acceptable in many, though not all, city-states. These differing attitudes about homosexual behavior reflected the complexity of Greek ideas of masculinity—of what made a man a man and what unmade him. For one thing, in Greek eyes a man had to be the one who took the lead in sex and never submitted to the control of another. In any case, a mentor was not supposed to exploit

The Masculine Ideal
This bronze statue of a male warrior-athlete made in the mid-fifth century B.C.E. was found in an ancient shipwreck off the coast of southern Italy. The figure's relaxed pose displays the asymmetry—the head looking to one side, the arms in different positions, the torso tilted—that characterized the change in the style of art from the Archaic Age to the Classical Age. The body shows the physical ideal that Greek men worked to achieve through daily workouts. (Eric Lessing/ Art Resource, NY.)

his younger partner just for sex or neglect his political education. Athenian society accepted the relationship as part of a complicated range of types of male bonding.

A new type of teachers called Sophists (wise men) came to Athens from elsewhere in Greece around the mid-fifth century B.C.E., at about the time that democracy became "radical." Sophists, who offered expensive instruction in public speaking, alarmed many people because what they taught seemed to threaten the stability of the democracy. Now, rich young men eager to become skilled political speechmakers no longer needed to learn from their family elders but could study with these foreign experts in the techniques of persuasion. People feared the techniques Sophists taught because charismatic public speakers could sway the assembly and the juries of radical democracy. Since codes of proper behavior, moral standards, and religious ideals were handed down in speech from generation to generation, a persuasive speaker could potentially wield as much power as an army of warriors. Sophists made people anxious especially because political leaders, such as Pericles, flocked to hear them and because the high tuition they charged restricted their knowledge to the wealthy.

The worry about Sophists was not just that their techniques taught speakers how to be dangerously persuasive; it was also that their ideas undermined traditional beliefs about religion and morality. One especially controversial Sophist was Protagoras, who arrived in Athens around 450 B.C.E. His ideas proved extremely upsetting, especially his agnosticism (the belief that human beings cannot know anything about the divine). When he said, "I cannot discover whether the gods exist, nor what their form is like, for there are many barriers to knowledge, [such as] the difficulty of the subject and the short span of human life," people worried that these ideas might provoke the gods' anger against Athens.

Equally controversial was Protagoras's denial of any absolute standard of truth: he asserted that every issue had two, irreconcilable sides. For example, he argued, if one person feeling a breeze thinks it warm, whereas another person thinks it cool, neither judgment can be absolutely correct because the wind simply is warm to one and cool to the other. Protagoras summed up his **subjectivism**—the belief that there is no absolute reality behind and independent of appearances—in the much-quoted opening of his work *Truth*: "Man is the measure of all things, of the things that are that they are, and of the things that are not that they are not." "Man" (*anthropos* in Greek, hence our word *anthropology*) in this passage refers to the individual human, male or female. Protagoras made the individual the sole judge of his or her own impressions.

This new way of thinking seemed to indicate that traditional human institutions and values were only matters of convention, custom, or law (*nomos*), not products of nature (*physis*), and that speakers should argue either side of a question with equal persuasiveness because truth was subjective. The combination of these two conclusions, many people worried, amounted to moral relativism, meaning that there were no absolute moral values. If this was true, then there could be no more shared public values. Protagoras tried to overcome such objections by insisting that his doctrines were not hostile to democracy, arguing that every person had an innate capability for "excellence" and that human survival depended on the rule of law based on a sense of justice. Members of the community, he explained, must be persuaded to obey the laws not because they are based on absolute truth, which does not exist, but because it was advantageous for people to live by them. A thief, for example, would have to be persuaded that the law forbidding theft was to his advantage because it protected his own property and the city-state in which he, like others, had to live in order to survive.

Other Sophists taught other disturbing ideas. One, for example, another friend of Pericles', offended believers in traditional religion by arguing that the sun was nothing more than a lump of flaming rock, not a god. Another Sophist invented an atomic theory of matter to explain how change was constant. Everything, he argued, consisted of tiny, invisible particles in eternal motion. Their random collisions caused them to combine and recombine in an infinite variety of forms. This physical explanation of the source of change, like the theory about the sun, implied that traditional religion, which explained events as the outcome of divine forces, was invalid. All of this made many people afraid that traditional ideas—and the success and stability that they seemed to have produced—were being destroyed.

Socrates and New Ideas on Ethics

The unique ideas of Socrates of Athens (469–399 B.C.E.), the most famous philosopher of the Golden Age, added to the tension that the appearance of the Sophists had provoked. Socrates was not a Sophist—he did not teach for money—but his views became well known because he devoted his life to spreading them through conversation. He rejected the notion that justice should be equated with the power to impose one's will on others. His passionate concern to discover valid guidelines for leading a just life and to prove that justice is better than injustice under all circumstances gave a new direction to Greek philosophy: an emphasis on ethics. Although other thinkers before him, especially poets and dramatists, had dealt with moral issues, Socrates was the first to make the ethics and morality of the individual a central concern for philosophy.

Socrates lived a life that attracted attention. He paid so little notice to his physical appearance and clothes that he seemed eccentric. Sporting a stomach, in his words, "somewhat too large to be convenient," he wore the same cheap cloak

Statuette of the Philosopher Socrates
The controversial Socrates, the most famous philosopher of Athens in the fifth century B.C.E., joked that he had a homely face and a bulging stomach. This small statue is an artist's impression of what Socrates looked like; we cannot be sure of the accuracy. Socrates was famous for his irony, and he may have purposely exaggerated his physical unattractiveness to show his disdain for ordinary standards of beauty, which valued a fit body, and his own emphasis on the quality of the soul as the true measure of a person's worth.
(© Copyright The Trustees of The British Museum.)

summer and winter and went barefoot in all weather. His tirelessness as a hoplite and his ability to outdrink anyone at a symposium amazed his companions. Unlike the Sophists, he lived in poverty and disdained material possessions, somehow managing to support a wife and several children. He may have inherited some money, but he certainly received gifts from wealthy admirers.

Socrates spent his time talking: conversing (and drinking) at symposia, strolling in the agora, or watching young men exercise in gymnasia. He wrote nothing; our knowledge of his ideas comes from others' writings, especially those of his pupil Plato (c. 428–348 B.C.E.). Plato portrays Socrates as a relentless questioner of his fellow citizens, foreign friends, and leading Sophists. Socrates' questions aimed at making his conversational partners examine the basic assumptions of their ways of life. Giving few answers, Socrates never directly instructed anyone; instead, he led them to draw conclusions in response to his probing questions, which picked apart their unexamined assumptions. Teaching this way is today called the **Socratic method**.

Socrates' indirect method of searching for the truth often made people unhappy because he forced them to conclude that they were ignorant of what they had assumed they knew very well. He argued that normal careers—pursuing success in politics or business or art—were excuses for avoiding genuine virtue. Socrates insisted that he was ignorant of the best definition of virtue, but that his wisdom consisted of knowing that he did not know. He vowed that he was trying to improve, not undermine, people's beliefs in morality, even though, as a friend put it, a conversation with Socrates made a man feel numb—just as if he had been stung by a stingray. Socrates especially wanted to use reasoning to discover universal standards justifying individual morality. He fiercely attacked the Sophists, who dismissed traditional morality as "chains that bind nature." This idea, he protested, equated human happiness with power and "getting more."

Socrates passionately believed that being just was more advantageous for people than being unjust and that morality was priceless because it guaranteed happiness. Essentially, he argued that just behavior, or virtue, was identical to knowledge, and that a true knowledge of justice would inevitably lead people to choose good over evil. They would therefore live truly happy lives, regardless of how rich or poor they were. Since Socrates believed that moral knowledge was all a person needed for the good life, he argued that no one knowingly behaved unjustly and that behaving justly was always in the individual's interest. It was simply ignorant to believe that the best life was the life of unlimited power to pursue whatever one desired. The most desirable human life was focused on virtue and guided by reason, not by dreams of personal gain.

Socrates' effect on many people was as disturbing as were the Sophists' doctrines questioning traditional morality. Socrates' attacks on his fellow citizens' ideas about the importance of wealth and public success made some men extremely upset because his ideas seemed to mean that people should not bother thinking about the community, only about their individual virtue. Unhappiest of all were the fathers whose sons, after listening to Socrates reduce someone to utter bewilderment, came home to try the same technique on their parents by arguing that the public accomplishments their family worked for were wrongheaded, even worthless. Men who experienced this reversal of the traditional educational hierarchy—fathers were supposed to educate sons—felt that Socrates was undermining the stability of society by making young men question Athenian traditions. The ancient sources fail to reveal what Athenian women thought of Socrates, or he of them. His thoughts about human capabilities and behavior could be applied to women as well as to men, and he probably believed that women and men both had the same basic capacity for justice.

People's worry that Socrates presented a danger to traditional society inspired the playwright Aristophanes to write his comedy *Clouds* (423 B.C.E.). He portrayed Socrates as a cynical Sophist operating a "thinking shop," who for a fee offered instruction in Protagoras-like techniques of making the weaker argument the stronger. When Socrates' curriculum transforms a youth into a public speaker arguing that a son has the right to beat his parents, his father burns down Socrates' school. None of these plot details were real; what was genuine was the fear that Socrates' uncompromising views on individual morality endangered the traditional practices of the community at a time when new ways of thought were angering many Athenians. Some people even believed that Socrates was an enemy of Athens's radical democracy, despite his serving heroically in the army, because some of the young men who associated with him were open supporters of oligarchy as the best form of government.

New Ideas in History and Medicine

One especially significant new idea that emerged in the Golden Age was to see the goal of history as the description and interpretation of the past based on a critical analysis of sources. Herodotus of Halicarnassus (c. 485–425 B.C.E.) and Thucydides of Athens (c. 455–399 B.C.E.) became Greece's most famous historians and established Western civilization's tradition of history writing. Herodotus wrote his groundbreaking work *Histories* (meaning "inquiries" in Greek), probably finishing it in the 420s B.C.E. It explained the Persian Wars as a clash between East and West; by Roman times he had been christened "the Father of History." Herodotus achieved an unprecedented depth in his book by giving it an investigative approach to evidence, a wide interest in human diversity, and a lively story. Herodotus searched for the origins of the Persian-Greek conflict both by delving deep into the past and by examining the cultural traditions of all the peoples involved. He recognized the relevance and the delight of studying other cultures as a component of historical investigation.

Thucydides wrote contemporary history influenced by what today is called realism in political science. His *History of the Peloponnesian War* (the generation-long war between Athens and Sparta that ended the Golden Age) made power politics, not divine intervention, the primary force in history. Deeply affected by the war's brutality, he used his personal experiences as a politician and military commander to make his history vivid and frank in describing human moral failings. His insistence that historians should spare no effort in seeking out the most reliable sources and evaluating their testimony with objectivity set a high standard for later writers.

Equally innovative and influential were the medical doctrines of Hippocrates of Cos, a fifth-century B.C.E. contemporary of Thucydides, who became Greece's most famous physician. He is remembered today in the oath bearing his name that doctors swear at the beginning of their professional careers. Hippocrates made great strides in putting medical diagnosis and treatment on a scientific basis. Earlier medicine had depended on magic and ritual. Hippocrates viewed the human body as an organism whose parts must be understood in relation to the whole. Hippocrates taught that the physician's most important duty was to base his knowledge on careful observation of patients and their response to remedies. Clinical experience, not theory, he insisted, was the best guide to effective treatments. Although various cults in Greek religion offered healing to worshippers, Hippocratic medical doctrine apparently made little or no mention of any role for the gods in illnesses and their treatments. Some attributed to him the view, profoundly influential in later times, that four humors (fluids) made up the human body: blood, phlegm, black bile, and yellow bile. This intellectual system corresponded to philosophers' division of the physical world into four parts: the elements earth, air, fire, and water. Health therefore depended on keeping the proper balance among them; being healthy was to be "in good humor."

Tragedy and Comedy as New Forms of Drama

The development of tragic drama was Golden Age Athens's most influential cultural innovation. By presenting shocking stories exploring tensions in the city-state, tragic plays inspired their large audiences to ponder the danger that arrogance, ignorance, and violence presented to Athens's democratic society. Following the tradition of Homer and Hesiod, Golden Age playwrights treated themes ranging from individual freedom and responsibility in the polis to the underlying nature of good and evil.

Tragedies were plays with plots presenting fierce conflicts among fiercely proud characters whose lives ended in disaster. These dramas were written in verse and used solemn language; they were often based on stories about the violent consequences of interactions between gods and humans told in myth. The plots often ended with a resolution to the trouble—but only after great suffering and death.

A successful tragedy presented a vivid spectacle. The actors wore rigid masks, dressed in striking costumes, and used broad gestures and booming voices to reach the upper tier of seats. A powerful voice was crucial to a tragic actor because words represented the heart of a tragedy, in which dialogue and long speeches were far more common than physical action. A chorus sang in unison between scenes of dialogue and performed intricate dance routines. Special effects were part of the spectacle. For example, a crane allowed actors playing the roles of gods to fly suddenly onto the stage.

The performance of Athenian tragedies took place over three days at an annual religious festival held during the daytime in a large outdoor theater sacred to Dionysus. In keeping with the competitive spirit characteristic of many events honoring the gods, Athens's government held a competition to choose three authors to present four plays each: three tragedies in a row (a trilogy), followed by a semicomic play. So important was a first-rate actor to a successful tragedy that performers were assigned by lottery to the playwrights to give all three an equal chance to have the finest cast. A great protagonist (the most important actor in a play) could become an international celebrity.

The prizes awarded to the authors, actors, and producers in the tragedy competition were modest, but the fame was enormous. As citizens, playwrights also fulfilled the normal military and political obligations of Athenian men. The best-known Athenian tragedians—Aeschylus (525–456 b.c.e.), Sophocles (c. 496–406 b.c.e.), and Euripides (c. 485–406 b.c.e.)—either served in the army or held public office at some point in their careers, or did both.

Theater of Dionysus at Athens
Tragedies and comedies produced at this theater in daytime festivals riveted the city's attention. The theater held about fifteen thousand spectators. In the Classical period, the seating, stage, and scenery were not yet permanent installations; the seating and stone stage building foundations are remnants of much later changes. What qualities do you think would have been most important in an actor under these conditions? (John Elk III/Bruce Coleman/Photoshot.)

Athenian tragedy was a public art form. Its performances were subsidized with public funds, and its plots explored the ethical problems of humans in conflict with the gods and with one another in a city-state. Even though most tragedies were based on stories that referred to a legendary time before city-states existed, such as tales of the Trojan War, the moral issues the plays explored always concerned the society and obligations of citizens in a city-state. To take only a few examples: In his trilogy *Oresteia* (458 B.C.E.), Aeschylus explains the importance of democratic Athens's court system by reworking the story of how the gods stopped the murderous violence in the family of Orestes, son of the Greek leader against Troy. The plays suggest that human beings have to learn by suffering but that the gods will provide justice in the long run. Sophocles' *Antigone* (441 B.C.E.) presents the pitiful story of the family of Oedipus of Thebes as a drama of harsh conflict between a courageous woman, Antigone, who insists on her family's moral obligation to bury its dead in obedience to divine command, and her uncle Creon, the city-state's stern male leader, who defends the need to preserve order and protect community values by prohibiting the burial of traitors. In a horrifying story of anger and suicide centered on one of the most famous heroines of Western literature, Sophocles deliberately exposes the right and wrong on each side of the conflict. His play offers no easy resolution to the possible conflict between divine and human laws. Euripides' *Medea* (431 B.C.E.) implies that the political order of a city-state depends on men treating their wives and families with honor and trust: when Medea's husband betrays her for a younger woman, she takes revenge by destroying their children and the community's political leadership with her magical powers.

Tragedies certainly appealed to audiences because they were entertainment, but they also had an educational function: to remind citizens that success created complex moral problems that could not be solved arrogantly or thoughtlessly. Spectators would have been aware that the central characters of the plays were figures who fell into ruin from positions of power and prestige like those enjoyed by the citizens of Athens at the head of its powerful "empire." The characters' reversals of fortune came about not because they were absolute villains but because, as humans, they could fail through a lethal combination of error, ignorance, and **hubris** (violent arrogance). Thoughtful spectators, we can imagine, thought about the warning implied by these plays that Athens's current power and prestige, managed as they were by humans, were hostage to the same forces that controlled the fates of the heroes and heroines of tragedy. The plays taught that Athenians needed to remember not to go too far in their pride in their city-state's political, social, and cultural accomplishments.

Golden Age Athens also developed comedy as another innovative form of public art. Written in verse and performed at religious festivals, comedies made direct comments about public policy, criticized current politicians and intellectuals by name, and devised plots and scenes of outrageous fantasy to make their points. An actor could fly to the gods on a giant beetle, for example, or the dancers in the chorus could dress as talking birds or dancing clouds.

Statuettes of Comic Actors
These little statues portray comic actors wearing the kinds of masks and costumes that became popular after Aristophanes and his contemporaries wrote their comedies in the fifth century B.C.E., and they give a vivid sense of the slapstick acting that characterized Greek comedy. In Aristophanes' day, the grotesque unreality of comic costumes would have been even more striking because attached below the waists of the male actors were large leather phalluses, which were props for all sorts of sex-related jokes. (Bildarchiv Preussischer Kulturbesitz/Art Resource, NY.)

The immediate goal of a comic playwright was to win the award for the festival's best comedy by creating beautiful poetry, raising laughs with constant jokes and puns, and mocking prominent men. Much of the humor concerned sex and bodily functions, described with explicit and imaginative profanity. Well-known male citizens were targeted for insults as cowardly or sexually effeminate. Women characters who were made fun of, however, seem to have been fictional.

Comedy's remarkable freedom of speech promoted frank, indeed brutal, commentary on current issues and personalities. Even during the Peloponnesian War, comic playwrights presented plays that criticized the city-state's policy, for example by recommending an immediate peace settlement. It was no accident that this energetic, critical dramatic form emerged in Athens at the same time as radical democracy, in the mid-fifth century B.C.E. The principle that all voters should have a stake in determining government policies evidently fueled a passion for using biting humor to keep the community's leaders from becoming arrogant and aloof. Athenian comedies often blamed particular political leaders for government policies that had been approved by the assembly, similar to the way ostracism singled out individuals for punishment. As the leading politician of radical democracy, Pericles came in for fierce criticism in comedy. Comic playwrights mocked his policies, his love life, and his looks ("Old Turnip Head" was a favorite insult).

The most remarkable of Aristophanes' comedies are those in which the main characters are powerful women who force the men of Athens to change their policy to preserve family life and the city-state. Most famous is *Lysistrata* (411 B.C.E.), named after the female lead character of the play. In it, the women of Athens and Sparta unite to force their husbands to end the Peloponnesian War. To make the men agree to a peace treaty, they first seize the acropolis, where Athens's financial reserves are kept, to prevent the men from spending them on the war. They then beat back an attack on their position by attacking the old men who have remained in Athens while the younger men are away from home fighting. When their husbands return from battle, the women refuse to have sex with them. This strike, which is portrayed in a series of overtly sexual episodes, finally coerces the men of Athens and Sparta to agree to a treaty.

Lysistrata presents women acting bravely and aggressively against men who seem bent on destroying traditional family life by staying away from home for long stretches while on military campaigns and ruining the city-state by prolonging a pointless war. Lysistrata insists that women have the intelligence and judgment to make political decisions: "I am a woman, and, yes, I have brains. And I'm not badly off for judgment. Nor has my education been bad, coming as it has from my listening often to the conversations of my father and the elders among the men." Her old-fashioned training and good sense allow her to see what needs to be done to protect the community. Like the heroines of tragedy, Lysistrata is a reactionary; she wants to put things back the way they were. To do that, however, she has to act like an impatient revolutionary. That irony well sums up the challenge that Golden Age Athens faced in trying to balance its faith in tradition with the energy of the period's innovation in so many areas.

> **REVIEW** How did new ideas threaten cherished traditions in the Golden Age?

The End of the Golden Age, 431–403 B.C.E.

A war between Athens and Sparta that lasted a generation (431–404 B.C.E.) ended the Athenian Golden Age. Today called the Peloponnesian War because it pitted Sparta's Peloponnesian League against Athens's Delian League, the war arose at least in part as a result of Pericles' policies. When in the 430s B.C.E. Sparta gave Athens an ultimatum—stop mistreating our allies—Pericles convinced the Athenian assembly to reject the demand as unfair because Sparta refused arbitration. In this way, the relations of Athens and Sparta with lesser city-states propelled the two powers over the brink into war.

The Peloponnesian War, 431–404 B.C.E.

The Peloponnesian War was so destructive because it lasted so many years; it was the longest war in Greek history. It took place above all because Spartan leaders feared that the Athenians would use their superior long-distance offensive weaponry—the

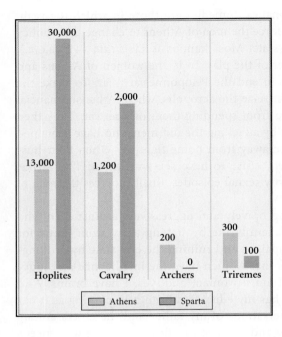

Taking Measure **Military Forces of Athens and Sparta at the Beginning of the Peloponnesian War**

These figures give estimates of the comparative strengths of the military forces of the Athenian side and the Spartan side when the Peloponnesian War broke out in 431 B.C.E. The numbers come from ancient historical sources—above all, the Athenian general and historian Thucydides, who fought in the war. The bar graphs reveal the different characteristics of the competing forces: Athens relied on its navy of triremes and its archers (the fifth-century B.C.E. equivalent of artillery and snipers). Sparta was preeminent in the forces needed for land battles—hoplites (heavily armed infantry) and cavalry (shock troops used to disrupt opposing infantry). These differences dictated the strategies and tactics of each side. Athens tried to launch surprise raids from the sea, and Sparta tried to force decisive confrontations on the battlefield.

naval forces of the Delian League—to destroy Spartan control over the Peloponnesian League (see "Taking Measure"). The duration of the struggle reflected the unpredictability of war and the consequences of the repeated refusal of the Athenian assembly to negotiate lasting peace terms when they had the chance.

Thucydides dramatically revealed the absolute refusal of the Athenians to find a compromise solution with these words of Pericles to the assembly:

> If we do go to war, never think that you went to war over a trivial affair. For you this trifling matter is the assurance and the proof of your determination. If you yield to their demands, they will immediately confront you with some larger demand, since they will think that you only gave way on the first point out of fear. But if you stand firm, you will show them that they have to deal with you as equals. . . . When our equals, without agreeing to arbitration of the matter under dispute, make claims on us as neighbors and state those claims as commands, it would be no better than slavery to give in to them, no matter how large or how small the claim may be.

Pericles convinced the Athenians to send their navy to raid enemy lands but to avoid all battles with the Spartan infantry, even when this meant abandoning the countryside and their rich properties there to be ravaged by enemy invasions. In the end, he predicted, the superior finances of Athens would enable it to win in a war of attrition. With his unyielding leadership, this strategy might have prevailed, but an unexpected disaster struck Athens soon after the start of the war.

An epidemic disease decimated the population for four years, killing thousands, including Pericles. The Athenians fought on, but they lost the clear vision for sacrificing their expectations of gain that Pericles' strategy had required; no one else was up to the task of leading Athens in the changed and unanticipated circumstances of a prolonged war. The generals after him followed increasingly risky plans, culminating in an overambitious campaign against Sparta's allies in Sicily, far to the west. Dazzling the assembly in 415 B.C.E. with the dream of conquering that rich island, Alcibiades, the most innovative and brashest commander of the war, persuaded the Athenians to launch their largest naval expedition ever by appealing to their expectations of victory and profit. His political rivals got him recalled from his command, however, and the invasion force suffered a catastrophic defeat in 413 B.C.E. (Map 2.3).

Map 2.3 The Peloponnesian War, 431–404 B.C.E.
During the first ten years of the war, most of the battles took place in mainland Greece. Sparta, whose armies usually avoided long-distance campaigns, shocked Athens with successful attacks against Athenian forces in northeastern Greece. In the war's next phase, Athens stunned the Greek world by launching a naval expedition against Spartan allies in Sicily. In the last ten years of the war, the action moved to the east, on and along the western coast of Anatolia and its islands. This was the western boundary of the Persian Empire, which helped the Spartans build a navy to defeat the Athenian fleet and win the war. **For more help analyzing this map, see the map activity for this chapter in the Online Study Guide at** bedfordstmartins.com/huntconcise.

The Spartans then launched the final phase of the war by establishing a permanent base of operations in the Athenian countryside for year-round raids. The agricultural economy was devastated, and revenues fell drastically when twenty thousand slave workers crippled production in Athens's publicly owned silver mines by deserting to the enemy. Distress over the war's losses led to a group of antidemocratic citizens briefly overturning the democracy in 411 B.C.E., but other citizens soon restored democratic government. Athens fought on. The end came when Persia sent money to help the Spartans finally build a strong navy. Aggressive Spartan action at sea forced Athens to surrender in 404 B.C.E. After twenty-seven years of near-continuous war, the Athenians were at the mercy of their enemies.

The Rule of the Thirty Tyrants, 404–403 B.C.E.

The aftermath of the war revealed that the accomplishments of Golden Age Athens had hidden a vicious disagreement over radical democracy. Following their victory, the Spartans went home after installing a regime of oligarchy-favoring Athenians to rule the city-state. Members of the social elite, they became known as the Thirty Tyrants because they murderously suppressed democratic opposition during an eight-month period of terror in 404–403 B.C.E. The speechwriter Lysias, for example, reported that the tyrants' thugs seized his brother for execution as a way of stealing the family's valuables, down to the gold earrings ripped from the ears of his brother's wife. Some of the oligarchs now terrorizing their neighbors were friends of Socrates, and people's belief that Socrates had taught these men to reject democracy created anger against him, even though he had refused to follow the orders of the tyrants to arrest a fellow citizen for execution. A resistance movement soon arose, violently expelled the Thirty Tyrants in 403 B.C.E. in a series of bloody street battles, and restored democracy.

This civil war made Athenians so angry at each other that continuing violence threatened to tear the community apart even after the restoration of democratic government. The assembly therefore proclaimed the first amnesty in Western history, a truce forbidding any official charges or revenge for crimes committed during the rule of the Thirty Tyrants. Athens's government was once again a functioning democracy, but its financial and military strength was shattered. Worse, its society harbored bitterness that no amnesty could fully dissolve. The end of the Golden Age left Athenians anxiously wondering how to remake their lives and restore the luster that their city-state's innovative accomplishments had produced in that wondrous period.

REVIEW What events and decisions contributed most to the outcome of the Peloponnesian War?

Conclusion

Two very long and very different wars framed the Greek Golden Age in the fifth century B.C.E. Twenty years of war against the Persians led to stunningly surprising Greek victories that produced significant long-term consequences: Sparta and

Mapping the West Greece, Europe, and the Mediterranean, c. 400 B.C.E.
No single power controlled the Mediterranean region at the end of the fifth century B.C.E. In the west, the
Phoenician city of Carthage and the Greek cities of Sicily and southern Italy were rivals for the riches to
be won by trade. In the east, the Spartans, made ambitious by their victory over Athens in the Peloponnesian War, tried to become an international power outside the mainland for the first time in their history by
sending campaigns into Anatolia and, they hoped, even farther east. This aggressive action aroused stiff
opposition from the Persians because it was a threat to their westernmost imperial provinces.

Athens, previously allies united to defend Greek freedom, became enemies; Athens
displaced Sparta as the leading city-state; and Athens, by dominating at sea militarily and commercially, reached a height of prosperity, international power, and proud
expectations unimaginable at the beginning of the century. The consequences of
this war against foreigners were beneficial for rich and poor alike because Athens
turned its naval empire into a profit-making enterprise when its allies lost the will
to defend themselves and the sea, swept clear of Persians, brought trade to Athens
from every corner of the Mediterranean. The recognition that the masses—meaning
the adult male citizens who rowed the imperial warships—gained through their war
service achieved political reality when elite leaders such as Pericles helped make
Athenian democracy "radical," motivated perhaps by a combination of genuine faith
in majority rule and the desire for the glory that popular leadership could bring.

    The riches of Golden Age Athens, which financed glorious monuments pro-
claiming Athenian gratitude to the gods who favored them, attracted people as well

as commerce, and with new people came new ideas. The ideas of the Sophists disturbed the buoyant and confident mood of the Golden Age because they seemed to threaten to bring down the wrath of the gods and to transform public speaking into a weapon that men with bad intentions could use to seduce the democratic masses into corruption. Even Socrates' endless conversations about justice—and who could be against justice?—seemed infuriating because they questioned everything that seemed normal and pleasant about life in a golden age.

Nearly three decades of war pitting Greek against Greek destroyed the Golden Age at the end of the century. The Athenians had become so accustomed to success that they could not adjust their pride and their expectations to the changed circumstances after their best leader's death, and they overextended themselves in the war, with disastrous consequences. The outcome of the Peloponnesian War made the playwrights seem like prophets who had warned about hubris in their tragedies and comedies. It is no wonder that these works of literature remain the most thought-provoking achievements of the Greek Golden Age.

CHAPTER REVIEW QUESTIONS
1. What were the most significant differences between Greece in the Archaic Age and Greece in the Golden Age?
2. What did Greeks in the Golden Age believe it was worth spending public funds to pay for and why?

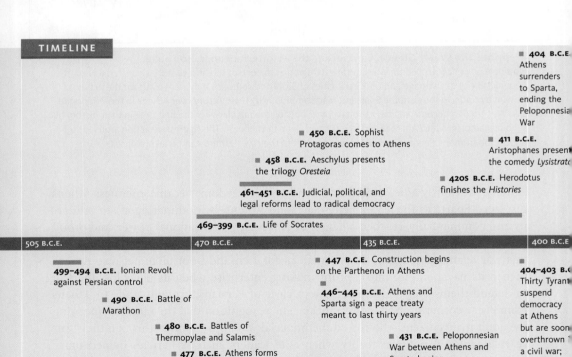

TIMELINE

- **404 B.C.E.** Athens surrenders to Sparta, ending the Peloponnesian War
- **450 B.C.E.** Sophist Protagoras comes to Athens
- **458 B.C.E.** Aeschylus presents the trilogy *Oresteia*
- **411 B.C.E.** Aristophanes presents the comedy *Lysistrata*
- **420s B.C.E.** Herodotus finishes the *Histories*
- **461–451 B.C.E.** Judicial, political, and legal reforms lead to radical democracy
- **469–399 B.C.E.** Life of Socrates

| 505 B.C.E. | 470 B.C.E. | 435 B.C.E. | 400 B.C.E |

- **499–494 B.C.E.** Ionian Revolt against Persian control
- **490 B.C.E.** Battle of Marathon
- **480 B.C.E.** Battles of Thermopylae and Salamis
- **477 B.C.E.** Athens forms the Delian League
- **447 B.C.E.** Construction begins on the Parthenon in Athens
- **446–445 B.C.E.** Athens and Sparta sign a peace treaty meant to last thirty years
- **431 B.C.E.** Peloponnesian War between Athens and Sparta begins
- **404–403 B.C.** Thirty Tyrants suspend democracy at Athens but are soon overthrown in a civil war; Athenian democracy is restored but weakened economically

For practice quizzes and other study tools, see the Online Study Guide at bedfordstmartins.com/huntconcise.

For primary-source material from this period, see Chapter 3 of *Sources of* THE MAKING OF THE WEST, Third Edition.

Suggested References

A major challenge in studying the Greek Golden Age is to understand how the period's nearly constant wars affected every part of life.

Blundell, Sue. *Women in Ancient Greece.* 1995.

Camp, John M. *The Archaeology of Athens.* 2001.

*Dillon, John, and Tania Gergel. *The Greek Sophists.* 2003.

*Grene, David, and Richmond Lattimore, eds. *The Complete Greek Tragedies.*

*Herodotus. *The Histories.* Trans. Aubrey de Sélincourt. Revised by John Marincola. New ed. 1996.

Lincoln, Bruce. *Religion, Empire, and Torture: The Case of Achaemenian Persia.* 2007.

Parker, Robert. *Athenian Religion: A History.* 1996.

Parthenon: http://www.perseus.tufts.edu/cgi-bin/vor?x=16&y=13&lookup=parthenon

Patterson, Cynthia B. *The Family in Greek History.* 1998.

*Strassler, Robert B., ed. *The Landmark Thucydides. A Comprehensive Guide to the Peloponnesian War.* 1996.

Thorley, John. *Athenian Democracy.* 2004.

Wees, Han van, ed. *War and Violence in Ancient Greece.* 2000.

From the Classical to the Hellenistic World

ABOUT 255 B.C.E., AN EGYPTIAN CAMEL TRADER (his name is lost) working abroad in Syria paid a scribe to write a letter to his Greek employer, Zeno, back in Egypt, to complain about his mistreatment by his foreman, Krotos, also a Greek:

Solving the Mystery of Egyptian Writing

The three kinds of writing on this stone found by Napoleon's army in 1799 C.E. near Rosetta, in Egypt's Nile River delta, unlocked the thousand-year mystery of how to read ancient Egyptian hieroglyphs. The three bands of text repeat the same message (praise for King Ptolemy V of Egypt decreed by priests in 196 B.C.E.) in three different scripts: at the top, hieroglyphs (Egypt's oldest writing system, c. 3100–3000 B.C.E.), then demotic (a cursive form of Egyptian invented around 600 B.C.E.), and finally Greek. Scholars in the nineteenth century C.E. deciphered the hieroglyphs by comparing them to the Greek version, which they could read. Most Egyptians, like the mistreated camel trader stranded in Syria, could not read Greek, and most Greeks living in Egypt under the rule of the Ptolemaic kings could not read Egyptian, so bilingual texts such as the Rosetta stone were necessary to reach the widest possible audience in Hellenistic Egypt. *(Art Resource, NY.)*

You know that when you left me in Syria with Krotos I followed all your instructions concerning the camels and behaved blamelessly towards you. But Krotos has ignored your orders to pay me my salary; I've received nothing despite asking him for my money over and over. He just tells me to go away. I waited a long time for you to come, but when I no longer had enough to live on and couldn't get help anywhere, I had to run away to keep from starving to death. . . . I am desperate summer and winter. . . . They have treated me with contempt because I am not a Greek. I therefore beg you, please, command them to pay me my salary so that I won't go hungry just because I don't know how to speak Greek.

The camel trader's situation—needing to beg for help from a foreigner who held power in his homeland—reflected the changes that had taken place in the eastern Mediterranean world as it moved from the Classical Age (500–323 B.C.E.) to the Hellenistic Age (323–30 B.C.E.). These changes resulted from the large-scale immigration of Greeks into the Near East and the resulting interaction between local ways of life and the newcomers' ways of life. War started these changes. Following the Peloponnesian War (431–404 B.C.E.), the Greek city-states fought each other to exhaustion, allowing the kingdom of Macedonia to dominate them. When the Macedonian king Alexander the Great (356–323 B.C.E.) conquered the Persian Empire, he settled Greeks in colonies from Egypt to Afghanistan to help administer his conquests. The movements of people that Alexander caused led to the changes characterizing the Hellenistic Age.

Scholars use the term **Hellenistic** to designate the period of Greek and Near Eastern history from Alexander's death in 323 B.C.E. to the death of Cleopatra VII, the last Macedonian queen of Egypt, in 30 B.C.E. *Hellenistic* indicates the mixed nature of the political, social, and cultural changes that Alexander set in motion. These consequences of his conquests brought Greek and Near Eastern traditions together. In politics, kingdoms became the greatest powers in the Greek world, dominating the city-states. Hellenistic kings hired Greeks to fill royal offices, man their armies, and run businesses throughout their Near Eastern territories. Immigrant Greeks, such as Zeno in Egypt, formed a social elite.

A new, multicultural society emerged in the eastern Mediterranean region as people combined Greek and Near Eastern traditions. Locals married Greeks, shared their religious traditions with the newcomers, taught them their agricultural and scientific knowledge, and learned Greek to win administrative jobs. Social tension between immigrants and locals never disappeared, but the blending of traditions and royal financial support promoted innovations in art, science, and religion. Philosophers developed new ideas as guides to life in a world seemingly dominated by chance.

The complex interaction of peoples and ideas that occurred in the Hellenistic period greatly influenced the Romans and later Western civilization. Hellenistic religious developments, for example, provided the background for Christianity. Hellenistic cultural achievements remained influential long after the glories of Greece's Golden Age had faded away.

CHAPTER FOCUS QUESTION What were the major political and cultural changes in the Hellenistic Age?

War and Disunity in Classical Greece, 400–350 B.C.E.

In the first half of the fourth century B.C.E., the Greek city-states continually fought one another to keep any one from becoming powerful enough to dominate. This international disunity exhausted the resources of even the richest city-states, especially because they were also internally fragmented. In Athens, the economy had gradually recovered after the Peloponnesian War, but greater prosperity did not reduce the hatred that democratic Athenians felt about the Thirty Tyrants' violent rule. This bitterness led to the execution of Socrates in 399 B.C.E. Outraged at Socrates' fate,

Plato and Aristotle created Greece's most famous philosophies about right and wrong and how human beings should live. The Spartans tried to turn their city-state into an international power, but their decision to collaborate with the Persian king stirred up fierce resistance. Ultimately, war and disunity made the Greeks too weak to prevent the expansion of their northern neighbor, the kingdom of Macedonia.

Postwar Athens and the Trial of Socrates

Athens in the early fourth century B.C.E. recovered some of its Golden Age prosperity but not its sense of confidence and unity. Economic conditions gradually improved as households and business owners revived trade and the production of goods in their homes and in small shops, such as metal foundries and pottery workshops. Businesses, usually family run, were small; the largest known was a shield-making company owning 120 slaves. The Peloponnesian War changed gender roles in the workforce because so many men who had been the family breadwinner died during the war. Without male providers, many war widows had to find work outside the home. It was in this postwar period that women and men began working together in commercial production for the first time, when weaving shops sprang up. Previously, only women had made cloth and had done so at home. Some women also carved out careers in the arts, especially painting and music.

Some families found ways to profit from women's skills. Socrates' friend Aristarchus, for example, became poverty-stricken supporting several widowed sisters, nieces, and female cousins. Socrates reminded his friend that his relatives knew how to make cloaks, shirts, capes, and smocks, "the work considered the best and most fitting for women." The women had been making clothing only for family members; Socrates suggested that they sell it for profit. The plan succeeded financially, but the women complained that Aristarchus was the only member of the household who ate without working. Socrates advised his friend to reply that the women should think of him as sheep viewed a guard dog—earning his food by keeping the wolves away.

Even in the improved postwar economy, most workers earned just enough to feed and clothe their families. They customarily ate two meals a day, a light lunch in midmorning and a heavier evening meal. Bread baked from barley provided the main part of their diet; only rich people could afford wheat bread. A family bought its bread from small bakery stands, often run by women, or made it at home. Most people ate greens, beans, onions, garlic, olives, fruit, and cheese with their bread; they had meat only at animal sacrifices paid for by the state. Everyone drank wine, diluted with water. Water was fetched from public fountains in jugs by women or slaves. All but the poorest families owned at least one or two slaves to do household chores and to look after the children.

The restored stability in the everyday lives of Athenians did not erase their memories of the murderous rule of the Thirty Tyrants and the civil war of 404–403 B.C.E. Socrates became the best-known victim of this hatred dividing Athenians when

Vase Painting of Women Fetching Water
This painting shows a scene from everyday Greek life: women filling water jugs at a covered public fountain to take back to their homes. Few Greek homes had running water, so it was the duty of freeborn and slave women in a household to gather water for drinking, cooking, washing, and cleaning. Prosperous cities built attractively decorated fountain houses, such as the one shown here, where a regular supply of fresh water was available from springs or was piped in through aqueducts. These fountains were popular spots for women's conversations outside the house. The women in this scene wear the long robes and hair coverings characteristic of the time. (William Francis Warden Fund. Photograph © 2011 Museum of Fine Arts, Boston [61.195].)

he was blamed for the violent crimes of his follower Critias, one of the tyrants. In fact, Socrates had put himself at risk by refusing to cooperate with the tyrants, but some prominent Athenians believed his philosophy had turned Critias into a traitor because Socrates questioned accepted ideas of what was proper behavior and was therefore believed to be hostile to democracy. Many Athenians apparently believed that Socrates' ideas that people should devote themselves to individual excellence and justice above any other concern meant that they should abandon their commitment to the city-state. Since the amnesty agreement blocked prosecution for offenses during the civil war, Socrates' opponents indicted him on a charge of impiety in 399 B.C.E. At his trial they accused him of not believing in the city-state's gods and of introducing new divinities, and also of turning young men away from Athenian moral traditions. When Socrates spoke in his own defense, he repeated his unyielding dedication to goading his fellow citizens into examining their unexamined assumptions about individual virtue. He vowed to remain their stinging gadfly. Socrates accepted his death sentence calmly because, as he put it, "nothing evil can happen to a good man, either in life or in death." He was executed in the customary way, with a poisonous drink concocted from powdered hemlock. Later sources report that many Athenians soon came to regret the execution of Socrates as a tragic mistake and a severe blow to their reputation as fair-minded citizens participating in a stable democracy.

The Philosophy of Plato and Aristotle

Tormented by anger and grief over Socrates' execution, his younger friend Plato (c. 429–348 B.C.E.) turned his back on marriage and a public career to become a philosopher. Plato felt driven to understand the nature of a world in which an evil fate could befall such a good man as Socrates. Plato's ideas on ethics and politics have remained central to philosophy and political science since his day, making him the most famous philosopher in Western civilization.

Plato established a philosophical "school," the Academy, in Athens around 386 B.C.E. that remained open for nine hundred years. The Academy was an informal association of educated people—mostly men but also including women—who studied philosophy, mathematics, and theoretical astronomy. Plato presented his ideas in written dialogues that read like plays instead of textbooks; he wanted them to make readers reflect thoughtfully on difficult philosophical questions. His views apparently changed over time—nowhere did he present a consistent set of doctrines.

Mosaic of Plato's Academy
This mosaic from the Roman period portrays philosophers (identified by their beards) at Plato's school in Athens holding discussions among themselves. Founded around 386 B.C.E., this school, called the Academy, became one of Greece's most famous and long-lasting organizations, attracting scholars and students until it closed around 530 C.E. The columns and tree express the Academy's harmonious blend of the natural and built environments, a setting meant to promote pleasant and productive discussions. (Erich Lessing/Art Resource, NY.)

Nevertheless, he always maintained one essential idea: moral virtues are universal and absolute, not relative.

To support this idea, Plato argued that virtues such as Goodness, Justice, Beauty, and Equality existed as realities he called Forms (or Ideas). He explained that the Forms are invisible, invariable, and eternal entities located in a higher realm beyond human existence. According to Plato, the Forms are the only true reality; what we experience through our senses in everyday life are only imperfect representations of these flawless realities, as if, he said, we were watching their shadows cast on the wall of a cave. His theory of Forms made **metaphysics**—the consideration of the ultimate nature of reality beyond the reach of the human senses—into a central issue for philosophers then and through the ages.

Plato's idea that humans possess immortal souls distinct from their bodies established the concept of **dualism**, a separation between spiritual and physical being. This notion influenced much of later philosophical and religious thought. Plato believed the proper goal for humans is to seek order and purity in their own souls by using reason to control their irrational desires, which are harmful. The desire to drink wine to excess, for example, is irrational because the drinker devalues the pain of the hangover that comes the next day. Finally, because the soul is immortal and the body is not, our present, impure existence is only one part of our true existence.

Plato presented the most famous version of his ideal society in his dialogue *The Republic*. This work, whose Greek title means "system of government," primarily concerns the nature of justice and the reasons people should be just. According to Plato, justice is impossible in a democracy and requires hierarchy. The trial of Socrates convinced Plato that most citizens are incapable of rising above ignorant self-interest. Plato ranked people in his ideal society by their ability to grasp the truth of the Forms. Women could rank as high as men because they possess the same virtues. To minimize distraction, the highest-ranking members of Plato's utopia are allowed to have neither private property nor individual families. These men and women are to live together in barracks, eat in mess halls, and exercise in the same gymnasia. They are to have sexual relations with various partners so that the best women can mate with the best men to produce the best children, who will be raised in a common environment by special caretakers. Those who achieve the highest level of knowledge in Plato's ideal society qualify to rule over it as philosopher-kings. Plato did not think such a society was truly possible, but he did believe that imagining it was important in teaching people to live justly. For this reason above all, he passionately believed the study of philosophy mattered to human life.

Plato was also influential because he trained an extremely famous pupil, Aristotle (384–322 B.C.E.). Aristotle created a practical philosophy for living a happy life and founded his own world-famous "school" in Athens in 335 B.C.E. There, he lectured with dazzling intelligence on nearly every branch of learning: biology, medicine, anatomy, psychology, meteorology, physics, chemistry, mathematics, music, metaphysics, rhetoric, political science, ethics, and literary criticism.

Aristotle's vast writings made him one of the most influential philosophers and scientists in Western civilization. His reputation rests on his development of rigorous systems of logical argument and his scientific investigation of the natural world. Creating a sophisticated system of logic, Aristotle established rules to tell the difference between a logically proven argument and a merely persuasive one. Furthermore, Aristotle insisted on explanations based on common sense rather than metaphysics. He denied the validity of Plato's theory of Forms, for example, on the grounds that the separate, unverifiable existence Plato asserted for them did not make sense. In scientific investigation, Aristotle believed that the best way to understand objects and beings was to observe them in their natural settings. The first scientist to try to collect all available information on animals, Aristotle recorded facts about more than five hundred different species, including insects. His recognition that whales and dolphins are mammals, which later writers on animals overlooked, was not rediscovered for another two thousand years.

Like Plato, Aristotle criticized democracy because it allowed uneducated instead of "better" people to control politics. Some of Aristotle's views justified inequalities characteristic of his time. He regarded slavery as natural, arguing that some people were by nature meant to be slaves because their souls lacked the rational part that should rule in a human. He also concluded, based on faulty notions of biology, that women were by nature inferior to men.

In ethics, Aristotle emphasized the need to develop habits of just behavior and not just good intentions. People should achieve self-control by training their minds to win out over instincts and passions. Self-control did not mean denying human desires and appetites; rather, it meant striking a balance between suppressing and heedlessly indulging physical yearnings, of finding "the mean." Aristotle claimed that the mind should rule in finding this balance because the intellect is the finest human quality and the mind is the true self—indeed, the godlike part of a person. Greek poets and dramatists had always emphasized the theme of moderation and humility as essential to human well-being, but Aristotle gave Western civilization the philosophical basis for achieving and valuing self-control in every individual.

The Fatal Weakening of Greece

The wars between city-states in the fifty years following the Peloponnesian War reduced Greece to a fatal state of weakness. In the 390s to 370s B.C.E., the Spartans did the most to provoke this fatal disunity by trying to conquer other city-states. Thebes, Athens, Corinth, and Argos responded by forming an anti-Spartan coalition because Spartan aggression threatened their interests at home and abroad. The Spartans counterbalanced the alliance by making a treaty with the Persian king. Abandoning their commitment to defend Greek freedom, the Spartans acknowledged the Persian ruler's right to control the Greek city-states of Anatolia—in return for permission to pursue their own power in Greece without Persian interference. This notorious treaty of 386 B.C.E., called the King's Peace, deprived the Anatolian Greeks of the freedom won in the Persian Wars. The Athenians rebuilt their military strength to combat Sparta. By 377 B.C.E., Athens had again become the leader of a naval alliance. This time, league members insisted that their rights be specified in writing to prevent any imperialistic Athenian behavior.

The Thebans became Greece's main land power in the 370s B.C.E. Attacking the Spartan homeland, they destroyed Sparta's power forever by freeing many helots. This Theban success so frightened the Athenians that they made a temporary alliance with the Spartans. Their combined armies confronted the Thebans in the battle of Mantinea in the Peloponnese in 362 B.C.E. Thebes won the battle but lost the war when its best general was killed and no capable replacement could be found.

The battle of Mantinea left the Greek city-states in powerless disunity. As the contemporary historian Xenophon said, "Everyone had supposed that the winners of this battle would be Greece's rulers and its losers their subjects; but there was only more confusion and disturbance in Greece after it than before." By the 350s B.C.E., then, the Greek city-states' struggle for domination over one another had left them in an impotent stalemate. This weakness opened the way for the rise of a new power—the kingdom of Macedonia, which threatened the Greeks' traditional independence.

REVIEW   How did daily life, philosophy, and the political situation change in Greece in the half-century following the Peloponnesian War (400–350 B.C.E.)?

Macedonia and Alexander the Great, 359–323 B.C.E.

Philip II, king of Macedonia (r. 359–336 B.C.E.), and his son and successor, Alexander the Great (r. 336–323 B.C.E.), took advantage of the Greek city-states' disunity to seize the leadership of Greece. That they transformed their previously weak kingdom into a superpower and conquered the Persian Empire ranks as one of the greatest achievements of leadership in ancient history. Their conquests marked the end of the Classical Age and propelled the cultural interactions of the Hellenistic Age.

Philip II and the Rise of Macedonian Power

The Macedonians' power sprang from the characteristics of their society and their ethnic pride. The Macedonian people demanded the freedom to tell their monarchs what needed to be changed, and a king could govern effectively only as long as he maintained the support of the other Macedonian men heading powerful families, who were the king's social equals and controlled large bands of followers. Fighting, hunting, and heavy drinking were these men's favorite pastimes. The king was expected to excel in these activities to prove he was capable of ruling. Queens and royal mothers received respect in this male-dominated society because they came from powerful families.

Macedonians thought of themselves as Greek by blood and took pride in their identity. They had their own language, but wealthy Macedonians learned to

Dancing Figures on a Gilded Bowl from Macedonia
Archaeologists discovered this large metal wine bowl, made of bronze plated with gold, in Macedonia. Its artistic style dates it to the 330s B.C.E. Wealthy Macedonian men at a Greek-style drinking party (symposium) used these expensive bowls to dilute wine so they could drink large amounts of it. The excited conditions of the two figures—a satyr (a half-man, half-horse creature) and a female worshipper of Dionysus, the god of wine and pleasure—express the ecstasy that the partygoers hoped to achieve. Since erect penises were shown frequently in Greek and Macedonian art associated with Dionysus, representing hopes for fertility and sexual pleasure, pictures like this were not regarded as obscene. (Thessaloniki, Archaeological Museum, © Archaeological Receipts Fund.)

speak Greek. Macedonians looked down on Greeks as being soft, but Greeks in turn scorned them as unsophisticated. The famed Athenian orator Demosthenes (384–322 B.C.E.) blasted Philip II as "not only not a Greek nor related to the Greeks, but not even a barbarian from a land worth mentioning; no, he's a plague from Macedonia, a region where you can't even buy a slave worth his salt."

Rivalry between kings and important families in Macedonia made it impossible to field a strong army until Philip became king. Indeed, kings so feared violence from their rivals that they stationed bodyguards outside the royal bedroom.

A military disaster brought Philip to the throne. The Illyrians, hostile neighbors to the north, had slaughtered the previous Macedonian king and four thousand troops. Philip restored the army's confidence by teaching the infantry an unstoppable new tactic. Arming his infantry with thrusting spears sixteen feet long and arranging them in a precisely aligned block formation (phalanx), he created dense rectangles of soldiers bristling with outstretched spears like a lethal porcupine. Using cavalry to disrupt the enemy's battle line and protect his own infantry's flanks, Philip smashed the Illyrians with his revived army.

Philip used diplomacy, bribery, and military action to turn Macedonia into an international power. A Greek contemporary said Philip "was never satisfied, extravagant—he did everything in a hurry . . . he never spared the time to reckon up his income and expenses." Philip found in Greek history the justification for making himself the leader of Greece: attack Persia to take revenge for the Persian Wars. Demosthenes complained that Greeks who did not resist the Macedonian king's plans were acting "as if Philip were a hailstorm, praying that he would not come their way, but not trying to do anything to head him off." Finally, Athens, Thebes, and some allies tried to block Philip, but in 338 B.C.E. the king and his Greek allies trounced the alliance's forces at the battle of Chaeronea in Boeotia. The defeated city-states were supposed to retain their internal freedom while becoming members of a military league under Philip's leadership. The course of later events showed the battle of Chaeronea to be a turning point in Greek history; although Philip promised the league city-states freedom from interference in their internal affairs, they had to yield to him their power to decide foreign policy. As it turned out, Greeks would never again regain the freedom to make such decisions on their own without some outside ruler looking over their shoulder.

Expansion of Macedonia under Philip II, r. 359–336 B.C.E.

The Conquests of Alexander the Great, 336–323 B.C.E.

Alexander III became king in 336 B.C.E. at age twenty, when an angry subordinate assassinated Philip II. Unconfirmed rumors speculated that Alexander's mother had arranged the murder. Alexander immediately killed potential rivals for the kingship and then quickly defeated Macedonia's enemies to the west and north. Next he forced the Greek city-states that had defected from the Macedonian-led league after Philip's death to rejoin. To demonstrate the price of disloyalty, in 335 B.C.E. he destroyed Thebes for rebelling.

In 334 B.C.E. Alexander launched the most astonishing military campaign in ancient history by leading a Macedonian and Greek army against the Persian

Empire to fulfill his father's dream of avenging Greece. Alexander's astounding success in conquering everything from Turkey to Egypt to Uzbekistan while still in his twenties earned him the title "the Great" in later ages and inspired countless legends. His greatness as a leader came from his ability to inspire his men to follow him into unknown lands, his genius in inventing solutions to difficult challenges on the battlefield, and his unlimited bravery. Alexander regularly rode his warhorse into the heart of the enemy's front line, sharing the danger of the common soldier. No one could miss him in his plumed helmet, vividly colored cloak, and armor polished to reflect the sun. He upset his principal adviser by giving away nearly all his property to create new landowners who would furnish troops. "What," the adviser asked, "do you have left for yourself?" "My hopes," Alexander replied. Those hopes came from his dream of becoming a warrior as splendid as Achilles in Homer's *Iliad;* he always slept with a copy of the epic and a dagger under his pillow.

Mosaic of Alexander the Great at the Battle of Issus
This large mosaic, which served as a floor in an upscale Roman house, was a copy of a famous earlier painting of the battle of Issus of 333 B.C.E. It shows Alexander the Great on his warhorse (at left) confronting the Persian king Darius in his chariot. Darius reaches out in horrified compassion for his warriors, who are sacrificing themselves to protect him. The original artist was an extremely skilled painter. Notice the dramatic foreshortening of the horse directly in front of Darius and the startling effect of the face of the dying warrior reflected in the polished shield just to the right of the horse. Alexander usually wore a helmet; why do you think the artist portrayed him bareheaded? (Erich Lessing/Art Resource, NY.)

Alexander displayed his heroic ambitions as his army advanced eastward through Persian territory (Map 3.1). In Anatolia, he visited Gordion, where an oracle had promised the lordship of Asia to whoever could untie a seemingly impenetrable knot of rope tying the yoke of an ancient chariot preserved in the city. The young king, so the story goes, cut the Gordian knot with his sword. When Alexander defeated the Persian king at the Battle of Issus in 333 B.C.E. and forced him to flee, leaving behind his wives and daughters, the Macedonian king treated the captured women with honor. Alexander's polite behavior toward the Persian royal women, showing that he wanted to behave like a noble ruler, won him respect from the peoples of the Persian Empire.

Alexander was a brilliant innovator in warfare. When Tyre, a fortified city on an island off the coast of the Levant, refused to surrender in 332 B.C.E., he built a massive stone pier as a platform for armored battering rams and catapults flinging boulders to breach the walls of the city. The capture of Tyre demonstrated to walled

Map 3.1 Conquests of Alexander the Great, r. 336–323 B.C.E.
The huge extent of Alexander's military campaigns in Asia made him a legend. From the time he led his army out of Macedonia and Greece in 334 B.C.E. until his death in Babylon in 323 B.C.E., he never stopped fighting. His careful intelligence gathering, combined with his charismatic and brilliant generalship, produced an unbroken string of victories. His skillful choice of regional administrators, his founding of garrison cities and colonies, and his preservation of local governing structures kept his conquests stable after he moved on. **For more help analyzing this map, see the map activity for this chapter in the Online Study Guide at** bedfordstmartins.com/huntconcise.

city-states that they could no longer hold out indefinitely against a siege and should simply surrender to Alexander immediately.

Alexander had a clear strategy for ruling a vast empire: establish colonies of Greeks and Macedonians in conquered territory but keep each area's traditional administrative system. The first new colony he established, in 331 B.C.E., was a city in Egypt on the Mediterranean coast to the west of the Nile River. He named it Alexandria, after himself. In Persia, he proclaimed himself king of Asia but left the existing Persian administrative system in place, even retaining some high-ranking Persian officials. That a Macedonian was now king of Persia hardly changed the lives of the local populations. They continued to send the same taxes to a still remote master, whom they rarely if ever saw.

Alexander's goals seem to have included becoming a legend by marching to the ends of the world. He led his forces northeast into lands previously unknown to Greeks (today Afghanistan and Uzbekistan) and even founded a city named Alexandria the Furthest to show that he had penetrated deeper into this region than any Persian king. When it proved impossible to capture the fast-moving locals, however, Alexander settled for an alliance sealed by his marriage to the local princess Roxane. He then headed east into India. Seventy days of marching through monsoon rains extinguished his soldiers' passion for conquest. In the spring of 326 B.C.E., they mutinied in western India and forced Alexander to turn around. A difficult march brought them back to Persia by 324 B.C.E. Alexander immediately began planning an invasion of the Arabian peninsula and, after that, North Africa.

Alexander's conquests changed him. He broke Philip's promise to the Greek city-states to respect their internal freedom when he ordered them to give citizenship to the many war-created exiles whose status as wandering, stateless persons was creating unrest. Even more startling was his announcement that he wished to receive the honors due a god. At first bewildered by these instructions, most Greek city-states soon complied by sending honorary religious delegations to him. A Spartan expressed the only prudent position on Alexander's deification: "If Alexander wishes to be a god, then we'll agree that he be called a god." Personal rather than political motives best explain Alexander's wish. He almost certainly had come to believe he was actually the son of Zeus; after all, Greek mythology contained many stories of Zeus mating with human females and producing children. Alexander's feats exceeded the bounds of human possibility, demonstrating that he had achieved godlike powers and therefore must be a god himself. Alexander's plans for more conquest ended when he died unexpectedly of an illness, made worse by heavy drinking, in Babylon in 323 B.C.E. Roxane gave birth to a child a few months after Alexander's death, but Alexander had made no plans for who should succeed him. The story goes that when his commanders asked him on his deathbed to whom he bequeathed his kingdom, he replied, "To the most powerful."

Historians disagree about almost everything concerning Alexander's character and goals. At one extreme is the opinion that he was a bloodthirsty monster interested only in endless conquest, while at the other is the claim that he was a visionary aiming to create a multiethnic world open to all cultures. The ancient sources suggest that Alexander had interlinked goals: the conquest and rule of the known world and the exploration and possible colonization of new territory beyond. Conquest through military action was a time-honored pursuit for Macedonian leaders and suited his restless, ruthless, and incredibly energetic nature. He included non-Macedonians in his administration and army because he needed their skills. His explorations benefited numerous scientific fields, from geography to botany, because he took along experts to collect and catalog the new knowledge they acquired; he regularly sent reams of new scientific information to his old tutor Aristotle. The far-flung cities that Alexander founded served as outposts to warn him about local uprisings. They also created new opportunities for trade in valuable goods such as spices that were not produced in the Mediterranean region.

An Athenian summed up the stunned reaction of many people to Alexander's deeds: "What strange and unexpected event has not occurred in our time? The life we have lived is no ordinary human one, but we were born to be an object of wonder to later ages." This prediction was accurate: stories of fabulous deeds attributed to Alexander became popular folktales throughout the world, reaching even distant regions where Alexander had never set foot, such as southern Africa. His legend as a warrior-hero lasted into later ages because his achievements seemed incredible. The most significant effect of his career was to bring the peoples of Greece and the Near East into closer interaction than ever before.

REVIEW   How were Philip II and his son Alexander able to establish such a vast empire?

The Hellenistic Kingdoms, 323–30 B.C.E.

The political, economic, and cultural changes of the Hellenistic period arose from the interaction of Greek and Near Eastern civilizations. These changes created tension between conquerors and subjects and had greater effect in some areas than in others. Greek ideas and practices had their biggest impact on the urban populations of Egypt and southwestern Asia. The many people who farmed in the countryside had much less contact with Greek ways of life.

The greatest political change came with the rise of new kingdoms, which turned many formerly independent Greeks into royal subjects. Commanders from Alexander's army created these kingdoms by seizing portions of his empire for themselves after his death and declaring themselves kings. Twenty years of war followed, until they finally established their families as dynasties ruling newly created Hellenistic kingdoms.

The Structure of the Hellenistic Kingdoms

Three major Hellenistic kingdoms arose from the division of Alexander's empire after his death (Map 3.2): Antigonus (c. 382–301 B.C.E.) took over in Anatolia, the Near East, Macedonia, and Greece; Seleucus (c. 358–281 B.C.E.) reigned in Babylonia

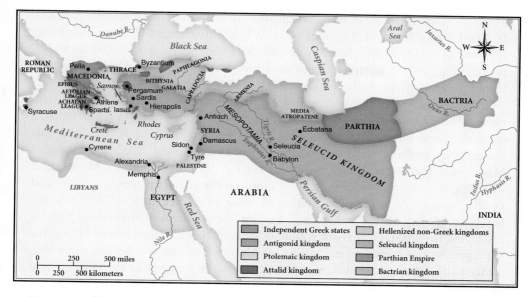

Map 3.2 Hellenistic Kingdoms, c. 240 B.C.E.
Monarchy became the dominant political system during the Hellenistic period in the areas of Alexander's former conquests. The Greek city-states kept their internal independence, but the kings controlled international policy. The biggest territorial changes to the three major kingdoms originally established by Alexander's successors were that by the mid-third century B.C.E., the Seleucids had given up their easternmost territories and the Attalid kingdom had carved out an independent local reign in western Anatolia.

and the East as far as India; and Ptolemy (c. 367–282 B.C.E.) controlled Egypt. These new rulers—historians call them the **successor kings** because they succeeded Alexander—had to create new kingdoms because they did not inherit their positions legitimately: they were self-declared monarchs with neither blood ties to any traditional royal family line nor any personal relationship to a particular territory. For this reason, historians characterize their rule as "personal monarchy."

By the middle of the third century B.C.E., these three kingdoms reached a balance of power. The Antigonid kingdom had been reduced to ruling Macedonia and controlling mainland Greece, whose city-states had to follow Antigonid foreign policy even though they retained certain internal freedoms. The Seleucid kingdom ruled in Syria and Mesopotamia but had lost Persia to the Parthians, a northern Iranian people, and the territory east of there to an Indian king. The Ptolemaic kingdom still ruled Egypt.

Conflicts frequently arose over contested border areas. The armies of the Ptolemaic and Seleucid kingdoms, for example, periodically battled over the Levant, just as the Egyptians and Hittites had done a thousand years earlier. The wars between the major kingdoms left openings for smaller, regional kingdoms to establish themselves.

The most famous of these was the kingdom of the Attalids in western Anatolia. In Central Asia (modern Afghanistan), Greek colonists settled by Alexander broke off from the Seleucid kingdom in the mid-third century B.C.E. to found their own regional kingdom in Bactria. It flourished for a century as a result of the trade in luxury goods between India and China and the Mediterranean world.

The success or failure of a successor king rested on his personal ability and power. The Hellenistic kings outside Macedonia realized they had to create political legitimacy and local support if their families were to continue to rule. For that reason, they included local traditions in their kingship. The Seleucids combined Macedonian with Near Eastern royal customs; the Ptolemies combined Macedonian with Egyptian. A letter from the city of Ilion (on the site of ancient Troy) summed up the situation of a successor king in its praise of a Seleucid king: "His rule depends mostly on his own excellence, and on the goodwill of his friends and on his forces." In truth, Hellenistic monarchy amounted to foreign rule over original local populations by kings and queens of Macedonian descent. Seleucus, for one, claimed this right as a universal truth: "It is not the customs of the Persians and other people that I impose upon you, but the law which is common to everyone, that what is decreed by the king is always just."

The survival of Hellenistic dynasties depended on their ability to create strong armies, effective administrations, and cooperative urban elites. Hellenistic armies and navies provided security against internal unrest as well as external enemies. To develop their forces, the Seleucid and Ptolemaic kings vigorously promoted immigration by Greeks and Macedonians, who received land grants in return for service as professional soldiers. When this source of manpower dried up, the kings had to employ more local men as troops. Military expenses eventually became a problem because the kings faced continual pressure to pay large numbers of mercenaries and because military technology had become so expensive. To compete effectively, a Hellenistic king had to build a fleet of warships propelled by hundreds of rowers and pay for giant artillery, such as catapults capable of flinging a projectile weighing 170 pounds a distance of nearly two hundred yards.

Hellenistic kings had to create large administrations to collect the revenues they needed. They recruited immigrant Greeks and Macedonians to be their top officials. Local men who wanted jobs as lower officials bettered their chances if they learned to read and write Greek in addition to their native language. This bilingualism qualified them to communicate official orders, especially tax laws, to farmers and crafts producers. Since Greeks and Macedonians generally saw themselves as too superior to mix with the locals, Greeks and non-Greeks tended to live in separate communities.

Agriculture and trade generated the wealth of the kingdoms, with cities as their economic and social hubs. Many Greeks and Macedonians lived in new cities founded by Alexander and his successors in Egypt and the Near East, but they also moved to old cities. Hellenistic kings promoted this urban emigration to build communities supportive of their rule. These rulers adorned their new cities with the traditional features of classical Greek city-states, such as gymnasia and theaters. Although these cities often had the political institutions of a city-state, such as councils and assemblies for citizen men, the requirement to follow royal policy limited their freedom. The kings treated the cities considerately because they needed the Greek and Macedonian urban elites to keep order and ensure a steady flow of tax revenues. Wealthy people had the crucial responsibility of collecting taxes from the surrounding countryside, as well as from their city, and sending the money on to the royal treasury. In turn, the kings honored and flattered members of the cities' social elites.

The kings' reliance on local elites led them to establish close relationships with well-to-do non-Greeks living in the old cities of Anatolia and the Near East, such as Sardis, Tyre, and Babylon. In addition, non-Greeks and non-Macedonians from eastern regions began moving westward to the new Hellenistic Greek cities in increasing numbers. Jews in particular moved from Palestine to Anatolia, Greece, and Egypt. The Jewish community eventually became an influential minority in Egyptian Alexandria, the most important Hellenistic city.

All the Hellenistic kingdoms eventually fell to the Romans. The Ptolemaic kingdom survived the longest. The end came when Queen

Hellenistic Architecture in the Jordanian Desert
This decorative front for a structure carved into a sheer rock cliff in probably the first century B.C.E. stands at the entrance to the ancient settlement of Petra, the capital of the Nabatean Arabs (in what is today Jordan). This desert people grew rich by controlling caravan trade from Asia across the deserts to the Mediterranean coast. In the Hellenistic spirit of cultural interaction, they took Greek architectural models and adapted them to express their own style. For example, this carved front has Greek triangular pediments but also includes a round gazebo to provide a break in the upper pediment. What do you think the visual effect of this innovation might have been as the sun moved through the day? (Z. Radovan, www.BibleLandPictures.com.)

Cleopatra VII, a descendant of Ptolemy and the last Macedonian to rule Egypt, chose the losing side in the Roman civil war between Mark Antony, her lover at the time, and the future emperor Augustus in the late first century B.C.E. In 30 B.C.E., an invading Roman army ended her reign and three centuries of Hellenistic monarchy.

Hierarchy in Hellenistic Society

Hierarchy became stronger in the Seleucid and Ptolemaic kingdoms. The royal family and the king's friends ranked highest. The Greek and Macedonian elites of the major cities ranked next. Just under them came the non-Greek wealthy elites of the cities, the leaders of large minority urban populations, and the traditional lords and princes of local groups who maintained their ancestral control over rural regions. Lowest of the free population were the masses of small merchants, artisans, and laborers. Slaves had no social status.

The growth of the kingdoms increased the demand for slave labor throughout the eastern Mediterranean. The centrally located island of Delos established a market where up to ten thousand slaves were bought and sold daily. The fortunate ones would become servants at court and live physically comfortable lives; the luckless ones would dig, and soon die, in the mines. Enslaved children often were taken far from home and put to work. A sales contract from 259 B.C.E. shows that Zeno, to whom the camel trader wrote, bought a girl about seven years old named Sphragis (Gemstone) to work in an Egyptian textile factory. This was not her first job. Originally from Sidon in the Levant, she had previously been the slave of a Greek mercenary soldier employed by Toubias, a Jewish cavalry commander in the Transjordan region.

The majority of the population continued to live in small villages. Most farmers were forced tenants on royal land who were not allowed to move away or stop working. Free peasants still worked their own small plots as well as the farms of wealthy landowners. Perhaps 80 percent of all adult men and women had to work the land to produce enough food to sustain the population. Men could also work as deckhands on the merchant ships that sailed the Mediterranean Sea and Indian Ocean. In the cities, the poor worked as small merchants, peddlers, and artisans.

The welfare of the masses depended on the generosity of the rich; without democracy, the poor had no political power to demand support. This strongly hierarchical arrangement reflected the top-down structure of Hellenistic society. Kings and queens intermittently helped the poor with distributions of food, and the wealthy increasingly followed their example. On the island of Samos, for example, rich citizens funded a foundation to distribute free grain. Many cities also began sponsoring doctors. Donor-sponsored schools sprang up in various cities, and sometimes girls as well as boys could attend.

Women's lives in the Hellenistic world depended on their social status. Hellenistic queens enjoyed enormous riches and high honor. Because the Ptolemaic

Egyptian-Style Statue of Queen Arsinoe II

Arsinoe II (c. 316–270 B.C.E.), daughter of King Ptolemy I and widow of the Macedonian successor king Lysimachus, married her brother Ptolemy II to unify the monarchy. Hailed as Philadelphoi (Brother-Loving), the couple set a precedent for brother-sister marriages in the Ptolemaic dynasty. One of the most remarkable women of the Hellenistic period, Arsinoe was the first Ptolemaic ruler whose image was placed in Egyptian temples as a "temple-sharing goddess." This eight-foot-tall, red granite statue portrays her in the traditional sculptural style of the pharaohs. (© Vatican Museums.)

royal family observed the Egyptian royal tradition of brother-sister marriage, daughters could rule alongside sons. For example, Arsinoe II (c. 316–270 B.C.E.), the daughter of Ptolemy I, first married the Macedonian successor king Lysimachus, who gave her four towns as her personal domain. After Lysimachus's death she married her brother Ptolemy II and exerted at least as much influence on Egyptian policy as he did. The virtues publicly praised in a queen reflected traditional Greek values for women. When the city of Hierapolis around 165 B.C.E. passed a decree honoring Queen Apollonis of the Attalid kingdom, for example, it praised her piety toward the gods, her reverence toward her parents, her distinguished conduct toward her husband, and her harmonious relations with her "beautiful children born in wedlock." Not all children were as fortunate as hers. Greeks continued to abandon infants they could not or would not raise—girls more often than boys, although Egyptians and Jews did not practice exposure (abandonment) of babies. Exposure differed from infanticide because the parents expected someone else to find the child and raise him or her, usually as a slave.

Some women achieved greater control over their own lives in the Hellenistic kingdoms. A woman of exceptional wealth could now enter public life by making donations or loans to her city and be rewarded with an official post in local government. In Egypt, women acquired greater say in the family because marriage contracts, the standard procedure, gradually evolved from an agreement between the groom and the bride's parents to one in which the bride made her own arrangements with the groom.

REVIEW What were the biggest challenges the Hellenistic kings faced in creating and running new states?

Hellenistic Literature, Art, Science, Philosophy, and Religion

Hellenistic literature, art, philosophy, science, and religion all reflected three principal characteristics of the age: the effects of royal wealth, the tendency of ordinary people to focus on private matters more than public life, and the increased interaction of diverse peoples. In keeping with the era's increasing hierarchy, the kings determined cultural developments by deciding which fields and which scholars and artists to support financially. The kings' status as sole rulers and the source of all law meant that authors and artists did not have freedom to criticize public policy and thus concentrated on individual emotions and aspects of private life. Nevertheless, royal support did produce an expansion and diversification of knowledge. Cultural interaction between Greek and Near Eastern traditions happened most prominently in language and religion. These developments greatly influenced the Romans; in this way, "captive Greece captured its fierce victor," the Roman poet Horace (65–8 B.C.E.) wrote, expressing the effect of Hellenistic culture on his own.

Patronage and Emotion in Literature and Art

The Hellenistic kings served as patrons financing writers and artists on a vast scale, competing with one another to lure the best ones to their capitals with magnificent salaries and benefits. The kings paid for many intellectual innovations but little technology, except for that which could be put to military use. The Ptolemies turned Alexandria into the Mediterranean's leading center of the arts. There they established the first scholarly research institute. Its massive library had the ambitious goal of trying to collect all the books (that is, manuscripts) in the world; it grew to hold half a million scrolls. Linked to it was a building in which the scholars dined together and produced encyclopedias of knowledge, such as *The Wonders of the World* and *On the Rivers of Europe* by Callimachus, a learned prose writer as well as a poet. The name of this building, the Museum (meaning "place of the Muses," the Greek goddesses of learning and the arts), is still used to designate institutions that preserve and promote knowledge. The output of the Alexandrian scholars was huge. The champion researcher was Didymus (c. 80–10 B.C.E.), nicknamed "Brass Guts" for having written nearly four thousand books; it is a sad commentary on the loss of ancient sources that not a single one has survived.

The writers and artists whom Hellenistic kings paid had to please their employers with their works. The poet Theocritus (c. 300–260 B.C.E.), for example, relocated from his home in Syracuse to the Ptolemaic court. In a poem praising his employer, the king, he spelled out their professional relationship: "The spokesmen of the Muses [that is, poets] celebrate King Ptolemy II in return for his benefactions." Theocritus and other poets succeeded by avoiding political subjects and stressing the division in society between the intellectual elite—to which the kings belonged—and the uneducated masses. Their poetry centered on individual emotions and broke new ground in demanding great intellectual effort, as well as emotional engagement, from the audience. Only people with a deep literary education could appreciate the allusions and complex references to mythology that these poets included in their elegant poems.

Theocritus was the first Greek poet to express the divide between town and countryside that was becoming a Hellenistic reality. The *Idylls,* his pastoral poems, emphasize the discontinuity between the elegant environment of the city and the simple life in the country, reflecting the fundamental social division of the Ptolemaic kingdom between the food consumers of the towns and the food producers of the countryside. He presented a city dweller's idealized dream that country life must be peaceful and stress-free; this fiction deeply influenced later literature.

Women poets made important contributions to literature in the Hellenistic period, apparently without any royal support. They excelled in writing **epigrams**, short poems originally meant for tombstones. Elegantly worded poems written by women from diverse regions of the Hellenistic world—Anyte of Tegea in the Peloponnese, Nossis of Locri in southern Italy, Moero of Byzantium—still survive. Women, from "companions" to respectable matrons, figured as frequent subjects in their work and expressed a wide variety of personal feelings, love above all. Nossis's poem on the power of "Eros" (Greek for "love"), for example, proclaimed, "Nothing is sweeter than Eros. All other delights are second to it—from my mouth I spit out even honey. And this Nossis says: whoever Aphrodite has not kissed knows not what sort of flowers are her roses." No Hellenistic literature presents the depth of human emotion better than the epigrams of the women poets.

Hellenistic drama mainly presented plays centered on individual emotions; writers no longer expressed open criticism of politics or contemporary leaders. Comic playwrights such as Menander (c. 342–289 B.C.E.), the most famous Hellenistic dramatist, composed plays with timeless plots concerning the trials and tribulations of fictional lovers. These comedies of manners, as they are called, proved enormously popular because, like modern situation comedies, they offered a humorous view of situations and feelings that occurred in daily life, cleverly made fun of social conditions, and usually had happy endings to resolve the troubles that energized the plot. Recent papyrus finds have allowed us to recover almost complete plays written by Menander and to appreciate his skill in depicting personality. No tragedies written in this period have survived intact, but we know that their plots could involve the interaction among peoples and cultures. Ezechiel, for example, a Jew living in Alexandria, wrote *Exodus,* a tragedy in Greek about Moses leading the Hebrews out of captivity in Egypt.

Hellenistic sculptors and painters also stressed human emotions. Classical-era artists had given their subjects' faces a serenity that represented an ideal rather than reality. Hellenistic artists portrayed individual emotions more naturally in a variety of types. In portrait sculpture, Lysippus's widely copied bust of Alexander the Great captured the young commander's passionate dreaminess. A sculpture by an unknown artist commemorated the third-century B.C.E. Attalid victory over the plundering Gauls (one of the Celtic peoples, called Galatians by the Greeks) by showing a defeated Gallic warrior stabbing himself after killing his wife to prevent her enslavement by the victors. A large-scale painting of Alexander battling the Persian

Dying Barbarians
Hellenistic artists excelled in portraying deeply emotional scenes such as this one of a Gallic warrior committing suicide after killing his wife to prevent their capture by the enemy after defeat in battle. The Gauls were one of the Celtic peoples, called Galatians by Greeks. Celtic women followed their men to the battlefield and willingly exposed themselves to the same dangers. The original statues (these are Roman imitations) were in bronze, forming part of a large sculptural group that Attalus I, king of Pergamum from 241 to 197 B.C.E., set up to commemorate his victory around 230 B.C.E. over the Gauls, who had moved into the region to conduct raids. Why do you think Attalus celebrated his victory by erecting a monument that portrayed the defeated enemy as brave and noble? **For more help analyzing this image, see the visual activity for this chapter in the Online Study Guide at** bedfordstmartins .com/huntconcise. (Erich Lessing/ Art Resource, NY.)

king Darius portrayed Alexander's intense concentration and Darius's horrified expression of concern for his dying men (see the illustration on page 95). The artist, probably either Philoxenus of Eretria or a Greek woman from Egypt named Helena (one of the first female artists known), used foreshortening and strong contrasts between shadows and highlights to increase the picture's emotional impact.

Hellenistic art differed from classical art in its social context. Works of classical art had been paid for by the city-states or by wealthy individuals to be displayed in public. Now sculptors and painters created their works primarily for royalty and the urban elites, who wanted to show they had artistic taste like the royal family.

A new diversity of subjects emerged in this Hellenistic art, showing humans in a wide variety of poses, mostly from private life. Hellenistic sculptors portrayed subjects never before shown: foreigners, drunkards, battered athletes, wrinkled old people. The female nude became a particular favorite. A statue of Aphrodite, which Praxiteles sculpted completely nude as an innovation in portraying this goddess, became so famous as a religious object and tourist attraction in the city of Cnidos that a foreign king offered to pay off the citizens' entire public debt if they would give him this work of art. They refused.

Innovation in Science

Scientific investigation of the physical world expanded so aggressively in the Hellenistic period that historians have dubbed it the Golden Age of ancient science. Various factors contributed to this flourishing of thought and discovery: Alexander's expedition had encouraged curiosity and increased knowledge about the extent and differing features of the world, royal wealth supported scientists financially, and the concentration of scientists in Alexandria paid by the Ptolemaic kings increased the exchange of ideas.

The greatest advances came in geometry and mathematics. Euclid, who taught in Alexandria around 300 B.C.E., made revolutionary progress in the analysis of two- and three-dimensional space. The usefulness of Euclidean geometry continues today. Archimedes of Syracuse (287–212 B.C.E.) was a mathematical genius who calculated the approximate value of pi and devised a way to manipulate very

Tower of the Winds
This forty-foot octagonal tower, built in Athens about 150 B.C.E., made use of scientific knowledge developed in Hellenistic Alexandria to tell time and predict the weather. Eight sundials, now missing, were carved on the wall to display the time year-round; a huge interior water clock showed hour, day, and phase of the moon; and a vane on the top showed wind direction. The carved figures represent the winds. Each figure's clothing reflects the typical weather coming from that direction, with the cold northern wind wearing boots and a heavy cloak, while the mild southern wind has bare feet and gauzy clothes. (The Art Archive/Dagli Orti.)

large numbers. He also invented hydrostatics (the science of the equilibrium of a fluid system) and mechanical devices, such as a screw for lifting water to a higher elevation. Archimedes' shout of delight—"I have found it" (*heureka* in Greek)—when he solved a problem while soaking in his bathtub lives on in the modern expression "Eureka!"

The sophistication of Hellenistic mathematics affected other fields that also required complex computations. About 280 B.C.E., Aristarchus of Samos became the first to propose the correct model of the solar system: the earth revolves around the sun, which is far larger and far more distant than it appears. Later astronomers rejected Aristarchus's heliocentric model in favor of the traditional geocentric one (with the earth at the center) because calculations based on the orbit he calculated for the earth failed to correspond to the observed positions of the planets. Aristarchus had made an unfortunate mistake: assuming a circular orbit instead of an elliptical one. Eratosthenes of Cyrene (c. 275–194 B.C.E.) pioneered mathematical geography. He calculated the circumference of the earth with astonishing accuracy by simultaneously measuring the length of the shadows of widely separated but identically tall structures.

The ideas and procedures of Hellenistic researchers gave Western scientific thought an important start toward the principle scientists now take for granted: the need to verify theory through observation and measurement in experiments. Hellenistic scientists maintained a spirit of discovery despite the difficulties imposed by technical limitations. Many experiments were not possible because no technology existed for the precise measurement of very short intervals of time. Measuring tiny quantities of matter was also next to impossible. The science of the age was as quantitative as it could be given these limitations. Ctesibius of Alexandria (b. c. 310 B.C.E.), a contemporary of Aristarchus's, invented the scientific field of pneumatics by creating machines operated by air pressure. He also built a working water pump, an organ powered by water, and the first accurate water clock. A later Alexandrian, Hero, continued the Hellenistic tradition of mechanical ingenuity by building a rotating sphere powered by steam. As in most of Hellenistic science, these inventions did not lead to uses in daily life. The scientists and their royal supporters were more interested in new theoretical discoveries than in practical results, and the metallurgical technology to produce the pipes, fittings, and screws needed to build powerful machines did not yet exist.

Military technology was the one area in which Hellenistic science produced practical inventions. The kings hired engineers to design powerful catapults and wheeled siege towers many stories high to batter down the defenses of walled cities. The most famous large-scale application of technology for nonmilitary purposes was the construction of a lighthouse three hundred feet tall (the Pharos) for the harbor at Alexandria. Using polished metal mirrors to reflect the light from a large bonfire, the lighthouse shone many miles out at sea. Grateful sailors regarded it as one of the wonders of the world.

Medicine also benefited from the Hellenistic desire for new knowledge. Increased contact between Greeks and people of the Near East made the medical knowledge of the ancient civilizations of Mesopotamia and Egypt better known in the West and promoted the study of human health and illness. Around 325 B.C.E., Praxagoras of Cos discovered the value of measuring the pulse in diagnosing illness. A bit later, Herophilus of Chalcedon (b. c. 300 B.C.E.), working in Alexandria, became the first scientist in the West to study anatomy by dissecting human cadavers and, it was rumored, the bodies of condemned criminals while they were still alive; he had this gruesome opportunity because the king authorized his research. Some of the anatomical terms Herophilus invented are still used. Other Hellenistic advances in understanding anatomy included the discovery of the nerves and nervous system.

As in science, however, Hellenistic medicine was limited by its inability to measure and observe things not visible to the naked eye. Unable to see what really occurred under the skin in living patients, for example, doctors thought many illnesses in women were caused by displacements of the womb, which they wrongly believed could move around in the body. These mistaken ideas could not be corrected because the technology to evaluate them did not yet exist.

New Personal Philosophies

New philosophies arose in the Hellenistic period asking the same question: what is the best way for humans to live? They recommended different paths to the same answer: individual humans must find personal serenity so that they feel free of the turbulence caused by forces beyond their control, especially chance. Greeks felt the need for a personal philosophy that would help them exist in a world in which they no longer had freedom because their fates ultimately rested in the hands of distant, unpredictable kings. It therefore seemed urgent, at least for those wealthy enough to spend time philosophizing, to look for personal, private solutions to the disturbing new conditions of life in the Hellenistic Age. More women than ever before joined in this philosophical quest.

Hellenistic philosophers concentrated not on metaphysics but on **materialism**, a doctrine explaining that only things made up of matter truly exist. It denied the concept of soul that Plato described and ignored any suggestion that nonmaterial phenomena could exist. Hellenistic philosophy was regularly divided into three related areas: *logic,* the process for discovering truth; *physics,* the fundamental truth about the nature of existence; and *ethics,* the way humans should achieve happiness and well-being as a consequence of logic and physics. The era's philosophical thought greatly influenced Roman thinkers and many important Western philosophers who followed them.

One of the two most significant new philosophical schools of thought was **Epicureanism**, named after its founder, Epicurus (341–271 B.C.E.). Epicurus admitted not only women but also slaves as regular members of his group. His lover, the "companion" Leontion, became well known for her treatise criticizing the views of Aristotle's most famous pupil, Theophrastus. Epicurus taught that people should above all be free of the fear of death because all matter consists of microscopic atoms in random movement and death is therefore nothing more than the painless separating of the body's atoms. Moreover, he insisted, human knowledge must be empirical—that is, derived from experience and perception. Despite what people say, he explained, the gods do not cause thunder, drought, and other natural events. The gods live far away in perfect peacefulness, paying no attention to human affairs. People, therefore, have no reason to fear the gods.

Epicurus believed people should pursue pleasure, but his notion of true pleasure had a special definition: the "absence of disturbance" from pain and everyday troubles, passions, and desires. A calm life spent with friends apart from the cares of the world could best provide this essential peace of mind. His teaching represented a serious challenge to the traditional ideal of Greek citizenship, which required men of means to participate in local politics and citizen women to engage in public religious cults.

The other important new Hellenistic philosophy, **Stoicism**, did not call for people to retire from public life. Its name derived from the Painted Stoa in Athens, where Stoic philosophers discussed their doctrines. Zeno (c. 333–262 B.C.E.), from Citium on Cyprus, founded Stoicism, but Chrysippus (c. 280–206 B.C.E.), from Cilicia in Anatolia, did the most to make it a complete guide to life. Stoics believed that life is fated but that people should still pursue virtue as their goal. Virtue, they said, consists of putting oneself in harmony with the divine, rational force of universal Nature by developing the virtues of good sense, justice, courage, and moderation. These doctrines applied to women as well as men. In fact, the Stoics advocated equal citizenship for women and doing away with marriage and families. Zeno even proposed unisex clothing as a way to obliterate unnecessary distinctions between women and men.

The belief that fate determines everything created the question of whether humans truly have free will. Employing some of the subtlest reasoning ever applied to this fundamental issue, Stoic philosophers concluded that purposeful human actions do have significance. Nature, itself good, does not prevent evil from occurring because virtue would otherwise have no meaning. What matters in life is the striving for good, not the result. A person should therefore take action against evil by, for example, participating in politics. To be a Stoic also meant to shun desire and anger while enduring pain and sorrow calmly, an attitude that yields the modern meaning of the word *stoic*. Through endurance and self-control, followers of Stoicism attained personal serenity. They did not fear death because they believed that people live over and over again infinitely, in a fashion identical to their present lives.

Numerous other philosophies emerged in the Hellenistic period to compete with Epicureanism and Stoicism. Some of them carried on the work of famous earlier thinkers such as Plato and Pythagoras. Still others struck out in new directions. Skeptics, for example, aimed at the same state of personal serenity as did Epicureans and Stoics, but from a completely different assumption about reality. Their ideas were influenced by the ascetic wise men (magi) encountered on Alexander the Great's expedition to India. Skeptics believed that secure knowledge about anything is impossible because the human senses yield contradictory information about the world. All people can do, they insisted, is depend on appearances while withholding judgment about their reality, hence our term *skeptical*.

The philosophers called Cynics boastfully rejected every convention of ordinary life, especially wealth and material comfort. They believed that humans should aim for complete self-sufficiency. Whatever is natural is good, they said, and can be done without shame before anyone. According to this idea, public defecation and fornication were acceptable, and women and men alike were free to have sex however and whenever they pleased. Above all, Cynics rejected traditional human behavior as ridiculous. The most famous early Cynic, Diogenes (d. 323 B.C.E.), from Sinope on the Black Sea, had a reputation for wearing borrowed clothes and sleeping in a giant storage jar. Almost as notorious was Hipparchia, a Cynic of the late fourth century B.C.E. She once bested an obnoxious philosophical opponent named Theodorus the Atheist with the following argument: "That which would not be considered wrong if done by Theodorus would also not be considered wrong if done by Hipparchia. Now if Theodorus strikes himself, he does no wrong. Therefore, if Hipparchia strikes Theodorus, she does no wrong." The name Cynic, which literally means "like a dog," reflects the ancient evaluation of this unconventional way of life. Our word *cynical* recalls the Cynics' biting criticism of what others regarded as normal.

Hellenistic philosophy reached a wider audience than ever before. Although the working poor had neither the leisure nor the money to attend philosophers' lectures, affluent members of society studied philosophy in growing numbers. Greek settlers took their interest in philosophy with them, even to the most remote Hellenistic cities. Archaeologists excavating a Hellenistic city located thousands of miles from Greece on the Oxus River in Afghanistan, for example, turned up a Greek philosophical text.

Hellenistic Religions

Religious ideas changed in the Hellenistic Age to reflect people's desire for a more personal experience. Sharing these new ideas became easier because a simplified version of Greek called **Koine** (meaning "shared" or "common") had become the international language of the eastern Mediterranean region; this was why the Egyptian camel trader stranded in Syria had to communicate in Greek. The most striking evidence of this development comes from Afghanistan. There, King Ashoka (r. c. 268–232 B.C.E.), who ruled most of the Indian subcontinent, used Greek as one of the languages in his public inscriptions introducing his subjects to Buddhist traditions of self-control, such as not eating meat. Local languages did not disappear in the Hellenistic kingdoms, however. In one region of Anatolia, people spoke twenty-two different languages.

The diversity of Hellenistic religions reflected the effects of cultural interaction between Greeks and local peoples in the Near East. The traditional cults of Greek religion remained popular and even spread farther, but new cults also arose in response to changing political and social conditions. As always in polytheistic religions, people could worship in both old and new cults. Those that had previously had only local significance, such as that of the Greek healing god Asclepius or the mystery cult of the

Egyptian goddess Isis, grew prominent all over the Hellenistic world. In many cases, Greek cults and local cults from the eastern Mediterranean influenced each other. Their beliefs meshed well because these cults shared many assumptions about how to remedy the troubles of human life. In other instances, local cults and Greek cults existed side by side, with some overlap. The inhabitants of villages in the Fayum district of Egypt, for example, continued worshipping their traditional crocodile god and mummifying their dead according to the old ways but also worshipped Greek deities.

New cults picked up a prominent theme of Hellenistic thought: anxiety about the relationship between individuals and the unpredictable power of chance (or luck). Although Greek religion had always been concerned with the unpredictability of life, the chaotic course of Greek history since the Peloponnesian War had made human existence seem more uncertain than ever. Since advances in astronomy had revealed the mathematical precision of the heavens, religion now had to address the seeming disconnect between that celestial uniformity and the shapeless chaos of life on earth. One increasingly popular approach to bridging that gap was to rely on astrology for guidance derived from the movement of the stars and planets, thought of as divinities. Another very common choice was to worship Tychê (Chance) as a god in the hope of securing good luck in life.

The most revolutionary approach in seeking protection from the unpredictable tricks of Tychê (Chance) was to pray for salvation from a king or queen regarded as a god, worshipped in what are known as **ruler cults**. Various populations established these cults to honor royal benefactors. The Athenians, for example, deified the Macedonians Antigonus and his son Demetrius as savior gods in 307 B.C.E., when these commanders liberated the city and bestowed magnificent gifts on it. Like most ruler cults, this one expressed both spontaneous gratitude and a desire to flatter the rulers in the hope of obtaining additional favors. Many cities in the Ptolemaic and Seleucid kingdoms created ruler cults for their kings and queens. An inscription put up by Egyptian priests in 238 B.C.E. describes the qualities appropriate to a divine king and queen:

> King Ptolemy III and Queen Berenice, his sister and wife, the Benefactor Gods, . . . have provided good government . . . and [after a drought] sacrificed a large amount of their revenues for the salvation of the population, and by importing grain . . . they saved the inhabitants of Egypt.

As these words make clear, the Hellenistic rulers' tremendous power and wealth gave them the status of gods among the ordinary people who depended on their generosity and protection in times of danger. The idea that a human being could be a god, present on earth to be a "savior" delivering people from evils, was firmly established and would prove influential later in Roman imperial religion and Christianity.

Healing divinities offered another form of protection to anxious individuals. People's faith in divine healing gave them hope that they could overcome the

Underground Labyrinth for Healing

This underground stone labyrinth formed part of the enormous healing sanctuary of the god Asclepius at Epidaurus in Greece. Patients traveled to the site from all over the Mediterranean world. They climbed down into the labyrinth, which was covered and dark, as part of their treatment, which involved reaching a trance state to receive dreams that provided instructions for their healing and, sometimes, miraculous surgery. (The Art Archive/Dagli Orti.)

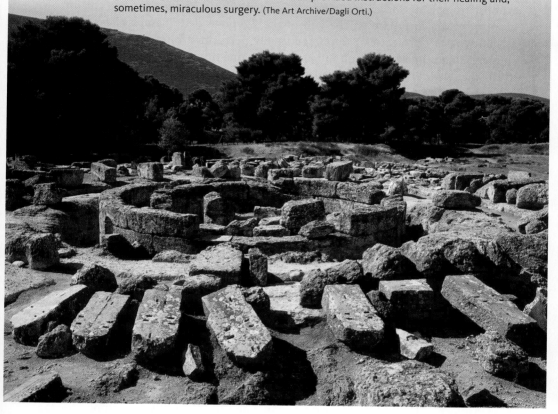

constant, unpredictable danger from disease. The cult of the god Asclepius, who offered cures for illness and injury at his many shrines, spread widely during the Hellenistic period. Suppliants seeking Asclepius's help would sleep in special dormitories at his shrines to await dreams in which he prescribed healing treatments. These prescriptions emphasized diet and exercise, but numerous inscriptions set up by grateful patients also testified to miraculous cures and surgery performed while the sufferer slept. The following example is typical:

> Ambrosia of Athens was blind in one eye. . . . She . . . ridiculed some of the cures [described in inscriptions in the sanctuary] as being incredible and impossible. . . . But when she went to sleep, she saw a vision; she thought the god was standing next to her. . . . He split open the diseased eye and poured in a medicine. When day came she left cured.

Mystery cults that promised secret knowledge as a key to salvation during life and after death grew even more popular. The cults of the Greek god Dionysus and, in particular, the Egyptian goddess Isis gained many followers in this period. The popularity of Isis, whose powers extended over every area of human life, received a boost from King Ptolemy I, who established a headquarters for her cult in Alexandria. He also promoted the cult of the Egyptian deity Sarapis, Isis's consort, as his dynasty's protector; Sarapis reportedly performed miracles of rescue from shipwreck and illness. The cult of Isis, who became the most popular female divinity in the Mediterranean, involved extensive rituals and festivals mixing features of Egyptian and Greek religion. Followers of Isis hoped, in return for a virtuous life, to gain the goddess's help against the demonic influence of Tychê (Chance); they also expected she would reward them with a happier fate after death. That an Egyptian deity such as Isis could achieve enormous popularity among Greeks (and Romans in later times) alongside the traditional gods of Greek religion is the best evidence of the cultural cross-fertilization characteristic of the Hellenistic world.

The history of Judaism in the Hellenistic period shows especially strong evidence of cultural interaction. King Ptolemy II had the Hebrew Bible translated into Greek (the Septuagint) in Alexandria in the early third century B.C.E. Many Jews, especially those living in the large Diaspora communities that had grown up in Hellenistic cities outside Palestine, adopted the Greek language and many aspects of Greek culture. Nevertheless, these Hellenized Jews largely retained the ritual practices and habits of life that defined traditional Judaism, and they did not worship Greek gods. The more traditional Jewish community in Palestine was controlled militarily and politically first by the Ptolemies and then by the Seleucids. Both kingdoms allowed the Jews to live according to their ancestral laws under the leadership of a high priest in Jerusalem.

Internal conflicts among Jews erupted in second-century B.C.E. Palestine over the amount of Greek influence that traditional Judaism could accept. The Seleucid king Antiochus IV (r. 175–163 B.C.E.) intervened in the conflict in support of the Jerusalem Jews who were most Greek-like in their ways. In 167 B.C.E., Antiochus converted the main Jewish temple there into a Greek temple and outlawed the practice of Jewish religious customs, such as circumcision and observing the Sabbath. A revolt led by Judah the Maccabee eventually won Jewish independence from the Seleucids after twenty-five years of war. The most famous episode of this revolt was the retaking of the Jerusalem temple and its rededication to the worship of the Jewish god, Yahweh—a triumphant moment celebrated by Jews ever since on the holiday of Hanukkah. That Greek culture attracted some Jews in the first place, however, provides a striking example of the transformations that affected many—though far from all—people of the Hellenistic world. By the time of the Roman Empire, one of those transformations would be Christianity, whose beliefs had roots in the cultural interaction of Hellenistic Jews and Greeks and their ideas on religion.

REVIEW   What were the main cultural changes that took place during the Hellenistic Age?

Conclusion

The transition in Greek history from the Classical Age to the Hellenistic Age produced changes just as significant as those that had taken place earlier during the transition from the Archaic Age to the Classical Age. New ideas emerged, new political systems arose, a leader of legendary fame shocked the world, and, most important, a new level of interaction between people in Greece and the Near East changed society and culture in those regions at a fundamental level. The uncertainty of the times stimulated creativity as well as anxiety.

Some of these changes were intended; others were not. As before, war and its unpredictable consequences had a tremendous influence extending far beyond simply who won on the battlefield. The aftermath of the protracted Peloponnesian

Mapping the West The Fall of the Hellenistic Kingdoms, to 30 B.C.E.
By 30 B.C.E. (the death of Cleopatra VII, the last Ptolemaic monarch of Egypt), the Roman republic had conquered or absorbed the Hellenistic kingdoms of the eastern Mediterranean. Competition for the tremendous wealth that Romans captured in this expansion helped fuel bitter and divisive feuds between Rome's most ambitious generals and political leaders. The territories of the former Hellenistic kingdoms became the main part of the eastern half of the Roman Empire.

War eroded the confidence and prosperity that had characterized the fifth century B.C.E. and left many people, especially in Athens, feeling angry about wartime atrocities and nostalgic for the supposedly golden days of the past. Later Western civilization benefited, however, because thinkers, especially Plato and Aristotle, responded to the troubles of the times by creating philosophical and scientific knowledge that was essential to understanding and dealing with the human condition.

Philip II, the Macedonian king, certainly intended to take advantage of the disunity of the Greek city-states to make his formerly insignificant land strong enough to topple the world's superpower, the Persian Empire. Alexander, however, was the one whose unsurpassed leadership allowed him to fulfill his father's dream of glory, winning lasting fame—still to be known as "the Great" more than two thousand years later!—without ever fully disclosing why he did what he did. By installing Greeks as administrators and guards all over the Near East, he set in motion the process that created the multicultural world of the Hellenistic Age.

The new Hellenistic kingdoms changed society and culture from the top down. To Greeks, these undemocratic and strictly hierarchical regimes demonstrated that freedom was precarious, even after centuries of being the standard for Greek political life. The kingdoms also showed that the concentration of money at the highest level of a hierarchical society—in the hands of the royal family—and its

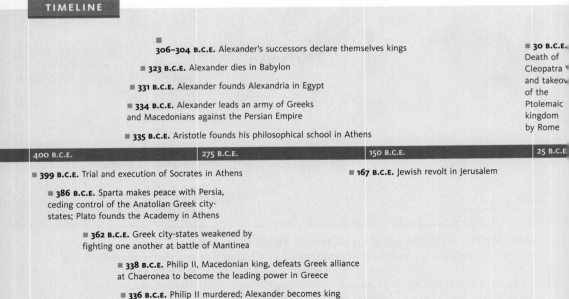

TIMELINE

306–304 B.C.E. Alexander's successors declare themselves kings

30 B.C.E. Death of Cleopatra and takeover of the Ptolemaic kingdom by Rome

323 B.C.E. Alexander dies in Babylon

331 B.C.E. Alexander founds Alexandria in Egypt

334 B.C.E. Alexander leads an army of Greeks and Macedonians against the Persian Empire

335 B.C.E. Aristotle founds his philosophical school in Athens

| 400 B.C.E. | 275 B.C.E. | 150 B.C.E. | 25 B.C.E |

399 B.C.E. Trial and execution of Socrates in Athens

167 B.C.E. Jewish revolt in Jerusalem

386 B.C.E. Sparta makes peace with Persia, ceding control of the Anatolian Greek city-states; Plato founds the Academy in Athens

362 B.C.E. Greek city-states weakened by fighting one another at battle of Mantinea

338 B.C.E. Philip II, Macedonian king, defeats Greek alliance at Chaeronea to become the leading power in Greece

336 B.C.E. Philip II murdered; Alexander becomes king

expenditure to finance research and art could vigorously push those activities in new, though not always freely chosen, directions. The kings and queens of the period also had a lasting effect on religion by creating the cult of the ruler as protector and savior, a doctrine that combined the human with the divine in a new way that would have a long history.

Philosophy remained more independent of the new political systems than any other activity, and its diversity reflects the sense of possibility, as well as the sense of unease, that characterized the Hellenistic Age. Tychê (Chance) seemed as powerful as Zeus or Isis, a view that made the world seem more open, more unpredictable, and more dangerous. Many people therefore turned to the new ideas of Hellenistic philosophers to find a personal guide to life.

> **CHAPTER REVIEW QUESTIONS**
> 1. What were the central political, social, and cultural developments of the Hellenistic world?
> 2. Compare life for people of all social classes in the Hellenistic kingdoms with that of people living in the Classical Greek city-states.

For practice quizzes and other study tools, see the Online Study Guide at bedfordstmartins.com/huntconcise.

For primary-source material from this period, see Chapter 4 of *Sources of THE MAKING OF THE WEST*, Third Edition.

Suggested References

Research on the transition from the Classical to the Hellenistic Mediterranean world focuses on the imaginative ways in which rulers, thinkers, and artists combined the old and the new, the familiar and the foreign, in the multicultural environment that emerged from the conquests of Alexander the Great.

*Aristotle. *Complete Works*. Ed. Jonathan Barnes. 1985.

Chaniotis, Angelos. *War in the Hellenistic World*. 2005.

Empereur, Jean-Yves. *Alexandria: Jewel of Egypt*. 2002.

Evans, J. A. S. *Daily Life in the Hellenistic Age: From Alexander to Cleopatra*. 2008.

Mikalson, Jon D. *Religion in Hellenistic Athens*. 1998.

*Plato. *The Collected Dialogues*. Ed. Edith Hamilton and Huntington Cairns. 1963.

*Plutarch. *The Age of Alexander*. Trans. Ian Scott-Kilvert. 1973.

Pollitt, J. J. *Art in the Hellenistic Age*. 1986.

Ptolemaic Egypt: http://www.houseofptolemy.org/

Rogers, Guy MacLean. *Alexander: The Ambiguity of Greatness*. 2004.

Sharples, R. W. *Stoics, Epicureans, and Sceptics: An Introduction to Hellenistic Philosophy*. 1996.

Snyder, Jane M. *The Woman and the Lyre: Women Writers in Classical Greece and Rome*. 1989.

The Rise of Rome

753–44 B.C.E.

ROMANS TREASURED LEGENDS about Rome's transformation from an isolated village in central Italy to the greatest power in the Western world. They especially loved stories about their first king, Romulus, because they remembered him as a dynamic leader. According to the legend known as the rape of the Sabine women, Romulus's Rome was a tiny settlement without enough women to bear children to work the fields and defend the community in war. The king therefore begged nearby peoples to allow Romans to intermarry with them. Everyone turned him down out of disrespect for Rome's poverty and weakness. Enraged, Romulus invited the neighboring Sabines to a religious festival and told Rome's men to kidnap the unmarried Sabine women. The kidnappers immediately married the women, promising to cherish them as beloved wives and new citizens. When the Sabine men then attacked Rome, the brides rushed into the bloody battle, yelling at their brothers, fathers, and new husbands to stop the slaughter by either laying down their weapons or killing all the women. The men immediately made peace and united their populations under Roman rule.

This legend taught that Rome had grown stronger by absorbing outsiders into its citizen body—sometimes violently, sometimes peacefully. Rome's growth became the ancient world's largest expansion of population and territory, as a people originally housed in a few huts slowly grew to a state that, after centuries of war and diplomacy, governed most of Europe, North Africa, Egypt, and the eastern Mediterranean. The social, cultural, political, legal, and economic traditions that the Romans developed forged closer connections among the diverse peoples of this vast region than ever existed before or since. Not even Alexander the Great equaled the

The Wolf Feeding Romulus and Remus

This bronze statue illustrates the legend that a she-wolf nursed the twins Romulus and Remus, the sons of the war god Mars and the founders of Rome. Romans treasured this story because it meant that Mars favored them so much that he sent a wild animal to save their founders after a tyrant forced the boys' mother to abandon them. The legend also reminded Romans of the violence of their origins: Romulus killed Remus in an argument over who would be Rome's leader. The wolf here is an Etruscan sculpture made in the fifth century B.C.E. The infants were added in the Renaissance. *(Scala/Art Resource, NY.)*

Romans in affecting the course of Western civilization. The history of Europe and its colonies, including the United States, has deep roots in Rome.

Roman culture originated in the traditions of ancient Italy's many peoples, but Greek literature, art, and thought deeply influenced Rome. Of course, Romans did not just passively absorb other civilizations' traditions or change them only in superficial ways, such as giving Latin names to Greek gods. Whatever Romans took over from others they adapted to their own purposes. The cultural interaction that so greatly influenced Rome was a kind of competition in innovation, rather than an "advanced" Greek culture improving a "primitive" Roman one.

Kings ruled Rome at first (c. 753–509 B.C.E.), but the majority of Roman history comes in two later periods of about five hundred years each—the republic and the empire. These terms refer to the system of government in each period. Under the republic (founded 509 B.C.E.), an oligarchy (the social elite) governed a limited democracy. Under the empire (founded after civil war in the late first century B.C.E.), monarchs (the Roman emperors) once again ruled.

Rome's greatest expansion came during the republic. Roman values under the republic emphasized service to the community, individual honor and public status, religion, the importance of laws, and shared decision making led by the elite. By the first century B.C.E., however, tension between these values had erupted into civil war because powerful individuals disagreed over how to govern the republic, and some placed their personal interests ahead of the common good.

CHAPTER FOCUS QUESTION How did traditional Roman values affect the rise and then the fall of the Roman republic?

Roman Social and Religious Traditions

One reason for Rome's amazing growth came from its citizens' belief that the gods wanted them to rule the world by military might and law and improve it through social and moral values. Romans therefore regulated their lives by traditional values stressing personal connections, social hierarchy, education for public service, and religious duties. Just as Greeks had emphasized excellence as a social value, Romans believed that men and women should show courage in all aspects of life. In public life, Roman men connected with one another as patron or client, each with obligations to the other. In private life, men as the heads of households held power over their children and slaves, but most wives lived independently of their husbands' control. In religion, the gods' power over human life meant that everyone had to pray for divine favor to protect the family and the community.

Values from the Past

Since Romans believed that their ancestors had handed down their values from ancient times, they referred to these values as **mos maiorum**, "the way of the ancestors." For Romans, "old-fashioned" meant "good because tested by long experience," while "new" suggested "dangerous because not tested by experience." They believed that the keys to Roman greatness lay in preserving and cherishing the ways of the past. Abandoning tradition was, they thought, equivalent to cultural suicide.

Roman tradition made honor the reward for right conduct, which required uprightness, faithfulness, and respect for others. Uprightness defined how a person related to others. In the second century B.C.E., the poet Lucilius defined it as "virtue":

> Virtue is to know the human relevance of each thing,
> To know what is humanly right and useful and honorable,
> And what things are good and what are bad, useless, shameful, and
>   dishonorable. . . .
> Virtue is to pay what in reality is owed to honorable status,
> To be an enemy and an opponent to bad people and bad values
> But a defender of good people and good values. . . .
> And, in addition, virtue is putting the country's interests first,
> Then our parents' interests, with our own third and last.

Faithfulness meant to keep one's obligations, no matter the cost. Failing to meet an obligation offended the community and the gods. Faithful women remained virgins before marriage and avoided adultery afterward. Faithful men kept their word, paid their debts, never had sex with another man's wife, and treated everyone justly—which did not mean treating everyone the same, but rather treating people appropriately according to whether they were equals, superiors, or inferiors.

Faithfulness was linked to the value of respect. Respect meant devotion to the gods, to one's own dignity, and to one's family, especially elders. Honoring the gods required worship, prayer, and sacrifices performed with strict purity. Respect for one's self meant maintaining self-control and displaying only limited emotion. So strict was this expectation that not even wives and husbands could kiss in public without seeming emotionally out of control. Respect also required never giving up, regardless of difficulties. Standing firm and overcoming all obstacles to do one's duty were fundamental Roman values.

Honor was the Romans' reward for living by those values. Women earned honor especially by bearing legitimate children and educating them morally. Honor for upper-class men brought concrete rewards: public recognition and, perhaps, election to government office. A man regarded as especially honorable commanded so much respect that others would obey him regardless of whether he held formal power over them. A man earning this much status was said to possess "authority."

Finally, Romans believed that family background influenced a person's values. Being born in an elite family was therefore a two-edged sword. It automatically carried greater status, but at the same time it imposed a stricter demand to behave morally. Originally, wealth had nothing to do with Roman moral virtue. Over time, however, it became overwhelmingly important to the elite to spend money in displays of conspicuous consumption, social entertainments, and gifts to the community. By the later centuries of the **Roman republic**, ambitious men required vast fortunes to buy honor, and they became willing to abandon other values to acquire riches.

The Patron-Client System

The hierarchy of Roman society depended on the **patron-client system**, a network of two-way personal relationships linking Romans to one another legally and morally. A patron was a man of superior status who was obliged to provide benefits to certain men of lower status, who paid special attention to him. These were his clients, who in return owed him duties. Both sets of obligations involved financial and political help. The network had multiple levels: a patron of others was often himself the client of a more distinguished man. A thoughtful patron would greet a social inferior as "my friend," not as "my client." A client, however, showed respect by addressing his superior as "my patron."

Benefits and duties made the relationship two-way. A patron provided benefits for his clients by giving gifts or loans in hard times, supporting them when they started political careers, and speaking for them in lawsuits. Clients paid duties to their patrons by lending money when patrons needed it to pay for public works or their daughters' expensive dowries, or by soliciting votes for their campaigns to be elected to public office. Since it was a mark of great status for a patron to have numerous clients crowding around him like a swarm of bees, he expected them to gather at his house early in the morning and accompany him to the forum, the city's public center. Prominent Romans needed a large house to accommodate a crowd of clients and to entertain social equals. A house crowded with visitors indicated social success.

These mutual obligations endured over generations. Ex-slaves, for example, who automatically became the clients of the masters who freed them, passed on this relationship to their children. Wealthy Romans could acquire clients among foreigners, sometimes even entire communities. By stressing duty and permanence, the patron-client system reflected the Roman idea that society depended on people faithfully keeping their obligations to one another.

The Roman Family

The family was the bedrock institution of Roman society because it taught values and determined the ownership of property. Men and women shared the duty of teaching values to their children, though by law the father possessed the *patria potestas* (power of a father) over his children of any age and over his slaves. This power gave him legal ownership of all the property acquired by his dependents. As long as he was alive, no son or daughter could own anything, accumulate money, or possess any independent legal standing—in theory. In actual life, adult children controlled personal property and money, and favored slaves might accumulate savings. Fathers also held legal power of life and death over these members of their households, but they

Sculpted Tomb of a Family of Ex-Slaves
The husband and wife sculpted on this tomb, which perhaps dates to the first century B.C.E., started life as slaves but gained their freedom and thus became Roman citizens. Their son, in the background holding a pet pigeon, was a free person. One of the remarkable features of Roman civilization, and a source of its demographic strength, was that it granted citizenship to ex-slaves. This family had done well enough financially to afford an expensive grave marker. The tablets the man is holding and the carefully groomed hairstyle of the woman are meant to show that their family was educated and stylish. What do you think it means that the couple are shown holding hands? (German Archeological Institute/Madeline Grimoldi.)

rarely exercised it on anyone except unwanted or deformed newborns. "Exposure"— abandoning babies so that they would die, be adopted, or be raised as slaves by strangers—was an accepted practice to control the size of families and dispose of physically imperfect infants. Baby girls probably suffered this fate more often than boys, as a family enhanced its power by investing its resources in its sons.

As the Roman value of shared decision making required, fathers regularly conferred with others on important family issues. Each Roman man identified a circle of friends and relatives, his "council," that he always consulted before making important decisions. A man considering whether to execute an adult member of his household, for example, would never have made the decision on his own. His council would recommend this violent exercise of a father's power only in the most extreme circumstances, as in 63 B.C.E. when a father had his son executed because the youth had committed treason by joining a conspiracy to overthrow the government.

Patria potestas did not allow a husband to control his wife because "free" marriages—in which the wife formally remained under her father's power for as long as he lived—eventually became common. Many Roman wives were relatively independent because their fathers were dead, and their husbands did not legally control their lives (four out of five parents died before their children reached age thirty). Legally, a woman needed a male guardian to conduct business for her, but guardianship became an empty formality by the first century B.C.E. As one legal expert said about Roman women's freedom of action, "The common belief, that because of their instability of judgment women are often deceived and that it is only fair to have them controlled by the authority of guardians, seems more false than true. For women of full age manage their affairs themselves." Upper-class women could express their opinions publicly. In 195 B.C.E., for example, they blocked Rome's streets for days until the men ended a wartime law meant to reduce tensions between rich and poor by limiting the amount of gold jewelry and fine clothing women could wear and where they could ride in carriages.

Roman women had to grow up fast to assume their duties as teachers of values to children and managers of their family's resources. Tullia, daughter of the famous first-century B.C.E. politician Marcus Tullius Cicero, was engaged at twelve, married at sixteen, and widowed by twenty-two. As a married Roman woman of wealth, she oversaw the household slaves, including wet nurses for infants; kept account books for the property she personally owned; and accompanied her husband to dinner parties—something Greek wives never did.

Sculpture of a Woman Running a Store
This relief sculpture shows a woman selling food from behind the counter of a shop while customers make purchases or converse with each other. Roman women could own property, so the woman may be the store owner. The man immediately to her right behind the counter could be her husband or a servant. Market areas in Roman towns were packed with small family-run stores that sold everything imaginable, much like the malls of today. (Art Resource, NY.)

Roman mothers won public honor for managing their households well and shaping their children's moral outlook. Cornelia, an aristocrat of the second century B.C.E., won extraordinary fame after her husband died by refusing an offer of marriage from the Ptolemaic king of Egypt so she could instead oversee the family estate and educate her surviving daughter and two sons. (Her other nine children had died.) The boys, Tiberius and Gaius Gracchus, grew up to be among the most influential and controversial officials of the late republic. Wealthy women such as Cornelia wielded political influence, if only indirectly, by expressing their opinions to the male members of their families. Marcus Porcius Cato, a famous second-century B.C.E. political leader, remarked on the behind-the-scenes reality of women's power: "All mankind rule their wives, we rule all mankind, and our wives rule us."

Women accumulated property both through inheritance and entrepreneurship. Recent archaeological discoveries suggest that by the late republic some women owned large businesses. Poor women, like poor men, toiled to help support their families by selling vegetables and trinkets from stands. More prosperous families crafted furniture or clothing at home, the location of most Roman production, with the men cutting, fitting, and polishing the wood, leather, and metal. The poorest women could earn money only as prostitutes, which was legal but disgraceful. Prenuptial agreements to outline the rights of both partners in marriage were common, and divorce was a simple matter, with fathers usually keeping the children.

Education: From Reading to Rhetoric

Education for both women and men aimed to make them supporters of traditional values and, for different purposes, effective speakers. Women learned the legends of Roman history so they could instill values in their children and speak well at dinner parties, and men so they could make effective speeches in court or political meetings, if they were rich enough to spend their time there. Most children were homeschooled; only the rich could afford to pay teachers. Wealthy parents bought literate slaves to teach their children. Often they chose Greek slaves so their children could be taught to speak Greek and read Greek literature. Elite Romans wanted to be bilingual and read Greek drama, philosophy, and history in the original language. They wanted to understand fully the lessons of Greek culture, which they respected for its great age and insight into the human condition. Repetition was the usual teaching technique. Teachers slapped and hit students to keep them attentive.

In upper-class families, both daughters and sons learned to read. Girls studied literature and perhaps music. Boys focused on physical training, fighting with weapons, and courageous actions. The highest level of an upper-class boy's education was rhetoric—skill in persuasive public speaking based on Greek models adapted to Roman purposes. Rhetorical training was crucial to a successful public career. A boy would accompany his father to trials and political gatherings. By listening to speeches, he would learn to imitate winning techniques. Cicero, Rome's most famous orator, agreed with his brother's advice that a young man must learn "to become an excellent public speaker. This is the way to control men at Rome, winning them over to your side and keeping them from harming you. You really have power when you are a man who can cause your rivals the greatest fears of meeting you [as a speaker] in a trial."

Religion in Public and Private

Romans worshipped many divinities that corresponded with Greek gods. Romans viewed their chief god, Jupiter (the equivalent of the Greek god Zeus), as a powerful, stern father. Juno (Greek Hera), queen of the gods, and Minerva (Greek Athena), goddess of wisdom, joined Jupiter as the three central gods of Rome's official public religion. These three gods shared Rome's most famous temple on the Capitoline hill at the center of the city.

The goal of Roman public religion was to preserve Rome's safety and prosperity. Priests were supposed to ensure the gods' goodwill toward the state, a crucial relationship the Romans called the *pax deorum* (peace of or with the gods). Men from the top of the social hierarchy served as priests by conducting sacrifices and presiding at festivals and other rituals conforming to ancestral tradition. They were not professionals who devoted their lives solely to religious activity, but rather citizens who performed a public service. The most important official, the *pontifex maximus* (highest priest), served as the head of state religion and the ultimate authority on religious matters affecting government. Rome's most prominent men sought this priesthood for its political influence.

Every official action was preceded by "taking the auspices"—seeking Jupiter's approval by observing natural "signs" such as the direction of the flights of birds, their eating habits, or the presence of thunder and lightning. Officials who made mistakes in this process were punished. Naval commanders, for example, "took the auspices" by feeding sacred chickens on their ships: if the birds ate energetically before a battle, Jupiter was thought to favor the Romans, and the battle could begin. Once during a fierce third-century B.C.E. sea battle, the commander Publius Claudius Pulcher grew frustrated when his chickens, probably seasick, refused to eat. Convinced that the gods nevertheless wanted him to attack, he finally hurled the birds overboard in a rage, sputtering, "Well then, let them drink!" When he suffered a huge defeat, he was fined very heavily.

Many official prayers requested the gods' help in growing crops, preventing disease, and spurring healthy reproduction for animals and people. In times of crisis, Romans brought in foreign gods to help them, such as the healing god Asclepius from Greece or the fertility goddess Cybele, the "Great Mother," from Asia Minor (the Roman term for Anatolia).

Romans supported many other cults with special guardian responsibilities. The shrine of Vesta, goddess of the hearth and a protector of the family, housed the official eternal flame of Rome, which Romans believed guaranteed the state's permanent existence. The Vestal Virgins—six unmarried women who were sworn to chastity at ages six to ten for terms of thirty years—kept the flame from going out. Their chastity symbolized Roman family values and thus the preservation of the republic itself. As Rome's only female priesthood, the Vestals earned high status and freedom from their fathers' control. If the flame went out, the Romans assumed that one of the women had broken her vow of chastity, and the disgraced Vestal was buried alive.

Romans performed many public and private rituals to seek divine help and also reinforce traditional values. For example, during the Lupercalia festival in February (the festival's name recalled the wolf, *luper* in Latin, that legend said had reared Romulus), naked young men streaked around the Palatine hill, lashing any women they met with strips of goatskin. Women who had not yet borne children would run out to be struck, believing this would make them fertile. At home, families maintained small shrines housing statuettes of their Penates (spirits of the household) and Lares (spirits of the ancestors), protectors of their well-being and moral traditions. Upper-class families hung death masks of famous ancestors in the main room of their homes and wore them at funerals to express the current generation's responsibility to live up

Household Religious Shrine from Pompeii
This colorfully painted shrine stood inside the entrance to a house at Pompeii known as the House of the Vettii, from the name of its owners. Successful businessmen, they spared no expense in decorating their home: with 188 frescoes (paintings done by applying pigments to damp plaster) adorning its walls, the interior blazed in a riot of color. This type of shrine for family religion, found in every Roman home, is called a lararium because it housed the Lares (spirits of the ancestors), who are shown here flanking a central figure representing the spirit (*genius*) of the father of the family. The snake, ready to drink from a bowl probably holding milk set out for it, also symbolizes a protective force. The scene sums up the role Romans expected their gods to play: providing protection and preventing bad luck. Why do you think Romans regarded snakes as symbols of divine protection? (Scala/Art Resource, NY.)

to the family's traditions. The Saturnalia festival in December turned the social order upside down to release tensions caused by the inequalities between masters and slaves. As a Roman author described the occasion, "People joyfully hold feasts all through the country and the towns, each owner acting as a waiter to his slaves." This temporary reversal of roles in fact emphasized slaves' ties to their owners by symbolizing patrons' benefits, which slaves were expected to repay with faithful service.

Social tradition, not religious belief, was the source of Roman morality. The shame of losing status by tarnishing one's reputation, and not the fear of divine punishment, was the reason to avoid immoral behavior. Romans gave human moral actions a religious dimension by representing their values, such as faithfulness or piety, as divinities with temples and cults. The principal Roman gods were more connected to national security and prosperity than to human morality, as Cicero explained: "We call Jupiter the Best (*Optimus*) and Greatest (*Maximus*) not because he makes us just or sober or wise but, rather, healthy, unharmed, rich, and prosperous."

REVIEW How did traditional values affect Roman society and beliefs?

From Monarchy to Republic, 753–287 B.C.E.

Rome's astounding growth from a tiny settlement into the Mediterranean's greatest power took centuries. During this slow process, the Romans reinvented their government and seized vast territories to provide land and revenues for a growing population. Rome's first government was a monarchy, the most common type of government in the ancient world. This rule by kings lasted from 753 to 509 B.C.E., when members of the social elite overthrew it in anger at the royal family's violent behavior. The elite then created a new political system—the republic—that lasted until almost the end of the first century B.C.E. The Roman republic, from the Latin *res publica* (meaning "the people's thing" or "the public business"), was based on male citizens making political decisions as a group and electing officials in assemblies organized by social hierarchy. Rome acquired land and population by winning aggressive wars and by absorbing other peoples. Its economic and cultural growth depended on contact with peoples around the Mediterranean.

Rule by Kings, 753–509 B.C.E.

Legend taught that kings ruled Rome from 753 to 509 B.C.E., but little reliable evidence exists for this period. The kings probably created the Senate, a body of advisers chosen from the city's leading men to serve as the ruler's council, in keeping with the Roman principle that decisions should be made in a group. The Senate advised Rome's leaders for two thousand years, as the government changed from a monarchy to a republic and back to a monarchy under the empire.

Rome's policy of making conquered outsiders into citizens or allies produced tremendous expansion, promoted ethnic diversity, and contrasted sharply with the exclusionary citizenship policies of Greek city-states. Another important Roman policy—also different from Greek tradition—was to grant citizenship to freed slaves. These freedmen and freedwomen, as ex-slaves were called, became clients of their former owners. They were barred from elective offices or military service but in all other ways possessed full civil rights, such as legal marriage. Their children enjoyed citizenship without any limitations. By the late republic, many Roman citizens were descendants of freed slaves.

Geography and contact with other cultures, especially Greek, drove Rome's initial growth. The city lay at the natural center of both Italy and the Mediterranean world. As the first-century B.C.E. historian Livy, our source for the heroic legends of early Rome, expressed it, "Gods and men chose this site for good reasons: all its advantages make it the best place in the world for a city destined to grow great." Those advantages were fertile farmland, control of a river crossing on the major north-south route in the peninsula, a nearby harbor on the Mediterranean Sea, and easy access to the surrounding areas in Italy. Most important, Rome was ideally situated for contact with the outside world. The Italian peninsula stuck out so far into the Mediterranean that east-west ship traffic naturally stopped in its ports (Map 4.1).

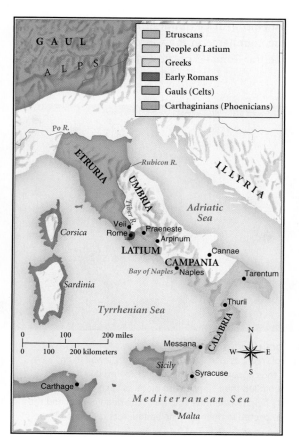

Map 4.1 Ancient Italy, c. 500 B.C.E. When the Romans ended the monarchy to found a republic in 509 B.C.E., they inhabited a relatively small territory in central Italy between the west coast and the mountain range that runs down the peninsula from north to south. Numerous different peoples lived in Italy at this time. The most prosperous occupied fertile agricultural land and sheltered harbors on the peninsula's west side. The early republic's most urbanized neighbors were the Etruscans to the north and the Greek city-states to the south and on the island of Sicily.

Ancient Italy was home to a diverse population, and the Romans' contact with their neighbors profoundly influenced their cultural development. The people of the region around Rome were poor villagers like the Romans and spoke the same Indo-European language, an early form of Latin. Flourishing Greek city-states dotted Italy to the south, however, and contact with them had the greatest effect on Rome. Greeks had established colonies in southern Italy from the 700s B.C.E. These settlements grew rich thanks to their ideal location for participating in international trade. Romans developed a love-hate relationship with Greeks, admiring their literature and art but despising their lack of military unity.

The Etruscans, a people north of the Tiber River, also influenced the Romans. They lived in prosperous, independent towns nestled on central Italian hilltops. Bright Etruscan wall paintings in tombs portray funeral banquets and games testifying to their society's splendor. Etruscans crafted fine artwork, jewelry, and sculpture, but they also imported luxury items from Greece and other Mediterranean lands. Most of the intact Greek vases known today, for example, were found in Etruscan tombs. The Etruscans' international contacts encouraged cultural interaction. Gold tablets inscribed in Etruscan and Phoenician reveal that in about 500 B.C.E., the Etruscans dedicated a temple to the Phoenician goddess Astarte, whom they had learned about by trading with Carthage. That city, founded in western North Africa (modern Tunisia) by Phoenicians around 800 B.C.E., dominated seaborne commerce in the western Mediterranean and by the third century B.C.E. had become the Romans' greatest rival.

Banquet Scene Painted in an Etruscan Tomb
Painted about 480–470 B.C.E., this brightly colored fresco at Tarquinia decorates a wall in an Etruscan tomb (known today as the Tomb of the Leopards, from the animals painted just above this scene). Wealthy Etruscan men and women filled their tombs with pictures such as these, which simultaneously represented the funeral feasts held to celebrate the life of the dead person and the social pleasures experienced in this life and expected in the next. The banqueters recline on their elbows in Greek style. (Scala/Art Resource, NY.)

The extent of Etruscan influence on Rome remains controversial. Until recently, scholars believed that the Etruscans conquered Rome and dominated it politically in the sixth century B.C.E. The Etruscans were also seen as more culturally refined, mainly because so much Greek art has been found at Etruscan sites. Etruscans were therefore assumed to have reshaped Roman culture during this period of supposed domination. New research, however, has revealed the independence of Romans in developing their own cultural traditions. They borrowed from Etruscans (as from Greeks) whatever appealed to them and adapted it to fit their local circumstances. Romans took over the Etruscans' procedures for religious rituals and adopted their magistrates' elaborate garments. They also learned Etruscan divination techniques for discovering the gods' will by identifying clues in the shapes of the internal organs of slaughtered animals. Romans may also have adopted from Etruscan society the tradition of wives joining husbands at dinner parties.

Many features of Roman culture previously thought to be the results of Etruscan influence were probably part of the ancient Mediterranean's shared cultural environment. The organization of the Roman army, a citizen militia of heavily armed infantry troops fighting in formation, reflected not just Etruscan tradition but also that of other peoples. The Romans' alphabet, which they first learned from the Etruscans, was Greek; the Greeks had acquired it through their contact with the Levant. The engineering necessary to urbanize Rome, once seen as exclusively Etruscan, did not come from one superior culture "instructing" another, less-developed one. Rather, at this time in Mediterranean history, similar cultural developments were under way in many places. The Romans, like so many others, found their own way in navigating this common cultural sea.

The Early Roman Republic, 509–287 B.C.E.

The social elite's hatred for kings created the Roman republic. Their belief that monarchy always turned into tyranny was expressed in Livy's story of the rape of Lucretia, the most famous legend about the creation of the republic. The assault on Lucretia, a chaste wife in the social elite, took place when the swaggering son of King Tarquin the Proud violently raped her to demonstrate his superior power. Despite pleas from her husband and father not to blame herself, she committed suicide after identifying her attacker.

Declaring themselves Rome's liberators from tyranny, her relatives and friends, led by Lucius Junius Brutus, expelled Tarquin in 509 B.C.E. They then created the republic, to ensure the sharing of power by the elite and to block rule by one man or family. Thereafter, the Romans prided themselves on living under a freer political system than that of their neighbors. The legend of the warrior Horatius at the bridge, for example, advertised the republic's dedication to national freedom. As Livy told the story, Horatius single-handedly blocked the Etruscan army's march on Rome when they wanted to put a king back in charge of the city. While hacking at his opponents, Horatius cursed them as slaves who had lost their freedom because they were ruled by arrogant kings. Horatius's legend made clear that Romans created the republic to prevent a leader from abusing power by ruling alone.

Conflict over which groups would control the republic persisted for over two hundred years after 509 B.C.E., in a process called the **struggle of the orders**. "Orders" refers to the two main divisions of the republic's social hierarchy, the patricians (a limited group of elite families) and the plebeians (the rest of Rome's citizen population). Patricians inherited their status by being born into one of the about 130 wealthy families controlling important religious activities. Some plebeians, however, were also rich, and they resented the patricians' arrogance in monopolizing elections to public office, banning intermarriage with plebeians, and advertising their social superiority by wearing special red shoes (later they changed to black footwear adorned with a shiny metal crescent). Above all, rich plebeians insisted they deserved the same influence in politics as patricians.

Economic and social discontent also inflamed the struggle. Poor plebeians demanded relief from crushing debts and a redistribution of farmland controlled by large landowners. To pressure the patricians, plebeians periodically took the extreme step of leaving the city (secession) and refusing to serve in the army. This tactic worked because they made up the majority of Rome's military. A secession provoked by a patrician's violence against a plebeian woman led to the earliest Roman laws, called the Twelve Tables from the bronze tablets on which they were engraved for display around 450 B.C.E. In Livy's words, these laws prevented the patrician government officials who judged most legal cases from "arbitrarily giving the force of law to their own preferences." So important did the Twelve Tables become as a symbol of the Roman commitment to justice for all citizens that for the next four hundred years, children were required to memorize them.

The Twelve Tables were only a first step toward greater sharing of legal and political power; that process occurred mainly by establishing the different and overlapping responsibilities of Rome's assemblies. At these outdoor meetings, adult male citizens elected officials, passed laws, decided government policies, and held some trials. Assemblies were only for voting, not discussion, but every session was preceded by a public gathering to hear speeches. Everyone, including women and noncitizens, could listen to these addresses. The crowd loudly expressed its agreement or disagreement by applauding or hissing. Speakers therefore had to pay close attention to public opinion in forming the proposals that they put before the male citizens who then voted them up or down in the assemblies. As a result, assemblies brought some democracy to the government of the Roman republic.

Assemblies were divided into voting groups according to the social hierarchy of status and wealth. Each group, not each individual, had a vote. A small group had the same vote as a large group (as in the U.S. Senate, in which each state has two votes regardless of size). The hierarchy of the voting groups in the Centuriate Assembly, which elected the major officials (consuls and praetors), reflected the organization of the army: it confined the huge population of men too poor to afford military weapons, the **proletarians**, to one group that cast only one out of the total of 193 votes.

The Plebeian Assembly excluded patricians and was grouped into thirty-five tribes based on where voters lived; it elected special officials (tribunes) responsible for protecting plebeians. It also passed resolutions called **plebiscites**, which were originally not recognized as law by patricians. The struggle of the orders finally ended in 287 B.C.E., when patricians agreed that plebiscites would have the status of laws. In a third grouping, the Tribal Assembly, patricians joined plebeians as voters grouped by residence. The Tribal Assembly, in which plebeians greatly outnumbered patricians, eventually became the republic's most important government institution for making policy, passing laws, and, until separate courts were created in the second century B.C.E., conducting trials.

Annually elected officials administered the republic's government. They served in groups, numbering from two to more than a dozen. The highest officials were consuls. Two consuls were elected each year, and their most important duty was commanding Rome's army. Winning a consulship was the greatest political honor a Roman man could achieve, and it bestowed high status on his descendants forever, entitling them to be called nobles. To be elected consul, a man traditionally had to work his way up the **ladder of offices**. After ten years of military service beginning at about age twenty, he would seek election as a quaestor, a financial administrator. Continuing to climb the ladder, he would next be elected to the board of aediles, officials overseeing the city's streets, sewers, aqueducts, temples, and markets. Each rung up the ladder was more competitive, and few men reached the next office, that of praetor, which performed judicial and military command duties. The most successful praetors then tried for the consulship. Ex-consuls could also compete to become one of the censors, prestigious senior officials elected every five years to conduct censuses of the citizen body and select new members of the three-hundred-man Senate, which advised the consuls (as it had the kings). The special role of the Senate in the republic's government made clear the Roman principle of making decisions through group agreement. The Senate had no authority to pass laws; it could only give advice. But its prestige was so enormous that no high official or assembly would disregard the senators' advice, unless they wished to start a political crisis. Following the Roman tradition that status should be visible, the senators wore special black high-top shoes and robes embroidered with a broad purple stripe.

The struggle of the orders also changed the balance of power among elective offices. The patricians tried to monopolize the highest ones, but through violent struggle from about 500 to 450 B.C.E., the plebeians forced them to yield a crucial concession: the creation of a special panel of ten annually elected officials called tribunes. Tribunes had the responsibility of blocking actions that would harm the plebeians and their property. The tribunate's purpose made it stand apart from regular ladder offices. Tribunes, who had to be plebeians, based their power on the sworn oath of the other plebeians to protect them against all attacks. This protected status, called sacrosanctity, allowed tribunes the right to use a veto (from the Latin meaning "I forbid") to stop the actions of officials, suspend elections, and even disregard the advice of the Senate. The tribunes' extraordinary power to halt government action sometimes made them the sources of bitter political disputes.

In the early republic, Roman values motivated men to compete for honor, not money, in pursuing a public career. By 367 B.C.E., the plebeians had forced their way fully into this competition by requiring that at least one consul every year must be a plebeian. Only well-off men could run for election because officials earned no salaries. On the contrary, they were expected to spend large sums to win popular support by entertaining the electorate with, for example, spectacles featuring gladiators (trained fighters) and wild beasts (such as lions imported from Africa). Once elected, magistrates from aediles to consuls were expected to benefit the people by paying for public works, such as roads, aqueducts, and temples. When Rome later won control of more and more overseas territory through warfare, the desire for the status that money could buy overcame the values of faithfulness and honesty. By the second century B.C.E., military officers could enrich themselves by seizing booty from enemies in successful foreign wars and by extorting bribes from the local people while administering conquered territory. They could then use their personal profits from war to finance the public works that promoted their political careers at home. In this way, acquiring money became more important in the late republic than winning honor through selfless public service.

Outrage over corrupt officials dismissing complaints about each other's conduct led to the creation of a court system with jury trials in the second century B.C.E. Since most officials were also senators, the Senate self-interestedly tried to have these juries be manned only by its members, while nonsenators agitated to be included. Both accusers and accused had to speak for themselves in court or have friends speak for them. Prominent men, usually senators with legal knowledge, played a central role as advisers in the Roman judicial system. These jurists, as they were called (from the Latin *jus, juris,* "law"), operated as private citizens, not official judges, in providing legal advice. This reliance on jurists reflected the Roman tradition of consulting a group of advisers to reach decisions. Roman law developed over centuries, sometimes adapting laws from other peoples, and became the basis for many later European legal codes still in use today.

These centuries of conflict between the orders produced overlapping political and judicial institutions. Several different assemblies voted on laws, while the Senate offered opinions that guided lawmaking. Legal cases could be decided by high-ranking magistrates, assemblies, or juries. Rome had no highest judicial authority, such as the U.S. Supreme Court, to resolve disputes about conflicting laws or verdicts. The republic's stability therefore depended on observing tradition, the mos maiorum. This reliance on tradition ensured that the most socially prominent and the richest Romans dominated government and society—because they defined the "way of the ancestors."

REVIEW   What issues fueled the struggle of the orders?

Roman Imperialism, Fifth to Second Centuries B.C.E.

During the fifth, fourth, and third centuries B.C.E., Rome fought war after war to expand in Italy until it became the most powerful state on the peninsula. In the third and second centuries B.C.E., Romans fought wars far from home in the west, the north, and the east, but above all they battled Carthage to the south. Their victories in these foreign wars won Rome an empire in Italy, Sicily, Sardinia, Corsica, Spain, North Africa, Greece, Asia Minor, and southern Gaul (France).

Rome's imperialist expansion transformed its culture and society. Astonishingly, Romans had no literature before about 240 B.C.E. Cultural interaction with others during overseas expansion stimulated Romans to write their first history and poetry and deeply influenced their art, especially portraits. Endless military campaigns far from home created stresses on family life and small farmers in the army, while the novel demands of ruling conquered territory undermined the government's stability. The importation of huge numbers of war captives to work as slaves on the estates of the rich put free laborers out of work. The conquests and spoils of war from Rome's great victories in the third and second centuries B.C.E. thus turned out to be a two-edged sword: they brought expansion and wealth, but their unexpected social and political consequences disrupted traditional values and the community's stability.

Roman Expansion in Italy

Fear, ambition, and need motivated Roman imperialism. Worries about national security made the senators recommend preemptive attacks against peoples perceived as enemies of Rome, and everyone longed to win plunder in war. Poorer soldiers hoped their gains would pull their families out of poverty. The elite longed to increase their riches and acquire glory as commanders, to promote their public careers. Finally, a growing population needed more land because the basis of the economy remained agriculture.

The Romans believed they were successful militarily because they respected the will of the gods. Cicero claimed, "We have defeated all the nations of the world, because we have realized that the world is directed and governed by the gods." Believing that the gods supported defensive wars as just, the Romans always insisted they fought only in self-defense, even when they attacked first. A devastating sack of Rome in 387 B.C.E. by Gauls (Celts) from beyond the Alps to the north proved only a temporary military setback. Celts were a diverse group of peoples living in what is today west-central Europe. Famously warlike, Celtic bands grew prosperous from raiding and control of trade routes north of Italy.

Rome and Central Italy, Fifth Century B.C.E.

Population growth forced some of them to look for new territory south of the Alps, and the Romans feared them as potential invaders.

By around 220 B.C.E., Rome controlled all of Italy south of the Po River. The Romans sometimes forced defeated opponents to give up large amounts of land or even enslaved them, but they also often struck generous peace terms with former enemies. Some defeated Italians even became Roman citizens, and no conquered Italian peoples had to pay taxes to Rome. All, however, had to send soldiers for future wars. These new allies then received a share of the booty, chiefly slaves and land, from victorious campaigns against a new crop of enemies. In this way, the Romans used the sharing of the profits of conquest to turn former opponents into partners, an arrangement that only made Rome more powerful.

To strengthen Italy's security, the Romans planted colonies of citizens and constructed roads up and down the peninsula to allow troops to march faster. These roads also connected the diverse peoples of Italy, speeding the creation of a more unified culture dominated by Rome. Latin, for example, became the common language.

Aqueduct at Nîmes in France
Like the Greeks, the Romans supplied fountains and public baths in their towns with water by constructing aqueducts. They excelled at building complex systems of tunnels, channels, and bridges to move water over great distances. One of the best-preserved sections of a major aqueduct is the so-called Pont du Gard near present-day Nîmes in France, erected in the late first century B.C.E. to serve the flourishing town of Nemausus. Built of stones fitted together without clamps or mortar, the span soars 160 feet high and is 875 feet long, carrying water from thirty-five miles away in a channel constructed to fall only one foot in height for every three thousand feet in length, so that the flow would remain steady but gentle. What sort of social and political organization would be necessary to construct such a system? (© Hubertus Kanus/Photo Researchers, Inc.)

Roman Roads, c. 110 B.C.E.

The wealth flowing from Rome's first two centuries of expansion in Italy attracted hordes of people to the city because these riches financed new aqueducts to provide fresh running water—a rarity in the ancient world—and a massive building program employing poor laborers. By around 300 B.C.E., perhaps 150,000 people lived within Rome's walls. Outside the city, about 750,000 free Roman citizens inhabited various parts of Italy on land taken from local peoples. Much conquered territory was declared public land, open to any Roman to use for grazing herds of cattle.

Roman Expansion outside Italy

The Romans' victories in three wars against the wealthy North African city of Carthage began their overseas empire. Also governed as a republic, Carthage by the third century B.C.E. controlled its own empire stretching across the northwest African coast, part of Libya, Sardinia, Corsica, Malta, and the southern portion of Spain. Geography therefore ensured that an expanding Rome would bump up against Carthage's interests, which depended on the sea. The Carthaginians had a strong fleet but had to hire mercenaries to field a sizable infantry. To Romans, Carthage seemed a dangerous rival, as well as a fine prize because of its riches. Roman hostility was also fueled by horror at the Carthaginian tradition of sacrificing infants in times of trouble in the belief that this would placate their gods.

The three wars with Carthage took Roman troops outside Italy and across the sea for the first time. They are called the Punic Wars, from the Roman term *Punici,* meaning "Phoenicians" (the ancestors of the Carthaginians). The First Punic War lasted for a generation (264–241 B.C.E.). Its bloody battles revealed why the Romans consistently conquered their rivals. In addition to being able to draw on the Italian population for reserves of manpower, they were prepared to lose as many troops, vote as much money, and fight as long as necessary to win. Previously unskilled at naval warfare, they spent vast sums to build warships to combat Carthage's experienced navy; they lost more than five hundred ships and 250,000 men while learning how to win at sea. (See "Taking Measure," page 138.)

Victory in the First Punic War made the Romans masters of Sicily, where they set up their first province (a foreign territory ruled and taxed by Roman officials). This innovation proved so profitable that they created another province by seizing the islands of Sardinia and Corsica from Carthage's control. Acquiring these foreign territories whetted the Romans' appetite for more, and they also feared a renewal of Carthage's power (Map 4.2). They therefore made alliances with local peoples in Spain, where the Carthaginians were expanding.

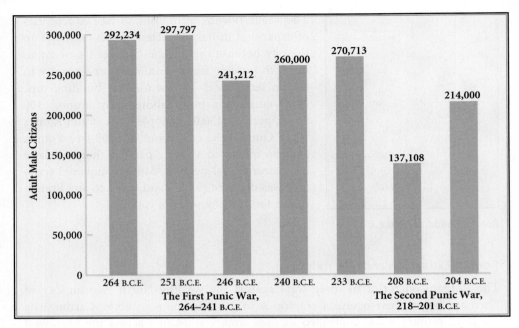

Taking Measure **Census Records of Adult Male Roman Citizens during the First and Second Punic Wars**

Livy (59 B.C.E.–17 C.E.) and Jerome (c. 347–420 C.E.) provided these numbers from Roman censuses conducted during and between the first two wars against Carthage. Only adult male citizens (the men eligible for Rome's regular army) were counted. The drop in the total for 246 B.C.E., compared with the total for 264 B.C.E., reflects losses in the First Punic War. The low total for 208 B.C.E. reflects losses in battle and defections by communities such as Capua in 216 B.C.E. Because the censuses did not include the Italian allies fighting on Rome's side, the numbers understate the wars' total casualties. Scholars estimate that the first two Punic Wars took the lives of nearly a third of Italy's adult male population— perhaps a quarter of a million soldiers.

The Senate's harsh warning to Carthage not to expand any further convinced the Carthaginians that another war was inevitable, so they decided to strike first. In the Second Punic War (218–201 B.C.E.), the Carthaginian general Hannibal shocked the Romans by marching troops and war elephants over the snowy Alps into Italy. After slaughtering a Roman army at the battle of Cannae in 216 B.C.E.—thirty thousand men died in the bloodiest defeat in Roman history—Hannibal tried to convince Rome's Italian allies to come over to his side. Disastrously for him, most Italians remained loyal to Rome. Hannibal's alliance with King Philip V of Macedonia forced the Romans to fight on a second front in Greece (their first presence in that region), but they refused to crack despite Hannibal's ravaging Italy for fifteen years before retreating to Africa in 203 B.C.E. The Romans finally won by invading the Carthaginians' homeland. Their general Scipio trained his soldiers to keep formation and then swivel out of the way of Hannibal's war elephants, even when facing dozens of the beasts charging so hard they shook the earth. The Romans punished the Carthaginians by forcing them to eliminate

Map 4.2 Roman Expansion, c. 500–44 B.C.E.
During the first two centuries of its existence, the Roman republic used war and diplomacy to extend its power north and south in the Italian peninsula. In the third and second centuries B.C.E., conflict with Carthage to the south and west and with the Hellenistic kingdoms to the east extended Roman power far outside Italy and led to the creation of provinces from Spain to Greece. The first century B.C.E. saw the conquest of Syria by Pompey and of Gaul by Julius Caesar. **For more help analyzing this map, see the map activity for this chapter in the Online Study Guide at** bedfordstmartins.com/huntconcise.

their navy, pay huge fines for fifty years, and hand over their rich territory in Spain, which became Roman provinces, valuable for their mines.

The Third Punic War (149–146 B.C.E.) broke out when the Carthaginians, who had revived financially, attacked an aggressive Roman ally in North Africa. After defeating Carthage for a third time, the Romans followed Cato's brutal advice: "We must destroy Carthage." After tearing down the city, they converted its territory into a province. This disaster did not obliterate Carthaginian language and culture, however, and under the Roman Empire this part of North Africa became renowned for its economic and intellectual vitality, which emerged from a combination of Roman and Punic traditions.

Rome's conquests in the Punic Wars led to the extension of Roman power to Greece and Asia Minor. After defeating King Philip for revenge and to prevent any threat of his invading Italy, the Romans proclaimed the "freedom of the Greeks" in 196 B.C.E. to show respect for Greece's traditional independence. The Greek cities

Plate Decorated with a War Elephant
This third-century B.C.E. plate from southern Italy depicts an Indian elephant followed by her calf. The adult animal carries on her back a fortified compartment for holding archers. War elephants were introduced to the Mediterranean after Alexander the Great fought against them in his campaign in India. Commanders used them to frighten and confuse the enemy with their size and loud bellowing. The Carthaginian general Hannibal shocked the Romans by bringing elephants over the treacherous passes of the Alps to invade Italy, but most of them died on the way. Armies eventually gave up on elephants because they were too expensive to feed and too difficult to control when panicked or wounded in battle. (Scala/Art Resource, NY.)

and federal leagues naturally interpreted the proclamation to mean they could behave as they liked; they thought that as "friends" of Rome, they were truly independent. They misunderstood. The Romans meant them to behave as clients and follow their new patrons' advice. Trouble developed because the two sides failed to realize that common and familiar words such as *freedom* and *friends* could carry very different meanings in different societies. To make the Macedonians and Greeks observe their obligations as clients, the Romans repeatedly sent armies to the region. Frustrated by continuing resistance, the Senate in 146 B.C.E. ordered the destruction of Corinth for asserting its independence and converted Macedonia and Greece into a province. In 133 B.C.E., the Attalid king of Pergamum boosted Roman power with an astonishing gift: he left his rich Asia Minor kingdom to Rome in his will. In 121 B.C.E., when the Greek city of Massilia on the southern coast of Gaul asked for protection against local Celts, the Romans made the lower part of Gaul across the Alps (modern France) into a province. By this date, then, Rome governed and profited from two-thirds of the Mediterranean region; only the easternmost Mediterranean lay outside its control (Map 4.2, page 139).

Greece's Influence on Rome's Literature, Philosophy, and Art

The wars that took Roman armies to Greece brought increased Greek cultural influence on Rome. In about 200 B.C.E., the first Roman historian used Greek to compose an account of Rome's foundation and the Punic War. Greece also directly inspired the earliest literature in Latin: an adaptation of Homer's *Odyssey* by a Greek ex-slave, written sometime after the First Punic War.

Actors in a Comedy

This relief sculpture dating to the first century B.C.E. shows actors portraying characters in one of the various kinds of comedies popular during the Roman republic. In this variety, which derived from Hellenistic Greek comedies, the actors wore exaggerated masks designating stock personality types and performed broad, slapstick skits. The plots ranged from comic versions of famous legends to stereotypes of common family problems. Here, on the right, an irresponsible son returns home after a night of drinking, supported by his slave and preceded by a hired female musician. On the left, his enraged father is restrained by a friend from beating the prodigal son with his cane. (Scala/Art Resource, NY.)

Many of the most famous early Latin authors were not native Romans, coming from all over Italy and also North Africa. Their widespread origins reveal the mixing of cultures under the republic. They all found inspiration in Greek literature. Roman comedies, for example, took their plots and standard characters from Hellenistic Greek comedies, which raised laughs by portraying family life and stereotyped personalities such as the boastful warrior and the obsessed lover.

Not all Romans applauded Greek influence. Cato, although he studied Greek himself, insisted that the "feeble" Greeks were corrupting the "sturdy" Romans. In the mid-second century B.C.E., he established Latin as an appropriate language for prose by publishing a history of Rome, *The Origins,* and instructions for running a large farm, *On Agriculture.* He glumly predicted that if the Romans ever became infected with Greek literature, they would lose their power. In fact, as is usual in cultural interactions, early Roman authors employed foreign models to express their own values in new ways. The epic poet Ennius, for example, adapted the traditions of Homer to compose his *Annals,* a long poem describing Roman history, but Ennius praised ancestral Roman tradition, as a much-quoted line demonstrates: "On the ways and the men of old rests the Roman commonwealth."

Later Roman writers also took inspiration from Greek literature. Lucretius (c. 94–55 B.C.E.), for example, published a long poem titled *On the Nature of Things* to argue that people should have no fear of death, which only inflamed "the running sores of life." His work's content followed closely the "atomic theory" of the nature of existence of the Greek philosopher Epicurus and described matter as composed of tiny, invisible particles. The poem explained that death meant only that the atoms temporarily forming a person's body once again separated, without pain or suffering. There could be no eternal punishment—or reward—after death because a person's soul, itself made up of atoms, dissolved along with the body.

Hellenistic Greek authors inspired Catullus (c. 84–54 B.C.E.), whose witty poems satirized prominent politicians for their sexual behavior and revealed his own disastrous love life. His most notorious erotic poems detailed his passion for a married woman named Lesbia, whom he begged to think only of immediate pleasures: "Let us live, my Lesbia, and love; the gossip of stern old men is not worth a cent. Suns can set and rise again; we, when once our brief light has set, must sleep one neverending night. Give me a thousand kisses, then a hundred, then a thousand more."

Cicero composed many essays on philosophy, ethics, theology, and political science that adapted Greek philosophy to Roman life. Retiring temporarily from active politics after Julius Caesar's victory in the civil war that destroyed the republic, Cicero in 45–44 B.C.E. wrote about his doctrine of ***humanitas*** (meaning "humanness" or "the quality of humanity"). This set of ideas expressed an ideal standard of human behavior based on the generous and honest treatment of others, a recognition of the uniqueness of each human being, and an abiding commitment to morality derived from natural law (the right that exists for all people by nature, independent of the differing laws and customs of different societies). Cicero's humanitas ideal has continued to influence thinkers to this day.

Greece also influenced Rome in art and architecture, from the style of sculpture and painting to the design of public buildings. As always, Romans adapted Greek models to their own purposes, especially in portrait sculpture. Hellenistic artists had pioneered the sculpting of realistic statues that showed the damage old age and stress did to the human body. These Greek statues, however, portrayed human stereotypes ("the old man" or "the drunken woman"), not specific people. Greek portrait sculpture, however, presented real individuals in the best possible light, much like a retouched photograph today.

Roman artists in the later republic transferred the Greek tradition of realistic sculpture to portraits. Roman sculptures of specific men did not conceal unflattering features such as protruding noses, receding chins, deep wrinkles, bald heads, and careworn eyes. Because either the men shown in the portraits or their families paid for their statues, they must have wanted the faces sculpted realistically—showing the toll of age and effort—to emphasize how hard the men had worked to serve "the people's thing" that was the republic. Portraits of women, however, were more idealized, perhaps to represent the traditional vision of a happy marriage. Portraits of children were not popular during the republic, perhaps because offspring were not seen as contributing to public life until they were grown.

Imperialism's Consequences for Republican Society

Rome's long wars abroad had the unintended consequence of disrupting Roman agriculture and creating social unrest. The years of conquest created hard times because a farmer absent on prolonged military expeditions had only two choices: relying on a hired hand or slave to manage his crops and animals, or having his wife take on what was traditionally men's work in the fields in addition to her usual domestic tasks. The story of the consul Regulus in the First Punic War reveals the severe problems a man's absence could cause. When the man who managed his four-acre farm died while the consul was away fighting Carthage, a hired hand ran off with all the farm's tools and livestock. Regulus begged the Senate to send a general to replace him so he could return home to save his wife and children from starving. Instead, the senators saved Regulus's family and property from ruin because they wanted to retain him as a commander in the field.

Ordinary soldiers received no such special aid, and these troubles hit poorer families particularly hard when in the second century B.C.E., for reasons that remain unclear, there was no longer enough farmland to support their children from generation to generation. Scholars have usually concluded that the rich had deprived the poor of land, but recent research suggests that the problem stemmed from a rapid growth in the population of young people. Not all regions of Italy suffered as severely as others, and some impoverished farmers and their families managed to remain in the countryside by working as day laborers for others. Whatever the cause of the rising number of people with no way to make a living, this change created a social crisis by the late second century B.C.E. Many homeless people migrated to Rome, where the men looked for work as menial laborers and the women sought piecework making cloth but were often forced into prostitution.

This influx of desperate, landless people swelled the poor population in Rome and created political conflict as ambitious politicians competed for their votes by promising welfare benefits. Fearing violent riots by the growing number of hungry poor in the capital, the government took on the task of importing food to calm them. By the late second century B.C.E., Rome was importing massive amounts of grain from abroad to support the city's masses. Their demand for rations of low-priced (and eventually free) grain distributed at the state's expense became one of the most explosive issues in late republican politics.

At the other end of the social hierarchy, Rome's elite reaped abundant rewards from imperialism. The increased need for commanders to lead overseas military campaigns allowed successful generals to enrich themselves and their families. By using their gains to finance public buildings, the elite enhanced their reputations while benefiting the general population. Building new temples, for example, was thought to increase everyone's security by pleasing the gods.

The financial troubles of small farmers enriched big landowners because they could buy bankrupt plots to create larger estates. They also illegally occupied public land carved from the territory of defeated peoples. The rich worked their large estates, called *latifundia,* with slaves as well as free laborers. Many free but poor

Bedroom in a Rich Roman House
This bedroom from about 40 B.C.E. was in the home of a wealthy Roman family near Naples. It was buried and preserved by the eruption of the volcano Vesuvius in 79 C.E. The bright paintings included a wide variety of outdoor scenes and architecture. The stone mosaic floor helped keep the house cool in the summer. (Image copyright © The Metropolitan Museum of Art/Art Resource, NY.)

Romans now found it hard to get work as laborers because the rich had acquired slave workers from the many people taken captive during the foreign wars. The growing size of the slave crews working on latifundia was a mixed blessing for their wealthy owners because the presence of so many slaves in one place led to periodic revolts, which required the army to suppress them.

The elite also profited from Rome's expansion by filling government offices in the new provinces, where they could enrich themselves if they ignored the traditional value of uprightness. Since Roman provincial officials ruled by martial law, no one in the provinces could curb a greedy governor's appetite for extracting money from the province's local peoples. Not all governors were corrupt, but some did use their unsupervised power to extort everything they could. Until jury trials were created, such offenders escaped punishment because in the Senate they and their colleagues would routinely excuse one another's crimes.

A new desire for luxury, financed by the fruits of expansion abroad, fractured the traditional values of moderation and frugality. Before, a general such as Manius Curius in the third century B.C.E. represented the ideal: despite his glorious military victories, legend said that he boiled turnips for his meals in a humble hut. Now, the elite acquired showy luxuries, such as large country villas for entertaining friends and clients, to proclaim their social superiority. Money had become more valuable to them than the good of "the people's thing."

> **REVIEW**   What were the intended and unintended consequences of Rome's creation of an empire?

The Destruction of the Republic, 133–44 B.C.E.

Ambitious leaders from the Roman elite destroyed the republic in civil war. The conflict had two main causes: fierce disagreements among these leaders about how much political influence and government support ordinary citizens should receive, and rivalry for individual glory. The tribunes Tiberius and Gaius Gracchus agitated for reforms to help poor Romans, whom they pitied for their bitter poverty and whose potential for rioting they feared. The brothers' opponents in the Senate resorted to murder to stop them. When Gaius Marius opened army service to the poor to boost his personal status, his creation of "client armies" undermined faithfulness to the republic. When the people's unwillingness to share citizenship with Italian allies sparked a war in Italy and the clashing ambitions of the "great men" Sulla, Pompey, and Julius Caesar burst into civil war, the republic shattered beyond repair.

The Gracchus Brothers and Political Violence

The brothers Tiberius and Gaius Sempronius Gracchus, sons of a famous elite family, won political support from poor citizens by promising a much higher level of government subsidies for them. Tiberius, the elder brother, spoke bluntly about the horrible lives of the landless poor, according to his second-century C.E. biographer Plutarch:

> The wild beasts that roam over Italy have their dens. . . . But the men who fight and die for Italy enjoy nothing but the air and light; without house or home they wander about with their wives and children. . . . They fight and die to protect the wealth and luxury of others; they are called masters of the world, and have not a lump of ground they call their own.

Tiberius was elected tribune for 133 B.C.E. Motivated by both compassion for these impoverished citizens and worry about their potential to use violence to try to improve their living conditions, he proposed reforms to give them financial support. The Senate strongly rejected his proposals. Tiberius then broke tradition by having the Plebeian Assembly pass laws contrary to the Senate's advice. He also violated tradition by running for reelection as tribune in consecutive years. In response,

Tiberius's own cousin led a band of senators and their clients in an ambush against him to, as they shouted, "save the republic." When they clubbed the tribune and many of his followers to death, their assault marked a turning point in the republic: murder now became a political tool.

Gaius, elected tribune for 123 B.C.E. and, in a dramatic break with tradition, for the following year as well, also pushed reforms that outraged the elite: land redistribution, subsidized grain prices, public works projects throughout Italy to provide employment for the poor, and colonies abroad to provide farms for the landless. Gaius's most revolutionary proposals were to grant Roman citizenship to many Italians and to establish new courts that would try senators accused of corruption as provincial governors. The new juries would be manned not by senators but by *equites* (equestrians, or knights). These were landowners from outside the city, wealthy businessmen whose choice of commerce over a public career set them apart from senators. Because they did not serve in the Senate, equestrians could convict corrupt senators without fear of peer pressure. Gaius's proposal marked the emergence of the equestrians as a political force in Roman politics and angered the Senate. When the senators blocked his plans, Gaius assembled an armed group to threaten them. They responded by instructing the consuls "to take all measures necessary to defend the republic," meaning violence. To escape execution, Gaius had one of his slaves cut his throat; the senators and their followers then murdered hundreds of Gaius's supporters.

The violent deaths of the Gracchus brothers and so many other citizens created a crisis in Roman politics. From then on, members of the elite divided themselves into two groups: "supporters of the common people" (*populares*) or "supporters of the best people" (*optimates*). Some identified with one side or the other based on genuine allegiance to its policies; others supported whichever side better promoted their own political advancement.

Gaius Marius and the First Client Armies

This crisis allowed a new kind of leader to arise: men from the elite but with no consul among their ancestors. Such men relied on sheer ability to force their way to fame, fortune, influence, and—their ultimate goal—election as consul. The most controversial of them was Gaius Marius (c. 157–86 B.C.E.), an equestrian from central Italy. Ordinarily, a man with his background had no chance of cracking the nobles' hold on the consulships. When Marius succeeded as a general against a rebel in Africa where nobles had failed, however, the people elected him consul for 107 B.C.E. In Roman terms, this election made him a "new man"—that is, the first man in the history of his family to become consul. Marius's further successes in great crises, especially against German tribes that attacked southern France and then Italy, led the people to elect him consul for six terms, including consecutive service. His career overturned Roman political tradition.

Marius became so famous that the Senate voted him a triumph, Rome's highest—and rarest—military honor. On the day of the ceremony, the general paraded through Rome in a chariot. His face was painted red for reasons Romans no longer remembered. Huge crowds cheered him, while his army teased him with off-color jokes to avert the evil eye at this moment of supreme glory. For a similar reason, a slave rode with him to keep whispering in his ear, "Look behind you, and remember that you are a mortal."

Ordinary citizens loved Marius for his reform of military service. Previously, only men with property were usually allowed to enroll as soldiers. Marius completed a growing trend by opening enlistment to proletarians, men who owned almost nothing. For them, serving in the army meant an opportunity to better their lot by acquiring plunder and a land grant to retire on.

This change created armies more tied to their commanders than to the community. Proletarian troops felt loyalty to commanders who led them to victory and then generously divided the plunder with them. Poor soldiers thus began to behave like an army of clients following their general as their patron and supporting his ambitions. Later generals used client armies in the political and personal disputes that destroyed the republic.

Sulla and Civil War

The first commander to do this was a noble named Lucius Cornelius Sulla (c. 138–78 B.C.E.). His opportunity came when Rome's Italian allies rebelled from 91 to 87 B.C.E. in frustration at their being denied citizenship. The Italians lost the war and 300,000 men, but they won the political battle: Romans granted citizenship to all freeborn peoples of Italy south of the Po River. Sulla's successful command in the war won him election as consul, and he then marched his client army against Rome to force the Senate to make him the commander in Asia Minor, to put down a serious rebellion there. The campaign would mean unimaginable plunder because Asia Minor had many wealthy cities. All Sulla's officers except one deserted him in horror, but his soldiers united behind him. Capturing Rome, Sulla murdered or exiled his opponents and let his men rampage through the city. He then led them off to Asia Minor, ignoring a summons to stand trial.

When Sulla returned victorious from Asia Minor, he devised a merciless procedure called proscription—posting a list of those supposedly guilty of treasonable crimes so that anyone could kill them without a trial. Because the property of those proscribed was confiscated, Sulla's followers listed the names of all those whose wealth they desired. The Senate in terror appointed Sulla dictator—an emergency office supposed to be held only temporarily—without any limitation of term. He reorganized the government in the interest of "the best people," his social class, by making senators the only ones allowed to judge cases against their colleagues and forbidding tribunes to offer legislation on their own or hold any other office after their terms.

Sulla died soon thereafter, but his bloody career revealed the sad fate of the traditional values of the republic. First, the definition of success in war had long ago changed from defending the community to acquiring profits for commanders and common soldiers alike. Second, the patron-client system had mutated to make poor soldiers feel stronger ties of obligation to their generals than to the republic. Finally, the traditional desire to win honor could now create political instability when a leader's desire for prestige and wealth overcame his desire to provide public service.

Pompey "the Great" and the First Triumvirate

The career of Gnaeus Pompey (106–48 B.C.E.) shows how weak the traditional restraints on a leader's power became after Sulla. Only twenty-three years old, Pompey gathered a private army from his father's clients to fight for Sulla. His spectacular victories made it impossible for Sulla to refuse his demand for a triumph. Awarding the supreme honor to such a young man, who had not held a single public office, shattered tradition, but as Pompey told Sulla, "People worship the rising, not the setting, sun."

By claiming the credit (the real victor was Marcus Licinius Crassus) for stopping a massive slave rebellion led by Spartacus, a fugitive gladiator who had terrorized southern Italy for two years and defeated consuls with his army of 100,000 escaped slaves, Pompey won election to the consulship in 70 B.C.E. without climbing the ladder of offices or reaching the legal age of forty-two. Three years later, he received unlimited powers to eradicate the pirates infesting the Mediterranean. He smashed them in a matter of months. This success made him wildly popular with the urban poor, who depended on a steady flow of imported grain; with wealthy shippers, who depended on safe sea-lanes; and with coastal communities that had suffered from the pirates' raids. Next he won the first Roman victories in the Levant and made Syria a province in 64 B.C.E., thereby ending the Seleucid kingdom and extending Rome's power to the eastern edge of the Mediterranean.

Pompey's victories were so amazing that people compared him to Alexander the Great and referred to him as *Magnus* (the Great). He boasted that he had increased Rome's provincial revenues by 70 percent and distributed plunder equal to twelve and a half years' pay to his soldiers. He treated foreign policy as his personal business. In the east he operated on his own and ignored the tradition of commanders consulting the Senate to decide on new political arrangements for conquered territories. He explained his attitude when replying to some foreigners who had objected to his actions as unjust: "Stop quoting the laws to us," he told them. "We carry swords."

Pompey's rivals in Rome tried to gain support by proclaiming their concern for the common people. By the 60s B.C.E., Rome's population had soared to over half a million, as farmers unable to make a living off the land flocked to the capital looking for day labor and government-provided food. Hundreds of thousands lived crowded together in shabby, multistory apartment buildings no better than slums and depended on subsidized grain as the basis of their meals. Work was hard to find. Danger haunted the crowded streets because the city had no police force. Even the propertied class was in trouble. Sulla's confiscations had produced a credit crunch and caused land values to crash by flooding the real estate market with properties for sale. Overextended investors were trying to borrow their way back to financial health, with no success.

In 60 B.C.E. Pompey joined his fiercest political rivals, Crassus and Julius Caesar, in an unofficial power-sharing arrangement called the **First Triumvirate** (a coalition of three men). They formed the alliance because none of them was strong enough to defeat the other two; by joining together, each could get at least part of what he wanted in political and military power. The triumvirate had no governing philosophy except self-interest; the arrangement's only cohesion came from personal connections. To cement his bond with Pompey, Caesar married his daughter, Julia, to Pompey in 59 B.C.E., even though she had been engaged to another man. Pompey then ordered his own daughter, who also had been engaged, to marry Julia's jilted fiancé. Through these marital connections, the two powerful rivals now had a common interest: the well-being of Julia, Caesar's only daughter and Pompey's new wife. (Pompey had earlier divorced his second wife after Caesar had allegedly seduced her.) Pompey and Julia apparently fell deeply in love, and as long as Julia lived, Pompey's affection for her restrained him from an outright break with her father.

The Rise and Fall of Julius Caesar

Julius Caesar (100–44 B.C.E.), born to one of Rome's oldest families and claiming the goddess Venus as his ancestor, had a brilliant military career that outshone even Pompey's. Most famously, in the 50s B.C.E. he achieved nearly ten years of victories—and swift recovery from defeats—against the fearsome Gauls in what is today France, which Caesar made into a Roman province. He awed his troops with his daring by crossing the channel to campaign even in Britain. His political enemies in Rome dreaded him even more as his military successes mounted, and the bond linking him to Pompey vanished in 54 B.C.E. when Julia died in childbirth. With Caesar's followers agitating to win the masses' support for his return to the capital, the two sides' rivalry exploded into violence. By the mid-50s B.C.E., political gangs of young men roamed the alleys of Rome in search of opponents to assault or murder. Street fighting reached such a level of violence in 53 B.C.E. that it prevented elections; no consuls could be chosen until the year was half over. The triumvirate completely dissolved that same year with the death of Crassus in battle in northern Mesopotamia. A year later, Caesar's enemies took the extraordinary step of having Pompey appointed sole consul. The traditions of republican government had crumbled.

When the Senate ordered Caesar to surrender his command and thus open himself to prosecution by his enemies, he led his army against Rome. As he crossed the Rubicon River, the official northern boundary of Italy, in early 49 B.C.E., he uttered the famous words signaling that he had chosen civil war: "The die is cast." Caesar's advance caused Pompey and most senators to flee to Greece to prepare to fight back. When Caesar led his army to Greece in 48 B.C.E., he nearly lost the war as his supplies ran out, but his soldiers remained loyal even when they were reduced to eating bread made from roots. When Pompey saw what his opponent's troops were willing to live on, he cried, "I am fighting wild beasts."

Coin Portrait of Julius Caesar

Julius Caesar (100–44 B.C.E.) was the first living Roman to have his portrait appear on a Roman coin. The images and words stamped on the front and back of Roman republican coins changed annually, chosen by the officials in charge of minting. Tradition mandated that only persons who had died could be shown (the same rule applies to U.S. currency), but after Caesar won the civil war in 45 B.C.E., he broke that tradition, as he did many others, to show that he was Rome's supreme leader. Here, he wears the laurel wreath of a conquering general. The realistic portrait conforms to late republican style. Caesar's wrinkled neck and careworn expression emphasize the suffering he endured—and imposed on others—to reach the pinnacle of success. Do you think a portrait is more impressive if it shows the person's blemishes or if it is idealized? **For more help analyzing this image, see the visual activity for this chapter in the Online Study Guide at** bedfordstmartins.com/huntconcise. (Bibliothèque nationale de France.)

Caesar defeated Pompey and then invaded Egypt, where he restored Cleopatra VII (69–30 B.C.E.) to the Egyptian throne. As intelligent as she was ruthless, Cleopatra charmed the invader into sharing her bed and supporting her rule. This attachment shocked Caesar's friends and enemies alike: they believed Rome should seize power from foreigners, not yield it to them. Still, so effective were Cleopatra's powers of persuasion that Caesar maintained the love affair and guaranteed her rule over a rich land that his army otherwise would have plundered.

By 45 B.C.E., Caesar had won the civil war but faced the problem of how to govern a shattered republic: only a popular leader ruling alone seemed capable of ending the cycle of violence, but the oldest tradition of the republic's elite was its hatred of monarchy. The second-century B.C.E. senator Cato, notorious for his advice in favor of destroying Carthage, had best expressed this feeling. "A king," he said, "is an animal that feeds on human flesh." Caesar's solution was to rule as king in everything but name. First, he had himself appointed dictator in 48 B.C.E.; by 44 B.C.E. he had become "dictator for an indefinite term," a startling break with tradition for an office meant to be short-term only. "I am not a king," he insisted, but the distinction was hard to recognize. Elections for offices continued, but Caesar controlled the results by recommending candidates to the assemblies, which his supporters dominated.

Acting as a sole ruler while carefully avoiding calling himself a monarch, Caesar introduced changes that he hoped would strengthen Rome and prevent violent unrest: a moderate cancellation of debts; a limitation on the number of people eligible for subsidized grain; a large program of public works, including the construction of public libraries; colonies for his veterans in Italy and abroad; the rebuilding of Corinth and Carthage as commercial centers; and a revival of the ancient policy of giving citizenship to non-Romans, such as the Gauls on the Italian side of the Alps. He also admitted non-Italians to the Senate when he expanded its membership from six hundred (the expanded size established by Sulla) to nine hundred.

Caesar prided himself on his clemency, the recipients of which were, by Roman custom, bound to be his grateful clients. In return, he received unprecedented honors, such as a special golden seat in the Senate house and the renaming of the seventh month of the year after him (July). He also regularized the Roman calendar by having each year include 365 days, a calculation based on an ancient Egyptian calendar that forms the basis of our modern one.

Julius Caesar's career and ideas made him the most popular and adored ruler among ordinary people in Roman history. What sort of government and society Rome would have developed if Caesar had lived longer is one of the most fascinating what-if questions in ancient history. But he was murdered soon after becoming "dictator for an indefinite term" because his rule outraged "the best people." They resented being dominated by one of their own, a "traitor" who had deserted to "the common people's" side. A band of senators formed a conspiracy, led by Caesar's former close friend Marcus Junius Brutus and inspired by the legend about Brutus's ancestor Lucius Junius Brutus having led the violent expulsion of Rome's original monarchy. They cut Caesar to pieces with daggers in the Senate house on March 15 (the Ides of March on the Roman calendar), 44 B.C.E. When his friend Brutus stabbed him, Caesar, according to some ancient reports, gasped his last words—in Greek: "You, too, my son?"

The "liberators," as the assassins called themselves, had no specific plan for reviving the republic. They apparently believed that it would automatically spring back to life, overlooking the horrible political violence of the previous forty years and the distortion of Roman values that it had brought. Panicked by the loss of their patron, the masses rioted at Caesar's funeral to vent their anger against the elite that had robbed them of their benefactor. Failing to form a united front, the elite resumed their feuds with one another. By 44 B.C.E., the republic was lost beyond recovery.

> **REVIEW**   How did the actions and policies of individual leaders destroy the republic?

Conclusion

From its beginnings in 509 B.C.E., the Roman republic flourished because its traditional values stressed the common good, it absorbed outsiders, and its small farmers produced agricultural surpluses. These surpluses supported a growing population, which supplied soldiers for a strong army that won an empire. Romans' willingness to endure tremendous losses of life and property—the proof that they valued faithfulness—helped make them unbeatable: Rome might lose battles but never wars. Because warfare brought profits, peace seemed a wasted opportunity. Elite commanders craved victories because they brought glory and riches to raise their status in Rome's social hierarchy.

Rome's long wars abroad had unexpected and harmful consequences at home. Many of Italy's rural poor farmers now found it impossible to make a living on the land. When desperate people flocked to Rome, they created political and social instability, especially with demands for food paid for with public money. Members of the elite disagreed over how to solve the problem and also increased their competition with each other for the career opportunities presented by constant war. These rivalries became unmanageable when successful generals began to extort advantages for themselves by acting as patrons to their client armies. In this hypercompetitive environment, violence became the ultimate action in political disputes. But violent actions provoked violent responses; community values were drowned in the blood of civil war. No reasonable Roman could have been optimistic about the chances for an enduring peace in the aftermath of Caesar's assassination in 44 B.C.E. That a sole ruler would forge such a peace less than fifteen years later would have seemed an impossible dream.

CHAPTER REVIEW QUESTIONS

1. Compare the political and social values of the Roman republic with those of the Classical Greek city-state.

2. What were the positive and negative consequences of war for the Roman republic?

For practice quizzes and other study tools, see the Online Study Guide at bedfordstmartins.com/huntconcise.

For primary-source material from this period, see Chapter 5 of *Sources of* THE MAKING OF THE WEST, Third Edition.

TIMELINE

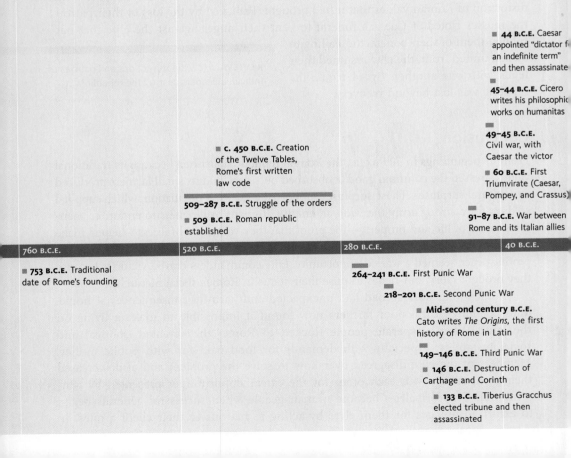

■ **44 B.C.E.** Caesar appointed "dictator for an indefinite term" and then assassinated

45–44 B.C.E. Cicero writes his philosophic works on humanitas

49–45 B.C.E. Civil war, with Caesar the victor

■ **60 B.C.E.** First Triumvirate (Caesar, Pompey, and Crassus)

91–87 B.C.E. War between Rome and its Italian allies

■ **c. 450 B.C.E.** Creation of the Twelve Tables, Rome's first written law code

509–287 B.C.E. Struggle of the orders

■ **509 B.C.E.** Roman republic established

760 B.C.E.   520 B.C.E.   280 B.C.E.   40 B.C.E.

■ **753 B.C.E.** Traditional date of Rome's founding

264–241 B.C.E. First Punic War

218–201 B.C.E. Second Punic War

■ **Mid-second century B.C.E.** Cato writes *The Origins*, the first history of Rome in Latin

149–146 B.C.E. Third Punic War

■ **146 B.C.E.** Destruction of Carthage and Corinth

■ **133 B.C.E.** Tiberius Gracchus elected tribune and then assassinated

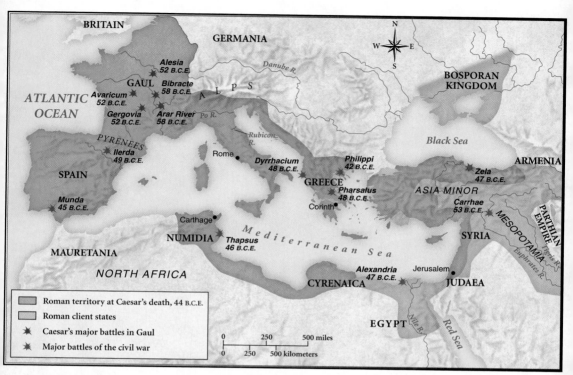

Mapping the West **The Roman World at the End of the Republic, c. 44 B.C.E.**
Upon Julius Caesar's assassination in 44 B.C.E., the territory that Rome would control during the coming centuries was almost complete. Caesar's young relative Octavian (the future Augustus) would conquer and add Egypt in 30 B.C.E. Geography and distance were the primary factors preventing further
expansion, which Romans never stopped thinking of as desirable even when practical difficulties made
this goal only a dream. The deserts of Africa and the Near East worked against expansion southward
or eastward, and trackless forests and fierce resistance from local inhabitants made expansion into
central Europe and the British Isles impossible to sustain.

Suggested References

Our knowledge of the political and economic changes in the Roman republic is being
revised by archaeological research linked to close study of the ancient literary sources.

Ashton, Sally-Ann. *Cleopatra and Egypt.* 2008.
Beard, Mary, et al. *Religions of Rome.* 2 vols. 1998.
Bradley, Keith. *Slavery and Society at Rome.* 1994.
*Caesar. *The Civil War.* Trans. John Carter. 1997.
*Cicero. *On the Good Life.* Trans. Michael Grant. 1971.
Daily life (and more): http://www.vroma.org/~bmcmanus/romanpages.html
Earl, Donald. *The Moral and Political Tradition of Rome.* 1967.
Gardner, Jane. *Women in Roman Law and Society.* 1986.
Goldsworthy, Adrian. *The Punic Wars.* 2000.
Lancel, Serge. *Carthage: A History.* Trans. Antonia Nevill. 1995.
Strong, Donald. *Roman Art.* 2d ed. 1988.

The Roman Empire

44 B.C.E.–284 C.E.

I N 203 C.E., VIBIA PERPETUA, wealthy and twenty-two years old, nursed her infant in a Carthage jail while awaiting execution for refusing to participate in traditional sacrifices for the Roman emperor's health and safety. One morning, the jailer dragged her off to see the local Roman governor, and Perpetua described in her journal what happened next:

Executing a Criminal in Public
This mosaic shows a convicted criminal being killed by a leopard at a public execution. Romans believed that serious criminals deserved disgraceful deaths before crowds of spectators. Martyrs charged with treason, like Perpetua, often were executed by being "condemned to the beasts." Here the prisoner is tied to a stake on a chariot so the handlers can push him into the face of the leopard to provoke an angry leap; wild animals frequently would not attack without such provocation. Dated to about Perpetua's time, c. 200 C.E., the mosaic covered a villa floor in North Africa, in what is today Libya. The villa's owner perhaps ordered this subject for his floor to show visitors that he had paid for the expensive spectacle that included this grisly execution. *(© Roger Wood/Corbis.)*

My father came carrying my son, crying "Perform the sacrifice; take pity on your baby!" Then the governor pleaded, "Think of your old father; show pity for your little child! Offer the sacrifice for the health of the emperor's family." "I refuse," I answered. "Are you a Christian?" asked the governor. "Yes." When my father would not stop trying to change my mind, the governor ordered him thrown to the ground and whipped with a rod. I felt sorry for my father; it seemed they were beating me. I pitied his pathetic old age.

The governor, reluctantly it seems, had Perpetua executed by being gored by a bull and stabbed by a gladiator. She died still proclaiming her faith in the new Christian religion and rejecting Rome's traditional religion of the imperial cult.

Perpetua's fate illustrates the continuing importance of tradition in Roman history after the fall of the republic. She died a criminal because she refused to observe "the way of the ancestors" by submitting to the demand that she prove her loyalty to Rome's government by making a sacrifice. Her refusal to act according to traditional values, though motivated by different reasons, recalled the refusal of Roman commanders in the late republic to value the community's needs over their personal ambitions. Their civil wars created a bloodbath following Julius Caesar's assassination in 44 B.C.E. After seventeen years of Roman fighting Roman, Augustus (63 B.C.E.–14 C.E.) restored peace in 27 B.C.E. by inventing a disguised monarchy, the **principate**, which claimed to restore traditional values. His new political and social system opened the pivotal period in Western civilization that we call the Roman Empire.

Romans welcomed the two centuries of relative peace that the principate brought, a period that historians call the **Pax Romana** (Roman peace). In the third century C.E., however, rivalry over who would be emperor reignited civil war, leading to economic crisis. By the 280s C.E., the Roman imperial government again desperately needed to transform its political system to restore traditional values of loyalty and public service. Diocletian, a military commander from the provinces, would begin that process by winning rule over the Roman world in 284 C.E.

CHAPTER FOCUS QUESTION   How did Augustus's new political system successfully keep the "Roman peace" for two centuries, and why did it fail in the third century?

Creating the "Roman Peace"

Inventing tradition takes time. Augustus developed his new political system gradually; as the biographer Suetonius said, Augustus "made haste slowly." The principate produced two centuries of peace, although its rulers periodically waged war to expand imperial territory, suppress rebellions, and repel invaders. Augustus succeeded in reinventing monarchy as an effective form of Roman government because he won the civil war and, during his long rule, found new ways to inspire loyalty by cashing in on the name bestowed on him by the Senate, "Father of His Country."

From Republic to Principate, 44–27 B.C.E.

The principate was born in blood. Julius Caesar's assassination in 44 B.C.E. set off another civil war between generals. The leading opponents were Mark Antony and Octavian (the future Augustus), Caesar's eighteen-year-old grandnephew, who by Caesar's will became his adopted son and heir. Octavian won the loyalty of Caesar's soldiers by taking his new father's name, making him a member of the Julian family, and by promising them rewards from their murdered general's wealth. Marching these veterans to Rome in 43 B.C.E., the teenager forced his election as consul without ever having been elected to any post on the ladder of offices, as tradition required.

Octavian, Antony, and a general named Lepidus then joined forces to eliminate rivals, especially Caesar's assassins. In late 43 B.C.E., the three formed the Second Triumvirate, which they forced the Senate to recognize as an official emergency panel for "rebuilding the state." With no checks on their power, they began to murder their enemies and confiscate the murdered men's property. Octavian and Antony soon forced Lepidus into retirement. Too ambitious to cooperate for long, especially because Antony thought the much younger Octavian should defer to him as his elder, they began a civil war with each other.

Antony made the eastern Mediterranean his base, joining forces with Cleopatra VII (69–30 B.C.E.), the Ptolemaic queen of Egypt who had earlier allied with Caesar. Enchanted by Cleopatra's wit and intelligence, Antony became her ally and lover. Skillfully playing on Romans' fear of foreign attack, Octavian rallied support by claiming that Antony planned to make Cleopatra queen of Rome. Octavian then persuaded the residents of Italy and the western provinces to swear a personal oath of loyalty to him, making them all his clients. In 31 B.C.E. Octavian's victory at the naval battle of Actium in northwestern Greece ended the war (Map 5.1). Cleopatra and Antony

Map 5.1 Expansion of the Roman Empire, 30 B.C.E.–117 C.E.
When Octavian (the future Augustus) captured Egypt in 30 B.C.E. after the suicides of Mark Antony and Cleopatra, he made a significant contribution to the economic strength of Rome because the land of the Nile provided huge amounts of grain and gold. Roman power now encircled the Mediterranean Sea (except for Mauretania, which remained technically under the rule of local kings with Roman approval until c. 44 C.E.). When the emperor Trajan took over the southern part of Mesopotamia in 114–117 C.E., imperial conquest reached its height: Rome's control had never before extended so far east. Hadrian, Trajan's successor, abandoned Mesopotamia, probably because it seemed too far away from Rome to defend. Egypt remained part of the empire until the Arab conquest in 642 C.E.

fled to Egypt, where they both committed suicide in 30 B.C.E., choosing to take their own lives to rob their enemy of celebrity hostages. The general stabbed himself first, bleeding to death in his lover's embrace. The queen then ended her life by letting a poisonous snake, a symbol of Egyptian royal authority, bite her. Octavian's capture of Egypt made him Rome's richest citizen and its unrivaled leader.

Augustus's "Restoration of the Republic," 27 B.C.E.–14 C.E.

Octavian justified his power by claiming that he had restored the republic and, as the Roman people's patron, protected them like a caring father. In 27 B.C.E. he announced that it was the duty of the Senate and the Roman people to preserve the republic now that he had ended the civil war. Awed by Octavian's power, the Senate begged him to do whatever was necessary to safeguard the "restored republic," granted him special civil and military powers, and gave him the honorary name **Augustus**, meaning "favored by the gods." Octavian had considered changing his name to Romulus, after Rome's legendary first king, but as a later historian wrote, "When he realized people thought this idea meant he wanted to be their king, he accepted the other title instead, as if he were more than human; for everything that is most treasured and sacred is called *augustus*." He was thereafter known as Augustus.

Augustus maintained the appearance of traditional republican government while in fact changing the structure of Roman political power. The reality of his system was that it was a monarchy masked as a restored and improved republic. To preserve at least the outward form of traditional government, Augustus continued the annual election of consuls and other officials, the passing of legislation in public assemblies, and respect for the Senate. He served several times as consul, the republic's premier official. So as not to break the tradition that no official should hold more than one post at a time, he had the Senate grant him the powers of a tribune without his actually holding the office. In this way, he possessed the authority to act and to compel citizens as if he were a tribune protecting the rights of the people, but he left the posts open for members of the plebeian elite to occupy, as they had done under the republic. Augustus also kept his own appearance "republican": he dressed and acted like a regular citizen.

Augustus masked his monarchy by taking the title "first man" (*princeps,* hence the term *principate* for his new political system). *Princeps* was the traditional honorary title for the leading senator. Using this as his only title of office was a cleverly calculated move. In the republic, the "first man" had guided Rome based on the respect (**auctoritas**) he had earned; he had no more formal power (*potestas*) than any other leader. By choosing the title *princeps,* Augustus appeared to carry on this valued tradition, but in reality he had taken control of the government. *Princeps* was, in fact, the title of the new kind of ruler that today we call the Roman emperor (from the Latin *imperator,* "commander"). Previously, no one could have exercised the powers of both consul and tribune simultaneously.

Cameo Celebrating Augustus

This cameo, about eight inches by nine inches, was carved early in the Roman Empire. The upper scene probably shows Augustus being crowned—for having saved Roman citizens—by a standing female figure representing the inhabited world. The seated female figure represents Rome and resembles Livia, Augustus's wife, his partner in rule. The man stepping out of the chariot is Tiberius, Livia's son and Augustus's choice to succeed him as princeps. Why do you think Tiberius carries a scepter like that held by Augustus? The lower scene shows defeated enemies subjected to Roman power. How do you think the lower scene relates to the upper scene? (Kunsthistorisches Museum, Wien.)

In 2 B.C.E. Augustus received the symbolic key to his power: the Senate declared him "Father of His Country." He announced that this was the greatest honor Rome could grant. He valued this title because it solidified his image of himself as princeps: a leader governing Romans like a father—stern but caring, requiring obedience and loyalty from his children, but dedicated to taking care of them in return.

The principate brought peace but had a fundamental weakness: the princeps could not automatically pass on his rule to his son. In regular monarchies, the ruler's son inherited his father's position and political legitimacy. Augustus had to create a new process to try to ensure a peaceful succession that would seem legitimate. He therefore said that the Senate would choose his successor, expecting, of course, that it would choose the person he nominated. This new system of succession later resulted in some violent struggles over who should become the next princeps. And since Augustus's successors did not have automatic legitimacy as rulers, they were always quick to suppress any sign of disloyalty or rebellion. Perpetua's refusal to sacrifice, for example, was considered treason and impiety, which was punishable by death, because it disrespected the princeps and angered the gods, thereby threatening the safety of the entire community.

Sources of Power and Legitimacy of the Principate

Augustus and his successors exercised supreme power because they controlled the army and the treasury. Augustus made the military the foundation of his power by turning the republican army—a part-time militia—into a full-time professional force under his command. He made the princeps into the troops' patron by establishing set lengths of service, regular pay, and substantial benefits upon retirement. To cover the added costs, Augustus imposed an inheritance tax on citizens. The rich hated this innovation, but the grateful army obeyed and protected the emperor. Another change Augustus made was to station soldiers—the **praetorian guard**—in Rome itself for the first time. These troops prevented rebellion in the capital and provided an imperial bodyguard, a visible reminder of the emperor's dominance.

To broadcast the political legitimacy he needed, Augustus communicated his image as "Father of His Country"—the patron of everyone in a father's traditional role as protector—with objects from coins to public buildings. As the only mass-produced source of official messages, coins functioned like modern political advertising. The most imposing evidence that Augustus provided of his generosity as a patron came from the mammoth buildings in Rome paid for by the fortune he had inherited from Caesar and then increased in war. The huge Forum of Augustus best illustrates his skill at communicating through bricks and stone (Figure 5.1). Its plaza was centered on a temple to Mars, the Roman god of war. Two-story colonnades stretched out from the temple like wings, sheltering statues of famous Roman heroes as inspirations to future leaders. Augustus's Forum provided a gathering place for religious rituals and ceremonies marking the passage into adulthood of upper-class boys, but it also stressed the themes he wanted to communicate about his new system: peace restored through victory, the foundation of a new age, devotion to the gods who had led Rome to victory, respect for tradition, and his unselfishness in spending money for the community. These messages communicated Augustus's justification for his rule.

Historians debate Augustus's motives for establishing the principate. Was he a cynical tyrant working to destroy the freedoms of the republic? Did he have no choice but to impose a disguised monarchy to reunite a society ripped apart by civil war? Perhaps it is best to see him as a revolutionary bound by tradition. His problem had been the one always facing Roman politicians—how to balance his own personal ambitions, the need for peace, and Rome's tradition of shared rule. Augustus's goals were stability, order, and legitimacy for his system, not political freedom for citizens. His strategy was to employ traditional values to justify changes, as in his reinvention of the meaning of the title "first man." Above all, he extended

Temple of Mars Ultor   Colonnades (porches) lined with columns   Statues of Roman heroes

Unroofed area

Figure 5.1 Cutaway Reconstruction of the Forum of Augustus
Augustus built this large forum (120 × 90 yards) to commemorate his victory over the assassins of his adoptive father, Julius Caesar. Dedicated in 2 B.C.E., its centerpiece was a marble temple dedicated to the god Mars Ultor ("the Avenger"). Inside the temple he placed statues of Mars, Venus (the divine ancestor of Julius Caesar), and Julius Caesar (as a god), as well as Caesar's sword and works of art. The two curved spaces flanking the temple featured statues of Aeneas and Romulus, Rome's founders. The porches stretching along the open courtyard housed other statues of Roman heroes. The ceremony marking teenage boys' passage into adulthood took place here, where they were surrounded by images of the valorous and glorious men whom they were expected to imitate.

the patron-client system to politics by making the emperor everyone's most important patron, possessing a father's moral authority to guide the lives of all.

Despite frequent illnesses, Augustus ruled until he died in his seventies in 14 C.E. The length of his rule, forty-one years, gave his innovations time to gradually become traditions. In explaining how Augustus managed to change the structure of Roman political power, the famous historian Tacitus observed that by the time Augustus died, "almost no one was still alive who had seen the republic." Augustus transformed republican Rome into imperial Rome by his long life, his military and financial innovations, his care for the capital's poor people, and his manipulation of the traditional vocabulary of politics to disguise his power and proclaim his legitimacy.

Life in Augustan Rome

Augustus's efforts to improve the lives of ordinary people helped make his rule secure. The problems were most serious in the capital city. Archaeology and literature let us sketch a picture of life in Augustan Rome. Although some of the sources refer to times after Augustus and to cities other than the capital, they nevertheless help us understand this period; economic and social conditions were essentially the same in all large cities throughout the early centuries of the empire.

The population of Augustan Rome—probably far over half a million—was vast for the ancient world. No European city would have nearly as many people again until London in the 1700s. The streets were packed: "One man jabs me with his elbow, another whacks me with a pole; my legs are smeared with mud, and from all sides big feet step on me" was the poet Juvenal's description of walking in Rome in the early second century C.E. To ease congestion in the narrow streets, wagon traffic was banned in the daytime. This regulation made nights noisy with the creaking of axles and the shouting of drivers caught in traffic jams.

Most urban residents lived in small apartments in multistory buildings called islands (so named because originally each building had an open strip around it). Outnumbering private homes by more than twenty to one, apartment buildings usually housed shops, bars, and simple restaurants on the first floor. Graffiti—political endorsements, personal insults, advertising, and messages of all kinds—covered many outside walls. The higher the floor, the cheaper were the apartments; the poorest people lived on the top floors in single rooms that they rented by the day. Aqueducts delivered fresh water to public fountains, but because apartments had no plumbing, residents had to lug buckets up the stairs. The wealthy few had piped-in water at ground level. Most tenants lacked bathrooms and had to use public latrines or pots for toilets at home. Some buildings had cesspits, or buckets could be carried down to the streets to be emptied by people who made their living collecting excrement. Lazy tenants flung the foul-smelling contents of these containers out the window.

Officials worked constantly to manage the sixty tons of human waste that Rome's population excreted every day. Augustus's administration improved the city's main sewer, but its untreated contents emptied directly into the Tiber River, which ran through the city. The technology for sanitary disposal of waste simply did not exist. People sometimes left human and animal corpses in the streets, to be gnawed by vultures and dogs until the city's officials had them removed. The poor were not the only people affected by such conditions; a stray mutt once brought a human hand to the table where Vespasian, who would be emperor from 69 to 79 C.E., was eating lunch. Flies buzzing everywhere and a lack of mechanical refrigeration contributed to frequent digestive illnesses; the most popular jewelry of the time was a charm to ward off stomach trouble. Although the wealthy could not eliminate such discomforts, they could make their lives more pleasant with luxuries such as snow rushed from the mountains to ice their drinks and slaves to clean their houses, which were built around courtyards and gardens to let in air and sunshine.

Public baths helped residents keep clean. Because admission fees were low and bath facilities were many, almost everyone could afford to go daily. Baths operated like modern health clubs, as centers for exercising and socializing as well as washing. Bathers progressed through a series of increasingly warm, humid areas until

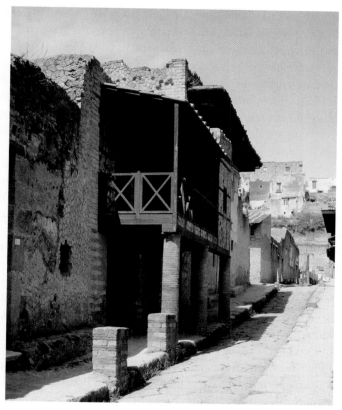

A Roman City Street
Like Pompeii, the prosperous town of Herculaneum, on the shore of the Bay of Naples, was frozen in time by the massive eruption of the neighboring volcano, Mount Vesuvius, in 79 C.E. A flood of mud from the eruption buried the town and preserved its buildings until they were excavated beginning in the eighteenth century. Typical of a Roman town, it had straight roads paved with large, flat stones and flanked by sidewalks. Balconies jutted from the upper stories of houses, offering residents a shady place to view the lively traffic in the urban streets below. Instead of having yards in front or back, houses often were built around a garden courtyard that was open to the sky. Why do you think urban homes were arranged in this way? (Scala/Art Resource, NY.)

they reached a sauna-like room. They swam naked in hot or cold pools. Men and women bathed apart, either in separate rooms or at different times of the day. Since doctors did not yet understand how infections were transmitted, the untreated pools could spread disease.

City residents faced hazards beyond infectious diseases that Augustus tried to reduce. Since Roman engineers, despite their skill in using concrete, brick, and stone as building materials, lacked the technology to calculate precisely how much weight their constructions could stand, apartment buildings could collapse. Augustus improved public safety by imposing a height limit of seventy feet on new apartment buildings. Fire presented the greatest risk; one of Augustus's most important innovations was to provide Rome with the first public fire department in Western history. He also established the first permanent police force, despite his fondness for stopping to watch the fistfights that often broke out in Rome's crowded streets. There were some downsides of city life the emperor could not change. Tenants routinely threw broken dishes and other trash from their apartment windows, to fall like missiles onto the streets below. "If you are walking to a dinner party in Rome," Juvenal warned, "you would be foolish not to make out your will first. For every open window is a source of potential disaster."

Augustus's most popular support for ordinary people was his guarantee of an adequate food supply. He took on this responsibility as Rome's patron and father, and he spent his personal fortune to pay for imported grain. Distributing grain at public expense to the capital's poor citizens had been a tradition for decades, but Augustus's welfare system expanded to an unprecedented 250,000 primary recipients, plus their families. This statistic suggests that between 600,000 and 700,000 people depended on the emperor for food to survive. Poor Romans usually boiled the grain to make a sticky soup, which they washed down with cheap wine. If they were lucky, they might have some beans, onions, or cheese on the side. The rich, as we learn from an ancient cookbook, ate costlier foods, such as roast pork or shellfish, served with pepper, a salty condiment, or a sweet-and-sour sauce made from honey and vinegar.

Augustus also took on moral responsibility for Roman society. By his time, many wealthy Romans were spending their money on luxuries and costly political careers rather than on raising children. Fearing that the decline in the birthrate would destroy the elite that Rome needed as officials, Augustus passed laws to strengthen marriage and encourage larger families by granting special legal privileges to the parents of three or more children. He made adultery a crime. So seriously did Augustus back these reforms that he exiled his own daughter—his only child—and a granddaughter for sex scandals. His laws had little effect, however, and the old elite families dwindled over the centuries. Recent research suggests that in every generation, up to three-fourths of senatorial-rank families lost their official status (by losing the wealth required for that designation) or died out. Equestrians and men from the provinces who won the ruler's favor took the place of these families in the social hierarchy and in the Senate.

The traditional Roman policy of granting citizenship to liberated slaves helped prevent a decline in the number of citizens. If a slave's descendants became wealthy, they could become members of the social elite. This possibility gave slaves reason to work harder and cooperate with their masters. Conditions of slavery varied widely according to occupation. Slaves in agriculture and manufacturing had harsh lives. Most such workers were men, although women might assist the foremen who managed gangs of rural laborers. The second-century novelist Apuleius wrote this grim description of slaves at work in a flour mill: "Through the holes in their ragged clothes you could see scars from whippings all over their bodies. Some wore only loincloths. Letters had been branded on their foreheads and shackles bound their ankles." Worse than the mills were the mines, where the foremen constantly flogged the miners to keep them digging out the metal ores in dangerous conditions.

Household slaves had an easier physical existence. Most Romans owned slaves to work in their homes, from one or two in modestly well-off families to large numbers in rich houses and, above all, the imperial palace. Domestic slaves were often women, working as nurses, maids, kitchen help, and clothes makers. Some male slaves ran businesses for their masters; to encourage them to work hard, masters allowed them to keep part of the profits to save toward purchasing their freedom someday. Women had less opportunity to earn money. Masters sometimes granted them tips for sexual favors, and female prostitutes (many of whom were slaves) could earn money for themselves. Slaves who managed to earn money would sometimes buy slaves themselves, thereby creating their own hierarchy. A male slave might buy a woman for a mate. They could then have an imitation of a normal family life, though a legal marriage was impossible because they remained their master's property, as did their children. If truly fortunate, slaves could slowly accumulate enough money to buy themselves from their masters or could be freed by their masters' wills. Some inscriptions on tombs testify to masters' affectionate feelings for slaves, but even household servants had to endure violent treatment if their masters were cruel. If they attacked their owners because of brutal treatment, the punishment was death.

Entertainment from the Emperor as Patron

The emperors believed they needed to pay for frequent public entertainment to demonstrate their generosity as patrons caring for their people's needs. They regularly provided mass spectacles featuring hunters killing fierce beasts, wild African animals such as lions mangling condemned criminals, mock naval battles in flooded arenas, gladiatorial combats, and chariot races. Spectators jammed stadiums for these violent shows, seated according to their social rank and gender following an Augustan law: the emperor and senators sat close to the action, while women and the poor sat in the upper tiers. These spectacles communicated a political message claiming legitimacy for the new system of government by showing that the emperor was generous in providing expensive entertainment for his subjects, powerful enough to command life-and-death exhibitions, and dedicated to preserving the social hierarchy.

Gladiatorial combats, which originated under the republic as part of extravagant funerals, became so popular under Augustus that they attracted crowds in the tens of thousands. Gladiators were war captives, criminals, slaves, or free volunteers who underwent long and expensive training to perform in these combats; most were men. Gladiatorial fights were bloody, but only captives and criminals usually fought to the death; professional fighters could have extended careers. To make the fights more exciting, gladiators used a variety of weapons. One favorite bout pitted a

Gladiators Sculpted on a Tomb
This relief sculpture, which adorned a tomb near Rome dating to about 30–10 B.C.E., shows gladiators competing in games held to honor the deceased. Gladiatorial combats originated as part of funeral ceremonies because they portrayed with dramatic energy the violent and inevitable struggle to avoid death. Only the very wealthy could afford to have gladiators perform at their funerals or in spectacles meant to win the people's favor. These gladiators represent a traditional form of fighter called provocator (challenger). A challenger, who fought gladiators only of the same type, used a short sword and a curved shield. He wore a metal belt cinching up a loincloth, forearm and lower-leg guards, a partial chest protector, and a plumed helmet. These men's muscular bodies show the great strength required to be a successful fighter. (Alinari/Art Resource, NY.)

lightly armored fighter, called a net man because he used a net and a trident, against a more heavily armored fish man, so named from the design of his helmet crest. Betting was a great attraction, and spectators could be rowdy. As one Christian Roman complained, "Look at the mob coming to the show—already they're out of their minds! Aggressive, mindless, already in an uproar about their bets! They all share the same suspense, the same madness, the same voice."

Champion gladiators won riches and celebrity but not social respectability. Early in the first century C.E., the senators became alarmed at what they regarded as the disgrace caused by members of the upper class fighting as gladiators. They therefore banned the elite and all freeborn women under age twenty from appearing in gladiatorial shows. Daughters trained by their gladiator fathers had first competed during the republic, and a few women continued to compete until the emperor Septimius Severus (r. 193–211 C.E.) banned them.

Gladiatorial shows, chariot races, and theater productions became an opportunity for ordinary citizens to express their feelings about city life to the emperors, who were expected to attend. On more than one occasion, for example, poorer Romans rioted at shows to protest a shortfall in the free grain supply. In this way, public entertainment served as a two-way form of communication between the ruler and the ruled.

Oratory, Literature, and Portrait Sculpture under the Emperor as Patron

Oratory, literature, and portrait sculpture changed under Augustus to serve the same goal as public entertainment: to express the legitimacy of his transformed system of government. Oratory—the skilled public speaking that was the highest attainment of Roman education—became more restricted. Under the republic, skill in making stinging speeches to criticize political opponents had been such a powerful weapon that it could catapult a "new man" like Cicero, who lacked social and military distinction, to international fame. Under the principate, the emperor's supremacy ruled out freewheeling public speech. Speakers used their skill to praise the emperor as the people's patron at public festivals staged to promote his image as a competent, compassionate, and legitimate ruler.

Education for oratory remained a privilege of wealthy boys. Rome had no free public schools, so the poor had to get basic learning from their parents. Most people had time only for training in practical skills. A character in a satire written at the time of the emperor Nero expressed this narrow attitude toward education: "I didn't study geometry and literary criticism and worthless junk like that. I just learned how to read the letters on signs and how to work out percentages, and I learned weights, measures, and the values of the different kinds of coins."

So much new literature emerged during the rule of Augustus that modern scholars call this period the Golden Age of Latin literature. The emperor himself composed verse and prose and served as the patron of a circle of writers and artists. His favorites were Horace and Virgil. Horace delighted audiences with the rhythms and wit of his short poems on public and private subjects. His poem celebrating Augustus's victory over Antony and Cleopatra at Actium became famous for its opening line, "Now it's time to drink!"

Virgil became the most popular poet of Augustus's time for his epic poem *The Aeneid,* which expresses both praise and subtle criticism of Augustus. Virgil took great pains with his poem, and it remained unfinished at his death. He wanted it burned, but Augustus preserved it. Inspired by Homer's *Iliad* and *Odyssey, The Aeneid* tells the story of the Trojan Aeneas, the most distant ancestor of the Romans. Although the poem describes how the gods supported Rome—in fact, Jupiter is portrayed as promising "imperial rule without limit"—it also describes the painful effort and sorrow that success required. The poem therefore speaks to the complex mix of gain and loss that followed Augustus's transformation of politics and society. Above all, *The Aeneid* provided a moral code for Romans at the time: no matter how tempting the emotional pull of revenge and pride, be merciful to the conquered but destroy the arrogant.

Authors had to be careful not to anger the emperor, their patron. Livy composed a lengthy history of Rome in which he recorded the ruthless actions of Augustus and his supporters. The emperor was unhappy, but he did not punish Livy because his history did explain that success and stability depended on traditional values of loyalty and self-sacrifice. By contrast, the poet Ovid was punished. In his witty poems *Art of Love* and *Love Affairs,* he mocked the emperor's laws on marriage and adultery with tongue-in-cheek tips for conducting secret love affairs and picking up other men's wives at festivals. His *Metamorphoses* (*Transformations*) undermined the idea of hierarchy as natural by telling bizarre stories of supernatural shape changes, with people becoming animals and confusion between the human and the divine. Augustus's anger at Ovid finally boiled over when the poet was rumored to be involved in a sex scandal involving the emperor's granddaughter. In 8 C.E., he exiled the poet to a bleak town on the Black Sea and exiled his granddaughter as well.

The style of portrait sculpture changed to reflect the emperor's wishes. Augustus used it to project a calm and competent image of himself as "restorer of the republic" and founder of a new age for Rome. When Augustus was growing up, portraits were starkly realistic, portraying the strain of human experience. The sculpture that Augustus ordered displayed a more idealized style, recalling classical Greek portraiture. In famous works of art such as the statue of himself at First Gate or the sculpted frieze on his Altar of Peace, Augustus had himself portrayed as serene and dignified, not careworn and sick as he often was.

REVIEW   How did Augustus bring peace to Rome and transform its political system?

First Gate Statue of Augustus
At six feet eight inches high, this statue stood a foot taller than its subject, Augustus, Rome's first emperor. Found at his wife's country villa at Prima Porta (First Gate), just outside the capital, the statue was probably a copy of a bronze original sculpted about 20 B.C.E., when Augustus was in his early forties. The sculptor showed him as a younger man, using the idealizing techniques of Greek art of the fifth and fourth centuries B.C.E. to emphasize the emperor's dignity. The sculpture is crowded with symbols that express the image of Augustus that he wanted to communicate. His bare feet hint that he was a near-divine hero, and the statue of Cupid, the son of Venus, refers to the Julian family's descent from that goddess. The carving on the breastplate shows a Parthian surrendering to a Roman soldier under the gaze of personified cosmic forces basking in the peace of Augustus's reign. **For more help analyzing this image, see the visual activity for this chapter in the Online Study Guide at** bedfordstmartins.com/huntconcise. (Scala/Art Resource, NY.)

Maintaining the "Roman Peace"

Augustus knew that the biggest threat to his "restored republic" was the kind of violent struggle for power among members of the social elite that had ruined the original republic. His solution was to train an heir from birth to take over as princeps, with the expectation that the Senate would give the new princeps the same powers that he had held. This strategy kept the rule in his family, called the Julio-Claudians, until Nero's death in 68 C.E., and it established the tradition that family dynasties ruled imperial Rome.

Augustus designed the principate to last by making the ruler's goals building loyalty, preventing unrest, financing the army and the administration of a vast territory of diverse provinces, and promoting Roman law and culture as universal standards, while allowing as much local freedom in the provinces as possible. The citizens, in return for their loyalty, expected the emperor to be a generous patron, but the difficulties of long-range communication imposed practical limits on the government's intervention in the lives of the empire's residents, for better or worse.

The Julio-Claudian Emperors, 14–68 C.E.

Augustus believed he needed to make monarchy Rome's permanent government to avoid civil war, but he could expect resistance from the elite if he did not appear to respect the republic's traditions. He therefore enlisted the Senate's cooperation in identifying his successor. He had no biological son, and one after another the young men he adopted died before he did. Finally, in 4 C.E., he adopted someone into the Julian family who would outlive him, his stepson Tiberius (42 B.C.E.–37 C.E.), a member of the Claudian family. Because Tiberius had been an excellent general, the army supported recommending him to the Senate as the next "first man." The senators approved Tiberius in this role after Augustus died in 14 C.E.; thus began the Julio-Claudian dynasty.

Tiberius's bitter personality made him unpopular, but he ruled for twenty-three years (r. 14–37 C.E.) because he had the most important qualification for succeeding as princeps: the army's loyalty. His long reign provided the stable transition period that the principate needed to establish the compromise between the elite and the emperor that made the monarchy workable. On the one hand, the traditional offices of consul, senator, and others continued, filled by the elite; on the other hand, the emperor decided who held office and determined law and policy. In doing this, everyone claimed that the government was still a republic.

Tiberius's reign revealed the problems that an unhappy emperor could create. Tiberius paid a steep personal price for becoming "first man" because, to strengthen their family ties, Augustus had forced him to divorce his beloved wife Vipsania and marry Augustus's daughter, Julia. This marriage was a disaster. Tiberius's bitterness and fear of rivals led him to spend the last decade of his rule away from Rome as a recluse on an island. His withdrawal from governing opened the way for abuses by officials in Rome and kept him from training his successor.

Tiberius named Augustus's great-grandson Gaius (12–41 C.E.), better known as Caligula (r. 37–41 C.E.), to be the next princeps. Although Caligula lacked the personal qualities and training necessary to be a worthy ruler, he still might have been successful because he knew about soldiering. (*Caligula* means "baby boots." Soldiers had given him that nickname as a child because he wore little leather shoes like theirs while growing up in the military camps his father commanded.) Unfortunately for Rome, however, Caligula paid attention only to his personal desires. Ruling through cruelty and violence, he drained the treasury to humor his whims. Suetonius labeled him a "monster." He frequently outraged the elite by fighting mock gladiatorial combats and appearing in public in women's clothing or costumes imitating gods. Two Praetorian Guard commanders murdered him in 41 C.E. to avenge personal insults.

After Caligula's assassination, the Senate debated the possibility of refusing to acknowledge a new "first man" and therefore restoring a true republic. They gave up, however, when Claudius (r. 41–54 C.E.), Augustus's grandnephew and Caligula's uncle, bought the Praetorian Guard's support with money and the soldiers threatened the senators. That Claudius became princeps by threat of force made it clear that the genuine republic would never return because the soldiers would always insist on having an emperor who would promote their interests. Claudius won wider support for his rule by making men from Gaul (France) members of the Senate. This change signaled that elites from provinces outside Italy would be the emperor's partners in governing. In return for keeping their regions peaceful and prosperous, they received offices at Rome. Claudius also changed imperial government by employing freed slaves as top administrators. Because these men owed their positions to the emperor, they could be expected to be loyal.

The last Julio-Claudian emperor was Nero (r. 54–68 C.E.). Only sixteen when he became "first man," Nero loved music and theater, not governing. The spectacular public festivals he sponsored and the cash he distributed to the poor in Rome kept him popular with the masses. A giant fire in 64 C.E. (the incident that led to the legend of Nero "fiddling while Rome burned") made the elite suspect that he had ordered the blaze to clear space for an enormous new palace. Nero outraged the senators by making them attend his singing performances and by bankrupting the treasury to pay for his building project and a trip to sing all over Greece. He raised money by faking charges of treason against senators and equestrians to seize their property. When military commanders in the provinces rebelled against his abuses, he had a servant help him cut his own throat, after wailing, "To die! And such a great performer!"

The Flavian Emperors, 69–96 C.E.

A year of civil war followed in 69 C.E.; four generals warred to become princeps in this "Year of the Four Emperors." Vespasian (r. 69–79 C.E.) won and began the dynasty of the Flavian family. The new emperor took two steps to minimize resistance. First, he had the Senate publicly recognize him as "first man" even though he was not a Julio-Claudian. Second, he encouraged the spread of the imperial cult (worship of the emperor as a living god and sacrifices for the welfare of the emperor's household) in the provinces outside Italy, where most of the empire's population lived. In promoting emperor worship, Vespasian was building on local traditions. In the eastern provinces, the Hellenistic kingdoms had long before established the tradition of worshipping royalty; provincials there had treated Augustus as a living god. The imperial cult communicated the same image of the emperor to people in the provinces as Rome's architecture and sculpture did to people in the city: he was larger than life, deserved loyalty, and provided aid and gifts as a patron. Because emperor worship was already well established in Greece and the ancient Near East, Vespasian concentrated on spreading it in the provinces of Spain, southern France, and North Africa. Italy, however, still had no temples to the living emperor. Traditional Romans looked down on the imperial cult as a provincial tradition. Vespasian, known for his wit, even muttered as he lay dying in 79 C.E., "Oh me! I think I'm becoming a god."

Vespasian's sons Titus (r. 79–81 C.E.) and Domitian (r. 81–96 C.E.) strengthened the principate with hardheaded financial policy, professional administration, and preemptive military campaigns on the frontiers. Titus sent relief to the populations of Pompeii and Herculaneum after a giant volcanic eruption of Mount Vesuvius buried their towns in 79 C.E., and he provided a fifty-thousand-seat stadium for public entertainments by finishing Rome's **Colosseum**, built on arches and outfitted with giant awnings to shade the crowd. This multistory amphitheater was deliberately constructed on the site of the former fishpond in Nero's Golden House to demonstrate the public-spiritedness of the new Flavian dynasty. Domitian balanced the budget and led the army north to hold the line against the Germanic tribes threatening the empire's frontier regions along the Rhine and Danube rivers—an area of conflict for centuries to come.

Domitian handled his success poorly, and his arrogance inspired hatred among the senators, to whom he once sent a letter announcing, "Our lord god, myself, orders you to do this." Enraged by the rebellion of a general in Germany, he executed numerous upper-class citizens as conspirators. Fearing Domitian would execute them, his wife and members of his court murdered him in 96 C.E. As Domitian's murder revealed, the principate had not solved monarchy's enduring weakness: rivalry for rule that was likely to explode into murderous conspiracy and destabilize succession. The danger of civil war always existed, whether generated by ambitious generals or by competition among the emperor's heirs. As Tacitus commented, emperors became like the weather: "We just have to wait for bad ones to pass and hope for good ones to appear."

The Five "Good Emperors" and the Roman Golden Age, 96–180 C.E.

Fortunately for Rome, politically better weather came with the next five emperors—Nerva (r. 96–98 C.E.), Trajan (r. 98–117 C.E.), Hadrian (r. 117–138 C.E.), Antoninus Pius (r. 138–161 C.E.), and Marcus Aurelius (r. 161–180 C.E.). Historians call them the five "good emperors" because they provided peaceful transfers of power for nearly a century. (The first four of them, lacking surviving sons, used adoption to pick capable successors.) The peace and prosperity of this period have led historians to refer to it as Rome's Golden Age. It marked the longest stretch in Roman history without a civil war since the second century B.C.E.

There were foreign wars and a major rebellion to fight during the Golden Age, however. Trajan fought fierce campaigns expanding Roman power northward across the Danube River into Dacia (today Romania) and eastward into Mesopotamia (Map 5.1, page 157). Hadrian earned the hatred of the Senate by executing several senators as alleged conspirators and punished a Jewish revolt by turning Jerusalem into a military colony. Aurelius spent many miserable years at war protecting the Danube region from outside attacks.

The foundations of the Golden Age were the loyalty of the army and the public service of the elites in the provinces. The army remained loyal because the emperors treated it well. To fulfill their obligations as the military's patrons, the emperors supplemented soldiers' regular pay with large bonuses. These financial rewards made a legionary career desirable, and enlistment counted as a privilege restricted to free male citizens. The army, however, also included auxiliary units of noncitizens from the provinces. Serving under Roman officers, they often picked up some Latin and Roman customs, and they improved life in the provinces by constructing public works. Upon discharge, they received Roman citizenship. In this way, the army served as an instrument for spreading a common way of life.

Most provinces needed relatively few garrison troops to keep them peaceful in this period. Even Gaul, which had bitterly resisted the Roman takeover, was now, according to a contemporary witness, "kept in order by 1,200 troops—hardly more soldiers than it has towns." Increasingly, the emperors stationed the legions (units of five thousand to six thousand troops) on the empire's northern and eastern frontiers to defend against potential invaders. During the course of the Golden Age, the emperors evidently concluded that the distance and the difficulty were too great to conquer new territory beyond the frontiers. This decision had an unintended long-term consequence: without the additional income that expansion brought in from plunder, prisoners of war sold into slavery, and additional taxes from conquered peoples, it became increasingly difficult to increase, or even maintain, the pay that kept the army loyal to the emperor.

A loyal army guaranteed the peace that promoted trade and tax revenues in the Golden Age. Long-distance trade for luxury goods such as spices and silk extended as far as India and China. Taxation of agricultural land in the provinces (Italy was exempt) provided the government's principal source of revenue. Most taxes collected in the provinces stayed there to pay for local projects. Most emperors under the early principate attempted to keep taxes low. As Tiberius put it when refusing a request for tax increases from provincial governors, "I want you to shear my sheep, not skin them alive." The imperial administration itself cost relatively little because it was small compared with the size of the population it governed: several hundred top officials governed about fifty million people. Senatorial and equestrian governors with small staffs ran the provinces, which eventually numbered about forty. In Rome, the emperor employed a substantial palace staff, but equestrian officials called prefects managed the city itself.

Voluntary public service by the elites in the provinces was key to the empire's financial health. Local officials called decurions (members of a municipal senate, later called curials) collected taxes due to the central government. They also personally guaranteed that their towns' expenses were covered. If a shortfall occurred in imperial tax collection or in the finances needed to support their towns, these wealthy men would make up the difference from their own pockets.

The status that civic positions brought made the elites willing to serve, despite the potential expense involved. Some received a priesthood in the imperial cult as a reward, an honor open to both men and women. All could hope to catch the emperor's ear for special help for their areas—for example, after an earthquake or flood. The system worked because it sprang from Roman tradition: the local social elites were the patrons of their communities but the clients of the emperor. As long as there were enough rich, public-spirited provincials participating in this system for its nonmonetary rewards, the principate remained financially stable by relying on the republic's tradition of public service.

Law and Population as Sources of Stability

The spread of Roman law and a healthy rate of reproduction in the population were major contributors to the stability of the Golden Age. Romans prided themselves on their ability to order their society through law. As Virgil said, their mission was "to establish law and order within a framework of peace." Even today, the influence of Roman law is still evident in most systems of law in Europe. Roman law was based on the principle of equity, which referred to accomplishing what was "good and fair" even if the letter of the law had to be disregarded. This principle meant, for example, that the intent of parties in a contract outweighed the words of their agreement and that the burden of proof lay with the accuser rather than the accused. The emperor Trajan ruled that no one should be convicted without clear evidence because it was better for a guilty person to go unpunished than for an innocent person to be condemned.

Roman notions of fairness required ranking people in "orders" according to their wealth. The elites in the highest orders made up a tiny portion of the population. Only about one person in fifty thousand had enough money to qualify for the senatorial order, the highest rank, while about one in a thousand belonged to the equestrian order, the next-highest rank. Different purple stripes on clothing identified these orders. The third-highest order consisted of decurions, the local officials in provincial towns.

This idea of ranking came to have important legal consequences under the empire because the emperors believed it promoted social stability. The social distinction between those designated as "better people" and those called "humbler people," which dated back to the republic, became a legal distinction under the principate. The "better people" included senators, equestrians, decurions, and retired army veterans. Everybody else—except slaves, who counted as property, not people—was consigned to the vastly larger group of "humbler people." The latter faced their worst disadvantage in court: the law imposed harsher penalties on them than on "better people" who committed the same crimes. "Humbler people" convicted of capital crimes were regularly executed by being crucified or torn apart by wild animals before a crowd of spectators. "Better people" rarely suffered the death penalty, but if they were condemned to death, they received a quicker and more dignified execution by the sword. "Humbler people" could be tortured in criminal investigations, even if they were citizens; "better people" usually avoided this fate. Romans regarded these differences as fair on the grounds that a person's higher status created a higher level of responsibility for the common good. As one provincial governor expressed it, "Nothing is less equitable than mere equality itself."

Law was crucial for maintaining order, but nothing mattered more to the stability and prosperity of the empire than steady population levels. Keeping up the birthrate was difficult, however, because doctors and midwives had only a few herbal medicines to treat pregnant women and infants. Complications at birth could easily lead to the mother's death because medical practitioners could not stop internal bleeding or cure infections. In addition, although they possessed carefully made instruments for surgery and physical examinations, they were seriously misinformed about pregnancy and reproduction. The upper-class government official Pliny, for example, sent the following report to the grandfather of his third wife, Calpurnia: "You will be very sad to learn that your granddaughter has suffered a miscarriage. She is a young girl and did not realize she was pregnant. As a result she was more active than she should have been and paid a high price." Likewise, gynecologists such as Soranus, who practiced in Rome during the reigns of Trajan and Hadrian, mistakenly recommended the days just after menstruation, when the woman's body was "not congested," as the best time to become pregnant. Soranus, following the common medical treatment of bleeding patients for various ailments, recommended treating exceptionally painful menstruation by drawing blood "from the bend of the arm." Doctors, often freedmen from Greece and other provinces, were considered of low status, unless they served the upper class.

As in earlier times, girls often wed in their early teens to have as many years as possible to bear children; their husbands would typically be around age thirty. Because so many babies died, families had to produce numerous offspring to keep from disappearing. The tombstone of Veturia, a soldier's wife married at age eleven, tells a typical story: "Here I lie, having lived for twenty-seven years. I was married to the same man for sixteen years and bore six children, five of whom died before I did." Richer families usually arranged marriages between spouses who hardly knew each other, although they could grow to love each other in a partnership devoted to family. The emphasis on childbearing in marriage brought many health hazards to women, but to remain single and childless represented social failure. Once children

Midwife's Sign Depicting Childbirth
Childbirth was a dangerous experience for women because of the chance of dying from internal bleeding. This terra-cotta sign from Ostia, the ancient port city of Rome, probably hung outside a midwife's rooms to announce her skill in aiding women in giving birth. It shows a pregnant woman clutching the sides of her chair and supported by another woman while the midwife crouches in front to help deliver the baby. The meaning of the sign was clear to people who were illiterate; a person did not have to be able to read to understand the services that the specialist inside could provide. (Scala/Art Resource, NY.)

were born, they were cared for by their mothers and by servants. Wealthy women routinely hired wet nurses to breast-feed their babies. When Romans wanted to control family size, they relied on female contraception through the use of vaginal sponges or drugs. Like the Greeks, they practiced exposure, more frequently for infant girls than for boys because sons were considered more valuable than daughters as future supporters and protectors of families.

The emperors and some members of the social elite did their best to support reproduction. The emperors aided needy children to encourage larger families, and wealthy people often adopted abandoned or orphaned children in their communities. One North African man gave enough money to support three hundred boys and three hundred girls each year until they grew up. The differing value afforded male and female children was also evident in some of these humanitarian programs, as boys often received more aid than girls.

Romanization in the Provinces

The principate changed the Mediterranean world deeply, but not evenly, by spreading Roman culture in the provinces. Historians call this process **Romanization**. Romanization was a two-way street; it did not mean the imposition of the conquerors' way of life, but rather interactions between the Romans and local peoples that produced new, mixed cultural traditions, from art to language to religion.

Romanization was more evident in some areas of the empire than in others. A wide diversity of peoples lived under Roman rule, speaking different languages, observing different customs, dressing in different styles, and worshipping different gods (Map 5.2). In the remote countryside, especially in the eastern sections of the empire, Romanization had only a modest effect on local customs. Where new cities sprang up, however, Roman influence increased. These communities sprouted up around Roman forts or grew from the settlements of army veterans the emperors had sprinkled throughout the provinces. They became especially influential in western Europe, permanently planting Latin (and the languages that would emerge from it) and Roman law and customs there. Modern cities such as Trier and Cologne in Germany started as Roman towns. As time passed, status gaps between the provinces and Italy lessened. Eventually, emperors came from the provinces; Trajan, from Spain, was the first.

Romanization in the western provinces raised people's standard of living as roads and bridges improved, trade increased, and agriculture flourished under the peaceful conditions provided by the army. Selling supplies to the troops brought new business to farmers and merchants. Greater prosperity under Roman rule made Romanization easier for provincials to accept, and local cultural traditions gradually merged with Roman ways of life.

In the eastern provinces, Romanization had less of a cultural effect. Large cities there, such as Alexandria in Egypt and Antioch in Syria, rivaled Rome in size and splendor (Map 5.1, page 157). In fact, compared with Rome, they boasted more single-family houses, fewer blocks of high-rise apartments, and equally magnificent temples. These cities had been flourishing for centuries and as a result tended to retain their Greek and Near Eastern traditions and languages. The eastern social elites did, however, easily accept the nature of Roman governance: the emperor was their patron, and they were his clients, with the mutual obligations this traditional relationship required. Provincial elites had long been accustomed to this kind of relationship with the ruler because Hellenistic kings had also ruled them in a paternalistic fashion. The non-Roman elites' willing cooperation in the task of governing the provinces was crucial for imperial stability and prosperity.

The continuing vitality of Greek culture and language in prosperous eastern cities supported a flourishing of Roman literature. Romantic adventure novels and satirical sketches were very popular. One of the best-known writers of the period was the essayist and philosopher Plutarch (c. 50–120 C.E.). His moral sense and taste for anecdotes made his works favorite reading well into modern times. The English dramatist William Shakespeare (1564–1616) based several of his plays on Plutarch's *Parallel Lives*, paired biographies of illustrious Greek and Roman men.

Latin literature also thrived in this period. Scholars rank the late first and early second centuries C.E. as its Silver Age, second only to the masterpieces of Augustan

Map 5.2 Natural Features and Languages of the Roman World

The Roman world had great variety in land, languages, and climate. People living there, estimated to have numbered as many as 55 million, spoke dozens of languages, many of which survived until the last years of the empire. The two predominant languages spoken by Roman citizens were Latin in the western part of the empire and Greek in the eastern part. Latin remained the language of law even in the eastern empire. Fields suitable for growing grain were the most valuable land feature because wheat and barley were the basis of the ancient diet. Vineyards and olive groves also were important. Wine was regarded as an essential beverage, and olive oil was the main source of fat for most people and the principal ingredient in soap, perfume, and other products for daily life. **For more help analyzing this map, see the map activity for this chapter in the Online Study Guide at** bedfordstmartins .com/huntconcise.

Roman Architecture in North Africa
The Roman town of Thysdrus (today El Djem in Tunisia) built this amphitheater for public entertainment in the early third century C.E. Seating 32,000 spectators (more than the town's total population), it imitated the larger Colosseum in Rome and was the seventh-biggest such building in the empire. Its arched walls soared more than a hundred feet high, and storerooms under the arena floor had three elevators to lift wild animals to the surface. Thysdrus also had a track for chariot racing and a smaller amphitheater. (Erich Lessing/Art Resource, NY.)

literature. The most famous authors wrote with acid wit, verve, and imagination. The historian Tacitus composed his *Annals* as a biting narrative of the Julio-Claudians, laying bare the ruthlessness of Augustus and the personal weaknesses of his successors. The satiric poet Juvenal skewered pretentious Romans and greedy provincials while hilariously describing the problems of being broke in the city. Apuleius intrigued readers with *The Golden Ass,* a sex-filled novel about a man turned into a donkey who regains his body and soul through the power of the Egyptian goddess Isis.

REVIEW   What were the strengths and weaknesses of Roman government and society during the principate after the rule of Augustus?

The Emergence of Christianity

The gradual rise of Christianity to become the leading religion among Romans, a process that took hundreds of years, was the ultimate proof that Romanization was a two-way process of cultural interaction because the new faith first emerged among non-Romans in the eastern part of the empire. The development of Christianity into a new religion separate from Judaism proved the most significant and enduring influence on later history that occurred during the Roman Empire.

Christianity emerged among a splinter group of Jews in Judaea, where, as elsewhere in the empire, Jews were allowed to practice their ancestral religion. The new faith attracted converts slowly; three centuries after the death of Jesus in 30 C.E., Christians remained a small minority. Christianity eventually spread because it had an appeal based on the career of Jesus, a message of salvation, an energetic sense of mission, a democratic openness in its early congregations, and a strong feeling of community.

The Teachings of Jesus

The new religion emerged from the life and teachings of Jesus (c. 4 B.C.E.–30 C.E.; see "The B.C.E./C.E. System for Dates" at the beginning of this book for an explanation of the date given for Jesus's birth). Christianity's background lay in Jewish history. By the time of Jesus's boyhood, some of his fellow Jews in Judaea were agitating for independence from Roman rule, making provincial officials fear rebellion. Jesus's career, therefore, took place in a troubled region. His execution was the standard Roman response to anyone they believed threatened peace and social order. In the two decades after his crucifixion, his devoted followers, particularly Paul of Tarsus, developed a new religion, now called Christianity, that expanded beyond the Jewish community in Palestine.

Christianity offered an answer to a troubling question about divine justice raised by the Jews' long history of defeat and exile: how could a just God allow the wicked to prosper and the righteous to suffer? The question had become prominent in the second century B.C.E., when persecution by the Seleucid king Antiochus IV (r. 175–164 B.C.E.) caused a bloody revolt. This war gave birth to the ideas called apocalypticism (from the Greek meaning "uncovering of the future"). According to this worldview, evil powers, divine and human, controlled the present world. Their rule would soon end, however, when God and his agents revealed their plan to conquer the forces of evil by sending the **Christ** (Greek for "anointed one"; in Hebrew, *Mashiah*, or in English *Messiah*) to win the great battle. A final judgment would follow, bringing eternal punishment for the wicked and eternal reward for the righteous. The apocalypticism that first inspired Jews living in Judaea under Roman rule later motivated Christians and Muslims.

Apocalyptic ideas became controversial around the time of Jesus's birth because most Judaean Jews were angry about Rome's control but disagreed about what their response should be. Some cooperated with their overlords, while others preached rejection of the non-Jewish world and its spiritual corruption. Their local ruler, installed by the Romans, was Herod the Great (r. 37–4 B.C.E.). His Greek style of life broke Jewish law, making him unpopular with his subjects despite his magnificent rebuilding of the holiest Jewish shrine, the great temple in Jerusalem. When a decade of unrest followed Herod's death, Augustus installed a Roman provincial government to oversee the region.

Palestine in the Time of Jesus, 30 C.E.

Jesus began his career as a teacher and healer in his native Galilee, the northern region of Palestine, during the reign of the emperor Tiberius. The books that would later become the Gospels, or the first four books of the Christian New Testament, offer the earliest accounts of his life and teachings; they were composed between about 70 and 90 C.E., decades after Jesus's death. Jesus himself wrote nothing down, and others' accounts of his words and deeds do not always agree on what he said or did. He taught mostly by telling parables, stories with an indirect moral or religious message.

All of the Gospels begin the story of Jesus's career with his baptism by John the Baptist, a prophet who urged people to repent before God's final judgment, which John preached was coming soon. John was executed by the Jewish ruler Herod Antipas, a son of Herod the Great whom the Romans supported; Herod Antipas feared that John's apocalyptic preaching might set off riots. After John's death, Jesus continued his mission by traveling around Judaea's countryside warning people to prepare spiritually for the coming of God's kingdom. Many saw Jesus as the Messiah, but he did not preach immediate revolt against the Romans. Instead, he taught that God's true kingdom was to be sought not on earth but in heaven. He stressed that this kingdom was open to believers regardless of their social status or sinfulness. His emphasis on God's love for humanity and people's responsibility to love one another reflected Jewish religious teachings, as in the first-century scholar Hillel's interpretation of the Hebrew Bible.

An educated Jew who perhaps knew Greek as well as Aramaic, the local language, Jesus realized that he had to reach the urban crowds to make an impact. Therefore, leaving the Galilean villages where he had started, he took his message to the Jewish population of Jerusalem, the region's main city. His miraculous healings and exorcisms and his powerful preaching created a sensation. His popularity attracted the attention of the Jewish authorities, who automatically assumed he aspired to political power. Fearing he might ignite a Jewish revolt, the Roman governor Pontius Pilate ordered his crucifixion, the usual punishment for rebellion, in Jerusalem in 30 C.E.

After Jesus's death, his followers reported that he had appeared to them in person. They proclaimed that God had miraculously raised him from the dead, and they set about convincing other Jews that Jesus was the promised savior and would soon return to judge the world and impose God's kingdom. Jesus's closest disciples, the twelve Apostles (Greek for "messengers"), considered themselves faithful Jews and continued to follow the commandments of Jewish law.

The Career of Paul of Tarsus

The conversion of Paul of Tarsus (c. 10–65 C.E.), a pious Jew of the Diaspora and also a Roman citizen who had previously attacked those who accepted Jesus as the Messiah, was the turning point in the development of Christianity as a new religion appealing to non-Jews. Around three years after Jesus's death, Paul experienced a spiritual vision on the road to Damascus in Syria, which he interpreted as a divine revelation. It inspired him to become a follower of Jesus as the Messiah, or Christ— a Christian, as members of the movement came to be known. According to Paul, Christians believed that Jesus was divine and his crucifixion was the ultimate sacrifice for the sins of humanity. Only by accepting this belief, Paul said, could people expect to win salvation in the world to come.

Seeking to win converts outside Judaea, in about 46 C.E. Paul began to travel to preach to Jews of the Diaspora and to Gentiles (non-Jews) who had adopted some Jewish customs in Syria, Asia Minor, and Greece (Map 5.3). Although Paul stressed the necessity of ethical behavior along traditional Jewish lines, especially

Map 5.3 Christian Populations in the Late Third Century C.E.
Christians remained a minority in the Roman world three hundred years after the crucifixion of Jesus. Certain areas of the empire, however, especially Asia Minor (western Turkey), where Paul of Tarsus had preached, had a concentration of Christians. Most Christians lived in cities and towns, where missionaries had gone to spread their message to crowds of curious listeners. *Paganus,* a Latin word meaning "country person" or "rural villager," came to mean a believer in traditional polytheistic cults— hence the term *pagan,* meaning "non-Christian," often found in modern works on this period.

the rejection of sexual immorality and polytheism, he also taught that converts did not need to obey all of Jewish law. To make conversion easier, Paul did not require men who became Christians to undergo the Jewish initiation rite of circumcision. This view, combined with his teachings that his congregations did not have to observe Jewish dietary restrictions or festivals, created great controversy and led to tensions with Jewish authorities in Jerusalem as well as with the followers of Jesus living there, who still believed that Christians had to follow Jewish law. Roman authorities arrested Paul as a criminal troublemaker; he was executed in about 65 C.E. Hatred of Roman rule in Palestine pushed the Jews to revolt in 66 C.E. When they were defeated in 70 C.E., their temple in Jerusalem was destroyed. This catastrophe meant that the Jewish community lost its religious center, and the separation of Christianity from Judaism begun by Paul gained momentum. In this way Christianity became a separate religion.

Paul's impact on early Christianity can be seen in the number of letters—thirteen—attributed to him in the twenty-seven writings brought together as the New Testament by around 200 C.E. Followers of Jesus came to regard the New Testament as having equal authority with the Hebrew Bible, which they then called the Old Testament. Because teachers such as Paul preached mainly in the cities to reach large crowds, congregations of Christians mostly sprang up in urban areas. Originally these groups had a democratic organization without much hierarchy. Women could be leaders in this early stage of Christianity, though not without controversy; many people believed that men should teach and women only listen. Still, early Christianity was diverse enough that a woman could found a congregation, as did Lydia at Philippi in Greece, or earn respect as a "deacon," as did Phoebe at Cenchreae, also in Greece.

The Development of Christianity as a New Religion

Christianity faced serious obstacles in developing as a new religion separate from Judaism. Roman officials, suspecting Christians of political disloyalty, sometimes persecuted them as traitors, especially for refusing to participate in the imperial cult (as happened to Perpetua). Christian leaders had to build an organization from scratch to administer their growing congregations. Also, they had to address the controversial question of whether women could be Christian leaders.

Most Romans in this period found Christians puzzling and irritating. In short, Christians seemed a threat to social order and peace with the gods. First, in contrast to Jews, Christians proclaimed a new faith rather than a traditional religion handed down from their ancestors. This broke with Roman tradition, in which anything new was seen as dangerous. Next, people feared that tolerating Christians would offend the gods of the official religion; Christians' denial of the old gods and of the emperor's cult seemed sure to provoke natural catastrophes. Christians furthermore aroused contempt because they proclaimed as their divine king a man whom the imperial government had crucified as a criminal. Finally, Christians were accused

Painting of a Sacred Banquet from a Roman Catacomb
Catacombs were the underground chambers Christians used for burials and meetings before their religion was officially recognized. Scenes such as this one seem simultaneously to represent actual meals held to remember the dead, banquets that the blessed dead were thought to have in their heavenly lives, and symbolic gatherings expressing a sense of community and mutual affection among believers. Seven people were usually shown, for reasons still not clear to historians. Women are prominently depicted here in the middle and at either end of the table. The woman at the left is presenting a goblet of wine to the banqueters. As the inscription suggests, she may be a personification of *agape*, the shared love that such sacred banquets commemorated. (© Held Collection/The Bridgeman Art Library.)

of cannibalism and sexual promiscuity because they symbolically ate the body and drank the blood of Jesus during secret communal dinners called Love Feasts, which men and women attended together.

Believing that Christians angered the traditional gods, Romans were quick to blame them for disasters. When a large portion of Rome burned in 64 C.E., Nero punished them as arsonists. As Tacitus wrote, the emperor had innocent Christians "covered with the skins of wild animals and torn to death by dogs, or fastened to crosses and set on fire to provide light at night." The cruelty of their punishment reportedly earned these Christians sympathy from Rome's population. After Nero, the government did not persecute Christians regularly or as a policy because no law specifically banned their religion. Nevertheless, Christians made easy victims for officials hunting for people to blame for crimes or disruptions in public order.

In response to persecution, Christians argued that Romans had nothing to fear from Christianity. They insisted that their faith taught respect for authority and a strict morality. It was not a foreign superstition but the true philosophy that combined the best features of Judaism and Greek thought and was thus a fitting religion for their diverse world. The theologian Tertullian pointed out that although

Christians could not worship the emperors, they did "pray to the true God for their [the emperors'] safety. We pray for a fortunate life for them, a secure rule, . . . a courageous army, a loyal Senate, a virtuous people, a world of peace."

Persecution did not stop Christianity. Tertullian proclaimed, "The blood of the martyrs is the seed of the Church." Christians like Perpetua regarded public trials and executions as an opportunity to become a **martyr** (Greek for "witness") to their faith and thus to strengthen Christians' sense of identity. Their belief that their deaths would lead directly to happiness in heaven allowed them to face painful torture with courage; some even became martyrs on purpose. For example, Ignatius, bishop of Antioch, begged Rome's congregation, which was becoming the most prominent Christian group, not to ask the emperor to show him mercy when he was condemned to die in the Colosseum early in the second century: "Let me be food for the wild animals [in the arena] through whom I can reach God," he pleaded. "I am God's wheat, to be ground up by the teeth of beasts so that I may be found pure bread of Christ." Most Christians tried their best to avoid becoming martyrs, but stories recording the martyrs' courage shaped the identity of this new religion as a faith that gave its believers the spiritual strength to endure great suffering.

The Organization of Hierarchy: Bishops and Women in the New Religion

Many first-century Christians expected that their troubles would end during their lifetimes because Jesus would return to pass judgment on the world and overturn the Roman Empire. When this expectation did not come true, believers began transforming their faith into a religion organized to survive indefinitely, instead of an apocalyptic offshoot of Judaism predicting the immediate end of the world. To make this change, they tried to achieve unity in their beliefs and created a hierarchical organization with bishops as leaders to impose order on congregations.

Unity proved impossible to achieve because early Christians constantly and fiercely disagreed about what they should believe, how they should live, and who had the authority to decide these questions. Some Christians believed they could observe Christ's teachings while keeping their jobs and regular lives. Others insisted it was necessary to withdraw from the everyday world to escape its evil, even abandoning their families and committing themselves to chaste celibacy. Many Christians believed they should not serve in the army because, as soldiers required to worship in the imperial cult, they would betray their faith. Controversy over such questions raged in the numerous congregations that arose in the early empire around the Mediterranean, from Gaul to Africa to the Near East (Map 5.3, page 181).

Although early Christians continued to disagree about doctrine, they realized that their new faith needed an organizational structure if it was to last. They therefore created bishops as religious officials with the authority to specify true doctrine and proper conduct. This was the most important development in organizing a hierarchy intended to preserve Christianity indefinitely. Bishops received their positions through the principle later called **apostolic succession**, which declares that Jesus's Apostles appointed the first bishops as their successors, granting these new officials the powers Jesus had originally given to the Apostles. Those men named as bishops by the Apostles in turn appointed their own successors, and so on. Bishops had the authority to ordain priests with the holy power to administer the sacraments, above all baptism and communion, which believers regarded as necessary for achieving eternal life. Bishops also controlled their congregations' memberships and finances (the money financing early churches came from members' gifts).

The bishops had the authority to define what was true doctrine (orthodoxy) and what was false (heresy), but Christians' disagreements over doctrine were too strong for the bishops to impose unity of belief. In this early stage, the occasional meetings of the bishops of different cities constituted the church's organization. Today it is common to refer to this loose organization as the early Catholic (meaning "universal") church, but even the bishops disagreed among themselves on what beliefs were proper.

A particularly bitter disagreement concerned women's role in the church. In the first congregations, women sometimes held leadership positions. After bishops were established atop the hierarchy, however, women usually were kept in inferior posts. This demotion reflected the view that in Christianity, as in Roman imperial society, women should be subordinate to men. Some congregations took a long time to accept this change, however, and some women still occupied leadership positions during the second and third centuries.

When leadership roles were closed off to them, many women chose not to marry, to demonstrate their devotion to Christ. This commitment to chaste celibacy gave them the power to control their bodies by removing their sexuality from the domination of men. Women choosing this special closeness to God were judged holy and socially superior by other Christians. By rejecting the traditional functions of wife and mother in favor of spiritual excellence, celibate Christian women achieved the independence and authority denied them in the outside world.

Competing Beliefs: Paganism and Philosophy

Most people during the time of the principate were polytheistic (worshipping multiple gods). Today such religious beliefs are labeled *paganism*. That modern term should not be taken to mean that ancient polytheists were immoral. In fact, their beliefs often taught strict moral purity.

Polytheistic worshippers prayed and sacrificed to try to win the favor of all the divinities that could affect human life. These divinities ranged from the traditional gods of the state cults, such as Jupiter and Minerva, to spirits thought to inhabit local groves and springs. International cults such as the Mysteries of Demeter and Persephone at Eleusis outside Athens remained popular. Polytheists never sought a unity of doctrine. They did agree, however, that the old gods favored and protected them and that the imperial cult added to their safety; the success and prosperity of the principate was the proof. Even people who found a more intellectually satisfying understanding of the world in philosophies such as Stoicism respected the traditional cults as symbols of divine protection for Rome. Christianity had to compete with the long and cherished traditions of polytheism to win converts.

The cult of the Egyptian goddess Isis reveals how polytheism could provide believers with a religious experience demanding a moral way of life and arousing strong personal emotions. Isis's cult had already attracted Romans by the time

Mithras Slaying the Bull

Hundreds of shrines to the mysterious god Mithras have been found in the Roman Empire, but the cult remains poorly known because almost no texts exist to explain it. To judge from the many representations in art—such as this wall painting from about 200 C.E., found in the shrine at Marino, south of Rome—the story of Mithras slaying a bull was a central part of the cult's identity. Scholars debate the symbolic meaning of the slaying shown here, in which a snake and a dog lick the bull's blood while a scorpion pinches its testicles. Most agree, however, that Mithras was derived, perhaps as late as the early imperial period, from the ancient Persian divinity Mithra. Only men could be worshippers, and many were soldiers. Earlier scholarly claims of the cult's popularity were exaggerated; its members numbered no more than 1 or 2 percent of the population. Mithraism probably involved complex devotion to astrology, with devotees ranked in grades, each grade protected by a different celestial body. (Scala/Art Resource, NY.)

of Augustus. He tried to suppress it because it was Cleopatra's religion, but Isis's reputation as a kind, compassionate goddess who relieved her followers' suffering made her cult too popular to crush. The Egyptians believed that her tears for starving people caused the Nile to flood every year and bring them good harvests. Her image was that of a loving mother, and in art she is often shown nursing her son. A central doctrine of her cult concerned the death and resurrection of her husband, Osiris. Isis promised her followers a similar hope for life after death.

Isis required her worshippers to behave righteously. Inscriptions put up in public by believers declared the goddess's standards for them by quoting her on her own work for justice: "I broke down the rule of tyrants; I put an end to murders; I caused what is right to be mightier than gold and silver." The main character of Apuleius's novel *The Golden Ass,* whom Isis rescues from his mistaken transformation into a donkey, expresses his intense joy after being spiritually reborn: "O holy and eternal guardian of the human race, who always cherishes mortals and blesses them, you care for the troubles of miserable humans with a sweet mother's love. Neither day nor night, nor any moment of time, ever passes by without your blessings." Other cults also required their believers to lead just lives. Inscriptions from remote villages in Asia Minor, for example, record the confessions of peasants to sexual sins for which their local god had imposed severe penance.

Many upper-class Romans found moral guidance in philosophy. Stoicism was the most popular. Stoics believed in self-discipline above all, and their code of personal ethics left no room for immoral conduct. As the philosopher Seneca explained, "It is easier to prevent harmful emotions from entering the soul than it is to control them once they have entered." Stoicism taught that a creative force combining reason, nature, and divinity directs the universe. Humans share in the essence of this universal force and find happiness and patience by living in harmony with it and always doing their duty. The emperor Marcus Aurelius, in his book *Meditations,* emphasized the Stoic belief that people exist for each other: "Either make them better, or just put up with them," he advised.

Christian and polytheist scholars argued over the merits of Christianity compared to traditional Greek philosophy. The theologian Origen, for example, argued that Christianity, because it was true, was a better guide to correct living than were Greek philosophical ideas. The philosopher Plotinus gave traditional Greek ideas new strength with his books on spiritual philosophy. These ideas, called **Neoplatonism** because their doctrines sprang from Plato's philosophy, influenced many educated Christians as well as polytheists. Neoplatonic religious ideas centered on a human longing to return to the universal Good from which human existence comes. By turning away from the life of the body through the study of philosophy, individual souls could rise to the level of the universal soul, becoming the whole of what as individuals they formed only a potential part. This mystical union with what the Christians would call God could be achieved only through strenuous self-discipline in personal morality as well as intellectual life. Neoplatonism's stress on spiritual purity gave it a powerful appeal

REVIEW   What beliefs and actions separated Christians from pagans?

to educated Christians. Like the cult of Isis or Stoicism, Neoplatonism provided guidance, comfort, and hope through good times or bad.

The Crisis of the Third Century

War, financial shortfalls, and natural disasters combined to create a crisis for the Roman Empire in the third century C.E. Attacks by outsiders on the northern and eastern frontiers forced the emperors to expand the army for defense. The rulers' attempts to find money to pay for these wars fueled inflation and crippled the economy. The public's outrage at these troubles encouraged ambitious generals to seek power by commanding personal armies, once again plunging Rome into civil war in a bloody replay of the destruction of the republic. Earthquakes and epidemics added to the crisis. By the end of the third century C.E., this combination of troubles had shredded the "Roman peace."

Defending the Frontiers

The emperors' supreme duty was to defend the empire. Throughout the principate, they sent military forces to repel invaders from the frontier regions. The most aggressive attackers were Germanic bands that often crossed the Danube and Rhine rivers for raiding. Their constant fighting against Roman troops turned these raiders into powerful armies, and they launched dangerous invasions during the reign of Marcus Aurelius (r. 161–180 C.E.). A major threat also emerged at the empire's eastern edge when a new dynasty, the Sasanids, defeated the Parthian Empire and reenergized the ancient Persian kingdom. By 227, Persia's military power forced the emperors to bring in legions to protect the rich eastern provinces, at the expense of the defense of the northern frontiers. Recognizing the courage of Germanic warriors, the emperors hired them as auxiliary soldiers for the Roman army and settled them on the frontiers as buffers against invasion. By around 200, the army had enrolled perhaps as many as 450,000 legionary and auxiliary troops (the size of the navy remains unknown).

Roman military life was tough. Training constantly, soldiers had to be fit enough to carry forty-pound packs up to twenty miles in five hours, swimming across rivers on the way. The emperors built many permanent forts for garrisons, but an army on the march constructed its own fort every night. Soldiers transported all the materials for a wooden-walled camp everywhere they went. As one ancient commentator noted during the republic, "Infantrymen were little different from loaded pack mules." At one camp in a frontier area, archaeologists found a supply of a million iron nails—ten tons in all. The same fort required seventeen miles of timber for its barracks walls. To outfit a legion with tents required 54,000 calves' hides.

Unlike the republic's wars of conquest, these defensive wars strained imperial finances because they did not bring in much plunder. By the third century C.E., the army had become a source of negative instead of positive cash flow to the treasury, and the economy had not expanded sufficiently to make up the difference. To make matters worse, inflation had driven up prices. A main cause of inflation under the principate may have been, ironically, the long period of peace, which promoted increased demand for the economy's relatively static production of goods and services.

In desperation at their financial problems, some emperors responded to rising prices by debasing imperial coinage in a vain attempt to cut government costs. **Debasement of coinage** meant putting less silver in each coin (there was no paper money) without changing its face value and therefore creating more cash with the same amount of precious metal (see "Taking Measure"). Merchants,

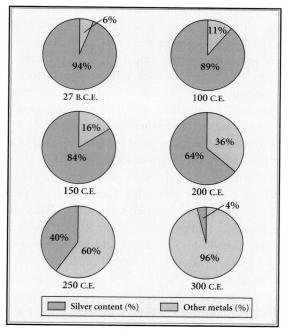

Taking Measure The Falling Value of Roman Imperial Coinage, 27 B.C.E.–300 C.E.
Ancient silver coinage derived its value from its metallic content; the less silver a coin had, the less it was worth. Emperors facing rising government and military expenses but flat or falling revenues tried to cut costs by debasing the coinage—reducing the amount of silver in each coin and increasing the amount of other, cheaper metals. These pie charts reveal the gradual debasement of Roman imperial coinage through the third century C.E., when military expenses apparently skyrocketed. By 300 C.E., coins contained only trace amounts of silver. Merchants and producers had to raise their prices for goods and services when they were being paid with currency that was increasingly less valuable. Thus debasement fueled inflation.

however, raised prices to make up for the reduced value of the debased coins. By 200 C.E., the debased coinage and inflation were ruining the imperial balance sheet and undermining public confidence in the imperial currency. As the soldiers kept demanding that their patrons, the emperors, pay them well, the situation only grew worse. The financial system fell into full collapse in the 250s and 260s.

The Severan Emperors and Financial and Political Catastrophe

Decisions by the emperor Septimius Severus (r. 193–211 C.E.) and his sons drove the imperial government into bankruptcy and instability. The father drained the treasury to satisfy the army, and his sons' murderous rivalry and reckless spending destroyed the government's stability. A soldier's soldier who came from North Africa, Severus became emperor in 193 C.E. after waging a civil war to get rid of the incompetent emperor currently holding power. To restore imperial prestige and acquire money through foreign conquest, Severus fought successful campaigns beyond the frontiers of the provinces, in Mesopotamia and northern Britain.

By this time, the soldiers were angry because inflation had eroded the value of their wages to practically nothing after they bought themselves basic supplies and clothing. They therefore expected the emperors to favor them with gifts of extra money. Severus spent large sums on such gifts, and he also decided to raise the soldiers' pay by one-third. The expanded size of the army made this raise more expensive than the treasury could afford and deepened inflation. The financial consequences of his policy, however, concerned Severus not at all. His deathbed advice to his sons in 211 C.E. was to "stay on good terms with each other, be generous to the soldiers, and pay no attention to anyone else."

Severus's sons undermined the principate's financial and political stability by following only the last two points of his advice. Caracalla (r. 211–217 C.E.) seized the throne for himself by murdering his brother, Geta. Caracalla's violent rule and limitless spending ended the peace and prosperity of the Roman Golden Age. He increased the soldiers' pay by another 40 to 50 percent and spent gigantic sums on building projects to display his glory, including the largest public baths Rome had ever seen, covering blocks and blocks of the city. The need for money to pay his out-of-control expenses put unbearable pressure on the provincial elites responsible for collecting taxes and on the citizens whom they squeezed for ever greater amounts.

In 212 C.E., Caracalla took his most famous step to try to fix the budget crisis: he granted Roman citizenship to almost every man and woman in imperial territory except slaves. His goal was to increase revenues from inheritance taxes and from fees for freeing slaves, which only citizens paid (noncitizens paid other taxes). The greater the number of citizens, he reasoned, the more money (most of it earmarked for the army) the empire would collect. Caracalla, who contemporaries whispered was insane, wrecked the imperial budget, setting in motion the ruinous inflation of the coming decades. Once when his mother criticized him for his excesses, he replied, as he drew his sword, "Never mind, we shall not run out of money as long as I have this."

The empire's financial troubles created political instability. When Macrinus, commander of the Praetorian Guard, murdered Caracalla in 217 C.E. to make himself emperor, Caracalla's female relatives bribed the army to overthrow Macrinus in favor of a young male relative. The restored Severan dynasty did not last long, however, and the assassination of the last Severan emperor in 235 C.E. began a half-century of civil wars that, compounded by natural disasters, destroyed the principate. For the next fifty years, emperors and generals constantly fought to rule. During this period of near anarchy, over two dozen men, often several at a time, held or claimed the throne. Their only qualification was their ability to lead an army and reward the troops for loyalty to their commander instead of to Rome.

The violence and financial distress caused by these civil wars made life miserable in many regions. Battling armies trampled farmers' fields searching for food, making it impossible to keep up normal agricultural production. City council members faced constantly rising demands for tax revenues from every new emperor, and the financial pressure destroyed their commitment to serving their communities. Foreign enemies took advantage of the Roman civil wars, invading from the east and north. Roman fortunes hit bottom in 260 C.E. when Shapur I, king of the Sasanid Empire of Persia, captured the emperor Valerian (r. 253–260 C.E.) while attacking the province of Syria. Imperial territory was in danger of splintering into breakaway regions. Even the tough and competent emperor Aurelian (r. 270–275 C.E.) could do no more to reduce the danger than recover Egypt and Asia Minor from Zenobia, the warrior-queen of Palmyra in Syria. He also had to encircle Rome with a massive wall to ward off surprise attacks by Germanic tribes smashing their way into Italy from the north.

Natural disasters worsened the crisis when strong earthquakes and epidemics struck some of the provinces in the mid-third century C.E. The population declined significantly as food supplies became less dependable, civil war killed soldiers and civilians alike, and infection flared over large regions. The loss of population meant fewer soldiers for the army, whose efficiency as a defense and police force had already declined because of the financial and political chaos. More frontier areas became vulnerable to raids, and roving bands of robbers became increasingly common within the imperial borders. Polytheists explained these horrible times in the traditional way: the state gods were angry. But why? The obvious answer seemed to be the presence of Christians, who denied the existence of the Roman gods and refused to participate in their worship. The emperor Decius (r. 249–251 C.E.) conducted systematic persecutions to eliminate Christians as a way to regain the goodwill of the gods. He justified the violence by calling himself "Restorer of the Cults," proclaiming, "I would rather see a rival to my throne than another bishop of Rome." He ordered all inhabitants of the empire to prove their loyalty to the

Mapping the West The Roman Empire in Crisis, c. 284 C.E.
By the early 280s C.E., the principate had been torn apart by the fifty years of civil war that had followed the end of the Severan dynasty. Imperial territory remained the same as in the time of Augustus
(Map 5.1, page 157), except for the loss of Dacia during the reign of Aurelian (r. 270–275 C.E.). Attacks
from the north and east had repeatedly penetrated the frontier regions, however. The Sasanid king
Shapur I (r. c. 240–270 C.E.), for example, temporarily held Antioch and captured the emperor Valerian
in 260 C.E. The public humiliation and death in captivity of the elderly imperial ruler indicate the
depths to which Roman fortunes sank in the third century C.E.

state by participating in a sacrifice to its gods. Christians who refused to sacrifice were killed.

These new persecutions did not end the civil war, financial failure, or diseases that had brought on the crisis. By the early 280s C.E., the empire was in danger of fragmenting. Remarkably, in 284 C.E. Diocletian would drag it back to safety in the same way Augustus had begun the principate: by creating a new form of authoritarian leadership.

> **REVIEW** What factors provoked the crisis in Roman government and society in the third century C.E.?

Conclusion

The creation of what we call the Roman Empire demonstrated the continuing and overwhelming importance of tradition as the Romans' guide to life. The new political system that governed the empire, the principate, could only be seen as legitimate if it was proclaimed a restoration of the republic, not a change for the better. Moreover, it also had to make plain the princeps's role in fulfilling the traditional paternalistic obligations of a patron toward his clients. For Romans, "back to the future" was a crucial principle of action.

The "restored republic" turned out to be a success for the majority of people in the empire, who enjoyed relative peace and prosperity for two centuries. It was only the elites that hated and feared the power of the emperor, at least until the Christians became numerous enough to attract unwanted attention from the authorities. Certainly, the diverse peoples of the vast empire did not all get along without prejudice or conflict. The rebellions of the Jews in Judaea provide violent evidence of how unpleasant Roman rule could seem to some. At the same time, it would be wrong to deny that the Roman army and Roman law did bring a stable and prosperous peace to a wider area of the world for a longer time than ever before in history. In the end, the principate failed for reasons that have brought down many governments over time: an inability to deal with the state's bottomless hunger for more revenue, and a failure to develop a system for consistently choosing good leaders and preventing them from abusing their power.

As focused as they were on the value of maintaining traditions, the Romans were also open to learning from cultural interaction with others. They realized that to survive and thrive in a dangerous world, it paid to be innovative in implementing tradition. The most influential innovation of the period, although it was very slow to develop, was the growth of Christianity as a separate religion from

Judaism and a competitor with paganism for the religious identity of the Roman population. Romans, like other ancient peoples, had always been deeply religious, and once they noticed that Christians existed, they took them and their beliefs very seriously. At first the reaction was hostile. How Christianity developed from a new faith that seemed to threaten the traditional "peace of the gods" to the source of most Romans' hope for divine protection and salvation is the central story of Roman history in the period following the principate.

CHAPTER REVIEW QUESTIONS

1. Compare the crisis in the first century B.C.E. that undermined the republic with the crisis in the third century C.E. that undermined the principate.
2. If you had been a first-century C.E. emperor, what would you have done about the Christians and why? What if you had been a third-century C.E. emperor?

For practice quizzes and other study tools, see the Online Study Guide at bedfordstmartins.com/huntconcise.

For primary-source material from this period, see Chapter 6 of *Sources of THE MAKING OF THE WEST,* Third Edition.

TIMELINE

■ **c. 33 C.E.** Paul of Tarsus becomes a Christian

27 B.C.E.–14 C.E.
Augustus's principate

■ **30 C.E.** Jesus of Nazareth crucified in Jerusalem

■ **44 B.C.E.** Julius Caesar's assassination reignites civil war

■ **8 C.E.** Augustus exiles the poet Ovid

50 B.C.E.	0	50 C.E.	100 C.E.

■ **2 B.C.E.** Senate proclaims Augustus "Father of His Country"

■ **64 C.E.** Nero blames Christians for great fire in Rome

■ **69 C.E.** Civil war in the "Year of the Four Emperors"

■ **70 C.E.** Jewish temple in Jerusalem destroyed

Suggested References

Modern scholarly work on the principate reveals how the emperors tried to create political legitimacy and social stability through a combination of military, religious, and artistic policy.

Ando, Clifford. *The Matter of the Gods: Religion and the Roman Empire.* 2008.

Denzey, Nicola. *The Bone Gatherers: The Lost Worlds of Early Christian Women.* 2007.

Futrell, Allison. *Blood in the Arena: The Spectacle of Roman Power.* 1997.

Galinsky, Karl. *Augustan Culture.* 1996.

Goldsworthy, Adrian. *The Complete Roman Army.* 2003.

*Kraemer, Ross Shephard. *Her Share of the Blessings: Women's Religion among Pagans, Jews, and Christians in the Greco-Roman World.* 1992.

MacMullen, Ramsay. *Christianizing the Roman Empire (A.D. 100–400).* 1984.

Roman emperors: http://www.roman-emperors.org/startup.htm

Roth, Roman, and Johannes Keller, eds. "Roman by Integration: Dimensions of Group Identity in Material Culture and Text." Special issue, *Journal of Roman Archaeology.* Suppl. no. 66. 2007.

*Suetonius. *The Twelve Caesars.* Trans. Robert Graves. 2003.

Syme, Ronald. *The Roman Revolution.* 1939; repr. 2002.

*Tacitus. *The Complete Works.* Trans. Alfred John Church and William Jackson Brodribb. 1964.

161–180 C.E. Germanic bands attack northern frontiers during the reign of Marcus Aurelius

250s–260s C.E. Imperial finances collapse from civil war, debased coinage, and inflation

150 C.E.   200 C.E.   250 C.E.   300 C.E.

■ **212 C.E.** Caracalla extends Roman citizenship to almost all free inhabitants of the provinces

■ **284 C.E.** Diocletian becomes emperor

6

The Transformation of the Roman Empire

284–600 C.E.

AN EGYPTIAN WOMAN NAMED ISIS wrote a letter to her mother in the third century that archaeologists discovered more than fifteen hundred years later in an excavation near the Nile River. Written in Greek on papyrus, the letter hints at the problems many people experienced during this troubled time.

Emperor Honorius as Christian Victor, c. 406
Both sides of this ivory diptych (folding tablet) depict Honorius, emperor of the western Roman Empire, as a military victor crediting Christ for his success. Petronius Probus presented this gift to the emperor to show his gratitude for being awarded the consulship, the empire's highest honor. On the left, Honorius holds a sign that says, "You will always conquer, in the name of Christ." On the right, he holds a shield and a scepter; a statuette of Victory standing on a globe offers him a victor's wreath. His clothing and armor identify him as a military leader; the inscription above his head proclaims him "Our Master, Always Augustus," while the circle around his head testifies to his special holiness. As this carving shows, Honorius, like other emperors, believed that he had divine backing for his army. In his case, it was not enough: the Goths sacked Rome only four years later. (Alinari/Art Resource, NY.)

Every day I pray to the lord Sarapis and his fellow gods to watch over you. I want you to know that I have arrived in Alexandria safely after four days. I send fond greetings to my sister and the children and Elouath and his wife and Dioscorous and her husband and children and Tamalis and her husband and son and Heron and Ammonarion and . . . Sanpat and her children. And if Aion wants to be in the army, let him come. For everybody is in the army.

The letter raises puzzling questions: What were the relationships between Isis and the people she mentions, with their mixture of Greek and Semitic names? Why had she gone to Alexandria? Why did Aion want to become a soldier? Why was "everybody" in the army? The answers, if we knew them, would surely relate to the economic and political crisis that gripped the Roman Empire in the third century. Perhaps financial troubles forced Isis to leave her village to seek work in the city. Perhaps Aion wanted to join the army to

197

earn wages; the emperors were always recruiting more soldiers. Perhaps everybody seemed to be in the army because there was continuous civil war.

Diocletian, emperor beginning in 284, reorganized the government and increased the authority of the emperor. Still, restoring peace and order proved difficult because religious tensions were growing between Christians and followers of traditional polytheistic cults, such as Isis the letter writer, named after the famous Egyptian goddess. Then, unexpectedly, early in the fourth century the emperor Constantine converted to Christianity. By the end of the fourth century, the new faith had become the official religion of Roman government, replacing the traditional gods.

Also at the end of the fourth century, the empire split permanently into western and eastern sections. In the west, non-Roman peoples began migrating into the region, transforming it—and themselves—politically and socially by replacing Roman provincial government with their own new kingdoms. By the fifth century, the weakening of Roman government in western Europe had divided that region into different states, anticipating Europe's modern nations. The provinces of the eastern Roman Empire remained economically vibrant and politically united, becoming (in modern terminology) the **Byzantine Empire** in the sixth century. There, the remaining part of the Roman Empire endured under Christian rule for centuries, until Turkish invaders finally conquered it in 1453.

CHAPTER FOCUS QUESTION   What were the sources of unity and the causes of division in the Roman Empire from the reign of the emperor Diocletian to the emergence of the Byzantine Empire in the sixth century?

Reorganizing the Empire

The emperors Diocletian (r. 284–305) and Constantine (r. 306–337) reorganized the Roman Empire and reinforced the emperor's authority to overcome the troubles that the third-century crisis had created. They differed radically, however, in their treatment of Christians and their attitude toward traditional Roman religion.

The Dominate and Imperial Reorganization

Diocletian ended the third-century crisis by imposing the strongest form of monarchy in Roman history and reorganizing the empire into administrative districts. He was an uneducated military man from outside Italy (Dalmatia, in what is now Croatia), but his exceptional leadership and intelligence propelled him through the ranks until the army made him emperor in 284. Diocletian proclaimed himself *dominus*—"master," what slaves called their owners—to replace Augustus's republican title, *princeps* ("first man"). Roman government from Diocletian onward is therefore called the **dominate** instead of the principate. Senators, consuls, and other traditional republican offices continued to exist, but the emperors held all the power. They reigned as autocrats— true sole rulers—and no longer tried to hide their supremacy, as Augustus had done when he invented the principate. To display their superiority, the emperors of the

Coin Portrait of Emperor Constantine

Constantine had these special, extra-large coins minted to show him as a Christian emperor. The jewels on his helmet and crown, the fancy bridle on his horse, and the scepter indicate his status as ruler, while his armor and shield show his military accomplishments. He proclaims his Christian rule with his scepter's new design—a cross with a globe—and the round badge sticking up from his helmet, which carries the monogram meaning "Christ." He had his soldiers paint this monogram on their shields to win God's favor in battle. (Staatliche Münzsammlung, Munich.)

dominate placed their throne on a raised platform, wore jeweled robes, and surrounded themselves with attendants and ceremony. Constantine wore a diadem—a purple headband sparkling with gems, a symbol of kingship avoided by earlier emperors out of respect for the Roman tradition that the ruler was a citizen, not a monarch. To demonstrate the ruler's superiority, a series of veils now separated palace waiting rooms from the inner space where the emperor listened to people's pleas for help. High-ranking officials received showy titles such as "most perfect" and wore special shoes and belts. The court of the dominate resembled the splendid court of the Great King of Persia a thousand years earlier (see the illustration on page 27). Diocletian, Constantine, and their successors believed that citizens were their subjects. The architecture of the dominate reflected its rulers' all-powerful status. Diocletian's public bath in Rome rivaled earlier emperors' buildings in the capital; its soaring vaults and domes covered a space more than three thousand feet long on each side.

The dominate also used religious language to mark the emperor's special status. The emperors added *et deus* (and God) to *dominus* as their title. Diocletian adopted the title Jovius, claiming Jupiter (Jove), the chief Roman god, as his ancestor. His titles signaled the elevated respect he now demanded from his subjects: he expected to be honored as magnificently as the gods.

The dominate's emperors made law. Relying on a personal staff that isolated them from the outside world, they no longer asked for advice from the elite. Their desire to maintain order led them to impose brutal punishments for crimes. For example, Constantine punished officials who did not keep what he called their "greedy hands" off bribes by having their hands "cut off by the sword"; the guardians of a young girl who allowed a lover to seduce her were punished by having molten lead poured into their mouths. The emperors of the dominate also widened the divide between poor and rich by making punishments even harsher for the large segment of the population legally known as "humbler people." Their laws excused those designated "better people" from most of the harshest penalties for the same crimes.

Map 6.1 Diocletian's Reorganization of 293
To try to prevent civil war and increase the emperor's authority, Emperor Diocletian reorganized the Roman Empire into four administrative districts, each governed by its own ruler. He also subdivided the provinces into smaller units and grouped them into twelve dioceses, each overseen by a regional administrator. This map shows the four districts as described in a book written by an imperial official around 360.

Diocletian decided that the empire could not be administered and defended from a single center (that is, Rome). In 293, he therefore divided imperial territory into four administrative districts, two in the west and two in the east (Map 6.1). Having no sons, he appointed three "partners" so that he and they could govern cooperatively in two pairs, each consisting of a senior "Augustus" and a junior "Caesar" as his adopted son and designated successor. Each partner controlled one of the four districts. To prevent disunity, the most senior partner—in this case Diocletian—served as supreme ruler (emperor) and was supposed to receive the loyalty of the others. This **tetrarchy** (rule by four), as modern scholars call it, was Diocletian's attempt to improve defense along the empire's long frontiers and to prevent a civil war over who should become the next emperor.

Diocletian also subdivided the provinces, nearly doubling their number to almost one hundred. He grouped them into twelve dioceses, each under the jurisdiction of a regional governor. To try to keep the governors from becoming powerful enough to threaten the emperors, Diocletian began the process of stripping them of their military authority, restricting them instead to overseeing legal and financial affairs. Generals were put in charge of the defense. Constantine completed this process of separating the provincial leaders' powers.

Although later emperors abandoned the tetrarchy, Diocletian's reorganization of provincial administration into a hierarchy continued. He also ended Rome's thousand years as the empire's capital city. Diocletian lived in Nicomedia, in Asia Minor, and did not even visit Rome until 303, nearly twenty years after he became emperor. He chose four new capitals (Nicomedia, Milan, Trier, and Sirmium; Map 6.1, page 200) for their usefulness as military command posts closer to the frontiers. Italy became just another region in the empire, on an equal footing with the other provinces and subject to the same taxation system, except for the tax-free district of Rome itself—the last trace of the city's former superiority.

Despite Diocletian's reforms, civil war broke out soon after he retired in 305. It took Constantine (r. 306–337), one of the "partners" ruling a region of the empire, almost twenty years to eliminate his rivals. He first proved his ability as a military commander by fighting barbarian tribes who were threatening the northern empire and then led his troops to victory in the civil war. The Roman Senate ultimately hailed him as "the greatest Augustus." His success in war and politics did not extend to his family life: he had one son executed and probably engineered the death of his wife, the empress, for reasons that were kept secret. Near the end of his reign, he named his remaining three sons as joint heirs, ordering them to rule as co-emperors. They failed as bloodily as had the sons of Septimius Severus a century earlier, plunging into war with one another. This civil war informally split the empire on a north-south line along the Balkan peninsula. In 395, the brothers Honorius and Arcadius divided the empire into western and eastern halves, ruling as co-emperors. This division launched the two parts of the empire toward different fates.

The Division of the Empire, c. 395

Each half of the empire had its own capital. Constantinople, near the mouth of the Black Sea, was the eastern capital. This city had been founded a thousand years before by Greeks and was known as Byzantium (today Istanbul, Turkey). Constantine reconstructed the city in 324 and renamed it Constantinople. He chose it for its geography: located on an easily fortified peninsula, it controlled routes for trade and troop movements. To give his "new Rome" the glory of the old capital, Constantine erected a forum, an imperial palace, a hippodrome for chariot races, and huge statues of the traditional gods. The eastern emperors inherited Constantinople as their capital; modern historians, recalling the city's ancient Greek name, use the term *Byzantine Empire* to refer to the eastern section of the original Roman Empire.

Geography determined the site of the western capital as well. The western emperor, Honorius (r. 395–423; see the illustration on page 196), wanted to keep the Alps between his territory and the raiders living to the north. In 404, he made Ravenna, a port on Italy's northeastern coast, the western capital because it was a naval base and an important commercial city. Walls and marshes protected it from attack by land, while its harbor kept it from being starved out in a siege. Although Ravenna never rivaled Constantinople in size or riches, the emperors built spectacular churches gleaming with multicolored mosaics there.

Financial Reform and Social Consequences

The empire's financial crisis proved Diocletian's biggest problem. He tried to improve revenues by creating new money, price controls, and a new taxation system. Unfortunately, Diocletian miscalculated in establishing values for his new coins and set off a financial panic that bred inflation in many regions. High prices caused people to hoard whatever goods they could buy, and hoarding drove prices even higher. "Hurry and spend all my money you have; buy me any kinds of goods at whatever prices they are available," wrote one official to his servant, fearing yet another decline in the value of the currency.

Diocletian tried to stop inflation by imposing price and wage controls in the worst-hit regions. His Edict on Maximum Prices blamed high prices on profiteers' "unlimited and crazed avarice," banned hoarding, and set limits on the prices that could legally be charged for about a thousand goods and services. The edict soon became ineffective, however, because merchants refused to cooperate, and government officials were unable to enforce it despite the threat of death or exile as the penalty for violations. In his final years, Diocletian revalued the currency to restore sound money and stable prices, but civil war under Constantine again weakened it. With the currency losing value, the emperors began collecting taxes not only in coin but also in goods. Recent research disputes whether this form of revenue actually replaced taxes paid in coin, as previous scholars believed, or served only as a way to impose higher property taxes, which had to be paid in coin as much as possible. By the end of the fourth century, however, it is clear that the government expected payment in gold and silver and that taxes rose, especially on the local elites. Taxes went mostly to support the army, which required enormous amounts of grain, meat, wine, horses, camels, and mules. The major sources of revenue were a tax on land, assessed according to its productivity, and a head tax on individuals.

The empire was too large for the emperor to enforce consistency in tax rates. In some areas, both men and women from about ages twelve to sixty-five paid the full tax; in others, women paid only one-half the tax assessment, or none at all. Workers in cities probably owed taxes only on their property. They periodically paid "in kind"—laboring without pay on public works projects such as cleaning municipal drains or repairing buildings. Urban businesspeople, from shopkeepers to prostitutes, paid taxes in coin. Members of the senatorial class were exempt from ordinary taxes but had to make other payments when the emperor demanded them.

Since the new tax system could work only if agricultural production remained stable and the government controlled the people liable for the head tax, Diocletian restricted the movement of tenant farmers (*coloni*), who formed the empire's economic base. Coloni had traditionally been free to move to different farms under different landlords. Now tenant farmers were increasingly tied to a particular plot, and their children were required to remain farmers.

The government also restricted workers in other essential occupations. Bakers, for example, could not leave their jobs, and anyone who acquired a baker's property had to assume that occupation. Bakers were essential in producing free bread for Rome's poor, a tradition begun under the republic to prevent food riots. Also, from Constantine's reign on, military service became a lifetime career that sons of soldiers inherited: they had to serve in the army.

The emperors in this period also announced oppressive regulations on the elites in the empire's towns. Almost all men in this class, known as **curials** (or decurions), were obliged sooner or later to serve as unsalaried city council members, who had to use their own funds if necessary to support the community. Their financial responsibilities ranged from maintaining the water supply to feeding troops, but their most expensive duty was covering shortfalls in taxes. The emperors' demands for increased revenue made this a crushing burden, compounding the damage to the curials that the third-century crisis had begun.

The tradition of public service by the elites broke down as wealthy people avoided it to escape financial ruin. To force curials to perform their obligations, the emperors ordered them not to move away from the towns where they had been born; they even had to ask official permission to travel. Forced service on a city council became one of the punishments for a minor crime. These laws made members of the elite try to win exemptions from public service by begging the emperor, bribing high-ranking officials, or taking up occupations that freed them from such obligations (such as being a soldier, an imperial administrator, or a church official). The most desperate people abandoned their homes and property.

The emperors' attempts to stabilize the empire by increasing its revenue also hurt nonelite citizens. The tax rate on land eventually reached one-third of its gross yield. This burden crushed poor farmers. They had to eat most of what they produced just to survive, save enough seed to plant the next crop, and then pay the high tax out of what was left. A bad harvest meant starvation. Conditions became so bad in fifth-century Spain, for example, that peasants openly revolted against imperial control. Financial troubles, especially severe in the west, kept the empire from ever regaining the prosperity of its Golden Age and worsened the friction between government and citizens.

Christianity: From Persecution to Conversion

The official position of Christianity in the Roman Empire changed completely from the reign of Diocletian to that of Constantine. Diocletian believed that Roman government needed to regain the goodwill of the pagan gods by promoting traditional religion and suppressing Christianity. He proclaimed, "The providence of the immortal gods has allowed superior, wise, and upright men in their wisdom to establish good and true principles. It is wrong to oppose these principles or to abandon the ancient religion for some new one."

Blaming Christians for angering the gods, Diocletian in 303 launched the **Great Persecution**. He expelled Christians from his administration, seized their property, tore down their churches, and executed them for refusing to participate in sacrifices. The policy was applied differently in different regions. In the western empire, the violence stopped after about a year; in the east, it continued for a decade. So gruesome were the public executions of martyrs that they aroused the sympathy of some polytheists.

Constantine changed the empire's religious history forever by converting to Christianity. He chose the new faith for the same reason that Diocletian had persecuted it: in the belief that he would receive divine protection for himself and the empire. During the civil war that he had to fight to become emperor after Diocletian resigned, Constantine had a vision in which he was promised the support of the Christian God. His biographer reported that Constantine had also seen a vision of Jesus's cross in the sky surrounded by the words "In this sign you shall be the victor." When Constantine defeated his main rival at the battle of the Milvian Bridge in Rome in 312, he proclaimed that God's miraculous power and goodwill had brought him the victory. He therefore declared himself a Christian emperor. After his conversion, Constantine did not outlaw polytheism or make Christianity the official religion. Instead, he announced religious toleration. The best statement of his new policy survives in the **Edict of Milan** of 313. It proclaimed free choice of religion for everyone and referred to the empire's protection by "the highest divinity"—a general term meant to satisfy both polytheists and Christians.

Constantine wanted to avoid angering polytheists because they still greatly outnumbered Christians, but he did all he could to promote his new religion. These goals called for a careful balancing act. For example, he returned all property seized during the Great Persecution to its Christian owners, but he had the treasury pay back those polytheists who had bought the confiscated property. When he made the Lord's Day a holy occasion each week on which no official business or manufacturing work could be performed, he called it Sunday in honor of two divinities, the Christian God and the pagan sun god. To beautify his new capital, Constantinople, he erected numerous statues of traditional gods around the city. He also respected Roman tradition by holding the office of pontifex maximus (highest priest), a position that all the emperors since Augustus had filled.

REVIEW   What changes did Diocletian and Constantine make to try to restore the peace and prosperity of the empire?

Relief Sculpture of Saturn from North Africa
This pillar shows the god known to the Romans
as Saturn and to the Carthaginians as Ba'al Ham-
mon (one of the gods of the Phoenician founders
of Carthage). This syncretism (identifying gods
as the same even though they carried different
names in different places) was typical of ancient
polytheism and allowed Roman and non-Roman
cults to merge. The smaller figure below the god is
sacrificing a sheep before an altar. The inscription
dates the pillar to 323, a decade after Constantine's
conversion to Christianity. Such objects testifying to
the continuing existence of polytheistic cults remained
common until the end of the fourth century, when the
Christian emperors succeeded in suppressing most public
activities of traditional religion. (© Copyright Martha Cooper/
Peter Arnold, Inc.)

Christianizing the Empire

Constantine's policy of religious toleration began the Christianization of the Roman
Empire. The process was slow and sometimes violent. Not until the end of the fourth
century did the emperors close the traditional gods' temples. Even after the vast majority of people in the empire had become Christians, some polytheists continued to
worship in private. Nevertheless, the transformation from a polytheist empire into a
Christian state was a turning point in global history.

Christianity as the Official Religion

It took a long time for the Christian emperors to make Christianity the official
religion of the empire because polytheists were serious believers. Polytheists and
Christians held some similar beliefs. Both believed spirits and demons had a powerful influence on daily life. Some people combined the religions. For example, a silver
spoon used in the worship of the polytheist forest spirit Faunus has been found

Mosaic of Christ as Sun God
This mosaic comes from a burial chamber in Rome that is now in the Vatican, under the basilica of St. Peter built by Constantine. It perhaps dates to the mid-third century. The depiction of Christ here is similar to a traditional polytheistic representation of the sun god, especially the Greek Apollo: with rays of light shining forth around his head as he rides in a chariot pulled by horses. This symbolism—God is light—reached back to ancient Egypt. Christian artists showed Jesus in this way because he said, "I am the light of the world" (John 8:12). The cloak flaring from Christ's shoulder suggests his movement across the sky. **For more help analyzing this image, see the visual activity for this chapter in the Online Study Guide at** bedfordstmartins.com/huntconcise. (Scala/Art Resource, NY.)

engraved with a fish, a common symbol of Christianity. (The Greek word for "fish," *ichthys,* was thought to be an acronym for the Greek words meaning "Jesus Christ the Son of God, the Savior.")

The differences between polytheists' and Christians' beliefs were much greater than their similarities, however. Above all was the fundamental difference between Christians' belief in one God and polytheists' belief in many gods. Polytheists still participated in festivals and sacrifices to their many gods. Why, they asked, did these joyous occasions not satisfy Christians' desire for contact with divinity? Polytheists also could not understand why Christians believed in a savior who had not established a new kingdom on earth and had been executed as a common criminal. The traditional gods, they insisted, had given a world empire to their worshippers. Moreover, they told Christians, cults such as that of the goddess Isis and philosophies such as Stoicism accepted only the pure of heart as followers. Christianity, by contrast, took in sinners. Why, puzzled polytheists wondered, would any righteous person want to associate with wrongdoers? In short, as one Greek philosopher remarked, Christians had no right to claim that they had the one true religion, for no one had ever discovered a single doctrine providing "the sole path to the liberation of the soul."

The slow pace of religious change revealed how strong polytheism remained in the fourth century, especially among the social elite. In fact, the emperor Julian

(r. 361–363) rebelled against his family's Christianity and tried to impose his philosophical brand of polytheism as Rome's official religion. This rejection of Christianity earned him the name Julian the Apostate (someone who turns against an established faith is called an **apostate**). Deeply religious, he believed in a supreme deity corresponding to the ideas of Greek philosophers: "This divine and completely beautiful universe, from heaven's highest sky to earth's lowest limit, is tied together by the continuous providence of god, has existed forever, and will last forever." Julian's restoration of the traditional gods ended when he died while invading Persia.

The Christian emperors who followed Julian worked to end polytheism. In 382, Gratian (r. 375–383 in the west) removed from the Senate in Rome the Altar of Victory, which Augustus had placed there to remind senators of Rome's success under its ancestral religion. Most important, Gratian stopped public funding for traditional sacrifices. Aurelius Symmachus, a polytheist senator who served as prefect (mayor) of Rome, objected to what he saw as an outrage against Rome's tradition of religious diversity. Protesting the emperors' moves against polytheism, he argued, "We all have our own way of life and our own way of worship. . . . So vast a mystery [as religious truth] cannot be approached by only one path."

Christianity finally replaced traditional polytheism as the state religion in 391, when the emperor Theodosius (r. 379–395 in the east) successfully banned all polytheist sacrifices, even if private individuals paid for the animals. He also made divination (predicting the future) by the inspection of animal entrails punishable as high treason and ordered that all polytheist temples be closed. Many shrines, however, such as the Parthenon in Athens, remained in use for a long time because the empire was too large for the emperors to enforce such laws at the local level. Temples were only gradually converted to churches during the fifth and sixth centuries. Non-Christian schools were not forced to close—the Academy, founded by Plato in Athens in the early fourth century B.C.E., endured for 140 years after Theodosius's reign—but Christians received advantages in government careers. Over time, non-Christians became outsiders in an empire ruled by Christian emperors.

Jews posed a special problem in the opinion of the Christian emperors. Like polytheists, Jews rejected the new official religion. Yet they seemed entitled to special treatment because Jesus had been a Jew and because previous emperors had allowed Jews to practice their religion. Fourth-century and later emperors placed legal restrictions on Jews. For example, they banned Jews from holding government jobs but still required them to take on the financial burdens of curials—without receiving the honor of curial status. By the late sixth century, they increased the pressure on Jews to convert to Christianity by barring them from making wills, receiving inheritances, or testifying in court. Although these developments began the long process that transformed Jews into second-class citizens in later European history, they did not destroy Judaism. Synagogues continued to exist in Palestine, where a few Jews still lived (most had been dispersed throughout the cities of the empire and the lands beyond the eastern border). The study of Jewish law and traditions flourished in this period, leading to the creation of books known as the Palestinian and the Babylonian Talmuds (collections of scholars' interpretations of Jewish law) and the scriptural commentaries of the Midrash (an explanation of the meaning of the Hebrew Bible). These works of religious scholarship provided guidance on how to live according to God's will and greatly influenced later Judaism.

With the emperors being Christians, soldiers could convert to Christianity and still serve in the army. Previously, Christian soldiers had sometimes created disciplinary problems. As one senior infantryman said in 298 at his court-martial for abandoning his duties, "A Christian serving the Lord Christ should not serve the affairs of this world." Once the emperors had become Christians, however, soldiers could justify military duty as supporting Christ.

Christianity's religious and social values helped it grow. It offered believers a strong sense of community in this world as well as the promise of salvation in the next. Wherever they went, Christians could find a warm welcome in the local congregation (Map 6.2). The new religion won converts by performing charitable works—in the tradition of Jews and some polytheist cults—especially in support of the poor, widows, and orphans. By the mid-third century, for example, Rome's congregation was supporting fifteen hundred widows and other poor people. Christianity's emphasis on taking care of others was especially important because people at that time had to depend mostly on friends and relatives for help; state-funded social services were rare.

Women were influential in spreading the new religion. Augustine (354–430), bishop of Hippo in North Africa and perhaps the most influential theologian in Western history, recognized women's contribution to the strengthening of Christianity in a letter he wrote to the unbaptized husband of a baptized woman: "O you men, who fear all the burdens imposed by baptism. The women are far better than you. Chaste and devoted to the faith, it is their presence in large numbers that causes the church to grow." Some women earned high status by giving their property to their congregations or by refusing marriage to dedicate themselves to Christ. Lifelong virgins and widows who chose not to remarry thus joined large donors as especially respected women. These women rejected the traditional social order, in which women were supposed to devote themselves to raising families. But even these holy women were excluded from leadership positions once the church's organization became a hierarchy of bishops matching the male-dominated hierarchy of the Roman world.

Once Christianity was the official religion, bishops became the emperors' partners in local rule, replacing the curials, whose numbers had shrunk drastically from the financial pressures the government had imposed on them but not on bishops. Bishops gained power because they could influence the emperor to direct government funds back to their regions. Regional councils of bishops appointed new bishops and tried to settle disputes over Christian doctrine. Bishops in the largest cities became the most powerful leaders in the church. The main bishop of Carthage, for example, supervised at least one hundred local bishops in the surrounding area. The

Map 6.2 The Spread of Christianity, 300–600
Christians were still a minority in the population of the Roman Empire in 300, although congregations existed in many cities and towns, especially in the eastern provinces. The emperor Constantine's conversion to Christianity in the early fourth century gave a boost to the new religion. It gained further strength during that century as the Christian emperors provided financial support and eliminated payments for the polytheist cults that had previously made up the state religion. By 600, the preaching of the church's missionaries and the money of the emperors had spread Christianity from one end of the empire to the other.

bishop of Rome became the church's supreme leader in the western empire. The eastern church never agreed that he controlled the entire Christian world, but his dominance in the west won him the title previously applied to many bishops: pope (from *pappas,* Greek for "father"), the name still used for the head of the Roman Catholic church.

The bishops of Rome quoted the New Testament to establish their leadership over other bishops. In the Book of Matthew (16:18–19), Jesus speaks to the Apostle Peter: "You are Peter, and upon this rock I will build my church. . . . I will entrust to you the keys of the kingdom of heaven. Whatever you bind on earth shall be bound in heaven. Whatever you loose on earth shall be loosed in heaven." Because Peter's name means "rock" in Greek and because Peter was believed to have been the first bishop of Rome, later bishops of Rome, believing they had inherited Peter's power, used this passage to justify their command over the church.

Conflict over Christian Beliefs

Christians had angry conflicts with one another about which beliefs were correct. The church's hierarchy of bishops struggled to create uniformity in beliefs and worship to ensure its members' spiritual purity and to maintain its authority over them. These leaders, however, disagreed about theology, too. Christians never achieved unity on what religious truth was.

Disputes flared over what should be orthodoxy (the official doctrines determined by councils of bishops; from the Greek for "correct thinking") as opposed to heresy (deviation from official doctrines; from the Greek for "private choice"). After Christianity became the official religion of the Roman government, the emperor became the top official responsible for enforcing the orthodox creed (a summary of beliefs). He used force against believers whom he regarded as heretics.

Questions about the nature of the Trinity of Father, Son, and Holy Spirit—defined in orthodoxy as a unified, coeternal, and identical divinity—caused the worst conflict. **Arianism**, for example, generated fierce controversy for centuries. Named after its founder, Arius (c. 260–336), a priest from Alexandria in Egypt,

Mosaic of a Family from Edessa in the Middle East

This mosaic, found in a cave tomb, depicts an upper-class family of Edessa in the late Roman imperial period. Edessa was the capital of the small kingdom of Osrhoëne, in northern Mesopotamia. The family's names are given in Syriac, the dialect of Aramaic spoken in their region, and their colorful clothing reflects local traditions. Rome took over the kingdom in 216, and it became famous in Christian history because its king Agbar (r. 179–216) was remembered as the first ruler to convert to Christianity, well before Constantine. By the early fourth century, the story had emerged that after Jesus's death and resurrection, he sent one of his disciples to Edessa, where the disciple painted a picture of Jesus that protected the city from its enemies. The Byzantine emperors proclaimed themselves the heirs of King Agbar and of Jesus's grant to the city of special divine protection. (Photo courtesy Thames & Hudson Ltd., London, from *Vanished Civilizations*, ed. Edward Bacon.)

this set of beliefs taught that Jesus as God's son had not existed eternally. Rather, God the Father had "begot" (created) his son from nothing and given him his special status. Thus Jesus was not coeternal with God and not identical to him in nature. This doctrine implied that the Trinity was divisible and that Christianity's monotheism was not absolute. Arianism found widespread support, perhaps because it eliminated the difficulty of understanding how a son could be as old as his father, and also because ranking the son as inferior to the father corresponded to regular family life. Arius used popular songs to make his views known, and people everywhere argued about the controversy. "When you ask for your change from a shopkeeper," one observer remarked in describing Constantinople, "he lectures you about the Begotten and the Unbegotten. If you ask how much bread costs, the reply is that 'the Father is superior and the Son inferior.'"

Other Christians became so angry about Arius's beliefs about Jesus that Constantine in 325 assembled 220 bishops at the Council of Nicaea to hammer out an agreement. The majority of bishops voted to crack down on Arianism: they banished Arius to the Balkan Mountains and declared that the Father and the Son were "of one substance" and coeternal. Arian's beliefs lived on: Constantine's third son, Constantius II (r. 337–361), favored Arianism, and his missionaries converted many of the barbarian immigrants who later came to live in the empire.

Nestorius, who became bishop of Constantinople in 428, disagreed with the orthodox doctrine of how Jesus's human and divine natures were related to his birth, insisting that his mother, Mary, gave birth to the human that became the temple for the divine. Nestorianism enraged orthodox Christians by rejecting Mary's title as *theotokos* (Greek for "bearer of God"). The bishops of Alexandria and Rome had Nestorius deposed and his doctrines officially rejected at councils held in 430 and 431; they condemned his writings in 435. Nestorian bishops in the eastern empire refused to accept these decisions, however, and they formed a separate church centered in Persia, where for centuries Nestorian Christians flourished under the tolerance of non-Christian rulers. They later became important agents of cross-cultural interaction by establishing communities that still endure in Arabia, India, and China.

The conflict over Donatism illustrates the bitterness of Christian conflicts over beliefs. Following the Great Persecution, in the fourth century a dispute arose in North Africa over whether to readmit to their old congregations those Christians who had cooperated with imperial authorities to avoid persecution. Some North African Christians felt these lapsed members should be forgiven, but the Donatists (followers of the North African priest Donatus) insisted that the church should not be polluted with such "traitors." Most important, Donatists insisted, unfaithful priests and bishops could not administer the sacraments. So angry was the conflict that it even divided Christian families. As one son threatened his mother, "I will join Donatus's followers, and I will drink your blood."

These fiery emotions made it difficult for bishops to enforce orthodoxy as religious truth. The Council of Chalcedon (a town on the outskirts of Constantinople) in 451 was the most important attempt to forge an agreement. Its conclusions on orthodoxy form the basis of what many Christians believe today: Jesus's divine and human natures were mixed within his person but nevertheless remained distinct. Monophysites (a Greek term meaning "single-nature believers") refused to agree, however, arguing that Jesus had only a single, divine nature. They split from the orthodox hierarchy in the sixth century to found independent churches in Egypt (the Coptic church), Ethiopia, Syria, and Armenia.

Augustine had the greatest influence on the doctrines of the western church. Born in North Africa in 354, he fathered a son by a mistress before converting to Christianity under the influence of his mother and Ambrose (c. 339–397), the powerful bishop of Milan. He became bishop of Hippo, but his reputation rests on his writings. By around 500, Augustine and other influential theologians such as Ambrose and Jerome (c. 345–420) had earned the informal title "church fathers" because their views were quoted as authoritative in disputes over orthodoxy. Augustine became the most famous of this group of patristic (from *pater,* Greek for "father") authors.

In his book *City of God,* a "large and difficult work" according to Augustine himself, he rejected the idea that Christianity guaranteed earthly success to Christians. Most important, he said, Christians were not responsible for the barbarian Alaric's sacking of Rome in 410, a disaster that polytheists claimed was the gods' punishment for Romans' abandoning their traditional religion. In addition, Augustine redefined the ideal state as a society of Christians. Not even Plato's doctrines offered a true path to purity, he insisted, because the true struggle for individuals was not between their emotions and reason, but between their desire for earthly pleasures and spiritual purity. The only existence with true meaning was in God's city.

Nevertheless, Augustine wrote, earthly law and government were required because humans were by nature imperfect. Humans lost their original perfection by inheriting a permanently sinful nature after Adam and Eve had disobeyed God in the Garden of Eden. This doctrine of original sin—a subject of theological debate since at least the second century—meant that people suffered from a hereditary moral disease that turned the human will into a corrupting force. Although far inferior to the divine ideal, civil government was necessary to impose moral order on the chaos of human life after the fall from grace in the Garden of Eden. The government therefore had a right to force people to remain united to the church, by violence if necessary.

In *City of God,* Augustine insisted that God's will lay behind the events of history, even if people found his will impossible to understand in detail. He explained that Christians could know with certainty only that God guided history toward an ultimate goal:

> To be truthful, I myself fail to understand why God created mice and frogs, flies and worms. Nevertheless, I recognize that each of these creatures is beautiful in its own way. For when I think about the body and limbs of any

living creature, where do I not find proportion, number, and order showing the unity of concord? Where one discovers proportion, number, and order, one should look for the craftsman.

Next to the nature of Christ, the question of how to understand and control sexual desire presented Christians with the toughest problem in the search for religious truth. Augustine became the most influential source of the belief that sex automatically involved human beings in evil and that they should therefore become ascetics (from the Greek *askesis,* meaning "training"), denying themselves all pleasure. Augustine knew from personal experience how difficult it was to accept this doctrine. In fact, he revealed in his autobiographical work *Confessions* that it took him a long time to pledge to go without sex as part of his conversion to Christianity.

Augustine advocated no sex as the purest choice for Christians because he believed that Adam and Eve's disobedience had forever ruined the original harmony that God had created between human will and human passions. According to Augustine, God punished his disobedient children by making sexual desire a corrupting force that humans could never completely control through will. Although Augustine declared the value of marriage in God's plan, he added that sexual intercourse even between loving spouses carried the sad reminder of humanity's fall from grace. A married couple should "lie down with a certain sadness" to the task of starting a pregnancy, the only acceptable reason for sex. Sexual pleasure could never be a human good.

This doctrine made virginity and avoidance of sex high virtues. In the words of Jerome, they counted as "daily martyrdom." This self-chosen holiness proved especially valuable for women in boosting their status in Christian society. Their sexual abstinence earned them such respect that they could demand privileges usually reserved for men, such as more education in Hebrew and Greek to read the Bible. By the end of the fourth century, sexual purity had become so significant for Christian virtue that congregations began to expect celibate male priests and bishops.

The Beginning of Christian Monasticism

Christian **asceticism** (the denial of pleasure, especially in regard to sex and food) reached its peak in monasticism. The word *monk* (from the Greek *monos,* meaning "single" or "solitary") describes the basis of monasticism: men and women withdrawing from society to live a life of extreme self-denial imitating Jesus's suffering, demonstrating their devotion to God, and praying for divine mercy on the world. The earliest monks lived alone, but soon they formed communities for mutual support in the pursuit of ascetic holiness (Map 6.2, page 209).

Polytheist and Jewish ascetics, motivated by philosophy and religion, had existed before. What made Christian monasticism different were the huge numbers of people it attracted and the high status monks earned. Leaving their families and congregations, they gave up sex, worshipped frequently, wore the roughest clothes, and ate barely enough to survive, aiming to win an inner peace isolated from daily concerns. They reported, however, that they constantly struggled against fantasies of earthly delights, dreaming of plentiful, tasty food more often than of sex.

The earliest Christian ascetics appeared in the late third century in Egypt. Antony (c. 251–356), from a well-to-do family, was among the first. One day, he abruptly abandoned all his property after hearing a sermon based on Jesus's advice to a rich young man to sell his possessions and give the proceeds to the poor (Matt. 19:21). Rejecting his duty to help his sister find a husband, he placed her in a home for unmarried women and spent his life alone in a barren region, demonstrating his excellence by worshipping God.

Monasticism appealed to its followers for many reasons, but above all because it gave ordinary people a way to achieve excellence and recognition. This opportunity seemed all the more valuable after Constantine's conversion and the end of the

Monastery of St. Catherine at Mount Sinai
Jews and Christians regarded this monastery in the desert at the foot of Mount Sinai (on the peninsula between Egypt and Arabia) as holy because Moses had received the Ten Commandments there during the Hebrews' wanderings after their exodus from Egypt. The Byzantine emperor Justinian supported the monastery to promote orthodoxy in a region dominated by Monophysite Christians. The monks at St. Catherine's gained a reputation for exceptional religious devotion: they spent much of their time repeating a simple prayer to Jesus over and over. The monastery obtained its name in the ninth century from a story about angels bringing the body of Catherine of Alexandria there. Catherine was said to have been martyred in the fourth century for refusing to marry the emperor because, in her words, she was the bride of Christ. (Erich Lessing/Art Resource, NY.)

persecutions. Becoming a monk—a living martyrdom—served as the substitute for a martyr's death and imitated the sacrifice of Christ. Individual, or eremetic (hence *hermit*), monks went to great lengths to win fame. In Syria, for example, "holy women" and "holy men" attracted great attention by their feats of endurance. One man lived atop a tall pillar for thirty years in the fifth century, preaching to people gathered below his perch. Egyptian Christians believed that their monks' religious devotion made them living heroes ensuring the annual flooding of the Nile, the duty once linked to the pharaohs' divine power. Exceptionally famous ascetics had even greater influence after death. Their relics—body parts or clothing—became treasured sources of protection and healing. Relics gave believers faith in God's favor by expressing the power of saints (people receiving special honor after their deaths as a reward for their holiness).

In about 323, Pachomius in Upper Egypt organized the first monastic community. In this "coenobitic" (seen-uh-BIT-ick), or "life in common," monasticism, male or female monks formed single-gender settlements to encourage one another along the hard road to holiness. Coenobitic monasticism became the primary form of Christian asceticism. Monasteries were often built close together to divide their labor, with women making clothing, for example, while men farmed.

All monasteries imposed military-style discipline, but they differed in the harshness of their rules and the amount of contact with the outside world. The most isolationist groups arose in the eastern empire, but the followers of Martin of Tours, an ex-soldier of the fourth century famed for his religious deeds, founded communities in the west as harsh as any eastern ones. Basil ("the Great") of Caesarea in Asia Minor started a different tradition in the fourth century: monasteries serving society. He required monks to perform charitable deeds, leading to the foundation of the first hospitals.

A milder, but still strict, code telling monks how to live became the standard in the west from the sixth century on, influencing almost every area of Catholic worship. Called the Benedictine rule after its creator, Benedict (c. 480–553) from Nursia in central Italy, this code prescribed a daily routine of prayers, scriptural readings, and manual labor. The rule divided the day into seven parts, each with a compulsory service of prayers and lessons, collectively called the Divine Office. Unlike harsher codes, Benedict's did not isolate the monks from the outside world or deprive them of sleep, adequate food, or warm clothing. Although his code gave the abbot (the head monk) full authority, it instructed him to listen to what every monk had to say before he decided important matters. The abbot was not allowed to beat the monks severely as punishment for breaking the rules. Communities of women, such as those founded by Basil's sister Macrina and Benedict's sister Scholastica, usually followed the rules of the male monasteries, with an emphasis on the modesty thought necessary for women.

The thousands of Christians who became monks thereafter joined monasteries for social as well as theological reasons. Some had been given as babies to monasteries by parents who could not raise them or were fulfilling religious vows, a practice called oblation. Jerome once gave this advice to a mother about her daughter:

> Let her be brought up in a monastery, let her live among virgins, let her learn to avoid swearing, let her regard lying as a sin against God, let her be ignorant of the world, let her live the angelic life, while in the flesh let her be without the flesh, and let her suppose that all human beings are like herself.

When she reaches adulthood as a virgin, he added, she should avoid the baths so she would not be seen naked or give her body pleasure by dipping in the warm pools. Jerome expressed traditional Roman values favoring males when he promised that God would reward the mother with the birth of sons to compensate for her dedicating her daughter to God. But he also said, "[As monks] we evaluate people's virtue not by their gender but by their character, and judge those to be worthy of the greatest glory who have given up both status and riches."

The monasteries' independence threatened the power of the church's hierarchy. Bishops did not like devoted members of their congregations withdrawing into monasteries, especially because they made donations to their new communities rather than to their local churches. Moreover, monks challenged bishops' authority because holy men and women earned their special status not by having it awarded by the church's leaders but by earning it through their own actions. Bishops and monks did share a spiritual goal—salvation and service to God. While polytheists had enjoyed immediate access to their gods, who were thought to visit the earth constantly, Christians worshipped a God outside this world. Monks bridged the gap between the human and the divine by asking God to be merciful to faithful believers.

REVIEW What were the major disputes among early Christians, and why were they so fierce?

Non-Roman (Barbarian) Kingdoms and the Western Roman Empire

The migrations and attacks of non-Roman peoples ("barbarians," according to Romans) into the western Roman Empire transformed politics, society, and the economy there. Two strong motives drove these diverse groups into Roman territory: to flee the brutal attacks of the Huns (nomads from the steppes of Central Asia) and to benefit from the empire's prosperity. By the 370s, the immigrants' presence had generated great violence in western Europe. As the imperial government's ability to maintain order weakened, these immigrants experienced great changes themselves, transforming from vaguely organized tribes into kingdoms with separate ethnic identities. By the 470s, one of their commanders ruled Italy. That political change has been said to mark the "fall of the Roman Empire." In fact, the lasting effects of the interactions of these non-Roman peoples with the diverse peoples of western Europe and North Africa are better understood as a gradual transformation that made them the heirs of the western Roman Empire and led to the formation of medieval Europe.

Migrations into and Attacks on the Empire

At first, the fourth-century emperors encouraged the migrations of barbarians into the empire. Like the earlier emperors, they recruited these foreign warriors for the Roman army. By the late fourth century, crowds of women and children had followed their men into the empire. The emperors' failure to either absorb the newcomers or expel them led to the fall of the Roman Empire.

Economic weakness from the third-century crisis lessened the emperors' ability to react to the migrations. They had demanded higher taxes during the crisis, forcing landowners to demand higher payments from their tenant farmers (coloni). Many of these tenants responded by illegally running away. Eventually, landowners also had to run away if they could not pay their taxes. This flight left farms deserted: as much as 20 percent of agricultural land lay unfarmed in the most seriously affected areas. The government pressed the farmers who remained to pay even more, but this only made more of them abandon their farms. In the end, the emperors' financial problems meant they could not hire enough soldiers to stop non-Roman peoples from immigrating into the empire.

Non-Roman groups crossed into Roman territory not in carefully planned invasions, but often fleeing for their lives. Fourth-century raids by the Huns drove them from their homelands east of the Rhine and north of the Danube. Mostly small groups of men, women, and children crossed the Roman border as refugees. Their future looked grim because they came with no political or military unity, no clear plan, and not even a shared sense of identity.

Loosely organized in democratic groups and often warring with one another, these diverse bands or tribes originally shared only similar languages and their terror of the Huns. The migrating groups developed different ethnic identities because the Roman government refused to accept them into Roman society. The newcomers therefore created their own kingdoms inside the imperial frontiers. Their desire for security forced them to develop a more tightly structured society to govern their new lands and gave them new identities.

Previously, these peoples had no experience organizing kingdoms. In their homelands, they had lived in small settlements as farmers, herders, and ironworkers. Most bands operated as chiefdoms, whose members could only be persuaded, not forced, to follow the chief. Chiefs maintained their leadership by leading warriors on successful raids to seize cattle and slaves and then giving gifts to their followers. Family life was patriarchal: men headed households and exercised authority over women, children, and slaves. Women earned respect by bearing children, and rich men could have more than one wife and perhaps concubines as well. A clear division of labor made women responsible for agriculture, pottery making, and the production of textiles, while men worked iron and herded cattle. Fighting and raiding were so prized by the men that when a man died, his grave was packed with weapons. Women had some rights of inheritance and could control property; married women received a marriage gift of one-third of their husbands' property.

Households were grouped into clans based on kinship through mothers as well as fathers. The members of a clan were supposed to keep peace among themselves, and violence against another clan member was the worst possible crime. Clans in turn grouped themselves into tribes, multiethnic coalitions that anyone could join. Different tribes identified themselves by their clothing, hairstyles, jewelry, weapons, religious cults, and oral stories.

Assemblies of free male warriors provided the tribes' only political organization. Tribal leaders' functions were mostly religious and military. Tribes tended to be unstable groupings with frequent bloody feuds between clans. Tribal law tried to set limits on the violence permitted in seeking revenge, but laws were oral, not written, and thus open to wide dispute.

Migrations into Roman territory surged when the Huns invaded eastern Europe in the fourth century. Related to the Xiongnu people who had attacked China and Persia, these Turkish-speaking nomads arrived on the Russian plains by 370. They excelled as raiders, launching cavalry attacks far and wide. With elongated skulls (from having been bound between boards in infancy), faces grooved with decorative scars, and arms bristling with tattoos, they terrified their victims. Their skill as horsemen made the Huns legendary. They could shoot their powerful bows while riding at full speed, and they could remain on horseback for days, sleeping atop their horses and packing snacks of raw meat between their thighs and the animal's back.

The eastern emperors in Constantinople bribed the Huns not to attack their territory. The Huns then abandoned their nomadic lifestyle and became landlords, cooperating among themselves to create an empire north of the Danube that forced local farmers to support these new masters. The Huns' most ambitious leader, Attila (r. c. 440–453), extended their domain from the Caspian Sea to the Alps and even farther west. He led attacks into Roman territory as far as Paris and into northern Italy. At Attila's death, the Huns lost their unity and faded from history. By this time, however, the terror that they inspired in the people living in eastern Europe had already started the migrations that transformed the western empire.

The bands that created a new identity as Visigoths after entering imperial territory were the first to experience what became the common pattern of the migrations. Some desperate and poorly organized group would plead with the emperor for protection from the Huns, and the empire would accept them in return for military service. Shredded by constant raids from the Huns, in 376 the Visigoths begged the eastern emperor, Valens (r. 364–378), to let them migrate into the Balkans. They received permission on condition that their warriors enlist in the Roman army to help fight the Huns. When greedy and incompetent Roman officers sent to help the refugee Visigoths instead mistreated them, the immigrants starved; the officials forced them to sell some of their own people into slavery in return for dogs to eat. The hungry Visigoths rebelled. In 378, they attacked and killed Valens in battle at Adrianople in Thrace (Map 6.3). The next eastern emperor, Theodosius I (r. 379–395), had to renegotiate the deal from a position of weakness. His concessions to the Visigoths

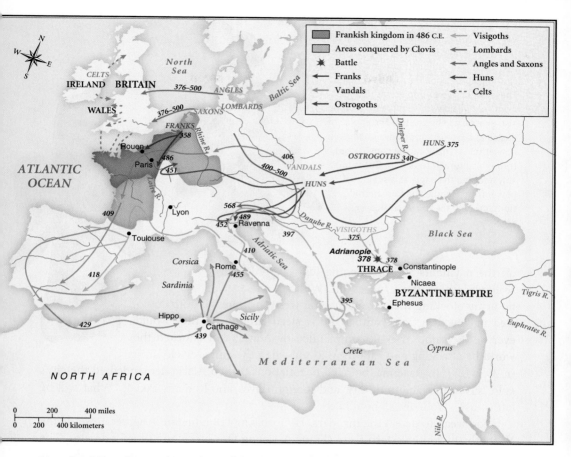

Map 6.3 Migrations and Invasions of the Fourth and Fifth Centuries

The movements of non-Roman peoples (barbarians) into imperial territory transformed the Roman Empire. These migrations began as early as the reign of Domitian (r. 81–96), but in the fourth century, they became a pressing problem for the emperors when the Huns' attacks pushed many multiethnic bands from their homelands in eastern Europe into the empire's northern provinces. Maps cannot really show dynamic processes such as migrations and invasions, and the arrows on this one do not mean that the newcomers came in an unbroken stream. The map does indicate, however, the variety of peoples involved, the wide extent of imperial territory they affected, and the concentration of their effects in the western section of the empire.

established the terms that other bands would seek for themselves and that would create new, self-conscious identities for them: permission to settle permanently inside the imperial borders, freedom to establish a kingdom under their own laws, the title of "federates of the empire" (allies expected to help protect Roman territory), and large annual payments from the emperors.

The eastern emperors soon realized, however, that they could not afford to keep such agreements. They therefore forced the migrating bands westward by cutting

Eagle Brooches (*Fibulae*) from Visigothic Spain
Visigothic women in their kingdom in Spain showed their new ethnic identity by their style of dress, in particular through the tradition of fastening their clothing at the shoulders with brooches. These expensive examples, fashioned from gold inlaid with semiprecious stones, also expressed elite status. The choice of eagles as a Gothic brooch design reveals how ethnic identity can be constructed through cultural interaction: Goths probably adopted the eagle as a symbol of power from Hunnic and Roman traditions. (Photo © The Walters Art Museum, Baltimore.)

off the payments and threatening full-scale war unless the refugees left. With no army blocking them from moving westward, the Visigoths traveled in that direction. Neither the western empire nor they would ever be the same. In 410, commanded by Alaric, they shocked the world by attacking and capturing Rome when the emperor Honorius (r. 395–423), in Ravenna, botched negotiations. When Alaric demanded all the city's gold, silver, movable property, and foreign slaves, the Romans asked, "What will be left to us?" "Your lives," he replied.

Too weak to defeat the invaders, Honorius in 418 reluctantly agreed to settle the Visigoths in southwestern Gaul (France), saving face by calling them federates. The Visigoths then completed their transition from tribal society to new kingdom by doing what no non-Roman group had done before: establishing an ethnic identity and organizing a state. They followed the model of Roman emperors by building mutually beneficial relations with local elites, including Romans. Elite Romans used time-tested ways of flattering their superiors to gain advantages. Sidonius Apollinaris, for example, a noble from Lyon, once purposely lost a backgammon game to the Visigothic king as a way of gaining a favor from the ruler. Honorius tried, without much success, to limit what he saw as barbarian influence on Roman citizens by ordering them not to adopt Visigothic clothing styles.

Historians still debate how the new non-Roman kingdoms financed their governments. The older view is that the newcomers became landowners by forcing Romans to turn over some of their land, slaves, and movable property to them. Recent scholarship argues that Roman taxpayers in the kingdoms did not have to give up land but were instead made directly responsible for paying the expenses of the non-Roman soldiers, who lived mostly in city garrisons. Whatever the arrangements were, the Visigoths found them so profitable that they later expanded into Spain.

Map 6.4 Peoples and Kingdoms of the Roman World, c. 526
The provinces of the Roman Empire had always been home to a population diverse in language and ethnicity. By the early sixth century, the territory of the western empire had fragmented into diverse political units as well. Italy and most of the former western provinces were kingdoms created and ruled by non-Roman peoples who had moved into former Roman territory over the past several centuries. The eastern empire (the Byzantine Empire) remained under the political control of the emperor in Constantinople. Justinian, who became Byzantine emperor in 527, made it his mission to try to reunite the eastern and western halves of the empire by force. How much do these states correspond to the modern boundaries of states in Europe? **For more help analyzing this map, see the map activity for this chapter in the Online Study Guide at** bedfordstmartins.com/huntconcise.

The western emperor's deal with the Visigoths motivated other groups to enter Roman territory to create kingdoms and identities (Map 6.4). The process was often violent. In 406, the Vandals, fleeing the Huns, fought their way all through Gaul to the Spanish coast. (The modern word *vandal,* meaning "destroyer of property," preserves their reputation for destruction.) In 429, eighty thousand Vandals crossed to North Africa, where they broke their agreement to become federates and captured the region with fierce attacks. Their new kingdom caused tremendous hardship for local Africans by confiscating property rather than allowing owners to make regular payments to the occupiers. The Vandals further weakened the western emperors by seizing North Africa's tax payments of grain and vegetable oil and disrupting the

Mosaic of Women Exercising
This picture covered a floor in a fourth-century country villa in Sicily that had more than forty rooms decorated with colorful mosaics. The women shown here were perhaps dancers getting in shape for performances, or gymnasts in a show. Members of the Roman elite built such large and expensive houses to try to protect their families from the troubles of the later Roman Empire. Often this strategy failed. Vandal invaders seriously damaged this villa. (Erich Lessing/Art Resource, NY.)

importation of grain to Rome. They also built a navy strong enough to threaten the eastern empire. In 455, the Vandals attacked and plundered Rome, proving the western imperial government was powerless.

Other small groups also managed to break off distant pieces of the weakened western empire. The most significant small band for later history was the Anglo-Saxons. Composed of Angles from what is now Denmark and Saxons from north-western Germany, this group invaded Britain in the 440s after the Roman army had been recalled from the province to defend Italy against the Visigoths. The Anglo-Saxons established their kingdoms by taking territory away from the local Celtic peoples and the remaining Roman inhabitants. Gradually, Anglo-Saxon culture replaced the local traditions of the island's eastern regions; the Celts there lost most of their language, and Christianity survived only in Wales and Ireland.

The Fall of the Roman Empire

The western empire's military weakness led to a change in leadership in 476 that has traditionally, but simplistically, been called the fall of the Roman Empire. In that year a non-Roman commander replaced the Roman emperor in the west, and no Roman would rule there ever again. The idea of a "fall" comes from the best-selling work that made it famous—*The Decline and Fall of the Roman Empire* by the English historian Edward Gibbon (1737–1794). The real story's details, however, reveal the complexity of the political transformation of the western empire under the pressure of non-Roman immigration. The weakness of the imperial army in the west had forced the western emperors to employ non-Roman officers to lead the defense of Italy. By the middle of the fifth century, one general after another decided who would serve as puppet emperor under his control. The last such unfortunate "emperor" was a boy. His father, a former aide to Attila, had rebelled against the emperor and raised his young son to the throne. He gave the child emperor the name Romulus Augustulus, meant to recall both Rome's founder and its first emperor. In 476, after a dispute over pay, soldiers murdered the father and deposed the boy. Pitied as an innocent child, Romulus was given a safe home and a generous pension. The rebels' leader, Odoacer, did not choose another western emperor. Instead, he had the Senate in Rome ask the eastern emperor to recognize his leadership in return for his recognizing the eastern emperor as sole emperor. Odoacer thereafter led Italy supposedly as the eastern emperor's assistant. In truth, he ruled independently.

Theodoric (r. 493–526), a non-Roman general from the eastern empire, overthrew Odoacer and established the Ostrogothic kingdom, which ruled Italy from the capital at Ravenna. He built legitimacy for his new state by preserving traditional Roman institutions, especially the Senate and the office of consul. Theodoric and his Ostrogothic nobles wanted to enjoy the empire's luxury and prestige, not destroy them. For this reason, modern scholars consider it more accurate to speak of the western empire's "transformation" than its "fall" (Map 6.4, page 221), even though the process was often violent.

An Arian Christian, Theodoric followed Constantine's example by announcing a policy of religious toleration: "No one can be forced to believe against his will." Many members of the Roman elite, such as the famous scholars Boethius and Cassiodorus, cooperated with Theodoric to try to establish stable government. Unfortunately, the Ostrogothic emperor executed Boethius, whom he had made a consul but later accused of disloyalty. While in prison, Boethius wrote the *Consolation of Philosophy,* a book that explained divine providence according to the ideas of Stoic and Neoplatonic philosophy, as well as those of Augustine. Boethius's scholarship became vastly influential in medieval Europe.

The Franks were a Germanic people who transformed Roman Gaul into Francia (from which the name *France* comes). They first moved into that region with the permission of the western emperor in the early fourth century. In 507, their king, Clovis (r. 485–511), overthrew the Visigothic king in southern Gaul with support from the eastern emperor. When the emperor named him an honorary Roman consul, Clovis celebrated this ancient honor by having himself crowned with a diadem in the style of the dominate's emperors. He carved out western Europe's largest new kingdom in what is today mostly France. This kingdom grew larger than the neighboring rival kingdoms of the Burgundians and Alamanni in eastern Gaul. Probably persuaded by his Christian wife, Clotilda, to believe that God had helped him defeat the Alamanni, Clovis proclaimed himself an orthodox Christian. To build stability, he forged good relations with Gaul's bishops, who helped him control the people in their regions.

Clovis's dynasty, called Merovingian after the legendary Frankish ancestor Merovech, lasted for another two hundred years, far longer than most other non-Roman royal families in the west. The Merovingian state anticipated the kingdom that emerged later as the forerunner of modern France. The Merovingians survived so long because their new state combined barbarian military might with Roman social and legal traditions.

The Transformation of the Western Empire

The political transformation of the western Roman Empire—the replacement of imperial government by non-Roman kingdoms—created a social transformation as well. Immigrants and Romans combined their traditions to establish new ways of living, above all law codes. Unfortunately, they failed to build a strong economy.

These transformations were meant to continue the empire's glory. The Visigoth king Athaulf (r. 410–415), having married a Roman noblewoman, explained his goals in this way:

> At the start I wanted to erase the Romans' name and turn their land into a Gothic empire, myself doing what Augustus had done. But I have learned that the Goths' freewheeling wildness will never accept the rule of law, and that a state with no law is no state. Thus, I have more wisely chosen another path to glory: reviving the Roman name with Gothic strength. I pray that future generations will remember me as the founder of a Roman restoration.

Roman law greatly influenced the new kings in their efforts to organize new states. The barbarians had never before had written laws. Now that they had transformed themselves into kings ruling Romans as well as their own people, they wanted legal codes to establish justice and order. The Visigothic kings were the first non-Roman leaders to create a written law code. Composed in Latin and dependent on Roman legal tradition, it made the payment of fines and compensation the primary method for resolving disputes.

Clovis also relied on written law in his Merovingian kingdom. His code, published in Latin, supported social order by setting clear penalties for specific crimes. In particular, he established a system of payments intended to defuse feuds between individuals and between clans. This system of penalties included **wergild**, the payment a murderer had to make as compensation for his crime. Most of the money was paid to the victim's kin, but the king received one-third of the amount.

Because law codes correspond to social values, the differing payments offer a glimpse of the relative social value of different categories of people in Clovis's kingdom. The penalty for murdering a woman of childbearing age, a boy under twelve, or a man in the king's service was a massive fine of six hundred gold coins, enough to buy six hundred cattle. The fine for murdering a woman past childbearing age (specified as sixty years), a young girl, or a freeborn man was two hundred gold coins; for murdering ordinary slaves, thirty-five.

The migrations and attacks that transformed the west harmed its already weak economy. The Vandals damaged many towns in Gaul. In the countryside, now outside the control of any central government, wealthy Romans from the social elite built villas on large estates staffed by tenants bound to the land like slaves. The owners of these estates operated them as self-sufficient units by producing all they needed, defending themselves against raids, and refusing to cooperate with imperial officials. The owners shunned membership on city councils and tax collection—the public services that had supplied the lifeblood of Roman administration—although the wealthiest boasted an annual income rivaling that of an entire region in the old western empire. The elite's withdrawal from public service withered Roman provincial government, and the new kingdoms never replaced the traditional services to the population.

A few provincial Romans helped transmit ancient learning to later ages. Cassiodorus, one of the scholars who had worked for Theodoric, founded a monastery on his ancestral estate in Italy in the 550s following his career in imperial administration. He gave the monks the task of copying manuscripts to preserve their contents as old texts disintegrated. His own book *Institutions,* composed to guide his monks, explained the respect for tradition that kept classical traditions alive: in prescribing the works a person of superior education should read, it included ancient secular texts as well as Scripture and Christian literature.

> **REVIEW**　What transformations took place in the Roman Empire from around 370 to the 550s?

The Byzantine (Eastern Roman) Empire

The eastern Roman Empire avoided the transformations that reshaped western Europe. Trade routes and diverse agriculture kept the east richer than the west, and the eastern emperors minimized the effect of the foreign migrations on their territory and blunted the aggression of the Sasanid kingdom in Persia with force, diplomacy, and bribery. By the early sixth century, the empire's eastern half had achieved such power, riches, and ambition that modern historians renamed it the Byzantine Empire; its emperors held power until 1453.

The Byzantine emperors saw themselves as continuing the Roman Empire and guarding its traditions against barbarians. Justinian (r. 527–565), the most famous of the early Byzantine emperors, took this mission so seriously that he bankrupted his treasury with wars to recover the western empire. He tried to impose religious orthodoxy to win God's support for his dream of reunifying the empire. One especially significant contribution of the early Byzantine Empire to later history was preserving classical literature and learning, which nearly disappeared in the west.

Byzantine Society

The Byzantine Empire enjoyed a prosperity that western Europe had lost. Members of the elite imported silk, precious stones, and expensive spices such as pepper from China and India. People of all kinds flocked to the empire's largest cities—Constantinople (the former Byzantium), Damascus, and Alexandria. There, churches with soaring domes testified to the Byzantines' confidence in God's power and favor.

The Byzantine emperors sponsored costly religious festivals and entertainments to rally public support. Rich and poor alike crowded city squares, theaters, and racetracks to enjoy the spectacles. Chariot racing aroused the hottest passions. Constantinople's residents divided themselves into competitive factions, called Blues and Greens after the racing colors of their favorite charioteers, which combined religious and sports rivalries: orthodox Christians became Blues, Monophysites Greens. They clashed as frequently over theological arguments as over race results.

The eastern emperors did everything they could to preserve traditional "Romanness." They feared their empire would become "barbarian," as in the west. They employed foreign mercenaries, but they tried to keep immigrant customs from influencing the empire's residents. They paid special attention to clothing. Eastern emperors banned Constantinople's residents from wearing barbarian-style outfits (especially heavy boots and clothing made from animal fur) instead of traditional Roman clothes (sandals or light shoes and robes). The Byzantines referred to themselves as "Romans" because they saw themselves as the heirs and protectors of Roman traditions. At the same time, they spoke Greek as their native language and used Latin only for government and military communication. (The Latin-speaking western empire referred to them as "Greeks.") Since Byzantine society was deeply multilingual and multiethnic, preserving an unchanging Roman identity was an impossible goal. Travelers around the empire heard countless languages, saw varying styles of dress, and encountered numerous ethnic groups.

For the Byzantines, Romanness included Christianity, but their theological diversity matched their ethnic variety. Bitter controversies over beliefs divided eastern Christians, and emperors joined forces with bishops to impose orthodoxy. They generally opted for words over swords to pressure heretics to accept orthodox theology, but they used violence when persuasion failed. Resorting to such extreme measures against fellow Christians was necessary, they believed, to save lost souls and preserve God's goodwill toward the empire.

In patriarchal Byzantine society, most women followed ancient Mediterranean tradition by focusing their lives on their households and minimizing contact with men outside that circle. Law barred women from many public functions, such as witnessing wills. Subject to the authority of their fathers and husbands, women veiled their heads (though not their faces) to show modesty. Christian theology made divorce more difficult than under Roman law and discouraged remarriage, even for widows. Stiffer legal penalties for sexual offenses also developed. Female prostitution remained legal, but emperors raised the penalties for people forcing girls or slave women to become prostitutes.

As always, women in the imperial family lived by different rules than ordinary women and could directly influence government. Theodora (c. 500–548), wife of the emperor Justinian, became the most influential and talked about of all Byzantine empresses. Using her brains and beauty to overcome her low social status (she was the daughter of a bear trainer and then an actress accused of performing pornographic scenes), she married Justinian and advised him in every part of his rule. She helped him make personnel choices for his administration, strongly pushed her religious views in the continuing disputes over Christian doctrine, and rallied her husband's courage in times of crisis. A high-ranking administrator judged her "superior in intelligence to any man."

Byzantine government made the social hierarchy more rigid than ever because it provided services according to people's wealth. It required piles of paperwork and fees for official transactions, from commercial permits to legal complaints. Without bribery, nothing got done. This arrangement benefited people with status and money: they used their social connections to get a hearing from the right official and used their wealth to pay bribes to get fast action.

The poor could not afford the bribes that government officials expected. Since interest rates were high, they had to take on backbreaking debt to raise the cash to pay officials to help them. This system saved the emperors money: they paid civil servants small salaries because bribes from the public supplemented their incomes. One official, for example, reported that he earned thirty times his annual salary in bribes during his first year in office. To keep unlimited extortion from destroying the system, the emperors published an official list of the maximum bribes that employees could demand. Overall, however, this kind of government generated enormous hostility among poorer subjects.

The Reign of Emperor Justinian, 527–565

Justinian dreamed of reuniting the empire as it had been under Augustus. Born in a small Balkan town, he rose rapidly in imperial service until 527, when he succeeded his uncle as emperor. During his reign, he launched military expeditions to win back western Europe and North Africa from the non-Roman kingdoms. His desire to build imperial glory led him to decorate Constantinople with magnificent and costly buildings. He was also an intellectual with a passion for law and theology. He pushed reforms meant to preserve social order based on hierarchy and maintain divine favor. Justinian's autocratic rule provoked both admiration and fear. The contemporary historian Procopius famously displayed this conflicted response to Justinian. Some of his works praised Justinian's bold initiatives in war and architecture, but Procopius's *Secret History* presented scandalous stories about the alleged cruelty and sexual immorality of Justinian and his wife, Theodora.

The huge expense of Justinian's plans led to social unrest. His taxes became so heavy and their collection so violent that they provoked a major riot in 532. Known as the Nika Riot, it erupted when the Blue and Green factions united against the emperor, shouting *"Nika! Nika!"* (Win! Win!). After nine days of violence that left much

Justinian and His Court in Ravenna
This mosaic centered on the Byzantine emperor Justinian (r. 527–565) is opposite Theodora's mosaic in San Vitale Church in Ravenna. Justinian and Theodora had finished building the church, which the Ostrogothic king Theodoric had started, to celebrate their successful campaign to restore Italy to the Roman Empire and retake control of the western capital, Ravenna. The soldiers at left remind viewers of the rulers' aggressive military policy in service of imperial unity. The presence of Maximianus, bishop of Ravenna, standing on Justinian's left and identified by name above his head stresses the theme of cooperation between bishops and emperors in ruling the world. (Scala/Art Resource, NY.)

of the capital in ashes, a panicky Justinian prepared to abandon his throne and flee. Theodora, however, showed the steel in her soul by telling him, "Once born, no one can escape dying, but for one who has held imperial power it would be unbearable to be a fugitive. May I never take off my imperial robes of purple, nor live to see the day when those who meet me will not greet me as their ruler." Shamed, Justinian called out his guard, who crushed the rebellion by slaughtering thirty thousand rioters.

In service to Justinian's plan to reunite the eastern and western empires, his generals defeated the Vandals and Ostrogoths after campaigns that lasted decades. At enormous expense, Justinian's armies reoccupied Italy, the Dalmatian coast, Sicily, Sardinia, Corsica, part of southern Spain, and western North Africa by 562. These successes temporarily restored the old empire's geography: Justinian's territory stretched from the Atlantic to the western edge of Mesopotamia (see "Mapping the West," page 233).

Theodora and Her Court in Ravenna
This mosaic was placed on one wall of the church of San Vitale in Ravenna, facing the matching scene of Theodora's husband, Justinian, and his attendants. Theodora (c. 500–548) wears the jewels, pearls, and rich robes characteristic of Byzantine rulers. She extends in her hands a gem-encrusted bowl, evidently a present to the church. Her gesture imitates the gift giving of the Magi to the baby Jesus, the scene illustrated on the hem of her garment. Like Honorius on page 196, a circle around her head indicates special holiness. (Scala/Art Resource, NY.)

These triumphs carried a tragic price: inflicting horrible damage on Europe and emptying Justinian's treasury. Italy endured the greatest damage, but the east suffered as Justinian demanded still more taxes to finance the western wars and bribe the Sasanids in Mesopotamia not to attack. The tax burden crippled the economy, leading to constant banditry in the countryside. Crowds poured into the capital from rural areas, seeking relief from poverty and robbers.

Natural disasters added to Justinian's troubles. In the 540s, an epidemic killed a third of the empire's inhabitants. A quarter of a million died in Constantinople alone, half the capital's population. This was only the first in a long series of diseases that erased millions of people in the eastern empire over the next two centuries. The loss of so many people created a shortage of army recruits, forced the emperors to hire expensive mercenaries, and left many farms vacant, thus hurting tax revenues.

The pressures on Justinian led him to strengthen his authority by emphasizing his closeness to God and his authority over the people. He had his artists portray the symbols of rule in a Christian context. A gleaming mosaic in his church at San Vitale in Ravenna, for example, displayed a dramatic vision of the emperor's role: Justinian standing at the center of the universe shoulder to shoulder with both the ancient Hebrew leader Abraham and Christ. In legal matters, Justinian proclaimed the emperor the "living law," reviving a Hellenistic royal doctrine.

Justinian's building program in Constantinople expressed his religious devotion and worldly power. Most spectacular of all was his magnificent reconstruction of Constantine's Church of the Holy Wisdom (Hagia Sophia). Its location facing the palace emphasized Justinian's combination of imperial and Christian authority. Creating a new design for churches, his architects erected a huge building on a square plan capped by a dome 107 feet across and soaring 184 feet above the floor. Its interior walls glowed like the sun from the light reflecting off their four acres of gold mosaics. Imported marble of every color added to the sparkling effect. When Justinian first entered his masterpiece, he remarked, "Solomon, I have outdone you," boasting that he had bested the glorious temple the ancient king had built for the Hebrews.

The Soaring Architecture of the Hagia Sophia
Golden mosaics originally reflected a dazzling light from the interior of the Hagia Sophia, the enormous Church of the Holy Wisdom, which the Byzantine emperor Justinian built in the 530s near his palace in Constantinople. A central dome, 184 feet high and supported by four arches resting on massive piers, capped the church's vast interior; the ring of windows at the base of the dome is just visible at the top of the picture. The Hagia Sophia became a mosque after the Turks captured the city in 1453; the large medallions contain religious quotations in Arabic. Now a museum, it continues to host people offering prayers. (© Adam Woolfitt/Corbis.)

Justinian's building up of the emperor's power made Constantinople still more important and reduced the local independence of the empire's other cities. Their councils ceased to govern; imperial officials took over instead. Provincial elites still had to ensure full payment of their areas' taxes, but they lost the compensating reward of deciding local matters. Now the imperial government made all decisions and determined people's social status. Men of property from the provinces who wanted a public career knew they could satisfy their ambitions only by joining the imperial administration.

To strengthen his authority, Justinian had the empire's laws codified to bring uniformity to the inconsistent decisions of earlier emperors. This collection of past decisions, intended to make legal cases go faster and provide class materials for law schools, influenced legal scholars for centuries. Justinian's experts also wrote a textbook for students that proclaimed the principles of a just life: "Live honorably, harm no one else, and give to each his own." This book remained on law school reading lists until modern times.

To win God's goodwill, Justinian enacted reforms to guarantee religious orthodoxy. Harshly enforcing laws against polytheists, he ordered them to be baptized or else lose their lands and official positions. He punished Christians whom he could not convince to accept his version of orthodoxy. In pursuit of sexual purity, his laws made sex between men illegal for the first time in Roman history. Homosexual marriage, apparently not uncommon earlier, had been officially prohibited in the fourth century, but penalties had never before been imposed on men engaging in homosexual activity. Previous emperors had simply taxed male prostitutes. The legal status of homosexual activity between women is unclear; it probably counted as criminal adultery for married women.

Justinian tried to unite orthodox and Monophysite Christians by revising the creed of the Council of Chalcedon, but church leaders in Rome and Constantinople had become too bitterly divided to agree on a unified church. The church's eastern and western divisions were by now launched on the diverging courses that would climax in a formal schism five hundred years later. Perhaps no emperor could have done better, but Justinian's drive for religious orthodoxy only drove Christians farther apart and worked against his dream of a reunited Roman world.

Preserving Classical Literature

The empire's Christianization endangered classical literature because many Christians thought its books were the work of the devil and because, as Christians became authors in great numbers, their works displaced the ancient texts of Greece and Rome as the most important literature of the age. Fortunately for later times, the Byzantine Empire helped preserve a significant fraction of the famous works of the past.

Classical texts survived because educated Christians kept reading ancient Greek and Roman literature. Byzantine scholars valued classical literature because they regarded it as the basis of a high-level education. Many of the classical works available today survived because they served as school texts in the eastern empire. A basic knowledge of famous pre-Christian classics was a requirement for a good career in government service, the goal of most ambitious students. In the words of an imperial decree from the fourth century, "No person shall obtain a post of the first rank unless it shall be shown that he excels in long practice of liberal studies, and that he is so polished in literary matters that words flow from his pen faultlessly."

The use of ancient rhetoric to present Christian theology also helped classical literature survive. When Ambrose, bishop of Milan in the fourth century, composed the first systematic description of Christian ethics for young priests, he imitated the great classical orator Cicero. Theologians employed the dialogue form pioneered by Plato to refute Christian heresies, and polytheist traditions in writing biography influenced the hugely popular Christian literature of saints' lives. Similarly, Christian artists used polytheist traditions to communicate their beliefs in paintings, mosaics, and carved reliefs. Artists showing Christ with a sunburst surrounding his head, for example, took their inspiration from polytheist depictions of the radiant sun as a god (see the illustration on page 206).

A technological innovation also helped preserve classical texts. Previously, scribes had written books on sheets made from thin animal skin or paper made from papyrus, gluing the sheets together and attaching rods at both ends to form scrolls. Readers had to unroll the scrolls to read them. For ease of use, Christians produced their literature in the form of codices, books with bound pages; codices (the plural of *codex*) became the standard form of book production in the Byzantine world. Because codices were less subject to damage from rolling and unrolling and could contain text more efficiently than scrolls, which were inefficient for long works, they aided the preservation of all forms of literature.

Despite the continuing importance of classical Greek and Latin literature in Byzantine education and rhetoric, its survival remained uncertain in a war-torn world governed by Christians. Knowledge of Greek in the transformed west faded so dramatically that almost no one could read the original versions of Homer's *Iliad* and *Odyssey*, the traditional foundations of a polytheist literary education. Latin fared better, and scholars such as Augustine and Jerome knew Rome's ancient literature extremely well. But they also saw its classics as too seductive because the pleasure of reading them could distract Christians from worshipping God. Jerome once had a nightmare of being condemned on Judgment Day for having been a Ciceronian instead of a Christian.

The closing around 530 of Plato's Academy, founded in Athens more than nine hundred years earlier, demonstrated the dangers for classical learning in the Byzantine world. This most famous of classical schools finally shut its doors when many of its scholars moved to Persia to escape restrictions on polytheists and its revenues dwindled because the Athenian elite, its traditional supporters, were increasingly Christianized. The Neoplatonist school at Alexandria, by contrast, continued. Its leader in the late sixth century, John Philoponus, was a Christian. In addition to Christian theology, Philoponus wrote commentaries on Aristotle's works. Some of his ideas anticipated those of Galileo a thousand years later. His work achieved the kind of blending of old and new that was one fruitful possibility of the transformation of the late Roman world—that is, he was a Christian subject of the Byzantine Empire in Egypt, heading a school founded long before by polytheists, studying the works of an ancient Greek philosopher as the inspiration for his innovative scholarship.

The tradition that the present should learn from the past would continue as Western civilization once again remade itself in medieval times.

REVIEW   What role did the emperor Justinian see himself playing in Roman history?

Conclusion

The Roman Empire splintered for reasons that no emperor was strong enough to overcome, once the finances of the state became too small to cover the expenses of defense against barbarian migrations and attacks. The vast size of the empire,

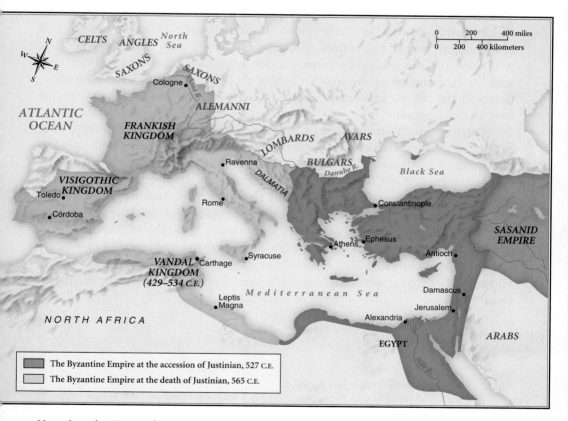

Mapping the West The Byzantine Empire and Western Europe, c. 600
Justinian employed brilliant generals and spent huge sums of money to reconquer Italy, North Africa, and part of Spain to reunite the western and eastern halves of the old Roman Empire. His wars to regain Italy and North Africa eliminated the Ostrogothic and Vandal kingdoms, respectively, but at a huge cost in effort, time (the war in Italy took twenty years), and expense. The resources of the eastern empire were so exhausted that following emperors could not maintain the reunification. By the early seventh century, the Visigoths had taken back all of Spain. Africa, despite serious revolts by local Berber tribes, remained under imperial control until the Arab conquest of the seventh century, but within five years of Justinian's death, the Lombards set up a new kingdom that controlled a large section of Italy. Never again would anyone attempt to reestablish a universal Roman Empire. Compare the political divisions on this map with those on the map at the end of Chapter 5 (page 192) showing Roman territory more than three centuries earlier.

a source of pride to Romans, was a double-edged sword because the length and distance of its frontiers made national defense expensive and difficult, and the traditional Roman desire for glory meant that pulling back voluntarily was not an option. Peoples outside the empire increasingly wanted to immigrate to live inside its territory, so as to share in its relative peace and prosperity.

In building their empire originally, Romans had made it stronger by absorbing outsiders and turning them into productive citizens. The emperors of the late Roman Empire failed to find a way to continue this policy, and the immigrants whom they mistreated or blocked eventually overwhelmed the western empire, so strong was the outsiders' motivation to flee danger in their homelands and find a better life in Roman lands. The barbarians who migrated into the empire from the north transformed themselves politically and changed life in the western half of the empire forever by combining Roman and non-Roman traditions, but they, too, failed to keep the peace, often warring with each other. The political and social transformation of the western half of the Roman Empire that some historians call the fall of the Roman Empire brought violence and uncertainty to the lives of many people.

Religion, which previously had been a force for unity in the Roman world, became a source of division and conflict in the later Roman Empire, both between pagans and Christians and between Christians and Christians. In the past, some scholars argued that Christian beliefs weakened the empire by lessening people's devotion to the state and its defense in favor of devotion to God. In truth, Christian emperors and armies fought just as ferociously as had the polytheistic military of earlier centuries. Moreover, the growing hierarchy of the church cooperated with the political rulers to try to keep social stability. If Christianity weakened the empire, it was because Christians disagreed so sincerely and so violently about what was religious truth that they had trouble cooperating in troubled times.

TIMELINE

- **325** Council of Nicaea
- **324** Constantine refounds Byzantium as Constantinople, the "new Rome"
- **c. 323** Pachomius in Upper Egypt establishes the first monasteries for men and women

- **440s** Anglo-Saxons take over Roman Britain
- **429** Vandals capture Roman North Africa after invading Spain
- **410** Visigoths sack Rome

- **c. 530** Plato's Academy in Athens clos
- **507** Clovis establishe Frankish kingdom in G

| 280 C.E. | 365 C.E. | 450 C.E. | 535 C.E |

- **284** Diocletian becomes Roman emperor
- **303** Diocletian begins Great Persecution of Christians
- **312** Constantine wins the battle of the Milvian Bridge in Rome and converts to Christianity

- **391** Theodosius bans polytheist sacrifice and closes the temples of traditional Roman religion
- **395** Roman Empire splits into western and eastern sections

- **451** Council of Chalcedon
- **476** "Fall of the Roman Empire" when the barbarian commander Odoacer deposes the final western emperor, Romulus Augustulus

Whatever the effect of the growth of Christianity on the Roman Empire might have been, its effect on later history is clear and huge. The conversion of Emperor Constantine to Christianity changed the course of the world, a change whose effects dominated the history of the Roman Empire from his time to that of Emperor Justinian, who spared no expense to try to fulfill the eastern empire's self-identified role as the heir to Rome's glory and the guardian of Rome's traditions. But not even Justinian's uncontrolled spending of the Byzantine Empire's money could hold the ancient Roman Empire together. A new European world was on the way, and its birth would be bloody.

> **CHAPTER REVIEW QUESTIONS**
> 1. What similarities existed between traditional Roman religion and Christianity as the official state religion?
> 2. Compare the fates of the eastern and western empires after they split apart.

For practice quizzes and other study tools, see the Online Study Guide at bedfordstmartins.com/huntconcise.

For primary-source material from this period, see Chapter 7 of *Sources of THE MAKING OF THE WEST,* Third Edition.

Suggested References

Recent research has deepened our appreciation of the complexity of the religious transformation of the Roman Empire and the emotional depths that the process stirred up for polytheists and Christians.

Brown, Peter. *The Body and Society: Men, Women, and Sexual Renunciation in Early Christianity.* 1988.

Byzantine Empire: http://www.fordham.edu/halsall/byzantium/

*Drew, Katherine Fischer, ed. *The Laws of the Salian Franks.* 1991.

Elsner, Jas. *Imperial Rome and Christian Triumph: The Art of the Roman Empire,* A.D. 100–450. 1998.

*Grubbs, Judith Evans. *Women and Law in the Roman Empire: A Sourcebook on Marriage, Divorce, and Widowhood.* 2002.

Halsall, Guy. *Barbarian Migrations and the Roman West.* 2007.

Heather, Peter. *The Fall of the Roman Empire.* 2005.

*Lee, A. D. *Pagans and Christians in Late Antiquity: A Sourcebook.* 2000.

Little, Lester K., ed. *Plague and the End of Antiquity: The Pandemic of 541–750.* 2006.

MacMullen, Ramsay. *Christianity and Paganism in the Fourth to Eighth Centuries.* 1997.

Odahl, Charles. *Constantine and the Christian Empire.* 2d ed. 2006.

Southern, Pat, and Karen R. Dixon. *The Late Roman Army.* 1996.

Islam, Byzantium, and the West

I N THE EIGHTH CENTURY, a Syrian monk named Joshua wrote about the first appearance of Islam in Roman territory: "The Arabs conquered the land of Palestine and the land as far as the great river Euphrates. The Romans fled," he marveled, then continued:

> The first king was a man among them named Muhammad, whom they also called Prophet because he turned them away from cults of all kinds and taught them that there was only one God, creator of the universe. He also instituted laws for them because they were much entangled in the worship of demons.

Dome of the Rock at Jerusalem
Rivaling the great churches of Christendom, the building in Jerusalem called the Dome of the Rock, built in 691, borrowed from late Roman and Byzantine forms even while asserting its Islamic identity. The columns and the capitals atop them, the round arches, the dome, and the mosaics are all from Byzantine models. But the strips of Arabic writing on the dome itself—and in many other parts of the building—assert Islamic doctrine.
(Erich Lessing/Art Resource, NY.)

Joshua was wrong about Muhammad leading the conquest of Palestine—Muhammad died in 632, six years before the fall of Palestine. But he was right to see the Arab movement as a momentous development. In the course of a few decades the Arabs conquered much of the Persian and Roman empires. Joshua was also right to emphasize Muhammad's teachings. It was the fervor of Islam that brought the Arabs out of Arabia and into the regions that hugged the Mediterranean in one direction and led to the Indus River in the other.

In the sixth century, as the western and eastern parts of the Roman Empire went their separate ways, a third power—Arab and Muslim—was taking shape. These three powers have continued in various forms to the present day. The western Roman Empire became today's western Europe. The eastern Roman Empire became Turkey, Greece, and some of eastern Europe, and it played a key role in shaping Russia. The Arab world endures in North Africa and the Middle East.

These diverse cultures share many of the same roots. All were heirs of Hellenistic and Roman traditions. All adhered to monotheism. The western and eastern halves of the Roman Empire had Christianity in common, although they differed at times

237

in interpreting it. Adherents of Islam, the Arab world's religion, believed in the same God as the Jews and Christians. They understood Jesus, however, as God's prophet rather than his son.

The history of the seventh and eighth centuries is a story of adaptation and transformation. Historians consider the changes in this period so remarkable that they speak of the end of one era—antiquity—and the beginning of another—the Middle Ages. They also find the changes in the eastern half of the Roman Empire so important that they use a new term—Byzantium or the Byzantine Empire, from the old Greek name for the city of Constantinople—to describe it.

During the period 600–750, the Islamic, Byzantine, and Western worlds combined elements of their ancient heritage with new values, interests, and conditions. The divergences among them resulted from disparities in geography and climate, material and human resources, skills, beliefs, and local traditions. But these differences should not obscure their fundamental similarities.

CHAPTER FOCUS QUESTION   What three cultures took the place of the Roman Empire, and to what extent did each of them both draw on and reject Roman traditions?

Islam: A New Religion and a New Empire

Islam, which means "submission to God" in Arabic, called for all believers to submit to the will of one God. It demanded a revolutionary change from the many warring tribes that populated the Arabian peninsula: unification into one community.

The first to teach Islam was Muhammad, a merchant turned holy man from the Arabian city of Mecca, a major oasis near the Red Sea. Many gods were worshipped in Arabia, but Muhammad recognized only one God, that of the Jews and Christians. He saw himself as God's last prophet, receiving and in turn repeating God's final words to humans. Invited by the city of Medina to come and mediate disputes, Muhammad exercised the powers of both a religious and a secular leader there. This dual role became the model for his successors, known as caliphs. Through a combination of persuasion and force, Muhammad and his coreligionists, the Muslims, converted most of the Arabian peninsula. By the time he died in 632, Islamic conquest and conversion had begun to move northward into Byzantine and Persian territories. In the next generation, the Muslims took over most of Persia and all of Egypt and were on their way across North Africa to Spain. Yet within the regions they conquered with such lightning speed, daily life went on much as before.

The Rise and Development of Islam, c. 610–632

In the seventh century, the Arabian peninsula was populated by both sedentary and nomadic peoples. By far the larger group was sedentary—people who lived in one place. Some were farmers; others lived in oases, where they raised dates (a highly prized food). Some oases were prosperous enough to support merchants and artisans.

The smaller group, the nomads (known as Bedouins), moved from place to place in the desert. They herded goats, sheep, or camels, and they survived largely from the products (leather, milk, and meat) of their animals. Warriors, the Bedouins raided one another for goods and women, valuing their honor highly and prizing bravery and generosity as well. Lacking written literature, they were proud of their oral culture of storytelling and poetry.

Islam began as a religion of the sedentary peoples, but it soon found support and military strength among the nomads. It began in Mecca, a major oasis and commercial center. More important, Mecca was also a religious center, home to a shrine called the Ka'ba, which contained the images of many gods. At the Ka'ba, war and violence among the various tribes that worshipped there were prohibited. The tribe that dominated Mecca, the Quraysh, controlled access to the shrine. The Quraysh taxed the pilgrims who flocked there and sold them food and drink. Visitors, assured of their security, bartered on the sacred grounds, transforming goods seized in raids into commodities of trade.

Mecca was the birthplace of Muhammad (c. 570–632). His early years were unpromising: orphaned at the age of six, he spent two years with his grandfather and then came under the care of his uncle, a leader of the Quraysh tribe. Eventually, Muhammad became a trader. At the age of twenty-five, he married Khadija, a rich widow who had once employed him. They had at least four daughters and lived (to all appearances) happily and comfortably. Yet Muhammad sometimes left home to spend time in a nearby cave in prayer and contemplation, practicing a type of piety similar to that of early Christians.

In about 610, on one such retreat, Muhammad heard a voice calling him to worship Allah, the God of the Jews and Christians. (*Allah* means "the God" in Arabic.) He accepted the call as coming from God. Over the next years he received messages that he understood to be divine revelation. Later, when they had been written down and arranged—a process that was completed in the seventh century, after Muhammad's death—these messages became the Qur'an, the holy book of Islam. The Qur'an, which means "recitation," is understood to be God's revelation as told to Muhammad by the angel Gabriel, then recited by Muhammad to others. It starts with the Fatihah, which is frequently also said as an independent prayer beginning as follows:

Arabia in Muhammad's Lifetime

> In the name of God
> The Compassionate the Caring
> Praise be to God.

Qur'an
More than a "holy book," the Qur'an represents the very words of God. Usually the text appeared on pages wider than they were long, perhaps to differentiate the Qur'an from other books. This particular example dates from the seventh or eighth century. It is written in Kufic script, a formal and majestic form of Arabic that scribes used for the Qur'an until the eleventh century. The round floral decoration on the right-hand page marks a new section of the text. (Copyright Biblioteca Ambrosiana.)

It continues with sections, or suras, of gradually decreasing length. These cover all of human experience and the life to come. For Muslims (literally, "those who submit to Islam") the Qur'an contains the foundations of history, prophecy, and the legal and moral code by which men and women should live.

The Qur'an emphasizes the nuclear family—a man, his wife, and their children—as the basic unit of Muslim society. Islam replaced the identity and protection of the tribe with a new identity: the ***ummah***, the community of believers who share both a belief in one God and a set of religious practices.

Stressing individual belief in God and adherence to the Qur'an, Islam has no priests or sacraments, although in time it came to have authoritative religious leaders who interpreted the Qur'an and related texts. The Ka'ba, with its many gods, had attracted numerous tribes from the surrounding area. Muhammad, with his one God, forged an even more universal religion.

The first to convert to Muhammad's faith were his wife, Khadija, and a few friends and members of his immediate family. Muhammad's insistence that the cults of other gods be abandoned in favor of one God brought him into conflict with leading members of the Quraysh, however, whose control over the Ka'ba had given them wealth and prestige. They insulted Muhammad and harassed his adherents.

Disillusioned with the people of Mecca, Muhammad looked elsewhere for groups that would be more receptive to his message. In particular, he expected support from Jews, whose monotheism, in Muhammad's view, prepared them for his own faith. When a few of Muhammad's converts from Medina promised to protect him if he joined them there, he eagerly accepted the invitation, in part because

Medina had a significant Jewish population. In 622, Muhammad immigrated to Medina, an oasis about two hundred miles north of Mecca. This journey, known as the Hijra, proved to be a crucial event for the new movement. At Medina, Muhammad found people ready to listen to his religious message and to regard him as the leader of their community. They expected him to act as a neutral and impartial judge in their interclan disputes. Muhammad's political position in the community set the pattern by which Islamic society would be governed thereafter: rather than simply adding a church to political and cultural life, Muslims made their political and religious institutions inseparable. After Muhammad's death, the year of the Hijra was named the first year of the Islamic calendar; it marks the beginning of the new Islamic era.*

Although successful in Medina, the Muslims felt threatened by the Quraysh in Mecca, who actively opposed the public practice of Islam. For this reason, Muhammad led raids against them. At the battle of Badr in 624, Muhammad and his followers killed forty-nine of the Meccan enemy, took numerous prisoners, and confiscated rich booty. In this way, traditional Bedouin plundering was grafted onto the Muslim duty of jihad.**

The battle of Badr was a great triumph for Muhammad, who was now able to consolidate his position at Medina, gaining new adherents and silencing doubters. The Jews at Medina had not converted to Islam as Muhammad had expected, however. Suspecting them of supporting his enemies, he expelled two Jewish tribes from Medina and executed the male members of another. Although Muslims had originally prayed in the direction of Jerusalem, the center of Jewish worship, Muhammad now had them turn in the direction of Mecca.

At the same time, Muhammad instituted new practices to define Islam as a unique religion. Among these were the *zakat*, a tax on possessions to be used for alms; the fast of Ramadan, which takes place during the ninth month of the Islamic year, the month in which the battle of Badr was fought; the *hajj*, an annual pilgrimage to Mecca that each Muslim is to try to accomplish at least once in his or her lifetime; and the *salat*, formal worship at least three times a day (later increased to five), which might include the *shahadah*, or profession of faith: "There is no god but God, and Muhammad is his Messenger." Detailed regulations for these practices, sometimes called the five pillars of Islam, were worked out in the eighth and early ninth centuries.

Meanwhile, the fierce rivalry between Mecca's tribes and Medina's Muslims began to spill over into the rest of the Arabian peninsula as both sides strove to win converts. Muhammad sent troops to subdue Arabs north and south. In 630, he

---

*Thus 1 A.H. (1 *anno Hegirae*, "year of the Hijra") on the Muslim calendar is equivalent to 622 C.E. on the Christian calendar.

**Jihad* means "striving" and is used in particular in the context of striving against unbelievers. In that sense, it is often translated as "holy war." But it can also mean striving against one's own worst impulses.

Map 7.1 Expansion of Islam, to 750
In little more than a century, Islamic armies conquered a vast region that included numerous different peoples, cultures, climates, and living conditions. Under the Umayyads, these disparate territories were administered by one ruler from his capital at Damascus. The uniting force was the religion of Islam itself, which gathered all believers into one community, the *ummah*.

entered Mecca with ten thousand men and took over the city, assuring the Quraysh of leniency and offering alliances with tribal leaders. By this time, the prestige of Islam was enough to convince tribes elsewhere to convert. Through a combination of force, conversion, and negotiation, Muhammad was able to unite many, though by no means all, Arabic-speaking tribes under his leadership by the time of his death two years later (Map 7.1).

Muhammad transformed Arab society. As Muhammad's converts "submitted" to Islam, they formed not a tribe but rather a community bound together by the worship of God. Women were accepted into this community, and their status was enhanced. Islam prohibited infanticide, the practice of killing unwanted babies, which had long been used largely against female infants. Men were allowed to have up to four wives at one time, but they were obliged to treat them equally. Wives received dowries and had certain inheritance rights. At first, Muslim women joined men during the salat. Beginning in the eighth century, however, women began to pray apart from men. Like Judaism and Christianity, Islam retained the practices of the patriarchal society in which it arose; women's participation in community life was limited.

Even though Islamic society was a new sort of community, in many ways it functioned as a tribe, or rather a "supertribe," obligated to fight common enemies, share plunder, and resolve peacefully any internal disputes. Muslims participated in group rituals, such as the salat and public recitations. The Qur'an was soon publicly sung by professional reciters, much as the old tribal poetry had been. Most significant for the eventual spread of Islam, Muslim men were warriors, and their armies reaped profits at the point of the sword. But this warfare differed from intertribal fighting; it was the "striving" (jihad) of people who were carrying out the injunction of God against unbelievers. "Strive, O Prophet," says the Qur'an, "against the unbelievers and the hypocrites, and deal with them firmly. Their final abode is Hell: And what a wretched destination!"

Muhammad's Successors, 632–750

Following his death, Muhammad's successors, the caliphs, conquered much of the Roman and Persian worlds. To the west, the Muslims attacked Byzantine territory in Syria with ease and moved into Egypt in the 640s (Map 7.1, page 242). To the east, they invaded the **Sasanid Empire**, defeating the Persians at the gates of their capital, Ctesiphon, in 637. All of Persia was in Muslim hands by 661. During the last half of the seventh century and the beginning of the eighth, Islamic rule extended from Spain to India. How were such conquests possible, especially in so short a time? First, Islamic forces came up against weakened empires. The Byzantine and Sasanid states were exhausted from fighting each other. The cities of the Middle East that had been taken by the Persians and retaken by the Byzantines were depopulated, their few survivors burdened with heavy taxes. Second, the Muslims were welcomed into both Byzantine and Sasanid territories by discontented groups. Many Monophysite Christians in Syria and Egypt, for example, had suffered persecution by the Byzantines and were glad to have new, Islamic overlords.

These were the external reasons for Islamic success. There were also internal reasons. Arabs had long been used to intertribal warfare; now, under the banner of jihad, Muslims exercised their skills as warriors not against one another but rather against unbelievers. Fully armed, on horseback, and employing camels in convoys, they seemed almost a force of nature. Where they conquered, the Muslims built garrison cities, from which soldiers requisitioned taxes and goods. Sometimes whole Arab tribes, including women and children, were imported to settle conquered territory, as happened in parts of Syria. In other regions, a small Muslim settlement, such as the one at Fustat in Egypt, sufficed to gather the spoils of conquest.

These successes hid tensions that developed within the Muslim leadership. Muhammad's death in 632 marked a crisis in the government of the new Islamic state, as different groups sought to promote their own successors. The first caliphs came not from the traditional tribal elite but from a new inner circle of men close to Muhammad and participants in the Hijra. The first two caliphs ruled without serious opposition, but the third, Uthman (r. 644–656), a member of the Umayyad

Arab Coin

The Arabs learned coinage and minting from the Persians and Byzantines whom they conquered. Although one branch of Islam barred depicting the human form, others were less condemning. Thus the Umayyads saw nothing wrong with imitating traditional coinage. The ruler depicted on this silver coin is wearing a headdress that echoes the one worn by the Sasanid ruler depicted on page 248. But the name of this type of coin, *dirham*, was not Persian but Greek, from *drachma*. The Umayyad fiscal system retained the old Roman land tax and was administered by Syrians, who had served Byzantine rulers in the same capacity.
(© Copyright, The Trustees of the British Museum.)

family and one of Muhammad's sons-in-law, aroused discontent among other clan members of the inner circle. They supported Uthman's rival, Ali, the husband of Muhammad's daughter Fatimah. When discontented soldiers murdered Uthman, civil war broke out between the Umayyads and Ali's faction. It ended in 661 when Ali was killed by one of his former supporters. The caliphate remained in Umayyad hands from 661 to 750.

Nevertheless, the *Shi'at Ali* (the faction of Ali) did not fade away. Ali's memory lived on among Shi'ite Muslims, who saw in him a symbol of justice and righteousness. For them, Ali's death was the martyrdom of the only true successor to Muhammad. They remained faithful to his dynasty, shunning the caliphs of the other Muslims (Sunni Muslims, as they were later called, from *Sunna,* the practices of Muhammad). The Shi'ites awaited the arrival of the true leader, the imam, who in their view could come only from the house of Ali. The Sunni-Shi'ite split remains a religious and political fact today.

Under the **Umayyad caliphate**, the Muslim world became a state, with its capital at Damascus. Borrowing from the institutions of the civilizations they had conquered, the Muslims issued coins and hired former Byzantine and Persian officials. They made Arabic a tool of centralization, imposing it as the official language on regions not previously united linguistically. Even so, the Islamic world was startlingly multiethnic. It included Arabs, Syrians, Egyptians, Iraqis, and other peoples. It was also multireligious, since Muslims tolerated other "people of the book" (meaning the Bible)—Jews and Christians of every sort. For many of these non-Muslims, the Muslim conquests brought a period of new settlement, urbanism, and literary and artistic flowering.

Peace and Prosperity in Islamic Lands

Ironically, the Islamic warriors brought peace. While the conquerors stayed within their fortified cities or built magnificent hunting lodges in the deserts of Syria, the conquered went back to work, to study, to play, and—in the case of Christians and

Jews, who were considered "protected subjects"—to worship as they pleased in return for the payment of a special tax. At Damascus, local artists and craftspeople worked on the lavish decorations for a mosque using Roman motifs. At Jerusalem, the shrine called the Dome of the Rock used Christian building models for its octagonal form and its interior arches (see the illustration on page 236).

During the seventh and eighth centuries, Muslim scholars wrote down the hitherto largely oral Arabic literature. They determined the definitive form for the Qur'an and compiled pious narratives about Muhammad, called hadith literature. Scribes wrote these works in exquisite calligraphy, handwriting that was also an art form. A literate class, composed mainly of the old Persian and Syrian elite who had now converted to Islam, created new forms of prose writing in Arabic. Employed as civil servants, they composed official documents for their new rulers. They also wrote essays on topics ranging from hunting to ruling. Umayyad poetry explored new worlds of thought and feeling. Patronized by the caliphs, who found in written poetry an important source of propaganda and a buttress for their power, the poets also reached a wider audience that delighted in their clever use of words, their satire, and their invocations of courage, piety, and sometimes erotic love:

> I spent the night as her bed-companion, each enamored of the other,
> And I made her laugh and cry, and stripped her of her clothes.
> I played with her and she vanquished me;
> I made her happy and I angered her.
> That was a night we spent, in my sleep, playing and joyful,
> But the caller to prayer woke me up.

Such poetry scandalized conservative Muslims, brought up on the sober tenets of the Qur'an. But this love poetry was a by-product of the new urban civilization of the Umayyad period, where wealth, cultural mix, and the confidence born of conquest inspired diverse and experimental literary forms. By the time the Umayyad caliphate ended in 750, Islamic civilization was multiethnic, urban, and sophisticated, a true heir of Roman and Persian traditions.

REVIEW How and why did the Muslims conquer so many lands in the relatively short period from 632 to 750?

Byzantium: A Christian Empire under Siege

While Islam was incorporating bits of Rome into its new empire, the Byzantines imagined that they were the continuators of Rome. Emperor Justinian (r. 527–565; (see page 227) had tried to re-create the old Roman Empire by conquest. On the surface he had succeeded. His empire once again included Italy, North Africa, and the Balkans. Vestiges of old Roman society persisted: an educated elite maintained its prestige, town governments continued to function, and old myths and legends were retold in poetry and depicted on silver plates and chests. By 600, however, the eastern empire had begun to undergo a transformation as striking as the one that had earlier remade the western empire. Historians call this reorganized empire the Byzantine Empire, or Byzantium.

From the last third of the sixth century, Byzantium was almost constantly at war, and its territory shrank drastically. Cultural and political change came as well. Cities—except for a few such as Constantinople—decayed, and the countryside became the focus of government and military administration. Following these shifts, the old elite largely disappeared, and classical learning gave way to new forms of education, mainly religious in content. The traditional styles of urban life, dependent on public gathering places and community spirit, faded away.

Wars on the Frontiers, c. 570–750

From about 570 to 750, the Byzantine Empire waged war against invaders on all fronts. Its first major challenge came from the east, from the Sasanid Empire of Persia. Its second came from new groups—Lombards, Slavs, Avars, Bulgars, and Muslims—who pushed into the empire. In the wake of these onslaughts, Byzantium was transformed.

The Persian challenge was the most predictable. Since the third century, the Sasanid kings and Roman emperors had fought sporadically but never with decisive effect on either side. In the middle of the sixth century, however, the Sasanids chose to concentrate their activities on the western half of their empire, Mesopotamia (today Iraq), nearer the Byzantine border (Map 7.2). Reforming the army, which previously had depended on nobles who could provide their own weapons, the Sasanid kings began to pay and arm new warriors drawn from the lower nobility. With the army more fully their own, the kings tried to re-create the Persian Empire of Darius and Xerxes (see page 48). Under Chosroes II (r. 591–628), the Persians invaded the Byzantine Empire in 603. By 613, they had taken Damascus; by 619, they dominated Egypt. In response, the Byzantine emperor Heraclius (r. 610–641) reorganized his army and by 627 had regained the lost territory. The chief outcome of these confrontations was the exhaustion of both sides.

The Byzantines could ill afford this weakness. From every side, new groups were pushing into their empire. The Lombards, a Germanic people, arrived in northern Italy in 568 and by 572 were masters of the Po valley and some inland regions in Italy's south, leaving the Byzantines only Bari, Calabria, and Sicily, as well as Rome and a narrow swath of land through Italy's middle called the Exarchate of Ravenna.

The Byzantines were equally weak in the face of the Slavs, Bulgars, and Avars just beyond the Danube River. The Slavs conducted lightning raids on the Balkan countryside (part of Byzantium at the time). Joined by the Avars—nomadic pastoralists and warriors—they attacked Byzantine cities as well. The Bulgars, entering what is now Bulgaria in the 670s, defeated the Byzantine army and in 681 forced the emperor to recognize the state they had carved out of formerly Byzantine territory. This Bulgar state crippled Byzantine influence in the Balkans and helped

Map 7.2 The Byzantine and Sasanid Empires, c. 600
Justinian hoped to re-create the old Roman Empire, but just a century after his death, Italy was largely conquered by the Lombards. Meanwhile, the Byzantine Empire had to contend with the Sasanid Empire to its east. In 600, these two major powers faced each other uneasily. Three years later, the Sasanid king invaded Byzantine territory. The resulting wars, which lasted until 627, exhausted both empires and left them open to invasion by the Arabs. By 700, the Byzantine Empire was quite small. Compare the inset map here with Map 7.1 (page 242). Where had the Muslims made significant conquests of Byzantine territory?

isolate Byzantium from western Europe. Avar and Slavic control of the Balkans effectively cut off trade and travel between Constantinople and the cities of the Dalmatian coast, and the Bulgar state threw a political barrier across the Danube River. Perhaps as a result of this physical separation, Byzantine historians ceased to be interested in the West, and eastern scholars no longer bothered to learn Latin. The two halves of the Roman Empire, once united, communicated very little in the seventh century.

While fighting these groups on their northern frontier, the Byzantines at the same time had to contend with the Arabs, whose military prowess was creating a new empire and spreading the new religion of Islam. In the hundred years between 630 and 730, Muslim armies succeeded in conquering much of the Byzantine Empire, at times attacking the walls of Constantinople itself. No wonder the patriarch of Jerusalem, chief bishop of the entire Levant, saw in the Arab onslaught the impending end of the world. "Behold," he said, "the Abomination of Desolation, spoken of by the Prophet Daniel, that stands in the Holy Place."

A Sasanid King

With its mighty horned headdress, this sixth- or seventh-century representation of a Sasanid ruler evokes the full majesty of a king of kings. A glance at The Great King of Persia on page 27 shows that traditional Persian sculpture was not, as here, three-dimensional. The new style is explained by the influence of Greek and Roman sculpture, despite the enmity between Sasanid Persia and Byzantium (heir of Greece and Rome) at the time. **For more help analyzing this image, see the visual activity for this chapter in the Online Study Guide at** bedfordstmartins.com/huntconcise. (Réunion des Musées Nationaux/Art Resource, NY.)

From an Urban to a Rural Way of Life

As Byzantine borders shrank, Byzantines in the conquered regions had to adjust to new rulers, while the rulers in turn accommodated their new subjects. Former Byzantines in Syria and Egypt who came under Arab rule adapted readily to their conquerors, paying them a special tax but practicing their Christian and Jewish religions in peace. In the cities, they continued practicing their professions in government, scholarship, and business; in the countryside, they stayed on their land and continued to farm. The Balkans experienced greater changes when Slavs and Bulgars came to dominate the peninsula: most cities disappeared, and local populations fled as the newcomers installed themselves on the land. Soon, however, the newcomers recognized the Byzantine emperor's authority, and they began to flirt with Christianity.

Some of the most radical transformations in seventh- and eighth-century Byzantine life occurred not in the conquered territories but in the shrunken empire itself. Under the ceaseless barrage of invaders, many towns, formerly bustling centers of trade and the imperial bureaucracy, vanished or became unrecognizable. The public activities of marketplaces, theaters, and town squares gave way to the private pursuits of table and hearth. Public baths, where people had once gossiped, made deals, and talked politics and philosophy, disappeared in most Byzantine towns—with the significant exception of Constantinople. Warfare reduced some cities to rubble, and when they were rebuilt, the limited resources available went to construct thick defensive walls and solid churches instead of large open marketplaces and baths. Markets moved to overcrowded streets that looked much like the open-air bazaars of the modern Middle East. People under siege sought

The Byzantine Empire, c. 700

protection at home or in churches and avoided public activities. In the Byzantine city of Ephesus, for example, citizens who built the new walls in the seventh century enclosed not the old public edifices but rather their homes and churches (Map 7.3).

Despite the general urban decay, Constantinople and a few other urban centers retained some of their old vitality. The manufacture and trade of fine silk textiles continued. Even though Byzantium's economic life became increasingly rural and barter based in the seventh and eighth centuries, the skills, knowledge, and institutions of urban workers remained. Centuries of devastating wars, however, prevented full use of these resources until after 750.

The social world of this shrunken Byzantium was small and local. Unlike Europe, where a rich and powerful elite dominated the agricultural economy, the Byzantine Empire of the seventh century was principally a realm of free and semi-free peasant farmers. They grew food, herded cattle, and tended vineyards on small plots of land. Farmers interacted mostly with members of their families or with monks at local monasteries; two or three neighbors were enough to ratify a land transfer. As Byzantine cities declined, the class of town councilors (curials), the elite who for centuries had mediated between the emperor and the people, disappeared. Now, on those occasions when farmers came into contact with the state—to

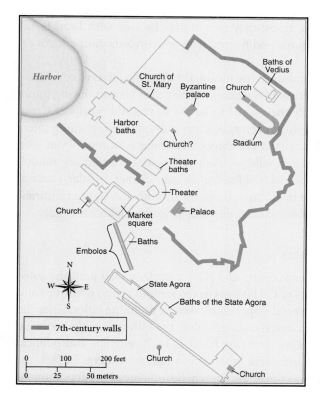

Map 7.3 Diagram of the City of Ephesus
Before the seventh century, Ephesus sprawled around its harbor. Nearest the harbor were baths and churches, including by 500 the bishop's church of St. Mary. To the south was the Embolos—a long, marble-paved avenue adorned with fountains, statues, and arcades and bordered by well-appointed homes. The earthquakes, plague, and invasions of the seventh century changed much. A seventh-century wall embraced the area around the harbor. The Embolos was neglected, and even within the narrow precinct protected by the new wall, baths were allowed to go to ruin, while people made their homes amid the debris. After the Arabs invaded, the bishop moved out of the city altogether.

pay taxes, for example—they felt the impact of the emperor or his representatives directly. There were no local protectors any longer.

Emperors, drawing on the still vigorous Roman legal tradition, promoted local, domestic life with imperial legislation. New laws strengthened the nuclear family by narrowing the grounds for divorce and setting new punishments for marital infidelity. Husbands and wives who committed adultery were whipped and fined, and their noses were slit. Abortion was prohibited, and new protections were set in place against incest with children. Mothers were given equal power with fathers over their offspring; if widowed, they became the legal guardians of their minor children and controlled the household property.

The shift from an urban-centered society to a rural way of life not only changed Byzantine social life and the economy but also affected the empire's military and cultural institutions. The Byzantine navy fought successfully at sea with its powerful weapon of "Greek fire," a mixture of crude oil and resin that was heated and projected via a tube over the water, where it burned and engulfed enemy ships. Determined to win wars on land as well, the imperial government tightened its control over the military by wresting power from other elite families and encouraging the formation of a middle class of farmer-soldiers.

In the seventh century, an emperor, possibly Heraclius, divided the empire into military districts called *themes* and put all civil as well as military matters in each district into the hands of one general. Landless men were lured to join the army with the promise of land and low taxes; they fought side by side with local farmers, who provided their own weapons and horses. The new organization effectively countered frontier attacks.

The disappearance of the old cultural elite meant a shift in the focus of education. Whereas the upper classes had cultivated the study of the pagan classics, hiring tutors or sending their children (primarily their sons) to school to read the works of Greek poets and philosophers, eighth-century parents of every class showed far more interest in giving their children, both sons and daughters, a religious education. Even with the decay of urban centers, cities and villages often retained an elementary school. There teachers used the Book of Psalms (the Psalter) as their primer. Secular, classical learning remained decidedly out of favor throughout the seventh and eighth centuries. Dogmatic writings, biographies of saints, and devotional works took center stage.

Religion, Politics, and Iconoclasm

The importance placed on religious learning and piety complemented both the autocratic imperial ideal and the powers of the bishops in the seventh century. Bishops and their clergy formed a rich and powerful upper class, even in declining cities. Since the spiritual and secular realms were considered inseparable, the bishops wielded political power in their cities, while Byzantine emperors ruled as both religious and political figures. In theory, empire and church were separate but interdependent. In fact, the emperor exercised considerable power over the church: he influenced the appointment of the chief religious official, the patriarch of Constantinople; he called church councils to determine dogma; and he regularly used bishops as local governors.

Bishops functioned as state administrators in their cities. They served as judges and tax collectors. They distributed food in times of famine or siege, provisioned troops, and set up military fortifications. As part of their charitable work, they cared for the sick and the needy. Theoretically, monasteries were under their control. In fact, however, monasteries were enormously powerful institutions that often defied the authority of bishops and even emperors. Because monks commanded immense prestige as the holiest of God's faithful, they could influence the many issues of church doctrine that shook the Byzantine church. Icons, which the monks supported, became the flash point of these controversies.

Icons are images of holy people—Christ, his mother (Mary), and the saints. To Byzantine Christians, icons were far more than mere representations; they were believed to possess holy power that directly affected people's daily lives as well as their chances for salvation. Many seventh-century Byzantines made icons the focus of their religious devotion. To them, the images were like the incarnation of divinity. Icons turned spirit into material substance by manifesting in physical form the holy person they depicted. Many Byzantines, especially monks, considered icons a necessary part of Christian piety.

Other Byzantines, however, detested icons. This was especially true of soldiers on the frontiers.

Icon of St. Peter
In this icon, produced by a Byzantine artist in the first half of the seventh century, the head and shoulders of St. Peter are nearly life-size. Seeing this image is like encountering the saint himself. In his right hand Peter holds the keys of the Kingdom of Heaven; with his left hand, he supports a staff topped by a cross. Above Peter are three medallions: Christ is in the center, flanked by the Virgin Mary and St. John. The golden halos unite the figures both artistically and religiously. (The Art Archive/ Kharbine-Tapabor/Boistesselin.)

Shocked by Arab triumphs, they became convinced that the cause of their misfortunes was the biblical injunction against graven (carved) images. When they compared their defeats to Muslim successes, they could not help but notice that Islam prohibited all visual representations of the divine. To these soldiers and others who shared their view, icons revived pagan idolatry and dishonored Christian divinity. As iconoclastic (anti-icon, or, literally, "icon-breaking") feeling grew, some churchmen became outspoken in their opposition to icons.

Byzantine emperors shared these religious objections, and they also had important political reasons for opposing icons. In fact, the issue of icons became a test of their authority. Icons represented intermediaries between worshippers and God; they undermined the emperor's exclusive place in the divine and temporal order. In addition, the emphasis on icons in monastic communities made monks potential threats to imperial power. The emperors hoped to use this issue to break the power of the monasteries. Above all, though, the emperors opposed icons because the army did, and they needed the support of their troops.

After Emperor Leo III ("the Isaurian"; r. 717–741) defeated the Arabs besieging Constantinople in 718, he turned his attention to consolidating his political position. In 726, officers of the imperial court tore down the great golden icon of Christ at the gateway of the palace and replaced it with a cross. This event marked the beginning of the period of **iconoclasm**. Soon afterward, Leo ordered all icons destroyed, a ban that remained in effect, despite much opposition, until 787. A modified ban would be revived in 815 and last until 843. Thereafter, icons again became an important part of Byzantine Christianity.

Iconoclasm had an enormous impact on daily life. At home, where people had their own portable icons, it forced changes in private worship: the devout had to destroy their icons or venerate them in secret. The ban on icons led to ferocious attacks on monasteries: splendid collections of holy images were destroyed; vast properties were confiscated; and monks, who were staunch defenders of icons, were ordered to leave their monasteries, give up their vocations, and marry. In this way iconoclasm destroyed communities that might otherwise have served as centers of resistance to imperial power. Reorganized and reoriented, Byzantium was ready to confront the Arabs with vigor.

REVIEW   What stresses did the Byzantine Empire endure in the seventh and eighth centuries, and how was iconoclasm a response to those stresses?

Western Europe: A Medley of Kingdoms

In contrast to Byzantium, where an emperor still ruled as the successor to Augustus and Constantine, drawing on an unbroken chain of Roman legal and administrative traditions, political power in the West was more diffuse. With the end of Roman imperial government in the western half of the empire, the region was divided into a number of kingdoms: Spain, Italy, England, and Gaul. The primary foundations of power and stability in all of these kingdoms were kinship networks, church patronage, royal courts, and wealth derived from land and plunder. Kings were important, to be sure; but in some places churchmen and rich magnates were even more powerful than royalty. As a focus of religious piety, icons were less important than the power of the saints as exercised through their relics—their bodies and body parts, even clothes and dust from their tombs. These relics represented and wielded the divine forces of God. Although the patterns of daily life and the procedures of government in western Europe remained recognizably Roman, they were also in the process of change, borrowing from and adapting to local traditions.

Frankish Kingdoms with Roman Roots

The most important kingdoms in post-Roman Europe were Frankish. During the sixth century, the Franks had established themselves as dominant in Gaul, and by the seventh century the limits of their kingdoms roughly approximated the eastern borders of present-day France, Belgium, Switzerland, and Luxembourg (Map 7.4). Moreover, their kings, the Merovingians (c. 485–751), had conquered many of the

Map 7.4 The Merovingian Kingdoms in the Seventh Century
By the seventh century, there were three powerful Merovingian kingdoms: Neustria, Austrasia, and Burgundy. The important cities of Aquitaine were assigned to one or another of these major kingdoms, while Aquitaine as a whole was assigned to a duke or other governor. Kings did not establish capital cities; they did not even stay in one place. Rather, they continually traveled throughout their kingdoms, making their power felt in person.

peoples beyond the Rhine, foreshadowing the contours of modern Germany. These northern and eastern regions were little Romanized, but the inhabitants of the rest of the Frankish kingdoms lived with bits and pieces of the ancient Roman Empire at their front doors.

Travel was difficult in this world of decaying roads and few amenities. Yet there were many travelers, such as pilgrims on their way to Rome or other shrines and traders transporting commodities and slaves—precious human cargo captured on the borders of the Christian world and sold to wealthy aristocrats, mainly in the Islamic world. Seventh-century travelers in western Europe relied mainly on river routes, for land travel was very slow, and even large groups of people on the roads were vulnerable to attacks by robbers. Such travelers passed through a very diverse landscape. Pilgrims returning north from a trip to Rome might take the Rhône River, passing Roman amphitheaters, farmland neatly and squarely laid out by Roman land surveyors, and great stone palaces and villas along the way. Although these sights would seem quite classical, if the travelers were observant, they would notice the absence of thriving cities. By the seventh century, Roman cities still served as the centers of church administration but no longer boasted commercial or cultural vitality. Depopulated, many of them survived as mere skeletons, with the exception of a few busy commercial centers like Arles and Marseille.

Continuing their journey north and a bit to the east, along the Mosel River, the travelers would pass through dense, nearly untouched forests and agricultural land more often used as pasture for animals than for cereal cultivation. Not much influenced by the Romans, these areas represented far more the farming and village settlement patterns of the barbarians. Yet even here some structures of the Roman Empire remained. Fortresses were still standing at Trier, and large stone villas, such as the one excavated by archaeologists near Douai, loomed over the humble wooden dwellings of the countryside.

Scattered here and there, independent peasants worked their own small plots as they had for centuries. But for the most part, semi-free peasant families settled on smallholdings. Each of these represented a family's manse—including a house, a garden, and cultivable land—for which the family often paid dues and owed labor services to an overlord. Some of these peasants were descendants of the coloni (tenant farmers) of the late Roman Empire; others were the sons and daughters of slaves; a few were people of free Germanic origin who for various reasons had come down in the world. At the lower end of the social scale, the status of barbarians and Romans had become identical.

Romans (or, more precisely, Gallo-Romans) and barbarians also had merged at the upper end of the social scale. Although people south of the Loire River continued to be called Romans and people to the north were called Franks, their cultures were strikingly similar: they shared languages, settlement patterns, and religious sensibilities. Many dialects—both Germanic and Latin-based—were spoken in the western kingdoms in the seventh century. But a man like Gregory, bishop of Tours

Stadium and Amphitheater at Arles
In what is today the south of France, the ruins of an amphitheater built by the Romans still dwarf the surrounding buildings of the modern city of Arles. This huge stadium was even more striking in the seventh century, when the city was impoverished and depopulated. Plague, war, and the dislocation of Roman trade networks forced most people to abandon the cities and live on the land. Only the bishop and his clergy—and individuals who could make a living servicing them—stayed in the cities. At Arles there were monasteries as well, and some of them were thriving. In the mid-sixth century, one of the female convents there housed perhaps two hundred nuns. (Bridgeman-Giraudon/Art Resource, NY.)

(r. 573–c. 594), could expect all of his readers to understand his rough Latin prose: "Though my speech is rude," he wrote,

> I have been unable to be silent as to the struggles between the wicked and the upright; and I have been especially encouraged because, to my surprise, it has often been said by men of our day, that few understand the learned words of the rhetorician but many the rude language of the common people.

Thus Gregory began his *Histories,* a valuable source of information about the Merovingian period. He was trying to evoke the sympathies of his readers, a traditional Roman rhetorical device, but he also expected that his "rude" Latin—the

Reliquary
Relics—saints' precious bodies, body parts, and often simply materials that came into contact with both—were housed in equally precious containers. This reliquary, made of cloisonné enamel (bits of enamel framed by metal), garnets, glass gems, and a cameo, is in the shape of a sarcophagus. On the back is the inscription "Theuderic the priest had this made in honor of Saint Maurice." Theuderic must have given the reliquary to the monastery of Saint-Maurice d'Agaune (today in Switzerland), which was renowned for its long and elaborate liturgy (its daily schedule of prayer) in the late seventh century. (Photo courtesy Thames and Hudson Ltd., London, from *The Dark Ages*, ed. David Talbot Rice.)

plain Latin of everyday speech—would be understood and welcomed by the general public.

Whereas Gallo-Roman aristocrats of the fourth and fifth centuries had lived in isolated villas with their wives, children, slaves, and servants, aristocrats of the seventh century lived in small villages surrounded by the huts of peasants, shepherds, and artisans. These villages, constructed mostly from wood or baked clay, were generally built near a waterway or forest or around a church for protection.

The cities shrank. At Tours, Gregory and his household and clerics still lived in the old Roman city center. But Tours's main focus was now outside the city walls, in a cemetery where a church had been built. The population of the surrounding countryside was pulled to this church as if to a magnet, for it housed the remains of the most important and venerated person in the locale: St. Martin, a fourth-century soldier turned monk. Martin was long dead, but his relics—his bones, teeth, hair, and clothes—could be found in the cemetery outside Tours, where he had served as bishop. In succeeding centuries, he remained a supernatural force for the entire region: a protector, healer, and avenger through whom God manifested divine power. In Gregory's view, for example, Martin's relics (or rather God *through* Martin's relics) had prevented armies from plundering local peasants. Martin was not the only one thought to have great supernatural power; all of God's saints were considered miracle workers.

In the classical world, the dead had been banished from the presence of the living; in the early medieval world, the holy dead held the place of highest esteem. There were no formal procedures for proclaiming saints, but influential community leaders, including local bishops, "recognized" holiness. When, for example, miracles were observed at the site of the supposed tomb of the martyr Benignus in Dijon, the common people went there to ask for help. But only after the martyr himself appeared to the local bishop in a vision, thus dispelling doubts about the occupant of the tomb, was Benignus recognized as a saint. Women as well as men might be considered saints: "[Our Savior] gave us as models [of sanctity] not only men, who fight [against sinfulness] as they should, but also women, who exert themselves in the struggle with success," wrote Gregory as a preface to his story of the nun Monegund, who lived with a few other ascetic women and whose miracles included curing tumors and helping paralyzed limbs move again.

Economic Activity in a Peasant Society

As a bishop, Gregory was aware of some of the sophisticated forms of economic activity in seventh- and eighth-century Europe, such as long-distance trade. Yet most people lived on the edge of survival. Studies of Alpine peat bogs show that from the fifth to the mid-eighth centuries, glaciers advanced and the average temperature in Europe dropped. This climate change spelled shortages in crops. Chronicles, histories, and saints' lives also describe crop shortages, famines, and diseases as a normal part of life. For the year 591 alone, Gregory reported that

> a terrible epidemic killed off the people in Tours and in Nantes. . . . In the town of Limoges a number of people were consumed by fire from heaven for having profaned the Lord's day [Sunday] by transacting business. . . . There was a terrible drought which destroyed all the green pasture. As a result there were great losses of flocks and herds.

An underlying reason for these calamities was the weakness of the agricultural economy. The dry, light soil of the Mediterranean region was easy to till, and wooden implements were no liability there. But in the north of Europe, where the soil was heavy, wet, and difficult to turn, the limitations of wooden implements meant a meager food supply. At the same time, agricultural work was not equitably or efficiently allocated and managed. A leisure class of landowning

Early Medieval Accounting
In the seventh century, grain production was marginal at best. To make sure that it got its share of the crops, at least one enterprising landlord, the monastery of St. Martin at Tours, kept a kind of ledger. This extremely unusual parchment sheet, dating from the second half of the seventh century, lists the amount of grain and wood owed to the monastery by its tenants. (Bibliothèque nationale de France.)

warriors and churchmen lived off the work of peasant men, who tilled the fields, and peasant women, who gardened, brewed, baked, and wove cloth.

Occasionally surpluses developed, either from peaceful agriculture or plunder in warfare, and these were traded, though rarely in an impersonal, commercial manner. Most economic transactions of the seventh and eighth centuries were part of a **gift economy**, a system of give-and-take: booty was taken, tribute was demanded, harvests were hoarded, and coins were minted, all to be redistributed to friends, followers, and dependents. Kings and other rich and powerful men and women amassed gold, silver, ornaments, and jewelry in their treasuries and grain in their storehouses to mark their power, add to their prestige, and demonstrate their generosity. Those benefiting from this bounty included religious people and institutions: monks and nuns in their monasteries, priests and bishops in their churches.

We still have a partial gift economy today. On holidays, for example, goods change hands for social purposes: to consecrate a holy event, to express love and friendship, to show off wealth and status. In the Merovingian world, the gift economy was the dynamic behind most of the occasions when goods and money changed hands.

However, some economic activity in the seventh century was purely commercial and impersonal. In the north of Europe, a thriving North Sea trade was beginning. Older trade networks still tied the West, which supplied slaves and raw materials such as furs and honey, to the East, which provided luxuries and manufactured goods such as silk and papyrus. Trade was a way for the Byzantine, Islamic, and western European descendants of the Roman Empire to keep in tenuous contact with one another. Seventh- and eighth-century sources speak of Byzantines, Syrians, and Jews as the chief intermediaries, many of them living in the still thriving port cities of the Mediterranean. Gregory of Tours associated Jews with commerce, complaining that they sold things "at a higher price than they were worth."

Contrary to Gregory's view, Jews were not involved only, or even primarily, in trade but were almost entirely integrated into every aspect of secular life in many regions of Europe. They used Hebrew in worship, but otherwise they spoke the same languages as Christians and used Latin in their legal documents. Their children were often given the same names as Christians (and, in turn, Christians often took Old Testament biblical names); they dressed like everyone else; they engaged in the same occupations. Many Jews planted and tended vineyards, in part because of the importance of wine in synagogue services, in part because the surplus could easily be sold. Some Jews were rich landowners, with slaves and dependent peasants working for them; others were independent peasants of modest means. Some Jews lived in towns with a small Jewish quarter, where their homes and synagogues were located. Most Jews, however, like their Christian neighbors, lived on the land. Only much later, in the tenth century, would their status change as they were driven from the countryside.

Women were also more fully integrated into society in Merovingian Gaul than they had been in the ancient world. Like Islamic women, those in the West received dowries and could inherit property. They also could be entrepreneurs; documents reveal at least one enterprising peasant woman who sold wine at Tours to earn additional money.

The Powerful in Merovingian Society

Monarchs and aristocrats were the powerful people in Merovingian society. Aristocrats included monks and bishops as well as laypeople. Holding power through hereditary wealth, status, and political influence, they lived off their estates—often scattered throughout Gaul—and the peasants who tilled the soil for them.

Along with administering their estates, many male aristocrats of the period spent their time honing their skills as warriors. Being a great warrior in Merovingian society, as in the otherwise very different world of the Bedouins, meant more than just fighting; it also meant perfecting the virtues necessary for leading armed men. Aristocrats affirmed their skills and comradeship in the hunt, proved their worth in the regular taking of booty, and rewarded their followers afterward at generous banquets. At these feasts, following the dictates of the gift economy, great lords combined fellowship with the redistribution of wealth as they gave abundantly to their followers.

Merovingian aristocrats also valued bedtime. The bed—and procreation—was the focus of marriage. Important both to the survival of aristocratic families and to the transmission of their property and power, marriage was an expensive institution. There was more than one form of marriage. In the most formal, the man gave a generous dowry of clothes, livestock, and land to his bride. After the marriage was consummated, he gave her a "morning gift" of furniture. Very wealthy men also might support one or more concubines, who enjoyed a less formal type of marriage, receiving a morning gift but no dowry. In this period, churchmen had many ideas about the value of marriages, but in practice they had little to do with the matter: people were married in their homes, not in a church.

Some sixth-century aristocrats still patterned their lives on those of the Romans, teaching their children Latin poetry and writing to one another in phrases borrowed from the classical poet Virgil. But already in the seventh century their spoken language, much like Gregory's, had become very different from ancient literary Latin. Some still learned Latin, but they cultivated it mainly to read the Psalms. Just as in Byzantium, a religious culture that emphasized Christian piety over the classics was developing in Europe.

The arrival on the continent of the Irish monk St. Columbanus (d. 615) in about 590 energized this heightened emphasis on religion. St. Columbanus's brand of monasticism, which stressed exile, devotion, and discipline, found much favor among the Merovingian elite. The monasteries that St. Columbanus established in both Gaul and Italy attracted local recruits from the aristocracy, some of them grown men and women. Others were young children, given to the monastery by their parents. This practice, called oblation, was not only accepted but often considered essential for the spiritual well-being of both the children and their families.

Bishops ranked among the most powerful men in Merovingian society. Gregory, for example, considered himself the protector of "his citizens" at Tours. When representatives of the king came to collect taxes, Gregory stopped them in their tracks, warning them that St. Martin would punish anyone who tried to tax his people. "That very day," Gregory reported, "the man who had produced the tax rolls caught a fever and died."

Like other aristocrats, many bishops were married. Church councils demanded celibacy, however, and as the overseers of priests, bishops were expected to be moral supervisors and refrain from sexual relations with their wives. Since bishops were ordinarily appointed late in life, long after they had raised a family, this restriction did not threaten the ideal of a procreative marriage.

Because unions bound together extended families rather than simply husbands and wives, noble parents determined whom their daughters were to marry. Women had some control over their lives, however. If they were widowed without children, they were allowed to sell, give away, exchange, or rent out their dowry estates as they wished. Moreover, men could give their female relatives property outright in written testaments. Fathers so often wanted to share their property with their daughters that an enterprising author created a formula for scribes to follow when drawing up such wills. It began:

> For a long time an ungodly custom has been observed among us that forbids sisters to share with their brothers the paternal land. I reject this impious law: I make you, my beloved daughter, an equal and legitimate heir in all my patrimony [inheritance].

Because of such bequests, dowries, and other gifts, many aristocratic women were very rich. Childless widows frequently gave grand and generous gifts from their vast possessions to the church. But a woman need not have been a widow to control enormous wealth. In 632, for example, the nun Burgundofara, who had never married, drew up a will giving to her monastery the land, slaves, vineyards, pastures, and forests she had received from her two brothers and her father. In the same will, she gave other properties near Paris to her brothers and a sister.

Though legally under the authority of her husband, a Merovingian woman often found ways to assert control over her life and her husband's life as well. Tetradia, wife of Count Eulalius, left her husband, taking all his gold and silver, because "he was in the habit of sleeping with the women-servants in his household . . . [and] neglected his wife. . . . As a result of his excesses, he ran into serious debt, and to meet this he stole his wife's jewelry and money." In a court of law, Tetradia was sentenced to repay Eulalius four times the amount she had taken from him, but she was allowed to keep and live on her own property.

Other women were able to exercise behind-the-scenes control through their sons. Artemia, for example, used the prophecy that her son Nicetius would become a bishop to prevent her husband from taking the bishopric himself. After Nicetius became a bishop (fulfilling the prophecy), he remained at home with his mother well into his thirties, working alongside the servants and teaching the younger children to read the Psalms.

Some Merovingian women exercised direct power. Some were abbesses, leaders of female monasteries and, sometimes, "double monasteries," which had separate facilities for men and women. These could be very substantial centers of population.

The convent at Laon, for example, had three hundred nuns in the seventh century. Because women lived in populous convents or were monopolized by rich men able to support several wives or mistresses at one time, unattached aristocratic women were scarce in society and therefore valuable.

Atop this aristocracy of men and women were the Merovingian kings, rulers of the Frankish kingdoms from about 485 to 751. The **Merovingian dynasty** owed its longevity to good political sense: it had allied itself with local lay aristocrats and ecclesiastical (church) authorities. The kings relied on these men to bolster their power, which was largely based on their tribal war leadership and access to the lion's share of plunder, as well as on their takeover of public lands and some of the legal framework of Roman administration. The kings' courts functioned as schools for the sons of the aristocracy, tightening the bonds between royal and aristocratic families. When kings sent officials—counts and dukes—to rule in their names in various regions of their kingdoms, these regional governors worked with and married into the aristocratic families who had long controlled local affairs.

Both aristocrats and kings had good reason to want a powerful royal authority. The king acted as arbitrator and intermediary for the competing interests of the aristocrats while taking advantage of local opportunities to appoint favorites and gain prestige by giving out land and privileges to supporters and religious institutions. Gregory of Tours's history of the sixth century is filled with stories of bitter battles between Merovingian kings, as royal brothers fought continuously over territories, wives, and revenues. Yet what seemed like royal weakness and violent chaos to the bishop was in fact one way the kings contained local aristocratic tensions, preventing them from spinning out of royal control. By the beginning of the seventh century, three relatively stable kingdoms had emerged: Austrasia to the northeast; Neustria to the west, with its capital city at Paris; and Burgundy, incorporating the southeast (Map 7.4, page 253). These divisions were so useful to local aristocrats and to the Merovingian dynasty alike that even when royal power was united in the hands of one king, Clothar II (r. 584–629), he made his son the independent king of Austrasia.

As the power of the Merovingian kings increased in the seventh century, so did the might of their chief court official, the mayor of the palace. In the following century, allied with the Austrasian aristocracy, one mayoral family would displace the Merovingian dynasty and establish a new royal line, the Carolingians.

Christianity and Classical Culture in the British Isles

The Merovingian kingdoms exemplify some of the ways in which Roman and non-Roman traditions combined; the British Isles show others. Ireland had never been part of the Roman Empire, but it was converted to Christianity early on, as were Roman Britain and parts of Scotland. Invasions by various Celtic and Germanic groups—particularly the Anglo-Saxons, who gave their name to England, "the land of the Angles"—redrew the religious boundaries. Ireland, largely free of invaders, remained Christian, as did Scotland, also relatively untouched by invaders. England, which emerged from the invasions as a mosaic of about a dozen kingdoms ruled by separate Anglo-Saxon kings, became largely pagan.

Christianity was introduced to Anglo-Saxon England from two directions. In the north, Irish monks brought their own brand of Christianity. Converted in the fifth century by St. Patrick and other missionaries, the Irish had rapidly evolved a church organization that corresponded to its rural clan organization. Abbots and abbesses, generally from powerful dynasties, headed monastic *familiae,* communities composed of blood relatives, servants, and slaves, as well as monks or nuns. Bishops were often under the authority of abbots, and monasteries rather than cities were the centers of population settlement in Ireland. Irish missionaries to England were monks, and they set up monasteries modeled on those at home.

In the south of England, Christianity came by way of missionaries sent by Pope Gregory the Great (r. 590–604) in 597. The missionaries, under the leadership of Augustine (not the same Augustine as the bishop of Hippo), intended to convert the king and people of Kent, the southernmost kingdom, and then work their way north. But Augustine and his party brought with them Roman practices that were at odds with those of Irish Christianity, stressing ties to the pope and the organization of the church under bishops rather than abbots. Using the Roman model, they divided England into dioceses, territorial units each headed by a bishop. At the insistence of the pope, England also got two archbishops—one at Canterbury, the other at York—to oversee the bishops. Augustine became archbishop of Canterbury. Because he was a monk, he set up a monastery right next to his cathedral, and it became a unique characteristic of the English church to have a community of monks attached to the bishop's church.

The British Isles

A major bone of contention between the Roman and Irish churches involved the calculation of the date of Easter, celebrated by Christians as the day on which Christ rose from the dead. The Roman church insisted that Easter fall on the first Sunday following the first full moon after the spring equinox. The Irish had a different method of determining Easter's date, and therefore they celebrated it on a different day. As everyone agreed that believers could not be saved unless they observed Christ's resurrection properly and on the right day, the conflict over dates was bitter. It was resolved by Oswy, king of Northumbria, who organized a meeting of churchmen, the Synod of Whitby, in 664. Convinced by the synod that Rome spoke with the voice of St. Peter, who was said in the New Testament to hold the keys to the kingdom of heaven, Oswy chose the Roman date. His decision paved the way for the triumph of the Roman brand of Christianity in England.

St. Peter was not the only reason the Anglo-Saxons favored Rome. To many English churchmen, Rome had great prestige because it was a treasure trove of knowledge, piety, and holy objects. Benedict Biscop (c. 630–690), the founder of two important English monasteries, made many difficult trips to Rome, bringing back relics, liturgical vestments, and even a cantor to teach his monks the proper melodies. Above all, he went to Rome to get books. At his monasteries in the north of England, he built up a grand library. In Anglo-Saxon England, as in Scotland and Ireland, all of which lacked a strong classical tradition from Roman times, a book was considered a precious object, to be decorated as finely as a garnet-studded brooch.

The Anglo-Saxons and Irish Celts had a thriving oral culture but extremely limited uses for writing. Books became valuable only when these societies converted to Christianity. Just as Islamic reliance on the Qur'an made possible a literary culture under the Umayyads, so Christian dependence on the Bible, liturgy, and ideas of the church fathers helped make England and Ireland centers of literature and learning in the seventh and eighth centuries. Archbishop Theodore (r. 669–690), who had studied at Constantinople and was one of the most learned men of his day, founded a school at Canterbury where students mined Latin, and even some Greek, manuscripts to comment on biblical texts. Men like Benedict Biscop soon sponsored other centers of learning, using texts from the classical past. Although women did not establish famous schools, many abbesses ruled over monasteries that stressed Christian learning. Here as elsewhere, Latin writings, even pagan texts, were studied diligently, in part because Latin was so foreign a language that mastering it required systematic and formal study. One of Benedict Biscop's pupils was Bede

Page from the Lindisfarne Gospels

This page from a lavishly illuminated manuscript was probably produced in the first third of the eighth century. For the monks at Lindisfarne, England, and elsewhere in the British Isles, books were precious objects, to be decorated much like pieces of jewelry. To introduce each of the four Gospels of the New Testament, the artist—who was also the scribe—produced three elaborate pages: the first was a "portrait" of the evangelist, the second a decorative "carpet" page, and the third the beginning of the text itself. The page depicted here is the beginning of the Gospel according to St. Matthew, which opens with the words "Liber generationis" ("The book of the generation [of Jesus]"). Note how elaborately the first letter, *L*, is treated and how the decoration gradually recedes, so that the last line, though still very embellished, is quite plain in comparison with the others. In this way, the layout of the book led the reader slowly and reverently into the Gospel itself. (© The British Library Board. Cotton Nero D.1.V, f.27.)

(673–735), an Anglo-Saxon monk and a historian of extraordinary breadth. Bede in turn taught a new generation of monks, many of whom became advisers to eighth- and ninth-century rulers.

Much of the vigorous pagan Anglo-Saxon oral tradition was adapted to Christian culture. In contrast to other European regions, where Latin was the primary written language in the seventh and eighth centuries, England made use of the vernacular—the language normally spoken by the people. Written Anglo-Saxon (or Old English) was used in every aspect of English life, from government to entertainment.

Unity in Spain, Division in Italy

In contrast to the British Isles, southern Gaul, Spain, and Italy had long been part of the Roman Empire and preserved many of its traditions. Nevertheless, as new peoples settled and fought over them, their histories diverged dramatically. When the Merovingian king Clovis defeated the Visigoths in 507, their vast kingdom, which had sprawled across southern Gaul and into Spain, was dismembered. By midcentury, the Franks came into possession of most of the Visigothic kingdom in southern Gaul.

In Spain the Visigothic king Leovigild (r. 569–586) established territorial control by military might. But no ruler could hope to maintain power there without the support of the Hispano-Roman population, which included both the great landowners and the leading bishops. Their backing was unthinkable while the Visigoths remained Arian Christians, but in 587 Leovigild's son Reccared (r. 586–601) took the necessary step, converting to Catholic Christianity. Two years later, at the Third Council of Toledo, most of the Arian bishops followed their king by announcing their conversion to Catholicism.

Thereafter, the bishops and kings of Spain cooperated to a degree unprecedented in other regions. The king gave the churchmen free rein to set up their own hierarchy (with the bishop of Toledo at the top) and to meet regularly at synods to regulate and reform the church. The bishops in turn supported their Visigothic king, who ruled as a minister of the Christian people. Rebellion against him was considered the same as rebellion against Christ. The Spanish bishops reinforced this idea by anointing the king, daubing him with holy oil in a ritual that paralleled the ordination of priests and demonstrated divine favor.

While the bishops adopted the king's cause as their own, their lay counterparts, the great landowners, helped supply the king with troops, allowing him to maintain internal order and repel his external enemies. Ironically, it was precisely the centralization and unification of the Visigothic kingdom that proved to be its undoing. When the Arabs arrived in 711, they needed only to kill the king, defeat his army, and capture Toledo to deal it a crushing blow.

By contrast, in Italy the Lombard king constantly faced a hostile papacy in the center of the peninsula and virtually independent dukes in the south. Theoretically

Lombard Italy, Early Eighth Century

royal officers, the dukes of Benevento and Spoleto in fact ruled on their own behalf. Although many Lombards were Catholics, others, including important kings and dukes, were Arians. The official religion varied with the ruler in power. Rather than signal a major political event, the conversion of the Lombards to the Catholic form of Christianity occurred gradually, ending only around the mid-seventh century. Partly as a result of this slow development, the Lombard kings, unlike the Visigoths, Franks, or even the Anglo-Saxons, never enlisted the wholehearted support of any particular group of churchmen.

Lacking a strong and united church to back them up, Lombard kings still had strengths. Chief among these were the traditions of leadership associated with the royal dynasty, the kings' military might, and their control over large estates and surviving Roman institutions in northern Italy. Although the Italian peninsula had been devastated by the wars between the Ostrogoths and the Byzantine Empire, the Lombard kings took advantage of the urban organization of Italian society and economy, assigning dukes to city bases and setting up a royal capital at Pavia. Recalling emperors like Constantine and Justinian, the kings built churches, monasteries, and other places of worship in the royal capital. They maintained city walls, issued laws, and minted coins. Revenues from tolls, sales taxes, port duties, and court fines filled their coffers, though their inability to revive the Roman land tax was a major weakness. The greatest challenge for the Lombard kings came from sharing the peninsula with Rome. As soon as the kings began to make serious headway into southern Italy against the duchies of Spoleto and Benevento, the pope began to fear for his own position.

In fact, the pope's position in Italy had long been uncertain. On the one hand, believing he was the successor of St. Peter and head of the church, he wielded real secular power. Pope Gregory the Great in many ways laid the foundations for the papacy's later spiritual and temporal triumphs. During his tenure, the pope became the greatest landowner in Italy; he organized the defenses of Rome and paid for its army; he heard court cases, made treaties, and provided welfare services. The missionary expedition he sent to England was only a small part of his involvement in the rest of Europe. A prolific author of spiritual works and biblical commentaries, Gregory summarized and simplified the ideas of church fathers like St. Augustine of Hippo, making them accessible to a wider audience. His practical handbook for the clergy, *Pastoral Rule,* was matched by practical reforms within the church: in Italy, for example, he tried to impose regular elections of bishops and to enforce clerical celibacy. On the other hand, even this pope was not independent. He was under the rule of the emperor, who lived in Constantinople.

Within a century, however, the situation changed as imperial authority began to unravel in Rome. In 691, Emperor Justinian II (r. 685–695) convened a council that determined 102 rules for the church. He sent them to Rome for papal endorsement. Most of the rules were unobjectionable, but Pope Sergius I (r. 687–701) was unwilling to agree to them as a whole because they permitted priestly marriage (which the Roman church did not want to allow) and prohibited fasting on Saturdays in Lent (which the Roman church required).

Outraged by Sergius's refusal, Justinian tried to arrest the pope, but Italian armies (theoretically under the emperor) came to the pontiff's aid, and Justinian's arresting officer hid under the pope's bed. The incident reveals that some local forces were already willing to rally to the side of the pope against the emperor. By now Constantinople's influence and authority over Rome was weak at best. Sheer distance, as well as diminishing imperial power in Italy, meant that the popes were in effect the leaders of the parts of Italy not controlled by the Lombards.

The gap between Byzantium and the papacy widened even more in the early eighth century when Emperor Leo III tried to increase the taxes on papal property to pay for his wars against the Arab invaders. The pope responded by leading a general tax revolt. Meanwhile, Leo's fierce policy of iconoclasm collided with the pope's tolerance of images. In the West, Christian piety hardly focused on icons, but the pope was not willing to allow sacred images and icons to be destroyed. He argued that holy images could and should be venerated, though not worshipped.

The pope's difficulties with the emperor were matched by increasing friction between the pope and the Lombards. The Lombard kings had gradually managed to bring under their control the duchies of Spoleto and Benevento, as well as part of the Exarchate of Ravenna. By the mid-eighth century, the popes feared that Rome would fall to the Lombards, and Pope Zachary (r. 741–752) looked northward for friends. He created an ally by sanctioning the deposition of the last Merovingian king and his replacement by the first Carolingian king, Pippin III ("the Short"; r. 751–768). In 753, Zachary's successor, Pope Stephen II (r. 752–757), called on Pippin to march to Italy with an army to fight the Lombards. Thus, events at Rome had a major impact on the history not only of Italy but of the Frankish kingdoms as well.

REVIEW   What were the similarities and differences among the kingdoms that emerged in western Europe, and how did their histories combine and diverge?

Conclusion

The Islamic world, Byzantium, and western Europe built on the legacies of Rome. Although Muslims were the newcomers to the Roman world, their religion, Islam, was influenced by Jewish and Christian monotheism, both with roots in Roman culture. Once the Muslim Arabs embarked on military conquests, they became the heirs of Rome in other ways: preserving Byzantine cities, hiring Syrian civil servants, and adopting Mediterranean artistic styles. Drawing on

Mapping the West Europe and the Mediterranean, c. 750
The major political event of the period 600–750 was the emergence of Islam and the creation of an
Islamic state that reached from Spain to the Indus River. The Byzantine Empire, once a great power,
was dwarfed—and half swallowed up—by its Islamic neighbor. To the west were fledgling barbarian
kingdoms, mere trifles on the world stage. The next centuries, however, would prove their resourceful-
ness and durability. **For more help analyzing this map, see the map activity for this chapter in the
Online Study Guide at** bedfordstmartins.com/huntconcise.

Roman and Persian traditions, the Umayyad dynasty created a powerful Islamic
state, with a culture that generally tolerated a wide variety of economic, religious,
and social institutions, so long as the conquered peoples paid taxes to their
Muslim overlords.

Byzantium directly inherited the central political institutions of Rome: its emperor
still called himself the Roman emperor; its cities, laws, and religion—Christianity—
were Roman. However, the changes of the seventh and eighth centuries—contraction
of territory, urban decline, disappearance of the old elite, and a ban on icons—
whittled away at this Roman character. By 750, Byzantium was less Roman than it
was a new, resilient political and cultural entity, a Christian state on the borders of
the new Muslim empire.

Western Europe also inherited—and transformed—Roman institutions. The Merovingian kings built on much-modified Roman traditions. In England, parts of the Roman legacy—Latin learning and the Christian religion—were largely imported. In Spain, the Visigothic kings converted from Arian to Roman Christianity. In Italy and at Rome itself, many of the traditions of the classical past endured.

Everywhere, the social hierarchy became simpler, with the loss of "middle" groups, like the curials in Byzantium, and the near-suppression of tribal affiliations among Muslims. Everywhere, religion was more tightly tied to politics than ever before. In Byzantium, the emperor was a religious force, presiding over the destruction of icons. In the Islamic world, the caliph was the successor to Muhammad, a religious and political leader. In western Europe, the kings allied with churchmen in order to rule. Despite their many differences, all of these leaders had a common understanding of their place in a divine scheme: they were God's agents on earth, ruling over God's people. In the next century they would consolidate their power. Little did they know that soon thereafter local elites would be able to assert greater authority than ever before.

CHAPTER REVIEW QUESTIONS

1. What were the similarities and the differences in political organization in the Islamic, Byzantine, and western European worlds in the seventh century?

2. Compare and contrast the role of religion in Islamic, Byzantine, and western European societies in the seventh century.

For practice quizzes and other study tools, see the Online Study Guide at bedfordstmartins.com/huntconcise.

For primary-source material from this period, see Chapter 8 of *Sources of THE MAKING OF THE WEST,* Third Edition.

TIMELINE

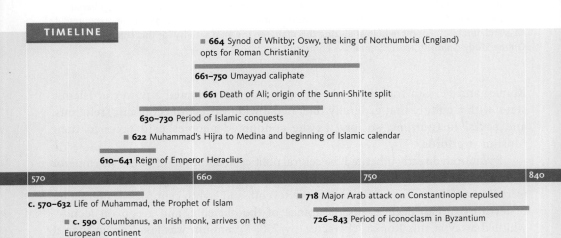

■ **664** Synod of Whitby; Oswy, the king of Northumbria (England) opts for Roman Christianity

661–750 Umayyad caliphate

■ **661** Death of Ali; origin of the Sunni-Shi'ite split

630–730 Period of Islamic conquests

■ **622** Muhammad's Hijra to Medina and beginning of Islamic calendar

610–641 Reign of Emperor Heraclius

| 570 | 660 | 750 | 840 |

c. 570–632 Life of Muhammad, the Prophet of Islam

■ **c. 590** Columbanus, an Irish monk, arrives on the European continent

590–604 Papacy of Gregory the Great

■ **597** Sent by Pope Gregory the Great, Augustine arrives in England to convert the Anglo-Saxons

■ **718** Major Arab attack on Constantinople repulsed

726–843 Period of iconoclasm in Byzantium

Suggested References

Taken together, early Islam is well covered by Berkey (for religion) and Kennedy (for politics). Ousterhout and Brubaker's book covers a crucial period in Byzantine history. Smith provides an excellent synthesis of developments in the West.

Berkey, Jonathan P. *The Formation of Islam: Religion and Society in the Near East, 600–1800.* 2003.

*Byzantium sourcebook: http://www.fordham.edu/halsall/sbook1c.html

Christie, Neil. *From Constantine to Charlemagne: An Archeology of Italy, AD 300–800.* 2006.

Connor, Carolyn L. *Women of Byzantium.* 2004.

*Gregory of Tours. *The History of the Franks.* Trans. Lewis Thorpe. 1976.

Heinzelmann, Martin. *Gregory of Tours: History and Society in the Sixth Century.* 2001.

Hen, Yitzhak. *Roman Barbarians: The Royal Court and Culture in the Early Medieval West.* 2007.

*Islamic History Sourcebook: http://www.fordham.edu/halsall/islam/islamsbook.html

Kennedy, Hugh. *The Prophet and the Age of the Caliphates: The Islamic Near East from the Sixth to the Eleventh Century.* 2d ed. 2004.

Ousterhout, Robert, and Leslie Brubaker, eds. *The Sacred Image East and West.* 1995.

Smith, Julia M. H. *Europe after Rome: A New Cultural History, 500–1000.* 2005.

Wickham, Chris. *Framing the Early Middle Ages: Europe and the Mediterranean, 400–800.* 2005.

8

Emperors, Caliphs, and Local Lords

750–1050

N 841, A FIFTEEN-YEAR-OLD BOY named William went to serve at the court of Charles the Bald, king of the Franks. William's father was Bernard, an extremely powerful noble. His mother was Dhuoda, a well-educated, pious, and able woman who administered the family's estates in the south of France while her husband occupied himself in court politics and royal administration. In 841, however, politics had become dangerous. King Charles was fighting with his brothers over his portion of the empire forged by his grandfather Charlemagne, and Bernard held a precarious position at the young king's court. In fact, William was sent to Charles's court as a kind of hostage, to ensure Bernard's loyalty. Anxious about her son, Dhuoda wrote a handbook of advice for him. There she told him where his loyalties ought to lie:

Carolingian Mother

This depiction of a nursing mother is a detail from a full-page illustration of the biblical story of the Creation and Fall in a Carolingian Bible manuscript made in the ninth century. The mother is Eve, cast out of the Garden of Eden and suckling her firstborn, Cain. Christian mothers had an important model in Mary, the mother of Jesus, and Eve's dignified placement within a bower of garlands may reflect this association. (© *The British Library Board. Add. 10546 f.5v det.*)

In the human understanding of things, royal and imperial appearance and power seem preeminent in the world, and the custom of men is to account those men's actions and their names ahead of all others. . . . But despite all this . . . I caution you to render first to him whose son you are special, faithful, steadfast loyalty as long as you shall live.

William heeded his mother's words, with tragic results: when Bernard ran afoul of Charles and was executed, William died in a failed attempt to avenge his father.

Dhuoda's handbook reveals the volatile political atmosphere of the mid-ninth century, and her advice to her son points to one of its causes: a crisis of loyalty.

Loyalty to emperors, caliphs, and kings—all of whom were symbols of unity cutting across regional and family ties—competed with allegiances to local authorities;

those, in turn, vied with family loyalties. Everywhere—in the Islamic world, Byzantium, and the West—the period 750–1050 would see first the rise of powerful central rulers and then their fall, as power fragmented and became more regional.

At Byzantium, military triumphs brought the emperors enormous prestige. A renaissance of culture and art took place at Constantinople. Even so, newly powerful families soon began to dominate the Byzantine countryside. In the Islamic world, a dynastic revolution in 750 ousted the Umayyads from the caliphate and replaced them with a new family, the **Abbasids**. Yet Abbasid power, too, began to ebb as regional Islamic rulers came to the fore. In the West, Charlemagne—a Frankish king from a new dynasty, the Carolingians—forged an empire that embraced most of Europe. But this new state, like the others, turned out to be fragile, disintegrating within a generation of Charlemagne's death. In the West, even more than in the Byzantine and Islamic worlds, power fell into the hands of local strongmen.

All along the fringes of these realms, new political entities began to develop, conditioned by the religion and culture of their more dominant neighbors. Russia grew up in the shadow of Byzantium, as did Bulgaria and Serbia. The West was more crucial for the development of central Europe. By the year 1050, the contours of modern Europe and the Middle East were dimly visible.

CHAPTER FOCUS QUESTION   What forces led to the dissolution—or weakening—of centralized governments in the period 750–1050, and what institutions took their place?

Byzantium's Renewed Strength and Influence

Between 750 and 850, Byzantium beat back Muslim attacks in Asia Minor and began to rebuild. After 850 it went on the offensive. Military victories brought new wealth and power to the imperial court, and the emperors supported a vast program of literary and artistic revival—the Macedonian renaissance—at Constantinople. But while the emperor dominated at the capital, a new landowning elite began to control the countryside. On its northern front, Byzantium helped create new Slavic realms.

Imperial Power

While the *themes*, with their territorial military organization, took care of attacks on Byzantine territory, new mobile armies made up of the best troops the emperor could muster moved aggressively outward beginning around 850. By 1025, the empire extended from the Danube in the north to the Euphrates in the south (Map 8.1). The Byzantines had not controlled so much territory since their wars with the Sasanid Persians four hundred years earlier.

Military victories gave new prestige to the army and the imperial court. The emperors drew revenues from vast and growing imperial estates. They could demand services and money from the population at will—requiring citizens to build bridges and roads, to offer lodging to the imperial retinue, and to pay taxes in cash. The emperors used their wealth to create a lavish court culture, surrounding themselves

Map 8.1 The Expansion of Byzantium, 860–1025
In 860, the Byzantine Empire was still only a fraction of its former size. To the west, it had lost most of Italy. To the east, it held only part of Asia Minor. On its northern flank, the Bulgarians had set up an independent state. By 1025, however, the empire had ballooned, its western half embracing all of the Balkans, its eastern arm extending around the Black Sea, and its southeastern fringe reaching nearly to Tripoli. The year 1025 marked the Byzantine Empire's greatest size after the rise of Islam. **For more help analyzing this map, see the map activity for this chapter in the Online Study Guide at** bedfordstmartins.com/huntconcise.

with servants, slaves, family members, and civil servants. Eunuchs (castrated men who could not pose a threat to the imperial line) were entrusted with some of the highest posts in government. From their powerful position, the emperors negotiated with other rulers, exchanging ambassadors and receiving and entertaining diplomats with elaborate ceremonies. One such diplomat, Liutprand, bishop of the northern Italian city of Cremona, reported on his audience with Emperor Constantine VII ("Porphyrogenitos"; r. 913–959):

> Leaning upon the shoulders of two eunuchs I was brought into the emperor's presence. At my approach [mechanical] lions began to roar and birds to cry out, each according to its kind. . . . After I had three times made obeisance to the emperor with my face upon the ground, I lifted my head, and behold! the

man whom just before I had seen sitting on a moderately elevated seat had now changed his raiment [clothes] and was sitting on the level of the ceiling. How it was done I could not imagine, unless perhaps he was lifted up by some such sort of device as we use for raising the timbers of a wine press.

Although Liutprand mocked this elaborate court ceremonial, it had a real function: to express the serious, sacred, concentrated power of imperial majesty.

The emperor's wealth relied on the prosperity of an agricultural economy organized for trade. Byzantine commerce depended on a careful balance of state regulation and individual enterprise. The emperor controlled craft and commercial guilds to ensure imperial revenues and a stable supply of valuable and useful commodities, while entrepreneurs organized most of the fairs held throughout the empire. Foreign merchants traded within the empire, either at Constantinople or in some border cities. Because this international trade intertwined with foreign policy, the Byzantine government considered trade a political as well as an economic matter. Emperors issued privileges to certain "nations" (as groups such as the Venetians, Russians, and Jews were called), regulating the fees they were obliged to pay and the services they had to render. At the end of the tenth century, for example, the Venetians bargained to reduce their customs dues per ship from thirty *solidi* (coins) to two; in return they promised to transport Byzantine soldiers to Italy whenever the emperor wished.

Imperial authority was not absolute, however. In the countryside, particularly in Anatolia, powerful families—often army generals but also members of the civil service and the church—bought and dominated huge tracts of land. Many peasants became dependents of these great landlords, tilling the soil without owning it. Although the new magnates were a potential counterweight to imperial power, they ordinarily believed that their interests coincided with the emperor's. They were glad to profit from imperial victories and the expansion of Byzantine territory.

The Macedonian Renaissance, c. 870–c. 1025

Flush with victory and recalling Byzantium's past glory, the emperors revived classical intellectual pursuits. Basil I (r. 867–886), who came from Macedonia, founded the imperial dynasty that presided over the so-called Macedonian renaissance (c. 870–c. 1025). The *renaissance** (French for "rebirth") was made possible by an intellectual elite—families which, even in the anxious years of the eighth century, had persisted in studying the classics despite the trend toward a simple religious education.

Now, with the empire slowly regaining its military eminence and with icons permanently restored in 843, the scholarly elite thrived again. Byzantine artists produced new works, and emperors and other members of the new court society, liberated from the sober taboos of iconoclasm, sponsored sumptuous artistic

---

*The word *renaissance* is commonly used in connection with a revival of classical art, languages, and culture in Italy during the period c. 1350–1500. However, it is also used for any artistic, intellectual, or cultural flowering nourished by classical traditions. It has both meanings in this book.

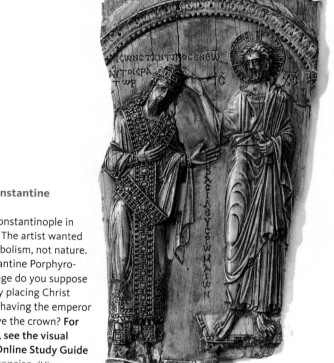

The Crowning of Emperor Constantine Porphyrogenitos
This ivory relief was carved at Constantinople in the middle of the tenth century. The artist wanted to emphasize hierarchy and symbolism, not nature. Christ is shown crowning Constantine Porphyrogenitos (r. 913–959). What message do you suppose the artist wanted to telegraph by placing Christ higher than the emperor and by having the emperor slightly incline his head to receive the crown? **For more help analyzing this image, see the visual activity for this chapter in the Online Study Guide at** bedfordstmartins.com/huntconcise. (Hirmer Fotoarchiv, Munich, Germany.)

productions. Emperor Constantine Porphyrogenitos wrote books about geography and history and financed the work of other scholars and artists. He even supervised the details of his craftspeople's products, insisting on exacting standards. "Who could enumerate how many artisans the Porphyrogenitos corrected? He corrected the stonemasons, the carpenters, the goldsmiths, the silversmiths, and the blacksmiths," wrote a historian supported by the same emperor's patronage.

The emperors were joined by other members of the imperial court, who also sponsored writers, philosophers, and historians. Scholars wrote summaries of classical literature, encyclopedias of ancient knowledge, and commentaries on classical authors. Others copied religious and theological manuscripts, such as sermons, liturgical texts, Bibles, and Psalters. They hoped to revive the intellectual and artistic achievements at the height of imperial Roman rule. But the Macedonian renaissance could not possibly succeed in this endeavor; too much had changed since the time of Justinian. Nevertheless, the renaissance permanently integrated classical forms into Byzantine political and religious life.

The Macedonian Renaissance
This manuscript illumination, made at Constantinople in the mid-ninth century, combines Christian and classical elements in a harmonious composition. David, author of the Psalms, sits in the center. Like the classical Orpheus, he plays music that attracts and tames the beasts. In the right-hand corner, a figure labeled "Bethlehem" is modeled on a lounging river or mountain god. Compare this image with The Crowning of Emperor Constantine Porphyrogenitos on page 275 and describe, using these two objects, the various styles and subject matters of the Macedonian renaissance. (Bibliothèque nationale de France.)

In Byzantium's Shadow: Bulgaria, Serbia, Russia

The shape of what was to become modern eastern Europe was created during the period 850–950. By 800, Slavic settlements dotted the area from the Danube River down to Greece and from the Black Sea to Croatia. The ruler of the Bulgarians, called the *khagan,* ruled over the largest realm, northwest of Constantinople.

The Balkans, c. 850–950

Under Khagan Krum (r. c. 803–814) and his son, Bulgarian rule stretched west to the Tisza River in modern Hungary. At about the same time as Krum's triumphant expansion, however, the Byzantine Empire began its own campaigns to conquer, convert, and control these Slavic regions, today known as the Balkans.

The Byzantine offensive to the north and west began under Emperor Nicephorus I (r. 802–811), who waged war against the Slavs of Greece in the Peloponnese, set up a new Christian diocese there, organized it as a new military theme, and forcibly resettled Christians in the area to counteract Slavic paganism. The Byzantines followed this pattern of conquest as they pushed northward. By 900, Byzantium ruled all of Greece.

Still under Nicephorus, the Byzantines launched a massive attack against the Bulgarians, took the chief city of Pliska, plundered it, burned it to the ground, and then marched against Krum's encampment in the Balkan Mountains. Krum took advantage of his position, however. He attacked the imperial troops, killed Nicephorus, and brought home the emperor's skull in triumph. Cleaned out and lined with silver, the skull served as the victorious Krum's drinking goblet. In 816, the two sides agreed to a peace that lasted for thirty years. But hostility remained, and intermittent skirmishes between the Bulgarians and Byzantines gave way to longer wars throughout the tenth century. Emperor Basil II (r. 963–1025) led the Byzantines in a slow, methodical conquest (1001–1018). Aptly called "the Bulgar-Slayer," Basil brought the entire region under Byzantine control and forced its ruler to accept the Byzantine form of Christianity. Around the same time, the Serbs, encouraged by Byzantium to oppose the Bulgarians, began to form the political community that would become Serbia.

Religion played an important role in the Byzantine conquest of the Balkans. In 863, the brothers Cyril and Methodius were sent as Christian missionaries from Byzantium to the Slavs. Well educated in both classical and religious texts, they spoke one Slavic dialect fluently and devised an alphabet for the Slavic language (which, until then, existed only orally) based on Greek forms. It was the ancestor of the Cyrillic alphabet used in Bulgaria, Serbia, and Russia today.

The region that would eventually become Russia lay outside the sphere of direct Byzantine rule in the ninth and tenth centuries. However, like Serbia and Bulgaria, it came under increasingly strong Byzantine cultural and religious influence. Vikings—Scandinavian adventurers who ranged over vast stretches of ninth-century Europe seeking trade, booty, and land—had penetrated Russia from the north and imposed their rule over the Slavs inhabiting the broad river valleys connecting the Baltic Sea with the Black Sea and thence with Constantinople. Like the Bulgars in Bulgaria, the Scandinavian Vikings gradually blended into the larger Slavic population. At the end of the ninth century, a chief named Oleg established control over most of the tribes in southwestern Russia and forced peoples farther away to pay him tribute. The tribal association that he created formed the nucleus of Kievan Russia, named for Kiev, the city that became the commercial center of the region and today is the capital of Ukraine.

The relationship between Kievan Russia and Byzantium began with war, developed through trade agreements, and was eventually sustained by religion. Around 905, Oleg launched a military expedition to Constantinople, forcing the Byzantines to pay a large fee and open their doors to Russian traders in exchange for peace. At the time, only a few Christians and Jews—and probably some Muslims—lived in Russia alongside a mainly pagan population. The Russians' conversion to Christianity was spearheaded by Vladimir (r. c. 980–1015), the grand prince of Kiev and all of Russia. Under the influence of the Byzantine emperor Basil II, Vladimir agreed to adopt the Byzantine form of Christianity. He took a variant of the name Basil in honor of the emperor and married the emperor's sister Anna; then he reportedly had all the people of his state baptized in the Dnieper River.

Vladimir's conversion represented a wider pattern. Slavic realms such as Moravia, Serbia, and Bulgaria adopted the Byzantine form of Christianity. Meanwhile, the rulers and peoples of Poland, Hungary, Denmark, and Norway were converted under the auspices of the Roman church. This development reinforced the emerging split between orthodox Byzantine Christianity in the eastern half of the former Roman Empire and Roman Catholicism in the west. Russia's conversion to the Byzantine form of Christianity was especially significant. Russia was geographically as close to the Islamic world as to the Christian; it could conceivably have become an Islamic land. By converting to Byzantine Christianity, Russia made itself the heir to Byzantium and its church, customs, art, and political ideology. Adopting Christianity linked Russia to the Christian world, but choosing Byzantine rather than Roman Christianity served to isolate Russia later from western Europe.

Wishing to counteract such isolation, Russian rulers at times sought to cement relations with central and western Europe, which were tied to Catholic Rome. Prince Iaroslav the Wise (r. 1019–1054) forged such links through his own marriage and the marriages of his sons and daughters to rulers and princely families in France, Hungary, and Scandinavia. Iaroslav encouraged intellectual and artistic developments to connect Russian culture to the classical past. But after his death, civil wars broke out, shredding what unity Russia had known. Massive invasions by outsiders, particularly from the east, further weakened Kievan rulers, who were eventually displaced by princes from northern Russia. At the crossroads of East and West, Russia could meet and adopt a great variety of traditions, but its situation also opened it to unremitting military pressures.

REVIEW Where and how did the Byzantine Empire expand during the period 750–1050?

The Caliphate and Its Fragmentation

A new dynasty of caliphs—the Abbasids—first brought unity and then, in their decline, fragmentation to the Islamic world. Caliphs continued to rule in name only, while regional rulers took over the real business of governing Islamic lands. Local traditions based on religious and political differences played an increasingly important role in people's lives. Yet even in the eleventh century, the Islamic world had a clear sense of its own unity, based on language, commerce, and intellectual achievements that crossed regional boundaries.

The Abbasid Caliphate, 750–c. 950

In 750, a civil war ousted the Umayyads and raised the Abbasids to the caliphate. The Abbasids found support in an uneasy coalition of Shi'ites (the faction loyal to Ali's memory) and non-Arabs who had been excluded from Umayyad government and now demanded a place in political life. The new regime signaled a revolution. The center of the Islamic state shifted from Damascus, with its roots in the Roman tradition, to Baghdad, a new capital city built by the Abbasids right next to Ctesiphon, which had been the Sasanid capital. Here the Abbasid caliphs followed Persian courtly models. They controlled a centralized government served by a staff of civil servants, and they appointed regional governors to carry out their policies at the local level.

From Baghdad, the Abbasid caliph Harun al-Rashid (r. 786–809) ruled over a flourishing empire. His contemporary Frankish ruler, Charlemagne, was impressed with the elephant Harun sent him as a gift, along with monkeys, spices, and medicines. But these items were mainstays of everyday commerce in Harun's Iraq. A mid-ninth-century list of imports listed "tigers, panthers, elephants, panther skins, rubies, white sandal[wood], ebony, and coconuts" from India as well as "silk, chinaware, paper, ink, peacocks, racing horses, saddles, felts, [and] cinnamon" from China.

The Abbasid dynasty began to decline after Harun's death. Obliged to support a huge army and an increasingly complex civil service, the Abbasids found their tax base inadequate. They needed to collect revenues from their provinces, such as Syria and Egypt, but the governors of those regions often refused to send the revenues. After Harun's caliphate, ex-soldiers, seeking better salaries, recognized different caliphs and fought for power in savage civil wars. The caliphs tried to bypass the regular army, made up largely of free Muslim foot soldiers, by turning to Turkish slaves—Mamluks—bought and armed to serve as mounted cavalry. But the caliphate's dwindling revenues could not sustain a loyal or powerful military force. In the tenth century the caliphs became figureheads only, as independent rulers established themselves in the various Islamic regions. For military support, many of these new rulers turned to independent military commanders who led Mamluk troops. Well paid to maintain their mounts and arms, many Mamluks gained renown and, after being freed by their masters, high positions at the courts of regional rulers. In the thirteenth century, some of them became rulers themselves.

Regional Diversity

A faraway caliph could not command sufficient allegiance from local leaders once he demanded more in taxes than he gave back in favors. The forces of fragmentation were strong in the Islamic world: it was, after all, based on the conquest of many diverse regions, each with its own deeply rooted traditions and culture. The Islamic religion, with its Sunni-Shi'ite split, also became

Fatimid Tableware
The elites under the Fatimid rulers cultivated a luxurious lifestyle that included dining on porcelain tableware, which was glazed and fired several times to produce an iridescent effect. Trade contacts with China inspired the Islamic world to mimic Chinese pottery. (© 2011 by Benaki Museum, Athens.)

a source of polarization. Western Europeans knew almost nothing about Muslims and ordinarily called them all Saracens (from the Latin for "Arabs") without distinction. But, in fact, as today, Muslims were of different ethnicities, practiced different customs, and identified with different regions. With the fragmentation of political and religious unity, each of the tenth- and early-eleventh-century Islamic states built on local traditions under local rulers (Map 8.2).

The most important and successful of these states was formed by the Fatimids, a group of Shi'ites who took their name from Fatimah, Muhammad's daughter and the wife of Ali. Allying with the Berbers in North Africa, the Fatimids established themselves in 909 as rulers in the region now called Tunisia. The Fatimid Ubayd Allah claimed to be not only the true imam (descendant of Ali) but also the *mahdi,* the "divinely guided" messiah, come to bring justice on earth. In 969, the Fatimids declared themselves rulers of Egypt, and eventually they controlled parts of North Africa, Arabia, and even Syria. Their dynasty lasted for about two hundred years.

While the Shi'ites dominated Egypt, Sunni Muslims ruled al-Andalus, the Islamic central and southern heart of Spain. Unlike the other independent Islamic states forged during the ninth and tenth centuries, the Spanish emirate of Córdoba (so called because its ruler took the secular title *emir,* "commander," and fixed his capital at Córdoba) was created near the start of the Abbasid caliphate, in 756. During the Abbasid revolution, Abd al-Rahman—a member of the Umayyad family—fled

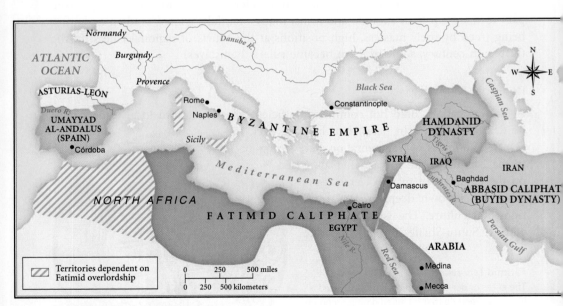

Map 8.2 Islamic States, c. 1000
A glance back at Map 7.1 (page 242) will quickly demonstrate the fragmentation of the once united Islamic caliphate. In 750, one caliph ruled territory stretching from Spain to India. In 1000, there was more than one caliphate—claimed by the Umayyads in Spain, the Fatimids based in Egypt, and the Abbasids in Iran—as well as several other ruling dynasties.

to North Africa, gathered an army, invaded Spain, and was declared emir after only one battle. He and his Umayyad successors ruled a broad range of peoples, including many Jews and Christians. After the initial Islamic conquest of Spain, the Christians there adopted so much of the new language and so many of the customs that Muslims called them Mozarabs, or "would-be Arabs." They were free to worship and live according to their own laws. Some Mozarabs were content with their status; others converted to Islam; still others intermarried with Muslims.

Abd al-Rahman III (r. 912–961) took the title of caliph, and the caliphate of Córdoba that he created lasted from 929 to 1031. Under Abd al-Rahman's rule, members of all religious groups in al-Andalus were given not only freedom of worship but also equal opportunity to rise in the civil service. The caliph also initiated important diplomatic contacts with Byzantine and European rulers, ignoring the weak and tiny Christian kingdoms squeezed into northern Spain. Yet under later caliphs, al-Andalus experienced the same political fragmentation that was occurring everywhere else. The caliphate of Córdoba broke up in 1031, and rulers of small, independent regions, called *taifas,* took power.

Although the regions of the Islamic world were culturally and politically diverse, they maintained a measure of unity through trade networks and language. Their principal bond was Arabic, the language of the Qur'an. At once poetic and sacred, Arabic was also the language of commerce and government from Baghdad to Córdoba. Moreover, despite political differences, borders were open: an artisan could move from Córdoba to Cairo; a landowner in North Africa might very well own property in al-Andalus; a young man from North Africa would think nothing of going to Iran to find a wife; a young girl purchased as a slave in Mecca might become part of a prince's harem in Baghdad. With few barriers to commerce (though every city and town had its own customs dues), traders regularly dealt in various, often exotic, goods.

Although the primary reason for these open borders was Islam itself, the openness extended to non-Muslims as well. The commercial activities of the Tustari brothers, Jewish merchants from southern Iran, were typical in the Arabic-speaking world. By 1026, the Tustaris had established a flourishing business in Egypt. Although they did not have "branch offices," informal contacts with friends and family allowed them to import fine textiles from Iran to sell in Egypt and to export Egyptian fabrics to sell in Iran.

The sophisticated Islamic society of the tenth and eleventh centuries supported networks even more vast than those of the Tustaris. Muslim merchants traded tin from England; salt and gold from Timbuktu in west-central Africa; amber, gold, and copper from Russia; and slaves from every region.

The Islamic Renaissance, c. 790–c. 1050

The dissolution of the caliphate into separate political entities multiplied the centers of learning and intellectual productivity. Unlike the Macedonian renaissance of Byzantium, which was concentrated in Constantinople, the Islamic renaissance occurred throughout the Islamic world. It was particularly dazzling in capital cities such as Córdoba, where tenth-century rulers presided over a brilliant court culture, patronizing scholars, poets, and artists. The library at Córdoba contained the largest collection of books in Europe at that time.

Elsewhere, as early as the eighth century, the Abbasid caliphs endowed research libraries and set up centers for translation. Scholars explored the writings of the ancients, including the classics of Persia, India, and Greece. Some read, translated, and commented on the works of ancient philosophers. Others worked on astronomy. Still others wrote on mathematics. Al-Khwarizmi (d. 850) wrote a book on algebra (the word itself is from the Arab *al-jabr*) and another on the Indian method of calculation, using the numbers 1, 2, and 3. He introduced the number zero, essential for differentiating 1 from 10, for example. When these numerals started to be used in western Europe in the twelfth century, they were called Arabic, as they are still known today.

The newly independent Islamic rulers supported science as well as mathematics. For example, Ibn Sina (980–1037), known in the West as Avicenna, wrote books on

A Dancing Constellation
The study of sciences such as medicine, physics, and astronomy flourished in the tenth and eleventh centuries in the cosmopolitan Islamic world. This whimsical depiction of Andromeda C, a constellation in the Northern Hemisphere, illustrates the *Book of Images of the Fixed Stars*, an astronomical treatise written around 965 by al-Sufi at the request of his pupil, the ruler of Iran. Al-Sufi drew from classical treatises, particularly the *Almagest* by Ptolemy. This copy of his book, probably made by his son in 1009, also drew on classical models for its illustrations. But instead of Greek clothing, Andromeda wears the pantaloons and skirt of an Islamic dancer. (Bodleian Library, University of Oxford; MS Marsh 144 page 167.)

logic, the natural sciences, and physics. His *Canon of Medicine* systematized earlier treatises and reconciled them with his own experience as a physician. Active in the centers of power, he served as vizier (prime minister) to various rulers.

Long before there were universities in the West, the Islamic world had important institutions of higher learning. Rich Muslims, generally of the ruling elite, demonstrated their piety and charity by establishing schools. Each school, or **madrasa**, was located within or attached to a mosque. Sometimes visiting scholars held passionate public debates at these schools. More regularly, professors conducted classes throughout the day on the interpretation of the Qur'an and other literary or legal texts. Students, all male, attended the classes that suited their achievement levels and interests. Most students paid a fee for learning, but there were also students who received scholarships.

At Byzantium and in the West, scholars were obliged to write on expensive parchment (made from animal skins); only the elite could afford their books. In the Islamic world, however, merchants, scholars, doctors, and others wrote on paper, which was inexpensive. The Islamic renaissance affected not just the very rich but a large and literate middle class.

> **REVIEW** What forces led to the fragmentation of the Islamic world in the tenth and eleventh centuries, and what factors nevertheless gave it a measure of unity?

The Creation and Division of a New European Empire

Just as in the Byzantine and Islamic worlds, so too in the West, the period 750–1050 began with the formation of a strong empire, ruled by one man. By the mid-ninth century, however, this empire began to fragment, as local rulers took power into their own hands. In 751 a new dynasty, the Carolingians, came to rule in a now united Frankish kingdom just one year after the Abbasids gained the caliphate in Iraq. Charlemagne, the most powerful of these Carolingian monarchs, conquered new territory, took the title of emperor, and presided over a revival of Christian classical culture known as the Carolingian renaissance. He ruled at the local level through counts and other military men. Nevertheless, the unity of the Carolingian Empire—based largely on conquest, a measure of prosperity, and personal allegiance to Charlemagne—was shaky. Its weaknesses were exacerbated by attacks from Viking, Muslim, and Magyar invaders. Charlemagne's successors divided his empire among themselves and saw it divided further as local leaders took defense—and rule—into their own hands.

The Rise of the Carolingians

The Carolingians were among many aristocratic families on the rise during the Merovingian period. Like the others, they were important landowners, but unlike the others, they gained exceptional power by monopolizing the position of "palace mayor"—a sort of prime minister—under the Merovingian kings. Charles Martel, palace mayor from 714 to 741, gave the name **Carolingian** (from *Carolus,* Latin for "Charles") to the dynasty. Renowned for defeating an invading army of Muslims from al-Andalus near Poitiers in 732, he also contended vigorously against other aristocrats who were carving out independent lordships for themselves. Charles and his family turned aristocratic factions against one another, rewarded followers, crushed enemies, and dominated whole regions by supporting monasteries that served as focal points for both religious piety and land donations.

The Carolingians also allied themselves with the Roman papacy and its adherents. They supported missionaries like the Anglo-Saxon Boniface (680–754), who went to areas on the fringes of the Carolingian realm as the pope's ambassador. To reform the local forms of Christianity that these regions had long ago adopted, Boniface set up a hierarchical church organization and founded monasteries dedicated to the Benedictine rule. His newly appointed bishops were loyal to Rome and the Carolingians. Charles Martel's son Pippin III (d. 768) turned to the pope even more directly. When he deposed the Merovingian king in 751, taking over the kingship himself, Pippin petitioned Pope Zachary to legitimize the act. The pope agreed. The Carolingians returned the favor a few years later when the pope asked for their help in defense against the hostile Lombards. That papal request signaled a major shift. Before 754, the papacy had been part of the Byzantine Empire; after that date, it turned to Europe for protection. Pippin launched a successful campaign against the Lombard king that ended in 756 with the so-called Donation of Pippin, a peace accord between the Lombards and the pope. The treaty gave back to the pope cities that had been taken by the Lombard king. The new arrangement recognized what the papacy had long ago created: a territorial "republic of St. Peter" ruled by the pope, not by the Byzantine emperor. Henceforth the fate of Italy would be tied largely to the policies of the pope and the Frankish kings to the north, not to the emperors of the East.

Partnership with the Roman church gave the Carolingian dynasty a Christian aura, expressed in symbolic form by anointment. Bishops rubbed holy oil on the foreheads and shoulders of Carolingian kings during their coronation ceremonies, imitating the Old Testament kings who had been anointed by God.

Charlemagne and His Kingdom, 768–814

The most famous Carolingian king was Charles (r. 768–814), called "the Great" (*le Magne* in Old French) by his contemporaries—thus Charlemagne. Epic poems portrayed Charlemagne as a just, brave, wise, and warlike king. Einhard, Charlemagne's courtier and younger contemporary, portrayed his ruler as the model of a Roman emperor. Some scholars at his court described him as another David, the anointed Old Testament king. Modern historians are less dazzled than his contemporaries were, noting that he was complex, contradictory, and sometimes brutal. He loved listening to readings from St. Augustine's *City of God* and supported major scholarly enterprises, yet he never learned to write. He was devout, building a beautiful chapel at his major residence at Aachen, yet he rejected the advice of churchmen when they told him to convert pagans rather than force baptism on them. He waged many successful wars, yet he thereby destroyed the buffer states surrounding the Frankish kingdoms, unleashing a new round of invasions even before his death. Behind these contradictions, however, lay a unifying vision. Charlemagne dreamed of an empire that would unite the military and intellectual traditions of the Roman and Germanic worlds with the legacy of Christianity. This vision lay at the core of his political activity, his building programs, and his support of scholarship and education.

During the early years of his reign, Charlemagne conquered lands in all directions (Map 8.3). He invaded Italy, seizing the crown of the Lombard kings and annexing northern Italy in 774. He then moved northward and began a long and difficult war against the Saxons, concluded only after more than thirty years of fighting. He forcibly annexed Saxon territory and converted the Saxon people to

Map 8.3 Expansion of the Carolingian Empire under Charlemagne
The conquests of Charlemagne temporarily united almost all of western Europe under one ruler. Although this great empire broke apart (the inset shows the divisions of the Treaty of Verdun), the legacy of that unity remained, even serving as one of the inspirations behind today's European Union.

Christianity through mass baptisms at the point of the sword. To the southeast, Charlemagne waged a campaign against the Avars, the people who had fought the Byzantines almost two centuries before. To the southwest, Charlemagne led an expedition to Spain, setting up a march, or military buffer region, between al-Andalus and his own realm. By the 790s, Charlemagne's kingdom stretched eastward across Germany, southeast to what is today Austria, and south to Spain and Italy.

Such power in the West was unheard of since the time of the Roman Empire. Charlemagne began to act according to the old Roman imperial model. He sponsored building programs to symbolize his authority, standardized weights and measures, and became a patron of intellectual and artistic efforts. He built a capital city at Aachen, complete with a church patterned on one built by Emperor Justinian at Ravenna in the sixth century. To discourage corruption, Charlemagne appointed special officials, called *missi dominici* (meaning "those sent out by the lord king"), to oversee his regional governors, the counts. The missi, who were lay aristocrats or bishops, traveled in pairs throughout the kingdom. As one of Charlemagne's capitularies (summaries of royal decisions) put it, the missi "are to make diligent inquiry wherever people claim that someone has done them an injustice, so that the missi fully carry out the law and do justice for everyone everywhere, whether in the holy churches of God or among the poor, orphans, or widows."

While Charlemagne was busy imitating Roman emperors through his conquests, building programs, legislation, and efforts at church reform, the papacy was beginning to claim imperial power for itself. At some point, perhaps in the 760s, members of the papal chancery, or writing office, created a document called the Donation of Constantine. It declared that the fourth-century Emperor Constantine had, upon his death, given the pope his crown, cloak, and military rank along with "all provinces, palaces, and districts of the city of Rome and Italy and of the regions of the West." (The document was much later proved a forgery.) The tension between the imperial claims of the Carolingians and those of the pope was heightened by the existence of an emperor at Constantinople who also had rights in the West.

Pope Leo III (r. 795–816) upset the delicate balance among these three powers. In 799, accused of adultery and perjury by a faction of the Roman aristocracy, Leo narrowly escaped being blinded and having his tongue cut out. He fled northward to seek Charlemagne's protection. Charlemagne had the pope escorted back to Rome under royal protection, and he soon arrived there himself to an imperial welcome orchestrated by Leo. On Christmas Day, 800, Leo put an imperial crown on Charlemagne's head, and the clergy and nobles who were present acclaimed the king "Augustus," the title of the first Roman emperor. The pope hoped in this way to exalt the king of the Franks, to downgrade the Byzantine ruler, and to claim for himself the role of "emperor maker."

About twenty years later, when Einhard wrote about this coronation, he said that the imperial title at first so displeased Charlemagne "that he stated that, if he had known in advance of the pope's plan, he would not have entered the church that day." In fact, Charlemagne did not use any title but king for more than a year afterward. But it is unlikely that he was completely surprised by the imperial title; his advisers certainly had been thinking about claiming it. He might have hesitated adopting it because he feared the reaction of the Byzantines, as Einhard went on to suggest, or he might have objected to the papal role in his crowning rather than to the crown itself. When Charlemagne finally did call himself emperor, after establishing a peace with the Byzantines, he used a long and revealing title: "Charles, the most serene Augustus, crowned by God, great and peaceful Emperor who governs the Roman Empire and who is, by the mercy of God, king of the Franks and the Lombards." According to this title, Charlemagne was not the Roman emperor crowned by the pope but rather God's emperor, who governed the Roman Empire along with his many other duties.

The Carolingian Renaissance, c. 790–c. 900

Charlemagne inaugurated—and his successors continued to support—a revival of learning designed to enhance the glory of the kings, educate their officials, reform the liturgy, and purify the faith. Like the renaissances of the Byzantine and Islamic worlds, the Carolingian renaissance resuscitated the learning of the past. Scholars studied Roman imperial writers such as Suetonius and Virgil; they read and commented on the works of the church fathers; and they worked to establish complete and accurate texts of everything they read and prized.

The English scholar Alcuin (c. 732–804), a member of the circle of scholars whom Charlemagne recruited to form a center of study, brought with him the traditions of Anglo-Saxon scholarship that had been developed by men such as Benedict Biscop and Bede. Invited to Aachen, Alcuin became Charlemagne's chief adviser, writing letters on the king's behalf, counseling him on royal policy, and tutoring the king's household, including the women and girls. Charlemagne's sister and daughter, for example, often asked Alcuin to explain passages from the Gospel to them. Charlemagne entrusted Alcuin with the task of preparing an improved edition of the Vulgate, the Latin Bible read in all church services.

The Carolingian renaissance depended on an elite staff of scholars such as Alcuin, yet its educational program had a broader impact. In one of his capitularies, Charlemagne ordered that the cathedrals and monasteries of his kingdom teach reading and writing to all who were able to learn. Some churchmen expressed the hope that schools for children (perhaps they were thinking of girls as well as boys) would be established even in small villages and hamlets. Although this dream was never realized, it shows that even before the Islamic world was organizing the madrasa system of schools, the Carolingians were thinking about the importance of religious education for more than a small elite.

Art, like scholarship, served Carolingian political and religious goals. Carolingian artists turned to models from Byzantium (perhaps some refugees from Byzantine iconoclasm joined them) and Italy to illustrate Gospels, Psalters, scientific treatises, and literary manuscripts.

The ambitious Carolingian program endured, even after the Carolingian dynasty had faded to a memory. The work of locating, understanding, and transmitting models of the past continued in a number of monastic schools. In the twelfth century, scholars would build on the foundations laid by the Carolingian renaissance. The very print of this textbook depends on one achievement of the period: modern letter fonts are based on the clear and beautiful letter forms, called Caroline minuscule, invented in the ninth century to standardize manuscript handwriting and make it more readable.

Charlemagne's Successors, 814–911

Charlemagne's son Louis the Pious (r. 814–840) was also crowned emperor, and he took his role as guarantor of the Christian empire even more seriously than his father did. He brought the monastic reformer Benedict of Aniane to court and issued a capitulary in 817 imposing a uniform way of life, based on the Benedictine rule, on all the monasteries of the empire. This moment marked the effective adoption of the Benedictine rule as the monastic standard in the West. Louis also regularized the practices of his notaries, who issued his documents and privileges, and he continued to use missi to administer justice throughout the realm.

In a new development of the coronation ritual, Louis's first wife, Ermengard, was crowned empress by the pope in 816. In 817, their firstborn son, Lothar, was given the title emperor and made co-ruler with his father. Their other sons, Pippin and Louis (later called Louis the German), were made subkings under imperial rule. Louis the Pious hoped in this way to ensure the unity of the empire while satisfying the claims of his and Ermengard's three sons. But Louis's plans were thwarted by events.

Ermengard died, and Louis married Judith, reputed to be the most beautiful woman in the kingdom. In 823, Judith and Louis had a son, Charles (later known as Charles the Bald, to whose court Dhuoda's son William was sent). The three sons of Ermengard, bitter over the birth of another royal heir, rebelled against their father and fought one another for more than a decade. Finally, after Louis the Pious's death in 840, the **Treaty of Verdun** (843) divided the empire among the three remaining brothers (Pippin had died in 838) in an arrangement that would roughly define the future political contours of western Europe (see the inset for Map 8.3, page 285). The western third, bequeathed to Charles the Bald, would eventually become France. The eastern third, handed to Louis the German, would become Germany. The "Middle Kingdom," which was given to Lothar along with the imperial title, had a different fate: parts of it were absorbed by France and Germany, and the rest eventually formed the modern states of the Netherlands, Belgium, Luxembourg, Switzerland, and Italy.

In 843, the European-wide empire of Charlemagne dissolved. Forged by conquest, it had been supported by a small group of privileged aristocrats with lands and offices stretching across the entire realm. Their loyalty—based on shared values, real friendship, expectations of gain, and formal ties of vassalage—was crucial to the success of the Carolingians. The empire had also been supported by an ideal, shared by educated laymen and churchmen alike, of conquest and Christian belief working together to bring good order to the earthly state. But powerful forces operated against the Carolingian Empire. Once the empire's borders were fixed and conquests ceased, the aristocrats could no longer hope for new lands and offices. They put down roots in

King David, Carolingian Style
In this sumptuously illustrated Bible made for King Charles the Bald, David plays the harp and dances on a cloud. Above and below him are his musicians with their instruments. Compare this view of David with the Byzantine image on page 276. (Bibliothèque nationale de France.)

particular regions and began to gather their own followers. Powerful local traditions such as different languages also undermined imperial unity. Finally, as Dhuoda revealed, some people disagreed with the imperial ideal. By asking her son to put his father before the emperor, she demonstrated her belief in the primacy of the family and the intimate and personal ties that bound it together. Dhuoda's ideal represented a new sensibility that saw real value in the breaking apart of Charlemagne's empire into smaller, more intimate local units.

Land and Power

The Carolingian economy, based on trade and agriculture, contributed to both the rise and the dissolution of the Carolingian Empire. At the outset, the empire's wealth came from land and plunder. After the booty from war ceased to pour in, the Carolingians still had access to money and goods. To the north, in Viking trading stations such as Haithabu (today Hedeby, in northern Germany), archaeologists have found Carolingian glass and pots alongside Islamic coins and cloth, evidence that the Carolingian economy intermingled with that of the Abbasid caliphate. Silver from the Islamic world probably came north up the Volga River through Russia to the Baltic Sea. There the coins were melted down, and the silver was traded to the Carolingians in return for wine, jugs, glasses, and other manufactured goods. The Carolingians turned the silver into coins of their own, to be used throughout the empire for small-scale local trade. The weakening of the Abbasid caliphate in the mid-ninth century disrupted this far-flung trade network and contributed to the weakening of the Carolingians at about the same time.

Land provided the most important source of Carolingian wealth and power. Like the landholders of the late Roman Empire and the Merovingian period, Carolingian aristocrats held many estates, scattered throughout the Frankish kingdom. But in the Carolingian period these estates were reorganized, and their productivity was carefully calculated. Modern historians often call these estates **manors**.

A typical manor was Villeneuve Saint-Georges, which belonged to the monastery of Saint-Germain-des-Prés (today in Paris) in the ninth century. Villeneuve consisted of arable fields, vineyards, meadows where animals could roam, and woodlands, all scattered about the countryside rather than connected in a compact unit. The land was not tilled by slave gangs, as had been the custom on the great estates of the Roman Empire, but rather by peasant families, each one settled on its own manse, which consisted of a house, a garden, and small sections of the arable land. The peasants farmed the land that belonged to them and also worked the demesne, the very large manse of the lord (in the case of Villeneuve, the lord was the abbey of Saint-Germain). These peasant farms marked a major social and economic development. Whereas agricultural slaves had worked in gangs on their owner's estates and had not been allowed to marry and have children, the peasants on Villeneuve and on other Carolingian estates normally lived with their families and could not be displaced from their manses. In this sense, the peasant household of the Carolingian period was the precursor of the modern nuclear family.

Peasants at Villeneuve practiced the most progressive sort of plowing, known as the three-field system, in which they farmed two-thirds of the arable land at one time. They planted one-third with winter wheat and one-third with summer crops, leaving the remaining third fallow, to restore its fertility. The crops sown and the fallow field were then rotated so that land use was repeated only every three years. This method of organizing the land produced larger yields (because two-thirds of the land was cultivated each year) than the still prevalent two-field system, in which only half of the arable land was cultivated one year, while the other half lay fallow.

All the peasants at Villeneuve were dependents of the monastery and owed dues and services to Saint-Germain. The peasants' obligations varied enormously. One family, for example, owed four silver coins, wine, wood, three hens, and fifteen eggs every year, and the men had to plow the fields of the demesne. Another family owed the intensive labor of working the vineyards. One woman was required to weave cloth and feed the chickens. Peasant women spent much time at the lord's house in the *gynaeceum*—the women's workshop, where they made and dyed cloth and sewed garments—or in the kitchens as cooks. Peasant men spent most of their time in the fields.

Manors organized on the model of Villeneuve were profitable. Like other lords, the Carolingians benefited from their extensive estates. Nevertheless, farming was still too primitive to return great surpluses. Further, as the lands belonging to the king were divided up in the wake of the partitioning of the empire and new invasions, Carolingian dependence on manors scattered throughout the kingdom proved to be a source of weakness.

Viking, Muslim, and Magyar Invasions, c. 790–955

Carolingian kings and counts confronted new groups—Vikings, Muslims, and Magyars—along their borders (Map 8.4). As royal sons fought one another and as counts and other powerful men sought to carve out their own principalities, some

Map 8.4 Viking, Muslim, and Magyar Invasions of the Ninth and Tenth Centuries

Bristling with multicolored arrows, this map suggests that western Europe was continually and thoroughly pillaged by invaders for almost two centuries. That impression is only partially true; it must be offset by several factors. First, not all the invaders came at once. The Viking raids were about over when the Magyar attacks began. Second, the invaders were not entirely unwelcome. The Magyars were for a time enlisted as mercenaries by the king of Italy, and some Muslims were allied to local lords in Provence. Third, the invasions, though widespread, were local in effect. Note, for example, that the Viking raids were largely limited to rivers and coastal areas.

allied with the newcomers, helping to integrate them swiftly into European society and political life.

The first of the new groups to attack the Carolingian Empire was the Vikings. The Franks called them Northmen; the English called them Danes. They were, in fact, much less united than their victims thought. When they began their voyages at the end of the eighth century, they did so in independent bands. Merchants and pirates at the same time, Vikings followed a chief, seeking profit, prestige, and land. Many traveled as families: husbands, wives, children, and slaves.

The Vikings perfected the art of navigation. They crossed the Atlantic in their longships, settling Iceland and Greenland and (about 1000 C.E.) landing on the coast of North America. Other Viking bands navigated the rivers of Europe. The Vikings were pagans, and to them monasteries and churches—with their reliquaries, chalices, and crosses—were storehouses of booty. "Never before," wrote Alcuin, who experienced one attack, "has such terror appeared in Britain as we have now suffered from a pagan race. . . . Behold the church of St. Cuthbert spattered with the blood of the priests of God, despoiled of all its ornaments."

The British Isles were the target of sporadic invasions by the Vikings from the eighth to the tenth centuries. From their fortified bases along the coast of Ireland, the Vikings attacked and plundered churches and monasteries. But they also established Dublin as a commercial center and, in the tenth century, began to intermarry with the Irish and convert to Christianity. In Scotland, the Scandinavians settled on the west coast. Meanwhile, by the 870s, they had settled the east coast of England, plowing the land and preparing to live on it. The region where they settled and imposed their own laws was later called the Danelaw.

In Wessex, the southernmost kingdom of England, King Alfred the Great (r. 871–899) bought time and peace by paying tribute and giving hostages to the

Viking Picture Stone
Picture stones—some very elaborate, others with simple incisions—were made on the island of Gotland, today part of Sweden, from the fifth to the twelfth centuries. This one, dating from the eighth or ninth century, has four interrelated scenes. The bottom scene is a battle between people defending a farm and archers outside. The woman in the enclosure above is either Gudrun mourning her brother Gunnar, who was thrown into a snake pit, or Sigyn, the faithful wife of the god Loke, catching in a bowl the venom that a snake pours down on her chained husband. The ship in the next scene is the ship of death that takes heroes to heaven. At the very top is heaven (Valhalla), where heroes hunt and feast for all eternity. (Photo: Raymond Hejdstrom.)

Danes. Such tribute, later called Danegeld, was collected as a tax that eventually became the basis of a relatively lucrative taxation system in England. Then in 878, Alfred led an army that, as his biographer put it, "gained the victory through God's will. He destroyed the Vikings with great slaughter and pursued those who fled . . . hacking them down." Thereafter, the pressures of invasion eased as Alfred reorganized his army, set up strongholds, and deployed new warships.

On the continent of Europe, the invaders set up trading posts and settled where they had originally raided. Beginning about 850, their attacks became well-organized expeditions for regional control. At the end of the ninth century, one contingent settled in the region of France that soon took the name Normandy, land of the Northmen. The new inhabitants converted to Christianity during the tenth century. Rollo, the Viking leader in Normandy, accepted Christianity in 911 when the Frankish king Charles the Simple (or Straightforward) formally ceded Normandy to him.

Normandy was not the only new Christian state created in the north during the tenth and eleventh centuries. Scandinavia itself was transformed with the creation of the powerful kingdom of Denmark. There had been kings in Scandinavia before the tenth century, but they had been weak, their power challenged by nearby chieftains. The Vikings had been led by these chieftains, each competing for booty to win prestige, land, and power back home. During the course of their raids, they and their followers came into contact with new cultures and learned from them. Meanwhile, the Carolingians and the English supported missionaries in Scandinavia. By the middle of the tenth century, the Danish kings and their people had become Christian. Following the model of the Christian kings to their south, the Danish kings built up an effective monarchy, with a royal mint and local agents who depended on them. By about 1000, the Danes had extended their control to parts of Sweden, Norway, and even England.

Far from Denmark, Muslims took advantage of Byzantium's early weakness. The dynasty that preceded the Fatimids in Egypt developed a navy that, over the ninth and tenth centuries, gradually conquered Sicily, which had been under Byzantine rule. By the middle of the tenth century, independent Islamic princes ruled all of Sicily. Around the same time, other raiders from North Africa set up bases on other Mediterranean islands, while pirates from al-Andalus built a stronghold in Provence (in southern France). Liutprand of Cremona was horrified:

[Muslim pirates from al-Andalus], disembarking under cover of night, entered the manor house unobserved and murdered—O grievous tale!—the Christian inhabitants. They then took the place as their own . . . [fortified it and] started stealthy raids on all the neighboring country. . . . Meanwhile the people of Provence close by, swayed by envy and mutual jealousy, began to cut one another's throats, plunder each other's substance, and do every sort of conceivable mischief. . . . [Furthermore, they called upon the Muslims] and in company with them proceeded to crush their neighbors.

In this way the Muslims, though outsiders, were drawn into local Provençal disputes. They were ousted only in 972, when they caused a scandal by capturing the holiest man of his era, Abbot Maieul of Cluny. Outraged, the count of Provence launched a successful attack against their hideout.

The last of the invaders were the Magyars. Nomadic people from the Urals (today northeastern Russia) who spoke a language unrelated to any other in Europe (except Finnish), the Magyars made their first appearance in the West around 899 in the Danube basin. Until then, the region had been predominantly Slavic, but the Magyars drove a wedge between the Slavs near the Frankish kingdom and those bordering on Byzantium. The Bulgarians, Serbs, and Russians, as we have seen, were driven into the Byzantine orbit, while the Slavs nearer the Frankish kingdom came under the influence of Germany.

From their bases in present-day Hungary, the Magyars raided far to the west, attacking Germany, Italy, and even southern Gaul frequently between 899 and 955. Then in 955, the German king Otto I defeated a marauding party of Magyars at the battle of Lechfeld. Otto's victory, his subsequent military reorganization of his eastern frontiers, and the cessation of Magyar raids around this time made Otto a great hero to his contemporaries. Historians today, however, think the containment of the Magyars had more to do with their internal transformation from nomads to farmers than with their military defeat.

The Viking, Muslim, and Magyar invasions were the final onslaught western Europe experienced from outsiders. In some ways they were a continuation of the invasions that had rocked the Roman Empire in the fourth and fifth centuries. Loosely organized in war bands, the new groups entered western Europe looking for wealth but stayed on to become absorbed in the region's post-invasion society.

REVIEW What were the strengths and weaknesses of the Carolingian institutions of government, warfare, and education?

After the Carolingians: The Emergence of Local Rule

The Carolingian Empire was too diverse to remain united. Although Latin was the language of official documents and most literary and ecclesiastical texts, few people spoke it; instead they used a wide variety of different languages and dialects. The king demanded loyalty from everyone, but most people knew only his representative, the local count. As the empire ceased to expand and was instead attacked by outsiders, the counts and other powerful regional rulers stopped looking to the king for new lands and offices and began to develop and exploit what they already had. They became powerful lords, commanding warriors and peasants, building castles, setting up markets, collecting revenues, and keeping the peace. A new warrior class of lords and **vassals** came to dominate post-Carolingian society.

Not all of Europe, however, came under the control of rural leaders. In northern and central Italy, where cities had never lost their importance, urban elites ruled over the surrounding countryside. Everywhere, kings retained a certain amount of power; in some places, such as Germany and England, they were extremely effective. Central European monarchies formed under the influence of Germany.* Nevertheless, throughout this period, it was local allegiances that mattered most to the societies of Europe.

Public Power and Private Relationships

Both kings and less powerful men commanded others by ensuring their personal loyalty. In the ninth century, the Carolingian kings had their *fideles,* "faithful men." Among these were the counts. In addition to a share in the revenues of their administrative district, the county, each count received benefices, later also called fiefs, which were temporary grants of land given in return for service. These short-term arrangements often became permanent when a count's son inherited the job and the fiefs of his father. By the end of the ninth century, fiefs could often be passed on to heirs.

In the wake of the invasions, more and more warriors were drawn into similar networks of dependency, but not with the king: they became the faithful men—the vassals—of local lords. From the Latin word for "fief" comes the word *feudal,* and some historians use the term *feudalism* to describe the social and economic system created by the relationship among vassals, lords, and fiefs.**

Medieval people often said that their society consisted of three groups: those who prayed, those who fought, and those who worked. Members of all these groups were involved in a hierarchy of dependency and linked by personal bonds, but the upper classes—the prayers (monks) and the fighters (knights)—were free. Their brand of dependency was prestigious, whether they were vassals, lords, or both. In fact, a typical warrior was lord of several vassals even while serving as the vassal of another lord. Monasteries normally had vassals to fight for them, and their abbots in turn were likely to be vassals of a king or other powerful lord.

Vassalage grew up as an alternative to public power and at the same time as a way to strengthen what little public power there was. Given the impoverished economic conditions of western Europe, its primitive methods of communication, and its lack of unifying traditions, kings relied on vassals who were personally loyal to them to muster troops, collect taxes, and administer justice. When in the ninth century the Carolingian Empire broke up politically and power fell into the hands of local lords, those lords, too, needed "faithful men" to protect them and carry

---

*Terms such as *Germany, France,* and *Italy* are used here for the sake of convenience. They refer to regions, not to the nation-states that would eventually become associated with those names.

**Many historians regard *feudalism* as a problematic term. Does it mean "anarchy"? Some historians have used it that way. Does it mean "a hierarchical scheme of lords and knights"? This is another common definition. And there are others as well. This imprecision has led some historians to drop the word altogether. Moreover, feudalism implies that one way of life dominated the Middle Ages, when in fact there were numerous social, political, and economic arrangements. For these reasons, *feudalism* rarely appears in *The Making of the West.*

out their orders. And vassals needed lords. At the low end of the social scale, poor vassals depended on their lords to feed, clothe, house, and arm them. They hoped that they would be rewarded for their service with a fief of their own, with which they could support themselves and a family. At the upper end of the social scale, vassals looked to lords to enrich them further.

Many upper-class laywomen participated in the society of fighters and prayers as wives and mothers of vassals and lords. A few women were themselves vassals, and some were lords (or, rather, ladies, the female counterpart). Other women entered convents and became members of the social group that prayed. Through its abbess, or a man standing in for her, a convent often had vassals as well. Many elite women engaged in property transactions, whether alone, with other family members, or as part of a group, such as a convent. (See "Taking Measure.")

Becoming a vassal involved both ritual gestures and verbal promises. In a ceremony witnessed by others, the vassal-to-be knelt and, placing his hands between the hands of his lord, said, "I promise to be your man." This act, known as homage, was followed by the promise of **fealty**—fidelity, trust, and service—which the vassal swore with his hand on a saint's relics or on a Bible. In many regions, the vassal and the lord kissed one another. In an age when many people could not read, a public ceremony such as this represented a visual and verbal contract. Vassalage bound the lord and vassal to one another with reciprocal obligations, usually military. Knights, as the premier fighters of the day, were the most desirable vassals.

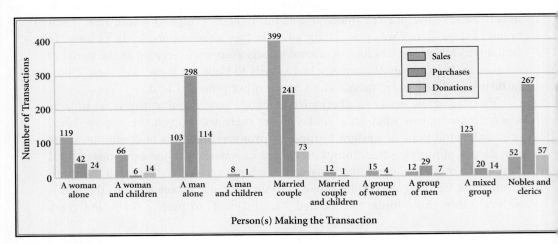

Taking Measure Sellers, Buyers, and Donors, 800–1000

How did ladies get their wealth, and what did they do with it? Two counties in northeastern Spain, Osona and Manresa, are particularly rich in documentation for the period 880–1000. We have 2,121 charters (legal documents) attesting to sales, purchases, and donations of land from this period. As the graph shows, few women purchased property, which suggests that they gained their land mainly through inheritance. As for what they did with it, by themselves they were more likely to sell property than men who were alone; as part of a married couple, they were often involved in sales. They were less likely than men to make donations, many of which went to churches or monasteries.

At the bottom of the social scale were those who worked—the peasants. In the Carolingian period, many peasants were free; they did not live on a manor, or if they did, they owed very little to its lord. But as power fell into the hands of local rulers, fewer and fewer peasants remained free. Rather, they were made dependent on lords, not as vassals but as **serfs**. Serfdom was a dependency separate from and completely unlike that of a vassal. Serfdom was not voluntary but inherited. No serf did homage or fealty to his lord; no serf kissed his lord as an equal. Vassals served their lords as warriors. Serfs worked as laborers on the land of their lord and paid him taxes and dues. Peasants constituted the majority of the population, but unlike knights, who were celebrated in song, they were barely noticed by the upper classes—except as a source of revenue. By the year 1000, though there were still some free peasants, many were serfs and therefore subject to a lord. Most important, they belonged to the land: when a lord sold a field to someone else, the serfs who cultivated that field got a new lord. They could not be sold apart from their land, but they were also not free to leave it.

New methods of cultivation and a slightly warmer climate helped transform the rural landscape, making it more productive and thus able to support a larger population. With a growing number of men and women to work the land, however, the lower classes now had more mouths to feed and faced the hardship of food shortages. Landlords began reorganizing their estates to run more efficiently. In the tenth century, the three-field system became more prevalent; heavy plows that could turn the heavy northern soils came into wider use; and horses (more effective than oxen) were harnessed to pull the plows. The result was surplus food and a better standard of living for nearly everyone.

In search of greater profits, some lords lightened the dues and services of peasants temporarily, giving them a chance to open up new lands by draining marshes and cutting down forests. Some landlords converted dues and labor services into money payments, a boon for both lords and peasants. Rather than receiving hens and eggs they might not need, lords now received money to spend on what they wanted. Peasants benefited as well because their taxes were fixed despite inflation. Thus, as the prices of their hens and eggs went up, they could sell them, reaping a profit in spite of the dues they owed their lords.

By the year 1000, many peasants lived in populous rural settlements, true villages. Surrounded by arable land, meadows, woods, and wasteland, villages developed a sense of community. Boundaries—sometimes real fortifications, sometimes simple markers—told nonresidents to keep out and to find shelter in huts located outside the village limits.

The church often formed the focal point of local activity. There people met, received the sacraments, drew up contracts, and buried their dead. Religious feasts and festivals joined the rituals of farming to mark the seasons. The church dominated the village in another way: men and women owed it a tax called a **tithe** (equivalent to one-tenth of their crops or income, paid in money or in kind), which was first instituted on a regular basis by the Carolingians.

Village peasants developed a sense of common purpose based on their interdependence, as they shared oxen or horses for the teams that pulled their village's plow or turned to village craftsmen to fix their wheels or shoe their horses. A sense of solidarity sometimes encouraged peasants to band together to ask for privileges as a group. Near Verona, in northern Italy, for example, twenty-five men living around the castle of Nogara in 920 joined together to ask their lord, the abbot of Nonantola, to allow them to lease plots of land, houses, and pasturage in return for a small yearly rent and the promise to defend the castle. The abbot granted their request.

Village solidarity could be compromised, however, by conflicting loyalties and obligations. A peasant in one village might very well have one piece of land connected with a certain manor and another bit of land on a different estate, and he or she might owe several lords different kinds of dues. Even peasants of one village working for one lord might owe him varied services and taxes for different pieces of land.

Obligations differed even more strikingly across the regions of Europe. The principal distinction was between free peasants—such as small landowners in Saxony and other parts of Germany, who had no lords—and serfs, who were especially common in France and England. In Italy, peasants ranged from small independent landowners to leaseholders (like the tenants at Nogara); most were both, owning a parcel in one place and leasing another nearby.

As the power of kings began to weaken, the system of peasant obligations became part of a larger system of local rule. When landlords consolidated their power over their manors, they collected not only dues and services but also fees for the use of their flour mills, bakehouses, and breweries. Some built castles—fortified strongholds—and imposed the even wider powers of the **ban**: the right to collect taxes, hear court cases, levy fines, and muster men for defense.

In France, for example, as the king's power waned, political control fell into the hands of counts and other princes. By the year 1000, castles had become the key to their power. In the south of France, power was so fragmented that each man who controlled a castle—a **castellan**—was a virtual ruler, although often with a very limited reach. In northwestern France, territorial princes, basing their rule on the control of many castles, dominated much broader regions. For example, Fulk Nera, count of Anjou (r. 987–1040), built more than thirteen castles and captured others from rival counts. By the end of his life, he controlled a region extending from Blois to Nantes along the Loire valley.

Castellans extended their authority by subjecting everyone near their castles to their bans. Peasants, whether they worked on a castellan's estates or not, had to pay him a variety of dues for his "protection" and judicial rights over them. Castellans also established links with wealthy landholders in the region, tempting or coercing them to become vassals. Lay castellans often supported local monasteries and controlled the appointment of local priests. But churchmen themselves sometimes held the position of territorial lord; a good example is the archbishop of Milan in the eleventh century.

The development of nearly independent local political units, dominated by a castle and controlled by a military elite, marks an important turning point in western Europe. Although this development did not occur everywhere simultaneously (and in some places it hardly occurred at all), the social, political, and cultural life of Europe was now dominated by landowners who saw themselves as military men and regional leaders.

Warriors and Warfare

Not all warriors were alike. At the top of this elite group were the kings, counts, and dukes. Below them, but on the rise, were the castellans; and still farther down the social scale were knights.

Nevertheless, they all shared a common lifestyle. High astride their horses, wearing shirts of chain mail and helmets of flat metal plates riveted together, knights and those above them marked a military revolution—a shift from a reliance on foot soldiers to a focus on cavalry. The war season started in May, when the grasses were high enough for horses to forage. Horseshoes allowed armies to move faster than ever before and to negotiate rough terrain previously unsuitable for battle. Stirrups, probably invented by Asiatic nomadic tribes, allowed the mounted warrior to hold his seat. This made it possible for knights to thrust at the enemy with heavy lances; the light javelin of ancient warfare was abandoned.

Lords and their vassals often lived together. In the lord's great hall they ate, enjoyed listening to music, songs, and stories, and bedded down for the night. They went out hunting together and went off to the battlefield as a group as well. More powerful vassals—counts, for example—lived on their own fiefs and hardly ever saw their lord (probably the king), except when doing homage and fealty—once during their lifetimes—or

Two Cities Besieged
In about 900, the monks of the monastery of St. Gall, in what is today Switzerland, produced a Psalter with numerous illuminations. The illustration for Psalm 59, which tells of King David's victories, used four pages. This page was the fourth. On the top level, David's army besieges a fortified city from two directions. On the right are foot soldiers, one of whom holds a burning torch to set the city afire. On the left are horsemen—led by their standard-bearer—with lances and bows and arrows. Within the city, four soldiers protect themselves with shields, while four other men seem to be cowering behind the city. In the bottom register, a different city burns fiercely (note the towers on fire). This city lacks defenders; the people within it are unarmed. Although this illumination purports to show David's victories, in fact it nicely represents the equipment and strategies of ninth-century warfare.
(Stiftsbibliothek St. Gallen, Switzerland.)

serving him in battle, for perhaps forty days a year. They themselves were lords of knightly vassals who were not married and who lived, ate, and hunted with them.

No matter how old they might be, unmarried knights who lived with their lords were called youths by their contemporaries. Such perpetual bachelors were something new, the result of a profound transformation in the organization of families and inheritance. Before the eleventh century, noble families recognized all their children as heirs and divided their estates accordingly. In the mid-ninth century, for example, one count and his wife willed their large estates, scattered from Belgium to Italy, to their four sons and three daughters. (True, they gave the boys far more than the girls, and the oldest boy far more than the others.)

By around the year 1000, French nobles, adapting to diminished opportunities for land and office and wary of fragmenting the estates they had, changed both the conception of the family and the way property passed to the next generation. Recognizing the overriding claims of one son, often the eldest, they handed down their entire inheritance to him. (In cases where the heir is indeed the eldest son, this system of inheritance is called primogeniture.) The heir, in turn, traced his lineage only through the male line, backward through his father and forward through his own eldest son. Such patrilineal families left many younger sons without an inheritance and therefore without the prospect of marrying and founding families. Instead, younger sons lived at the courts of the great as "youths," or they joined the church as clerics or monks. The development of territorial rule and patrilineal families went hand in hand, as fathers passed down to one son not only manors but titles, castles, and the authority of the ban.

Patrilineal inheritance tended to bypass daughters and so tended to work against the interests of aristocratic women. In families without sons, however, widows and daughters did inherit property. Wives often acted as lords of estates when their husbands were at war. Moreover, all aristocratic women played an important role in this warrior society, whether in the monastery (where they prayed for the souls of their families) or through their marriages (where they helped forge alliances between their own and their husbands' families).

Highly militarized, post-Carolingian society was almost constantly at war. Warfare benefited territorial rulers in the short term, but in the long run their revenues suffered, as armies plundered the countryside and sacked walled cities. Bishops, who were themselves from the class of lords and warriors, worried about the dangers to church property. Peasants cried out against wars that destroyed their crops or forced them to join regional infantries. Monks and religious thinkers were appalled at violence that was not in the service of an anointed king. By the end of the tenth century, all classes clamored for peace.

Sentiments against local violence came together in a movement called the **Peace of God**, which began in the south of France and by 1050 had spread over a wide region. Meetings of bishops, counts, and lords, and often crowds of lower-class men and women, set forth the provisions of this peace. "No man in the counties or bishoprics shall seize a horse, colt, ox, cow, ass, or the burdens which it carries. . . . No one shall seize a peasant, man or woman," ran the decree of one council held in 990. Anyone who violated this peace was to be excommunicated: cut off from the community of the faithful, denied the services of the church and the hope of salvation.

The peace proclaimed at local councils like this limited some violence but did not address the problem of conflict between armed men. A second set of agreements, the Truce of God, soon supplemented the Peace of God. The truce prohibited fighting between warriors at certain times: on Sunday because it was the Lord's Day, on Saturday because it was a reminder of Holy Saturday, on Friday because it symbolized Good Friday, and on Thursday because it stood for Holy Thursday. Enforcement of the truce fell to the local knights and nobles, who swore over saints' relics to uphold it and to fight anyone who broke it.

The Peace of God and Truce of God were only two of the ways in which men and women contained and defused violent confrontations in the tenth and eleventh centuries. At times, lords and their vassals mediated wars and feuds in assemblies called *placita*. In other instances, monks or laymen tried to find solutions to disputes that would leave the honor of both parties intact. Rather than try to establish guilt or innocence, winners or losers, these methods of adjudication often resulted in compromises on both sides.

Political Communities in Italy, England, and France

The political systems that emerged in the wake of the breakup of the Carolingian Empire were as varied as the regions of Europe. In Italy, cities were the centers of power, still reflecting, though feebly, the political organization of ancient Rome. In England, strong kings came to the fore. In France, as we have seen, great lords dominated the countryside; there the king was relatively weak.

Whereas in France great landlords built their castles in the countryside, in northern and central Italy they often constructed their family seats within the walls of cities. Churches, often as many as fifty or sixty, also were built within city walls, the proud work of rich laypeople or bishops. From their perches within the cities, the great landholders of Italy, both lay and religious, dominated the countryside. Italian cities also functioned as important marketplaces. Peasants sold their surplus goods there; artisans and merchants lived within the walls; foreign traders offered their wares there. These members of the lower classes were supported by the noble rich, who in Italy even more than elsewhere depended on cash to satisfy their desires. In the course of the ninth and tenth centuries, both servile and free tenants became renters who paid in currency.

Social and political life in Italy favored a familial organization somewhat different from the patrilineal families of France. To prevent the partitioning of their properties among heirs, families organized themselves by formal contract into *consorteria*, in which all male members shared the profits of the family's inheritance and all women were excluded. The consorterial family was like a blood-related corporation, a social unit on which early Italian businesses and banks would later be modeled.

Whereas Italy was urban, England was rural. In the face of the Viking invasions in England, King Alfred of Wessex (r. 871–899) developed new mechanisms of royal government, instituting reforms that his successors continued. He fortified settlements throughout Wessex and divided the army into two parts. The duty of one was to defend the fortifications (or *burhs*); the other operated as a mobile unit. Alfred also started a navy. These military innovations cost money, and the assessments fell on peasants' holdings.

Alfred sought to strengthen his kingdom's religious integrity as well as its regional fortifications. In the ninth century, people interpreted invasions as God's punishment for their sins. Alfred began a program of religious reform and renewal by bringing scholars to his court to write and to educate others. Above all, Alfred wanted to translate key religious works from Latin into Anglo-Saxon. He was determined to "turn into the language that we can all understand certain books which are the most necessary for all men to know." Alfred and scholars under his guidance translated works by church fathers such as Gregory the Great and St. Augustine. Even the Psalms, until now sung only in Hebrew, Greek, and Latin, were rendered into Anglo-Saxon. In most of ninth- and tenth-century Europe, Latin remained the language of scholarship and writing, separate from the language people spoke. In England, however, the vernacular—the common spoken language—was also a literary language. With Alfred's work giving it greater legitimacy, Anglo-Saxon came to be used alongside Latin for both literature and royal administration.

Alfred's reforms strengthened not only defense, education, and religion but also royal power. He consolidated his control over Wessex and fought the Danish kings, who by the mid-870s had taken Northumbria, northeastern Mercia, and East Anglia. Eventually, as he fought the Danes who were pushing south and west, he was recognized as king of all the English not under Danish rule. He issued a law code, the first by an English king since 695. Unlike earlier codes, drawn up for each separate kingdom of England, Alfred's laws were drawn from and intended for all the English kingdoms. In this way, Alfred became the first king of all the English.

Alfred's successors rolled back Danish rule in England. "Then the Norsemen departed in their nailed ships, bloodstained survivors of spears," wrote one poet about a battle the Vikings lost in 937. But many Vikings remained. Converted to Christianity, their great men joined Anglo-Saxons

England in the Age of King Alfred, 871–899

in attending the English king at court. As peace returned, new administrative subdivisions—shires (counties) and hundreds (districts)—were established throughout England for judicial and taxation purposes. The powerful men of the kingdom swore fealty to the king, promising to be enemies of his enemies, friends of his friends. England was united and organized to support a strong ruler.

Alfred's grandson Edgar (r. c. 959–975) commanded all the possibilities early medieval kingship offered. He was the sworn lord of all the great men of the kingdom. He controlled appointments to the English church and sponsored monastic reform. In 973, following the continental fashion, he was anointed. The fortifications of the kingdom were in his hands, as was the army, and he took responsibility for keeping the peace by proclaiming certain crimes—arson and theft—to be under his special jurisdiction and mobilizing the machinery of the shire and the hundred to find and punish thieves.

Despite its apparent centralization, England was not a unified state in the modern sense, and the king's control was often weak. Many royal officials were great landowners who (as on the continent) worked for the king because doing so was in their best interest. When it was not, they allied with different claimants to the throne. This political fragility may have helped the Danish king Cnut (or Canute) to conquer England. As king of England from 1017 to 1035, Cnut reinforced the already strong connections between England and Scandinavia while keeping intact much of the administrative, ecclesiastical, and military apparatus already established in England by the Anglo-Saxons (Map 8.4, page 291). By Cnut's time Scandinavian traditions had largely merged with those of the rest of Europe, and the Vikings were no longer an alien culture.

French kings had a harder time than the English coping with the invasions because their realm was much larger. They had no chance to build up their defenses slowly

The Kingdom of the Franks under Hugh Capet, 987–996

from one powerful base. During most of the tenth century, Carolingian kings alternated on the throne with kings from another family. As the Carolingian dynasty waned, the most powerful men of the kingdom—dukes, counts, and important bishops—at last came together to elect as king Hugh Capet (r. 987–996), a lord of considerable prestige yet relatively little power. His election marked the end of Carolingian rule and the beginning of the new **Capetian dynasty**, which would hand down the royal title from father to son until the fourteenth century.

In the eleventh century, the reach of the Capetian kings was limited by territorial lordships in the vicinity. The king's scattered but substantial estates lay in the north of France, in the region around Paris—the Île-de-France (literally, "island of France"). His castles and his vassals were there. Independent castellans, however, controlled areas nearby. In the sense that he was a neighbor of castellans and not much more powerful militarily than they, the king of the Franks—who would only later take the territorial title "king of France"—was just another local strongman. Yet the Capetian kings enjoyed considerable prestige. They were anointed with holy oil, and they represented the idea of unity inherited from Charlemagne. Most of the counts, at least in the north of France, became their vassals. They did not promise to obey the king, but they did vow not to try to kill or depose him.

Emperors and Kings in Central and Eastern Europe

In contrast with the development of territorial lordships in France, Germany's fragmentation hardly began before it was reversed. Five duchies (regions ruled by dukes) emerged in Germany in the late Carolingian period, each much larger than the counties and castellanies of France. With the death in 911 of the last Carolingian king in Germany, Louis the Child, the dukes elected one of themselves as king over all. Then, as the Magyar invasions increased, the dukes gave the royal title to the powerful duke of Saxony, Henry I (r. 919–936), who proceeded to set up fortifications and reorganize his army, crowning his efforts with a major defeat of a Magyar army in 933. Otto I (r. 936–973), the son of Henry I, was an even greater military hero. His defeat of the Magyar forces in 955 gave him prestige and helped solidify his dynasty. In 951, he marched into Italy and took the Lombard crown. Against the Slavs, with whom the Germans shared a border, Otto set up marches (military buffers) from which he could make expeditions and hold off counterattacks. After the pope crowned him emperor in 962, he claimed the Middle Kingdom carved out by the Treaty of Verdun and cast himself as the agent of Roman imperial renewal.

The Ottonian Empire, 936–1002

Otto's victories brought tribute, plunder, plum positions to disburse, and lands to give away, ensuring him a following among the great men of the realm. His successors, Otto II (r. 961–983), Otto III (r. 983–1002)—not surprisingly, the dynasty is called the "Ottonian"—and Henry II (r. 1002–1024), built on his achievements.

Granted power by the magnates, the kings gave back in turn: they distributed lands and appointed their aristocratic supporters to duchies, counties, and bishoprics. Always, however, their decisions were tempered by hereditary claims and plenty of lobbying by influential men at court and at the great assemblies that met with the king to hammer out policies. The role of kings in appointing bishops and archbishops was particularly important because bishoprics, unlike counties and duchies, could not be inherited. Otto I created new eastern bishoprics, endowing them with extensive lands and subjecting the local peasantry to their overlordship.

Otto III Receiving Gifts

This triumphal image is from a book of Gospels made for Otto III (r. 983–1002). The crowned women on the left are personifications of the four parts of Otto's empire: Sclavinia (the Slavic lands), Germania (Germany), Gallia (Gaul), and Roma (Rome). Each holds a gift in tribute and homage to the emperor, who sits on a throne holding the symbols of his power (an orb and scepter). He is flanked by representatives of the church (on his right) and the army (on his left). Why do you suppose the artist separated the image of the emperor from that of the women? What does the body language of the women tell you about the relations that Otto wanted to portray between himself and the parts of his empire? Can you relate this manuscript, which was made in 997–1000, to Otto's conquest over the Slavs in 997? (Bayerische Staatsbibliothek, Munich.)

In some areas of Germany, bishops gained the power of the ban: they collected revenues, took over the rights of justice, and called men to arms. Answering to the king and furnishing him with troops, the bishops became royal officials while also carrying out their pastoral and religious duties. German kings claimed the right to select bishops (usually with the consent of the cathedral clergy) and to "invest" them by participating in the ceremony that installed them in office. Bishops and archbishops joined the king at court: many had been schooled there in their youth, while in their more mature years, they taught new young clergy as well as princes and noblewomen.

Like all the strong rulers of the day, whether in Europe or in the Byzantine and Islamic worlds, the Ottonians presided over a renaissance of learning. For example, the tutor of Otto III was Gerbert (later Pope Sylvester II), the best-educated man of his time. Gerbert knew how to calculate with Arabic numerals. He spent "large sums of money to pay copyists and to acquire [books]," as he put it. He studied the classics as models of rhetoric and argument, and he reveled in logic and debate. Not only did churchmen and kings support Ottonian scholarship, but to an unprecedented extent noblewomen in Germany also acquired an education and participated in the intellectual revival. Aristocratic women spent much of their wealth on learning. Living at home with their kinsfolk and servants or in convents that provided them with comfortable private apartments, noblewomen studied and wrote books. They also supported other artists and scholars.

The German kings' policies played a crucial role in the political communities on Germany's eastern border. Hand in hand with the papacy, the Ottonians fostered the emergence of Christian monarchies aligned with the Roman church in the regions that today constitute the Czech and Slovak republics, Poland, and Hungary. The Czechs, who lived in the region of Bohemia, converted under the rule of Václav (r. 920–929), who thereby gained recognition in Germany as the duke of Bohemia. He and his successors did not become kings, remaining politically within the German sphere. Václav's murder by his younger brother made him a martyr and the patron saint of Bohemia, a symbol around which later movements for independence rallied.

The Poles gained a greater measure of independence than the Czechs. In 966, Mieszko I (r. 963–992), the leader of the Slavic tribe known as the Polanians, accepted baptism to head off the attacks that the Germans were already mounting against pagan Slavic peoples along the Baltic coast and east of the Elbe River. Busily engaged in bringing the other Slavic tribes of Poland under his control, he skillfully shifted his alliances with various German princes to suit his needs. In 991, Mieszko placed his realm under the protection of the pope, establishing a tradition of Polish loyalty to the Roman church. Mieszko's son Boleslaw the Brave (r. 992–1025) greatly extended Poland's boundaries, at one time or another ruling from the Bohemian border to Kiev. In 1000, he gained a royal crown with papal blessing.

Hungary's case was similar to that of Poland. The Magyars settled in the region known today as Hungary. They became landowners, using the native Slavs to till the soil. At the end of the tenth century, the Magyar ruler Stephen I (r. 997–1038) accepted Christianity. In return, German knights and monks helped him consolidate his power and convert his people. According to legend, the crown placed on Stephen's head in 1000 or 1001, like Boleslaw's crown, was sent to him by the pope. To this day, the crown of St. Stephen remains the most hallowed symbol of Hungarian nationhood.

Symbols of rulership such as crowns, consecrated by Christian priests and accorded a prestige almost akin to saints' relics, were among the most vital institutions of royal rule in central Europe. The economic basis for the power of central European rulers gradually shifted from slave raids to agriculture. This change encouraged a proliferation of regional centers of power that challenged monarchical rule. From the eleventh century onward, all the medieval Slavic states would face a constant problem of internal division.

REVIEW   After the dissolution of the Carolingian Empire, what political systems developed in western, northern, eastern, and central Europe, and how did these systems differ from one another?

Conclusion

In 800, the model of the Roman Empire was still powerful: whether in Europe, at Byzantium, or in the Islamic world, political systems were centralized, monarchical, and imperial. Byzantine emperors writing their learned books, Abbasid caliphs holding court in their resplendent new palace at Baghdad, and Carolingian emperors issuing their directives for reform to the missi dominici all mimicked the Roman

Mapping the West Europe and the Mediterranean, c. 1050
"The Empire" here refers to the area ruled by the Ottonian emperors. But the clear borders and distinct colors of the "states" on this map distort an essential truth: none of them had centralized governments that controlled whole territories, as in modern states. Instead, there were numerous regional rulers within each, and there were numerous overlapping claims of jurisdiction. The next centuries would show both the weaknesses and the surprising strengths of this fragmentation.

emperors. Yet these rulers confronted tensions and regional pressures that tended to decentralize political power. Byzantium felt this fragmentation least, yet even there the emergence of a new elite led to decentralization and the emperor's loss of control over the countryside. In the Islamic world, economic crisis, religious tension, and the ambitions of powerful local rulers decisively weakened the caliphate and opened the way to separate successor states. In western Europe, powerful independent land-owners strove with greater or lesser success (depending on the region) to establish themselves as effective rulers. By 1050, the states that would become those of modern Europe began to form.

Local conditions determined political and economic organizations. Between 900 and 1000, for example, French society was transformed by the development of territorial lordships, patrilineal families, and ties of vassalage. These factors figured less prominently in Germany, where a central monarchy remained, buttressed by churchmen and conquests to the east. We shall see in the next chapter, however, how fragile this centralization was to be.

CHAPTER REVIEW QUESTIONS

1. How were the Byzantine, Islamic, and European economies similar? How did they differ? How did these economies interact?

2. Compare the effects of the barbarian invasions into the Roman Empire with the effects of the Viking, Muslim, and Magyar invasions into the Carolingian Empire.

For practice quizzes and other study tools, see the Online Study Guide at bedfordstmartins.com/huntconcise.

For primary-source material from this period, see Chapter 9 of *Sources of THE MAKING OF THE WEST*, Third Edition.

TIMELINE

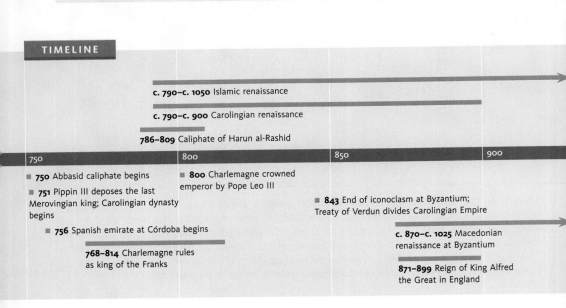

c. 790–c. 1050 Islamic renaissance

c. 790–c. 900 Carolingian renaissance

786–809 Caliphate of Harun al-Rashid

750	800	850	900

- **750** Abbasid caliphate begins
- **751** Pippin III deposes the last Merovingian king; Carolingian dynasty begins
- **756** Spanish emirate at Córdoba begins
- **768–814** Charlemagne rules as king of the Franks
- **800** Charlemagne crowned emperor by Pope Leo III
- **843** End of iconoclasm at Byzantium; Treaty of Verdun divides Carolingian Empire
- **c. 870–c. 1025** Macedonian renaissance at Byzantium
- **871–899** Reign of King Alfred the Great in England

Suggested References

Excellent recent biographies allow for interesting comparisons of rulers: Becher's *Charlemagne*, Cooperson's *al-Ma'mun* (an important Abbasid caliph), and Nelson's *Charles the Bald*. Many primary sources for the Carolingian period are translated by Paul Dutton. Political disintegration used to be seen as a bad thing, but recent historians, such as Duby and Head and Landes, value the diversity and local developments that it permitted.

Becher, Matthias. *Charlemagne.* 2003.

Byzantine art: http://historylink101.com/lessons/art_history_lessons/ma/byzantine_art.htm

Cooperson, Michael. *Al-Ma'mun.* 2005.

Duby, Georges. *The Early Growth of the European Economy: Warriors and Peasants from the Seventh to the Twelfth Century.* Trans. H. B. Clark. 1974.

*Dutton, Paul Edward. *Carolingian Civilization: A Reader.* 2d ed. 2004.

Franklin, Simon, and Jonathan Shepard. *The Emergence of Rus, 750–1200.* 1996.

Garland, Lynda. *Byzantine Empresses: Women and Power in Byzantium,* A.D. *527–1204.* 1999.

Head, Thomas, and Richard Landes, eds. *The Peace of God: Social Violence and Religious Response in France around the Year 1000.* 1992.

McCormick, Michael. *Origins of the European Economy: Communications and Commerce,* A.D. *300–900.* 2001.

Moore, R. I. *The First European Revolution, c. 970–1215.* 2000.

Nelson, Janet. *Charles the Bald.* 1987.

*Psellus, Michael. *Fourteen Byzantine Rulers: The Chronographia.* Trans. E. R. A. Sewter. 1966.

■ **955** Otto I defeats Magyars   ■ **c. 1000** Beginning of the age of the castellans in France

| 950 | 1000 | 1050 | 1100 |

963–1025 Reign of Byzantine emperor Basil II ("the Bulgar-Slayer")

969–1171 Fatimid dynasty in Egypt

The Flowering of
the Middle Ages

N THE MIDDLE OF THE TWELFTH CENTURY, a sculptor was hired to add friezes depicting scenes from the Old and New Testaments to the facade of the grand new hilltop cathedral at Lincoln, England. He portrayed in striking fashion the deaths of the poor man Lazarus and the rich man Dives. Their fates could not have been more different. While Lazarus was carried to heaven by two angels, a contented-looking devil poked Dives and two other rich men straight into the mouth of hell—headfirst.

Dives and Lazarus
At the time this sculpted depiction of the rich man Dives (bottom) and the poor man Lazarus (top) was made, the town of Lincoln was expanding both within and outside its Roman walls. Within the walls were the precincts of the fishmongers, the grain sellers, and the poultry merchants. Outside the walls were the bakers, the soapmakers, and the salt sellers. The town was highly attuned to moneymaking—both its pleasures and its dangers. *(Conway Library, Courtauld Institute of Art, London.)*

The sculptor's work reflected a widespread change in attitudes toward money. In the Carolingian and post-Carolingian period, wealth was considered, in general, a very good thing. Rich kings were praised for their generosity, sumptuous manuscripts were highly prized, and splendid churches like Charlemagne's chapel at Aachen were widely admired. This view changed over the course of the eleventh century. A new money economy, burgeoning cities, and the growth of a well-heeled merchant and trading class led many observers to condemn wealth and to emphasize its corrupting influence. Even participants in the new economy shared this perspective: Lincoln's new cathedral was built right next to a marketplace, and its twelfth-century bishops—who were themselves rich men—wanted to warn moneymaking parishioners about the perils of wealth.

The most salient feature of the period 1050–1200 was increasing wealth. Cities, trade, and agricultural production swelled. The resulting worldliness met with a wide variety of responses. Some people tried to flee the new commercial society; others tried to reform it; and still others embraced, enjoyed, or tried to

311

understand it. Within one century, the development of a profit economy transformed western European communities. Many villages and fortifications became cities where traders, merchants, and artisans conducted business. Although most people still lived in less populated, rural areas, their lives were touched in many ways by the new cash economy. Economic concerns drove changes within the church, where a movement for reform gathered steam. Money helped redefine the role of the clergy, while popes, kings, and princes came to exercise new forms of power. At the same time, city dwellers began to demand their own governments. Monks, nuns, and clerics reformulated the nature of their communities, seeking newly intense spiritual lives. All of these developments inspired (and in turn were inspired by) new ideas, new forms of scholarship, and new methods of inquiry. The rapid pace of religious, political, and economic change was matched by new developments in thought, learning, and artistic expression.

CHAPTER FOCUS QUESTION How important was the new commercial economy to church reform, centralizing monarchies, and new forms of scholarship and piety?

The Commercial Revolution

As the population of Europe expanded in the eleventh century, cities, long-distance trade networks, local markets, and new business arrangements meshed to create a profit-based economy. With improvements in agriculture and more land in cultivation, the great estates of the eleventh century produced surpluses that helped feed, and therefore made possible, a new urban population. The result was the **commercial revolution** of the Middle Ages. It produced the institutions that would be the direct ancestors of modern business and commerce.

Centers of Commerce and Commercial Life

New commercial centers developed around castles and monasteries and within the walls of ancient towns. Great lords in the countryside—including monasteries—were eager to take advantage of the profits generated by their estates. In the late tenth century, they had reorganized their lands for greater productivity, encouraged their peasants to cultivate new land, and converted services and dues to money payments. Now with ready cash, they not only fostered the development of fairs—temporary markets where they and their peasants could sell their surpluses and buy other goods—but also encouraged traders and craftspeople to settle down near them. The lords gained at each step: their purchases brought them an enhanced lifestyle and greater prestige, while they charged merchants tolls and sales taxes, which yielded even greater profits from trade. Sometimes markets formed just outside the walls of older cities; these gradually merged into new and enlarged urban communities as town walls were built around them to protect the inhabitants. At other times informal country markets came to be housed in permanent structures. Along the Rhine and in other river valleys, cities sprang up to service the merchants who traversed the route between Italy and the north (Map 9.1).

By the mid-twelfth century rural life was increasingly organized for the marketplace in many regions of western Europe. This opened up opportunities for both peasants and lords, but it also burdened some with unwelcome obligations. Great lords hired trained, literate agents to administer their estates, calculate profits and

Map 9.1 Medieval Trade Routes in the Eleventh and Twelfth Centuries
In the medieval world, bulk goods from the north (furs, fish, and wood) were traded for luxury goods from the south (ivory, spices, olive oil, and ceramics). Already regions were beginning to specialize. England, for example, supplied raw wool, and Flanders (Ypres, Ghent) specialized in turning that wool into cloth and shipping it to the fairs of Champagne (whose capital was Troyes) or Germany. Italian cities channeled goods from the Muslim and Byzantine worlds northward and exported European goods southward and eastward.

losses, and make marketing decisions. Some offered special privileges to peasants who would do the backbreaking work of plowing marginal land. In Flanders, where land was regularly inundated by seawater, the great monasteries sponsored drainage projects, and newly dug canals linking the cities to the agricultural regions let boats ply the waters to nearly every nook and cranny of the region.

The new initiatives supported an increasing population. On old estates the rise in population strained the manse organization that had developed in Carolingian Europe, where each household was settled on the land that supported it. In the twelfth century, twenty peasant families might live on what had been, in the tenth century, the manse of one family. With the manse supporting so many more people, labor services and dues had to be recalculated, and peasants and their lords often turned services and dues into money rents, payable once a year. With this change, peasant men gained more control over their plots: they could sell them, will them to their sons, or even designate a small portion for their daughters. However, they had to pay high fees for these privileges.

Business Arrangements

The development of commerce reflected changing attitudes toward money. In the gift economy, exchanges of land and money were components of ongoing relationships. Kings offered treasures to their followers, peasants gave dues to their lords, and pious donors presented land to the saintly patrons of churches, all in the expectation of long-term relationships. In the new market economy, which thrived on the profit motive, arrangements were less personal. They often relied on written contracts and calculations of the profitability of a particular business venture.

Although the new business agreements took many forms, they had the common purpose of bringing people together to pool their resources and finance larger enterprises. Some of these arrangements were temporary, such as those that supported a commercial sea voyage. Others were permanent. In Italy, for example, a *compagnia* was formed when families invested their wealth in trade. The compagnia gave its members joint and unlimited liability for all losses and debts. This provision enhanced family solidarity, as each member was responsible for the debts of all the others; but it also risked bankrupting entire households.

The commercial revolution fostered the development of contracts for sales, exchanges, and loans. Loans were the most problematic. In the Middle Ages, as now, interest payments were the chief inducement for an investor to supply money. To circumvent the church's ban on usury (profiting from loans), interest was often disguised in contracts as a penalty for "late payment." The new willingness to finance business enterprises with loans signaled a changed attitude toward credit: risk was acceptable if it brought profit.

Contracts and partnerships were just two of the ways in which money resources were pooled to make large-scale productive enterprises and new industries possible. In fact, light industry began in the eleventh century. One of the earliest products to benefit from new industrial technologies was cloth. Water mills powered machines such as flails to clean and thicken cloth and presses to extract oil from fibers. Machines were also used to exploit raw materials more efficiently: new deep-mining technology provided Europeans with hitherto untapped sources of metals. At the same time, forging techniques improved, and iron was for the first time regularly used for agricultural tools and plows. This in turn made for better farming, and better farming fed the commercial revolution. Metals were also used for weapons, armor, and coins.

Whether fashioned by machines or handworkers, products relied on the expertise of artisans able to finish the cloth, mint the coins, and forge the weapons. To regulate and protect their products and trades, craftspeople and others involved in commerce formed **guilds**—local social, religious, and economic associations whose members plied the same trades. By the late twelfth century, guilds had become corporations defined by statutes and rules. They controlled their membership and determined dues, working hours, wages, and standards for materials and products. Producing wool cloth involved numerous guilds— shearers, weavers, fullers (people who beat the cloth to make it bulkier), and dyers. These guilds generally worked under the supervision of the merchant guild that imported the raw wool. Some guilds were more prestigious than others; in Florence, for example, professional guilds of notaries and judges ranked above craft guilds.

Within each guild of artisans or merchants existed another kind of hierarchy. Apprentices were at the bottom, journeymen and (less often) journeywomen (journey being a term for workers paid by the day) in the middle, and masters at the top. Apprentices were boys and occasionally girls placed under the tutelage of a master for a number of years to learn a trade. Once trained, the apprentice became a simple day laborer working for a wage. Journeywomen earned far less than journeymen and were active in fewer trades. Even the men's careers were precarious; only a few of them would become masters—the ones who dominated the offices and policies of the guild, hired the day laborers, and recruited and educated the apprentices.

Rural labor was not organized into guilds. But here, too, work was transformed by the commercial revolution. The most important change was in the work that women did. Formerly occupied with grinding grain, women gradually found

Comb for Wool
This stout wooden comb, which was used in the first half of the eleventh century to remove the tangles in raw wool, had two sets of teeth. (Collection Musée dauphinois [inv.90.14.81], Grenoble—France.)

this task taken over by water- and animal-powered mills. Instead, women turned to spinning, producing the wool threads that were then used by male weavers operating heavy looms in the towns.

Self-Government for the Towns

Guilds were one way townspeople expressed their mutual concerns and harnessed their collective energies. Movements for self-government were another. Townspeople banded together for protection and freedom.

Both to themselves and to outsiders, townspeople seemed different. Trades-people, artisans, ship captains, innkeepers, and money changers did not fit into the old categories of medieval types—those who pray, those who fight, and those who work. Just knowing they were different gave townspeople a sense of solidarity with one another. But practical reasons also contributed to their feeling of common purpose: they lived in close quarters with one another, and they shared a mutual interest in reliable coinage, laws to facilitate commerce, freedom from servile dues and services, and independence to buy and sell as the market dictated. Already in the early twelfth century, the king of England granted to the citizens of Newcastle-upon-Tyne the privilege that any unfree peasant who lived there unclaimed by his lord for a year and a day would thereafter be a free person. To townspeople, freedom meant having their own officials and law courts. They petitioned the political powers that ruled them—bishops, kings, counts, castellans—for the right to govern themselves. Often they formed **communes**, sworn associations of townspeople that generally cut across the boundaries of rich and poor, merchants and craftspeople, clergy and laity.

Collective movements for urban self-government emerged especially in Italy, France, and Germany. Italian cities were centers of regional political power even before the commercial revolution. Castellans constructed their fortifications in the cities, and bishops ruled the countryside from behind city walls. The commercial revolution swelled Italian cities with tradespeople, whose interest in self-government was often fueled by religious as well as economic concerns. At Milan in the second half of the eleventh century, popular discontent with the archbishop, who effectively ruled the city, led to numerous armed clashes. In 1097, the Milanese succeeded in transferring political power from the archbishop and his clergy to a government of leading men of the city who called themselves consuls. The title recalled the government of the ancient Roman republic, affirming the consuls' status as representatives of the people. Like the archbishops' power before, the consuls' rule extended beyond the town walls into the *contado,* the outlying countryside.

Outside Italy, movements for city independence took place within the framework of larger kingdoms or principalities. Such movements were sometimes violent, as at Milan, but at other times they were peaceful. For example, William Clito, who claimed the county of Flanders (today in Belgium), willingly granted the citizens of Saint-Omer the rights they asked for in 1127 in return for their support of his claims. He recognized them as legally free, gave them the right to mint coins, allowed them their own laws and courts, and lifted certain tolls and taxes.

REVIEW   What new professions and institutions arose as a result of the commercial revolution?

Church Reform and Its Aftermath

The commercial revolution affected the church. Bishops ruled over many cities. Kings appointed many bishops. Local lords installed priests in their parish churches. Churchmen gave gifts and money to these secular powers for their offices. Now, with the commercial revolution sensitizing them to the crasser uses of money, some people took offense at this mingling of sacred and secular. The impulse to "free the church from the world" was as old as the origins of monasticism, but beginning in the tenth century and more insistently in the eleventh, reformers demanded that the church as a whole remodel itself and become free of secular entanglements.

This freedom was from the start as much a matter of power as of religion. Most people had long believed that their ruler—whether king, duke, count, or castellan— reigned by the grace of God and had the right to control the churches in his territory. But by the second half of the eleventh century, more and more people saw a great deal wrong with secular power over the church. They looked to the papacy to lead the movement of church reform. The most important moment came in 1075, when Pope Gregory VII called on King Henry IV, who claimed rulership in both Germany and Italy, to end his appointment of churchmen. This demand brought about a major civil war in Germany and a great upheaval in the distribution of power everywhere. By the early 1100s, a reformed church, with the pope at its head, had become institutionalized, penetrating into areas of life never before touched by churchmen. Church reform began as a way to free the church from the world, but in the end the church was equally involved in the new world it had helped to create.

Beginnings of the Reform Movement

The idea of freeing the church from the world began in the tenth century with no particular program and only a vague idea of what it might mean. At the Benedictine monastery of Cluny, for example, which was founded in 910, there was no organized program of reform. Nevertheless, the founders of the monastery, the duke and duchess of Aquitaine, wanted to "free" it from the world. They achieved this goal by endowing the monastery with property but then giving it and its worldly possessions to St. Peter and St. Paul. In this way, they put control of the monastery into the hands of the two most powerful heavenly saints. They designated the pope, as the successor of St. Peter, to be the monastery's worldly protector if anyone should bother or threaten it. The whole notion of "freedom" at this point was very vague. But Cluny's prestige was great because of its status as St. Peter's property and because of the elaborate round of prayers that its monks carried out with scrupulous devotion.

The Cluniac monks fulfilled the role of "those who pray" in a way that dazzled their contemporaries. Through their prayers they seemed to guarantee the salvation of all Christians. Rulers, bishops, rich landowners, and even serfs (if they could) gave Cluny donations of land, joining their contributions to the land of St. Peter. Powerful men and women called on the Cluniac monks to reform new monasteries along the Cluniac model.

The abbots of Cluny came to see themselves as reformers of the world as well. They believed in clerical celibacy, preaching against the prevailing norm that let parish priests and even bishops marry. They also thought that the laity could be reformed, become more virtuous, and cease their oppression of the poor. In the eleventh century, the Cluniacs began to link their program of internal monastic and external worldly reform to the papacy. They asked the popes to help them when Cluniac lands were encroached upon by bishops and laypeople at the same time as the papacy itself was becoming interested in reform.

Around the time when the Cluniacs were joining their fate to that of the popes, a small group of clerics and monks in Germany began calling for systematic reform within the church. They buttressed their arguments with new interpretations of canon law—the laws decreed over the centuries at church councils and by bishops and popes. They concentrated on two breaches of those laws: clerical marriage and **simony** (buying church offices).

Emperor Henry III (r. 1039–1056) supported the reformers. Taking seriously his position as the anointed of God, Henry felt responsible for the well-being of the church in his empire. He denounced simony and personally refused to accept money or gifts when he appointed bishops to their posts. When in 1046 three men, each representing a different faction of the Roman aristocracy, claimed to be pope, Henry, as ruler of Rome, traveled to Italy to settle the matter. The Synod of Sutri (1046), over which he presided, deposed all three popes and elected another. In 1049, Henry appointed Leo IX (r. 1049–1054) to the papacy.

This appointment marked an unanticipated turning point for the emperor when Leo set out to reform the church under papal, rather than imperial, control. He traveled to France and Germany, holding councils to condemn simoniac bishops (bishops guilty of simony). He sponsored the creation of a canon law textbook, the *Collection in 74 Titles,* which emphasized the pope's power. To the papal court, Leo brought the most zealous reformers of his day: Humbert of Silva Candida, Peter Damian, and Hildebrand (later Pope Gregory VII).

At first, Leo's claims to new power over the church hierarchy were ignored by clergy and secular rulers alike. But Leo insisted, and gradually his view prevailed. He maintained it in the Byzantine world as well. In 1054, Leo sent Humbert of Silva Candida to Constantinople on a diplomatic mission to argue for the new, lofty claims of the pope. Furious at the contemptuous way he was treated by the patriarch, Humbert excommunicated him and soon afterward condemned the entire Greek Orthodox Church. In retaliation, the patriarch and his bishops excommunicated Humbert and his party, threatening them with eternal damnation. Clashes between the two churches had occurred before and had been patched up, but this one, called the **Great Schism** (1054), proved insurmountable.* Thereafter, the Roman Catholic and Greek Orthodox churches were largely separate.

Later popes continued Leo's program to expand papal power. When military adventurers from Normandy began carving out states for themselves in southern Italy, the popes in nearby Rome felt threatened. After waging unsuccessful war against the interlopers, the papacy made the best of a bad situation by granting the Normans Sicily and parts of southern Italy as a fief, turning its former enemies into vassals. Similarly, the papacy participated in wars in Spain, where it supported Christians against the dominant Muslims. The political fragmentation of al-Andalus into small, weak taifas (independent, Muslim-ruled principalities) made it seem fair game to the Christians to the north. Slowly the idea of the *reconquista*, the Christian reconquest of Spain, took shape, fed by religious fervor as well as worldly ambition.

Gregorian Reform and the Investiture Conflict, 1073–1085

The papal reform movement is above all associated with Pope Gregory VII (r. 1073–1085) and is therefore often called the **Gregorian reform**. Gregory began as a lowly Roman cleric, Hildebrand, with the job of administering the papal estates and rose slowly in the hierarchy. A passionate advocate of papal primacy (the theory that the pope was head of the church), he was not afraid to clash with Emperor Henry IV (r. 1056–1106) over leadership of the church. In his view, the emperor was just a layman who had no right to meddle in church affairs—an astonishing thought at the time, given the religious and spiritual roles associated with rulers.

Henry IV had been brought up in the traditions of his father, Henry III, a pious church reformer who considered it part of his duty to appoint bishops and even popes to ensure the well-being of both church and state. Henry IV believed that he and his bishops—who were, at the same time, his most valuable supporters and administrators—were the rightful leaders of the church. He had no intention of allowing the pope to become head of the church.

The great confrontation between Gregory and Henry began over the appointment of the archbishop of Milan. Gregory disputed Henry's right to "invest" the archbishop (put him into office). In the investiture ritual, the emperor or his representative symbolically gave the church and the land that went with it to the priest, bishop, or archbishop chosen for the job. When, in 1075, Henry invested his own candidate as archbishop of Milan, Gregory called on Henry to "give more respectful attention to the master of the Church"; he meant St. Peter and his living

---

*The mutual excommunications led to a permanent breach between the churches that largely remained in effect until 1965, when Pope Paul VI and Patriarch Athenagoras I made a joint declaration regretting "the offensive words" and sentences of excommunication on both sides, deploring "the effective rupture of ecclesiastical communion," and expressing the hope that the "differences between the Roman Catholic Church and the Orthodox Church" would be overcome in time.

representative, Gregory himself. In reply, Henry and the German bishops called on Gregory to resign from the papacy. This was the beginning of what historians delicately call the **Investiture Conflict** or Investiture Controversy. In fact, it was a war. In February 1076, Gregory called a synod that both excommunicated Henry and suspended him from office, authorizing anyone in Henry's kingdom to rebel against him. The German princes (as German aristocrats were called) saw an opportunity to increase their power; they threatened to elect another king.

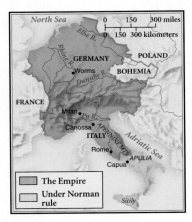

The World of the Investiture Conflict, c. 1075–1122

His fortunes low, Henry traveled to intercept Gregory, who was journeying northward to join the rebellious princes. In early 1077, the king and pope met at Canossa, high in central Italy's Apennine Mountains. Gregory was inside a fortress there; Henry stood outside as a penitent—barefoot in the cold and snow. The gesture was an astute move by Henry because no priest could refuse absolution to a penitent; Gregory had to lift the excommunication and receive Henry back into the church. But Gregory had the advantage of making the king humble himself before the majesty of the pope.

Although Henry was technically back in the fold, nothing of substance had been resolved, and civil war began. The princes elected an antiking (a king chosen illegally), and Henry and his supporters elected an antipope. From 1077 to 1122, papal and imperial armies waged intermittent war. Long after the original antagonists, Gregory and Henry, had died, the Concordat of Worms (1122) ended the fighting with a compromise that relied on a conceptual distinction between two parts of the investiture ceremony—the spiritual (in which a man received the symbols of his clerical office) and the secular (in which he received the symbols of the material goods that would allow him to function). Under the terms of the Concordat of Worms, in the first part of the ceremony, a churchman would give the bishop the ring and staff (symbols of church office). In the second part, the emperor or his representative would touch the bishop with a scepter, a symbolic gesture that stood for the land and other possessions that went with his office. Elections of bishops in Germany would take place "in the presence of the emperor"—that is, under his influence. In Italy, the pope would have a comparable role.

Superficially, nothing much had changed; secular rulers would continue to have a part in choosing and investing churchmen. In fact, however, almost no one any longer claimed that the king was head of the church. Just as the new investiture ceremony broke the ritual into spiritual and secular parts, so too it implied a new notion of kingship that separated it from priesthood. The Investiture Conflict did not produce the modern distinction between church and state—that would develop only very slowly—but it set the wheels in motion.

The most important changes brought about by the Investiture Conflict were on the ground: the political landscape in both Italy and Germany was irrevocably transformed. In Germany, the princes consolidated their lands and their positions at the expense of royal power. They gradually became virtual monarchs within their own principalities; the emperor, though retaining his title, eventually became a figurehead. In Italy, the emperor lost power to the cities.

The Italian communes were formed in the crucible of the war between the pope and the emperor. In fierce communal struggles, city factions, motivated in part by local grievances but often claiming to fight on behalf of the papal or the imperial cause, created their own governing bodies, as in Milan. In the course of the twelfth century, northern Italian cities became used to self-government.

The Sweep of Reform

Church reform involved much more than the clash of popes, emperors, and their supporters. It penetrated deeply into the daily lives of ordinary Christians, in part through the church's new emphasis on the sacraments—the regular means (according to the Catholic church) by which God's heavenly grace infused mundane existence. Eleventh-century church reformers began the process—which continued into the thirteenth century—of emphasizing the importance of the sacraments and the special nature of the priest, whose chief role was to administer them.

In the sacrament of marriage, for example, the effective involvement of the church in the wedding of a man and woman came only after the Gregorian reform. Not until the twelfth century did people regularly come to be married by a priest, and only then did churchmen assume jurisdiction over marital disputes, not simply in cases involving royalty but also in those of lesser aristocrats. At the same time, churchmen began to stress the sanctity of marriage. Hugh of St. Victor argued that marriage was the union of a man and woman who loved one another.

The reformers also proclaimed the special importance of the sacrament of the Mass, holy communion through the body and blood of Christ. Gregory VII called the Mass "the greatest thing in the Christian religion." No layman, no matter how powerful, and no woman of any sort could perform anything equal to it, for the Mass was the key to salvation.

The new emphasis on the difference between the priest (who could celebrate Mass) and the laity (who could not) led to vigorous enforcement of an old element of church discipline: the celibacy of priests. The demand for a celibate clergy had far-reaching significance for the history of the church. It distanced western clerics even farther from their eastern Orthodox counterparts (whose priests did not practice celibacy), exacerbating the Great Schism of 1054. It also broke with traditional local practice, for clerical marriage was customary in many places in Europe. Gregorian reformers exhorted every cleric in higher orders, from the humble parish priest to the exalted bishop, to refrain from marriage or to abandon his wife. In 1123 the pope proclaimed all clerical marriages invalid.

The rule about clerical marriages was only one in a veritable explosion of canon law. Canon law had begun simply as rules determined at church councils or papal declarations. Attempts to gather together and organize these laws had been made before the eleventh century. But the proliferation of rules during that century, along with the desire of Gregorians to clarify church law as they saw it, made a systematic collection even more necessary. This was supplied in about 1140 by the *Concordance of Discordant Canons,* also known as the *Decretum,* a landmark work by Gratian, a monk who taught law at Bologna in northern Italy. Gratian gathered thousands of passages from the decrees of popes and councils with the intention of showing their harmony. If he found any "discord," he strove to show how they applied to different situations. A bit later a different legal scholar revised and expanded the *Decretum,* adding Roman law to the mix. Meanwhile, the papacy itself was gradually developing its own court of law to hear cases and rule on petitions.

Before the Gregorian reform the papacy had been relatively powerless and much loved; afterward, it was very powerful and often resented. A satire written about 1100, in the style of the Gospels, made bitter fun of the costs of bringing cases to the papal court:

> There came to the court a certain wealthy clerk, fat and thick, and gross, who in the sedition [rebellion] had committed murder. He first gave to the dispenser, second to the treasurer, third to the cardinals. But they thought among themselves that they should receive more. The Lord Pope, hearing that his cardinals had received many gifts, was sick, nigh unto death. But the rich man sent to him a couch of gold and silver and immediately he was made whole.

With his law courts, bureaucracy, and financial apparatus, the pope had become a monarch.

Early Crusades and Crusader States

Asserting itself as head of the Christian church and leader of its reform movement, the papacy sometimes supported and proclaimed holy wars to advance the cause of Christianity. The most important of these were the crusades. Combinations of war and pilgrimage—the popular practice of making a pious voyage to a sacred shrine to petition for help or cure—the early crusades sent armed European Christians into battle against Muslims in the Holy Land, the place where Christ had lived and died.

The crusaders established several tiny states in the Levant, holding on to them precariously until 1291. Although the crusades ultimately "failed," in the sense that the crusaders did not succeed in permanently retaining the Holy Land for Christendom, they were a pivotal episode in Western civilization. They marked the first stage of European overseas expansion—what later would become imperialism.

The First Crusade (1096–1099) began with the entry of the Seljuk Turks into Asia Minor (Map 9.2). In the 1050s, taking advantage of the political fragmentation of the Muslim world, the Seljuks, converts to Sunni Islam, captured Baghdad, subjugated the caliphate, and began to threaten Byzantium. The difficulties the Byzantine emperor Romanus IV had in pulling together an army to attack the Turks in 1071 reveal how weak his position had become. Unable to muster Byzantine troops, Romanus had to rely on a mercenary army made up of Normans, Franks, Slavs, and even Turks. In 1071, this motley force met the Seljuks at Manzikert, in what is today eastern Turkey. The battle was a disaster for Romanus: the Seljuks routed his army and captured him. Manzikert marked the end of Byzantine domination in the region. The Turks, gradually settling in Asia Minor, extended their control across the Byzantine Empire and beyond, all the way to Jerusalem, which had been under Muslim control since the seventh century.

In 1095, the Byzantine emperor Alexius I appealed for help to Pope Urban II (r. 1088–1099), hoping to get new mercenary troops for a fresh offensive. Urban II

Map 9.2 The First Crusade, 1096–1099
The First Crusade was a major military undertaking that required organization, movement over both land and sea, and enormous resources. Four main groups were responsible for the conquest of Jerusalem. One group began at Cologne, in northern Germany; another group started from Blois, in France; a third originated to the west of Provence; and a fourth launched ships from Brindisi, at the heel of Italy. All joined up at Constantinople, where their leaders negotiated with Alexius I for help and supplies in return for a pledge of vassalage to the emperor. **For more help analyzing this map, see the map activity for this chapter in the Online Study Guide at** bedfordstmartins.com/huntconcise.

chose to interpret the request in his own way. That year, at the Council of Clermont (in France), Urban moved outside the church and addressed an already excited throng:

> Oh, race of Franks, race from across the mountains, race beloved and chosen by God. . . . Let hatred depart from among you, let your quarrels end, let wars cease, and let all dissensions and controversies slumber. Enter upon the road to the Holy Sepulcher; wrest that land from the wicked race, and subject it to yourselves.

The crowd reportedly responded with one voice: "God wills it." Urban's call gave the papacy a new position of leadership, one that complemented in a military arena the place the popes had gained in the church hierarchy.

Men and women, rich and poor, young and old, heeded Urban's call. They abandoned their homes and braved the rough journey to the Holy Land to fight for their God. They also went because they wanted land and booty. Some knights joined the expedition because they were obligated to follow their lord. Although women were discouraged from going on the crusade, some crusaders were accompanied by their wives. Other women went as servants. Children, old men, and women, not able to fight, made the cords for siege engines—giant machines used to hurl stones at enemy fortifications. As more crusades were undertaken during the twelfth century, the transport and supply of these armies became a lucrative business for the commercial classes of maritime Italian cities such as Venice.

A Crusader and His Wife
How do we know that the man on the left is a crusader? On his shirt is a cross, the sign worn by all men going on the crusades. In his right hand is a pilgrim's staff, a useful reminder that the crusades were sometimes considered less a matter of war than of penance and piety. What does the embrace of the crusader's wife imply about marital love in the twelfth century?
(© Musée Lorrain, Nancy/Photo: P. Mignot.)

The main objective of the First Crusade—to take the Holy Land from the Muslims and subject it to Christian rule—was accomplished largely because of Muslim disunity. After nearly a year of ineffectual attacks, the crusaders took Antioch on June 28, 1098. The following year, on July 15, 1099, they seized Jerusalem. By 1109 they had carved out several tiny states in the Holy Land.

Because the crusader states were created by conquest, they were treated as lordships. The rulers granted fiefs to their own vassals, and some of these men in turn gave portions of their holdings as fiefs to some of their own vassals. Since most Europeans went home after the First Crusade, the rulers who remained learned to coexist with the indigenous population, which included Muslims, Jews, and Greek Orthodox Christians. They encouraged a lively trade at their ports, which received merchants from Italy, Byzantium, and Islamic cities. The main concern of these rulers, however, was military. They set up castles and recruited knights from Europe. So organized for war was this society that it produced a new and militant kind of monasticism: the Knights Templar, who vowed themselves to poverty and chastity. But rather than withdraw into the cloister, the Templars, whose name came from their living quarters in the area of the former Jewish temple at Jerusalem, devoted themselves to warfare. Their first mission—to protect the pilgrimage routes from Palestine to Jerusalem—soon diversified. They manned the town garrisons of the crusader states and transported money from Europe to the Holy Land. In this way the Templars became enormously wealthy, with branch "banks" in major cities across Europe.

The Crusader States, 1109

The presence of the Templars did not prevent the Seljuks from taking the city of Edessa in 1144. The event marked the slow but steady shrinking of the crusader states. New crusades were called, but none was successful. The Second Crusade (1147–1149) came to a disastrous end. After besieging the walls of Damascus for only four days, the crusaders, whose leaders could not keep the peace among themselves, gave up and went home. Soon the Muslims took all of Syria, and under the leadership of Saladin (1138–1193), they took Jerusalem in 1187. This in turn led to the call for the Third Crusade (1189–1192). Led by the greatest rulers of Europe—Emperor Frederick I, Philip II of France, Leopold of Austria, and Richard I of England—the Third Crusade nevertheless accomplished little, and the crusader states were reduced to a few tiny outposts.

Jews as Strangers

The same militant piety that inspired the crusades was turned against Jews. Sentiment against Jews grew over time. Once the Roman Empire became Christian, Jews

Krak-des-Chevaliers
The Hospitallers, a religious military order much like the Templars, built this imposing castle in 1142 on the site of a Muslim fortification in Syria. A large community of perhaps fifty monk-knights and their hired mercenaries lived there. To the northeast (in back of the complex seen here) was a fortified village that served the needs of the castle. Peasants raised grain, which was ground by a windmill on one wall of the castle. For water, there were reservoirs to catch the rain, wells, and an aqueduct (visible on the right). Twelve toilets connected to a common drain. The monks worshiped in a chapel within the inner walls. The outer walls, built of masonry, completely enclosed the inner buildings, making Krak one of the most important places for refuge and defense in the crusader states. (Maynard Owen Williams/ National Geographic Image Collection.)

were prohibited by Roman law from owning Christian slaves or marrying Christian women. Church laws added to these restrictions. Socially isolated and branded as outcasts, Jews served as scapegoats who helped define the larger society as orthodox. But only at the end of the eleventh century did severe persecution begin.

Forced out of the countryside during the eleventh century by castellans and other regional rulers, most Jews ended up in the cities as craftsmen or merchants. But they were not allowed into guilds, and many were therefore pushed into the one profession that Christians could not practice, moneylending. Jews thus provided capital for the developing commercial society, whose Christian members were prohibited from charging interest by the Bible's restrictions against usury.

Many Jews lived in the flourishing commercial region of the Rhineland. Under Henry IV, Jews in Speyer and elsewhere in the Empire received protection from the local bishop (an imperial appointee) in return for paying a tax. Within these cities, the Jews lived in their own neighborhoods, in tightly knit communities focused on their synagogues. Synagogues served not only as houses of worship but also as schools and community centers. Jews also participated in the life of the larger Christian community. Archbishop Anno of Cologne dealt with Jewish moneylenders, and other Jews in Cologne were allowed to trade their wares at the fairs there.

Among the earliest anti-Jewish attacks were those directed against these Rhineland Jews. Some of the crusaders of the First Crusade declared it ridiculous to attack Muslims when other infidels lived in their own backyards. "That's doing our work backward," they said, as they moved into the Rhineland to force conversions or to kill. Some Jews found refuge with bishops or in the houses of Christian friends, but in many cities—Metz, Speyer, Worms, Mainz, and Cologne—they were massacred.

In the course of the twelfth century, Jews were attacked elsewhere as well. European rulers claimed Jews as their serfs and Jewish property as their own. King Henry II of England (r. 1154–1189) imposed new and arbitrary taxes on the Jewish community. In France, persecuting Jews and confiscating their property benefited both the treasury and the authoritative image of the king. Early in the reign of the French king Philip II, known as Philip Augustus (r. 1180–1223), royal agents surprised Jews at Sabbath worship in their synagogues and seized their goods, demanding that they redeem their own property for a large sum of money. Shortly thereafter, Philip canceled 80 percent of all debts owed to Jews; the remaining 20 percent was to be paid directly to the king. About a year later, in 1182, Philip expelled the Jews from the Île-de-France. When he allowed them to return in 1198, he permitted them to be only moneylenders or money changers, taxed and monitored by royal officials.

Limiting Jews to moneylending in an increasingly commercial economy and then persecuting them served the interests of lords in debt to Jewish creditors. For example, in 1190, local nobles orchestrated a brutal attack on the Jews of York, England. Their purpose was to rid themselves of their debts and of the Jews to whom they owed money. Churchmen, too, used credit in a money economy but resented the fiscal obligations it imposed. With their drive to create centralized territorial states and their desire to make their authority known

The Jew as Other
Medieval artists often portrayed people not as individuals but rather as "types" that could be identified by physical markers. In the second half of the twelfth century, Jews were increasingly portrayed as looking different from Christians. This illustration shows clerics borrowing money from a Jew. What physical features do all the clerics have in common? (Be sure to look at the clothes as well as the hairstyles.) What distinguishes the layman (standing behind the Jew) from the clerics? The Jew is identified by his pointed hat. In fact, however, Jews did not regularly wear this type of hat until they were forced to do so in some regions of Europe in the late thirteenth century. (Bayerische Staatsbibliothek, Munich.)

and felt, powerful rulers of Europe—churchmen and laymen alike—exploited and coerced Jews while drawing upon and encouraging widespread anti-Jewish feeling. Although Jews must have looked exactly like Christians in reality, Jews now became clearly identified in sculpture and in drawings by markers such as conical hats and, increasingly, demeaning features.

Attacks against Jews were inspired by more than resentment against Jewish money and the desire for power and control. They also grew out of the codification of Christian religious doctrine and Christians' anxiety about their own institutions. For example, in the twelfth century, church leaders promulgated a newly rigorous definition of the Eucharist, declaring that when the bread and wine were blessed by the priest during Mass, they became the true body and blood of Christ. For some believers this meant that Christ, wounded and bleeding, lay on the altar. Miracle tales sometimes reported that the elements of the Eucharist bled. Reflecting Christian anxieties about the presence of real flesh on the altar, sensational stories—originating in clerical circles but soon widely circulated—told of Jews who secretly sacrificed Christian children in a morbid revisiting of the crucifixion of Jesus. This charge, called "blood libel" by historians, led to massacres of Jews in cities in England, France, Spain, and Germany. Jews had no rituals involving blood sacrifice at all, but they were convenient and vulnerable scapegoats for Christian guilt and anxiety.

REVIEW   What were the causes and consequences of the Gregorian reform?

The Revival of Monarchies

Attacks on Jews reveal the ugly side of a wider development: kings and other rulers were enhancing and consolidating their power. They created new and revived old ideologies to justify their power; they hired officials to work for them; and they found vassals and churchmen to support them. The money that flowed into their treasuries from the new urban economy increased their effectiveness.

Byzantium in Its Prime

The First Crusade was an unanticipated result of a monarchical revival at Byzantium. In 1081, ten years after the disastrous battle at Manzikert, the energetic soldier Alexius Comnenus (r. 1081–1118) seized the imperial throne. He faced considerable unrest in Constantinople, whose populace suffered from a combination of high taxes and rising living costs. In addition, the Byzantine Empire was under attack on every side—by Normans in southern Italy, Seljuk Turks in Asia Minor, and new groups in the Balkans. But Alexius managed to turn actual and potential enemies against one another.

When Alexius asked Pope Urban II to supply him with some western troops to fight his enemies, he was shocked and disappointed to learn that crusaders rather than mercenaries were on the way. But Alexius had to make the best of what he could get. For his army, he could no longer rely on the *theme* system. He had to use mercenaries and to call on the great magnates of his realm to join him with their own troops. In return for their services he gave these nobles *pronoia* grants, lifetime possession of large imperial estates and their dependent peasants. Beyond his military needs, the emperor found support in the patriarch and Byzantine clergy, for emperor and church depended on each other to suppress heresy and foster orthodoxy. The emperors of the Comnenian dynasty (1081–1185) thus gained a measure of increased imperial power, but at the price of important concessions to the nobility.

In the eleventh and twelfth centuries, Constantinople remained a rich, sophisticated, and highly cultured city. Sculptors and other artists strove to depict ideals of human beauty and elegance. Churches built during the period were decorated with elaborate depictions of the cosmos. Significant innovations occurred in Byzantine scholarship and literature. The Neoplatonic tradition of late antiquity had always influenced Byzantine religious and philosophical thought, but now scholars renewed their interest in the wellsprings of classical Greek philosophy, particularly Plato and Aristotle. The revival of these writings in eleventh- and twelfth-century Byzantium would have profound consequences for both eastern and western European civilization in the centuries to come as ancient Greek thought gradually penetrated scholarly circles.

Norman and Angevin England

In Europe, the twelfth-century kings of England were the most powerful monarchs before 1200 because they ruled their whole kingdom by right of conquest. When the Anglo-Saxon king Edward the Confessor (r. 1042–1066) died childless in 1066, the duke of Normandy, William (1027–1087), claimed the throne of England. Gathering a force recruited from many parts of France, he launched an invasion. His armies clashed with those of another claimant to the throne, Harold, at Hastings on October 14, 1066. In one of history's rare decisive battles, William won and took over the realm.

Some people in England gladly supported William, considering his victory a verdict from God and hoping to be granted a place in the new order themselves. But William, known to posterity by the epithet "the Conqueror," wanted to

Norman Conquest of England, 1066

replace, not assimilate, the Anglo-Saxons. In the course of William's reign, families from continental Europe almost totally supplanted the English aristocracy. And although the English peasantry remained—now with new lords—the peasants were

Bayeux "Tapestry"
This famous "tapestry" is misnamed; it is really an embroidery, 231 feet long and 20 inches wide, created to tell the story of William's conquest of England from his point of view. In this detail, Norman archers are lined up at the bottom. Above them, Norman knights on horseback attack English foot soldiers wielding long battle-axes. Who seems to be winning? **For more help analyzing this image, see the visual activity for this chapter in the Online Study Guide at** bedfordstmartins.com/huntconcise. (Tapisserie de Bayeux. By special permission of the City of Bayeux, France.)

severely shaken. A twelfth-century historian claimed to record William's deathbed confession:

> I have persecuted [England's] native inhabitants beyond all reason. Whether gentle or simple, I have cruelly oppressed them; many I unjustly disinherited; innumerable multitudes, especially in the county of York, perished through me by famine or the sword.

Modern historians estimate that one out of five people in England died as a result of the Norman conquest and its immediate aftermath.

Although the Normans destroyed a generation of English men and women, they preserved and extended some Anglo-Saxon institutions, retaining the old administrative divisions and legal system of shires (counties) and hundreds (districts; see page 302). The Normans also drew from continental institutions. They created a system of vassalage culminating in the king and buttressed by his castles, just as French kings were trying to do at about the same time (see page 334). But because all of England was the king's by conquest, he could treat it as his booty. William kept about 20 percent of the land for himself and divided the rest, distributing it in large but scattered fiefs to a relatively small number of his barons and family members, lay and ecclesiastical, as well as to some lesser men, such as personal servants and soldiers. In turn, these men and their vassals owed the king military service along with certain dues, such as reliefs (money paid upon inheriting a fief) and aids (payments made on important occasions).

Those were the revenues expected from the nobles, but the king of England commanded the peasantry as well. In 1086, twenty years after his conquest, William ordered a survey and census of England, popularly called Domesday because, like the records of people judged at doomsday, it provided facts that could not be appealed. It was the most extensive inventory of land, livestock, taxes, and population that had yet been compiled in Europe.

The Norman conquest tied England to the languages, politics, institutions, and culture of France and Flanders. Modern English is an amalgam of Anglo-Saxon and Norman French. English commerce was linked to the wool industry in Flanders. St. Anselm (1033–1109), the archbishop of Canterbury (England), was born in Italy and was the abbot of a monastery in Normandy before crossing the English Channel. The barons of England retained their estates in Normandy and elsewhere, and the kings of England often spent more time on the continent than they did on the island. When William's son Henry I (r. 1100–1135) died without male heirs, civil war erupted: the throne of England was fought over by two French counts.

The eventual outcome of that civil war (1139–1153) was the accession to the English throne of Henry II (r. 1154–1189),* Henry I's grandson. He was not only count of Anjou (his father was Count Geoffrey of Anjou) but also, by an astute marriage to Eleanor of Aquitaine in 1152, duke of Aquitaine. His father, who had conquered Normandy, had named Henry duke there, and Henry also exercised hegemony over Poitou and Brittany. Although technically a vassal of the king of France (as a result of his continental lands), Henry in effect ruled a territory that stretched from England to the south of France (Map 9.3).

Henry's marriage to Eleanor brought him both a huge duchy and a feisty queen, who bore him the sons he needed to maintain his dynasty. Before her marriage to Henry, Eleanor had been married to King Louis VII of France. Louis had the marriage annulled because she bore him only daughters. Nevertheless, as queen of France, Eleanor enjoyed an important position. She disputed with St. Bernard, the most renowned churchman of the day, and she accompanied her husband on the Second Crusade, bringing more troops than he did. She determined to separate from Louis even before he considered leaving her. Married to Henry, she had much less power. After plotting unsuccessfully against Henry with one of their sons, she spent most of her time, until her husband's death in 1189, confined under guard at Winchester Castle.

As king of England, Henry immediately set to work to undo the damage to the monarchy caused by the civil war, during which the English barons and high churchmen had gained new privileges and powers, building private castles

---

*Henry II is known as the first Angevin (from *Anjou*) king of England because by inheritance, he was count of Anjou. But the dynasty he began also has another name. His father, Count Geoffrey of Anjou, was nicknamed *Plantagenet*, from *genet*, a shrub that he liked, and historians sometimes use that name to refer to the entire dynasty. Thus Henry II was the first Plantagenet as well as the first Angevin king of England.

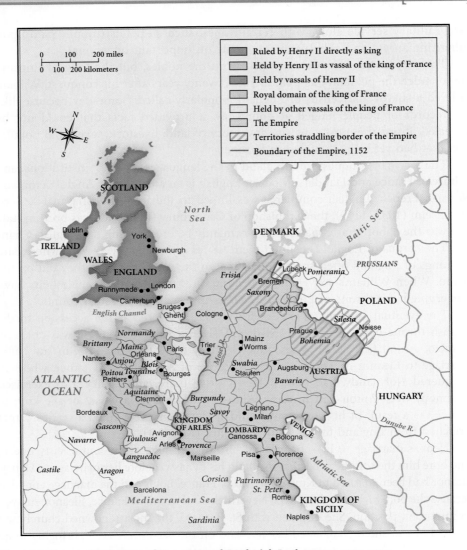

Map 9.3 Europe in the Age of Henry II and Frederick Barbarossa, 1150–1190
The second half of the twelfth century was dominated by two men, King Henry II and Emperor Frederick Barbarossa. Of the two, Frederick seemed to control more land, but this was deceptive. Although he was emperor, he had great difficulty ruling the territory that was theoretically part of his empire. Frederick's base was in central Germany, and even there he had to contend with powerful vassals. Henry II's territory was more compact but also more surely under his control.

as symbols of their strength. Henry destroyed or confiscated the new castles and regained crown lands. Then he proceeded to extend monarchical power, above all by imposing royal justice.

Henry's judicial reforms built on an already well-developed English system. The Anglo-Saxon kings had established royal district courts and appointed sheriffs to police the shires, call up men to fight, and haul criminals into court. The Norman kings retained these courts, which all the free men of the shires were summoned to attend. To these institutions, Henry II added a system of judicial visitations called eyres (from the Latin *iter*, "journey"). Under this system, royal justices made regular trips to every locality in England. Henry declared that some crimes, such as murder, arson, and rape, were so heinous as to violate the "king's peace," no matter where they were committed. The king required local representatives of the knightly class to meet during each eyre and either give the sheriff the names of those suspected of committing crimes in the vicinity or arrest the suspects and hand them over to the royal justices. During the eyres, the justices also heard cases between individuals, today called civil cases. Free men and women (that is, people of the knightly class or above) could bring their disputes over matters such as inheritance, dowries, and property claims to the king's justices. Earlier courts had generally relied on duels between litigants to determine verdicts. Henry's new system offered a different option—an inquest under royal supervision.

The new system was praised for its efficiency, speed, and effectiveness by the king's supporters. They might have added that the king also quickly gained a large treasury. The exchequer, as the financial bureau of England was called, recorded all the fines paid for judgments and the sums collected for writs. The amounts, entered on parchment sewn together and stored as rolls, became the Receipt Rolls and Pipe Rolls, the first of many such records of the English monarchy and an indication that writing had become a mechanism for institutionalizing royal power in England.

The stiffest opposition to Henry's extension of royal courts came from

Hanging Thieves
The development of common law in England meant mobilizing royal agents to bring charges and arrest people throughout the land. In 1124, the royal justice Ralph Basset hanged forty-four thieves. It could not have been very shocking in that context to see, in this miniature from around 1130, eight thieves hanged for breaking into the shrine of St. Edmund. Under Henry II, all cases of murder, arson, and rape were considered crimes against the king himself. The result was not just the enhancement of the king's power but also new definitions of crime, more thorough policing, and more systematic punishments. Even so, hanging was probably no more frequent than it had been before. (Pierpont Morgan Library/Art Resource, NY.)

the church, where a separate system of trial and punishment had long been available to the clergy and to others who enjoyed church protection. The punishments that these courts meted out were generally quite mild. Jealous of their prerogatives, churchmen refused to submit to the jurisdiction of Henry's courts, and the ensuing contest between Henry and his archbishop, Thomas Becket (1118–1170), became the greatest battle between church and state in the twelfth century. Their conflict over jurisdiction simmered for six years, until Henry's henchmen murdered Thomas, unintentionally transforming him into a martyr. Although Henry's role in the murder remained ambiguous, he had to do public penance for the deed largely because of the general outcry. In the end, both church courts and royal courts expanded to address the concerns of an increasingly litigious society.

Praising the King of France

The twelfth-century kings of France were much less obviously powerful than their English and Byzantine counterparts. Yet they, too, took part in the monarchical revival. Louis VI ("the Fat"; r. 1108–1137), so heavy that he had to be hoisted onto his horse with a crane, was a tireless defender of royal power. We know a good deal about him because his contemporary and close associate, Suger (1081–1152), abbot of Saint-Denis, wrote Louis's biography. When Louis set himself the task of consolidating his rule in the Île-de-France, Suger portrayed the king as a righteous hero. He thought of the king as the head of a political hierarchy in which Louis had rights over the French nobles because they were his vassals or when they broke the peace.

Suger also believed that Louis had a religious role: to protect the church and the poor. He viewed Louis as another Charlemagne, a ruler for all society, not merely an overlord of the nobility. Louis waged war to keep God's peace. To be sure, the Gregorian reform had made its mark: Suger did not claim Louis was head of the church. Nevertheless, he emphasized the royal dignity and its importance to the papacy. When a pope happened to arrive in France, Louis, not yet king, and his father, Philip I (r. 1052–1108), bowed low, but (recalled Suger) "the pope lifted them up and made them sit before him like devout sons of the apostles. In the manner of a wise man acting wisely, he conferred with them privately on the present condition of the church." Here the pope was shown needing royal advice.

When Louis VI died in 1137, Suger's notion of the might and right of the king of France reflected reality in an extremely small area. Nevertheless, Louis laid the groundwork for the gradual extension of royal power in France. As the lord of vassals, the king could call upon his men to aid him in times of war (though the great ones sometimes disregarded his wishes and chose not to help). As a king and landlord, he could obtain many dues and taxes. Officials enforced his royal laws and collected taxes. With money and land, Louis could dispense the favors and give the gifts that added to his prestige and his power. Louis VI and Suger together created the territorial core and royal ideal of the future French monarchy. Louis's grandson Philip Augustus would build on this foundation, greatly expanding the territory of the French monarchy in the thirteenth century.

Remaking the Empire

The Investiture Conflict and the civil war it generated (1075–1122) strengthened the German princes and weakened the emperors. For decades, the princes enjoyed near independence, building castles on their properties and establishing control over whole territories. To ensure that the emperors who succeeded Henry V (r. 1106–1125) would be weak, the princes supported only rulers who agreed to give them new lands and powers. A ruler's success depended on his ability to juggle the many conflicting interests of his own royal and imperial offices, his family, and the German princes. He also had to contend with the increasing influence of the papacy and the Italian communes, which were forging alliances with one another and with the German princes, preventing the consolidation of power under a strong German monarch during the first half of the twelfth century.

Weakness at the top, however, meant constant warfare among princely factions. Eventually the German princes became exhausted by conflict and in 1152 elected Frederick I ("Barbarossa"; r. 1152–1190) as the first Hohenstaufen king of Germany. He was an impressive man with a striking red-blond beard (hence *Barbarossa,* or "red-beard") and a firm sense of his position. Frederick affirmed royal rights even when he handed out duchies and allowed others to name bishops, because in return for these political powers he required the princes to concede formally and publicly that they held their rights and territories from him as their lord. By making them his vassals—though with nearly royal rights within their principalities—Frederick defined the princes' relationship to the German king: they were powerful yet personally subordinate to him. In this way, Frederick hoped to save the monarchy and to coordinate royal and princely rule, thus ending Germany's chronic civil wars. Frederick used the lord-vassal relationship to give himself a free hand to rule while placating the princes.

Since the Investiture Conflict, the emperor had ruled Italy in name only. The communes of the northern cities guarded their liberties jealously, and the pope considered Italy his own sphere of influence. Frederick's territorial base north of Italy (in Swabia) and his designs on northern Italy threatened those interests (Map 9.3, page 332). Some historians have criticized Frederick for "entangling" himself in Italy, but Frederick's title was *emperor,* a position that demanded he intervene there. To fault him for not concentrating on Germany is to blame him for lacking modern wisdom, which knows from hindsight that European polities developed into nation-states, such as France, Germany, and Italy. There was nothing inevitable about the development of nation-states, however, and Frederick should not be condemned for failing to see into the future. In addition, control of Italy made sense even for Frederick's effectiveness in Germany. His base in

Swabia together with northern Italy would give him a compact and central territory. Moreover, the flourishing commercial cities of Italy would make him rich. Taxes on agricultural production there alone yielded thirty thousand silver talents annually, an incredible sum.

By alternately negotiating with and fighting against the great cities of northern Italy, especially Milan, Frederick achieved military control there in 1158. No longer able to make Italian bishops royal governors, as German kings had done earlier—the Investiture Conflict had effectively ended that practice—Frederick insisted that the communes be governed by magistrates from outside the communes who were appointed (or at least authorized) by him. Here is where Frederick made his mistake: the heavy hand of these officials, many of them from Germany, created enormous resentment. By 1167, most of the cities of northern Italy had joined with Pope Alexander III (r. 1159–1181) to form the Lombard League against Frederick. Defeated at the battle of Legnano (near Milan) in 1176, Frederick made peace with Alexander and withdrew most of his forces from Italy. The battle marked the triumph of the city over the crown in Italy, which would not have a centralized government until the nineteenth century; Italy's political history would instead be that of its various regions and their dominant cities.

The Courtly Culture of Europe

With the consolidation of territory, wealth, and power in the second half of the twelfth century, kings, barons, princes, and their wives and daughters created a newly opulent court culture. For the first time on the European continent, poems and songs were written in the vernacular, the spoken language, rather than in Latin. They celebrated the lives of the nobility and were meant to be read aloud or sung as entertainment. Already at the beginning of the twelfth century, Duke William IX of Aquitaine (1071–1126), the grandfather of Eleanor of Aquitaine, had written lyric poems in Occitan, the vernacular spoken in southern France. Perhaps influenced by love poetry in Arabic and Hebrew from al-Andalus, his own poetry in turn provided a model for poetic forms that gained great popularity. The final four-line stanza of one such poem demonstrates the composer's skill with words:

> Per aquesta fri e tremble,
> quar de tan bon' amor l'am;
> qu'anc no cug qu'en nasques
>   semble
> en semblan de gran linh n'Adam.

> For this one I shiver and tremble,
> I love her with such a good love;
> I do not think the like of her was
>   ever born
> in the long line of Lord Adam.

The rhyme scheme of this poem appears to be simple—*tremble* rhymes with *semble*, *l'am* with *n'Adam*. But the poem has five earlier verses, each six lines long and all containing the *-am*, *-am* rhyme in the fourth and sixth lines, while every other line within each verse rhymes as well. The whole scheme is dazzlingly complex.

William was followed by other troubadours—lyric poets who wrote in Occitan (Figure 9.1). Whether male or female, their subject was love. The Contessa de Dia (flourished c. 1160) wrote about her unrequited love for a man:

> So bitter do I feel toward him
> whom I love more than anything.
> With him my mercy and fine manners [*cortesia*] are in vain.

The key to troubadour verse was the notion of *cortesia* (courtesy), which referred to the refinement of people living at court and to their struggle to achieve an ideal of virtue.

Historians and literary critics used to use the term *courtly love* to emphasize one of the themes of courtly literature: the poet expresses overwhelming love for a beautiful married noblewoman who is far above him in status and utterly unattainable. But this was only one of many aspects of love that the troubadours sang about. Some boasted of sexual conquests; others played with the notion of equality between lovers; still others preached that love was the source of virtue. The overall theme of this literature was not courtly love but the power of women. No wonder Eleanor of Aquitaine and other aristocratic women patronized the troubadours: they enjoyed the image that the poetry gave them of themselves. Nor was that image a delusion.

Figure 9.1 Troubadour Song: "I Never Died for Love"
This music is the first part of a song that the troubadour poet Peire Vidal wrote sometime between 1175 and 1205. It has been adapted here for the treble clef. There is no time signature, but the music may easily be played by calculating one beat for each note, except for the two-note slurs, which fit into one beat together.

There were many powerful female lords in southern France. They owned property, had vassals, led battles, decided disputes, and entered into and broke political alliances as their advantage dictated. Both men and women appreciated troubadour poetry, which recognized and praised women's power even as it eroticized it.

From southern France the lyric love song spread to Italy, northern France, England, and Germany—regions where Occitan was a foreign language. Similar poetry appeared in other vernacular languages: the *minnesingers* (literally, "love singers") sang in German; the *trouvères* sang in the Old French of northern France. Some poets wrote much longer works—long heroic poems focused on war (later called epics) or equally long romantic poems about love (later called romances). Romances, often inspired by the legend of King Arthur, reached the zenith of their popularity during the late twelfth and early thirteenth centuries. A good example is *Lancelot* by Chrétien de Troyes (c. 1150–1190). The hero, in love with Queen Guinevere, the wife of his lord, King Arthur, will do anything for her. When she sees him, the greatest knight in Christendom, fighting in a tournament, she tests his love for her by asking him to do his "worst." The poor knight is then obliged to lose all his battles until she changes her mind.

Lancelot was the perfect chivalric knight. The word *chivalry* derives from the French word *cheval* (horse); the fact that the knight was a horseman marked him as a warrior of the most prestigious sort. Perched high on his mount, his heavy lance couched in his right arm, the knight was an imposing and menacing figure. Chivalry made him gentle—except to his enemies on the battlefield. The chivalric hero was a knight constrained by a code of refinement, fair play, piety, and devotion to an ideal. Historians debate whether real knights lived up to the codes implicit in epics and romances, but there is no doubt that they liked to imagine themselves that way.

> **REVIEW**   What new sources and institutions of power became available to rulers in the twelfth century?

New Forms of Scholarship and Religious Experience

The commercial revolution, the newly organized church, and the revived monarchies of the twelfth century set the stage for the growth of schools and for new forms of scholarship. Money and career opportunities attracted unheard-of numbers of young men to city schools. Worldly ambitions, however, were equaled by spiritual ones. The movement for church reform stressed the importance of the church and its beliefs. Many students and teachers in the twelfth century sought knowledge to make their faith clearer and deeper.

Other people in the twelfth century, however, sought to avoid schools and commerce. Some found refuge in the measured ceremonies and artistic splendor of Benedictine monasteries such as Cluny. Others considered these vast monastic complexes to be ostentatious and worldly. Rejecting the opulence of cities and the splendor of well-endowed monasteries alike, some pursued a monastic life of poverty, while others, like St. Francis, rejected even the shelter of the cloister.

Schools, Scholars, and the New Learning

Schools had been connected to monasteries and cathedrals since the Carolingian period. They served to train new recruits to become either monks or priests. Some were better endowed with books and masters (teachers) than others; a few developed a reputation for a certain theological approach or specialized in a certain branch of learning, such as literature, medicine, or law. By the end of the eleventh century, the best schools were generally in the larger cities: Reims, Paris, Bologna, Montpellier. Eager students flocked to them. Teachers at cathedral schools found themselves forced to find larger halls to accommodate the crush of students. Other teachers simply declared themselves "masters" and set up shop by renting a room. If they could prove their mettle in the classroom, they had no trouble finding paying students.

Because schools had hitherto been the training ground for clergymen, all students not only were male but also were considered clerics, whether or not they had been ordained. Many students went from school to school, sampling the offerings of different teachers. They could take to the roads because the consolidation of castellanies, counties, and kingdoms made violence against travelers less frequent. Urban centers soon responded to the needs of transients with markets, taverns, and lodgings. Using Latin, Europe's common language, students could drift from, say, Italy to Spain, Germany, England, and France, wherever a noted master had settled. Along with crusaders, pilgrims, and merchants, students made the roads of Europe very crowded indeed.

What the students sought above all was knowledge of the seven liberal arts. Grammar, rhetoric, and logic (or dialectic) belonged to the

A Teacher and His Students
This miniature, which illustrates the hierarchical relationship between students and teachers in the twelfth century, appears in a late-twelfth-century manuscript of a commentary written by Gilbert (d. 1154), bishop of Poitiers. Although some considered Gilbert's ideas in this commentary to be heretical, he escaped condemnation. The artist asserts Gilbert's orthodoxy by depicting him with a halo, in the full dress of a bishop, speaking from his throne. Below Gilbert are three of his disciples, also with halos. The artist's positive view of Gilbert is echoed by modern historians, who recognize Gilbert as a pioneer in his approach to scriptural commentary. (Bibliothèque municipale de Valenciennes.)

"beginning" arts, the so-called trivium. Logic, involving the technical analysis of texts as well as the application and manipulation of mental constructs, was a transitional subject leading to the second, higher part of the liberal arts, the quadrivium. This comprised four areas of study that we might call theoretical math and science: arithmetic, geometry, music (theory rather than practice), and astronomy. Of all these subjects, logic excited the most intense interest. Medieval students and masters were convinced that logic clarified every issue, even questions about the nature of God. With logic, they thought, one could prove that what one believed on faith was in fact true. At the end of the twelfth century, some Western scholars took advantage of Islamic achievements. At Islamic centers in Spain and Sicily the Greek texts of Aristotle, with their sophisticated logic, had already been translated into Arabic and closely commented on. Now Christian scholars translated the Arabic texts into Latin, making Aristotle and other ancient writers their own.

After studying the liberal arts, some students went on to study medicine, theology, or law. At Bologna, for example, students studied Lombard, Roman, and canon law. Men skilled in canon law served popes and bishops; popes, kings, princes, and communes all found that Roman law, which claimed the emperor as its source, justified their claims to power. The University of Paris, established at the very end of the twelfth century, concentrated on theology. Montpellier, in the south of France, was noted for its medical education. With books expensive and hard to find, lectures were the chief method of communication. These were centered on important texts: the teacher read an excerpt aloud, delivered his commentary on it, and disputed any contrary commentaries that rival teachers might have proposed. Students committed the lectures to memory.

Universities functioned as guilds, with the teachers in the role of masters and the students in the position of apprentices (except at Bologna, where the students, usually older men experienced in administration, had their own guild). Like guilds, they set prices (in this case, fees), determined standards (in this case, the knowledge that had to be learned), and regulated discipline. Given generous privileges by both popes and kings, who valued the services of scholars, universities were sometimes at odds with townspeople. It is common to speak of "town against gown"—the "gown" referring to the garb worn by the students and masters (and imitated by the American graduation gown). Students could be rowdy and worse; townspeople resented a self-governing body of transients in their midst. Yet pub owners, innkeepers, food purveyors, and landlords benefited from the patronage of students and masters, and generally town-gown relations were good.

The remarkable renewal of scholarship in the twelfth century had an unexpected benefit: we know a great deal about the men—and a few of the women—involved in it because they wrote so much, often about themselves. Three important figures typify the scholars of the period: Abelard and Heloise, who embraced the new learning wholeheartedly and retired to monasteries only when forced to do so, and Hildegard of Bingen, who spent most of her life happily in a cloister yet wrote knowingly about the world.

Peter Abelard (1079–1142) was one of the twelfth century's greatest thinkers. Turning his back on a career as a warrior and lord, he studied in Paris and soon began to write influential works on ethics, logic, and theology. Around 1120 he prepared a textbook for his students, the *Sic et Non* (*Yes and No*), unusual because it presented opposing positions on various subjects without reconciling them. Abelard challenged his students to make sense of the conflicts and resolve the contradictions themselves.

Abelard's fame as a teacher was such that a Parisian cleric named Fulbert gave him room and board and engaged him as tutor for Heloise (c. 1100–c. 1163/1164), Fulbert's niece. Brought up under her uncle's guardianship, Heloise had been sent as a young girl to a convent school, where she received a thorough education in Latin and Christian literature. Her uncle hoped to continue her education at home by hiring Abelard. Abelard, however, became her secret lover as well as her tutor. "Our desires left no stage of love-making untried," wrote Abelard in his *Historia calamitatum* (*Story of My Calamities*), his autobiographical account. When Heloise became pregnant, Abelard insisted they marry. They did so clandestinely, informing only a very few, such as Fulbert, for the new emphasis on clerical celibacy meant that Abelard's professional success and prestige would have been compromised if news of his marriage were made public. After they were married, Heloise and Abelard rarely saw one another. Suspecting that Abelard had abandoned his niece, Fulbert plotted a cruel punishment: he paid a servant to castrate Abelard. Soon after, husband and wife entered separate monasteries.

For Heloise, separation from Abelard was a lasting misfortune. For Abelard, however, the loss of Heloise and even his castration were not the worst disasters of his life. The cruelest blow came later, and it was directed at his intellect. He wrote a book that applied "human and logical reasons" (as he put it) to the Trinity. The book was condemned at the Council of Soissons in 1121, and he was forced to throw it into the flames, page by page. Bitterly weeping at the injustice, Abelard lamented, "This open violence had come upon me only because of the purity of my intentions and love of our Faith which had compelled me to write." Abelard had written the treatise on the Trinity for his students, maintaining that "words were useless if the intelligence could not follow them, [and] that nothing could be believed unless it was first understood." For Abelard, logic was the key to knowledge, and knowledge the key to faith.

Unlike Abelard and Heloise, Hildegard of Bingen (1098–1179) did not attend the city schools or learn under one of their scholars. Placed in a German convent at age eight, she received her schooling there and took vows as a nun. In 1136, she was elected abbess of the convent. Shortly thereafter, very abruptly, she began to write and to preach. She was probably the only woman authorized by the church to preach in her day.

Writing and preaching were the sudden external manifestations of an inner life that had been extraordinary from the beginning. Even as a child, Hildegard had experienced visions—of invisible things, of the future, and (always) of a special kind of light. These visions were intermingled with pain and sickness. Only in her forties did Hildegard interpret her sickness and her visions as gifts from God. In her *Scivias*

(*Know the Ways of the Lord,* 1151), Hildegard described some of her visions and explained their meaning. She interpreted them as containing nothing less than the full story of creation and redemption, a **summa** (compendium) of church doctrine.

Benedictine Monks and Artistic Splendor

Hildegard's contentment within the confines of her cloister was characteristic of many Benedictine monks and nuns. Known as black monks and nuns because they dyed their robes black, the Benedictines reached the height of their popularity in the eleventh century. Monasteries often housed hundreds of monks; convents for nuns were usually less populated. Cluny was one of the largest monasteries, with some four hundred brothers in the mid-eleventh century.

The chief occupation of the monks, as befitted (in their view) citizens of heaven, was prayer. The black monks and nuns devoted themselves to singing psalms and other prayers specified in the Benedictine rule, adding to them still more psalms. The rule called for chanting the entire Psalter—150 psalms—over the course of a week, but some monks, like those at Cluny, chanted that number in a day. Such prayer was neither private nor silent. Black monks had to know not only the words but also the music that went with their prayers. This was plainchant, also known as Gregorian chant, which consisted of melodies, each sung in unison, without

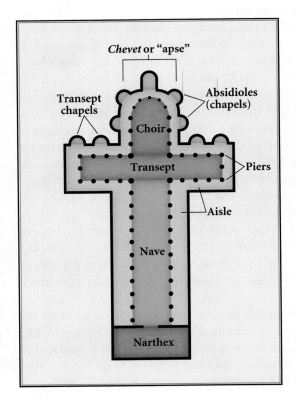

Figure 9.2 Floor Plan of a Romanesque Church
As churchgoers entered a Romanesque church, they passed through the narthex, an anteroom decorated with sculptured depictions of important scenes from the Bible. Walking through the portal of the narthex, they entered the church's nave, at the east end of which—just after the crossing of the transept and in front of the choir—was the altar, the focus of the Mass. Walking down the nave, they passed tall, massive piers leading up to the vault (roof) of the nave. Each of these piers was decorated with sculpture, and the walls were brightly painted. Romanesque churches were both lively and colorful (because of their decoration) and solemn and somber (because of their heavy stones and massive scale).

accompaniment. Although plainchant was rhythmically free, lacking a regular beat, its melodies ranged from extremely simple to highly ornate and embellished. By the twelfth century, a large repertoire of melodies had grown up—at first through oral composition and transmission and then in written notation, which was invented in the ninth century.

The **Romanesque** church—so called because its round arches and other architectural elements reminded modern art historians of Roman buildings—was the place in which black monks spent most of the day chanting the psalms. Built of stone, it might be small or large, but it was always decorated with inventive sculpture and/or wall paintings. The various parts of the church—the chapels in the *chevet*, or "apse" (at the east end of the building), for example—were treated as discrete units, retaining the forms of cubes, cones, and cylinders (Figure 9.2).

In such a setting, gilded reliquaries and altars made of silver, precious gems, and pearls were the fitting accoutrements of worship. Prayer, liturgy, and music in this way complemented the gift economy: richly clad in vestments of the finest materials, intoning the liturgy in the most splendid of churches, monks and priests offered up the gift of prayer to God; in return they begged for the gift of salvation of their souls and the souls of all the faithful.

New Monastic Orders of Poverty

Not everyone agreed that such opulence pleased God. At the end of the eleventh century, the new commercial economy and the profit motive that fueled it led many to reject wealth and to embrace poverty as a key element of religious life. The Carthusian order founded by Bruno of Cologne was one such group. Settling far from any city, each

Painted Vault
This fresco of Christ as ruler of the universe, his hand raised in a gesture of blessing, is one of many paintings in the Romanesque church of San Isidore de León, built in northwest Spain in the eleventh century. Surrounding Christ are the symbols of the four evangelists: the ox for Luke, the lion for Mark, the eagle for John, and the man for Matthew. (The Art Archive.)

monk took a vow of silence and lived as a hermit in his own small hut. Occasionally the monks gathered for prayer in a common prayer room, or oratory. When not engaged in prayer or meditation, the Carthusians copied manuscripts. They considered this task part of their religious vocation, a way to preach God's word with their hands rather than their mouths. The Carthusian order grew slowly. Each monastery was limited to only twelve monks, the number of Christ's Apostles.

The Cistercians, by contrast, expanded rapidly. Rejecting even the luxury of dyeing their robes, they left them the original color of wool—hence their nickname, white monks. The Cistercian order began as a single monastery, Cîteaux (in Latin, Cistercium) in France, founded in 1098. It grew rapidly under the leadership of St. Bernard (c. 1090–1153), abbot of the important Cistercian monastery Clairvaux. Despite the Cistercian order's official repudiation of female houses, many convents followed its lead and adopted its customs. Women were as eager as men to live the life of simplicity and poverty that they believed the Apostles had enjoyed and endured.

Although the Cistercians held up the Benedictine rule as the foundation of their customs, they elaborated a style of life all their own, largely governed by the goal of simplicity. Cistercian churches, though built of stone, were initially unlike the great Romanesque churches of the Benedictines. They were remarkably standardized; the church and the rest of the buildings of one Cistercian monastery were almost exactly like those of the others (Figure 9.3). The churches were small, made of smoothly hewn, undecorated stone. Wall paintings and sculpture were prohibited. Illuminated by the pure white light that came through clear glass windows, Cistercian houses were luminous, cool, and serene.

There were two sorts of white monks: *conversi,* or "lay brothers," toiled in the fields; choir monks dedicated themselves to private prayer and contemplation and to monastic administration. By the end of the twelfth century, the Cistercians had a closely monitored network of houses, and each year the Cistercian abbots met to hammer out legislation for all of them. The abbot of the motherhouse (or founding house) visited the daughter houses annually to make sure the legislation was being followed. Each house, whether mother or daughter, had large and highly organized farms and grazing lands called granges. Cistercian monks spent much of their time managing their estates and flocks, both of which were yielding handsome profits by the end of the twelfth century. Clearly part of the agricultural and commercial revolutions of the Middle Ages, the Cistercian order made managerial expertise a part of the monastic life.

At the same time, the Cistercians elaborated a spirituality of intense personal emotion. As Bernard said:

Often enough when we approach the altar to pray our hearts are dry and lukewarm. But if we persevere, there comes an unexpected infusion of grace, our breast expands as it were, and our interior is filled with an overflowing love.

Figure 9.3 Floor Plan of a Cistercian Monastery
Cistercian monasteries seldom deviated much from this standard plan, which perfectly suited their double lifestyle: one half for the lay brothers, who worked in the fields; the other half for the monks, who spent their days praying. This plan shows the first floor. Above were dormitories: the lay brothers slept above their cellar and refectory; the monks slept above their chapter house (where the rule of St. Benedict was read to them), common room, and room for novices. No one had a private bedroom, just as the rule prescribed.

The Cistercians emphasized not only human emotion but also Christ's and Mary's humanity. While pilgrims continued to stream to the tombs and reliquaries of saints, the Cistercians dedicated all their churches to the Virgin Mary (for whom they had no relics) because for them she signified the model of a loving mother. Indeed, the Cistercians regularly used maternal imagery (as Bernard's description invoking the metaphor of a flowing breast illustrates) to describe the nurturing care provided to humans by Jesus himself. The Cistercians' God was approachable, human, protective, even mothering.

Similar views of God were held by many who were not members of the Cistercian order. Their spirituality signaled wider changes. For example, around 1099, St. Anselm wrote a theological treatise titled *Why God Became Man*, in which he argued that since man had sinned, only a sinless man could redeem him. St. Anselm's work represented a new theological focus on the redemptive power of human charity, including that of Jesus as a human being.

Religious Fervor and Dissent

Christ's humanity became the focus of men and women of every age and every walk of life. They made Christ's childhood, agony, death, and presence in the Eucharist—the bread and wine that became the body and blood of Christ in the

Saint-Savin-sur-Gartempe

The nave of the church of Saint-Savin was built between 1095 and 1115. Its barrel (or tunnel) vault is typical of Romanesque churches, as is its sense of liveliness, variety, and color. The columns, decorated with striped or wavy patterns, are topped by carved capitals, each one different from the next. The entire vault is covered with frescoes painted in shades of brown, ocher, and yellow depicting scenes from the Old Testament. What were the purposes of such decorations? (Bridgeman-Giraudon/Art Resource, NY.)

Eberbech

Compare the nave of Eberbech, a Cistercian church built between 1170 and 1186, with the nave of Saint-Savin. What at Saint-Savin appears full of variety and color is here subdued by order and calm. There are no wall paintings in a Cistercian church, no variegated columns—nothing that might distract the worshipper. Yet a close look reveals subtle points of interest. How has the architect played with angles, planes, and light in the vaulting? Are the walls utterly smooth? What decorative elements can you see on the massive piers between the arches? (akg-images/ Stefan Drechsel.)

Mass—the most important experiences of their own lives. They punctuated their daily routines with scriptural reading, fasting, and charity. New religious groups sprouted in the towns and cities. Some of this intense religiosity developed into official, orthodox movements within the church; other religious movements so threatened established doctrine that church leaders declared them heretical.

St. Francis (c. 1182–1226) founded the most famous orthodox religious movement of the day—the Franciscans. Francis was a child of the commercial revolution. Expected to follow his well-to-do father in the cloth trade at Assisi in Italy, Francis experienced doubts, dreams, and illnesses, which spurred him to religious self-examination. In time, he renounced his family's wealth, dramatically marking the decision by casting off all his clothes and standing naked before his father, a crowd of spectators, and the bishop of Assisi. Francis then put on a simple robe and went about preaching penance to anyone who would listen. Adopting the life of a mendicant (one who begs for his livelihood), he accepted no money (only hospitality), walked without shoes, wore only one coarse tunic, and refused to be cloistered. Intending to follow the model of Christ, he received, as his biographers put it, a miraculous gift of grace: the stigmata, bleeding sores corresponding to the wounds Christ suffered on the cross.

By all accounts Francis was a spellbinding speaker, and he attracted many followers. Recognized as a religious order by the pope, the Brothers of St. Francis (or **friars**, from the Latin term for "brothers") spent their time preaching, ministering to lepers, and doing manual labor. Eventually they dispersed, setting up fraternal groups throughout Italy and then in France, Spain, the Holy Land, Germany, and England. Unlike the Carthusians and Cistercians, who had rejected cities, the friars sought town life, preaching to urban crowds and begging for their daily bread. St. Francis converted both men and women. In 1212, a young noblewoman named Clare formed the nucleus of a community of pious women, which became the Order of the Sisters of St. Francis. At first the women worked alongside the friars, but the church disapproved of their activities in the world, and soon Franciscan sisters were confined to cloisters under the Benedictine rule.

Clare was one of many women who sought a new kind of religious expression. In northern Europe at the end of the twelfth century, laywomen who lived together in informal pious communities were called Beguines. Without permanent vows or an established rule, the Beguines chose to be celibate (though they were free to leave and marry) and often made their living by weaving cloth or working with the sick and old. Although their daily occupations were ordinary, the Beguines' private, internal lives were often emotional and ecstatic, infused with the combined imagery of love and religion so pervasive in both monasteries and courts.

More hardheaded was St. Dominic (1170–1221), founder of the Dominicans, an order of friars patterned very closely on the Franciscans. Like Francis, Dominic and his followers rejected material riches and instead went about on foot, preaching and begging. Their initial audience was not the men and women of the Italian cities, however, but rather the people of southern France, where new doctrines that contradicted those officially accepted by the church—and therefore labeled "heretical"—had become very popular.

Dominic and his friars were responding to an unprecedented explosion of heresies, part of the ferment of ideas and experiments in social life that were characteristic of medieval city growth. Among the most visible of the heretics were the dualists, who saw the world torn between two great forces—one good, the other evil. Dualism became a prominent ingredient in religious life in Italy and the Rhineland by the end of the twelfth century. Another center of dualism was Languedoc, an area of southern France; there the dualists were called Albigensians, a name derived from the Languedoc town of Albi.

Described collectively as Cathars, or "Pure Ones," the Albigensians, like other dualists, believed that the devil had created the material world. Therefore they renounced the world, rejecting wealth, sex, and meat. Their repudiation of sex reflected some of the attitudes of eleventh-century church reformers (whose orthodoxy, however, was never in doubt), and their rejection of wealth echoed the same concerns that moved the Cistercians to worship in plain churches and St. Francis to embrace poverty. In many ways the dualists simply took these attitudes to an extreme. But unlike orthodox reformers, they also challenged the efficacy and value of the church hierarchy. Cathars considered themselves followers of Christ's original message, but the church called them heretics.

The church also condemned other, nondualist groups as heretical, not on doctrinal grounds but because these groups allowed their lay members to preach, challenging the authority of the church hierarchy. In Lyon (in southeastern France) in the 1170s, for example, a rich merchant named Waldo decided to take literally the Gospel message "If you wish to be perfect, then go and sell everything you have, and give to the poor" (Matt. 19:21). The same message had inspired countless monks and would worry the church far less several decades later, when St. Francis established his new order. But when Waldo went into the street and gave away his belongings, announcing, "I am not really insane, as you think," he scandalized not only the bystanders but the church as well. Refusing to retire to a monastery, Waldo and his followers, men and women called Waldensians, lived in poverty and went about preaching, quoting the Gospel in the vernacular so that everyone would understand. But the papacy rebuffed Waldo's bid to preach freely, and the Waldensians— denounced, excommunicated, and expelled from Lyon—wandered to Languedoc, Italy, northern Spain, and the Mosel valley (in Germany).

REVIEW   How did the money economy affect religious life?

Conclusion

The commercial revolution and the building boom it spurred profoundly changed the look of Europe. Thriving cities of merchants and artisans brought trade, new wealth, and new institutions to the West. Mutual and fraternal organizations like the commune, the compagnia, and the guilds expressed and reinforced the solidarity and economic interests of city dwellers.

Mapping the West Major Religions in the West, c. 1200
The broad washes of color on this map tell a striking story: by 1150, there were three major religions, each corresponding to a broad region. To the west, north of the Mediterranean Sea, Catholic Christianity held sway; to the east, the Greek Orthodox church was ascendant; all along the southern Mediterranean, Islam triumphed. Only a few places defied this logic: one was the crusader states, a tiny outpost of Catholics who ruled over a largely Muslim population. What this map does not show are the details: Jewish communities in many cities, lively varieties of Islamic beliefs within the Muslim world, communities of Coptic Christians in Egypt, and scattered groups of heretics in Catholic lands.

Political centralization accompanied economic growth, as kings and popes exerted their authority and tested its limits. The Gregorian reform pitted the emperor against the pope, and two separate political hierarchies emerged: the secular and the ecclesiastical. The two might cooperate, as Suger and Louis VI showed in their mutual respect, admiration, and dependence. But they might also clash, as Becket did with Henry II. Secular and religious leaders developed new and largely separate systems of administration, reflecting the new distinctions that separated clergy from laity. Although in some ways growing apart, the two groups never worked together so closely as in the crusades, military pilgrimages inspired by the pope and led by lay lords.

The commercial economy, political stability, and ecclesiastical needs fostered the growth of schools and the achievements of new scholarship. Young men sought learning to enhance their careers and bring personal fulfillment; women gained excellent educations in convents. Logic fascinated some students because it seemed to clarify the nature of both the world and God. Others, such as St. Bernard, felt that faith could not be analyzed.

While the black monks added to their hours of worship, built lavish churches, and devoted themselves to the music of the plainchant, the white monks insisted on an intense, interior spiritual life in a monastery shorn of decoration. Other reformers, such as Bruno of Cologne, sought isolation and hardship. These reformers rejected urban society yet unintentionally reflected it: the Cistercians

TIMELINE

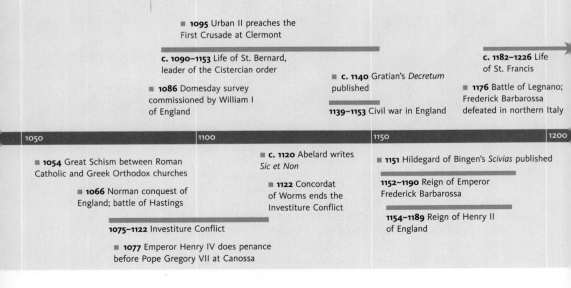

- **1095** Urban II preaches the First Crusade at Clermont

c. 1090–1153 Life of St. Bernard, leader of the Cistercian order

- **1086** Domesday survey commissioned by William I of England

- **c. 1140** Gratian's *Decretum* published

1139–1153 Civil war in England

c. 1182–1226 Life of St. Francis

- **1176** Battle of Legnano; Frederick Barbarossa defeated in northern Italy

1050   1100   1150   1200

- **1054** Great Schism between Roman Catholic and Greek Orthodox churches

- **1066** Norman conquest of England; battle of Hastings

1075–1122 Investiture Conflict

- **1077** Emperor Henry IV does penance before Pope Gregory VII at Canossa

- **c. 1120** Abelard writes *Sic et Non*

- **1122** Concordat of Worms ends the Investiture Conflict

- **1151** Hildegard of Bingen's *Scivias* published

1152–1190 Reign of Emperor Frederick Barbarossa

1154–1189 Reign of Henry II of England

were as anxious as any tradesman about the success of their granges, and the Carthusians were dedicated to their books. With the Franciscans and Dominicans, as well as heretical groups such as the Cathars, laypeople were drawn to participate actively in a deeply felt imitation of Christ's life and sufferings. Yet this new piety, paired with new power, contributed to the persecution of Jews and the periodic call for crusades against Muslims.

> **CHAPTER REVIEW QUESTIONS**
> 1. What were the similarities and differences between the powers wielded by the Carolingian kings and those wielded by twelfth-century rulers?
> 2. Contrast the purposes and the institutions of the gift economy discussed in Chapter 7 with those of the new profit economy.

For practice quizzes and other study tools, see the Online Study Guide at bedfordstmartins.com/huntconcise.

For primary-source material from this period, see Chapters 10 and 11 of *Sources of* THE MAKING OF THE WEST, Third Edition.

Suggested References

All aspects of the Gregorian reform are treated in the succinct book by Miller. The crusades, always a popular topic, have two new historians in Asbridge and Tyerman. Little's book on the commercial economy and religious movements is a classic.

Asbridge, Thomas. *The First Crusade: A New History.* 2004.

Bartlett, Robert. *England under the Norman and Angevin Kings, 1075–1225.* 2000.

Boynton, Susan. *Shaping a Monastic Identity: Liturgy and History at the Imperial Abbey of Farfa, 1000–1125.* 2006.

Clanchy, Michael. *Abelard: A Medieval Life.* 1997.

Hildegard of Bingen: http://www.healingchants.com/hvb_links.html

Hudson, John. *The Formation of the English Common Law: Law and Society in England from the Norman Conquest to Magna Carta.* 1996.

Little, Lester K. *Religious Poverty and the Profit Economy in Medieval Europe.* 1978.

*Lopez, Robert S., and Irving W. Raymond, eds. *Medieval Trade in the Mediterranean World.* 1955.

Miller, Maureen C. *Power and the Holy in the Ages of the Investiture Conflict.* 2005.

Thomas, Hugh M. *The Norman Conquest: England after William the Conqueror.* 2008.

Tyerman, Christopher. *God's War: A New History of the Crusades.* 2006.

Wheeler, Bonnie, and John Carmi Parsons, ed. *Eleanor of Aquitaine: Lord and Lady.* 2003.

The Medieval Search for Order

1200–1340

I N THE SECOND HALF of the thirteenth century, a wealthy patron asked a Parisian workshop specializing in manuscript illuminations to decorate Aristotle's *On the Length and Shortness of Life*. Most Parisian illuminators knew very well how to illustrate the Bible, liturgical books, and the writings of the church fathers. But Aristotle was a Greek who had lived before the time of Christ, and he was skeptical about the possibility of an afterlife. His treatise on the length of life ended with death. The artists in the workshop ignored this fact, however, and illustrated Aristotle's work as if he had believed in the immortal soul. As shown in the illustration opposite, the workshop artists decorated an initial (the first letter of a word) in the book with a depiction of the Christian Mass for the dead, a rite that is performed for the eternal salvation of the soul. In this way, they subtly but surely made Aristotle part of the orderly system of Christian belief and practice.

In Europe during the period 1200–1340, people at all levels, from workshop artists to kings and popes, expected to find order and unity in a world they believed was created by God. Sometimes their search for order led to compromise and adaptation, as in the case of the artists illustrating Aristotle's work. As medieval thinkers, writers, musicians, and artists reconciled faith with reason, they discovered the commonalities in the sacred and secular realms. Because of this, historians sometimes speak of the "medieval synthesis."

The quest for order also led to new institutions of power and control. Kings insisted on ruling whole territories and everyone within them. Although the often competing needs of kings and their subjects led to the development of representative

Christianizing Aristotle
This illumination was created for a thirteenth-century Latin translation of Aristotle's *On the Length and Shortness of Life*. Although Aristotle did not believe in the eternity of the soul, the artists nevertheless placed a depiction of the Christian Mass for the dead in one of the book's initials, in this way revealing their conviction that the ancient teachings of Aristotle and Christian practice worked together. (© *Biblioteca Apostolica Vaticana [Vatican] Vat. Lat. 2071, f. 297.*)

353

political institutions, rulers used these institutions to increase their control over their realms. Church laws were promulgated to regulate the lives of both clergy and laity. Throughout the period, the church sought to stamp out heresy, which led to the **Inquisition** and the persecution of whole communities of dissidents. In addition, as the conquests of the Mongols—invaders of China as well as the West—opened up new trade routes, more crusades were launched to bring everyone into the Christian fold.

Conflict also arose between church and state. In the mid-thirteenth century, the pope sought to destroy the emperor and very nearly did so. At the end of the century, the French and English kings sought to diminish the pope's power and succeeded quite well. Thus the end result of the desire for order was in many cases not unity, harmony, and synthesis, but rather discord.

> **CHAPTER FOCUS QUESTION**   In what areas of life did thirteenth-century Europeans try to impose order, and how successful were these attempts?

War, Conquest, and Settlement

In the thirteenth and early fourteenth centuries, Europeans aggressively moved outward in nearly all directions. While some warriors pushed north and east on the Baltic coast, others attacked Constantinople, and still others pursued the reconquista of Spain. In the south of France and in Sicily, crusaders with the pope's blessing waged war against people whom the church declared to be heretics, including a Christian king. Far beyond Europe's eastern fringes, merchants like Marco Polo traveled to and settled in lands ruled by the Mongols.

The Northern Crusades

Long before the twelfth century, the peoples living along the Baltic coast—partly pagan, mostly Slavic- or Baltic-speaking—had learned to glean a living and a profit from the inhospitable soil and climate. Through fishing and trading, they supplied the rest of Europe and Russia with slaves, furs, amber, wax, and dried fish. Like the Vikings, they combined commercial competition with outright raiding. The Danes and the Saxons (that is, the Germans in Saxony) both benefited and suffered from their presence.

When St. Bernard began to preach the Second Crusade in Germany, he discovered that the Germans were eager to attack unbelievers—the ones right next door to them! St. Bernard pressed the pope to add these northern heathens to the list of those against whom holy war should be launched, and he urged their conversion or extermination. Thus began the Northern Crusades, which continued intermittently until the early fifteenth century.

The king of Denmark and the duke of Saxony launched the first phase of the Northern Crusades. Their initial attacks were uncoordinated; in some instances they even fought each other. Then, in key raids in the 1160s and 1170s, the two leaders worked together briefly to bring much of the region west of the Oder River under their control. They took some land outright—the Saxon duke apportioned conquered territory to his followers, for example—but more often the Slavic princes surrendered and had their territories reinstated once they became vassals of the Christian rulers.

In 1198, Pope Innocent III (r. 1198–1216) declared a crusade against the Livs, even farther to the north and east. A military order—the Order of Sword Brothers, later supplanted by the Teutonic Knights—was set up to lead crusading armies, and a bishopric, the see of Riga, was established at the mouth of the Dvina River. The native populations were obliged to submit, whether by material inducements (the crusaders helped the Livs raid the Estonians, for example) or by sheer force. Repeatedly they agreed to a truce and baptism, and just as repeatedly they rebelled. In some areas, the crusaders resorted to scorched-earth tactics. By 1300, they had secured Livonia, Prussia, Estonia, and Finland. Only Lithuania managed to resist conquest and conversion (Map 10.1).

Though less well known than the crusades to the Holy Land, the Northern Crusades had far more lasting effects: they settled the Baltic region with German-speaking lords and peasants, and they forged a permanent relationship between the very north of Europe and its neighbors to the south and west. With the Baltic dotted with churches and monasteries and its peoples dipped into baptismal waters, the region would gradually adopt the institutions of western medieval society—cities, guilds, universities, castles, and manors.

The Capture of Constantinople

Four years after calling the crusade against the Livs, Pope Innocent III declared the Fourth Crusade (1202–1204) to the Holy Land. He hoped to reverse the failures of the Second and Third Crusades, but attitudes and circumstances beyond his control took over the new enterprise. Prejudice, religious zeal, and opportunism had become characteristic of western European dealings with the Byzantine Greeks. These attitudes help explain what happened from 1202 to 1204. The crusading army turned out to be far smaller than had been expected. Its leaders could not pay the Venetians, who had fitted out a large fleet of ships in anticipation of carrying multitudes of warriors across the Mediterranean to Jerusalem. The Venetians seized the opportunity to exact a different form of payment by convincing the crusade's leaders to attack Zara, a Christian city that was Venice's competitor in the Adriatic (Map 10.1, page 356). The Venetians then set their sights on Constantinople, hoping to control it and gain a commercial monopoly there. They persuaded the crusaders to join them on behalf of Alexius, a member of the ousted imperial family. Alexius claimed the Byzantine throne and promised the crusaders that he would reunite the eastern and western churches and fund the expedition to the Holy Land. Most of the crusaders convinced themselves that the cause was noble. "Never," wrote a contemporary, "was so great an enterprise undertaken by any people since the creation of the world."

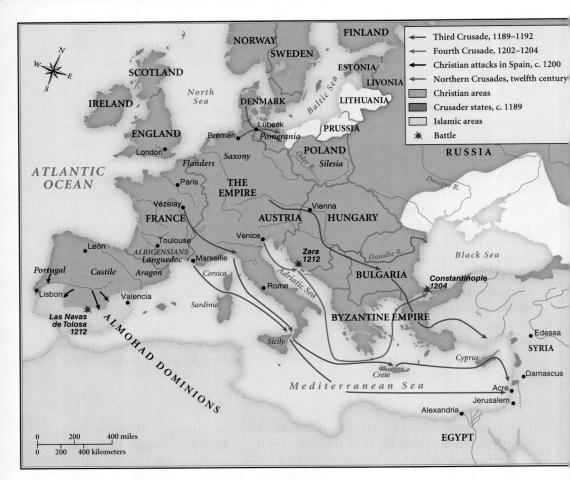

Map 10.1 Crusades and Anti-Heretic Campaigns, 1150–1204
Europeans aggressively expanded their territory during the second half of the twelfth century. To the north, German knights pushed into the lands bordering the Baltic Sea; to the south, Spanish warriors moved into the remaining strip of al-Andalus; to the east, new crusades were undertaken to shore up the tiny European outpost in the Holy Land. Although most of these aggressive activities had the establishment of Christianity as at least one motive, the conquest of Constantinople in 1204 had no such justification. It grew in part out of general European hostility toward Byzantium but mainly out of Venice's commercial ambitions.

The siege of Constantinople lasted nearly a year. Finally, on April 12, 1204, the city fell to the crusaders. Their deal with Alexius had broken down, and the crusaders brutally sacked Constantinople, killing residents and plundering treasure and relics. When one crusader discovered a cache of relics, a chronicler recalled, "he plunged both hands in and, girding up his loins, he filled the folds of his gown with the holy booty of the Church." The loss of that "holy booty" was, for the Byzantines, a great tragedy. The bishop of Ephesus wrote:

And so the streets, squares, houses of two and three stories, sacred places, nunneries, houses for nuns and monks, sacred churches, even the Great Church of God and the imperial palace, were filled with men of the enemy, all of them maddened by war and murderous in spirit. . . . [T]hey tore children from their mothers and mothers from their children, and they defiled the virgins in the holy chapels, fearing neither God's anger nor man's vengeance.

But to the Europeans, it was the Byzantines' just deserts.

Pope Innocent condemned the looting of Constantinople, but he also took advantage of it, ordering the crusaders to stay there for a year to consolidate their gains. The crusade leaders chose one among themselves, Baldwin of Flanders, to be Byzantine emperor, and he, the other princes, and the Venetians parceled out the Byzantine Empire. This new Latin Empire of Constantinople lasted until 1261, when the Byzantines recaptured the city and some of its outlying territory. No longer a strong state after 1204, Byzantium was always overshadowed and hemmed in by the military might of the Muslims and Europeans.

Popes continued to call crusades to the Holy Land until the mid-fifteenth century, but the Fourth Crusade marked the last major mobilization of men and leaders. Working against these expeditions were new values that placed a premium on the *interior* pilgrimage of the soul and celebrated rulers who stayed home to care for their people. The crusades to the Holy Land served as an outlet for religious fervor, ambition, prejudice, and aggression, but they had very little lasting positive effect. They managed to stimulate the European economy slightly, and they inspired a vast literature of songs and chronicles. Such achievements must be weighed against the lives lost on both sides and the religious polarization and prejudices that the crusades fed upon and fortified. The bitterest fruit of the crusades was the destruction of Byzantium. The Latin conquest of Constantinople in 1204 irrevocably weakened the one buffer state standing between Europe and Islam.

The Spanish Reconquista Advances

By 1200, Christian Spain had achieved the political configuration that would last for centuries: to the east was the kingdom of Aragon, to the west was Portugal, and in between was Castile, which in 1230 merged with León (Map 10.2). The leaders of these kingdoms competed for territory and power. Above all, they sought an advantage against the Muslims, who still ruled a strip of southern Spain. The reconquista, which had begun against the Muslim taifas (small, independent Muslim states) continued in full force, aided by Muslim disunity. The taifas not only were in competition with one another but also were beset from the south by the Almoravids and, after 1147, the Almohades, Muslims from North Africa. Claiming religious purity, these Berber groups declared their own holy war against al-Andalus. These simultaneous threats caused alliances within Spain to be based on political as well

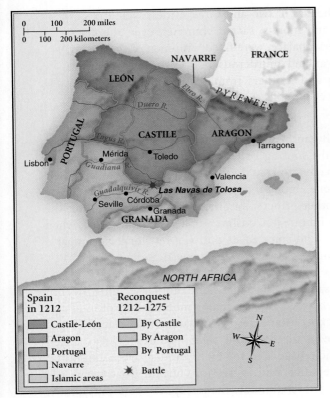

Map 10.2 The Reconquista Triumphs, 1212–1275

A major turning point in the reconquista was the battle of Las Navas de Tolosa (1212). This marked not only the defeat of the Muslims but also the triumph of Castile, which had originally been a tributary of León. In the course of the twelfth century, Castile became a power in its own right; in 1230, León and Castile merged into one kingdom. During the thirteenth century, Castile-León (and, to a lesser extent, Portugal and Aragon) conquered most of the rest of the Iberian peninsula, leaving only Granada under Islamic rule.

as religious considerations. The Muslim ruler of Valencia, for example, declared himself a vassal of the king of Castile and bitterly opposed the Berber expansion.

The crusading ideal, however, held no room for such subtleties. During the 1140s, armies under the command of the Christian kings of Portugal, Castile, and Aragon scored resounding victories against Muslim cities. Enlisting the aid of crusaders on their way to the Holy Land in 1147, the king of Portugal promised land, plunder, and protection to all who would help him attack Muslim-controlled Lisbon. His efforts succeeded, and Lisbon's Muslim inhabitants fled or were slain, its Mozarabic bishop (the bishop of the Christians living under Muslim rule) was killed, and a crusader from England was set up as bishop. In the 1170s, the Almohades conquered the Muslim south and advanced toward the cities taken by the Christians, but their exertions had no lasting effect. In 1212, a crusading army of Spaniards led by the kings of Aragon and Castile defeated the Almohades decisively at Las Navas de Tolosa. "On their side 100,000 armed men or more fell in the battle," the king of Castile wrote afterward, "but of the army of the Lord . . . incredible though it may be, unless it be a miracle, hardly 25 or 30 Christians of our whole army fell. O what happiness! O what thanksgiving!" The turning point in the reconquista had been reached (Map 10.2). The Almohades continued to lose strength, and Christian armies marched from victory to victory. Mérida fell in 1230, Córdoba in 1236, and Seville in 1248. By 1275, all that remained of Muslim-controlled Spain was a thin wedge of territory around Granada.

Reconquista

In the north of Spain, Christians adopted the figure of St. James, considered the Apostle to Spain, as the supernatural leader of their armies against the Muslims to the south. On this tympanum (the space within the archway over a door) from the cathedral of St. James (Santiago) at Compostela, James is shown as a knight on horseback, holding a flag and a sword. He was known as "the Moor-Slayer," or slayer of Muslims. (Institut Amatller de Arte Hispanico. Arxiu Mas.)

Putting Down the Heretics in Their Midst

In the thirteenth century, church and secular powers combined not only to conquer pagans and Muslims on the borders of Europe but also to stamp out heresy in their midst. The papacy declared crusades against the dualist Albigensians of southern France and even against a reigning emperor, Frederick II.

The Dominican efforts against the Cathar Albigensians (see page 348) were not effective enough to wipe out the movement. In 1208, the murder of a papal legate (an official representative of the pope) in southern France prompted Pope Innocent III to demand that princes from the north of France take up the sword, invade Languedoc, seize the land from the heretics, and populate it with orthodox Christians. This Albigensian Crusade (1209–1229) marked the first time the pope offered warriors fighting an enemy in Christian Europe all the spiritual and temporal benefits of a crusade to the Holy Land. Innocent suspended the crusaders' monetary debts and promised that their sins would be forgiven after forty days' service.

Like all crusades, the Albigensian Crusade had political as well as religious dimensions. It pitted southern French princes with Cathar connections against northern French leaders eager to demonstrate their piety and win new possessions. After twenty years of fighting, leadership of the crusade was taken over in 1229 by

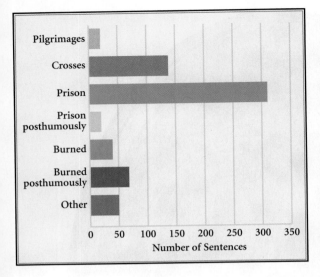

Taking Measure Sentences Imposed by an Inquisitor, 1308–1323
How harsh was the Inquisition? Did its agents regularly burn people alive? How frequently did they imprison people or order them to wear crosses on their clothing? The register of offenses and punishments kept by Bernard Gui, an inquisitor in Languedoc from 1308 to 1323, shows that only a relatively small number of people were burned alive. Of the 633 punishments handed down by Gui's tribunal, nearly half of the guilty were sentenced to prison, usually for life. Those listed as having been burned or sent to prison posthumously died before their sentences could be carried out.

the Capetian kings of France. Southern resistance was broken, and Languedoc was brought under the French crown.

Meanwhile, the papacy set up the Inquisition in southern France to discover undetected heretics. The Inquisition was a legal proceeding. First the inquisitors typically called the people of a district to a "preaching," where they gave a sermon and promised clemency to those who confessed their heresy promptly. Then, at a general inquest, they questioned each man and woman who seemed to know something about heresy: "Have you ever seen any heretics . . . ? Have you heard them preach? Attended any of their ceremonies? Adored heretics?" The judges assigned relatively lenient penalties to those who were not aware that they held heretical beliefs and to heretics who quickly recanted. But others were punished, even if they recanted. (See "Taking Measure.") Anyone who died while still a heretic could not be buried in consecrated ground—cemeteries specially blessed and set apart for believers. Raymond VII, count of Toulouse, saw the body of his father, who died excommunicated, rot in its coffin as the pope denied all requests for a Christian burial. Houses where heretics had resided or even simply entered were burned, and the sites were turned into garbage dumps. Children of heretics could not inherit any property or become priests, even if they adopted orthodox views.

In the thirteenth century, for the first time, long-term imprisonment became a tool to repress heresy, even if the heretic confessed:

We, friars of the Order of Preachers . . . deputed as inquisitors of heretical depravity in the city and diocese of Toulouse by apostolic authority: . . . It is our will, because they [certain named men and women] have rashly transgressed against God and holy church in the ways aforesaid [by seeing heretics, adoring them, hearing their preaching, and believing them to be good], that they be thrust into perpetual prison to do condign [appropriate] penance, and we command them to remain there in perpetuity. . . . However, we grant permission to Raymond Sabbatier to remain with his father, who is an invalid and who, it is reported, is a Catholic and a poor man, as long as his father shall live.

Raymond's privilege was quite unusual.

The inquisitors also used imprisonment to force people to recant, to give the names of other heretics, or to admit a plot. One heretic, for example, confessed to participating in a wicked (and imaginary) meeting of lepers who planned to poison all the wells. As the quest for religious order and conformity spawned wild fantasies of deviance, the inquisitors pinned their paranoia on real people.

The Inquisition created a new group—penitent heretics—who lived on the margins of Christian society. Forced to wear huge yellow fabric crosses sewn on the front and back of their shirts, they were publicly disgraced. Moreover, every Sunday and every feast day penitent heretics had to attend church twice; and during religious processions these men and women were required to join with the clergy and the faithful, carrying large branches in their hands as a sign of their penance.

One "heretic" was an emperor: Frederick II (r. 1212–1250). Innocent III—the pope who called the Fourth Crusade, the crusade against the Livs, and the Albigensian Crusade—had given the imperial crown to Frederick, but his successors regretted this bitterly. Like his grandfather Frederick Barbarossa, Frederick II, who was king of Sicily as well as Germany, sought to control Italy. This policy was intolerable to the papacy, which had its own ambitions on the peninsula.

Frederick was an amazing ruler: his contemporaries called him *stupor mundi,* "wonder of the world." Heir to two cultures, Sicilian on his mother's side and German on his father's, he cut a worldly and sophisticated figure. In Sicily, he moved easily within a diverse culture of Jews, Muslims, and Christians. There he could play the role of all-powerful ruler. In Germany, where Christian princes—often churchmen with military retinues—were acutely aware of their rights and privileges, he was less at home.

Frederick had a three-pronged imperial strategy. First, to ensure that opponents in Germany would not hound him, he granted the princes important concessions, finalized in 1232. These privileges allowed the German princes to turn their principalities into virtually independent states. Second, Frederick revamped the government of Sicily to give himself more control and yield greater profits. His *Constitutions of Melfi* (1231), an eclectic body of laws, called for nearly all court cases to be heard by royal justices, regularized commercial privileges, and set up a system of taxation. Third, Frederick sought to enter Italy through Lombardy, as his grandfather had done (Map 10.3).

The papacy followed Frederick's every move, excommunicating him a number of times. The most serious of these condemnations came in 1245, when the pope and other churchmen, assembled at the Council of Lyon, excommunicated and

Map 10.3 Europe in the Time of Frederick II, r. 1212–1250
King of Sicily and Germany and emperor as well, Frederick ruled over territory that encircled—and threatened—the papacy. Excommunicated several times, Frederick spent much of his career fighting the pope's forces. In the process, he conceded so much power to the German princes that the emperor thenceforth had little power in Germany. Meanwhile, rulers of smaller states, such as England, France, and Castile-León, were increasing their power and authority. **For more help analyzing this map, see the map activity for this chapter in the Online Study Guide at** bedfordstmartins.com/huntconcise.

deposed Frederick, absolving his vassals and subjects of their fealty to him and forbidding anyone to support him. "He has deservedly become suspect of heresy," the council intoned, explaining that "he has despised and continues to despise the keys of the church [the symbol of St. Peter and thus of the pope], causing the sacred rites to be celebrated or rather . . . to be profaned. . . . Besides, he is joined in odious friendship with the Saracens [Muslims]." By 1248, papal legates were preaching a crusade against Frederick and all his followers. Two years later, Frederick died.

The fact that Frederick's vision of the Empire failed is of less long-term importance than the way it failed. His concessions to the German princes meant that Germany would remain divided under numerous regional princes until the nineteenth century. Between 1254 and 1273, the princes kept the German throne empty. Splintered into factions, they elected two different foreigners, who spent their time fighting each other. In one of history's strange twists, it was during this low point of the German monarchy that the term *Holy Roman Empire* was coined.

In 1273, the princes at last united and elected a German, Rudolf (r. 1273–1291), whose family, the Habsburgs, was new to imperial power. Rudolf used the imperial title to help him gain Austria for his dynasty, but he did not try to fulfill the meaning of the imperial title in Italy. For the first time, the word *emperor* was freed from its association with Italy and Rome. For the Habsburgs, the title Holy Roman Emperor was prestigious but otherwise meaningless. In 1356 the reigning emperor published the Golden Bull,* which named the seven German princes who henceforth were to be the electors of the emperor. They included three churchmen (the archbishop of Mainz was one) and four laymen (including the duke of Saxony). The office of "king of the Romans," as the emperor was called, was completely divorced from papal power, and Germany was henceforth to be ruled by the princes.

Italy at the End of the Thirteenth Century

As for Italy, Frederick's failure meant that the cities of northern Italy would continue their independent course, while the papacy ensured that Frederick's heirs would not continue to rule in Sicily. The popes called on other rulers to take over the island—first Henry III of England and then Charles of Anjou. Forces loyal to Frederick's family turned to the king of Aragon (Spain). That move left two enduring claimants to Sicily's crown—the royal family of Aragon and the house of Anjou—and it spawned a long war impoverishing the region.

In the struggle between pope and emperor, the pope had clearly won. The moment marked a high point in the political power of the medieval papacy. Nevertheless, some agreed with Frederick II's view that by tampering with secular matters the popes had demeaned and sullied their office: "These men who feign holiness," Frederick had sneered, are "drunk with the pleasures of the world." Scattered throughout Germany were people who believed that Frederick was a divine scourge sent to overpower a materialistic papacy. The papacy won the war against Frederick, but at a cost. Even the saintly king of France criticized the popes for doing "new and unheard of things." By making its war against Frederick part of its crusade against heresy, the papacy came under attack for using religion as a political tool.

---

*Official documents issued by emperors and popes are called *bulls* because they were often authenticated by a *bulla,* or seal. This document was called the Golden Bull because of its golden seal.

The Mongol Takeover

Europeans were not the only warring society in the thirteenth century. To the east, the Mongols (sometimes called Tatars or Tartars) created an aggressive army under the leadership of Chingiz (or Genghis) Khan and his sons. In part, economic necessity impelled them out of Mongolia: climatic change had reduced the grasslands that sustained their animals and their nomadic way of life. But they were also inspired by Chingiz's hope of conquering the world. In the 1230s, the Mongols began concerted attacks on Europe—in Russia, Poland, and Hungary—where weak native princes were no match for the Mongols' formidable armies and tactics. Only the death of their Great Khan, Chingiz's son Ogodei (1186–1241)—styled the khagan, or "khan of khans"—and disputes over his succession prevented a concentrated assault on Germany. In the 1250s, the Mongols took Iran, Iraq, and Syria.

The Mongols' sophisticated and devastating military tactics contributed to their overwhelming success. Organizing their campaigns at meetings held far in advance of a planned attack, they devised two- and three-flank operations. The invasion of Hungary, for example, was two-pronged: one division of the Mongol army arrived from Russia, while the other moved through Poland and Germany. Many Hungarians perished in the assault as the Mongols, fighting mainly on horseback and wielding heavy lances and powerful bows whose arrows traveled far and penetrated deeply, crushed the Hungarian force of mixed infantry and cavalry (Map 10.4). Although the Mongols were beaten off, everyone expected them to attack again. In desperation, King Béla IV of Hungary appealed to the pope: "Most of the kingdom of Hungary has been reduced to a desert by the scourge of the Tartars [Mongols], and it is surrounded like a sheepfold by different infidel peoples." Luckily for Béla, the second attack never came. But Hungary was now a frontier not between two versions of Christianity (eastern and Roman Catholic), but between the east and the west.

Russia was a different story. There the Mongols established long-term control. At Vladimir, in the north, they broke through the walls of the city and burned the people huddled for protection in the cathedral. In 1240, they captured Kiev and made the mouth of the Volga River the seat of their power. The Mongols dominated Russia's principalities for about two hundred years.

The Mongol Empire in Russia, later called the **Golden Horde** (*golden* probably from the color of their leader's tent; *horde* from a Turkic word meaning "court"), adopted much of the native government apparatus. The Mongols standardized the collection of taxes and the recruitment of troops by basing them on a population census, and they allowed Russian princes to continue ruling as long as they paid homage and tribute to the khan. Although the Mongols of the Golden Horde converted to Islam, they exempted the Russian church from taxes in return for prayers for their leaders.

The Mongols changed the political configuration of Europe and Asia. Willing to deal with Westerners, they welcomed European missionaries and traders. The

Map 10.4 The Mongol Invasions, to 1259
The Mongols were the first people to tie the eastern world to the west. Their conquest of China, which took place at about the same time as their invasions of Russia and Iran, opened up trade relations across regions formerly separated by language, religion, and political regimes.

most famous of these travelers was Marco Polo (1254–1324), son of a merchant family from Venice. Marco's father and uncle had already been to China once, and Marco joined them on their second expedition. He stayed in China for nearly two years, but others stayed even longer. In fact, evidence suggests that an entire community of Venetian traders lived in the city of Yangzhou in the mid-fourteenth century.

Merchants paved the way for missionaries. Friars (preachers to the cities of Europe) became missionaries to new continents as well. In 1289, the pope made the Franciscan John of Monte Corvino his envoy to China. Preaching in India along the way, John arrived in China four or five years after setting out, converting one local ruler and building a church. A few years later, now at Beijing, he boasted that he had converted six thousand people, constructed two churches, and translated the New Testament and the Psalter into the native language.

Pietro Vesconte's World Map, c. 1320
The Polo family knew how to travel from Venice to China not because they were guided by maps, but because they were led by local escorts. Most of the maps available in their day were symbolic rather than accurate. Pietro Vesconte's world map is partly in that old style, but it also shows a growing interest in precision. Note, for example, the "rhumb lines" that crisscross the map. These were carefully constructed as a series of equidistant spokes radiating from a point, each indicating a wind direction. Vesconte was copying "portolan charts," the most scientific maps of his day, which gave accurate indications of land and water shapes to help sailors navigate.
(© The British Library Board. Add. 27376 ff.187v-188.)

The long-term effect of the Mongols on the west was to open up new land routes to the east that helped bind together the regions of the known world. Travel stories such as Marco Polo's inspired others to seek out the fabulous riches—textiles, ginger, ceramics, copper—of China and other places in the east. In a sense, the Mongols initiated the search for exotic goods and missionary opportunities that culminated in the European "discovery" of a new world, the Americas.

REVIEW   Where and how did the desire for order and uniformity lead to aggressive military action during the period 1200–1340?

Politics of Order and Control

In the thirteenth century, Europeans for the first time spoke of their rulers not as kings of peoples (for example, king of the Franks) but as kings of territories (for example, king of France). This new designation reflected an important new element in medieval rulership. However strong earlier rulers had been, their political power had been personal, depending on ties of kinship, friendship, and vassalage. Now their power was territorial, touching all who lived within the borders of their states. This new conception, reinforced by renewed interest in Roman legal concepts and supplemented by old-fashioned personal networks, served as a foundation for strong, central rule—most strikingly in western Europe but in central and eastern Europe as well.

France: From Acorn to Oak

Even with the achievements of Louis VI, the French monarchy remained weak, a realm surrounded by powerful neighbors. This changed under Philip Augustus

(r. 1180–1223), whose acquisitive policies toward Jews (see page 327) were matched by his territorial ambitions. When Philip first came to the throne, the royal domain,

The Consolidation of France under Philip Augustus, r. 1180–1223

the Île-de-France, was sandwiched between territory controlled by the counts of Flanders, Champagne, and Anjou. By far the most powerful ruler on the European continent was King Henry II of England, who was both count of Anjou and duke of Normandy. He also held the duchy of Aquitaine through his wife while exercising hegemony over Poitou and Brittany.

Henry and the counts of Flanders and Champagne vied to control the young king of France. Philip, however, quickly learned to play them off against one another. Contemporaries were astounded when Philip successfully gained territory to the north and west. Most important, he gained Normandy and nearby counties from Henry II's son King John in 1204. Then he made good on his claim at the decisive battle of Bouvines in 1214.

Pivotal forces led to the extension of the French king's power and the territorial integrity of France. The Second Crusade (1147–1149) had brought together many French lords as vassals of the king and united them against a common foe. The language they spoke was becoming increasingly uniform and "French." This in itself did not create a larger French kingdom, however. That came about through royal strategy. Rather than give his new territories out as fiefs, Philip determined to govern them himself.* In Normandy, in particular, he demanded that the aristocrats become his vassals, and he sent his officials to collect taxes and hear cases. Philip also instituted a new kind of French administration, based on writing. Before his day, most French royal arrangements were committed to memory rather than to parchment. If decrees were written at all, they were saved by the recipient, not by the government. For example, when a monastery wanted a confirmation of its privileges from the king, its own scribes wrote the document for its archives to preserve the monastery against possible future challenges. The king did keep some documents, which generally followed him in his travels like personal possessions. But in 1194, in a battle with the king of England, Philip lost his meager cache of documents along with much treasure when he had to abandon his baggage train. After 1194, the king had all his decrees written down, and he established permanent repositories in which to keep them.

---

*Philip was particularly successful in imposing royal control in Normandy. Later French kings gave most of the other territories to collateral members of the royal family.

Map 10.5 France under Louis IX, r. 1226–1270
Louis IX did not expand his kingdom as dramatically as his grandfather Philip Augustus had done. He was greatly admired nevertheless, for he was seen by contemporaries as a model of Christian charity, piety, and justice. After his death, Louis IX was recognized as a saint and thus posthumously enhanced the prestige of the French monarchy.

To do the daily work of government, Philip relied on members of the lesser nobility—knights and clerics, many of whom were "masters" educated in the city schools of France. They served as officers of his court; as *prévôts* (provosts), who oversaw the king's estates and collected his taxes; and as *baillis* (bailiffs; called seneschals in the south), who supervised the provosts and functioned as regional judges, presiding over courts that met monthly and making the king's power felt locally as never before.

Under Philip's grandson Louis IX (r. 1226–1270), the Capetian monarchy reached the height of its prestige if not its power. Louis was revered not because he was a military leader, but because he was an administrator, judge, and "just father" of his people. On warm summer days, he would sit under a tree in the woods near his castle at Vincennes, on the outskirts of Paris, hearing disputes and dispensing justice personally. He used his administrators to impose royal law and justice throughout his kingdom. Over the city of Paris he appointed a salaried officer who could be supervised and fired if necessary. During his reign, the influence of the parlement of Paris, the royal court of justice, increased significantly. Originally a changeable and movable body, part of the king's personal entourage when he dealt with litigation, it was now permanently housed in Paris and staffed by professional judges who heard cases and recorded their decisions. Unlike his grandfather Philip, Louis did not try to expand his territory. He inherited a large kingdom that included Poitou and Languedoc (gained during the Albigensian Crusade)(Map 10.5), and he was content. Although the king of England attacked him continually to try to regain territory lost under Philip, Louis remained unprovoked. Rather than prolong the fighting, he conceded a bit and made peace. At the same time, Louis was a zealous crusader. He took seriously the need to defend the Holy Land when most of his contemporaries were weary of the idea.

Louis was respectful of the church and the pope; he accepted limits on his authority in relation to the church and never claimed power over spiritual matters. Nevertheless, Louis vigorously maintained the dignity of the king and his rights. He expected royal and ecclesiastical power to work in harmony, and he refused to let the church dictate how he should use his temporal authority. When French bishops wanted royal officers to support the church's sentences of excommunication, Louis declared that he would authorize his officials to do so only if he were given full knowledge of each case so that he could judge them for himself. Louis's biographer described the scene that followed:

> After consulting together the prelates informed the king that they would not give him such knowledge, since this was solely a matter for the ecclesiastical court. The king replied that he in his turn would not give them knowledge of such matters as fell within his jurisdiction, nor order his officers to compel all excommunicated persons to obtain absolution. . . . "For if I did so," he added, "I should be acting contrary to God's laws and the principles of justice."

As a result, royal and ecclesiastical power would work side by side, neither subservient to the other.

It is easy for historians to fault Louis for his policies toward Jews. His hatred of them was well known. He did not exactly advocate violence against them, but he sometimes subjected them to arrest, canceling the debts that Christians owed to them (but collecting part of those debts into the royal treasury) and confiscating their belongings. In 1253, he ordered Jews to live "by the labor of their hands" or leave France. He meant that they should no longer lend money, in effect taking away their only means of support. Louis's contemporaries did not criticize him for his policies; if anything, his hatred of Jews enhanced his reputation.

In fact, many of Louis's contemporaries considered him a saint, praising his care for the poor and sick, the pains and penances he inflicted on himself, and his regular participation in church services. In 1297, Pope Boniface VIII canonized him as St. Louis. The result was enormous prestige for the French monarchy. This prestige, joined with the renown of Paris as the center of scholarship and the repute of French courts as the epitome of chivalry, made France the cultural model of Europe.

England: Crisis and Consolidation

What the French king gained the English king lost. Henry II had been very strong, and his son Richard I (r. 1189–1199) was called "the Lion-Hearted" for his boldness. Under these men, the English monarchy was powerful and rich. Its power derived largely from its judicial and administrative apparatus. Its wealth came from court fees, income from numerous royal estates both in England and on the continent, taxes from cities, and customary feudal dues (called aids) collected from barons and knights. These aids were extraordinary taxes, demanded (traditionally) by the king on occasions such as the knighting of his eldest son and the marriage of his eldest daughter. Enriched by the commercial economy of the late twelfth century, the English kings encouraged their knights and barons not to serve them personally in battle but instead to pay the king a tax called scutage in lieu of service. The monarchs preferred to hire mercenaries both as troops to fight external enemies and as policemen to enforce the king's will at home.

But Richard died young, and his brother and heir, John (r. 1199–1216), lost badly to Philip Augustus. John was widely disliked by his contemporaries, who accused him of asserting his will in a high-handed way. But to understand John, it is necessary to appreciate how desperate he was to keep his continental possessions. After he lost his northern French territories to Philip, John did everything he could to add to the crown revenues so he could pay for an army to fight the French. He forced his vassals to pay ever-increasing scutages and extorted money in the form of new feudal aids. He compelled the widows of his vassals to marry men of his choosing or pay him a hefty fee if they refused. John's heavy investment in this war effort, however, could not prevent the defeat of his army at the battle of Bouvines in 1214, and this defeat caused discontented English barons to rebel openly against the king. At Runnymede in June 1215, John was forced to agree to the charter of baronial liberties that has come to be called Magna Carta, "Great Charter."

The English barons intended Magna Carta (so named to distinguish it from a smaller charter issued around the same time concerning the royal forests) to be a conservative document defining the "customary" obligations and rights of the nobility and forbidding the king to break from these customs without consulting his barons. "No widow shall be forced to marry so long as she wishes to live without a husband," it declared, continuing:

> No scutage or aid shall be imposed in our kingdom unless by common counsel of our kingdom, except for [the customary purposes:] ransoming our person, for making our eldest son a knight, and for once marrying our eldest daughter.

In its most famous clause, Magna Carta provided that

> no free man shall be arrested or imprisoned or disseised [deprived of his property] or outlawed or exiled or in any way victimized, neither will we attack him or send anyone to attack him, except by the lawful judgment of his peers or by the law of the land.

Thus Magna Carta established that all free men in the land had certain customs and rights in common and that the king had to uphold those customs and rights. In this way, it documented the subordination of the king to custom, implying that the king was not above the law. Magna Carta shows that the growth of royal power was matched by the self-confidence of the English barons, certain of their rights and eager to articulate them.

When it was drawn up, Magna Carta applied only to a small elite—the "free men" of the realm. It did not promise a jury trial by peers to everyone, nor did it secure the rights of Englishmen in general. But in the course of time, the definition of *free men* expanded to include all the king's subjects, and the rights guaranteed by Magna Carta came to be understood as applying to all.

Papal Monarchy

As the kings of France and England were gaining newly precise roles, so too were the popes. Innocent III was the most powerful, respected, and prestigious of the medieval popes. The first pope to have a university training, Innocent had studied theology at Paris and law at Bologna. From theology, he learned to tease new meaning out of the pope's position: he thought of himself as ruling in the place of Christ the King. In his view, secular kings and emperors existed to help the pope. From law, Innocent gained his conception of the pope as lawmaker and of law as an instrument of moral reformation.

Utilizing the traditional method of declaring church law, Innocent convened and presided over a council in 1215 at the pope's Lateran Palace in Rome. Known as the Fourth Lateran Council, it aimed to reform not only the clergy but also the laity. Innocent and the other assembled churchmen hoped to create a well-ordered society united under the authority of the church.

For laymen and laywomen, perhaps the most important canons of the Fourth Lateran Council concerned the sacraments, the rites the church believed Jesus had instituted to confer sanctifying grace. One canon required Christians to attend Mass and confess their sins to a priest at least once a year. At the same time, the council explained with new precision the transformation of bread and wine (the Eucharist) in the Mass. In the twelfth century, a newly rigorous understanding of this transformation had already been publicized, according to which Christ's body and blood were truly contained in the sacrament that looked like bread and wine on the altar.

The Fourth Lateran Council not only declared this to be dogma (authoritative teaching) but also explained it by using a technical term coined by twelfth-century scholars. The bread and wine were *transubstantiated*: although the Eucharist continued to *look* like bread and wine, with its consecration during the Mass the bread became the actual flesh and the wine the real blood of Christ. The council's emphasis on this potent event strengthened the role of the priesthood, for only a priest could celebrate this mystery (that is, transform the bread and wine into Christ's body and blood) through which God's grace was transmitted to the faithful.

Innocent III wanted the council to condemn Christian men who had intercourse with Jewish women and then claimed "ignorance" as their excuse. But the council went even further, requiring all Jews to advertise their religion by some outward sign: "We decree that [Jews] of either sex in every Christian province at all times shall be distinguished from other people by the character of their dress in public." Like all church rules, this canon took effect only when local rulers enforced it. In many instances, they did so with zeal, not so much because they were eager to humiliate Jews but rather because they could make money selling exemptions to Jews who were willing to pay to avoid the requirements. Nonetheless, sooner or later Jews almost everywhere had to wear a badge as a sign of their second-class status. In southern France and in a few places in Spain, Jews were supposed to wear round badges. In England, the city of Salisbury demanded that they wear special clothing. In Vienna, they were told to put on pointed hats (see the illustration on page 327).

The Fourth Lateran Council's longest decree blasted heretics: "Those condemned as heretics shall be handed over to the secular authorities for punishment." If the secular authority did not "purge his or her land of heretical filth," the heretic was to be excommunicated. If he had vassals, they were to be released from their oaths of fealty, and the heretic's land was to be taken over by orthodox Christians. Rulers heeded these demands. Already some had taken up arms against heretics in the Albigensian Crusade (1209–1229). The Fourth Lateran Council was also responsible for setting up the Inquisition.

The council's mission to regulate and Christianize lay behavior was carried forward by Dominican and Franciscan friars. Both orders focused on travel, preaching, and poverty—vocations that brought them into cities and towns. Soon their members dominated the fledgling city universities and were sending into the community friar-preachers trained by them. Townspeople flocked to such preachers because they wanted to know how the Christian message applied to their daily lives. They were concerned, for example, about the ethics of moneymaking, sex in marriage, and family life. In turn, the preachers represented the front line of the church. They

Friars and Usurers

How did the friars treat money? As this illustration shows, they fled it. In fact, the founder of the Franciscans, St. Francis, refused to touch money. At first, the friars begged for food and shelter. Even when their numbers grew and they began forming communities and living in monasteries, they insisted on personal poverty while ministering to city dwellers. In this illumination from about 1250, a Franciscan (in light-colored robes) and a Dominican (in black) reject offers from two usurers, whose profession they are thus shown to condemn. Other friars, however, including Thomas Aquinas, worked out justifications for some of the urban moneymaking professions. (Bibliothèque nationale de France.) **For more help analyzing this image, see the visual activity for this chapter in the Online Study Guide at** bedfordstmartins.com/huntconcise.

A Lady and Her Loving Falcon
This sumptuous velvet and silk pouch, made by an embroideress in about 1320, shows a lady in the position of falconer. The falcon, a bird ordinarily used as an aid in hunting, is here depicted as the lady's lover. He is flying toward her to place a crown of greenery on her head while she touches him tenderly on the shoulder. In her other hand she holds the leash with which she trained him. (© Musée de Tissus, Lyon.)

met the laity on their own turf and taught them to bend their activities to church teachings. Many members of the lay community became "tertiaries" of the orders, adopting lives of simplicity, prayer, and works of charity yet continuing to live in the world, raising families and tending to the tasks of daily life. Even kings became tertiaries.

The third orders were not the only outlets for lay piety. In particular, women throughout Europe found a great variety of religious refuges. As in previous centuries, powerful families founded nunneries, especially within urban areas. These were primarily for the daughters of the wealthy. Ordinary women found different modes of religious expression. Some were attracted by the quiet life and rapturous mysticism of the Beguines; others found comfort in the life of charity and service of women's mendicant orders, such as those connected to the Franciscans; and still others lived happily as wives and mothers, punctuating their domestic duties with religious devotions. Elisabeth of Hungary, who married a German prince at the age of fourteen, raised three children. At the same time, she devoted her life to fasting, prayer, and service to the poor.

Of course, many women were not as devout as Elisabeth. In the countryside, they cooked their porridge, brewed their ale, and raised their children. They attended church regularly, but only on major feast days or for "churching"—the ritual of purification after a pregnancy. In the cities, women who scratched out a meager living sometimes made pilgrimages to relic shrines to seek divine help or cures. Religion was part of these women's lives but did not dominate them.

The church's attempt to define and control the Eucharist had some unintended consequences for a number of women who made religion the focus of their lives. The new emphasis on the transformed bread and wine induced these pious women to eat nothing but the Eucharist. One such woman, Angela of Foligno, reported that the consecrated bread swelled in her mouth, tasting sweeter than any other food. In the minds of these holy women, Christ's crucifixion was the literal sacrifice of his body, to be eaten by sinful men and women as the way to redeem themselves. Renouncing all other food became part of a life of service to others, as many of these devout women gave the food they refused to eat to the poor. Even if not engaged in community service, holy women felt that their suffering itself was a work of charity, helping to release souls from purgatory, the place where (the church taught) souls were cleansed of their sins.

The Kings Triumph

The Fourth Lateran Council was the high-water mark of the medieval papacy. However, the growing prestige and actual jurisdiction of secular rulers changed the balance of power between church and state in the course of the thirteenth century. At the end of that century, when the pope clashed with the kings of France and England, the kings were the clear winners, and the papacy lost both prestige and power.

The clash began over taxing the clergy. The French king Philip IV (r. 1285–1314), known as Philip the Fair, and the English king Edward I (r. 1272–1307) financed their wars (mainly against one another) by taxing the clergy along with everyone else. The new principle of national sovereignty that they were claiming led them to assert jurisdiction over all people, even churchmen, who lived within their borders. For the pope, however, the principle at stake was his role as head of the clergy. In response to clerical taxation, Boniface VIII (r. 1294–1303) declared that only the pope could authorize such taxes. Threatening to excommunicate kings who taxed prelates without papal permission, he called upon clerics to disobey any such royal orders.

Edward and Philip reacted swiftly. Taking advantage of the important role that English courts played in protecting the peace, Edward declared that all clerics who refused to pay their taxes would be considered outlaws—literally, "outside the law." Clergymen who were robbed, for example, would have no appeal against their attackers; if accused of crimes, they would have no defense in court. Relying on a different strategy, Philip forbade the exportation of precious metals, money, or jewels, effectively sealing the French borders. Immediately the English clergy cried out for legal protection, while the papacy itself clamored for the revenues it had long enjoyed from French pilgrims, litigants, and travelers. Boniface was forced to back down, conceding in 1297 that kings had the right to tax the clergy of their kingdoms in emergencies.

But the crisis was not over. In 1301, Philip the Fair tested his jurisdiction in southern France by arresting the bishop of Pamiers on a charge of treason for slandering the king by comparing him with an owl, "the handsomest of birds which is worth absolutely nothing." Imprisoning a bishop violated the principle, maintained both by the pope and by French law, that a clergyman was not subject to lay justice. Boniface reacted angrily, and Philip seized the opportunity to ridicule and humiliate the pope, orchestrating a public relations campaign against him. Boniface's reply, a bull titled *Unam Sanctam* (1302), intensified the situation by declaring bluntly "that it is altogether necessary to salvation for every human creature to be subject to the Roman Pontiff." At meetings of the king's inner circle, Philip's agents declared Boniface a false pope, accusing him of sexual perversion, various crimes, and heresy. In 1303, royal agents, acting under Philip's orders, invaded Boniface's palace at Anagni (southeast of Rome) to capture the pope, bring him to France, and try him. Fearing for the pope's life, however, the people of Anagni joined forces and drove the French agents out of town. Boniface died shortly thereafter, but the king had made his power felt. The next two popes pardoned Philip and his agents for their actions.

Just as Frederick II's defeat showed the weakness of the Empire, so Boniface's humiliation showed the limits of the papacy. The two powers that claimed "universal" authority had little weight in the face of the new, limited, but tightly controlled national states. After 1303, popes continued to criticize kings, but their words had less and less impact. In the face of powerful medieval states such as France, Spain, and England—supported by vast revenues, judicial apparatuses, representative institutions, and even the loyalty of churchmen—the papacy could make little headway. The delicate balance between church and state, a hallmark of the years of Louis IX, broke down by the end of the thirteenth century.

In 1309, forced from Rome by civil strife, the papacy settled at Avignon, a city technically in the Holy Roman Empire but very close to, and influenced by, France (Map 10.5, page 368). Here the popes remained until 1378. Italians called the

Boniface VIII
The sculptor who depicted Pope Boniface VIII made him young, majestic, authoritative, sober, and calm. Yet Boniface could not have been very calm, for his authority was challenged at every turn. (Scala/Art Resource, NY.)

period from 1309 to 1378 the Babylonian captivity, likening the popes' absence from Rome to the ancient Israelites' exile to Babylon (2 Kings 25:11). The Avignon popes, many of them French, established a sober and efficient organization that took in regular revenues and gave the papacy more say than ever before in the appointment of churchmen. They would, however, slowly abandon the idea of leading all of Christendom and would tacitly recognize the growing power of the secular states to regulate their internal affairs.

Power Shifts in the Italian Communes

During the thirteenth century, the Italian communes continued to extend their control over the surrounding countryside as independent city-states. While generally presenting a united front to outsiders, factions within the communes fought for control and its spoils. In the early thirteenth century, these factions represented noble families. In the course of the century, however, newer groups, generally though not exclusively from the non-noble classes, attempted to seize the reins of government in the communes. The *popolo* (people), as such groups were called, incorporated members of city associations such as craft and merchant guilds, parishes, and the commune itself. In fact, the popolo was a kind of alternative commune, a sworn association in each city that dedicated itself to upholding the interests of its members. Armed and militant, the popolo demanded a share in city government, particularly to gain a voice in matters of taxation. In 1222 at Piacenza, for example (see "Mapping the West," page 389), the popolo won half the government offices; a year later, they and the nobles worked out a plan to share the election of their city's *podestà,* or "chief executive." Such power sharing often resulted from the popolo's struggle for rights. In some cities, however, nobles overcame and dissolved the popolo, while in others the popolo virtually excluded the nobles from government. Constantly confronting one another—quarreling, feuding, and compromising—these factions turned Italian cities into centers of civil discord.

Weakened by this constant friction, the communes were tempting prey for great regional nobles who, allying with one or another faction, established themselves as *signori* (singular *signore,* "lord") of the cities, keeping the peace at the price of repression. In these circumstances, the commune gave way to the *signoria* (a state ruled by a signore), and one family began to dominate the government. The communes ceased to exist, and many Italian cities fell under the control of despots. The fate of Piacenza was typical. First dominated by nobles, its commune had granted the popolo a voice by 1225. By midcentury, however, the signore's power had eclipsed that of both the nobles and the popolo.

New-Style Associations amid the Monarchies

Although the thirteenth century was the age of newly strong signori or monarchs, there were some exceptions. Under the leadership of Lübeck, the cities of northern Germany trading between the Baltic and North seas banded together to form the

Hanseatic League (or Hanse). It was one fruit of the Northern Crusades; even the Teutonic Knights were members. Merchants in these cities dominated the northern grain trade, and their control over this commodity gave them power. They were able to declare embargoes against enemies and monopolies for themselves. Throughout the thirteenth and fourteenth centuries, the Hanseatic League dominated the Baltic region.

Similarly independent were the self-governing peasant and town communes in the high Alpine valleys that became the united Swiss Confederation. In 1291, the peasants of Uri, Schwyz, and Unterwalden swore a perpetual alliance against their oppressive Habsburg overlord. After defeating a Habsburg army in 1315, these free peasants took the name "Confederates" and developed a new alliance that would become Switzerland. In the process, the Swiss enshrined their freedom in the legend of William Tell, their national hero, who was forced by a Habsburg official to prove his archery skills by shooting an apple placed on the head of his own son. This act so outraged the citizens that they rose up against Habsburg rule. By 1353, the important cantons of Lucerne, Zurich, and Bern had joined the confederation. It continued to acquire new members into the sixteenth century, defeating armies sent by different princes to undermine its liberties.

Swiss cantons in 1291
Swiss cantons added 1332–1353
- - - Contemporary border of Switzerland

Lake Constance
Basel
Zurich
Lucerne Zug Schwyz
Unter-walden Uri Glarus
Fribourg Bern
Lake Geneva

0   25   50 miles
0 25 50 kilometers

Growth of the Swiss Confederation, to 1353

The Birth of Representative Institutions

Monarchies found it useful to embrace groups beyond the narrow elite of the aristocracy. One of the ways in which Philip the Fair orchestrated his public relations campaign against Pope Boniface was to convene representatives of the clergy, nobles, and townspeople to explain, justify, and propagandize his position. This new assembly, which met at Paris in 1302, was the ancestor of the Estates General, which would meet sporadically for centuries thereafter—for the last time in 1789, at the beginning of the French Revolution. (In France, the various orders—clergy, nobles, and commoners—were called estates.) After Philip's agents declared Boniface a false pope, the king sent his commissioners to the various provinces of France to convene local meetings to repeat his charges against Boniface and gain support. Clergy, local nobles, townspeople, and even villagers attending these meetings almost unanimously denounced the pope.

As in France, representative institutions elsewhere began as political tools with which rulers hoped to broaden their support. All across Europe—from Spain to Poland, from England to Hungary—rulers summoned parliaments. These assemblies grew out of the ad hoc advisory sessions kings customarily held with their nobles and clergy, men who informally represented the two most powerful classes, or "orders," of medieval society. Although these bodies differed from place to place, the impulse behind their creation was similar. They began (as in France) as assemblies where kings celebrated their royal power and prestige and where the "orders" simply assented to royal policy. In the thirteenth century, the advisory sessions became solemn, formal meetings of representatives of the "orders" to the kings' chief councils—the precursors of parliamentary sessions. Eventually these bodies became organs through which people not ordinarily at court could articulate their wishes.

One of the earliest such representative institutions was created in Castile-León (part of present-day Spain). Sometimes the king of Castile-León called together only the clergy and nobles, but other times he sent for representatives of the towns, especially when he wanted the help of town militias. As townsmen gradually began to participate regularly in advisory sessions called *cortes,* kings came to depend on them and their support. In turn, commoners became more fully integrated into the work of royal government. Because of their wealth, they were crucial to this work. Enriched by plunder from the reconquista, the villages of Castile-León had become major commercial centers, dominating the countryside. Town leaders—called *caballeros villanos,* or "city horsemen," because they were rich enough to fight on horseback—monopolized municipal offices. In 1188, when King Alfonso IX (r. 1188–1230) summoned townsmen to the cortes, the city caballeros served as their representatives, agreeing to Alfonso's plea for military and financial support and for help in consolidating his rule. Once convened at court, these wealthy townsmen joined bishops and noblemen in formally counseling the king and assenting to royal decisions. Beginning with Alfonso X (r. 1252–1284), Castilian monarchs regularly called on the cortes to participate in major political and military decisions and to assent to new taxes to finance them.

The English Parliament* also developed as a tool of royal government. In this case, however, the king's control was complicated by the power of the barons, manifested, for example, in Magna Carta. In the twelfth century, King Henry II had consulted prelates and barons at Great Councils, using these parliaments as his tool to ratify and gain support for his policies. Although Magna Carta had nothing to do with such councils, the barons thought the document gave them an important and permanent role in royal government as the king's advisers and a solid guarantee of their customary rights and privileges. When Henry III (r. 1216–1272) was crowned at the age of nine, he was king in name only for the first sixteen years of his reign. During that period, England was governed by a council consisting of a few barons, professional administrators, and a papal legate. Though not quite "government by Parliament," this council set a precedent for baronial participation in government.

---

*Although *parliament* and *parlement* are very similar words, both deriving from the French word *parler* (to speak), the institutions they named were very different. The Parlement of France was a law court, whereas the English Parliament, though beginning as a court to redress grievances, had by 1327 become above all a representative institution. The major French representative assembly, later called the Estates General, first convened at the beginning of the fourteenth century.

An English parliament that included commoners came into being in the midst of war and as a result of political weakness. Henry so alienated nobles and commoners alike by his wars, debts, choice of advisers, and demands for money that the barons threatened to rebel. At a meeting at Oxford in 1258, they forced Henry to dismiss his foreign advisers; to rule with the advice of a Council of Fifteen, chosen jointly by the barons and the king; and to limit the terms of his chief officers. However, this new government was also torn apart by disputes among the barons, and civil war erupted in 1264. At the battle of Lewes in the same year, the leader of the baronial opposition, Simon de Montfort (c. 1208–1265), routed the king's forces, captured the king, and became England's de facto ruler. Because only a minority of the barons followed Simon, he sought new support by convening a parliament in 1265. He summoned not only the earls, barons, and churchmen who backed him but also representatives from the towns—the "commons"—and he appealed for their help. Thus, for the first time, the English commons were given a voice in government. Simon's brief rule ended that very year, and Henry's son Edward I became a rallying point for royalists (backers of the king). Edward's constant need for new revenues led him to call regular sessions of Parliament. Without meaning to do so, he solidified its role as a regular institution of royal government in England. Thus, in England, representative government emerged out of the interplay between royal initiatives and baronial revolts.

> **REVIEW**   Compare the administrative tools of the papal monarchy with those of secular monarchies in France, England, and Spain.

The Medieval Synthesis

Just as the church wanted to regulate worldly life in accordance with God's plan for salvation, so contemporary thinkers, writers, musicians, and artists sought to harmonize the secular with the sacred realms. Scholars wrote treatises that reconciled faith with reason, poets and musicians sang of the links between heaven and earth, and artists expressed the same ideas in stone and sculpture and on parchment. In the face of many contradictions, all of these groups were largely successful in communicating an orderly image of the world.

Scholasticism: Harmonizing Faith and Reason

Scholasticism was the culmination of the method of logical inquiry and exposition pioneered by masters like Peter Abelard (see page 341). In the thirteenth century, the method was used to summarize and reconcile all knowledge. Many of the thirteenth-century scholastics (those who practiced scholasticism) were members of the Dominican and Franciscan orders and taught in the universities. On the whole, they were confident that knowledge obtained through the senses and reason was compatible with knowledge known through faith and revelation. One of their goals was to demonstrate this harmony. The scholastic summa (plural summae), or summary of knowledge, was a systematic exposition of the answer to every possible question about human morality, the physical world, society, belief, action, and theology.

The method of the summa borrowed much of the vocabulary and many of the rules of logic outlined by Aristotle. Even though Aristotle was a pagan, scholastics considered his coherent and rational body of thought the most perfect that human reason alone could devise. Because they had the benefit of Christ's revelations, scholastics considered themselves able to take Aristotle's philosophy one step further and reconcile human reason with Christian faith. Confident in their method and conclusions, scholastics embraced the world and its issues.

Some scholastics considered questions about the natural world. Albertus Magnus (c. 1200–1280) was a major theologian who also contributed to the fields of biology, botany, astronomy, and physics. His reconsideration of Aristotle's views on motion led the way to distinctions that helped scientists in the sixteenth and seventeenth centuries arrive at the modern notion of inertia.

One of Albertus's students was St. Thomas Aquinas (c. 1225–1274), perhaps the most famous scholastic. Huge of build and renowned for his composure in debate, Thomas came from a noble Italian family that had hoped to see him become a powerful bishop rather than a poor university professor. When he was about eighteen years old, he defied his family's wishes and joined the Dominicans. Soon he was studying at Cologne with Albertus. At thirty-two he became a master at the University of Paris. Like many other scholastics, Thomas considered Aristotle "the Philosopher," the authoritative voice of human reason, which he sought to reconcile with divine revelation in a universal and harmonious scheme. In 1273, he finished his monumental *Summa Theologiae* (sometimes called *Summa Theologica*), intended to cover all important topics, human and divine. Thomas divided these topics into questions, exploring each one thoroughly and systematically, and concluding each question with a decisive position and a refutation of opposing views.

Many of Thomas's questions spoke to the keenest concerns of his day. He asked, for example, whether it was lawful to sell something for more than it was worth. Thomas arranged his argument systematically, quoting first authorities that seemed to declare every sort of selling practice, even deceptive ones, to be lawful. This was the *sic* (or "yes") position. Then he quoted an authority that opposed selling something for more than it was worth. This was the *non*. Following that, he gave his own argument, prefaced by the words "I answer that." Unlike Abelard, whose method left differences unresolved, Thomas wanted to harmonize the two points of view, so he pointed out that price and worth depended on the circumstances of the buyer and seller, and he concluded that charging more than a seller had originally paid could be legitimate at times.

For townspeople engaged in commerce and worried about biblical prohibitions on moneymaking, Thomas's ideas about selling practices addressed burning questions. Hoping to go to heaven as well as reap the profits of their business ventures, laypeople listened eagerly to preachers who delivered their sermons in the vernacular but who based their ideas on the Latin summae of Thomas and other scholastics. Thomas's conclusions aided townspeople in justifying their worldly activities. In his own day, Thomas Aquinas was a controversial figure, and his ideas, emphasizing reason, were by no means universally accepted. In Thomas's view, God, nature, and reason were in harmony, so Aristotle's arguments could be used to explore both the human and the divine orders.

The work of the thirteenth-century scholastics to unite the secular with the sacred continued for another generation after Thomas. Yet at the beginning of the fourteenth century, fissures began to appear. In the summae of John Duns Scotus (c. 1266–1308), for example, the world and God were less compatible. John, whose name "Duns Scotus" betrays his Scottish origin, was a Franciscan who taught at both Oxford and Paris. For John, human reason could know truth only through the "special illumination of the uncreated light"—that is, by divine illumination. This was a Neoplatonic idea that had long inspired medieval thinkers. But unlike his predecessors, John believed that this illumination came not as a matter of course but only when God chose to intervene. John and others sometimes experienced God as willful rather than reasonable. Human reason could not soar to God; God's will alone determined whether a person could know him. In this way, John separated the divine and secular realms.

Like John, William of Ockham (c. 1285–1349), an English Franciscan who was one of the most eminent theologians of his age, rejected any confident synthesis of Christian doctrine and Aristotelian philosophy. Ockham believed that universal concepts had no reality in nature but instead existed only as mere representations, names in the mind—a philosophy that came to be called nominalism. Perceiving and analyzing such concepts as "man" or "papal infallibility" offered no assurance that the concepts expressed truth. Observation and human reason were limited as means to understanding the universe and knowing God. Ockham's insistence that the simplest explanation was the best came to be known as "Ockham's razor." Where human reason left off, God's covenant with his faithful took over.

New Syntheses in Writing and Music

Thirteenth-century writers and musicians, as confident in their powers as any king or scholastic, presented complicated ideas and feelings as harmonious and unified syntheses. Writers explored the relations between this world and the next; musicians found ways to bridge sacred and secular forms of music.

Dante Alighieri (1265–1321), perhaps the greatest vernacular poet of the Middle Ages, harmonized the scholastic universe with the mysteries of faith and the poetry of love. Born in Florence in a time of political turmoil, Dante incorporated the heroes and villains of his day into his most famous poem, the *Commedia*, written between 1313 and 1321. Later known as the *Divine Comedy*, Dante's poem describes the poet taking an imaginary journey from Hell to Purgatory and finally to Paradise. The poem is an allegory in which every person and object must be understood at more than one level. At the most literal level, the poem is about Dante's travels. At a deeper level, it is about the soul's search for meaning and enlightenment and its ultimate discovery of God in the light of divine love. Just as Thomas Aquinas thought that Aristotle's logic could lead to important truths, so Dante used the pagan poet Virgil as his guide through Hell and Purgatory. And just as Thomas believed that faith went beyond reason to even higher truths, so Dante found a new guide representing earthly love to lead him through most of Paradise. This guide was Beatrice, a Florentine girl with whom Dante had fallen in love as a boy and whom he never forgot. But only the Virgin Mary, representing faith and divine love, could bring Dante to the culmination of his journey—a blinding and inexpressibly awesome vision of God:

> What I then saw is more than tongue can say.
> Our human speech is dark before the vision.
> The ravished memory swoons and falls away.

Dante's poem electrified a wide audience. By elevating one dialect of Italian—the language that ordinary Florentines used in their everyday lives—to a language of exquisite poetry, Dante was able to communicate the scholastics' harmonious and optimistic vision of the universe in an even more exciting and accessible way. So influential was his work that it is no exaggeration to say that modern Italian is based on Dante's Florentine dialect.

Other writers of the period used different methods to express the harmony of heaven and earth. The anonymous author of *Quest of the Holy Grail* (c. 1225), for example, wrote about the adventures of the knights of King Arthur's Round Table to convey the doctrine of transubstantiation and the wonder of the vision of God. In *The Romance of the Rose,* begun by one author (Guillaume de Lorris, a poet in the romantic tradition) and finished by another (Jean de Meun, a poet in the scholastic tradition), a lover seeks the rose, his true love. In the long dream that the poem describes, the narrator's search for the rose is thwarted by personifications of love, shame, reason, abstinence, and so on. They present him with arguments for and against love, not incidentally commenting on people of the poets' own day. In the end, sexual love is made part of the divine scheme—and the lover plucks the rose.

Musicians, like poets, developed new forms that bridged sacred and secular subjects in the thirteenth and fourteenth centuries. This connection appears in the most distinctive musical form of the thirteenth century, the motet (from the French *mot,* meaning "word"). The motet is an example of **polyphony**, music that consists of two or more melodies performed simultaneously. Before about 1215, most polyphony was sacred; purely secular polyphony was not common before the fourteenth century. The motet, a unique merging of the sacred and the secular, evidently originated in Paris, the center of scholastic culture as well.

The typical thirteenth-century motet has three melody lines (or "voices"). The lowest, usually from a liturgical chant melody, has no words and may have been played on an instrument rather than sung. The remaining melodies have different texts, either Latin or French (or one of each), which are sung simultaneously. Latin texts are usually sacred, whereas French ones are secular, dealing with themes such as love and springtime. In one example, the top voice chirps in quick rhythm about a lady's charms ("Fair maiden, lovely and comely; pretty maiden, courteous and pleasing, delicious one"); the middle voice slowly and mournfully laments the "malady" of love; and the lowest voice sings a liturgical melody. The motet thus weaves the sacred (the chant melody in the lowest voice) and the secular (the French texts in the upper voices) into a sophisticated tapestry of music.

Like the scholastic summae, motets were written by and for a clerical elite. Yet they incorporated the music of ordinary people, such as the calls of street vendors and the boisterous songs of students. In turn, they touched the lives of everyone, for polyphony influenced every form of music, from the Mass to popular songs that entertained and diverted laypeople and churchmen alike.

Complementing the motet's complexity was a new notation for rhythm. Until the thirteenth century, musical notation could indicate pitch but had no way to denote the duration of the notes. In that century, music theorists developed increasingly precise methods to indicate rhythm. Franco of Cologne, for example, in his *Art of Measurable Song* (c. 1280), used different shapes to mark the number of beats each note should be held. His system became the basis of modern musical notation. Because each note could now be allotted a specific duration, written music could express new and complicated rhythms. The music of the thirteenth century reflected both the melding of the secular and the sacred and the possibilities for greater order and control.

The Order of High Gothic

Just as polyphonic music united the sacred with the secular, so **Gothic** architecture, sculpture, and painting expressed the order and harmony of the universe. The term *Gothic* was originally used to belittle medieval art and architecture, but it now refers with admiration to a particular style used in the twelfth to fifteenth centuries. Its chief characteristic is the use of pointed arches, which began as architectural motifs but were soon adopted in every art form. Gothic churches appealed to the senses the way that scholastic argument appealed to human reason: both were designed to lead people to knowledge that touched the divine. Being in a Gothic church was a foretaste of heaven.

Gothic architecture began around 1135, with the project of Abbot Suger, the close associate of King Louis the Fat (see page 334), to remodel portions of the church of Saint-Denis. Suger's rebuilding of Saint-Denis was part of the fruitful melding of royal and ecclesiastical interests and ideals in the north of France. At the west end of his church, the point where the faithful entered, Suger decorated the portals with figures of Old Testament kings, queens, and patriarchs, signaling the links between the present king and his illustrious predecessors. Within the church, Suger rebuilt the *chevet,* or apse, using pointed arches and stained glass to let in light, which he believed would transport the worshipper from the "slime of earth" to the "purity of Heaven." Suger thought that the Father of lights, God himself, "illuminated" the minds of the beholders via the light that filtered through the stained-glass windows. Soon the style that Suger pioneered was taken up across northern France and then, in the 1250s, as French culture gained enormous prestige under Louis IX, all across

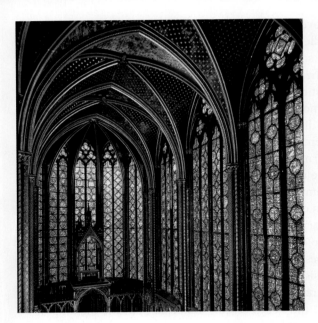

French Gothic: Sainte-Chapelle
Gothic architecture opened up the walls of the church to windows, as may be seen at Sainte-Chapelle, the private chapel of the French king Louis IX (St. Louis) in Paris. Consecrated in 1248, it was built to house Christ's crown of thorns and other relics of the Passion. This photo shows the interior of the upper chapel looking east. Filled with "stained" glass—the colors were added to the ingredients of the glass before they were heated, melted, and blown—the windows glow like jewels. Moreover, each has a story to tell: the life of Christ, major events from the Old Testament, the lives of saints. Compare the use of windows, walls, vault, and piers here with that of the Romanesque church Saint-Savin on page 346.
(Bridgeman-Giraudon/Art Resource, NY.)

Europe. Gothic was an urban architecture, reflecting—in its towering heights, jewel-like windows, and bright ornaments—the aspirations, pride, and confidence of rich and powerful merchants, artisans, and bishops. A Gothic church, usually a cathedral (the bishop's principal church), was the focal point of a city.

Building Gothic cathedrals was a community project, enlisting the labor and support of an entire urban center. New cathedrals required a small army of quarrymen, builders, carpenters, and glass cutters. Bishops, papal legates, and clerics planned and helped pay for these grand churches, but townspeople also generously financed them and filled them to attend Mass and visit relics. Guilds raised money to pay for stained-glass windows that depicted and celebrated their own patron saints. In turn, towns made money when pilgrims came to visit relics, and sightseers arrived to marvel at their great churches. At Chartres, near Paris, for example, which had the relic of the Virgin's tunic, crowds thronged the streets, the poor buying small lead figures of the Virgin, the rich purchasing wearable replicas of her tunic. Churches were centers of commercial activity. In their basements, wine merchants plied their trade, while other vendors sold goods outside.

The technologies that made Gothic churches possible were all known before the twelfth century. But Suger's church showed how they could be brought together to achieve a particularly dazzling effect. Gothic techniques included ribbed vaulting, which gave a sense of precision and order; pointed arches, which produced a feeling of soaring height; and flying buttresses, which took the weight of the vault off the walls (Figure 10.1). The buttresses permitted much of the wall to be cut away and the open spaces to be filled with glass.

Figure 10.1 Elements of a Gothic Cathedral
Bristling on the outside with stone flying buttresses, the Gothic cathedral was lofty and serene on the inside. The buttresses, which held the weight of the vault, allowed Gothic architects to pierce the walls with windows running the full length of the church. Within, thick piers anchored on sturdy bases became thin columns as they mounted over the triforium and clerestory (windows), blossoming into ribs at the top. Whether plain or ornate, the ribs gave definition and drew attention to the high, pointed vault.

Romanesque church exteriors, with their massive walls and clearly articulated parts, prepare visitors for what they will see within (see Figure 9.2, page 342). Gothic cathedrals, however, surprise. The exterior of a Gothic church has an opaque, bristling, and forbidding look owing to the dark surface of its stained glass and its flying buttresses. The interior, however, is just the opposite. It is all soaring lightness, harmony, and order. Just as a scholastic presented his argument with utter clarity, so the interior of a Gothic church revealed its structure through its skeleton of ribbed vaults and piers. And just as a scholastic bridged the earthly and celestial realms, so the cathedral elicited a response beyond reason, evoking a sense of awe.

By the mid-thirteenth century, Gothic architecture had spread from France to other European countries. Yet the style varied by region, most dramatically in Italy. The outer walls of the cathedral at Orvieto, for example, are built of alternate bricks of light and dark color, providing texture instead of glass and light; the vault over the large nave is round rather than pointed, recalling the Roman aqueducts that could still be seen in Italy when the builders were designing the cathedral. With no flying buttresses and relatively little portal sculpture, Italian Gothic churches convey a spirit of austerity.

Gothic art, both painting and sculpture, echoed and decorated the Gothic cathedral. Gothic sculpture differed from earlier church sculpture in its naturalism and monumentality. Romanesque sculpture played upon a flat surface; Gothic figures were liberated from their background. Sculpted in the round, they turned, moved, and interacted with one another. The positions of the figures, the people they represented, and the ways in which they interacted were meant to be "read" like a scholastic summa, for Gothic sculpture often depicted complex stories or scenes. The south portal complex of Chartres cathedral is a good example. Each massive doorway tells a separate story through sculpture: the left depicts the martyrs, the right the confessors, and the center the Last Judgment. Like Dante's *Divine Comedy,* these portals taken together show the soul's pilgrimage from the suffering of this world to eternal life.

Like Gothic architecture, Gothic sculpture began in France and was adopted, with many variations, elsewhere in Europe during the thirteenth century. The German sculptor who carved the tympanum (the half-circle form) over the south portal of Strasbourg's cathedral (see page 387) was particularly interested in emotional expression. As the Virgin Mary dies, the figures around her bend and gesture, showing their grief with their hands and faces.

By the early fourteenth century, the expressive sculptures so prominent in architecture were reflected in painting as well. This new style is evident in the work of Giotto (1266–1337), a Florentine artist who helped change the emphasis of painting, which had been predominantly symbolic, decorative, and intellectual. For example, Giotto filled the walls of a private chapel at Padua with paintings depicting scenes of Christ's life. Here he experimented with the illusion of depth. Giotto's figures, appearing weighty

German Gothic: Strasbourg

The Virgin Mary is mourned in this tympanum over the portal of the Strasbourg cathedral's south transept (the arm that crosses the church from north to south). Here, in German Gothic, the emphasis is on emotion and expressivity. Notice the depiction of Mary, with her bedclothes agitated and her body contorted. Why do you suppose Christ stands in the center of the tympanum, as if he is one of the mourners? What is he holding in the crook of his arm? (Hint: The souls of the dead are often shown as miniature people.) (Foto Marburg/Art Resource, NY.)

and voluminous, express a range of emotions as they seem to move across interior and exterior spaces (see page 388). In bringing sculptural realism to a flat surface, Giotto stressed three-dimensionality, illusional space, and human emotion. By melding earthly sensibilities with religious themes, Giotto found yet another way to bring together the natural and divine realms.

> **REVIEW**   How did artists, architects, musicians, and scholastics try to link this world with the divine?

Conclusion

In the thirteenth and early fourteenth centuries, western Europeans sought order through control. They aggressively expanded outward, from the Baltic to Gibraltar. They sacked Constantinople in 1204 and proclaimed their own emperor. They treated the Mongol hegemony in the east as an opportunity for trade and missionary work.

Powerful territorial kings and princes created new bureaucratic institutions. They hired staffs to handle their accounts, record acts, collect taxes, issue writs, and preside over courts. Flourishing cities, a growing money economy, and trade

Giotto, *Birth of the Virgin*
Giotto's depiction of the Virgin Mary's birth pays attention to the homey details of a thirteenth-century Florentine aristocratic household. The baby is bathed and swaddled by maidservants in the bottom tier, while above she is handed to her mother, St. Anne, who reaches out eagerly for the child. (The Art Archive/Scrovegni Chapel, Padua/Dagli Orti [A].)

and manufacturing (see Chapter 9) provided the finances necessary to support the personnel now used by medieval governments. The universities became the training grounds for the new administrators as well as for urban preachers.

Both the church and the state became more assertive. The Fourth Lateran Council was an attempt to regulate intimate aspects of the lives of all, even lay-people and non-Christians. The conflict between Boniface and Philip showed how the French king could galvanize his subjects—even his clergy—on behalf of the interests of the state. In England, where John agreed to Magna Carta, it was the barons who helped forge a notion of government that transcended the king. By contrast, the artists and architects of the time sought to bring together two separate entities—the worldly and the divine.

New power, new piety, and new exclusivity arose in a society both more confident and less tolerant. Crusaders fought against an increasing variety of foes, not only in the Holy Land but also in Spain, in southern France, and on Europe's northern frontiers. With heretics voicing criticism and maintaining their beliefs, the

Mapping the West Europe, c. 1340
The Empire, now called the Holy Roman Empire, still dominated the map of Europe in 1340, but the emperor himself had little power. Each principality—often each city—was ruled separately and independently. To the east, the Ottoman Turks were just beginning to make themselves felt. In the course of the next century, they would disrupt the Mongol hegemony and become a great power.

church, led by the papacy, defined orthodoxy and declared dissenters its enemies. Jews, who had once been fairly well integrated into the Christian community, were treated ambivalently, alternately used and abused. The Baltic peoples became targets for new evangelical and armed zeal; the Greeks became the butt of envy, hostility, and finally enmity. Confident and aggressive, the leaders of Christian Europe in the thirteenth and early fourteenth centuries attempted to impose their rule, legislate morality, and create a unified worldview impregnable to attack. But the drive for order would soon be challenged by economic and political crises and epidemic disease.

CHAPTER REVIEW QUESTIONS
1. Why was Innocent III more successful than Boniface VIII in carrying out his objectives?
2. Compare the origins and outcomes of the challenges faced by Boniface VIII with those confronted by Gregory VII in the eleventh century.

For practice quizzes and other study tools, see the Online Study Guide at bedfordstmartins.com/huntconcise.

For primary-source material from this period, see Chapters 11 and 12 of *Sources of THE MAKING OF THE WEST,* Third Edition.

Suggested References

Bartlett takes up the physical expansion of Europe, while Dante and Thomas Aquinas demonstrate its intellectual range. Bynum deftly ties together religious, theological, and gender issues. The politics of the period always had religious implications, and religious movements always had political ramifications, as Jordan and Moore show in different ways.

Bartlett, Robert. *The Making of Europe: Conquest, Colonization, and Cultural Change, 950–1350.* 1993.

Bergreen, Laurence. *Marco Polo: From Venice to Xanadu.* 2007.

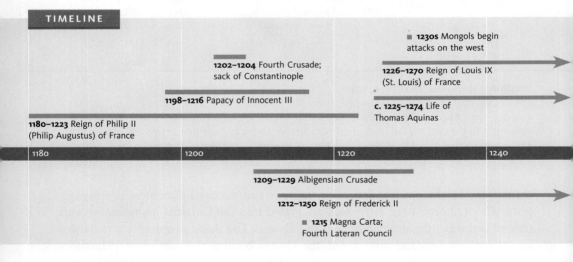

TIMELINE

1230s Mongols begin attacks on the west

1202–1204 Fourth Crusade; sack of Constantinople

1226–1270 Reign of Louis IX (St. Louis) of France

1198–1216 Papacy of Innocent III

c. 1225–1274 Life of Thomas Aquinas

1180–1223 Reign of Philip II (Philip Augustus) of France

| 1180 | 1200 | 1220 | 1240 |

1209–1229 Albigensian Crusade

1212–1250 Reign of Frederick II

1215 Magna Carta; Fourth Lateran Council

Burnham, Louisa A. *So Great a Light, So Great a Smoke: The Beguin Heretics of Languedoc.* 2008.

Bynum, Caroline Walker. *Holy Feast and Holy Fast: The Religious Significance of Food to Medieval Women.* 1987.

*Dante. *The Divine Comedy.* Many editions; recommended are translations by Mark Musa, John Ciardi, and Robert Pinsky.

Jones, Philip J. *The Italian City-State: From Commune to Signoria.* 1997.

Jordan, William Chester. *The French Monarchy and the Jews: From Philip Augustus to the Last Capetians.* 1989.

Moore, R. I. *The Formation of a Persecuting Society: Power and Deviance in Western Europe, 950–1250.* 2d ed. 2007.

O'Callaghan, Joseph F. *The Cortes of Castile-León, 1188–1350.* 1989.

Rubin, Miri. *Corpus Christi: The Eucharist in Late Medieval Culture.* 1991.

*Thomas Aquinas, *Summa Theologiae* (English translation): http://www.newadvent.org/summa/

Tolan, John Victor. *Sons of Ishmael: Muslims through European Eyes in the Middle Ages.* 2008.

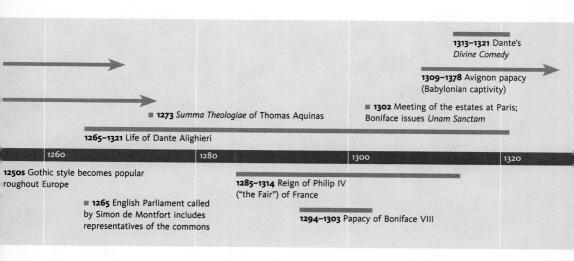

1313–1321 Dante's *Divine Comedy*

1309–1378 Avignon papacy (Babylonian captivity)

1273 *Summa Theologiae* of Thomas Aquinas

1302 Meeting of the estates at Paris; Boniface issues *Unam Sanctam*

1265–1321 Life of Dante Alighieri

1260   1280   1300   1320

1250s Gothic style becomes popular throughout Europe

1285–1314 Reign of Philip IV ("the Fair") of France

1265 English Parliament called by Simon de Montfort includes representatives of the commons

1294–1303 Papacy of Boniface VIII

11

Crisis and Renaissance

1340–1500

 N 1453, THE OTTOMAN TURKS turned their cannons on Constantinople and blasted the city's walls. The fall of Constantinople, which spelled the end of the Byzantine Empire, was an enormous shock to Europeans. Some, like the pope, called for a crusade against the Ottomans. Others, like the writer Lauro Quirini, sneered, calling the Turks "a barbaric, uncultivated race, without established customs, or laws, [who live] a careless, vagrant, arbitrary life."

But the Ottomans didn't consider themselves uncultivated or arbitrary. In fact, they shared many of the values and tastes of the Europeans who were so hostile to them. Sultan Mehmed II employed European architects to construct his new palace, the Topkapi Saray, in the city that was once called Constantinople and was now normally called Istanbul. He also commissioned the Venetian Gentile Bellini to paint his portrait. In this, he was no different from the most fashionable European rulers of the day.

Portrait of Mehmed II
The Ottoman ruler Mehmed II (r. 1451–1481) saw himself as a Renaissance patron of the arts, and he called upon the most famous artists and architects of the day to work for him. The painter of this portrait, Gentile Bellini, was from a well-known family of artists in Venice and served at Mehmed's court in 1479–1480. The revival of portraiture, so characteristic of Renaissance tastes, was as important to the Turkish sultans as to European rulers. *(Erich Lessing/Art Resource, NY.)*

Mehmed's actions and interests sum up the three main features of the period 1340–1500: a crisis in the global order, as the Ottomans created a new and long-lived state; political consolidation; and the artistic and cultural movement known as the Renaissance.

During this period a series of crises struck Europe. The disease known as the **Black Death** tore at the fabric of communities and families, though survivors and their children reaped the benefits of higher wages and better living standards. The **Hundred Years' War**, fought between France and England from 1337 to 1453, brought untold misery to the French countryside. Following their conquest of Constantinople, the Ottoman Turks penetrated far into the Balkans. And a crisis in the church, called the **Great Schism**, pitted pope against pope and divided Europe into separate camps.

These crises were met and overcome in large measure through the policies of newly consolidated states. New political entities such as Poland-Lithuania and Muscovy rose to prominence. France and England became centralized monarchies. Italy's political mosaic began to coalesce into five territorial states. And the Iberian kingdoms of Portugal and Spain expanded European domination to Africa, Asia, and the Americas.

Meeting the needs of men and women in crisis while often catering to the wishes of newly rich and powerful rulers, the Renaissance—a word that means "rebirth" and refers to the revival of classical culture—gave Europe new styles of living, ruling, and thinking. A new vocabulary drawn from classical literature, as well as astonishing new forms of art and music based on ancient precedents, were used both to confront and to mask the crises of the day.

CHAPTER FOCUS QUESTION What were the roles of the newly consolidated states of Europe in both the crises of the period and the Renaissance?

Crisis: Disease, War, and Schism

The crises began in the mid-fourteenth century. The Black Death decimated the population; the Hundred Years' War buffeted France, England, and the Low Countries; and the Ottoman Turks began their conquest of formerly Byzantine territory. Soon two and then three rival popes divided the church. In the wake of these crises, many ordinary folk sought solace in new forms of piety, some of them heretical.

Economic Contraction and the Black Death

Bad weather and overpopulation contributed to a series of famines at the beginning of the fourteenth century. Population growth meant that peasants had to divide their plots into ever smaller parcels or farm marginal land. Their income and the quality of their diet eroded. In the great urban centers, where thousands depended on steady employment and cheap bread, a bad harvest, always followed by sharply rising food prices, meant hunger and eventual famine.

A cooling of the European climate also contributed to the crisis in the food supply. Europe entered a colder period, with a succession of severe winters beginning in 1315. Crop failures were widespread. In many cities of northwestern Europe, the price of bread tripled, and thousands starved to death. The Great Famine (1315–1322) left many people hungry, sick, and weak.

At midcentury, a terrible disease, later called the Black Death (1346–c. 1350), hit Europe. Possibly bubonic plague, possibly another as yet unidentified disease, the Black Death attacked the region between the Black and Caspian seas in 1346 (Map 11.1). In 1347, many members of the Genoese colony in Caffa, in the Crimea, fell to the disease, which then traveled westward, to Byzantium, the Middle East, the North African coast, and Europe. By January 1348, the Black Death had infected southern Italy and France. Soon it spread to all of Italy, the Balkans, and most of

Legend:
- 1347
- Jan. 1348
- June 1348
- 1349
- 1350
- 1351 and later
- Few or no plague deaths
- ✱ Center of urban revolt
- Rural uprisings

Map 11.1 Advance of the Black Death
The gradual but deadly spread of the Black Death followed the roads and waterways of Europe. **For more help analyzing this map, see the map activity for this chapter in the Online Study Guide at** bedfordstmartins.com/huntconcise.

France. The disease then crept northward to Germany, England, and Scandinavia, reaching the Russian city of Novgorod around 1350.

Nothing like this had struck Europe before. Inhabitants of cities, where crowding and filth increased the chances of contagion, died in massive numbers. Florence lost almost two-thirds of its population of ninety thousand; Siena, like most cities visited by the disease, lost half its people. Rural areas suffered fewer deaths, but regional differences were pronounced. (See "Taking Measure," page 396.) Further outbreaks of the disease, though not called the Black Death, occurred in Europe in 1361, 1368–1369, 1371, 1375, 1390, and 1405. They continued, with longer dormant intervals, into the eighteenth century.

In some places, responses to the Black Death were immediate and practical. At the Italian city of Pistoia in 1348, for example, the government decreed that no citizen could go to nearby Pisa or Lucca, nor could people from those cities enter

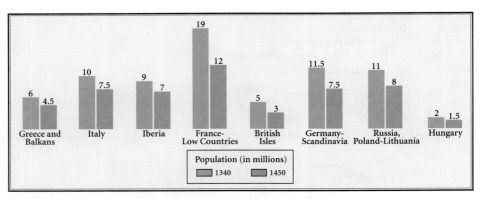

Taking Measure Population Losses and the Black Death, 1340–1450
This bar chart dramatically represents the impact of the Black Death and the recurrence of the disease between 1340 and 1450. More than a century after the Black Death, none of these regions of Europe had made up for the population losses. The hardest-hit areas were France and the Low Countries, which also suffered from the devastations of the Hundred Years' War.

Pistoia; in effect, Pistoia established a quarantine. In the same set of ordinances, the Pistoians, thinking that "bad air" brought the disease, provided for better sanitation, declaring that "butchers and retailers of meat shall not stable horses or allow any mud or dung in the shop or other place where they sell meat." Elsewhere reactions were religious. The archbishop of York in England tried to prevent the disease from entering his diocese by ordering "that devout processions [be] held every Wednesday and Friday in our cathedral church."

Some people took more extreme measures. Lamenting their sins—which they believed had brought on the Black Death and other calamities—and attempting to placate God, groups of men and women wandered from city to city with whips in their hands. Entering a church, they took off their shirts or blouses, lay down one by one on the church floor, and, according to the chronicler Henry of Hervordia (d. 1370),

> one of them would strike the first with a whip, saying, "May God grant you remission [forgiveness] of all your sins. Arise." And he would get up, and do the same to the second, and all the others in turn did the same. When they were all on their feet, and arranged two by two in procession, two of them in the middle of the column would begin singing a hymn in a high voice, with a sweet melody.

Churchmen did not approve of the flagellants, as these people were called, because they took on the preaching and penance that was supposed to be done by the clergy. Nevertheless, the flagellants aroused popular sympathy wherever they went. The religious enthusiasm they inspired often culminated in violence against Jews, as rumors circulated that Jews were responsible for the Black Death. Old charges that Jews were plotting to "wipe out all the Christians with poison and had poisoned wells and springs everywhere," as one Franciscan friar put it, revived. In Germany especially thousands of Jews were slaughtered. Many fled to Poland, which was less affected by the Black Death and where the authorities welcomed Jews as productive taxpayers. In western and central Europe, however, the persecutions impoverished Jews.

Preoccupation with death led to the popularity of a theme called the Dance of Death as a subject of art, literature, and performance. It featured a procession of people of every age, sex, and rank making their way to the grave. Preachers and poets talked and wrote on the theme. Yet at the same time the Black Death helped inspire this bleak view of the world, it brought new opportunities for those who survived its murderous path. With a smaller population to feed, less land was needed for farming. Marginal land that had been cultivated was returned to pasture, meadow, or forest. Landlords diversified their products. Wheat had been the favored crop before the Black Death, but barley—the key ingredient in beer—turned out to be more profitable afterward. Animal products continued to fetch a high price, and some landlords switched from farming to animal husbandry.

These changes in agriculture meant a better standard of living. The peasants and urban workers who survived the Black Death were able to negotiate better working conditions or higher wages from their landlords or employers. With more money to spend, people could afford a better and more varied diet that included beer and meat. Even commoners could now afford finery, a fact that threatened to erase the lines between the nobles and everyone else. Many Italian cities passed laws to prohibit ostentatious dress among every class of citizens. These laws were generally ineffective, however, as families continued to announce their rank and prestige by wearing lavish clothes.

Each attack of the disease brought with it, a few years later, a slight jump in the birthrate. It is unlikely that women became more fertile. Rather, the cause of the increased birthrate was more subtle: with good employment opportunities, couples married at younger ages and with greater frequency than they had previously. "After the end of the epidemic," one chronicler wrote, "the men and women who stayed alive did everything to get married."

The Black Death also had an effect on patterns of education. The survivors' children needed schooling, but the disease spared neither the students nor the professors of the old universities. As the disease ebbed, new local colleges and universities were built, partly to train a new generation for the priesthood and partly to satisfy local donors—many of them rulers—who, riding on a sea of wealth left behind by the dead, wanted to be known as patrons of education. Thus, in 1348, in the midst of the Black Death, Holy Roman Emperor Charles IV chartered a university at Prague. The king of Poland founded Cracow University, and a Habsburg duke created the University of Vienna. Rather than travel to Paris or Bologna, young men living east of the Rhine River now tended to study closer to home.

The Hundred Years' War, 1337–1453

In France, the misery wrought by disease was compounded by the devastation of war. Since the Norman invasion of England in the eleventh century (see page 329), the king of England had held land on the continent. The French kings continually

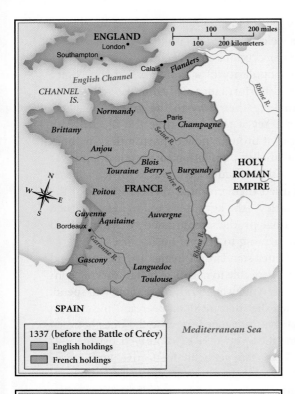

0   100   200 miles
0   100   200 kilometers

ENGLAND
London
Southampton
Calais Flanders
English Channel
CHANNEL IS.
Normandy
Paris Champagne
Seine R.
Brittany
Anjou
Blois Berry
Touraine Burgundy
HOLY ROMAN EMPIRE
Poitou FRANCE
Rhine R.
Loire R.
Guyenne
Aquitaine Auvergne
Bordeaux
Garonne R.
Rhône R.
Gascony
Languedoc
Toulouse
SPAIN
Mediterranean Sea

1337 (before the Battle of Crécy)
English holdings
French holdings

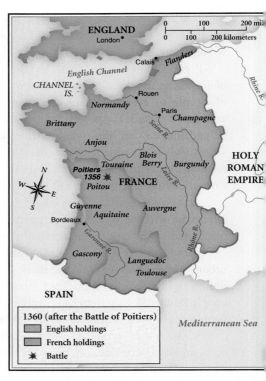

0   100   200 mi
0   100   200 kilometers

ENGLAND
London
Calais Flanders
English Channel
CHANNEL IS.
Normandy
Rouen
Paris Champagne
Seine R.
Brittany
Anjou
Blois Berry
Touraine Burgundy
HOLY ROMAN EMPIRE
Poitiers 1356
Poitou FRANCE
Rhine R.
Loire R.
Guyenne
Aquitaine Auvergne
Bordeaux
Garonne R.
Rhône R.
Gascony
Languedoc
Toulouse
SPAIN
Mediterranean Sea

1360 (after the Battle of Poitiers)
English holdings
French holdings
★ Battle

0   100   200 miles
0   100   200 kilometers

ENGLAND
London
Calais Flanders
English Channel
Agincourt 1415
Amiens
CHANNEL IS.
Normandy
Rouen
Paris Reims
Champagne
Seine R.
Brittany
Domrémy
HOLY ROMAN EMPIRE
Orléans
Anjou
Chinon
Blois Berry
Touraine Bourges
Duchy of Burgundy
County of Burgundy
Poitiers
Poitou FRANCE
Loire R.
Guyenne
Aquitaine Auvergne
Bordeaux
Garonne R.
Rhône R.
Gascony
Languedoc
Toulouse
SPAIN
Mediterranean Sea

c. 1429 (after the Siege of Orléans)
English holdings
French holdings
Burgundian lands allied with England to 1435
★ Battle
← Route taken by Joan of Arc, 1429–1431

0   100   200 mi
0   100   200 kilometers

ENGLAND
London
Calais Flanders
English Channel
CHANNEL IS.
Normandy
Paris
Champagne
Seine R.
Brittany
HOLY ROMAN EMPIRE
Anjou
Blois Berry
Touraine Duchy of Burgundy
Poitou FRANCE
Loire R.
Guyenne
Aquitaine Auvergne
Bordeaux
Garonne R.
Rhône R.
Gascony
Languedoc
Toulouse
SPAIN
Mediterranean Sea

1453 (end of war)
English holdings
French holdings
Burgundian lands reconciled with France after 1435

chipped away at it, however, and by the beginning of the fourteenth century England retained only the area around Bordeaux, called Guyenne. In 1337, after a series of challenges and skirmishes, King Philip VI of France declared Guyenne to be his; King Edward III of England in turn declared himself king of France. The Hundred Years' War had begun.

The war had four phases (Map 11.2). The first three saw the progressive weakening of French power, the strengthening of England, and the creation of a new kingdom, Burgundy, which for a crucial time allied itself with England. The fourth phase, which began when King Henry V (r. 1413–1422) of England invaded France and achieved a great victory at the battle of Agincourt in 1415, ended in a complete reversal and the ousting of the English from the continent for good.

That reversal was largely begun by a woman, Joan of Arc (1412–1431). The sixteen-year-old arrived at the court of the dauphin (the uncrowned king of France) wearing armor, riding a horse, and leading a small army. Full of charisma and confidence at a desperate hour, Joan convinced the dauphin that she had been sent by God. She was allowed to fight (and win) a battle at Orléans in 1429. At her urging and under her leadership, the dauphin traveled deep into enemy territory to be anointed and crowned King Charles VII at the cathedral in Reims, following the tradition of French monarchs. Despite Joan's victory at Orléans and the anointing of Charles, the French allowed her to be captured and turned over to the English in 1431. Tried as a witch, she was burned at the stake. But her bad luck was matched by French good fortune. The duke of Burgundy recognized Charles VII as king of France, and Charles entered Paris in 1437. Skirmish by skirmish, the English were driven from French soil.

The Hundred Years' War drew other countries into its vortex. Mercenaries for both sides came from Germany, Switzerland, and the Netherlands; the best crossbowmen came from Genoa. The textile workers of Flanders rose up against their French-leaning count when the war cut off their supply of raw wool. In 1369, the marriage of the heiress of Flanders and the duke of Burgundy created a powerful new state, the duchy of Burgundy, which allied itself with England until 1435. Then, riding the wave of French victories, it switched sides. The dukes of Burgundy created a glittering court, a center of art and culture, but their state was short-lived. Clashing with the Swiss Confederation, the duchy of Burgundy began to fall apart in 1474.

The French chronicler Jean Froissart, writing around 1400, considered the Hundred Years' War to be a chivalric adventure. But even Froissart had to admit that the armies were made up mainly of mercenaries rather than knights. These men, who fought for pay and plunder, cared nothing about the king for whom they were

Map 11.2 The Hundred Years' War, 1337–1453
During the Hundred Years' War, English kings, aided by the new state of Burgundy, contested the French monarchy for the domination of France. For many decades, the English seemed to be winning, but the French prevailed in the end.

Joan of Arc, c. 1430
Painted in the style of the French-Flemish school, this manuscript illustration contrasts the metallic hardness of Joan's armor and sword with the soft, fluttering banner depicting God and two angels. With her right hand upturned and clasping a sword, and her left turned down to support the banner, Joan strikes a perfect pose as a messenger of God, similar to the angels depicted above. **For more help analyzing this image, see the visual activity for this chapter in the Online Study Guide at** bedfordstmartins.com/huntconcise**.** (© akg-images, London.)

supposed to be fighting. They formed "Free Companies" and during lulls in the war lived off the French countryside, terrorizing the peasants and exacting "protection" money.

Some of the soldiers recruited by both sides, both mercenaries and nonmercenaries, were archers. The French archers tended to use crossbows, whose heavy, deadly arrows were released by a mechanism that even a townsman could master. The English employed longbows, which could shoot five arrows for every one launched with a crossbow. Gunpowder was introduced during this war, and cannons were forged. Handguns also were beginning to be used, their effect about equal to that of crossbows.

The Spoils of War
This illustration from Jean Froissart's *Chronicles* depicts soldiers pillaging a conquered city. During the Hundred Years' War, looting became the main source of income for mercenary troops and contributed to the general misery of late-medieval society. Food, furniture, and even everyday household items were taken. (Bibliothèque nationale de France.)

By the end of the war, chivalry was only a dream (though one that continued to inspire soldiers even up to the First World War). Heavy artillery and foot soldiers, tightly massed together in formations of many thousands of men, were the face of the new military. The army was becoming more professional and centralized. In the 1440s the French king created a permanent army of mounted soldiers, paying them wages and subjecting them to regular inspection.

The outbreak of the Hundred Years' War led to popular revolts. Although the Flemish count supported France, the townspeople, dependent on England for the raw wool they wove into cloth, revolted in 1338. The count fled to France, but discord among and within the towns allowed his successor to return in 1348. Revolts continued to flare up thereafter, but the new count allowed the towns a measure of self-government, maintained some distance from French influence, and managed on the whole to keep the peace. Later, as we have seen, Flanders became part of the duchy of Burgundy, an ally of England.

In France, the Parisians chafed against the high taxes they were forced to pay to finance the war. When the English captured the French king John at the battle of Poitiers in 1356, Étienne Marcel, provost of the Paris merchants, and other disillusioned members of the estates of France (the representatives of the clergy, nobility, and commons) met in Paris to discuss political reform, the incompetence of the French army, and taxes. Under Marcel's leadership, the Parisians took control of the city. In response, the royal army blockaded Paris and cut off its food supply. Later that year, Marcel was assassinated, and the Parisian revolt came to an end.

In that same year, 1358, the French peasants, weary of the Free Companies that were ravaging the countryside and disgusted by the military incompetence of the nobility, rose up in protest. Their revolt, derisively called the Jacquerie (from the word *jacque*, or "peasant"), was quickly put down by the nobility.

Similar revolts took place in England. Wat Tyler's Rebellion started as an uprising in much of southern and central England after royal agents tried to collect a poll tax (a tax on each household) to finance the Hundred Years' War. Refusing to pay and refusing to be arrested, the commons (peasants and small householders) rose up in rebellion in 1381. They massed in various groups and marched to London to see the king, whom they professed to support. There they made a radical demand: an end to serfdom. Although the rebellion was put down and its leaders executed, the death knell of serfdom in England had been sounded, as the peasants returned home to bargain with their lords for better terms.

Finally, the Hundred Years' War started a period of financial hard times. During the war, the English king Edward III borrowed heavily from the largest Italian banking houses, the Bardi and Peruzzi of Florence. With many of their assets tied up in loans to the English monarchy, the Italian bankers had no choice but to extend more credit, hoping to recover their initial investments. In the early 1340s, however, Edward defaulted, and the once illustrious houses went bankrupt. Meanwhile, diminished production and trade eventually caused turmoil in northern Europe and a crisis for financiers in the Low Countries. Bruges, the financial center of northwestern Europe, saw its power fade during the fifteenth century when several of its money changers went bankrupt.

The Ottoman Conquests

The rise of the Ottoman Turks, a new Islamic group, was the most astonishing development of the late thirteenth century, when they began a holy war against Byzantium. Under Osman I (r. 1280–1324), who gave the dynasty its name, and his successors, the Ottomans became a formidable force in Anatolia and the Balkans, where political disunity opened the door for their advances (Map 11.3). By the end of the fourteenth century, they had reduced the Byzantine Empire to the city of Constantinople, Thessalonika, and a narrow strip of land in modern-day Greece. Farther to the west, the Ottomans defeated a joint Hungarian-Serbian army at the Maritsa River (1364), alerting Europe for the first time to the threat of an Islamic

Map 11.3 Ottoman Expansion in the Fourteenth and Fifteenth Centuries
The Balkans were the major theater of expansion for the Ottoman Empire. The Byzantine Empire was reduced to the city of Constantinople and surrounded by the Ottomans before its final fall in 1453.

invasion. Pope Urban V called vainly for a crusade. In the Balkans, the Ottomans skillfully exploited Christian disunity, playing local interests against one another. An Ottoman army, allied with the Bulgarians and some Serbian princes, won the battle of Kosovo (1389), destroying the last organized Christian resistance south of the Danube. (Even today the battle remains a rallying cry for Serbian nationalists.) The Ottomans secured control of southeastern Europe after 1396, when they crushed a crusading army summoned by Pope Boniface IX.

After Mehmed II (r. 1451–1481) ascended the Ottoman throne, he laid siege to Constantinople in 1453. The Byzantine capital, a city of 100,000, could muster only six thousand defenders (including a small contingent of Genoese) against an Ottoman force estimated at between 200,000 and 400,000 men. The city's walls were no match for fifteenth-century cannons. The last Byzantine emperor, Constantine XI ("Palaeologos"), died in battle, some sixty thousand residents were carried off into slavery, and the city was sacked. Mehmed entered Constantinople in triumph and rendered thanks to God in Justinian's Church of the Holy Wisdom (Hagia Sophia), which he turned into a mosque.

Mehmed wanted to be the new ruler of the Roman Empire—a Muslim Roman Empire. We have seen that he turned to the west for his artistic commissions, such as his Topkapi palace and his portrait. The Ottoman sultan employed Christian slave children raised as Muslims to be his Janissaries, the backbone of the Ottoman army. At the sultan's court, Christian women were prominent in the harem, and as a consequence many Ottoman princes had Greek or Serbian mothers. Christian princes and converts to Islam served in the emerging Ottoman administration. In conquered areas, existing religious and social structures remained intact when local people accepted Ottoman overlordship and paid taxes. Only in areas of persistent resistance did the Ottomans drive out or massacre the inhabitants, settling Turkish tribes in their place. A distinctive pattern of Balkan history was therefore established

The Siege of Constantinople, 1453
Bertrandon de la Broquiere wrote his *Overseas Voyage* in the 1430s for the duke of Burgundy, who was contemplating a new crusade against the Turks. "I will discuss the means and the men necessary to break their power and defeat them in battle and gain their territory," he wrote, adding, "I don't think it would be very hard to break and defeat them, given their lack of arms." Within two decades, however, the Turks had taken Constantinople. When an artist was commissioned around 1455 to illustrate Bertrandon's work, he or she chose to show the siege. In this picture, you can see the tents of the Turkish captains, their cannons and cannonballs just behind them, and, across the water, the city of Constantinople with its doomed defenders. (Bibliothèque Nationale, Paris/The Bridgeman Art Library.)

at the beginning of the Ottoman conquest: extremely diverse ethnic and religious communities were woven together into the fabric of an efficient central state.

The Great Schism, 1378–1417

Even as war and disease threatened Europeans' material and physical well-being, a crisis in the church, precipitated by a scandal in the papacy, tore at their spiritual life. The move of the papacy from Rome to Avignon in 1309 (see page 375) had caused an outcry, especially among Italians, distraught by the election of French popes and anxious to see the papacy return to Rome. Some critics, such as Marsilius of Padua, were disillusioned with the institution of the papacy itself. Marsilius, a physician and lawyer by training, argued in *The Defender of the Peace* (1324) that the source of all power lay within the people: "The law-making power or the first and real effective source of law is the people or the body of citizens or the prevailing part of the people according to its election or its will expressed in general convention by vote." Applied to the papacy, Marsilius's argument meant that Christians themselves formed the church and that the pope should be elected by a general council representing all Christians.

When Pope Gregory XI (r. 1370–1378) left Avignon to return to Rome in 1377, the scandal of the Avignon papacy seemed to be over. But Rome itself presented a problem. Glad to have the papacy back, the Romans were determined never to lose it again. When the cardinals—many of whom came from Spain, Italy, and France—met to elect Gregory's successor, the Roman popolo, who controlled the city, demanded that they choose a Roman: "A Roman! A Roman! A Roman or at least an Italian! Or else we'll kill them all." Expecting to gain an important place in papal government, the cardinals chose an Italian, who took the name Urban VI. But Urban had no intention of kowtowing to the cardinals. Instead, he exalted the power of the pope and began to reduce the cardinals' wealth and privileges. The cardinals from France decided that they had made a big mistake. Many left Rome for a meeting at Anagni, where they claimed that Urban's election had been irregular and called on him to resign. When he refused, they elected a Frenchman as pope. He took the name Clement VII and soon moved his papal court back to Avignon, but not before he and Urban had excommunicated each other. The Great Schism (1378–1417) had begun.

All of Europe was drawn into the dispute. The king of France supported Clement; the king of England favored Urban. Some European states—Burgundy, Scotland, and Castile, for example—lined up on the side of France. Others—the Holy Roman Empire, Poland, and Hungary—supported Urban. Portugal switched sides four times, depending on which alliance offered it the most advantages. Each pope declared that those who followed the other were to be deprived of the rights of church membership; in effect, everyone in Europe was excommunicated by one or the other of the popes.

Contrary to the ideas of Marsilius, church law said that only a pope could summon a general council of the church—a sort of parliament of high churchmen. But given the state of confusion in Christendom, many intellectuals argued that the crisis justified calling a general council to represent the body of the faithful, even against the wishes of an unwilling pope—or popes. They spearheaded the conciliar movement—a movement to have the cardinals or the Holy Roman Emperor call a council.

In 1408, long after Urban and Clement had passed away, the conciliar movement succeeded when cardinals from both sides met and declared their resolve "to pursue the union of the Church . . . by way of abdication of both papal contenders." With support from both England and France, the cardinals called for a council to be held at Pisa in 1409. Both popes refused to attend, and the council deposed them, electing a third pope, Alexander V. The "deposed" popes refused to budge, even though most of the European powers abandoned them. Alexander's successor, John XXIII, turned to the emperor to arrange for another council.

The Council of Constance (1414–1418) met to resolve the papal crisis and to institute church reforms. The delegates deposed John XXIII and accepted the resignation of the pope at Rome. After long negotiations with rulers still supporting the Avignon pope, all allegiance to him was withdrawn, and he was deposed. The council then elected Martin V, who was recognized as pope by every important ruler of Europe. The Great Schism had come to an end.

New Forms of Piety and Heresy

The Great Schism, along with the miseries of disease and war, caused enormous anxiety among ordinary Christians. Worried about the salvation of their souls, pious men and women eagerly sought new forms of religious solace. The plenary indulgence—full forgiveness of sins, which had been originally offered to crusaders who died while fighting for the cause—was now offered to those who made a pilgrimage to Rome or one of the other designated holy places during declared Holy Years. Sins could be wiped away through confession and contrition, but some guilt remained that could be removed only through good deeds or in purgatory. As the idea of purgatory—the place where sins were fully purged—took full form, new indulgences were offered for good works to reduce the time there. Thus, for example, the duchess of Brittany was granted a hundred days off her purgatorial punishments when she allowed the Feast of Corpus Christi to be preached in her chapel. Lesser folk might obtain indulgences in more modest ways.

Both clergy and laity became more interested than ever in the education of young people as a way to deepen their faith and spiritual life. The Brethren of the Common Life—laypeople, mainly in the Low Countries, who devoted themselves to pious works—set up a model school at Deventer, and humanists in Italy emphasized primary school education. Priests were expected to teach the faithful the basics of the Christian religion.

Home was also a place for devotion. Portable images of Mary, the mother of God, and of the life and passion of Christ proliferated. They were meant to be contemplated by ordinary Christians at convenient moments throughout the day. People purchased or commissioned copies of Books of Hours, which contained prayers to be said on the appropriate day at the hours indicated in the Benedictine rule. Books of Hours included calendars, sometimes splendidly illustrated with depictions of the seasons and labors of the year. Other illustrations reminded readers of the life and suffering of Christ.

On the streets of towns, priests marched in dignified processions, carrying the sanctified bread of the Mass—the very body of Christ—in tall, splendid containers called monstrances, which trumpeted the importance and dignity of the Eucharistic wafer. Like images of the Lord's life and crucifixion, the monstrance emphasized Christ's body. Christ's blood was perhaps even more important. It was considered "wonderful blood," the blood that had brought people's redemption. The image of a bleeding, crucified Christ was seen repeatedly in depictions of the day. Viewers were meant to think about Christ's pain and feel it themselves, mentally participating in his death on the cross. Flagellants, as we have seen, literally drew their own blood.

Religious anxieties, intellectual dissent, and social unrest combined to create new heretical movements in England and Bohemia. In England the Lollards (a derisive name given to them by their opponents, from the Middle Dutch *lollaerd*, or "mumbler") were inspired by the Oxford scholar John Wycliffe (c. 1330–1384), who had come to believe that the true church was the community of believers rather than the clerical hierarchy. Wycliffe criticized monasticism, excommunication, and the Mass. He wanted people to read the Bible in the vernacular rather than in Latin, arguing that true believers, not corrupt priests, formed the church.

Wycliffe's followers included scholars and members of the gentry (lesser nobles), as well as artisans and other humbler folk. His supporters translated the Bible into English and produced many sermons to publicize his views. They influenced the priest John Ball, one of the leaders of Wat Tyler's Rebellion. Ball rallied the crowds with the chant "When Adam dug and Eve spun / Who then was the gentleman?" From questioning the church hierarchy, some Lollards advanced to challenging social inequality of every sort. After Wycliffe's death, the Lollards were persecuted in England. Groups of them remained underground, only to reemerge with the coming of the Reformation (see Chapter 12).

The Bohemian Hussites—named after one of their leaders, Jan Hus (1372?–1415)—had greater success. Their central demand—that the faithful receive not just the bread (the body) but also the wine (the blood) at Mass—brought together several passionately held desires and beliefs. The blood of Christ was particularly important to the devout, and the Hussite call to allow the laity to drink the wine from the chalice reflected this focus on its redemptive power. Furthermore, the call for communion in both bread and wine signified a desire for equality. Bohemia was an exceptionally divided country, with an urban German-speaking elite, including merchants, artisans, bishops, and scholars, and a Czech-speaking nobility and peasantry that was beginning to seek better opportunities. (Hus himself was a Czech of peasant stock who became a professor at the University of Prague.) When priests celebrated Mass, they had the privilege of drinking the wine. The Hussites, who were largely Czech laity, wanted the same privilege and, with it, recognition of their dignity and worth.

Condemned by the church as a heretic, Hus was protected by the Bohemian nobility until he was lured to the Council of Constance by the Holy Roman Emperor Sigismund "to justify himself before all men." Though promised safe conduct, Hus was arrested when he arrived at the council. After refusing to recant his views, he was declared a heretic and burned at the stake.

Hus's death caused an uproar, and his movement became a full-scale national revolt of Czechs against Germans. Sigismund called crusades against the Hussites, but all of his expeditions were soundly defeated. Radical groups of Hussites organized several new communities in southern Bohemia at Mount Tabor, named after the New Testament spot where the transfiguration of Christ was thought to have taken place (Matt. 7:1–8). Here the radicals attempted to live according to the example of the first Apostles. They recognized no secular lord, gave women some political rights, and created a simple liturgy in the Czech language. Negotiations with Sigismund and his successor led by 1450 to the Hussites' tentative incorpora-

The Hussite Revolution, 1415–1436

tion into the Bohemian political system and the right to receive communion in "both kinds" (wine and bread). The Hussites made Bohemia intensely aware of its Czech, rather than its German, identity.

REVIEW   What crises did Europeans confront in the fourteenth and fifteenth centuries, and how did they handle them?

The New Map of Europe

As both a symptom and a result of these crises, political consolidation was taking place all across Europe in the period 1340–1500. As we have seen, the Ottoman Empire joined European powers in the Balkans. Eastern Europe took shape when the capital of the Holy Roman Empire moved to Prague and the duke of Lithuania married the queen of Poland, uniting those two states. In western Europe, the union of Aragon and Castile via the marriage of their respective rulers created Spain. In England and France, consolidation meant the strengthening of the central monarchies. The few states that organized and maintained themselves as republics—Switzerland, Venice, and Florence—were run by elites. Nowhere was the consolidation of the period clearer than in Italy. In 1340 it was dotted with numerous small city-states. By 1500 it was dominated by five major powers: Milan, Venice, and Florence in the north, the papacy in the middle, and the kingdom of Naples in the south.

New States in Eastern Europe

In the eastern half of the Holy Roman Empire, Bohemia gained new status as the seat of the Luxembourg imperial dynasty (Emperor Sigismund was its last representative). This development bred a religious and political crisis when the Hussites clashed with Sigismund. The chief beneficiary of the violence was the nobility, both Catholic and Hussite, but they quarreled among themselves, especially about who should be king. No Joan of Arc appeared to declare the national will, and most of Europe considered Bohemia a heretic state.

Farther north, it was the cities rather than the landed nobility that held power. Allied cities, such as the Hanseatic League (see page 376), were common. By the fourteenth century, the Hanseatic League linked the Baltic coast with Russia, Norway, the British Isles, France, and even (via imperial cities like Augsburg and Nuremberg) the cities of Italy. When threatened by rival powers in Denmark and Norway in 1367–1370, the league waged war and won the peace. In the fifteenth century it confronted new rivals and began a long and slow decline.

To the east of the Hanseatic cities, two new monarchies took shape in north-eastern Europe: Poland and Lithuania. Poland had begun to form in the tenth century. Powerful nobles soon dominated it, and Mongol invasions devastated the land. But recovery was under way by 1300. Unlike almost every other part of Europe, Poland expanded demographically and economically during the fourteenth century. Jews migrated there to escape persecution in western Europe, and both Jewish and German settlers helped build thriving towns like Cracow. Monarchical consolidation began thereafter.

On Poland's eastern flank was Lithuania, the only major holdout from Christianity in eastern Europe. As it expanded into southern Russia, however, its grand dukes flirted with both the Roman Catholic and Orthodox churches. In 1386, Grand Duke Jogailo (c. 1351–1434), taking advantage of a hiatus in the Polish ruling dynasty, united both states when he married Queen Jadwiga of Poland, received a Catholic baptism, and was elected by the Polish nobility as King Wladyslaw II ("Jagiello"). As part of the negotiations prior to these events, he promised to convert Lithuania, and after his coronation he sent churchmen there to begin the long, slow process. The union of Poland and Lithuania lasted, with some interruptions, until 1772 (Map 11.4, page 410).

Powerful States in Western Europe

Four powerful states dominated western Europe during the fifteenth century. The kingdom of Spain and the duchy of Burgundy were created by marriage; the newly powerful kingdoms of France and England were forged in the crucible of war. By the end of the century, however, Burgundy had disappeared, leaving three exceptionally powerful monarchies.

Decades of violence on the Iberian peninsula ended when Isabella of Castile and Ferdinand of Aragon married in 1469 and restored law and order in the decades that followed. Castile was the powerhouse, with Aragon its lesser neighbor and Navarre a pawn between the two. When the king and queen joined forces, they ruled together over their separate dominions, allowing each to retain its traditional laws and privileges. The union of

Unification of Spain, Late Fifteenth Century

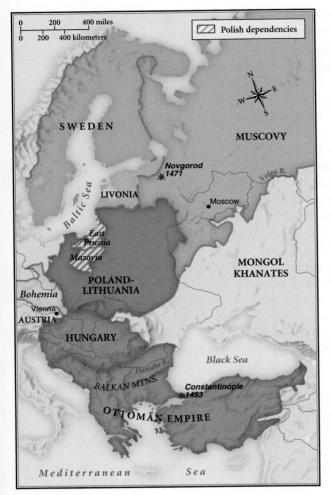

Map 11.4 Eastern Europe in the Fifteenth Century
Crucial to the new political developments of the fifteenth century was the rise of Muscovy and Poland-Lithuania.

Castile and Aragon was the first step toward a united Spain and a centralized monarchy there.

Relying on a lucrative taxation system, pliant meetings of the cortes (the representative institution that voted taxes), and an ideology that glorified the monarchy, Ferdinand and Isabella consolidated their power. They had an extensive bureaucracy to handle financial matters and a well-staffed writing office. They sent their own officials to rule over towns that had previously been self-governing, and they established regional courts of law.

Once Ferdinand and Isabella established their rule over Castile and Aragon, they sought to impose religious uniformity and purity. First they began systematically persecuting the *conversos* (converts)—Jews who had converted to Christianity in the aftermath of vicious attacks on Jews at Seville, Córdoba, Toledo, and other Spanish towns in 1391. During the first half of the fifteenth century they and their descendants (still called conversos, even though their children had been born and baptized in the Christian faith) took advantage of the opportunities open to educated Christians, in many instances rising to high positions in both the church and the state and marrying into "Old Christian" families. The conversos' success bred resentment, and their commitment to Christianity was questioned as well.

Local massacres of conversos began even before Isabella and Ferdinand married. In 1467, for example, two conversos in Toledo were hanged "as traitors and captains of the heretical conversos." The terms "traitors" and "heretical" are telling: because conversos were technically no longer Jews, their persecution was justified by branding them as heretics who undermined the monarchy. In 1478, Ferdinand and Isabella set up the Inquisition in Spain to continue, on behalf of the crown, what the towns had started. Treating the conversos as heretics, the inquisitors imposed harsh sentences, expelling or burning most of them. That was not enough (in the view of the monarchs) to purify the land. In 1492, Ferdinand and Isabella decreed that all Jews in Spain must convert or leave the country. Some did convert, but the experiences of the former conversos soured most on the prospect, and many Jews—perhaps 150,000—left Spain, scattering around the Mediterranean.

Meanwhile, Ferdinand and Isabella determined to defeat Granada, the last Muslim stronghold in Spain. Disunity within Granada's ruling family allowed the conquest to proceed, and in January 1492—just a few months before they expelled the Jews—Ferdinand and Isabella made their triumphal entry into the Alhambra, the former residence of the Muslim king of Granada. Although they initially promised freedom of religion to the Muslims who chose to remain, the royal couple also provided a fleet of boats to evacuate those who chose exile. In 1502, they demanded that all Muslims adopt Christianity or leave the kingdom.

United with less tumult, the duchy of Burgundy—created when the duke of Burgundy and heiress of Flanders married in 1369—was nevertheless disunited linguistically and geographically. Its success and expansion in the fifteenth century were the result of military might and careful statecraft. Soon, however, Burgundy fell to the militias of its neighbors. The chief importance of the duchy of Burgundy was its support of the arts; the dukes were great patrons of Renaissance culture.

By contrast, France, one of Burgundy's neighbors, became more powerful in the years before 1500. It made a quick recovery from the Hundred Years' War and expanded under Louis XI (r. 1461–1483). Soon after most of Burgundy fell to him, Louis also inherited much of southern France. After he inherited claims to the duchy of Milan and the kingdom of Naples, he was ready to invade Italy. By the end of the century, France had doubled its territory, assuming boundaries close to its modern ones, and was looking to expand even further.

To strengthen royal power at home, Louis promoted industry and commerce, imposed permanent salt and land taxes, maintained western Europe's first standing army (created by his predecessor), and suspended the meetings of the estates, which included the clergy, the nobility, and representatives from the major towns of France. The French kings had already increased their power with important concessions from the papacy. In addition, the Pragmatic Sanction of Bourges (1438) had asserted the superiority of a general church council over the pope. Claiming special sacredness because of their anointment, the kings established what would come to be known as Gallicanism (after Gaul, the ancient Roman name for France), in which the French king would effectively control ecclesiastical revenues and the appointment of French bishops.

The experience of England was only slightly less fortunate. The Hundred Years' War led to intermittent civil wars that came to be called the Wars of the Roses (1460s–1485). They ended with the victory of Henry Tudor, who took the title of Henry VII (r. 1485–1509). Though long, the Wars of the Roses caused relatively little damage; the battles were generally short, and, in the words of one chronicler, "neither the country, nor the people nor the houses, were wasted, destroyed or demolished, but the calamities and misfortunes of the war fell only upon the soldiers, and especially on the nobility."

As a result, the English economy continued to grow during the fifteenth century. The cloth industry expanded considerably, and the English used much of the raw wool they had been exporting to the Low Countries to manufacture goods at home. London merchants, taking a vigorous role in trade, also assumed greater political prominence, not only in governing London but also as bankers to kings and members of Parliament. In the countryside the landed classes—the nobility, the gentry (the lesser nobility), and the yeomanry (free farmers)—benefited from rising farm and land-rent income as the population increased slowly but steadily. The Tudor monarchs took advantage of the general prosperity to bolster both their treasury and their power.

It did not matter whether a state was run by a monarch or a small elite; consolidation was the watchword. Switzerland, Venice, and Florence were republics that prided themselves on traditions of self-rule. At the same time, however, they were in every case dominated by elites—or even by one family.

In the late thirteenth century, Swiss cantons had formed an alliance that eventually became the Swiss Confederation (see page 377). Though not united by a comprehensive constitution, the Swiss Confederation was nevertheless an effective political force. Wealthy merchants and tradesmen dominated the cities of the confederation, and in the fifteenth century they managed to supplant the landed nobility. At the same time, the power of the rural communes gave some ordinary folk political importance. No king, duke, or count ever became head of the confederation. In its fiercely independent stance against the Holy Roman Empire, it became a symbol of republican freedom. Yet it was also dominated by the wealthy. Poor Swiss foot soldiers made their living by hiring themselves out as mercenaries, fueling the wars of kings in the rest of Europe.

Similarly, Venice proudly proclaimed itself a republic but was ruled by a small elite. Built on a lagoon, Venice by 1400 ruled an extensive empire. Its merchant ships plied the waters stretching from the Black Sea to the Mediterranean and out to the Atlantic Ocean, and it had an excellent navy. Now, for the first time, it turned its attention inland, looking to conquer the cities of northern Italy. In the early fifteenth century, Venice took over Brescia, Verona, Padua, Belluno, and many other cities, eventually coming up against the equally powerful city-state of Milan to its west. Between 1450 and 1454, two coalitions—one led by Milan, the other by Venice—fought for territorial control of the eastern half of northern Italy. Financial exhaustion and fear of an invasion by France or the Ottoman Turks led to the Peace of Lodi in 1454. With that peace, it was clear that Italy was no longer a collection of small cities and their contados (the surrounding countryside) but a country of large, territorial city-states.

It is no accident that the Peace of Lodi was signed one year after the Ottoman conquest of Constantinople; Venice wanted to redirect its might against the Turks. But the Venetians also knew that peace was good for business; they traded with the Ottomans, and the two powers influenced each other's art and culture. Gentile Bellini's portrait of Mehmed is a good example of the importance of Venetian artists at the Ottoman court.

Venice was never ruled by a signore (lord). Far from being a hereditary monarch, the doge—the leading magistrate at Venice—was elected by the Great Council. But that council itself was dominated by the most important families. It is unclear why the lower classes at Venice did not rebel and demand their own political power, as happened in so many other Italian cities. The answer may be that Venice's foundation on water demanded so much central planning, citywide effort to maintain buildings and services, and the dedication of public funds to provide the population with necessities that it fostered a greater sense of community than could be found elsewhere.

Florence, like Venice, was also a republic. Unlike Venice, it came to be ruled by one family. Also unlike Venice, its society and political life were turbulent, as social classes and political factions competed for power. The most important of these civil uprisings was the Ciompi Revolt of 1378. Named after the wool workers (*ciompi*), laborers so lowly they had not been allowed to form a guild, the revolt led to the creation of a guild, along with a new distribution of power in the city. By 1382, however, the upper classes were once again monopolizing the government, and now with even less sympathy for the commoners.

By 1434, the Medici family had become the dominant power in Florence. The patriarch of this family, Cosimo de' Medici (1389–1464), founded his political power on the wealth of the Medici bank, which handled papal finances and had numerous branch offices in Italian and northern European cities. Backed by this money, Cosimo took over Florentine politics. He determined which men could take public office, and he established new committees made up of men loyal to him to govern the city. He kept the old forms of the Florentine constitution intact, governing behind the scenes not by force but through a broad consensus among the ruling elite.

Cosimo's grandson Lorenzo the Magnificent (1449–1492), who assumed power in 1467, bolstered the regime's legitimacy with his patronage of the humanities and arts. He himself was a poet and avid collector of antiquities. He intended to build a grand library made of marble at his palace but died before it was completed. More successful was his sculpture garden, which he filled with ancient works. Serving on various Florentine committees in charge of building, renovating, and adorning the churches of the city, Lorenzo employed important artists and architects to work on his own palaces as well. He probably encouraged the young Michelangelo; he certainly patronized the poet Angelo Poliziano, whose verses inspired Botticelli's *Birth of Venus* (see the illustration on page 421). No wonder writers and poets sang his praises.

But the Medici family also had enemies. In 1478, Lorenzo narrowly escaped an assassination attempt, and his successor was driven out of Florence in 1494. The Medici returned to power in 1512, only to be driven out again in 1527. In 1530, the republic fell for good as the Medici once again took power, this time declaring themselves dukes of Florence.

The Tools of Power

Whether monarchies, duchies, or republics, the newly consolidated states of the fifteenth century exercised their power more thoroughly than ever before. Sometimes they reached into the intimate lives of their subjects or citizens.

A good example of the ways in which governments peeked into people's lives—and picked their pockets—is the Florentine *catasto*. This was an inventory of households within the city and its outlying territory made for the purposes of taxation in 1427. The Domesday survey conducted in England in 1086 had been the most complete census of its day. But the catasto bested Domesday in thoroughness and inquisitiveness. It inquired about names, types of houses, and animals. It asked people to identify their trades, and their answers reveal the levels of Florentine society, ranging from agricultural laborers with no land of their own to soldiers, cooks, grave diggers, scribes, merchants, doctors, wine dealers, innkeepers, and tanners. The catasto inquired about private and public investments, real estate holdings, and taxable assets. Finally, it turned to the sex of the head of the family, his or her age and marital status, and the number of mouths to feed in the household. An identification number was assigned to each household.

The catasto shows that in 1427 Florence and its outlying regions had a population of more than 260,000. Although the city itself had only thirty-eight thousand inhabitants (about 15 percent of the total population), it held 67 percent of the wealth. Some 60 percent of Florentine households belonged to the "little people"—artisans and small merchants. The "fat people" (*popolo grosso,* what we would call the upper middle class) made up 30 percent of the urban population and included wealthy merchants, leading artisans, notaries, doctors, and other professionals. At the bottom of the hierarchy were slaves and servants, largely women from the surrounding countryside employed in domestic service. At the top, a tiny elite of wealthy patricians, bankers, and wool merchants controlled the state and owned more than one-quarter of its wealth. This was the group that produced the Medici family.

Most Florentine households consisted of at least six people, not all of whom were members of the family. Wealthier families had more children, while childless couples existed almost exclusively among the poor. The rich gave their infants to wet nurses to breast-feed, while the poor often left their children to public charity. Florence was rightly proud of its orphanage: it both provided for the city's poorer children and was built in the newest and finest Renaissance style.

> **REVIEW**   What were the chief political entities in the year 1500, and how did they come to be so powerful?

New Forms of Thought and Expression: The Renaissance

Whether monarchies, principalities, or republics, states throughout Europe used their new power and money to foster Renaissance writers, artists, and musicians. Most textbooks divide the period 1340–1500 into two chapters, one covering the crises and the other the Renaissance. But this is misleading; both phenomena happened at the same time. In many ways, the Renaissance was a response to the crises. It revived elements of the classical past—the Greek philosophers before Aristotle, Hellenistic artists, and Roman rhetoricians—in order to deal with contemporary issues. Humanists modeled their writing on the Latin of Cicero, architects looked back to ancient notions of public space, artists adopted classical forms, and musicians used classical texts. Yet they were very much involved in the movements of their own day.

Renaissance Humanism

Humanism was a literary and linguistic movement—an attempt to revive classical Latin (and later Greek), as well as the values and sensibilities that came with the language. It began among men and women living in the Italian city-states, where many saw parallels between their urban, independent lives and the experiences of the city-states of the ancient world. Humanism was a way to confront the crises—and praise the advances—of the fourteenth through sixteenth centuries. Humanists wrote poetry, history, moral philosophy, and grammar books, all patterned on classical models.

A good example of the aim of humanists is provided by three delegates to the Council of Constance—Cincius Romanus, Poggius Bracciolinus, and Bartholomaeus Politianus. One day they decided to take time off from the council for a "rescue mission." Cincius described the escapade to one of his Latin teachers back in Italy:

> In Germany there are many monasteries with libraries full of Latin books. This aroused the hope in me that some of the works of Cicero, Varro, Livy, and other great men of learning, which seem to have completely vanished, might come to light if a careful search were instituted. A few days ago, [we] went by agreement to the town of St. Gall. As soon as we went into the library [of the monastery there], we found *Jason's Argonauticon,* written by C. Valerius Flaccus in verse that is both splendid and dignified and not far removed from poetic majesty. Then we found some discussion in prose of a number of Cicero's orations.

Cicero, Varro, Livy, and Valerius Flaccus were pagan Latin writers. Even though Cincius and his friends were working for Pope John XXIII, they loved the writings of the ancients, whose Latin was, in their view, "splendid and dignified," unlike the Latin that was used in their own time, which they found debased and faulty. They saw themselves as the resuscitators of ancient language, literature, and culture. Cincius continued:

> When we carefully inspected the nearby tower of the church of St. Gall in which countless books were kept like captives and the library neglected and infested with dust, worms, soot, and all the things associated with the destruction of books, we all burst into tears. . . . Truly if this library could speak for itself, it would cry loudly: ". . . Snatch me from this prison. . . ." There were in that monastery an abbot and monks totally devoid of any knowledge of literature. What barbarous hostility to the Latin tongue! What damned dregs of humanity!

The monks were barbarians, and Cincius and his companions were heroic raiders swooping in to liberate the captive books.

That Cincius was employed by the pope yet considered the monks of St. Gall barbarians was no oddity. Most humanists combined sincere Christian piety with their new appreciation of the pagan past. Besides, they needed to work in order to live, and they took employment where they found it. Some humanists worked for the church, others were civil servants, and still others were notaries. A few were rich men who had a taste for literary subjects.

The first humanist, most historians agree, was Francis Petrarch (1304–1374). He was born in Arezzo, a town about fifty miles southeast of Florence. As a boy, he moved around a lot (his father was exiled from Florence), ending up in the region of Avignon, where he received his earliest schooling and fell in love with classical literature. After a brief flirtation with legal studies at the behest of his father, Petrarch gave up law and devoted himself to writing poetry, in both Italian and Latin. When writing in Italian, he drew on the traditions of the troubadours, dedicating poems of longing to an unattainable and idealized woman named Laura. When writing in Latin, he was much influenced by classical poetry.

On the one hand, a boyhood in Avignon made Petrarch sensitive to the failings of the church: he was the writer who coined the phrase "Babylonian captivity." On the other hand, he took minor religious orders there, which afforded him a modest living. Struggling between what he considered a life of dissipation (he fathered two children out of wedlock) and a religious vocation, he resolved the conflict at last in his book *On the Solitary Life,* in which he claimed that the solitude needed for reading the classics was akin to the solitude practiced by those who devoted themselves to God. For Petrarch, humanism was a vocation, a calling.

Less famous, but for that reason perhaps more representative of humanists in general, was Lauro Quirini (1420–1475?), the man who (as we saw at the start of this chapter) considered the Turks to be barbarians. Educated at the University of

Padua, Quirini eventually got a law degree there. He wrote numerous letters and essays, corresponding with other humanists on topics such as the nature of the state and the character of true nobility. He spent the last half of his life in Crete, where he traded various commodities—alum, cloth, wine, Greek books. Believing that the Ottomans had destroyed the libraries of Constantinople, he wrote to Pope Nicholas V, "The language and literature of the Greeks, invented, augmented, and perfected over so long a period with such labor and industry, will certainly perish." But the fact that he himself participated in the lively trade of Greek books proved his prediction wrong.

If Quirini represents the ordinary humanist, Giovanni Pico della Mirandola (1463–1494) was perhaps the most flamboyant. Born near Ferrara of a noble family, Pico received a humanist education at home before going on to Bologna to study law and to Padua to study philosophy. Soon he was picking up Hebrew, Aramaic, and Arabic. A convinced eclectic, he thought that Jewish mystical writings supported Christian Scriptures, and in 1486 he proposed that he publicly defend at Rome nine hundred theses drawn from diverse sources. The church found some of the theses heretical, however, and banned the whole affair. But Pico's *Oration on the Dignity of Man*, which he intended to deliver before his defense, summed up the humanist view of humanity: the creative individual, armed only with his (or her) "desires and judgment," could choose to become a boor or an angel. Humanity's potential was unlimited.

Christine de Pisan (c. 1365–c. 1430) exemplifies a humanist who chose to fashion herself into a writer and courtier. Born in Venice and educated in France, Christine de Pisan was married and then widowed young. Forced to support herself, her mother, and her three young children, she began to write poems inspired by classical models, depending on rich patrons to admire her work and pay her to write more. Many members of the upper nobility supported her, including Duke Philip the Bold of Burgundy, Queen Isabelle of Bavaria, and the English earl of Salisbury. But this cast of characters did not mean she sided with the English during the Hundred Years' War. On the contrary, she lamented the violence on all sides, and Joan of Arc's early victories inspired her to write a hymn to "the Maid":

> We've never heard
> About a marvel quite so great,
> For all the heroes who have lived
> In history can't measure up
> In bravery against the Maid.

Even more political was the humanist Niccolò Machiavelli (1469–1527), whose small handbook *The Prince* (1513) argued that the state was an artifice of human creation to be conquered, shaped, and administered by princes according to the principles of power politics. Was it better for a ruler to be loved or feared by his subjects? Machiavelli answered coldly: "It may be answered that one should wish to be both, but, because it is difficult to unite them in one person, it is much safer to be feared than loved." Today the word *Machiavellian* means "coldly calculating": the end justifies the means.

Some historians deny Machiavelli the status of a humanist. But when he wrote in *The Prince* about his study of the ancients, he was identifying himself with the humanist movement. His contemporaries certainly considered him one, appointing him (in 1498) chancellor of Florence, a position normally held by humanists.

Through their activities as educators, writers, and civil servants, professional humanists gave new vigor to the humanist curriculum of grammar, rhetoric, poetry, history, and moral philosophy. By the end of the fifteenth century, the Renaissance was a European-wide phenomenon, and the humanist agenda—a good command of classical Latin, with perhaps some knowledge of Greek—had come to be one of the requirements of an educated person.

The invention of the printing press in the 1440s by a German goldsmith named Johannes Gutenberg made the world of letters more accessible to a literate audience. The key to Gutenberg's innovation was movable type—reusable metal letters, numbers, and various other characters. The typesetter arranged the characters by hand, page by page, to create a printable text. The surface of the type was inked, and sheets of paper pressed against the type picked up an impression of the text. Numerous copies could be made with only a small amount of human labor. This was a revolutionary departure from the old practice of copying by hand, making possible the mass production of identical books and pamphlets.

The printing press depended on paper production. The art of papermaking came to Europe from the Islamic world (which had borrowed it from China). By the fourteenth century, paper mills were operating in Italy, producing paper that was more fragile but much cheaper than parchment or vellum, the animal skins that Europeans had previously used for writing. To produce paper, old rags were soaked in a chemical solution, beaten by mallets into a pulp, washed with water, treated, and dried in sheets—a method that still produces good-quality paper today.

After the 1440s, printing spread rapidly from Germany to other European countries. The German cities of Cologne, Strasbourg, Nuremberg, and Augsburg all had major presses. In 1467, two German printers established the first press in Rome and produced twelve thousand volumes in five years, a feat that previously would have required a thousand scribes working full-time. By 1480, many Italian cities had established their own presses. In the 1490s, the German city of Frankfurt am Main became an international meeting place for printers and booksellers. The Frankfurt Book Fair, where printers from different nations exhibited their newest titles, represented a major international cultural event and remains an unbroken tradition to this day.

The invention of mechanical printing gave rise to a communications revolution as significant as the widespread use of the personal computer today. The multiplication of standardized texts altered the thinking habits of Europeans by freeing individuals from having to memorize everything they learned; it made possible the relatively speedy and inexpensive dissemination of knowledge; and it created a wider community of scholars, no longer dependent on personal patronage or church sponsorship for texts. Printing facilitated the free expression and exchange of ideas, and its disruptive potential did not go unnoticed by political and ecclesiastical authorities. Emperors and bishops in Germany, the homeland of the printing industry, moved quickly to issue censorship regulations.

The Prestige of Renaissance Art

The lure of the classical past was as strong in the arts as in literature. Architects and artists admired ancient Athens and Rome and drew on their traditions. At the same time, they modified classical models, combining them with medieval forms. Working for patrons—churchmen, secular rulers, rich patrons, or republican governments— Renaissance artists used both past and present to express the patriotism, religious piety, and prestige of their benefactors.

The change was clear even on the streets of the cities. Medieval cities had grown without planning: streets turned back on themselves; churches sat cheek by jowl with private houses. In the Renaissance, however, the whole city was reimagined as a place of order and harmony. The Florentine architect Leon Battista Alberti (1404–1472) proposed that each building in a city be proportioned to fit harmoniously with all the others and that city spaces allow for all necessary public activities: there should be market squares, play areas, and grounds for military exercises. In Renaissance cities, the agora and forum (the public spaces of the classical world) appeared once again, but in a new guise, as the piazza (a plaza or open square). Architects carved out spaces around their new buildings, and they built graceful covered walkways (porticos) of columns and arches. The artist Pietro Perugino (1445–1523) depicted Christ giving the keys of the kingdom of heaven to the Apostle Peter in an idealized city piazza, at the center of which was a perfectly proportioned church.

The same principles applied to the architecture of the Renaissance court. At Urbino, Duke Federico, a great patron of humanists and artists, commissioned a new palace. The architect, probably Luciano Laurana, designed its courtyard as a public space, a sort of piazza within a palace. A city had both public and private spaces; similarly, public rooms at the ducal palace gave way to a modest space for the duke's private quarters: a bedroom, a bathroom, a chapel, and, most important, his study, filled with books.

The Gothic cathedral of the Middle Ages was a cluster of graceful spikes and soaring arches. Renaissance architects appreciated its vigor and energy, but they tamed it with regular geometrical forms inspired by classical buildings. Classical forms were applied to previously built structures as well as new ones. Florence's Santa Maria Novella, for example, had been a typical Gothic church when it was first built. But when Alberti, the man who believed in public spaces and harmonious buildings, was commissioned to replace its facade, he drew on Roman temple forms.

Powerful groups within the cities, whether guilds, communes, or princely families, sponsored the new art. In 1400, the Florentines held a competition for new bronze doors for their baptistery. The entry of Lorenzo Ghiberti (1378?–1455) depicted the sacrifice of Isaac, the Old Testament story in which God tests Abraham's

Pietro Perugino, *Christ Giving the Keys to St. Peter*
This fresco on one of the side walls of the Sistine Chapel in the papal palace at Rome (now the Vatican) depicts the transfer of power in Christ's church. Inspired by the architecture of the ancient world, Perugino set the action in a large piazza flanked by Roman triumphal arches. (© Vatican Museums and Galleries, Vatican City, Italy/The Bridgeman Art Library.)

faith by ordering him to sacrifice his son. Cast in one piece, a major technological feat at the time, it shows a young, nude Isaac modeled on a classical sculpture. At the same time, Ghiberti drew on medieval models for his depiction of Abraham. In this way, he gracefully melded old and new elements—and won the contest.

In addition to using the forms of classical art, Renaissance artists also mined the ancient world for new subjects. Venus, the Roman goddess of love and beauty, had numerous stories attached to her name. At first glance, *The Birth of Venus* (page 421) by Sandro Botticelli (c. 1445–1510) seems simply an illustration of the tale of Venus's rise from the sea. In fact, however, Botticelli's work is much more complicated, drawing on the ideas of Marsilio Ficino (1433–1499) and the poetry of Angelo Poliziano (1454–1494). According to Ficino, Venus was "humanitas"—the essence of the humanities. For Poliziano, she was

> fair Venus, mother of the cupids.
> Zephyr bathes the meadow with dew
> spreading a thousand lovely fragrances:
> wherever he flies he clothes the countryside
> in roses, lilies, violets, and other flowers.

In Botticelli's painting, Zephyr, one of the winds, blows, while Venus receives a fine robe embroidered with leaves and flowers.

Sandro Botticelli, *The Birth of Venus*
Venus had been depicted in art before Botticelli's painting, but he was the first artist since antiquity to portray her in the nude. (© Galleria degli Uffizi, Florence, Italy/Giraudon/The Bridgeman Art Library.)

The Sacrifice of Isaac and *The Birth of Venus* show some of the ways in which Renaissance artists used ancient models. Other artists perfected perspective—the illusion of three-dimensional space—to a degree that even classical antiquity had not anticipated. The development of the laws of perspective accompanied the introduction of long-range weaponry, such as cannons. In fact, some artists who excelled in using perspective, such as Leonardo da Vinci (1452–1519), were military engineers as well. In Leonardo's painting *The Annunciation* (page 422), sight lines meeting at a point on the horizon open wide precisely where the angel kneels and Mary responds in surprise.

Ghiberti, Botticelli, and Leonardo were all Italian artists. While they were creating their works, a northern Renaissance was taking place as well. At the court of France during the Hundred Years' War, kings commissioned portraits of themselves—sometimes unflattering ones—just as Roman leaders had once commissioned their own busts. Soon it was the fashion for everyone who could afford it to have his or her portrait made, as naturalistically as possible. Compare the image of Joan of Arc on page 400 with the painting of the Virgin Mary and Chancellor Nicolas Rolin completed by the Dutch artist Jan van Eyck around 1433 (see page 423). The artist who depicted Joan wanted to show a young woman dressed

Leonardo da Vinci, *The Annunciation*
Working with a traditional Christian theme (the moment when the angel Gabriel announced to the Virgin Mary that she would give birth to Christ), Leonardo produced a work of great originality, drawing the viewer's eye from a vanishing point in the distance to the subject of the painting. The ability to subordinate the background to the foreground was a great contribution of Renaissance perspective.
(Scala/Ministero per i Beni e le Attività Culturali/Art Resource, NY.)

in armor—any young woman. The image was meant to be symbolic. By contrast, van Eyck and his patron wanted to show a particular person, Nicolas Rolin. The very wrinkles of Rolin's neck proclaim his individuality. Though shown in a pious pose, Rolin is the key figure in the picture; the Virgin and baby Jesus sit a bit to the back and in the shadows. Meanwhile, the grand view of a city spreads out behind them, underscoring Rolin's stature in the community. Van Eyck was a master of perspective, and he used it here to emphasize Rolin's gravity and importance. Rolin was indeed an eminent man: he worked for the duke of Burgundy and was the founder of a hospital at Beaune and a religious order of nurses to serve it. Van Eyck conveyed his prominence in this portrait.

The Music of the Courts

Patrons of the new arts also used music to add glamour and glory to their courts and reputations. Renaissance rulers spent as much as 6 percent of their annual revenue to support musicians and composers. The Avignon papacy, in its own way one such court, was a major sponsor of sacred music. Whether secular or religious, music was appreciated for its ability to express the innermost feelings of the individual.

Every proper court had its own musicians. Some served as chaplains, writing music for the ruler's private chapel—the place where his court and household heard Mass. When Josquin Desprez (1440–1521) served as the duke of Ferrara's chaplain,

Jan van Eyck, *The Virgin of Chancellor Rolin*
Van Eyck portrays the Virgin and Chancellor Rolin as if they were contemporaries sharing a nice chat. Only the angel, who is placing a crown on the Virgin's head, suggests that something out of the ordinary is happening. (Erich Lessing/Art Resource, NY.)

he wrote a Mass that used the musical equivalents of the letters of the duke's name (the Italian version of *do re mi*) as its theme. Isabella d'Este (1474–1539), the daughter of the duke, employed her own musicians—singers, woodwind and string players, percussionists, and keyboard players—while her husband, the duke of Mantua, had his own band. When her brother sent her poems to copy, she had her favorite musician set them to music. This was one of the ways in which humanists and musicians worked together: the poems that interested composers and rulers alike were of the newest sort, patterned on classical forms. Isabella particularly favored Petrarch's poems.

The church, too, was a major sponsor of music. Every feast required music, and the papal schism inadvertently encouraged more musical production than usual, as rival popes tried to best one another in the realm of pageantry and sound. Churches needed choirs, and many composers got their start as choirboys. But that job could last well into adulthood. In the fourteenth century, the men who sang in the choir at Reims, for example, received a yearly stipend and an extra fee every time the choir sang the Mass and the liturgical offices of the day.

When the composer Johannes Ockeghem, chaplain for three French kings, died in 1497, his fellow musicians vied in expressing their grief in song. Josquin Desprez was among them, and his composition illustrates how the addition of classical elements to very traditional musical forms enhanced music's emotive power. Josquin's work combines personal grief with religious liturgy and the feelings expressed in classical elegies. The piece uses five voices. Inspired by classical mythology, four of the voices sing in the vernacular French about the "nymphs of the wood" coming together to mourn. But the fifth voice intones the words of the liturgy: "Requiescat in pace" (May he rest in peace). At the very moment in the song when the four vernacular voices lament Ockeghem's burial in the dark ground, the liturgical voice sings of the heavenly light. The contrast makes the song more moving. By drawing on the classical past, Renaissance musicians found new ways in which to express emotion.

REVIEW How and why did Renaissance humanists, artists, and musicians revive classical traditions?

On the Threshold of Global History

Only in the fifteenth century did Europe become a major player in world history. Before the maritime explorations of Portugal and Spain, Europe had remained at the periphery of world events. Fourteenth-century Mongols had been more interested in conquering China and Persia—lands with sophisticated cultures—than in invading Europe; Persian historians of the early fifteenth century dismissed Europeans as "barbaric Franks"; and China's Ming dynasty rulers, who sent maritime expeditions to Southeast Asia and East Africa around 1400, seemed unaware of Europeans, even though Marco Polo and other Italian merchants had appeared at the court of the preceding Mongol Yuan dynasty.

In the fifteenth century, Portuguese and Spanish vessels, followed a century later by English, French, and Dutch ships, sailed across the Atlantic, Indian, and Pacific oceans, bringing with them people, merchandise, crops, and diseases in a global exchange that would shape the modern world. For the first time, the people of the Americas were brought into contact with a larger historical force that threatened to destroy not only their culture but also their existence. European exploitation and conquest defined this historical era of transition from the medieval to the modern world, as Europeans left the Baltic and the Mediterranean for wider oceans.

The Divided Mediterranean

In the second half of the fifteenth century, the Mediterranean Sea, which had dominated medieval maritime trade, began to lose its preeminence to the Atlantic Ocean. To win control over the Mediterranean, the Ottomans embarked on an ambitious naval program to transform their empire into a major maritime power. War and piracy disrupted the flow of Christian trade: the Venetians mobilized all their resources to fight off Turkish advances, and the Genoese largely abandoned the eastern Mediterranean for trade opportunities presented by the Atlantic.

Mediterranean trade used ships made with relatively backward naval technology. The most common ship, the galley—a flat-bottomed vessel propelled mainly by oarsmen with the help of a sail—dated from the time of ancient Rome. Most galleys could not withstand open-ocean voyages, although Florentine and Genoese galleys did make long journeys to Flanders and England, hugging the coast for protection. The galley's dependence on human labor was a more serious handicap. Because prisoners of war and convicted criminals toiled as oarsmen on both Christian and Muslim ships, victory in war or the enforcement of criminal penalties was crucial to a state's ability to float large numbers of galleys. Slaves, too, sometimes provided the necessary labor.

Portuguese Confrontations

The exploration of the Atlantic began with the Portuguese (Map 11.5). By 1415, they had captured Ceuta on the Moroccan coast, establishing a foothold in Africa. Thereafter, Portuguese voyages sailed farther down the West African coast. By midcentury, a chain of Portuguese forts reached Guinea, protecting the trade in gold and slaves. At home, the royal house of Portugal financed the fleets, with crucial roles played by Prince Peter, regent between 1440 and 1448; his more famous younger brother Prince Henry the Navigator; and King John II. As a governor of the noble crusading Order of Christ, Henry financed many voyages out of the order's revenues. Private monies also helped, as leading Lisbon merchants participated in financing the gold and slave trades off the Guinea coast.

In 1455, Pope Nicholas V authorized Portuguese overseas expansion, praising King John II's crusading spirit and granting him and his successors a monopoly on trade with inhabitants of the newly "discovered" regions. In 1487–1488, Bartholomeu Dias took advantage of the prevailing winds in the South Atlantic to reach the Cape of Good Hope. A mere ten years later (1497–1499), under the captainship of Vasco da Gama, a Portuguese fleet rounded the cape and reached Calicut, India, center of the spice trade. By 1517, a chain of Portuguese forts dotted the Indian Ocean. In 1519, Ferdinand Magellan, a Portuguese sailor in Spanish service, led the first expedition to circumnavigate the globe.

In many ways a continuation of the struggle against the Muslims on the Iberian peninsula, Portugal's maritime voyages displayed that country's mixed motives of piety, glory, and greed. The sailors dreamed of finding gold mines in West Africa and a mysterious Christian kingdom established by a mythical "Prester John." They hoped to reach the spice-producing lands of South and Southeast Asia by sea and to bypass the Ottoman Turks, who controlled the traditional land routes between Europe and Asia.

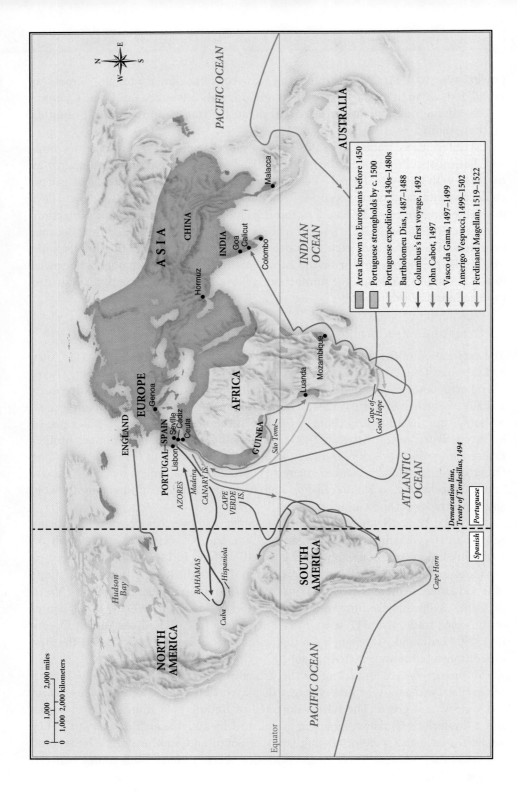

PACIFIC OCEAN

AUSTRALIA

Area known to Europeans before 1450
Portuguese strongholds by c. 1500
Portuguese expeditions 1430s–1480s
Bartholomeu Dias, 1487–1488
Columbus's first voyage, 1492
John Cabot, 1497
Vasco da Gama, 1497–1499
Amerigo Vespucci, 1499–1502
Ferdinand Magellan, 1519–1522

A S I A

CHINA

INDIA
Goa
Calicut
Colombo

Malacca

Hormuz

INDIAN
OCEAN

Mozambique

Luanda

AFRICA

Cape of
Good Hope

EUROPE
Genoa

ENGLAND

PORTUGAL–SPAIN
Seville
Lisbon
Gádiz
Ceuta

GUINEA

São Tomé

Madeira
AZORES
CANARY IS.
CAPE
VERDE
IS.

ATLANTIC
OCEAN

*Demarcation line,
Treaty of Tordesillas, 1494*

Spanish | Portuguese

BAHAMAS
Hispaniola
Cuba

Hudson
Bay

NORTH
AMERICA

SOUTH
AMERICA

Cape Horn

PACIFIC OCEAN

Equator

N
E
W S

0   1,000   2,000 miles
0   1,000   2,000 kilometers

The new voyages depended for their success on several technological break-throughs. The lateen (triangular) sail permitted ships to tack against headwinds. Light caravels and heavy galleons, however different in size, were alike in using more than one mast and sail, harnessing wind—rather than human—power to move them. Better charts, maps, and instruments made long-distance voyages less risky.

After the voyages of Christopher Columbus, Portugal's interests clashed with those of Spain. Mediated by Pope Alexander VI, the 1494 Treaty of Tordesillas reconciled Portugal and Spain by dividing the Atlantic world between the two royal houses. A demarcation 370 leagues west of the Cape Verde Islands divided the Atlantic Ocean, reserving for Portugal the western coast of Africa and the route to India and giving Spain the oceans and lands to the west. Unwittingly, this agreement also allowed Portugal to claim Brazil in 1500, which Pedro Álvares Cabral (1467–1520) accidentally "discovered" on his voyage to India.

The Voyages of Columbus

Historians agree that Christopher Columbus (1451–1506) was born of Genoese parents; beyond that, we have little accurate information about this man who brought together the history of Europe and the Americas. In 1476, he arrived in Portugal, apparently a survivor in a naval battle between a Franco-Portuguese and a Genoese fleet. In 1479, he married a Portuguese noblewoman. He spent the next few years mostly in Portuguese service, gaining valuable experience in regular voyages down the west coast of Africa. In 1485, after the death of his wife, Columbus settled in Spain.

Fifteenth-century Europeans already knew that Asia lay beyond the vast Atlantic Ocean, and *The Travels of Marco Polo,* written more than a century earlier, still exerted a powerful hold on European images of the East. Columbus read it many times, along with other travel books, and proposed to sail west across the Atlantic to reach the lands of the khan, unaware that the Mongol Empire had already collapsed in eastern Asia. Vastly underestimating the distances, he dreamed of finding a new route to the East's gold and spices and partook of the larger European vision that had inspired the Portuguese voyages. (His critics had a much more accurate idea of the globe's size and of the difficulty of the venture. No one believed that the

Map 11.5 Early Voyages of World Exploration
At the end of the fifteenth century, Europeans began moving aggressively across the globe. Beginning with initial forays along the African coast, their voyages soon widened out to transatlantic crossings and, by 1522, the circumnavigation of the world. The web of arrows on this map suggests an earth bound together by many threads, and this is partly true, for never again would the two halves of the globe be isolated. At the same time, the threads pulled in one direction only—toward the Europeans. Africa was exploited for gold and slaves, while the discovery of precious metals fueled the explorations and settlements of Central and South America.

world was flat!) After the Portuguese and French monarchs rejected his proposal, Columbus found royal patronage with the recently proclaimed Catholic monarchs Isabella of Castile and Ferdinand of Aragon. In August 1492, equipped with a modest fleet of three ships and about ninety men, Columbus set sail across the Atlantic. His contract stipulated that he would claim Castilian sovereignty over any new land and inhabitants and share any profits with the crown.

Reaching what we know today as the Bahamas on October 12, Columbus mistook the islands to be part of the East Indies, not far from Japan and "the lands of the Great Khan." As the Castilians explored the Caribbean islands, they encountered communities of peaceful Indians, the Arawaks, who were awed by the Europeans' military technology, not to mention their appearance. Exchanging gifts of beads and broken glass for Arawak gold—an exchange that convinced Columbus of the trusting nature of the Indians—the crew established peaceful relationships with many communities. Yet despite many positive entries in the ship's log referring to Columbus's personal goodwill toward the Indians, the Europeans' objectives were clear: find gold, subjugate the Indians, and propagate Christianity.

Excited by the prospect of easy riches, many flocked to join Columbus's second voyage. When Columbus departed Cádiz in September 1493, he commanded seventeen ships that carried between twelve hundred and fifteen hundred men, many believing all they had to do was "load the gold into the ships." Failing to find the imaginary gold mines and spices, however, the colonial enterprise quickly switched its focus to finding slaves. Columbus and his crew first enslaved the Caribs, enemies of the Arawaks; in 1494, Columbus proposed a regular slave trade based in Hispaniola. The Spaniards exported enslaved Indians to Spain, and slave traders sold them in Seville. Soon the Spaniards began importing sugarcane from the Portuguese island of Madeira and forced large numbers of Indians to work on plantations to produce more sugar for export to Europe. Columbus himself was edged out of this new enterprise. When the Spanish monarchs realized the vast potential for material gain that lay in their new dominions, they asserted direct royal authority by sending officials and priests to the Americas, which were later named after the Italian Amerigo Vespucci, who led a voyage across the Atlantic in 1499–1502.

Columbus's place in history embodies the fundamental transformations of his age. A Genoese in the service of Portuguese and Spanish employers, Columbus's career illustrates the changing balance between the Mediterranean and the Atlantic. His voyages of 1492–1493 would eventually draw a triangle of exchange among Europe, the Americas, and Africa, an exchange gigantic in its historical impact and its human cost.

A New Era in Slavery

During the Middle Ages and Renaissance, female slaves served as domestic servants in wealthy Mediterranean homes, and male slaves toiled in the galleys of Ottoman and Christian fleets. Some were captured in war or by piracy; others, Africans, were

Dürer's Engraving of Katharina, an African Woman
Like other artists in early-sixteenth-century Europe, Albrecht Dürer would have seen in person Africans who were living in Portugal and Spain as students, servants, and slaves. (Foto Marburg/Art Resource, NY.)

sold by African and Bedouin traders to Christian buyers. In western Asia, impoverished parents sometimes sold their children into servitude. Many people in the Balkans became slaves when their land was devastated by Ottoman invasions. Slaves were Greek, Slav, European, African, and Turk.

The Portuguese maritime voyages changed this picture. From the fifteenth century on, Africans increasingly filled the ranks of slaves. Exploiting warfare in West Africa, the Portuguese traded in gold and "pieces," as African slaves were called, a practice condemned at home by some conscientious clergy. Critical voices, however, could not deny the enormous profits the slave trade brought to Portugal. Most slaves toiled on the sugar plantations of the Portuguese Atlantic islands and in Brazil. A fortunate few labored as domestic servants in Portugal, where African freedmen and slaves, some 35,000 in the early sixteenth century, constituted almost 3 percent of the population, a much higher percentage than in other European countries. In the Americas, slavery would flourish as an institution of exploitation.

Europeans in a New World

In 1500, on the eve of European invasion, the native peoples of the Americas were divided into many sedentary and nomadic societies. Among the settled peoples, the largest political and social organizations were in the Mexican and Peruvian highlands. The Aztecs and Incas ruled over subjugated Indian populations in their respective empires. With an elaborate religious culture and a rigid social and political hierarchy, the Aztecs and Incas based their civilizations in large urban capitals.

The Spanish explorers organized their expeditions to the mainland from a base in the Caribbean. Two prominent leaders, Hernán Cortés (1485–1547) and Francisco Pizarro (c. 1475–1541), gathered men and arms and set off in search of gold. Catholic priests accompanied the fortune hunters to bring Christianity to allegedly uncivilized peoples and thus to justify brutal conquests. His small band swollen by peoples who had been subjugated by the Aztecs, Cortés captured the Aztec capital, Tenochtitlán, in 1519. To the south, Pizarro conquered the Andean highlands, exploiting a civil war between rival Incan kings. By the mid-sixteenth century, the Spanish Empire stretched unbroken from Mexico to Chile.

Not to be outdone by the Spaniards, other European powers joined the scramble for gold in the New World. In 1500, a Portuguese fleet led by Pedro Álvares Cabral landed in Brazil, but Portugal did not begin colonizing there until 1532, when it established a permanent fort on the coast. In North America, the French went in search of a "northwest passage" to China. By 1504, French fishermen had appeared in Newfoundland. Thirty years later, Jacques Cartier led three voyages that explored the St. Lawrence River as far as Montreal. An early attempt in 1541 to settle Canada failed because of the harsh winter and Indian hostility, and John Cabot's 1497 voyage to find a northern route to Asia also failed. More permanent settlements in Canada and the present-day United States would succeed only in the seventeenth century.

REVIEW   Which European countries led the way in maritime expansion, and what were their motives?

Conclusion

Confronted by disease, economic contraction, war, popular uprisings, and a disgraced papacy, Europe's ruling classes grasped the reins of power ever more tightly, creating more centralized and institutionalized states. Muscovy and Poland-Lithuania formed in the east, while western European kings, dukes, and even republics consolidated their rule.

Surrounding themselves with artists, musicians, and humanists, these new-style rulers supported the Renaissance—an attempt to resuscitate the classical past for the purposes of the present. The Renaissance, which emphasized human potential and achievement, was one of Europe's most brilliant periods of artistic activity, one that glorified both God and humanity. Inspired by ancient models, Renaissance humanists

Mapping the West Renaissance Europe, c. 1500
By 1500, the shape of early modern Europe was largely set. It would remain stable until the eighteenth century, except for the disappearance of an independent Hungarian kingdom, which was conquered by the Ottomans in 1529.

revived classical literary style, Renaissance architects planned cities as well as buildings, Renaissance artists demonstrated a new appreciation for the human body and the illusion of depth, and Renaissance musicians invented new forms of polyphony. The Renaissance began mainly in the city-states of Italy, but it spread throughout much of Europe. At the courts of great kings and dukes, even the Ottoman sultan, Renaissance music, art, and literature served as a way to celebrate the grandeur of rulers who controlled more of the apparatuses of government—armies, artillery, courts, and taxes—than ever before.

Political consolidation fueled intense competition among the European powers for more land, money, and glory. Rulers paid explorers to expand their frontiers, first to Africa and then across the Atlantic Ocean to the Americas, ushering in the first period of global history. Few at the time would have guessed that Europe would soon enter yet another period of turmoil, one brought about not by demographic and economic collapse but by a profound crisis of conscience that the brilliance of Renaissance civilization had tended to obscure.

CHAPTER REVIEW QUESTIONS
1. How did Renaissance states differ from medieval monarchies?
2. How did the Ottomans' impact on Europe differ from the Mongols'?

For practice quizzes and other study tools, see the Online Study Guide at bedfordstmartins.com/huntconcise.

For primary-source material from this period, see Chapters 13 and 14 of *Sources of THE MAKING OF THE WEST*, Third Edition.

TIMELINE

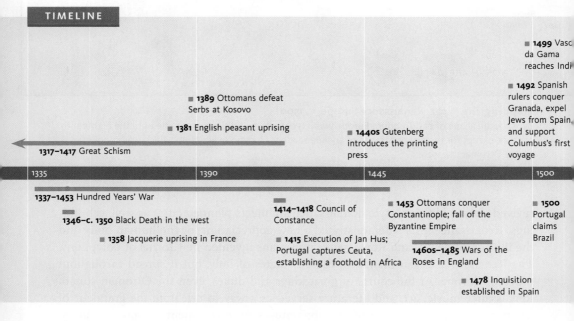

- **1499** Vasco da Gama reaches India

- **1492** Spanish rulers conquer Granada, expel Jews from Spain, and support Columbus's first voyage

- **1389** Ottomans defeat Serbs at Kosovo

- **1381** English peasant uprising

- **1440s** Gutenberg introduces the printing press

1317–1417 Great Schism

| 1335 | 1390 | 1445 | 1500 |

1337–1453 Hundred Years' War

1346–c. 1350 Black Death in the west

- **1358** Jacquerie uprising in France

1414–1418 Council of Constance

- **1415** Execution of Jan Hus; Portugal captures Ceuta, establishing a foothold in Africa

- **1453** Ottomans conquer Constantinople; fall of the Byzantine Empire

1460s–1485 Wars of the Roses in England

- **1478** Inquisition established in Spain

- **1500** Portugal claims Brazil

Suggested References

The old view of historians associated the Renaissance primarily with Florence, but now the Renaissance is seen as a European movement (Kirkpatrick, Knecht) and even part of Ottoman culture (Jardine and Brotton). Similarly, the traditional view of "Europe discovering the world" has been replaced by a more nuanced and complex discussion (Abulafia) that includes non-European views and uses Asian, African, and Mesoamerican sources.

Aberth, John. *From the Brink of the Apocalypse: Confronting Famine, War, Plague, and Death in the Later Middle Ages.* 2001.

Abulafia, David, ed. *The Discovery of Mankind: Atlantic Encounters in the Age of Columbus.* 2008.

Bisaha, Nancy. *Creating East and West: Renaissance Humanists and the Ottoman Turks.* 2004.

*Froissart, Jean. *Chronicles.* Trans. Geoffrey Brereton. 1968.

*Horrox, Rosemary, ed. and trans. *The Black Death.* 1994.

Jardine, Lisa, and Jerry Brotton. *Global Interests: Renaissance Art between East and West.* 2000.

Jordan, William Chester. *The Great Famine: Northern Europe in the Early Fourteenth Century.* 1996.

Kirkpatrick, Robin. *The European Renaissance, 1400–1600.* 2002.

Knecht, R. J. *The French Renaissance Court, 1483–1589.* 2008.

Plague and public health in Renaissance Europe: http://jefferson.village.virginia.edu/osheim/intro.html

Renaissance art in Italy: http://witcombe.sbc.edu/ARTHrenaissanceitaly.html

Russell-Wood, A. J. R. *A World on the Move: The Portuguese in Africa, Asia, and America, 1415–1808.* 1992.

Thomas, Hugh. *Rivers of Gold: The Rise of the Spanish Empire, from Columbus to Magellan.* 2003.

Struggles over Beliefs

HILLE FEIKEN LEFT THE NORTHERN GERMAN CITY of Münster on June 16, 1534, elegantly dressed, bedecked with jewels, and determined to kill. Münster, which religious radicals had declared a holy city, lay under siege by armies loyal to the local Catholic bishop—her intended victim. Hille crossed enemy lines and tried to persuade the commander of the besieging troops to take her to the bishop, promising to reveal a secret means of recapturing the city. When a defector from her camp recognized Hille and betrayed her, she was beheaded.

Hille Feiken belonged to the religious group known as **Anabaptists**, who wanted to form a holy community separate from the rest of society. Anabaptists organized in response to the Protestant Reformation, which was set in motion by the German friar Martin Luther in 1517 and quickly became a sweeping movement to uproot church abuses and restore early Christian teachings. Supporters of Luther were called **Protestants**, those who protested. Inspired by Luther and then by other reformers, ordinary men and women across much of Europe attempted to remake their heaven and earth. Their stories intertwined with bloody struggles among princes for domination in Europe, an age-old conflict now complicated by the clash of rival faiths.

Vincenzo Catena, *Judith*
The Book of Judith tells the story of a beautiful young Israelite who presents herself to Holofernes, the general of an army besieging Jerusalem. His guard lowered by wine and Judith's charms, Holofernes falls victim to Judith, who assassinates him and cuts off his head, thus frightening off the enemy and saving her people. In this painting from the 1520s, the Venetian artist Vincenzo Catena conveys Judith's strength, beauty, and commitment to her task—one that Hille Feiken sought to reenact so that she might free her own besieged city of Münster. *(akg-images/ Cameraphoto.)*

Struggles over religious beliefs frequently erupted into armed confrontation, culminating in the Thirty Years' War of 1618–1648, which devastated the lands of central Europe. The orgy of mutual destruction in this war left no winners in the religious struggle, and the cynical manipulation of religious issues by both Catholic and Protestant leaders showed that political interests eventually outweighed those of religion. The extreme violence of religious conflict pushed rulers and political thinkers to seek other, non-religious grounds for governmental authority. Few would argue for genuine toleration

435

of religious differences, but many began to insist that the interests of states had to take priority over the desire for religious conformity.

Although particularly dramatic and deadly, the church-state crisis was only one of a series of upheavals that shaped this era. After decades of rapid economic and population growth in the sixteenth century, a major economic downturn led to food shortages, famine, and disease in the first half of the seventeenth century. An upheaval in worldviews was also in the making, catalyzed by increasing knowledge of the new worlds discovered overseas and in the heavens. The development of new scientific methods of research would ultimately reshape Western attitudes toward religion and state power, as Europeans desperately sought alternatives to wars over religious beliefs.

CHAPTER FOCUS QUESTION Why did struggles over religious beliefs in the sixteenth and seventeenth centuries provoke such violence?

The Protestant Reformation

Since the mid-fifteenth century, many clerics had tried to reform the church from within, criticizing clerical abuses and calling for moral renewal, but their efforts came up against the church's inertia and resistance. At the beginning of the sixteenth century, widespread popular piety and anticlericalism existed side by side, fomenting a volatile mixture of need and resentment. A young German friar, tormented by his own religious doubts, was to become the spokesman for a generation. From its origins as a theological dispute, Martin Luther's reform movement sparked explosive protests. By the time he died in 1546, half of western Europe had renounced allegiance to the Roman Catholic church. Christian unity fractured, opening the way not only to widespread turmoil but also to a host of new attitudes about the nature of religious and political authority.

Popular Piety and Christian Humanism

Numerous signs pointed to an intense spiritual anxiety among the laity. New shrines sprang up, reports of miracles multiplied, and prayer books sold briskly. Critics complained that the church gave external behavior more weight than spiritual intentions. In receiving the sacrament of penance—one of the central pillars of the Roman church—sinners were expected to examine their consciences, sincerely confess their sins to a priest, and receive forgiveness. In practice, however, some priests abused their authority by demanding sexual or monetary favors in return for forgiveness. Priests also sold **indulgences**, which according to doctrine could alleviate suffering in purgatory after death. The faithful were supposed to earn indulgences by performing certain religious tasks—going on pilgrimage, attending Mass, doing holy works. The sale of indulgences as a substitution for performing good works suggested that the church was more interested in making money than in saving souls.

Dissatisfaction with the official church prompted some Christian intellectuals to link their scholarship to the cause of social reform and to dream of ideal societies based on peace and morality. The Dutch scholar Desiderius Erasmus (c. 1466–1536) and the English lawyer Thomas More (1478–1535) stood out as representatives of these Christian humanists, who, unlike Italian humanists, placed their primary emphasis on Christian piety. Each established close links to the powerful. Erasmus was on intimate terms with kings and popes, and his fame spread across Europe. More became lord chancellor to England's king Henry VIII.

Erasmus advocated a simple piety devoid of greed and the lust for power, but he also promoted the new humanist learning. To this end he devoted years to translating a new Latin edition of the New Testament from the original Greek. He argued ironically in *The Praise of Folly* (1509) that the wise appeared foolish, because modesty, humility, and poverty had few adherents in this world. Although Erasmus mocked the clergy's corruption and Christian princes' bloody ambitions, he emphasized the role of education in reforming individuals and through them society as a whole. Even ordinary table manners drew his attention. In the *Colloquies* (1523), a compilation of Latin dialogues intended as language-learning exercises, he advised his cultivated readers not to pick their noses at meals and not to speak while stuffing their mouths. Challenged by angry younger men and radical ideas once the Reformation took hold, Erasmus chose Christian unity over reform and schism. He died in the Swiss city of Basel, isolated from the Protestant community and condemned by many in the Catholic church, who found his writings too critical of the church's authority.

Erasmus's good friend Thomas More, to whom *The Praise of Folly* was dedicated,* met with even greater suffering for his beliefs. He would later pay with his life for upholding conscience over political expediency. Inspired by the recent voyages of discovery, More's best-known work, *Utopia* (1516), describes an imaginary ideal place that offered a stark contrast to his own society. Because utopians enjoyed public schools, communal kitchens, hospitals, and nurseries, they had no need for money. Greed and private property disappeared in this world. Dedicated to the pursuit of knowledge and natural religion, Utopia knew neither crime nor war (*Utopia* means both "no place" and "best place" in Greek). Despite a few oddities—voluntary slavery, for instance, and strictly controlled travel—Utopia seemed a paradise compared with the increasing violence in a Europe divided by religion.

Martin Luther and the German Nation

Like Erasmus and More, Martin Luther (1483–1546) pursued a life of scholarship, but a personal crisis of faith led him to break with the Roman church and establish a competing one. The son of a miner, Luther abandoned his studies in the law to enter the Augustinian order. The choice of a monastic life did not resolve Luther's doubts about his own salvation. Appalled at his own sense of sinfulness and the weakness of human nature, he lived in terror of God's justice despite frequent confessions and penance.

---

*The Latin title *Encomium Moriae* (*The Praise of Folly*) was a pun on More's name and the Latin word meaning "folly."

A pilgrimage to Rome only deepened his unease with the institutional church. Sent to study theology by a sympathetic superior, Luther gradually came to new insights through his study of Scripture. He later described his breakthrough experience:

> At last, by the mercy of God, meditating day and night, I gave heed to the context of the words [in Romans 1:17], namely, "In [the Gospel] the righteousness of God is revealed, as it is written, 'He who through faith is righteous shall live.'" There I began to understand that the righteousness of God is that by which the righteous live by a gift of God, namely by faith.

Luther soon came into conflict with the church authorities. In 1516, the new archbishop ordered the sale of indulgences to help cover the cost of constructing St. Peter's Basilica in Rome and also to defray his expenses in pursuing his election. Such blatant profiteering outraged many, including Luther, who now served as professor of theology at the University of Wittenberg. In 1517, Luther composed ninety-five theses—propositions for an academic debate—that questioned indulgence peddling and the purchase of church offices. Once they became public, the theses unleashed a torrent of pent-up resentment and frustration among the laypeople. This apparently ordinary academic dispute soon engulfed the Holy Roman Empire in conflict.

As Luther developed his ideas more fully, rupture became inevitable. In 1520, he published three treatises that laid out his theological position, attacked the papacy in Rome as the embodiment of the Antichrist, and called upon the German princes to reform the church themselves. Luther insisted that faith alone, not good works or penance, could save sinners from damnation. Faith came from the believer's personal relationship with God, which he or she cultivated through individual study of Scripture. Ordinary laypeople thus made up "the priesthood of all believers," who had no need of a professional caste of clerics to show them the way to salvation. The attack on the church's authority could not have been more dramatic.

Luther Triumphs over His Catholic Opponents
This 1521 woodcut by Matthias Gnidias shows Martin Luther, Bible in hand, standing above his Catholic opponent, the Franciscan friar Thomas Murner, who is depicted here as the biblical monster Leviathan. The monster breathes "ignis, fumus, & sulphur"—fire, smoke, and sulfur. The vertical Latin caption declares that the Lord will visit the earth with his sword and kill the monster. Both Protestants and Catholics used woodcuts and illustrations extensively as propaganda to appeal to the vast majority of people who were illiterate.

From Rome's perspective, the "Luther Affair," as church officials called it, was essentially a matter of clerical discipline. Rome ordered Luther to obey his superiors and keep quiet. But the church establishment had seriously misjudged the extent of Luther's influence. Luther's ideas, published in numerous German and Latin editions, spread rapidly throughout the Holy Roman Empire, unleashing forces that Luther himself could not control. Social, nationalist, and religious protests fused into an explosive mass very similar to the Czech revolution that Jan Hus had inspired a century earlier. Like Hus, Luther appeared before an emperor: in 1521, he defended his faith before Charles V (r. 1520–1558), the newly elected Holy Roman Emperor, who at the age of nineteen was the ruler of the Low Countries, Spain, Spain's Italian and New World dominions, and the Austrian Habsburg lands. At the Imperial Diet of Worms, the formal assembly presided over by this powerful ruler, Luther shocked Germans by declaring his admiration for the Czech heretic. But unlike Hus, Luther did not suffer martyrdom because he enjoyed the protection of his local lord, the elector of Saxony (one of the seven German princes entitled to elect the Holy Roman Emperor). Luther also had the support of many literate townspeople who were eager to read the Scriptures for themselves.

What began as an urban movement turned into a war in the countryside in 1525. The church was the largest landowner in the Holy Roman Empire: about one-seventh of the empire's territory consisted of ecclesiastical principalities in which bishops and abbots exercised both secular and churchly power. Peasants had to pay taxes to both the church and their lords. In the spring of 1525, many peasants in southern and central Germany rose in rebellion, sometimes inspired by wandering preachers. Urban workers and artisans joined the peasant bands, plundering monasteries, refusing to pay church taxes, and demanding village autonomy, the abolition of serfdom, and the right to appoint their own pastors. In Thuringia, the rebels were led by an ex-priest, Thomas Müntzer (1468?–1525), who promised to chastise the wicked and thus clear the way for the Last Judgment.

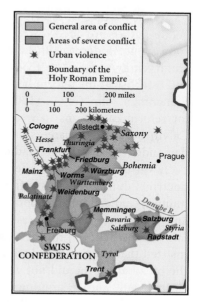

The Peasants' War, 1525

The uprising of 1525, known as the Peasants' War, split the reform movement. In Thuringia, Catholics and reformers joined hands to kill Müntzer and crush his supporters. All over the empire, princes rallied their troops to defeat the peasants and hunt down their leaders. By the end of 1525, more than 100,000 rebels had been killed and others maimed, imprisoned, or exiled. Luther had tried to mediate, criticizing the princes for their brutality toward the peasants but also warning the rebels against mixing religion and social protest.

The Progress of the Reformation

1517	Martin Luther disseminates ninety-five theses attacking the sale of indulgences and other church practices
1520	Reformer Huldrych Zwingli breaks with Rome
1525	Radical reformer Thomas Müntzer killed in the Peasants' War
1529	Lutheran German princes protest the condemnation of religious reform by Charles V; genesis of the term *Protestants*
1534	English Parliament establishes King Henry VIII as head of the Anglican church, severing ties to Rome
1534–1535	Anabaptists control the city of Münster, Germany, in a failed experiment to create a holy community
1541	John Calvin and his followers take control in Geneva, making that city the center of Calvinist reforms

Luther believed that rulers were ordained by God and thus must be obeyed even if they were tyrants. The kingdom of God belonged not to this world but to the next. When the rebels ignored his appeal to stop, Luther called on the princes to destroy "the devil's work" and slaughter the rebels. Fundamentally conservative in its political philosophy, the Lutheran church would henceforth depend on established political authority for its protection.

Emerging as the champions of an orderly religious reform, many German princes eventually confronted Emperor Charles V, who supported Rome. In 1529, Charles declared the Roman Catholic faith the empire's only legitimate religion. Proclaiming their allegiance to the reform cause, the Lutheran German princes protested and thus came to be called Protestants.

Huldrych Zwingli and John Calvin

While Luther provided the religious leadership for northern Germany, the south soon came under the influence of reformers based in Switzerland. In 1520, Huldrych Zwingli (1484–1531), the son of a Swiss village leader, broke with Rome and established his reform headquarters in German-speaking Zurich. In 1541, the Frenchman John Calvin (1509–1564) made French-speaking Geneva his center for reform campaigns in western Europe (Map 12.1). Like Luther, Zwingli and Calvin began their careers as priests, but in contrast to their predecessor, they demanded an even more radical break with the Roman Catholic church, especially on the question of the sacrament of communion. According to Catholic doctrine, during the Mass officiated by a priest the bread and wine of holy communion changed into the body and blood of Christ. Luther believed that the body and blood were actually present in the bread and wine, but only because of the faith of the believer, not because a priest officiated. Zwingli pushed further and insisted that the bread and wine simply symbolized Christ's union with believers; the bread and wine did not change in substance. Calvin took a position between Zwingli and Luther, arguing that the sacrament of communion was more than just symbolic but insisting that it was entirely in God's power, dependent neither on the priest nor on the individual's faith. All efforts to mediate between these positions failed.

Map 12.1 The Spread of Protestantism in the Sixteenth Century
The Protestant Reformation divided northern and southern Europe. From its heartland in the Holy Roman Empire, the Reformation spread to Scandinavia, England, and Scotland and made considerable inroads into the Low Countries, France, eastern Europe, the Swiss Confederation, and even parts of northern Italy. While the Mediterranean countries remained loyal to Rome, religious divisions characterized the landscape of Europe from the British Isles in the west to Poland in the east.

In Zurich, Zwingli tolerated no dissent. When laypeople secretly set up their own new sect, called Anabaptists, Zwingli immediately attacked them. The Anabaptists believed that only adults had the free will to truly understand and accept baptism and therefore had to be rebaptized (*anabaptism* means "rebaptism"). How could a baby knowingly choose Christ? Rebaptism symbolized the Anabaptists' determination to withdraw from a social order corrupted, as they saw it, by power and evil. They therefore rejected the authority of courts and magistrates and refused to bear arms or swear oaths of allegiance. When persuasion failed to convince them, Zwingli urged Zurich magistrates to impose the death sentence.

Anabaptism spread quickly from Zurich to many cities in southern Germany, despite the Holy Roman Empire's general condemnation of the movement in 1529. In 1534, one incendiary Anabaptist group, believing that the end of the world was imminent, seized control of the northwestern German town of Münster. Proclaiming themselves a community of saints and imitating the ancient Israelites, they were initially governed by twelve elders and later by Jan of Leiden, a Dutch Anabaptist tailor who claimed to be the prophesied leader—a second "King David."

The Münster Anabaptists abolished private property and dissolved traditional marriages, allowing men, like Old Testament patriarchs, to have multiple wives, to the chagrin of many women. In 1535, Münster fell to a combined Protestant and Catholic army. Many Anabaptists died in battle or, like Hille Feiken, were executed. The remnants of the Anabaptist movement survived under the determined pacifist leadership of the Dutch reformer Menno Simons (1496–1561), whose followers were eventually named Mennonites.

As a young priest, Calvin had believed it might be possible to reform the Roman Catholic church from within, but gradually he came to share Luther and Zwingli's conviction that only fundamental change could restore the true religion. While Calvin moved toward the Protestant position, his homeland of France experienced increasing turmoil over religion. On Sunday, October 18, 1534, in the so-called Affair of the Placards, Parisians found church doors posted with broadsheets denouncing the Catholic Mass. The government arrested hundreds of French Protestants and executed scores of them, precipitating the flight into exile of many others, including Calvin.

Calvin did not intend to settle in Geneva, but when he stopped there, a local reformer threatened him with God's curse if he did not stay and help organize reform in the city. After intense conflict between the supporters of reform, many of whom were French refugees, and the opposition, led by the traditional elite families, the Calvinists triumphed in 1541. Geneva soon followed the precepts laid out in Calvin's great work, *The Institutes of the Christian Religion,* first published in 1536. Calvin followed the other Protestant reformers in insisting that God is almighty and humans cannot earn their salvation by good works, and then he went a step further, arguing that no Christian can be certain of salvation. With his doctrine of **predestination**, Calvin asserted that God had foreordained every man, woman, and child to salvation or damnation—even before the creation of the world. Only God knew who was among the "elect."

In practice, however, Calvinist doctrine demanded rigorous discipline: the knowledge that a small group of "elect" would be saved should guide the actions of the godly in an uncertain world. Fusing church and society into what followers named the Reformed church, Geneva became a single theocratic community, in which dissent was not tolerated. The Genevan magistrates arrested the Spanish physician Michael Servetus when he passed through in 1553 because he had published books attacking Calvin and questioning the doctrine of the Trinity, the belief shared by virtually all Christians that God exists in three persons—the Father, Son (Christ), and Holy Spirit. Servetus was executed at Calvin's insistence. Geneva quickly became the new center of the Reformation, sending out pastors trained for mission work and exporting books that taught Calvinist doctrines. The Calvinist movement spread to France, the Netherlands, England, Scotland, the German states, Poland, Hungary, and eventually New England, becoming the established form of the Reformation in many of these countries (Map 12.1, page 441).

Protestantism in England

Until 1527, England's king Henry VIII (r. 1509–1547) firmly opposed the Reformation, even receiving the title "Defender of the Faith" from Pope Leo X for a treatise Henry wrote against Luther. Henry's family problems changed his mind. Henry had married Catherine of Aragon (d. 1536), the daughter of Ferdinand and Isabella of Spain and the aunt of Charles V, and the marriage had produced a daughter, Princess Mary (known as Mary Tudor). Henry wanted a male heir to consolidate the rule of his Tudor dynasty, and he had fallen in love with Anne Boleyn, a lady-in-waiting at court and a strong supporter of the Reformation. In 1527, Henry asked the reigning pope, Clement VII, to declare his eighteen-year marriage to Catherine invalid on the grounds that she was the widow of his older brother, Arthur. Arthur and Catherine's marriage, which apparently was never consummated, had been annulled by Pope Julius II. When Henry failed to secure a papal dispensation for his divorce, he chose two Protestants as his new loyal servants: Thomas Cromwell (1485–1540) as chancellor and Thomas Cranmer (1489–1556) as archbishop of Canterbury. Under their leadership the English Parliament declared Henry's marriage to Catherine invalid, allowing him to marry Anne Boleyn; passed the Act of Supremacy of 1534, establishing Henry as the head of the Anglican church (the Church of England); and began confiscating the properties of the Catholic monasteries. Henry thus doubled his revenues.

By 1536, Henry had grown tired of Anne Boleyn, who had given birth to the future Queen Elizabeth I but had produced no sons. The king, who would go on to marry four other wives but father only one son, Edward (by his third wife, Jane Seymour), had Anne beheaded on the charge of adultery, an act that he defined as treason. Thomas More, once Henry's chancellor, had been executed in 1535 for treason—in his case, for refusing to recognize Henry as "the only supreme head on earth of the Church of England"—and Cromwell suffered the same fate in 1540 when he lost favor. After Henry's death in 1547, the Anglican church, nominally

Elizabeth Regina.

2. PARALIPOM. 6.

Domine Deus Israel, non est similis tui Deus in cælo & in terra, qui pacta custodis & misericordiam cum seruis tuis, qui ambulant coram te in toto corde suo.

Queen Elizabeth I of England
The Anglican (Church of England) Prayer Book of 1569 included a hand-colored print of Queen Elizabeth saying her prayers. As queen, Elizabeth was also the official head of the Church of England (the scepter or sword at her feet symbolizes her power). She named bishops and made final decisions about every aspect of church governance. **For more help analyzing this image, see the visual activity for this chapter in the Online Study Guide at** bedfordstmartins.com/ huntconcise. (HIP/Art Resource, NY.)

Protestant, still retained much traditional Catholic doctrine and ritual. But the principle of royal supremacy in religious matters would remain a lasting feature of Henry's reforms.

When Henry's Protestant son, Edward VI (r. 1547–1553), died at age sixteen, his half sister Mary Tudor (r. 1553–1558) succeeded him, and the Catholic Mass was spontaneously restored in most places without bloodshed. Mary intended to reestablish Catholicism and the authority of Rome, but she lost popularity when she ordered some three hundred Protestants burned at the stake as heretics, including Cranmer. Hundreds more fled. In 1554 she married the Catholic king of Spain, Philip II, which prompted a brief and unsuccessful rebellion. When Mary died in 1558, Anne Boleyn's daughter, Elizabeth, came to the throne and the Anglican cause again gained momentum. As Elizabeth I (r. 1558–1603) moved to solidify her personal power and the authority of the Anglican church, she had to squash uprisings by Catholics in the north and at least two serious plots against her life. She also had to hold off Calvinist **Puritans**, who pushed for more reform, and Spain's Philip II, who first wanted to be her husband and then, failing that, planned to invade her country to restore Catholicism.

The Puritans were strict Calvinists who opposed all vestiges of Catholic ritual in the Church of England. After Elizabeth became queen, many Puritans returned from exile abroad, but Elizabeth resisted their demands for drastic changes in Anglican ritual and governance. She had assumed control as "supreme governor" of the Church of England, and she therefore appointed all bishops. The Church of England's Thirty-nine

Articles of Religion, issued in 1563, incorporated elements of Catholic ritual along with Calvinist doctrines. Puritan ministers angrily denounced the Church of England's "popish attire . . . and a thousand more abominations." Puritans tried to undercut the bishops' authority by placing control of church administration in the hands of the local congregation. Elizabeth rejected this Calvinist "presbyterianism." The Puritans nonetheless steadily gained influence. Known for their emphasis on strict moral lives, the Puritans tried to close the theaters and Sunday fairs and insisted that every father "make his house a little church" by teaching the children to read the Bible. The precise nature of church government would remain a subject of contention for generations to come.

Elizabeth made the most of her limited means and consolidated the country's position as a Protestant power. In her early years, she held out the prospect of marriage to many political suitors but never married. She cajoled Parliament with references to her female weaknesses, but she showed steely-eyed determination in protecting the monarchy's interests. Her chosen successor, James I (r. 1603–1625), came to the throne as king of Scotland, England, and Ireland. Elizabeth left James secure in a kingdom of growing stature in world politics.

Reshaping Society through Religion

For all their differences over doctrine and church organization, the Protestant reformers shared a desire to instill greater discipline in Christian worship and in social behavior. As a consequence, they advocated changes in education and marriage to create a God-fearing, pious, and orderly Christian society. Some of these efforts grew out of developments that stretched back to the Middle Ages, but others, such as an emphasis on literacy, appeared first in Protestant Europe.

Prior to the Reformation, the Latin Vulgate was the only Bible authorized by the church; as a result, priests interpreted the Bible for their parishioners. In 1522, Martin Luther translated Erasmus's Greek New Testament into German because he believed that everyone should read the Bible for him- or herself. Within twelve years, printers published more than 200,000 copies of it, an immense number for the time. In 1534, Luther completed a German translation of the Old Testament. Inspired by Luther's example during a visit to Wittenberg, the Englishman William Tyndale (1495–1536) translated the Bible into English. After he had his translation printed in Germany and the Low Countries, Tyndale smuggled copies into England in 1526, while England was still Catholic.

Although the vernacular Bible was a prized possession in many Protestant households, Bible reading did not become widespread until the 1600s. To educate children in the new religious principles and replace the late medieval church schools, the Protestant reformers set up state school systems. Luther urged the German princes to use the proceeds of confiscated church properties to establish primary schools in every parish for boys and girls ages six to twelve. The Protestant churches also developed a secondary system of higher schools for boys, called gymnasia (from the Greek *gymnasion*), in which the study of Greek and Latin classics and religious instruction prepared future pastors, scholars, and officials for university study.

Like the reforms of education, Protestant efforts to reshape marriage reflected their concern to discipline individual behavior and institute an orderly Christian society. Protestant magistrates established marital courts, passed new marriage laws, closed brothels, and inflicted harsher punishments for sexual deviance. Under canon law, the Catholic church recognized any promise made between two consenting adults (with the legal age of twelve for females, fourteen for males) as a valid marriage. In rural areas and among the urban poor, most couples simply lived together as common-law husband and wife, and some couples never even registered with the church. Protestant governments declared a marriage illegitimate if the partners failed to register their marriage with a local official and a pastor. They usually also required parental consent, thus giving parents immense power in regulating marriage and the transmission of family property.

Taught to become obedient spouses and affectionate companions in Christ, women approached this new sexual regime with ambivalence. The new laws stipulated that women could seek divorce for desertion, impotence, and flagrant abuse, although in practice the marital courts encouraged reconciliation. These improvements came at a price, however: Protestant women were expected to be obedient wives, helpful companions, and loving mothers, but they could no longer join the convent and pursue their own religious paths outside the family. Luther's wife, Katharina von Bora, typified the new ideal Protestant woman. A former nun, she accepted her prescribed role in a patriarchal household: once married, Katharina ran the couple's household, feeding their children, relatives, and student boarders. Although she deferred to Luther—she addressed him as "Herr Doktor"—she nonetheless defended a woman's right as an equal in marriage. Other Protestant

The Disciplined Home
Proper table manners reflected discipline and morality in the godly household, an ideal of the religious reformers of the sixteenth century. The householder, the father-patriarch, leads his wife and children in prayer before a meal. The orderly behavior parallels the comfort (oven, smoked-glass windows, chandeliers, timbered ceiling, and cabinets) of a well-off patrician family. (Staatsbibliothek Bamberg, Germany.)

women spoke out even more decisively. Katharina Zell, wife of the Strasbourg reformer Matthew Zell, wrote hymns, fed the sick and imprisoned, and denounced the intolerance of the new Protestant clergy. Rebuking one for his persecution of dissenters, she wrote, "You young fellows tread on the graves of the first fathers of this church in Strasbourg and punish all who disagree with you, but faith cannot be forced." She also insisted that women should have a voice in religious affairs.

Catholic Renewal and Missionary Zeal

Reacting to the waves of Protestant challenge, the Catholic church mobilized for defense in a movement that is called by some the Counter-Reformation and by others Catholic Reform. Pope Paul III (r. 1534–1549) convened a general church council to codify church doctrine, and he personally approved the founding of new religious orders to undertake aggressive missionary efforts. The Council of Trent (Map 12.1, page 441) met intermittently between 1545 and 1563, when it concluded its work. Its decisions shaped the essential character of Catholicism until the 1960s. Emphatically rejecting the major Protestant positions, the council reasserted the supremacy of clerical authority over the laity and reaffirmed that the bread and wine of communion actually become Christ's body and blood. It required that all weddings take place in churches and be registered by the parish clergy and explicitly refused to allow divorce. All hopes of reconciliation between Protestants and Catholics faded.

Most important of the new Catholic religious orders was the Society of Jesus. Its founder was Ignatius of Loyola (1491–1556), a Spanish nobleman and charismatic former military officer, who abandoned his quest for military glory in favor of serving the church. Ignatius soon attracted other young men to his side, and in 1540 the pope recognized his small band of Jesuits. Over time, the Jesuits founded hundreds of colleges in Spain, Portugal, France, Italy, the German states, Hungary, Bohemia, and Poland. Among their alumni would be princes, philosophers, lawyers, churchmen, and officials—the elite of Catholic Europe. In 1544 the pope recognized a new order for women, the Company of Saint Ursula, known as the Ursulines, who devoted themselves to the education of girls. Together these new religious orders restored the confidence of the faithful in the dedication and power of the Catholic church.

Catholic missionaries set sail throughout the globe to bring Roman Catholicism to Africans, Asians, and native Americans. They saw their effort as proof of the truth of Roman Catholicism and the success of their missions as a sign of divine favor, both particularly important in the face of Protestant challenge. To ensure rapid Christianization, European missionaries focused initially on winning over local elites. A number of young African nobles went to Portugal to be trained in theology. Catholic missionaries preached the Gospel to Confucian scholar-officials in China and to the samurai (the warrior aristocracy) in Japan. Measured in numbers alone, the Catholic missionary enterprise seemed highly successful: by the second half of the sixteenth century, vast multitudes of native Americans had become

The Portuguese in Japan
In this sixteenth-century Japanese black-lacquer screen painting of Portuguese missionaries, the Jesuits are dressed in black and the Franciscans in brown. At the lower left corner is a Portuguese nobleman depicted with exaggerated "Western" features. The Japanese considered themselves lighter in skin color than the Portuguese, whom they classified as "barbarians." In turn, the Portuguese classified Japanese (and Chinese) as "whites." The perception of ethnic differences in the sixteenth century depended less on skin color than on clothing, eating habits, and other cultural signals. Color classifications were unstable and changed over time. By the late seventeenth century, Europeans no longer regarded Asians as "white." (The Granger Collection, NY.)

Christians at least in name, and thirty years after Francis Xavier's 1549 landing in Japan, the Jesuits could claim over 100,000 Japanese converts.

After an initial period of relatively little racial discrimination, the Catholic church in the Americas and Africa adopted strict rules based on color. For example, the first Mexican Ecclesiastical Provincial Council in 1555 declared that holy orders were not to be conferred on Indians, mestizos (people of mixed European-Indian parentage), or mulattoes (people of mixed European-African heritage), groups deemed "inherently unworthy of the sacerdotal [priestly] office." Europeans reinforced their sense of racial superiority with their perception of the "treachery" that native Americans and Africans exhibited whenever they resisted domination. Frustrated in his efforts to convert Brazilian Indians, a Jesuit missionary wrote to his superior in Rome in 1563 that "for this kind of people it is better to be preaching with the sword and rod of iron." The Dominican Bartolomé de Las Casas (1474–1566) criticized the treatment of the Indians in Spanish America, yet even he argued that Africans should be imported in order to relieve the indigenous peoples, who were being worked to death.

> **REVIEW**   In what ways did Luther, Zwingli, and Calvin challenge the Roman Catholic church?

State Power and Religious Conflict, 1500–1618

Even as religious disputes heightened the potential for conflict within Europe, the European powers continued to fight their traditional dynastic wars and still faced the military threat posed by the Muslim Ottoman Turks in the east. But these wars did not long deflect attention from increasing divisions within European countries. Rulers viewed religious divisions as a dangerous challenge to the unity of their realms and the stability of their regimes; a subject could very well swear greater allegiance to God than to his lord. Yet rulers often proved powerless to stem the rising tide of religious strife. Lutheranism flourished in the northern German states and Scandinavia; Calvinism spread from its headquarters in the Swiss city of Geneva all the way to England and Poland-Lithuania. The rapid expansion of Lutheranism and Calvinism created deadly political conflicts between Protestants and Catholics.

Wars among the Habsburgs, Valois, and Ottomans

While the Reformation was taking hold in the German states, the Catholic powers of Spain and France fought each other for the domination of Europe (Map 12.2). French claims over Italian territories sparked conflict in 1494, but the ensuing Italian Wars soon involved most Christian monarchs and the Muslim Ottoman sultan as well. Despite some spectacular and bloody turns of fortune, no one power ultimately emerged victorious. In 1525, the troops of the Habsburg emperor Charles V crushed the French army at Pavia, Italy, and captured the French king Francis I (r. 1515–1547). Charles treated Francis as an honored guest but held him in Spain until he agreed to renounce his claims to Italy. Furious at this humiliation, Francis repudiated the agreement the moment he returned to France, reigniting the conflict. In 1527, Charles's troops invaded and then pillaged Rome to punish the pope for allying with the French. Among the imperial troops were German Protestant mercenaries, who pillaged Catholic churches. The sack of Rome shocked the Catholic church hierarchy and helped turn it toward renewal.

Charles could not crush the French in one swift blow because he also had to counter the Muslim Ottomans in Hungary and along the Mediterranean coast. The Ottoman Empire reached its height of power under Sultan Suleiman I ("the

Map 12.2 The Habsburg-Valois-Ottoman Wars, 1494–1559
As the dominant European power, the Habsburg dynasty fought on two fronts: a religious war against the Islamic Ottoman Empire and a political war against the French Valois, who challenged Habsburg hegemony. The Mediterranean, the Balkans, and the Low Countries all became theaters of war.

Magnificent"; r. 1520–1566). In 1526, a Turkish force destroyed the Hungarian army at Mohács. Three years later, the Ottoman army laid siege to Vienna; though unsuccessful, the siege shocked Christian Europe. In 1535, Charles V tried to capture Tunis, the lair of North African pirates under Ottoman rule. Desperate to overcome Charles's superior forces in Europe, Francis I eagerly forged an alliance with the Turkish sultan. The Turkish fleet besieged Nice, on the southern coast of France, to help the French wrest it from imperial occupiers. Francis even ordered all inhabitants of nearby Toulon to vacate their town so that he could turn it into a Muslim colony for eight months, complete with a mosque and slave market. The Franco-Turkish alliance, however brief, showed that the age-old idea of a Christian crusade against Islam had to make way for a new political strategy that considered religion as but one factor in power politics.

In 1559, the French king finally acknowledged defeat and signed the peace treaty of Cateau-Cambrésis. By then, years of conflict had drained the treasuries of all the monarchs. Fueled by warfare, armies grew in size, firepower became ever more deadly, and costs soared. For example, heavier artillery pieces meant that the rectangular walls of medieval cities had to be transformed into fortresses with

The Siege of Vienna, 1529
This illustration from an Ottoman manuscript of 1588 depicts the Turkish siege of Vienna (the siege guns can be seen in the center of the picture). Sultan Suleiman I ("the Magnificent") led an army of more than 100,000 men against Vienna, the capital of the Austrian Habsburg lands. Several attacks on the city failed, and the Ottomans withdrew in October 1529. They maintained control over Hungary, but the logistics of moving so many men and horses kept them from advancing any farther west into Europe. (The Art Archive/Topkapi Museum, Istanbul/Dagli Orti.)

jutting forts and gun emplacements. Charles V boasted the largest army in Europe—but he could not make ends meet with the proceeds from taxation, the sale of offices, and even outright confiscation. Charles and his French opponents both relied on private bankers for funds to make ends meet. Bankers, like the Fugger family of the southern German imperial city of Augsburg, charged as much as 14 to 18 percent interest on their loans and amassed huge fortunes.

French Wars of Religion

During the 1540s and 1550s, one-third of the French nobles converted to Calvinism, usually influenced by noblewomen who protected pastors, provided money and advice, and helped found schools and establish relief for the poor. As many as twelve hundred Reformed churches were established, especially in southern and western France. The Catholic Valois monarchy tried to maintain a balance of power between Catholics and Calvinists. Francis I and his successor, Henry II (r. 1547–1559), both succeeded to a degree. But when Henry was accidentally killed during a jousting tournament, the weakened monarchy could no longer hold together the fragile realm. Henry was succeeded first by his fifteen-year-old son, Francis II, who died in 1560, and then by his ten-year-old son, Charles IX (r. 1560–1574).

Catherine de Médicis (1519–1589), the Italian wife of Henry II, acted as regent for her young son. She first urged limited toleration for the Calvinists—called **Huguenots** in

France—in an attempt to maintain political stability, but she could not prevent the eruption of civil war between Catholics and Huguenots in 1562. Although a Catholic herself,

Protestant Churches in France, 1562

Catherine desperately tried to play the Catholic and Huguenot factions off against each other so that neither would dominate. To this end, she arranged the marriage of her daughter Marguerite to Henry of Navarre, head of the Bourbon family, which had converted to Calvinism. Just four days after the wedding in August 1572, assassins tried but failed to kill one of the Huguenot nobles allied with the Bourbons, Gaspard de Coligny. Panicked at the thought of Huguenot revenge and perhaps herself implicated in the botched plot, Catherine convinced her son to order the killing of leading Huguenots. On St. Bartholomew's Day, August 24, a bloodbath began, fueled by years of growing animosity between Catholics and Protestants. In three days, Catholic mobs murdered three thousand Huguenots in Paris. Thousands more died in the provinces over the next six weeks. The pope joyfully ordered the church bells rung throughout Catholic Europe; Spain's Philip II wrote Catherine that it was "the best and most cheerful news which at present could come to me." Protestants and Catholics alike now saw the conflict as an international struggle for survival that required aid to coreligionists in other countries. In this way, the French Wars of Religion paved the way for wider international conflicts over religion in the future.

The religious division in France grew even more dangerous when Charles IX died and his brother Henry III (r. 1574–1589) became king. Like his brothers before him, Henry III failed to produce an heir. Next in line to succeed the throne was none other than the Calvinist Bourbon leader Henry of Navarre. Because Henry III saw an even greater threat to his authority in a newly formed Catholic League, which had requested Spain's help in rooting out Protestantism in France, he took action against the league. In 1588, he summoned two prominent league leaders to a meeting and had his men kill them. A few months later a fanatical monk stabbed Henry III to death, and Henry of Navarre became Henry IV (r. 1589–1610), despite Spain's attempt to block his way with military intervention.

The new king soon concluded that to establish control over the war-weary country, he had to place the interests of the French state ahead of his Protestant faith. In 1593, Henry IV publicly embraced Catholicism, reputedly explaining his conversion with the phrase "Paris is worth a Mass." In 1598, he made peace with Spain and issued the Edict of Nantes, in which he granted the Huguenots a large measure of religious toleration. The approximately 1.25 million Huguenots became a legally protected minority within an officially Catholic kingdom of some 20 million people. Protestants were free to worship in specified towns and were allowed their own troops, fortresses, and even courts. Few believed in religious toleration, but Henry IV followed the advice of those neutral Catholics and Calvinists called *politiques* who urged him to give priority to the development of a durable state. Although their opponents hated them for their compromising spirit, the politiques believed that religious disputes could be resolved only in the peace provided by strong government.

The Edict of Nantes ended the French Wars of Religion, but Henry still needed to reestablish monarchical authority. He used court festivities and royal processions to rally subjects around him, and he developed a new class of royal officials to counterbalance the fractious nobility. In exchange for an annual payment, officials who had purchased their offices could pass them on to heirs or sell them to someone else. By buying offices that eventually ennobled their holders, rich middle-class merchants and lawyers could become part of a new social elite known as the nobility of the robe (named after the robes that magistrates wore, much like those judges wear today). New income raised by the increased sale of offices reduced the state debt and helped Henry build the base for a strong monarchy. His efforts did not, however, prevent his own assassination in 1610 after nineteen unsuccessful attempts.

Challenges to Habsburg Power

Charles V proved more successful at fending off the Turks and subduing the French than he did at resolving growing religious conflicts inside his empire. After the Imperial Diet of Regensburg in 1541 failed to patch up the theological differences between Protestants and Catholics, Charles secured papal support for a war against the Schmalkaldic League, a powerful alliance of Lutheran princes and cities. Charles's army occupied the German imperial cities in the south, restoring Catholic patricians and suppressing the Reformation wherever they triumphed. In 1547, Charles defeated the Schmalkaldic League armies at Mühlberg and captured the leading Lutheran princes. Jubilant, he proclaimed the Interim, which restored Catholics' right to worship in Protestant lands while still permitting Lutherans to celebrate their own services. Riots broke out in many cities as resistance to the Interim spread. Charles's victory proved short-lived, for after one of his former allies, Duke Maurice of Saxony, joined the other side, the princes revived the war in 1552 and chased a surprised, unprepared, and practically bankrupt emperor back to Italy.

Forced to negotiate, Charles V agreed to the Peace of Augsburg in 1555. The settlement recognized the Lutheran church in the empire; accepted the secularization of church lands but kept the remaining ecclesiastical territories (mainly the bishoprics) for Catholics; and, most important, established the principle that all princes, whether Catholic or Lutheran, enjoyed the sole right to determine the religion of their lands and subjects. Significantly, the agreement excluded Calvinist, Anabaptist, and other dissenting groups from the settlement. The Peace of Augsburg preserved a fragile peace in central Europe until 1618, but the exclusion of Calvinists planted the seeds of future conflict.

Exhausted by constant war and depressed by the disunity in Christian Europe, Charles V resigned his many thrones in 1555 and 1556, leaving his Netherlandish-Burgundian and Spanish dominions to his son, Philip II, and his Austrian lands to his brother, Ferdinand, who was also elected Holy Roman Emperor to succeed Charles. Retiring to a monastery in southern Spain, the once powerful Christian monarch spent his last years quietly seeking salvation. Although Philip II of Spain (r. 1556–1598) ruled over fewer territories than his father, his inheritance still left him the most powerful ruler in Europe (Map 12.3). In addition to the western Habsburg lands in

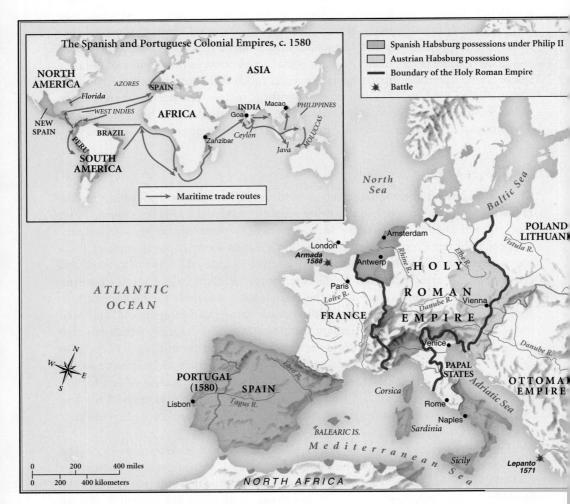

Map 12.3 The Empire of Philip II, r. 1556–1598
The Spanish king Philip II drew revenues from a truly worldwide empire. In 1580, he was the richest European ruler, but the demands of governing such far-flung territories eventually drained many of his resources. **For more help analyzing this map, see the map activity for this chapter in the Online Study Guide at** bedfordstmartins.com/huntconcise.

Spain and the Netherlands, he had inherited all the Spanish colonies recently settled in the New World of the Americas. In 1580, when the king of Portugal died without a direct heir, Philip took over this neighboring realm with its rich empire in Africa, India, and the Americas. Gold and silver funneled from the colonies supported his campaigns against the Ottoman Turks and French and English Protestants.

A deeply devout Catholic, Philip II came to the Spanish throne at age twenty-eight, determined to restore Catholic unity in Europe and lead the Christian defense against the Muslims. In 1571, Philip joined with Venice and the papacy to defeat the Turks in a great sea battle off the Greek coast at Lepanto. But Philip could not rest on his laurels. Between 1568 and 1570, the Moriscos—Muslim converts to Christianity who remained secretly faithful to Islam—had revolted in the south of Spain, killing ninety priests and fifteen hundred Christians. The victory at Lepanto destroyed any prospect that the Turks might come to their aid, yet Philip

nonetheless forced fifty thousand Moriscos to leave their villages and resettle in other regions. In 1609, his successor, Philip III, ordered their expulsion, and by 1614 some 300,000 Moriscos had been forced to relocate to North Africa.

The Calvinists of the Netherlands were less easily intimidated than the Moriscos: they were far from Spain and accustomed to being left alone. In 1566, Calvinists in the Netherlands attacked Catholic churches, smashing stained-glass windows and statues of the Virgin

Philip II of Spain
The king of Spain is shown here (kneeling in black) with his allies at the battle of Lepanto, the doge of Venice on his left and Pope Pius V on his right. El Greco painted this canvas, sometimes called *The Dream of Philip II*, in 1578 or 1579. The painting is typically mannerist in the way it crowds figures into every available space, uses larger-than-life or elongated bodies, and creates new and often bizarre visual effects. What can we conclude about Philip II's character from the way he is depicted here? (© National Gallery, London/Art Resource, NY.)

Mary. Philip sent an army, which executed more than eleven hundred people during the next six years. When resistance revived, the Spanish responded with more force, culminating in November 1576, when Philip's armies sacked Antwerp, then Europe's wealthiest commercial city. In eleven days of horror known as the Spanish Fury, the Spanish soldiers slaughtered seven thousand people. Shocked into response, the ten Catholic southern provinces joined with the seven Protestant northern provinces and expelled the Spaniards. In 1579, however, the Catholic southern provinces returned to the Spanish fold. Despite the assassination in 1584 of William of Orange, the leader of the anti-Spanish forces, Spanish troops never regained control in the north.

Spain would not formally recognize Dutch independence until 1648, but by the end of the sixteenth century the Dutch Republic was a self-governing state sheltering a variety of religious groups. The princes of Orange (whose name came from family lands near the city of Orange, in southern France) resembled a ruling family in the Dutch Republic, but their powers paled next to those of local interests. Urban merchant and professional families known as regents controlled the towns and provinces. Each province (Holland was the most populous of the seven provinces) governed itself and sent delegates to the one common institution, the States General. Well situated for maritime commerce, the Dutch Republic developed a thriving economy based on shipping and shipbuilding. By 1670, the Dutch commercial fleet was larger than the English, French, Spanish, Portuguese, and Austrian fleets combined.

The Netherlands during the Revolt, c. 1580

The Dutch Republic tolerated more religious diversity than the other European states. One-third of the Dutch population remained Catholic, and the secular authorities allowed Catholics to worship as they chose in private. Because Protestant sects could generally count on toleration from local regents, they remained peaceful. The Dutch Republic also had a relatively large Jewish population because many Jews had settled there after being driven out of Spain and Portugal. From 1597, Jews could worship openly in their synagogues. This openness to various religions helped make the Dutch Republic one of Europe's chief intellectual and scientific centers in the seventeenth and eighteenth centuries.

The brief marriage of Philip II to Mary Tudor (Mary I of England) did not produce an heir, but it gave him reason to resist England's return to Protestantism. When Mary died, Elizabeth rejected Philip's proposal of marriage and eventually provided funds and troops to the Dutch rebels. Philip bided his time as long as Elizabeth remained unmarried and her Catholic cousin Mary Stuart—better known as Mary, Queen of Scots—stood next in line to inherit the English throne. In 1567,

Scottish Calvinists forced Mary to abdicate the throne of Scotland in favor of her year-old son, James (eventually James I of England), who was then raised as a Protestant. The Scottish Calvinists feared Mary's connections to Catholic France; her mother was French and devoutly Catholic, and Mary had earlier been married to France's Francis II (who died in 1560). After her abdication, Mary spent nearly twenty years under house arrest in England, fomenting plots against Elizabeth. In 1587, when Mary's letter offering her succession rights to Philip was discovered, Elizabeth overcame her reluctance to execute a fellow monarch and ordered Mary's beheading.

In response, Pope Sixtus V decided to subsidize a Catholic crusade under Philip's leadership against the heretical queen. At the end of May 1588, Philip II sent his armada (Spanish for "fleet") of 130 ships from Lisbon toward the English Channel. The English scattered the Spanish Armada by sending blazing fireships into its midst. A great gale then forced the Spanish to flee around Scotland. By the time the Armada limped home in September, half the ships had been lost and thousands of sailors were dead or starving. Protestants throughout Europe rejoiced. A Spanish monk lamented, "Almost the whole of Spain went into mourning." When Philip II died in 1598, his great empire was beginning to lose its luster. The costs of fighting the French, the Dutch, and the English had mounted, and an overburdened peasantry could no longer pay the taxes required to meet rising expenses. In his novel *Don Quixote* (1605), the Spanish writer Miguel de Cervantes (who had himself been wounded at Lepanto and been held captive in Algiers, then served as a royal tax collector) captured the sadness of Spain's loss of grandeur. His hero, a minor nobleman, reads so many romances and books of chivalry that he loses his wits and wanders the countryside hoping to re-create the heroic deeds of times past.

REVIEW   How did the power of states depend on unity in religion?

The Thirty Years' War and the Balance of Power, 1618–1648

In 1618, a new series of violent conflicts between Catholics and Protestants erupted in the Holy Roman Empire. The final and most deadly of the wars of religion, the Thirty Years' War eventually drew in most of the European states. By the end of the war in 1648, many central European lands lay in ruins and many rulers were bankrupt. Reformation and Counter-Reformation had shattered the Christian humanist dream of peace and unity. The Thirty Years' War brought the preceding religious conflicts to a head and by its very violence effectively removed religion from future European disputes. Although religion still divided people *within* various states, after 1648 religion no longer provided the rationale for wars *between* European states. Out of the carnage would emerge centralized and powerful states that made increasing demands on ordinary people.

Origins and Course of the War

The fighting that devastated central Europe had its origins in religious, political, and ethnic divisions within the Holy Roman Empire. The Austrian Habsburg emperor and four of the seven electors who chose him were Catholic; the other three electors were Protestant. The Peace of Augsburg of 1555 was supposed to maintain the balance between Catholics and Lutherans, but it had no mechanism for resolving conflicts. Tensions rose as the Jesuits won many Lutheran cities back to Catholicism and as Calvinism, unrecognized under the agreement, made inroads into Lutheran areas. By 1613, two of the three Protestant electors had become Calvinists. When the Catholic Habsburg heir Archduke Ferdinand was crowned king of Bohemia in 1617, he began to curtail the religious freedom previously granted to Protestants. Protestants wanted to build new churches; Ferdinand wanted to stop them. Tensions boiled over when two Catholic deputy governors tried to dissolve the meetings of Protestants.

On May 23, 1618, a crowd of angry Protestants surged up the stairs of the royal castle in Prague, trapped the two Catholic deputies, dragged them screaming for mercy to the windows, and hurled them to the pavement below. Because they landed in a dung heap, the deputies survived. Although no one died, this "defenestration" (from the French for "window," *la fenêtre*) of Prague touched off a new cycle of conflict. The Czechs, the largest ethnic group in Bohemia, established a Protestant assembly to spearhead resistance. A year later, when Ferdinand was elected emperor (as Ferdinand II, r. 1619–1637), the rebellious Bohemians deposed him and chose in his place the young Calvinist Frederick V of the Palatinate (r. 1616–1623). A quick series of clashes ended in 1620 when the imperial armies defeated the

Israel ex. Cum Privil Reg.

The Horrors of the Thirty Years' War

The French artist Jacques Callot produced this etching of the Thirty Years' War as part of a series called The Miseries and Misfortunes of War (1633). It shows the rape, torture, and pillaging inflicted by soldiers on noncombatants they found in their path. (The Granger Collection, NY.)

outmanned Czechs at the battle of White Mountain, near Prague (Map 12.4). Like the martyrdom of the religious reformer Jan Hus in 1415, White Mountain became an enduring symbol of the Czechs' desire for self-determination. They would not gain their independence until 1918.

White Mountain did not end the war. Private mercenary armies (armies for hire) began to form during the fighting, and the emperor had virtually no control over them. In 1625, a Czech Protestant, Albrecht von Wallenstein (1583–1634), offered to raise an army for the Catholic emperor and soon had in his employ 125,000 soldiers, who occupied and plundered much of Protestant Germany with the emperor's approval. In response, the Lutheran king of Denmark, Christian IV (r. 1596–1648), invaded to protect the Protestants and to extend his own influence.

Map 12.4 The Thirty Years' War and the Peace of Westphalia, 1648
The Thirty Years' War involved many of the major continental European powers. The arrows marking invasion routes show that most of the fighting took place in central Europe, in the lands of the Holy Roman Empire. The German states and Bohemia sustained the greatest damage during the fighting. None of the combatants emerged unscathed because even ultimate winners such as Sweden and France depleted their resources of men and money.

Wallenstein's forces defeated him. Emboldened by his general's victories, Ferdinand issued the Edict of Restitution in 1629, which outlawed Calvinism in the empire and reclaimed Catholic church properties confiscated by the Lutherans.

With Protestant interests in serious jeopardy, Gustavus Adolphus (r. 1611–1632) of Sweden marched into Germany in 1630. A Lutheran by religion, he also hoped to gain control over trade in northern Europe, where he had already ejected the Poles from present-day Latvia and Estonia. Poland and Lithuania had joined in a commonwealth (common state) in 1569, and many Polish and Lithuanian nobles converted to Lutheranism or Calvinism, but this did not ensure common cause with Sweden. Gustavus's highly trained army of some 100,000 soldiers made Sweden, with a population of only one million, the supreme power of northern Europe, even more powerful than Russia, which had barely recovered from the "Time of Troubles" that had followed on the rule of Tsar Ivan IV (r. 1533–1584). Known as "Ivan the Terrible" because of his rages, during one of which he killed his son and heir, Ivan had initiated Russian expansion eastward into Siberia, but his moves westward had run up against the Poles and the Swedes.

Although Gustavus had religious motives for intervening in German affairs, events soon showed that power politics trumped religious interests. The Catholic French government under the leadership of Louis XIII (r. 1610–1643) and his chief minister, Cardinal Richelieu (1585–1642), offered to subsidize Gustavus—and the Lutheran ruler accepted. The French hoped to counter Spanish involvement in the war and win influence and perhaps territory in the Holy Roman Empire. Gustavus defeated the imperial army and occupied the Catholic parts of southern Germany before he was killed at the battle of Lützen in 1632 (Map 12.4, page 459). Once again the tide turned, but this time it swept Wallenstein with it. Because Wallenstein was rumored to be negotiating with Protestant powers, Ferdinand dismissed his general and had his henchmen assassinate Wallenstein.

France openly joined the fray in 1635 by declaring war on Spain and soon after forged an alliance with the Calvinist Dutch to aid them in their struggle for independence from Spain. The two Catholic powers, France and Spain, pummeled each other. The Swedes kept up their pressure in Germany, the Dutch attacked the Spanish fleet, and a series of internal revolts shook the cash-strapped Spanish crown. In 1640, peasants in the rich northeastern province of Catalonia rebelled, overrunning Barcelona and killing the viceroy; the Catalans resented government confiscation of their crops and demands that they house and feed soldiers on their way to the French frontier. The Portuguese revolted in 1640 and proclaimed independence. In 1643, the Spanish suffered their first major defeat at French hands. Although the Spanish were forced to concede independence to Portugal (part of Spain only since 1580), they eventually suppressed the Catalan revolt.

France, too, faced exhaustion after years of rising taxes and recurrent revolts. In 1642, Richelieu died. Louis XIII followed him a few months later and was succeeded by his five-year-old son, Louis XIV. With the queen mother, Anne of Austria, serving as regent and depending on the Italian cardinal Mazarin for advice, French politics once again moved into a period of instability, rumor, and crisis. All sides were ready for peace.

Effects of Constant Fighting

When peace negotiations began in the 1640s, they did not come a moment too soon for the ordinary people of Europe. Some towns faced up to ten or eleven prolonged sieges during the fighting. In 1648, as negotiations dragged on, a Swedish army sacked the rich cultural capital of Prague, plundered its churches and castles, and effectively eliminated it as a center of culture and learning. Even worse suffering took place in the countryside. Peasants fled their villages, which were often burned down. War and intermittent outbreaks of plague cost some German towns one-third or more of their population. One-third of the inhabitants of Bohemia also perished.

Soldiers did not fare all that much better. Governments increasingly short of funds often failed to pay the troops, and frequent mutinies, looting, and pillaging resulted. Armies attracted all sorts of displaced people desperately in need of provisions. In the last year of the Thirty Years' War, the Imperial-Bavarian Army had 40,000 men entitled to draw rations—and more than 100,000 wives, prostitutes, servants, children, maids, and other camp followers forced to scrounge for their own food. The bureaucracies of early-seventeenth-century Europe simply could not cope with such demands: armies and their hangers-on had to live off the countryside.

Peace of Westphalia, 1648

The comprehensive settlement finally provided by the Peace of Westphalia—named after the German province where negotiations took place—would serve as a model for resolving conflict among warring European states. For the first time, a diplomatic congress addressed international disputes, and the signatories to the treaties guaranteed the resulting settlement. A method still in use, the congress was the first to bring all parties together, rather than two or three at a time.

France and Sweden gained most from the Peace of Westphalia. Although France and Spain continued fighting until 1659, France replaced Spain as the prevailing power on the European continent and acquired parts of Alsace, a region on its eastern border that would remain a source of conflict between French and German rulers well into the twentieth century. Baltic conflicts would not be resolved until 1661, but Sweden took several northern territories from the Holy Roman Empire (Map 12.4, page 459).

The Habsburgs lost the most. The Spanish Habsburgs recognized Dutch independence after eighty years of war. The Swiss Confederation and the German princes demanded autonomy from the Austrian Habsburg rulers of the Holy Roman Empire. Each German prince gained the right to establish Lutheranism, Catholicism, or Calvinism in his state, a right denied to Calvinist rulers by the earlier Peace of Augsburg. The independence ceded to German princes sustained political divisions that would remain until the nineteenth century. After losing considerable territory

.he west, the Austrian Habsburgs turned eastward to concentrate on restoring
.holicism to Bohemia and wresting Hungary from the Turks.

The Peace of Westphalia permanently settled the distributions of the main religions
.the Holy Roman Empire: Lutheranism would dominate in the north, Calvinism in
.e area of the Rhine River, and Catholicism in the south (see "Mapping the West,"
.age 477). In the future, warfare between European states would be undertaken for
.reasons of national security, commercial ambition, or dynastic pride rather than to
enforce religious uniformity. As the politiques of the late sixteenth century had hoped,
state interests now outweighed motivations of faith in political affairs.

Growth of State Authority

Warfare increased the reach of states: as the size of armies increased, governments
needed more men, more money, and more supervisory officials. Most armies in the
1550s had fewer than 50,000 men, but Gustavus Adolphus had 100,000 men under
arms in 1631. In France, the rate of land tax paid by peasants doubled in the eight years
after France joined the Thirty Years' War. In addition to raising taxes, governments
deliberately depreciated the value of the currency, which often resulted in inflation
and soaring prices; sold new offices; and manipulated the embryonic stock and bond
markets. When all else failed, they declared bankruptcy. The Spanish government, for
example, did so three times in the first half of the seventeenth century.

As the demand for soldiers and for the money to supply them rose, the number
of state employees multiplied, paperwork proliferated, and appointment to office
began to depend on university education in the law. Monarchs relied on advisers who
began to take on the role of modern prime ministers. As the French king Louis XIII's
chief minister, Richelieu arranged support for the Lutheran Gustavus even though
Richelieu was a cardinal of the Catholic church. His priority was **raison d'état** (reason of state)—that is, the state's interest above all else. Richelieu silenced Protestants
within France because they had become too independent, and he crushed noble and
popular resistance to Louis's policies. He set up intendants—delegates from the king's
council dispatched to the provinces—to oversee police, army, and financial affairs.
Richelieu and his intendants still had to contend with the thousands of officials who
had bought their offices and therefore owned them as personal property.

To justify the growth of state authority and the expansion of government
bureaucracies, rulers carefully cultivated their royal images. James I of England
explicitly argued that he ruled by divine right and was accountable only to God:
"Kings are not only God's lieutenant on earth, but even by God himself they are
called gods." Words rarely sufficed to make the point, however, and rulers used
displays at court to overawe their subjects. Already in the 1530s, the French court of
Francis I had numbered sixteen hundred people, including officials, guards, cooks,
physicians, librarians, musicians, dwarfs, and animal trainers. When the court
changed residence, which it did frequently, no fewer than eighteen thousand
horses were required to transport the people, furniture, and documents—not to

mention the dogs and falcons for the royal hunt. Hunting and mock battles honed the military skills of the male courtiers. Francis once staged a mock combat at court involving twelve hundred "warriors," and he led a party to lay siege to a model town during which several players were accidentally killed.

Just as soldiers had to learn new drills for combat, courtiers had to learn to follow precise rituals. In his influential treatise *The Courtier* (1528), the Italian diplomat Baldassare Castiglione (1478–1529) depicted the ideal courtier as a gentleman who spoke in a refined language and carried himself with nobility and dignity in the service of his prince and his lady. Spain's king Philip IV (r. 1621–1665) translated this notion of courtesy into detailed regulations that set the wages, duties, and ceremonial functions of every courtier. State funerals, public festivities, and court displays, like the acquisition of art and the building of sumptuous palaces, served to underline the power and glory of the ruler.

> **REVIEW**   Why did a war fought over religious disputes result in stronger states?

From Growth to Recession

The Protestant Reformation started in a period of economic growth, but by the time of the Thirty Years' War recession had set in. In the sixteenth century, despite religious and political turbulence, population grew, doubling in Spain and increasing 70 percent in England. The supply of precious metals swelled, too. Spanish gold imports from the American colonies peaked in the 1550s, silver in the 1590s (see "Taking Measure"). The flood of gold and silver fueled an astounding inflation in food prices in western Europe—400 percent in the sixteenth century. When recession

Taking Measure   The Rise and Fall of Silver Imports to Spain, 1550–1660
Gold and silver from the New World enabled the king of Spain to pursue aggressive policies in Europe and around the world. At what point did silver imports, shown here, reach their highest level? Was the fall in silver imports precipitous or gradual? What can we conclude about the resources available to the Spanish king?

struck after 1600, all the economic indicators slumped: silver imports declined; textile production collapsed; agricultural prices dropped. Overall, Europe's population may actually have declined, from 85 million in 1550 to 80 million in 1650.

Causes and Consequences of Economic Crisis

Historians have long disagreed about the causes of the early-seventeenth-century recession. Some cite the inability of agriculture to support a growing population by the end of the sixteenth century. Others blame the Thirty Years' War, the states' demands for more taxes, the irregularities in money supply resulting from rudimentary banking practices, or the waste caused by middle-class expenditures in the desire to emulate the nobility. To this list of causes, recent researchers have added climate change. Global cooling translated into advancing glaciers, falling temperatures, and great storms, like the one that blocked the escape of the Spanish Armada. Bad harvests, food shortages, and famine followed in short order.

Economic crisis dramatically altered the rural landscape. As prices began to stagnate and population growth slowed, farmers converted grain-growing land to pasture or vineyards. In some places, peasants abandoned their villages and left

The Life of the Poor
This mid-seventeenth-century painting by the Dutch artist Adriaen Pietersz van de Venne depicts the poor peasant weighed down by his wife and child. An empty food bowl signifies their hunger. In retrospect, this painting seems unfair to the wife: she is shown in clothes that are not nearly as tattered as her husband's and is portrayed as a burden rather than as a helpmate in hard times. In reality, many poor men abandoned their homes in search of work, leaving their wives behind to cope with hungry children and what remained of the family farm. (Allen Memorial Art Museum, Oberlin College, Mrs. F. F. Prentiss Fund, 1960.)

land to waste, as had happened during the plague epidemic of the late fourteenth century. The only country that emerged relatively unscathed from this downturn was the Dutch Republic, principally because it had long excelled in agricultural innovation. Inhabiting Europe's most densely populated area, the Dutch developed systems of field drainage, crop rotation, and animal husbandry that provided high yields of grain for both people and animals. After the Dutch, the English fared best; unlike the Spanish, the English never depended on New World gold and silver, and unlike most continental European countries, England escaped the direct impact of the Thirty Years' War.

When grain harvests fell short, peasants immediately suffered because outside of England and the Dutch Republic, grain had replaced more expensive meat as the essential staple of most Europeans' diets. Peasants lived on bread, soup with a little fat or oil, peas or lentils, garden vegetables in season, and only occasionally a piece of meat or fish. Usually the adverse years differed from place to place, but from 1594 to 1597 most of Europe suffered from shortages that triggered revolts from Ireland to Muscovy. To head off social disorder, the English government drew up a new Poor Law in 1597 that required each community to support its poor. Many other governments also increased relief efforts.

Most people, however, did not respond to their dismal circumstances by rebelling or mounting insurrections. They simply left their huts and hovels and took to the road in search of food and charity. Overwhelmed officials recorded pitiful tales of suffering. Women and children died while waiting in line for food at convents or churches. Husbands left their wives and families to search for better conditions in other parishes or even other countries. Those left behind might be reduced to eating chestnuts, roots, bark, and grass. In eastern France in 1637, a witness reported, "The roads were paved with people. . . . Finally it came to cannibalism." Eventually compassion gave way to fear as these hungry vagabonds, who sometimes banded together to beg for bread, became more aggressive, occasionally threatening to burn a barn if they were not given food.

Successive bad harvests led to malnutrition, which weakened people and made them more susceptible to such epidemic diseases as the plague, typhoid fever, typhus, dysentery, smallpox, and influenza. Disease did not spare the rich, although many epidemics hit the poor hardest. The plague was feared most: in one year it could kill up to half a town or village's population, and it struck with no discernible pattern. Nearly 5 percent of France's population died in the plague epidemic of 1628–1632.

Economic crisis heightened the contrast between prosperity and poverty. In England, the Dutch Republic, northern France, and northwestern Germany, the peasantry was disappearing: improvements gave some peasants the means to become farmers who rented substantial holdings, produced for the market, and in good times enjoyed relative comfort and higher status. Those who could not afford to plant new crops such as buckwheat or to use techniques that ensured higher yields became simple laborers with little or no land of their own. One-half to four-fifths of the peasants in Europe did not have enough land to support a family.

They descended deeper into debt during difficult times and often lost their land to wealthier farmers or to city officials intent on developing rural estates.

Families reacted almost immediately to economic crisis. During bad harvests, they postponed marriages and had fewer children. When hard times passed, more people married and had more children. But even in the best of times, one-fifth to one-quarter of all children died in their first year, and half died before age twenty. Ten percent of women died in childbirth, and even in the richest homes childbirth often occasioned an atmosphere of panic. It might be assumed that families would have more children to compensate for high death rates, but from around 1600 to 1800, families in all ranks of society started to limit the number of children. Because methods of contraception were not widely known, they did this for the most part by marrying later; the average age at marriage during the seventeenth century rose from the early twenties to the late twenties. The average family had about four children. Poorer families seem to have had fewer children, wealthier ones more. Peasant couples, especially in eastern and southeastern Europe, had more children than urban couples because cultivation still required intensive manual labor.

The consequences of late marriage were profound. Young men and women were expected to put off marriage (and sexual intercourse) until their mid- to late twenties—if they were among the lucky 50 percent who lived that long and not among the 10 percent who never married. Because both the Reformation and the Counter-Reformation stressed sexual fidelity and abstinence before marriage, the number of births out of wedlock was relatively small (2 to 5 percent of births); premarital intercourse was generally tolerated only after a couple had announced their engagement.

The Economic Balance of Power

Just as the recession produced winners and losers among ordinary people, it also created winners and losers among the competing states of Europe. The seventeenth-century downturn ended the dominance of Mediterranean economies, which had endured since the time of the Greeks and Romans, and ushered in the new powers of northwestern Europe with their growing Atlantic economies. With expanding populations and geographical positions that promoted Atlantic trade, England and the Dutch Republic vied with France to become the leading mercantile powers. Northern Italian industries were eclipsed; Spanish commerce with the New World dropped. Amsterdam replaced Seville, Venice, Genoa, and Antwerp as the center of European trade and commerce. The plague also had differing effects. Whereas central Europe and the Mediterranean countries took generations to recover from its ravages, northwestern Europe quickly replaced its lost population, no doubt because this area's people had suffered less from the effects of the Thirty Years' War and from the malnutrition related to the economic crisis.

All but the remnants of serfdom had disappeared in western Europe, but in eastern Europe nobles reinforced their dominance over peasants, and the burden of serfdom increased. The price rise of the sixteenth century had prompted Polish and eastern German nobles to expand their holdings and step up their production of grain for western markets. Although noble landlords lost income in the economic downturn of the first half of the seventeenth century, their peasants gained nothing. Those who were already dependent became serfs—completely tied to the land. In Muscovy, the complete enserfment of the peasantry would eventually be recognized in the Code of Laws in 1649. Although enserfment produced short-term profits for landlords, in the long run it retarded economic development in eastern Europe and kept most of the population in a stranglehold of illiteracy and hardship.

Competition for colonies overseas intensified because many European states, including Sweden and Denmark, hoped it would tip the balance of power in their favor. According to the doctrine of mercantilism, governments should sponsor policies to increase national wealth and make sure new sources of wealth did not fall into the hands of their competitors. To this end, rulers chartered private joint-stock companies to enrich investors by importing fish, furs, tobacco, and precious metals, if they could be found, and to develop new markets for European products. Because Spain and Portugal had divided among themselves the rich spoils of South America, other prospective colonizers had to carve niches in seemingly less hospitable places, especially North America and the Caribbean. Eventually the English, French, and Dutch would dominate commerce with these colonies (Map 14.1, page 524).

What began as a competition for national wealth between trading companies soon evolved, sometimes by accident, into permanent colonies with whole new communities. Originally, the warm climate of Virginia made it an attractive destination for the Pilgrims, a small English sect that, unlike the Puritans, attempted to separate from the Church of England. But the *Mayflower*, which sailed for Virginia with Pilgrim emigrants, landed far to the north in Massachusetts, where in 1620 the settlers founded New Plymouth Colony. As the religious situation for English Puritans worsened, wealthier people became willing to emigrate, and in 1629 a prominent group of Puritans incorporated themselves as the Massachusetts Bay Company. They founded a virtually self-governing colony headquartered in Boston.

Colonization gradually spread. Migrating settlers, including dissident Puritans, soon founded new settlements in Connecticut and Rhode Island. Catholic refugees from England established a much smaller colony in Maryland. By the 1640s, the English North American colonies had more than fifty thousand people—not including the Indians, whose numbers had been decimated by epidemics and wars—and the foundations of representative government in locally chosen colonial assemblies.

By contrast, French Canada had only about three thousand European inhabitants by 1640. Because the French government refused to let Protestants emigrate from France and establish a foothold in the New World, it denied itself a ready population for the settling of permanent colonies abroad. Both England and France turned their attention to the Caribbean in the 1620s and 1630s when they occupied the islands of the West Indies after driving off the native Caribs. These islands would prove ideal for a plantation economy of tobacco and sugarcane.

REVIEW What were the consequences of economic recession in the early 1600s?

A Clash of Worldviews

The countries that moved ahead economically in this period—England, the Dutch Republic, and to some extent France—turned out to be the most receptive to new secular worldviews. Although secularization did not entail a loss of religious faith, it did prompt a search for nonreligious explanations for political authority and natural phenomena. During the late sixteenth and early seventeenth centuries, art, political theory, and science all began to break some of their bonds with religion. A "scientific revolution" was in the making. Yet traditional attitudes such as belief in magic and witchcraft did not disappear. People of all classes accepted supernatural explanations for natural phenomena, a view only gradually and partially undermined by new ideas.

The Arts in an Age of Religious Conflict

A new form of artistic expression—professional theater—developed to express secular values in this age of conflict over religious beliefs. In previous centuries, traveling companies made their living by playing at major religious festivals. In London, Seville, and Madrid, the first professional acting companies performed before paying audiences in the 1570s. A huge outpouring of playwriting followed. The Spanish playwright Lope de Vega (1562–1635) alone wrote more than fifteen hundred plays. Between 1580 and 1640, three hundred English playwrights produced works for a hundred different acting companies. Theaters did a banner business despite Puritan opposition in England and Catholic objections in Spain. Shopkeepers, apprentices, lawyers, and court nobles crowded into open-air theaters to see everything from bawdy farces to profound tragedies.

The most enduring and influential playwright of the time was the Englishman William Shakespeare (1564–1616), son of a glovemaker, who wrote three dozen plays and acted in one of the chief troupes. Shakespeare never referred to religious disputes in his plays and did not set the action in contemporary England. Yet his works clearly reflected the political concerns of his age: the nature of power and the crisis of authority. Three of his greatest tragedies—*Hamlet* (1601), *King Lear* (1605), and *Macbeth* (1606)—show the uncertainty and even chaos that result when power is misappropriated or misused. In each play, family relationships are linked to questions about the legitimacy of government, just as they were for Elizabeth I herself. Hamlet's mother marries the man who murdered his royal father and usurped the crown; Macbeth's wife persuades him to murder the king and seize the throne. Like many real-life people, Shakespeare's tragic characters found little peace in the turmoil of their times.

Although many rulers commissioned paintings on secular subjects for their own uses, religion still played an important role in painting, especially in Catholic Europe. The popes competed with secular rulers to hire the most talented painters and sculptors. Pope Julius II, for example, engaged the Florentine Michelangelo Buonarroti (1475–1564) to paint the walls and ceiling of the Sistine Chapel and to prepare a tomb and sculpture for himself. Michelangelo's talents served to glorify a papacy under siege, just as other artists burnished the images of secular rulers.

In the late sixteenth century, the artistic style known as **mannerism** departed abruptly from the Renaissance perspective of painters like Michelangelo. An almost theatrical style, mannerism allowed painters to distort perspective to convey a message or emphasize a theme. The most famous mannerist painter, El Greco, created new and often strange visual effects. The religious intensity of his pictures shows that faith still motivated many artists, as it did much political conflict.

The most important new style was the **baroque**, which featured exaggerated lighting, intense emotions, release from restraint, and even a kind of artistic sensationalism. *Baroque* was not used as a label by people living at the time; in the eighteenth century, art critics coined the word to mean shockingly bizarre, confused, and extravagant, and until the late nineteenth century, art historians and collectors largely disdained the baroque style. Closely tied to the Counter-Reformation, this style melodramatically reaffirmed the emotional depths of the Catholic faith and glorified both church and monarchy. The first great baroque painter was Peter Paul Rubens (1577–1640). Born in the Spanish Netherlands and trained in Italy, Rubens painted vivid, exuberant pictures on religious themes. The style spread from Rome to other Italian states and then into central Europe, Spain, and the Spanish Netherlands. The Spanish built baroque churches in their American colonies as part of their massive conversion campaign. The great Dutch Protestant painters of the next generation, such as Rembrandt van Rijn (1606–1669),

sometimes used biblical subjects, but their pictures were more realistic and focused on everyday scenes. Many of them suggested the Protestant concern for an inner life and personal faith rather than the public expression of religiosity.

Differences in musical style also reflected religious divisions. The new Protestant churches developed their own distinct music, which differentiated their worship from the Catholic Mass. Unlike

Baroque Painting

The baroque painter Peter Paul Rubens used monumental canvases like this one from the Antwerp cathedral to celebrate the Catholic religion. Known as *The Elevation of the Cross*, this painting from 1610 to 1611 shows one of the most important moments in the story of the crucifixion of Jesus. (© Onze Lieve Vrouwkerk, Antwerp Cathedral, Belgium/The Bridgeman Art Library.)

Catholic services, for which professional musicians sang in Latin, Protestant services invited the entire congregation to sing, thereby encouraging participation. Martin Luther, an accomplished lute player, composed many hymns in German, including "Ein' feste Burg" ("A Mighty Fortress"). Protestants sang hymns before going into battle, and Protestant martyrs sang before their executions.

A new secular musical form, the opera, grew up parallel to the baroque style in the visual arts. First influential in the Italian states, opera combined music, drama, dance, and scenery in a grand sensual display, often with themes chosen to please the ruler and the aristocracy. Like Shakespeare, opera composers often turned to familiar stories their audiences would recognize and readily follow. One of the most innovative composers of opera was Claudio Monteverdi (1567–1643), whose work contributed to the development of both opera and the orchestra. His earliest operatic production, *Orfeo* (1607), was the first to require an orchestra of about forty instruments and to include instrumental as well as vocal sections.

The Natural Laws of Politics

In reaction to the wars over religious beliefs, jurists and scholars not only began to defend the primacy of state interests over those of religious conformity but also insisted on secular explanations for politics. Machiavelli had pointed in this direction with his prescriptions for Renaissance princes in the early sixteenth century, but the intellectual movement gathered steam in the aftermath of the religious violence unleashed by the Reformation. Religious toleration could not take hold until government could be organized on some principle other than one king, one faith. The French *politiques* Michel de Montaigne and Jean Bodin and the Dutch jurist Hugo Grotius started the search for those principles.

Michel de Montaigne (1533–1592) was a French magistrate who resigned his office in the midst of the wars of religion to write about the need for tolerance and open-mindedness. Although himself a Catholic, Montaigne painted on the beams of his study the words "All that is certain is that nothing is certain." In short and pointed essays filled with personal reflection, he revived the ancient doctrine of skepticism, which held that total certainty is never attainable—a doctrine, like toleration of religious differences, that was repugnant to Protestants and Catholics alike, both of whom were certain that their religion was the right one. Montaigne also questioned the common European habit of calling newly discovered peoples in the New World barbarous and savage: "Everyone gives the title of barbarism to everything that is not in use in his own country."

The French Catholic lawyer Jean Bodin (1530–1596) sought systematic secular answers to the problem of disorder in *The Six Books of the Republic* (1576). Comparing the different forms of government throughout history, he identified three basic types of sovereignty: monarchy, aristocracy, and democracy. Only strong monarchical power offered hope for maintaining order, he insisted. Bodin rejected any doctrine of the right to resist tyrannical authority: "I denied that it was the function of a good man or of a good citizen to offer violence to his prince for any reason, however great a tyrant he might be" (and, it might be added, whatever his ideas on religion). Bodin's ideas helped lay the foundation for absolutism, the idea that the monarch should be the sole and uncontested source of power. Nonetheless, the very discussion of types of governments in the abstract implied that they might be subject to choice rather than simply being God given, as most rulers maintained.

During the Dutch revolt against Spain, the jurist Hugo Grotius (1583–1645) gave new meaning to the notion of "natural law"—laws of nature that give legitimacy to government and stand above the actions of any particular ruler or religious group. Grotius argued that natural law stood beyond the reach of either secular or divine authority; it would be valid even if God did not exist. By this account, natural law—not Scripture, religious authority, or tradition—should govern politics. Such ideas got Grotius into trouble with both Catholics and Protestants. When the Dutch Protestant government arrested him, his wife helped him escape from prison by hiding him in a chest of books. Grotius was one of the first to argue that international conventions should govern the treatment of prisoners of war and the making of peace treaties.

At the same time that Grotius expanded the principles of natural law, many jurists worked on codifying the huge amount of legislation and jurisprudence devoted to legal forms of torture. Most states and the courts of the Catholic church used torture when the crime was serious and the evidence seemed to point to a particular defendant but no definitive proof had been established. The judges ordered torture—hanging the accused by the hands with a rope thrown over a beam, pressing the legs in a leg screw, or just tying the hands very tightly—to extract a confession, which had to be given with a medical expert and notary present and had to be repeated without torture. Children, pregnant women, the elderly, aristocrats, kings, and even professors were exempt.

Grotius's conception of natural law directly challenged the use of torture. To be in accord with natural law, Grotius argued, governments had to defend natural rights, which he defined as life, body, freedom, and honor. Grotius's ideas would influence John Locke and the American revolutionaries of the eighteenth century. Although Grotius did not encourage rebellion in the name of natural law or rights, he did hope that someday all governments would adhere to these principles and stop killing their own and one another's subjects in the name of religion. Natural law and natural rights would play an important role in the founding of constitutional governments from the 1640s forward and in the establishment of various charters of human rights in our own time.

The Scientific Revolution

Although the Catholic and Protestant churches encouraged the study of science and many prominent scientists were themselves clerics, the search for a secular, scientific method of determining the laws of nature eventually challenged the traditional accounts of natural phenomena. A revolution in astronomy undermined the view of the second-century Greek astronomer Ptolemy, endorsed by the Catholic church, which held that the sun revolved around the earth. Remarkable advances took place in medicine, too, which laid the foundations for modern anatomy and pharmacology. Conflicts between the new science and religion followed almost immediately, but toward the end of the seventeenth century Isaac Newton provided a new mathematical explanation for movement both on earth and in the heavens. It made the **scientific method** the new standard of truth.

The traditional account derived from Ptolemy put the earth at the center of the cosmos. Above the earth were fixed the moon, the stars, and the planets in concentric crystalline spheres; beyond these fixed spheres dwelt God and the angels. The sun revolved around the earth, the heavens were perfect and unchanging, and the earth was "corrupted." In 1543, the Polish clergyman Nicolaus Copernicus (1473–1543) attacked the Ptolemaic account in his treatise *On the Revolution of the Celestial Spheres*. He argued that it was mathematically simpler to calculate orbits if the earth and planets revolved around the sun, a view known as **heliocentrism** (a sun-centered universe).

Copernicus's views began to attract widespread attention in the early seventeenth century, when astronomers systematically collected evidence that undermined the Ptolemaic view. A leader among them was the Danish astronomer Tycho Brahe (1546–1601), whose observations of a new star in 1572 and a comet in 1577 called into question the Aristotelian view that the universe was unchanging. Brahe still rejected heliocentrism, but the assistant he employed when he moved to Prague in 1599, Johannes Kepler (1571–1630), was converted to the Copernican view. Kepler continued Brahe's collection of planetary observations and used the evidence to develop his three laws of planetary motion, published between 1609 and 1619. Kepler's laws provided mathematical backing for heliocentrism and directly challenged the claim long held, even by Copernicus, that planetary motion was circular. Kepler's first law stated that the orbits of the planets were ellipses, with the sun always at one focus of the ellipse.

The Italian Galileo Galilei (1564–1642) provided more evidence to support the heliocentric view and also challenged the doctrine that the heavens were perfect and unchanging. In 1609, he developed an improved telescope and then observed the earth's moon, four satellites of Jupiter, the phases of Venus (a cycle of changing physical appearances like that of the moon), and sunspots. The moon, the planets, and the sun were no more perfect than the earth, he insisted, and the shadows he could see on the moon could only be the product of hills and valleys like those on earth. Because he recognized the utility of the new science for everyday projects and hoped to appeal to a lay audience of merchants and aristocrats, Galileo was the first scientist to publish his studies in the vernacular (Italian) rather than in Latin.

Since his discoveries challenged the Bible as well as the commonsensical view that the sun rose and set while the earth stood still, Galileo's work alarmed the Catholic church. In 1616, the church forbade Galileo to teach that the earth moved and in 1633 accused him of not obeying the earlier order. Forced to appear before the Inquisition, he agreed to publicly recant his assertion that the earth moved to save himself from torture and death. Afterward he lived under house arrest and could publish his work only in the Dutch Republic, which had become a haven for scientists and thinkers who challenged conventional ideas.

Startling breakthroughs took place in medicine, too. Until the mid-sixteenth century, medical knowledge in Europe had been based on the writings of the second-century Greek physician Galen, a contemporary of Ptolemy. In the same year that Copernicus challenged the traditions of astronomy (1543), the Flemish scientist Andreas Vesalius (1514–1564) did the same for anatomy. He published a new illustrated anatomical text, *On the Construction of the Human Body,* that revised Galen's work by drawing on public dissections in the medical faculties of European universities. Theophrastus Bombastus von Hohenheim, better known as Paracelsus (1493–1541), went even further than Vesalius. He burned Galen's text at the University of Basel, where he was a professor of medicine. Paracelsus experimented with new drugs, performed operations (at the time most academic physicians taught medical theory, not practice), and pursued his interests in magic, alchemy, and astrology. He helped establish the modern science of pharmacology.

The Englishman William Harvey (1578–1657) also used dissection to examine the circulation of blood within the body, demonstrating how the heart worked as a pump. The heart and its valves were "a piece of machinery," Harvey claimed. They obeyed mechanical laws just as the planets and earth revolved around the sun in a mechanical universe. Nature could be understood by experiment and rational deduction, not by following traditional authorities.

In the 1630s, the European intellectual elite began to accept the new scientific views. Ancient learning, the churches and their theologians, and even cherished popular beliefs seemed to be undermined by a new standard of truth—the scientific method, which was based on systematic experiments and rational deduction. Two men were chiefly responsible for spreading the prestige of the scientific method, the English politician Sir Francis Bacon (1561–1626) and the French mathematician and philosopher René Descartes (1596–1650). Respectively, they represented the two essential processes of the scientific method: (1) inductive reasoning through observation and experimental research and (2) deductive reasoning from self-evident principles.

In *The Advancement of Learning* (1605), Bacon attacked reliance on ancient writers and optimistically predicted that the scientific method would lead to social progress. The minds of the medieval scholars, he said, had been "shut up in the cells of a few authors (chiefly Aristotle, their dictator) as their persons were shut up in the cells of monasteries and colleges." Knowledge, in Bacon's view, must be empirically based—that is, gained by observation and experiment. Claiming that God had called the Catholic church "to account for their degenerate manners and ceremonies," Bacon looked to the Protestant English state, which he served as lord chancellor, for leadership on the road to scientific advancement.

Although Descartes agreed with Bacon's denunciation of traditional learning, he saw that the attack on tradition might only replace the dogmatism of the churches with the skepticism of Montaigne—that nothing at all was certain. A Catholic who served in the Thirty Years' War, Descartes insisted that human reason could not only unravel the secrets of nature but also prove the existence of God. He aimed to establish the new science on more secure philosophical foundations, those of mathematics and logic. Not coincidentally, Descartes invented analytic geometry. In his *Discourse on Method* (1637), he argued that mathematical and mechanical principles provided the key to understanding all of nature, including the actions of people and states. All prior assumptions must be repudiated in favor of one elementary principle: "I think, therefore I am." Everything else could—and should—be doubted, but even doubt showed the certain existence of someone thinking. Begin with the simple and go on to the complex, he asserted, and believe only those ideas that present themselves "clearly and distinctly." Although Descartes hoped to secure the authority of both church and state, his reliance on human reason alone irritated authorities, and his books were banned in many places. He moved to the Dutch Republic to work in peace. Scientific research, like economic growth, became centered in the northern, Protestant countries, where it was less constrained by church control.

Building on the work of Copernicus, Kepler, and Galileo, the English scientist Isaac Newton (1642–1727) finally synthesized astronomy and physics with his **law of universal gravitation**, further enhancing the prestige of the new science. Yet Newton also aimed to reconcile faith and science. By proving that the physical universe followed rational principles, Newton argued, scientists could prove the existence of God and so liberate humans from doubt and the fear of chaos. Newton applied mathematical principles to formulate three physical laws: (1) in the absence of external force, an object in motion continues in a straight line; (2) the rate of change in the motion of an object is a result of the forces acting on it; and (3) the action and reaction between two objects are equal and opposite. The basis of Newtonian physics thus required understanding mass, inertia, force, velocity, and acceleration—all key concepts in modern science.

Extending these principles to the entire universe in his masterwork, *Principia Mathematica* (1687), Newton united celestial and terrestrial mechanics—astronomy and physics—with his law of universal gravitation. This law holds that every body in the universe exerts over every other body an attractive force directly proportional to the product of their masses and inversely proportional to the square of the distance between them. The law of gravitation explained Kepler's elliptical planetary orbits just as it accounted for the motion of ordinary objects on earth. Once set in motion, the universe operated like clockwork, with no need for God's continuing intervention. Gravity, though a mysterious force, could be expressed mathematically. Not all scientists accepted Newton's theories immediately, but within a couple of generations his work was preeminent, partly because of experimental verification. His breakthroughs remained the basis for all physics until the advent of relativity theory and quantum mechanics in the early twentieth century.

Magic and Witchcraft

Despite the new emphasis on clear reasoning, observation, and independence from past authorities, science had not yet become entirely separate from magic. Paracelsus and Newton studied alchemy alongside other scientific pursuits; magic and science were still closely linked. In a world in which most people believed in astrology, magical healing, prophecy, and ghosts, it is hardly surprising that many of Europe's learned people also firmly believed in witchcraft, the exercise of magical powers gained by a pact with the devil. The same Jean Bodin who argued against religious fanaticism insisted on death for witches—and for those magistrates who would not prosecute them. In France alone, 345 books and pamphlets on witchcraft appeared between 1550 and 1650. Trials of witches peaked in Europe between 1560 and 1640, the very time of the celebrated breakthroughs of the new science. Montaigne was one of the few to speak out against executing accused witches. "It is taking one's conjectures rather seriously to roast someone alive for them," he wrote in 1580.

Belief in witches was not new in the sixteenth century. Witches had long been thought capable of almost anything: passing through walls, flying through the air, destroying crops, and causing personal catastrophes from miscarriage to demonic possession. What was new was the official persecution, justified by the notion that witches were agents of Satan whom the righteous must oppose. In a time of economic crisis, plague, warfare, and the clash of religious differences, witchcraft trials provided an outlet for social stress and anxiety, legitimated by state power. At the same time, the trials seem to have been part of the religious reform movement itself. Denunciation and persecution of witches coincided with the spread of reform, both Protestant and Catholic. The trials concentrated especially in the German lands of the Holy Roman Empire, the boiling cauldron of the Thirty Years' War.

The victims of the persecution were overwhelmingly female: women accounted for 80 percent of the accused witches in about 100,000 trials in Europe and North

Giving a Child to Satan
This woodcut from Francesco Maria Guazzo's *Compendium Maleficarum* of 1608 shows witches giving a child to the devil. Many believed that witches made a pact with the devil to carry out his evil deeds. (The Art Archive/Dagli Orti [A].)

America during the sixteenth and seventeenth centuries. About one-third were sentenced to death. Before 1400, when witchcraft trials were rare, nearly one-half of those accused had been men. Two Catholic clergymen compiled a guide for detecting witches, the *Malleus Maleficarum* (Hammer of Witches), which was published in 1486 and reissued countless times in the sixteenth and seventeenth centuries. Official descriptions of witchcraft oozed lurid details of sexual orgies, incest, homosexuality, and cannibalism, in which women acted as the devil's sexual slaves. Social factors help explain the prominence of women among the accused. The poorest and most socially marginal people in most communities were elderly spinsters and widows. Because they were thought likely to hanker after revenge on those more fortunate, they were singled out as witches.

Witchcraft trials declined when scientific thinking about causes and effects raised questions about the evidence used in court: how could judges or jurors be certain that someone was a witch? The tide turned everywhere at about the same time, as physicians, lawyers, judges, and even clergy came to suspect that accusations were based on popular superstition and peasant untrustworthiness. In 1682, a French royal decree treated witchcraft as fraud and imposture, meaning that the law did not recognize anyone as a witch. In 1693, the jurors who had convicted twenty witches in Salem, Massachusetts, recanted, claiming, "We justly fear that we were sadly deluded and mistaken." The Salem jurors had not stopped believing in witches; they had simply lost confidence in their ability to identify them. When physicians and judges had believed in witches and persecuted them officially, with torture, witches had gone to their deaths in record numbers. But when the same groups distanced themselves from popular beliefs, the trials and the executions stopped.

REVIEW How could belief in witchcraft and the rising prestige of the scientific method coexist?

Conclusion

The witchcraft persecutions reflected the traumas of these times of religious war and economic decline. Marauding armies combined with economic depression, disease, and the threat of starvation to shatter the lives of many ordinary Europeans, while religious conflicts shaped the destinies of every European power in this period. These conflicts began with the Protestant Reformation, which dispelled forever the Christian humanist dream of peace and unity, and came to a head from 1618 to 1648 in the Thirty Years' War, which cut a path of destruction through central Europe and involved most of the European powers. Shocked by the effects of religious violence, European rulers agreed to a peace that effectively removed disputes between Catholics and Protestants from the international arena.

The growing separation of political motives from religious ones did not mean that violence or conflict had ended, however. Struggles for religious uniformity within states would continue, though on a smaller scale. Bigger armies required more state involvement, and almost everywhere rulers emerged from these decades

Mapping the West The Religious Divisions of Europe, c. 1648
The Peace of Westphalia recognized major religious divisions within Europe that have endured for the most part to the present day. Catholicism dominated in southern Europe, Lutheranism had its stronghold in northern Europe, and Calvinism flourished along the Rhine River. In southeastern Europe, the Islamic Ottoman Turks accommodated the Greek Orthodox Christians under their rule but bitterly fought the Catholic Austrian Habsburgs for control of Hungary.

of conflict with expanded powers. The growth of state power directly changed the lives of ordinary people: more men went into the armies, and most families paid higher taxes. The constant extension of state power is one of the defining themes of modern history; religious warfare gave it a jump start.

For all their increased power, rulers could not control economic, social, or intellectual trends, much as they often tried. The economic downturn of the seventeenth century produced unexpected consequences for European states even while it made life miserable for many ordinary people. Economic power and vibrancy shifted from the Mediterranean world to the northwest because the countries of northwestern Europe—England, France, and the Dutch Republic especially—suffered less from the fighting of the Thirty Years' War and recovered more quickly from the loss of population and production during bad times.

In the face of violence and uncertainty, some began to look for secular alternatives in art, politics, and science. Although it would be foolish to claim that everyone's mental universe changed because of the clash between religious and secular worldviews, a truly monumental shift in attitudes had begun. Secularization combined a growing interest in nonreligious forms of art, such as theater and opera; the search for nonreligious foundations of political authority; and the establishment of the scientific method as the standard of truth. Proponents of these changes did not renounce their religious beliefs or even hold them less fervently, but they did insist that attention to state interests and scientific knowledge could serve as a brake on religious violence and popular superstitions. The search for order in the aftermath of religious warfare would continue in the decades to come.

CHAPTER REVIEW QUESTIONS

1. How did the balance of power in Europe shift between 1500 and 1648? What were the main reasons for the shift?
2. Relate the new developments in the arts and sciences to the political and economic changes in this period of crisis.

TIMELINE

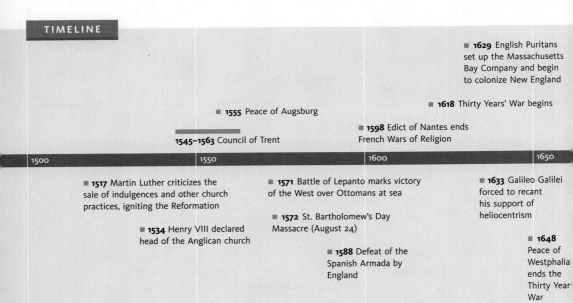

1629 English Puritans set up the Massachusetts Bay Company and begin to colonize New England

1618 Thirty Years' War begins

1555 Peace of Augsburg

1598 Edict of Nantes ends French Wars of Religion

1545–1563 Council of Trent

1500   1550   1600   1650

1517 Martin Luther criticizes the sale of indulgences and other church practices, igniting the Reformation

1571 Battle of Lepanto marks victory of the West over Ottomans at sea

1633 Galileo Galilei forced to recant his support of heliocentrism

1534 Henry VIII declared head of the Anglican church

1572 St. Bartholomew's Day Massacre (August 24)

1588 Defeat of the Spanish Armada by England

1648 Peace of Westphalia ends the Thirty Year War

For practice quizzes and other study tools, see the Online Study Guide at bedfordstmartins.com/huntconcise.

For primary-source material from this period, see Chapters 14 and 15 of *Sources of THE MAKING OF THE WEST,* Third Edition.

Suggested References

Religion, warfare, science, witchcraft, and the travails of everyday life have all been the subject of groundbreaking research, yet the personalities of individual rulers still make for great stories, too.

Benedict, Philip. *Christ's Churches Purely Reformed: A Social History of Calvinism.* 2002.

Bonney, Richard. *The Thirty Years' War.* 2002.

Braudel, Fernand. *The Mediterranean and the Mediterranean World in the Age of Philip the Second.* Trans. Siân Reynolds. 2 vols. 1972, 1973.

Briggs, Robin. *Witches and Neighbors: The Social and Cultural Context of European Witchcraft.* 1996.

*Diefendorf, Barbara B. *The Saint Bartholomew's Day Massacre: A Brief History with Documents.* 2009.

Erasmus: The Praise of Folly and Other Writings. Trans. Robert M. Adams. 1989.

Galileo Project: http://galileo.rice.edu

Hsia, R. Po-chia. *The World of the Catholic Renewal.* 1997.

Jacob, James. *The Scientific Revolution.* 1998.

Luther's life and thought: http://www.luther.de/en

Lynn, John A. *Women, Armies, and Warfare in Early Modern Europe.* 2008.

Patterson, Benton Rain. *With the Heart of a King: Elizabeth I of England, Philip II of Spain, and the Fight for a Nation's Soul and Crown.* 2007.

State Building and the Search for Order

1648–1690

DURING A WEEK IN MAY 1664, King Louis XIV of France organized a series of entertainments for his court at Versailles, where he had recently begun the construction of a magnificent new palace. More than six hundred members of his court attended the series of spectacles called "The Delights of the Enchanted Island." The carefully orchestrated activities opened with an elaborate parade of the king and his courtiers, accompanied by an eighteen-foot-high float in the form of a chariot dedicated to Apollo, the Greek god of the sun and Louis's personally chosen emblem. During the week, the king's favorite artists presented works prepared especially for the occasion, including ballets, plays, and musical concerts. Equestrian tournaments, visits to the king's personal collection of wild animals and birds, and a huge fireworks display captivated the audience. Every detail of the festivities appeared in an official program published the same year.

Louis XIV and His Bodyguards
One of Louis XIV's court painters, Adam Frans van der Meulen, depicted the king arriving at the Palace of Versailles, still under construction (the painting dates from 1669). None of the gardens, pools, or statues had yet been installed. Louis is the only figure facing the viewer, and his dress is much more colorful than that of anyone else in the painting. *(Réunion des Musées Nationaux/Art Resource, NY.)*

Louis XIV spared no expense in promoting his image, especially to those most dangerous to him, the leading nobles of the kingdom. Other rulers either followed his example or explicitly rejected it, but they could not afford to ignore it. All governments faced the daunting task of rebuilding authority after the wars over religion and the economic recession of the early seventeenth century. As part of his campaign to emphasize his majesty, Louis encouraged leading nobles to dispense huge sums to entertain him and his court. He always spent even more in order to show that he was richer and more powerful than any noble or than any other monarch.

Louis XIV's model of state building was known as **absolutism**, a system of government in which the ruler claimed sole and uncontestable power. Although

481

absolutism exerted great influence, especially in central and eastern Europe, it faced competition from **constitutionalism**, a system in which the ruler had to share power with parliaments made up of elected representatives. Constitutionalism led to weakness in Poland-Lithuania, but it provided a strong foundation for state power in England, the English North American colonies, and the Dutch Republic. Constitutionalism triumphed in England, however, only after one king had been executed as a traitor and another had been deposed.

Whether absolutist or constitutionalist, states faced similar challenges to state building in the mid-seventeenth century. Competition in the international arena required resources, and all states raised taxes, provoking popular protests and even rebellions. The wars over religion that had culminated in the Thirty Years' War (1618–1648) left many economies in dire straits, and, even more significant, they created a need for new explanations of political authority. Monarchs still relied on religion to justify their divine right to rule, but they increasingly sought secular defenses of their powers, too. Absolutism and constitutionalism were the two main responses to the threat of disorder and breakdown left as a legacy of the wars over religion.

The search for order took place not only at the level of states and rulers but also in intellectual, cultural, and social life. Thomas Hobbes and John Locke famously sought to ground political authority in a **social contract**. Artists looked for ways of glorifying power and expressing order and symmetry in their work. As states consolidated their power, elites endeavored to distinguish themselves more clearly from the lower orders. The upper classes emulated the manners developed at court and tried in every way to distance themselves from anything viewed as vulgar or lower-class. Officials, clergy, and laypeople all worked to reform the poor, now seen as a major source of disorder.

CHAPTER FOCUS QUESTION   What were the chief differences between absolutism and constitutionalism?

Louis XIV: Model of Absolutism

The French king Louis XIV (r. 1643–1715) personified the absolutist ruler who in theory shared his power with no one. Louis personally made all important state decisions and left no room for dissent. In 1651, he reputedly told the Paris high court of justice, *"L'état, c'est moi"* (I am the state), emphasizing that state authority rested in him personally. Louis cleverly manipulated the affections and ambitions of his courtiers, chose as his ministers middle-class men who owed everything to him, built up Europe's largest army, and snuffed out every hint of religious or political opposition. Yet the absoluteness of his power should not be exaggerated. Like all other rulers of his time, Louis depended on the cooperation of many others: local officials who enforced his decrees, peasants and artisans who joined his armies and paid his taxes, creditors who loaned crucial funds, and nobles who joined court festivities organized to glorify the king rather than stay at home and cause trouble.

The Fronde, 1648–1653

Louis XIV built on a long French tradition of increasing centralization of state authority, but before he could extend it, he had to weather a series of revolts known as the **Fronde**. Derived from the French word for a child's slingshot, the term was used by critics to signify that the revolts were mere child's play. In fact, they posed an unprecedented threat to the French crown. Louis was only five when he came to the throne in 1643 upon the death of his father, Louis XIII. Louis XIV's mother, Anne of Austria, and her Italian-born adviser and rumored lover, Cardinal Mazarin (1602–1661), ruled in the young monarch's name. To meet the financial pressure of fighting the Thirty Years' War and then even after the peace to keep up a draining war against Spain, Mazarin sold new offices, raised taxes, and forced creditors to extend loans to the government. In 1648, a coalition of his opponents presented him with a charter of demands that, if granted, would have given the **parlements** (high courts) a form of constitutional power with the right to approve

The Fronde, 1648–1653

new taxes. Mazarin responded by arresting the coalition's leaders. He soon faced a series of revolts that at one time or another involved nearly every social group in France and lasted until 1653.

Faced with barricades in the streets of Paris, Anne took Louis and fled the city. As civil war threatened, Mazarin and Anne agreed to compromise with the parlements. The nobles then tried to reassert their own claims to power by raising private armies. The middle and lower classes chafed at the constant tax increases and in some places organized revolts. Conflicts erupted throughout the kingdom, and rampaging soldiers devastated rural areas and disrupted commerce. Neither the nobles nor the judges of the parlements really wanted to overthrow the king; they simply wanted a greater share in power. But Louis XIV never forgot the humiliation and uncertainty that marred his childhood. Years later he recalled an incident in which a band of Parisians had invaded his bedchamber to determine whether he had fled the city, and he declared the event an affront not only to himself but also to the state. His own policies as ruler would be designed to prevent the repetition of any such revolts.

Court Culture as an Element of Absolutism

When Cardinal Mazarin died in 1661, Louis XIV decided to rule without a first minister. He described the dangers of his situation in memoirs he wrote later for his son's instruction: "Everywhere was disorder. My Court as a whole was still very far removed from the sentiments in which I trust you will find it." Typically quarrelsome, the French nobles had long exercised local authority by maintaining their own fighting forces, meting out justice on their estates, arranging jobs for underlings, and resolving their own conflicts through dueling.

Louis set out to domesticate the warrior-nobles by replacing violence with court ritual. Using a systematic policy of bestowing pensions, offices, honors, gifts, and the threat of disfavor or punishment, he made himself the center of French power and culture. The aristocracy soon vied for his favor, attended the ballets and theatricals he put on, and learned the rules of etiquette he supervised. Great nobles competed for the honor of holding his shirt when he dressed, foreign ambassadors squabbled for places near him, and royal mistresses basked in the glow of his personal favor. Louis de Rouvroy, duke of Saint-Simon (1675–1755), complained, "There was nothing he [Louis XIV] liked so much as flattery . . . the coarser and clumsier it was, the more he relished it." Madame de Lafayette described the effects on court life in her novel *The Princess of Cleves* (1678): "The Court gravitated around ambition. Nobody was tranquil or indifferent—everybody was busily trying to better his or her position by pleasing, by helping, or by hindering somebody else."

Louis XIV used every form of art—mock battles, theatrical performances, paintings, sculpture, poetry, medals, histories, even the ritual of his dinner—to enhance his personal prestige. Calling himself "the Sun King," Louis adorned his palace with statues of Apollo and emulated the style of the ancient Roman emperors. The king's officials treated the arts as a branch of government. Louis's ministers set up royal academies of dance, painting, architecture, and music and took control of the Académie Française (French Academy), which to this day decides on correct usage of the French language. A royal furniture workshop at the Gobelins tapestry works on the outskirts of Paris turned out the delicate and ornate pieces whose style bore the king's name. Louis's government also regulated the number and locations of theaters and closely censored all forms of publication.

Music and theater enjoyed special prominence. Louis commissioned operas to celebrate royal marriages, baptisms, and military victories. The king himself danced in ballets if a role seemed especially important. Playwrights presented their new plays directly to the court. Pierre Corneille and Jean-Baptiste Racine wrote tragedies set in Greece or Rome that celebrated the new aristocratic virtues that Louis aimed to inculcate: a reverence for order and self-control.

Louis glorified his image through massive public works projects as well. Military facilities, such as veterans' hospitals and fortified towns on the frontiers, represented his military might. Urban improvements, such as the reconstruction of the Louvre palace in Paris, proved his wealth. But his most ambitious project was the construction of a new palace at Versailles, twelve miles from the turbulent capital. Building began in the 1660s, and by 1685, the frenzied effort engaged 36,000 workers, not including the thousands of troops who diverted a local river to supply water for pools and fountains. Even the gardens reflected the spirit of Louis XIV's rule: their geometrical

The Palace of Versailles
This painting by Jean-Baptiste Martin from the late seventeenth century gives a good view of one section of the palace and especially the geometrically arranged gardens. (Réunion des Musées Nationaux/ Art Resource, NY.)

arrangements and clear lines showed that art and design could tame nature and that order and control defined the exercise of power. Versailles symbolized Louis's success in reining in the nobility and dominating Europe. Other monarchs eagerly mimicked French fashion and often conducted their business in French.

By the time Louis actually moved from the Louvre to Versailles in 1682, he had reigned as monarch for thirty-nine years. Fifteen thousand people crowded into the palace's apartments, including all the highest military officers, the ministers of state, and the separate households of each member of the royal family. After the death of his queen in 1683, Louis secretly married his mistress, Françoise d'Aubigné, marquise de Maintenon, and conducted most state affairs from her apartments at the palace. De Maintenon's opponents at court complained that she controlled all the appointments, but her efforts focused on her own projects, including her favorite: the founding in 1686 of a royal school for girls from impoverished noble families. She also inspired one of Louis XIV's most fateful decisions—to root out any alternatives to Roman Catholicism.

Enforcing Religious Conformity

Louis believed that he ruled by divine right. As Bishop Jacques-Benigne Bossuet (1627–1704) explained, "We have seen that kings take the place of God." Louis believed it was his duty as God's lieutenant to bring his subjects to the one true religion. He first focused on the Jansenists, Catholics whose doctrines and practices resembled some aspects of Protestantism. Following the posthumous publication of the book *Augustinus* (1640) by the Flemish theologian Cornelius Jansen (1585–1638), the Jansenists stressed the need for God's grace in achieving salvation. They emphasized the importance of original sin and insisted on an austere religious practice. Prominent among the Jansenists was Blaise Pascal (1623–1662), a mathematician of genius, who wrote his *Provincial Letters* (1656–1657) to defend Jansenism against charges of heresy. Many judges in the parlements likewise endorsed Jansenist doctrines.

Some questioned Louis's understanding of the finer points of Catholic doctrine. According to his German-born sister-in-law, Louis himself "has never read anything about religion, nor the Bible either, and just goes along believing whatever he is told." Louis rejected any teaching that gave priority to considerations of individual conscience over the demands of the official church hierarchy. He insisted on obedience to authority. Therefore, in 1660 he began enforcing various papal bulls (decrees) against Jansenism and closed down Jansenist theological centers. Jansenists were forced underground for the rest of his reign.

After many years of escalating pressure on the Calvinist Huguenots, Louis revoked the Edict of Nantes in 1685 and eliminated all of the Calvinists' rights. Louis considered the edict (1598), by which his grandfather Henry IV granted the Protestants religious freedom and a degree of political independence, a temporary measure, and he fervently hoped to reconvert the Huguenots to Catholicism. He closed their churches and schools, purged all Calvinists from official positions, and forced Calvinist ministers into exile even while refusing to let ordinary Protestants leave. Nonetheless, at least 150,000 Huguenots refused to submit and fled to England, Brandenburg-Prussia, or the Dutch Republic. Refugee Calvinists soon wrote essays and books denouncing Louis XIV's absolutism. Protestant European countries were shocked by this crackdown on religious dissent and would cite it when they went to war against Louis.

Extending State Authority at Home and Abroad

Louis XIV could not have enforced his religious policies without the services of a nationwide **bureaucracy**. The word *bureaucracy*—a network of state officials carrying out orders according to a regular and routine line of authority—comes from *bureau*, the French word for "desk," which came to mean "office," in the sense of both a physical space and a position of authority. Louis extended the bureaucratic forms his predecessors had developed, especially the use of intendants, officials who held their positions directly from the king rather than owning their offices. Louis handpicked them to represent his will against entrenched local interests such as the parlements, provincial estates, and noble governors. The intendants reduced local powers over finances and insisted on more efficient tax collection. Despite the doubling of taxes in Louis's reign, the local rebellions that had so beset the crown from the 1620s to the 1640s subsided in the face of these better-organized state forces.

Louis's success in consolidating his authority depended on hard work, an eye for detail, and an ear to the ground. In his memoirs he explained his priorities:

> to be well-informed on an infinite number of matters about which we are supposed to know nothing; to elicit from our subjects what they hide from us with the greatest care; to discover the most remote opinions of our courtiers and the most hidden interests of those who come to us with quite contrary professions [claims].

To gather all this information, Louis relied on a series of talented ministers, usually of modest origins, who gained fame, fortune, and even noble status by serving the king. Most important among them was Jean-Baptiste Colbert (1619–1683), the son of a wool merchant turned royal official. Colbert had managed Mazarin's personal finances and worked his way up under Louis XIV to become controller general, the head of royal finances, public works, and the navy.

Colbert followed the policy of **mercantilism**, which held that governments must intervene to increase national wealth by whatever means possible. Such government intervention inevitably increased the role and eventually the number of bureaucrats needed. Under Colbert, the French government established overseas trading companies, granted manufacturing monopolies, and standardized production methods for textiles, paper, and soap. A government inspection system regulated the quality of finished goods and compelled all craftsmen to organize into guilds, in which masters could supervise the work of the journeymen and apprentices. To protect French production, Colbert rescinded many internal customs fees while enacting high tariffs on foreign imports. To compete more effectively with England and the Dutch Republic, Colbert also subsidized shipbuilding, a policy that dramatically expanded the number of seaworthy vessels. Such mercantilist measures aimed to ensure France's prominence in world markets and to provide the resources needed to fight wars against its increasingly long list of enemies. Although later economists questioned the value of this state intervention in the economy, nearly every government in Europe embraced mercantilism.

Colbert's mercantilist projects extended to Canada, where in 1663 he took control of the trading company that had founded New France. He transplanted several thousand peasants from western France to the present-day province of Quebec, which France had claimed since 1608, and he sent fifteen hundred soldiers to fend off the Iroquois, who regularly raided French fur-trading convoys. Shows of French military force, including the burning of Indian villages and winter food supplies, forced the Iroquois to make peace, and from 1666 to 1680 French traders moved westward with minimal interference. In 1672, the fur trader Louis Jolliet and Jesuit missionary Jacques Marquette reached the upper Mississippi River and traveled downstream as far as Arkansas. In 1684, the French explorer Sieur de La Salle ventured all the way down to the Gulf of Mexico, claiming a vast territory for Louis XIV and calling it Louisiana after him. Louis and Colbert encouraged colonial settlement as part of their rivalry with the English and Dutch in the New World.

Colonial settlement occupied only a small portion of Louis XIV's attention, however, for his main foreign policy goal was to extend French power in Europe. In pursuing this purpose, he inevitably came up against the Spanish and Austrian Habsburgs, whose lands encircled his. To expand French power, Louis needed the biggest possible army. The ministry of war centralized the organization of French troops. Barracks built in major towns received supplies from a central distribution system. The state began to provide uniforms for the soldiers and to offer veterans some hospital care. A militia draft instituted in 1688 supplemented the army in times of war and enrolled 100,000 men. Louis's wartime army could field a force as large as that of all his enemies combined.

Louis gained new enemies as he tried to expand the territory under his rule. In 1667–1668, in the first of his major wars after assuming personal direction of French affairs, Louis defeated the Spanish armies but had to make peace when England, Sweden, and the Dutch Republic joined the war. In the Treaty of Aix-la-Chapelle in 1668, he gained control of towns on the border of the Spanish Netherlands (Map 13.1). Pamphlets sponsored by the Habsburgs accused Louis of aiming for "universal monarchy," or domination of Europe.

In 1672, Louis XIV opened hostilities against the Dutch because they stood in the way of his acquisition of more territory in the Spanish Netherlands. He declared war again on Spain in 1673. By now the Dutch had allied themselves with their former Spanish masters to hold off the French. Louis also marched his troops into territories of the Holy Roman Empire, provoking many of the German princes to join with the emperor, the Spanish, and the Dutch in an alliance against Louis, now denounced as a "Christian Turk" for his imperialist ambitions. But the French armies more than held their own. Faced with bloody yet inconclusive results on the battlefield, the parties agreed to the Treaty of Nijmegen of 1678–1679, which ceded several Flemish towns and Franche-Comté to Louis (Map 13.1, page 489). These territorial additions were costly: French government deficits soared, and increases in taxes touched off the most serious antitax revolt of Louis's reign in 1675.

Louis had no intention of standing still. Heartened by the Habsburgs' seeming weakness, he pushed eastward, seizing the city of Strasbourg in 1681 and invading the province of Lorraine in 1684. Lorraine would remain a subject of contention between France and its neighbors for nearly three centuries. In 1688, Louis attacked some of the small German cities of the Holy Roman Empire and was soon involved in a long war against a coalition made up of England, Spain, Sweden, the Dutch Republic, the Austrian emperor, and various German princes. Between 1689 and 1697, the coalition fought Louis to a stalemate. When hostilities ended in the Treaty of Rijswijk in 1697, Louis returned many of his conquests made since 1678, with

Map 13.1 Louis XIV's Acquisitions, 1668–1697
Every ruler in Europe hoped to extend his or her territorial control, and war was often the result. Louis XIV steadily encroached on the Spanish Netherlands to the north and the lands of the Holy Roman Empire to the east. Although coalitions of European powers reined in Louis's grander ambitions, he incorporated many neighboring territories into the French crown.

the exception of Strasbourg (Map 13.1). Louis never lost his taste for war, but his enemies learned how to set limits on his ambitions.

Louis was the last French ruler before Napoleon to accompany his troops to the battlefield. In later generations, as the military became more professional, French rulers left the fighting to their generals. Although Louis had managed to suppress the private armies of his noble courtiers, he constantly promoted his own military prowess in order to keep his noble officers under his sway. He had miniature battle scenes painted on his high heels and commissioned tapestries showing his military processions into cities, even those he did not take by force. He seized every occasion to assert his supremacy, insisting that other fleets salute his ships first.

War required money and men, which Louis obtained by expanding state control over finances, conscription into the army, and military supply. Thus absolutism and warfare fed each other, as the bureaucracy created new ways to raise and maintain an army and the army's success in war justified the expansion of state power. But constant warfare also eroded the state's resources. Further administrative and legal reform, the elimination of the buying and selling of offices, and the lowering of taxes—all were made impossible by the need for more money.

The playwright Corneille wrote, no doubt optimistically, "The people are very happy when they die for their kings." What is certain is that the wars touched many peasant and urban families. The people who lived on the routes leading to the battlefields had to house and feed soldiers; only nobles were exempt from this requirement. Everyone, moreover, paid the higher taxes that were necessary to support the army. By the end of Louis's reign, one in six Frenchmen had served in the military.

REVIEW   How "absolute" was the power of Louis XIV?

Absolutism in Central and Eastern Europe

Central and eastern European rulers saw in Louis XIV a powerful model of absolutist state building. Yet they did not blindly emulate the Sun King, in part because they confronted conditions peculiar to their regions. The ruler of Brandenburg-Prussia had to rebuild lands ravaged by the Thirty Years' War and unite far-flung territories. The Austrian Habsburgs needed to govern a mosaic of ethnic and religious groups while fighting off the Ottoman Turks. The Russian tsars wanted to extend their power over a large but relatively impoverished empire. The great exception to absolutism in eastern Europe was Poland-Lithuania, where a long crisis virtually destroyed central authority and sucked much of eastern Europe into its turbulent wake.

Brandenburg-Prussia and Sweden: Militaristic Absolutism

Brandenburg-Prussia began as a puny state on the Elbe River, but it would have a remarkable future. In the nineteenth century, it would unify the disparate German states into modern-day Germany. The ruler of Brandenburg was an elector, one of the seven German princes entitled to select the Holy Roman Emperor. Since the sixteenth century, the ruler of Brandenburg had also controlled the duchy of East Prussia; after 1618, the state was called Brandenburg-Prussia. Despite meager resources, Frederick William of Hohenzollern, the Great Elector of Brandenburg-Prussia (r. 1640–1688), succeeded in welding his scattered lands into an absolutist state.

Pressured first by the necessities of fighting the Thirty Years' War and then by the demands of reconstruction, Frederick William determined to force his territories' estates (representative institutions) to grant him a dependable income. The Great Elector struck a deal with the Junkers (nobles) of each land: in exchange for allowing him to collect higher taxes to support his growing army, he gave them complete control over the peasants. The tactic worked. By the end of his reign the estates met only on ceremonial occasions.

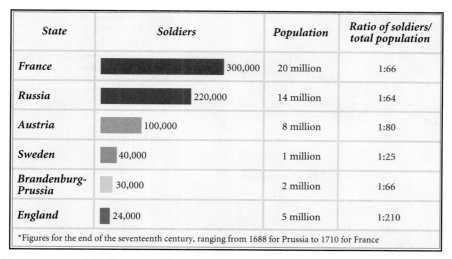

State	Soldiers	Population	Ratio of soldiers/ total population
France	300,000	20 million	1:66
Russia	220,000	14 million	1:64
Austria	100,000	8 million	1:80
Sweden	40,000	1 million	1:25
Brandenburg-Prussia	30,000	2 million	1:66
England	24,000	5 million	1:210

*Figures for the end of the seventeenth century, ranging from 1688 for Prussia to 1710 for France

Taking Measure The Seventeenth-Century Army
The figures in this chart are only approximate, but they tell an important story. What conclusions can we draw about the relative weight of the military in the different European states? Why would England's army have been so much smaller than the other states'? Is the absolute or the relative size of the military the more important indicator?

Supplied with a steady income, Frederick William could devote his attention to military and bureaucratic consolidation. Over forty years he expanded his army from eight thousand to thirty thousand men (see "Taking Measure"). The army mirrored the rigid domination of nobles over peasants that characterized Brandenburg-Prussian society: peasants filled the ranks, and Junkers became officers. Nobles also took positions as bureaucratic officials, but military needs always had priority. The Great Elector named special war commissars to take charge not only of military affairs but also of tax collection. To hasten military dispatches, he also established one of Europe's first state postal systems.

As a Calvinist ruler, Frederick William disdained the ostentation of the French court, even while following the absolutist model of centralizing state power. He boldly rebuffed Louis XIV by welcoming twenty thousand French Huguenot refugees after Louis's revocation of the Edict of Nantes. In pursuing policies that promoted state power, Frederick William adroitly switched sides in Louis's wars and would stop at almost nothing to crush resistance at home. In 1701, his son Frederick I (r. 1688–1713) persuaded Holy Roman Emperor Leopold I to grant him the title "king in Prussia." Prussia had arrived as an important power (Map 13.2).

Across the Baltic, Sweden also stood out as an example of absolutist consolidation. In the Thirty Years' War, King Gustavus Adolphus's superb generalship and highly trained army had made Sweden the supreme power of northern Europe. The huge but sparsely populated state included not only most of present-day Sweden but also Finland, Estonia, half of Latvia, and much of the Baltic coastline of modern Poland

Map 13.2 State Building in Central and Eastern Europe, 1648–1699
The Austrian Habsburgs had long contested the Ottoman Turks for dominance of eastern Europe, and by 1699 they had pushed the Turks out of Hungary. In central Europe, the Austrian Habsburgs confronted the growing power of Brandenburg-Prussia, which had emerged from relative obscurity after the Thirty Years' War to begin an aggressive program of expanding its military and its territorial base. As emperor of the Holy Roman Empire, the Austrian Habsburg ruler governed a huge expanse of territory, but the emperor's control was in fact only partial because of guarantees of local autonomy.

and Germany. The Baltic, in short, was a Swedish lake. After Gustavus Adolphus died, his daughter Queen Christina (r. 1632–1654) conceded much authority to the estates. Absorbed by religion and philosophy, Christina eventually abdicated and converted to Catholicism. Her successors temporarily made Sweden an absolute monarchy.

Absolutism in Sweden (as in neighboring Denmark-Norway) took the form of the estates standing aside while the king led the army on lucrative foreign campaigns. The aristocracy went along because it staffed the bureaucracy and reaped war profits. Though intrigued by French culture, Sweden also gleamed with national pride. In 1668, the nobility demanded the introduction of a distinctive national costume: should Swedes, they asked, "who are so glorious and renowned a nation . . . let ourselves be led by the nose by a parcel of French dancing-masters"? Sweden spent the forty years after 1654 continuously warring with its neighbors. By the 1690s, war expenses began to outrun the small Swedish population's ability to pay, threatening the continuation of absolutism.

An Uneasy Balance: Austrian Habsburgs and Ottoman Turks

Holy Roman Emperor Leopold I (r. 1658–1705) ruled over a variety of territories of different ethnicities, languages, and religions, yet in ways similar to his French and Prussian counterparts, he gradually consolidated his power. Like all the Holy Roman emperors since 1438, Leopold was an Austrian Habsburg. He was simultaneously duke of Upper and Lower Silesia, count of Tyrol, archduke of Upper and Lower Austria, king of Bohemia, king of Hungary and Croatia, and ruler of Styria and Moravia (Map 13.2, page 492). Some of these territories were provinces in the Holy Roman Empire; others were simply ruled from Vienna as Habsburg family holdings.

Leopold needed to build up his armies and state authority in order to defend the Holy Roman Empire's international position, which had been weakened by the Thirty Years' War, and to push back the Ottoman Turks, who steadily encroached from the southeast. The emperor and his closest officials took control over recruiting, provisioning, and strategic planning and worked to replace the mercenaries hired during the Thirty Years' War with a permanent standing army that promoted professional discipline. To pay for the army and to staff his growing bureaucracy, Leopold had to gain the support of local aristocrats and chip away at the powers of the provincial institutions. Intent on replacing Bohemian nobles who had supported the 1618 revolt against Austrian authority, the Habsburgs promoted a new nobility made up of Czechs, Germans, Italians, Spaniards, and even Irish, who used German as their common tongue, professed Catholicism, and loyally served the Austrian dynasty. Bohemia became a virtual Austrian colony. "You have utterly destroyed our home, our ancient kingdom," lamented a Czech Jesuit in 1670, addressing Leopold. "Of smiling towns you have made straggling villages." Austrian censors prohibited publication of this protest for over a century.

In addition to holding Louis XIV in check on his western frontiers, Leopold confronted the ever-present challenge of the Ottoman Turks to his east. In 1683, the Turks once again pushed all the way to the gates of Vienna and laid siege to the Austrian capital. After reaching this high-water mark, however, Turkish power ebbed. With the help of Polish cavalry, the Austrians finally broke the siege and turned the tide in a major counteroffensive. By the Treaty of Karlowitz of 1699, the Ottoman Turks surrendered almost all of Hungary to the Austrians (Map 13.2, page 492).

Hungary's "liberation" from the Turks came at a high price. The fighting laid waste vast stretches of Hungary's central plain, and the population may have declined as much as 65 percent since 1600. To repopulate the land, the Austrians settled large communities of foreigners: Romanians, Croats, Serbs, and Germans. Magyar (Hungarian) speakers became a minority, and the seeds were sown for the poisonous nationality conflicts that would take place in nineteenth- and twentieth-century Hungary, Romania, and Yugoslavia.

The Siege of Vienna, 1683
This detail from a painting by Franz Geffels shows the camp of the Ottoman Turks. The Turkish armies surrounded Vienna on July 14, 1683. Jan Sobieski led an army of Poles that joined with Austrian and German forces to beat back the Turks on September 12. (© The Art Archive/ Corbis.)

Once the Turks had been beaten back, Austrian rule over Hungary tightened. In 1687, the Habsburg dynasty's hereditary right to the Hungarian crown was acknowledged by the Hungarian diet, a parliament revived by Leopold in 1681 to gain the support of Hungarian nobles. The diet was dominated by nobles who had amassed huge holdings in the liberated territories. They formed the core of a pro-Habsburg Hungarian aristocracy that would buttress the dynasty until it fell in 1918. As the Turks retreated from Hungary, Leopold systematically rebuilt churches, monasteries, roadside shrines, and monuments in the flamboyant Austrian baroque style.

The Ottoman Turks also pursued state consolidation, but in a very different fashion from the Europeans. The Ottoman state extended its authority through a combination of settlement and military control. Hundreds of thousands of Turkish families moved with Turkish soldiers into the Balkan peninsula in the 1400s and 1500s. As locals converted to Islam, administration passed gradually into their hands. In the Ottoman homeland of Anatolia, the sultans, the Ottoman rulers, were often challenged by mutinous army officers. Despite frequent palace coups and assassinations, the Ottoman state survived by hiring restive peasants as mercenaries and by playing bureaucratic elites off one another. This constantly shifting social and political system explains how the coup-ridden Ottoman state could appear "weak" in Western eyes and still pose a massive military threat on Europe's southeastern borders. In the end, the Ottoman state lasted much longer than Louis XIV's absolute monarchy.

Russia: Foundations of Bureaucratic Absolutism

Seventeenth-century Russia seemed a world apart from the Europe of Louis XIV. Straddling Europe and Asia, it stretched across Siberia to the Pacific Ocean. Western visitors either sneered or shuddered at the "barbarism" of Russian life, and Russians reciprocated by nursing deep suspicions of everything foreign. But under the surface, Russia was evolving along paths much like the rest of absolutist Europe; the tsars increased their power by surmounting internal disorder and coming to an accommodation with noble landlords.

When Tsar Alexei (r. 1645–1676) tried to extend state authority by imposing new administrative structures and taxes in 1648, Moscow and other cities erupted in bloody rioting. The government immediately doused the fire. In 1649, Alexei convoked the Assembly of the Land (consisting of noble delegates from the provinces) to consult on a sweeping law code to organize Russian society in a strict social hierarchy that would last for nearly two centuries. The code of 1649 assigned all subjects to a hereditary class according to their current occupation or state needs. Slaves and free peasants were merged into a serf class. As serfs they could not change occupations or move; they were tightly tied to the soil and to their noble masters. To prevent tax evasion, the code also forbade townspeople to move from the community where they resided. Nobles owed absolute obedience to the tsar and were required to serve in the army, but in return no other group could own estates worked by serfs. Serfs became the chattel of their lords, who could sell them like horses or land. Their conditions of life differed little from those of the slaves on the plantations in the Americas.

Some peasants resisted enserfment. In 1667, Stenka Razin led a huge rebellion in southern Russia that promised liberation from "the traitors and bloodsuckers of the peasant communes"—the great noble landowners, local governors, and Moscow courtiers. Razin was a Cossack, the name given to bandit gangs consisting of runaway serfs and poor nobles in southern Russia and Ukraine. Captured four years later by the tsar's army, Razin was dismembered, his head and limbs publicly displayed and his body thrown to the dogs. Thousands of his followers also suffered grisly deaths, but his memory lived on in folk songs and legends. Landlords successfully petitioned for the abolition of the statute of limitations on runaway serfs and for harsh penalties against those who harbored runaways. The increase in Russian state authority went hand in hand with the enforcement of serfdom.

To extend his power and emulate his western rivals, Tsar Alexei wanted a bigger army, exclusive control over state policy, and a greater say in religious matters. The size of the army increased dramatically from 35,000 in the 1630s to 220,000 by the end of the century (see "Taking Measure," page 491). The Assembly of the Land, once an important source of noble consultation, never met again after 1653. In 1666, the Russian Orthodox church reaffirmed the tsar's role as God's direct representative on earth and took action against a religious group called the Old Believers, who rejected church efforts to bring Russian worship in line with Byzantine tradition. Whole communities of Old Believers starved or burned themselves to death rather than submit. Religious schism opened a gulf between the Russian people and the crown.

Stenka Razin in Captivity
After leading a revolt of thousands of serfs, peasants, and members of non-Russian tribes of the middle and lower Volga region, Razin was captured by Russian forces and led off to Moscow, where he was executed in 1671. He has been the subject of songs, legends, and poems ever since. (RIA Novosti.)

The tsar's emulation of western rivals extended to culture, too. Alexei set up the first Western-style theater in the Kremlin, and his daughter Sophia translated French plays. Nobles and ordinary citizens commissioned portraits of themselves instead of buying only religious icons. The most adventurous nobles began to wear German-style clothing. A long struggle over Western influence had begun.

Poland-Lithuania Overwhelmed

Unlike the other eastern European powers, Poland-Lithuania did not follow the absolutist model. Decades of war weakened the monarchy and made the great nobles into practically autonomous warlords. They used the parliament and demands for constitutionalism to stymie monarchical power. The result was a precipitous slide into political disarray and weakness.

In 1648, Ukrainian Cossack warriors revolted against the king of Poland-Lithuania, inaugurating two decades of tumult known as the Deluge. In 1654, the Cossacks offered Ukraine to Russian rule, provoking a Russo-Polish war that ended in 1667 when the tsar annexed eastern Ukraine and Kiev. Sweden, Brandenburg-Prussia, and Transylvania sent armies to seize territory, too. As much as a third of the Polish population eventually perished in the fighting. The once prosperous Jewish and Protestant minorities suffered great losses: some 56,000 Jews were killed by either the Cossacks, Polish peasants, or Russian troops. One rabbi wrote, "We were slaughtered each day, in a more agonizing way than cattle: they are butchered quickly, while we were being executed slowly." Surviving Jews moved from towns to shtetls (Jewish villages), where they could survive only by petty trading, moneylending, tax gathering, and tavern leasing—activities that fanned peasant anti-Semitism. Desperate for protection amid the war, most Protestants backed the violently anti-Catholic Swedes, and the victorious Catholic majority branded them as traitors, forcing some Protestants to seek refuge as far away as the Dutch Republic and England. In Poland-Lithuania, once an outpost of religious toleration, it came to be assumed that a good Pole was a Catholic.

The commonwealth revived briefly when Jan Sobieski (r. 1674–1696) was elected king. He gained a reputation throughout Europe when he led 25,000 Polish cavalrymen into battle in the siege of Vienna in 1683. His cavalry helped rout the Turks and turned the tide against the Ottomans. Married to a politically shrewd French princess, Sobieski openly admired Louis XIV's France. Despite his efforts to rebuild the monarchy, he could not halt Poland-Lithuania's decline into powerlessness.

Elsewhere the ravages of war had created opportunities for kings to increase their power, but in Poland-Lithuania the great nobles gained all the advantage. They dominated the Sejm (parliament), and to maintain an equilibrium among themselves, they each wielded an absolute veto power. This "free veto" constitutional system soon deadlocked parliamentary government. The monarchy lost its room to maneuver, and with it much of its remaining power. An appalled Croat visitor in 1658 commented, "Among the Poles there is no order in the state. . . . Everybody who is stronger thinks to have the right to oppress the weaker, just as the wolves and bears are free to capture and kill cattle. . . . Such abominable depravity is called by the Poles 'aristocratic freedom.'" The Polish version of constitutionalism fatally weakened the state and made it prey to its neighbors.

> **REVIEW** Why did absolutism succeed everywhere in eastern Europe except Poland-Lithuania?

Constitutionalism in England

In the second half of the seventeenth century, western and eastern Europe began to move in different directions. In general, the farther east one traveled, the more absolutist the style of government (with the exception of Poland-Lithuania) and the greater the gulf between landlord and peasant. In eastern Europe, nobles lorded over their serfs but owed almost slavish obedience in turn to their rulers. In western Europe, even in absolutist France, serfdom had almost entirely disappeared, and nobles and rulers alike faced greater challenges to their control. The greatest challenges of all would come in England.

This outcome might seem surprising, for the English monarchs enjoyed many advantages compared with their continental rivals: they needed less money for their armies because they had stayed out of the Thirty Years' War, and their island kingdom was in theory easier to rule because they governed a relatively homogeneous population only one-fourth the size of France's with few regional institutions to block the ruler's will. Yet the English rulers failed in their efforts to install absolutist policies. The English revolutions of 1642–1660 and 1688–1689 overturned two kings, confirmed the constitutional powers of an elected parliament, and laid the foundation for the idea that government must guarantee certain rights under the law.

England Turned Upside Down, 1642–1660

Disputes about the right to levy taxes and the nature of authority in the Church of England had long troubled the relationship between the English crown and Parliament. For over a hundred years, wealthy English landowners had been accustomed to participating in government through Parliament and expected to be consulted on royal policy. Although England had no one constitutional document, customary procedures and a variety of laws, judicial decisions, charters, and petitions granted by the king regulated relations between king and Parliament. When Charles I tried to assert his authority over Parliament, a civil war broke out. It set in motion an unpredictable chain of events, which included an extraordinary ferment of religious and political ideas. Some historians view the English civil war of 1642–1646 as the last great war of religion because it pitted Puritans against those trying to push the Anglican church toward Catholicism, but it should be considered the first modern revolution because it gave birth to democratic political and religious movements.

Charles I (r. 1625–1649) inherited the problems that had been left by his father, James I, and James's predecessor, Elizabeth I. Elizabeth had defended the crown's right to regulate religion, but neither she nor James definitively reined in the Puritans. In addition, James antagonized Parliament by selling monopolies and titles to raise money and by relying increasingly on the advice of his favorite courtier, George Villiers, rumored to be his lover. Charles consequently faced an increasingly aggressive Parliament when he inherited the throne. In 1628, Parliament forced Charles to agree to the Petition of Right, by which he promised not to levy taxes without its consent. Charles hoped to avoid further interference with his plans by simply refusing to call Parliament into session between 1629 and 1640.

Religious tensions brought conflicts over the king's authority to a head. The Puritans had long agitated for the removal of any vestiges of Catholicism, but Charles, married to a French Catholic, moved in the opposite direction. With Charles's encouragement, the archbishop of Canterbury, William Laud (1573–1645), imposed increasingly elaborate ceremonies on the Anglican church. Angered by these moves toward "popery," the Puritans poured forth vituperative pamphlets and sermons. In response Laud hauled them before the feared Court of Star Chamber, a special court consisting of handpicked members of the king's council. The Court of Star Chamber came to stand for royal tyranny and religious persecution because it rode roughshod over the regular judicial process and imposed its own penalties. The court ordered harsh sentences for Laud's Puritan critics; they were whipped, pilloried, and branded and even had their ears cut off and their noses split. When Laud tried to apply his policies to Scotland, however, they backfired completely. The stubborn Presbyterian Scots rioted against the imposition of bishops and a prayer book modeled on the Anglican Book of Common Prayer. In 1640 the Scots invaded the north of England and defeated Charles's army. To raise money, Charles called Parliament into session and unwittingly opened the door to a constitutional and religious crisis.

Reformers in the House of Commons (the lower house of Parliament) seized the opportunity to undo what they saw as the growing royal tyranny of the 1630s. Parliament removed Laud from office, ordered the execution of an unpopular royal commander, abolished the Court of Star Chamber, repealed recently levied taxes, and provided for a parliamentary assembly at least once every three years, thus establishing a constitutional check on royal authority. Moderate reformers expected to stop there and resisted Puritan pressure to abolish bishops and eliminate the Anglican prayer book. But their hand was forced in January 1642, when Charles and his soldiers invaded Parliament and tried unsuccessfully to arrest those leaders who had moved to curb his power. Faced with mounting opposition within London, Charles withdrew from the city and prepared to fight.

The ensuing civil war between king and Parliament lasted four years (1642–1646) and divided the country. The king's army of royalists, known as Cavaliers, enjoyed the most support in northern and western England. The parliamentary forces, called Roundheads because they cut their hair short, had their stronghold in the southeast, including London. Although Puritans dominated on the parliamentary side, they were divided about the proper form of church government: the Presbyterians wanted a Calvinist church with some central authority, whereas the Independents favored entirely autonomous congregations free from other church government (hence the term *congregationalism,* often associated with the Independents). Putting aside their differences for the sake of military victory, the Puritans united under an obscure member of the House of Commons, the country gentleman Oliver Cromwell (1599–1658). Cromwell was one of the generals of the New Model Army, so called because it was a disciplined national force rather than a hodgepodge of local militias. The New Model Army defeated the Cavaliers at the battle of Naseby in 1645. Charles fled to Scotland but was turned over by the Scots in 1647.

Although the civil war between king and Parliament had ended in victory for Parliament, divisions within the Puritan ranks now came to the fore: the Presbyterians dominated Parliament, but the Independents controlled the army. The disputes between elites drew lower-class groups into the debate. When Parliament tried to disband the

England during the Civil War, 1642–1646

New Model Army in 1647, disgruntled soldiers protested. Called Levellers because of their insistence on leveling social differences, the soldiers took on their officers in a series of debates about the nature of political authority. The Levellers demanded that Parliament meet annually, that members be paid so as to allow common people to participate, and that all male heads of households be allowed to vote. Their ideal of political participation excluded servants, the propertyless, and women but offered access to artisans, shopkeepers, and modest farmers. Cromwell and other army leaders rejected the Levellers' demands as threatening to property owners. Cromwell insisted, "You have no other way to deal with these men but to break them in pieces. . . . If you do not break them they will break you."

Just as political differences between Presbyterians and Independents helped spark new political movements, so too did their conflicts over church organization foster the emergence of new religious doctrines. The new sects had in common only their emphasis on the "inner light" of individual religious inspiration and a disdain for hierarchical authority. Their emphasis on equality before God and greater participation in church governance appealed to the middle and lower classes. The Baptists, for example, insisted on adult baptism because they believed that Christians should choose their own church and that every child should not automatically become a member of the Church of England. Quaker men pointedly refused to take off their hats as a sign of respect to men in authority. Manifesting their religious experience by trembling, or "quaking," the Quakers believed that anyone, man or woman, inspired by a direct experience of God could preach.

Parliamentary leaders feared that the new sects would overturn the whole social hierarchy. Rumors abounded, for example, of naked Quakers running through the streets waiting for a "sign." Some sects did advocate sweeping change. Diggers promoted rural communism—collective ownership of all property. Seekers and Ranters questioned just about everything. A few men advocated free love. In keeping with their notions of equality and individual inspiration, many of the new sects provided opportunities for women to become preachers and prophets. Women also presented petitions, participated prominently in street demonstrations, distributed tracts, and occasionally even dressed as men, wearing swords and joining armies. The outspoken women in new sects like the Quakers underscored the threat of a social order turned upside down. These developments convinced the political elite that tolerating the new sects would lead to skepticism, anarchy, and debauchery.

At the heart of the continuing political struggle was the question of what to do with the king, who tried to negotiate with the Presbyterians in Parliament. In late 1648, Independents in the army purged the Presbyterians from Parliament, leaving a "rump" of about seventy members. This Rump Parliament then created a high court to try Charles I. The court found him guilty of attempting to establish "an unlimited and tyrannical power" and pronounced a death sentence. On January 30, 1649, Charles was beheaded before an enormous crowd, which reportedly groaned as one when the axe fell. Although many had objected to Charles's autocratic rule, few had wanted him killed. For royalists, Charles immediately became a martyr, and reports of miracles, such as the curing of blindness by the touch of a handkerchief soaked in his blood, soon circulated. In 1650, the dead king's son Charles (the future Charles II) allied with Scottish royalists, but Cromwell's forces routed them. Charles escaped to France.

Printed in the year Year, of the Hang-mans down-fall, 1649.

Execution of Charles I
This print of the execution of the English king Charles I on January 30, 1649, appeared on the first page of the fictitious confessions of his executioner, Richard Brandon, who supposedly claimed to feel pains in his own neck from the moment he cut off Charles's head. (© British Library, London, UK/The Bridgeman Art Library.)

The Rump Parliament abolished the monarchy and the House of Lords (the upper house of Parliament). It set up a republic with Cromwell as head of the Council of State. Cromwell did not tolerate dissent from his policies. He saw the hand of God in events and himself as God's agent. When plans for mutiny within the army were discovered, Cromwell had the perpetrators executed. Although Cromwell allowed the various Puritan sects to worship rather freely and permitted Jews with needed skills to return to England for the first time since the thirteenth century, Catholics could not worship publicly, nor could Anglicans use the Book of Common Prayer. The elites, many of whom were still Anglicans, were troubled by Cromwell's religious policies but pleased to see some social order reestablished.

The new regime aimed to extend state power just as Charles I had before. Cromwell laid the foundation for a Great Britain made up of England, Wales, Ireland, and Scotland by reconquering Scotland and subduing Ireland. Anti-English rebels in Ireland had seized the occasion of troubles between king and Parliament to revolt in 1641. When Cromwell's position was secured in 1649, he went to Ireland with a large force and easily defeated the rebels, massacring whole garrisons and their priests. He encouraged expropriating the lands of the Irish "barbarous wretches," and Scottish immigrants resettled the northern county of Ulster. This seventeenth-century English conquest left a legacy of bitterness that the Irish even today call "the curse of Cromwell." In 1651, Parliament turned its attention overseas, putting mercantilist ideas into practice in the first Navigation Act, which allowed imports only if they were carried on English ships or came directly from the producers of goods. The Navigation Act was aimed at the Dutch, who dominated world trade; Cromwell tried to carry the policy further by waging naval war on the Dutch from 1652 to 1654.

At home, however, Cromwell faced growing resistance. His wars required a budget twice the size of Charles I's, and his increases in property taxes and customs duties alienated landowners and merchants. In 1653, when the Rump Parliament considered disbanding the army, Cromwell abolished Parliament in a military coup and made himself Lord Protector. His regime came to be known as the Protectorate. Cromwell silenced his critics by banning newspapers and using networks of spies and mail readers to keep tabs on his enemies. Cromwell's death in 1658 revived the prospect of civil war and political chaos. In 1660, a newly elected, staunchly Anglican Parliament invited Charles II, the son of the executed king, to return from exile. The period between the regicide of Charles I and the restoration of Charles II came to be known as the Interregnum (literally, "between reigns").

The Restoration and the "Glorious Revolution" of 1688

The traditional monarchical form of government was reinstated in 1660, restoring the king to full partnership with Parliament. Charles II (r. 1660–1685) promised to extend religious toleration, especially to Catholics, with whom he sympathized. Yet in the first years of his reign more than a thousand Puritan ministers lost their positions, and after 1664, attending a service other than one conforming with the Anglican prayer book was illegal. Natural disasters also marred the early years of the restoration of the monarchy. The plague stalked London's rat-infested streets in May 1665 and claimed more than thirty thousand victims by September. Then in 1666, the Great Fire swept the city, causing cataclysmic destruction. The crown now had a city as well as a monarchy to rebuild.

The restoration of monarchy made some in Parliament fear that the English government would come to resemble French absolutism. This fear was not unfounded. In 1670, Charles II made a secret agreement, soon leaked, with Louis XIV in which he promised to announce his conversion to Catholicism in exchange for money for a war against the Dutch. Charles never proclaimed himself a Catholic, but in his Declaration of Indulgence (1673) he did suspend all laws against Catholics and Protestant dissenters. Parliament refused to continue funding the Dutch war unless Charles rescinded his Declaration of Indulgence. Asserting its authority further, Parliament passed the Test Act in 1673, requiring all government officials to profess allegiance to the Church of England and in effect disavow Catholic doctrine. Then in 1678, Parliament precipitated the so-called Exclusion Crisis by explicitly denying the throne to a Roman Catholic. This action was aimed at the king's brother and heir, James, an open convert to Catholicism. Charles refused to allow it to become law.

The dynastic crisis over the succession of a Catholic gave rise to two distinct factions in Parliament: the Tories, who supported a strong, hereditary monarchy

Great Fire of London, 1666

This painting shows the three-day fire at its height. The writer John Evelyn described the scene in his diary: "All the sky was of a fiery aspect, like the top of a burning oven, and the light seen above 40 miles round about for many nights. God grant mine eyes may never behold the like, who now saw above 10,000 houses all in one flame; the noise and cracking and thunder of people, the fall of towers, houses, and churches, was like an hideous storm." Everyone in London at the time felt overwhelmed by the catastrophe, and many attributed it to God's punishment for the upheavals of the 1640s and 1650s. (Museum of London.)

and the restored ceremony of the Anglican church, and the Whigs, who advocated parliamentary supremacy and toleration for Protestant dissenters such as Presbyterians. The Tories favored James's succession despite his Catholicism, whereas the Whigs opposed a Catholic monarch. The loose moral atmosphere of Charles's court also offended some Whigs, who complained tongue in cheek that Charles was father of his country in much too literal a fashion (he had fathered more than one child by his mistresses but had produced no legitimate heir).

Upon Charles's death, James succeeded to the throne as James II (r. 1685–1688). James pursued pro-Catholic and absolutist policies even more aggressively than his brother. When a male heir—who would take precedence over James's two adult Protestant daughters and be reared a Catholic—was born, Tories and Whigs banded together. They invited the Dutch ruler William, prince of Orange and the husband of James's older daughter, Mary, to invade England. James fled to France, Parliament declared that he had abdicated, and hardly any blood was shed. Parliament offered the throne jointly to William (r. 1689–1702) and Mary (r. 1689–1694) on the condition that they accept a bill of rights guaranteeing Parliament's full partnership in a constitutional government.

In the Bill of Rights (1689), William and Mary agreed not to raise a standing army or to levy taxes without Parliament's consent. They also agreed to call meetings of Parliament at least every three years, to guarantee free elections to parliamentary seats, and to abide by Parliament's decisions and not suspend duly passed laws. The agreement gave England's constitutional government a written, legal basis by formally recognizing Parliament as a self-contained, independent body that shared power with the rulers. Victorious supporters of the coup declared it the **Glorious Revolution**. Constitutionalism had triumphed over absolutism in England.

The propertied classes who controlled Parliament prevented any resurgence of the popular turmoil of the 1640s. The Toleration Act of 1689 granted all Protestants freedom of worship, though non-Anglicans were still excluded from the universities; Catholics got no rights but were often left alone to worship privately. When the Catholics in Ireland rose to defend James II, William and Mary's troops brutally suppressed them. With the Whigs in power and the Tories in opposition, wealthy landowners now controlled political life throughout the realm. Differences between the factions had become minor; the Tories simply enjoyed less access to the king's patronage.

REVIEW   What differences over religion and politics caused the conflict between king and Parliament in England?

Other Outposts of Constitutionalism

When William and Mary came to the throne in England in 1689, the Dutch and English put aside the rivalries that had brought them to war against each other in 1652–1654, 1665–1667, and 1672–1674. Under William, the Dutch Republic and England together led the coalition that blocked Louis XIV's efforts to dominate continental Europe. The two states had much in common: oriented toward commerce, especially overseas, they were the successful exceptions to absolutism in Europe. Also among the few outposts of constitutionalism in the seventeenth century were the English North American colonies, which developed representative government while the English were preoccupied with their revolutions at home. Constitutionalism was not the only factor shaping this Atlantic world; as constitutionalism developed in the colonies, so too did the enslavement of black Africans as a new labor force.

The Dutch Republic

When the Dutch Republic gained formal independence from Spain in 1648, it had already established a decentralized, constitutional state. Rich merchants called regents effectively controlled the internal affairs of each province and through the Estates General (an assembly made up of deputies from each province) named the *stadholder,* the executive officer responsible for defense and for representing the state at all ceremonial occasions. They almost always chose one of the princes of the house of Orange, but the prince of Orange resembled a president more than a king.

The decentralized state encouraged and protected trade, and the Dutch Republic soon became Europe's financial capital. The Bank of Amsterdam offered interest rates less than half those available in England and France. Praised for their industriousness, thrift, and cleanliness—and maligned as greedy, dull "butterboxes"—the Dutch dominated overseas commerce with their shipping (Map 13.3). They imported products from all over the world: spices, tea, and silk from Asia; sugar and tobacco from

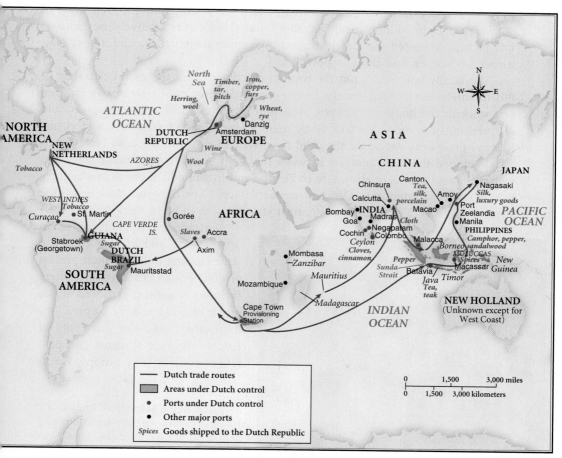

Map 13.3 Dutch Commerce in the Seventeenth Century
Even before gaining formal independence from Spain in 1648, the Dutch had begun to compete with the Spanish and Portuguese all over the world. In 1602, a group of merchants established the Dutch East India Company, which soon offered investors an annual rate of return of 35 percent on the trade in spices with countries located on the Indian Ocean. Global commerce gave the Dutch the highest standard of living in Europe and soon attracted the envy of the French and English. **For more help analyzing this map, see the map activity for this chapter in the Online Study Guide at** bedfordstmartins.com/huntconcise.

the Americas; wool from England and Spain; timber and furs from Scandinavia; grain from eastern Europe. A widely reprinted history of Amsterdam that appeared in 1662 described the city as "risen through the hand of God to the peak of prosperity and greatness. . . . The whole world stands amazed at its riches."

The Dutch rapidly became the most prosperous and best-educated people in Europe. Middle-class people supported the visual arts, especially painting, to an unprecedented degree. In the town of Delft, with a population of thirty thousand, for example, two-thirds of the households owned paintings. Whereas in other countries, kings, nobles, and churches bought art, Dutch buyers were merchants, artisans, and shopkeepers. Engravings, illustrated histories, and oil paintings, even those of the widely acclaimed Rembrandt van Rijn (1606–1669), were relatively inexpensive. The pictures reflected the Dutch interest in familiar daily details: children at play, winter landscapes, and ships in port.

The family household, not the royal court, determined the moral character of this intensely commercial society. Dutch society fostered public enterprise for men and work in the home for women, who were expected to filter out the greed and materialism of commercial society by maintaining domestic harmony and virtue. Relative prosperity decreased the need for married women to work, so Dutch society developed the clear contrast between middle-class male and female roles that would become prevalent elsewhere in Europe and in America more than a century later. As one contemporary Dutch writer explained, "The husband must be on the street to practice his trade; the wife must stay at home to be in the kitchen."

Extraordinarily high levels of urbanization and literacy created a large reading public. Dutch presses printed books censored elsewhere (printers or authors censored in one province simply shifted operations to another), and the University of Leiden attracted students and professors from all over Europe. Dutch

A Typical Dutch Scene from Daily Life
Jan Steen painted *The Baker Arent Oostwaard and His Wife* in 1658. Steen ran a brewery and tavern in addition to painting, and he was known for his interest in the details of daily life. Dutch artists popularized this kind of "genre" painting, which showed ordinary people at work and play. **For more help analyzing this image, see the visual activity for this chapter in the Online Study Guide at** bedfordstmartins.com/ huntconcise. (Rijksmuseum, Amsterdam.)

tolerance extended to the works of Benedict Spinoza (1633–1677), a Jewish philosopher and biblical scholar who was expelled by his synagogue for alleged atheism but was left alone by the Dutch authorities. Spinoza strove to reconcile religion with science and mathematics, but his work scandalized many Christians and Jews because he seemed to equate God and nature. Like nature, Spinoza's God followed unchangeable laws and could not be influenced by human actions, prayers, or faith.

Dutch learning, painting, and commerce all enjoyed wide renown in the seventeenth century, but this luster proved hard to maintain. The Dutch lived in a world of international rivalries in which strong central authority gave their enemies an advantage. Though inconclusive, the naval wars with England drained the state's revenues. Even more dangerous were the land wars with France, which continued into the eighteenth century. The Dutch survived these challenges but increasingly depended on alliances with other powers, such as England. By the end of the seventeenth century, the regent elite had become more exclusive, more preoccupied with ostentation, less tolerant of deviations from strict Calvinism, and more concerned with imitating French styles than with encouraging their own.

Freedom and Slavery in the New World

The French and English also increasingly overshadowed the Dutch in the New World colonies. While the Dutch concentrated on shipping, including the slave trade, the French and English established settler colonies that would eventually provide fabulous revenues to the home countries. Many European governments encouraged private companies to vie for their share of the slave trade, and slavery began to take clear institutional form in the New World in this period. While whites found in the colonies greater political and religious freedom than in Europe, they subjected black Africans to the most degrading forms of bondage.

After the Spanish and Portuguese had shown that African slaves could be transported and forced to labor in South and Central America, the English and French endeavored to set up similar labor systems in their new Caribbean island colonies. White planters with large tracts of land bought African slaves to work fields of sugarcane, and as they gradually built up their holdings, the planters displaced most of the original white settlers, who moved to mainland North American colonies. After 1661, when Barbados instituted a slave code that stripped all Africans of rights under English law, slavery became codified as an inherited status that applied only to blacks. The result was a society of extremes: the very wealthy whites—about 7 percent of the population in Barbados—and the enslaved, powerless black majority. The English brought little of their religious or constitutional practices to the Caribbean. Other Caribbean colonies followed a similar pattern of development. Louis XIV promulgated a "black code" in 1685 to regulate the legal status of slaves in the French colonies. Although one of his aims was to prevent non-Catholics from owning slaves in the French colonies, the code had much the same effect as the English codes on the slaves themselves: they had virtually no legal rights.

The highest church and government authorities in Catholic and Protestant countries alike condoned the gradually expanding slave trade. The governments of England, France, Spain, Portugal, the Dutch Republic, and Denmark all encouraged private companies to traffic in black Africans. The Dutch West India Company was the most successful of them in this period. In the early 1600s, about 9,000 Africans were exported from Africa to the New World every year; by 1700, this figure had increased to 25,000 annually. Historians advance several different reasons for the increase in the slave trade: some claim that improvements in muskets made European slavers more formidable; others cite the rising price of slaves, which made their sale more attractive to Africans; still others focus on factors internal to Africa, such as the increasing size of African armies and their use of muskets in fighting and capturing other Africans for sale as slaves. Whatever the reason, the way had been prepared for the development of an Atlantic economy based on slavery.

Virtually left to themselves during the upheavals in England, the fledgling English colonies in North America developed representative government on their own. Almost every colony had a governor and a two-house legislature. The colonial legislatures constantly sought to increase their power and resisted the efforts of Charles II and James II to reaffirm royal control. William and Mary reluctantly allowed emerging colonial elites more control over local affairs. The social and political elite among the settlers hoped to impose an English social hierarchy dominated by rich landowners. Ordinary immigrants to the colonies, however, took advantage of plentiful land to carve out their own farms using white servants and, later in some colonies, African slaves.

For native Americans, the expanding European presence meant something else altogether. They faced death through unfamiliar diseases and warfare and the accelerating loss of their homelands. Unlike white settlers, native Americans believed that land was a divine gift provided for their collective use and not subject to individual ownership. As a result, Europeans' claims that they owned exclusive land rights caused frequent skirmishes. In 1675–1676, for instance, three tribes allied under Metacomet (called King Philip by the English) threatened the survival of New England settlers, who savagely repulsed the attacks and sold their captives as slaves. Whites portrayed native Americans as conspiring villains and sneaky heathens, akin to Africans in their savagery.

REVIEW How could outposts of constitutionalism coexist with slavery?

The Search for Order in Elite and Popular Culture

While freedom and slavery simultaneously took root in the New World, the conflict between absolutist and constitutional forms of government in Europe was giving rise to profound new thinking about the foundations of the political order. Concerns about order were not limited to politics. Poetry, painting, and architecture reflected those preoccupations, too. As European states, both absolutist and constitutional, expanded their powers, elites worked to distinguish themselves from the lower classes. They developed new codes of correct behavior for themselves and tried to teach order and discipline to their social inferiors.

Social Contract Theory: Hobbes and Locke

Two figures stood out prominently in the debates over the foundations of political authority: Thomas Hobbes and John Locke. Their writings helped shape the modern subject of political science. Hobbes justified absolute authority; Locke provided the rationale for constitutionalism. Yet both argued that all authority came not from divine right but from a social contract between citizens.

Thomas Hobbes (1588–1679) was a royalist who sat out the English civil war of the 1640s in France, where he tutored the future king Charles II. Returning to England in 1651, he published his masterpiece, *Leviathan,* in which he argued for unlimited authority in a ruler. Absolute authority could be vested in either a king or a parliament; it had to be absolute, he insisted, in order to overcome the defects of human nature. Believing that people are essentially self-centered and driven by the "right to self-preservation," Hobbes made his case by referring to science, not religion. To Hobbes, human life in a state of nature—that is, any situation without firm authority—was "solitary, poor, nasty, brutish, and short." He believed that the desire for power and natural greed would inevitably lead to unfettered competition. Only the assurance of social order could make people secure enough to act according to law; consequently, giving up personal liberty, he maintained, was the price of collective security. Rulers derived their power, he concluded, from a contract by which people gave up their natural rights to an absolute authority that guaranteed their rights in society.

Hobbes's notion of rule by an absolute authority left no room for political dissent or nonconformity, and it infuriated both royalists and supporters of Parliament. He enraged royalists by arguing that authority came not from divine right but from the social contract between citizens. Parliamentary supporters resisted Hobbes's claim that rulers must possess absolute authority to prevent the greater evil of anarchy; they believed that a constitution should guarantee shared power between king and parliament and protect individual liberties. Like Machiavelli before him, Hobbes became associated with a cynical, pessimistic view of human nature, and future political theorists often began their arguments by refuting Hobbes.

Rejecting both Hobbes and the more traditional royalist defenses of absolute authority, John Locke (1632–1704) used the notion of a social contract to provide a foundation for constitutionalism. Locke experienced political life firsthand as the physician, secretary, and intellectual companion of the earl of Shaftesbury, a leading English Whig. In 1683, Locke fled with Shaftesbury to the Dutch Republic when Charles II clamped down on those conspiring to prevent his Catholic brother from succeeding him. There Locke continued work on his *Two Treatises of Government,* which, when published in 1690, served to justify the Glorious Revolution of 1688. Locke's position was thoroughly anti-absolutist. He denied the divine right of kings and ridiculed the common royalist idea that political power in the state mirrored the father's authority in the family. Like Hobbes, he posited a state of nature that applied to all people. Unlike Hobbes, he thought people were reasonable and the state of nature peaceful.

Locke insisted that government's only purpose was to protect life, liberty, and property, a notion that linked economic and political freedom. Ultimate authority rested in the will of a majority of men who owned property, and government should be limited to its basic purpose of protection. A ruler who failed to uphold his part of the social contract between the ruler and the populace could be justifiably resisted, an idea that would become crucial for the leaders of the American Revolution a century later. For England's landowners, however, Locke helped validate a revolution that consolidated their interests and ensured their privileges in the social hierarchy.

Locke defended his optimistic view of human nature in the immensely influential *Essay concerning Human Understanding* (1690). He denied the existence of any innate ideas and asserted instead that each human is born with a mind that is a tabula rasa (blank slate). Everything humans know, he claimed, comes from sensory experience, not from anything inherent in human nature. Locke's views promoted the belief that "all men are created equal," a belief that challenged absolutist forms of rule and ultimately raised questions about women's roles as well. Not surprisingly, Locke devoted considerable energy to rethinking educational practices; he believed that education crucially shaped the human personality by channeling all sensory experience. Although he himself owned shares in the Royal African Company and justified slavery, Locke's writings were later used by abolitionists in their campaign against slavery.

Freedom and Order in the Arts and Sciences

Hobbes and Locke were not alone in wrestling with the conflicts between desires for greater freedom and the need for reassuring order. The French mathematician Blaise Pascal vividly captured the fear of chaos in his *Pensées* (*Thoughts*) of 1660: "I look on all sides, and I see only darkness everywhere. Nature presents to me nothing which is not a matter of doubt and concern. . . . It is incomprehensible that God should exist, and incomprehensible that He should not exist." Poets, artists, and scientists all tried to make sense of the individual's place within what Pascal called "the eternal silence of these infinite spaces."

The English Puritan poet John Milton (1608–1674) responded to the challenge by giving priority to individual liberty. In 1643, in the midst of the civil war between king and Parliament, he published writings in favor of divorce. When Parliament enacted a censorship law aimed at such literature, Milton countered in 1644 with one of the first defenses of freedom of the press, *Areopagitica* (*Tribunal of Opinion*). Forced into retirement after the restoration of the monarchy, Milton published in 1667 his epic poem *Paradise Lost*. He used Adam and Eve's Fall to meditate on human freedom and the tragedies of rebellion. Although Milton wanted to "justify the ways of God to man," his Satan, the proud angel who challenges God, is so compelling as to be heroic. Individuals must learn the limits of their freedom, Milton seems to say, and yet the

Gian Lorenzo Bernini, *Ecstasy of St. Teresa of Ávila*

This ultimate statement of baroque sculpture captures all the drama and even sensationalism of a mystical religious faith. Bernini based the figures in this piece, created around 1650, on a vision reported by St. Teresa in which she saw an angel: "In his hands I saw a great golden spear, and at the iron tip there appeared to be a point of fire. This he plunged into my heart several times so that it penetrated my entrails. When he pulled it out I felt that he took them with it, and left me utterly consumed by the great love of God." (Scala/Art Resource, NY.)

desire for liberty remains essential to their nature as humans, creating at times a tragic discord.

The dominant artistic styles on the continent, the baroque and the classical, both submerged the individual in a grander design, emphasizing the majesty of authority. The baroque style proved to be especially suitable for public displays of faith and power that overawed individual beholders. The combination of religious and political purposes in baroque art is best exemplified in the architecture and sculpture of Gian Lorenzo Bernini (1598–1680), the papacy's official artist. His architectural masterpiece was the gigantic square facing St. Peter's Basilica in Rome (1656–1671). His use of freestanding colonnades and a huge open space is meant to impress the individual observer with the power of the popes and the Catholic religion.

Bernini sculpted tombs and statues for the popes and private patrons. In 1665, Louis XIV hired Bernini to plan the rebuilding of the Louvre palace in Paris but then rejected his ideas as incompatible with French tastes. Although France was a Catholic country, French painters, sculptors, and architects, like their patron Louis XIV, preferred the standards of **classicism** to those of the baroque. French artists developed classicism to be a national style, distinct from the baroque style that was closely associated with France's enemies, the Austrian and Spanish Habsburgs. As its name suggests, classicism reflected the ideals of the art of antiquity; geometric shapes, order, and harmony of lines took precedence over the sensuous, exuberant, and emotional forms of the baroque. Rather than being overshadowed by the sheer power of emotional display, in classicism the individual could be found at the intersection of converging, symmetrical, straight lines. These influences were apparent in the work

French Classicism

This painting by Nicolas Poussin, *Discovery of Achilles on Skyros* (1649–1650), shows the French interest in classical themes and ideals. In the Greek story, Thetis dresses her son Achilles as a young woman and hides him on the island of Skyros so that he will not have to fight in the Trojan War. When a chest of treasures is offered to the women, Achilles reveals himself (he is the figure on the far right) because he cannot resist the sword. In telling the story, Poussin emphasizes harmony and almost a sedateness of composition, avoiding the exuberance and emotionalism of the baroque style. (Photograph © 2011 Museum of Fine Arts, Boston.)

of the leading French painters of the period, Nicolas Poussin (1594–1665) and Claude Lorrain (1600–1682), both of whom worked in Rome and tried to re-create classical Roman values in their mythological scenes and Roman landscapes.

Art might also serve the interests of science. One of the most skilled illustrators of insects and flowers was Maria Sibylla Merian (1646–1717), a German-born painter-scholar whose engravings were widely celebrated for their brilliant realism and microscopic clarity. Merian sought her own version of freedom by separating from her husband and joining a sect called the Labadists (after its French founder, Jean de Labadie), whose members did not believe in formal marriage ties and established a colony in the northern Dutch province of Friesland. After moving there with her daughters, Merian went with missionaries from the sect to the Dutch colony of Surinam in South America and painted watercolors of the exotic flowers, birds, and insects she found in the jungle around the cocoa and sugarcane plantations. In the seventeenth century, many women became known for their still lifes and especially their paintings of flowers. Paintings by the Dutch artist Rachel Ruysch, for example, fetched higher prices than works by Rembrandt.

Because of their exclusion from most universities, women only rarely participated in the new scientific discoveries. In 1667, nonetheless, the English Royal Society invited Margaret Cavendish—a writer of poems, essays, letters, and philosophical treatises—to attend a meeting to watch the exhibition of experiments. She attacked the use of telescopes and microscopes because she detected in the new experimentalism a mechanistic view of the world that exalted masculine prowess and challenged the Christian belief in free will. She nonetheless urged the formal education of women, complaining that "we are kept like birds in cages to hop up and down in our houses." She insisted, "Many of our Sex may have as much wit, and be capable of Learning as well as men."

Scientists needed freedom to publish their results, as Galileo had discovered, yet they also required support in order to carry out their work. As the scientific revolution of Galileo, Kepler, and Newton steadily gained new adherents, rulers seized upon the potential for enhancing their prestige and glory. Various German princes funded the work of Gottfried Wilhelm Leibniz (1646–1716), one of the inventors, along with Newton, of calculus. A lawyer, diplomat, and scholar who wrote about metaphysics, logic, and history, Leibniz, like Milton, ultimately wanted to explain the ways of God to humans. His most controversial view was that we live in the best of all possible worlds because it was created by a perfect God. Leibniz did not intend to expound a mindless optimism. He thought of God as like a mathematician who aims to solve problems in the simplest and most elegant fashion. Many modern scientific principles, such as the conservation of energy, followed from Leibniz's view. Leibniz also helped establish scientific societies in the German states. Government involvement in science was greatest in France, where it became an arm of mercantilist policy. In 1666, Jean-Baptiste Colbert founded the Royal Academy of Sciences, which supplied fifteen scientists with government stipends.

Women and Manners

Philosophers, poets, and painters all imaginatively explored the place of the individual within a larger whole, but real-life individuals had to learn to navigate their own social worlds. Manners—the learning of individual self-discipline—were essential skills of social navigation, and women usually took the lead in teaching them. Under the tutelage of their mothers and wives, nobles learned to hide all that was crass and to maintain a fine sense of social distinction. In some ways, aristocratic men were expected to act more like women. Just as women had long been expected to please men, now aristocratic men had to please their monarch or patron by displaying proper manners and conversing with elegance and wit. Men as well as women had to master the art of pleasing, which included a facility with foreign languages (especially French), skill in dance, a taste for fine music, and attention to dress.

As part of the evolution of new aristocratic ideals, nobles learned to disdain all that was lowly. The upper classes began to reject popular festivals and fairs in favor of private theaters, where seats were relatively expensive and behavior was formal. Clowns and buffoons now seemed vulgar; the last king of England to keep a court fool was Charles I. The greatest French playwright of the seventeenth century, Molière (the pen name of Jean-Baptiste Poquelin, 1622–1673), wrote sparkling comedies of manners that revealed much about the new aristocratic behavior. Molière's play *The*

Middle-Class Gentleman, first performed at the royal court in 1670, revolves around the yearning of a rich, middle-class Frenchman, Monsieur Jourdain, to learn to act like a *gentilhomme* (meaning both "gentleman" and "nobleman" in French). By making fun of Jourdain's outlandish aspirations, the play seems to have been an attempt to reassure the nobles at court: only true nobles by blood could hope to act like nobles. But the play also shows how the middle classes were learning to emulate the nobility: if one could learn to *act* nobly through self-discipline, could not anyone with some education and money pass himself off as noble?

As Molière's play demonstrates, new attention to manners trickled down from the court to the middle class. A French treatise on manners from 1672 explained:

> If everyone is eating from the same dish, you should take care not to put your hand into it before those of higher rank have done so. . . . Formerly one was permitted . . . to dip one's bread into the sauce, provided only that one had not already bitten it. Nowadays that would be a kind of rusticity. Formerly one was allowed to take from one's mouth what one could not eat and drop it on the floor, provided it was done skillfully. Now that would be very disgusting.

The key words "rusticity" and "disgusting" reveal the association of unacceptable social behavior with the peasantry, dirt, and repulsion. Courtly manners often permeated the upper reaches of society by means of the salon, an informal gathering held regularly in private homes and presided over by a socially eminent woman. In 1661, one French author claimed to have identified 251 Parisian women as hostesses of salons. Although the French government occasionally worried that these gatherings might be seditious, the three main topics of conversation were love, literature, and philosophy. Hostesses often worked hard to encourage the careers of budding authors. Before publishing a manuscript, many authors would read their compositions to a salon gathering. Corneille, Racine, and even Bishop Bossuet sought female approval for their writings.

Women who wrote on their own faced many obstacles. Marie-Madeleine Pioche de la Vergne, known as Madame de Lafayette, wrote several short novels that were published anonymously because it was considered inappropriate for aristocratic women to appear in print. After the publication of *The Princess of Cleves* in 1678, she denied having written it. Hannah Wooley, the English author of many books on domestic conduct, published under the name of her first husband. Women were known for writing wonderful letters, many of which circulated in handwritten form; hardly any appeared in print during the authors' lifetimes. In the 1650s, despite these limitations, French women began to turn out best sellers in a new type of literature, the novel. Their success prompted the philosopher Pierre Bayle to remark in 1697 that "our best French novels for a long time have been written by women."

The new importance of women in the world of manners and letters did not sit well with everyone. Although the French writer François Poulain de la Barre (1647–1723), in a series of works published in the 1670s, used the new science to assert the equality of women's minds, most men resisted the idea. Clergymen, lawyers, scholars, and playwrights attacked women's growing public influence. Women, they complained, were corrupting forces and needed restraint. Women were accused of raising "the banner of prostitution in the salons, in the promenades, and in the streets." Molière wrote plays denouncing women's pretension to judge literary merit. English playwrights derided learned women by creating characters with names such as Lady Knowall, Lady Meanwell, and Mrs. Lovewit. A real-life target of the English playwrights was Aphra Behn (1640–1689), one of the first professional woman authors, who supported herself as a journalist and also wrote plays and poetry. Her short novel *Oroonoko* (1688) tells the story of an African prince mistakenly sold into slavery. The story was so successful that it was adapted by playwrights and performed repeatedly in England and France for the next hundred years. Behn responded to her critics by arguing that there was "no reason why women should not write as well as men."

Reforming Popular Culture

The illiterate peasants who made up most of Europe's population had little or no knowledge of political theory, philosophy, or novels, no matter who authored them. Their culture had three main elements: the skills needed to work at farming or in a trade; popular forms of entertainment such as village fairs and dances; and their religion, which shaped every aspect of life and death. In the seventeenth century the division between elite and popular culture widened as elites insisted on their difference from the lower orders and pushed forward the ongoing effort to instill religious and social discipline in their social inferiors.

Building upon campaigns against popular "paganism" that began during the sixteenth-century Protestant and Catholic reform movements, Protestant and Catholic churches alike pushed hard to change popular religious practices. Puritans in England tried to root out maypole dances, Sunday village fairs, gambling, taverns, and bawdy ballads because they interfered with sober observance of the Sabbath. In Lutheran Norway, pastors denounced a widespread belief in the miracle-working powers of St. Olaf. The word *superstition* previously meant "false religion" (Protestantism was a superstition for Catholics, Catholicism for Protestants). In the seventeenth century, it took on its modern meaning of irrational fears, beliefs, and practices, which anyone educated or refined would avoid. *Superstition* became synonymous with popular or ignorant beliefs.

The Catholic campaign against superstitious practices found a ready ally in Louis XIV. While he reformed the nobles at court through etiquette and manners, Catholic bishops in the French provinces trained parish priests to reform their flocks by using catechisms in local dialects and insisting that parishioners attend Mass. The church faced a formidable challenge. One bishop in France complained in 1671, "Can you believe that there are in this diocese entire villages where no one has even heard of Jesus Christ?" In some places, believers sacrificed animals to the Virgin Mary, prayed to the new moon, and worshipped at the sources of streams as in pre-Christian times.

Like its Protestant counterpart, the Catholic campaign against ignorance and superstition helped extend state power. Clergy, officials, and local police worked together to limit carnival celebrations (festivities before the beginning of Lent that often had a riotous character), to regulate pilgrimages to shrines, and to replace

Corpus Christi Procession in Peru
The Catholic campaign against paganism extended to Spanish possessions in the New World. This painting shows a Catholic procession by Incas that took place in the late 1670s in Cuzco, Peru. The Inca in front is wearing his native dress; he is followed by a float and religious figures carrying traditional Catholic imagery. (Museo del Arzobispo, Cuzco, Peru.)

"indecent" images of saints with more restrained and decorous ones. In Catholicism, the cult of the Virgin Mary and devotions closely connected with Jesus, such as the Holy Sacrament and the Sacred Heart, took precedence over the celebration of more popular saints who seemed to have pagan origins or were credited with unverified miracles. Reformers everywhere tried to limit the number of feast days on the grounds that they encouraged lewd behavior.

The campaign for more disciplined religious practices helped generate a new attitude toward the poor. Poverty previously had been closely linked with charity and virtue in Christianity: it was a Christian duty to give alms to the poor, and Jesus and many of the saints had purposely chosen lives of poverty. In the sixteenth and seventeenth centuries, the upper classes, the church, and the state increasingly regarded the poor as dangerous, deceitful, and lacking in character. "Criminal laziness is the source of all their vices," wrote a Jesuit expert on the poor. The courts had previously expelled beggars from cities; now local leaders, both Catholic and Protestant, tried to reform their character. In the sixteenth century, local and state officials began to levy taxes for more organized poor relief; after the mid-seventeenth century officials began to transform hospitals into houses of confinement for beggars. In Catholic France, upper-class women's religious associations, known as confraternities, set up asylums that confined prostitutes (by arrest if necessary) and rehabilitated them. Confraternities also founded hospices where orphans learned order and respect. Such groups advocated harsh discipline as the cure for poverty.

Although hard times had increased the numbers of poor people and the rates of violent crime as well, the most important changes were attitudinal. The elites wanted to separate the very poor from society either to change them or to keep them from contaminating others. Hospitals became holding pens for society's unwanted

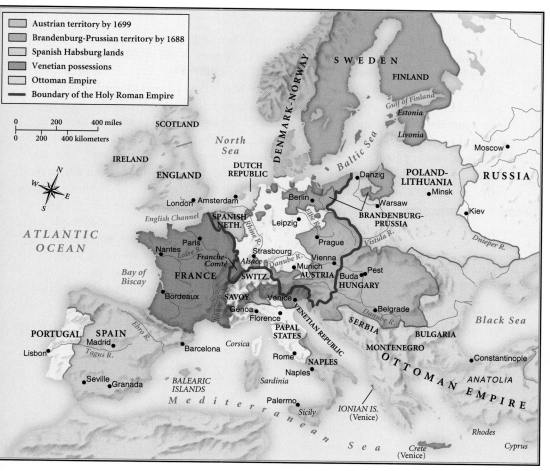

Mapping the West Europe at the End of the Seventeenth Century
Size was not necessarily an advantage in the late 1600s. Poland-Lithuania, a large country on the map, had been fatally weakened by internal conflicts. In the next century it would disappear entirely. While the Ottoman Empire still controlled an extensive territory, outside of Anatolia its rule depended on intermediaries. The Austrian Habsburgs had pushed the Turks out of Hungary and back into the Balkans. The tiny Dutch Republic, meanwhile, had become very rich through international commerce and was the envy of far larger nations.

members, where the poor joined the disabled, the incurably diseased, and the insane. The founding of hospitals demonstrates the connection between these attitudes and

state building. In 1676, Louis XIV ordered every French city to establish a hospital, and his government took charge of their finances. Other rulers soon followed the same path.

> **REVIEW** In what ways did elite and popular culture become more separate during the second half of the seventeenth century?

Conclusion

The search for order in the wake of religious warfare and political upheaval took place on various levels, from the reform of the disorderly poor to the establishment of more regular bureaucratic routines in government. The biggest factor shaping the search for order was the growth of state power. Whether absolutist or constitutionalist in form, seventeenth-century states all aimed to penetrate more deeply into the lives of their subjects. They wanted more men for their armed forces, higher taxes to support their projects, and more control over foreign trade, religious dissent, and society's unwanted.

Some tearing had begun to appear, however, in the seamless fabric of state power. In England, the Dutch Republic, and the English North American colonies, property owners successfully demanded constitutional guarantees of their right to participate in government. In the eighteenth century, moreover, new levels of economic growth and the appearance of new social groups would exert pressures on the European state system. The success of seventeenth-century rulers created the political and economic conditions in which their critics would flourish.

CHAPTER REVIEW QUESTIONS

1. What are the most important differences between absolutism and constitutionalism as political systems?
2. Why was the search for order a major theme in science, politics, and the arts during the second half of the seventeenth century?

For practice quizzes and other study tools, see the Online Study Guide at bedfordstmartins.com/huntconcise.

For primary-source material from this period, see Chapter 16 of *Sources of THE MAKING OF THE WEST*, Third Edition.

TIMELINE

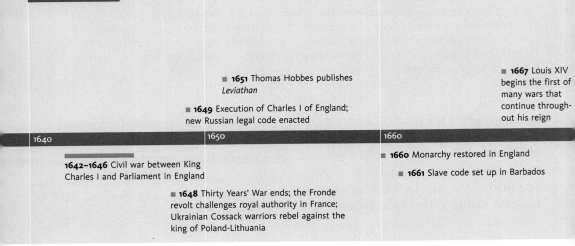

1651 Thomas Hobbes publishes *Leviathan*

1649 Execution of Charles I of England; new Russian legal code enacted

1667 Louis XIV begins the first of many wars that continue throughout his reign

1640   1650   1660

1642–1646 Civil war between King Charles I and Parliament in England

1648 Thirty Years' War ends; the Fronde revolt challenges royal authority in France; Ukrainian Cossack warriors rebel against the king of Poland-Lithuania

1660 Monarchy restored in England

1661 Slave code set up in Barbados

Suggested References

Recent studies have insisted that absolutism could never be entirely absolute because the king depended on collaboration to enforce his policies. Some of the best sources for Louis XIV's reign are the letters written by important noblewomen.

Barkey, Karen. *The Ottoman Route to State Centralization.* 1994.

*Beik, William. *Louis XIV and Absolutism: A Brief Study with Documents.* 2000.

Brook, Timothy. *Vermeer's Hat: The Seventeenth Century and the Dawn of the Global World.* 2008.

Cowart, Georgia. *The Triumph of Pleasure: Louis XIV and the Politics of Spectacle.* 2008.

Cromwell, Oliver: http://www.olivercromwell.org/

Davis, Natalie Zemon. *Women on the Margins: Three Seventeenth-Century Lives.* 1995.

*Forster, Elborg, trans. *A Woman's Life in the Court of the Sun King: Elisabeth Charlotte, Duchesse d'Orléans.* 1984.

France in America (site of the Library of Congress on French colonies in North America): http://international.loc.gov/intldl/fiahtml/fiatheme.html#track1

Hill, Christopher. *The World Turned Upside Down: Radical Ideas during the English Revolution.* 1972.

Kotilaine, Jarmo, and Marshall Poe, eds. *Modernizing Muscovy: Reform and Social Change in Seventeenth-Century Russia.* 2004.

*Pincus, Steven C. A. *England's Glorious Revolution, 1688–1689: A Brief History with Documents.* 2006.

Versailles: http://www.chateauversailles.fr

Wilkinson, Richard. *Louis XIV.* 2007.

■ **1670** Molière's play *The Middle-Class Gentleman* first performed at the French court

■ **1678** Marie-Madeleine Pioche de la Vergne (Madame de Lafayette) anonymously publishes *The Princess of Cleves*

■ **1688** Parliament forces James II to abdicate and invites the daughter of James II, Mary, and her husband, William of Orange, to take the English throne in the "Glorious Revolution"

| 1670 | 1680 | 1690 |

■ **1683** Austrian Habsburgs break the Turkish siege of Vienna

■ **1685** Louis XIV revokes toleration for French Protestants granted by the Edict of Nantes

■ **1690** John Locke publishes *Two Treatises of Government* and *Essay concerning Human Understanding*

The Atlantic System and Its Consequences

JOHANN SEBASTIAN BACH (1685–1750), composer of mighty organ fugues and church cantatas, was not above amusing his Leipzig audiences, many of them university students. In 1732 he produced a cantata about a young woman in love with coffee. Her old-fashioned father rages that he won't find her a husband unless she gives up the fad. She agrees, secretly vowing to admit no suitor who will not promise in the marriage contract to let her brew coffee whenever she wants. Bach offers this conclusion:

The cat won't give up its mouse,
Girls stay faithful coffee-sisters
Mother loves her coffee habit,
Grandma sips it gladly too—
Why then shout at the daughters?

Bach's era might well be called the age of coffee. European travelers at the end of the sixteenth century had noticed Middle Eastern people drinking a "black drink," *kavah*. Few Europeans sampled it at first, and the Arab monopoly on its production kept prices high. This changed around 1700 when the Dutch East India Company introduced coffee plants to Java and other Indonesian islands. Coffee production then spread to the French Caribbean, where African slaves provided the plantation labor. In Europe, imported coffee spurred the development of a new kind of meeting place: London's first coffeehouse opened in 1652, and the idea spread quickly to other European cities. Coffeehouses became gathering places for men to drink, read newspapers, and talk politics. Even Isaac Newton had his favorite coffeehouse. As a London newspaper commented in 1737, "There's scarce an Alley in City and Suburbs but has a Coffeehouse in it, which may be called the School of Public Spirit, where every Man over Daily and Weekly Journals, a Mug, or a Dram . . . devotes himself to that glorious one, his Country."

London Coffeehouse

This gouache (a variant on watercolor painting) from about 1725 depicts a scene from a London coffeehouse located in the courtyard of the Royal Exchange (merchants' bank). Middle-class men, wearing wigs, read newspapers, drink coffee, smoke pipes, and discuss the news of the day. The coffeehouse draws them out of their homes into the new public sphere. (© *British Museum, London, England/The Bridgeman Art Library.*)

521

European consumption of coffee, tea, chocolate, and other novelties increased dramatically as European nations forged worldwide economic links. At the center of this new world economy was the **Atlantic system**, which bound together western Europe, Africa, and the Americas. Europeans bought slaves in western Africa, transported and sold them in their colonies in North and South America and the Caribbean, bought commodities such as coffee and sugar produced by the new colonial **plantations**, and then sold the goods in European ports for refining and reshipment. This Atlantic system first took clear shape in the early eighteenth century; it was the hub of European expansion all over the world.

Coffee drinking was one example among many of the new social and cultural patterns that took root between 1690 and 1740. Improvements in agricultural production at home reinforced the effects of trade overseas; Europeans now had more disposable income for "extras," and they spent their money not only in the new coffeehouses and cafés that sprang up all over Europe but also on newspapers, musical concerts, paintings, and novels. A new middle-class public began to make its presence felt in every domain of culture and social life, creating a new public sphere that would ultimately transform the nature of politics on both sides of the Atlantic.

Although the rise of the Atlantic system gave Europe new prominence in the global context, European rulers still focused most of their political, diplomatic, and military energies on their rivalries within Europe. A coalition of countries succeeded in containing French aggression, and a more balanced diplomatic system emerged. In eastern Europe, Prussia and Austria had to contend with the rising power of Russia under Peter the Great. In western Europe, both Spain and the Dutch Republic declined in influence but continued to vie with Britain and France for colonial spoils in the Atlantic. The more evenly matched competition among the great powers encouraged the development of diplomatic skills and drew attention to public health as a way of encouraging population growth.

In the aftermath of Louis XIV's revocation of the Edict of Nantes in 1685, a new intellectual movement known as the **Enlightenment** began to germinate. French Protestant refugees began to publish works critical of absolutism in politics and religion. Increased prosperity, the growth of a middle-class public, and the decline in warfare after Louis XIV's death in 1715 all fostered the development of this new critical spirit. Fed by the popularization of science and the growing interest in travel literature, the Enlightenment encouraged greater skepticism about religious and state authority. Building on the growth of the new public sphere, eventually the movement would question almost every aspect of social and political life in Europe. The Enlightenment began in western Europe in those countries—Britain, France, and the Dutch Republic—most affected by the new Atlantic system. It, too, was a product of the age of coffee.

CHAPTER FOCUS QUESTION   What were the most important consequences of the growth of the Atlantic system?

The Atlantic System and the World Economy

European ships had been circling the globe since the early 1500s, and European colonization had dramatically altered the landscape and populations of the Americas, yet only in the 1700s did Europe draw most of the rest of the world into its economic orbit. Western European trading nations sent ships loaded with goods to buy slaves from local rulers on the western coast of Africa; transported the slaves to the colonies in North and South America and the Caribbean and sold them to the owners of plantations producing coffee, sugar, cotton, and tobacco; and bought the raw commodities produced in the colonies and shipped them back to Europe, where they were refined or processed and then sold to other parts of Europe and the world. This Atlantic system and the growth of international trade helped create a new consumer society.

Slavery and the Atlantic System

Spain and Portugal had dominated Atlantic trade in the sixteenth and seventeenth centuries, but in the eighteenth century European trade in the Atlantic rapidly expanded and became more systematically interconnected (Map 14.1). By 1650, Portugal had already sent 200,000 African slaves to Brazil to work on the new sugar plantations (large tracts of lands farmed by slave labor). Realizing that plantations producing staples for Europeans could bring fabulous wealth, the European powers grew less interested in the dwindling trade in precious metals and more eager to colonize. Large-scale planters of sugar, tobacco, and coffee displaced small farmers who relied on one or two servants. Planters and their plantations won out because slave labor was cheap and therefore able to produce mass quantities of commodities at low prices.

State-chartered private companies from Portugal, Spain, France, Britain, the Dutch Republic, Prussia, and even Denmark exploited the 3,500-mile coastline of West Africa for slaves. Before 1675, most blacks taken from Africa had been sent to Brazil or Spanish America on Portuguese ships, but by 1725 more than 60 percent of African slaves landed in the Caribbean (Figure 14.1), and more and more of them were carried on British or French ships. All in all, 90 percent of the slaves were transported by Portuguese, British, or French ships. After 1700, the plantation economy also began to expand on the North American mainland. The numbers stagger the imagination. More than 11 million Africans were transported to the Americas before the slave trade began to wind down after 1850. Some 1.4 million died during the passage across the ocean. Many traders gained spectacular wealth, but companies did not always make profits. The English Royal African Company, for example, delivered 100,000 slaves to the Caribbean and imported 30,000 tons of sugar to Britain, yet lost money after the few profitable years following its founding in 1672.

The balance of white and black populations in the New World colonies was determined by the staples produced. New England merchants and farmers bought few slaves because they did not own plantations. Blacks—both slave and free—made

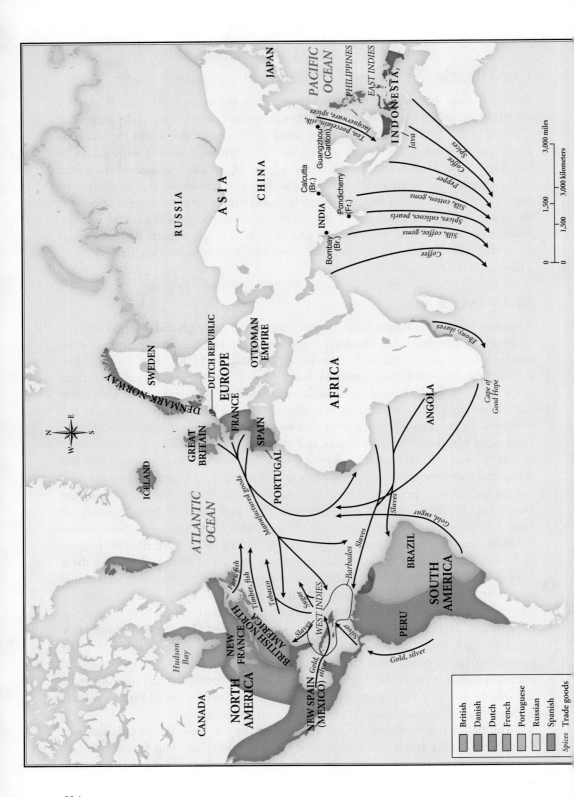

Map 14.1 European Trade Patterns, c. 1740

By 1740, the European powers had colonized much of North and South America and incorporated their American colonies into a worldwide system of commerce centered on the slave trade and plantation production of staple crops. Europeans still sought spices and luxury goods in China and the East Indies, but outside of Java, few Europeans had settled permanently in these areas. How did control over colonies determine dominance in this period? **For more help analyzing this map, see the map activity for this chapter in the Online Study Guide at** bedfordstmartins.com/huntconcise.

up only 3 percent of the population in eighteenth-century New England, compared with 60 percent in South Carolina. On the whole, the British North American colonies contained a higher proportion of African Americans from 1730 to 1765 than at any other time in American history. The imbalance of whites and blacks was even more extreme in the Caribbean. In the early 1700s, the British sugar islands had a population of about 150,000 people, only 30,000 of them Europeans. The remaining 80 percent were African slaves, as most indigenous people died fighting Europeans or the diseases they brought.

Enslaved women and men suffered terribly. Most had been sold to European traders by Africans from the west coast who acquired them through warfare or kidnapping. The vast majority were between fourteen and thirty-five years old. Before they were crammed onto ships for the three-month transatlantic trip, their heads were shaved, they were stripped naked, and some were branded with red-hot irons. Men and women were separated. Men were shackled with leg irons. Sailors and officers raped the women whenever they wished and beat those who refused their

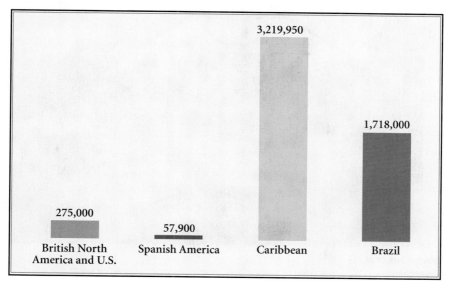

Figure 14.1 African Slaves Imported into American Territories, 1701–1800

During the eighteenth century, planters in the newly established Caribbean colonies imported millions of African slaves to work the new plantations. The vast majority of African slaves transported to the Americas ended up either in the Caribbean or in Brazil.

advances. In the cramped and appalling conditions aboard ship, as many as one-fourth of the slaves died in transit.

Once they landed, slaves were forced into degrading and oppressive conditions. As soon as masters bought slaves, they gave them new names, often only first names, and in some colonies branded them as personal property. Slaves had no social identities of their own; they were expected to learn their master's language and to do any job assigned. Slaves worked fifteen- to seventeen-hour days and were fed only enough to keep them on their feet. Brazilian slaves consumed more calories than the poorest Brazilians do today, but that hardly made them well fed. The death rate among slaves was high, especially in Brazil, where quick shifts in the weather, lack of clothing, and squalid living conditions made them susceptible to a variety of deadly illnesses.

Not surprisingly, despite the threat of torture or death on recapture, slaves sometimes ran away. In Brazil, runaways hid in *quilombos* (hideouts) in the forests or backcountry. When the quilombo of Palmares was discovered and destroyed in 1695, it had thirty thousand fugitives, who had formed their own social organization complete with elected kings and councils of elders. Outright revolt was uncommon,

Caribbean Sugar Mill
This seventeenth-century engraving of a sugar mill, or grinder, makes the work seem much less difficult than it was in practice. Slaves cut the sugarcane and then hauled it from the fields to the mill, where it was crushed. Many slaves lost fingers or hands in the process. The slaves then collected the juice (bottom center) and carried it to the boilers (bottom left and right). The sap was poured into molds and dried. The bricks of raw sugar were then exported to Europe for refining. (The Granger Collection, NY.)

especially before the nineteenth century, but other forms of resistance included stealing food, breaking tools, and feigning illness or stupidity. Slaveholders' fears about conspiracy and revolt lurked beneath the surface of every slave-based society. In 1710, the royal governor of Virginia reminded the colonial legislature of the need for unceasing vigilance: "We are not to Depend on Either Their Stupidity, or that Babel of Languages among 'em; freedom Wears a Cap which Can Without a Tongue, Call Togather all Those who Long to Shake off the fetters of Slavery." Masters defended whipping and other forms of physical punishment as essential to maintaining discipline. Laws called for the castration of a slave who struck a white person.

Plantation owners often left their colonial possessions in the care of agents and collected the revenue to live as wealthy landowners back home, where they built opulent mansions and gained influence in local and national politics. William Beckford, for example, was sent from Jamaica to England to attend school as a young boy. When he inherited sugar plantations and shipping companies from his father and older brother, he moved the headquarters of the family business to London in the 1730s to be close to the government and financial markets. His holdings formed the single most powerful economic interest in Jamaica, but he preferred to live in England, where he could collect art for his many luxurious homes, hold political office (he served as lord mayor of London and in Parliament), and even lend money to the government.

The slave trade permanently altered consumption patterns for ordinary people. Sugar had been prescribed as medicine before the end of the sixteenth century, but the development of plantations in Brazil and the Caribbean made it a standard food item. By 1700, the British sent home fifty million pounds of sugar a year, a figure that doubled by 1730. During the French Revolution of the 1790s, sugar shortages would become a cause for rioting in Paris. Equally pervasive was the spread of tobacco. By the 1720s, Britain imported two hundred shiploads of tobacco from Virginia and Maryland every year, and men of every country and class smoked pipes or took snuff.

The traffic in slaves disturbed many Europeans. As a government memorandum to the Spanish king explained in 1610, "Modern theologians in published books commonly report on, and condemn as unjust, the acts of enslavement which take place in provinces of this Royal Empire." Between 1667 and 1671, the French Dominican monk Father Du Tertre published three volumes in which he denounced the mistreatment of slaves in the French colonies.

In the 1700s, however, slaveholders began to justify their actions by demeaning the mental and spiritual qualities of enslaved Africans. White Europeans and colonists sometimes described black slaves as animal-like, akin to apes. A leading New England Puritan asserted this about black slaves: "Indeed their *Stupidity* is a *Discouragement*. It may seem, unto as little purpose, to *Teach*, as to *wash an Aethiopian* [Ethiopian]." One of the great paradoxes of this time was that talk of liberty and self-evident rights, especially prevalent in Britain and its North American colonies, coexisted with the belief that some people were meant to be slaves. Although Christians believed in principle in a kind of spiritual equality between blacks and whites, the churches often defended or at least did not oppose the inequities of slavery.

World Trade and Settlement

The Atlantic system helped extend European trade relations across the globe. The textiles that British shippers exchanged for slaves on the west coast of Africa, for example, were manufactured in India and exported by the British East India Company, a government-chartered joint-stock company that ended up virtually ruling India. As much as one-quarter of the British exports to Africa in the eighteenth century were actually reexports from India. To expand its trade in the rest of the world, Europeans seized territories and tried to establish permanent settlements. The eighteenth-century extension of European power prepared the way for western global domination in the nineteenth and twentieth centuries.

In contrast to the sparsely inhabited trading outposts in Asia and Africa, the colonies in the Americas bulged with settlers. The British North American colonies, for example, contained about 1.5 million nonnative (that is, white settler and black slave) residents by 1750. While the Spanish competed with the Portuguese for control of South America, the French competed with the British for control of North America. Spanish and British settlers came to blows over the boundary between the British colonies and Florida, which was held by Spain.

Local economies shaped colonial social relations. Men in French trapper communities in Canada, for example, had little in common with the men and women of the plantation societies in Barbados or Brazil. Racial attitudes also differed from place to place. The Spanish and Portuguese tolerated intermarriage with the native populations in both America and Asia. Sexual contact, both inside and outside marriage, fostered greater racial variety in the Spanish and Portuguese colonies than in the French and British territories (though mixed-race people could be found everywhere). By 1800, **mestizos**, children of Spanish men and Indian women, accounted for more than a quarter of the population in the Spanish colonies, and many of them aspired to join the local elite. Greater racial diversity seems not to have improved the treatment of slaves, however, which was probably harshest in Portuguese Brazil.

Where intermarriage between colonizers and natives was common, conversion to Christianity proved most successful. Although the Indians maintained many of their native religious beliefs, the majority of Indians in the Spanish colonies had come to consider themselves Catholics by 1700. Indian carpenters and artisans in the villages produced innumerable altars, retables (painted panels), and sculpted images to adorn their local churches, and individual families put up domestic shrines. Yet the clergy remained overwhelmingly Spanish: the church hierarchy concluded that the Indians' humility and innocence made them unsuitable for the priesthood.

In the early years of American colonization, many more men than women emigrated from Europe. At the end of the seventeenth century, the gender imbalance began to decline but remained substantial. Two and a half times as many men as women were among the immigrants leaving Liverpool, England, between 1697 and 1707, for example. Women who emigrated as indentured servants ran great risks: if they did not die of disease during the voyage, they might end up giving birth to illegitimate children (the fate of at least one in five servant women) or being virtually sold into marriage.

The uncertainties of life in the American colonies provided new opportunities for European women and men willing to live outside the law, however. In the 1500s and 1600s, the English and Dutch governments had routinely authorized pirates to prey on the shipping of their rivals, the Spanish and Portuguese. Then, in the late 1600s, English, French, and Dutch bands made up of deserters and crews from wrecked vessels began to form their own associations of pirates, especially in the Caribbean. Called **buccaneers** from their custom of curing strips of beef, called *boucan* by the native Caribs of the islands, the pirates governed themselves and preyed on everyone's shipping without regard to national origin. After 1700, the colonial governments tried to stamp out piracy. As one English judge argued in 1705, "A pirate is in perpetual war with every individual and every state. . . . They are worse than ravenous beasts."

White settlements in Africa and Asia remained small and almost insignificant, except for their long-term potential. Europeans had little contact with East Africa and almost none with Africa's vast interior. A few Portuguese trading posts in Angola and Dutch farms on the Cape of Good Hope provided the only toeholds for future expansion. In China, the emperors had welcomed Catholic missionaries at court in the seventeenth century, but the priests' credibility diminished as they squabbled among themselves and associated with European merchants, whom the Chinese considered pirates. "The barbarians [Europeans] are like wild beasts," one Chinese official concluded. In 1720, only one thousand Europeans resided in Guangzhou (Canton), the sole place where foreigners could legally trade for spices, tea, and silk (Map 14.1, page 524).

Europeans exercised more influence in India and Java, in the East Indies. Dutch coffee production in Java and nearby islands increased phenomenally in the early 1700s, and many Dutch settled there to oversee production and trade. In India, Dutch, British, French, Portuguese, and Danish companies competed for spices, cotton, and silk. By the 1740s the British and French had become the leading rivals in India, just as they were in North America. Both countries extended their power as India's Muslim rulers lost control to local Hindu princes, rebellious Sikhs, invading Persians, and their own provincial governors. A few thousand Europeans lived in India, though many thousands more soldiers were stationed there to protect them. The staple of trade with India in the early 1700s was calico—lightweight, brightly colored cotton cloth that caught on as a fashion in Europe.

Europeans who visited India were especially struck by what they viewed as exotic religious practices. In a book published in 1696 of his travels to western India, an Anglican minister described fakirs (religious ascetics), "some of whom show their devotion by a shameless appearance, and walking naked." Such writings increased European interest in the outside world, but they also fed a European sense of superiority that helped excuse violent forms of colonial domination.

India Cottons and Trade with the East
This colored cotton cloth (now faded with age) was painted and embroidered in Madras, in southern India, in the late 1600s. The male figure with the mustache may be a European, but the female figures are clearly Asian. Europeans, especially the British, discovered that they could make big profits on the export of Indian cotton cloth to Europe. They also traded Indian cotton in Africa for slaves and sold large quantities in the colonies. (V&A Images/Victoria and Albert Museum, London.)

The Birth of a Consumer Society

Worldwide colonization produced new supplies of goods, from coffee to calico, and population growth in Europe fueled demand for them. Beginning first in Britain, then in France and the Italian states, and finally in eastern Europe, population surged, growing by about 20 percent between 1700 and 1750. The gap between a fast-growing northwestern Europe and a more stagnant southern and central Europe now diminished as regions that had lost population during the seventeenth-century downturn recovered. Cities in particular grew. Between 1600 and 1750, London's population more than tripled, and Paris's more than doubled.

Although contemporaries could not have realized it then, this was the start of the modern "population explosion." It appears that a decline in the death rate, rather than a rise in the birthrate, explains the turnaround. Three main factors contributed to this decline in the death rate: better weather and hence more bountiful harvests, improved agricultural techniques, and the plague's disappearance after 1720.

By the early eighteenth century, the effects of economic expansion and population growth brought about a **consumer revolution**. The British East India Company began to import into Britain huge quantities of calico. British imports of tobacco doubled between 1672 and 1700. At Nantes, the center of the French sugar trade, imports quadrupled between 1698 and 1733. Tea, chocolate, and coffee became virtual necessities. In the 1670s, only a trickle of tea reached London, but by 1720 the East India Company sent 9 million pounds to England—a figure that rose to 37 million pounds by 1750. In 1700, England had two thousand coffeehouses; by 1740, every English country town had at least two. Paris got its first cafés at the end of the seventeenth century; Berlin opened its first coffeehouse in 1714; Bach's Leipzig boasted eight coffeehouses by 1725.

The birth of consumer society did not go unnoticed by eyewitnesses. In the English economic literature of the 1690s, writers began to express a new view of humans as consuming animals with boundless appetites. Such opinions gained a wide audience with the appearance of Bernard Mandeville's poem *Fable of the Bees* (1705), which argued that private vices might have public benefits. Mandeville insisted that pride, self-interest, and the desire for material goods (all Christian vices) in fact promoted economic prosperity: "every part was full of Vice, Yet the whole mass a Paradise." Many authors attacked the new doctrine of consumerism, and the French government banned the poem's publication. But Mandeville had captured the essence of the emerging market for consumption.

> **REVIEW**   How is consumerism related to slavery?

New Social and Cultural Patterns

The impact of the Atlantic system and world trade was most apparent in the cities, where people had more money for consumer goods and more opportunities to participate in new public activities. But rural changes also had significant long-term influence, as a revolution in agricultural techniques made it possible to feed more and more people with a smaller agricultural workforce. As population increased, more people moved to the cities, where they found themselves caught up in innovative urban customs such as attending musical concerts and reading novels. Along with a general increase in literacy, these activities helped create a new public sphere ready to respond to new styles and new ideas. Social and cultural changes were not uniform across Europe, however; as usual, people's experiences varied depending on whether they lived in wealth or poverty, in urban or rural areas, or in eastern or western Europe.

The Agricultural Revolution

Although Britain, France, and the Dutch Republic shared the enthusiasm for consumer goods, Britain's domestic market grew most quickly. In Britain, as agricultural output increased 43 percent over the course of the 1700s, the population increased by 70 percent. The British imported grain to feed the growing population, but they also benefited from the development of techniques that together constituted an

agricultural revolution. No new machinery propelled this revolution—just more aggressive attitudes toward investment and management. The Dutch and Flemish had pioneered many of these techniques in the 1600s, but the British took them further.

Four major changes occurred in British agriculture that eventually spread to other countries. First, farmers increased the amount of land under cultivation by draining wetlands and by growing crops on previously uncultivated common lands (acreage maintained by the community for grazing). Second, farmers who could afford to do so consolidated smaller, scattered plots into larger, more efficient units. Third, livestock raising became more closely linked to crop growing, and the yields of each increased. (See "Taking Measure.") For centuries, most farmers had rotated their fields in and out of production to replenish the soil. Now farmers planted carefully chosen fodder crops such as clover and turnips that added nutrients to the soil, thereby eliminating the need to leave a field fallow (unplanted) every two or three years. With more fodder available, farmers could raise more livestock, which in turn produced more manure to fertilize grain fields. Fourth, selective breeding of animals combined with the increase in fodder to improve the quality and size of herds. New crops had only a slight impact. Potatoes, for example, were introduced

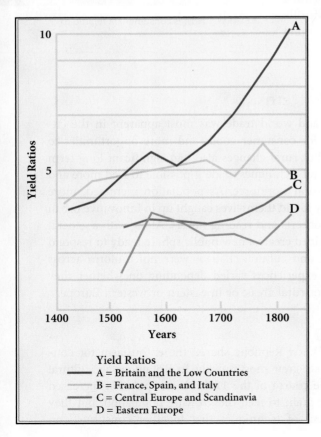

Taking Measure Relationship of Crop Harvested to Seed Used, 1400–1800

The impact and even the timing of the agricultural revolution can be seen in this figure, based on yield ratios (the number of grains produced for each seed planted). Britain, the Dutch Republic, and the Austrian Netherlands all experienced huge increases in crop yields after 1700. Other European regions lagged behind right into the 1800s. What are the economic and social consequences of having a higher crop yield?

Yield Ratios

A = Britain and the Low Countries
B = France, Spain, and Italy
C = Central Europe and Scandinavia
D = Eastern Europe

to Europe from South America in the 1500s, but because people feared they might cause leprosy, tuberculosis, or fevers, they were not grown in quantity until the late 1700s. By the 1730s and 1740s, agricultural output had increased dramatically, and prices for food had fallen because of these interconnected innovations.

Changes in agricultural practices did not benefit all landowners equally. The biggest British landowners consolidated their holdings in the "enclosure movement." They put pressure on small farmers and villagers to sell their land or give up their common lands. The big landlords then fenced off ("enclosed") their property. Because enclosure eliminated community grazing rights, it frequently sparked a struggle between the big landlords and villagers, and in Britain it normally required an act of Parliament. Such acts became increasingly common in the second half of the eighteenth century, and by the century's end six million acres of common lands had been enclosed and developed. "Improvers" produced more food more efficiently and thus supported a growing population.

Contrary to the fears of contemporaries, small farmers and cottagers (those with little or no property) were not forced off the land all at once. But most villagers could not afford the litigation involved in resisting enclosure, and small landholders consequently had to sell out to landlords or farmers with larger plots. Landlords with large holdings leased their estates to tenant farmers at constantly increasing rents, and tenant farmers in turn employed cottagers as salaried agricultural workers. In this way the English peasantry largely disappeared, replaced by a more hierarchical society of big landlords, enterprising tenant farmers, and poor agricultural laborers.

The new agricultural techniques spread slowly from Britain and the Low Countries (the Dutch Republic and the Austrian Netherlands) to the rest of western Europe. Outside a few pockets in northern France and the western German states, however, subsistence agriculture (producing just enough to get by rather than surpluses for the market) continued to dominate farming in western Europe and Scandinavia. In southwestern Germany, for example, 80 percent of the peasants produced no surplus because their plots were too small. Unlike the populations of the highly urbanized Low Countries (where half the people lived in towns and cities), most Europeans, western and eastern, eked out an existence in the countryside.

In eastern Europe, the condition of peasants worsened in the areas where landlords tried hardest to improve their yields. To produce more for the Baltic grain market, aristocratic landholders in Prussia, Poland, and parts of Russia drained wetlands, cultivated moors, and built dikes. They also forced peasants off lands the peasants worked for themselves, increased compulsory labor services (the critical element in serfdom), and began to manage their estates directly. Some eastern landowners grew fabulously wealthy. The Potocki family in the Polish Ukraine, for example, owned three million acres of land and had 130,000 serfs. In parts of Poland and Russia, the serfs hardly differed from slaves in status, and their "masters" ran their huge estates much like American plantations.

Social Life in the Cities

Because of emigration from the countryside, cities grew in population and consequently exercised more influence on culture and social life. Between 1650 and 1750, cities with at least 10,000 inhabitants increased in population by 44 percent. From the eighteenth century onward, urban growth would be continuous. Along with the general growth of cities, an important south-to-north shift occurred in the pattern of urbanization. Around 1500, half of the people in cities of at least 10,000 residents could be found in the Italian states, Spain, or Portugal; by 1700, the urbanization of northwestern and southern Europe was roughly equal. Eastern Europe, despite the huge cities of Istanbul and Moscow, was still less urban than western Europe. London was by far the most populous European city, with 675,000 inhabitants in 1750; Berlin had 90,000 people, Warsaw only 23,000.

Many landowners kept a residence in town, so the separation between rural and city life was not as extreme as might be imagined, at least not for the very rich. At the top of the ladder in the big cities were the landed nobles. Some of them filled their lives only with conspicuous consumption of fine food, extravagant clothing, coaches, books, and opera; others held key political, administrative, or judicial offices. However they spent their time, these rich families employed thousands of artisans, shopkeepers, and domestic servants. Many English peers (the highest-ranking nobles) had thirty or forty servants at each of their homes.

The middle classes of officials, merchants, professionals, and landowners occupied the next rung down on the social ladder. London's population, for example, included about twenty thousand middle-class families (constituting, at most, one-sixth of the city's population). In this period, the middle classes began to develop distinctive ways of life that set them apart from both the rich noble landowners and the lower classes. Unlike the rich nobles, the middle classes lived primarily in the cities and towns, even if they owned small country estates. They ate more moderately than nobles but much better than peasants or laborers. For breakfast, the British middle classes ate toast and rolls and, after 1700, drank tea. Dinner, served midday, consisted of roasted or boiled beef, mutton, poultry, or pork, and vegetables. Supper was a light meal of bread and cheese with cake or pie. Beer was the main drink in London, and many families brewed their own. Even children drank beer because of the lack of fresh water.

In contrast to the gigantic and sprawling countryseats of the richest English peers, middle-class houses in town had about seven rooms, including four or five bedrooms and one or two living rooms, still many more than the homes of poor agricultural workers. New household items reflected society's increasing wealth and its exposure to colonial imports. By 1700, the middle classes of London typically had several mirrors, a coffeepot and coffee mill, numerous pictures and ornaments, a china collection, and several clocks. Life for the middle classes on the European continent was quite similar, though wine replaced beer in France.

Below the middle classes came the artisans and shopkeepers (most of whom were organized in professional guilds), then the journeymen, apprentices, servants, and laborers. At the bottom of the social scale were the unemployed poor, who survived on intermittent work and charity. Women married to artisans and shopkeepers often kept the accounts, supervised employees, and ran the household. Every home from the middle classes to the upper classes employed servants; artisans and shop-keepers frequently hired them, too. Women from poorer families usually worked as domestic servants until they married. Four out of five domestic servants in the city were female. In large cities such as London, the servant population grew faster than the population of the city as a whole.

Social status in the cities was readily visible. Wide, spacious streets graced rich districts; the houses had gardens, and the air was relatively fresh. In poor districts, the streets were narrow, dirty, dark, humid, and smelly, and the houses were damp and crowded. The poorest people were homeless, sleeping under bridges or in abandoned homes. A Neapolitan prince described his homeless neighbors as "lying like filthy animals, with no distinction of age or sex." In some districts, rich and poor lived in the same buildings; the poor clambered up to shabby, cramped apartments on the top floors.

Like shelter, clothing was a reliable social indicator. The poorest workingwomen in Paris wore woolen skirts and blouses of dark colors over petticoats, bodice, and corset. They also donned caps of various sorts, cotton stockings, and shoes (probably their only pair). Workingmen dressed even more drably. Many occupations could be recognized by their dress: no one could confuse lawyers in their dark robes with masons or butchers in their special aprons, for example. People higher on

Vauxhall Gardens, London
This hand-colored print from the mid-1700s shows the newly refurbished gardens near the Thames River. Prosperous families show off their brightly colored clothes and listen to a public concert by the orchestra seated just above them. These activities helped form a more self-conscious public.
(© Bibliothèque des Arts Décoratifs, Paris, France/The Bridgeman Art Library.)

the social ladder were more likely to sport a variety of fabrics, colors, and unusual designs in their clothing and to own many different outfits. Social status was not an abstract idea; it permeated every detail of daily life.

Public Hygiene and Health Care

The growth of cities created new challenges for public hygiene. Cities were notoriously unhealthy because excrement (animal and human) and garbage accumulated where people lived densely packed together. Paris seemed to a visitor "so detestable that it is impossible to remain there" because of the smell. Even the facade of the Louvre palace was soiled by the contents of night commodes that servants routinely dumped out of windows every morning. Only the wealthy could escape walking in mucky streets, by hiring men to carry them in sedan chairs or drive them in coaches.

After investigating specific cities, medical geographers urged government campaigns to improve public sanitation. Everywhere, environmentalists gathered and analyzed data on climate, disease, and population, searching for correlations to help direct policy. As a result of these efforts, local governments undertook such measures as draining low-lying areas, burying refuse, and cleaning wells, all of which eventually helped lower the death rates from epidemic diseases.

Hospitals and medical care underwent lasting transformations. Founded originally as charities concerned foremost with the moral worthiness of the poor, hospitals gradually evolved into medical institutions that defined patients by their diseases. The process of diagnosis changed as physicians began to use specialized Latin terms for illnesses. The gap between medical experts and their patients increased, as physicians now also relied on postmortem dissections in the hospital to gain better knowledge, a practice most patients' families resented. Press reports of body snatching and grave robbing by surgeons and their apprentices outraged the public well into the 1800s.

Despite the change in hospitals, individual health care remained something of a free-for-all in which physicians competed with bloodletters, itinerant venereal disease doctors, bonesetters, druggists, midwives, and "cunning women," who specialized in home remedies. The medical profession, with nationwide organizations and licensing, had not yet emerged, and no clear line separated trained physicians from quacks. Physicians often followed popular prescriptions for illnesses because they had nothing better to offer. Patients were as likely to die of diseases caught in the hospital as to be cured there. Antiseptics were nearly unknown.

The various "medical opinions" about childbirth highlight the confusion people faced. Midwives delivered most babies, though they sometimes encountered criticism even from within their own ranks. One consulting midwife complained that ordinary midwives in Bristol, England, made women in labor drink a mixture of leek juice and their husbands' urine. By the 1730s, female midwives faced competition from male midwives, who were known for using instruments such as forceps to pull babies out of the birth canal. Women rarely sought a physician's help in giving birth, however; they preferred the advice and assistance of trusted local midwives. In any case, trained physicians were few in number and almost nonexistent outside cities.

Hardly any infectious diseases could be cured, though inoculation against smallpox spread from the Middle East to Europe in the early eighteenth century, thanks largely to the efforts of Lady Mary Wortley Montagu, who learned about the technique while living in Constantinople. After 1750, physicians developed successful procedures for wide-scale vaccination, although even then many people resisted the idea of inoculating themselves with a disease. Other diseases spread quickly in the unsanitary conditions of urban life. Ordinary people washed or changed clothes rarely, lived in overcrowded housing with poor ventilation, and got their water from contaminated sources, such as refuse-filled rivers.

Until the mid-1700s, most people considered bathing dangerous. Public bathhouses had disappeared from cities in the sixteenth and seventeenth centuries because they seemed a source of disorderly behavior and epidemic illness. In the eighteenth century, even private bathing came into disfavor because people feared the effects of contact with water. Fewer than one in ten newly built private mansions in Paris had baths. Bathing was hazardous, physicians insisted, because it opened the body to disease. One manners manual of 1736 admonished, "It is correct to clean the face every morning by using a white cloth to cleanse it. It is less good to wash with water, because it renders the face susceptible to cold in winter and sun in summer." The upper classes associated cleanliness not with baths but with frequently changed linens, powdered hair, and perfume, which was thought to strengthen the body and refresh the brain by counteracting corrupt and foul air.

The New Public Sphere

Cities may have been unhealthy, but they promoted the development of a new public sphere that rested in the first instance on the spread of literacy. City people were more literate than peasants. Protestant countries appear to have been more successful at promoting education and literacy than Catholic countries, perhaps because of the Protestant emphasis on Bible reading. Widespread popular literacy was first achieved in the Protestant areas of Switzerland and in Presbyterian Scotland, and rates were also very high in the New England colonies and the Scandinavian countries. In France, literacy doubled in the eighteenth century thanks to the spread of parish schools, but still only one in two men and one in four women could read and write. Despite the efforts of some Protestant German states to encourage primary education, primary schooling remained woefully inadequate almost everywhere in Europe: few schools existed, teachers received low wages, and no country had yet established a national system of control or supervision.

Despite the deficiencies of primary education, a new literate public arose, especially among the middle classes of the cities. More books and periodicals were published than ever before. England and the Dutch Republic led the way in this powerful outpouring of printed words. The trend began in the 1690s and gradually accelerated. In 1695, the English government allowed the licensing system through which it controlled publications to lapse, and new newspapers and magazines appeared almost immediately. The first London daily newspaper came out in 1702, and in

1709 Joseph Addison and Richard Steele published the first literary magazine, the *Spectator*. They devoted their magazine to the cultural improvement of the increasingly influential middle class. By the 1720s, twenty-four provincial newspapers were published in England. In the London coffeehouses, an edition of a single newspaper might reach ten thousand male readers. Women did their reading at home.

Newspapers on the continent lagged behind and often consisted mainly of advertising with little critical commentary. France, for example, had no daily paper until 1777. The new literate public did not just read newspapers; its members now pursued an interest in painting, attended concerts, and besieged booksellers in search of popular novels. Because increased trade and prosperity put money into the hands of the growing middle classes, the new public sphere began to compete with the churches, rulers, and courtiers as chief patrons of new work. As the public for the arts expanded, printed commentary on them emerged, setting the stage for the appearance of political and social criticism. New artistic tastes thus had effects far beyond the realm of the arts.

Developments in painting reflected the tastes of the new public. The **rococo** style challenged the hold of the baroque and classical schools, especially in France. Like the baroque, the rococo emphasized irregularity and asymmetry, movement and curvature, but it did so on a much smaller, subtler scale. Many rococo paintings depicted scenes of intimate sensuality rather than the monumental, emotional grandeur favored by classical and baroque painters. Personal portraits and pastoral paintings took the place of heroic landscapes and large ceremonial canvases. Rococo

Rococo Painting

This painting by the Venetian artist Rosalba Carriera (1675–1757) is titled *Africa*. The young black girl wearing a turban represents the African continent. Carriera was known for her use of pastels. In 1720, she journeyed to Paris, where she became an associate of Antoine Watteau and helped inaugurate the rococo style in painting. Why might the artist have chosen to paint an African girl? **For more help analyzing this image, see the visual activity for this chapter in the Online Study Guide at** bedfordstmartins.com/huntconcise. (Gemälde-galerie Alte Meister, Staatliche Kunstsammlungen Dresden.)

paintings adorned homes as well as palaces and served as a form of interior decoration rather than as a statement of piety. Its decorative quality made rococo art
an ideal complement to newly discovered materials such as stucco and porcelain,
especially the porcelain vases now imported from China.

Rococo was an invented word (from the French word *rocaille,* meaning "shell-
work") and originally a derogatory label meaning "frivolous decoration." But the
great French rococo painters, such as Antoine Watteau (1684–1721) and François
Boucher (1703–1770), were much more than mere decorators. Although both
emphasized the erotic in their depictions, Watteau captured the melancholy side of
a passing aristocratic style of life, and Boucher painted middle-class people at home
during their daily activities. Both painters thereby contributed to the emergence of
new sensibilities in art that increasingly attracted a middle-class public.

Music as well as art grew in popularity. The first public music concerts were
performed in England in the 1670s, becoming much more regular and frequent
in the 1690s. City concert halls typically seated about two hundred, but the relatively high price of tickets limited attendance to the better-off. Music clubs provided
entertainment in smaller towns and villages. In continental Europe, Frankfurt organized the first regular public concerts in 1712; Hamburg and Paris began holding
them within a few years. Opera continued to spread in the eighteenth century;
Venice had sixteen public opera houses by 1700, and Covent Garden opera house
opened in London in 1732.

The growth of a public that appreciated and supported music had much the
same effect as the extension of the reading public: like authors, composers could now
begin to liberate themselves from court patronage and work for a paying audience.
This development took time to solidify, however, and court or church patrons still
commissioned much eighteenth-century music. Bach, a German Lutheran, wrote
his *St. Matthew Passion* for Good Friday services in 1729 while he was organist and
choirmaster for the leading church in Leipzig. He composed secular works (like
the "Coffee Cantata" quoted at the beginning of this chapter) for the public and a
variety of private patrons.

The composer George Frederick Handel (1685–1759) was among the first to
grasp the new directions in music. He began his career playing second violin in
the Hamburg opera orchestra and then moved to Britain in 1710, where he eventually turned to composing oratorios, a form he introduced in Britain. The oratorio
combined the drama of opera with the majesty of religious and ceremonial music
and featured the chorus over the soloists. Handel's most famous oratorio, *Messiah*
(1741), reflects his personal, deeply felt piety but also his willingness to combine
musical materials into a dramatic form that captured the enthusiasm of the new
public. In 1740, a poem published in the *Gentleman's Magazine* exulted, "His art so
modulates the sounds in all, / Our passions, as he pleases, rise and fall." Music had
become an integral part of the new public sphere.

But nothing captured the imagination of the new public more than the novel,
the literary genre whose very name underscored the eighteenth-century taste for

novelty. Over three hundred French novels appeared between 1700 and 1730. During this unprecedented explosion, the novel took on its modern form and became more concerned with individual psychology and social description than with the picaresque adventures popular earlier (such as Cervantes's *Don Quixote*). The novel's popularity was closely tied to the expansion of the reading public, and novels were available in serial form in periodicals or from the many booksellers who popped up to serve the new market.

Women figured prominently in novels as characters, and women writers abounded. The English novel *Love in Excess* (1719) quickly reached a sixth printing, and its author, Eliza Haywood (1693?–1756), earned her living turning out a stream of novels with titles such as *Persecuted Virtue, Constancy Rewarded,* and *The History of Miss Betsy Thoughtless*—all showing a concern for the proper place of women as models of virtue in a changing world. Haywood had first worked as an actress when her husband deserted her and her two children, but she soon turned to writing plays and novels. In the 1740s, she began publishing a magazine, the *Female Spectator,* which argued in favor of higher education for women.

Haywood's male counterpart was Daniel Defoe (1660?–1731), a merchant's son who had a diverse and colorful career as a manufacturer, political spy, novelist, and social commentator. Defoe's novel about a shipwrecked sailor, *Robinson Crusoe* (1719), portrayed the new values of the time: to survive, Crusoe had to meet every challenge with fearless entrepreneurial ingenuity. He had to be ready for the unexpected and be able to improvise in every situation. He was, in short, the model for the new man in an expanding economy. Crusoe's patronizing attitude toward the black man Friday now draws much critical attention, but his discovery of Friday shows how the fate of blacks and whites had become intertwined in the new colonial environment.

Religious Revivals

Despite the novel's growing popularity, religious books and pamphlets still sold in huge numbers, and most Europeans remained devout, even as their religions were changing. In this period, a Protestant revival known as **Pietism** rocked the complacency of the established churches in the German Lutheran states, the Dutch Republic, and Scandinavia. Pietists believed in a mystical religion of the heart; they wanted a more deeply emotional, even ecstatic religion. They urged intense Bible study, which in turn promoted popular education and contributed to the increase in literacy. Many Pietists attended catechism instruction every day and also went to morning and evening prayer meetings in addition to regular Sunday services.

Catholicism also had its versions of religious revival. A Frenchwoman, Jeanne Marie Guyon (1648–1717), attracted many noblewomen and a few leading clergymen to her own Catholic brand of Pietism, known as Quietism. Claiming miraculous visions and astounding prophecies, she urged a mystical union with God through prayer and simple devotion. Despite papal condemnation and intense controversy within Catholic circles in France, Guyon had followers all over Europe.

Even more influential were the Jansenists, who gained many new adherents to their austere form of Catholicism despite Louis XIV's harassment and repeated condemnation by the papacy (see page 486). Under the pressure of religious and political persecution, Jansenism took a revivalist turn in the 1720s. At the funeral of a Jansenist priest in Paris in 1727, the crowd that flocked to the grave claimed to witness a series of miraculous healings. Within a few years, a cult formed around the priest's tomb, and clandestine Jansenist presses reported new miracles to the reading public. When the French government tried to suppress the cult, one enraged wit placed a sign at the tomb that read, "By order of the king, God is forbidden to work miracles here." Some believers fell into frenzied convulsions, claiming to be inspired by the Holy Spirit through the intercession of the dead priest. After midcentury, Jansenism became even more politically active as its adherents joined in opposition to crown policies on religion.

> **REVIEW** What were the social and political consequences of the agricultural revolution?

Consolidation of the European State System

The spread of Pietism and Jansenism reflected the emergence of a middle-class public that now participated in every new development, including religion. The middle classes could pursue these interests because the European state system gradually stabilized. Warfare settled three main issues between 1690 and 1740: a coalition of powers held Louis XIV's France in check on the continent; Great Britain emerged from the wars against Louis as the preeminent maritime power; and Russia defeated Sweden in the contest for supremacy in the Baltic. After Louis XIV's death in 1715, Europe enjoyed the fruits of a more balanced diplomatic system, in which warfare became less frequent and less widespread. States could then spend their resources establishing and expanding control over their own populations, both at home and in their colonies.

French Ambitions Thwarted

Lying on his deathbed in 1715, the seventy-six-year-old Louis XIV watched helplessly as his accomplishments continued to unravel. Not only had his plans for territorial expansion been thwarted, but his incessant wars had exhausted the treasury, despite new taxes. In 1689, Louis's rival, William III, prince of Orange and king of England and Scotland (r. 1689–1702), had set out to forge a European alliance that eventually included Britain, the Dutch Republic, Sweden, Austria, and Spain. The allies fought Louis to a stalemate in the War of the League of Augsburg, sometimes called the Nine Years' War (1689–1697), and when hostilities resumed four years later, they finally put an end to Louis's expansionist ambitions.

The War of the Spanish Succession (1701–1713) broke out when the mentally and physically feeble Charles II (r. 1665–1700) of Spain died without a direct heir. The Spanish succession could not help but be a burning issue. Even though Spanish power had declined steadily since Spain's golden age in the sixteenth century, Spain still had extensive territories in Italy and the Netherlands and colonies overseas. Before Charles died, he named Louis XIV's second grandson, Philip, duke of Anjou, as his heir, but the Austrian emperor Leopold I refused to accept Charles's deathbed will. In the ensuing war, the French lost several major battles and had to accept disadvantageous terms in the Peace of Utrecht of 1713–1714 (Map 14.2). Although Philip was recognized as king of Spain, he had to renounce any future claim to the French crown, thus barring unification of the two kingdoms. Spain surrendered its territories in Italy and the Netherlands to the Austrians and Gibraltar to the British; France ceded possessions in North America (Newfoundland, the Hudson Bay area, and most of Nova Scotia) to Britain. France no longer threatened to dominate European power politics.

At home, Louis's policy of absolutism had fomented bitter hostility. Nobles fiercely resented his promotions of commoners to high office. The duke of Saint-Simon complained that "falseness, servility, admiring glances, combined with a dependent and cringing attitude, above all, an appearance of being nothing without him, were the only ways of pleasing him." On his deathbed, Louis XIV gave his blessing and some sound advice to his five-year-old great-grandson and successor, Louis XV (r. 1715–1774): "My child, you are about to become a great King. Do not imitate my love of building nor my liking for war."

After being named regent, the duke of Orléans (1674–1723), nephew of the dead king, revived some of the parlements' powers and tried to give leading nobles a greater say in political affairs. Financial problems plagued the regency as they would beset all succeeding French regimes in the eighteenth century. In 1719, the regent appointed the Scottish financier John Law to the top financial position of controller general. Law founded a trading company for North America and a state bank that issued paper money and stock (without them, trade depended on the available supply of gold and silver). The bank was supposed to offer lower interest rates to the state, thus cutting the cost of financing the government's debts. The value of the stock rose rapidly in a frenzy of speculation, only to crash a few months later. With it vanished any hope of establishing a state bank or issuing paper money for nearly a century.

France finally achieved a measure of financial stability under the leadership of Cardinal Hercule de Fleury (1653–1743), the most powerful member of the government after the death of the regent. Fleury aimed to avoid adventure abroad and keep social peace at home; he balanced the budget and carried out a large project for road and canal construction. Colonial trade boomed. Peace and the acceptance of limits on territorial expansion inaugurated a century of French prosperity.

British Rise and Dutch Decline

The English and Dutch had formed a coalition against Louis XIV under their joint ruler, William III, who was simultaneously stadholder of the Dutch Republic and, with his English wife, Mary (d. 1694), ruler of England, Wales, Scotland, and Ireland. After William's death in 1702, the English and Dutch went their separate ways. Dutch imperial power declined, even though Dutch merchants still controlled a substantial

Map 14.2 Europe, c. 1715

Although Louis XIV succeeded in putting his grandson Philip on the Spanish throne, France emerged from the War of the Spanish Succession considerably weakened. France ceded large territories in Canada to Britain, which also gained key Mediterranean outposts from Spain as well as a monopoly on providing slaves to the Spanish colonies. Spanish losses were catastrophic: Philip had to renounce any future claim to the French crown and give up considerable territory in the Netherlands and Italy to the Austrians.

portion of world trade. English relations with Scotland and Ireland were complicated by the problem of succession: William and Mary had no children. To ensure a Protestant succession, Parliament ruled that Mary's sister, Anne, would succeed William and Mary and that the Protestant house of Hanover in Germany would succeed Anne if she had no surviving heirs. Catholics were excluded. When Queen Anne (r. 1702–1714) died leaving no children, the elector of Hanover, a Protestant great-grandson of James I, consequently became King George I (r. 1714–1727). The house of Hanover—renamed the house of Windsor during World War I in response to anti-German sentiment—still occupies the British throne.

Support from the Scots and Irish for this solution did not come easily because many in Scotland and Ireland supported the claims to the throne of the deposed Catholic king, James II, and, after his death in 1701, his son James Edward. Out of fear of this Jacobitism (from the Latin *Jacobus,* "James"), Scottish Protestant leaders agreed to the Act of Union of 1707, which abolished the Scottish Parliament and affirmed the Scots' recognition of the Protestant Hanoverian succession. The Scots agreed to obey the Parliament of Great Britain, which would include Scottish members in the House of Commons and the House of Lords. A Jacobite rebellion in Scotland in 1715, aiming to restore the Stuart line, was suppressed (Map 14.2, page 543). The threat of Jacobitism nonetheless continued into the 1740s.

The Irish, 90 percent of whom were Catholic, proved even more difficult to subdue. When James II went to Ireland in 1689 to raise a Catholic rebellion against the new monarchs of England, William III responded by taking command of the joint English and Dutch forces and defeating James's Irish supporters. James fled to France, and the Catholics in Ireland faced yet more confiscation and legal restrictions. By 1700, Irish Catholics, who in 1640 had owned 60 percent of the land in Ireland, owned just 14 percent. The Protestant-controlled Irish Parliament passed a series of laws limiting the rights of the Catholic majority: Catholics could not bear arms, send their children abroad for education, establish Catholic schools at home, or marry Protestants. Catholics could not sit in Parliament, nor could they vote for its members unless they took an oath renouncing Catholic doctrine. These and a host of other laws reduced Catholic Ireland to the status of a colony. One British official commented in 1745, "The poor people of Ireland are used worse than negroes." Most of the Irish were peasants who lived in primitive housing and subsisted on a meager diet that included no meat.

The Parliament of Great Britain was soon dominated by the Whigs. In Britain's constitutional system, the monarch ruled with Parliament. The crown chose the ministers, directed policy, and supervised administration, while Parliament raised revenue, passed laws, and represented the interests of the people to the crown. The powers of Parliament were reaffirmed by the Triennial Act of 1694, which provided that Parliament must meet at least once every three years (this was extended to seven years in 1716, after the Whigs had established their ascendancy). Only 200,000 propertied men could vote, out of a population of more than five million people, and not surprisingly, most members of Parliament came from the landed gentry. In fact, a few hundred families controlled all the important political offices.

George I and George II (r. 1727–1760) relied on one man, Sir Robert Walpole (1676–1745), to help them manage their relations with Parliament. From his position as first lord of the treasury, Walpole made himself into first, or "prime," minister, leading the House of Commons from 1721 to 1742. Although appointed initially by the king, Walpole established an enduring pattern of parliamentary government in which a prime minister from the leading party guides legislation through the House of Commons. Walpole also built a vast patronage machine that dispensed government jobs to win support for the crown's policies. Walpole's successors relied more and more on the patronage system and eventually alienated not only the Tories but also the middle classes in London and even the North American colonists.

The partisan division between the Whigs, who had supported the Hanoverian succession and the rights of dissenting Protestants, and the Tories, who had backed the Stuart line and the Anglican church, did not hamper Great Britain's pursuit of economic, military, and colonial power. In this period, Britain became a great power on the world stage by virtue of its navy and its ability to finance major military involvement in the wars against Louis XIV. The founding in 1694 of the Bank of England—which, unlike the French bank, endured—enabled the government to raise money at low interest for foreign wars. By the 1740s, the government could borrow more than four times what it could in the 1690s.

Sir Robert Walpole at a Cabinet Meeting
Sir Robert Walpole and George II developed the institution of the cabinet, which brought together the important heads of government departments. Walpole's cabinet was the ancestor of modern cabinets in Great Britain and the United States. How might discussions in the new coffeehouses (shown in the illustration on page 520) have influenced the kinds of decisions made by Walpole and his cabinet? (The Fotomas Index, U.K./The Bridgeman Art Library.)

By contrast, the Dutch Republic, one of the richest and most influential states of the seventeenth century, saw its power eclipsed in the eighteenth. When William of Orange (William III of England) died in 1702, he left no heirs, and for forty-five years the Dutch lived without a stadholder. The merchant ruling class of some two thousand families dominated the Dutch Republic more than ever, but they presided over a country that counted for less in international power politics. In some areas, Dutch decline was only relative. The Dutch population was not growing as fast as populations elsewhere, for example, and the Dutch share of the Baltic trade decreased from 50 percent in 1720 to less than 30 percent by the 1770s. After 1720, the Baltic countries—Prussia, Russia, Denmark, and Sweden—began to ban imports of manufactured goods to protect their own industries, and Dutch trade in particular suffered. The output of Leiden textiles dropped to one-third its 1700 level by 1740. Shipbuilding, paper manufacturing, tobacco processing, salt refining, and pottery production all dwindled as well. The biggest exception to the downward trend was trade with the New World, which increased with escalating demands for sugar and tobacco. The Dutch shifted their interest away from great-power rivalries toward those areas of international trade and finance where they could establish an enduring presence.

Russia's Emergence as a European Power

The commerce and shipbuilding of the Dutch and English so impressed the Russian tsar Peter I (r. 1689–1725) that he traveled incognito to their shipyards in 1697 to learn their methods firsthand. Known to history as Peter the Great, he dragged Russia kicking and screaming all the way to great-power status. Although he came to the throne while still a minor (on the eve of his tenth birthday), grew up under the threat of a palace coup, and enjoyed little formal education, his accomplishments soon matched his seven-foot-tall stature. Peter transformed public life in Russia and established an absolutist state on the Western model. His **Westernization** efforts ignited an enduring controversy: did Peter set Russia on a course of inevitable Westernization required to compete with the West, or did he forever and fatally disrupt Russia's natural evolution into a distinctive Slavic society?

Peter reorganized government and finance on Western models and, like other absolute rulers, strengthened his army. With ruthless recruiting methods, which included branding a cross on every recruit's left hand to prevent desertion, he forged an army of 200,000 men and equipped it with modern weapons. He created schools for artillery, engineering, and military medicine and built the first navy in Russian history. Not surprisingly, taxes tripled.

The tsar allowed nothing to stand in his way. He did not hesitate to use torture and executed thousands. He allowed a special regiment of guards unprecedented power to expedite cases against those suspected of rebellion, espionage, pretensions to the throne, or just "unseemly utterances against him." Opposition to his policies reached into his own family. When his only son, Alexei, allied himself with Peter's critics, the young man was thrown into prison, where he mysteriously died.

Peter the Great
In this painting by Gottfried Danhauer (1680–1733/7), the Russian tsar appears against the backdrop of his most famous battle, Poltava. The angel holds a laurel wreath, a symbol of victory, over his head. (© Tretyakov Gallery, Moscow, Russia/The Bridgeman Art Library.)

To control the often restive nobility, Peter insisted that all noblemen engage in state service. The Table of Ranks (1722) classified them into military, administrative, and court categories, a codification of social and legal relationships in Russia that would last for nearly two centuries. All social and material advantages now depended on serving the crown. Because the nobles lacked a secure independent status, Peter could command them to a degree that was unimaginable in western Europe. State service was not only compulsory but also permanent. Moreover, the male children of those in service had to be registered by the age of ten and begin serving at fifteen. To increase his authority over the Russian Orthodox church, Peter allowed the office of patriarch (supreme head) to remain vacant, and in 1721 he replaced it with the Holy Synod, a bureaucracy of laymen under his supervision. To many Russians, Peter was the Antichrist incarnate.

With the goal of Westernizing Russian culture, Peter set up the first greenhouses, laboratories, and technical schools and founded the Russian Academy of Sciences. He ordered translations of Western classics and hired a German theater company to perform the French plays of Molière. He replaced the traditional Russian calendar with the Western one,* introduced Arabic numerals, and in 1703 brought out the first public newspaper. He ordered his officials and the nobles to shave their beards and dress in Western fashion, and he even issued precise regulations about the suitable style of jacket, boots, and cap (generally French or German). He published a book on manners for young noblemen and experimented with dentistry on his courtiers.

Peter built a new capital city, named St. Petersburg after him. It symbolized Russia opening to the West. Construction began in 1703 in a Baltic province that had been recently conquered from Sweden. By the end of 1709, forty thousand recruits a year

---

*Peter introduced the Julian calendar, then still used in Protestant but not Catholic countries. Later in the eighteenth century, Protestant Europe abandoned the Julian for the Gregorian calendar. Not until 1918 was the Julian calendar abolished in Russia, at which point it had fallen thirteen days behind Europe's Gregorian calendar.

found themselves assigned to the projects there. Peter ordered skilled workers to move to the new city and commanded all landowners possessing more than forty serf households to build houses there. In the 1720s, a German minister described the city "as a wonder of the world, considering its magnificent palaces . . . and the short time that was employed in the building of it." By 1710, the permanent population of St. Petersburg reached eight thousand. At Peter's death in 1725, it had forty thousand residents.

As a new city far from the Russian heartland around Moscow, St. Petersburg represented a decisive break with Russia's past. Peter widened that gap by every means possible. At his new capital, he tried to improve the traditionally denigrated, secluded status of women by ordering them to dress in European styles and appear publicly at his dinners for diplomatic representatives. Imitating French manners, he decreed that women attend his new social salons of officials, officers, and merchants for conversation and dancing. A foreigner headed every one of Peter's new technical and vocational schools, and for its first eight years the new Academy of Sciences included no Russians. Every ministry was assigned a foreign adviser. Upper-class Russians learned French or German, which they often spoke even at home. Such changes affected only the very top of Russian society, however. The mass of the population had no contact with the new ideas and ended up paying for the innovations either in ruinous new taxation or by building St. Petersburg, a project that cost the lives of thousands of workers. Serfs remained tied to the land, completely dominated by their noble lords.

Despite all his achievements, Peter could not ensure his succession. In the thirty-seven years after his death in 1725, Russia endured six different rulers, including a boy of twelve, an infant, and an imbecile. Recurrent palace coups weakened the monarchy and enabled the nobility to loosen Peter's rigid code of state service. In the process, the status of the serfs only worsened. They ceased to be counted as legal subjects; the criminal code of 1754 listed them as property. They not only were bought and sold like cattle but also had become legally indistinguishable from them. Westernization had not yet touched their lives.

Changes in the Balance of Power in the East

Peter the Great's success in building up state power changed the balance of power in eastern Europe. Overcoming initial military setbacks, Russia eventually defeated Sweden and took its place as the leading power in the Baltic region. Russia could then turn its attention to eastern Europe, where it competed with Austria and Prussia. Formerly mighty Poland-Lithuania became the playground for great-power rivalries.

Sweden had dominated the Baltic region since the Thirty Years' War and did not easily give up its preeminence. In 1700, when Peter the Great formed an anti-Swedish coalition with Denmark, Saxony, and Poland, Sweden's Charles XII (r. 1697–1718) stood up to the test. Still in his teens at the beginning of the Great Northern War, Charles first defeated Denmark, then destroyed the new Russian army, and quickly marched into Poland and Saxony. After defeating the Poles and occupying Saxony, Charles invaded Russia. Here Peter's rebuilt army finally defeated him at the battle of Poltava (1709).

The Russian victory resounded everywhere. The Russian ambassador to Vienna reported, "It is commonly said that the tsar will be formidable to all Europe, that he will be a kind of northern Turk." Prussia and other German states joined the anti-Swedish alliance, and when Charles XII died in battle in 1718, the Great Northern War finally came to an end. By the terms of the Treaty of Nystad (1721), Sweden ceded its eastern Baltic provinces—Livonia, Estonia, Ingria, and southern Karelia—to Russia. Sweden also lost territories on the north German coast to Prussia and the other allied German states (Map 14.3). An aristocratic reaction against Charles XII's incessant demands for war supplies swept away Sweden's absolutist regime, essentially removing Sweden from great-power competition.

Prussia had to make the most of every military opportunity, as it did in the Great Northern War, because it was much smaller in size and population than Russia, Austria, or France. King Frederick William I (r. 1713–1740) doubled the size of the Prussian army; though much smaller than the armies of his rivals, it was the best trained and most up-to-date force in Europe. By 1740, Prussia had Europe's highest proportion of men at arms (1 of every 28 people, versus 1 in 157 in France and 1 in 64 in Russia) and the highest proportion of nobles in the military (1 in 7 noblemen, as compared with 1 in 33 in France and 1 in 50 in Russia).

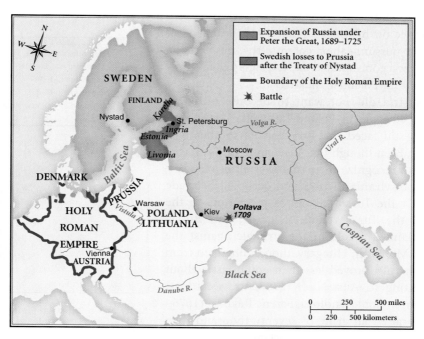

Map 14.3 Russia and Sweden after the Great Northern War, 1721
After the Great Northern War, Russia supplanted Sweden as the major power in the north. Although Russia had a much larger population from which to draw its armies, Sweden made the most of its advantages and gave way only after a great military struggle.

The army so dominated life in Prussia that the country earned the description "a large army with a small state attached." So obsessed was Frederick William with his soldiers that the five-foot-five-inch-tall king formed a regiment of "giants," the Grenadiers, composed exclusively of men over six feet tall. Royal agents scoured Europe trying to find such men and sometimes kidnapped them right off the street. Frederick William, "the Sergeant King," was one of the first rulers to wear a military uniform as his everyday dress. He subordinated the entire domestic administration to the army's needs. He also installed a system for recruiting soldiers by local district quotas. He financed the army growth by subjecting all the provinces to an excise tax on food, drink, and manufactured goods and by increasing rents on crown lands. Prussia was now poised to become one of the major players on the continent of Europe.

During the War of the Polish Succession (1733–1735), Prussia stood on the sidelines, content to watch the bigger powers fight each other. The war showed how the balance of power had changed since the heyday of Louis XIV: France had to maneuver within a complex great-power system that now included Russia, and Poland-Lithuania no longer controlled its own destiny. When the king of Poland-Lithuania died in 1733, France, Spain, and Sardinia went to war against Austria and Russia, each side supporting rival claimants to the Polish throne. After Russia drove the French candidate out of Poland-Lithuania, France agreed to accept the Austrian candidate. In exchange, Austria gave the province of Lorraine to the French candidate, the father-in-law of Louis XV, with the promise that the province would pass to France on his death. France and Britain went back to pursuing their colonial rivalries. Prussia and Russia concentrated on shoring up their influence within Poland-Lithuania.

Austria did not want to become mired in a long struggle in Poland-Lithuania because its armies still faced the Turks on its southeastern border. Even though the Austrians had forced the Turks to recognize their rule over all of Hungary and Transylvania in 1699 and occupied Belgrade in 1717, the Turks did not stop fighting. In the 1730s, the Turks retook Belgrade, and Russia now claimed a role in the struggle against the Turks. Moreover, Hungary, though liberated from Turkish rule, proved less than enthusiastic about submitting to Austria. In 1703, the wealthiest Hungarian noble landlord, Ferenc Rákóczi (1676–1735), raised an army of seventy thousand men who fought for "God, Fatherland, and Liberty"

Austrian Conquest of Hungary, 1657–1730

until 1711. They forced the Austrians to recognize local Hungarian institutions, grant amnesty, and restore confiscated estates in exchange for confirming hereditary Austrian rule.

The Power of Diplomacy and the Importance of Numbers

No single power emerged from the wars of the first half of the eighteenth century clearly superior to the others, and the idea of maintaining a balance of power guided both military and diplomatic maneuvering. The Peace of Utrecht had explicitly declared that such a balance was crucial to maintaining peace in Europe, and in 1720 a British pamphleteer wrote, "There is not, I believe, any doctrine in the law of nations, of more certain truth . . . than this of the balance of power." It was the universal law of gravitation of European politics. This system of equilibrium often rested on military force, such as the leagues formed against Louis XIV or the coalition against Sweden. All states counted on diplomacy, however, to resolve issues even after fighting had begun.

To meet the new demands placed on it, the diplomatic service, like the military and financial bureaucracies before it, had to develop regular procedures. The French set a pattern of diplomatic service that the other European states soon imitated. By 1685, France had embassies in all the important capitals. Nobles of ancient families served as ambassadors to Rome, Madrid, Vienna, and London, whereas royal officials were chosen for Switzerland, the Dutch Republic, and Venice. Most held their appointments for at least three or four years, and all went off with elaborate written instructions that included explicit statements of policy as well as full accounts of the political conditions of the country to which they were posted. The ambassador selected and paid for his own staff. This practice could make the journey to a new post very cumbersome, because the staff might be as large as eighty people, and they brought along all their own furniture, pictures, silverware, and tapestries. It took one French ambassador ten weeks to get from Paris to Stockholm.

By the early 1700s, French writings on diplomatic methods were read everywhere. François de Callières's manual *On the Manner of Negotiating with Sovereigns* (1716) insisted that sound diplomacy was based on the creation of confidence, rather than deception: "The secret of negotiation is to harmonize the real interests of the parties concerned." Callières believed that the diplomatic service had to be professional— that young attachés should be chosen for their skills, not their family connections. These sensible views did not prevent the development of a dual system of diplomacy, in which rulers issued secret instructions that often negated the official ones sent by their own foreign offices. Secret diplomacy had some advantages because it allowed rulers to break with past alliances, but it also led to confusion and, sometimes, scandal, for the rulers often employed unreliable adventurers as their confidential agents. Still, the diplomatic system in the early eighteenth century proved successful enough to ensure a continuation of the principles of the Peace of Westphalia (1648): in the midst of every crisis and war, the great powers would convene and hammer out a written agreement detailing the requirements for peace.

Adroit diplomacy could smooth the road toward peace, but success in war still depended on sheer numbers—of men and muskets. Because each state's strength depended largely on the size of its army, the growth and health of the population increasingly entered into government calculations. The publication in 1690 of the

Englishman William Petty's *Political Arithmetick* quickened the interest of government officials everywhere. Petty offered statistical estimates of human capital—that is, of population and wages—to determine England's national wealth. In 1727, Frederick William I of Prussia founded two university chairs to encourage population studies, and textbooks and handbooks advocated state intervention to improve the population's health and welfare.

> **REVIEW**   What were the consequences of the stabilization of the balance of power in Europe at the start of the eighteenth century?

The Birth of the Enlightenment

Economic expansion, the emergence of a new consumer society, and the stabilization of the European state system all generated optimism about the future. The intellectual corollary was the Enlightenment, a term used later in the eighteenth century to describe the loosely knit group of writers and scholars who believed that human beings could apply a critical, reasoning spirit to every problem they encountered in the world. The new secular, scientific, and critical attitude first emerged in the 1690s, scrutinizing everything from the absolutism of Louis XIV to the traditional role of women in society. After 1740, criticism took a more systematic turn as writers provided new theories for the organization of society and politics, but even by the 1720s and 1730s, established authorities realized they faced a new set of challenges.

The Popularization of Science and the Challenges to Religion

The writers of the Enlightenment glorified the geniuses of the new science and championed the scientific method as the solution for all social problems. One of the most influential popularizations was the French writer Bernard de Fontenelle's *Conversations on the Plurality of Worlds* (1686). Presented as a dialogue between an aristocratic woman and a man of the world, the book made the Copernican, sun-centered view of the universe available to the literate public. By 1700, mathematics and science had become fashionable pastimes in high society, and the public flocked to lectures explaining scientific discoveries. Journals complained that scientific learning had become the passport to female affection: "There were two young ladies in Paris whose heads had been so turned by this branch of learning that one of them declined to listen to a proposal of marriage unless the candidate for her hand undertook to learn how to make telescopes." Such writings poked fun at women with intellectual interests, but they also demonstrated that women now participated in discussions of science.

Interest in science spread in literate circles because it offered a model for all forms of knowledge. As the prestige of science increased, some developed a skeptical attitude toward attempts to enforce religious conformity. A French Huguenot refugee from Louis XIV's persecutions, Pierre Bayle (1647–1706), launched an internationally influential campaign against religious intolerance from his safe haven in the Dutch Republic. His *News from the Republic of Letters* (first published

A Budding Scientist
In this engraving, *Astrologia*, by the Dutch artist Jacob Gole (c. 1660–1723), an upper-class woman looks through a telescope to do her own astronomical investigations. Women were not allowed to attend university classes in any European country, yet the Italian Laura Bassi (1711–1778) still managed to become a professor of physics at the University of Bologna. Because many astronomical observatories were set up in private homes rather than public buildings or universities, wives and daughters of scientists could make observations and even publish their own findings. (Bibliothèque nationale de France.)

in 1684) bitterly criticized the policies of Louis XIV and was quickly banned in Paris and condemned in Rome. After attacking Louis XIV's anti-Protestant policies, Bayle took a more general stand in favor of religious toleration. No state in Europe officially offered complete tolerance, though the Dutch Republic came closest with its tacit acceptance of Catholics, dissident Protestant groups, and open Jewish communities. In 1697, Bayle published the *Historical and Critical Dictionary,* which cited all the errors and delusions that he could find in past and present writers of all religions. Even religion must meet the test of reasonableness: "Any particular dogma, whatever it may be, whether it is advanced on the authority of the Scriptures, or whatever else may be its origins, is to be regarded as false if it clashes with the clear and definite conclusions of the natural understanding [reason]." Although Bayle claimed to be a believer himself, his insistence on rational investigation seemed to challenge the authority of faith. As one critic complained, "It is notorious that the works of M. Bayle have unsettled a large number of readers, and cast doubt on some of the most widely accepted principles of morality and religion." Bayle asserted, for example, that atheists might possess moral codes as effective as those of the devout. Bayle's *Dictionary* became a model of critical thought in the West.

Other scholars challenged the authority of the Bible by subjecting it to historical criticism. Discoveries in geology in the early eighteenth century showed that marine fossils dated immensely farther back than the biblical flood. Investigations of miracles, comets, and oracles, like the growing literature against belief in witchcraft, urged the use of reason to combat superstition and prejudice. Comets, for example, should not be considered evil omens just because such a belief had been passed on from earlier generations. Defenders of church and state published books warning of the dangers of the new skepticism. The spokesman for Louis XIV's absolutism, Bishop Bossuet, warned that "reason is the guide of their choice, but reason only brings them face to face with vague conjectures and baffling perplexities." Human beings, the traditionalists held, were simply incapable of subjecting everything to reason, especially in the realm of religion.

State authorities found religious skepticism particularly unsettling because it threatened to undermine state power, too. The extensive literature of criticism was not limited to France, but much of it was published in French, and the French government took the lead in suppressing the more outspoken works. Forbidden books were then often published in the Dutch Republic, Britain, or Switzerland and smuggled back across the border to a public whose appetite was only whetted by censorship.

The most influential writer of the early Enlightenment was a Frenchman born into the upper middle class, François-Marie Arouet, known by his pen name, Voltaire (1694–1778). In his early years, Voltaire suffered arrest, imprisonment, and exile, but he eventually achieved wealth and acclaim. His tangles with church and state began in the early 1730s, when he published his *Letters concerning the English Nation* (the English version appeared in 1733), in which he devoted several chapters to Newton and Locke and used the virtues of the British as a way to attack Catholic bigotry and government rigidity in France. Impressed by British toleration of religious dissent (at least among Protestants),Voltaire spent two years in exile in Britain when the French state responded to his book with yet another order for his arrest.

Voltaire also popularized Newton's scientific discoveries in his *Elements of the Philosophy of Newton* (1738). The French state and many European theologians considered Newtonianism threatening because it glorified the human mind and seemed to reduce God to an abstract, external, rationalistic force. So sensational was the success of Voltaire's book on Newton that a hostile Jesuit reported, "The great Newton was, it is said, buried in the abyss, in the shop of the first publisher who dared to print him. . . . M. de Voltaire finally appeared, and at once Newton is understood or is in the process of being understood; all Paris resounds with Newton, all Paris stammers Newton, all Paris studies and learns Newton." The success was international, too. Before long, Voltaire was elected a fellow of the Royal Society in London and in Edinburgh, as well as to twenty other scientific academies. Voltaire's fame continued to grow, reaching truly astounding proportions in the 1750s and 1760s (see Chapter 15).

Travel Literature and the Challenge to Custom and Tradition

Just as scientific method could be used to question religious and even state authority, a more general skepticism also emerged from the expanding knowledge about the world outside of Europe. During the seventeenth and eighteenth centuries, accounts of travel to exotic places dramatically increased as travel writers used the contrast between their home societies and other cultures to criticize the customs of European society.

In their travels to the new colonies, visitors sought something resembling "the state of nature"—that is, ways of life that preceded sophisticated social and political organization—although they often misinterpreted different forms of society and politics as having no organization at all. Travelers to the Americas found "noble savages" (native peoples) who appeared to live in conditions of great freedom and equality; they were "naturally good" and "happy" without taxes, lawsuits, or much organized government. In China, in contrast, travelers found a people who enjoyed prosperity and an ancient civilization. Christian missionaries made little headway in China, and visitors had to admit that China's religious systems had flourished for four or five thousand years with no input from Europe or from Christianity. The basic lesson of travel literature in the 1700s, then, was that customs varied: justice, freedom, property, good government, religion, and morality all were relative to the place. One critic complained that travel encouraged free thinking and the destruction of religion: "Some complete their demoralization by extensive travel, and lose whatever shreds of religion remained to them. Every day they see a new religion, new customs, new rites."

Travel literature turned explicitly political in Montesquieu's *Persian Letters* (1721). Charles-Louis de Secondat, baron of Montesquieu (1689–1755), the son of an eminent judicial family, was a high-ranking judge in a French court. He published *Persian Letters* anonymously in the Dutch Republic, and the book went into ten printings in just one year—a best seller for the times. In the book, Montesquieu tells the story of two Persians, Rica and Usbek, who leave their country "for love of knowledge" and travel to Europe. They visit France in the last years of Louis XIV's reign, writing of the king: "He has a minister who is only eighteen years old, and a mistress of eighty. . . . Although he avoids the bustle of towns, and is rarely seen in company, his one concern, from morning till night, is to get himself talked about." Other passages ridicule the pope. Beneath the satire, however, is a serious investigation into the foundation of good government and morality. Montesquieu chose Persians for his travelers because they came from what was widely considered the most despotic of all governments, in which rulers had life-and-death powers over their subjects. In the book, the Persians constantly compare France to Persia, suggesting that the French monarchy itself might verge on despotism.

The paradox of a judge publishing an anonymous work attacking the regime that employed him demonstrates the complications of the intellectual scene in this period. Montesquieu's anonymity did not last long, and soon Parisian society lionized him. In the late 1720s, he sold his judgeship and traveled extensively in Europe, including an eighteen-month stay in Britain. In 1748, he published a widely influential work on comparative government, *The Spirit of Laws*. The Vatican soon listed both *Persian Letters* and *The Spirit of Laws* in its index of forbidden books.

Raising the Woman Question

Many of the letters exchanged in *Persian Letters* focus on women, marriage, and the family because Montesquieu considered the position of women a sure indicator of the nature of government and morality. Although he was not a feminist, his depiction of Roxana, the favorite wife in Usbek's harem, struck a chord with many readers. Roxana revolts against the authority of Usbek's eunuchs and writes a final letter to her husband announcing her impending suicide: "I may have lived in servitude, but I have always been free, I have amended your laws according to the laws of nature, and my mind has always remained independent." Women writers used the same language of tyranny and freedom to argue for concrete changes in their status.

The most systematic of these women writers was the English author Mary Astell (1666–1731), the daughter of a businessman and herself a supporter of the Tory party and the Anglican religious establishment. In 1694, she published *A Serious Proposal to the Ladies,* in which she advocated founding a private women's college to remedy women's lack of education. Addressing women, she asked, "How can you be content to be in the World like Tulips in a Garden, to make a fine *shew* [show] and be good for nothing?" Astell argued for intellectual training based on Descartes's principles, in which reason, debate, and careful consideration of the issues took priority over custom or tradition. Her book was an immediate success: five printings appeared by 1701. In later works, such as *Reflections upon Marriage* (1706), Astell criticized the relationship between the sexes within marriage: "If Absolute Sovereignty be not necessary in a State, how comes it to be so in a family? . . . *If all Men are born free,* how is it that all Women are born slaves?" Her critics accused her of promoting subversive ideas and of contradicting the Scriptures.

The influence of such views should not be overestimated. Most male writers unequivocally stuck to the traditional view of women, which held that women were less capable of reasoning than men and therefore did not need systematic education. Such opinions often rested on biological suppositions. The long-dominant Aristotelian view of reproduction held that only the male seed carried spirit and individuality. At the beginning of the eighteenth century, however, scientists began to undermine this belief. More physicians and surgeons began to champion the doctrine of ovism—that the female egg was essential in making new humans. During the decades that followed, male Enlightenment writers would continue to debate women's nature and appropriate social roles.

REVIEW   What were the main issues in the early decades of the Enlightenment?

Conclusion

Europeans crossed a major threshold in the first half of the eighteenth century. They moved silently but nonetheless momentously from an economy governed by scarcity and the threat of famine to one of ever increasing growth and the prospect of continuing improvement. Expansion of colonies overseas and economic development

Mapping the West Europe in 1740
By 1740 Europe had achieved a kind of diplomatic equilibrium in which no one power predominated. But the relative balance should not deflect attention from important underlying changes. Spain, the Dutch Republic, Poland-Lithuania, and Sweden had all declined in power and influence, while Great Britain, Russia, Prussia, and Austria had solidified their positions, each in a different way. France's ambitions had been thwarted, but the combination of a large army and rich overseas possessions made France a major player for a long time to come.

at home created greater wealth, longer life spans, and higher expectations for the future. In these better times for many, a spirit of optimism prevailed. People could now spend money on newspapers, novels, and travel literature as well as on coffee, tea, and cotton cloth. Participants in the growing public sphere avidly followed the latest trends in religious debates, art, and music. Everyone did not share equally in the benefits: slaves toiled in abjection in the Americas; serfs in eastern Europe found themselves ever more closely bound to their noble lords; and rural folk almost everywhere tasted few fruits of consumer society.

Politics, too, changed as population and production increased and cities grew. Experts urged government intervention to improve public health, and states found it in their interest to settle many international disputes by diplomacy, which itself became more regular and routine. The consolidation of the European state system allowed a tide of criticism and new thinking about society to swell in Great Britain and France and begin to spill throughout Europe. Ultimately, the combination of the Atlantic system and the Enlightenment would give rise to a series of Atlantic revolutions.

CHAPTER REVIEW QUESTIONS

1. How did the rise of slavery and the plantation system change European politics and society?
2. Why did the Enlightenment begin just at the moment that the Atlantic system took shape?

For practice quizzes and other study tools, see the Online Study Guide at bedfordstmartins.com/huntconcise.

For primary-source material from this period, see Chapter 17 of *Sources of THE MAKING OF THE WEST,* Third Edition.

TIMELINE

■ **1709** Joseph Addison and Richard Steele publish the first edition of the *Spectator* in England

■ **1703** Peter the Great of Russia begins the construction of St. Petersburg and founds the first Russian newspaper

■ **1699** Turks forced to recognize Habsburg rule over Hungary and Transylvania

1690	1700	1710

■ **1690s** Beginning of the rapid development of plantations in the Caribbean

■ **1694** Bank of England established; Mary Astell's *A Serious Proposal to the Ladies* argues for the founding of a private women's college

■ **1697** Pierre Bayle publishes the *Historical and Critical Dictionary,* detailing errors of religious writers

1713–1714 Peace of Utrecht, followir the War of the Spanish Succession (1701–1713)

■ **1714** Elector of Hanover becomes King George I of England

■ **1715** Death of Louis XIV

Suggested References

A new Web site on the slave trade offers the most up-to-date information about the workings of the Atlantic system. The definitive study of the early Enlightenment is the book by Hazard, but many others have contributed biographies of individual figures or studies of women writers.

Bach's Leipzig, 1725–1750: http://www.baroquemusic.org/bachleipzig.html

Black, Jeremy. *European Warfare in a Global Context, 1660–1815.* 2007.

Blackburn, Robin. *The Making of New World Slavery: From the Baroque to the Modern, 1492–1800.* 1997.

Brewer, John. *The Sinews of Power: War, Money, and the English State, 1688–1783.* 1990.

Cracraft, James. *The Revolution of Peter the Great.* 2003.

Handel's Messiah: The New Interactive Edition (CD-ROM). 1997.

Hazard, Paul. *The European Mind: The Critical Years, 1680–1715.* 1990.

*Hill, Bridget. *The First English Feminist: Reflections upon Marriage and Other Writings by Mary Astell.* 1986.

Hunt, Margaret R. *The Middling Sort: Commerce, Gender, and the Family in England, 1680–1780.* 1996.

*Jacob, Margaret C. *The Enlightenment: A Brief History with Selected Readings.* 2000.

Pearson, Roger. *Voltaire Almighty: A Life in Pursuit of Freedom.* 2005.

Slave trade: http://www.slavevoyages.org/tast/index.faces

War of the Spanish Succession: http://www.spanishsuccession.nl/

■ **1721** Treaty of Nystad; Montesquieu publishes *Persian Letters* anonymously in the Dutch Republic; Robert Walpole becomes the first prime minister of Great Britain

■ **1720** Last outbreak of bubonic plague in western Europe

1719 Daniel Defoe publishes *Robinson Crusoe*

■ **1741** George Frederick Handel composes *Messiah*

| 1720 | 1730 | 1740 |

■ **1733** Voltaire's *Letters concerning the English Nation* attacks French intolerance and narrow-mindedness

1733–1735 War of the Polish Succession

The Promise of Enlightenment

I N THE SUMMER OF 1766, Empress Catherine II ("the Great") of Russia wrote to Voltaire, one of the leaders of the Enlightenment:

> It is a way of immortalizing oneself to be the advocate of humanity, the defender of oppressed innocence. . . . You have entered into combat against the enemies of mankind: superstition, fanaticism, ignorance, quibbling, evil judges, and the powers that rest in their hands. Great virtues and qualities are needed to surmount these obstacles. You have shown that you have them: you have triumphed.

Catherine the Great
In this portrait by the Danish painter Vigilius Eriksen, the Russian empress Catherine the Great is shown on horseback (c. 1762), much like any male ruler of the time. Born Sophia Augusta Frederika of Anhalt-Zerbst in 1729, Catherine was the daughter of a minor German prince. When she married the future tsar Peter III in 1745, she promptly learned Russian and adopted Russian Orthodoxy. Peter, physically and mentally frail, proved no match for her. In 1762, she staged a coup against him and took his place when he was killed. *(Erich Lessing/Art Resource, NY.)*

Over a fifteen-year period Catherine corresponded regularly with Voltaire, a writer who at home in France found himself in constant conflict with church and state authorities. Her admiring letter shows how influential Enlightenment ideals had become by the middle of the eighteenth century.

Catherine's letter aptly summed up Enlightenment principles: progress for humanity could be achieved only by rooting out the wrongs left by superstition, religious fanaticism, ignorance, and outmoded forms of justice. Enlightenment writers used every means at their disposal—from encyclopedias to novels to personal interaction with rulers—to argue for reform. Everything had to be examined in the clear light of reason, and anything that did not promote the improvement of humanity was to be jettisoned. As a result, Enlightenment writers attacked the legal use of torture to extract confessions, favored the spread of education to eliminate ignorance, supported religious toleration, and criticized censorship by state or church. The book trade and new places for urban socializing, such as coffeehouses and Masonic lodges (social clubs organized around the rituals of masons' guilds), spread these ideas within a new elite of middle- and upper-class men and women.

Rulers pursued Enlightenment reforms that they believed might enhance state power, but they feared changes that might unleash popular discontent. For example, Catherine aimed to bring Western culture and reforms to Russia, but when faced with a massive uprising of the serfs, she not only suppressed the revolt but also increased the nobles' power over their serfs. All reform-minded rulers faced similar potential challenges to their authority.

Even though the movement for reform had its limits, governments now needed to respond to a new force: public opinion. Rulers wanted to portray themselves as modern, open to change, and responsive to the segment of the public that was reading newspapers and closely following political developments. Enlightenment writers appealed to public opinion, but they still looked to rulers to effect reform. Writers such as Voltaire expressed little interest in the future of peasants or lower classes; they favored neither revolution nor political upheaval. Yet their ideas paved the way for something much more radical and unexpected. The American Declaration of Independence in 1776 showed how lofty Enlightenment goals could be translated into democratic political practice. After 1789, democracy would come to Europe as well.

CHAPTER FOCUS QUESTION   What was the influence of Enlightenment ideals on public opinion and on European rulers?

The Enlightenment at Its Height

The Enlightenment emerged as an intellectual movement before 1740 but reached its peak only in the second half of the eighteenth century. The writers of the Enlightenment called themselves **philosophes** (French for "philosophers"), but that term is somewhat misleading. Whereas philosophers generally concern themselves with theoretical questions (for example, "What is truth?"), the philosophes were public intellectuals dedicated to solving the real problems of the world. They wrote on subjects ranging from current affairs to art criticism, and they wrote in every conceivable format. The Swiss philosophe Jean-Jacques Rousseau, for example, wrote a political tract, a treatise on education, a constitution for Poland, an analysis of the effects of the theater on public morals, a best-selling novel, an opera, and a notorious autobiography.

The philosophes wrote for an educated public of readers who snatched up every Enlightenment book they could find at their local booksellers, even when rulers or churches tried to forbid publication. Between 1740 and 1789, the Enlightenment acquired its name and, despite heated conflicts between the philosophes and state and religious authorities, gained support in the highest reaches of government.

The Men and Women of the Republic of Letters

Although *philosophe* is a French word, the Enlightenment was distinctly cosmopolitan; philosophes could be found from Philadelphia to Moscow. The philosophes considered themselves part of a grand "republic of letters" that transcended national political boundaries. They were not republicans in the usual sense—that is, people who supported representative government and opposed monarchy. What united them were the ideals of reason, reform, and freedom. In 1784, the German philosopher Immanuel Kant summed up the program of the Enlightenment in two Latin words: *sapere aude,* "dare to know"—have the courage to think for yourself.

The philosophes used reason to attack superstition, bigotry, and religious intolerance, which they considered the chief obstacles to free thought and social reform. "Once fanaticism has corrupted a mind," Voltaire proclaimed, "the malady is almost incurable. . . . The only remedy for this epidemic malady is the philosophical spirit." Enlightenment writers did not necessarily oppose organized religion, but they strenuously objected to religious intolerance. They believed that the systematic application of reason could do what religious belief could not: improve the human condition by pointing to needed reforms. Reason meant critical, informed, scientific thinking about social issues and problems. Many Enlightenment writers collaborated on a new multivolume *Encyclopedia,* published between 1751 and 1772, that

Bookbinding
In this plate from the *Encyclopedia,* the various stages in bookbinding are laid out from left to right. Binding was not included in the sale of books; owners had to order leather bindings from a special shop. The man at (a) is pounding the pages to be bound on a marble block. The woman at (b) is stitching the pages with a special frame. The worker at (c) cuts the pages, and at (d) the volumes are pressed to prevent warping. In what ways is this illustration representative of the aims of the *Encyclopedia*?

aimed to gather together knowledge about science, religion, industry, and society. The chief editor of the *Encyclopedia,* Denis Diderot (1713–1784), explained the goal: "All things must be examined, debated, investigated without exception and without regard for anyone's feelings."

The philosophes believed that the spread of knowledge would encourage reform in every aspect of life, from the grain trade to the penal system. The philosophes wanted freedom of the press and freedom of religion, which they considered "natural rights" guaranteed by "natural law." In their view, progress depended on these freedoms. As Voltaire asserted, "I quite understand that the fanatics of one sect slaughter the enthusiasts of another sect . . . [but] that Descartes should have been forced to flee to Holland to escape the fury of the ignorant . . . these things are a nation's eternal shame."

Most philosophes, like Voltaire, came from the upper classes, yet Rousseau's father was a modest watchmaker in Geneva, and Diderot was the son of a cutlery maker. The French noblewoman Émilie du Châtelet (1706–1749) was one of the rare female philosophes. She wrote extensively about the mathematics and physics of Leibniz and Newton. (Her lover Voltaire learned much of his science from her.) Few of the leading writers held university positions, except those who were German or Scottish. Universities in France were dominated by the clergy and unreceptive to Enlightenment ideas.

Enlightenment ideas developed instead through personal contacts; through letters that were hand-copied, circulated, and sometimes published; through informal readings of manuscripts; and through letters to the editor and book reviews in periodicals. **Salons**—informal gatherings usually sponsored by middle-class or aristocratic women—gave intellectual life an anchor outside the royal court and the church-controlled universities. Best known was the Parisian salon of Madame Marie-Thérèse Geoffrin (1699–1777), a wealthy middle-class widow who had been raised by her grandmother and married off at fourteen to a much older man. She brought together the most exciting thinkers and artists of the time; her social gatherings provided a forum for new ideas and an opportunity to establish new intellectual contacts. In the salon, the philosophes could discuss ideas they might hesitate to put into print and thus test public opinion and even push it in new directions. Madame Geoffrin corresponded extensively with influential people across Europe, including Catherine the Great. One Italian visitor commented, "There is no way to make Naples resemble Paris unless we find a woman to guide us, organize us, *Geoffrinize* us."

Women's salons helped galvanize intellectual life and reform movements all over Europe. Wealthy Jewish women created nine of the fourteen salons in Berlin at the end of the eighteenth century, and in Warsaw Princess Zofia Czartoryska gathered around her the reform leaders of Poland-Lithuania. Middle-class women in London used their salons to raise money to publish women's writings. Salons could be tied closely to the circles of power: in France, for example, Louis XV's mistress, Jeanne-Antoinette Poisson, first made her reputation as hostess of a salon frequented by Voltaire and Montesquieu. When she became Louis XV's mistress in 1745, she gained the title Marquise de Pompadour and turned her attention to influencing artistic styles by patronizing architects and painters.

Conflicts with Church and State

Madame Geoffrin did not approve of discussions that attacked the Catholic church, but elsewhere voices against organized religion could be heard. Criticisms of religion required daring because the church, whatever its denomination, wielded enormous power in society, and most influential people considered religion an essential foundation of good society and government. Defying such opinion, the Scottish philosopher David Hume (1711–1776) boldly argued in *The Natural History of Religion* (1755) that belief in God rested on superstition and fear rather than on reason.

Before the scientific revolution, nearly every European believed in God. After Newton, however, and despite Newton's own deep religiosity, people could conceive of the universe as an eternally existing, self-perpetuating machine in which God's intervention was unnecessary. In short, such people could become either **atheists**, who did not believe in any kind of God, or **deists**, who believed in God but gave him no active role in earthly affairs. For the first time, writers claimed the label *atheist* and disputed the common view that atheism led inevitably to immorality.

Deists continued to believe in a benevolent, all-knowing God who had designed the universe and set it in motion. But deists usually rejected the idea that God directly intercedes in the functioning of the universe, and they often criticized the churches for their dogmatic intolerance of dissenters. Voltaire was a deist, and in his popular *Philosophical Dictionary* (1764) he attacked most of the claims of organized Christianity, both Catholic and Protestant. Christianity, he argued, had been the prime source of fanaticism and brutality among humans. Throughout his life, Voltaire's motto was *Écrasez l'infâme*—"Crush the infamous thing" (the "thing" being bigotry and intolerance). French authorities publicly burned his *Philosophical Dictionary*.

Criticism of religious intolerance involved more than simply attacking the churches. Critics also had to confront the states to which churches were closely tied. In 1761, a judicial case in Toulouse provoked throughout France an outcry that Voltaire soon joined. When the son of a local Calvinist was found hanged (he probably committed suicide), authorities accused his father, Jean Calas, of murdering him to prevent his conversion to Catholicism. (Since Louis XIV's revocation of the Edict of Nantes in 1685, it had been illegal to practice Calvinism publicly in France.) The all-Catholic parlement of Toulouse tried to extract the names of accomplices through torture—using a rope to pull up Calas's arm while weighting down his feet and then by pouring pitchers of water down his throat (now known as "water boarding")—and then executed him by breaking every bone in his body. Voltaire launched a successful crusade to rehabilitate Jean Calas's good name and to restore the family's properties, which had been confiscated after his death. Voltaire's efforts eventually helped bring about the extension of civil rights to French Protestants and encouraged campaigns to abolish the legal use of torture.

Critics also assailed state and church support for European colonization and slavery. One of the most popular books of the time was the *Philosophical and Political History of European Colonies and Commerce in the Two Indies,* published in 1770 by Abbé Guillaume Raynal (1713–1796), a French Catholic clergyman. Raynal and his collaborators described in excruciating detail the destruction of native populations by Europeans and denounced the slave trade. Raynal was forced into exile, and his work was banned by both the Catholic church and the French government, but the Enlightenment belief in natural rights led many others to denounce slavery. An article in the new *Encyclopedia* proclaimed, "There is not a single one of these hapless souls . . . who does not have the right to be declared free . . . since neither his ruler nor his father nor anyone else had the right to dispose of his freedom." Some Enlightenment thinkers, however, took a more ambiguous or even negative view. Hume judged blacks to be "naturally inferior to . . . whites," concluding, "There never was a civilized nation of any other complexion than white."

Enlightenment critics of church and state advocated reform, not revolution. Although Voltaire, for example, lived near the French-Swiss border in case he had to flee arrest, he made a fortune from financial speculations, wrote a glowing history called *The Age of Louis XIV* (1751), and lived to be celebrated in his last years as a national hero even by many former foes. Other philosophes also lived respectably, believing that published criticism, rather than violent action, would bring about necessary reforms. As Diderot said, "We will speak against senseless laws until they are reformed; and, while we wait, we will abide by them." Those few who lived long enough to see the French Revolution in 1789 resisted its radical turn, for the philosophes generally regarded the lower classes—"the people"—as ignorant, violent, and prone to superstition, hence in need of leadership from above. They pinned their hopes on educated elites and enlightened rulers.

Despite the philosophes' preference for reform, in the long run their books often had a revolutionary impact. For example, Montesquieu's widely reprinted *Spirit of the Laws* (1748) warned against the dangers of despotism, opposed the divine right of kings, and favored constitutional government. In his somewhat rosy view, Great Britain was "the one nation in the world which has political liberty as the direct object of its constitution." His analysis of British constitutionalism inspired French critics of absolutism and would greatly influence the American revolutionaries.

The Individual and Society

In previous centuries, questions of theological doctrine and church organization had been the main focus of intellectual and even political interest. The Enlightenment writers shifted attention away from religious questions toward the secular study of society and the individual's role in it. In this way, the Enlightenment advanced the secularization of European political life that had begun after the Wars of Religion of the sixteenth and seventeenth centuries. At the same time, it laid the foundations for the social sciences of the modern era.

Just as Newton had used his reason to penetrate the laws of nature, so too the philosophes hoped to use reason to discern the laws of social life. But they did not necessarily agree about the conclusions to be drawn. Among the many different approaches were two that proved enduringly influential, those of the Scottish philosopher Adam Smith and the Swiss writer Jean-Jacques Rousseau. Smith provided a theory of modern capitalist society and devoted much of his energy to defending free markets as offering the best way to maximize individual efforts. The modern discipline of economics took shape around the questions raised by Smith. Rousseau set out the principles of a more communitarian philosophy, one that emphasized the needs of the community over those of the individual. His work led both toward democracy and toward communism and continues to inspire heated debate in political science and sociology. A closer look at these two thinkers will demonstrate the breadth and depth of Enlightenment thought.

Adam Smith (1723–1790) optimistically believed that individual interests naturally harmonized with those of the whole society. To explain how this natural harmonization worked, he published *An Inquiry into the Nature and Causes of the Wealth of Nations* in 1776. Smith insisted that individual self-interest, even greed, was quite compatible with society's best interest: the market served as an "invisible hand" ensuring that individual interests would be synchronized with those of the whole society. "By pursuing his own interest," the merchant "frequently promotes that of the society more effectually than when he really intends to promote it."

Smith rejected the prevailing mercantilist views that the general welfare would be served by accumulating national wealth through agriculture or the hoarding of gold and silver. Instead, he argued that the division of labor in manufacturing would increase productivity and generate more wealth for society and well-being for the individual. To maximize the effects of market forces and the division of labor, Smith endorsed a concept called **laissez-faire** (that is, "to leave alone") to free the economy from government intervention and control. He insisted that governments eliminate all restrictions on the sale of land, remove restraints on the grain trade, and abandon duties on imports. He believed that free international trade would stimulate production everywhere and thus ensure the growth of national wealth. He argued:

> The natural effort of every individual to better his own condition, when suffered to exert itself with freedom and security, is so powerful a principle, that it is alone, and without any assistance, not only capable of carrying the society to wealth and prosperity, but of surmounting a hundred impertinent obstructions with which the folly of human laws too often encumbers its operations.

Governments should restrict themselves to providing "security"—that is, national defense, internal order and a secure framework for market activity, and public works.

Much more pessimistic about the relation between individual self-interest and the good of society was Jean-Jacques Rousseau (1712–1778). In Rousseau's view, society itself threatened natural rights or freedoms: "Man is born free, and everywhere he is in chains." Rousseau first gained fame by writing a prizewinning essay in 1749 in which he argued that the revival of science and the arts had corrupted social morals, not improved them. This startling conclusion seemed to oppose some of the Enlightenment's most cherished beliefs. Rather than improving society, he claimed, science and art raised artificial barriers between people and their natural state. Rousseau's works extolled the simplicity of rural life over urban society. Although he participated in the salons, Rousseau always felt ill at ease in high society, and he periodically withdrew to live in solitude far from Paris. Paradoxically, his "solitude" was often paid for by wealthy upper-class patrons, who lodged him on their estates, even as his writings decried the upper-class privilege that made his efforts possible.

Rousseau explored the tension between the individual and society in various ways, including his widely influential work on education, *Émile* (1762), in which a boy develops practical skills and independent thinking under the guidance of his

Jean-Jacques Rousseau
This eighteenth-century engraving of Rousseau shows him in his favorite place, outside in nature, where he walked, read, and, in this case, collected plants. Rousseau claimed that he came to his most important insights while taking long walks, and in *Émile* he underlines the importance of physical activity for children. (© Private Collection/The Bridgeman Art Library.)

tutor. In *The Social Contract* (1762), Rousseau proposed a political solution to the tension between the individual and society. Whereas earlier he had argued that society corrupted the individual by taking him out of nature, in this work Rousseau insisted that individual moral freedom could be achieved only by learning to subject one's individual interests to "the general will"—that is, to the good of the community. Individuals did this by entering into a social contract, not with their rulers but with one another. If everyone followed the general will, then all individuals would be equally free and equally moral because they lived under a law to which they had all consented.

These arguments threatened the legitimacy of eighteenth-century governments. Rousseau derived his social contract from human nature, not from history, tradition, or the Bible. He implied that people would be most free and moral under a republican form of government with direct democracy, and his abstract model included no reference to differences in social status. He roundly condemned slavery: "To decide that the son of a slave is born a slave is to decide that he is not born a man." Not surprisingly, authorities in both Geneva and Paris banned *The Social Contract* for undermining political authority. Rousseau's works would become a kind of political bible for the French revolutionaries of 1789, and his attacks on private property would inspire the communists of the nineteenth century such as Karl Marx. Rousseau's rather mystical concept of the general will remains controversial. The "greatest good of all," according to Rousseau, was liberty and equality, but he also insisted that the individual could be "forced to be free" by the terms of the social contract. He provided no legal protections for individual rights. In other words, Rousseau's particular version of democracy did not guarantee the individual freedoms so important to Adam Smith.

Spreading the Enlightenment

The Enlightenment flourished in places where the new public sphere provided an eager audience for ideas of constitutionalism and reform. Where constitutionalism and the guarantee of individual freedoms were most advanced, as in Great Britain and the Dutch Republic, the movement had less of an edge because there was, in a sense, less need for it. Scottish and English writers concentrated on economics, philosophy, and history rather than politics or social relations. Dutch printers made money publishing the books that were forbidden in France. In British North America, Enlightenment ideas helped stiffen growing colonial resistance to British rule after 1763. In places with small middle classes, such as Spain, the Italian states, and Russia, governments successfully suppressed writings they did not like. Italian philosophes, such as the Milanese penal reformer Cesare Beccaria (1738–1794), got moral support from their French counterparts in the face of stern censorship at home.

The hot spot of the Enlightenment was France. French writers published the most daring critiques of church and state and suffered the most intense harassment and persecution. Voltaire, Diderot, and Rousseau all faced arrest, exile, or even imprisonment. The Catholic church and royal authorities routinely forbade the publication of their books, and the police arrested publishers who ignored their warnings. Yet the French monarchy was far from the most autocratic in Europe, and Voltaire, Diderot, and Rousseau all were revered as cultural heroes. France seems to have been curiously caught in the middle during the Enlightenment: with fewer constitutional guarantees of individual freedom than Great Britain, it still enjoyed much higher levels of prosperity and cultural development than most other European countries. In short, French elites had reason to complain, the means to make their complaints known, and a government torn between the desires to censor dissident ideas and to appear open to modernity and progress.

The government in France controlled publishing—all books had to get official permission—but not as tightly as in Spain, where the Catholic Inquisition made up its own list of banned books, or in Russia, where Catherine the Great allowed no opposition. In the 1760s and 1770s, a growing flood of works printed abroad poured into France and circulated underground. In the Dutch Republic and Swiss cities, private companies made fortunes smuggling illegal books into France over mountain passes and back roads. Foreign printers provided secret catalogs of their offerings and sold their products through booksellers who were willing to market forbidden texts for a high price—among them not only philosophical treatises of the Enlightenment but also pornographic works and pamphlets (some by Diderot) lampooning the Catholic clergy and leading members of the royal court.

Whereas the French philosophes often took a violently anticlerical and combative tone, their German counterparts avoided direct political confrontations with authorities. Gotthold Lessing (1729–1781) complained in 1769 that Prussia was still "the most slavish society in Europe" in its lack of freedom to criticize government policies. As a playwright, literary critic, and philosopher, Lessing promoted religious toleration of Jews and spiritual emancipation of Germans from foreign, especially French, models of culture, which still dominated. Lessing also introduced the German Jewish writer Moses Mendelssohn (1729–1786) into Berlin salon society. Mendelssohn labored to build bridges between German and Jewish culture by arguing that Judaism was a rational and undogmatic religion. He believed persecution and discrimination against the Jews would end as reason triumphed.

Reason was also the chief focus of the most influential German thinker of the Enlightenment, Immanuel Kant (1724–1804). A university professor who lectured on everything from economics to astronomy, Kant wrote one of the most important works in the history of Western philosophy, *The Critique of Pure Reason* (1781). He admired Adam Smith and especially Rousseau, whose portrait he displayed proudly in his lodgings. Just as Smith founded modern economics and Rousseau modern political theory, Kant in *The Critique of Pure Reason* set the foundations for modern philosophy. In this complex book, Kant established the doctrine of *idealism,* the belief that true understanding can come only from examining the ways in which ideas are formed in the mind. Ideas are shaped, Kant argued, not just by sensory information (a position central to *empiricism,* a philosophy based on John Locke's writings) but also by the operation on that information of mental categories such as space and time. In Kant's philosophy, these "categories of understanding" were neither sensory nor supernatural; they were entirely ideal and abstract and located in the human mind. For Kant the supreme philosophical questions—Does God exist? Is personal immortality possible? Do humans have free will?—were unanswerable by reason alone. But like Rousseau, Kant insisted that people could achieve true moral freedom only by living in society and obeying its laws.

The Limits of Reason: Roots of Romanticism and Religious Revival

In reaction to what some saw as the Enlightenment's excessive reliance on the authority of human reason, a new artistic movement called **romanticism** took root. Although it would not fully flower until the early nineteenth century, romanticism traced its emphasis on individual genius, deep emotion, and the joys of nature to thinkers like Rousseau who had scolded the philosophes for ignoring those aspects of life that escaped and even conflicted with the power of reason. Rousseau's autobiographical *Confessions,* published posthumously in 1782, caused an immediate sensation because it revealed so much about his inner emotional life, including his sexual longings and his almost paranoid distrust of other Enlightenment figures.

The appeal to feelings and emotions also increased interest in the occult. In the 1780s, a charismatic Austrian physician turned "experimenter," Franz Mesmer, awed crowds of aristocrats and middle-class admirers with his demonstrations in Paris of "animal magnetism." He passed a weak electrical current through tubs filled with water or iron filings, around which groups of his disciples sat, holding hands; with this process of "mesmerism" he claimed to cure their ailments. (The word *mesmerize,* meaning "hypnotize" or "hold spellbound," is derived from Mesmer's name.)

A novel by the German writer Johann Wolfgang von Goethe (1749–1832) captured the early romantic spirit with its glorification of emotion. *The Sorrows of Young Werther* (1774) tells of a passionate youth who reveres nature and rural life and is unhappy in love. When the woman he loves marries someone else, he falls into deep melancholy and eventually kills himself. Reason cannot save him. The book spurred a veritable Werther craze: there were Werther costumes, Werther engravings and embroidery, Werther medallions, and a perfume called Eau de Werther. Tragically, there were even a few imitations of Werther's suicide. The young Napoleon Bonaparte, who was to build an empire for France, claimed to have read Goethe's novel seven times.

Religious revivals underlined the limits of reason in a different way. Much of the Protestant world experienced an "awakening" in the 1740s. In the German states, Pietist groups founded new communities, and in the British North American colonies, revivalist Protestant preachers drew thousands of fervent believers in a movement called the Great Awakening. In North America, bitter conflicts between revivalists and their opponents in the established churches prompted the leaders on both sides to set up new colleges to support their beliefs. These included Princeton, Columbia, Brown, and Dartmouth, all founded between 1746 and 1769.

George Whitefield
One of the most prominent preachers of the Great Awakening in the British North American colonies was the English Methodist George Whitefield, painted here by John Wollaston in 1742. Whitefield visited the North American colonies seven times, sometimes for long periods, and drew tens of thousands of people to his dramatic and emotional open-air sermons. (National Portrait Gallery, London.)

Revivalism also stirred eastern European Jews at about the same time. Israel ben Eliezer (1698–1760) laid the foundation for Hasidism in the 1740s and 1750s. He traveled the Polish countryside offering miraculous cures and became known as the Ba'al Shem Tov (meaning "Master of the Good Name") because he used divine names to effect healing and bring believers into closer personal contact with God. He emphasized mystical contemplation of the divine, rather than study of Jewish law, and his followers, the **Hasidim** (Hebrew for "most pious" Jews), often expressed their devotion through music, dance, and fervent prayer. Their practices soon spread all over Poland-Lithuania.

Most of the waves of Protestant revivalism ebbed after the 1750s, but in Great Britain the movement known as **Methodism** continued to grow. John Wesley (1703–1791), the Oxford-educated son of an Anglican cleric, founded Methodism, a term evoked by Wesley's insistence on strict self-discipline and a methodical approach to religious study and observance. In 1738, Wesley began preaching a new brand of Anglicanism, with some similarities to Calvinism, that emphasized an intense personal experience of salvation and a life of thrift, abstinence, and hard work. Traveling all over the British Isles, Wesley would mount a table or a box to speak to the ordinary people of the village or town. He slept in his followers' homes and treated their illnesses with various remedies, including small electric shocks for nervous diseases. (Wesley eagerly followed Benjamin Franklin's experiments with electricity.)

In fifty years, Wesley preached forty thousand sermons, an average of fifteen a week. When the Anglican authorities refused to let him preach in the churches, Wesley began to ordain his own clergy. Nevertheless, during Wesley's lifetime the Methodist leadership remained politically conservative. Wesley himself denounced political agitation in the 1770s because, he said, it threatened to make Great Britain "a field of blood" ruled by "King Mob."

> **REVIEW** Why was France the center of the Enlightenment, and in what ways was it surprising that the philosophes and new ideas flourished there?

Society and Culture in an Age of Enlightenment

Religious revivals and the first stirrings of romanticism show that all intellectual currents did not flow in the same channel. Similarly, some social and cultural developments manifested the influence of Enlightenment ideas, but others did not. The traditional leaders of European societies—the nobles—responded to Enlightenment ideals in contradictory fashion: many simply reasserted their privileges and resisted the influence of the Enlightenment, but an important minority embraced change and actively participated in reform efforts. The expanding middle classes saw in the Enlightenment a chance to make their claim for joining society's governing elite. They bought Enlightenment books, joined Masonic lodges, and patronized new styles in art, music, and literature. The lower classes were more affected by economic growth. Continuing population increases contributed to a rise in prices for basic goods. At the same time, peasants had to face rising rents, which created resentment of upper-class privileges.

The Nobility's Reassertion of Privilege

Nobles made up about 3 percent of the European population, but their numbers and way of life varied greatly from country to country. At least 10 percent of the population in Poland and 7 to 8 percent in Spain was noble, in contrast to only 2 percent in Russia and between 1 and 2 percent in the rest of western Europe. Many Polish and Spanish nobles lived in poverty; a title did not guarantee wealth. The wealthiest European nobles luxuriated in almost unimaginable opulence. Many of the English peers, for example, owned more than ten thousand acres of land (the average western European peasant owned about five acres), invested widely in government bonds and trading companies, kept several country residences with scores of servants as well as houses in London, and occasionally even had their own private orchestras, libraries of expensive books, greenhouses for exotic plants, kennels of pedigree dogs, and collections of antiques, firearms, and scientific instruments.

In the face of the commercialization of agriculture and the inflation of prices, European aristocrats converted their remaining legal rights (called *seigneurial dues,* from the French *seigneur,* for "lord") into money payments and used them to support an increasingly expensive lifestyle. Peasants felt the squeeze as a result. French peasants, for instance, paid a wide range of dues to their landlords—including payments to grind grain at the lord's mill, bake bread in his oven, and press grapes in his winepress—and various inheritance taxes on the land. In addition, peasants had to work on the public roads without compensation for a specified number of days every year. They also paid taxes to the government on salt, an essential preservative, and on the value of their land; customs duties if they sold produce or wine in town; and the tithe on their grain (one-tenth of the crop) to the church.

In Britain, the landed gentry could not claim these same onerous dues from their tenants, but they fiercely defended their exclusive right to hunt game. The game laws kept the poor from eating meat and helped protect the social status of the rich. The gentry enforced the game laws themselves by hiring gamekeepers who hunted down poachers and even set traps for them in the forests. According to the law, anyone who poached deer or rabbits while armed or disguised could be sentenced to death. After 1760, the number of arrests for breaking the game laws increased dramatically. In most other countries, too, hunting was the special right of the nobility and a cause of deep popular resentment.

Even though Enlightenment writers sharply criticized nobles' insistence on special privileges, most aristocrats maintained their marks of distinction. The male court nobility continued to sport swords, plumed hats, makeup, and powdered hair; middle-class men wore simpler and more somber clothing. Aristocrats had their own seats in church and their own quarters in the universities. Frederick II ("the Great") of Prussia (r. 1740–1786) made sure that nobles dominated both the army officer corps and the civil bureaucracy. Catherine II of Russia (r. 1762–1796) granted the nobility vast tracts of land, the exclusive right to own serfs, and exemption from personal taxes and corporal punishment. Her Charter of the Nobility of 1785 codified these privileges in exchange for nobles' political subservience to the state. In many countries, including Spain and France, the law prohibited aristocrats from engaging directly in retail trade. In Austria, Spain, the Italian states, Poland-Lithuania, and Russia, most nobles consequently cared little about Enlightenment ideas; they did not read the books of the philosophes and feared reforms that might challenge their dominance of rural society.

In France, Britain, and the western German states, however, the nobility proved more open to the new ideas. Among those who personally corresponded with Rousseau, for example, half were nobles, as were 20 percent of the 160 contributors to the *Encyclopedia*. It had not escaped their notice that Rousseau had denounced inequality. In his view, it was "manifestly contrary to the law of nature . . . that a handful of people should gorge themselves with superfluities while the hungry multitude goes in want of necessities."

The Middle Class and the Making of a New Elite

The Enlightenment offered middle-class people an intellectual and cultural route to social improvement. The term *middle class* referred to the middle position on the social ladder; middle-class families did not have legal titles like the nobility above them but did not work with their hands like the peasants, artisans, or workers below them. Most middle-class people lived in towns or cities and earned their living in the professions—as doctors, lawyers, or lower-level officials—or through investment in land, trade, or manufacturing. In the eighteenth century, the ranks of the middle class—also known as the bourgeoisie (after *bourgeois,* the French word for "city dweller")—grew steadily in western Europe as a result of economic expansion. In France, for example, the overall population grew by about one-third in the 1700s, but the bourgeoisie nearly tripled in size. Although middle-class people had many reasons to resent the nobles, they also aspired to be like them.

Nobles and middle-class professionals mingled in Enlightenment salons and joined the new Masonic lodges and local learned societies. The members of Masonic lodges were known as **Freemasons** because that was the term given to apprentice masons when they were deemed "free" to practice as masters of their guild. The Freemasons quickly lost any connection to guild life, however; they held secret rituals and meetings devoted to philanthropy and the discussion of new ideas. Although not explicitly political in aim, the lodges encouraged equality among members, and both aristocrats and middle-class men could join. Members wrote constitutions for their lodges and elected their own officers, thus promoting a direct experience of constitutional government.

Freemasonry arose in Great Britain and spread eastward: the first French and Italian lodges opened in 1726; Frederick II of Prussia founded a lodge in 1740; and after 1750, Freemasonry spread in Poland, Russia, and British North America. In France, women set up their own Masonic lodges. Despite the papacy's condemnation of Freemasonry in 1738 as subversive of religious and civil authority, lodges continued to multiply throughout the eighteenth century because they offered a place for socializing outside of the traditional channels and a way of declaring one's interest in the Enlightenment and reform. In short, Freemasonry offered a kind of secular religion. After 1789 and the outbreak of the French Revolution, conservatives would blame the lodges for every kind of political upheaval, but in the 1700s many high-ranking nobles became active members and saw no conflict with their privileged status.

Shared tastes in travel, architecture, and the arts helped strengthen the links between nobles and members of the middle class. "Grand tours" of Europe often led upper-class youths to the recently discovered Roman ruins at Pompeii and Herculaneum in Italy. The excavations aroused enthusiasm for the neoclassical style in architecture and painting, which began pushing aside the rococo and the long dominant baroque. Urban residences, government buildings, furniture, fabrics, wallpaper, and even pottery soon reflected the neoclassical emphasis on purity and clarity of forms. The English potter Josiah Wedgwood (1730–1795) almost single-handedly created a mass market for domestic crockery by appealing to middle-class desires to emulate the rich and royal. His designs of special tea sets for the British queen, for Catherine the Great of Russia, and for leading aristocrats allowed him to advertise his wares as fashionable. By 1767, he claimed that his Queensware pottery

Neoclassical Style
In this Georgian interior of Syon House on the outskirts of London, various neoclassical motifs are readily apparent: Greek columns, Greek-style statuary on top of the columns, and Roman-style mosaics in the floor. The Scottish architect Robert Adam created this room for the duke of Northumberland in the 1760s. Adam had spent four years in Italy and returned to London in 1758 to decorate homes in the "Adam style," meaning the neoclassical manner. (© The Fotomas Index, U.K./ The Bridgeman Art Library.)

had "spread over the whole Globe," and indeed by then his pottery was being marketed in France, Russia, Venice, the Ottoman Empire, and British North America.

This period also supported artistic styles other than neoclassicism. Frederick II of Prussia built himself a palace in the earlier rococo style; gave it a French name, Sans-souci (meaning "worry-free"); and filled it with paintings and sculptures by the French masters of the rococo. The new emphasis on emotion and family life was reflected in a growing taste for moralistic family scenes in painting. The paintings of Jean-Baptiste Greuze (1725–1805), much praised by Diderot, depicted ordinary families at moments of domestic crisis. Such subjects appealed in particular to the middle-class public, which now attended the official painting exhibitions in France that were held regularly every other year after 1737.

Although wealthy nobles still patronized Europe's leading musicians, music too began to reflect the broadening of the elite, and the spread of Enlightenment ideals as classical forms replaced the baroque style. Complex polyphony gave way to melody, which made music more accessible to the ordinary listener. The first subscription concerts open to the public took place in London in the 1670s and in Frankfurt in 1712, and the German city of Leipzig opened the first public orchestra hall in 1781. The public concert gradually displaced the private recital, and a new attitude toward "the classics" developed: for the first time in the 1770s and 1780s, concert groups began to play older music rather than simply playing the latest commissioned works. This laid the foundation for what we still call classical music today—that is, a repertory of the greatest music of the eighteenth and early nineteenth centuries. Because composers now created works that would be performed over and over again as part of a classical repertory, rather than occasional pieces for

Jean-Baptiste Greuze, *Broken Eggs* (1756)
Greuze made his reputation as a painter of moralistic family scenes. In this one, an old woman (perhaps the mother) confronts the lover of a young girl and points to the eggs that have fallen out of a basket. The broken eggs are a symbol of lost virginity. Denis Diderot praised Greuze's work as "morality in paint," but the paintings often had an erotic subtext. (© Francis G. Mayer/Corbis.)

the court or noble patrons, they deliberately attempted to write lasting works. As a result, the major composers began to produce fewer symphonies: the Austrian composer Franz Joseph Haydn (1732–1809) wrote more than one hundred symphonies, but his successor Ludwig van Beethoven (1770–1827) would create only nine.

The two supreme masters of the new musical style of the eighteenth century show that the transition from noble patronage to classical concerts was far from complete. The Austrians Haydn and Wolfgang Amadeus Mozart (1756–1791) both wrote for noble patrons, but by the early 1800s their compositions had been incorporated into the canon of concert classics all over Europe. Incredibly prolific, both excelled in combining lightness, clarity, and profound emotion. Both also wrote numerous Italian operas, a genre whose popularity continued to grow: in the 1780s, the Papal States alone boasted forty opera houses. Haydn spent most of his career working for a Hungarian noble family, the Eszterházys. Asked why he had written no string quintets (at which Mozart excelled), he responded simply, "No one has ordered any."

Interest in reading, like attending public concerts, took hold of the middle classes. Shaped by coffeehouses, Masonic lodges, and public concerts more than by formal schooling, the new reading public fueled a frenzied increase in publication. By the end of the eighteenth century, six times as many books were being published in the German states, for instance, as at the beginning of the century. One Parisian author commented that "people are certainly reading ten times as much in Paris as they did a hundred years ago." Provincial towns in Britain, France, the Dutch Republic, and the German states published their own newspapers; by 1780, thirty-seven English towns had local newspapers. Newspapers advertised arithmetic, dancing, and drawing lessons—and potions to induce abortions and cures for venereal disease. Lending libraries multiplied, and in England especially, even small villages housed book clubs. Women benefited as much as men from the spread of print. As one Englishman observed, "By far the greatest part of ladies now have a taste for books."

The novel had become a respectable and influential genre. Among the most widely read novels were those of the English printer and writer Samuel Richardson (1689–1761). In *Clarissa Harlowe* (1747–1748), a long novel in eight volumes, Richardson tells the story of a young woman from a heartless upper-class family who is torn between her family's choice of a repulsive suitor and her attraction to Lovelace, an aristocratic rake. Although she runs off with Lovelace to escape her family, she resists his advances; after being drugged and raped by Lovelace—despite the frantic pleas of readers of the first volumes to spare her—Clarissa dies of what can only be called a broken heart. One woman complained to Richardson, "I verily believe I have shed a pint of tears, and my heart is still bursting." Richardson claimed that he wrote *Clarissa Harlowe* as a kind of manual of virtuous female conduct, yet critics nonetheless worried that novels undermined morals with their portrayals of lowlife characters, the seductions of virtuous women, and other examples of immoral behavior.

Although he himself grew up reading novels with his father, Rousseau discouraged novel reading in *Émile*. Still, he helped change attitudes in the new elite toward children by offering an educational approach for gently drawing the best out of children rather than repressing their natural curiosity and love of learning. Paintings now showed individual children playing at their favorite activities rather than formally posed with their families. Books about and for children became popular. *The Newtonian System of the Universe Digested for Young Minds*, by "Tom Telescope," was published in Britain in 1761 and reprinted many times. Toys, jigsaw puzzles, and clothing designed for children all appeared for the first time in the 1700s. At the same time, however, the Enlightenment's emphasis on reason, self-control, and childhood innocence made parents increasingly anxious about their children's sexuality. Moralists and physicians wrote books about the evils of masturbation, "proving" that it led to physical and mental degeneration and even madness. One English writer linked masturbation to debility of body and of mind; infertility; epilepsy; loss of memory, sight, and hearing; distortions of the eyes, mouth, and face; a pale, sallow, and bluish complexion; wasting of the limbs; idiotism; and death itself. While the Enlightenment thus encouraged excessive concern about children being left to their own devices, it nevertheless taught the middle and upper classes to value their children and to expect their improvement through education.

Life on the Margins

Even more than worrying about their children, the upper and middle classes worried about the increasing numbers of poor people. Although booming foreign trade—French colonial trade, for example, increased tenfold in the 1700s—fueled a dramatic economic expansion, the results did not necessarily trickle all the way down the social scale. The population of Europe grew by nearly 30 percent, with especially striking gains in England, Ireland, Prussia, and Hungary. Even though food production increased, shortages and crises still occurred periodically. Prices went up in many countries after the 1730s and continued to rise gradually until the early nineteenth century; wages in many trades rose as well, though less quickly than prices. Peasants who produced surpluses to sell in local markets and shopkeepers and artisans who could increase their sales to meet growing demand prospered. But those at the bottom of the social ladder—day laborers in the cities and peasants with smallholdings—lived on the edge of dire poverty, and when they lost their land or work, they either migrated to the cities or wandered the roads in search of food and work. In France alone, 200,000 workers left their homes every year in search of seasonal employment elsewhere. At least 10 percent of Europe's urban population depended on some form of charity.

The growing numbers of poor people overwhelmed local governments and created fears about rising crime. In some countries, officials sent beggars and vagabonds to workhouses. The expenses for running these overcrowded institutions increased 60 percent in England between 1760 and 1785. After 1740, most German towns began to set up workhouses that were part workshop, part hospital, and part prison. Such institutions also appeared for the first time in Boston, New York, and Philadelphia. To supplement the inadequate system of religious charity, offices for the poor, public workshops, and workhouse-hospitals, the French government created *dépôts de mendicité,* or "beggar houses," in 1767. The government sent people to these new workhouses to labor in manufacturing, but most were too weak or sick to work, and 20 percent of them died within a few months of incarceration.

Those who were able to work or keep their land fared better. An increase in literacy, especially in the cities, allowed some lower-class people to participate in new tastes and ideas. One French observer insisted, "These days, you see a waiting-maid in her backroom, a lackey in an ante-room reading pamphlets. People can read in almost all classes of society." In France, however, only 50 percent of men and 27 percent of women could read and write in the 1780s (although that was twice the rate of a century earlier). Literacy rates were higher in England and the Dutch Republic, much lower in eastern Europe. About one in four Parisians owned books, but the lower classes overwhelmingly read religious books, as they had in the past.

Whereas the new elite might attend salons, concerts, or art exhibitions, peasants enjoyed their traditional forms of popular entertainment, such as fairs and festivals, and the urban lower classes relaxed in cabarets and taverns. Sometimes pleasures were cruel. In Britain, bullbaiting, bearbaiting, dogfighting, and cockfighting were all common forms of entertainment that provided opportunities for organized gambling. Even "gentle" sports frequented by the upper classes had their violent side, showing that the upper classes had not become so different as they sometimes thought. Cricket matches, whose rules were first laid down in 1744, were often accompanied by brawls among fans (not unlike soccer matches today, though on a much smaller scale). Many British enjoyed what one observer called a "battle royal with sticks, pebbles and hog's dung."

As population increased and villagers began to move to cities to better their prospects, sexual behavior changed, too. The rates of births out of wedlock soared, from less than 5 percent of all births in the seventeenth century to nearly 20 percent at the end of the eighteenth. Historians have disagreed about the causes and meaning of this change. Some detect in this pattern a sign of sexual liberation and the beginnings of a modern sexual revolution: as women moved out of the control of their families, they began to seek their own sexual fulfillment. Others view this change more bleakly, as a story of seduction and betrayal: family and community pressure had once forced a man to marry a woman pregnant with his child, but now a man could abandon a pregnant lover by simply moving away.

Increased mobility brought freedom for some women, but it also aggravated the vulnerability of those newly arrived in cities from the countryside. Desperation, not reason, often ruled their choices. Women who came to the city as domestic servants had little recourse against masters or fellow servants who seduced or raped them. The result was a startling rise in abandoned babies. Most European cities established foundling hospitals to care for abandoned children in the 1700s, but infant and child mortality was 50 percent higher in such institutions than for children brought up at home. For women of this era who wanted to terminate a pregnancy, the options were limited and usually handled in secrecy. Some women tried herbs, laxatives, or crude surgical means of abortion; a few, usually servants who would lose their jobs if their employers discovered they had borne a child, resorted to infanticide. Reformers criticized the harshness of laws against infanticide, but they showed no mercy for "sodomites" (as male homosexuals were called), who in some places, in particular the Dutch Republic, were systematically persecuted and imprisoned or even executed. Male homosexuals attracted the attention of authorities because they had begun to develop networks and special meeting places. The stereotype of the effeminate, exclusively homosexual male seems to have appeared for the first time in the eighteenth century, perhaps as part of a growing emphasis on separate roles for men and women.

REVIEW   What were the major differences in the impact of the Enlightenment on nobles, the middle classes, and the lower classes?

State Power in an Era of Reform

Rulers turned to Enlightenment-inspired reforms to improve life for their subjects and gain commercial or military advantage over rival states. Historians label many of the sovereigns of this time **enlightened despots** or enlightened absolutists, for they aimed to promote Enlightenment reforms without giving up their absolutist powers. Catherine the Great's admiring relationship with Voltaire showed how even the most absolutist rulers championed reform when it suited their own goals. Foremost among those goals was the expansion of a ruler's territory.

War and Diplomacy

Europeans no longer fought devastating wars over religion that killed hundreds of thousands of civilians; instead, professional armies and navies battled for control of overseas empires and for dominance on the European continent. Rulers continued to expand their armies; the Prussian army, for example, nearly tripled in size between 1740 and 1789. Widespread use of flintlock muskets required deployment in long lines, usually three men deep, with each line in turn loading and firing on command. Military strategy became cautious and calculating, but this did not prevent the outbreak of hostilities. The instability of the European balance of power resulted in two major wars, a diplomatic reversal of alliances, and the partition of Poland-Lithuania among Russia, Austria, and Prussia.

The War of the Austrian Succession (1740–1748) broke out when Holy Roman Emperor Charles VI died in 1740 without a male heir. Most European rulers recognized the emperor's chosen heiress, his daughter Maria Theresa, because Charles's Pragmatic Sanction of 1713 had given women the right to inherit the Habsburg crown lands. The new king of Prussia, Frederick II, who had just succeeded his father a few months earlier in 1740, saw his chance to grab territory and immediately invaded the rich Austrian province of Silesia. France joined Prussia in an attempt to further humiliate its traditional enemy Austria, and Great Britain allied with Austria to prevent the French from taking the Austrian Netherlands (Map 15.1). French and British colonials in North America soon fought each other all along their boundaries, enlisting native American auxiliaries. Britain tried but failed to isolate the French Caribbean colonies during the war, and hostilities broke out in India, too. Maria Theresa (r. 1740–1780) survived only by conceding Silesia to Prussia in order to split the Prussians off from France. The Peace of Aix-la-Chapelle of 1748 recognized Maria Theresa as the heiress to the Austrian lands, and her husband, Francis I, became Holy Roman Emperor, thus reasserting the integrity of the Austrian Empire.

In 1756, a major reversal of alliances reshaped relations among the great powers. Prussia and Great Britain signed a defensive alliance, prompting Austria to overlook two centuries of hostility and ally with France. Austrian and French willingness to put aside their long-standing dynastic rivalry in favor of more immediate strategic

Map 15.1 The War of the Austrian Succession, 1740–1748
The accession of a twenty-three-year-old woman, Maria Theresa, to the Austrian throne gave the new king of Prussia, Frederick II, an opportunity to invade the province of Silesia. France joined on Prussia's side, Great Britain on Austria's. In 1745, the French defeated the British in the Austrian Netherlands and helped instigate a Jacobite uprising in Scotland. The rebellion failed, and British attacks on French overseas shipping forced the French to negotiate. The peace treaties guaranteed Frederick's conquest of Silesia, which soon became the wealthiest province of Prussia. France came to terms with Great Britain to protect its overseas possessions; Austria had to accept the peace settlement after a formal public protest.

interests prompted some to call this a "diplomatic revolution." Russia and Sweden soon joined the Franco-Austrian alliance. When Frederick II invaded Saxony, an ally of Austria, with his bigger and better-disciplined army, the long-simmering hostilities between Great Britain and France over colonial boundaries flared into a general war that became known as the Seven Years' War (1756–1763).

Fighting soon raged around the world (Map 15.2). The French and British battled on land and sea in North America (where the conflict was called the French and Indian War), the West Indies, and India. The two coalitions also fought each other in central Europe. At first, in 1757, Frederick the Great surprised Europe with a spectacular victory at Rossbach in Saxony over a much larger Franco-Austrian army. But in time, Russian and Austrian armies encircled his troops. Frederick despaired: "I believe all is lost. I will not survive the ruin of my country." A fluke of history saved him. Empress Elizabeth of Russia (r. 1741–1762) died and was succeeded by the mentally unstable Peter III, a fanatical admirer of Frederick and things Prussian. Peter withdrew Russia from the war. (He was soon mysteriously murdered, probably at the instigation of his wife, Catherine the Great.) In separate peace treaties with Russia and Austria, Frederick kept all his territory, including Silesia.

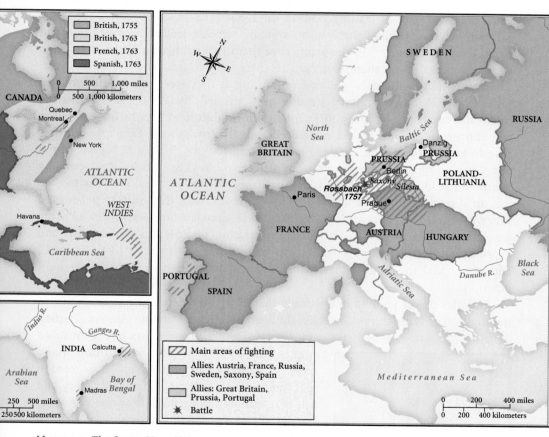

Map 15.2 The Seven Years' War, 1756–1763
In what might justly be called the first worldwide war, the French and British fought each other in Europe, the West Indies, North America, and India. Skirmishing in North America helped precipitate the war, which became more general when Austria, France, and Russia allied to check Prussian influence in central Europe. The treaty between Austria and Prussia simply restored the status quo in Europe, but the changes overseas were much more dramatic. Britain gained control over Canada and India but gave back to France the West Indian islands of Guadeloupe and Martinique. Britain was now the dominant power of the seas. **For more help analyzing this map, see the map activity for this chapter in the Online Study Guide at** bedfordstmartins.com/huntconcise.

The Anglo-French overseas conflicts ended more decisively than the continental land wars. British naval superiority, fully achieved only in the 1750s, enabled Great Britain to rout the French in North America, India, and the West Indies. In the Treaty of Paris of 1763, France ceded Canada to Great Britain and agreed to remove its armies from India, in exchange for keeping its rich West Indian islands. Eagerness to avenge this defeat would motivate France to support the British North American colonists in their War of Independence just fifteen years later.

Although Prussia suffered great losses in the Seven Years' War—some 160,000 Prussian soldiers died either in action or of disease—the army helped vault Prussia to the rank of leading powers. In 1733, Frederick II's father, Frederick William I, had instituted the "canton system," which enrolled peasant youths in each canton (or district) in the army, gave them two or three months of training annually, and allowed them to return to their family farms the rest of the year. They remained "cantonists" (reservists) as long as they were able-bodied. In this fashion, the Prussian military steadily grew in size. By 1740, Prussia had the third- or fourth-largest army in Europe even though it was tenth in population and thirteenth in land area. Under Frederick II, Prussia's military expenditures rose to two-thirds of the state's revenue. Almost every nobleman served in the army, paying for his own support as an officer and buying a position as company commander. Once retired, the officers returned to their estates, coordinated the canton system, and served as local officials. In this way, the military permeated every aspect of rural society, fusing army and agrarian organization. The army gave the state great power, but the militarization of Prussian society also had a profoundly conservative effect: it kept the peasants enserfed to their lords, and it blocked the middle classes from access to estates or high government positions.

Prussia's power grew so dramatically that in 1772 Frederick the Great proposed the division of large chunks of Polish-Lithuanian territory among Austria, Prussia, and Russia. Despite the protests of the Austrian empress Maria Theresa that the partition would spread "a stain over my whole reign," she agreed to split one-third of Poland-Lithuania's territory and half of its people among the three powers. Austria feared growing Russian influence in Poland and in the Balkans, where Russia had been successfully battling the Ottoman Empire. Conflicts among Catholics, Protestants, and Orthodox Christians in Poland were used to justify this cynical move. Russia took over most of Lithuania, effectively ending the large but weak Polish-Lithuanian commonwealth.

The First Partition of Poland, 1772

Dividing Poland, 1772
In this contemporary depiction, Catherine the Great, Joseph II, and Frederick II point on the map to the portion of Poland-Lithuania each plans to take. The artist makes it clear that Poland's fate rested in the hands of neighboring rulers, not its own people. Can you infer the sentiments of the artist from the content of this engraving? (Mansell/Time Life Pictures/Getty Images.)

State-Sponsored Reform

In the aftermath of the Seven Years' War, all the belligerents faced pressing needs for more money to fund their growing armies, to organize navies to wage overseas conflicts, and to counter the impact of inflation. To make tax increases more palatable to public opinion, rulers appointed reform-minded ministers and gave them a mandate to modernize government. As one adviser to Joseph II of Austria (r. 1780–1790) put it, "A properly constituted state must be exactly analogous to a machine . . . and the ruler must be the foreman, the mainspring . . . which sets everything else in motion." Such reforms always threatened the interests of traditional groups, however, and the spread of Enlightenment ideas aroused sometimes unpredictable desires for more change.

Legal reform, both of the judicial system and of the often disorganized and irregular law codes, was central to the work of many reform-minded monarchs. Although Frederick II favored all things French in culture—he insisted on speaking French in his court and prided himself on his personal friendship with Voltaire—he made Prussian justice the envy of Europe. His institution of a uniform civil justice system created the most consistently administered laws and efficient judiciary of the time. Joseph II also ordered the compilation of a unified law code, a project that required many years for completion. Catherine II of Russia began such an undertaking even more ambitiously. In 1767, she called together a legislative commission of 564 deputies and asked them to consider a long document called the *Instruction,* which represented her hopes for legal reform based on the ideas of Montesquieu and the Italian writer Cesare Beccaria. Montesquieu had insisted that any punishment should fit the crime; he also criticized the use of torture and brutal corporal punishment. In his influential book *On Crimes and Punishments* (1764), Beccaria argued that laws should be printed for everyone to read and administered in rational procedures, that torture should be abolished as inhumane, and that the accused should be presumed innocent until proven guilty. Despite much discussion and hundreds of petitions and documents about local problems, little came of Catherine's commission because the monarch herself—despite her regard for Voltaire and his fellow philosophes—proved ultimately unwilling to see through far-reaching legal reform.

Rulers everywhere wanted more control over church affairs, and they used Enlightenment criticisms of the organized churches to get their way. In Catholic countries, many government officials resented the influence of the Jesuits, the major Catholic teaching order. The Jesuits trained the Catholic intellectual elite, ran a worldwide missionary network, enjoyed close ties to the papacy, and amassed great wealth. Critics mounted campaigns against the Jesuits in many countries, and by the early 1770s the Society of Jesus had been dissolved in Portugal, France, and Spain. In 1773, Pope Clement XIV (r. 1769–1774) agreed under pressure to disband the order, an edict that held until a reinvigorated papacy restored the society in 1814. Joseph II of Austria not only applauded the suppression of the Jesuits but also required Austrian bishops to swear fidelity and submission to him. Under Joseph, the Austrian state supervised seminaries, reorganized diocesan boundaries, abolished contemplative monastic orders, and confiscated their property to pay for education and poor relief.

Enlightened absolutists also tried to gain greater state authority over education, even while extending education to the lower classes. Joseph II launched the most ambitious educational reforms of the period. In 1774, once the Jesuits had been disbanded, the General School Ordinance in Austria ordered state subsidies for local schools, which the state would regulate. By 1789, one-quarter of the school-age children attended school. In Prussia, the school code of 1763 required all children between the ages of five and thirteen to attend school. Although not enforced uniformly, the Prussian law demonstrated Frederick II's belief that modernization depended on education. Catherine II of Russia also tried to expand elementary education—and the education of women in particular—and founded engineering schools.

No ruler pushed the principle of religious toleration as far as Joseph II of Austria, who became Holy Roman Emperor and co-regent with his mother, Maria Theresa, in 1765 and then ruled alone after 1780. In 1781, he granted freedom of religious worship to Protestants, Orthodox Christians, and Jews. For the first time, these groups were allowed to own property, build schools, enter the professions, and hold political and military offices. The efforts of other rulers to extend religious toleration proved more limited. Louis XVI signed an edict in 1787 restoring French Protestants' civil rights—but still they could not hold political office. Great Britain continued to deny Catholics freedom of open worship and the right to sit in Parliament. Most European states limited the rights and opportunities available to Jews. In Russia, only wealthy Jews could hold municipal office, and in the Papal States, the pope encouraged forced baptism. The leading philosophes opposed the persecution of Jews in theory but often treated them with undisguised contempt. Diderot's comment was all too typical: Jews, he said, bore "all the defects peculiar to an ignorant and superstitious nation."

Limits of Reform

When enlightened absolutist leaders introduced reforms, they often faced resistance from groups threatened by the proposed changes. The most contentious area of reform was agricultural policy. Whereas Frederick II and Catherine II reinforced the authority of nobles over their serfs, Joseph II tried to remove the burdens of serfdom in the Habsburg lands. In 1781, he abolished the personal aspects of serfdom: serfs could now move freely, enter trades, or marry without their lords' permission. Joseph abolished the tithe to the church, shifted more of the tax burden to the nobility, and converted peasants' labor services into cash payments.

The Austrian nobility furiously resisted these far-reaching reforms. When Joseph died in 1790, his brother Leopold II had to revoke most reforms to appease the nobles. On his deathbed, Joseph recognized the futility of many of his efforts; as his epitaph he suggested, "Here lies Joseph II, who was unfortunate in all his enterprises." Prussia's Frederick II, like Joseph, encouraged such agricultural innovations as planting potatoes and turnips (new crops that could help feed a growing population), experimenting with cattle breeding, draining swamplands, and clearing forests. But Prussia's noble landlords, the Junkers, continued to expand their estates at the expense of poorer peasants, and Frederick did nothing to ameliorate serfdom except on his own domains.

Reforming ministers also tried to stimulate agricultural improvement in France. Unlike most other western European countries, France still had about 100,000 serfs; though their burdens weighed less heavily than those in eastern Europe, serfdom did not entirely disappear until 1789. A group of economists called the **physiocrats** urged the French government to deregulate the grain trade and make the tax system more equitable to encourage agricultural productivity. In the interest of establishing a free market, they also insisted that urban guilds be abolished because they prevented free entry into the trades. Their proposed reforms applied the Enlightenment emphasis on individual liberties to the economy; Adam Smith took up many of the physiocrats' ideas in his writing in favor of free markets. The French government heeded some of this advice and gave up its system of price controls on grain in 1763, but it had to reverse this decision in 1770 when grain shortages caused a famine.

French reform efforts did not end there. To break the power of the parlements (the thirteen high courts of law that had led the way in opposing royal efforts to increase and equalize taxation), Louis XV appointed a reform-minded chancellor who in 1770 replaced the parlements with courts in which the judges no longer owned their offices and thus could not sell them or pass them on as an inheritance. Justice would then be more impartial. Nevertheless, the judges of the displaced parlements aroused widespread opposition to what they portrayed as tyrannical royal policy. The furor calmed down only when Louis XV died in 1774 and his successor, Louis XVI (r. 1774–1792), yielded to aristocratic demands and restored the old parlements. Louis XV died one of the most despised kings in French history, resented both for his high-handed reforms and for his private vices. Underground pamphlets lampooned him, describing his final mistress, Madame du Barry, as a prostitute who pandered to the elderly king's well-known taste for young girls. This often pornographic literature linked despotism to the supposedly excessive influence of women at court.

Louis XVI tried to carry out part of the program suggested by the physiocrats, and he chose one of their disciples, Jacques Turgot (1727–1781), as his chief minister. Turgot pushed through several edicts that again freed the grain trade, suppressed many guilds, converted the peasants' forced labor on roads into a money tax payable by all landowners, and reduced court expenses. He also began making plans to introduce a system of elected local assemblies, which would have made government much more representative. Faced with broad-based resistance led by the parlements and his own courtiers, as well as with riots against rising grain prices, Louis XVI dismissed Turgot, and one of the last possibilities to overhaul France's monarchy collapsed.

The failure of reform in France paradoxically reflected the power of Enlightenment ideas; everyone now endorsed Enlightenment ideals but used them for different ends. The nobles in the parlements blocked the French monarchy's reform efforts using the very same Enlightenment language spoken by the crown's ministers. But unlike Austria, the other great power that faced persistent aristocratic resistance to reform, France had a large middle-class public that was increasingly frustrated by the failure to institute social change, a failure that ultimately helped undermine the monarchy itself. Where Frederick II, Catherine II, and even Joseph II used reform to bolster the efficiency of absolutist government, attempts at change in France backfired. French kings found that their ambitious programs for reform succeeded only in arousing unrealistic hopes.

REVIEW   What prompted enlightened absolutists to undertake reforms in the second half of the eighteenth century?

Rebellions against State Power

Although traditional forms of popular discontent had not disappeared, Enlightenment ideals and reforms changed the rules of the game in politics. Governments had become accountable for their actions to a much wider public sphere than ever before. In Britain and France, ordinary people rioted when they perceived government as failing to protect them against food shortages. The growth of informed public opinion had its most dramatic consequences in the North American colonies, where a struggle over the British Parliament's right to tax turned into a full-scale war for independence. The American War of Independence showed that once put into practice, Enlightenment ideals could have revolutionary implications.

Food Riots and Peasant Uprisings

Population growth, inflation, and the extension of the market system put added pressure on the already beleaguered poorest classes of people. Seventeenth-century peasants and townspeople had rioted to protest new taxes. In the last half of the eighteenth century, the food supply became the focus of political and social conflict. Poor people living in the villages and towns believed it was the government's responsibility to ensure that they had enough food, and many governments did stockpile grain to make up for the occasional bad harvest. At the same time, in keeping with Adam Smith's and the French physiocrats' free-market proposals, governments wanted to allow grain prices to rise with market demand, because higher profits would motivate producers to increase the supply of food.

Free trade in grain meant selling to the highest bidder even if that bidder was a foreign merchant. In the short run, in times of scarcity, big landowners and farmers could make huge profits by selling grain outside their hometowns or villages. This practice enraged poor farmers, agricultural workers, and city wageworkers, who could not afford the higher prices. Lacking the political means to affect policy, they could enforce their desire for old-fashioned price regulation only by rioting. Most did not pillage or steal grain, but rather forced the sale of grain or flour at a "just" price and blocked the shipment of grain out of their villages to other markets. Women often led these "popular price fixings," as they were called in France, in desperate attempts to protect the food supply for their children.

Such food riots occurred regularly in Britain and France in the second half of the eighteenth century. One of the most turbulent was the so-called Flour War in France in 1775. Turgot's deregulation of the grain trade in 1774 caused prices to rise in several provincial cities. Rioting spread from there to the Paris region, where villagers attacked grain convoys heading to the capital city. Local officials often ordered merchants and bakers to sell at the price the rioters demanded, only to find themselves arrested by the central government for overriding free trade. The government brought in troops to restore order and introduced the death penalty for rioting.

Frustrations with serfdom and hopes for a miraculous transformation provoked the Pugachev rebellion in Russia beginning in 1773. An army deserter from the southeast frontier region, Emelian Pugachev (1742–1775) claimed to be Tsar Peter III, the dead husband of Catherine II. Pugachev's appearance seemed to confirm peasant hopes for a "redeemer tsar" who would save the people from oppression. He rallied around him Cossacks like himself who resented the loss of their old

The Pugachev Rebellion, 1773

tribal independence. Now increasingly enserfed or forced to pay taxes and endure army service, these nomadic bands joined with other serfs, rebellious mineworkers, and Muslim minorities. Catherine dispatched a large army to squelch the uprising, but Pugachev eluded them, and the fighting spread. Nearly three million people eventually participated, making this the largest single rebellion in the history of tsarist Russia.

When Pugachev urged the peasants to attack the nobility and seize their estates, hundreds of noble families perished. Foreign newspapers called it "the revolution in southern Russia" and offered fantastic stories about Pugachev's life history. Finally, the army captured the rebel leader and brought him in an iron cage to Moscow, where he was tortured and executed. In the aftermath, Catherine tightened the nobles' control over their serfs and harshly punished those who dared to criticize serfdom.

A Cossack

Emelian Pugachev and many of his followers were Cossacks, Ukrainians who set up nomadic communities of horsemen to resist outside control, whether from the Turks, Poles, or Russians. This eighteenth-century engraving captures the common view of Cossacks as horsemen always ready for battle but with a fondness for music, too. **For more help analyzing this image, see the visual activity for this chapter in the Online Study Guide at** bedfordstmartins.com/huntconcise. (© The Bridgeman Art Library.)

Public Opinion and Political Opposition

Peasant uprisings might briefly shake even a powerful monarchy, but the rise of public opinion as a force independent of court society caused more enduring changes in European politics. Across much of Europe and in the North American colonies, demands for broader political participation reflected Enlightenment notions about individual rights. Aristocratic bodies such as the French parlements, which had no legislative role like that of the British Parliament, insisted that the monarch consult them on the nation's affairs, and the new educated elite wanted more influence, too. Newspapers began to cover daily political affairs, and the public learned the basics of political life, despite the strict limits on political participation in most countries.

Monarchs turned to public opinion to seek support against aristocratic groups that opposed reform. Gustavus III of Sweden (r. 1771–1792) called himself "the first citizen of a free people" and promised to deliver the country from "insufferable aristocratic despotism." Shortly after coming to the throne, Gustavus proclaimed a new constitution that divided power between the king and the legislature, abolished the use of torture in the judicial process, and ensured some freedom of the press.

In France, both the parlements and the monarch appealed to the public through the printed word. The crown hired writers to make its case; the magistrates of the parlements wrote their own rejoinders. French-language newspapers published in the Dutch Republic provided many people in France with detailed accounts of political news and also gave voice to pro-parlement positions. One of the new French-language newspapers printed inside France, *Le Journal des Dames (The Ladies' Journal)*, was published by women and mixed short stories and reviews of books and plays with demands for more women's rights.

The Wilkes affair in Great Britain showed that public opinion could be mobilized to challenge a government. In 1763, during the reign of George III (r. 1760–1820), John Wilkes, a member of Parliament, attacked the government in his newspaper, *North Briton,* and sued the crown when he was arrested. He won his release as well as damages. When he was reelected, Parliament denied him his seat, not once but three times.

The Wilkes episode soon escalated into a major campaign against the corruption and social exclusiveness of Parliament, complaints the Levellers had first raised during the English revolutions of the late 1640s. Newspapers, magazines, pamphlets, handbills, and cheap editions of Wilkes's collected works all helped promote his cause. Those who could not vote demonstrated for Wilkes. In one incident, eleven people died when soldiers broke up a huge gathering of his supporters. The slogan "Wilkes and Liberty" appeared on walls all over London. Middle-class voters formed the Society of Supporters of the Bill of Rights, which circulated petitions for Wilkes; they gained the backing of about one-fourth of all the voters. The more determined Wilkesites proposed sweeping reforms of Parliament, including more frequent elections, more representation for the counties, the elimination of "rotten boroughs" (election districts so small that they could be controlled by one big patron), and restrictions of pensions used by the crown to gain support. These demands would be at the heart of agitation for parliamentary reform in Britain for decades to come.

Popular demonstrations did not always support reforms. In 1780, the Gordon riots devastated London. They were named after the fanatical anti-Catholic crusader Lord George Gordon, who helped organize huge marches and petition campaigns against a bill the House of Commons passed to grant limited toleration to Catholics. The demonstrations culminated in a seven-day riot that left fifty buildings destroyed and three hundred people dead. Despite the continuing limitation on voting rights in Great Britain, British politicians were learning that they could ignore public opinion only at their peril.

Political opposition also took artistic forms, particularly in countries where governments restricted organized political activity. A striking example of a play with a political message was *The Marriage of Figaro* (1784) by Pierre-Augustin Caron de Beaumarchais (1732–1799), a watchmaker, a judge, a gunrunner in the American War of Independence, and a French spy in Britain. *The Marriage of Figaro* was first a hit at court, when Queen Marie-Antoinette had it read for her friends. But when her husband, Louis XVI, read it, he forbade its production on the grounds that "this man mocks at everything that should be respected in government." When finally performed publicly, the play caused a sensation. The chief character, Figaro, is a clever servant who gets the better of his noble employer. When speaking of the count, he cries, "What have you done to deserve so many rewards? You went to the trouble of being born, and nothing more." Two years later, Mozart based an equally famous but somewhat tamer opera on Beaumarchais's story.

Revolution in North America

Oppositional forms of public opinion came to a head in Great Britain's North American colonies, where the result was American independence and the establishment of a republican constitution that stood in stark contrast to most European regimes. The successful revolution was the only blow to Britain's increasing dominance in world affairs in the eighteenth century, and as such it was another aspect of the power rivalries existing at that time. Yet many Europeans saw the American War of Independence, or the American Revolution (1775–1783), as a triumph for Enlightenment ideas. As one German writer exclaimed in 1777, an American victory would give "greater scope to the Enlightenment, new keenness to the thinking of peoples and new life to the spirit of liberty."

The American revolutionary leaders had been influenced by a common Atlantic civilization; they participated in the Enlightenment and shared political ideas with the opposition Whigs in Britain. Supporters demonstrated for Wilkes in South Carolina and Boston, and the South Carolina legislature donated a substantial sum to the Society of Supporters of the Bill of Rights. In the 1760s and

1770s, both British and American opposition leaders became convinced that the British government was growing increasingly corrupt and despotic. British radicals wanted to reform Parliament so the voices of a broader, more representative segment of the population would be heard. The colonies had no representatives in Parliament, and the colonists claimed that "no taxation without representation" should be allowed. Indeed, they denied that Parliament had any jurisdiction over the colonies, insisting that the king govern them through colonial legislatures and recognize their traditional British liberties. The failure of the "Wilkes and Liberty" campaign to produce concrete results convinced many Americans that Parliament was hopelessly tainted and that they would have to stand up for their rights as British subjects.

The British colonies remained loyal to the crown until Parliament's encroachment on their autonomy, and the elimination of the French threat at the end of the Seven Years' War transformed colonial attitudes. Unconsciously perhaps, the colonies had begun to form a separate nation. Their economies generally flourished in the eighteenth century, and between 1750 and 1776 their population almost doubled. More slaves were imported during that quarter-century than at any other time in American history. With the British clamoring for lower taxes and the colonists paying only a fraction of the tax rate levied on the Britons at home, Parliament passed new taxes, including the Stamp Act in 1765, which required a special tax stamp on all legal documents and publications. After violent rioting in the colonies, the tax was repealed, but in 1773 a new Tea Act revived colonial resistance, which culminated in the so-called Boston Tea Party of 1773. Colonists dressed as Indians boarded British ships and dumped the imported tea (by this time an enormously popular beverage) into Boston's harbor. The British government tried to clamp down on the unrest, but British troops in the colonies soon found themselves fighting locally organized militias.

Political opposition in the American colonies turned belligerent when Britain threatened to use force to maintain control. In 1774, the First Continental Congress convened, composed of delegates from all the colonies, and unsuccessfully petitioned the crown for redress. The next year the Second Continental Congress organized an army with George Washington in command. After actual fighting had begun, in 1776, the congress proclaimed the Declaration of Independence. An eloquent statement of the American cause written principally by Thomas Jefferson, a delegate from Virginia, the Declaration of Independence was couched in the language of universal human rights, which enlightened Europeans could be expected to understand. George III denounced the American "traitors and rebels." But European newspapers enthusiastically reported on every American response to "the cruel acts of oppression they have been made to suffer." Two years after the Declaration was issued, France boosted the American cause by entering on the colonists' side in 1778. Spain, too, saw an opportunity to check the growing power of Britain, though without actually endorsing American independence out of fear of the response of its Latin American colonies. Spain declared war on Britain in 1779. The following year, Britain declared war on the Dutch Republic in retaliation for Dutch support of the rebels. The worldwide conflict that resulted was more than Britain could handle. The American colonies achieved their independence in the peace treaty of 1783.

The newly independent states still faced the challenge of republican self-government. The Articles of Confederation, drawn up in 1777 as a provisional constitution, proved weak because they gave the central government few powers. In 1787, a constitutional convention met in Philadelphia to draft a new constitution. It established a two-house legislature, an indirectly elected president, and an independent judiciary. The Constitution's preamble insisted explicitly, for the first time in history, that government derived its power solely from the people and did not depend on divine right or on the tradition of royalty or aristocracy. The new educated elite of the eighteenth century had now created a government based on a "social contract" among male, property-owning, white citizens. It was by no means a complete democracy, and women and slaves were excluded from political participation. But the new government represented a radical departure from European models. In 1791, the Bill of Rights, outlining the essential rights (such as freedom of speech) that the government could never overturn, was appended to the Constitution. Although slavery continued in the American republic, the new emphasis on rights helped fuel a movement for its abolition in both Britain and the United States.

Interest in the new republic was greatest in France. The U.S. Constitution and various state constitutions were published in French with commentary by leading thinkers. Even more important in the long run were the effects of the American war. Dutch losses to Great Britain aroused a widespread movement for political reform in the Dutch Republic, and debts incurred by France in supporting the American colonies would soon force the French monarchy to the edge of bankruptcy and then to revolution. Ultimately, the entire European system of royal rule would be challenged.

REVIEW   Why did public opinion become a new factor in politics in the second half of the eighteenth century?

Conclusion

The American Revolution was the most profound practical result of the general European movement known as the Enlightenment. When Thomas Jefferson looked back many years later on the Declaration of Independence, he said he hoped it would be "the signal of arousing men to burst the chains under which monkish ignorance and superstition had persuaded them to bind themselves."

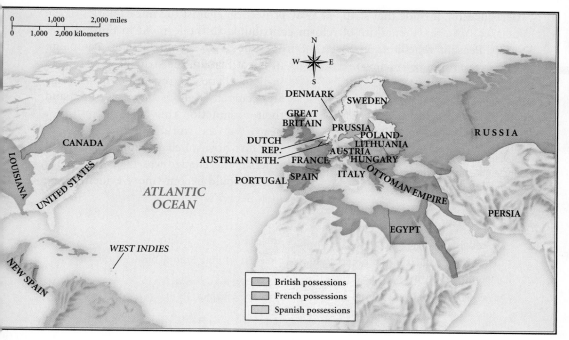

Mapping the West Europe and the World, c. 1780
Although Great Britain lost control over its North American colonies, which became the new United States, European influence on the rest of the world grew dramatically in the eighteenth century. The slave trade linked European ports to African slave-trading outposts and to plantations in the Caribbean, South America, and North America. The European countries on the Atlantic Ocean benefited most from this trade. Yet almost all of Africa, China, and Japan and large parts of India still resisted European incursion, and the Ottoman Empire, with its massive territories, still presented Europe with a formidable military challenge.

What began as a cosmopolitan movement of a few intellectuals in the first half of the eighteenth century reached a relatively wide audience among the educated elite of men and women. The spirit of reform swept from the salons and coffeehouses into the halls of government. Reasoned, scientific inquiry into the causes of social misery and laws defending individual rights and freedoms gained adherents everywhere.

For most Europeans, however, Enlightenment remained a promise rather than a reality. Rulers such as Catherine the Great had every intention of retaining their full, often unchecked, powers, even as they corresponded with leading philosophes, announced support for their causes, and entertained them at their courts. Moreover, would-be reformers often found themselves thwarted by the resistance of nobles, by the priorities rulers gave to waging wars, or by popular resistance to deregulation of trade that stripped away protection against the uncertainties of the market. Yet even the failure of reform contributed to the ferment in Europe after 1770. Peasant rebellions in eastern Europe, the "Wilkes and Liberty" campaign in Great Britain, the struggle over reform in France, and the revolution in America all occurred at about the same time, and their conjunction convinced many Europeans that the world was in fact changing. Just how much it had changed, and whether the change was for better or for worse, would become more evident in the next decades.

CHAPTER REVIEW QUESTIONS

1. Why would rulers feel ambivalent about the Enlightenment, supporting reform on the one hand, while clamping down on political dissent on the other?

2. Which major developments in the second half of the eighteenth century ran counter to the influence of the Enlightenment?

For practice quizzes and other study tools, see the Online Study Guide at bedfordstmartins.com/huntconcise.

For primary-source material from this period, see Chapter 18 of *Sources of THE MAKING OF THE WEST*, Third Edition.

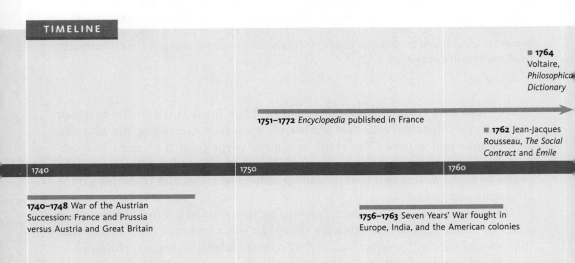

TIMELINE

■ **1764** Voltaire, *Philosophical Dictionary*

1751–1772 *Encyclopedia* published in France

■ **1762** Jean-Jacques Rousseau, *The Social Contract* and *Émile*

1740   1750   1760

1740–1748 War of the Austrian Succession: France and Prussia versus Austria and Great Britain

1756–1763 Seven Years' War fought in Europe, India, and the American colonies

Suggested References

The interpretive study by Gay remains useful, but the Kors volumes offer the most up-to-date views on the Enlightenment. As the autobiography of Equiano (Allison) shows, the influence of new ideas spread far and wide.

*Allison, Robert J., ed. *The Interesting Narrative of the Life of Olaudah Equiano.* 2006.

Beales, Derek. *Enlightenment and Reform in Eighteenth-Century Europe.* 2005.

Cash, Arthur H. *John Wilkes: The Scandalous Father of Civil Liberty.* 2006.

Catherine the Great: http://russia.nypl.org/level4.html

Gay, Peter. *The Enlightenment: An Interpretation.* 2 vols. 1966, 1969.

Hull, Isabel V. *Sexuality, State, and Civil Society in Germany, 1700–1815.* 1996.

Kors, Alan Charles, ed. *Encyclopedia of the Enlightenment.* 4 vols. 2003.

Lessing, Gotthold Ephraim. *Nathan the Wise.* Ed. Ronald Schechter. 2004.

McMahon, Darrin M. *Enemies of the Enlightenment: The French Counter-Enlightenment and the Making of Modernity.* 2001.

Mozart Project: http://www.mozartproject.org

*Rakove, Jack N. *Declaring Rights: A Brief History with Documents.* 1998.

Seven Years' War: http://www.historyworld.net/wrldhis/PlainTextHistories.asp?historyid=aa66

Thompson, E. P. *Whigs and Hunters: The Origin of the Black Act.* 1975.

Venturi, Franco. *The End of the Old Regime in Europe, 1768–1776: The First Crisis.* Trans. R. Burr Litchfield. 1989.

*Voltaire. *Candide.* Ed. and trans. Daniel Gordon. 1999.

Voltaire Foundation: http://www.voltaire.ox.ac.uk

■ **1787** Delegates from the states draft a new U.S. Constitution

■ **1776** American Declaration of Independence from Great Britain; Adam Smith, *The Wealth of Nations*

■ **1785** Catherine the Great's Charter of the Nobility grants nobles exclusive control over their serfs in exchange for subservience to the state

■ **1775** Flour War in France

1770	1780	1790

■ **1770** Louis XV of France fails to break the power of the French law courts

■ **1772** First partition of Poland

■ **1773** Pugachev rebellion of Russian peasants

■ **1780** Joseph II of Austria assumes sole power and undertakes wide-reaching reform; Gordon (anti-Catholic) riots in London

■ **1781** Immanuel Kant, *The Critique of Pure Reason;* Leipzig opens first public orchestra hall

The French Revolution and Napoleon

1789–1815

ON OCTOBER 5, 1789, a crowd of several thousand women marched in a drenching rain twelve miles from the center of Paris to Versailles. They demanded the king's help in securing more grain for the hungry and his reassurance that he did not intend to resist the emerging revolutionary movement. Joined by thousands of men who came from Paris to reinforce them, they broke into the royal family's private apartments the next morning. To prevent further bloodshed—two of the royal bodyguards had already been killed and their heads paraded on pikes—the king agreed to move his family and his government back to Paris. A dramatic procession guarded by thousands of ordinary men and women made its slow way back to the city. The people's proud display of cannons and pikes underlined the fundamental transformation that was occurring. The women's march to Versailles had forced the king of France to respond to their grievances. The French monarchy was in danger, and if such a powerful and long-lasting institution could come under fire, could any monarch of Europe rest easy?

Women's March to Versailles
Thousands of prints broadcast the events of the French Revolution to the public in France and elsewhere. They varied from fine art engravings signed by the artists to anonymous simple woodblock prints. This colored etching shows a crowd of armed women marching to Versailles on October 5, 1789, to confront the king. The sight of armed women frightened many observers and demonstrated that the Revolution was not only a men's affair.
(The Granger Collection, NY.)

The French Revolution first grabbed the attention of the entire world because it seemed to promise universal human rights, constitutional government, and broad-based political participation. In the words of its most famous slogan, it pledged "Liberty, Equality, and Fraternity" for all. The revolutionaries did not stop with the establishment of constitutional monarchy, however: they abolished nobility, executed the king and queen, established a republic for the first time in French history, and gave the vote to almost all adult men. At the same time, the Revolution inaugurated a new cycle of violence and intimidation. When the revolutionaries encountered resistance to their programs, they set up a government of terror to compel

599

obedience. Some historians therefore see in the French Revolution the origins of modern totalitarianism—that is, governments that try to control every aspect of life, including daily activities, while limiting all forms of political dissent.

The Revolution might have remained a strictly French affair if war had not involved the rest of Europe. After 1792, huge French republican armies, fueled by patriotic nationalism, marched across Europe. These campaigns promised Europeans liberation from traditional monarchies, but in the end they delivered old-fashioned conquest and annexation benefiting France. Nevertheless, French victories spread revolutionary ideas far and wide, from the colonies in the Caribbean, where the first successful slave revolt established the republic of Haiti, to Poland and Egypt.

The army's success ultimately undermined the republic and made possible the rise of Napoleon Bonaparte, a remarkable young general from the French-controlled island of Corsica, who brought France more wars, more conquests, and a form of military dictatorship. By 1812, Emperor Napoleon I ruled over an empire greater than any Europe had seen since Roman times. Eventually, resistance to the French armies and the ever-mounting costs of military glory toppled him, but not before he had established himself as an almost mythic figure. The French Revolution produced many surprises; Napoleon Bonaparte was the most astonishing of them.

CHAPTER FOCUS QUESTION Did Napoleon represent the continuation or end of the French Revolution?

The Revolution of Rights and Reason

France was not the only country experiencing upheaval. Between 1787 and 1789, revolts in the name of liberty also broke out in the Dutch Republic, the Austrian Netherlands (present-day Belgium and Luxembourg), and Poland. At the same time, the newly independent United States of America prepared a new federal constitution. Historians have sometimes referred to these revolts as the "Atlantic revolutions" because so many protest movements arose in countries on both sides of the North Atlantic in the late 1700s. Internal divisions and external interference doomed the Dutch, Belgian, and Polish revolts: the Prussians invaded the Dutch Republic and restored the stadholder, the Austrian emperor Leopold II reinstated Austrian authority in Belgium, and Catherine the Great engineered the failure of the new Polish constitution of 1791. Not only was France the richest, most powerful, and most populous state in western Europe, but its revolution lasted longer, brought about more startling changes, and caused more violence. It shaped European politics for generations afterward.

Origins of the French Revolution, 1787–1789

On the surface the French monarchy in the late 1780s seemed as strong as ever. After suffering humiliation at the hands of the British in the Seven Years' War (1756–1763), the French had regained international prestige by supporting the victorious

Americans. Success came at a high price, however. About half of the French national budget went to paying interest on the debt that had accumulated over the years of involvement in the American War of Independence. In contrast to Great Britain, which had a national bank to help raise loans for the government, the French government lived off relatively short-term, high-interest loans from private sources, including Swiss banks, government annuities, and advances from tax collectors. For years the French government had been trying unsuccessfully to modernize the tax system to make it more equitable. The peasants bore the greatest burden of taxes and resented the exemptions enjoyed by the nobles and clergy. Private contractors collected many taxes and pocketed a large share of the proceeds. With the growing support of public opinion, the bond and annuity holders from the middle and upper classes now demanded a clearer system of fiscal accountability.

Faced with budget shortfalls and growing criticism of Queen Marie-Antoinette's personal spending, Louis XVI (r. 1774–1792) tried every available avenue to raise funds. In 1787, he submitted proposals for reform to the Assembly of Notables, a group of handpicked nobles, clergymen, and officials. When this group refused to cooperate, the king presented his plan for a more uniform land tax to his old rival, the parlement of Paris. When it too refused, he ordered the parlement judges into exile in the provinces. Overnight, the judges (members of the nobility because of the offices they held) became popular heroes for resisting the king's "tyranny"; in reality, however, the judges, like the notables, wanted reform only on their own terms. Louis finally gave in to demands that he call a meeting of the **Estates General**, which had last met 175 years before.

The calling of the Estates General electrified public opinion. Who would determine the fate of the nation? There were three estates, or orders, in the Estates General. The deputies in the First Estate represented some 100,000 clergy of the Catholic church, which owned about 10 percent of the land and collected its own taxes (the tithe) on peasants. The deputies of the Second Estate represented the nobility, about 400,000 men and women who owned about 25 percent of the land and collected seigneurial dues and rents from their peasant tenants. The deputies of the Third Estate represented everyone else, at least 95 percent of the nation. In 1614, at the last meeting of the Estates General, each order had voted separately, and either the clergy or the nobility could therefore veto any decision of the Third Estate. Before the elections to the Estates General in 1789, the king agreed to double the number of deputies for the Third Estate (making them equal in number to the other two combined), but he left it to the Estates General to decide whether the estates would continue to vote separately by order rather than by individual head. Voting by order would conserve the traditional powers of the clergy and nobility; voting by head would give the Third Estate an advantage because many clergymen and even some nobles sympathized with the Third Estate.

In this excited political climate, the state's censorship apparatus broke down. Pamphleteers by the hundreds denounced the traditional privileges of the nobility and clergy and called for voting by head rather than by order. In the winter and

REVEIL DU TIERS ETAT.

Ma feinte, il étoit tems que je me réveillasse, car l'opression de mes fers me donnoient le cauchemar un peu trop fort.

The Third Estate Awakens

This print, produced after the fall of the Bastille (notice the two heads raised on pikes outside the prison), shows a clergyman (First Estate) and a nobleman (Second Estate) alarmed by the awakening of the commoner (Third Estate). The Third Estate breaks the chains of oppression and arms itself to battle for its rights. In what ways does this print draw attention to the social conflicts that lay behind the political struggles in the Estates General? **For more help analyzing this image, see the visual activity for this chapter in the Online Study Guide at** bedfordstmartins.com/huntconcise. (Réunion des Musées Nationaux/Art Resource, NY.)

spring of 1789, thousands of men (and a few women by proxy) held meetings to elect deputies and write down their grievances. The effect was immediate. Although educated men dominated the meetings at the regional level, the humblest peasants also voted in their villages and burst forth with complaints, especially about taxes. As one villager lamented, "The last crust of bread has been taken from us." The grievance lists demanded fairer distribution of taxes, constitutional recognition of rights, revision of the law codes, and a variety of other reforms. The meetings and the compiling of grievances raised expectations that the Estates General would help the king to solve all the nation's ills.

These new hopes soared just at the moment France experienced a dangerous food shortage. Bad weather damaged the harvest of 1788, causing bread prices to rise in many places in the spring and summer of 1789 and threatening starvation for the poorest people. A serious slump in textile production had been causing massive unemployment since 1786. Hundreds of thousands of textile workers were out of work and hungry, adding another volatile element to an already tense situation.

When some twelve hundred deputies journeyed to the king's palace of Versailles for the opening of the Estates General in May 1789, many readers avidly followed the developments in newspapers that sprouted up overnight. Although most nobles insisted on voting by order, the deputies of the Third Estate refused to proceed on that basis. After six weeks of stalemate, on June 17, 1789, the deputies of the Third Estate took unilateral action and declared themselves and whoever would join them the National Assembly, in which each deputy would vote as an individual. Two days later, the clergy voted by a narrow margin to join them. Barred from their meeting hall on June 20, the deputies met on a nearby tennis court and swore an oath not to disband until they had given France a constitution that reflected their newly declared authority. This "tennis court oath" expressed the determination of the Third Estate to carry through a constitutional revolution.

At first Louis appeared to agree to the new representative assembly, but he also ordered thousands of soldiers to march to Paris. The deputies who supported the new National Assembly feared a plot by the king and high-ranking nobles to arrest them and disperse the Assembly. "Everyone is convinced that the approach of the troops covers some violent design," one deputy wrote home. Their fears were confirmed when on July 11 the king fired Jacques Necker, his finance minister and the one high-ranking official regarded as sympathetic to the deputies' cause.

The furious reaction in Paris to Necker's dismissal and the threat of military force changed the course of the French Revolution. When the news spread, the common people in Paris began to arm themselves and attack places where either grain or arms were thought to be stored (Map 16.1). A deputy in Versailles reported home: "Today all of the evils overwhelm France, and we are between despotism, carnage, and famine." On July 14, 1789, an armed crowd marched on the Bastille, the fortified prison that symbolized royal authority. After a chaotic battle in which one hundred armed citizens died, the prison officials surrendered. The angry crowd shot and stabbed the governor of the prison and flaunted his head on a pike.

The fall of the Bastille (an event now commemorated as a French national holiday) set an important precedent. The common people showed themselves willing to intervene violently at a crucial political moment. All over France, food riots turned into local revolts. Local governments were forced out of power and replaced by committees of "patriots" loyal to the revolutionary cause. The patriots relied on newly formed National Guard units composed of civilians. One of their first duties was to calm the peasants in the countryside, who feared that the beggars and vagrants crowding the roads might be part of an aristocratic plot to starve the people by burning crops or barns. In some places, the **Great Fear** (the term used by historians to describe this rural panic) turned into peasant attacks on aristocrats or on seigneurial records of peasants' dues kept in the lord's château. The king's

Map 16.1 Revolutionary Paris, 1789

The French Revolution began with the fall of the Bastille on July 14, 1789. The huge fortified prison was located in a working-class neighborhood on the eastern side of the city. Before attacking the Bastille, crowds had torn down many of the customs booths located in the wall of the Farmers General (the private company in charge of tax collection) and had taken the weapons stored in the Hôtel des Invalides, a veterans' hospital on the western side of the city where the upper classes lived. During the Revolution, executions took place on the Place de la Révolution, now called the Place de la Concorde.

government began to crumble. One of Louis XVI's brothers and many other leading aristocrats fled into exile. In Paris, the Marquis de Lafayette, a hero of the American War of Independence and a noble deputy in the National Assembly, became commander of the new National Guard. The Revolution thus had its first heroes, its first victims, and its first enemies.

From Monarchy to Republic

Until July 1789, the French Revolution followed a course much like that of the protest movements in the Low Countries. Unlike the Dutch and Belgian uprisings, however, the French Revolution did not come to a quick end. The French revolutionaries first tried to establish a constitutional monarchy based on the Enlightenment principles of human rights and rational government. This effort failed when the king attempted to raise a counterrevolutionary army. When war broke out in 1792, new tensions culminated in a second revolution on August 10, 1792,

Fall of the Bastille
The Bastille prison is shown here in all its imposing grandeur. The moment depicted is that of the surrender of the fortress's governor, Bernard René de Launay. Because so many of the besieging citizens
had been killed (only one of the defenders died), popular anger ran high, and de Launay was to be
the sacrificial victim. As the hastily formed citizens' guard marched him off to city hall, huge crowds
taunted and spat at him. When he lashed out at one of the men nearest him, he was stabbed, shot,
and then beheaded. The head was displayed as a trophy on a pike held high above the crowd. Royal
authority had been successfully challenged and even humiliated. (The Granger Collection, NY.)

that deposed the king and established a republic in which all power rested in an
elected legislature.

Before drafting a new constitution, the deputies of the National Assembly had
to confront growing violence in the countryside, as the Great Fear sparked peasant
attacks on their lords' castles and records. In response to peasant unrest, on the
night of August 4, 1789, noble deputies announced their willingness to give up their
tax exemptions and seigneurial dues. By the end of the night, amid wild enthusiasm,
dozens of deputies had come to the podium to relinquish the tax exemptions of
their own professional groups, towns, or provinces. The National Assembly decreed
the abolition of what it called "the feudal regime"—that is, it freed the few remaining serfs and eliminated all special privileges in matters of taxation, including all
seigneurial dues on the land (a few days later, the deputies insisted on financial
compensation for some of these dues, but most peasants refused to pay). The peasants had achieved their goals. The Assembly also mandated equality of opportunity

in access to official posts. Talent, rather than birth, was to be the key to success. Enlightenment principles were beginning to become law.

Three weeks later, the deputies drew up the **Declaration of the Rights of Man and of the Citizen** as a preamble to the constitution. In words reminiscent of the American Declaration of Independence, whose principal author, Thomas Jefferson, was in Paris at the time, it proclaimed, "Men are born and remain free and equal in rights." The Declaration granted freedom of religion, freedom of the press, equality of taxation, and equality before the law. By pronouncing all "men" free and equal, the Declaration immediately created new dilemmas. Did women have equal rights with men? What about free blacks in the colonies? How could slavery be justified if all men were born free? Did religious toleration of Protestants and Jews include equal political rights? Women never received the right to vote during the French Revolution, though Protestant and Jewish men did. Women were theoretically citizens under civil law but without the right to full political participation.

Some women did not accept their exclusion, viewing it as a betrayal of the promised new order. In addition to joining demonstrations, such as the march to Versailles in October 1789 described at the beginning of this chapter, women wrote petitions, published tracts, and organized political clubs to demand more participation. In her Declaration of the Rights of Women of 1791, Olympe de Gouges (1748–1793) played on the language of the official Declaration to make the point that women should also be included. In Article I, she announced, "Woman is born free and lives equal to man in her rights." Unresponsive to such calls for women's equality, the National Assembly gave voting rights only to white men who paid a minimum level of taxation. The constitution defined them as the "active citizens"; all others were "passive."

Despite these limitations, France became a constitutional monarchy, in which the king served simply as the leading state functionary. A one-house legislature was responsible for making laws. The king could hold up the enactment of laws but could not veto them absolutely. The nobles not only lost their tax exemptions, but on June 19, 1790, the Assembly abolished all titles of nobility. The deputies replaced the old administrative divisions of the provinces with a national system of eighty-three regional departments (*départements*) with identical administrative and legal structures. All officials were elected; no offices could be bought and sold. The deputies also abolished the old taxes and replaced them with new ones that were supposed to be uniformly levied. The National Assembly had difficulty collecting taxes, however, because many people had expected a substantial cut in the tax rate. The new administrative system survived, nonetheless, and these departments are still the basic units of the French state today.

When the deputies turned to reforming the Catholic church, they created enduring conflicts. Motivated partly by the ongoing financial crisis, the Assembly confiscated all the church's property and promised to pay clerical salaries in return. The Civil Constitution of the Clergy passed in July 1790 set pay scales for the clergy and provided that the voters elect their own parish priests and bishops just as they elected other officials. Impounded church property served as a guarantee for the new paper money, called assignats, issued by the government. The government began to sell the church lands to the highest bidders in state auctions. The sales increased the landholdings of wealthy city dwellers and prosperous peasants but cut the ground out from under the assignats. Convinced that monastic life encouraged idleness and a decline in the nation's population, the deputies also outlawed any future monastic vows and encouraged monks and nuns to return to private life on state pensions.

Faced with resistance to these changes, the National Assembly in November 1790 required all clergy to swear an oath of loyalty to the Civil Constitution of the Clergy. Pope Pius VI in Rome condemned the constitution, and half of the French clergy refused to take the oath. The oath of allegiance permanently divided the Catholic population, which had to choose between loyalty to the old church and commitment to the Revolution with its "constitutional" church. The revolutionary government passed laws against the clergy who refused to take the oath, forcing some into exile and executing others as traitors. Riots and demonstrations led by women confronted many of the oath-taking priests who showed up to replace those who refused.

Louis XVI deeply resented the new limits on his powers and in particular the changes imposed on the Catholic church. On June 20, 1791, the royal family escaped in disguise from the Tuileries palace in Paris and fled to the eastern border of France, where they hoped to gain support from the Austrian emperor Leopold II (r. 1790–1792), the brother of Marie-Antoinette. The plans went awry when a postmaster recognized the king from his portrait on the new French money, and the royal family was arrested at Varennes, forty miles from the border with the Austrian Netherlands. The National Assembly tried to depict this incident as a kidnapping, but the "flight to Varennes" touched off demonstrations in Paris against the royal family, whom some now regarded as traitors. Cartoons depicting the royal family as animals being returned "to the stable" circulated among the public.

The constitution finally completed in 1791 provided for the immediate election of the new Legislative Assembly. The status of the king might have remained uncertain if war had not intervened, but by early 1792 everyone seemed intent on war with Austria. Louis and Marie-Antoinette hoped that war would lead to the definitive defeat of the Revolution, whereas the deputies in the new Assembly who favored a republic believed that war would reveal the king's treachery and lead to his downfall. On April 20, 1792, Louis declared war on Austria. Prussia immediately entered on the Austrian side. Thousands of French aristocrats, including two-thirds of the army officer corps, had already emigrated, including both the king's brothers, and they were gathering along France's eastern border in expectation of joining Leopold's counterrevolutionary army.

When fighting broke out in 1792, all the powers expected a brief and relatively contained war. Instead, it would continue despite brief interruptions for the next twenty-three years. War had an immediate radicalizing effect on French politics. When the French armies proved woefully unprepared for battle, the authority of the Legislative Assembly came under fire. In June 1792, an angry crowd invaded the hall of the Assembly in Paris and threatened the royal family. When the Prussians crossed the border and advanced on Paris, the Prussian commander, the duke of Brunswick, issued a manifesto announcing that Paris would be destroyed if the royal family suffered any violence.

The ordinary people of Paris did not passively await their fate. Known as **sans-culottes** (without breeches)—because men who worked with their hands wore long trousers rather than the knee breeches of the upper classes—they had followed every twist and turn in revolutionary fortunes. Political clubs had multiplied since the founding in 1789 of the first and most influential of them, the **Jacobin Club**, named after the former monastery in Paris where the club first met. Every local district in Paris had its club, where men and women listened to the news of the day and discussed their opinions. Faced with the threat of military retaliation and frustrated with the inaction of the Legislative Assembly, the sans-culottes organized an insurrection on August 10, 1792, and attacked the Tuileries palace, where the king resided. The Legislative Assembly ordered new elections, this time by universal male suffrage (no wealth qualifications as in the constitution of 1791), for a National Convention that would write a new constitution.

Before the National Convention could meet, violence exploded again in early September 1792 when the Prussians approached Paris. Hastily gathered mobs stormed the overflowing prisons to seek out traitors who might help the enemy. In an atmosphere of near hysteria, eleven hundred inmates were killed, including many innocent people. The princess of Lamballe, one of the queen's favorites, was hacked to pieces, and her mutilated body was displayed beneath the windows where the royal family was kept under guard. These "September massacres" showed the dark side of popular revolution, in which the common people demanded instant revenge on supposed enemies and conspirators.

The Execution of Louis XVI

When it met, the National Convention abolished the monarchy and, on September 22, 1792, established the first republic in French history. The republic would answer only to the people, not to any royal authority. The new government faced a dire situation. It was supposed to write a new constitution for the republic while fighting a war with external enemies and confronting increasing resistance at home. The Revolution had divided the population: for some, it had not gone far enough toward providing food, land, and retribution against enemies; for others, it had gone too far by dismantling the church and the monarchy. The French people had never known any government other than monarchy. Only half the population could read and write at even a basic level. In this situation, symbolic actions became very important. Any public sign of monarchy was at risk, and revolutionaries soon pulled down statues of kings and burned reminders of the former regime.

The fate of Louis XVI and the future direction of the republic divided the deputies elected to the National Convention. Most of the deputies were middle-class lawyers and professionals who had developed their ardent republican beliefs in the national network of Jacobin Clubs. After the fall of the monarchy in August 1792, however, the Jacobins divided into two factions: the Girondins and the Montagnards. The Girondins (named after a department in southwestern France, the Gironde, which provided some of its leading orators) resented the growing power of Parisian militants and tried to appeal to the departments outside Paris. The Montagnards (French for "men of the mountain," so called because they sat in the highest seats) were closely allied with the Paris militants and willing to enact the extreme measures urged on them by the sans-culottes.

The first showdown between the Girondins and the Montagnards occurred during the trial of the king in December 1792. Although the Girondins agreed that the king was guilty of treason, many of them argued for clemency, exile, or a popular referendum on his fate. After a long and bitter debate, the deputies voted by a very narrow majority to execute the king. Louis XVI went to the guillotine on January 21, 1793, sharing the fate of Charles I of England in 1649. "We have just convinced ourselves that a king is only a man," wrote one newspaper, "and that no man is above the law." The Girondins lasted only a few months longer. On June 2, 1793, twenty-nine Girondin deputies were arrested after militants in Paris organized an armed demonstration against them and invaded the National Convention. Dissent, even among republicans, could now prove fatal.

The Execution of King Louis XVI
Louis XVI was executed by order of the National Convention on January 21, 1793. In this print, the executioner shows the severed head to the National Guard arranged in orderly silence around the scaffold. (Mary Evans Picture Library.)

European elites reacted with horror to the execution of Louis XVI. The British government suppressed the many corresponding societies made up of democrats and reformers who had established links with the Paris Jacobins and charged some of their leaders with sedition. Ireland posed even greater problems to the British government because Catholics and Presbyterians, both excluded from the vote, joined together in the Society of United Irishmen in 1791. In the United States, opinion fiercely divided on the virtues of the French Revolution. In Sweden, when Gustavus III (r. 1771–1792) was assassinated by a nobleman, the king's son and heir, Gustavus IV (r. 1792–1809), believed that the French Jacobins had sanctioned the killing. Spain's royal government suppressed all news from France, fearing that it might ignite the spirit of revolt. This fear was not misplaced; even in Russia, for instance, 278 outbreaks of peasant unrest occurred between 1796 and 1798. One Russian landlord complained, "This is the self-same . . . spirit of insubordination and independence, which has spread through all Europe."

REVIEW Why did the French Revolution not stop with the installation of a constitutional monarchy?

The British Reaction to the French Revolution
In this caricature, James Gillray satirizes the French version of liberty. Gillray produced thousands of political caricatures. How would you interpret the message of this print? (© Copyright The Trustees of The British Museum.)

Terror and Resistance

The execution of the king and the arrest of the Girondins did not end the new regime's problems. The continuing war required ever more men and money, and the introduction of a national draft provoked massive resistance in some parts of France. The new republic's armies fought not only in Europe and within France but also in the Caribbean, where a major slave uprising threatened French control. In response to growing pressures, the National Convention set up a highly centralized government designed to provide food, direct the war effort, and punish counterrevolutionaries. Thus began the **Terror**, in which the guillotine became the most terrifying instrument of a government that suppressed almost every form of dissent. The leader of this government, Maximilien Robespierre (1758–1794), aimed to create a "Republic of Virtue," in which the government would teach, or force, citizens to become virtuous republicans through a massive program of political reeducation. These policies only increased divisions, which ultimately led to Robespierre's fall from power and to a dismantling of government by terror.

The Guillotine
Before 1789, only nobles were decapitated if condemned to death; commoners were usually hanged. J. I. Guillotin, a professor of anatomy and a deputy for the Third Estate in the National Assembly, first proposed equalization of the death penalty. He also suggested that a mechanical device be constructed for decapitation, leading to the instrument's association with his name. The Assembly decreed decapitation as the death penalty in June 1791. Another physician, A. Louis, actually invented the guillotine. Its use began in April 1792 and did not end until 1981, when the French government abolished the death penalty. Although it was invented to make death equal and painless, the guillotine disturbed many observers; its mechanical operation and efficiency—the executioner merely pulled up the blade by a cord and then released it—seemed somehow inhumane. Nonetheless, the guillotine fascinated as much as it repelled. Reproduced in miniature, painted on snuffboxes and china, worn as jewelry, and even serving as a toy, the guillotine became part of popular culture, celebrated as the people's avenger by supporters of the Revolution and vilified as the preeminent symbol of the Terror by opponents. (Réunion des Musées Nationaux/Art Resource, NY.)

Robespierre, War, and Slavery

Setting the course for government and the war increasingly fell to the twelve-member Committee of Public Safety, set up by the Convention on April 6, 1793. When Robespierre, one of the Montagnards, was elected to the committee three months later, he became in effect its guiding spirit and the chief spokesman of the Revolution. A lawyer from northern France known as "the incorruptible" for his stern honesty and fierce dedication to democratic ideals, Robespierre remains one of the most controversial figures in world history because of his association with the Terror. In September 1793, another demonstration organized by Parisian militants demanded that the Convention "put Terror on the agenda." Although he originally opposed the death penalty and the war (he also opposed slavery), Robespierre took the lead in implementing emergency measures, including death for those, such as the Girondins, who opposed the committee's policies. At the same time, he maneuvered to clamp down on popular demonstrations.

Like many other educated eighteenth-century men, Robespierre read the classics of republicanism, from the ancient Roman writers Tacitus and Plutarch to the Enlightenment thinkers Montesquieu and Rousseau. But he took them a step further. He spoke eloquently about "the theory of revolutionary government" as "the war of liberty against its enemies." He defended the people's right to democratic government, while in practice he supported many measures that restricted their liberties. He personally favored a free-market economy, as did almost all middle-class deputies, but in this time of crisis he was willing to enact price controls and requisitioning. The Convention had organized paramilitary bands called "revolutionary armies" to hunt down hoarders and political suspects, and on September 29, 1793, it established the General Maximum on wages and the prices of thirty-nine essential commodities. In a speech to the Convention, Robespierre explained the necessity of a government by terror: "The first maxim of your policies must be to lead the people by reason and the people's enemies by terror. . . . Without virtue, terror is deadly; without terror, virtue is impotent." *Terror* was not an idle term; it seemed to imply that the goal of democracy justified what we now call totalitarian means—that is, the suppression of all dissent.

The Committee of Public Safety did everything possible to ensure its control. It sent deputies out "on mission" to purge unreliable officials and organize the war effort. In the first universal draft of men in history, every unmarried man and childless widower between the ages of eighteen and twenty-five was declared eligible for conscription. Revolutionary tribunals set up in Paris and provincial centers tried political suspects. In October 1793, the Revolutionary Tribunal in Paris convicted Marie-Antoinette of treason and sent her to the guillotine. The Girondin leaders were also guillotined, as was Olympe de Gouges. The government confiscated all the property of convicted traitors.

The government won its greatest success on the battlefield. As of April 1793, France faced war with Austria, Prussia, Great Britain, Spain, Sardinia, and the Dutch

Republic—all fearful of the impact of revolutionary ideals on their own populations. To face this daunting coalition of forces, the French republic tapped a new and potent source of power—nationalist pride—in decrees mobilizing young and old alike: "The young men will go to battle; married men will forge arms and transport provisions; women will make tents and clothing and serve in hospitals; children will make bandages." Forges were set up in the parks and gardens of Paris to produce thousands of guns, and citizens everywhere helped collect saltpeter, a rock salt used to make gunpowder.

The powers allied against France squandered their best chance for victory in 1793, when the French army verged on chaos because of the emigration of noble officers and the problems of integrating new draftees. At that moment, Prussia, Russia, and Austria were preoccupied once again with Poland. Catherine the Great abolished Poland's constitution of 1791 and joined with Prussia in gobbling up generous new slices of Polish territory in the second partition of 1793 (Map 16.2). When Tadeusz Kościuszko (1746–1817), an officer who had been a foreign volunteer in the War of American Independence, tried to lead a nationalist uprising, Catherine's army struck again. This time, Russia, Prussia, and Austria wiped Poland completely off the map in the third partition of 1795. "The Polish question" would plague international relations for more than a century, as Polish rebels flocked to any international upheaval that might undo the partitions.

While Russia, Prussia, and Austria feasted on Poland, France regrouped and by the end of 1793 had amassed through the new national draft a huge fighting force of 700,000 men. The French first stopped the advance of the allied powers and then moved into the territories of its enemies, aiming to carry the gospel of

Map 16.2 The Second and Third Partitions of Poland, 1793 and 1795
In 1793, Prussia took over territory that included 1.1 million Poles, while Russia gained 3 million new inhabitants. Austria gave up any claims to Poland in exchange for help from Russia and Prussia in acquiring Bavaria. In the final division of 1795, Prussia absorbed an additional 900,000 Polish subjects, including those in Warsaw; Austria incorporated 1 million Poles and the city of Cracow; Russia gained another 2 million Poles. The three powers determined never to use the term *Kingdom of Poland* again. How had Poland fallen prey to the other powers?

revolution and republicanism to the rest of Europe. The French army proved less successful in the faraway Caribbean colonies, in part because the armed forces in place were small and in part because the British navy controlled the seas. Twice the size in land area of the neighboring British colonies, the French Caribbean colonies also produced nearly twice as much revenue in exports. The slave population had doubled in the French colonies in the twenty years before 1789. St. Domingue (present-day Haiti) was the most important French colony. Occupying the western half of the island of Hispaniola, it was inhabited in 1789 by approximately 465,000 slaves, 30,000 whites, and 28,000 free people of color, whose primary job was to apprehend runaway slaves and ensure plantation security.

Despite the efforts of a Paris club called the Friends of Blacks, most French revolutionaries did not consider slavery a pressing problem in 1789. As one deputy explained, "This regime [in the colonies] is oppressive, but it gives a livelihood to several million Frenchmen. This regime is barbarous but a still greater barbarity will result if you interfere with it without the necessary knowledge."

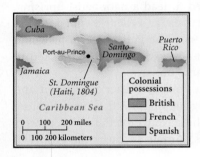

St. Domingue on the Eve of the Revolt, 1791

In August 1791, slaves in northern St. Domingue organized a large-scale revolt. To restore authority over the slaves, the Legislative Assembly in Paris granted civil and political rights to the free people of color. This action infuriated white planters and merchants, and in 1793 they signed an agreement with Great Britain, now France's enemy in war, declaring British sovereignty over St. Domingue. To complicate matters further, Spain, which controlled the rest of the island and had entered on Great Britain's side in the war with France, offered freedom to individual slave rebels who joined the Spanish army as long as they agreed to maintain the slave regime for other blacks.

The few thousand French republican troops on St. Domingue were outnumbered, and to prevent complete military disaster, the French commissioner freed all the slaves in his jurisdiction in August 1793 without permission from the government in Paris. In February 1794, the National Convention formally abolished slavery and granted full rights to all black men in France's colonies. These actions had the desired effect. One of the ablest black generals allied with the Spanish, the ex-slave François Dominique Toussaint L'Ouverture (1743–1803), changed sides and committed his troops to the French. The French eventually appointed Toussaint governor of St. Domingue as a reward for his efforts.

The Republic of Virtue, 1793–1794

Even while war raged in Europe and the Caribbean, Robespierre and the Committee of Public Safety encouraged efforts to win hearts and minds to the republic back home. Songs—especially the new national anthem, "La Marseillaise" (named after the soldiers from the city of Marseille who first sang it)—placards, posters, pamphlets, books, engravings, paintings, sculpture, even everyday crockery, chamber pots, and playing cards conveyed republican slogans and symbols. Foremost among them was the figure of Liberty (an early version of the Statue of Liberty now in New York harbor), which appeared on coins and bills, on letterheads and seals, in engravings and paintings, and as statues in festivals. Hundreds of new plays were produced, and old classics were revised. To encourage the production of patriotic and republican works, the government sponsored state competitions for artists to "awaken the public spirit and make clear how atrocious and ridiculous were the enemies of liberty and of the Republic."

At the center of this elaborate cultural campaign were revolutionary festivals that first emerged in 1789 with the spontaneous planting of liberty trees in villages and towns. The Festival of Federation on July 14, 1790, marked the first anniversary of the fall of the Bastille. Under the Convention, the well-known

Representing Liberty
Liberty was always represented by a female figure because in French the noun is gendered feminine (*la liberté*). This painting, *La Liberté,* by a woman, Jeanne-Louise (Nanine) Vallain, from 1793–1794, captures the usual attributes of liberty: she is soberly seated, wearing a Roman-style toga and holding a pike with a Roman liberty cap on top. Her Roman appearance signals that she is not a contemporary Frenchwoman but rather the representation of an abstract quality. The fact that she holds an instrument of battle suggests that women might have been active participants. The Statue of Liberty in New York harbor, given to the United States by the French, is a late-nineteenth-century version of the same figure, but without any suggestion of battle. (Musée de la Révolution Française, Vizille. On loan from the Musée du Louvre. Inv. MRFD1986-4. Oil on cloth.)

painter Jacques-Louis David (1748–1825), who was a deputy and an associate of Robespierre, took over festival planning. David aimed to destroy the mystique of monarchy and to make the republic sacred. His Festival of Unity on August 10, 1793, for example, celebrated the first anniversary of the overthrow of the monarchy. In front of the statue of Liberty built for the occasion, a bonfire consumed the crowns and scepters of royalty, while a cloud of three thousand white doves rose into the sky.

Some hoped the festival system would replace the Catholic church altogether. They initiated a campaign of **de-Christianization** that included closing churches (Protestant as well as Catholic), selling many church buildings to the highest bidder, and trying to force even those clergy who had taken the oath of loyalty to abandon their clerical vocations and marry. Great churches became storehouses for arms or grain, or their stones were sold off to contractors. The medieval statues of kings on the facade of Notre Dame cathedral were beheaded. Church bells were dismantled and church treasures melted down for government use. In the ultimate step in de-Christianization, extremists tried to establish a cult of reason to supplant Christianity. The Committee of Public Safety halted the de-Christianization campaign because the deputies feared it would turn rural, devout populations against the republic.

In principle, the best way to ensure the future of the republic was through the education of the young. The Convention voted to make primary schooling free and compulsory for both boys and girls. It took control of education away from the Catholic church and tried to set up a system of state schools at the primary and secondary levels, but it lacked trained teachers to replace those the Catholic religious orders provided. As a result, opportunities for learning how to read and write may have diminished. In 1799, only one-fifth as many boys enrolled in the state secondary schools as had studied in church schools ten years earlier.

Although many of the ambitious republican programs failed, almost all aspects of daily life became politicized, even colors. The tricolor—the combination of red, white, and blue that was to become the flag of France—was devised in July 1789, and by 1793 everyone had to wear a cockade (a badge made of ribbons) with the colors. Using formal forms of speech—*vous* for "you" or the title *monsieur* or *madame*—might identify someone as an aristocrat; true patriots used the informal *tu* and *citoyen* or *citoyenne* (citizen) instead. Some people changed their names or gave their children new names. Biblical and saints' names, such as Jean, Pierre, Joseph, or Marie, gave way to names recalling heroes of the ancient Roman republic (Brutus, Gracchus, Cornelia), revolutionary heroes, or flowers and plants. Such changes symbolized adherence to the republic and to Enlightenment ideals rather than to Catholicism.

Even the measures of time and space were revolutionized. In October 1793, the Convention introduced a new calendar to replace the Christian one. Year I dated from the beginning of the republic on September 22, 1792. Twelve months of exactly thirty days each received new names derived from nature—for example,

Pluviôse (roughly equivalent to February) recalled the rain (*la pluie*) of late winter. Instead of seven-day weeks, ten-day *décades* provided only one day of rest every ten days and pointedly eliminated the Sunday of the Christian calendar. The five days left at the end of the calendar year were devoted to special festivals called *sans-culottides.* The calendar remained in force for twelve years despite continuing resistance to it. More enduring was the new metric system based on units of ten that was invented to replace the hundreds of local variations in weights and measures. Other countries in Europe and throughout the world eventually adopted the metric system.

Successive revolutionary legislatures also changed the rules of family life. The state took responsibility for all family matters away from the Catholic church. Birth, death, and marriage registration now happened at city hall, not the parish church. Marriage became a civil contract and as such could be broken. The new divorce law of September 1792 was the most far-reaching in Europe: a couple could divorce by mutual consent or for reasons such as insanity, abandonment, battering, or criminal conviction. Thousands of men and women took advantage of the law to dissolve unhappy marriages, even though the pope had condemned the measure. (In 1816, the government revoked the right to divorce.) In one of its most influential actions, the National Convention passed a series of laws that created equal inheritance among all children in a family, including girls. A father's right to favor one child, especially the oldest male, was considered aristocratic and hence antirepublican.

Resisting the Revolution

By intruding into religion, culture, and daily life, the republic inevitably provoked resistance. Shouting curses against the republic, uprooting liberty trees, carrying statues of the Virgin Mary in a procession, hiding a priest who would not take the loyalty oath, singing a royalist song—all these actions expressed discontent with the new symbols, rituals, and policies. Many women, in particular, suffered from the hard conditions of life that persisted in this time of war, and they had their own ways of dissenting. Long breadlines in the cities exhausted the patience of women, and police spies reported their constant grumbling, which occasionally turned into spontaneous demonstrations or riots over high prices or food shortages. Other forms of resistance were more individual. One young woman, Charlotte Corday, assassinated the outspoken deputy Jean-Paul Marat in July 1793. Corday fervently supported the Girondins, and she considered it her patriotic duty to kill the Montagnard deputy who, in the columns of his paper *The Friend of the People,* had constantly demanded more heads and more blood.

Organized resistance broke out in many parts of France. The arrest of the Girondin deputies in June 1793 sparked in several departments insurrections that if coordinated might have threatened the central government in Paris. But the army promptly dispatched the rebels. After the government retook the city of Lyon, one of the centers of the revolt, the deputy "on mission" there ordered sixteen hundred houses demolished. Special courts sentenced almost two thousand people to death. The name of the city was changed to Ville Affranchie (Liberated Town).

In the Vendée region of western France, resistance turned into full-scale civil war. Between March and December 1793, peasants, artisans, and weavers joined under noble leadership to form the Catholic and Royal Army. One rebel group explained its motives: "They [the republicans] have killed our king, chased away our priests, sold the goods of our church, eaten everything we have and now they want to take our bodies [in the draft]." The uprising took two different forms: in the Vendée itself, a counterrevolutionary army organized to fight the republic; in nearby Brittany, resistance took the form of guerrilla bands, which united to attack a target and then quickly melted into the countryside. Great Britain provided money and underground contacts for these attacks.

For several months in 1793, the Vendée rebels stormed the largest towns in the region. Both sides committed atrocities. At the small town of Machecoul, for example, the rebels massacred more than a hundred republicans, including administrators and National Guard members; many were tied together, shoved into freshly dug graves, and shot. By the fall, however, republican soldiers had turned back the rebels. A republican general wrote to the Committee of Public Safety claiming, "There is no more Vendée, citizens, it has perished under our free sword along with its women and children. . . . Following the orders that you gave me I have crushed children under the feet of horses, massacred women who at least . . . will engender no more brigands." "Infernal columns" of republican troops marched through the region to restore control, military courts ordered thousands executed, and republican soldiers massacred thousands of others. In one especially gruesome incident, the deputy Jean-Baptiste Carrier supervised the drowning of some two thousand Vendée rebels, including a number of priests. Barges loaded with prisoners were floated onto the Loire River near Nantes and then sunk. Controversy still rages about the rebellion's death toll. Estimates of rebel deaths alone range from about 20,000 to 250,000 and higher. Many thousands of republican soldiers and civilians also lost their lives. Even the low estimates reveal the carnage of this catastrophic confrontation between the republic and its opponents.

The Fall of Robespierre and the End of the Terror, 1794–1799

In the atmosphere of fear of conspiracy that these outbreaks fueled, Robespierre tried simultaneously to exert the Convention's control over popular political activities and to weed out opposition among the deputies. The Convention cracked down on popular clubs and societies in the fall of 1793. First to be suppressed were women's political clubs. Founded in early 1793, the Society of Revolutionary Republican Women played a very active part in sans-culottes politics. The society urged harsher measures against the republic's enemies and insisted that women have a voice in politics even if they did not have the vote. The Convention abolished women's political clubs in order to limit agitation in the streets. The deputies called on biological arguments about natural differences between the sexes to bolster their case. As one argued, "Women are ill suited for elevated thoughts and serious meditations."

In the spring of 1794, the Committee of Public Safety moved against its critics in Paris and among deputies in the Convention. Most of those critics were once Montagnards themselves. First, a handful of men labeled "ultrarevolutionaries"—in fact a motley collection of local Parisian politicians—were arrested and executed. Next came the other side, the "indulgents," so called because they favored moderation of the Terror. Included among them was the popular deputy Georges-Jacques Danton (1759–1794), once a member of the Committee of Public Safety and a friend of Robespierre despite the striking contrast in their personalities. Danton was the Revolution's most flamboyant orator and, unlike Robespierre, was a high-living, high-spending, excitable politician. At every turning point in national politics, his booming voice had swayed opinion in the National Convention. Now, under government pressure, the Revolutionary Tribunal convicted him and his friends of treason and sentenced them to death.

With the arrest and execution of these leaders in Paris, the prophecies of doom for the Revolution seemed about to be realized. "The Revolution," as one of the Girondin victims of 1793 had remarked, "was devouring its own children." Even after the major threats to the committee's power had been eliminated, the Terror continued and in some cases worsened. A law passed in June 1794 denied the accused the right of legal counsel, reduced the number of jurors necessary for conviction, and allowed only two judgments: acquittal or death. The category of political crimes expanded to include "slandering patriotism" and "seeking to inspire discouragement." Ordinary people risked the guillotine if they expressed any discontent. The rate of executions in Paris rose from five a day in the spring of 1794 to twenty-six a day in the summer. The political atmosphere darkened even though the military situation improved. At the end of June, French armies decisively defeated the main Austrian army and advanced through the Austrian Netherlands to Brussels and Antwerp. The emergency measures for fighting the war were working, yet Robespierre and his inner circle had made so many enemies that they could not afford to loosen the grip of the Terror.

The Terror hardly touched many parts of France, but overall the experience was undeniably traumatic. Across the country, the official Terror cost the lives of at least 40,000 French people, most of them living in the regions of major insurrections or near the borders with foreign enemies, where suspicion of collaboration ran high. As many as 300,000 people—one out of every fifty French people—went to prison as suspects between March 1793 and August 1794. The toll for the aristocracy and the clergy was especially high. Many leading nobles perished under the guillotine, and thousands emigrated. Thirty thousand to forty thousand clergy who refused to take the oath of allegiance emigrated, at least two thousand (including many nuns) were executed, and thousands were imprisoned. Clergy were singled out in particular in the civil war zones: 135 priests were massacred at Lyon in November 1793, and 83 were shot in one day during the Vendée revolt. Yet many victims of the Terror were peasants or ordinary working people.

The final crisis of the Terror came in July 1794. Conflicts within the Committee of Public Safety and the National Convention left Robespierre isolated. On July 27, 1794 (9 Thermidor, Year II, according to the revolutionary calendar), Robespierre appeared before the Convention with yet another list of deputies to be arrested. Many feared they would be named, and they shouted him down and ordered him arrested along with his followers on the committee, the president of the Revolutionary Tribunal in Paris, and the commander of the Parisian National Guard. An armed uprising led by the Paris city government failed to save Robespierre when most of the National Guard took the side of the Convention. Robespierre tried to kill himself with a pistol but only broke his jaw. The next day, he and scores of followers went to the guillotine.

The men who led the attack on Robespierre in Thermidor (July 1794) did not intend to reverse all his policies, but that happened nonetheless because of a violent backlash known as the **Thermidorian Reaction**. Newspapers attacked the Robespierrists as "tigers thirsting for human blood." The new government released hundreds of suspects and arranged a temporary truce in the Vendée. It purged Jacobins from local bodies and replaced them with their opponents. It arrested some of the most notorious "terrorists" in the National Convention and put them to death. Within the year, the new leaders abolished the Revolutionary Tribunal and closed the Jacobin Club in Paris. Popular demonstrations met severe repression. In southeastern France, in particular, the "White Terror" replaced the Jacobins' "Red Terror." Former officials and local Jacobin leaders were harassed, beaten, and often murdered by paramilitary bands that had tacit support from the new authorities. Those who remained in the National Convention prepared yet another constitution in 1795, setting up a two-house legislature and an executive body—the Directory—headed by five directors.

Between 1795 and 1799, the Directory government maintained itself by alternately purging royalists and Jacobins who did well in the yearly elections of deputies. While politically weak at home, the government continued the Convention's largely successful war effort abroad. In 1794 the reconstituted French army invaded the Austrian Netherlands, which France then annexed. In 1795 the French swarmed into the Dutch Republic, abolished the office of stadholder, and—with the revolutionary penchant for renaming—created the new Batavian Republic, a satellite of France. The Cisalpine Republic (northern Italy), Helvetic Republic (Switzerland), and Roman Republic soon followed. Ironically, however, these triumphs would ultimately bring to power the man who would dismantle the republic itself.

REVIEW   What factors can explain the Terror? To what extent was it simply a response to a national emergency or a reflection of deeper problems with the French Revolution?

The Rise and Fall of Napoleon Bonaparte

The story of the rise of Napoleon Bonaparte (1769–1821) is one of the most remarkable in Western history. It would have seemed astonishing in 1795 that the twenty-six-year-old son of a Corsican noble would within four years become the supreme ruler of France and one of the greatest military leaders in world history. In 1795, he was a penniless artillery officer, only recently released from prison as a presumed Robespierrist. Continuing warfare, the upheavals caused in the rest of Europe by the impact of the French Revolution, and political divisions within the republican leadership gave Bonaparte the opportunity to change the course of history. Yet because his power rested on his military prowess, in the end he could not survive defeat on the battlefield.

Creating an Authoritarian State

The Directory regime never succeeded in establishing a firm center that could appeal to a majority of voters. In Paris bands of young dandies picked fights with known Jacobins and disrupted theater performances with loud antirevolutionary songs. All over France, people banded together and petitioned to reopen churches closed during the Terror. If necessary, they broke into a church to hold services with a priest who had been in hiding or with a lay schoolteacher who was willing to say Mass. Amid increasing political instability, generals like Bonaparte became practically independent, and the troops felt greater loyalty to their units and generals than to the republic. Military victories made the army a parallel and rival force to the state.

Thanks to some early military successes and links to Parisian politicians, Bonaparte was named commander of the French army in Italy in 1796. His astounding success in the Italian campaigns of 1796–1797 launched his meteoric career. With an army of fewer than fifty thousand men, he defeated the Piedmontese and the Austrians. He molded the army into his personal force by paying the soldiers in cash taken as tribute from the newly conquered territories. He mollified the Directory government by sending home wagonloads of Italian masterpieces, which were added to Parisian museum collections (most are still there) after being paraded in victory festivals.

In 1798, the Directory set aside its plans to invade England, gave Bonaparte command of the army raised for that purpose, and sent him across the Mediterranean Sea to Egypt, away from the Parisian centers of power. The French had encouraged the Irish to time a rebellion to coincide with their planned invasion, and when the French went elsewhere, the British mercilessly repressed the revolt. Thirty thousand people were killed. Twice as many regular British troops (seventy thousand) as fought in any of the major continental battles against Napoleon were required to put down the Irish rebellion.

The Directory government hoped that French occupation of Egypt would strike a blow at British trade by cutting the route to India and thus compensate France for its losses there years before. Bonaparte took France's leading scientists with him on the expedition, and his soldiers discovered a slab of black basalt dating

Napoleon as Military Hero

In this painting from 1800–1801, *Napoleon Crossing the Alps at St. Bernard,* Jacques-Louis David reminds the French of Napoleon's heroic military exploits. Napoleon is a picture of calm and composure, while his horse shows the fright and energy of the moment. David painted this propagandistic image shortly after one of his former students went to the guillotine on a trumped-up charge of plotting to assassinate the new French leader. The former organizer of republican festivals during the Terror, David became a kind of court painter for the new regime. (Réunion des Musées Nationaux/Art Resource, NY.)

from 196 B.C.E. written in both hieroglyphic and Greek. Called the Rosetta stone after a nearby town, it enabled scholars to finally decipher the hieroglyphs used by the ancient Egyptians. Once the army disembarked in Egypt, however, the British admiral Horatio Nelson destroyed the French fleet while it was anchored in Aboukir Bay. With his army pinned down after its initial successes, Napoleon slipped out of Egypt and made his way secretly across the Mediterranean to southern France.

In October 1799, Bonaparte arrived in Paris at just the right moment. Resistance to the Directory was growing, and many government leaders wanted to revise the constitution of 1795. Disillusioned members of the government saw in Bonaparte's return an occasion to overturn the constitution. On November 9, 1799 (18 Brumaire, Year VIII, by the revolutionary calendar), the conspirators within the Directory government persuaded the legislature to move out of Paris to avoid an alleged Jacobin plot. But when Bonaparte stomped into the meeting hall the next day and demanded changes in the constitution, he was greeted with cries of "Down with the dictator." His quick-thinking brother Lucien, president of the Council of Five Hundred (the lower house), saved Bonaparte's coup by summoning troops guarding the hall and claiming that the deputies had tried to assassinate the popular general. The soldiers ejected the deputies, and a hastily assembled legislature voted to abolish the Directory and establish a new three-man executive called the consulate.

The deputies of the legislature who engineered the coup d'état of 18 Brumaire picked Bonaparte as one of three provisional consuls because he was a famous general. But under the new constitution of 1799, he was named **First Consul**, a title revived from the ancient Roman republic, with the right to pick the Council of State, which drew up all laws. Millions had abstained from voting on the new constitution, which eliminated direct elections for deputies and granted no independent powers to the three houses of the legislature. Bonaparte and his advisers chose the legislature's members out of a small pool of "notables." Inside France, political apathy had overtaken the original enthusiasm for revolutionary ideals. Bonaparte's coup appeared to be just the latest in a long line of upheavals in revolutionary France. Within the year, however, Bonaparte had set France on a new course toward an authoritarian state.

Bonaparte's most urgent task was to reconcile to his regime Catholics who had been alienated by revolutionary policies. Though nominally Catholic, Napoleon held no deep religious convictions. "How can there be order in the state without religion?" he asked cynically. "When a man is dying of hunger beside another who is stuffing himself, he cannot accept this difference if there is not an authority who tells him: 'God wishes it so.'" In 1801, a concordat with Pope Pius VII (r. 1800–1823) ended a decade of church-state conflict. The pope validated all sales of church lands, and Catholicism was officially recognized as the religion of "the great majority of French citizens." (The state continued to pay the salaries of clergymen, both Catholic and Protestant.) The pope thus brought the huge French Catholic population back into the fold, and Napoleon gained the pope's support for his regime.

Napoleon centralized state power more effectively than kings or revolutionaries had before him. He personally appointed prefects to directly supervise local affairs in every department. He created the Bank of France to facilitate government borrowing and relied on gold and silver coinage rather than paper money. He severely limited political expression, refusing to allow those who opposed him to meet in clubs or influence elections. A decree reduced the number of newspapers in Paris from seventy-three to thirteen (and then finally to four), and the newspapers that remained became government mouthpieces. Government censors had to approve all operas and plays, and they banned "offensive" artistic works even more frequently than their royal predecessors. The minister of police, Joseph Fouché, a leading figure in the Terror, kept political dissidents under constant surveillance. When a bomb attack on Napoleon's carriage failed in 1800, Fouché suppressed evidence of a royalist plot and instead arrested hundreds of former Jacobins. More than one hundred of them were deported and seven hundred imprisoned.

The one place that escaped Napoleon's grasp was St. Domingue. The vicious fighting and flight of whites during the slave revolt had left the island's economy in ruins. In 1800 the plantations produced one-fifth of what they had in 1789. In 1802 Napoleon sent French armies to regain control of St. Domingue and reimpose slavery. They arrested Toussaint and transported him to France, where he died in prison. His arrest prompted the English romantic poet William Wordsworth (1770–1850) to write of him:

> There's not a breathing of the common wind
> That will forget thee; thou hast great allies;
> Thy friends are exultations, agonies,
> And love, and man's unconquerable mind.

Toussaint became a hero to abolitionists everywhere, a potent symbol of black struggles to win freedom. The remaining black generals defeated Napoleon's armies, which had been weakened by yellow fever, and in 1804 proclaimed the Republic of Haiti.

France itself proved more pliable. In 1802, Napoleon set up a referendum to approve him as First Consul for life, and then in 1804, with the pope's blessing, he crowned himself Emperor Napoleon I. Like the kings who preceded him, Napoleon cultivated personal symbolism. His face and name adorned coins, engravings, histories, paintings, and public monuments. His favorite painters embellished his legend by depicting him as a warrior-hero of mythic proportions. Believing that "what is big is always beautiful," Napoleon embarked on ostentatious building projects that would outshine even those of Louis XIV. Government-commissioned architects built the Arc de Triomphe, the Stock Exchange, fountains, and even slaughterhouses. In his imperial court, Napoleon staged his entrances carefully to maximize his personal presence: his wife and courtiers were dressed in regal finery, and he was announced with great pomp—but he usually arrived dressed in a simple military uniform with no medals.

Toussaint L'Ouverture
The leader of the St. Domingue slave uprising appears in his general's uniform, sword in hand. This portrait appeared in one of the earliest histories of the revolt, Marcus Rainsford's *Historical Account of the Black Empire of Hayti* (London, 1805). Toussaint, a former slave who educated himself, fascinated many of his contemporaries in Europe as well as the New World by turning a chaotic slave rebellion into an organized and ultimately successful independence movement. (North Wind Picture Archives.)

Napoleon also worked hard at establishing his reputation as an efficient administrator with broad intellectual interests. He met frequently with scientists, jurists, and artists, and stories abounded of his unflagging energy. To assist him, Napoleon relied on men who had served with him in the army. His chief of staff, Alexandre Berthier, for example, became minister of war, and the chemist Claude Berthollet, who had organized the scientific part of the expedition to Egypt, became vice president of the Senate in 1804. Napoleon's bureaucracy was based on a patron-client relationship, with Napoleon as the ultimate patron. Some of Napoleon's closest associates married into his family.

The New Paternalism

"Authority," declared Napoleon's adviser Abbé Emmanuel-Joseph Sieyès, "must come from above and confidence from below." Napoleon applied this basic military model to all of French society. Combining aristocratic and revolutionary values in a new social hierarchy that rewarded merit and talent, Napoleon used the Senate to dispense his patronage and personally chose as senators the nation's most illustrious generals, ministers, prefects, scientists, rich men, and former nobles. In 1802, he took a step toward creating a new nobility by founding the Legion of Honor, 95 percent of whose members in 1814 were military men. In 1808, Napoleon introduced a complete hierarchy of noble titles, ranging from princes down to barons and chevaliers. Titles could be inherited, but all Napoleonic nobles served the state in one way or

Napoleon's Coronation as Emperor
In *The Coronation of Napoleon and Josephine* (1805–1807), Jacques-Louis David shows Napoleon crowning his wife at the ceremony in 1804. Napoleon orchestrated the entire event and took the only active role in it. Pope Pius VII gave his blessing to the ceremony (he can be seen seated behind Napoleon), but Napoleon crowned himself. What is the significance of Napoleon crowning himself? (Erich Lessing/Art Resource, NY.)

another. To go along with their new titles, Napoleon gave his favorite generals huge fortunes, often in the form of estates in the conquered territories.

Napoleon's own family reaped the greatest benefits. He made his older brother, Joseph, ruler of the newly established kingdom of Naples in 1806; the same year he installed his younger brother Louis as king of Holland. He proclaimed his twenty-three-year-old stepson Eugène de Beauharnais viceroy of Italy in 1805 and established his sister Caroline and brother-in-law General Murat as king and queen of Naples in 1808, when he moved Joseph to the throne of Spain. Napoleon wanted to establish an imperial succession, but he lacked an heir. In thirteen years of marriage, his wife, Josephine, had borne no children, so in 1809 he divorced her and in 1810 married the eighteen-year-old Princess Marie-Louise of Austria. The next year she gave birth to a son, to whom Napoleon immediately gave the title "king of Rome."

Napoleon believed that authority in the family and the workplace had to be reestablished in the same way that he had reasserted the authority of the state. The critical element in his vision of paternalism was the new **Civil Code** of 1804. Napoleon succeeded where previous governments had failed in unifying and standardizing France's local law codes. Called the Napoleonic Code as a way of further exalting his image, it defined and ensured property rights, guaranteed religious liberty, and provided equal legal treatment for all adult males. At the same time, however, the code sharply curtailed women's rights. The law obligated a husband to support his wife, but he alone controlled any property held in common. A wife could not sue in court, sell or mortgage her own property, or contract a debt without her husband's consent. Divorce was still possible, but a wife could petition for divorce only if her husband brought his mistress to live in the family home. In contrast, a wife convicted of adultery could be imprisoned for up to two years. The code's framers saw these discrepancies as a way to reinforce the family and make women responsible for private virtue, while leaving public decisions to men. The French code was imitated in many European and Latin American countries and in the French colony of Louisiana, where it had a similar negative effect on women's rights. Not until 1965 did French wives gain legal status equal to that of their husbands.

The Civil Code also reinforced a father's control over his children, which revolutionary legislation had limited. For example, children under age sixteen who refused to follow their fathers' commands could be sent to prison for up to a month with no hearing of any sort. At the same time, the code required fathers to provide for their children's welfare. Napoleon himself encouraged the foundation of private charities to help indigent mothers, and one of his decrees made it easier for women to abandon their children anonymously to a government foundling hospital. Napoleon hoped such measures would discourage abortion and infanticide, especially among the poorest classes in the fast-growing urban areas. The new paternalism extended to relations between employers and employees. The state required all workers to carry a work card attesting to their good conduct, and it prohibited all workers' organizations.

Napoleon continued the central government's patronage of science and intellectual life but once again put his own distinctive paternalist stamp on these activities. He closely monitored the research institutes established during the Revolution, sometimes intervening personally to achieve political conformity. Napoleon aimed to modernize French society through science, but he could not tolerate criticism. He considered most writers useless or dangerous, "good for nothing under any government." Some of the most talented French writers of the time had to live in exile. The best known of them was Germaine de Staël (1766–1817). When explaining his desire to banish her, Napoleon exclaimed, "She is a machine in motion who stirs up the salons." While exiled in the German states, Madame de Staël wrote a novel, *Corinne* (1807), whose heroine is a brilliant woman thwarted by a patriarchal system, and *On Germany* (1810), an account of the important new literary currents east of the Rhine. Her books were banned in France.

Despite Napoleon's accommodation with the pope, many royalists and Catholics still criticized him as an impious usurper. François-René de Chateaubriand

Germaine de Staël
One of the most fascinating intellectuals of her time, Anne-Louise Germaine de Staël seemed to irritate Napoleon more than any other person did. The daughter of Louis XVI's finance minister, Jacques Necker, and the wife of a Swedish diplomat, Madame de Staël frequently criticized Napoleon's regime. She published best-selling novels and influential literary criticism, and whenever allowed to reside in Paris, she encouraged the intellectual and political dissidents from Napoleon's regime. (Réunion des Musées Nationaux/Art Resource, NY.)

(1768–1848) admired Napoleon as "the strong man who has saved us from the abyss," but he preferred monarchy. In his view, Napoleon had not properly understood the need to defend Christian values against the Enlightenment's excessive reliance on reason. Chateaubriand wrote his *Genius of Christianity* (1802) to draw attention to the power and mystery of faith. He warned, "It is to the vanity of knowledge that we owe almost all our misfortunes. . . . The learned ages have always been followed by ages of destruction."

"Europe Was at My Feet": Napoleon's Military Conquests

Building on innovations introduced by the republican governments before him, Napoleon revolutionized the art of war with tactics and strategies based on a highly mobile army. Napoleon attributed his military success "three-quarters to morale" and the rest to leadership and superiority of numbers at the point of attack. Conscription provided the large numbers: 1.3 million men ages twenty to twenty-four were drafted between 1800 and 1812, another million in 1813–1814. Military service was both a patriotic duty and a means of social mobility. The men who rose through the ranks to become officers were young, ambitious, and accustomed to the new ways of war. Consequently, the French army had higher morale than the armies of other powers, most of which rejected conscription as too democratic and continued to restrict their officer corps to the nobility. Only in 1813–1814 did French morale plummet, as the military tide turned against Napoleon.

When Napoleon came to power in 1799, desertion was rampant, and the generals competed with one another for predominance. Napoleon united all the armies into one Grand Army under his personal command. By 1812, he commanded 700,000 troops. In any given battle, between 70,000 and 180,000 men, not all of them French, fought for France. Napoleon inspired almost fanatical loyalty. A brilliant strategist who carefully studied the demands of war, he outmaneuvered nearly all his opponents. He gathered the largest possible army for one great and decisive battle and then followed with a relentless pursuit to break enemy morale altogether. He fought alongside his soldiers in some sixty battles and had nineteen horses shot out from under him. One opponent said that Napoleon's presence alone was worth 50,000 men.

One of Napoleon's greatest advantages was the lack of coordination among his enemies. Britain dominated the seas but did not want to field huge land armies. The French republic had already established satellite regimes in the Netherlands and Italy, which served as a buffer against the big powers to the east—Austria, Prussia, and Russia. By maneuvering diplomatically and militarily, Napoleon could usually take these on one by one. After reorganizing the French armies in 1799, for example, Napoleon won striking victories against the Austrians at Marengo and Hohenlinden in 1800, forcing them to agree to peace terms. Once the Austrians had withdrawn, Britain agreed to the Treaty of Amiens in 1802, effectively ending hostilities in Europe for a time. Napoleon considered the peace with Great Britain merely a truce, however, and it lasted only until 1803. When the attempt to retake St. Domingue failed, Napoleon abandoned his plans to extend his empire to the Western Hemisphere and sold the Louisiana Territory to the United States in 1803.

France's Retreat from America

When war resumed in Europe, the British navy once more proved its superiority by defeating the French and their Spanish allies in a huge naval battle at Trafalgar off the Spanish coast in 1805. France lost many ships; the British lost no vessels, but their renowned admiral Lord Horatio Nelson died in the battle. On land, however, Napoleon remained invincible. In 1805, Austria took up arms again when Napoleon demanded that it declare neutrality in the conflict with Britain. Napoleon promptly captured 25,000 Austrian soldiers at Ulm in Bavaria in 1805. After marching on to Vienna, he again trounced the Austrians, who had been joined by their new ally, Russia. The battle of Austerlitz, often considered Napoleon's greatest victory, was fought on December 2, 1805, the first anniversary of his coronation.

After maintaining neutrality for a decade, Prussia declared war on France. In 1806, the French promptly destroyed the Prussian army at Jena and Auerstadt. In 1807, Napoleon defeated the Russians at Friedland. Personal negotiations between Napoleon and the young tsar Alexander I (r. 1801–1825) resulted in a humiliating settlement imposed on Prussia, which paid the price for temporary reconciliation between France and Russia. The Treaties of Tilsit turned Prussian lands west of the Elbe River into the kingdom of Westphalia under Napoleon's brother Jerome, and Prussia's Polish provinces became the duchy of Warsaw. Alexander recognized Napoleon's conquests in central and western Europe and promised to help him against the British in exchange for Napoleon's support against the Turks. Neither party kept the bargain. Napoleon once again had turned the divisions among his enemies in his favor.

Wherever the Grand Army conquered, Napoleon's influence soon followed. By annexing some territories and setting up others as satellite kingdoms with much-reduced autonomy, Napoleon attempted to colonize large parts of Europe. He brought the disparate German and Italian states together to rule them more effectively and to exploit their resources for his own ends. In 1806, he established the Confederation of the Rhine, which soon included almost all the German states except Austria and Prussia. The Holy Roman Emperor gave up his title, held since the thirteenth century, and became simply the emperor of Austria. Napoleon established three units in Italy: the territories directly annexed to France and the satellite kingdoms of Italy and Naples. Italy had not been so unified since the Roman Empire.

Consolidation of the German and Italian States, 1812

Napoleon forced French-style reforms on both the annexed territories, which were ruled directly from France, and the satellite kingdoms, which were usually ruled by one or another of Napoleon's relatives but with a certain autonomy. Napoleon brought in French experts to work with handpicked locals to abolish serfdom, eliminate seigneurial dues, introduce the Napoleonic Code, suppress monasteries, subordinate church to state, and extend civil rights to Jews and other religious minorities. Reactions to these innovations were mixed. Napoleon's chosen rulers often made real improvements in roads, public works, law codes, and education. Yet tax increases and ever-rising conscription quotas also fomented discontent. The annexed territories and satellite kingdoms paid half the French war expenses. Napoleon's brother Louis would not allow conscription in his kingdom of the Netherlands because the Dutch had never had compulsory military service. In 1810, Napoleon annexed the satellite kingdom because his brother had become too sympathetic to Dutch interests.

Napoleon's victories forced defeated rulers to rethink their political and cultural assumptions. After suffering a crushing military defeat in 1806, Prussian king Frederick William III (r. 1797–1840) appointed a reform commission, and on its recommendation he abolished serfdom. Peasants gained their personal independence from their noble landlords, who could no longer sell them to pay gambling debts, for example, or refuse them permission to marry. Yet the lives of the former serfs remained bleak; they were left without land, and their landlords no longer had to care for them in hard times. The king's advisers also overhauled the army to make the high command more efficient and to open the way for the appointment of middle-class officers. Prussia instituted these reforms to try to compete with the French, not to promote democracy. As one reformer wrote to Frederick William, "We must do from above what the French have done from below."

Reform received lip service in Russia. Tsar Alexander I had gained his throne after an aristocratic coup deposed and killed his autocratic and capricious father, Paul (r. 1796–1801). In the early years of his reign, the remorseful young ruler created Western-style ministries, lifted restrictions on importing foreign books, and founded six new universities. There was even talk of drafting a constitution. But none of these efforts reached beneath the surface of Russian life, and by the second decade of his reign, Alexander began to reject the Enlightenment spirit that his grandmother Catherine the Great had instilled in him.

Napoleon's Fall

Despite Napoleon's repeated successes on the battlefield, his empire ultimately failed because it was based on a contradiction: Napoleon tried to reduce almost all of Europe to the status of colonial dependents even though Europe had long consisted of independent states. His actions resulted in a great upsurge of the nationalist feeling that has dominated European politics to the present.

The one power always standing between Napoleon and total dominance of Europe was Great Britain. The British ruled the seas and financed anyone who would oppose Napoleon. In an effort to bankrupt this "nation of shopkeepers" by choking its trade, Napoleon inaugurated the **Continental System** in 1806. It prohibited all commerce between Great Britain and France as well as between Great Britain and France's dependent states and allies. After an initial decline in British exports and industrial production, the system proved impossible to enforce, and widespread smuggling brought British goods into the European market. British industrial growth resumed; calico-printing works, for example, quadrupled their production. The temporary protection from British competition could not make up for French losses in the port cities, whose trade with the Caribbean colonies had been disrupted by war and Haitian independence.

Smuggling British goods was only one way of opposing the French. Resistance to French demands for money or for draftees eventually prompted that patriotic defense of the nation known as nationalism. In southern Italy, opposition led to the formation of a network of secret societies, called the *carbonari* (charcoal burners), which got its name from the practice of marking each new member's forehead with a charcoal mark. Throughout the nineteenth century, the carbonari played a leading role in Italian nationalism. In the German states, intellectuals wrote passionate defenses of the virtues of the German nation and of the superiority of German literature. A thriving press, the multiplication of Masonic lodges and literary clubs, and a resurgence of intellectual life in the German universities all eventually connected with anti-French nationalism.

No nations bucked under Napoleon's reins more than Portugal and Spain. In 1807, Napoleon sent 100,000 troops through Spain to invade Portugal, forcing the royal family to flee to the Portuguese colony of Brazil. But fighting continued, aided by a British army. When Napoleon got his brother Joseph named king of Spain in place of the senile Charles IV (r. 1788–1808), the Spanish clergy and nobles raised bands of peasants to fight the French occupiers. The peasants hated French requisitioning of their food supplies; Spanish nobles feared revolutionary reforms. The Spanish Catholic church spread anti-French propaganda that equated Napoleon with heresy. As the former archbishop of Seville wrote to the archbishop of Granada in 1808, "You realize that we must not recognize as king a free-mason, heretic, Lutheran, as are all the Bonapartes and the French nation." Even Napoleon's taking personal command of French forces failed to quell the Spanish. Germaine de Staël commented that Napoleon "never understood that a war might be a crusade. . . . He never reckoned with the one power that no arms could overcome—the enthusiasm of a whole people."

Despite opposition, Napoleon controlled more territory by 1812 than any European ruler had since Roman times (see "Mapping the West," page 635). Only two major European states remained fully independent—Great Britain and Russia—but once allied they would successfully challenge his dominion and draw many other states to their side. Britain sent aid to the Portuguese and Spanish rebels, while Russia once again prepared for war. Tsar Alexander I made peace with the Ottoman Turks and allied himself with Great Britain and Sweden. In 1812, Napoleon invaded Russia with 250,000 horses and 600,000 men, including contingents of Italians, Poles, Swiss, Dutch, and Germans. This daring move proved to be his undoing.

Napoleon followed his usual strategy of trying to strike quickly, but the Russian generals avoided confrontation and retreated eastward, destroying anything that might be useful to the invaders. In September, on the road to Moscow, Napoleon finally engaged the main Russian force in the gigantic battle of Borodino. French casualties were 30,000 men, including 47 generals; the Russians lost 45,000. Once again the Russians retreated, leaving Moscow undefended. Napoleon entered the deserted city, but the victory turned hollow when the departing Russians set the wooden city on fire. Within a week, three-fourths of it had burned to the ground. Alexander refused to negotiate, and French morale plunged with worsening problems of supply. Weeks of constant marching in the dirt and heat had worn down the foot soldiers, who were dying of disease or deserting in large numbers.

In October, Napoleon began his retreat; in November came the cold. Napoleon himself reported that on November 14 the temperature fell to 24 degrees Fahrenheit. A German soldier in the Grand Army described trying to cook fistfuls of raw bran with snow to make something like bread. For him the retreat was "the indescribable horror of all possible plagues." Within a week, the Grand Army lost 30,000 horses and had to abandon most of its artillery and food supplies. Russian forces harassed the retreating army, now more pathetic than grand. By December, only 100,000 troops remained, one-sixth the original number, and the retreat had turned into a rout: the Russians had captured 200,000 soldiers, including 48 generals and 3,000 other officers.

Napoleon had made a classic military mistake that would be repeated by Adolf Hitler in World War II: fighting a war on two distant fronts simultaneously. The Spanish war tied up 250,000 French troops and forced Napoleon to bully Prussia and Austria into supplying soldiers of dubious loyalty for the Moscow campaign. They deserted at the first opportunity. The fighting in Spain and Portugal also worsened the already substantial logistical and communications problems involved in marching to Moscow.

Napoleon's humiliation might have been temporary if the British and Russians had not successfully organized a coalition to complete the job. Napoleon still had resources at his command; by the spring of 1813 he had replenished his army with another 250,000 men. With British financial support, Russian, Austrian, Prussian, and Swedish armies met the French outside Leipzig in October 1813 and defeated Napoleon in the Battle of the Nations. One by one, Napoleon's German allies deserted him to join the German nationalist "war of liberation." The Confederation of the Rhine dissolved, and the Dutch revolted and restored the prince of Orange. Joseph Bonaparte fled Spain, and a combined Spanish-Portuguese army under British command invaded France. In only a few months, the allied powers crossed the Rhine and marched toward Paris. In March 1814, the French Senate deposed Napoleon, who abdicated when his remaining generals refused to fight. Napoleon went into exile on the island of Elba off the Italian coast. His wife, Marie-Louise, refused to accompany him. The allies restored to the throne Louis XVIII (r. 1814–1824), the brother of Louis XVI (whose son was known as Louis XVII even though he died in prison in 1795 without ever ruling).

Napoleon had one last chance to regain power. Lacking a solid base of support, Louis XVIII tried to steer a middle course by granting a charter that established a British-style monarchy with a two-house legislature and guaranteed civil rights. But he was caught between returning émigré nobles who demanded a complete restoration of their lands and powers and those who had supported either the republic or Napoleon during the previous twenty-five years. Sensing an opportunity, Napoleon escaped from Elba in early 1815 and, landing in southern France, attracted cheering crowds and former soldiers to his side. The period known as the Hundred Days (the length of time between his escape and his final defeat) had begun. Louis XVIII fled across the border, waiting for help from France's enemies.

Napoleon quickly moved his reconstituted army into present-day Belgium. At first it seemed that he might succeed in separately fighting the two armies arrayed against him—a Prussian army and a joint force of Belgian, Dutch, German, and British troops led by Sir Arthur Wellesley (1769–1852), the duke of Wellington. But the Prussians evaded him and joined with Wellington at Waterloo. Completely routed, Napoleon had no choice but to abdicate again. This time the victorious allies banished him permanently to the remote island of St. Helena, far off the coast of West Africa, where he died in 1821 at the age of fifty-two.

REVIEW   Why was Napoleon able to gain control over so much of Europe?

Conclusion

The cost of Napoleon's rule was high: 750,000 French soldiers and 400,000 others from annexed and satellite states died fighting for the French between 1800 and 1815. The losses among those attempting to stop Napoleon were at least as high, but no military figure since Alexander the Great in the fourth century B.C.E. had made such an impact on world history. Napoleon's plans for a united Europe, his insistence on spreading the legal reforms of the French Revolution, his model of an authoritarian state, and even his inadvertent awakening of national sentiment set the agenda for European history in the modern era.

The revolutionary cataclysm permanently altered the political landscape of Europe. The French executed their king as a traitor and set up Europe's first republic with universal male suffrage and a written guarantee of "the rights of man." Ordinary people marched in demonstrations, met in clubs, and in the case of men, voted in national elections for the first time. They got their first taste of democracy. But the ideals of universal education, religious toleration, and democratic participation could not prevent the institution of new forms of government terror to persecute, imprison, and kill dissidents. The French revolutionary experiment thus led to democracy *and* to a kind of totalitarianism. The French used the new spirit of national pride to inspire a huge citizen army, but the army conquered other peoples and gave a leading general the chance to take power for himself. Napoleon in turn created yet another new form of rule with a long history in the modern era: a police state in which the generals played a leading political role. Napoleon suppressed all other meaningful political participation and offered in its place law and order and modernization from above. Like many other authoritarian rulers after him, however, Napoleon could not maintain his position once he lost in battle.

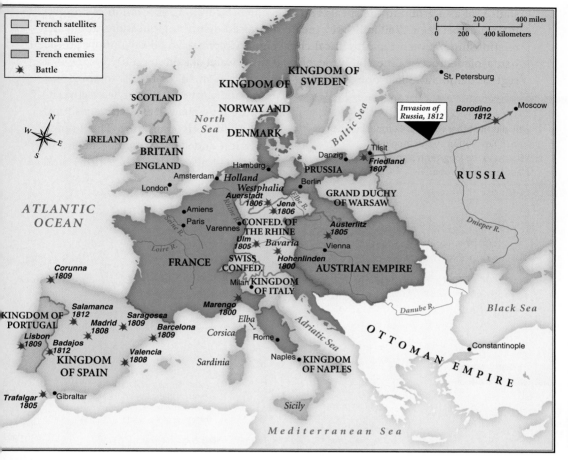

Mapping the West Europe under Napoleonic Domination, 1812

In 1812, Napoleon had at least nominal control of almost all of western Europe. Even before he made his fatal mistake of invading Russia, however, his authority had been undermined in Spain and seriously weakened in the Italian and German states. His efforts to extend French power sparked resistance almost everywhere. As Napoleon insisted on French domination, local people began to think of themselves as Italian, German, or Dutch. Thus, Napoleon inadvertently laid the foundations for the nineteenth-century spread of nationalism. **For more help analyzing this map, see the map activity for this chapter in the Online Study Guide at** bedfordstmartins.com/huntconcise.

As events unfolded between 1789 and 1815, the French Revolution became *the* model of modern revolution and in the process set the enduring patterns of all modern politics. Republicanism, democracy, terrorism, nationalism, and military dictatorship all took their modern forms during the French Revolution. Even the terms *left* and *right* got their political meaning in this period: "the left" was a reference to deputies who favored extensive change and sat together in seats to the speaker's left in 1789; deputies who preferred a more cautious and conservative stance sat as a group to the speaker's right. The breathtaking succession of regimes in France between 1789 and 1815 inevitably raised disturbing questions about the relationship between rapid political change and violence. Do all revolutions in the name of democracy inevitably degenerate into wars of conquest or terror? Is a regime democratic if it does not allow poor men, women, or blacks to vote? Is a militaristic, authoritarian style of government the only answer to divisive political conflicts in a time of war? The French Revolution and its aftermath—the era of Napoleon—raised these questions and many more.

CHAPTER REVIEW QUESTIONS
1. Why did the other rulers of Europe find the French Revolution so threatening?
2. What was the long-term significance of Napoleon for Europe?

For practice quizzes and other study tools, see the Online Study Guide at bedfordstmartins.com/huntconcise.

For primary-source material from this period, see Chapters 19 and 20 of *Sources of THE MAKING OF THE WEST,* Third Edition.

TIMELINE

■ **1805** British naval forces defeat the French at the battle of Trafalgar; Napoleon wins his greatest victory at the battle of Austerlitz

■ **1794** France annexes the Austrian Netherlands; abolition of slavery in French colonies; Robespierre falls, ending the Terror

■ **1815** Napoleon defeated a Waterloo and exiled to island o St. Helena where he dies in 182

■ **1804** Napoleon crowns himself emperor of France and issues the Civil Code

■ **1793** Second partition of Poland by Prussia and Russia; Louis XVI of France executed for treason

■ **1801** Napoleon signs a concordat with the pope

1785	1795	1805	1815

■ **1789** French Revolution begins

■ **1795** Third (final) partition of Poland

■ **1810** Germaine de Staël publishes *On Germany*

■ **1791** Slave revolt in St. Domingue (Haiti)

■ **1799** Napoleon Bonaparte comes to power in a coup

■ **1812** Napoleon invades Russia

■ **1792** Start of war between France and the rest of Europe; second revolution of August 10 overthrows French monarchy

Suggested References

The most influential book on the meaning of the French Revolution is still the classic study by Tocqueville, who insisted that the Revolution continued the process of state centralization undertaken by the monarchy. Recent works on Napoleon show how powerfully his armies affected every European state.

Andress, David. *The Terror: The Merciless War for Freedom in Revolutionary France.* 2006.

Beaucour, Fernand Emile, Yves Laissus, and Chantal Orgogozo. *The Discovery of Egypt.* Trans. Bambi Ballard. 1990.

Bell, David A. *The First Total War: Napoleon's Europe and the Birth of Warfare as We Know It.* 2007.

*Blaufarb, Rafe. *Napoleon: A Symbol for an Age; A Brief History with Documents.* 2008.

Censer, Jack R., and Lynn Hunt. *Liberty, Equality, Fraternity: Exploring the French Revolution* (includes CD-ROM of images and music). 2001. See also the accompanying Web site: http://www.chnm.gmu.edu/revolution

Cole, Juan. *Napoléon's Egypt: Invading the Middle East.* 2007.

*Dubois, Laurent, and John D. Garrigus. *Slave Revolution in the Caribbean, 1789–1804: A Brief History with Documents.* 2006.

Englund, Steven. *Napoleon: A Political Life.* 2004.

Furet, François. *Interpreting the French Revolution.* Trans. Elborg Forster. 1981.

Godineau, Dominique. *The Women of Paris and Their French Revolution.* Trans. Katherine Streip. 1998.

*Hunt, Lynn, ed. *The French Revolution and Human Rights: A Brief Documentary History.* 1996.

*Levy, Darline Gay, Harriet Branson Applewhite, and Mary Durham Johnson, eds. *Women in Revolutionary Paris, 1789–1795.* 1979.

Napoleon Foundation: http://www.napoleon.org

Palmer, R. R. *The Age of the Democratic Revolution: A Political History of Europe and America, 1760–1800.* Vol. 2, *The Struggle.* 1964.

Tocqueville, Alexis de. *The Old Regime and the French Revolution.* Trans. Stuart Gilbert. 1955. Originally published 1856.

17

Industrialization and Social Ferment

1815–1850

I N 1830, THE LIVERPOOL AND MANCHESTER RAILWAY LINE opened in England to the cheers of crowds and the congratulations of government officials, including the duke of Wellington, the hero of Waterloo and now prime minister. The thirty-mile-long line required an act of Parliament and cost the private company formed to build it some £800,000, twice the original estimate. The sum was enormous; by contrast, the engine man earned only £54 a year. In the excitement of the opening, some of the dignitaries gathered on a parallel track. Another engine, George Stephenson's *Rocket,* approached at high speed—the engine could go as fast as twenty-seven miles per hour. Most of the gentlemen scattered to safety, but former cabinet minister William Huskisson fell and was hit. He died within a few hours, the first official casualty of the newfangled railroad.

The New Railroad
This engraving by H. Pyall from 1831 shows the entrance of the Liverpool and Manchester Railway Line at Edge Hill in Liverpool. The engine seems quaint to us now, but at the time it impressed everyone with its size and speed. Even upper-class men and women flocked to see the new engine in operation. Railroads immediately became the symbol of the industrial age, as well as its driving force. (*Getty Images.*)

Dramatic and expensive, railroads were the most striking symbol of the new industrial age. Industrialization and its by-product rapid urban growth fundamentally altered political conflicts, social relations, cultural concerns, and even the landscape itself. So great were these changes that they are collectively labeled the Industrial Revolution. Although this revolution did not take place in a single decade like the French Revolution, the introduction of steam-driven machinery, large factories, and a new working class transformed life in the Western world. Peasants and workers streamed into the cities. The population of London grew by 130,000 people in the 1830s alone; Berlin more than doubled between 1819 and 1849; and Paris expanded by 120,000 just between 1841 and 1846. To many observers, overcrowding, disease, prostitution, crime, and drinking all seemed to be on the increase as a result.

Although Europeans longed for peace and stability in the aftermath of the Napoleonic whirlwind, they lived in a world that was deeply unsettled by two parallel revolutions: the French Revolution and the Industrial Revolution. Social and political ferment prompted the development of a whole spectrum of ideologies to explain the meaning of the changes taking place. **Ideology**, a word coined during the French Revolution, refers to a coherent set of beliefs about the way a society's social and political order should be organized. Conservatism, nationalism, liberalism, socialism, and communism each offered their adherents a doctrine that explained social change and advocated a political program to confront it.

The claims of the new ideologies, the revolutionary legacy, and the new problems created by industrialization and urbanization all posed pressing challenges to rulers. After the Congress of Vienna (1814–1815) settled the boundaries of post-Napoleonic Europe and established conservatism as a kind of official ideology on the continent, restored monarchs tried to limit challenges to their rule. Despite their efforts, political revolts broke out sporadically in the 1820s and again in 1830. Most of these revolts failed, except in Latin America and Greece, where new nations emerged. Demands for social and political change came to a head in 1848, when the rapid transformation of European society provided the combustible material for a new set of revolutionary outbreaks more consuming than any since 1789.

CHAPTER FOCUS QUESTION How did the Industrial Revolution create new social and political conflicts?

The Industrial Revolution

French and British writers of the 1820s introduced the term *Industrial Revolution* to capture the drama of contemporary economic change and to draw a parallel with the French Revolution. But unlike the French upheaval, the Industrial Revolution did not have definite dates that marked its beginning or end. From their first appearance in Great Britain in the second half of the eighteenth century, steam-driven machines, large factories, and a new working class spread fitfully across Europe and eventually to the rest of the world. In the first half of the nineteenth century, many Europeans began to take notice of the acceleration of **industrialization** and urbanization and often complained of the consequences.

Roots of Industrialization

British inventors had been steadily perfecting and adapting steam engines for five decades before George Stephenson built his *Rocket*. A key breakthrough took place in 1776, when James Watt adapted the existing model to make a more efficient steam engine for pumping water from coal mines and for driving machinery in textile factories. Since coal fired the steam engines that drove the new textile machines, innovations tended to reinforce each other. This kind of synergy built on previous changes in the textile industry. In 1733, the Englishman John Kay had patented the flying shuttle, which weavers operated by pulling a cord that drove the shuttle to either side of the loom, enabling them to "throw" yarn across the loom rather than draw it back and forth by hand. When the flying shuttle came into widespread use in the 1760s, weavers began producing cloth more quickly than spinners could produce thread. The resulting shortage of spun thread propelled the invention of machines to speed the process of spinning. The spinning jenny and water frame, a power-driven spinning machine, were introduced in the 1760s. In the following decades, water frames replaced thousands of women spinners working at home by hand. Using the engines produced by Watt and his partner, Matthew Boulton, Edmund Cartwright designed a mechanized loom in the 1780s, which when perfected could be run by a small boy and yield fifteen times the output of a skilled adult weaver working a handloom. By the end of the century, all the new power machinery was assembled in large factories that hired semiskilled men, women, and children to replace skilled weavers.

Several factors interacted to make England the first site of the Industrial Revolution. Because population increased by more than 50 percent in England in the second half of the eighteenth century, manufacturers had an incentive to produce more and cheaper cotton cloth. England had a good supply of private investment capital from overseas trade and commercial profits, ready access to raw cotton from the plantations of its Caribbean colonies and the southern United States, and the necessary natural resources at home, such as coal and iron. Good opportunities for social mobility and relative political stability in the eighteenth century provided an environment that fostered the pragmatism of the English and Scottish inventors who designed the machinery. These early industrialists shared a culture of informal scientific education through learned societies and popular lectures (one of the prominent forms of the Enlightenment in Britain). Manufacturers proved eager to introduce steam-driven machinery to increase output and gradually established factories to house the new machines and concentrate the labor of their workers. The agricultural revolution of the eighteenth century had enabled England to produce food more efficiently, freeing some agricultural workers to move to the new manufacturing centers. Cotton textile production skyrocketed.

Elsewhere in Europe, textile manufacturing—long a linchpin in the European economy—expanded in the eighteenth century even without the introduction of new machines and factories. Textile production increased because of the spread of the "putting-out" or "domestic" system. Under the putting-out system, manufacturers supplied the raw materials, such as woolen or cotton fibers, to families working at home. The mother and children washed the fibers and carded and combed them. Then the mother and older daughters spun them into thread. The father, assisted by the children, wove the cloth. The cloth was then "finished" (bleached, dyed, smoothed, and so on) under the supervision of the manufacturer in a large workshop, located either in town or in the countryside. This system had existed in the textile industry for hundreds of years, but in the eighteenth century it grew dramatically, and it included not only textiles but also the manufacture of products such as glassware, baskets, nails, and guns. The spread of the domestic system of manufacturing is sometimes called proto-industrialization to signify that the process helped pave the way for the full-scale Industrial Revolution. Because of this expansion, ordinary people began to wear underclothes and nightclothes, both rare in the past. White, red, blue, yellow, green, and even pastel shades of cotton now replaced the black, gray, or brown of traditional woolen clothing.

Engines of Change

Steam-driven engines took on a dramatic new form in the 1820s, when the English engineer George Stephenson perfected an engine to pull wagons along iron tracks. The idea of a railroad was not new: iron tracks had been used since the seventeenth century to haul coal from mines in wagons pulled by horses. Railroads, however, developed only after Stephenson's invention of a steam-powered locomotive. In the 1830s, railroad building became a new industry throughout Europe (see "Taking Measure"). Belgium, newly independent in 1830, opened the first continental railroad in 1835 with state bonds backed by British capital. Railroads grew spectacularly in the United States in the 1830s and 1840s as well, and the British also began to

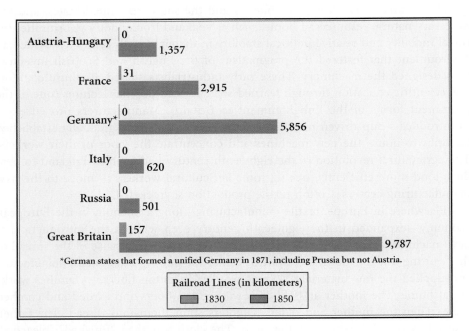

Austria-Hungary   0   1,357
France   31   2,915
Germany*   0   5,856
Italy   0   620
Russia   0   501
Great Britain   157   9,787

*German states that formed a unified Germany in 1871, including Prussia but not Austria.

Railroad Lines (in kilometers)
█ 1830   █ 1850

Taking Measure Railroad Lines, 1830–1850
Great Britain quickly extended its lead in building railroads. The extension of commerce and, before long, the ability to wage war would depend on the development of effective rail networks. These statistics might be taken as predicting a realignment of power within Europe after 1850. What do the numbers say about the relative positions of Germany (the German states, including Prussia but excluding Austria), Austria-Hungary, and France?

build railroads in India. In all, the world had 23,500 miles of track by midcentury, the vast majority of them in Europe.

Railroad building spurred both industrial development and state power (see "Mapping the West," page 679). Placed on the new tracks, steam-driven carriages could transport people and goods to the cities and link coal and iron deposits to the new factories. Governments everywhere participated in the construction of railroads, which depended on private and state funds to pay for the massive amounts of iron, coal, heavy machinery, and human labor required to build and run them. One-third of all investment in the German states in the 1840s went into railroads. Some people expected social and political change to follow. One German entrepreneur confidently predicted, "The locomotive is the hearse which will carry absolutism and feudalism to the graveyard." But the most obvious effects could be seen in the demand for iron products. Until the 1840s, cotton had led industrial production, but afterward iron and coal began to count more and more.

Steam-powered engines made Great Britain the world leader in manufacturing. By midcentury, more than half of Britain's national income came from manufacturing and trade. The number of steamboats in Britain increased from two in 1812 to six hundred in 1840. Between 1840 and 1850, steam power doubled in Britain and increased even more rapidly elsewhere in Europe, as those adopting British inventions strove to catch up. Although Britain consciously tried to protect its industrial supremacy, thousands of British engineers defied laws against the export of machinery or the emigration of artisans. The best known of them, John Cockerill, set up a machine works in Belgium that was soon selling its products as far east as Poland and Russia. Cockerill claimed to know about every innovation within ten days of its appearance in Britain.

Only slowly, thanks to such pirating of British methods and to new technical schools, did most continental European countries begin closing the gap. Belgium became the fastest-growing industrial power on the continent. Between 1830 and 1844, the number of steam engines in Belgium quadrupled, and Belgians exported seven times as many steam engines as they imported. Even so, by 1850 continental Europe still lagged almost twenty years behind Great Britain in industrial development.

Formation of the Working Class

Steam-driven machines first brought workers together in factories in the textile industry. By 1830, more than one million people in Britain depended on the cotton industry for employment, and cotton cloth constituted 50 percent of the country's exports. The rapid expansion of the British textile industry had as its colonial corollary the destruction of the hand-manufacture of textiles in India. The British put high import duties on Indian cloth entering Britain and kept such duties very low for British cloth entering India. The figures are dramatic: in 1813, the Indian city of Calcutta exported to England £2 million of cotton cloth; by 1830, Calcutta was importing from England £2 million of cotton cloth. When Britain abolished slavery in its Caribbean colonies in 1833, British manufacturers began to buy raw cotton in the southern United States, where slavery still flourished.

Factories drew workers from the urban population surge, which had begun in the eighteenth century and now accelerated. The population of such new industrial cities as Manchester and Leeds increased 40 percent in the 1820s alone. Historians long thought that factory workers came from the countryside, pushed off the land by the field enclosures of the 1700s. But recent studies have shown that the number of agricultural laborers actually increased during industrialization in Britain, suggesting that a growing birthrate created a larger population and fed workers into the new factory system. A system of employment that resembled family labor on farms or in putting-out, or cottage, industries also developed in the new factories. Entire families came to toil for a single wage, although family members performed different tasks. Workdays of twelve to seventeen hours were typical, even for children, and the work was grueling.

As urban factories grew, their workers gradually came to constitute a new socio-economic class with a distinctive culture and traditions. Like *middle class,* the term *working class* came into use for the first time in the early nineteenth century. It referred to the laborers in the new factories. In the past, workers had labored in isolated trades: water and wood carrying, gardening, laundry, and building. In contrast, factories brought people together with machines, under close supervision by their employers.

Factory Work
This 1836 depiction of the mechanized spinning of cotton in England captures the dangers of child labor: the child (lower right) is sweeping even while the machine works. The print does not portray the churning noise and swirling dust of the workplace, but it does show how machines could produce thread much more efficiently than individuals working on their own. Do you think the artist aimed to provide a positive or a negative picture of factory work? (Mary Evans Picture Library.)

Workers soon developed a sense of common interests and organized societies for mutual help and political reform. From these would come the first labor unions.

In 1811 and 1812, bands of handloom weavers, fearing their displacement by machines, wrecked factory machinery and burned mills in the Midlands, Yorkshire, and Lancashire. To restore order and protect industry, the British government sent in an army of twelve thousand regular soldiers and made machine wrecking punishable by death. The rioters were called Luddites, after the fictitious figure Ned Ludd, whose signature appeared on their manifestos. (The term is still used to describe those who resist new technology.)

Other British workers focused their organizing efforts on reforming Parliament, whose members were chosen in elections dominated by the landowning elite. One reformer complained that the members of the House of Commons were nothing but "toad-eaters, gamblers, public plunderers, and hirelings." Reform clubs held large open-air meetings, and ordinary people eagerly bought cheap newspapers that clamored for change. In August 1819, sixty thousand people attended an illegal meeting held in St. Peter's Fields in Manchester. When the local authorities sent the cavalry to arrest the speaker, panic resulted. Eleven people were killed and many hundreds were injured in what was soon labeled the Peterloo massacre (combining St. Peter's with Waterloo, the battle that had ended Napoleon's reign only four years before). An alarmed government passed the Six Acts, which forbade large political meetings and restricted press criticism, suppressing the reform movement for a decade.

Despite increasing industrial growth, factory workers remained a minority everywhere. In the 1840s, factories in England employed only 5 percent of the workers, in France 3 percent, and in Prussia 2 percent. Most workers, both men and women, continued to toil at home in cottage industries. In the 1840s, for example, two-thirds of the manufacturing workers in Prussia and Saxony labored at home for contractors or merchants who supplied raw materials and then sold the finished goods. Some peasants kept their options open by combining factory work with agricultural labor. They worked in agriculture during the spring and summer and in manufacturing in the fall and winter. Unstable industrial wages made such arrangements essential. Some new industries idled periodically: for example, iron forges stopped for several months when the water level in streams dropped, and blast furnaces shut down for repairs several weeks every year. In hard times, factory owners simply closed their doors until demand for their goods improved.

Even though factories employed only a small percentage of the population, they attracted much attention because they created both unheard-of riches and new forms of poverty. "From this filthy sewer pure gold flows," wrote the French aristocrat Alexis de Tocqueville after visiting Manchester in the 1830s. "Here humanity attains its most complete development and its most brutish, here civilization works its miracles and civilized man is turned almost into a savage." Studies by physicians set the life expectancy of workers in Manchester at just seventeen years in 1840 (partly because of high rates of infant mortality), compared to the average life span of forty years throughout England. Visitors invariably complained about the smoke and soot. One American visitor to Britain in the late 1840s described how "in the manufacturing town, the fine soot or *blacks* darken the day, give white sheep the color of black sheep, discolor the human saliva, contaminate the air, poison many plants, and corrode monuments and buildings."

Authorities worried in particular about the effects on families. A doctor in the Prussian town of Breslau (population 111,000 in 1850), for example, reported that in working-class districts "several persons live in one room in a single bed, or perhaps a whole family, and use the room for all domestic duties, so that the air gets vitiated [polluted]. . . . Their diet consists largely of bread and potatoes." In Great Britain, the Factory Act of 1833 outlawed the employment of children under the age of nine in textile mills. It also limited the workdays of children ages nine to thirteen to nine hours a day and those ages thirteen to eighteen to twelve hours. Adults worked even longer hours. When investigating commissions showed that women and young children, sometimes under age six, were hauling coal trucks through low, cramped passageways in coal mines, Parliament passed the Mines Act of 1842 prohibiting the employment of women and girls underground. In 1847, the Central Short Time Committee, one of Britain's many social reform organizations, successfully pressured Parliament to limit the workday of women and children to ten hours. Countries in continental Europe followed Britain's lead, but since most did not insist on government inspection, enforcement was lax.

The advance of industrialization in eastern Europe was slow, in large part because serfdom still survived there, hindering labor mobility and tying up investment capital. As long as peasants were legally tied to the land as serfs, they could not migrate to the new factory towns, and landlords felt little incentive to invest their income in manufacturing. The problem was worst in Russia, where industrialization had hardly begun and would not take off until the end of the nineteenth century. Nevertheless, even in Russia signs of industrialization could be detected: raw cotton imports (a sign of a growing textile industry) increased sevenfold between 1831 and 1848, and the number of factories doubled, along with the size of the industrial workforce.

Urbanization and Its Consequences

Industrial development spurred urban growth wherever factories were located in or near cities, yet cities grew even with little industry. Here, too, Great Britain led the way: half the population of England and Wales lived in towns by 1850, while in France and the German states the urban population was only about a quarter of the total. In the 1830s and 1840s, many European cities ballooned. Massive rural emigration, rather than births to women already living in cities, accounted for this remarkable increase. Europe's population grew by nearly 100 percent between 1800 and 1850, yet agricultural yields increased by only 30 to 50 percent. City life and new factories beckoned those faced with hunger and poverty, including emigrants from other lands: thousands of Irish emigrated to English cities, Italians went to French cities, and Poles flocked to German cities. Since the construction of new housing could not keep up with population growth, overcrowding was inevitable. In 1847 in

St. Giles, the Irish quarter of London, 461 people lived in just twelve houses. Men, women, and children huddled together on piles of filthy, rotting straw or potato peels because they had no money for fuel to keep warm.

Severe crowding worsened already dire sanitation conditions. Residents dumped refuse into streets or courtyards, and human excrement collected in cesspools under apartment houses. At midcentury, London's approximately 250,000 cesspools were emptied only once or twice a year. Water was scarce and had to be fetched daily from nearby fountains. Despite the diversion of water from provincial rivers to Paris and a tripling of the number of public fountains, Parisians had enough water for only two baths annually per person (the upper classes enjoyed more baths, the lower classes fewer). In London, private companies that supplied water turned on pumps in the poorer sections for only a few hours three days a week. In rapidly growing British industrial cities such as Manchester, one-third of the houses contained no latrines. Human waste ended up in the rivers that supplied the cities' drinking water. The horses that provided transportation inside the cities left droppings everywhere, and city dwellers often kept chickens, ducks, goats, pigs, geese, and even cattle, as well as dogs and cats, in their houses. The result was, as one observer noted, a "universal atmosphere of filth and stink."

Such conditions made cities prime breeding grounds for disease. In 1830–1832 and again in 1847–1851, devastating outbreaks of **cholera** swept across Asia and Europe, touching the United States as well in 1849–1850. Today we know that a waterborne bacterium causes cholera, but at the time no one understood the disease and everyone feared it. The usually fatal illness induced violent vomiting and diarrhea and left the skin blue. While cholera particularly ravaged the crowded, filthy neighborhoods of rapidly growing cities, it also claimed many rural and some well-to-do victims. In Paris, 18,000 people died in the 1832 epidemic and 20,000 in that of 1849; in London, 7,000 died in each epidemic; and in Russia, the epidemics were catastrophic, claiming 250,000 victims in 1831–1832 and 1 million in 1847–1851.

Rumors and panic followed in the wakes of epidemics such as cholera. In Paris in April 1832, a crowd of workers attacked a central hospital, believing the doctors were poisoning the poor and using cholera as a hoax to cover up the conspiracy. Eastern European peasants burned estates and killed physicians and officials. Though devastating, cholera did not kill as many people as tuberculosis, Europe's deadliest disease. Tuberculosis took its victims one by one, however, and therefore had less impact on social relations.

Reformers believed that overcrowding among the poor led not only to disease but also to sexual promiscuity, illegitimacy, and crime. A physician visiting Lille, France, in 1835 wrote of "individuals of both sexes and of very different ages lying together, most of them without nightshirts and repulsively dirty. . . . The reader will complete the picture." Officials collected statistics on illegitimacy that seemed to bear out these fears: one-quarter to one-half of the babies born in the big European cities in the 1830s and 1840s were illegitimate, and alarmed medical men wrote about thousands of infanticides. Between 1815 and the mid-1830s in France, 33,000 babies were abandoned at foundling hospitals every year. Middle-class observers linked sexual disorder with drinking and crime. Beer halls and pubs dotted the urban landscape. One London street boasted of twenty-three pubs in three hundred yards. Police officials estimated that London had 70,000 thieves and 80,000 prostitutes. A Swiss pastor warned of the consequences of lower-class poverty: "Their hearts seethe with hatred of the well-to-do; their eyes lust for a share of the wealth about them; their mouths speak unblushingly of a coming day of retribution."

Reforming the Social Order

Government reports, medical accounts, and fictionalized depictions prompted reformers to organize to help the poor. Charitable impulses often went hand in hand with attempts to impose order and discipline on lower-class families deemed to be lacking in both. Although women's professional opportunities were severely limited, they took a prominent role in charitable and reform work. Catholic religious orders, which by 1850 enrolled many more women than men, ran schools, hospitals, leper colonies, insane asylums, and old-age homes. New Catholic orders, especially for women, were established, and Catholic missionary activity overseas increased.

Protestant women in Great Britain and the United States established Bible, missionary, and female reform societies by the hundreds. Many societies dedicated themselves to reforming prostitutes and castigating their male clients. Others promoted missionary activity in other parts of the world. In the British colony of India, Protestant missionaries argued for the reform of Hindu customs. *Sati*—the burning of widows on the funeral pyres of their husbands—was abolished by the British administration of India in 1829. Protestant and Catholic missionary activity would become an arm of European imperialism and cultural influence in the nineteenth century.

Religiously motivated reformers first had to overcome the perceived indifference of the working classes. Less than 10 percent of the workers in cities attended religious services. To combat such indifference, British religious groups launched the Sunday school movement, which reached its zenith in the 1840s. By 1851, more than half of all working-class children between the ages of five and fifteen were attending Sunday schools, which taught children how to read at a time when few working-class children could go to school during the week. Many Sunday schools were run by Methodists, who followed the teachings of John Wesley (1703–1791). The Methodists, or Wesleyans, gradually separated from the Church of England and in the early decades of the nineteenth century attracted thousands of members in huge revival meetings that lasted for days. Shopkeepers, artisans, agricultural laborers, miners, and workers in cottage industries, both male and female, flocked to the new denomination.

Social reformers elsewhere also saw education as one of the main prospects for uplifting the poor and the working class. In 1833, the French government passed an education law that required every town to maintain a primary school, pay a teacher, and provide free education to poor boys. The law's author, François Guizot, explained the government's attitude: "Ignorance renders the masses turbulent and ferocious."

Girls' schools were optional. By the late 1830s, 60 percent of children attended primary school in France, still less than in Protestant Prussia, where 75 percent of children went to school. Popular education remained woefully undeveloped in most of eastern Europe. Peasants were specifically excluded from the few primary schools in Russia.

Catholics and Protestants alike promoted the **temperance movement** to fight the "pestilence of hard liquor." The first temperance societies had appeared in the United States as early as 1813, and by 1835 the American Temperance Society claimed 1.5 million members. Temperance advocates saw drunkenness as a sign of moral weakness and a threat to the social order. One German temperance advocate insisted, "One need not be a prophet to know that all efforts to combat the widespread and rapidly spreading pauperism will be unsuccessful as long as the common man fails to realize that the principal source of his degradation and misery is his fondness of drink." Yet temperance societies also attracted working-class people who shared the desire for respectability.

Organizations such as the Society for the Prevention of Cruelty to Animals tried to eliminate popular blood sports such as cockfighting and bearbaiting. Their members believed that such entertainments encouraged violent behavior outside the arena. By the end of the 1830s, bullbaiting had been abandoned in Great Britain. "This useful animal," rejoiced one reformer in 1839, "is no longer tortured amidst the exulting yells of those who are a disgrace to our common form and nature." Other blood sports died out more slowly, and efforts in other countries generally lagged behind those of the British.

When private charities failed to meet the needs of the poor, governments often intervened. Great Britain sought to control the costs of public welfare by passing a new poor law in 1834, called by its critics the "Starvation Act." The law required that all able-bodied persons receiving relief be placed in workhouses, with husbands separated from wives and parents from children. Workhouse life was designed to be as unpleasant as possible so that poor people would move on to regions of higher employment. British women from all social classes organized anti–poor law societies to protest the separation of mothers from their children in the workhouses.

Many women viewed charitable work as the extension of their domestic roles: they promoted virtuous behavior and morality and thus improved society. Yet women's social reform activities concealed a paradox. According to the set of beliefs that historians call the doctrine or ideology of **domesticity**, women should live their lives entirely within the domestic sphere; they should devote themselves to the home, not public activities. The English poet Alfred, Lord Tennyson, captured this view in a popular poem published in 1847: "Man for the field and woman for the hearth; / Man for the sword and for the needle she. . . . All else confusion." Many believed that maintaining proper and distinct roles for men and women was critically important to maintaining social order in general.

Most women had little hope of economic independence. The notion of a separate, domestic sphere for women prevented them from pursuing higher education, work in professional careers, or participation in politics through voting or holding office—all activities deemed appropriate only to men. Laws everywhere codified the subordination of women. Many countries followed the model of Napoleon's Civil Code, which classified married women as legal incompetents along with children, the insane, and criminals.

Distinctions between men and women were most noticeable in the privileged classes. Whereas boys attended secondary schools, most middle- and upper-class girls still received their education at home or in church schools, where they were taught to be religious, obedient, and accomplished in music and languages. As men's fashions turned practical—long trousers and short jackets of solid, often dark colors; no makeup (previously common for aristocratic men); and simply cut hair rather than wigs—women continued to dress for decorative effect, now with tightly corseted waists that emphasized the differences between female and male bodies. Middle- and upper-class women had long hair that required hours of brushing and pinning up, and they wore long, cumbersome skirts. Advice books written by women detailed the tasks that such women undertook in the home: maintaining household accounts, supervising servants, and organizing social events.

Scientists reinforced stereotypes. Once considered sexually insatiable, women were now described as incapacitated by menstruation and largely uninterested in sex, an attitude that many equated with moral superiority. Thus was born the "Victorian" woman, a figment of the largely male medical imagination. Physicians and scholars considered women mentally inferior. In 1839, Auguste Comte, an influential early French sociologist, wrote, "As for any functions of government, the radical inaptitude of the female sex is there yet more marked . . . and limited to the guidance of the mere family."

Novels by women often revealed the bleaker side of women's situations. *Jane Eyre* (1847), a novel by the English writer Charlotte Brontë, describes the difficult life of an orphaned girl who becomes a governess, the only occupation open to most single middle-class women. Although she is in an economically weak position, Jane Eyre refuses to achieve respectability and security through marriage, the usual option for women. The French novelist George Sand (Amandine-Aurore Dupin, 1804–1876) took her social criticism a step further. She announced her independence in the 1830s by dressing like a man and smoking cigars. Like many other women writers of the time, she published her work under a male pseudonym while creating female characters who prevail in difficult circumstances through romantic love and moral idealism. Sand's novel *Indiana* (1832), about an unhappily married woman, was read all over Europe. Her notoriety made the term *George-Sandism* a common expression of disdain for independent women.

Whether by women or men, novels proved to be the art form best suited to portraying the new society and its social ills. Thanks to increased literacy, the spread of reading rooms and lending libraries, and serialization in newspapers and journals, novels reached a large reading public and helped shape public awareness. Unlike the fiction of the eighteenth century, which had focused on individual personalities, the great novels of the 1830s and 1840s specialized in the description of social life in all its varieties. Manufacturers, financiers, starving students, workers, bureaucrats, prostitutes, underworld figures, thieves, and aristocratic men and women filled the pages of works

George Sand

In this lithograph by Alcide Lorentz (1842), George Sand is shown in one of her notorious masculine costumes. Sand published numerous works, including novels, plays, essays, travel writing, and an autobiography. She actively participated in the revolution of 1848 in France, writing pamphlets in support of the new republic. (The Granger Collection, NY.)

by popular writers such as Honoré de Balzac and Charles Dickens. Pushing himself to exhaustion and a premature death to get out of debt, the French writer Balzac (1799–1850) cranked out ninety-five novels and many short stories.

The English author Charles Dickens (1812–1870) worked with a similar frenetic energy and for much the same reasons. When his father was imprisoned for debt in 1824, the young Dickens took a job in a shoe-polish factory. After working briefly as a political journalist, he began publishing novels, many of which drew attention to the poverty and misery produced by industrialization and urbanization. In *The Old Curiosity Shop* (1841), for example, he depicts the Black Country, the manufacturing region west and northwest of Birmingham, as a "cheerless region" and a "mournful place," in which tall chimneys "made foul the melancholy air." In addition to publishing such enduring favorites as *Oliver Twist* (1838) and *A Christmas Carol* (1843), he set up a home for homeless women and personally ran it for twelve years. For Dickens, the ability to portray the problems of the poor went hand in hand with a personal commitment to reform.

> **REVIEW**   Why were cities seen as dangerous places?

New Ideologies

Although reform organizations grew rapidly in the 1830s and 1840s, many Europeans found them insufficient to answer the questions raised by industrialization and urbanization. How did the new social order differ from the earlier one, which was less urban and less driven by commercial concerns? Who should control this new order? Should governments try to moderate or accelerate the pace of change? New ideologies such as liberalism and socialism offered competing answers to these questions and provided the platform for new political movements. This was an era of "isms"—conservatism, liberalism, socialism, nationalism, and romanticism.

Conservatism

The French Revolution and Napoleonic domination of Europe had shown contemporaries that government could be changed overnight, that the old hierarchies could be overthrown in the name of reason, and that even Christianity could be written off or at least profoundly altered with the stroke of a pen. The potential for rapid change raised many questions about the proper sources of authority. Kings and churches could be restored and former revolutionaries locked up or silenced, but the old order no longer commanded automatic obedience. The old order was now merely *old*, no longer "natural" and "timeless." It had been ousted once and therefore might fall again. People insisted on having reasons to believe in their "restored" governments. The political doctrine that justified the restoration was **conservatism**.

Conservatives benefited from the disillusionment that permeated Europe after 1815. In the eyes of most Europeans, Napoleon had become a tyrant who ruled in his own interests. Conservatives believed it was crucial to analyze the roots of such tyranny so that established authorities could use their knowledge of history to prevent its recurrence. They saw a logical progression in recent history: the Enlightenment based on reason led to the French Revolution, with its bloody guillotine and horrifying Terror, which in turn spawned the authoritarian and militaristic Napoleon. Conservative intellectuals therefore either rejected Enlightenment principles or at least subjected them to scrutiny and skepticism.

The most influential spokesman of conservatism was Edmund Burke (1729–1799), the British critic of the French Revolution. He argued that the revolutionaries erred in thinking they could construct an entirely new government based on reason. Government, Burke said, had to be rooted in long experience, which evolved over generations. All change must be gradual and must respect national and historical traditions.

Like Burke, later conservatives believed that religious and other major traditions were an essential foundation for any society. Conservatives blamed the French Revolution's attack on religion on the skepticism and anticlericalism of such Enlightenment thinkers as Voltaire, and they defended both hereditary monarchy and the authority of the church, whether Catholic or Protestant. Only the church, the state, and the family, rather than the individualistic "rights of man," could provide an enduring social order. Faith, history, and tradition must fill the vacuum left by the failures of reason and excessive belief in individual rights. Across Europe, these views were taken up and elaborated by government advisers, professors, and writers.

Liberalism

The adherents of **liberalism** defined themselves in opposition to conservatives on one end of the political spectrum and revolutionaries on the other. Nineteenth-century liberals should not be confused with those of the present day. In the nineteenth century, liberals emphasized constitutionalism and free trade above all else. They generally applauded the social and economic changes produced by the Industrial Revolution, while opposing the violence and excessive state power promoted by the French Revolution. The leaders of the rapidly expanding middle class, composed of manufacturers, merchants, and professionals, favored liberalism.

The foremost exponent of early-nineteenth-century liberalism was the English philosopher and jurist Jeremy Bentham (1748–1832). He called his brand of liberalism "utilitarianism" because he held that the best policy is the one that produces "the greatest good for the greatest number" and is thus the most useful, or utilitarian. Bentham's criticisms spared no institution; he railed against the injustices of the British parliamentary process, the abuses of the prisons and the penal code, and the educational system.

Bentham and many other liberals joined the abolitionist movement, which intensified between the 1790s and 1820s. Agitation by groups such as the London Society for Effecting the Abolition of the Slave Trade succeeded in gaining a first victory in 1807 when the British House of Lords voted to abolish the slave trade. The abolitionists' efforts finally bore fruit in 1833 when Britain abolished slavery in all its colonies.

British liberals pushed for two major reforms in addition to the abolition of slavery: expansion of the electorate to give representation to a broader segment of the middle class and repeal of the **Corn Laws**, or tariffs on foreign grain. They gained their first goal in the Reform Bill of 1832. When the Tories in Parliament resisted the proposed extension of the right to vote, liberals and their supporters organized mass demonstrations. The Reform Bill passed after the king threatened to create enough new peers to obtain its passage in the House of Lords. Although the number of male voters increased by about 50 percent, only one in five Britons could now vote, and voting still depended on holding property. Nevertheless, the bill gave representation to new cities in the industrial north for the first time and set a precedent for further widening suffrage.

When landholders in the House of Commons thwarted efforts to lower grain tariffs, two Manchester cotton manufacturers set up the Anti–Corn Law League. The league denounced the landlords as "blood-sucking vampires" and attracted working-class backing by promising lower food prices. The league established local branches, published newspapers and the journal *The Economist* (founded in 1843 and now one of the world's most influential periodicals), and campaigned in elections. The league eventually won the support of the Tory prime minister Sir Robert Peel, whose government repealed the Corn Laws in 1846.

Liberalism had less appeal in continental Europe, except in France, because industrial growth was slower and the middle classes smaller than in Britain. French liberals agitated for greater freedom of the press and a broadening of the vote. The flamboyant Hungarian nationalist Lajos Kossuth (1802–1894) grabbed every opportunity to publicize American democracy and British political liberalism, all in a fervent nationalist spirit. Considered subversive ideas in Russia, Western liberal writings, as well as all books about the United States, were banned by Tsar Nicholas I (r. 1825–1855). He sent nearly ten thousand people a year into exile in Siberia as punishment for their political activities.

Socialism and the Early Labor Movement

Socialism took up where liberalism left off. Socialists believed that the liberties advocated by liberals benefited only the middle class—the owners of factories and businesses—not the workers. They sought to reorganize society totally rather than to reform it piecemeal through political measures. Many were utopians who believed that ideal communities are based on cooperation rather than competition. Like Thomas More, whose book *Utopia* (1516) gave the movement its name, the utopian socialists believed that society would benefit all its members only if private property ceased to exist.

Socialists criticized the new industrial order for dividing society into two classes: the new middle class, or capitalists, who owned the wealth; and the working class, their downtrodden and impoverished employees. Such divisions tore the social fabric, and as their name suggests, the socialists aimed to restore harmony and cooperation through social reorganization. Three early socialists helped instigate the movement: Robert Owen, Claude Henri de Saint-Simon, and Charles Fourier.

Robert Owen (1771–1858) founded British socialism. A successful Welsh-born manufacturer, Owen bought a cotton mill in New Lanark, Scotland, in 1800 and began to set up a model factory town, where workers labored only ten hours a day (instead of seventeen, as was common). He moved to the United States in the 1820s to establish a community in Indiana named New Harmony. The experiment collapsed after three years, a victim of internal squabbling. Nonetheless, Owen's experiments and writings inspired the movement for producer cooperatives (businesses owned and controlled by their workers), consumer cooperatives (stores in which consumers owned shares), and a national trade union.

Claude Henri de Saint-Simon (1760–1825) and Charles Fourier (1772–1837) were Owen's contemporaries in France. Saint-Simon was a noble who had served as an officer in the American War of Independence and lost a fortune speculating in national property during the French Revolution. Fourier traveled as a salesman for a Lyon cloth merchant. Both shared Owen's alarm about the effects of industrialization on social relations. Saint-Simon coined the terms *industrialism* and *industrialist* to define the new economic order and its chief organizers. He believed that work, the central element in the new society, should be controlled not by politicians but by scientists, engineers, artists, and industrialists. To correct the abuses of the new industrial order, Fourier urged the establishment of communities that were part garden city and part agricultural commune; all jobs would be rotated to maximize happiness. The emancipation of women was essential to Fourier's vision of a harmonious community: "The extension of the privileges of women is the fundamental cause of all social progress."

Women participated actively in the socialist movements of the day, even though socialist men often shared the widespread prejudice against women's political activism. In Great Britain, many women joined the Owenites and helped form cooperative societies and unions. They defended women's working-class organizations against the complaints of men in the new societies and trade unions. As one woman wrote, "Do not say the unions are only for men. . . . 'Tis a wrong impression, forced on our minds to keep us slaves!" As women became more active, Owenites agitated for women's rights, marriage reform, and popular education. In 1832, Saint-Simonian women founded a feminist newspaper in France, *The Free Woman.* Some followers of Saint-Simon's brand of socialism developed a quasi-religious cult with elaborate rituals and a "he-pope" and "she-pope," or ruling father and mother. They lived and worked together in cooperative arrangements and scandalized some by advocating free love.

The French activist Flora Tristan (1801–1844) devoted herself to reconciling the interests of male and female workers. She had seen the "frightful reality" of London's poverty and made a reputation reporting on British working conditions. Tristan published a stream of books and pamphlets urging male workers to address women's unequal status, arguing that "the emancipation of male workers is *impossible* so long as women remain in a degraded state." She advocated the Universal Union of Men and Women Workers.

Even though most male socialists ignored Tristan's plea for women's participation, like her they worked to found working-class associations. French socialist Pierre-Joseph Proudhon (1809–1865) urged workers to form producers' associations so that they could control the work process and eliminate profits made by capitalists. His 1840 book *What Is Property?* argues that property is theft: labor alone is productive, and rent, interest, and profit are unjust.

After 1840, some socialists began to call themselves **communists**, emphasizing their desire to replace private property with communal, collective ownership. The two most influential communists were Karl Marx (1818–1883) and Friedrich Engels (1820–1895), both sons of prosperous German-Jewish families that had converted to Christianity. Marx studied philosophy at the University of Berlin, edited a liberal newspaper until the Prussian government suppressed it, and then left for Paris, where he met Engels. While working in the offices of his wealthy family's cotton manufacturing interests in Manchester, England, Engels had been shocked into writing *The Condition of the Working Class in England in 1844* (1845), a sympathetic depiction of industrial workers' dismal lives. In Paris, where German and eastern European intellectuals could pursue their political interests more freely than at home, Marx and Engels organized the Communist League, in whose name they published *The Communist Manifesto* (1848). It eventually became the touchstone of Marxist and communist revolution all over the world.

Limited as was the influence of Marx and Engels in the 1840s, they had already begun their lifework of scientifically understanding the "laws" of capitalism and fostering revolutionary organizations. Their principles and analysis of history were in place: communists, the *Manifesto* declared, must aim for "the downfall of the bourgeoisie [capitalist class] and the ascendancy of the proletariat [working class], the abolition of the old society based on class conflicts and the foundation of a new society without classes and without private property." Marx and Engels embraced industrialization because they believed it would eventually bring on the proletarian revolution and lead inevitably to the abolition of exploitation, private property, and class society.

Socialism accompanied, and in some places incited, an upsurge in working-class organization in western Europe. In 1824, the British government repealed laws prohibiting labor unions, though it maintained restrictions on strikes. Other European rulers forbade unions. Artisans and skilled workers in France formed mutual aid societies that provided insurance, death benefits, and education. In eastern and central Europe, socialism and labor organization—like liberalism—had less impact than in western Europe. Cooperative societies and workers' newspapers did not appear in the German states until 1848. Working-class organization, even in limited form, struck fear in the hearts of many in the upper classes. A British newspaper exclaimed in 1834, "The trade unions are, we have no doubt, the most dangerous institutions that were ever permitted to take root."

Nationalism

Nationalists could be liberals, socialists, or even conservatives. In the nineteenth century, **nationalism** began as a radical or revolutionary movement and then evolved in a more conservative direction over time. Nationalism holds that all peoples derive their identities from their nations, which are defined by common language, shared cultural traditions, and sometimes religion. When such "nations" do not coincide with state boundaries, as they often did not in the nineteenth and twentieth centuries, nationalism can produce violence and warfare as different national groups compete for control over territory.

The French showed the power of national feeling in their revolutionary and Napoleonic wars, but they also provoked nationalism in the people they conquered. Once Napoleon and his satellite rulers departed, nationalist sentiment turned against other outside rulers—the Ottoman Turks in the Balkans, the Russians in Poland, and the Austrians in Italy. Intellectuals took the lead in demanding unity and freedom for their peoples. They collected folktales, poems, and histories and prepared grammars and dictionaries of their native languages (Map 17.1). Students, middle-class professionals, and army officers formed secret societies to promote national independence and constitutional reform.

Nationalist aspirations were especially explosive for the Austrian Empire, which included a variety of peoples united only by their enforced allegiance to the Habsburg emperor. The empire included three main national groups: the Germans, who made up one-fourth of the population; the Magyars of Hungary (which included Transylvania and Croatia); and the Slavs, who together formed the largest group in the population but were divided into different nationalities such as Poles, Czechs, Croats, and Serbs. The empire also included Italians in Lombardy and Venetia and Romanians in Transylvania. The Austrian government under the Habsburg emperor Francis I (r. 1792–1835) tried to keep nationalist impulses in check with the help of a secret police force set up on the Napoleonic model.

Students in some German states established nationalist student societies, or *Burschenschaften*. In 1817, they held a mass rally at which they burned books they did not like, including Napoleon's Civil Code. One of their leaders, Friedrich Ludwig

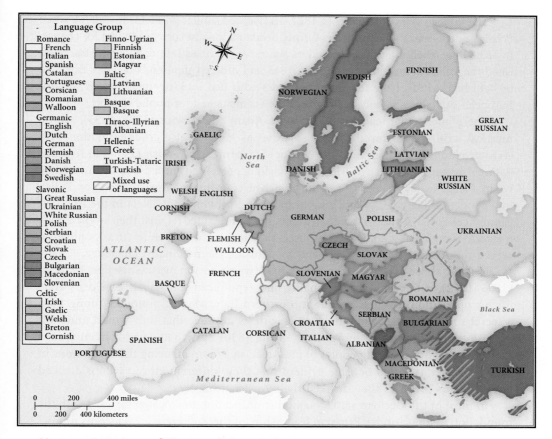

Map 17.1 Languages of Nineteenth-Century Europe
Even this detailed map of linguistic diversity understates the number of different languages and dialects spoken in Europe. In Italy, for example, few Italians spoke Italian as their first language. Instead, they spoke local dialects such as Piedmontese or Ligurian, and some might have spoken better French than Italian if they came from the regions bordering France. How does the map underline the inherent contradictions of nationalism in Europe? What were the consequences of linguistic diversity within national borders? Keep in mind that even in Spain, France, and Great Britain, linguistic diversity continued right up to the beginning of the 1900s.

Jahn, spouted such xenophobic (antiforeign) slogans as "If you let your daughter learn French, you might just as well train her to become a whore." The Austrian government, led by its chief minister, Prince Klemens von Metternich (1773–1859), was convinced that the Burschenschaften in the German states and the carbonari in Italy were linked in an international conspiracy. In 1820, when a student assassinated the playwright August Kotzebue because he ridiculed the student movement, Metternich convinced the leaders of the biggest German states to pass the Karlsbad Decrees dissolving the student societies and more strictly censoring the press. No evidence of a conspiracy was found, but Metternich's efforts to nip dissent in the bud worked.

The Russian tsar Alexander I (r. 1801–1825) faced similar problems in Poland, when Polish students and military officers formed secret nationalist societies to plot for change. In 1830, they rebelled against Alexander's successor, Nicholas I. In reprisal, the tsar abolished the Polish constitution granted in 1815 and ordered thousands of Poles executed or banished. Most of the ten thousand Poles who fled took up residence in western European capitals, especially Paris, where they campaigned for public support.

Their intellectual leader was the poet Adam Mickiewicz (1798–1855), whose mystical writings portrayed the Polish exiles as martyrs of a crucified nation with an international Christian mission. Mickiewicz formed the Polish Legion to fight for national restoration, but rivalries and divisions prevented united action until 1846, when Polish exiles in Paris tried to launch a coordinated insurrection for Polish independence. Plans for an uprising in the Polish province of Galicia in the Austrian Empire collapsed, however, when peasants instead revolted against their noble Polish masters. Slaughtering some two thousand aristocrats, a desperate rural population served the Austrian government's end by defusing the nationalist challenge.

One of those most touched by Mickiewicz's vision was Giuseppe Mazzini (1805–1872), a fiery Italian nationalist and republican journalist. Exiled in 1831 for his opposition to Austrian rule in northern Italy, Mazzini founded Young Italy, a secret society that attracted thousands with its message that Italy would touch off a European revolutionary movement. In the 1830s and 1840s, nationalism spread among the many different peoples of the Austrian Empire. During the revolutions of 1848, however, it would become evident that these different ethnic groups disliked each other as much as they disliked their Austrian masters.

In most of the German states, economic unification took a step forward with the foundation in 1834, under Prussian leadership, of the *Zollverein,* or "customs union." Economist Friedrich List argued that the elimination of tariffs within the borders of the union would promote industrialization and cooperation and enable the union to compete with the rest of Europe. German nationalists sought a government uniting German-speaking peoples, but they could not agree on its boundaries. Austria was not part of the Zollverein. Would the unified German state include both Prussia and the Austrian Empire? If it included Austria, what about the non-German territories of the Austrian Empire? And could the powerful and conservative kingdom of Prussia coexist in a unified German state with other, more liberal but smaller states? These questions would vex German history for decades to come.

In Russia, nationalism took the form of opposition to Western ideas. Russian nationalists, or Slavophiles (lovers of the Slavs), opposed the "Westernizers," who wanted Russia to follow Western models of industrial development and constitutional government. The Slavophiles favored maintaining rural traditions infused by the values of the Russian Orthodox church. Only a return to Russia's basic historical principles, they argued, could protect the country against the corrosion of rationalism and materialism. Slavophiles sometimes criticized the regime, however, because they believed the state exerted too much power over the church. The conflict between Slavophiles and Westernizers continues to shape Russian cultural and intellectual life to the present day.

Nationalism also played a significant role in Ireland. The Irish had struggled for centuries against English occupation, but Irish nationalists developed strong organizations only in the 1840s. In 1842, a group of writers founded the Young Ireland movement that aimed to recover Irish history and preserve the Gaelic language (spoken by at least one-third of the peasantry). Daniel O'Connell (1775–1847), a Catholic lawyer and landowner who sat in the British House of Commons, hoped to force the British Parliament to repeal the Act of Union of 1801, which had made Ireland part of Great Britain. In 1843, London newspapers reported "monster meetings" that drew crowds of as many as 300,000 people in support of repeal of the union. In response, the British government arrested O'Connell and convicted him of conspiracy. More radical leaders, who preached insurrection against the English, replaced him.

Romanticism

More an artistic movement than a true ideology, romanticism glorified nature, emotion, genius, and imagination. It proclaimed these as correctives to the Enlightenment and to classicism in the arts, challenging the reliance on reason, symmetry, and cool, geometric spaces. Classicism idealized models from Roman history; romanticism turned to folklore and medieval legends. Classicism celebrated orderly, crisp lines; romantics sought out all that was wild, fevered, and disorderly. Chief among the romantic arts were poetry, painting, and music, which captured the deep-seated emotion characteristic of romantic expression. George Gordon, Lord Byron (1788–1824), explained his aims in writing poetry:

> For what is Poesy but to create
> From overfeeling, Good and Ill, and aim
> At an external life beyond our fate,
> And be the new Prometheus of new man.

Prometheus was the mythological figure who brought fire from the Greek gods to human beings. Byron did not seek the new Prometheus among the men of industry; he sought him within his own "overfeeling," his own intense emotions.

Romantic poetry elevated the wonders of nature almost to the supernatural. Nature, wrote the English poet William Wordsworth (1770–1850), "to me was all in all." It allowed him to sing "the still, sad music of humanity." Like many poets of his time, Wordsworth greeted the French Revolution with joy. In his poem "French Revolution" (1809), he remembered his early enthusiasm: "Bliss was it in that dawn to be alive." But gradually he became disenchanted with the revolutionary experiment and celebrated British nationalism instead. In 1816, he published a poem to commemorate the "intrepid sons of Albion [England]" who had died at the battle of Waterloo.

Romanticism in painting often expressed anxiety about the coming industrial order while idealizing nature. These concerns came together in an emphasis on the natural landscape. The German romantic painter Caspar David Friedrich (1774–1840) depicted scenes—often in the mountains, far from any factory—that captured the romantic

Caspar David Friedrich, *Wanderer above the Sea of Fog* (1818) Friedrich, a German romantic painter, captured many of the themes most dear to romanticism: melancholy, isolation, and individual communion with nature. He painted trees reaching for the sky and mountains stretching into the distance. Nature to him seemed awesome, powerful, and overshadowing of human perspectives. The French sculptor David d'Angers said of Friedrich, "Here is a man who has discovered the tragedy of landscape." (© Hamburger Kunsthalle, Hamburg/The Bridgeman Art Library.)

fascination with the sublime power of nature. Friedrich hated the new modern world and considered industrialization a disaster. The English painter Joseph M. W. Turner (1775–1851) depicted his vision of nature in mysterious, misty seascapes, anticipating later artists by blurring the outlines of objects. The French painter Eugène Delacroix (1798–1863) chose contemporary as well as medieval scenes of great turbulence to emphasize light and color and to break away from what he saw as "the servile copies repeated *ad nauseam* in academies of art." Critics denounced the new techniques as "painting with a drunken broom." To broaden his experience of light and color, Delacroix traveled in the 1830s to North Africa and painted many exotic scenes in Morocco and Algeria.

Architects of the period sought to recapture a preindustrial world. When the British Houses of Parliament were rebuilt after they burned down in 1834, the architect Sir Charles Barry constructed them in a Gothic style reminiscent of the Middle Ages. This medievalism was taken even further by A. W. N. Pugin, who prepared the Gothic details for the Houses of Parliament. In his polemical book *Contrasts* (1836), Pugin denounced modern conditions and compared them unfavorably with those in the 1400s. To underline his view, Pugin wore medieval clothes at home.

The towering presence of the German composer Ludwig van Beethoven (1770–1827) in early-nineteenth-century music helped establish the direction for musical romanticism. His music, according to one leading German romantic, "sets in motion the lever of fear, of awe, of horror, of suffering, and awakens just that infinite longing which is the essence of Romanticism." Beethoven's symphonies conveyed the impression of growth, a metaphor for the organic process with an emphasis on the natural that was dear to the romantics. For example, his Sixth Symphony, the *Pastoral* (1808), used a variety of instruments to represent sounds heard in the country. Some of his work was explicitly political. His Ninth Symphony (1824), for example, employed a chorus to sing the German poet Friedrich Schiller's verses in praise of universal human solidarity.

If any common political thread linked the romantics, it was support for nationalist aspirations, especially through the search for the historical origins of national identity. The Polish composer and pianist Frédéric Chopin (1810–1849) became a powerful champion for the cause of his native land with music that incorporated Polish folk rhythms and melodies. Lord Byron died fighting for Greek independence. The career of the writer Sir Walter Scott (1771–1832) exemplifies the romantic obsession with history and national identity. He published Scottish ballads that he heard as a child, but after achieving immediate success with his poetry, he switched to historical novels, a genre that he helped create. *Rob Roy* (1817), for example, tells of Scottish resistance to the English in the early eighteenth century. Scott used novels to bring history to life for readers all over Europe. One contemporary critic claimed that "there is more history in the novels of Walter Scott than in half of the historians."

> **REVIEW**   Why did ideologies have such a powerful appeal in the 1830s and 1840s?

Restoration, Revolt, and Revolution

When Napoleon went off to his permanent exile on St. Helena, those allied against him breathed a collective sigh of relief. Revolution, it seemed, had finally been defeated. Even as Napoleon had made his last desperate bid for power, his enemies were meeting in the Congress of Vienna (1814–1815) to decide the fate of post-revolutionary Europe. Many of Europe's monarchs hoped to nullify revolutionary and Napoleonic reforms and "restore" their old regimes. Revolts in the 1820s and especially in 1830 weakened the Vienna settlement, and then a massive series of uprisings in 1848 threatened to demolish it altogether.

The Congress of Vienna and Restoration Europe

The Congress of Vienna produced a new equilibrium that relied on cooperation among the major powers while guaranteeing the status of smaller states. Besides redrawing the boundaries of France and determining who would rule each nation, the congress had to decide the fate of Napoleon's duchy of Warsaw, the German province of Saxony, the Netherlands, the states once part of the Confederation of the Rhine, and various Italian territories. All had either changed hands or been created during the wars. These issues were resolved by face-to-face negotiations among representatives of the five major powers: Austria, Russia, Prussia, Britain, and France.

The Congress of Vienna
An unknown French engraver caricatured the efforts of the diplomats at the Congress of Vienna, complaining that they used the occasion to divide up Europe. What elements in this engraving make it a caricature? (Copyright © Wien Museum.)

With its aim to arrange a long-lasting, negotiated peace endorsed by all parties—both winners and losers—it also established a new framework for international relations based on periodic meetings, or congresses, between the major powers. This congress system, or "concert of Europe," helped prevent another major war until the 1850s, and no conflict comparable to the Napoleonic wars would occur until 1914.

Austria's Metternich took the lead in negotiations. Although his penchant for womanizing made him a security risk in the eyes of the British Foreign Office (he even had an affair with Napoleon's younger sister), he worked with the British prime minister Robert Castlereagh (1769–1822) to ensure a moderate agreement that would check French aggression yet maintain France's great-power status. Metternich and Castlereagh believed that France must remain a major player so that no one European power might dominate the others. In this way, France could help Austria and Britain counter the ambitions of Prussia and Russia.

When the French army failed to oppose Napoleon's return to power in the Hundred Days, the allies took away all territory conquered by France since 1790 and required France to pay an indemnity and support an army of occupation until it was paid. The goal of the congress was to achieve postwar stability by establishing secure states with guaranteed borders (Map 17.2). Where possible, the congress simply restored traditional rulers, as in Spain and the Italian states. The great powers decided to turn Napoleon's duchy of Warsaw into a new Polish kingdom but made

Map 17.2 Europe after the Congress of Vienna, 1815
The Congress of Vienna forced France to return to its 1789 borders. The Austrian Netherlands and the Dutch Republic were united in a new kingdom of the Netherlands; the German states were joined in the German Confederation, which built on Napoleon's Confederation of the Rhine; and Napoleon's duchy of Warsaw became the kingdom of Poland, with the tsar of Russia as king.

the tsar of Russia its king. (Poland would not regain its independence until 1918.) The former Dutch Republic and the Austrian Netherlands, both annexed to France in the preceding years, now united as the new kingdom of the Netherlands under the restored stadholder. Prussia gained territory in Saxony and on the left bank of the Rhine to compensate for its losses in Poland. To make up for its losses in Poland and Saxony, Austria reclaimed the Italian provinces of Lombardy and Venetia and the Dalmatian coast. Austria now presided over the German Confederation, which replaced the defunct Holy Roman Empire and also included Prussia.

The lesser powers were not forgotten. The kingdom of Piedmont-Sardinia took Genoa, Nice, and part of Savoy. Sweden obtained Norway from Denmark but had to accept Russia's conquest of Finland. Finally, various international trade issues were resolved. At the urging of Great Britain, the congress agreed to condemn in principle the slave trade, abolished by Great Britain in 1807. In reality, however, the slave trade continued in many places until the 1840s.

To impart spiritual substance to this very calculated political settlement, Tsar Alexander proposed the Holy Alliance, which would ensure divine assistance in upholding religion, peace, and justice. Prussia and Austria signed the agreement, but Great Britain refused to accede to what Castlereagh called "a piece of sublime mysticism and nonsense." Pope Pius VII also refused on the grounds that the papacy needed no help in interpreting Christian truth. Despite the reassertion of traditional religious principles, the congress had in fact given birth to a new diplomatic order: in the future, the legitimacy of states depended on the treaty system, not on divine right. It was clear that traditional rule could not just be restored in most places. Too much had changed during the French Revolution and the Napoleonic wars.

Religion did play a significant role, nonetheless, in the effort to revive traditional values. Many Europeans felt that the French Revolution and Napoleonic domination had undermined the religious fabric of society. Restoration, for most rulers, meant renewing the authority of the Catholic church as well. In France, the church sent missionaries to hold open-air "ceremonies of reparation" to express repentance for the outrages of the Revolution. In Rome, the papacy reestablished the Jesuit order, which had been disbanded during the Enlightenment. In the Italian states and Spain, governments used religious societies of laypeople to combat the influence of reformers and nationalists. For conservative rulers, religion was a necessary foundation for political and social order.

The First Cracks in the Vienna Settlement

Attempts to restore traditional rule soon provoked resistance. After Ferdinand VII regained the Spanish crown in 1814, he had foreign books and newspapers confiscated at the frontier and allowed the publication of only two newspapers. In 1820, disgruntled soldiers demanded that Ferdinand proclaim his adherence to the constitution of 1812, which he had abolished in 1814. Ferdinand stalled for time, and in 1823 a French army invaded with the consent of the other Vienna powers to support him. His government then tortured and executed hundreds of rebels; thousands were imprisoned or forced into exile. Nothing was spared to crush dissent.

Hearing of the Spanish uprising, rebellious soldiers in the kingdom of Naples joined forces with the carbonari and demanded a constitution. But when a new parliament met, it broke down over internal disagreements. The promise of reform sparked rebellion in the northern Italian kingdom of Piedmont-Sardinia, where rebels urged Charles Albert, the young heir to the Piedmont throne, to fight the Austrians for Italian unification. He vacillated, and in 1821, after the rulers of Austria, Prussia, and Russia met and agreed on intervention, the Austrians defeated the rebels in Naples and Piedmont (Map 17.2, page 663). Despite the opposition of

Great Britain, which condemned the "indiscriminate" suppression of revolutionary movements, Metternich convinced the other powers to agree to his muffling of the Italian opposition to Austrian rule.

Aspirations for constitutional government surfaced in Russia when Alexander I died in 1825. On the December day that the troops assembled in St. Petersburg to take an oath of loyalty to Alexander's brother Nicholas as the new tsar, rebel officers insisted that the crown belonged to another brother, Constantine, whom they hoped would be more favorable to constitutional reform. Constantine, though next in the line of succession after Alexander, had refused the crown. The soldiers nonetheless raised the cry "Long live Constantine; long live the Constitution." Soldiers loyal to Nicholas easily suppressed the outnumbered Decembrists (so called after the month of their uprising). For the next thirty years, Nicholas I used a new political police force to spy on potential opponents and stamp out rebelliousness.

The Ottoman Turks faced growing nationalist challenges in the Balkans, but the European powers feared that supporting them would encourage a rebellious spirit at home. The Serbs nonetheless revolted against Turkish rule and won virtual independence by 1817. An uprising by Greek peasants sparked a wave of mutual atrocities in 1821 and 1822. In retaliation for the killing of many Turks, the Ottoman authorities hanged the Greek patriarch (head of the Greek Orthodox church), and in the areas they still controlled, the Turks pillaged churches, massacred thousands of men, and sold the women into slavery.

Nationalistic Movements in the Balkans, 1815–1830

Western opinion turned against the Turks; Greece, after all, was the home of Western civilization. While the great powers negotiated, Greeks and pro-Greece committees around the world sent food and military supplies; a few enthusiastic European and American volunteers even joined the Greeks. The Greeks held on until the great powers were willing to intervene. In 1827, a combined force of British, French, and Russian ships destroyed the Turkish fleet at Navarino Bay, and in 1828 Russia declared war on the Turks and advanced close to Istanbul. The Treaty of Adrianople (1829) gave Russia a protectorate over the Danubian principalities (now part of Romania) and provided for a conference among representatives of Britain, Russia, and France, all of whom had broken with Austria in support of the Greeks. In 1830, Greece was declared an independent kingdom under the guarantee of the three powers. Nationalism, with the support of European public opinion, had opened a hole in Metternich's system.

Greek Independence

From 1836 to 1839, the Greek painter Panagiotis Zographos worked with his two sons on a series of scenes depicting the Greek struggle for independence from the Turks. The response was so favorable that one Greek general ordered lithographic reproductions for popular distribution. Nationalistic feeling could thus be encouraged even among those who were not directly touched by the struggle. Here the Turkish sultan Mehmet the Conqueror, exulting over the fall of Constantinople in 1453, views a row of Greeks under the yoke, a sign of submission. **For more help analyzing this image, see the visual activity for this chapter in the Online Study Guide at** bedfordstmartins.com/huntconcise. (The Visual Connection.)

Across the Atlantic, national revolts also succeeded after a series of bloody wars of independence. Taking advantage of the upheavals in Spain and Portugal that had begun under Napoleon, restive colonists from Mexico to Argentina rebelled. Their most important leader was Simón Bolívar (1783–1830), the son of a slave owner, who was educated in Europe on the works of Voltaire and Rousseau. With help from newly independent Haiti and in exchange for agreeing to abolish slavery, Bolívar liberated the lands of northern South America (Venezuela, Colombia, Ecuador, Panama, and eventually Peru and Bolivia) from Spanish rule (Map 17.3). Although Bolívar fancied himself a Latin American Napoleon, he had to acquiesce to the formation of a series of independent republics between 1821 and 1823, even in Bolivia, which is named after him. At the same time, Brazil (then still a monarchy) separated from Portugal. The United States recognized the new states, and in 1823 President James Monroe (1758–1831) announced his Monroe Doctrine, closing the Americas to European intervention—a prohibition that depended on

Map 17.3 Latin American Independence, 1804–1830
Napoleon's occupation of Spain and Portugal seriously weakened the hold of those countries on their Latin American colonies. Despite the restoration of the Spanish and Portuguese rulers in 1814, most of their colonies successfully broke away in a wave of rebellions between 1811 and 1830. **For more help analyzing this map, see the map activity for this chapter in the Online Study Guide at** bedfordstmartins .com/huntconcise.

British naval power and British willingness to declare neutrality. The Vienna powers were able to maintain their settlement only in areas where they could intervene militarily.

The Revolutions of 1830

Although the restored Bourbon monarchy in France worked in concert with the other great powers to maintain the Vienna settlement, at home it had to confront the legacy of twenty-five years of upheaval. Louis XVIII (r. 1814–1824) tried to ensure a measure of continuity by maintaining Napoleon's Civil Code and confirming the rights of ownership to church lands sold during the revolutionary period. He created a parliament composed of the Chamber of Peers, nominated by the king, and the Chamber of Deputies, elected by highly restricted suffrage (fewer than 100,000 voters in a population of 30 million). The Ultras (ultraroyalists) pushed for a more complete repudiation of the revolutionary past, including the abolition of divorce. When an assassin killed Louis XVIII's nephew in 1820, the Ultras demanded even more extreme measures.

The Ultras got the ear of the king when Charles X (r. 1824–1830), the younger brother of Louis XVIII, succeeded to the throne. He pushed through the Law of

Indemnity in 1825 to compensate nobles for the loss of their lands during the French Revolution. At the same time, he insisted on the Law of Sacrilege, imposing the death penalty for offenses such as stealing religious objects from churches. He ultimately dissolved the legislature and imposed strict censorship. Spontaneous demonstrations in Paris led to fighting on July 26, 1830. After three days of street battles in which 500 citizens and 150 soldiers died, a group of moderate liberal leaders, fearing the reestablishment of a republic, agreed to offer the crown to Charles X's cousin Louis-Philippe, duke of Orléans.

Charles X went into exile in England, and the new king extended political liberties and voting rights. Although the number of voting men nearly doubled, it remained minuscule. Such reforms did little for the poor and working classes, who had manned the barricades in July. Dissatisfaction with the 1830 settlement boiled over in Lyon in 1831, when a silk workers' strike over wages turned into a rebellion that died down only when the army arrived. Revolution had broken the hold of those who wanted to restore the pre-1789 monarchy and nobility, but it had gone no further than installing a more liberal, constitutional monarchy.

The success of the July revolution in Paris ignited the Belgians, whose country had been annexed to the kingdom of the Netherlands in 1815. Differences in traditions, language, and religion separated the largely Catholic Belgians from the Dutch. King William of the Netherlands appealed to the great powers for help, but Great Britain and France opposed intervention and invited Russia, Austria, and Prussia to a conference that guaranteed Belgium independence in exchange for its neutrality in international affairs. Belgian neutrality would remain a cornerstone of European diplomacy for a century.

European Influence Overseas

When the new Latin American republics abolished slavery in the 1820s and 1830s, they helped put slavery back on the European agenda. Despite British efforts to end the European slave trade, more than 3 million slaves were transported to the Americas between 1801 and 1850, and slavery still continued even in the British colonies. As many as 350,000 British women signed one major petition to Parliament demanding the abolition of slavery in the British colonies. Parliament finally agreed in 1833. In France, the new government of Louis-Philippe took strong measures against clandestine slave traffic, virtually ending French participation in the slave trade during the 1830s. Slavery was abolished in the remaining French Caribbean colonies in 1848.

Slavery did not disappear immediately just because the major European powers had given it up. Although the transatlantic trade in slaves dwindled away after 1850, human bondage continued unabated in Brazil, Cuba (still a Spanish colony), and the United States. Some American reformers supported abolition, but it remained a minority movement. Like serfdom in Russia, slavery in the Americas involved a quagmire of economic, political, and moral problems that worsened over time.

As Europeans turned their interest away from the plantation colonies of the Caribbean toward colonies in Asia and Africa, they developed new forms of colonial rule. Colonialism became **imperialism**—a term first coined in the mid-nineteenth century. Colonialism most often led to the establishment of settler colonies, direct rule by Europeans, slave labor from Africa, and the wholesale destruction of indigenous peoples. In contrast, imperialism usually meant more indirect forms of economic exploitation and political rule. Europeans still aimed to derive economic profit from their colonies, but now they also wanted to reform colonial peoples in their own image.

In the 1830s and 1840s, France and Britain continued to extend their influence across the globe. Using the pretext of an insult to its envoy, France invaded the North African country of Algeria in 1830 and after a long military campaign established political control over most of the region in the next two decades. By 1850, more than seventy thousand French, Italian, and Maltese colonists had settled in Algeria, often confiscating the lands of native peoples. Eventually France would not only incorporate Algeria into France but also try to assimilate its native population to French culture. France also imposed a protectorate government over the South Pacific island of Tahiti.

Although the British granted Canada greater self-determination in 1839, they extended their dominion elsewhere by annexing Singapore (1819), an island off the Malay peninsula, and New Zealand (1840). They also increased their control in India through the administration of the East India Company, a private group of merchants chartered by the British crown. The British educated a native elite to take over much of the day-to-day business of administering the country and used native soldiers to augment their military control. By 1850, only one in six soldiers serving Britain in India was European.

The East India Company also tried to establish a regular trade with China in **opium**, a drug long known for its medicinal uses but increasingly bought in China as a recreational drug. Bypassing the efforts of the Chinese government to ban the import of opium, British traders smuggled opium grown in India into China and, by bribing local officials, built up a flourishing market. When in 1839 the Chinese authorities expelled British merchants from southern China, Britain retaliated by bombarding Chinese coastal cities, beginning the First Opium War. In 1842, it dictated to a defeated China the Treaty of Nanking, by which the British forced the opening of four more Chinese ports to Europeans, took sovereignty over the island of

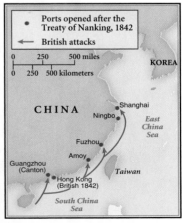

The First Opium War, 1839–1842

Hong Kong, received a substantial war indemnity, and were assured of a continuation of the opium trade. The complaints of religious groups in Britain fell on deaf ears.

The Revolutions of 1848

Imperialist ventures abroad continued even as the revolutionary legacy revived again in Europe in 1848. As in 1789, food shortages and constitutional crises fueled the rebellion, but now class tensions and nationalist impulses sparked outbreaks in capitals across Europe. Crop failures in many countries threatened the food supply, and food prices shot skyward. In the best of times, urban workers paid 50 percent of their income for a diet consisting largely of bread or potatoes; now even those foods were beyond workers' means. Overpopulation hastened famine in some places, especially Ireland, where an airborne blight destroyed the potato crop in 1846, 1848, and 1851. Out of a population of eight million, as many as one million people died of starvation and disease. Corpses lay unburied on the sides of roads, and whole families were found dead in their cottages, half-eaten by dogs. Hundreds of thousands emigrated to England, the United States, and Canada.

High food prices also drove down the demand for manufactured goods, resulting in increased unemployment. Industrial workers' wages had been rising—in the German states, for example, wages rose an average of 5.5 percent in the 1830s and 10.5 percent in the 1840s—but the cost of living rose about 16 percent each decade, canceling out wage increases. Seasonal work and regular unemployment were already the norm when the crisis of the late 1840s intensified the uncertainties of urban life. "The most miserable class that ever sneaked its way into history" is how Friedrich Engels described underemployed and starving workers in 1847.

The Irish Famine
Contemporary engravings such as this one from 1847 drew attention to the plight of Irish peasants when a blight infected potato plants, destroying Ireland's single most important staple crop. In this illustration, a girl turns up the ground looking for potatoes, while a starving boy looks dazed. The artist reported seeing six dead bodies nearby. (The Granger Collection, NY.)

The specter of hunger tarnished the image of established rulers and amplified voices critical of them. Louis-Philippe's government had blocked all moves for electoral reform, and in February 1848, a campaign for reform sponsored by the liberal opposition turned into a revolution. At first the police and the army dispersed the demonstrators who took to the streets on February 22, 1848. The next day, however, forty or fifty people died when panicky soldiers opened fire on the crowd. On February 24, faced with fifteen hundred barricades and a furious populace, Louis-Philippe abdicated and fled to England. A hastily formed provisional government declared France a republic once again.

The new republican government issued liberal reforms—an end to the death penalty for political crimes, the abolition of slavery in the colonies, and freedom of the press—and agreed to introduce universal adult male suffrage despite misgivings about political participation by peasants and unemployed workers. To address the gnawing problem of unemployment, the government allowed Paris officials to organize a system of "national workshops" to provide those out of jobs with construction work. When women protested their exclusion, the city set up a few workshops for women workers, albeit with wages lower than men's. To meet a mounting deficit, the provisional government then levied a 45 percent surtax on property taxes, alienating peasants and landowners.

The establishment of the republic politicized many segments of the population. Scores of newspapers and political clubs revived grassroots democratic fervor; meeting in concert halls, theaters, and government auditoriums, clubs became a regular attraction for the citizenry. Women also formed clubs, published women's newspapers, and demanded representation in national politics. Street-corner activism alarmed middle-class liberals and conservatives. To maintain control, the republican government paid some unemployed youths to join a mobile guard with its own uniforms and barracks. Tension between the government and the workers in the national workshops rose; class warfare loomed like a thunderstorm on the horizon.

Revolutions of 1848

1848

February	Revolution in Paris; proclamation of a republic
March	Insurrections in Vienna, German cities, Milan, and Venice; autonomy movement in Hungary; Charles Albert of Piedmont-Sardinia declares war on Austrian Empire
May	Frankfurt parliament opens
June	Austrian army crushes revolutionary movement in Prague; June Days end in defeat of workers in Paris
July	Austrians defeat Charles Albert and Italian forces
November	Insurrection drives the pope out of Rome
December	Francis Joseph becomes Austrian emperor; Louis-Napoleon elected president of France

1849

February	Rome declared a republic
April	Frederick William of Prussia rejects crown of united Germany offered by Frankfurt parliament
July	Roman republic overthrown by French intervention
August	Russian and Austrian armies combine to defeat Hungarian forces

Faced with rising radicalism in Paris and other big cities, the voters elected a largely conservative National Assembly in April 1848, which immediately appointed a five-man executive committee to run the government and deliberately excluded known supporters of workers' rights. Suspicious of all demands for rapid change, the deputies dismissed a petition to restore divorce and voted down woman suffrage, 899 to 1. When the numbers enrolled in the national workshops in Paris rocketed from a predicted 10,000 to 110,000, the government ordered the workshops closed to new workers, and on June 21 it directed that those already enrolled move to the provinces or join the army.

The workers of Paris responded to these measures on June 23 by taking to the streets in the tens of thousands. In the June Days, as the following week came to be called, the government summoned the army, the National Guard, and the newly recruited mobile guard to fight the workers. Provincial volunteers came to help put down the workers, who had been depicted as lazy ruffians intent on destroying order and property. One observer breathed a sigh of relief: "The Red Republic [red being associated with demands for socialism] is lost forever; all France has joined against it. The National Guard, citizens, and peasants from the remotest parts of the country have come pouring in." The republic's army crushed the protesters; more than 10,000 were killed or injured, 12,000 were arrested, and 4,000 eventually were convicted and deported.

When the National Assembly adopted a new constitution calling for a presidential election in which all adult men could vote, the electorate chose Louis-Napoleon Bonaparte, nephew of the dead emperor. Bonaparte got more than 5.5 million votes out of some 7.4 million cast. He had lived most of his life outside France, and the leaders of the republic expected him to follow their tune. In uncertain times, the Bonaparte name promised something to everyone. Even many workers supported him because he had no connection with the blood-drenched June Days.

In reality, Bonaparte's election spelled the end of the Second Republic, just as his uncle had dismantled the first one, established in 1792. In 1852, on the forty-eighth anniversary of Napoleon I's coronation as emperor, Louis-Napoleon declared himself Emperor Napoleon III (r. 1852–1870). (Napoleon I's son died and never became Napoleon II, but Napoleon III wanted to create a sense of legitimacy and so used the Roman numeral III.) Political division and class conflict had proved fatal to the Second Republic. Although the revolution of 1848 never had a period of terror like that in 1793–1794, it nonetheless ended in a similar fashion, with an authoritarian government that played monarchists and republicans off against each other.

The Parisian uprising galvanized Italian nationalists. Armed demonstrators took on the Austrians in Milan and actually drove them out of Venice. Peasants in the south occupied their landowners' estates, while across central Italy the poor and

The Divisions of Italy, 1848

unemployed rose up against local rulers. But class tensions and regional differences still stood in the way of Italian national unity. Some nationalists favored a loose federation; others wanted a monarchy under Charles Albert of Piedmont-Sardinia; still others urged rule by the pope. A few shared Mazzini's Young Italy movement vision of a republic with a strong central government. Many leaders of national unification spoke Italian only as a second language; most Italians spoke regional dialects.

As king of the most powerful Italian state, Charles Albert played a central role. After some hesitation caused by fears of French intervention, he led a military campaign against Austria. It failed, partly because of dissension over goals and tactics among the nationalists. Although Austrian troops defeated Charles Albert in the north in the summer of 1848, democratic and nationalist forces prevailed at first in the south. In the fall, the insurgents drove the pope from the city, and in February 1849 they declared Rome a republic. For the next few months republican leaders, such as Mazzini and Giuseppe Garibaldi (1807–1882), congregated in Rome to organize the new republic. These efforts faltered in July when foreign powers intervened. The new president of republican France, Louis-Napoleon Bonaparte, sent an expeditionary force to secure the papal throne for Pius IX (r. 1846–1878). Mazzini and Garibaldi fled. Although revolution had been defeated in Italy, the memory of the Roman republic and the commitment to unification remained, and they would soon emerge again with new force.

News of the revolution in Paris also provoked popular demonstrations in the German states. "My heart beat with joy. The monarchy had fallen. Only a little blood had been shed for such a high stake, and the great watchwords Liberty, Equality, Fraternity were again inscribed on the banner of the movement." So responded one Frankfurt woman to Louis-Philippe's overthrow. The Prussian army's efforts to clear the square in front of Berlin's royal palace on March 18, 1848, provoked panic and street fighting around hastily assembled barricades. The next day the crowd paraded wagons loaded with dead bodies under King Frederick William IV's window, forcing him to salute the victims killed by his own army. In a state of near collapse, the king promised to call an assembly to draft a constitution and adopted the German nationalist flag of black, red, and gold.

The goal of German unification soon took precedence over social reform or constitutional changes within the separate states. In March and April 1848, most of the German states agreed to elect delegates to a federal parliament at Frankfurt that would attempt to unite Germany. Local princes and even the more powerful kings of Prussia and Bavaria seemed to totter. In Bavaria, students marched to "La Marseillaise" and called for a republic. Yet the revolutionaries' weaknesses soon became apparent. The eight hundred delegates to the Frankfurt parliament had little practical political experience: "a group of old women," one socialist called them; a "Professors Parliament" was the common sneer. These delegates had no access to an army, and they dreaded the demands of the lower classes for social reforms.

Unemployed artisans and workers smashed machines; peasants burned landlords' records and occasionally attacked Jewish moneylenders; women established clubs and newspapers to demand their emancipation from "perfumed slavery." The advantage lay with the princes, who retained legal authority and control over the armed forces. The most powerful German states, Prussia and Austria, expected to determine whether and how Germany should unite. While the Frankfurt parliament laboriously prepared a liberal constitution for a united Germany—one that denied self-determination to Czechs, Poles, and Danes within its proposed German borders—the Prussian king Frederick William IV (r. 1840–1860) recovered his confidence. First his army crushed the revolution in Berlin in the fall of 1848. Prussian troops then intervened to help other local rulers put down the last wave of democratic and nationalist insurrections in the spring. In April 1849, when the Frankfurt parliament finally concluded its work, offering the emperorship of a constitutional, federal Germany to the king of Prussia, Frederick William contemptuously refused this "crown from the gutter."

Events followed a similar course in the Austrian Empire. Just as Italians were driving the Austrians out of their lands in northern Italy and Magyar nationalists were demanding political autonomy for Hungary, on March 13, 1848, a student-led demonstration for political reform in Vienna turned into rioting, looting, and machine breaking. Metternich resigned, escaping to England in disguise. The Austrian emperor Ferdinand I (r. 1835–1848) promised a constitution, an elected parliament, and the end of censorship. Beleaguered authorities in Vienna could not refuse Magyar demands for home rule, and the Hungarian nationalist Lajos Kossuth became a minister in the new Hungarian government.

Ethnic, political, and social conflicts divided the revolutionaries. The Magyars were the largest ethnic group in Hungary but still did not make up 50 percent of the population, which included Romanians, Slovaks, Croats, and Slovenes, who preferred Austrian rule to domination by local Magyars. The new Hungarian government alienated the other nationalities when it imposed the Magyar language on them. Fears of peasant insurrection prompted the Magyar nationalists around Kossuth to abolish serfdom, but this measure alienated the largest noble landowners. In Prague, Czech nationalists convened a Slav congress as a counter to the Germans' Frankfurt parliament and called for a reorganization of the Austrian Empire that would recognize the rights of ethnic minorities. Such assertiveness by non-German peoples provoked German nationalists to protest on behalf of German-speaking people in areas with a Czech or Magyar majority.

The Austrian government slowly took advantage of these divisions. To quell peasant discontent and appease liberal reformers, it abolished all remaining peasant obligations to the nobility in March 1848. Rejoicing country folk soon lost interest in the revolution. Military force finally broke up the revolutionary movements. The first blow fell in Prague in June 1848. General Prince Alfred von Windischgrätz, the military governor, bombarded the city into submission when a demonstration led to violence (including the shooting death of his wife, watching from a window). After another uprising in Vienna a few months later, Windischgrätz marched 70,000 soldiers into the capital and set up direct military rule. In December, the Austrian monarchy came back to life when the eighteen-year-old Francis Joseph (r. 1848–1916), unencumbered by promises extracted by the revolutionaries from his now feeble uncle Ferdinand, assumed the imperial crown after intervention by leading court officials. In the spring of 1849, General Count Joseph Radetzky defeated the last Italian challenges to Austrian power in northern Italy, and his army moved east, joining with Croats and Serbs to take on the Hungarian rebels. In August, the Austrian army teamed up with Tsar Nicholas I, who marched into Hungary with more than 300,000 Russian troops. Hungary was put under brutal martial law. Kossuth sought refuge in the United States. Social conflicts and ethnic divisions weakened the revolutionary movements from the inside and gave the Austrian government the opening it needed to restore its position.

The Aftermath of 1848

The revolutionaries of 1848 failed to achieve most of their goals, but their efforts left a profound mark on the political and social landscape. Between 1848 and 1851, the French served a kind of republican apprenticeship that prepared the population for another, more lasting republic after 1870. No French government could henceforth rule without extensive popular consultation. In Italy, the failure of unification did not stop the spread of nationalist ideas and the rooting of demands for democratic participation. In the German states, the revolutionaries of 1848 turned nationalism from an academic idea into a popular movement. The very idea of the Frankfurt parliament and the insistence on brandishing a German national flag at demonstrations showed that German nationalism had become a practical reality. The initiation of artisans, workers, and journeymen into democratic clubs increased political awareness in the lower classes and helped prepare them for broader political participation. Almost every German state had a constitution and a parliament after 1850. The spectacular failures of 1848 thus hid some important successes.

The absence of revolution in 1848 was just as significant as its presence. No revolution occurred in Great Britain, the Netherlands, or Belgium, the three places where industrialization and urbanization had developed most rapidly. In Great Britain, the prospects for revolution actually seemed quite good. Many British workers joined in **Chartism**, a movement that aimed to transform Britain into a democracy. In 1838, political radicals had drawn up the People's Charter, which demanded universal manhood suffrage, vote by secret ballot, equal electoral districts, annual elections, and the elimination of property qualifications for and the payment of stipends to members of Parliament. Chartists denounced their opponents as seeking "to keep the people in social slavery and political degradation." Many women took part by founding female political unions, setting up Chartist Sunday schools, organizing boycotts of unsympathetic shopkeepers, and joining Chartist temperance associations. Nevertheless, the People's Charter refrained from calling for woman suffrage because the movement's leaders feared that doing so would alienate potential supporters.

The Chartists organized a massive campaign during 1838 and 1839, with large public meetings, fiery speeches, and torchlight parades. Presented with petitions for the People's Charter signed by more than a million people, the House of Commons refused to act. In response to this rebuff from middle-class liberals, the Chartists

The Revolution of 1848 in Eastern Europe
This painting by an unknown artist shows Ana Ipatescu leading a group of Romanian revolutionaries in Transylvania in opposition to Russian rule. In April 1848, local landowners began to organize meetings. Paris-educated nationalists spearheaded the movement, which demanded the end of Russian control and various legal and political reforms. By August, the movement had split between those who wanted independence only and those who were pushing for the end of serfdom and for universal manhood suffrage. In response, the Russians invaded Moldavia, and the Turks moved into Walachia. By October, the uprising was over. Russia and Turkey agreed to control the provinces jointly. (The Art Archive.)

allied themselves in the 1840s with working-class strike movements in the manufacturing districts and associated with various European revolutionary movements.

Inspired by the outbreak of nearly simultaneous revolutions in 1848, the Chartists mounted several gigantic demonstrations to force Parliament into granting all adult males the vote. But Parliament refused and no uprising occurred, in part because the government had already proved its responsiveness. The middle classes in Britain had been co-opted into the established order by the Reform Bill of 1832, and the working classes had won parliamentary regulation of children's and women's work.

The other notable exception to revolution among the great powers was Russia, where Tsar Nicholas I maintained a tight grip through police surveillance and censorship. The Russian schools, limited to the upper classes, taught Nicholas's three most cherished principles: autocracy (the unlimited power of the tsar), orthodoxy (obedience to the church in religion and morality), and nationality (devotion to Russian traditions). These provided no space for political dissent. Social conditions also fostered political passivity: serfdom continued in force, and the slow rate of industrial and urban growth created little discontent.

For all the differences between countries, some developments touched them all. European states continued to expand their bureaucracies. For example, in 1750 the Russian government employed approximately 10,500 functionaries; a century later it needed almost 114,000. New government agencies such as the British urban police forces (10,000 strong in the 1840s) intruded increasingly in ordinary people's lives. States wanted to take children out of the fields and factories where they worked with their families and educate them. And in some German cities, the police reported people who cleared snow off their roofs after the permitted hour or smoked in the streets, reflecting the expansion of government powers.

Although much had changed, the aristocracy remained the dominant power in most places. As army officers, aristocrats put down revolutionary forces. As landlords, they continued to dominate the rural scene and control parliamentary bodies. They also held many official positions in the state bureaucracies. One Italian princess explained, "There are doubtless men capable of leading the nation . . . but their names are unknown to the people, whereas those of noble families . . . are in every memory." Aristocrats kept their authority by adapting to change: they entered the bureaucracy and professions, turned their estates into moneymaking enterprises, and learned how to invest shrewdly.

The reassertion of conservative rule hardened gender definitions. Women everywhere had participated in the revolutions, especially in the Italian states, where they had joined armies in the tens of thousands and applied household skills to making bandages, clothing, and food. Schoolgirls in Prague had thrown desks and chairs out windows and helped build students' barricades. Many women in Paris had supported the new republic and seized the occasion of greater political openness to demand women's rights, only to experience isolation as their claims were denied by most republican men. Men in the revolutions of 1848 almost always defined universal suffrage as a male right. When workingmen gained the vote and women did not, the notion of separate spheres penetrated even into working-class life: political participation became one more way to distinguish masculinity from femininity. As conservatives returned to power, all signs of women's political activism disappeared. The French feminist movement, the most advanced in Europe, fell apart after the June Days, when the increasingly conservative republican government forbade women to form political clubs and arrested and imprisoned two of the most outspoken women leaders for their socialist activities.

In May 1851, Europe's most important female monarch presided over a midcentury celebration of peace and industrial growth that helped dampen the still smoldering fires of revolutionary passion. Queen Victoria (r. 1837–1901), who herself promoted the notion of domesticity as women's sphere, opened the international Exhibition of the Works of Industry of All Nations in London on May 1. A monument of modern iron and glass architecture had been constructed to house the display; the building

The Crystal Palace, 1851
George Baxter's lithograph shows the exterior of the main building for the Exhibition of the Works of Industry of All Nations in London. It was designed by Sir Joseph Paxton to gigantic dimensions: 1,848 feet long, 456 feet wide, and 135 feet high—772,784 square feet of ground-floor area covering no less than 18 acres. (© Maidstone Museum and Art Gallery, Kent, England/The Bridgeman Art Library.)

was more than a third of a mile long and so tall that it was erected over the trees of its Hyde Park site. Soon people referred to it as the Crystal Palace; its nine hundred tons of glass created an aura of fantasy, and the abundant goods from all nations inspired satisfaction and pride. One German visitor described it as "this miracle which has so suddenly appeared to dazzle the inhabitants of our globe." In the place of revolutionary fervor, the Crystal Palace offered a government-sponsored spectacle of what industry, hard work, and technological imagination could produce.

REVIEW   Why did the revolutions of 1848 fail?

Conclusion

Many of the six million people who visited the Crystal Palace display traveled there on railroads and wore the cheaper cotton clothing produced by workers in mechanized textile factories. They had not forgotten the threat of disease, fears of overpopulation, and lingering popular resentments. The revolutions of 1848, in particular, had brought to the surface the profound tensions within a European society in transition toward industrialization and modernization. Industrialization and urbanization continued; workers developed more extensive organizations; and liberals, conservatives, and socialists fought over the pace of reform.

Mapping the West Industrialization in Europe, c. 1850
Industrialization first spread across northern Europe in a band that included Great Britain, northern France and the region around Lyon, Belgium, the northern German states, the region around Milan in northern Italy, and Bohemia. Much of Scandinavia and southern and eastern Europe did not participate in this first phase of industrial development. Although railroads were not the only factor in promoting industrialization, the map makes clear the interrelationship between railroad building and the development of new industrial sites of coal mining and textile production.

The Congress of Vienna had sought to clamp a lid on the various forces that threatened political and social order, and for some time the major powers succeeded in holding back demands for change. Nationalist aspirations, desires for constitutional rights, and calls for social reform proved impossible to contain, however, and revolts and revolutions repeatedly broke through. Confronted with these prospects, elites hoped to find alternatives that would be less threatening to the established order. This search for alternatives became immediately evident over the next two decades in the question of national unification in Germany and Italy. National unification would hereafter depend on what the Prussian leader Otto von Bismarck would call "blood and iron," not speeches and parliamentary resolutions.

CHAPTER REVIEW QUESTIONS

1. Which of the ideologies of this period had the greatest impact on political events? How can you explain this?
2. In what ways might industrialization be considered a force for peaceful change rather than a revolution? (Hint: Consider the situation in Great Britain.)

TIMELINE

■ **1839** First Opium War between Britain and China begins

■ **1824** Ludwig van Beethoven composes his Ninth Symphony

■ **1834** German customs union (*Zollverein*) established under Prussian leadership

■ **1820** Revolt of liberal army officers against the Spanish crown; Karlsbad Decrees abolish German student societies and tighten press censorship

■ **1833** Factory Act regulates the work of children in Great Britain; slavery abolished in the British Empire

■ **1851** Crystal Palace exhibition in London

| 1815 | 1827 | 1839 | 1851 |

1814–1815 Congress of Vienna

■ **1825** Russian army officers demand constitutional reform in the Decembrist uprising

■ **1846** Famine strikes Ireland; Britain repeals the Corn Laws; peasant insurrection in the Austrian province of Galicia

■ **1819** Peterloo massacre in Manchester, England

■ **1830** Liverpool and Manchester Railway Line opens in England; Greece gains independence from Ottoman Turks; France invades and begins conquest of Algeria; rebels overthrow Charles X of France and install Louis-Philippe; cholera epidemic begins in Europe

■ **1847** Charlotte Brontë, *Jane Eyre*

■ **1831** Belgium becomes an independent country

■ **1848** Last great wave of Chartist demonstrations in Britain; Karl Marx and Friedrich Engels, *The Communist Manifesto*; revolutions of 1848 throughout Europe; slavery abolished in French colonies; serfdom ended in Austrian Empire

■ **1832** British Parliament passes the Reform Bill

For practice quizzes and other study tools, see the Online Study Guide at bedfordstmartins.com/huntconcise.

For primary-source material from this period, see Chapters 20 and 21 of *Sources of THE MAKING OF THE WEST,* Third Edition.

Suggested References

The spread of industrialization has elicited much more historical interest than the process of urbanization because the analysis of industrialization occupied a central role in Marxism. The Web site Gallica, produced by the National Library of France, offers a wealth of imagery and information on French cultural history.

Davidoff, Leonore, and Catherine Hall. *Family Fortunes: Men and Women of the English Middle Class, 1780–1850.* 1987.

Dickens Project: http://humwww.ucsc.edu/dickens

Gallica: Images and Texts from Nineteenth-Century French-Speaking Culture: http://gallica.bnf.fr

Hobsbawm, E. J. *The Age of Revolution, 1789–1848.* 1996.

Johnson, Paul. *The Birth of the Modern: World Society, 1815–1830.* 1991.

Kahan, Alan S. *Liberalism in Nineteenth-Century Europe: The Political Culture of Limited Suffrage.* 2003.

Kramer, Lloyd S. *Nationalism: Political Cultures in Europe and America, 1775–1865.* 1998.

Laven, David, and Lucy Riall, eds. *Napoleon's Legacy: Problems of Government in Restoration Europe.* 2000.

*Marx, Karl, and Frederick Engels. *The Communist Manifesto: With Related Documents.* Ed. John E. Toews. 1999.

McLean, Stuart. *The Event and Its Terrors: Ireland, Famine, Modernity.* 2004.

Mokyr, Joel. *The Enlightened Economy: An Economic History of Britain, 1700–1850.* 2009.

Murray, Christopher John, ed. *Encyclopedia of the Romantic Era, 1760–1850.* 2004.

*Pollard, S., and C. Holmes. *Documents of European Economic History.* Vol. 1, *The Process of Industrialization, 1750–1870.* 1968.

Romantic Chronology: http://english.ucsb.edu:591/rchrono

Sperber, Jonathan. *The European Revolutions, 1848–1851.* 2d ed. 2005.

Thompson, E. P. *The Making of the English Working Class.* 1964.

Constructing the Nation-State

IN 1859, THE NAME "VERDI" suddenly appeared scrawled on walls across the disunited cities of the Italian peninsula. The graffiti seemed to celebrate the composer Giuseppe Verdi, whose operas thrilled crowds of Europeans. Verdi was a particular hero among Italians, however, for his stories of downtrodden groups struggling against tyrannical government seemed to refer specifically to them. As his operatic choruses thundered out calls to rebellion in the name of the nation, Italian audiences were sure that Verdi meant for them to throw off Austrian and papal rule and unite in a reborn Roman Empire. Yet the graffiti was doubly political, a call to arms in the days before mass media. For VERDI also formed an acronym for Vittorio Emmanuele Re ("king") d'Italia, and in 1859 it summoned Italians to unite immediately under Victor Emmanuel II, king of Piedmont-Sardinia—the one leader with a nationalist, modernizing profile. The graffiti was good publicity, for the very next year Italy united as a result of warfare and hard bargaining by political realists.

Aïda Poster

Aïda (1871), Giuseppe Verdi's opera of human passion and state power, became a staple of Western culture. As the opera played across Europe, it brought Europeans into a common cultural orbit. Written to celebrate the opening of the Suez Canal, Aïda also celebrated Europe's better access to Asian resources provided by the new waterway. As the poster shows, the opera ushered in another wave of Egyptomania—the craze for Egyptian styles and objects. (Madeline Grimoldi.)

After the failed revolutions of 1848, European statesmen and the politically conscious public increasingly rejected the politics of idealism in favor of **Realpolitik**—a politics of tough-minded realism aimed at strengthening the state and tightening social order. Realpolitikers disliked the romanticism and high-minded ideas of the revolutionaries. Instead they put their faith in power politics, a strong national economy, and the use of violence to attain their goals. Two particularly skilled practitioners of Realpolitik, the Italian Camillo di Cavour and the Prussian Otto von Bismarck, succeeded in unifying Italy and Germany, respectively, not by consensus but by war and diplomacy. Most leading figures of these decades, enmeshed like Verdi's operatic heroes in power politics, strengthened their states by harnessing the forces of nationalism and liberalism.

Making modern nation-states and empires during these momentous decades was complicated. Continued economic development was crucial, and entrepreneurs produced a host of new inventions, new procedures, and new ways of doing business. A growing sense of national identity and common purpose was forged by both culture and government policy. As productivity and wealth increased, governments took vigorous steps to improve their rapidly growing cities, monitor public health, and promote national loyalty. State support for cultural developments ranging from public schools to opera productions helped establish a common fund of knowledge and even shared political beliefs. Authoritarian leaders such as Bismarck and the new French emperor Napoleon III believed that a better quality of life would not only calm revolutionary impulses and build state power but also quiet political opponents.

Culture built a sense of belonging. Reading novels, attending operas and art exhibitions, and visiting the newly fashionable world's fairs created a greater sense not only of being French or German or British but also of being European. Cultural works increasingly rejected romanticism, featuring instead realistic aspects of daily life. Artists painted nudes in shockingly blunt ways, eliminating dreamy poses. Russian author Leo Tolstoy depicted the bleak life of soldiers in the Crimean War, which erupted in 1853 between the Russian and Ottoman empires, while his countryman Fyodor Dostoevsky wrote of criminals and murders in urban neighborhoods. **Realism** in the arts paralleled that in politics.

Realpolitik focused on outcomes in building strong nations with far less concern for the costs to ordinary people. Strengthening nation-states involved global expansion and stamping out resistance to it. At home, governments uprooted neighborhoods in favor of constructing public buildings, roads, and parks. The process of nation building was often brutal, bringing foreign wars, arrests, and even civil war—all the centerpieces of many Verdi operas. In 1871, an uprising of Parisians challenged the central government's violent intrusion into everyday life. The powerful Western state did not spring up spontaneously during these years. Instead, its growth depended on shrewd policy, deliberate warfare, and new inroads into the lives of people around the world. Realpolitik relied on all of these factors, as well as on a modern climate of opinion that valued realism and hard facts.

CHAPTER FOCUS QUESTION   How did the creation and strengthening of nation-states change European politics, society, and culture in the mid-nineteenth century?

The End of the Concert of Europe

The revolutions of 1848 had weakened the concert of Europe, driving out its architect, Klemens von Metternich, and allowing the forces of nationalism to flourish. It became more difficult for countries to control their competing ambitions and act together. In addition, the dreaded revival of Bonapartism in the person of Napoleon III (Louis-Napoleon, the nephew of Napoleon I) added to European instability as

France reasserted itself. One of Napoleon's direct targets was Russia, formerly a mainstay of the concert of Europe. To limit Russia's and Austria's grip on power, France helped engineer the Crimean War of 1853–1856, which reduced these two states' authority over Europe as a whole.

Napoleon III and the Quest for French Glory

Louis-Napoleon Bonaparte encouraged the resurgence of French grandeur and the cult of his famous uncle as part of nation building. "There are certain men who are born to serve as a means for the march of the human race," he wrote. "I consider myself to be one of these." Louis-Napoleon used political coups to rise from president of the Second Republic to emperor. Arresting opponents in towns and cities, he declared himself Emperor Napoleon III (r. 1852–1870) and proclaimed the Second Empire on December 2, 1852—the anniversary of Napoleon I's own ascension to power.

Napoleon III acted as Europe's schoolmaster, showing its leaders how to combine economic liberalism and nationalism with authoritarian rule. Cafés where men might discuss politics were closed, and a rubber-stamp legislature, the Corps législatif, made representative government a charade. Imperial style replaced republican simplicity. Napoleon's opulent court dazzled the public, and the emperor cultivated a masculine image of strength and majesty by wearing a military uniform (like his namesake) and conspicuously maintaining mistresses. Napoleon's wife, Empress

Napoleon III and Eugénie Receive the Siamese Ambassadors
At a splendid gathering of their court, Emperor Napoleon III, Empress Eugénie, and their son and heir greet ambassadors from Siam, whose exoticism and servility before the French imperial family are the centerpiece of this depiction. Amid the grandeur of the Napoleonic dynasty, the West towers above the East. (Bridgeman-Giraudon/Art Resource, NY.)

Eugénie, followed middle-class norms by serving as a devoted mother to her only son and supporting many volunteer charities. The authoritarian, apparently old-fashioned order imposed by Napoleon satisfied many in the countryside that the radicalism of 1848 was under control.

Yet Napoleon III simultaneously pushed for a modern economy, and he promoted industrial growth, public works programs, and jobs, which lured the middle and working classes away from radical politics. The magnificent rebuilding of Paris made France prosper. Empress Eugénie wore lavish gowns, encouraging French silk production and keeping Paris at the center of the lucrative fashion trade. The regime also reached a free-trade agreement with Britain and backed an innovative investment bank, the Crédit Mobilier. Such new institutions led the way in financing railroad expansion, and railway mileage increased fivefold during Napoleon's reign. During the economic downturn of the late 1850s, he wooed support by allowing working-class organizations to exist and introducing features of democratic government. Although some historians have judged Napoleon III to be devious because of these abrupt changes, he made practical responses to economic change.

On the international scene, Napoleon III's main goals were to overcome the containment of France imposed by the Congress of Vienna and to acquire international glory like a true Bonaparte. To realign European politics in France's favor, Napoleon pitted France first against Russia in the Crimean War, then against Austria in the War of Italian Unification (1860–1861), and finally against Prussia in the Franco-Prussian War (1870–1871). Beyond Europe, Napoleon's army continued to enforce French rule in Algeria and Southeast Asia and tried to install Habsburg emperor Francis Joseph's brother Maximilian as ruler of Mexico and ultimately of all Central America (a plan that displayed French weakness in 1867 when Mexican forces executed Maximilian). Napoleon's foreign policy transformed relations among the great powers by causing a breakdown in the international system of peaceful diplomacy established at the Congress of Vienna. While his encouragement of projects like the Suez Canal to connect the Mediterranean and the Red Sea proved visionary, his push for worldwide influence eventually destroyed him. The French overthrew him after Prussia easily defeated his army in 1870.

The Crimean War, 1853–1856: Turning Point in European Affairs

Napoleon first flexed his diplomatic muscles in the Crimean War, which began as a conflict between the Russian and Ottoman empires. Russia continued to build state power by expanding further into Asia and the Middle East. In particular, Tsar Nicholas I eyed territory in the Ottoman Empire, fast becoming known as "the sick man of Europe" because of its declining political authority. Napoleon III encouraged Nicholas to be more aggressive, and in October 1853 war erupted between the two eastern empires (Map 18.1).

The Crimean War drew in other states and undid Europe's balance of power as set in the Congress of Vienna. Napoleon III convinced Austria to remain neutral

Map 18.1 The Crimean War, 1853–1856
The most destructive war in Europe between the Napoleonic wars and World War I, this conflict drew attention to the competing ambitions around territories of the declining Ottoman Empire. Importantly for state building in these decades, it fractured the alliance of conservative forces from the Congress of Vienna, allowing Italy and Germany to come into being as unified states and permitting Napoleon III to pursue his ambitions for France. **For more help analyzing this map, see the map activity for this chapter in the Online Study Guide at** bedfordstmartins .com/huntconcise.

during the war, thus fracturing the conservative Russian-Austrian coalition that had checked French ambitions since 1815. The Austrian government was concerned that defeat of the Ottomans would bring Russian expansion into the Balkans. To protect their Mediterranean routes to Asia, the British prodded the Ottomans to stand up to Russia, but in the fall of 1853, the Russians blasted the wooden Turkish ships to bits at the Ottoman port of Sinope on the Black Sea. In 1854, France and Great Britain, enemies in war for more than a century, declared war on Russia to defend the Ottoman Empire's sovereignty and territories. Their own interests, however, were their main motivation.

Faced with attacking the massive Russian Empire, the allies settled for limited military goals focused on capturing the Russian naval base at Sevastopol, on the Black Sea in the Crimea. Even so, the Crimean War was spectacularly bloody. British and French troops landed in the Crimea in September 1854 and waged a long siege of Sevastopol, which fell after a year of savage and costly combat. Generals on both sides demonstrated their incompetence, and governments failed to provide combatants with even minimal supplies, sanitation, or medical care. The war claimed a massive toll. A million men died, more than two-thirds from disease and starvation.

In the midst of this unfolding catastrophe, Alexander II (r. 1855–1881) ascended the Russian throne after the death of his father, Nicholas I, in 1855. With casualties mounting, the new tsar asked for peace. As a result of the Peace of Paris, signed in March 1856, Russia lost the right to base its navy in the Black Sea or in the Straits of Dardanelles (the strait between Europe and Asia Minor), which were declared neutral waters. Moldavia and Walachia (which soon merged to form Romania) became autonomous Turkish provinces under the victors' protection.

Some historians have called the Crimean War one of the most senseless conflicts in modern history, because competing claims in southeastern Europe could have been settled by diplomacy had it not been for Napoleon III's driving ambition. Yet the war was full of consequence. New technologies were introduced into warfare: the railroad, shell-firing cannons, breech-loading rifles, and steam-powered ships. The relationship of the home front to the battlefront was beginning to change with the use of the telegraph and increased press coverage. Home audiences received news from the Crimea more rapidly and in more detail than ever before. Reports of incompetence, poor sanitation, and the huge death toll outraged the public, inspiring some civilians, such as Florence Nightingale, to head for the front lines to help. Nightingale seized the moment to escape the confines of middle-class domesticity by organizing a battlefield nursing service to care for the British sick and wounded. Through her tough-minded organization of nursing units, she made sanitary conditions for soldiers a priority and pioneered nursing as a profession. More immediately, the war accomplished Napoleon III's goal of ending Austria's and Russia's direction of European affairs. It thus undermined their ability to control European politics and thereby contain the forces of liberalism and nationalism.

The Spirit of Reform in Russia

Defeat in the Crimean War forced Russia on the path of long-overdue reform. Hundreds of peasant insurrections had erupted during the decade before the war. Serf defiance ranged from malingering while at forced labor to boycotting vodka in protest of the heavy tax on it. "Our own and neighboring households were gripped with fear," one aristocrat reported, because everyone expected a massive serf uprising. The Russian economy stagnated compared with western Europe. Old-fashioned farming techniques depleted the soil and led to food shortages, and the nobility was often contemptuous of ordinary people. Works of art, such as novelist Ivan Turgenev's sympathetic portrayals of serfs and depictions of openly brutal masters in *A Hunter's Sketches* (1852), contributed to the spirit of reform. A Russian translation of Harriet Beecher Stowe's antislavery novel *Uncle Tom's Cabin* (1852) also hit home. When Russia lost the Crimean War, the educated public, including some government officials, found the poor performance of serf armies a disgrace and the system of serf labor a liability.

Confronted with the need for change, Alexander acted. Educated and widely traveled, he ushered in what came to be known as the age of Great Reforms, granting Russians new rights from above as a way of preventing violent action from below. The most dramatic reform was the emancipation of almost fifty million serfs beginning in 1861. By the terms of emancipation, communities of former serfs, headed by male village elders, received grants of land. Each community, called a **mir**, had full power to allocate this land among individuals and to direct their economic activity. Thus, although emancipation partially laid the groundwork for a modern labor force in Russia, communal landowning and decision making prevented the free movement of country people who could otherwise have become an industrial labor force. More burdensome to them, peasants were not given land

Emancipation of the Russian Serfs
This trading card was used as a marketing gimmick by businesspeople hoping to push their new products—in this case, canned meat. They were given away by the thousands in stores and traded just as baseball cards are today. Historical scenes were popular subjects for the cards. This one shows the emancipation of the serfs in Russia, which was a major event to people across Europe. Note that the caption is in French, the language used by many in Europe's upper classes, including those in Russia, who would have consumed this product. The emancipation is presented as a wholly beneficial act with no drawbacks, such as the immense debt imposed on former serfs. (Mary Evans Picture Library.)

along with their personal freedom; they were forced to "redeem" the land they farmed by accepting long-term government loans, which in turn reimbursed the big landowners. The best land remained in the hands of the nobility, and most peasants ended up actually owning less land than they had farmed as serfs. These conditions, especially the huge burden of debt and regulations, slowed Russian agricultural development for decades. Even so, idealistic reformers believed the emancipation of the serfs produced miraculous results. As one reformer put it, "The people are without any exaggeration transfigured from head to foot. . . . The look, the walk, the speech, everything is changed."

The state also reformed local administration, the judiciary, and the military. The government set up zemstvos—regional councils through which aristocrats could direct neglected local matters such as education and public health. Aristocratic control ensured that zemstvos would remain conservative but also offer some balance to the authoritarian central government. Simultaneously, judicial reform gave all Russians, even former serfs, access to modern civil courts, rather than leaving them at the mercy of a landowner's version of justice. The Western principle of equality of all persons before the law, regardless of social rank, was introduced in Russia for the first time. Military reform followed in 1874, when the government replaced the twenty-five-year period of service with a six-year term and focused on educating Russian troops in an effort to match the efficiency of soldiers elsewhere in western Europe.

Alexander's reforms helped landowners be more effective in the market, just as enclosures and emancipation had done much earlier in western Europe. At the same time, the changes diminished the privileges of the nobility, leaving their authority weakened and sparking family conflict. "An epidemic seemed to seize upon [noble] children . . . an epidemic of fleeing from the parental roof," one observer noted. Rejecting aristocratic leisure, youthful rebels from the upper classes valued practical activity and sometimes identified with peasants and workers. Some formed communes where they hoped to do humble manual labor; others turned to higher education, especially the sciences. Daughters of the nobility rebelled by cutting their hair short, wearing black, and escaping from home through phony marriages so they could study in western European universities. This rejection of traditional norms led Turgenev to label radical youths *nihilists* (from the Latin for "nothing"), a term that meant a lack of belief in any values whatsoever. In fact, they represented the defiant spirit growing in Russian society.

Reform also inspired resistance among the more than one hundred minority nationalities in the Russian Empire. Aristocratic and upper-class Poles staged an uprising in 1863, but Alexander II's army regained control of the Russian section of Poland by 1864. The government then intensified repression and **Russification**—a tactic meant to reduce the threat of future rebellions by minorities within the empire by forcing them to adopt the Russian language and culture. In this era of the Great Reforms, the tsarist regime only partially succeeded in developing the administrative, economic, and civic institutions of the nation-state. The tsar and his inner circle tightly controlled the government, allowing few to share power. In imperial Russia, autocracy and the continued abuse of many in the population slowed the development of the sense of citizenship forming elsewhere in the West, while it increased the urge to revolt.

REVIEW   What were the main results of the Crimean War?

War and Nation Building

Dynamic leaders in the German and Italian states used the opportunity offered by the weakened concert of Europe to unify their countries through warfare. When national disunity threatened, the United States also waged a bloody civil war to maintain its integrity, which opened the way for dynamic economic growth. Historians sometimes treat the rise of powerful nation-states such as Italy, Germany, and the United States as part of an inevitable process, but millions of individuals, especially those living in rural areas, maintained a local sense of identity even as nation building was taking place and national sentiment was on the rise.

Cavour, Garibaldi, and the Process of Italian Unification

Despite the failed revolutions of 1848 in the Italian states, hope for national unification, or Risorgimento (rebirth), remained strong, aided by diplomatic instability across Europe. This time the kingdom of Piedmont-Sardinia, in the economically modernizing north of Italy, drove the unification process. The kingdom rallied to the operas of Verdi, but its nation-building efforts depended on the construction of railroads and a modern army, along with military help from France.

The architect of the new Italy was the pragmatic Camillo di Cavour (1810–1861), prime minister of the kingdom of Piedmont-Sardinia from 1852 until his death. A rebel in his youth, the young Cavour had conducted agricultural experiments on his aristocratic father's land. He organized steamship companies, played the stock market, and inhaled the spirit of modernization during his travels to Paris and London. As prime minister, he pushed the development of a healthy Piedmontese economy, a modern army, and a liberal political climate as the foundation of Piedmont-Sardinia's claim to lead the unification process (Map 18.2).

To unify Italy, however, Piedmont-Sardinia would have to confront Austria, which governed the provinces of Lombardy and Venetia and exerted a strong influence over most of the peninsula. Cavour turned for help to Napoleon III, who in the summer of 1858 promised French assistance in exchange for the city of Nice and the region of Savoy. Napoleon additionally expected that France rather than Austria would influence the peninsula thereafter. Sure of French help, Cavour provoked the Austrians into invading northern Italy in April 1859. The cause of Piedmont-Sardinia's monarchy now became the cause of nationalist Italians everywhere, even those who had supported romantic republicanism in 1848. Using the newly built Piedmontese railroad to move troops, the French and Piedmontese armies achieved rapid victories. Suddenly fearing the growth of Piedmont as a potential competing force, Napoleon independently signed a peace treaty with Austria that gave Lombardy but not Venetia to Piedmont-Sardinia. The rest of Italy remained disunited, and Cavour's nationalist ambitions were not yet realized.

Napoleon's plans for the controlled liberation of Lombardy and Venetia and a partitioned peninsula were derailed as support for Piedmont continued to swell across Italy. Ousting their rulers, citizens of states in the center of Italy (except Rome, which French troops occupied) elected to join Piedmont. In May 1860, Giuseppe Garibaldi (1807–1882), a committed republican and veteran of the revolutions of 1848, set sail from Genoa with a thousand red-shirted volunteers (many of them teenage boys) to liberate Sicily, where peasant revolts against landlords and the corrupt government were under way. In the autumn of 1860, the army of King Victor Emmanuel of Piedmont-Sardinia and "Garibaldi's Thousand" joined forces in Naples (Map 18.2, page 692). Although some of Garibaldi's supporters still clamored for social reform and a republic, he threw his support to the king. In 1861, the kingdom of Italy was proclaimed, with Victor Emmanuel as ruler (r. 1861–1878).

Map 18.2 Unification of Italy, 1859–1870
The many states of the Italian peninsula had different languages, ways of life, and economic interests. In the north, the kingdom of Piedmont-Sardinia had much to gain from a unified market and a more extensive labor pool. Although the armies of King Victor Emmanuel and Garibaldi unified these states into a single country, it would take decades to construct a culturally, socially, and economically connected nation.

Exhausted by a decade of overwork, Cavour died within months of leading the unification, leaving lesser men to organize the new Italy. Consensus among Italy's elected leaders was hard to achieve once the war was over, and admirers of Cavour, such as Verdi (who had been made a senator), quit the quarrelsome political scene. The wealthy commercial north and impoverished agricultural south remained at odds over basic policies (as they do even today). Finally, Venetia and Rome, under Austrian and French control, respectively, remained outside Italy's borders. Amid

Seamstresses of the Red Shirts
Sewing uniforms and making battle flags, European women like these Italian volunteers saw themselves as contributors to the nation. Donating their domestic skills and raising the next generation of citizens to be patriotic, many nineteenth-century women participated in nation building as "republican mothers." (akg-images/Electa.)

these strains, the legend of an Italian struggle for freedom symbolized by the figure of Garibaldi and his Red Shirts became a powerful unifying force even though it sentimentalized the Realpolitik that had made unification possible. Many citizens of the new country took pride in the Italian nation based on this and other national myths.

Bismarck and the Realpolitik of German Unification

The most momentous act of nation building for the future of Europe was the creation of a united Germany in 1871. This, too, was the product of Realpolitik, undertaken once the concert of Europe was smashed and the champions of the status quo were defeated. Employing the old military order to wage war, yet with the support of economic modernizers who saw the benefits of a single national market, the Prussian state brought a vast array of cities and kingdoms under its control within just one decade. From then on, Germany prospered, continuing to consolidate its economic and political might. By the end of the century, it would be the foremost continental power.

The architect of a unified Germany was Otto von Bismarck (1815–1898). Bismarck came from a traditional Junker (Prussian landed nobility) family on his father's side; his mother's family included high-ranking bureaucrats of the middle class. At university, the young Bismarck had gambled and womanized, interested only in one academic course, on the economic foundations of politics. After failing in the civil service, he worked to modernize operations on his landholdings while leading an otherwise rowdy life. His marriage to a sober Lutheran woman gave him new purpose. In the 1850s, his diplomatic service to the Prussian state made him increasingly angry about the Habsburg grip on German affairs. Establishing Prussia as a respected and dominant power became his cause.

In 1862, William I (king of Prussia, r. 1861–1888; German emperor, r. 1871–1888) appointed Bismarck prime minister in hopes that he would crush the growing power of the liberals in the Prussian parliament. The liberals, representing the prosperous professional and business classes, had gained parliamentary strength at the expense of conservative landowners during the decades of industrial expansion. Indeed, the liberals' wealth was crucial to Prussia's growing power. Desiring Prussia to be like western Europe, Prussian liberals advocated the extension of political rights and increased civilian control of the military. By contrast, William, along with members of the traditional Prussian elite such as Bismarck, rejected the western European model. Bismarck simply rammed through programs to build the army and thwart civilian control. "Germany looks not to Prussia's liberalism, but to its power," he proclaimed. "The great questions of the day will not be settled by speeches and majority decisions—that was the great mistake of 1848 and 1849—but by iron and blood."

After his triumph over the parliament, Bismarck led Prussia into a series of wars—against Denmark in 1864, Austria in 1866, and France in 1870. Using war as a political tactic, he kept the disunited German states from choosing Austrian leadership and instead united them around Prussia. Bismarck drew Austria into a joint war with Prussia against a rebellious Denmark in 1864 over Denmark's proposed incorporation of the provinces of Schleswig and Holstein, with their partially German populations. Their joint victory resulted in an agreement that Prussia would administer Schleswig and Austria would oversee Holstein. Such an arrangement stretched Austria's geographic interests far from its central European base.

Austria proved weaker than Prussia, as the Habsburgs lagged in economic development and suffered from a swelling national debt and the discontent of its many national minorities. Bismarck, however, so encouraged Habsburg pretensions of grandeur and influence that Austria disputed the administration of Schleswig and Holstein and, in the summer of 1866, confidently declared war on Prussia, with the support of most of the German Confederation. Within seven weeks, the modernized Prussian army, using railroads and fast breech-loading rifles against the outdated Austrian military, won decisively. The masterful victory allowed Bismarck to drive Austria from the German Confederation and create the North German Confederation, led by Prussia (Map 18.3).

To bring the remaining German states into Prussia's orbit, Bismarck next moved to entrap France in a war. During the Austro-Prussian War, Bismarck had suggested to Napoleon III that his neutrality would bring France territory, thus heating up nationalist sentiments in both France and Germany. The atmosphere became even more charged when Spain proposed a minor Prussian prince to fill its vacant throne. This candidacy threatened France with Prussian rulers on two of its borders. Bismarck used the occasion to stir up nationalist feelings in Prussia and France by editing a diplomatic communication (known as the Ems telegram) to make it look as if the king of Prussia had insulted France over the succession issue. His release of the revised version to journalists inflamed the French public into demanding

Map 18.3 Unification of Germany, 1862–1871
In a complex series of diplomatic maneuvers, Otto von Bismarck welded disunited kingdoms and small states into a major continental power independent of the other dominant German dynasty, the Habsburgs. Prussia's use of force unified Germany politically, and almost immediately that unity unleashed the new nation's economic potential. An aristocratic and agrarian elite remained firmly in power, but a rapidly growing working class would soon become a political force to be reckoned with.

war against Prussia. The French parliament gladly declared war on July 19, 1870, setting in motion the alliances Prussia had created with the other German states. The Prussians captured Napoleon III with his army on September 2, 1870, and the Second Empire fell two days later.

With Prussian forces still besieging Paris, in January 1871 in the Hall of Mirrors at Versailles, King William of Prussia was proclaimed the kaiser (or emperor) of a new, imperial Germany. By the terms of the peace signed in May 1871, France lost the rich industrial provinces of Alsace and Lorraine to

Emperor William I of Germany, 1871
The defeat of France in the Franco-Prussian War ended with the king of Prussia being proclaimed emperor of a unified Germany. Otto von Bismarck, who had orchestrated the wars of unification, appropriately appears in this artistic rendering as the central figure attired in heroic white. The event in the French palace of Versailles symbolized the militaristic and antagonistic side of state building, especially the Franco-German rivalry that would disastrously motivate European politics in the future. (akg-images, London.)

Germany and paid a multibillion-franc indemnity. Without French protection for the papacy, Rome became part of Italy. Germany was now poised to dominate continental politics.

Prussian military might served as the foundation for German state building, and a complex constitution ensured the continued political dominance of the aristocracy and monarchy despite the growing wealth of the business classes. The kaiser, who remained Prussia's king, controlled the military and appointed Bismarck to the powerful position of imperial chancellor. The Reichstag, an assembly elected by universal male suffrage, ratified all budgets. Bismarck accorded constitutional rights such as suffrage in the belief that the masses would uphold the monarchy out of their fear of modernizing businessmen, whom Bismarck opposed as a source of "liberal power." He balanced this move with an electoral system in Prussia in which votes from the upper classes counted more than votes from the lower classes. He had little to fear from liberals, however. Dizzy with German military success, they came to support the blend of economic progress, constitutionalism, and militaristic nationalism that Bismarck represented.

Francis Joseph and the Creation of the Austro-Hungarian Monarchy

The Austrian monarchy took a different approach to nation building, proving that there was no one model for the modern nation-state. Just as the Crimean War left Russia searching for solutions to its social and political problems, so the confrontation with Cavour and Bismarck left the Habsburg Empire struggling to keep its standing in a rapidly changing Europe. The Habsburg Empire emerged from the revolutions of 1848 renewed by the ascension of Francis Joseph (r. 1848–1916), who favored absolutist rule. A tireless worker, Francis Joseph enhanced his authority through stiff, formal court ceremonies, playing to people's fascination with the lavish trappings of royalty. Although the emperor stubbornly resisted change, official standards of honesty and efficiency improved, and the government promoted local education. The German language was used by the administration and taught by the schools, but the government respected the rights of national minorities such as Czechs and Poles to receive education and to communicate with officials in their native tongues. Above all, the government abolished most internal customs barriers, boosted railway construction, and attracted foreign capital. The capital city, Vienna, underwent extensive rebuilding, and people found jobs as industrialization progressed, if unevenly.

In the fast-moving nineteenth century, the emperor could not match Bismarck in modern nation building; too much of the old regime remained as a roadblock. The Catholic church had nearly a free hand in education and in civil institutions such as marriage, and wealthy businessmen lacked influence in such important policy matters as taxation and finance. After Prussia's victory over Francis Joseph's armies in 1866, the most disaffected but wealthiest part of the empire, Hungary, became the key to stability, even to the empire's existence. The leaders of the Hungarian agrarian elites forced the emperor to accept a **dual monarchy**—that is, Magyar home rule over the Hungarian kingdom. This agreement restored the Hungarian parliament and gave it control of internal policy (including the right to decide how to treat Hungary's national minorities). Although the Habsburg emperor Francis Joseph was crowned

The Austro-Hungarian Monarchy, 1867

king of Hungary and Austro-Hungarian foreign policy was coordinated from Vienna, the Hungarians mostly ruled themselves after 1867 and hammered out common policies such as tariffs in negotiations with Vienna. These negotiations were mostly bitter, weakening the process of nation building.

A second weakness in the dual monarchy was that it was designed specifically to address Hungarian demands. In doing so, it strengthened the voices of Czechs, Slovaks, and at least half a dozen other national groups in the Habsburg Empire wanting the same kind of self-rule. The Czechs, who helped the empire advance industrially, failed to gain Hungarian-style liberties. More menacing, some of the dissatisfied ethnic groups turned to **Pan-Slavism**—the transnational unity of all ethnic Slavs—and looked beyond the borders of Austria-Hungary to Russia, the largest Slavic country, to achieve this. With so many competing ethnicities, the Austro-Hungarian monarchy remained a dynastic, or princely, state in which people were ultimately loyal to the Habsburg dynasty but had difficulty relating to one another as members of a single nation.

Political Stability through Gradual Reform in Great Britain

In contrast to the turmoil in continental Europe, Britain appeared the model of liberal progress. By the 1850s, the monarchy symbolized domestic tranquillity and stability. Unlike their predecessors, Queen Victoria (r. 1837–1901) and her husband, Prince Albert, were considered models of middle-class virtue. Britain's parliamentary system steadily brought more men into the political process. Economic prosperity fortified peaceful political reform, except in Ireland, where suffering and failure to achieve justice continued. An evolving but focused party system helped in decision making. The Tory Party changed into the Conservatives, many of whose policies favored the aristocracy. Nonetheless, the Conservatives still went along with the liberal consensus in support of economic development and representative government. Skilled politician William Gladstone, who would serve four terms as prime minister, helped the Whigs and several other political groups become the Liberals. In 1867, the Conservatives, led by Benjamin Disraeli, passed the Second Reform Bill, which made a million more men eligible to vote.

Political parties supported reforms because citizens now formed pressure groups to influence national policies. The Law Amendment Society and the Social Science Association, for example, lobbied for laws to improve social conditions. Women's groups advocated the Matrimonial Causes Act of 1857, which facilitated divorce, and the Married Women's Property Act of 1870, which allowed married women to own property and keep the wages they earned. Plush royal ceremonies helped critics, activists, and, more important, different social classes bond as one people. Whereas previous monarchs' sexual scandals had caused riots, the monarchy of Queen Victoria and Prince Albert, with its newly invented celebrations of royal marriages, anniversaries, and births, drew respectful crowds. Promoting the monarchy in this way was so successful that the term *Victorian* came to symbolize almost the entire century and could refer to anything from manners to political institutions. Yet Britain's politicians were as devoted to Realpolitik as were those in Germany, Italy, or France, endorsing violence to expand their overseas empire and control Ireland. The violence was far beyond the view of most British people, however, allowing them to imagine their nation as peaceful, advanced, and united.

Queen Victoria and Prince Albert
In the mid-nineteenth century, rulers started using the new photographic technology to portray themselves as respectable and distinguished figures. Queen Victoria and her husband were expert publicists, often posing as an ordinary middle-class couple and the epitome of domestic order, in marked contrast to their often scandalous royal predecessors. Photos of them were sold or given away on small cards called *cartes de visite*, which many leaders used to spread their fame. (The Royal Collection © 2009 Her Majesty Queen Elizabeth II.)

Civil War and Nation Building in the United States and Canada

In North America, increasing nationalism and powerful economic growth characterized the nation-building experience. The United States experienced the midcentury as a period of unprecedented and destructive upheaval born of nation building. It had a far more democratic political culture than existed in Europe, including almost universal white male suffrage, a rowdy independent press, and mass political parties, all of which upheld the view that sovereignty came from the people.

The United States continued to expand its territory to the west (Map 18.4). In 1848, victory in a war with Mexico almost doubled the size of the country. Texas was officially annexed, and large portions of California and the Southwest extended the borders of the United States into former Mexican land. Politicians and ordinary citizens alike favored removing the native Indian peoples from these western lands. Complicating matters, however, was the question of whether the U.S. West would be settled by free white farmers or whether southern slaveholders could bring in their slaves. The issue polarized the country. In the North, the new Republican Party emerged to demand "free soil, free labor, free men," although few Republicans endorsed the abolitionists' demand to end slavery.

With the 1860 election of Republican Abraham Lincoln to the presidency, most of the slaveholding states of the South seceded to form the Confederate States of

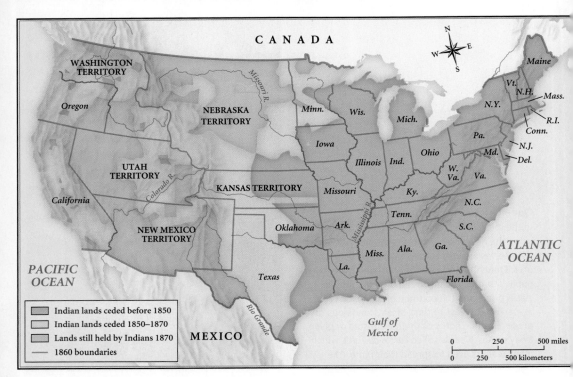

Map 18.4 U.S. Expansion, 1850–1870

Like Russia, the United States expanded into adjacent regions to create a continental nation-state, conquering indigenous peoples and taking over their territories. The United States' treatment of those whose lands it took was different from that of Russia, however. Native American peoples were herded into small, confined spaces called reservations so that settlers could take for themselves thousands of square miles for farming and other enterprises. Gradually, some native Americans acquired the right to vote, and the U.S. government granted full citizenship to all native Americans in 1925.

America. Under Lincoln's leadership, the North fought a civil war against the South to restore the Union. Lincoln did not initially aim to abolish slavery, but in January 1863 his Emancipation Proclamation came into force as a wartime measure, officially freeing all the slaves in the Confederate states and turning the war into a fight not only for the Union but also for liberation from slavery. After the summer of 1863, the superior industrial strength and military might of the North overpowered and physically destroyed much of the South. In April 1865, the North won even as a Confederate sympathizer assassinated Lincoln. Constitutional amendments ended slavery and promised political rights for African American men.

Northerners welcomed their victory as the triumph of American values, but racism remained entrenched throughout the United States. By 1871, southern whites began regaining control of state politics, often by organized violence. The end of northern occupation of the South in 1877 put on hold the promise of rights for blacks for nearly a century. Nonetheless, in ending slavery, the Union victory opened the way to a more coherent national government and economic advancement beyond the old Atlantic system based on slave plantation production.

The North's triumph also had profound effects elsewhere in North America. For one thing, it allowed the reunited United States to help defeat Napoleon III in Mexico in 1867. The United States also eyed the annexation of Canada in retribution for Britain's bias toward the Confederacy (due to British dependence on southern cotton). To head off this threat, the British government allowed Canadians to form a united, self-governing dominion. According dominion status answered Canadians' appeals for home rule, lessened domestic opposition to Britain's control of Canada, and advanced the cause of Canadian national unity.

> **REVIEW**   What varying roles did warfare play in nineteenth-century nation building?

Industry and Nation Building

Behind the growing power of European states lay the dramatic development of economic and technological power. Industry turned out an unbelievable array of new products, and the wages of many workers increased. Beginning in 1873, however, downturns in business threatened both businesspeople and the working class. Businesspeople sought remedies in new managerial techniques and a revolutionary marketing institution—the department store. Governments played their part by changing business law and supporting the drive for global profits. The steady advance of industry, global trade, and the consumer economy further transformed people's daily lives.

Industrial Innovation

Industrial, technological, and commercial innovation abounded in nineteenth-century Europe to back the ambitions of the nation-state. New products ranging from the bicycle, typewriter, and telephone to the internal combustion engine were striking proof of industrial progress. Alongside independent tinkerers and inventor-manufacturers were sophisticated engineers—for example, Karl Benz of Germany and Armand Peugeot of France—who invented revolutionary technologies such as the gasoline engine. Electricity began to provide the power to light everything from private drawing rooms to government office buildings. To fuel growth, the leading industrial nations mined and produced massive quantities of coal, iron, and steel during the 1870s and 1880s. The production of iron increased from 11 million to 23 million tons. Steel output in the industrial nations grew just as impressively, increasing from 500,000 to 11 million tons in the 1870s and 1880s. Manufacturers used the metal to build the more than 100,000 locomotives that pulled trains during these years—trains that transported 2 billion people annually.

Historians used to contrast a "second" Industrial Revolution, with its concentration on heavy industrial products, with the "first" Industrial Revolution of the eighteenth and early nineteenth centuries, in which innovations in textile making and the use of steam energy predominated. But many historians now believe this distinction applies mainly to Britain. In countries where industrialization came later, the two stages occurred simultaneously. Numerous textile mills were installed on the European continent later than in Britain, for instance, at the same time that blast furnaces were being constructed. Industrialization led to the decline of cottage production in traditional crafts like weaving. Domestic production, or "outwork," persisted in garment making, metalwork, and "finishing trades" such as porcelain painting and button polishing. Urban families painted tin soldiers, wrapped chocolate, and made cheese boxes. Factory owners liked to employ outworkers because the low piece rates forced them to work extremely long days. A German seamstress at her new home sewing machine reported that she "pedaled at a stretch from six o'clock in the morning until midnight. . . . At four o'clock I got up and did the housework and prepared meals." This coexistence of home and factory enterprise has continued through all the changes in manufacturing to the present day.

Industrial innovations also changed agriculture. Chemical fertilizers boosted crop yields, and reapers and threshers mechanized harvesting. In the 1870s, Sweden produced a cream separator, the first step toward mechanizing dairy farming. Wire fencing and barbed wire replaced wooden fencing and stone walls, both of which were labor-intensive to create. Refrigeration, developed during this period, allowed fruits, vegetables, and meat to be transported long distances without spoiling, thus diversifying and increasing the urban food supply. Tin from colonial trade facilitated large-scale commercial canning, which made many foods available year-round to people in cities.

During these decades, Britain's rate of industrial growth slowed as its entrepreneurs remained wedded to older, successful technologies. Two countries began surpassing Britain in technical education, innovation, and industrial development: Germany and the United States. Profiting from the acquisition of resource-rich Alsace and Lorraine after the Franco-Prussian War, German businesses invested in research and began to mass-produce goods that other countries had originally manufactured. Germany also spent as much money on education as on its military in the 1870s and 1880s. This investment resulted in highly skilled engineers and technical workers, whose productivity enabled Germany's electrical and chemical engineering capabilities to soar. The United States began an intensive exploitation of its vast natural resources, including coal, ore, gold, and oil. Whereas German accomplishments rested more on state promotion of industrial efforts, innovative entrepreneurs, such as Andrew Carnegie in iron and steel and John D. Rockefeller in oil, drove U.S. growth. Most other countries trailed the three leaders in the pervasiveness of industry.

French industry grew steadily, but French businesses remained smaller than those in Germany and the United States. Although France had some huge mining, textile, and metallurgical establishments, many French businessmen retired early to imitate the still enviable aristocratic way of life. Industrial development in Spain, Austria-Hungary, and Italy was primarily a local phenomenon. Austria-Hungary had densely industrialized areas around Vienna and in Styria and Bohemia, but the rest of the country remained tied to traditional, unmechanized agriculture. The Italian government spent more on building Rome into a grand capital than it invested in economic growth. A mere 1.4 percent of Italy's 1872 budget went to education and science, compared with 10.8 percent in Germany. The commercial use of electricity helped Scandinavians, who were poor in coal and ore, to industrialize in the last third of the nineteenth century and become leaders in the use of hydroelectric power. Russia's industrialization was slowed by the terms of the emancipation of the serfs, but it was fostered by the new railroad lines and the development of metallurgy and mining late in the nineteenth century.

Facing Economic Crisis

Economic conditions were far from rosy throughout the 1870s and 1880s despite industrial innovation. In 1873, prosperity abruptly gave way to a severe economic depression, followed by almost three decades of economic fluctuations featuring sharp downturns. People of all classes lost their jobs or businesses or faced long stretches of unemployment or bankruptcy. Because economic ties bound industrialized western Europe to international markets, recession affected the economies of such diverse regions as Australia, South Africa, California, Newfoundland, and the West Indies.

By the 1870s, as industry gained in influence, industrial and financial setbacks—not agricultural ones, as in the past—were sending the economy into a long tailspin. Businesspeople faced real problems. First, the start-up costs of new enterprises skyrocketed. Textile mills had required relatively modest amounts of capital in comparison with factories producing steel and iron. Industrialization had become what modern economists call *capital-intensive* rather than *labor-intensive*: industrial growth required the purchase of expensive machinery, not merely the hiring of more workers. Second, the distribution and consumption of goods were inadequate to sustain industrial growth, in part because businessmen kept wages so low despite rising productivity that workers could afford little besides food. Industrialists had made their fortunes by emphasizing production, not consumption. The series of slumps refocused entrepreneurial efforts on building sales.

Governments took steps to address the economic crisis. New laws established the limited liability corporation, which protected businesspeople from personal responsibility for a firm's debts and thus encouraged investment. Before limited liability, owners were personally responsible for the debts of a bankrupt business. In one case in England, a former partner who failed to have his name removed from a legal document after leaving the business remained responsible to creditors when the company went bankrupt. He lost everything he owned except a watch and the equivalent of $100. By reducing personal risk, limited liability made investors more confident about financing businesses. Public financing in stocks also helped raise vast amounts of new capital. Early stock exchanges had dealt mainly in government bonds and in government-sponsored enterprises such as railroads. By the end of the century, stock markets traded heavily in industrial corporate stock, thus raising money from a larger pool of private capital than before.

Another way businesses met the crisis was to band together in cartels and trusts to control prices and competition. Cartels were organizations of industries powerful enough to set prices; they flourished particularly in the German chemical, iron, coal, and electric industries. A single German coal cartel founded in the 1890s eventually dominated more than 95 percent of coal production in Germany. Trusts appeared first in the United States. In 1882, John D. Rockefeller created the Standard Oil Trust by acquiring stock from many different oil companies and placing it under the direction of trustees. The trustees then controlled so much of the companies' stock that they could set prices for the entire industry and even dictate to the railroads the rates for transporting the oil. While praising competition and free trade, the directors of cartels and trusts were actually limiting the free market. Soon governments began to do the same by imposing import tariffs.

Much of Europe had adopted free trade after midcentury, but during the recessions of the 1870s, the resulting huge trade deficits caused when imports exceed exports had soured many Europeans on the concept. A country with a trade deficit had less capital available to invest internally. Fewer jobs were created, and the chances of social unrest increased. Farmers in many European countries were hurt when improvements in transportation made it possible to import perishable foods, such as cheaper grain from the United States and Ukraine. With broad popular support, governments approved tariffs throughout these decades to prevent competition from foreign goods.

A Revolution in Business Practices

Industrialists also tried to minimize the damage of economic downturns by revolutionizing the everyday operations of their businesses. A generation earlier, a factory owner was directly involved in every aspect of his business and often learned to run the firm through trial and error. In the late 1800s, industrialists began to hire managers to run their increasingly complex day-to-day operations. Managers who specialized in sales and distribution, finance, or the purchase of raw materials made decisions in their areas of expertise. Other managers dealt with the factory floor, determining skill levels for each task. Managers used the concept of skill (based on the old craft traditions) to segment or divide the labor force according to levels of skill and thus levels of pay. The trend toward breaking down and separating work processes into discrete tasks advanced with the management revolution. For example, builders came to employ excavators, scaffolders, and haulers to do the "dirty work," hiring fewer highly paid carpenters. At the same time, skill levels were often arbitrary. When women were assigned certain tasks, for instance, those tasks were said to require less skill. Thus when women ran weaving machines in some mills, the job was considered an unskilled job worth lower pay; when men performed the same job in other mills, it was considered a higher-skilled job.

The rise of management led to the emergence of a white-collar service sector of office workers such as secretaries, file clerks, and typists to guide the flow of business information. Banks, railroads, insurance companies, and government-run telegraph and telephone companies all needed armies of white-collar employees. Workers with mathematical skills and literacy acquired in the new public primary schools staffed this service sector, which also provided clean work for educated, middle-class women. Whether to support themselves or to help pay the growing cost of raising and educating children, unmarried and an increasing number of married women of the respectable middle class took jobs despite the relatively new ideology of domesticity for women. Employers, as one put it, found in the new women workers a "quickness of eye and ear, and the delicacy of touch" essential to office work. By hiring women for newly created clerical jobs, business and government contributed further to a dual labor market in which certain categories of jobs were predominantly male and others were overwhelmingly female. White-collar work gradually became the domain of cheap female labor. In the absence of competition, businesses in the service sector boosted their profits by paying women low wages—much less than they would have had to pay men for the same work.

Finally, the rise of consumer capitalism magnified the scale of consumption, just as industrial capitalism had revolutionized the scale of production. The principal institution of this change was the department store. Founded after midcentury in large cities, department stores gathered such an impressive variety of goods in one place that consumers popularly called them "marble palaces" or "the eighth wonder of the world." Created by daring entrepreneurs, department stores eventually replaced the single-item stores that people entered knowing clearly what they wanted to purchase. Instead, these modern palaces stimulated consumer whims and desires with lavish displays spilling over railings and counters in glorious disarray. Shoppers no longer bargained rationally over prices; now they reacted to sales, a new marketing technique that could incite a buying frenzy. Because most men lacked the time for shopping expeditions, department stores appealed mostly to women, who came out of their domestic sphere into a new public role. Attractive salesgirls, another variety of service workers, were hired to inspire customers to buy. Glossy mail-order catalogs brought to rural households both necessities and exotic items from the faraway dream world of the city.

REVIEW   What were the major economic changes in the West between 1850 and 1880?

Interior of Au Coin de la Rue (c. 1870)
This Parisian department store, not the grandest or first of its kind, shows the typical cascade of goods displayed on railings and balconies. The abundance of textiles and carpets sparked shoppers' imaginations, inciting them to let go of thrift and wander wherever their fancy took them, among many counters and displays, until they had overspent. (© Stefano Bianchetti/Corbis.)

Nation Building through Social Order

Government officials and reformers worked to establish social unity and order in an attempt to make political unity stronger. With an array of new improvements and policies, they also hoped to offset the violent changes of the nation-building process. Population rose dramatically and cities grew crowded as the nineteenth century progressed, leading officials across Europe to attend to public health and safety. Many liberal theorists advocated a laissez-faire government that left social and economic life largely to private enterprise. Nevertheless, confident in the benefits of European institutions in general, bureaucrats and reformers paid more attention to citizens' lives and, with the help of missionaries and explorers, spread European power and policies to the farthest reaches of the globe. Some of these efforts met violent resistance both within Europe and outside it.

Ordering Cities and the Countryside

European cities became the backdrop for displays of state power and national solidarity; thus efforts to improve sanitation, control disease, and beautify the landscape redounded to the state's credit. In 1857, Francis Joseph ordered the destruction of the old Viennese city walls and replaced them with boulevards lined with major public buildings such as an opera house and government offices. Such buildings showed off national wealth and power, and the broad boulevards allowed crowds to observe royal pageantry. These wider roads were also easier for troops to navigate than the twisted, narrow medieval streets that in 1848 had concealed insurrectionists in cities such as Vienna and Paris—an advantage that convinced some otherwise reluctant officials to approve the expense. Impressive parks and public gardens showed the state's control over nature, helped order people's leisure time, and inspired respect for the nation-state's achievements.

One effect of renovated cities was to highlight class differences. Construction first required destruction: buildings and entire neighborhoods of housing for the poor disappeared, and thousands of city dwellers were dislocated. The boulevards often served as boundaries marking rich and poor sections of the city. In Paris, the process of urban change was called **Haussmannization**, named for the prefect Georges-Eugène Haussmann, who implemented a grand design that included

Museums and Nation Building

The Kunsthistorisches Museum (Museum of Fine Arts) in Vienna was part of a huge rebuilding project that beautified the city with wide boulevards and grand public buildings. Art museums such as the one shown here represented the cultural wealth of the state and allowed citizens to take pride in this wealth while they routinely strolled the streets to view it.
(ullstein—imagebroker.net.)

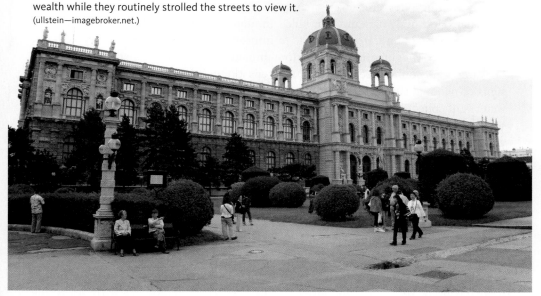

eighty-five miles of new city streets, many lined with showy dwellings for the wealthy. The size and spaciousness of the many new banks and insurance companies built in London, one architect believed, "help[ed] the impression of stability," thus creating social order. The civic pride resulting from urban rebuilding would replace rebelliousness.

Yet amid redevelopment and beautification, serious problems loomed. Repeated epidemics of diseases such as cholera mowed down city dwellers and gave the strong impression of social decay. Poor sanitation allowed typhoid bacteria to spread through sewage and into water supplies, infecting rich and poor alike. In 1861, Britain's Prince Albert died of typhus, commonly known as a "filth disease." Unregulated urban slaughterhouses and tanneries; heaps of animal excrement in chicken coops, pigsties, and stables; human waste alongside buildings; and garbage everywhere facilitated the spread of disease. The stench of cities alone made sanitation a top priority.

Scientific research, increasingly undertaken in public universities and hospitals, provided the means to promote public health and control disease. France's Louis Pasteur, whose three young daughters had died of typhus, advanced the germ theory of disease. Seeking a method to prevent wine from spoiling, Pasteur began his work in the mid-1850s by studying fermentation. He found that the growth of living organisms caused fermentation, and he suggested that certain organisms—bacteria and parasites—might be responsible for human and animal diseases. Pasteur demonstrated that heating foods such as wine and milk to a certain temperature, a process soon known as pasteurization, killed these organisms and made food safe. English surgeon Joseph Lister applied the germ theory to medicine. He connected Pasteur's theory of bacteria to infection and developed antiseptics for treating wounds and preventing puerperal fever, a condition that was caused by the dirty hands of physicians and midwives and that killed innumerable women after childbirth.

Governments undertook projects to improve sewer and other sanitary systems, including the straightening of rivers to eliminate marshes and other stagnant pools of water that could breed disease. Citizens often prized such improvements as signs of national superiority. In Paris, sewage flowed into newly built underground, watertight collectors. In addition, Haussmann piped in water from uncontaminated sources in the countryside to provide each household with a secure supply. Such ventures were imitated throughout Europe: the Russian Empire's port city Riga (now in Latvia), for example, organized its first water company in 1863. To prevent devastating floods and the persistence of disease-ridden marshlands, governments rerouted and straightened rivers such as the Rhine and built canals. Alongside such grand projects were those affecting the details of everyday life. When public toilets for men became a feature of modern cities, for instance, women petitioned governments for similar facilities. On the lookout for disease and sanitary dangers, the average person became more aware of smells and the foul air that had been an accepted part of daily life for thousands of years. To show that they were becoming more "civilized," the middle and lower-middle classes bathed more regularly, mirroring in their own lives the quest of governments for order.

Expanding the Reach of Bureaucracy

Improved sanitation meant a more active role for the state, and bureaucracies expanded in these years to direct nation building and the drive for social order. The nation-state required citizens to follow a growing catalog of regulations as government authority reached further into the realm of everyday life. The censuses that Britain, France, and the United States had begun early in the nineteenth century became routine in most other countries as well. Censuses provided the state with personal details of citizens' lives, such as age, occupation, marital status, residential patterns, and fertility. Governments used these data for a variety of endeavors, ranging from setting quotas for military conscription to predicting needs for new prisons. Reformers like Florence Nightingale, who gathered statistics to support sanitary reform, believed that such quantitative information made government less susceptible to corruption and inefficiency. In 1860, Sweden introduced the income tax, which opened an area of private life—one's earnings from work or investment—to government scrutiny.

To bring about their vision of social order, many governments also expanded their regulation and investigation of prostitution. Venereal disease, especially syphilis, was common and, like typhus, infected individuals and whole families. Officials blamed prostitutes, not their clients, for its spread. The police picked up suspect women, who were examined for syphilis and incarcerated for treatment. As states began monitoring prostitution and other social matters such as public health and housing, they had to add departments and agencies. In 1867, Hungary's bureaucracy handled fewer than 250,000 individual cases, ranging from health to poverty issues; twenty years later, it handled more than a million.

Schooling and Professionalizing Society

An emphasis on knowledge and objective standards changed the professions and raised their status. Growing numbers of middle-class doctors, lawyers, managers, and journalists employed solid information in their work. The middle classes argued that civil service jobs should be awarded according to talent and skill rather than automatically going to those of aristocratic birth or with political connections. In Britain, a civil service law passed in 1870 required competitive examinations to ensure competency in government posts—a system long used in China. Governments began to allow professional people to influence state policy and determine rules for admission to "the professions." Such legislation had both positive and negative effects: groups could set high standards, but some otherwise qualified people were prohibited from working because they lacked the established credentials. The medical profession, for example, gained the authority to license physicians, but it tried to block experienced midwives from attending childbirths. Science became the province of the trained specialist rather than the experienced amateur.

Nation building required major improvements in the education of all citizens, professional or not. "We have made Italy," one Italian official announced. "Now we have to make Italians." Education was one way of bringing citizens to hold common beliefs and values. Bureaucrats and professionals called for radical changes in the curriculum and faculty of schools—from kindergarten to university—to make the general population more fit for citizenship and more useful in furthering economic progress. Expansion of the electorate and lower-class activism prompted one British aristocrat to say of the common people, whom he feared as they gained influence, "We must now educate our masters!" Governments thus introduced compulsory schooling to reduce illiteracy, at a level of more than 65 percent in Italy and Spain in the 1870s and even higher in eastern Europe (see "Taking Measure"). As ordinary people were allowed to vote, books taught them about the responsibilities of citizenship and provided the practical knowledge they needed to participate in an industrial society.

Education reform was not easy. At midcentury, religious authorities supervised schools and charged tuition, making primary education an option chosen only by prosperous or religious parents. After the 1850s, national politicians felt that their states could not afford masses of ignorant citizens, whose backwardness one French official blamed on parish priests. In 1861, an English commission on education concluded that instead of the Bible, "the knowledge most important to a labouring man is that of the causes which regulate the amount of his wages, the hours of his work, the regularity of his employment, and the prices of what he consumes." Replacing religion was a challenge for the increasingly knowledge-based nation.

Enforcing school attendance was another. Although the Netherlands, Sweden, and Switzerland had functioning primary school systems before midcentury, many parents in these and other countries resisted sending their children to school. Farm families depended on children to perform chores and believed that work in the

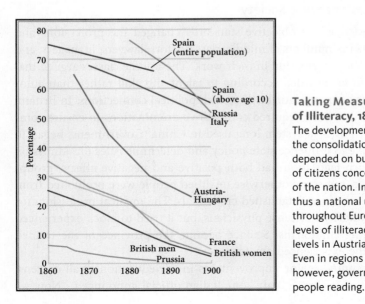

Taking Measure The Decline of Illiteracy, 1850–1900
The development of mass politics and the consolidation of the nation-state depended on building a cohesive group of citizens concerned with the progress of the nation. Increasing literacy was thus a national undertaking that varied throughout Europe, ranging from the low levels of illiteracy in Prussia to the high levels in Austria-Hungary and Russia. Even in regions of high levels of illiteracy, however, governments successfully got people reading.

fields or the household provided the best education. Urban homemakers needed their children to fetch water, dispose of waste, tend the younger children, and scavenge for household necessities such as stale bread from bakers. Yet some of the poor joined a craze for learning, which made traveling lecturers, public forums, reading groups, and debating societies popular among the middle and working classes.

Secondary and university education also expanded, yet remained even more of a luxury. In authoritarian countries such as Russia, advanced education, including education in science and technology, was often suspect because it empowered the young with information and taught them to think for themselves. Reformers pushed for more advanced and more complex courses for young women as part of nation building. In France and Russia, for example, government leaders themselves saw that "public education has had in view only half the population—the male sex," as the Russian minister of education wrote to Tsar Alexander II in 1856. They started secondary- and university-level courses for women as part of their programs to make women more interesting wives and better mothers and to control the modernization of society. In Britain, the founders of two women's colleges, Girton (1869) and Newnham (1871) at Cambridge University, believed that exacting standards in women's higher education would provide an example of a modern curriculum and also raise the low standards of scholarship prevalent in the men's colleges of Cambridge and Oxford at the time. Nonetheless, higher education for women remained controversial, as many people felt that knowledge of religion, sewing, and deportment was adequate for women.

Education also opened professional doors to women, who came to attend universities—in particular medical schools—in Zurich and Paris in the 1860s. Despite the complaint that their practice of medicine would weaken the system of separate spheres, women doctors thought they would bring feminine values to health care and also get better results, because their women patients would be more open with them than with male doctors. The need for knowledgeable citizens also offered opportunities for large numbers of women to enter teaching, a field once dominated by men. Hundreds of women founded nurseries, kindergartens, and primary schools based on the Enlightenment idea that learning starts at an early age. In Italy, women founded schools as a way to expand knowledge and teach civics lessons, thus providing a service to the nation. Yet many men opposed the idea of women teaching. "I shudder at philosophic women," wrote one German critic of female kindergarten teachers. Seen as radical because it brought middle-class women out of the home, the cause of early childhood education, or the "kindergarten movement," was as controversial as other education reforms.

Spreading National Power and Order beyond the West

In an age of nation building and industrial development, colonies took on new importance because they were seen to add to the power of the nation-state. This benefit led Great Britain, France, and Russia to expand their political control and rule colonies directly rather than through trading companies. Sometimes they offered social and cultural services such as schools. For instance, in the 1850s and 1860s Russian officials promoted the expansion of Russia's borders to gain control over nomadic tribes in central and eastern Asia. The Russian government then instituted educational and religious programs, such as instruction in the Russian language and in the beliefs of the Orthodox church, as a means to strengthen social order.

Great Britain, the era's mightiest imperial power, made a dramatic change of course toward political rule abroad as part of nation building during these decades. Before the 1850s, British liberals desired commercial gain from colonies, but believing in laissez-faire, they kept government involvement in colonial affairs minimal. In India, the East India Company worked across the subcontinent on Britain's behalf, and many regional rulers awarded the company commercial advantages. Since the eighteenth century, the East India Company had gained control over various kingdoms on the Indian subcontinent and had built railroads throughout the countryside to make commerce and revenue collecting more efficient. As commerce with Britain grew, many Indian merchants became wealthy. Other local men enlisted in the British-run Indian army, which became one of the largest standing armies in the world.

European expansion, including Britain's, was contested around the world, and in 1857 Indian troops, both Muslim and Hindu, violently rebelled when a rumor spread that Britain would force them to use ammunition cartridges greased with cow and pig fat, which violated the Hindu ban on beef and the Muslim prohibition of pork. This was not their main grievance, though. The soldiers, more generally angered at widening British control, stormed and conquered the old Mughal capital of Delhi and declared the independence of the Indian nation—an uprising that became known as the Indian Rebellion of 1857.

Indian Resistance, 1857

Simultaneously, civil rebellions erupted among leaders who were being displaced and the general populace who backed them against "the tyranny and oppression of the infidel and treacherous English." The rani (queen) Lakshmibai, widow of the ruler of the state of Jhansi in central India, led a separate military revolt when the East India Company tried to take over her lands after her husband died. As the British brutally crushed the rebels, Indian nationalism was born. Victorious, the British government took direct control of India in 1858, and the British Parliament declared Queen Victoria the empress of India in 1876.

A system of rule emerged in which close to half a million Indians governed a region the British called India under the supervision of a few thousand British men. Indians also collected taxes and distributed patronage. Colonial rule meant both outright oppression and more subtle intervention in everyday life. British production of cheap goods forced the impoverishment of such artisans as Indian hand-loom weavers, who had once dominated international markets. The British aimed to divert colonial populations into the production of cheap raw materials such as wheat, cotton, and jute to supply their industries. Nonetheless, some Indians benefited from improved sanitation and medicine and chose to accept British arguments against Indian customs such as infanticide, child marriage, and *sati*—a widow's self-immolation on her husband's funeral pyre. Others found Europe's scientific values attractive and, ironically, also came to appreciate that British rule brought a kind of unity to the many separate princedoms, thus laying the foundation for Indian nationalism.

French political expansion was similarly complex. The French government pushed to control Cochin China (modern southern Vietnam) in the 1860s. But missionaries in the area, ambitious French naval officers stationed in Asia, and even some local peoples pulled the French government further into the region. Like the British, the French brought improvements, such as the Mekong Delta project that increased the amount of cultivated land and spurred rapid growth of the food supply. Sanitation and public health programs proved a mixed blessing, because they led to population growth that strained other resources. Furthermore, landowners and French imperialists siphoned off most of the profits from economic improvement. The French also undertook a cultural mission to transform cities such as Saigon with tree-lined boulevards and other signs of Western urban life as they were doing in France itself. French literature, theater, and art diverted not only colonial officials but also upper-class Indochinese.

In this age of Realpolitik, the Crimean War had shown the great powers that the Mediterranean basin was crucial to expansion. Napoleon III, remembering his uncle's campaign in Egypt, took an interest in building the Suez Canal, which would dramatically shorten the route to Asia. The canal was completed in 1869, and as "canal fever" spread, Verdi composed the opera *Aïda* (set in ancient Egypt) in celebration. Great Britain and France were especially eager to do business with Egypt, where the combined value of imports and exports had jumped from 3.5 million Egyptian pounds in 1838 to 21 million in 1880 (and would grow to 60 million in 1913). European financial investment in the region also rose, first in ventures such as the Suez Canal in the 1860s and then in the laying of thousands of miles of railroad tracks and the creation of telegraph systems. Improvement-minded rulers in Asia and Africa paid dearly in 12 percent interest rates on loans for such projects. The completion of harbors, dams, canals, and railroads increased the Middle East's desirability as a market for European exports and as an intermediate stop on the way to trade with Asia. Having invested in the Suez Canal and in other commercial development, the British and French soon took over the Egyptian treasury to secure their own financial investments, and after invading Egypt in 1882, the British effectively took over the government, despite heated parliamentary opposition at home. Britain reshaped the Egyptian economy from a system based on multiple crops that maintained the country's self-sufficiency to one that emphasized the production of a few crops—mainly cotton, raw silk, wheat, and rice—that were especially useful to Europe. Local landowners and moneylenders also profited from these agricultural changes, while the bulk of the rural population barely eked out an existence.

The rest of the Mediterranean felt the heightened presence of the European powers. Driving deep into North Africa, the French army occupied all of Algeria by 1870, when the number of European immigrants to that region reached one-quarter million. French rule in Algeria as elsewhere brought profits to those dealing in European goods. Local leaders made money building railroads and government buildings and sometimes sent their children to European-style schools. Many local peoples, however, resisted the invasions and died from European-spread diseases. By 1872, the native population in Algeria had declined by more than 20 percent from five years earlier. As a further guarantee of their Mediterranean claims, the French occupied neighboring Tunisia in 1881. Western businessmen flooded the region with cheap goods, driving artisans from their trades and into low-paid work on railroads or in tobacco factories. Instead of basing wage rates on gender (as they did at home), Europeans used ethnicity and religion to segment the workforce, paying Muslims less than Christians and Arabs less than other ethnic groups.

The vastness of China allowed it to escape complete takeover, but traders and missionaries from European countries, carrying their message of Christian salvation, made inroads for the Western powers. Missionaries directed the Christian message to a population of 430 million, which had nearly doubled since the last century. Defeat in the Opium Wars caused an economic slump and helped generate the mass opposition movement known as the Taiping (Heavenly Kingdom). Headed by a leader who claimed to be the brother of Jesus, the movement attracted millions of followers who wanted an end to the ruling Qing dynasty, the expulsion of foreigners, more equal treatment of women, and land reform. By the mid-1850s, the Taiping controlled half of China. The threatened Qing regime promised the British and French greater influence in exchange for aid in defeating the Taiping. More than 20 million Chinese died in the resulting civil war (compared with 600,000 dead in the U.S. Civil War). When peace finally came in 1864, Western governments controlled much of the Chinese customs service and had almost unlimited access to the country.

Japan alone was able to escape European domination but not its influence. Through Dutch traders at Nagasaki, the Japanese had become keenly aware of the industrial, military, and commercial innovations of European society. In 1854, when the Japanese agreed to open the country to foreign trade, contacts with Europe had already given the Japanese a healthy appetite for Western knowledge and goods, including its superior weaponry. In 1867, reformers overthrew a government that resisted change, and in 1868 they enacted the **Meiji Restoration**. The word *Meiji* pointed to the "enlightened rule" of the new emperor whom the reformers had installed. Its goal was to combine "Western science and Eastern values" as a way of "making new"—hence, a combination of restoration and innovation. The new regime established Japan as a modern, technologically powerful state free from Western control.

Contesting the Nation-State at Home

Europeans did not simply sit by as the growing nation-state disrupted their lives. A better-informed working class protested the upheavals in everyday life caused when cities were ripped apart for improvement and when the growth of factories destroyed people's livelihoods. Workers' organizations slowly reemerged after their repression in the 1850s, and new theories arose to explain the growing power of the nation-state and the spread of industry on which the state depended. Increasingly educated by public schools, urban workers frequented cafés and pubs to hear news and discuss economic and political changes.

Many of the most outspoken labor activists were artisans, struggling to survive in the new industrializing climate. They were attracted either by the ideas of political theorist and former printer Pierre-Joseph Proudhon or by anarchist thought. In the 1840s, Proudhon proclaimed, "Property is theft," suggesting that ownership robbed workers of their rightful share of the earth's benefits. He opposed the centralized state and proposed that society be organized instead around natural groupings of men (but not women, who should work in seclusion at home for their husbands' comfort) in artisans' workshops. These workshops and a central bank crediting each worker for his labor would replace government and would lead to a "mutualist" social organization. **Anarchism** maintained that the existence of the state was the root of social injustice. According to the Russian nobleman and anarchist leader Mikhail Bakunin, the slightest infringement on freedom, especially by the central state and its laws, was unacceptable. Anarchists thus advocated the destruction of all state power, an increasingly attractive platform in this age of the expanding nation-state.

Political theorist and labor organizer Karl Marx opposed both mutualism and anarchism. These doctrines, he insisted, were wrongheaded, lacking the sound, scientific basis of his own theory, subsequently called **Marxism**. Marx's analysis, explained most notably in his book *Das Kapital* (*Capital*), adopted the liberal idea, dating back to John Locke in the seventeenth century, that human existence was defined by the requirement to work as a way of fulfilling basic needs such as food and shelter. Published between 1867 and 1894, *Das Kapital* was based on mathematical calculations of production and profit that would justify Realpolitik for the working classes. Marx held that the fundamental organization of any society, including its politics and culture, derived from the relationships arising from work or production. This idea, known as materialism, meant that the foundation of a society rested on class relationships—such as those between slave and master, serf and nobleman, or worker and capitalist. Marx called the class relationships that developed around work the "mode of production"—for instance, slavery, feudalism, or capitalism. He rejected the liberal focus on individual rights and emphasized instead the unequal class relations caused by those who had taken from the workers control of the means of production—that is, the capital, land, or factories—necessary to fulfill basic human needs.

Marx, like the politicians around him, took a tough-minded and realistic look at society as a whole. When a wave of strikes erupted in the late 1860s—in France alone, forty thousand workers participated in strikes in 1869, followed by more than eighty-five thousand in 1870—Marx saw struggle, not the warmhearted cooperation proposed by Proudhon or the utopian socialists (see page 654), as the means for bringing about change. Workers' awareness of their oppression would produce class consciousness among those in the same predicament and ultimately lead them to revolt against their exploiters—the capitalists, or bourgeoisie. Capitalism would be overthrown by these workers—the proletariat—bringing about a socialist society.

Marx saw the uprisings in France as the Franco-Prussian War ended in 1871 as a sign that his predictions were coming true. As the Prussians laid siege to Paris in 1870–1871, causing death and starvation in the bitter cold, the besieged Parisians rose up and demanded new republican liberties, new systems of work, and a more balanced distribution of power between the central government and the localities. To counter what they saw as the despotism of the centralized government, they declared themselves a self-governing commune on March 28, 1871. One issue behind the unrest was the nation-state's takeover of city life. As urban renovation displaced tens of thousands of workers from their homes in the heart of the city, homelessness and chaos embittered many Parisians against the state. Other French municipalities declared themselves communes as well, in an attempt to form a decentralized nation of independent, confederated units run by local citizens, not bureaucrats.

In the Paris Commune's two months of existence, its forty-member council, National Guard, and many other improvised offices found themselves at cross-purposes. Trying to maintain "communal" instead of "national" values, Parisians quickly developed a wide array of political clubs, local ceremonies, and self-managed, cooperative workshops. Women workers, for example, banded together to make National Guard uniforms on a cooperative rather than a profit-making basis. Beyond liberal political equality, the Commune proposed to liberate the worker and ensure "the absolute equality of women laborers." Thus a *commune* in contrast to a *republic* was meant to bring about social revolution. Communards, however, often disagreed about how specifically to change society. Mutualism, feminism, international socialism, and anarchism were but a few of the proposed avenues to social justice.

In the meantime, the provisional government that succeeded the defeated Napoleon III struck back to reinstitute national order. On May 21, 1871, the army

Woman Incendiary
The Paris Commune galvanized women activists, many of whom hoped to reform social conditions. After the fall of the Commune, women Communards were denigrated as half-clothed degenerates, using gender disorder to highlight the disorderliness of the Commune's resistance to the state. (© Bibliothèque nationale, Paris, France/The Bridgeman Art Library.)

entered Paris. In a week of fighting, both Communards and the army set the city ablaze (the Communards did so to slow the progress of government troops), and both sides executed hostages. Ultimately, however, the well-supplied French national army won. In the wake of victory, the army shot tens of thousands of citizens found on the streets. Parisian insurgents, one citizen commented, "deserved no better judge than a soldier's bullet." The Communards had fatally promoted a kind of antistate in an age of growing national power, and soon a different interpretation of the Paris Commune emerged: it was the work of the *pétroleuse,* or "woman incendiary"—a case of women running mad, crowding the streets in frenzy and fury. Within a year, writers were blaming the burning of Paris on women— "shameless slatterns, half-naked women, who kindled courage and breathed life into arson." Revolutionary men later became heroes in the history books, but women in political situations were characterized as "sinister females, sweating, their clothing undone, [who] passed from man to man."

The Franco-Prussian War, the Paris Commune, and the civil war were all horrendous blows from which France struggled to recover. The keys to restoring order in France after 1871 were instilling family values, fortifying religion, and claiming that the Commune had resulted from the collapsed boundaries between the male political sphere and the female domestic sphere. Karl Marx disagreed: he analyzed the Commune as a class struggle of workers attacking capitalist interests, which were protected by the centralized state. In the struggle against the Commune, the nation-state once again showed its strengthening muscle.

REVIEW   How did nation-states expand their reach, and what resistance did they face?

The Culture of Social Order

Artists and writers of the mid-nineteenth century had reactions to the expanding nation-state as complex as those of people in Europe and around the world. In one way, artists took a remarkable turn by adopting a realistic style in cultural works in the 1850s to 1870s that paralleled Realpolitik. After 1848, many artists and writers expressed anger about political repression and economic growth. They saw daily life as filled with commercial values and organized by mindless officials. Unlike the romantics of the first half of the century, artists of the second half often had trouble seeing ordinary people as heroic. "How tired I am of the ignoble workman, the inept bourgeois, the stupid peasant, and the odious priest," wrote French novelist Gustave Flaubert. Rejecting romanticism, he described ordinary people in a new style called realism. Intellectuals proposed theories called **positivism** and Darwinism, which also took a cold, hard look at society. It was a stark realism similar to that which statesmen applied to politics.

The Arts Confront Social Reality

Culture helped the cause of national unity. The reading public devoured biographies of political leaders, past and present, and credited daring heroes with creating the triumphant nation-state. As literacy spread, readers of all classes responded to the mid-nineteenth-century novel and to an increasing number of artistic, scientific, and natural history exhibitions sponsored by the nation-state. While reading the same novels or attending exhibitions, citizens were schooled to appreciate the artistic style called realism and, more generally, to embrace their shared national heritage.

A well-financed press and commercially minded publishers produced an age of best sellers out of the craving for realism—or true-to-life portrayals of society without romantic or idealistic overtones. The novels of Charles Dickens appeared in serial form in newspapers, and each installment attracted buyers eager for the latest plot twist. His characters, drawn from contemporary English society, included starving orphans, grasping lawyers, and ruthless opportunists. *Hard Times* (1854) depicts the grinding poverty and ill health of workers alongside the heartlessness of businessmen. Novelist George Eliot (the pseudonym of Mary Ann Evans) deeply probed private, "real-life" dilemmas in works such as *The Mill on the Floss* (1860) and *Middlemarch* (1871–1872). Describing rural society, high and low, Eliot allowed Britons to see one another's predicaments, wherever they lived. She knew the pain of ordinary life from her own experience: she was a social outcast because she lived with a married man; despite her fame, she was not received in polite society. These popular novels showed a hard reality and thus helped form a shared culture among people in distant parts of a nation much as state institutions did.

French writers also scorned dreams of political utopias and ideal beauty. Gustave Flaubert's *Madame Bovary* (1857) tells the story of a bored doctor's wife whose life is filled with romantic fantasies. She has one love affair after another and becomes so hopelessly indebted buying gifts for her lovers that she commits suicide. *Madame Bovary* scandalized French society for its frank picture of women's sexuality but attracted a wide readership. Poet Charles-Pierre Baudelaire wrote explicitly about sex; in *Les Fleurs du mal*

(*Flowers of Evil*, 1857), he expressed sexual passion and described drug- and wine-induced fantasies. French authorities brought charges against both Flaubert and Baudelaire for these violations of social convention. At issue was social and artistic order. "Art without rules is no longer art," the prosecutor maintained, as both were found guilty.

During the era of the Great Reforms, Russian writers debated whether western European values were harming Russian culture. Rather than dividing the nation, this discussion about Russian culture united people around a national issue. Adopting one viewpoint, Ivan Turgenev created a powerful novel of Russian life, *Fathers and Sons* (1862), a story of nihilistic children rejecting not only parental authority but also their parents' spiritual values in favor of science and facts. Expressing another point of view, Fyodor Dostoevsky in *The Possessed* (1871–1872) and other works showed the dark, ridiculous, and neurotic side of nihilists, thus holding up Turgenev as a softheaded romantic. Dostoevsky's highly intelligent characters in *Crime and Punishment* (1866) are often personally tormented and condemned to lead absurd, even criminal lives. He used these antiheroes to emphasize spirituality and traditional Russian values, but he gave his works a "realistic" spin by planting such values in ordinary, often seedy people.

Visual artists had a different relationship to their governments than did writers, yet many also depicted society in harsh terms. Artists usually depended on government support rather than sales to thousands of readers. Leaders such as Britain's Prince Albert purchased works for official collections and for themselves. Having artwork chosen for display at government-sponsored exhibitions was another way for artists to gain prominence and earn a living. Officially appointed juries selected works of art to be exhibited and then chose prizewinners from among them. Hundreds of thousands of people from all classes attended these exhibitions.

After 1848, artists began rejecting romantic conventions idealizing ordinary folk and grand historic events. Instead, painters like French artist Gustave Courbet portrayed weary laborers at backbreaking work because, as he stated, an artist should "never permit sentiment to overthrow logic." Édouard Manet broke with romantic conventions of the nude. His *Olympia* (1865) depicts a white courtesan lying on her bed, attended by a black woman. This disregard for the classical traditions of showing women in dreamy poses or mythical settings was too much for the critics; one called *Olympia* "a sort of female gorilla." Shocking at first, graphic portrayals that shattered comforting illusions were a feature of realism.

Artistic realism faced a challenge from photography—a challenge that found its response in the 1860s to 1890s in a new style called **impressionism**. Manet coined the term to reflect artists' attempts to capture a single moment by focusing on the ever-changing light and color found in everyday vision. Using splotches and dots, impressionists moved away from the precise realism of earlier painters. Claude Monet, for example, was fascinated by the way light transformed an object, and he often portrayed the same place—a bridge or a railroad station—at different times of day. Dutch-born painter Vincent Van Gogh used vibrant colors in great swirls to capture sunflowers and the starry night sky. Such distortions of reality made the impressionists' visual style seem outrageous to those accustomed to realism, but others enthusiastically greeted impressionism's luminous quality as more real than realism. Industry contributed to the

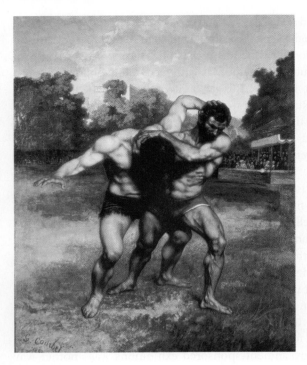

Gustave Courbet, *Wrestlers* **(1850)**
Courbet painted his dirty, grunting
wrestlers in the realist style, which
rejected the dreamy romanticism of
revolutionary Europe. These muscular
men sum up the resort to physical
struggle during these state-building
decades and convey the art world's
recognition that Realpolitik had taken
over the governance of society.
(© Museum of Fine Arts, Budapest, Hungary/
The Bridgeman Art Library.)

new style, as factories produced paint from chemicals rather than plants in a wider, more intense spectrum of colors.

In both composition and style, impressionists borrowed heavily from Asian art, knowledge of which rapidly spread in Europe as the West extended its reach. The concept of the fleetingness of situations came from a centuries-old Japanese concept called *mono no aware* (sensitivity to the fleetingness of life). The color, line, and delicacy of Japanese art (which many impressionists collected) is evident in Monet's later paintings of water lilies, his studies of wisteria, and even his re-creation of a Japanese garden at his home in France. Similarly, American artist Mary Cassatt used the two-dimensionality of Japanese art in her work. Some of the characters in her paintings, though European, look Japanese. Van Gogh sometimes filled the background of portraits with copies of intensely colored Japanese prints.

Artists also commented on the changing economic scene, especially the fact that a growing segment of service workers did less physical work and had more energy for leisure. French painter Georges Seurat, for example, depicted the newly created parks with their walking paths and Sunday bicyclists; white-collar workers carrying books or newspapers paraded in their store-bought clothing. Degas focused on portraying women—from ballet dancers to laundrywomen—in various states of exertion and fatigue. Van Gogh, avoiding the intense colors he typically used for the countryside, depicted the gray outskirts of cities, where industries were often located and where the desperately poor lived.

Unlike most of the visual arts, opera was commercially profitable, accessible to most classes of society, and thus an effective means of reaching the public. Verdi used musical theater to contrast noble ideals with the deadly effects of power, and the lure of passion with the need for social order. The German composer Richard Wagner, the most musically innovative composer of this era, hoped to revolutionize opera by combining music and drama to arouse the audience's fear, awe, and engagement. A gigantic cycle of four operas, *The Ring of the Nibelung* (1854–1874), reshaped ancient German myths into a modern, nightmarish allegory of a world doomed by its obsessive pursuit of money and power and redeemable only through unselfish love. Another of his operas, *The Mastersingers of Nuremberg* (1867), was a nationalistic tribute to German culture, and like the arts elsewhere, it helped unite individuals into a public with a shared, if debated, cultural experience.

Religion and Secular Order

The expansion of state power set the stage for clashes over the role of organized religion in the nation-state. Should religion have the same hold on government and public life as in the past, thus competing with loyalty to the nation? In the 1850s, many politicians supported religious institutions and attended religious services because they were another source of order. Simultaneously, some nation builders, intellectuals, and economic liberals rejected the competing worldview and authority of established churches, particularly Roman Catholicism. Bismarck was one of these. Believing that the church slowed the development of nationalist sentiment, he mounted a full-blown *Kulturkampf* (culture war) against Catholic influence in 1872. Mercilessly attacking the church, the German government expelled the Jesuits in 1872, increased state power over the clergy in Prussia in 1873, and introduced obligatory civil marriage in 1875. Bismarck, however, overestimated his ability to manipulate politics, for both conservatives and Catholics objected to religious repression in the name of state building.

The Catholic church felt assaulted by a growing rationalism that was supposed to replace religious faith and by the state building in Italy and Germany that competed for people's traditional loyalty. In addition, nation building had resulted in the extension of liberal rights to Jews, whom many Christians considered enemies. Attacking reform and changing values, Pope Pius IX (r. 1846–1878) issued *The Syllabus of Errors* (1864), and in 1870 the First Vatican Council approved the dogma of papal infallibility. This teaching proclaimed that the pope spoke divinely revealed truth on issues of morality and faith. Eight years later, a new pope, Leo XIII (r. 1878–1903), began the process of reconciliation with modern politics by encouraging up-to-date scholarship in Catholic institutes and universities and by accepting aspects of democracy. Leo's ideas marked a dramatic turn, ending the Kulturkampf and calming worried Catholics across Europe.

Religious doctrine continued to have powerful popular appeal, but the place of organized religion in society was changing. Church attendance declined among workers and artisans, but many people in the upper and middle classes and most of the peasantry remained faithful. The Orthodox church of Russia and eastern Europe, with its Pan-Slavic appeal, fostered nationalism among Serbs and became a rallying point. Women's spirituality intensified, and Roman Catholic and Russian Orthodox religious orders of women increased in size and number. Men, by contrast, were falling away from religious devotion. In 1858, an outburst of popular religious fervor, especially among women, followed a young peasant girl's visions of the Virgin Mary at Lourdes in southern France. Bernadette Soubirous said that Mary told her to drink from the ground, at which point a spring appeared. Crowds besieged the area to be cured of ailments by the waters of Lourdes. In 1867, less than ten years later, a railroad line was laid to Lourdes to enable millions of pilgrims to visit the shrine on church-organized trips. The Catholic church thus showed that it was up-to-date, willing to use modern means such as railroads and medical verification of miraculous cures to make Lourdes itself the center of a brisk commercial as well as religious culture.

At nearly the same time as Bernadette's vision, the English naturalist Charles Darwin published *On the Origin of Species* (1859), which challenged the Judeo-Christian worldview that humanity was the creation of God. Darwin argued that life had taken shape over countless millions of years before humans existed and that human life was the result of this slow development, called evolution. Instead of believing that God had miraculously brought the universe and all life into being in six days as described in the Bible, Darwin held that human life had developed from

lower forms through a battle for survival, and through the selection of sexual partners, more-evolved individuals passed their natural strength to the next generation. In a perpetual challenge to meet the forces of nature, Darwin suggested, some species die out, and those with better-adapted characteristics survive. A highly respectable Victorian gentleman, Darwin announced that the Bible gave a "manifestly false history of the world." Darwin's theories also undermined certain liberal, secular beliefs. The Enlightenment,

Darwin Ridiculed, c. 1860
Charles Darwin's theories claimed that humans had evolved from animal species and rejected the long-standing explanation of a divine human origin. His scientific ideas so diverged from people's beliefs that cartoonists made fun of both the respectable Darwin and his theory. Despite the controversy, evolution withstood the test of further scientific study. **For more help analyzing this image, see the visual activity for this chapter in the Online Study Guide at** bedfordstmartins.com/ huntconcise. (Hulton Archive/Getty Images.)

for example, had glorified nature as tranquil and noble and viewed human beings as essentially rational. The theory of **natural selection**, in which the fittest survive, suggested that human society is one in which combative individuals and groups constantly fight one another.

Darwin's findings and other innovative biological research placed religious views under attack. Working with pea plants in his monastery garden in the 1860s, Gregor Mendel determined the principles of heredity, from which the science of genetics later developed. Investigation into the female reproductive cycle led other scientists to discover the principle of spontaneous ovulation—the automatic release of the egg by the ovary whether sexual intercourse took place or not. This discovery caused theorists to conclude that men had aggressive and strong sexual drives because reproduction depended on their sexual arousal. In contrast, the spontaneous and regular release of the egg independent of emotions indicated that women were passive and lacked sexual feeling.

Darwin added to this social commentary. The legal, political, and economic privilege of white European men in the nineteenth century, he maintained, was natural because they were more highly evolved than white women or people of color. Despite his belief in a common ancestor for people of all races, Darwin held that people of color, or "lower races," were far behind whites in intelligence and civilization. As for women, "the chief distinction in the intellectual powers of the two sexes," Darwin declared, "is shewn by man's attaining to a higher eminence in whatever he takes up." The school of Social Darwinism developed its own version of evolutionary theory to lobby for racist, sexist, and nationalist policies. Social Darwinist arguments were influential in the years to come.

From Natural Science to Social Science

Darwin's thought motivated the search for alternatives to the idea that the social order was created by God. French social philosopher Auguste Comte developed positivism—a theory claiming that the careful study of facts would generate accurate and useful, or "positive," laws of society. Comte's *System of Positive Politics, or Treatise on Sociology* (1851) proposed that social scientists construct knowledge of the political order as they would construct understanding of the natural world—that is, through observation and objective study. This idea inspired people to believe they could solve the problems resulting from economic and social change. To accomplish this goal, tough-minded reformers founded study groups and scientifically oriented associations to dig up social facts such as statistics on poverty or the conditions of working-class life. Comte encouraged women's participation in reform because he saw "womanly" compassion and scientific public policy to be equally important to producing social harmony. Positivism led not only to women's increased public activism but also to the growth of the social sciences.

The celebrated English philosopher John Stuart Mill used Comte's theories to promote widespread reform and mass education. In his political essay *On Liberty*

(1859), Mill argued for the improvement of society generally, but he also expressed concern that "superior" people not be brought down or confined by the will of the masses. Influenced by his wife, Harriet Taylor Mill, he advocated rights for women and introduced a woman suffrage bill into the House of Commons after her death. The bill's defeat prompted Mill to publish *The Subjection of Women* (1869), which presented the family as maintaining an older kind of order lacking modern concepts of rights and freedom. Mill exposed women's cheerful obedience in marriage as a sham. To make women appear "not a forced slave, but a willing one," he said, they were trained not to value their own talent and independence but to embrace "submission." Critiquing the century's basic beliefs about men's and women's roles, *The Subjection of Women* became an internationally celebrated argument for the rights of women.

The progressive side of Mill's social thought was soon lost in a flood of Social Darwinist theories and became one among several visions of social order—all of them claiming to be scientific and thus true. The theories of Mill, Comte, Darwin, and others influenced later national debates over policy in the West. Inspired by the social sciences, policymaking came to rely on statistics and fact gathering to produce realistic, hardheaded appraisals for the purpose of building strong, unified nations.

REVIEW   What were the results of applying the scientific method to social thought?

Conclusion

Throughout modern history, the development of nation-states and the economic prosperity on which they depended has been neither inevitable nor uniform nor peaceful. This was especially true in the nineteenth century, when ambitious politicians and determined bureaucrats used a variety of methods to transform very different countries into effective nation-states. Nation building was most dramatic in Germany and Italy, where states unified through military force and where people of opposing political opinions ultimately agreed that national unity should be the primary goal. Compelled by military defeat to shake off centuries of tradition, the Austrian and Russian monarchs instituted reforms as a way of keeping their systems in place. The Habsburg Empire became a dual monarchy that raised the level of disunity. Reforms in Russia left the authoritarian monarchy intact but partially transformed the social order.

After decades of romantic fervor, realism in politics and the industrial economy became a much-celebrated principle, which spread to cultural matters as well. Proponents of realism such as Darwin and Marx developed theories disturbing to those who maintained an Enlightenment faith in social and political harmony. Realist novels and artworks jarred polite society and, like the operas of Verdi, portrayed dilemmas of the times. Growing government administrations set policies that were meant to bring order but often brought disorder and resistance, including the Taiping uprising, the Indian Rebellion, and the Paris Commune—all of

Mapping the West Europe and the Mediterranean, c. 1880
European nation-states consolidated their power by building unified state structures and by developing the means to foster social and cultural integration of the diverse peoples within their borders.
They also were rapidly expanding outside their boundaries, extending the economic and political reach
of the nation-state. North Africa and the Middle East—parts of the declining Ottoman Empire—had
particular appeal to Europeans because of their natural resources and their potential for further
European settlement. They also provided a gateway to the rest of the world.

them challenging European nation building. When the ordinary people of the Paris Commune rose up to protest the loss of French power and prestige in the Franco-Prussian War, they also defied the trend toward economic modernity and state building. Their actions raised difficult questions. How far should the power of the state extend in both domestic and international affairs? Would nationalism be a force for war or for peace? As these issues ripened, the next decades would see continued economic advancement, growing competition for global power, and unprecedented changes that ultimately would lead to a major war. All of these were the result of successes in nation building.

CHAPTER REVIEW QUESTIONS

1. Some would call the decades between 1850 and 1880 a period of order, while others would call it a period of disorder. Which characterization would you choose and why?

2. What ingredients contribute to the "realism" historians see in the events and actions of this period?

TIMELINE

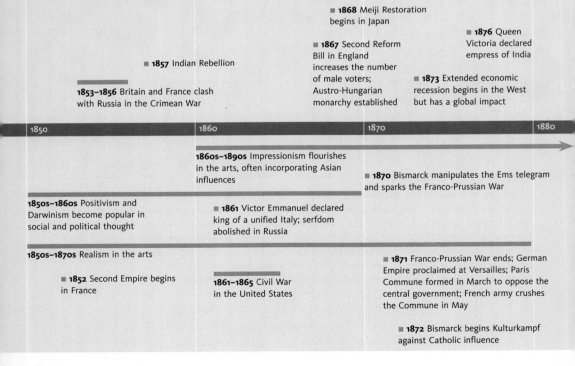

1869–1871 Women's colleges founded at Cambridge University

1868 Meiji Restoration begins in Japan

1867 Second Reform Bill in England increases the number of male voters; Austro-Hungarian monarchy established

1876 Queen Victoria declared empress of India

1857 Indian Rebellion

1873 Extended economic recession begins in the West but has a global impact

1853–1856 Britain and France clash with Russia in the Crimean War

1850   1860   1870   1880

1860s–1890s Impressionism flourishes in the arts, often incorporating Asian influences

1870 Bismarck manipulates the Ems telegram and sparks the Franco-Prussian War

1850s–1860s Positivism and Darwinism become popular in social and political thought

1861 Victor Emmanuel declared king of a unified Italy; serfdom abolished in Russia

1850s–1870s Realism in the arts

1871 Franco-Prussian War ends; German Empire proclaimed at Versailles; Paris Commune formed in March to oppose the central government; French army crushes the Commune in May

1852 Second Empire begins in France

1861–1865 Civil War in the United States

1872 Bismarck begins Kulturkampf against Catholic influence

For practice quizzes and other study tools, see the Online Study Guide at
bedfordstmartins.com/huntconcise.

For primary-source material from this period, see Chapters 22 and 23 of
Sources of THE MAKING OF THE WEST, Third Edition.

Suggested References

Nation building has produced a varied literature ranging from studies of royalty
as unifying figures to histories of the arts and industry. Bayly's book puts the
development of the Western nation-state into a world history perspective.

Bayly, C. A. *The Birth of the Modern World, 1780–1914: Global Connections and Comparisons.* 2004.

Blackbourn, David. *The Conquest of Nature: Water, Landscape, and the Making of Modern Germany.* 2006.

*Darwin, Charles. *Autobiography.* 1969.

Eichner, Carolyn. *Surmounting the Barricades: Women in the Paris Commune.* 2004.

Eley, Geoff. *Forging Democracy: A History of the Left in Europe, 1850–2000.* 2002.

Faust, Drew Gilpin. *This Republic of Suffering: Death and the American Civil War.* 2008.

Gross, Michael B. *The War against Catholicism: Liberalism and the Anti-Catholic Imagination in Nineteenth-Century Germany.* 2005.

Homans, Margaret. *Royal Representations: Queen Victoria and British Culture, 1837–1876.* 1998.

Kaufman, Suzanne. *Consuming Visions: Mass Culture and the Lourdes Shrine.* 2005.

King, Jeremy. *Budweisers into Czechs and Germans: A Local History of Bohemian Politics, 1848–1948.* 2002.

Papayanis, Nicholas. *Planning Paris before Haussmann.* 2004.

Rappaport, Erika. *Shopping for Pleasure: Women in the Making of London's West End.* 2000.

Rappaport, Helen. *No Place for Ladies: The Untold Story of Women in the Crimean War.* 2007.

Roy, Tapti. *The Raj of the Rani.* 2007.

*Seacole, Mary. *Wonderful Adventures of Mrs. Seacole in Many Lands.* 1857.

Stites, Richard. *Serfdom, Society, and the Arts in Imperial Russia.* 2005.

Victorian Web: http://www.victorianweb.org

Empire, Modernity, and the Road to War

c. 1880–1914

I N THE FIRST DECADE of the twentieth century, a wealthy young Russian man traveled from one country to another to find relief from a common ailment of the time called neurasthenia. Its symptoms included fatigue, lack of interest in life, depression, and sometimes physical sickness. In 1910, the young man encountered Sigmund Freud, a Viennese doctor whose unconventional treatment—eventually called **psychoanalysis** took the form of conversations about the patient's dreams, sexual experiences, and everyday life. Over the course of four years, Freud uncovered his patient's deeply hidden fear of castration disguised as a fear of wolves—thus the name "Wolf-Man," by which he is known to us. Freud worked his cure, as the Wolf-Man himself put it, "by bringing repressed ideas into consciousness."

The Wolf-Man could be said to represent his time. Born into a family that owned vast estates, he reflected the growing prosperity of Europeans, though on a grander scale than most. Countless individuals were troubled, even mentally disturbed like the Wolf-Man, and suicide was not uncommon. The Wolf-Man's own sister and father died from intentional drug overdoses. At the turn of the century, Europeans raised questions about family life, gender relationships, empire, religion, and the consequences of technology. Every sign of imperial wealth brought on a sense of Europe's decline. British writer H. G. Wells saw in this era "humanity upon the

Edvard Munch, *The Scream* (1893)
In some of his paintings, Norwegian artist Edvard Munch captured the spirit of the turn of the century using delightful pastel colors to convey the leisured life of people strolling in the countryside. But modern life at this time also had its tortured side, which Munch was equally capable of portraying. *The Scream* is seen as emblematic of the torments of modernity as the individual turns inward, driven by neuroses, self-destructive impulses, and even madness. While some people, like the two figures in the background, could react calmly to whatever modern life had to offer, others, like the screamer, agonized over every turn of events. It can also be suggested that the screamer, like Europe, was traveling the road to World War I. *(Scala/Art Resource, NY. © 2010 The Munch Museum/The Munch-Ellingsen Group/Artists Rights Society [ARS], NY.)*

wane . . . the sunset of mankind." Gloom filled the pages of many a book and upset the lives of individuals like the Wolf-Man.

Conflict rattled the world as a growing number of powers, including Japan, fought their way into even more territories and took political control. As the race for worldwide empire continued—most notably in Africa—colonized peoples developed liberation movements to become independent, like their oppressors. While the great powers fought to dominate people around the world, the competition for empire fueled an arms race that threatened to turn Europe, the "most civilized" continent in the world according to its leaders, into a savage battleground. In domestic politics, militant nationalism fueled anti-Semitism and ethnic hatred. Women suffragists along with politically disadvantaged groups such as the Slavs and Irish demanded full rights, even as political assassinations and public brutality swept away the liberal values of tolerance and rights.

Those were just some of the conflicts associated with **modernity**—a term often used to describe the faster pace of life, the rise of mass politics, and the decline of a rural social order that were so visible in the West from the late nineteenth century on. The word *modernity* also refers to the celebrated "modern" art, music, science, and philosophy of this period. Although many people today admire the brilliant qualities of the modern arts, some people at the time were offended, even outraged, by the new styles and sounds. Freud's theory that sexual drives exist even in the youngest children shocked early-twentieth-century people. Middle-class faith in artistic and scientific progress was tested, and just as the Wolf-Man was finishing his treatment in June 1914, all the tensions that had been building nationally and internationally were coming to a head. The Wolf-Man rejoiced at the end of June 1914 that "he could now leave Vienna a healthy man." Yet the political, social, and diplomatic friction of the past few decades was about to erupt into World War I—one of the most horrific wars the world has ever seen.

CHAPTER FOCUS QUESTION How did developments in social and intellectual life, imperial expansion, and politics at the turn of the twentieth century produce instability and set the backdrop for war?

The Challenge of Empire

Imperialism surged in the last third of the nineteenth century and increasingly caused conflict in the early twentieth century. Colonies provided investments and crucial markets for some businesses, and heated rivalry among nations fueled competition for territory in Africa and Asia. The imperialism of these decades is called "new" because of the rush to rule more territories directly rather than just control trade with them. But the situation was complicated and the distribution of benefits uneven. Late in the century, for example, French colonies bought 65 percent of France's exports of soap, and imperialism provided huge numbers of jobs to people in European port cities. Yet Europeans did not benefit uniformly from the search for new markets, which often proved more costly than profitable. Whether they benefited or not, taxpayers in all parts of a nation paid for colonial armies, increasingly costly weaponry, and colonial administrators. Although imperialism was supposed to advance peaceful "civilization," this wave of "new imperialism" actually intensified international tensions. In securing India's borders, for example, the British faced Russian expansion in Afghanistan and China. Generating conflict around the world, imperial competition even made areas of Europe, such as the Balkans, more volatile than ever as states struggled for control of disputed territory.

Motives for imperialism were complex. Goals such as fostering national might and Christianizing peoples often proved difficult to achieve. Governments worried that imperialism—because of its expense and the constant possibility of war—might weaken rather than strengthen them. The French statesman Jules Ferry argued that France "must keep its role as the soldier of civilization." But it was unclear whether imperialists should emphasize soldiering—that is, conquest and conflict—or the goal of exporting culture and religion. Hoping to Christianize colonized peoples, European missionaries ventured to newly occupied areas of Africa and Asia. A woman missionary working among the Tibetans reflected a common view when she remarked that the native peoples were "going down, down into hell, and there is no one but me . . . to witness for Jesus amongst them." Europeans were confident of their religious and cultural superiority and thus fought their way into distant countries, undermining age-old civilizations.

The Scramble for Africa

After the British takeover of the Egyptian government in the 1880s, European commerce with sub-Saharan Africa turned into political rule, as one territory after another fell to European military force. Europeans' principal objective was obtaining Africa's raw materials, such as palm oil, cotton, diamonds, cocoa, and rubber. Additionally, Britain wanted the southern and eastern coasts of Africa secure for stopover ports on the route to Asia. The British, French, Belgians, Portuguese, Italians, and Germans competed to dominate peoples, land, and resources—"the magnificent cake of Africa," as King Leopold II of Belgium put it (Map 19.1). Driven by insatiable greed, Leopold claimed the Congo region of central Africa (Map 19.2, page 734), competing with France for that territory and inflicting on local Africans unparalleled acts of cruelty. German chancellor Otto von Bismarck, who saw colonies mostly as political bargaining chips, established German control over Cameroon and a section of East Africa. Faced with competition, the British poured millions of pounds into conquering the continent "from Cairo to Cape Town," as the slogan went, and the French cemented their hold on large portions of West Africa.

The scramble for Africa escalated tensions in Europe, prompting Bismarck to call a conference of European nations at Berlin. The fourteen nations at the conference, held in a series of meetings in 1884 and 1885, decided that their settlements along the African coast guaranteed their rights to the interior territory as well. This

MADEIRA IS. (Port.)

CANARY IS. (Sp.)

N W E S

OTTOMAN EMPIRE

Mediterranean Sea

ALGERIA TUNISIA

MOROCCO

TRIPOLI

Suez Canal

Cairo [4]

EGYPT

ARABIA

S A H A R A

TIBESTI

Nile R.

Red Sea

RIO DE ORO

SENEGAL

GAMBIA

TUKULOR EMPIRE [2]

Niger R.

BORNU

L. Chad WADAI

SOKOTO SULTANATE

RABIH

MAHDIST STATE

White Nile R.

Blue Nile R.

Gulf of Aden

BR. SOMALIA

ETHIOPIA

GUINEA

SIERRA LEONE

LIBERIA

SAMORI'S EMPIRE

DAHOMEY

ASANTE

TOGO

GOLD COAST

YORUBA

[3]

CAMEROON

São Tomé (Port.)

GABON

CABINDA

Ubangi R.

Congo R.

EQUATORIA

BUGANDA

CONGO FREE STATE

TIPPU TIB'S DOMAIN

L. Victoria

L. Tanganyika

INDIAN OCEAN

SULTANATE OF ZANZIBAR

ATLANTIC OCEAN

ANGOLA

CHOKWE DOMAIN

MSIRI'S KINGDOM

L. Nyasa

Zambezi R.

PORTUGUESE EAST AFRICA (MOZAMBIQUE)

Madagascar

GERMAN SOUTHWEST AFRICA

[1]

SOUTH AFRICAN REPUBLIC (TRANSVAAL)

MERINA (HOVA) KINGDOM

WALVIS BAY

KALAHARI DESERT

BRIT. BECHUANALAND

Limpopo R.

Orange R.

ORANGE FREE STATE

ZULULAND

NATAL

CAPE COLONY

BASUTOLAND

Cape Town

British	Routes of Colonial Expansion
French	[1] Route of Rhodes's British S. African Company, 1890
German	
Italian	[2] French expansion into West Africa, 1883-1896
Portuguese	
Spanish	[3] British expansion into Nigeria, 1880-1902
Ottoman	
Nominally Ottoman; British controlled	[4] British invasion and occupation of Egypt, 1882
Non-European regimes (including Boer republics)	
Boundary of the Congo Free State	

0   500   1,000 miles

0   500   1,000 kilometers

agreement led to the strictly linear dissection of the continent; geographers and diplomats cut across local boundaries of African culture and ethnic life (Map 19.2). The Berlin conference also banned the sale of alcohol and controlled the sale of arms to native peoples. The Berlin settlement was supposed to reduce bloodshed and to calm growing concerns about European ambitions in Africa, but the greedy Europeans continued to plunder the continent and terrorize its people. The popular appetite for news of imperialist ventures grew, too.

Industrial technology provided the powerful guns, railroads, steamships, and medicines that made Western penetration of all the continents possible. The gunboats that forced the Chinese to open their borders to opium in the 1830s played a part in forcing African ethnic groups to give up their independence. Quinine and guns were also an important factor in African conquest. Before the development of medicinal quinine in the 1840s and 1850s, the deadly tropical disease malaria decimated many European groups setting out for exploration or military conquest, giving Africa the nickname "the White Man's Grave." Treating malaria with quinine, extracted from cinchona bark from the Andes, radically cut death rates among missionaries, traders, and soldiers.

While quinine saved lives, the technology to take lives advanced with improvements to the breech-loading rifle and the development of the machine gun between 1862 and the 1880s. Europeans took advantage of these developments, while also carrying on a brisk trade selling inferior guns to Africans along the coast. As a result of this trade, as well as the fact that peoples in the interior still used bows and arrows, Muslim slave traders and European Christians alike were able to crush African resistance with their superior firepower. "The whites did not seize their enemy as we do by the body, but thundered from afar," claimed one local African resister. "Death raged everywhere."

This destructive capacity had a great effect in southern Africa, where farmers of European descent and immigrant prospectors, rather than military personnel, battled African peoples for control of the frontier regions of the Transvaal, Natal, Orange Free State, and Cape Colony (Map 19.1, page 732). The Dutch had moved into the area in the seventeenth century, but the British had gained control by 1815. Thereafter, descendants of the Dutch, called Boers (Dutch for "farmers"), were joined by British immigrants in seizing farmland and mineral resources from the natives. British businessman and politician Cecil Rhodes, sent to South Africa for his health just as diamonds were being discovered in 1870, cornered the diamond

Map 19.1 **Africa, c. 1890**
The scramble for Africa entailed an expansion of European trading practices, which until approximately 1880 generally were limited to the coastline. The effort to conquer, penetrate economically, and rule the interior would result in a map of the continent that made sense only to the imperial powers (Map 19.2, page 734). This map divided ethnic groups and created colonial entities that had nothing to do with Africans' sense of geography, patterns of settlement, or political organization.

Map 19.2 Africa in 1914

Uprisings intensified in Africa in the early twentieth century as Europeans tried to consolidate their rule through bureaucratization and military action and to extract more wealth from the continent. While the Europeans were putting down rebellions against their rule, a pan-African movement arose, attempting to unite Africans as one people. As in Asia and the Middle East, the more the colonial powers tried to impose their will, the greater the political forces that took shape against them.

market, moved into gold mining, and claimed a huge amount of African territory with the help of the British government. His ambition for Britain and for himself was boundless. "I contend that we are the finest race in the world," he explained, "and that the more of the world we inhabit the better it is."

Social Darwinism justified the treatment of Africans. While Europeans credited China and India with a scientific and artistic heritage, Africans were seen as valuable only for their manual labor, despite their many accomplishments in other areas such as dyeing fabrics, building roads, and designing architecture. By confiscating Africans' land, Europeans forced native people to work for them to earn a living and pay the taxes they imposed. Subsistence agriculture, often performed by women and slaves, declined in favor of mining and farming cash crops. Standards of living dropped for Africans who lost their land without realizing the Europeans were claiming permanent ownership.

Tensions among whites escalated, too, when in 1896 the British experienced a bloody defeat after Rhodes directed his right-hand man, Dr. Leander Jameson, to lead a raid into the Transvaal. The goal was to stir up enough trouble between the Boers and the more recent immigrants from Britain that the British would be justified in taking over the Transvaal and Orange Free State, which the Boers controlled. The Boers, however, easily routed the raiders, striking a blow at British imperial pride. The British did not accept this loss. From 1899 to 1902, they fought the South African War, also called the Boer War, in the Transvaal and Orange Free State. Britain finally won that conflict in 1902 and annexed the disputed area, but the cost of the war—in money, destruction, and loss of life—horrified many Britons and caused them to see imperialism as a burden.

Imperial Newcomers

The bloodiness of the South African War was not the only challenge to the sense that this new imperialism was Europe's destiny. Europeans' confident approach to imperialism was also weakened by the rise of Japan as a power after the Meiji Restoration of 1868. Japan escaped the "new" European imperialism by rapidly transforming itself into a modern industrial nation with its own imperial agenda. "All classes high and low shall unite in vigorously promoting the economy and welfare of the nation," the new regime pronounced. The Japanese embraced knowledge from other countries, and in the 1870s deputations traveled to Europe and the United States to study technological and industrial developments. Western dress became the rule at the imperial court, and when a fire destroyed Tokyo in 1872, a European directed the rebuilding of the city in Western architectural style.

The new Japanese government, led by some of the old samurai, or warrior elite, crushed massive rebellions against modernization. It also merged older samurai traditions, such as spiritual discipline and the drive to excel, with a technologically

Modernization in Japan
Like the West, Japan bustled with commerce and industry thanks to improved and expanding transportation. Railroads, ships, and a range of new inventions such as the rickshaw speeded goods and individuals within cities, across the country, and ultimately to new, foreign destinations. The Japanese traveled widely to learn about ongoing technological innovation. (Rue des Archives/The Granger Collection, NY.)

modern military and sponsorship of trade. The state stimulated economic development by building railroads and shipyards, establishing financial institutions, and encouraging heavy industries such as mining and shipping. In Japan, unlike the rest of Asia, Western-style accomplishments became a patriotic goal.

Like its Western models, Japan started intervening elsewhere in Asia, ultimately provoking war with its powerful neighbors China and Russia. In 1894 the Japanese defeated the Chinese in the brief Sino-Japanese War, which in 1895 ended China's domination of Korea. Japan's imperial ambitions next clashed with those of the European powers. Pushing into eastern Asia, the Russians had built the Trans-Siberian Railroad through Manchuria, sent millions of Russian settlers eastward, and sponsored anti-Japanese groups in Korea. In 1904 Japan attacked tsarist forces at Port Arthur (Map 19.3). The Russian military proved inept in the ensuing yearlong Russo-Japanese War. In an astonishing display of poor leadership, Russia's Baltic Fleet sailed halfway around the globe, only to be destroyed in the battle of Tsushima Strait (1905). Opening an era of Japanese domination in East Asian politics, the victory was the first by a non-European nation over a European great power in the modern age. As one British general observed of the Russian defeat, "I have today seen the most stupendous spectacle it is possible for the mortal brain to conceive—Asia advancing, Europe falling back." Japan went on to annex Korea in 1910 and to target other areas for colonization.

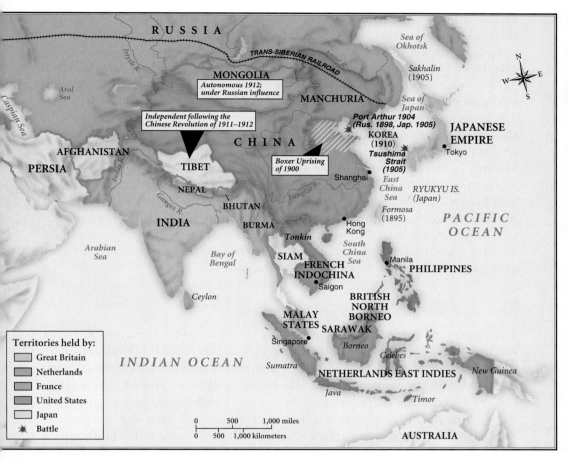

Map 19.3 Imperialism in Asia, 1894–1914
Most of the modernizing states converged on Asia. The established imperialists came to blows in
East Asia as they struggled for influence in China and encountered a formidable new rival—Japan.
Simultaneously, liberation movements like that of the Boxers in China were taking shape, committed
to throwing off restraints imposed by foreign powers. In 1911, Sun Yat-Sen overthrew the Qing dynasty
and set the country on a different course. **For more help analyzing this map, see the map activity for
this chapter in the Online Study Guide at** bedfordstmartins.com/huntconcise.

There were other troublesome newcomers to the imperial table. Almost simultaneously, Spain lost Cuba, Puerto Rico, and the Philippines following its defeat by
the United States in the Spanish-American War of 1898. Urged on by the expan-
sionist-minded Theodore Roosevelt, then assistant secretary of the navy, and a fiery
press, the United States went to war against Spain, claiming it was doing so to help
the independence movements in Cuba and the Philippines. Instead of allowing the
independence that victory promised, the United States then waged a bloody war

against the Philippines who did not want another imperial ruler. British writer Rudyard Kipling encouraged the United States to "take up the white man's burden" by bringing the benefits of Western civilization to those liberated from Spain. However, reports of American brutality in the Philippines, where some 200,000 people were massacred, further disillusioned the Western public, who liked to imagine native peoples joyously welcoming the bearers of "civilization."

Emerging European powers had an emotional stake in obtaining colonies. In the early twentieth century, Italian public figures aimed to restore Italy to its ancient position of world domination by conquering Africa. After a disastrous war against Ethiopia in 1896, Italy won a costly victory over the Ottomans in Libya. Germany, foremost among the new competitors for empire, met with some success, as German bankers and businessmen prospered across Asia, the Middle East, and Latin America. In colonial skirmishes, however, the Germans, like the British and French, met with humiliation and constant problems. As Italy and Germany pursued new territory, the rules set for imperialism at the Berlin conference a generation earlier gave way to heated rivalry and nationalist passion.

Growing Resistance to Colonial Domination

The Japanese military victories over the Qing in China and the Romanovs in Russia within a single decade had wide-ranging repercussions. Uprisings began in China after its 1895 defeat by Japan, as drought and famine brought additional suffering to everyday life. Peasants organized into secret societies to restore Chinese integrity and especially to defeat the foreigners who, they believed, were causing their misery. One such organization was the Society of the Righteous and Harmonious Fists, or Boxers, whose members maintained that ritual boxing would protect them from a variety of evils, including bullets. Encouraged by the Qing government and desperate because of spreading famine, the Boxers rebelled in 1900, killing missionaries and Chinese Christians. The forces of eight colonial powers put down the Boxer Uprising and required the Chinese to pay a huge indemnity in addition to forcing a wider foreign military occupation. The Boxer Uprising thoroughly discredited the Qing dynasty and led to its overthrow by a group of revolutionaries in 1911, which declared China a republic the next year. The group's leader, Sun Yat-Sen, who had been educated in Hawaii and Japan, combined Western concepts and traditional Chinese values, including correctness in behavior between governors and the governed and modern economic reform. Sun's stirring leadership and changes brought about by the revolution threatened Western channels of trade and domination.

Meanwhile, opposition to control by outsiders was spreading in India. In 1885, the Indian elite founded the Indian National Congress, which challenged Britain's right to rule, but the Japanese victory over Russia stimulated Indian politicians to take a more radical course. The anti-British Hindu leader B. G. Tilak preached noncooperation: "We shall not give them assistance to collect revenue and keep

The Foreign Pig Is Put to Death
The Boxers sought to fortify the Chinese government against powerful threats to China's survival. As in this image from the uprising, they used brightly colored placards to spread information about their goals and their successes to build support among the Chinese population. The Boxers felt that the presence of foreigners had caused a series of disasters, including the abandonment of traditional Chinese religion, the flow of wealth from the country, and natural disasters such as famine that seemed to be taking place with greater frequency. This depiction shows the Boxers' harsh judgment of foreigners and their Chinese allies: they are pigs to be killed. **For more help analyzing this image, see the visual activity for this chapter in the Online Study Guide at** bedfordstmartins.com/huntconcise.
(© The Bridgeman Art Library.)

peace. We shall not assist them in fighting beyond the frontiers or outside India with Indian blood and money." Tilak promoted Hindu customs, asserted their distinctiveness from British ways, and inspired violent rebellion in his followers. This brand of nationalism broke with the earlier form based on assimilating to British culture and promoting gradual change. Trying to repress Tilak, the British sponsored a rival nationalist group, the Muslim League, in an attempt to divide Muslim nationalists from Hindus in the Congress. Britain hoped to maintain power by appeasing the upper and middle classes with concessions of partial representation and voting based on ownership of property. But Britain's hold on India was weakening.

Revolutionary nationalism was also undermining the Ottoman Empire, which for centuries had controlled much of the Mediterranean. Rebellions plagued Ottoman rule, and the Ottoman state itself lost its effectiveness. Sultan Abdul Hamid II tried to revitalize the multiethnic empire by using Islam to counteract the rising nationalism of the Serbs, Bulgarians, and Macedonians, just as the Habsburgs used Catholicism in Austria-Hungary. Instead, he unintentionally provoked Turkish nationalism in Constantinople itself. Turkish nationalists rejected the sultan's pan-Islamic platform and built their movement on the uniqueness of their culture, history, and language, as many European ethnic groups were doing. They hoped to change the word *Turk* from one of derision to one of pride and purged their language of Arabic and Persian words. Additionally, Japan's victory over Russia electrified these nationalists with the vision of a modern Turkey becoming "the Japan of the Middle East." In 1908, a group called the Young Turks took control of the government in Constantinople.

The Young Turks' triumph motivated other ethnic and nationalist groups in the Middle East and the Balkans to demand self-rule as well. But in order not to lose control over the extensive Ottoman territories, the Young Turks brutally tried to suppress the uprisings in Egypt, Syria, and the Balkans that their own success had encouraged. The nationalist rebellions became part of the tumult shaping international relations in the decade before World War I, upsetting the Europeans' vision of stable domination over the rest of the world.

REVIEW   What changes occurred in Europe's relationships with the rest of the world between the early nineteenth and the early twentieth centuries?

Modern Life in an Age of Empire

As empire made the world an interconnected, industry-driven marketplace, it transformed everyday culture and society. Success in manufacturing and foreign ventures created millionaires, and consumers in the West could purchase goods that poured in from around the world. Many Europeans grew healthier, partly because of an improved diet and partly because of the efforts of reformers who sponsored government programs aimed at promoting the fitness they saw as necessary for citizens of imperial powers. Opportunities for mobility arose as Europeans modernized global communication with steamships and intercontinental railroads. Working people's experience of the internationalizing force of imperialism was different from that of the middle class. Increasingly from the mid-nineteenth century on, millions facing political or economic insecurity migrated from country to city and back and, as frequently, left their homelands for the United States, Canada, Australia, Argentina, Brazil, and Siberia.

While European power grew, the accepted social order in the home weakened. Western ideals of a comfortable family life flourished because of Europe's improved standard of living, but a falling birthrate, a rising divorce rate, and growing activism for marriage reform provoked intense debate about values. Although still widely condemned, homosexuality became acknowledged as a way of life and the topic of politics. Middle-class women took jobs and became active in public life to such an extent that some feared the disappearance of distinct gender roles. Debate over changing gender roles and private life contributed to rising social tensions.

Life in the "Best Circles"

Profits from empire and industrial expansion enlarged the ranks of the upper class, or "best circles," so called because of their members' wealth, education, and social status. People in the best circles came from the aristocracy, which retained much of its power, but increasingly aristocrats had to share their position with new millionaires from the upper middle class. In fact, the very distinction between aristocrat and bourgeois became blurred, as monarchs gratefully bestowed aristocratic titles on wealthy businesspeople for their contributions to the nation. Moreover, poorer aristocrats were only too willing to offer their children in marriage into the families of the newly rich. Such arrangements brought much-needed money to old established families and the glamour of an aristocratic title to upstarts. Thus Jeanette Jerome, daughter of a wealthy New York financier, married Britain's Lord Randolph Churchill (their son Winston later became Britain's prime minister). Millionaires without official connections to the aristocracy abandoned the thrifty ways of a century earlier in order to build palatial villas and engage in flashy displays of wealth. To justify their success, the wealthy quoted Social Darwinist principles that their prosperity resulted from their natural superiority over the poor.

Upper-class men bonded around hunting, a favorite leisure-time activity, which was reshaped by imperial contact. For centuries, aristocrats had pursued fox and bird hunting locally; now big-game hunting in Asia and Africa became the rage. European hunters forced native Africans, who traditionally depended on hunting for income or food and for group unity, to work as guides, porters, and domestics on hunts. Mastering foreign activities like big-game hunting, Europeans brought exotic specimens back to Europe for zoological exhibits and natural history museums, all of which flourished during this period as signs that they could master not only territory but culture as well.

People in the best circles saw themselves as an imperial elite, and upper-class women devoted themselves to maintaining rigid standards of social conduct. Members of the upper class did their best to exclude inferiors by controlling their children's social lives, especially by preventing girls' sexual activity and relationships with the lower classes. Upper-class men had liaisons with working-class women, because a double standard judged promiscuity normal for men and immoral for women. Few upper-class men thought of marrying these women, though. Parents still arranged many marriages directly, and "visiting days" brought eligible young people together to help ensure correct matrimonial decisions.

Instead of working for pay, upper-class women devoted themselves to having children, directing staffs of servants, and maintaining standards of social conduct. Furnishings in fashionable homes displayed imperial treasures such as Oriental carpets, bamboo furniture, and Chinese porcelains. With the importation of azaleas, rhododendrons, and other plants from around the world, lavish flower gardens replaced parks and lawns. Being an active consumer of fashionable clothing was also a time-consuming activity for women. In contrast to men's plain garments, upper-class women's clothing was elaborate, ornate, and dramatic, featuring constricting

Tiger Hunting in the Punjab
Big-game hunting became the imperial sport of choice, as shown in this colorful Indian painting. European and American hunters adopted the sport from local Asians and Africans, who had previously depended on the hunt for their livelihood. Now these Asians and Africans served the Western amateurs, many of whom were in wretched physical shape and inexperienced in hunting big game. Nonetheless, Western manliness was coming to depend on such feats, as imperialists saw those who continued the old aristocratic foxhunt as effeminate. Some Western women enjoyed hunting, too. As a chivalrous gesture, men would let women issue the coup de grace, or death shot, should a tiger materialize during the hunt.
(V & A Images, London/Art Resource, NY.)

corsets, long voluminous skirts, bustles, and low-cut necklines for evening wear. Women took their roles seriously by keeping detailed accounts of their expenditures and monitoring their children's religious and intellectual development. In addition, they tried to offset the drabness of industrial life with art and music. One Hungarian observer wrote, "The piano mania has become almost an epidemic in Budapest as well as Vienna." Some upper-class women also engaged in religious and philanthropic activities to aid lower-class women and children.

Although middle-class professionals could sometimes mingle with people at the apex of society, especially in charity work, their lives remained more modest. They usually employed at least one servant, which created the illusion of leisure for middle-class women, who in fact worked hard to maintain their homes. Professional men working at home did so from the best-appointed room. Middle-class domesticity substituted cleanliness and polish for upper-class conspicuous consumption.

The middle classes pointed to their hard work, along with their bathing with soap, as a sign of their racial superiority over colonized peoples, who actually labored to produce the raw materials for goods such as soap.

The "Best Circles" Transformed

Despite the well-being of the middle and upper classes, urgent concerns over population, marriage, and sexuality were hotly discussed from the 1880s on. The staggering population increases of the eighteenth century continued through the nineteenth century (see "Taking Measure"), and rural people crowded into cities. Germany increased in size from 41 million people in 1871 to 64 million in 1910; tiny Denmark grew from 1.7 million in 1870 to 2.7 million in 1911. Improvements in sanitation and public health that extended longevity and reduced infant mortality contributed to the growth. To cope with their bulging populations, Berlin, Budapest, and Moscow were torn down and rebuilt, following the earlier lead of Vienna and Paris. The German government reconstructed Berlin with new roadways and mass-transport systems as the capital's population grew to more than four million. Rebuilding was not confined to the most powerful states, however. Balkan cities such as Sofia, Belgrade, and Bucharest gained tree-lined boulevards, public buildings, and improved sanitation.

While the absolute size of the population was rising in the West, the birthrate (measured in births per thousand people) was actually falling. The birthrate had been decreasing in France since the eighteenth century; other European countries began experiencing a decline late in the nineteenth century. The Swedish birthrate dropped

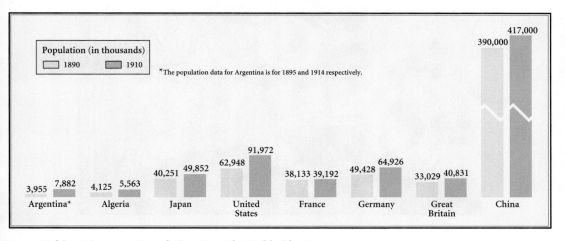

Taking Measure Population Growth Worldwide, 1890–1910
Countries in the West underwent a demographic revolution in these decades as birthrates declined sharply. Nevertheless, population soared in many countries because of improved health and immigration. Exceptions were China and other regions suffering the effects of imperialism, as well as France, where growth stagnated because the French had drastically curtailed reproduction early in the nineteenth century.

from 35 births per thousand people in 1859 to 24 per thousand in 1911. Even populous Germany went from 40 births per thousand in 1875 to 27 per thousand in 1913.

Industrialization and urbanization helped bring about this change. Farm families needed fewer hands because agricultural machinery was taking the place of human laborers, causing individual couples to practice birth control to limit family size. The use of new birth-control practices spread through cities to villages, cutting Europe's birthrate dramatically—a trend that would encompass most of the globe by the end of the twentieth century. In cities, pamphlets and advice books supplied information about coitus interruptus—the withdrawal method of preventing pregnancy. Industrial technology also played a role in curtailing reproduction: condoms, improved after the vulcanization of rubber in the 1840s, proved fairly reliable in preventing conception. In the 1880s, Aletta Jacobs, a Dutch physician, opened the first birth-control clinic, which specialized in promoting the new, German-invented diaphragm. Abortions were not uncommon.

The wider use of birth control stirred controversy. Critics accused middle-class women, whose fertility was falling most rapidly, of holding a "birth strike." Anglican bishops condemned birth control as "demoralizing to character and hostile to national welfare." Politicians worried about a crisis in masculinity that would put military strength at risk. In the United States, Theodore Roosevelt, who

A Large Czech Family

This photograph of a rural family in Czechoslovakia shows the differences that were coming to distinguish urban from rural people. Although even a farm family, especially in eastern Europe, might proudly display technology such as a new phonograph, it might not practice family limitation, which was gradually reducing the size of urban households. In eastern Europe, several generations often lived together, especially in rural areas. How many generations do you see in this image? (© Scheufler Collection/Corbis.)

became president in 1901, blamed middle-class women's selfishness for the population decline, calling it "one of the most unpleasant and unwholesome features of modern life." The quality of those who were giving birth worried activists. If the best circles had fewer children, politicians asked, what would society look like when peopled mostly by the "worst" classes? Racism and nationalism grew. The decline in fertility, one German nationalist warned, would fill the country with "alien peoples, above all Slavs and probably East European Jews as well." The political climate grew heated around the population question.

Reformers thought that improving conditions within marriage would raise the quality of children born. Many educated Europeans believed in eugenics—a set of ideas about the importance of producing "superior" people through selective breeding and of preventing the disabled and those from other ethnicities and races from polluting one's nation. As a famed Italian criminologist put it, people from "lower" groups were not humans but "orangutans." Eugenicists wanted increased fertility for "the fittest" and sterilization, or at least limited fertility, for "degenerates." Women of the better classes, reformers felt, would have more children if the disadvantages of marriage were removed and wives gained the legal right to their own wages and property. To this end, Sweden made men's and women's control over property equal in marriage and allowed women to work without their husbands' permission. Other countries legalized divorce. Reformers believed that divorce would allow unhappy couples to separate and undertake new, more loving—and thus more fertile—marriages.

The conditions of women's lives varied throughout Europe. For example, a greater number of legal reforms occurred in western Europe; however, women could get university degrees in Austrian universities long before they could at Oxford or Cambridge. In much of rural eastern Europe, the father's power over the extended family remained almost absolute. According to a survey of family life in eastern Europe in the early 1900s, fathers married off their children so young that 25 percent of women in their early forties had been pregnant more than ten times. Yet reform of everyday customs did occur, as community control gave way to individual practice in some places. For instance, in some Balkan villages, a kind of extended-family system called the *zadruga,* in which several nuclear families shared a common great house, survived from earlier times. By the turn of the century, individual couples had developed a degree of privacy by building one-room sleeping dwellings surrounding the great house. In addition, among the middle and upper classes of eastern Europe, many grown children were coming to believe they had the right to select a marriage partner, not just accept the spouse their parents chose for them.

The spread of empire and rapid social change set the stage for even bolder behaviors among some middle-class women. Adventurous women traveled the globe to promote Christianity, earn money, or obtain knowledge of other cultures. The increasing availability of white-collar jobs for educated women meant that more of them could afford to adopt an independent way of life. The so-called **new woman** dressed more practically with fewer petticoats and looser corsets, biked through

Sydney Grundy, *The New Woman* (1900)
By the opening of the twentieth century, the "new woman" had become a much-discussed phenomenon. Artists painted portraits of this independent creature, while playwrights such as Henrik Ibsen depicted her ambition to throw off the wifely role—or at least to shape that role more to her own personality. The new woman was also well educated: she had been to university or was working as a journalist or in a profession such as law or medicine. (© Private Collection/The Stapleton Collection/The Bridgeman Art Library.)

city streets and down country lanes, lived apart from her family in a women's club or apartment, and supported herself financially. Italian educator Maria Montessori, for example, went to medical school and secretly gave birth to an illegitimate child. Not surprisingly the growing number of women living on their own led to criticism. The "new woman," German philosopher Friedrich Nietzsche wrote, had led to the "uglification of Europe."

Sexual identity also fueled debate. A popular book in the new field of "sexology," which discussed sex scientifically, was *Sexual Inversion* (1894) by Havelock Ellis. Ellis, a British medical doctor, proposed a new personality type—the homosexual—identifiable by such traits as effeminate behavior and interest in the arts in males and physical passion for members of their own sex in both males and females. Homosexuals joined the discussion, calling for recognition that they composed a natural "third sex" and were not just people behaving sinfully. Some maintained that homosexuals were members of an "intermediate" sex, possessing both male and female qualities, and were thus of a higher order.

The issue became explosive when in the spring of 1895, Irish playwright Oscar Wilde was sentenced to two years in prison for indecency—a charge that referred to his sexual affairs with young men. After Wilde's conviction, the press went wild. "Open the windows! Let in the fresh air!" one newspaper rejoiced at the conviction. Between 1907 and 1909, German newspapers broadcast the courts-martial of men in Kaiser William II's closest circle who were condemned for homosexuality and transvestitism. Amid growing concern over population and family values, the government assured the public that William's own family life "provides the entire country with a fine model." Heterosexuality thus took on patriotic overtones: the accused homosexual elite in Germany was said by journalists to "emasculate our courageous master race." Despite their less-than-tolerant outcomes, these cases paved the way for growing sexual openness in the next generations and made sexual issues regular weapons in politics.

Working People's Strategies

For centuries, working people had migrated from countryside to city and from country to country to make a living. By the end of the nineteenth century, empire and economic change were spurring millions more to emigrate (Figure 19.1). Older port cities of Europe, such as Riga, Marseille, and Hamburg, offered jobs in global trade; new colonies provided land, jobs for soldiers and administrators, and the possibility of unheard-of wealth in diamonds, gold, and other natural resources.

Europeans left their homes for a variety of reasons. In parts of Europe, the land simply could not support so rapidly expanding a population. Sicilians by the hundreds of thousands left the eroded soil of their island to find work in the industrial cities of North and South America. Between 1840 and 1920, one-third of all European emigrants came from the British Isles, especially Ireland, first because of the potato famine and then because landlords drove them from their farms to get higher rents from newcomers. Between 1886 and 1900, half a million Swedes, out of a population of 4.75 million, quit their country. Millions of rural Jews, especially in

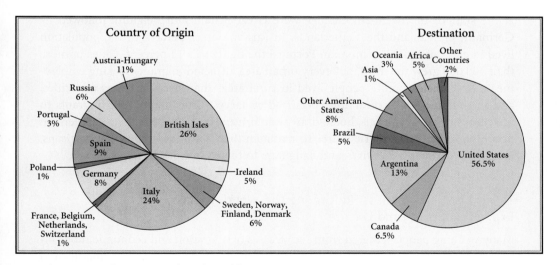

Figure 19.1 European Emigration, 1881–1910

The suffering caused by economic change and political persecution motivated people from almost every European country to leave their homes for greater security elsewhere. North America attracted nearly two-thirds of these migrants, many of whom had heard reports of vast quantities of available land in Canada and the United States. Both countries were known for following the rule of law and for economic opportunity in urban as well as rural areas.

eastern Europe, left their villages for economic reasons, but Russian Jews also fled as vicious mobs attacked their communities, even murdering some of them. These ritualized attacks, called pogroms, were scenes of horror.

As news of opportunity abroad reached Europe, migrants headed to North and South America, Australia, and New Zealand. The railroad and steamship made journeys across Europe and then across the ocean more affordable and faster, although most migrants traveled in steerage, with no comforts. Once established elsewhere, migrants frequently sent money back home and thus remained part of the family economy. Nationalist commentators in Slovakia, Poland, Hungary, and other parts of eastern and central Europe bemoaned the loss of ethnic vigor, but peasants themselves welcomed the arrival of "magic dollars" from their relatives. Migrants appreciated the chance to begin anew without the deprivation and social constraints of the Old World. One settler in the United States was relieved to escape the skimpy peasant meal of rye bread and herring. "God save us from . . . all that is Swedish," he wrote home sourly.

Migration out of Europe often meant the end of the old ways of life. Workers had to learn new languages and compete for jobs in unfamiliar cities, where they formed the cheapest labor pool. Women who worked in the home, however, tended to keep to themselves, preserving traditional ways. More isolated, they might never learn the new language or abandon their peasant dress. Their husbands and children were more likely to leave the past behind, as they faced the challenges of a new world.

Internal migration from rural areas to European cities—more common than international migration—accelerated urbanization. The most urbanized countries at the start of the twentieth century were Great Britain and Belgium, followed by Germany, France, and the Netherlands. In Russia, only 7 percent of the population lived in cities of 10,000 or more; in Portugal the figure was 12 percent. Cities of more than 100,000 grew the most, but every urban area attracted migrants seeking employment. Nevertheless, more people lived in rural areas than lived in towns and cities, and migration back to rural areas occurred at harvest time. Temporary migrants to the cities worked as masons, horse-drawn cab drivers, or factory hands to supplement declining income from agriculture. To maintain their status as independent artisans, hand-weavers sent their wives and daughters to towns to work in factories.

Toward National Fitness: Reforming the Working Class, Expanding Sports and Leisure

Many working people suffered from the stresses of migration and economic modernization, and in an age of Social Darwinist concerns about national fitness, middle- and upper-class reformers worked to address these problems. Settlement houses, clinics, and maternal and child wellness societies seemed to spring up overnight in cities. Young men and women, often from universities, eagerly took up residence in poor neighborhoods to study and help the people there. Belief in the scientific approach to solving social problems, as well as compassion for the poor, led them to seek the causes of social ills and their solutions. The Fabian Society in London, an organization established in 1884, undertook studies to determine the course of socialist reform based on planning rather than revolution. The Fabians helped found the Labour Party in 1893 to make social improvement a political cause. Religious fervor also shaped reform efforts. Some Protestants and Catholics across Europe countered growing secularization with increased missionary efforts among the urban poor at home. The Catholic church in Hungary, for example, channeled some of its efforts away from its traditional constituency in villages and toward ministering to workers in cities.

To make the poor more fit in a competitive world, philanthropists and government agencies intervened more and more in the lives of working-class families. They sponsored health clinics and milk centers to provide good medical care and food for children, and they instructed mothers in child care, including breast-feeding—an important way, reformers maintained, to promote infant health. Some schools distributed free lunches, medicine, and clothing, and some health care professionals began to spread birth-control information in the belief that small families were more likely to survive the rigors of urban life. Other reformers believed that the sexual exploitation of women would increase if the likelihood of pregnancy were overcome so easily. Government officials and charity workers, considering themselves the creators of "wise social legislation," believed they had the right to enter working-class apartments whenever they wanted. Such interfering pressured poor, overworked mothers to adopt middle-class norms for their children—such as providing them with "respectable" shoes and clothing, which they could not afford.

Fearing that women were not producing healthy enough children and were stealing jobs from men, reformers pushed for "protective" legislation. Such legislation barred women across Europe from night work and "dangerous" jobs (such as florist), allegedly for health reasons, even though medical statistics demonstrated that women became sick on the job less often than men. The new laws made the task of earning a living harder by blocking women's access to well-paid work.

Officials also promoted competitive sports and healthy leisure-time activities to build national fitness and provide some relief from the stresses of daily life. As nations competed for territory and economic markets, team sports arose, eventually replacing village games. Soccer, rugby, and cricket drew mass followings and helped integrate migrants, as well as people from the lower and upper classes, into a common national culture. Large audiences drawn from all classes backed their favorite teams, and competitive sports began to be seen as valuable promoters of national strength and spirit. Newspapers reported the results of all sorts of new contests, including the Tour de France bicycle race, sponsored by tire makers who wanted to prove the superiority of their products. Team sports further differentiated male and female spheres and thus promoted a social order based on distinctions between the sexes. Some team sports for women emerged—soccer, field hockey, and rowing—but women generally were encouraged to engage in individual sports. "Riding improves the temper, the spirits and the appetite," wrote one sportswoman; others practiced yoga. Rejecting the idea of women's natural frailty, reformers introduced

Anglo-Indian Polo Team

Team sports underwent rapid development during the imperial years, as spectators rooted for the success of their sports teams in the same spirit they rooted for their armies abroad. Some educators believed that team sports formed the male character, making men more effective soldiers. In cricket, soccer, and other sports, city challenged city, nation challenged nation, and race challenged race. Although mixed-race teams were generally unusual, they were more common in polo, because the British learned the sport from the Indians. (Hulton Archive/Getty Images.)

exercise and gymnastics into schools for girls, often with the idea that they would strengthen young women for motherhood and thus help build the nation-state.

The middle classes saw leisure pursuits such as mountain climbing as building mental and physical skills. Working-class people adopted middle-class habits by joining clubs for bicycling, touring, and hiking. Laborers and their families also sought the benefits of fresh air and exercise by visiting the beach, taking the train into the countryside, and enjoying day trips on river steamships. Clubs that sponsored trips often had names such as "The Patriots" or "The Nationals," again associating physical fitness with national strength. The new emphasis on healthy recreation gave people a greater sense of individual freedom and power and thereby fostered a sense of citizenship based less on constitutions and rights than on an individual nation's exercise of raw power. A farmer's son in the 1890s boasted that with a bicycle, "I was king of the road, since I was faster than a horse."

Sciences of the Modern Self

Scientists and Social Darwinists found cause for alarm not only in the condition of the working class but also in modern society's complaints about fatigue and irritability. Such illnesses originated in the "nerves," they reasoned, which were overstimulated by the pace and demands of urban living. A rash of books in the 1890s discussed the blossoming of nervous illnesses, such as that suffered by the Wolf-Man and his family. The most widely translated of them, *Degeneration*, written by Hungarian-born physician Max Nordau, saw increasingly bizarre modern art, male lethargy, and female hysteria as symptoms of a general downturn in the human species. The Social Darwinist prescription for curing such mental decline was imperial adventure, renewed virility, and increased childbearing.

Some researchers attempted to quantify and classify mental characteristics. Scientific study of the origins of criminal traits created the field of criminology. French psychologist Alfred Binet designed intelligence tests that he claimed could measure the capacity of the human mind more accurately than schoolteachers could. In Russia, physiologist Ivan Pavlov proposed that conditioning mental reflexes—that is, causing a subject to associate a desired response with a previously unrelated stimulus—could modify behavior. His experiments, especially his success in changing the behavior of a dog, formed the basis of modern psychology.

Sigmund Freud (1856–1939) devised an approach to treating modern anxieties that, he claimed, avoided traditional moralizing about human behavior. He became convinced that individuals were far from rational. Dreams, he explained in *The Interpretation of Dreams* (1900), reveal an unseen, repressed part of the personality—the "unconscious"—where all sorts of desires are more or less hidden. Freud also believed that the human psyche is made up of three competing parts: the *ego,* the part that is most in touch with reality; the *id* (or libido), the part that governs instincts and sexual energy; and the *superego,* the part that serves as the conscience. Like Darwin's ideas, Freud's notions challenged the widespread liberal belief, dating from the Enlightenment, in a rational self that peacefully acts in its own best interest.

Freud shocked many of his contemporaries by insisting that all children have a sexual drive from the moment of birth. He believed that many sexual impulses have to be rigorously repressed for the individual to attain maturity and for society to remain civilized. Attaining one's adult sexual identity is always a painful process, he maintained, because it depends on repressing infantile urges, which include bisexuality and incest. Thus the Wolf-Man's nightmare of white wolves outside his window symbolized his unresolved sexual fears and feelings. Freud also claimed that certain aspects of gender roles—such as motherhood—are "normal" and that throughout their lives, women in general achieve far less than men do, becoming neurotic when they strive to excel. At the same time, he believed that adult gender identity results not from anatomy alone (motherhood is not the only way to be female) but from the inescapable mental processing of life experiences as well. He thus made gender more complicated than simple biology would suggest. Finally, Freud's psychoanalytic theory maintained that girls and women have powerful sexual feelings, an assertion that broke with ideas of women's passionlessness.

The influence of psychoanalysis was complex and widespread. Two mainstays of psychoanalysis—free association of ideas and interpretation of dreams—derived from African and Asian influences on Freud's thought. The "talking cure," as it was quickly

Freud's Office in London
Sigmund Freud's therapy room, where his patients experienced the "talking cure," was filled with imperial "trophies" such as Oriental rugs and African art. Freud himself was fascinated by shamanism, trances, and other non-Western medical practices, as well as by drug-induced mental states. Freud fled to England in 1938 to escape the Nazis. (Mary Evans Picture Library/Sigmund Freud copyrights.)

labeled, gave rise to a general acceptance of talking out one's problems. As psychoanalysis became an accepted means of recovering mental health, terms such as *neurosis, unconscious,* and *libido* came into widespread use and could apply to anyone, not just the mentally ill. On the one hand, Freud was a meticulous scientist, examining symptoms, urging attention to the most minute evidence from everyday life, and demanding that sexual life be regarded with a rational rather than a religious eye. On the other hand, he was pessimistic: he abandoned the optimism of Enlightenment science and instead theorized that humans were motivated by irrational drives toward death and destruction and that these drives shaped society's collective mentality. Freud would later interpret the devastation of World War I as proof of his bleak theories.

REVIEW What social changes were transforming Europe at the start of the twentieth century?

Modernity and the Revolt in Ideas

Toward the beginning of the twentieth century, intellectuals and artists so completely rejected long-standing beliefs and established artistic forms that they ushered in a new era. In science the theories of Albert Einstein and other researchers established shocking new truths in physics. Artists and musicians who produced deliberately outrageous works were, like Freud, heavily influenced by advances in science and the progress of empire. Their blending of the scientific and the irrational, and of forms from the West and non-West, helped launch the disorienting revolution in ideas and creative expression that we now identify collectively as **modernism**.

The Challenge to Positivism

Late in the nineteenth century, many philosophers and social thinkers suddenly rejected the century-old belief that using scientific methods would uncover enduring social laws. This belief, called positivism, had emphasized the permanent nature of fundamental laws and had motivated reformers' attempts to perfect legislation based on studies of society. Challenging positivism, some critics declared that because human experience is ever changing, there are no constant or enduring social laws. German political theorist Max Weber maintained that the sheer number of factors involved in policymaking would often make a decisive action by bureaucrats impossible. In times of crisis, a charismatic leader might take power because of his ability to act simply on intuition. These turn-of-the-century thinkers, called relativists and pragmatists, influenced thinking about society throughout the twentieth century.

The most radical among the scholars was the German philosopher Friedrich Nietzsche (1844–1900), who early in his career distinguished between the "Apollonian," or rational, side of human existence and the "Dionysian" side, with its expression of more primal urges. Nietzsche believed that people generally prefer rational, Apollonian explanations of life because the powerful Dionysian sense of death and love, as found in Greek tragedy, is too disturbing. He maintained that all assertions of scientific fact and theory are mere illusions, that knowledge of nature is only a mathematical, linguistic, or artistic representation. Truth, Nietzsche insisted, thus exists only in the representation itself, for humans can never experience unfiltered knowledge of nature or reality. This aspect of Nietzsche's philosophy powerfully questioned scientific certainty.

Much of Nietzsche's writing took the form of aphorisms—short, disconnected statements of truth or opinion—rather than the long, sustained argument common to traditional Western philosophy. Nietzsche used aphorisms to give the impression that his ideas were a single individual's unique perspective, not universal truths that thinkers since the Enlightenment had claimed were attainable. Nietzsche was convinced that late-nineteenth-century Europe was witnessing the decline of dogmatic truths such as those found in religion. Thus, he announced, "God is dead, we have killed him." Far from arousing dread, the death of God, according to Nietzsche, would give birth to a joyful quest for new "poetries of life" to replace worn-out religious and middle-class rules. Nietzsche believed that an uninhibited, dynamic "superman," free from traditional moralizing, would replace the rule-bound middle-class person. On his death, however, Nietzsche's sister edited his attacks on middle-class values into attacks on Jews. She revised his complicated concepts about each individual's "will to power" and the "superman" so as to appeal to nationalists, imperialists, and militarists, all of whom he actually hated.

Revolutionizing Science

While philosophers questioned the ability of traditional science to provide timeless truths, scientific inquiry itself flourished, and the sciences gained in prestige. Around the turn of the century, however, discoveries by pioneering researchers shook the foundations of traditional scientific certainty and challenged accepted knowledge about the nature of the universe. In 1896, Antoine Becquerel discovered radioactivity. He also suggested the mutability of elements by the rearrangement of their atoms. French chemist Marie Curie and her husband, Pierre Curie, isolated the elements polonium and radium, which are more radioactive than the uranium Becquerel used. From these and other discoveries, scientists concluded that atoms are not solid, as had long been believed, but are composed of subatomic particles moving about a core. In a paper published in 1900, German physicist Max Planck announced his influential quantum theorem, stating that energy is delivered in irregular packets that he later called quanta, not in a steady stream.

In this atmosphere of discovery, physicist Albert Einstein (1879–1955) proclaimed his special theory of relativity in 1905. According to this theory, space and time are not absolute categories but instead vary according to the vantage point of the observer. Only the speed of light is constant. That same year, Einstein also suggested that the solution to problems in Planck's quantum theorem lay in considering light both as little packets *and* as waves. Einstein later proposed yet another blurring of two distinct physical properties, mass and energy. He expressed this equivalence in the formulation $E = mc^2$, or energy equals mass times the square of the speed of light. In 1916, Einstein published his general theory of relativity, which connected the force, or gravity, of an object with its mass and proposed a fourth mathematical dimension to the universe. Much more lay ahead once Einstein's theories of energy were applied to technology: television, nuclear power, and, within forty years, atomic bombs.

The findings of Planck, Einstein, and others were not immediately accepted, because long-standing scientific truths were at stake. Einstein, like Planck, struggled against mainstream science and its professional institutions. As a female scientist, Marie Curie faced such resistance that even after she became the first person ever to receive a second Nobel Prize (1911), the prestigious French Academy of Science turned down her candidacy for membership, claiming that a woman could simply not have done such outstanding work. Acceptance of all these scientists' discoveries gradually came, and Max Planck institutes were established in German cities, streets across Europe were named after Marie Curie, and Einstein's name became synonymous with *genius*. These scientists achieved what historians call a paradigm shift—that is, in the face of staunch resistance, they transformed the foundations of science.

Marie Curie and Her Daughter
The recipient of two Nobel Prizes, Marie Curie traveled from Poland to western Europe to study science. Her extraordinary career made her the epitome of the "new woman." Her daughter, Irene Joliot-Curie, followed her into the field and also won a Nobel Prize. Both women died of leukemia caused by their exposure to radioactive materials. (ACJC—Fund Curie et Joliot-Curie.)

Modern Art

Conflicts between traditional values and new ideas also raged in the arts, as artists created an array of competing styles and many rejected the historic and realistic scenes still favored by powerful patrons in government and public museums. Abandoning the soft colors of impressionism as too subtle for a dynamic industrial society, a group of Parisian artists exhibiting in 1905 combined blues, greens, reds, and oranges so intensely that they were called fauves, literally "wild beasts." A leader of the short-lived fauvism, Henri Matisse soon struck out in a new direction, targeting the expanding class of white-collar workers. Matisse dreamed of "an art . . . for every mental worker, be he businessman or writer, like an appeasing influence, like a mental soother, something like a good armchair in which to rest from physical fatigue."

French artist Paul Cézanne initiated one of the most powerful and enduring trends in modern art. Cézanne used rectangular daubs of paint to portray his geometric vision of dishes, fruit, drapery, and the human body. He accentuated the lines and planes found in nature instead of presenting nature as people saw it in everyday life. Following in Cézanne's footsteps, Spanish artist Pablo Picasso developed a style called cubism. Its radical emphasis on planes and surfaces converted humans into bizarre, almost unrecognizable forms. Picasso's painting *Les Demoiselles d'Avignon* (1907) depicts the bodies of the *demoiselles,* or young ladies (prostitutes in this case), as fragmented and angular, with their faces modeled on African masks. Picasso's work showed the profound influences of African, Asian,

Pablo Picasso, *Les Demoiselles d'Avignon* (1907)
Whereas impressionists had borrowed heavily from Asian art, many artists in Picasso's time looked to
Africa for inspiration. In *Les Demoiselles d'Avignon,* Picasso used the elongated, angular limbs found in
African carvings, while the faces resemble African masks. He borrowed these forms even as Europeans
were declaring the superiority of their civilization to that of Africa. (Digital Image © The Museum of Modern
Art/Licensed by Scala/Art Resource, NY. © 2010 Estate of Pablo Picasso/Artists Rights Society [ARS], NY.)

and South American art, but his use of these features was less decorative and more
brutal than Matisse's, for example. Like explorers, botanists, and foreign journalists,
he was bringing knowledge of the empire into the imperial homeland.

Across Europe, artists mixed political criticism, even outrage, with the radical
stylistic changes in their work. Anarchists wanted to "show the people how hideous
is their actual life," and Picasso, who had spent his youth in the heart of working-
class Barcelona, a hotbed of anarchist thought, aimed to reflect this goal in his art.
In 1912, Picasso and the French painter Georges Braque devised a new kind of
collage that incorporated bits of newspaper, string, and other useless objects. The
effect was a work of art that appeared to be made of trash. The newspaper clippings
Picasso included described battles and murders, suggesting that Western civilization was not as refined as it claimed to be. In eastern and central Europe, artists
criticized the growing nationalism that determined official purchases of sculpture

and painting. "The whole empire is littered with monuments to soldiers and monuments to Kaiser William of the same conventional type," one German artist complained. In response, groups of avant-garde artists in Vienna and Berlin created art that was critical of boastful nationalism.

Scandinavian and eastern European artists produced tormented works. Like the vision of Freud, their style of portraying inner feelings, called expressionism, broke with middle-class optimism. Norwegian painter Edvard Munch aimed "to make the emotional mood ring out again as happens on a gramophone." In his painting *The Scream* (1895), he used twisting lines and a depiction of a tortured human form to convey the horror of modern life that many artists perceived. The "Blue Rider" group of artists, including German avant-garde artist Gabriele Münter and Russian painter Wassily Kandinsky, used geometric forms and striking colors to express an inner, spiritual truth. Kandinsky is often credited with producing the first fully abstract paintings around 1909; shapes in these paintings no longer resemble actual objects but are meant to express abstract reality and deep feelings. The expressionism of Austrian painter Oskar Kokoschka was even more intense, displaying ecstasy, horror, and hallucinations. As a result, his work—like that of other expressionists and cubists before World War I—was a commercial failure in an increasingly complex marketplace that featured not only museum curators but also professional dealers—"experts" like the professionals in medicine and law.

Only one innovative style was an immediate commercial success: **art nouveau** (new art) won approval from governments, critics, and the masses. Creating everything from dishes and advertising posters to streetlamps and even entire buildings in this new style, designers manufactured beautiful things for the general public. As one French official said about the first version of art nouveau coins issued in 1895, "Soon even the most humble among us will be able to have a masterpiece in his pocket." Adapted from Asian design principles, art nouveau was meant to offset the harshness of factory and office work with images drawn from nature. The impersonality of machines was replaced by intertwined vines and flowers and the softly curving bodies of female nudes intended to soothe the viewer psychologically—an idea that contrasted directly with Picasso's artistic vision. Art nouveau was the notable exception to the public outcries over innovations in the visual arts.

The Revolt in Music and Dance

"Astonish me!" was the motto of modern dance and music, both of which shocked audiences in the concert halls of Europe. American dancer Isadora Duncan took Europe by storm at the turn of the century when, draped in a flowing garment, she danced barefoot in the first performance of modern dance. Her sophisticated style was nonetheless called primitive because it no longer followed the steps of classical ballet. Experimentation with forms of bodily expression animated the Russian Ballet's 1913 performance of *The Rite of Spring* by Igor Stravinsky, the tale of an orgiastic dance to the death performed to ensure a harvest. The dance troupe struck awkward poses and danced to rhythms intended to sound primitive. At the work's premiere in Paris, one journalist reported that "the audience began shouting its indignation. . . . Fighting actually broke out among some of the spectators." Such controversy made *The Rite of Spring* a box-office hit, although critics called its choreographer a "lunatic" and the music itself "the most discordant composition ever written."

Composers had been rebelling against Western traditions for several decades, producing music that was disturbing rather than pretty. Having heard Asian musicians at international expositions, French composer Claude Debussy transformed his style to reflect non-European musical patterns and wrote articles in praise of Asian harmonies. Italian composer Giacomo Puccini used non-Western subject matter for his opera *Madame Butterfly*, which debuted in 1904. Like the bizarre representations of reality in cubism, the works of Austrian composer Richard Strauss upset convention by using several keys simultaneously in his compositions and thus distorting familiar musical patterns. Strauss's operas *Salome* (1905) and *Elektra* (1909) reflect the modern fascination with violence and obsessive passion. A newspaper critic claimed that the notes in Strauss's dissonant music "spit and scratch and claw each other like enraged panthers."

The early orchestral work of Austrian composer Arnold Schoenberg, who also wrote cabaret music to earn a living, shocked even Strauss. In his book *Theory of Harmony* (1911), Schoenberg proposed eliminating tonality altogether; a decade later he devised a new twelve-tone scale. "I am aware of having broken through all the barriers of a dated aesthetic ideal," Schoenberg wrote of his music. But new aesthetic models distanced artists like Schoenberg from their audiences, separating high from low culture even more and ending the support of many in the upper classes, who found this music simply unpleasant. "Anarchist! Nihilist!" shouted Schoenberg's audiences, showing their distaste for modernism and using political terms to characterize the arts.

REVIEW   What changes in intellectual life upset accepted cultural standards at the start of the twentieth century?

The Birth of Mass Politics

Alongside these disturbances in intellectual life, the political atmosphere heated up. On the one hand, liberal opinions led to political representation for workingmen. Networks of communication, especially the development of journalism, created a common fund of political knowledge that made mass political participation possible. On the other hand, political activists were no longer satisfied with the liberal rights sought by reformers a century earlier, and some strenuously opposed them. Militant nationalists, anti-Semites, socialists, suffragists, and others demanded changes that challenged liberal values. Traditional elites, resentful of the rising middle classes and urban people, aimed to slow constitutional processes and reverse the development of city life. Mass politics soon threatened national unity, especially in central and eastern Europe, where governments often answered reformers' demands with repression.

The Growing Power of Labor

Mass politics arose from a combination of the right to vote accorded to men across Europe before World War I and the rise of popular activism, especially among working people. In the fall of 1879, William Gladstone (1809–1898), leader of the British Liberal Party, which was then out of power, waged an experimental electoral campaign across the country. Speaking before thousands of working men and women, he advocated a way of life based on "honest, manful, humble effort" in the middle-class tradition of "hard work." Newspapers publicized his trip, further building interest in politics and helping him become prime minister. The Reform Act of 1884 doubled the British electorate to around 4.5 million men, including many urban workers and artisans, whose votes reduced traditional aristocratic influence. This move reflected the universal manhood suffrage already granted in France and Germany; much of Europe would follow suit before World War I.

Journalism helped forge a broad national community of up-to-date citizens by providing information (and misinformation) about politics and world events. The invention of mechanical typesetting and the production of newsprint from wood pulp lowered the costs of printing; the telegraph and the telephone allowed reporters to communicate news to their papers almost instantly. Once literary in content, daily newspapers now emphasized sensational news, using blaring headlines and gruesome details—particularly about murders, sexual scandals, and sagas of the empire—to sell papers. In the hustle and bustle of industrial society, one editor wrote, "you must strike your reader right between the eyes." Elites complained that the sensational press was another sign of social decay, but for up-and-coming working- and middle-class people, journalism offered another career option.

Political activism took many forms in the late nineteenth century. Housewives, who often acted in support of strikers, protested against high food prices by confiscating merchants' goods and selling them at what they considered a fair price. "There should no longer be either rich or poor," argued organized Italian peasant women. "All should have bread for themselves and for their children. We should all be equal." Women took other kinds of action, too, building working-class solidarity in neighborhoods. When landlords evicted tenants, women would gather in the streets, and as soon as the ousted families' household goods were removed from their rooms, the women would carry them back inside. Meeting on doorsteps or at fountains, laundries, pawnshops, and markets, women initiated rural newcomers into urban ways and developed class unity.

In the last third of the nineteenth century, workers also organized formal unions, which attracted the allegiance of millions. Unions demanded a say in working conditions and aimed, as one union's rule book put it, "to ensure that wages . . . always follow the rises in the price of basic commodities." After the Paris Commune, many businessmen and governments viewed striking workers as threatening, but strong unions appealed to some industrialists because the unions could make strikes more predictable (or even prevent them) and present demands more coherently.

From the 1880s on, collective action for higher pay, lower prices, and better working conditions increased. In 1888, for example, hundreds of young women who made matches in London struck to end the fining system, under which they could be penalized an entire day's wages for being a minute or two late to work. This system, the "match girls" maintained, helped companies reap profits of more than 20 percent. Newspapers and philanthropists picked up the strikers' story, helping them win their case. Soon after, London dockworkers and gasworkers went on strike to protest their working conditions. Across Europe, the number of strikes and demonstrations rose from 188 in 1888 to 289 in 1890. Fearing destructive acts, governments increasingly responded with armed force, even though most strikes were about the conditions of everyday life for workers and not political revolution.

Working-class political parties developed from unions. Craft-based unions of skilled artisans, such as carpenters and printers, were the most active and cohesive, but from the mid-1880s on, a new unionism attracted transport workers, miners, match girls, and dockworkers. These new unions were nationwide groups with salaried managers who could plan massive general strikes across the trades with common goals such as the eight-hour workday. They could thus paralyze an entire nation. Large unions in the industrialized countries of Europe, like cartels and trusts, increasingly influenced business practices. They were joined by working-class parties—the Labour Party in England, the Socialist Party in France, and the Social Democratic Parties in Sweden, Hungary, Austria, and Germany—most of which were inspired by Marxist theories. Germany was home to the largest socialist party in Europe after 1890.

Those who accepted Marx's assertion that "workingmen have no country" also founded an international movement to address workers' common interests across national boundaries. In 1889, some four hundred socialists from across Europe met in Paris to form the **Second International**, a federation of working-class organizations and political parties that replaced the First International, started by Marx before the Paris Commune. As socialists were elected to parliaments, some members of the Second International worried that their participation in government would produce helpful reform of conditions generally that would slow their ultimate goal of revolution. The preference for evolutionary tactics rather than the violent overthrow of government was known as reformism. To avoid the dangers in reformism, some socialists refused seats in government even when they were elected.

The Second International was also determined to rid the organization of anarchists, who flourished in the less industrial parts of Europe, including Russia, Italy, and Spain. In these countries, the anarchist movement got strong support from peasants, small property owners, and day laborers, for whom Marxist theories of worker-controlled factories had less appeal. In an age of tough international competition in agriculture, many rural people hoped for a life free from the control of large landowners and government. Many advocated extreme tactics, including physical violence and even murder. "We want to overthrow the government . . . with violence since it is by the use of violence that they force us to obey," wrote one Italian anarchist. In the 1880s, anarchists bombed stock exchanges, parliaments, and businesses, and by the 1890s they were assassinating heads of state—violence that members of the socialist movement believed to be counterproductive.

Workingwomen joined unions and political parties, but in much smaller numbers than men. Not able to vote in national elections, they had little reason to join political parties. Women also were usually responsible for housework in addition to their paying jobs and so had little time for meetings. In addition, their low wages barely allowed them to survive, much less pay party or union dues. Many workingmen also opposed women's presence in these organizations. Contact with women would mean "suffocation," one Russian workingman believed, and end male union members' sense of being "comrades in the revolutionary cause." The shortage of women's voices in unions and political parties paralleled women's exclusion from government; it helped make the middle-class belief in separate spheres part of a working-class ideology, too. Marxist leaders continued to maintain that injustice to women was caused by capitalism and would disappear in a socialist society. As a result, although working-class organizations wanted women's support, they did not take seriously women's concerns about issues such as lower wages and sexual harassment.

Popular community activities that intertwined politics and everyday life built worker solidarity. The gymnastic and choral societies that had once united Europeans in nationalistic fervor now served working-class goals. Songs emphasized worker freedom, progress, and eventual victory. Socialist gymnastics, bicycling, and marching societies rejected competition and prizes as middle-class preoccupations, but they valued physical fitness for helping workers in the "struggle for existence"—a reflection of the spread of Darwinian thinking to all levels of society. Workers also held festivals and gigantic parades, most notably on May 1, a centuries-old holiday that the Second International now claimed as a labor holiday. Like religious processions of an earlier time, parades fostered unity, and as a result governments frequently banned such public gatherings, calling them a public danger.

Political persecution forced some working-class groups to operate in exile. The Russian government, for instance, outlawed political parties and imprisoned activists. The foremost Russian activist, V. I. Lenin (1870–1924), who would take power during the Russian Revolution of 1917, migrated to western Europe after his release from confinement in Siberia in 1900. He earned his place among Russian Marxists there with his hard-hitting journalism and political intrigue. Lenin developed the theory that a highly disciplined socialist elite would lead a lightly industrialized Russia into socialism. At a 1903 party meeting of Russian Marxists, he maneuvered his opponents into walking out, leaving his supporters in control of the party. Thereafter, his faction was known as the Bolsheviks, from the Russian word for "majority," which they had briefly formed. Their goal was to suppress the Mensheviks, the dominant voice in Russian Marxism until Lenin outmaneuvered them. Neither of these factions, however, had as large a constituency within Russia as the Socialist Revolutionaries, whose objective was to politicize peasants rather than industrial workers as the foundation of revolution. All these groups prepared for the revolutionary moment through study, propaganda efforts, and organizing—not through the electoral politics successfully employed elsewhere in Europe.

Rights for Women and the Battle for Suffrage

Singly and in groups, women continued to agitate against their exclusion from the benefits of liberalism, such as the rights to vote and own property (including their own wages) if married. Laws in France, Austria, and Germany made women's attendance at political meetings a crime. German women focused not only on obtaining these rights but also on widening opportunities for women's education. Their activism aimed to achieve the German cultural ideal of *Bildung*—the belief that education can strengthen character and that individual development has public importance. In several countries, women continued to monitor the regulation of prostitution. Their goal was to prevent prostitutes from being imprisoned on suspicion of having syphilis when men with syphilis faced no such incarceration. Other women took up pacifism as their special cause. Many of them were inspired by Bertha von Süttner's popular book *Lay Down Your Arms* (1889), which emphasized the terror inflicted on women and families by the ravages of war.

By the 1890s, many women's rights activists decided to focus on a single issue—the right to vote—as the most effective way to correct the problems caused by male privilege. Thereafter suffragists created major organizations involving millions of activists, paid officials, and permanent offices. British suffrage leader Millicent Garrett Fawcett (1847–1929) and other women pressured members of Parliament for the vote and participated in national and international congresses on behalf of suffrage. Similarly, American suffragist Susan B. Anthony (1820–1906) traveled throughout the United States to speak at rallies, raised money to support the movement, and founded the International Woman Suffrage Association in 1904. The movement's leadership argued that despite men's promises to protect women in exchange for their inequality, the system of male chivalry had led to exploitation and abuse. "So long as the subjection of women endures, and is confirmed by law and custom, . . . women will be victimized," a leading suffragist claimed. Other activists believed that women had the values needed to counterbalance masculine qualities in the running of society. The characteristics that came from mothering were as necessary in shaping a country's destiny as were the qualities that stemmed from industry and business, they declared.

Women's rights activists were generally, though not exclusively, from the middle classes. Free from the need to earn a living, they simply had more time to be activists and to study the works of feminist theorists such as Harriet Taylor and John Stuart Mill. They attended theater productions by playwrights such as the Norwegian Henrik Ibsen, whose heroine Nora (*A Doll's House,* 1879) walks out on a loveless and oppressive marriage. Some working-class women also participated, although many saw suffrage for women as less important than their economic concerns. Textile workers in Manchester, England, however, combined calls for social and economic reform and put together a vigorous suffrage movement connecting the vote to improved working conditions.

Woman Suffrage in Finland
In 1906, Finnish women became the first women in Europe to receive the vote in national elections when the Socialist Party—usually opposed to feminism as a middle-class rather than a working-class project—supported woman suffrage. The Finnish vote elated activists in the West, now linked by many international organizations, because it showed that more than a century of lobbying for reform could lead to gains. (Mary Evans Picture Library.)

In 1906, suffragists achieved their first major victory when the Finnish parliament granted women the vote. But the failure of parliaments to enact similar legislation elsewhere in Europe led some suffragists to violence. In Britain, Emmeline Pankhurst (1858–1928) and her daughters founded the Women's Social and Political Union (WSPU) in 1903 in the belief that women would accomplish nothing unless they threatened men's property. Starting in 1907, WSPU members staged parades in English cities, and in 1909 they began a campaign of violence, blowing up railroad stations, slashing works of art, and chaining themselves to the gates of Parliament. Disguising themselves as ordinary shoppers, they carried little hammers in their hand warmers to smash the plate-glass windows of department stores and shops. Parades and demonstrations made suffrage a public spectacle, provoking attacks on the marchers by outraged men. Arrested for disturbing the peace, the marchers went on hunger strikes in prison. Like striking workers, these women were willing to use confrontational tactics in order to obtain rights.

Liberalism Tested

Governments in western Europe, where liberal institutions seemed well entrenched, sought to control turn-of-the-century conflicts with practical policies that often struck at liberalism's very foundations. Some ended laissez-faire trade policies by instituting protective tariffs; others expanded social welfare programs. Both approaches were a break with the liberal idea that societies should develop freely without government interference. In 1905, the British Liberal Party won a solid majority in the House of Commons and pushed for social legislation to gain working-class support. "We are keenly in sympathy with the representatives of Labour," one Liberal politician announced. "We have too few of them in the House of Commons." The National Insurance Act of 1911 set up a program of unemployment assistance funded by new taxes on the wealthy, and Parliament eliminated the long-standing veto power of the predominantly aristocratic House of Lords.

The Irish question tested British commitment to still other liberal values: autonomy, opportunity, and individual rights. Despite the Irish receiving the secret ballot, the political climate in Ireland remained explosive because of the repressive tactics of absentee landlords, many of them English and Protestant. These landlords evicted unsuccessful and prosperous tenants alike so they could raise the rents of newcomers. In the 1890s, new groups formed to foster Irish culture as a way of challenging what they saw as Britain's continuing colonization of the country. In 1901, the circle around the modernist poet William Butler Yeats and the charismatic patriot and actress Maud Gonne founded the Irish National Theater to present Irish rather than English plays. Gonne took Irish politics into everyday life by opposing British efforts to gain support from the young. Every time an English monarch visited Ireland, he or she held special receptions for children. Gonne and other Irish volunteers sponsored competing events, handing out candies and other treats for patriotic youngsters. Promoters of an "Irish way of life" encouraged speaking Gaelic instead of English, singing Gaelic songs, and supporting Catholicism instead of Anglicanism. This cultural agenda gained political force with the founding in 1905 of Sinn Fein (We Ourselves), a group that strove for complete Irish independence. In 1913, Parliament finally approved home rule for Ireland; the outbreak of World War I prevented the legislation from taking effect, though it hardly killed Irish dreams of independence.

Italian nation builders, left with a towering debt from unification and with widespread pockets of discontent, drifted rapidly away from liberalism's moorings in solid industrial development and the rule of law. Corruption plagued Italy's constitutional monarchy, which had developed neither the secure parliamentary system of Britain nor the authoritarian monarchy of Germany to guide its growth. To forge national unity in the 1890s, Italian prime ministers used patriotic rhetoric and imperial adventure such as skirmishes in Ethiopia, culminating in the crushing defeat in 1896. Riots and strikes, followed by armed government repression, erupted in Italy, until Giovanni Giolitti, who served as prime minister for three terms between 1903 and 1914, adopted a policy known as *trasformismo* (from the Italian word for "transform"), by which he used bribes, public works programs, and other benefits to localities to influence their deputies in parliament. Political opponents called Giolitti "the Minister of the Underworld" and accused him of preferring to buy the votes of local bosses instead of spending money to develop the Italian economy. He hoped to calm unrest in the industrializing cities of Turin and Milan and in the depressed agrarian south by instituting social welfare programs and, in 1912, nearly complete manhood suffrage.

Anti-Semitism, Nationalism, and Zionism in Mass Politics

The real crisis for the liberal political values of equal citizenships and tolerance came in the two decades leading up to World War I, when many politicians used anti-Semitism and nationalism to win elections. They told voters that Jews were responsible for the difficulties of modern life and that anti-Semitism and increased patriotism would fix all of society's problems. Voters from all levels of society responded enthusiastically, agreeing that Jews were the villains and that the nation-state was the hero in the armed struggle to survive. In republics and monarchies alike, anti-Semitism and militant nationalism played key roles in mass politics by leading to the creation of a radical right committed to combating the radical left of social democracy. The new radical right shattered the older notion of nationalism as pride in constitutions, rights, and the rule of law. Liberals had hoped that voting by the masses would make politics more harmonious as parliamentary debate and compromise smoothed out class and other differences. The new politics as shaped by right-wing leaders—usually representatives of the agrarian nobility, the aristocratically controlled military, and highly placed clergy—dashed those hopes by making politics loud, emotional, and hateful.

The most notorious instance of anti-Semitism occurred in France, where the Dreyfus Affair sorely tested the principle of equal citizenship. The French Third Republic, formed after France's defeat in the Franco-Prussian War, was fragile, with the liberal alliance of businessmen, shopkeepers, professionals, and rural property owners who backed republican government opposed by the aristocracy, military, and Catholic church. The latter groups hoped that the Third Republic, like the earlier two, would be overthrown. Economic downturns and government corruption made the republic even more vulnerable, and the press stirred things up by attributing failures of almost every kind to French Jews. Despite an excellent system of primary education promoting literacy and rational thinking, the public tended to agree.

Amid rising anti-Semitism, a Jewish captain in the French army, Alfred Dreyfus, was charged with spying for Germany in 1894. Dreyfus had attended elite schools and become an officer in the French military, whose upper ranks were traditionally aristocratic, Catholic, and monarchist. The military produced manufactured evidence to gain Dreyfus's conviction and exile to the harsh fortress on Devil's Island. Even though the espionage continued after his arrest, the government stubbornly upheld his guilt. Then several newspapers received proof that the army had used false testimony and fabricated documents to convict Dreyfus. In 1898, the celebrated French novelist Émile Zola published "J'accuse" ("I Accuse") on the front page of a Paris daily, exposing how military lies and cover-ups had created the illusion of Dreyfus's guilt. The article revealed the names of the guilty parties and called for the return of a government based on honesty and the rule of law. "I have but one passion, that of Enlightenment," wrote Zola. "J'accuse" led to public riots, quarrels among families and friends, and denunciations of the army, which eroded public confidence in the republic and in French institutions. The government finally pardoned Dreyfus in 1899, dismissed the aristocratic and Catholic officers held

LE JUGEMENT DERNIER

AH! LA SALE BÊTE!

Public Opinion in the Dreyfus Affair: "Ah! The Dirty Beast!"
The French army used forged documents and perjured testimony to convict Captain Alfred Dreyfus of espionage. In a climate of escalating anti-Semitism, the conviction of a Jew struck many in the public as yet another narrow escape for the country. Only intense detective work by pro-Dreyfus activists and lobbying by Dreyfus's family convinced republican leaders that the system of equal rights was imperiled not by Dreyfus but by the bigotry of the army and those right-wing politicians who had trumped up the case against him. (© Musée Carnavalet/Roger Viollet/The Image Works.)

responsible, and outlawed teaching by religious orders to ensure a public school system that honored toleration and the rule of law. Nonetheless, the Dreyfus Affair made anti-Semitism a standard political tool by showing the effectiveness of hate-filled slogans in mainstream politics.

The ruling elites in Germany also used anti-Semitism to gain political support from those who feared the consequences of Germany's sudden and overwhelming industrialization. Bismarck tried to woo the working class with an array of social programs such as accident and disability insurance while out-lawing the Social Democratic Party. The agrarian elites, who controlled the highest reaches of government, lost ground as agriculture declined as a force in Germany's economy. The agrarian elites came to loathe both vibrant industry and the working class as better jobs drew rural people away from the land. As one Berlin newspaper noted, "The agrarians' hate for cities . . . blinds them to the simplest needs and the most natural demands of the urban population."

These conservatives and a growing radical right claimed that Jews, who made up less than 1 percent of the German population, were responsible for the disruption of traditional society and charged them with being the main beneficiaries of economic change. In the 1890s, nationalist and anti-Semitic pressure groups flourished, denouncing not only Jews and "new women" but also Social Democrats, whom they branded as internationalist and unpatriotic. In the 1890s, the new Agrarian League fueled the fears of small farmers by accusing Jews of causing agricultural booms and busts. Hate-filled slogans and violent expressions of nationalism, rather than rational proposals to solve problems of economic change, became regular features of political campaigns.

Politicians in Austria-Hungary, the dual monarchy, also used militant nationalism and anti-Semitism to win votes, but here the presence of many ethnic groups meant competing nationalisms and thus greater complexity in the politics of hate. Foremost among the nationalists were the Hungarians, who wanted autonomy for themselves while forcibly imposing the Magyar language and culture on all other ethnic groups within Hungary itself. This policy was called Magyarization, from the name of the dominant Hungarian ethnic group. Nationalist demands for greater Hungarian influence rested on two pieces of evidence: Budapest's importance as a thriving industrial city and the massive exportation of grain from the vast estates of the Hungarian nobility—both of which, it was claimed, saved the monarchy's finances. Yet political chaos within Hungary resulted from Magyar domination there, as Slovaks, Romanians, and Ruthenians protested horrendous labor conditions and tens of thou-

Principal Ethnic Groups in Austria-Hungary, c. 1900

sands of others demanded the vote. In the face of this resistance, Hungary intensified Magyarization, even decreeing that all tombstones be engraved in the Magyar language.

Hungarian nationalism led other nationalists to intensify their own demands for rights in the dual monarchy. Croats, Serbs, and other Slavic groups in the south called for equality with the Hungarians. The central government allowed the Czechs more influence in the government because of growing industrial prosperity in their region. But every step favoring the Czechs provoked outrage from the traditionally dominant ethnic Germans in the region. When Austria-Hungary decreed in 1897 that government officials in the Czech region would have to speak Czech as well as German, the Germans rioted, further straining political stability.

Tensions mounted as politicians in Vienna linked the growing power of Hungarian and Czech politicians to Jews. Karl Lueger, whose newly formed Christian Social Party attracted aristocrats, Catholics, artisans, shopkeepers, and white-collar workers, had great success with this new brand of politics. In hate-filled speeches, Lueger hurled abuse at Jews and non-German groups, appealing to those people for whom modern life meant a loss of privilege and security. Lueger's ethnic nationalism and anti-Semitism threatened the multinationalism on which Austria-Hungary was based. His attacks were so effective at getting votes—he was elected mayor of Vienna in 1895—that a widening range of politicians made anti-Semitism an integral part of their election campaigns, calling Jews the "sucking vampire" of modernity and blaming them for any and all problems. Thus politics moved from parliaments to the streets, inflaming the atmosphere with racism.

Like Christians and people of other religions, Jews often differed from one another based on social class and education. Jews in many parts of Europe had responded to increasing legal tolerance by moving out of Jewish neighborhoods, intermarrying with Christians, and in some cases converting to Christianity—practices known as assimilation. Many educated Jews favored the classical culture of the German Empire over the Catholic ritual promoted by Austria-Hungary. Still, many accomplished and prosperous Jews, including Sigmund Freud, flourished amid the cosmopolitan culture of Vienna and Budapest. By contrast, less fortunate Jews, such as those in Russia and Romania, were increasingly targeted for persecution, legally disadvantaged, and forced to live in ghettos. Jews from these countries might seek refuge in the cities of central and eastern Europe or migrate to countries around the world. By 1900, Jews were prominent in cultural and economic affairs in cities across the continent and discriminated against, even victimized, in more rural areas.

Amid vast migration and continued persecution, a spirit of Jewish nationalism arose, as Jews began organizing resistance to pogroms and anti-Semitic politics, and intellectuals drew on Jewish folklore and history to establish a national identity similar to that of European nations. In the 1880s, Ukrainian physician Leon Pinsker, seeing the Jews' lack of national territory as fundamental to the persecution heaped on them, advocated the migration of Jews to Palestine—a goal known as **Zionism**. Theodor Herzl, strongly influenced by Pinsker, called not simply for migration but for the creation of a Jewish nation-state. A Hungarian-born Jew, Herzl experienced anti-Semitism firsthand as a Viennese journalist and writer in Paris during the Dreyfus Affair. With the support of poorer eastern European Jews, he succeeded in calling the first International Zionist Congress in Basel, Switzerland (1897), which endorsed settlement in Palestine and helped gain financial backing from the Rothschild banking family. By 1914, some eighty-five thousand Jews had resettled in Palestine.

Threats to the Russian Empire

Politics were equally explosive in Russia, where anti-Semitism escalated and internal affairs seemed in disarray. Russia was one of the few European countries without a constitutional government, and reform-minded Russian youths increasingly turned to revolutionary, even terrorist groups for solutions to political and social problems. Writers fueled an intense debate over Russia's future. Leo Tolstoy, author of the epic *War and Peace* (1869), opposed the revolutionaries' desire to overturn the social order, promoting the cause of spiritual regeneration instead. His novel *Anna Karenina* (1877) is the story not only of an impassioned, adulterous love affair but also of a landowner who, like Tolstoy himself, rejects modernization and idealizes the peasantry's simple values. Radicals, however, sought to change Russia by violent action rather than by spiritual uplift, and in 1881 one of them killed Tsar Alexander II in a bombing attack. Although his death failed to provoke the peasant uprising the terrorists expected, the assassination reflected Russian discontent.

Alexander III (r. 1881–1894) rejected his father's legacy of liberal reform and unleashed further repression of religious and ethnic minorities. He gave the police almost unchecked power. Intensified Russification further alienated nationalities such as the Poles and turned the once loyal German middle and upper classes of the Baltic provinces against Russian rule. But the main victims of Alexander's policies were the five million Russian Jews, confined since the eighteenth century to the Pale of Settlement, the restricted territory in which they were permitted to live. Distinctive language, dress, and isolation made them easy targets in an age when the Russian government was enforcing cultural uniformity and national identity. Government officials also encouraged people to blame Jews for heavy taxes and living costs—though the true cause was the policy of raising taxes to pay for industrialization.

When Alexander III's son Nicholas II took the throne in 1894, the empire faced mounting difficulties. Taught as a child to hate Jews, Nicholas II (r. 1894–1917) stepped up the persecutions, and many high officials eagerly endorsed anti-Semitism to gain his favor. Pogroms became a regular feature of the Easter holiday in Russia, and Nicholas increasingly limited how Jews could earn a living. Simultaneously, uprooted Russians settled much of Siberia, and the government sponsored industrialization, especially the growth of transport and manufacturing. Industrialization, however, produced urban unrest as Marxist and other activists incited workers to demand better conditions. In 1903, skilled workers led strikes in Baku, where the participation of Armenians and Tatars showed how urbanization and Russification could actually bring diverse ethnicities together to challenge—not support—the autocratic regime.

The tense situation exploded into revolution during the Russo-Japanese War. In January 1905, a crowd gathered outside the tsar's Winter Palace in St. Petersburg to try to make Nicholas aware of the brutal conditions under which they suffered. Instead of allowing the demonstration to pass, troops guarding the palace shot into the crowd, killing hundreds and wounding thousands. News of this event, referred to as Bloody Sunday, moved workers across Russia to rebel. They struck over wages, working hours, and factory conditions and demanded political representation in the government. Workers rejected the leadership of both Social Democrats and Social Revolutionaries and instead organized their own councils, called soviets. In June, sailors on the battleship *Potemkin* mutinied. In October, a massive railroad strike brought rail transportation to a halt, and the Baltic territories and Transcaucasia rebelled. In November, uprisings broke out in Moscow. Professionals, the upper

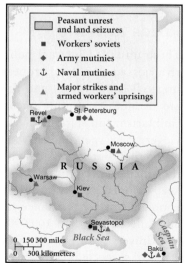

The Russian Revolution of 1905

classes, and women joined the assault on autocracy, with a series of demands including the creation of a representative legislature. They believed that the monarchy's reliance on censorship and a secret police force had relegated Russia to the ranks of the most backward nation-states.

The tsar finally yielded to the violence and created a representative body called the Duma. Although very few Russians could vote for representatives to the Duma, its mere existence, along with the new right to debate issues in public, liberalized government and allowed people to present their grievances to a more responsive body. Political parties took shape, and the Revolution of 1905 drew to a close. But people soon wondered whether anything had really changed. From 1907 to 1917, the Duma convened, but twice when the tsar disliked its recommendations, he simply sent the delegates home. Nicholas did have a successful administrator in Prime Minister Pyotr Stolypin, who tried to eliminate rural discontent by ending the mir system of communal farming, canceling the peasants' redemption payments for the land they farmed, and making loans available to peasants for the purchase of land. Although these reforms did not eradicate rural poverty, they did allow people to move to the cities in search of jobs, and they created a larger group of independent peasants. Meanwhile, another round of strikes broke out, culminating in a general strike in St. Petersburg in 1914. The imperial government and the conservative nobility still had no solution to the social turmoil, and their refusal to share power and introduce true political reform left the way open to an even greater upheaval in 1917.

REVIEW   What were the major changes in political life between 1880 and 1914?

Roads to World War I

These unsettled internal politics throughout Europe kept nerves on edge, while rivalries among the European powers over empire intensified. As a result of imperial competition, one British economist wrote in 1902, "Diplomatic strains are of almost monthly occurrence between the Powers." Nationalism swelled: "militarism run stark mad" was how one U.S. official described the scene in 1914. Government spending on what people called the "arms race" stimulated European economies, but while stockpiles of arms temporarily promoted economic growth, they menaced the future. Europe was jittery, waging a growing number of wars to keep colonial peoples in line. In German East Africa, for example, colonial forces countered native resistance in 1905 with a scorched-earth policy, which eventually killed more than 100,000 Africans (Map 19.2, page 734). The French closed the University of Hanoi, executed Indochinese intellectuals, and deported thousands of suspected nationalists to maintain a tenuous grip on Indochina (Map 19.3, page 737). By 1914, a hostile international scene, militant nationalism in the Balkan states, and conflicts in domestic politics came together, driving Europeans toward mass destruction.

Competing Alliances and Clashing Ambitions

As the twentieth century opened, an alliance system first established by Bismarck to ensure the peaceful consolidation of the new German Empire and to maintain European stability was changing rapidly. Anxious about the Balkans and Russian leadership of the Slavs, Austria-Hungary had entered a defensive alliance with Germany in 1879. The **Dual Alliance**, as it was called, offered protection against Russia, which appeared to threaten Hungarian control of its Slavic peasantry. In 1882, Italy joined this partnership (called the Triple Alliance thereafter), largely because of Italy's imperial rivalries with France. Bismarck also signed the Reinsurance Treaty (1887) with Russia to check Habsburg dreams of having a free hand against this rival for Slavic loyalty. Bismarck intended these alliances to show that Germany was now a "satisfied" nation and one that would prevent further disruptive wars.

Bismarck's delicate alliance system started unraveling, however, when the blustering but deeply insecure Kaiser William II came to power in 1888. Advisers flattered the twenty-nine-year-old into thinking that Bismarck was a bother, even a rival to his own creativity. William II (r. 1888–1918) dismissed Bismarck in 1890. An ardent supporter of German nationalism, the kaiser saw Austria-Hungary as closely connected because of its German dynasty and thus let the alliance with Russia lapse, driving the Russians to form an alliance with the French. William then became "dissatisfied" with Germany's international status and inflamed rather than calmed the diplomatic atmosphere. He used the opportunity presented by the defeat of France's ally Russia in the Russo-Japanese War to contest French claims in Morocco, boldly landing his own ship in Morocco in 1905 to challenge French predominance. To resolve what became known as the First Moroccan Crisis, an international conference met in Spain in 1906. William expected Britain to side with Germany over its traditional rival France, but instead of awarding Germany Morocco, the powers supported French rule. The French and British military, faced with German aggression in Morocco, drew closer together. When the French finally took over Morocco in 1911, Germany triggered the Second Moroccan Crisis by sending a gunboat to the port of Agadir and demanding concessions from France. This time no power, not even Austria-Hungary, backed the German move.

The backdrop to William's aggressive demands was the competition for empire between France and Britain, which seemed to rule out an alliance between the two powers. Constant rivals in Africa, they had been on the brink of war in 1898, at a town in the Sudan called Fashoda (Map 19.2, page 734), when France withdrew. At that point, both nations decided it was in their own best interests to try to get along. To prevent another Fashoda, they entered into secret agreements, the first of which (1904) guaranteed British claims in Egypt and French claims in Morocco. This agreement marked the beginning of the British-French alliance called the **Entente Cordiale**. After the First Moroccan Crisis, the British and French planned for the coordination of their forces in case of war. In 1907, Britain and Russia put aside their rivalries to allow Russia to join what became the Triple Entente among

France, Britain, and Russia. Thus two opposing alliance systems were now in place. Smarting from its setbacks on the world stage, Germany reconsidered its role in continental Europe.

The Balkans, in the meantime, loomed as a site for competing ambitions on the part of the great powers and among the Balkan states themselves. Germany's bold territorial claims, along with uncertainty about alliances, unsettled Europe, particularly the Balkans. German statesmen began envisioning the creation of a **Mitteleuropa** that included central Europe, the Balkans, and Turkey under German rule. Russia, however, saw itself as the protector of the Slavs in that same region and wanted to replace the Ottomans as the major Balkan power. Meanwhile, Austria-Hungary swiftly annexed Bosnia-Herzegovina during the Young Turk revolt in 1908. This was part of its plan to control more Balkan ethnicities in order to dilute the power of any one ethnicity in the kingdom (Map 19.4).

The nineteenth century had seen the rise of nationalism and ethnicity as the basis for the development of independent nation-states in the Balkans, however, and by the early twentieth century, Balkan states, composed of several ethnicities as well as Orthodox Christians, Roman Catholics, and Muslims, sought more Ottoman and Habsburg territory and went to war to obtain it. In the First Balkan War (1912), Serbia, Bulgaria, Greece, and Montenegro joined forces to gain Macedonia and Albania from the Ottomans. The victors divided up their booty but soon turned against one another. In the Second Balkan War (1913), Serbia, Greece, and Montenegro contested Bulgarian gains in the first war. The quick victory of these allies increased Austria-Hungary's dismay at Serbia's rising power. Grievances between the Serbs and the Habsburgs, who feared that any disturbance in the Balkan balance of power would encourage ethnic rebellion at home, now seemed irreconcilable, and the angry Serbs looked to Russia for help. The situation tempted strategists on all sides to think hopefully that a quick war there—something like Bismarck's wars—could resolve this tension and uncertainty.

The Race to Arms

At the turn of the twentieth century, these and other rivalries and the drive for national greatness made constant readiness for war seem increasingly necessary. On the seas and in foreign lands, the colonial powers battled to establish control, and they developed railroad, telegraph, and telephone networks everywhere to move troops and encourage commerce. Governments began to draft ordinary citizens for periods of two to six years into large standing armies, in contrast to the smaller eighteenth-century forces that had served the more limited military goals of the time. By 1914, escalating tensions in Europe boosted the annual intake of draftees: Germany, France, and Russia called up 250,000 or more troops each year. Per capita expenditures on the military rose in all the major powers between 1890 and 1914; the proportion of national budgets devoted to defense in 1910 was lowest in Austria-Hungary at 10 percent and highest in Germany at 45 percent.

Map 19.4 The Balkans, 1908–1914
Balkan peoples—mixed in religion, ethnicity, and political views—were successful in developing and asserting their desire for independence, especially in the First Balkan War (1912), which claimed territory from the Ottoman Empire. Their increased autonomy sparked rivalries among them and continued to attract attention from the great powers. Three empires in particular—the Russian, Ottoman, and Austro-Hungarian—simultaneously sought greater influence in the region, which became a powder keg of competing ambitions.

The modernization of weaponry also transformed warfare. Swedish arms manufacturer Alfred Nobel patented dynamite and developed a kind of gunpowder that improved the accuracy of guns and reduced the amount of smoke they produced, resulting in a less clouded battlefield environment. Breakthroughs in the chemical industry led to improvements in long-range artillery, which by 1914 could fire on targets as far as six miles away. Military leaders devised strategies to protect their armies from overwhelming firepower. Munitions factories across Europe manufactured ever-growing stockpiles of howitzers, Mauser rifles, and Hotchkiss machine guns. Used in the South African and Russo-Japanese wars, these new weapons had shown that military offensives were more difficult to win than in the past because neither side could overcome such accurate and forceful firepower. Military leaders also had devised new strategies to protect armies from this firepower, including the use of trenches and barbed wire.

Naval construction also played a major role in both the arms race and nationalist politics. In 1905, the British launched the HMS *Dreadnought,* a warship with unprecedented firepower and the centerpiece of a program to update the British navy by constructing at least seven battleships per year. Germany followed British naval building step by step and made itself a force to be feared not just on land but also at sea. The German military encouraged William II to view the navy as the essential ingredient in making Germany a world power and directed him to the writings of U.S. naval theorist Alfred Thayer Mahan. Mahan's argument that command of the seas determined international power encouraged Germany to build naval bases as far away as the Pacific. The German drive to build battleships strengthened Britain's alliance with France in the Entente Cordiale, as all the powers dramatically raised their annual naval spending. The Germans announced the fleet buildup as "a peaceful policy," but like British naval expansion, it led only to a worsening international climate and intense competition in weapons manufacture.

Public relations campaigns promoted the great powers' military buildup. When critics of the arms race suggested a temporary "naval holiday" to stop British and German shipbuilding, British officials put out a news release warning that such a move "would throw innumerable men on the pavement." Nationalist groups and boosters of empire lobbied for military spending, while governments publicized large navies as beneficial to trade and industry. When Germany's Social Democrats questioned the use of increased taxes to fund this buildup and their heavy burden on workers, the press criticized the party as unpatriotic. The Conservative Party in Great Britain, eager for more battleships, made popular the slogan "We want eight and we won't wait." One military leader captured the enthusiasm for war at the time, even among the public at large. When asked in 1912 about his predictions for war and peace, he responded enthusiastically, "We shall have war. I will make it. I will win it." Everything was in place for war—alliances, stocks of armaments, war plans, mass armies, and a boiling pot of animosities and tensions—in the summer of 1914.

REVIEW   What major factors made Europe set for war by 1914?

Conclusion

By 1914, Europe as a whole was ripe for a major conflict and had feverishly prepared for it, even as the Wolf-Man was completing his treatment with Freud in that summer—"a cured man," he called himself. Imperialism and the arms race had stimulated militant nationalism and brought many Europeans to favor war over peace.

Mapping the West Europe at the Outbreak of World War I, August 1914
Each of the European powers expected a swift victory when war broke out. Many were convinced that
war would bring them great advantages over their rivals in trade and empire, including the chance to
expand their territories. But if the powers appeared well prepared and invincible at the start of the
war, relatively few would survive the conflict intact.

The rapid pace of change had helped blaze the path to war. Facing continuing violence
in politics, grating new trends in the arts, and problems in society, Europeans had
come to believe that war would set events back on the right course and save them
from the perils of modernity. Disturbances in private life and challenges to tradition posed by new technologies and modern urban life would disappear, it was

believed, in the flames of war. "Like men longing for a thunderstorm to relieve them of the summer's sultriness," wrote one Austrian official, "so the generation of 1914 believed in the relief that war might bring." Such a possibility caused many Europeans to rejoice as war approached. But instead of bringing the refreshment of summer rain, the war that erupted in the summer of 1914 opened an era of political turmoil, widespread suffering, massive human slaughter, and even greater doses of modernity.

CHAPTER REVIEW QUESTIONS
1. How did changes in society at the beginning of the twentieth century affect the development of mass politics?
2. How did cultural changes affect politics between 1880 and 1914?

For practice quizzes and other study tools, see the Online Study Guide at bedfordstmartins.com/huntconcise.

For primary-source material from this period, see Chapters 23 and 24 of *Sources of THE MAKING OF THE WEST*, Third Edition.

Suggested References

New studies of imperialism show increasing conquest, the creation of an international economy, and the social and cultural impulses behind imperial expansion. The University of Pennsylvania's African Studies Center Web site looks at African history, politics, and culture. New forms of art and philosophy and the rise of mass politics

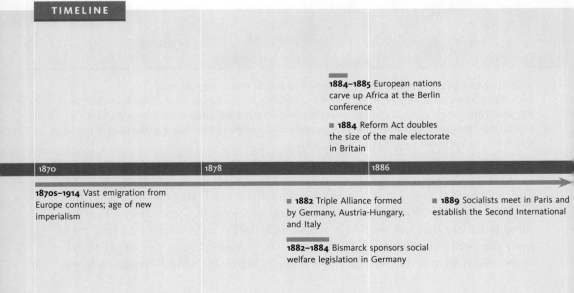

TIMELINE

1884–1885 European nations carve up Africa at the Berlin conference

■ **1884** Reform Act doubles the size of the male electorate in Britain

1870   1878   1886

1870s–1914 Vast emigration from Europe continues; age of new imperialism

■ **1882** Triple Alliance formed by Germany, Austria-Hungary, and Italy

■ **1889** Socialists meet in Paris and establish the Second International

1882–1884 Bismarck sponsors social welfare legislation in Germany were central to the challenges Europe faced, but the question of why war broke out remains widely debated.

African Studies Center: http://www.sas.upenn.edu/African_Studies/AS.html

Cain, P. J., and A. G. Hopkins. *British Imperialism, 1688–2000.* 2002.

Childs, Peter. *Modernism.* 2008.

Davis, Mike. *Late Victorian Holocausts: El Niño Famines and the Making of the Third World.* 2001.

Hermann, David G. *The Arming of Europe and the Making of the First World War.* 1997.

Hull, Isabel. *Absolute Destruction: Military Culture and the Practices of War in Imperial Germany.* 2005.

Kaplan, Morris B. *Sodom on the Thames: Sex, Love, and Scandal in Wilde Times.* 2005.

Koven, Seth. *Slumming: Sexual and Social Politics in Victorian London.* 2004.

Marchand, Suzanne, and David Lindenfeld, eds. *Germany at the Fin de Siècle: Culture, Politics, and Ideas.* 2004.

Moch, Leslie Page. *Moving Europeans: Migration in Western Europe since 1650.* 2003.

Nineteenth- and twentieth-century philosophy: http://www.epistemelinks.com/index.asp

Reagin, Nancy. *Sweeping the German Nation: Domesticity and National Identity in Germany, 1870–1945.* 2006.

Reeder, Linda. *Widows in White: Migration and the Transformation of Rural Italian Women, Sicily, 1880–1920.* 2003.

Stanislawski, Michael. *Zionism and the Fin-de-Siècle: Cosmopolitanism and Nationalism from Nordau to Jabotinsky.* 2001.

Streets, Heather. *Martial Races: The Military, Race and Masculinity in British Imperial Culture, 1857–1914.* 2004.

Zahra, Tara. *Kidnapped Souls: National Indifference and the Battle for Children in the Bohemian Lands, 1900–1948.* 2008.

■ **1908** Young Turks revolt against rule by the sultan in the Ottoman Empire

■ **1901** Irish National Theater established by the circle around Maud Gonne and William Butler Yeats

■ **1907** Pablo Picasso launches cubism

■ **1906** Women receive the vote in Finland; international conference held in Spain to resolve the First Moroccan Crisis

■ **1900** Sigmund Freud, *The Interpretation of Dreams*

■ **1905** Revolution erupts in Russia; violence forces Nicholas II to establish an elected body, the Duma; Albert Einstein publishes his special theory of relativity

1894   1902   1910   1918

1894–1899 Dreyfus Affair lays bare anti-Semitism in France

■ **1903** Emmeline Pankhurst founds the Women's Social and Political Union to fight for woman suffrage in Great Britain

■ **1911** Second Moroccan Crisis

1899–1902 South African War

1911–1912 Revolutionaries overthrow the Qing dynasty and declare China a republic

■ **1904** French and British form the Entente Cordiale

1912–1913 First and Second Balkan Wars

1904–1905 Russo-Japanese War

20

War, Revolution, and Reconstruction

1914–1929

JULES AMAR FOUND HIS TRUE VOCATION in World War I. A French expert on making industrial work more efficient, Amar switched focus after 1914. As hundreds of thousands of men returned from the battlefront missing body parts, plastic surgery and the construction of masks and other devices to hide deformities developed rapidly. Amar devised artificial limbs and appendages in these traumatic years that would allow wounded soldiers to return to everyday life by "mak[ing] up for a function lost, or greatly reduced." He designed arms that featured hooks, magnets, and other mechanisms with which the veteran could hold a cigarette, play the violin, and, most important, work with tools such as typewriters. Mangled by the weapons of modern technological warfare, the survivors of World War I would be made whole, it was thought, by technology such as Amar's.

Amar dealt with the human tragedy of the "Great War," so named by contemporaries because of its staggering human toll—forty million wounded or killed in battle. The Great War did not settle problems or restore social order as the European powers hoped it would. Instead, the war produced political chaos, overturning the Russian, German, Ottoman, and Austro-Hungarian empires. The crushing burden of war on the European powers accelerated the rise of the United States, while service in the war intensified the demands of colonized peoples for freedom. Many soldiers remained actively fighting long into what was supposed to be peacetime, while others had been so militarized that they longed for a life that was more like wartime.

Grieving Parents

Before World War I, the German artist Käthe Kollwitz gained her artistic reputation with woodcuts of hand-loom weavers, whose livelihoods were threatened by industrialization. From 1914 on, she depicted the suffering and death that swirled around her, and never with more somber force than in these two monuments to her son Peter, who died on the western front in the first months of the war. Today one can still visit his burial place in Vladslo, Belgium, to see this father and mother mourning their loss, like millions across Europe in those heartbreaking days.

(© *John Parker Picture Library.* © *2010 Artists Rights Society [ARS], NY/VG Bild-Kunst, Bonn.*)

World War I transformed society, too. A prewar feeling of doom and decline gave way to postwar cynicism. Many Westerners turned their backs on politics and attacked life with wild gaiety in the Roaring Twenties, snapping up new consumer goods, escaping their daily routines with entertainment provided by films and radio, and enjoying once forbidden personal freedoms. Others found reason for hope in the new political systems the war made possible: Soviet communism and Italian **Fascism**. Modern communication technologies such as radio gave politicians the means to promote a mass politics that, ironically, was often antidemocratic, militaristic, and eventually dictatorial.

A war that was long anticipated and even welcomed in some quarters as a remedy for modernity destabilized Europe and the world far into the following decades. From statesmen to ordinary citizens, many Europeans like Amar found themselves dealing year after year with the aftermath of the war. Some devoted their peacetime efforts to making war-ravaged society function normally; others planned to tap into the forces of militarism that the war had so glorified.

CHAPTER FOCUS QUESTION   What political, social, and economic impact did World War I have during the conflict, immediately after it, and through the 1920s?

The Great War, 1914–1918

June 28, 1914, began as an ordinary day for Austria's archduke Francis Ferdinand and his wife, Sophie, as they ended a state visit to Sarajevo in Bosnia-Herzegovina. Wearing full military dress, the archduke was riding in a motorcade to bid farewell to various officials when a group of young Serbian nationalists threw bombs in an unsuccessful assassination attempt. The full danger did not register, and after a stop the archduke and his wife set out again. In the crowd was another armed nationalist, Gavrilo Princip, who for several weeks had traveled clandestinely to reach this destination, dreaming of reuniting his homeland of Bosnia-Herzegovina with Serbia. The unprotected and unsuspecting couple became Princip's victims, as he shot them both dead. Within weeks, the assassination led to all-out war. The ground had been prepared with long-standing alliances, the development of strategies for war, and the buildup of new military weapons such as heavy artillery, machine guns, and the airplane. Given recent experience, most people felt the conflict would be short and decisive. The unforeseen happened, however, and the war lasted for more than four years. It was a **total war**, mobilizing entire societies and producing the unbelievable horror that made it "great."

War Erupts

The Habsburg government saw the assassination as an opportunity to defeat Serbia once and for all. German statesmen and military leaders agreed, urging the Austrians to stand firm and repeating promises of support in case of war. Evidence showed that

Archduke Francis Ferdinand and His Wife in Sarajevo, June 1914
Archduke Francis Ferdinand, heir to the Austro-Hungarian monarchy, was a thorn in the side of many politicians because he did not want to favor Hungarian interests over other ethnic interests in his kingdom. His own family life was also unusual for royalty in those days: his wife, Sophie, and he had married for love and did not like to be apart. They were traveling together to Bosnia-Herzegovina in 1914 when they were assassinated. That event helped produce the outbreak of World War I. (Mary Evans Picture Library.)

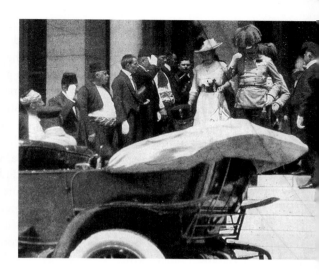

Princip had received arms and information from Serbian officials who directed a terrorist organization from within Serbia's government. The Austrians demanded that the Serbs publicly condemn terrorism, suppress terrorist groups, and allow Habsburg officials to participate in the investigation of the crime. The ultimatum was severe. "You are setting Europe ablaze," the Russian foreign minister told the Habsburgs in light of the humiliating demands. Yet the Serbs were conciliatory, accepting all the terms except one—the participation of Austrian officials in the investigation. Kaiser William II was pleased, declaring this "a great moral success for Vienna! All reason for war is gone." His relief was premature. Confident of German backing, Austria-Hungary used Serbia's resistance to that one demand as the pretext for declaring war on July 28.

Some European statesmen tried hard to avoid war. Tsar Nicholas II and Kaiser William exchanged letters asking each other not to go to war. The British foreign secretary proposed an all-European conference, but with no success. Germany backed Austria-Hungary fully in hopes of convincing France and Britain to stay out of the war, which, German officials believed, would keep Russia from mobilizing. At the same time, however, German military leaders were determined to fight a short, preemptive war that would result in territorial gains leading to their goal of creating a Mitteleuropa. As an additional incentive, the war would allow these leaders to declare martial law in Germany and as a result justify the arrest of the leadership of the German Social Democratic Party, which threatened conservative rule.

Even as some governments were torn over what to do, the European press caught war fever. Like the press, military leaders, especially in Germany and Austria-Hungary, promoted mobilization rather than diplomacy in the last days of July. The Austrians declared war and then ordered mobilization on July 31, believing Russia would not dare intervene. But Nicholas II ordered the Russian army to mobilize in defense of Serbia—Russia's Slavic ally. Having encouraged the Austrians to attack Serbia, the German general staff mobilized on August 1.

Germany's war strategy was based on the Schlieffen Plan, named after its author, Alfred von Schlieffen, a former chief of the general staff. The plan outlined a way to combat antagonists on two fronts by concentrating on one foe at a time. First would come a rapid and concentrated German blow to the west against Russia's ally France, which would lead to France's defeat in six weeks. Accompanying that strike would be a light holding action to the east. With France beaten, German armies in the west would then be deployed against Russia, which, German war planners believed, would be slow to mobilize. The attack on France would proceed through Belgium, whose neutrality was guaranteed by the European powers. Events did not occur as the Germans hoped. The Belgian government rejected an ultimatum to allow the uncontested passage of the German army through the country, and Germany's subsequent violation of Belgium's neutrality brought Britain into the war on the side of Russia and France, which was already mobilizing in support of its ally Russia.

The Conflict Widens

World War I pitted two sets of opponents formed roughly out of the alliances developed during the previous fifty years. On one side stood the Central Powers (Austria-Hungary and Germany), which had evolved from Bismarck's Triple Alliance. On the other side stood the Allies (France, Great Britain, and Russia), which had emerged as a bloc from the Entente Cordiale between France and Great Britain and from the 1890s treaties between France and Russia. Italy, originally part of the Triple Alliance, joined the Allies in 1915. The war soon expanded globally as well. In late August 1914, Japan, eager to extend its empire into China, lined up with the Allies. In the fall, the Ottoman Empire united with the Central Powers against its traditional enemy, Russia.

Both sides fought with the same ferocious hunger for power, prestige, and prosperity that had inspired imperialism. Germany aspired to a far-flung empire to be gained by annexing Russian territory and incorporating parts of Belgium, France, and Luxembourg. Some German leaders wanted to annex Austria-Hungary as well. Austria-Hungary hoped to retain its great-power status in the face of competing nationalisms within its borders. Among the Allies, Russia wanted to reassert its status as a great power and as the protector of the Slavs by adding a reunified Poland to the Russian Empire and by taking formal leadership of other Slavic peoples. The French craved territory, especially the return of resource-rich Alsace and Lorraine, taken after the Franco-Prussian War. The British sought to cement their hold on Egypt and the Suez Canal and to secure the rest of their world empire. By the Treaty of London (1915), France and Britain promised Italy territory in Africa, Asia Minor, the Balkans, and elsewhere in return for joining the Allies.

The colonies provided massive assistance and were also battlegrounds. Some one million Africans, one million Indians, and more than one million men from the British Commonwealth served on the battlefronts. The imperial powers also conscripted uncounted numbers of colonists as forced laborers both at home and on the battlefronts. Colonial troops fought on European battlefields and also played a major role in fighting across North and sub-Saharan Africa. Relying on Arab, African, and Indian troops, the British waged a successful war on Ottoman lands in the Middle East, menacing Germany's longtime interests by taking Baghdad in 1917 and also taking Palestine, Syria, and Mesopotamia.

Unprecedented use of machinery helped determine the course of the war. In August 1914, weapons such as machine guns and fast breech-loading rifles; military vehicles such as airplanes, battleships, and submarines; and motorized transport (cars and railroads) were all at the armies' disposal. New technologies such as chlorine gas, tanks, and bombs were developed between 1914 and 1918. Countries differed, however, in their experience with and access to large quantities of these weapons. British generals knew the destructive capacity of the weapons because of their colonial wars; the Germans were far more advanced in strategy and weaponry than either the Russians or the Austrians. The war itself became a lethal testing ground, as both new and old weapons were used, often ineffectively. Many officers on both sides believed in a "cult of the offensive," which called for spirited attacks and high troop morale. Despite the availability of newer, more powerful war technology, an old-fashioned vision of warfare made many officers unwilling to abandon sabers, lances, bayonets, and cavalry charges. In the face of massive firepower, the cult of the offensive would cost millions of lives.

Battlefronts

The first months of the war crushed any hope of a quick victory. All the major armies mobilized rapidly. Guided by the Schlieffen Plan, the Germans quickly reached Luxembourg and Belgium, but the plan fell apart when the Belgians resisted, slowing the German advance and allowing British and French troops to reach the northern front after the French had mistakenly fallen for German diversionary moves on the eastern border. In September, British and French armies engaged the Germans along the Marne River in France. Neither side could defeat the other, and casualties were shocking: in the first three months of the war, more than 1.5 million men fell on the western front alone. Firepower turned what was supposed to be an offensive war of movement into a stationary standoff along a line stretching from the North Sea through Belgium and northern France to Switzerland (Map 20.1). Deep within opposing lines of trenches dug along this western front, soldiers lived a nightmarish existence.

On the eastern front, the "Russian steam-roller"—so named because of the number of men mobilized, some twelve million in all—drove far more quickly than expected into East Prussia. The Russians believed that no army could withstand their massive numbers, no matter how ill equipped and poorly trained they were. Their success was short-lived. The Germans crushed the tsar's army in East Prussia

Map 20.1 The Fronts of World War I, 1914–1918

Fighting on all fronts destroyed portions of Europe's hard-won industrial and agricultural capacity. Because the western front remained relatively stationary, the devastation of land and resources in northern and eastern France was especially intense. Men engaged in trench warfare developed an intense comradeship based on their mutual suffering.

and then turned south to Galicia. Victory made heroes of military leaders Paul von Hindenburg and Erich Ludendorff. Despite victories, German triumphs in the east had failed to knock out the Russians and had also undermined the Schlieffen Plan by removing forces from the west before the western front had been won.

The war at sea proved equally indecisive. Confident of Britain's superior naval power, the Allies blockaded ports to prevent supplies from reaching Germany and Austria-Hungary. Kaiser William and his advisers planned a massive submarine, or U-boat (*Unterseeboot*, "underwater boat"), campaign against Allied and neutral shipping around Britain and France. In May 1915, German submarines sank the British passenger ship *Lusitania* and killed 1,198 people, including 124 Americans. Despite U.S. outrage, President Woodrow Wilson maintained a policy of neutrality; Germany, unwilling to provoke Wilson further, called off unrestricted submarine warfare. In May 1916, the navies of Germany and Britain finally clashed in the North Sea at Jutland. Though inconclusive, this battle demonstrated that the German fleet could not master British sea power (Map 20.1, page 784).

Ideas of a negotiated peace were discarded. "No peace before England is defeated and destroyed," the kaiser railed against his cousin King George V. "Only amidst the ruins of London will I forgive Georgy." French leaders called for a "war to the death." The general staffs on both sides continued to prepare fierce attacks several times a year. Indecisive campaigns opened with heavy artillery pounding enemy trenches and gun emplacements. Troops then responded to the order to go "over the top," scrambling out of their trenches, usually to be mowed down by machine-gun fire from defenders secure in their own trenches. On the western front, the French assaulted the Germans in the north throughout 1915 in an attempt to drive them from the industrial regions. They accomplished little, and casualties of 100,000 or more during a single campaign became commonplace. On the eastern front, Russian armies captured parts of Galicia in the spring of 1915 and lumbered toward Hungary. The Central Powers struck back in Poland later that year, bringing the front closer to Petrograd (formerly St. Petersburg), the Russian capital.

The next year was even more disastrous. To cripple French morale, the Germans launched massive assaults on the fortress at Verdun, firing as many as a million shells in a single day. Combined French and German losses totaled close to a million men. Nonetheless, the French held. Hoping to relieve their allies, the British unleashed an artillery assault on German trenches in the Somme region in June 1916. In several months of battle, 1.25 million men were killed or wounded, but the final result was a stalemate. By the end of 1916, the French had suffered more than 3.5 million casualties. To help the Allies engaged at Verdun and the Somme, the Russians struck again, driving into the Carpathian Mountains, recouping territory, and menacing the Habsburg Empire. Only the German army stopped the Russian advance.

Had military leaders thoroughly dominated the scene, historians judge, all armies would have been demolished in nonstop offensives by the end of 1915. Yet ordinary soldiers in this war were not automatons in the face of what seemed to them suicidal orders. Informal agreements among troops to avoid battles allowed some battalions to go for long stretches with hardly a casualty. Enemies facing each other across the trenches frequently ate their meals in peace even though the trenches were within a hand grenade's reach. Throughout the war, soldiers on opposing sides fraternized, playing an occasional game of soccer, shouting to each other across the battlefield, and making gestures not to fight. A British veteran of the trenches explained to a new recruit that the Germans "don't want to fight any more than we do, so there's a kind of understanding between us. Don't fire at us and we'll not fire at you." Burying enemy dead in common graves with their own fallen comrades, many ordinary soldiers came to feel more warmly toward enemies who shared the trench experience than toward uncomprehending civilians back home.

Newly forged bonds of male companionship relieved some of the misery of trench life and aided survival. Facing the danger and deprivations of the frontline experience weakened traditional class distinctions. In some cases, upper-class officers and working-class recruits became friends in that "wholly masculine way of life uncomplicated by women," as one soldier put it. Soldiers picked lice from each other's bodies and clothes, tended each other's blistered feet, and came to love each other, sometimes even passionately. This sense of community would survive the war and influence postwar politics.

Troops of colonial soldiers from Asia and Africa had different experiences. Often these soldiers were put in the front ranks where the risks were greatest. They suffered from the rigors of totally unfamiliar climates and strange food, as well as from the ruin inflicted by Western war technology. Yet like class divisions, racial barriers sometimes fell—for instance, when European soldiers took pains to alleviate the distress

War in the Trenches
Men at the front developed close friendships as they lived with daily discomfort and death and the horrors of modern technological warfare. Some of the complexities of trench warfare appear in this image showing soldiers rescuing their fallen comrades after fighting at Bagatelle in northern France. (Getty Images.)

the cold inflicted on colonial troops. The perspectives of colonial soldiers changed, too. "What miserable crowned head was able to order such horrors?" wrote one corporal from West Africa. These troops saw their "masters" completely undone and "uncivilized," for when fighting did break out, the trenches became a veritable hell of shelling and sniping, flying body parts, blinding gas, and rotting cadavers. Some soldiers became hysterical or shell-shocked; others became cynical or lost hope. "It might be me tomorrow," a young British soldier wrote to his mother in 1916. "Who cares?" Soldiers who had gone to war to escape ordinary life in industrial society learned, as one German put it, "that in the modern war . . . the triumph of the machine over the individual is carried to its most extreme form." They took this hard-won knowledge into battle, pulling their comrades back when an offensive seemed lost or too costly.

The Home Front

World War I took place off the battlefield, too. Total war meant the involvement of civilians in essential war industries manufacturing the shells and machine guns, poisonous gases, bombs and airplanes, and eventually tanks that were the backbone of technological warfare. Increased production of coffins, canes, wheelchairs, and artificial limbs (devised by the likes of Jules Amar) also was required. Because the war would have failed utterly without them, civilians had to work overtime for, believe in, and sacrifice for victory. To keep the war machine operating smoothly, governments oversaw factories, transportation systems, and resources ranging from food to coal to textiles. Before the war, such tight government control would have outraged many liberals, but now it was accepted as a necessary condition for victory.

At first, political parties put aside their differences. Many socialists and working-class people who had criticized the military buildup announced their support for the war. For decades, socialist parties had preached that "workingmen have no country" and that nationalism was an ideology meant to keep workers disunited and subjected to their employers. In August 1914, however, the socialist rank and file, along with most of the party leaders, became as patriotic as the rest of society. Feminists divided over whether to maintain their traditional condemnation of war or to support the war effort. Although many feminists actively opposed the conflict, Emmeline Pankhurst and her daughter Christabel were among those who became militant nationalists, even changing the name of their suffrage paper to *Britannia*. Parties representing the middle class dropped their distrust of socialists and the working class. In the name of victory, national leaders wanted to end political divisions of all kinds. "I no longer recognize [political] parties," William II declared on August 4, 1914. "I recognize only Germans." Ordinary people, even those who had been on the receiving end of discrimination, came to believe that a new day of unity was dawning. One rabbi proudly echoed the kaiser: "In the German fatherland there are no longer any Christians and Jews, any believers and disbelievers, there are only Germans."

Governments mobilized the home front with varying degrees of success. All countries were caught without ready replacements for the heavy losses of weapons and military equipment and soon felt the shortage of food and labor as well. War ministries set up boards to allocate labor on the home front and the battlefront and to give industrialists financial incentives to encourage productivity. The Russian bureaucracy, however, only cooperated halfheartedly with industrialists and other groups that could aid the war effort. In several countries, emergency measures allowed the drafting of both men and women for military or industrial service. Desperate for factory workers, the Germans forced Belgian citizens to move to Germany, housing them in prison camps. In rural Russia, Austria-Hungary, Bulgaria, and Serbia, youths, women, and old men struggled to sustain farms without government help.

Throughout Europe, governments passed sedition laws that made it a crime to criticize the war or official policies. To ensure civilian acceptance of longer working hours and shortages of consumer goods, governments created propaganda agencies to advertise the war as a patriotic mission to resist villainous enemies. British propagandists fabricated atrocities that the German "Huns" supposedly committed against Belgians, and German propaganda warned that French African troops would rape German women if Germany was defeated. In Russia, Nicholas II changed the German-sounding name of the capital *St. Petersburg* to the Russian *Petrograd* as another patriotic move. World War I inflicted greater danger on civilians than mind control. Maintaining that Armenians in the Ottoman Empire

War Propaganda, 1915

"Never Forget!" screams the headline of this propaganda poster depicting an assaulted woman in despair. Intended to create outrage against the Germans, the poster suggests what German passage through neutral Belgium came to be called— "the rape of Belgium." Propaganda offices for the Allies sent out reports of women attacked and children massacred as the German armies moved through Belgian territory. **For more help analyzing this image, see the visual activity for this chapter in the Online Study Guide at** bedfordstmartins .com/huntconcise. (Mary Evans Picture Library.)

were plotting against the Central Powers, the Ottomans drove those Armenians living in Turkey from their homes, forcing them into landlessness where they starved or driving them into concentration camps or on long marches during which they simply died or were murdered. The Allies also caused the deaths of civilians en masse when they created famines by blockading the Syrian provinces of the Ottoman Empire in hopes that people there would rebel or die of starvation.

Extreme persecution of civilians along with the frightening propaganda often carried in the press made a compromise peace unlikely. Nonetheless, some individuals worked to end the war. In 1915, activists in the international women's movement met in The Hague to call for peace. "We can no longer endure . . . brute force as the only solution of international disputes," declared Dutch physician Aletta Jacobs. Many of these women spent the remainder of the war meeting with statesmen to urge them to seek peace, but with little success. In Austria-Hungary, nationalist groups agitating for ethnic self-determination hampered the empire's war effort. The Czechs undertook a vigorous anti-Habsburg campaign at home and abroad, while in the Balkans, the Croats, Slovenes, and Serbs formed a committee to plan a "South Slav" state independent of Austria-Hungary or any other power. The Allies encouraged such independence movements as part of their strategy to defeat the Habsburgs.

The war upset the social order as well as the political one. In the war's early days, many women lost their jobs when luxury shops, textile factories, and other nonessential establishments closed. But governments and businesses soon recognized the amount of labor it would take to wage a technological war. As more and more men left for the trenches, many women who had lost their jobs in nonessential businesses, as well as many low-paid domestic workers, took higher-paying jobs in formerly restricted munitions and metallurgical industries. In Warsaw women drove trucks, and in London they worked as streetcar conductors. Some young women nursed the wounded near the front lines.

Women's assumption of men's jobs looked to many like a sign of social disorder. In the words of one metalworker, women were "sending men to the slaughter." Men feared that women would remain in the workforce after the war, robbing men of their breadwinner role. Many people, even some women, objected to women's loss of femininity. "The feminine in me decreased more and more, and I did not know whether to be sad or glad about this," wrote one Russian nurse about wearing rough male clothing near the battlefield. Others criticized young female munitions workers for squandering their pay on ribbons and jewelry. The heated prewar debates over the "new woman" and gender roles returned.

Although soldiers from different backgrounds often felt bonds of solidarity in the trenches, difficult wartime conditions increasingly pitted civilians against one another on the home front. Whereas workers toiled longer hours while eating less, many in the upper classes still bought fancy food and fashionable clothing on the

A New Workforce in Wartime
With men at the front, women moved into factory work, doing jobs from which they had been unofficially barred before the war, as shown in this French photograph. In addition, tens of thousands of forced laborers from the colonies were moved to Europe to replace men sent to the front. The experience of forced labor during the war and service at the front politicized colonial peoples, fortifying independence movements in the postwar period. (Roget Viollet/Getty Images.)

black market (outside the official system of rationing). Governments allowed many businesses to make high rates of profit, a policy that made the cost of living soar and contributed to social tensions. Shortages of staples such as bread, sugar, and meat grew worse; Germans called the brutal winter of 1916–1917 "the turnip winter" because turnips were often the only food available. A German roof workers' association pleaded for relief: "We can no longer go on. Our children are starving." Reviving prewar hatred, some people blamed Jews for shortages. Colonial populations suffered the most oppressive working conditions. The French forcibly transported some 100,000 Vietnamese to work in France for the war effort. Africans also faced grueling forced labor along with skyrocketing taxes and prices. Civilian suffering during the war, whether in the colonies or at home in Europe, laid the groundwork for ordinary people to take political action.

REVIEW   What factors contributed to making World War I a total war?

Protest, Revolution, and War's End, 1917–1918

By 1917, the situation was becoming desperate for everyone—the military, civilians, and politicians. Discontent on the home front started shaping the course of the war. Neither patriotic slogans before the war nor propaganda during it had prepared people for wartime suffering. Across Europe civilians rebelled, soldiers mutinied, and nationalist struggles continued to plague Britain and Austria-Hungary. Soon full-fledged revolution was sweeping Europe, toppling the Russian dynasty and threatening not just war but civil war as well.

War Protests

On February 1, 1917, the German government, hard-pressed by public clamor over mounting casualties and by the military's growing control over decision making, resumed unrestricted submarine warfare. The military promised that this campaign would end the war in six months by cutting off food and military supplies being sent to Britain and thus forcing the island nation to surrender before the United States could come to its rescue. Britain responded by mining its harbors and the seas and by developing the convoy system of shipping, in which a hundred or more warships and freighters traveling together could drive off German submarines. The Germans' gamble not only failed to defeat the British but also brought the United States into the war in April 1917 after German U-boats sank several American ships.

Political opposition increased in Europe, deteriorating living conditions sparked outright revolt by civilians, and the war effort threatened to fail, causing governments to send out peace feelers. Irish nationalists attacked government buildings in Dublin on Easter Monday 1916 in an effort to gain Ireland's independence from Britain. Ill-prepared, the rebels were easily defeated, and many of them were executed. In the cities of Italy, Russia, Germany, and Austria, women rioted to get food for their families. As inflation mounted, tenants conducted rent strikes, and factory hands and white-collar workers alike walked off the job. Amid these protests, Austria-Hungary secretly asked the Allies for a negotiated peace to avoid a total collapse of the empire. In the summer of 1917, the German Reichstag made overtures to the Allies for a "peace of understanding and permanent reconciliation of peoples." In January 1918, President Woodrow Wilson issued his **Fourteen Points**, a blueprint for a nonvindictive peace settlement held out to war-weary citizens of the Central Powers. By that time, however, French soldiers were mutinying against bloody and fruitless offensives, and in Russia wartime protests turned into outright revolution. "We are living on a volcano," warned one Italian politician in the spring of 1917.

Revolution and Civil War in Russia

The volcano erupted in Russia, which of all the warring nations had sustained the greatest number of casualties—7.5 million by 1917. Slaughter on the eastern front drove hundreds of thousands of peasants into the Russian interior, spreading hunger, homelessness, and disease. In March 1917, crowds of workingwomen swarmed the streets of Petrograd demanding relief from harsh conditions. They soon fell in with protestors commemorating International Women's Day and were then joined by factory workers and other civilians. Russia's economic underdevelopment hampered the government's ability to provide basic necessities on the home front. Instead of remaining loyal to the tsar, many soldiers were bitter about the massive casualties caused by their inferior weapons and their leaders' foolhardy tactics.

The incompetence of the government and Nicholas II's stubborn resistance to change had made the war even worse in Russia than elsewhere. Unlike other heads of state, Nicholas failed to unite the bureaucracy and the people in a single-minded wartime effort. Grigori Rasputin, a combination holy man and charlatan, manipulated Nicholas and his wife, Alexandra, by claiming to control their son's hemophilia. Rasputin's disastrous influence on state matters led influential leaders to question rather than support the government. The riots erupted in March 1917, and in a week Nicholas abdicated, as the three-hundred-year-old Romanov dynasty came to an abrupt end.

Aristocratic and middle-class politicians from the old Duma formed a new administration called the **Provisional Government**. At first, hopes were high that under the Provisional Government, as one revolutionary poet put it, "our false, filthy, boring, hideous life should become a just, pure, merry, and beautiful life." To survive, the Provisional Government had to pursue the war successfully, manage internal affairs better, and set government on a firm constitutional footing to establish its credibility. However, it did not rule alone, because other political forces developed during the Revolution. Among them were **soviets**—elected councils of workers and soldiers—which competed with the government for political support. Born during the Revolution of 1905, the soviets in 1917 campaigned to end the deference society usually paid the wealthy and military officers, urged respect for workers and the poor, and temporarily gave an air of celebration to the current political upheaval. The peasants, also competing for power, began to confiscate landed estates and withhold agricultural products from the market because consumer goods, for which they would normally exchange food, were lacking. As a result, urban food shortages worsened.

In hopes of further destabilizing Russia, the Germans in April 1917 provided safe rail transportation for Lenin and other prominent Bolsheviks in exile to return to Russia through German territory. Lenin had devoted his entire existence to bringing about socialism through the force of his small band of Bolsheviks. Upon his return to Petrograd, he issued the April Theses, a radical document that called for Russia to withdraw from the war, for the soviets to seize power on behalf of workers and poor peasants, and for all private land to be nationalized. The Bolsheviks aimed to supplant the Provisional Government with the slogans "All power to the soviets" and "Peace, land, and bread."

Lenin Addressing the Second All-Russian Congress of Soviets
In the spring of 1917, the German government craftily let Lenin and other Bolsheviks travel from their exile in Switzerland back to the scene of the unfolding revolution in Russia. A committed revolutionary instead of a political reformer, Lenin used oratory and skillful maneuvering to convince many in the soviets to follow him in overthrowing the Provisional Government, taking Russia out of the war, and implementing his brand of communism. (RIA Novosti.)

Time was running out for the Provisional Government, which saw a battlefield victory as the only way to ensure its survival. On July 1, the Russian army attacked the Austrians in Galicia but was defeated once again (Map 20.1, page 784). The new prime minister, Aleksandr Kerensky, used ringing oratory to arouse patriotism, but he lacked the political skills to create an effective wartime government. In November, the Bolshevik leadership, urged on by Lenin, seized power on behalf of the soviets while simultaneously asserting its own right to form a government. In January 1918, elections for a constituent assembly failed to give the Bolsheviks a plurality, so the party used troops to take over the government completely. The Bolsheviks seized town and city administrations, and in the winter of 1918–1919, the new government, observing Marxist doctrine, abolished private property and nationalized factories in order to increase production. The Provisional Government had allowed both men and women to vote in 1917, making Russia the first great power to legalize universal suffrage. This was a hollow privilege, once the Bolsheviks limited candidates to chosen members of the Communist Party.

The Bolsheviks asked Germany for peace and agreed to the Treaty of Brest-Litovsk (March 1918), which placed vast regions of the old Russian Empire under German occupation (Map 20.2). Because the loss of millions of square miles put Petrograd at risk, the Bolsheviks relocated the capital to Moscow. They formally adopted the name Communists (taken from Marx's writings) to distinguish themselves from the socialists or Social Democrats. Lenin called the catastrophic terms of the treaty "obscene," but he accepted them not only because he had promised to bring peace to Russia but also because he believed that the rest of Europe would soon rebel against the war and overthrow the capitalist order.

A full-blown civil war now broke out in Russia, with the pro-Bolsheviks (or "Reds") facing an array of antirevolutionary forces (the "Whites"). Among the

Map 20.2 The Russian Civil War, 1917–1922

Nationalists, aristocrats, middle-class citizens, and property-owning peasants tried to combine their interests to defeat the Bolsheviks, but they failed to create an effective political consensus. The result was more suffering for ordinary people, whose agricultural products were confiscated to fight the civil war. The Western powers and Japan also sent in troops to put down this revolution that so threatened the economic and political order.

Whites, the tsarist military leadership, composed mainly of landlords and supporters of aristocratic rule, used whatever troops it could muster. Businessmen whose property had been nationalized and liberal intellectuals soon lent their support to the Whites. Many non-Russian nationalities, formerly brought into the empire through force, fought the Bolsheviks because they saw this as a chance for independence. Before World War I ended, Russia's former allies, notably the United States, Britain, France, and Japan, landed troops in the country both to block the Germans and to stop the Bolsheviks. The counterrevolutionary groups lacked a strong leader and unified goals, however. Instead, the groups competed with one another: the pro-tsarist forces, for example, alienated those wanting independent nation-state status, such as the Ukrainians, Estonians, and Lithuanians, by stressing the goal of restoring the Russian Empire. Even with the presence of Allied troops, the opponents of revolution could not defeat the Bolsheviks without a common purpose or a unified command.

The civil war shaped Russian communism. Leon Trotsky, Bolshevik commissar of war, built the highly disciplined Red Army by ending democratic procedures, such as the election of officers, which had originally attracted soldiers to Bolshevism. Lenin and Trotsky introduced the policy of war communism, whereby urban workers and troops moved through the countryside, brutally seizing grain from the peasants to feed the civil war army and workforce. The Cheka (secret police) imprisoned political opponents and black marketers and often shot them without bothering with a trial. The bureaucracy, the Cheka, and the Red Army all grew in size and strength. The result was a more authoritarian government—a development that broke with Marx's promise that revolution would bring a "withering away" of the state.

As the Bolsheviks clamped down on opposition during the bloody civil war, they organized their supporters to foster revolutionary Marxism across Europe. In March 1919, they founded the Third International, also known as the Comintern (Communist International), to replace the old Second International with a centralized organization dedicated to preaching communism. By mid-1921, the Red Army had defeated the Whites in the Crimea, the Caucasus, and the Muslim borderlands in central Asia. After ousting the Japanese from Siberia in 1922, the Bolsheviks were in charge of a state as multinational as the old Russian Empire had been (Map 20.2, page 794). Although the revolution had brought down the inept Romanovs and the privileged aristocracy, the civil war and the resulting hunger and disease took millions of lives. Meanwhile, the Bolsheviks had made brutality, which was at odds with socialist promises for a humane and flourishing society, their political style.

Ending the War, 1918

With Russia out of the war, Europe's leaders faced a new balance of military force. In the spring of 1918, the Central Powers made one final attempt to smash through the Allied lines, but the offensive ground to a bloody halt within weeks. By then, the British and French had started making limited but effective use of tanks supported by airplanes. Although the first tanks were cumbersome, their ability to withstand machine-gun fire made offensive attacks possible. In the summer of 1918, the Allies, now reinforced by the Americans, pushed back the Germans all along the western front and headed toward Germany. The German armies, suffering more than two million casualties between spring and summer, rapidly disintegrated.

By October 1918, the desperate German command had helped create a civilian government to take over on the home front. As these inexperienced politicians took power, they were also taking the blame for the defeat. Shifting the blame from the military, the generals proclaimed themselves still fully capable of winning the war. Weak-willed civilians, they claimed, had dealt the military a "stab in the back" that would force Germany's surrender. Amid this outright lying, naval officers called for a final sea battle, but the order triggered a mutiny against what sailors saw as a suicide mission. The sailors' revolt spread to workers in Berlin, Munich, and other major German cities. The uprisings led Social Democratic politicians to declare a German republic in an effort to prevent a revolution. At the end of October, the Czechs and Slovaks declared an independent state, and the Croatian parliament simultaneously announced Croatia's independence. On November 9, 1918, Kaiser William II fled as the Central Powers collapsed on all fronts. Finally, on November 11, 1918, an armistice was signed, and the guns fell silent.

In the course of four years, European civilization had been sorely tested, if not shattered. Conservative figures put the battlefield toll at ten million deaths and thirty million wounded, incapacitated, or doomed eventually to die of their wounds. In every European combatant country, industrial and agricultural production had plummeted, and much of the reduced output had been put to military use. Parts of Asia, Africa, and the Americas, which depended on European trade, felt the painful impact of Europe's decline. In 1918 and 1919, the weakened global population suffered an influenza epidemic that left as many as one hundred million more dead.

Moral questioning filled the media and private discussions alike. Soldiers returning home flooded the book market with their memoirs, trying to give meaning to their experiences. Whereas many had begun by emphasizing heroism and glory, others were cynical and bitter by war's end. They insisted that the fighting had been absolutely meaningless. Total war had drained society of resources and population and had sown the seeds of future catastrophes.

REVIEW   Why did people revolt during World War I, and what turned revolt into outright revolution in Russia?

The Search for Peace in an Era of Revolution

The war was over, but revolutionary fervor now swept the continent of Europe, especially in the former empires of Germany and Austria-Hungary. Until 1921, a widespread triumph for socialism seemed plausible; many of the newly independent peoples of eastern and central Europe fervently supported socialist principles. The revolutionary mood infected workers and peasants in Germany, too. In contrast, many liberal and right-wing opponents hoped for a political order based on military authority of the kind they had relied on during the war. Faced with uprisings by radicals from both right and left, diplomats from around the world arrived in Paris in January 1919 to negotiate the terms of peace, often without recognizing the fact that the war was still going on, not only in city streets where soldiers were bringing the war home, but also in people's hearts.

Europe in Turmoil

Urban citizens and returning soldiers ignited the protest that swept Europe in 1918 and 1919. In January 1919, the red flag of socialist revolution flew from the city hall in Glasgow, Scotland, while in cities of the collapsing Austro-Hungarian monarchy, workers set up councils to direct factory production and influence politics. After the armistice, soldiers in many parts of Europe did not disband but instead formed volunteer armies, preventing a return to peacetime politics.

Germany was especially unstable, partly because of the shock of defeat. Independent socialist groups and workers' councils fought the dominant Social Democrats for control of the government, and workers and veterans took to the streets to demand food and back pay. Whereas in 1848 revolutionaries had marched to city hall or the king's residence, these protesters took over newspapers and telegraph offices to control the flow of information. One of the most radical socialist factions, the Spartacists, was led by cofounders Karl Liebknecht and Rosa Luxemburg. Unlike Lenin, the two Spartacist leaders favored political uprisings that would give workers political experience rather than simply following an all-knowing party leadership. They shared Lenin's dislike of parliamentary politics, but they argued for direct worker control of institutions.

Social Democratic leader Friedrich Ebert, who headed the new government, rejected revolution and supported the creation of a parliamentary republic to replace the monarchy. Splitting with his former socialist allies, he called on the German army and the Freikorps—a roving paramilitary band of students, demobilized soldiers, and others—to suppress the workers' councils and demonstrators. He thus appeared to endorse the idea that political differences could be settled with violence. "The enthusiasm is marvelous," wrote one young soldier. "No mercy's shown. We shoot even the wounded. . . . We were much more humane against the French in the field." Members of the Freikorps hunted down Luxemburg and Liebknecht and murdered them.

Violence continued even as a constituent assembly meeting in the city of Weimar in February 1919 approved a constitution and founded a parliamentary republic called the **Weimar Republic**. The military leadership dreamed of a restored monarchy and rebelled. "As I love Germany, so I hate the Republic," wrote one officer. Facing a military coup by Freikorps officers, Ebert called for a general strike. This action blocked a takeover by showing the lack of popular support for a military regime. In so doing, the Weimar Republic set a dangerous precedent: it relied on street violence and paramilitary groups rather than parliaments to solve political problems.

Revolutionary activism surged and was smashed. Late in the winter of 1919, leftists proclaimed "soviet republics"—governments led by workers' councils—in Bavaria and Hungary. Volunteer armies and troops soon put the soviets down. The Bolsheviks tried to establish a Marxist regime in Poland in the belief that its people wanted a workers' revolution. Instead, the Poles resisted and drove the Red Army back in 1920, while the Allied powers rushed supplies and advisers to Warsaw (Map 20.2, page 794). Though this and other revolts failed, they provided further proof that total war had let loose political and social disorder.

The Paris Peace Conference, 1919–1920

As political turmoil plagued peoples from Berlin to Moscow, the Paris Peace Conference opened in January 1919. Visions of communism spreading westward haunted the conference, but the assembled statesmen were also focused on the reconstruction of a secure Europe and the status of Germany. Leaders such as French premier Georges Clemenceau had to satisfy their angry citizens, who demanded revenge or, at the very least, money to rebuild and pay their nation's war debts. France had lost 1.3 million people—almost an entire generation of young men—as well as more than a million buildings, six thousand bridges, and thousands of miles of railroad tracks and roads. Great Britain's representative, Prime Minister David Lloyd George, had caught the mood of the British public by campaigning in 1918 with slogans such as "Hang the kaiser." The Italians arrived on the scene demanding the territory promised to them in the 1915 Treaty of London. Meanwhile, U.S. president Woodrow Wilson, head of the new world power that had helped achieve the Allied victory, had his own agenda. His Fourteen Points, on which the truce had been based, were steeped in the language of freedom and called for open diplomacy, arms reduction, and the right for nationality groups to have their own government.

The Fourteen Points did not represent the mood of the victors. Allied propaganda had made the Germans seem like inhuman monsters, and many citizens in the Allied countries demanded a harsh peace. In addition, some military experts feared that Germany was using the armistice only as an opportunity to regroup for more warfare. Indeed, the German people widely refused to admit that their army had lost the war. Eager for army support, Ebert had given returning soldiers a victors' welcome: "As you return unconquered from the field of battle, I salute you." Wilson's former allies campaigned to make him look naive and unrealistic. "Wilson bores me with his Fourteen Points," Clemenceau complained. "Why, the good Lord himself has only ten."

Nevertheless, the Fourteen Points persuaded Germans that the settlement would not be vindictive. Wilson's commitment to *settlement* as opposed to *surrender* wisely recognized that Germany was still the strongest state on the continent, and he pushed for a treaty that balanced the strengths and interests of all the European powers. Economists and other experts accompanying Wilson to Paris agreed that if Germany was dealt with harshly and humiliated, it might soon become vengeful and chaotic—a lethal combination.

After six months, the statesmen and their teams of experts produced the **Peace of Paris** (1919–1920), a cluster of individual treaties that shocked the countries that had to accept them. The treaties separated Austria from Hungary, reduced Hungary by almost two-thirds of its inhabitants and three-quarters of its territory, broke up the Ottoman Empire, and treated Germany severely (Map 20.3). They replaced the Habsburg Empire with a group of small, internally divided, and relatively weak states: Czechoslovakia, Poland, and the Kingdom of the Serbs, Croats, and Slovenes, soon renamed Yugoslavia. After a century and a half of partition, Poland was reconstructed from parts of Russia, Germany, and Austria-Hungary; one-third of its population was ethnically non-Polish. The statesmen in Paris also created the Polish Corridor, which connected Poland to the Baltic Sea and separated East Prussia from the rest of Germany. In general, the new states were politically and economically weak. Austria and Hungary were left reeling at their loss of territory and resources.

The Treaty of Versailles, the centerpiece of the Peace of Paris, dealt specifically with Germany. Under this treaty, France recovered Alsace and Lorraine, and the Allies would temporarily occupy the left, or western, bank of the Rhine River and the coal-rich Saar basin. Wilson accepted his European allies' expectations that Germany would pay substantial reparations for civilian damage during the war. The specific amount was set in 1921 at the crushing sum of 132 billion gold marks. Germany also had to reduce its army, almost eliminate its navy, stop manufacturing offensive weapons, and deliver a large amount of free coal each year to Belgium and France. Furthermore, it was forbidden to have an air force and had to give up its colonies. The average German saw in these terms an unmerited humiliation that was compounded by Article 231 of the treaty, which described Germany's "responsibility" for damage "imposed . . . by the aggression of Germany and her allies." Outraged Germans interpreted this as a "war guilt" clause, which blamed Germany for the war and allowed the victors to collect reparations from their economically developed country rather than from the ruined Austria. War guilt made Germany an outcast in the community of nations.

Besides redrawing the map of Europe, the Peace of Paris set up an organization called the **League of Nations**, whose members had a joint responsibility for maintaining peace—a principle called collective security. It was supposed to replace the divisive secrecy of prewar power politics. As part of Wilson's vision, the league would guide the world toward disarmament and arbitrate its members' disputes. The U.S. Senate, rejecting the idea of collective security, failed to ratify the peace settlement and refused to join the league. Moreover, Germany and Russia were initially excluded from the league and thus were blocked from working cooperatively with the league.

The covenant, or charter, of the League of Nations also organized the administration of the former colonies and territories of Germany and the Ottoman Empire —such as Togo, Cameroon, Syria, and Palestine—through a system of mandates (see "Mapping the West," page 821). The European powers exercised political control, or

Map 20.3 Europe and the Middle East after the Peace Settlements of 1919–1920
The political landscape of central, eastern, and east-central Europe changed dramatically as a result of the Russian Revolution and the Peace of Paris. The Ottoman, German, Russian, and Austro-Hungarian empires were either broken up into multiple small states or reduced in size. The settlement bred resentment among Germans, Austrians, and Hungarians and created a group of weak, struggling nations in the heartland of Europe. The victorious powers took over much of the oil-rich Middle East.
For more help analyzing this map, see the map activity for this chapter in the Online Study Guide at
bedfordstmartins.com/huntconcise.

mandates, over these territories, while local leaders retained limited authority. The league covenant justified the mandate system as providing governance by "advanced nations" over territories "not yet able to stand by themselves under the strenuous conditions of the modern world." The people in these territories, many of whom had served on the battlefield during the war, were enraged by the mandates and began to challenge the claims of their European masters. They had seen how savage and degraded these people who claimed to be racially superior leaders of global culture could be. "Never again will the darker people of the world occupy just the place they had before," the African American leader W. E. B. Du Bois predicted in 1918. Yet the mandate system kept imperialism alive, and like the Peace of Paris, it aroused anger and resistance.

Economic and Diplomatic Consequences of the Peace

Just as wartime conditions, including military action, continued after the armistice, so the Peace of Paris posed problems in the 1920s and beyond. Western leaders faced two related issues in the aftermath of the war: economic recovery and preserving peace. In regard to economic recovery, France, the hardest hit by the war and billions of dollars in debt to the United States, estimated that Germany owed it at least $200 billion. Britain, by contrast, had not been physically devastated and was worried instead about maintaining its empire and restoring trade with Germany, not about exacting huge reparations to rebuild. Both, however, were dependent on German funds to pay their war debts to the United States because European income from world trade had plunged during the war.

Germany claimed that the demand for reparations strained its government, which was already facing political upheaval. But Germany's economic problems had not begun with the Peace of Paris but with the kaiser's policy of not raising taxes, especially on the rich, to pay for the war, leaving the new German republic with a staggering war debt. Now this republic, an experiment in democracy, needed to win over its citizens, not anger them by hiking taxes. When Germany refused in 1921 to present a realistic payment scheme to the former Allies, the French occupied several cities in the Ruhr basin until a settlement was reached.

At odds with the powers to the west, the German government turned to eastern Europe for support. Germany reached an agreement on establishing economic ties with Russia, which was desperate for western trade, in the Treaty of Rapallo (1922). Meanwhile, Germany's relations with powers to the west continued to deteriorate. In 1923, after Germany defaulted on coal deliveries, the French and Belgians sent troops into the Ruhr, planning to use its abundant resources to recoup their wartime expenditures. Urged on by the German government, the people there fought back, shutting down production by staying home from work. The government printed trillions of marks to support the workers and to pay its own war debts, with practically worthless currency. Soon Germany was experiencing staggering inflation, which not only demoralized its citizens but also gravely threatened the international economy. At one point, a single U.S. dollar was worth 4.42 trillion marks, and wheelbarrows of money were required to buy a turnip. Negotiations to resolve this chaos resulted in the Dawes Plan (1924) and the Young Plan (1929), which reduced payments to more realistic levels and restored the German currency. In the meantime, people's savings had been wiped out, and more and more Germans were turning against their democratic government.

In addition to economic recovery, a second burning issue involved ensuring a lasting peace. Statesmen determined that peace needed disarmament, a return of Germany to the community of European nations, and security for the new countries of eastern Europe. Hard diplomatic bargaining produced two plans in Germany's favor. At the Washington Conference in 1921, the United States, Great Britain, Japan, France, and Italy agreed to reduce their numbers of battleships and to stop constructing new ones for ten years. Four years later, in 1925, the League of Nations sponsored a meeting of the great powers, including Germany, at Locarno, Switzerland. The Treaty of Locarno provided Germany with a seat in the league as of 1926. In return, Germany agreed not to violate the borders of France and Belgium and to keep the nearby Rhineland demilitarized (unfortified by troops).

To the east, statesmen feared German attempts to regain territory lost to Poland, to form a merger with Austria, or to launch aggression against the states spun off from Austria-Hungary (Map 20.3, page 800). To meet this threat, Czechoslovakia, Yugoslavia, and Romania formed the Little Entente in 1920–1921—a collective security agreement to protect themselves from Germany and Russia. Then, between 1924 and 1927, France allied itself with the Little Entente and with Poland. In 1928, sixty nations, including the major European powers, Japan, and the United States, signed the Kellogg-Briand Pact, which formally rejected international violence. The pact lacked any guarantee or mechanism for enforcement and thus resembled, as one critic put it, "an international kiss."

The publicity surrounding the international agreements during the 1920s sharply contrasted with old-style diplomacy, which had been conducted in secret and subject to little public scrutiny. The development of a system of open, collective security suggested a diplomatic revolution that would promote international peace. Yet openness in negotiations also allowed diplomats to feed the press reports designed to provoke the masses. For example, the press and politicians whipped German citizens into a nationalist fury whenever Germany's diplomats appeared to compromise, even though compromise actually helped undo the Treaty of Versailles. Right-wing journalists who hated republican government used international meetings such as the one at Locarno to fire up political hatreds and undermine the goal of collective security.

REVIEW   What were the major outcomes of the postwar peacemaking process?

A Decade of Recovery: Europe in the 1920s

During the 1920s, towns and villages built their monuments to the Great War, and battlefield tourism sprang up for veterans and for families in search of a son's or father's resting place. The wartime spirit endured in words and phrases from the battlefield that became part of everyday speech. Before the war, the word *lousy* had meant "lice-infested," but English-speaking soldiers returning from the trenches now applied it to anything bad. Raincoats became *trench coats,* and military terms such as *bombarded* and *rank and file* entered civilian talk. Maimed, disfigured veterans were present everywhere, and while some received prostheses designed by Jules Amar, others without limbs were sometimes carried in baskets—hence the expression *basket case.*

Total war had generally strengthened military values and authoritarian government. Four autocratic governments—those in Germany, Austria-Hungary, Russia, and the Ottoman Empire—had collapsed as a result of the war, but whether these states would become workable democracies remained a burning question. During the war, the European economy lost many of its international markets to India, Canada, Australia, Japan, and the United States. Now worldwide economic competition with these new players also threatened European recovery. Although contemporaries referred to the 1920s as the Roaring Twenties and the Jazz Age, the sense of cultural release masked the serious problems of restoring social stability and implementing democracy. The real challenge of the 1920s was coming to terms with the grim legacy of the war.

Changes in the Political Landscape

The collapse of autocratic governments and the widespread extension of suffrage to women brought political turmoil as well as the expansion of democracy. Women's suffrage resulted in part from decades of activism, but many men in government claimed that suffrage was a "reward" for women's war efforts. In the first postwar elections, women were voted into parliaments, and the impression grew that they had also made extraordinary gains in the workplace. French men pointedly denied women the vote, however, insisting that women would use their votes to bring back the rule of kings and priests. (Only at the end of World War II did France and Italy extend suffrage to women.) The welfare state also expanded, with payments being made to veterans and to victims of workplace accidents. These

Women Gain Suffrage in the West	
1906	Finland
1913	Norway
1915	Denmark, Iceland
1917	Netherlands, Russia
1918	Czechoslovakia, Great Britain (limited suffrage)
1919	Germany
1920	Austria, United States
1921	Poland
1925	Hungary (limited suffrage)
1945	Italy, France
1971	Switzerland

benefits stemmed from the belief that more evenly distributed wealth, sometimes called economic democracy, would prevent the outbreak of revolution.

The trend toward economic democracy was not easy to maintain, as the cycles of boom and bust that had characterized the late nineteenth century reemerged. A short postwar boom prompted by reconstruction and consumer spending was followed by an economic downturn that was most severe between 1920 and 1922. By the mid-1920s, many of the economic opportunities for women had disappeared, and they made up a smaller percentage of the workforce than in 1913. Veterans were especially angered by economic insecurity after their years of enduring the war's horrors, and skyrocketing unemployment resulted in more anger toward governments.

The new republics of eastern Europe were especially unprepared for hard economic times and were poorly equipped to compete in the world market. None but Czechoslovakia had a mature industrial sector, and agricultural techniques were often primitive. But more pressing problems hampered them. Vast migrations occurred as some one million people escaped the civil war in Russia and 800,000 soldiers from the defeated Whites searched for safety. Two million people fled Turkey, Greece, and Bulgaria because the postwar settlement called for the new nations to be built along "nationality" lines. One statesman called this "a great unmixing of populations." Hundreds of thousands of migrants landed in new nations with populations most closely resembling their own ethnic groups. Hungary, for example, had to receive 300,000 people of Magyar ethnicity who were no longer welcome in Romania, Czechoslovakia, or Yugoslavia. Most of these refugees lacked land or jobs. They had nothing to do "but loaf and starve," one English reporter observed of refugees in Bulgaria, and as a result conflict and chaos haunted postwar eastern Europe.

National Minorities in Postwar Poland

A reunified Poland showed how postwar turmoil could destroy the new nation's parliamentary democracy. One-third of the population consisted of Ukrainians, Belorussians, Germans, and other ethnic minorities—many of whom had grievances against the dominant Poles. Religious, dynastic, and cultural traditions also divided the Poles, who for 150 years had been split among Austria, Germany, and Russia. Polish reunification occurred without a common currency, political structure, or language. Even the railroad tracks were not a standard size. Under a new constitution that professed equal rights for all ethnicities and religions, the Sejm (parliament) tried to divide large estates among the peasantry, but declining crop prices and overpopulation made life in the countryside difficult. The economic downturn brought strikes and violence in 1922–1923. Ultimately former military leader Jozef Pilsudski responded to the disorder with a coup in 1926—a strongman solution that would become more common elsewhere in Europe and the world.

Germany was a different case, although it too received a flood of refugees from the east. Although the German economy picked up and Germany became a center of experimentation in the arts, political life remained unstable because so many people felt nostalgia for imperial glory and associated the Versailles treaty with the Weimar Republic. Extremist politicians heaped daily abuse on Weimar's parliamentary government. A wealthy newspaper and film tycoon called anyone cooperating with the parliamentary system "a moral cripple." Right-wing parties favored violence rather than consensus building, and nationalist gangs murdered democratic leaders and Jews. The Communists, feeling their muscle, jumped into street brawls too.

Support for the far right came from wealthy landowners and businessmen, white-collar workers whose standard of living had dropped during the war, and members of the lower-middle and middle classes hurt by inflation. Bands of discontented youths and veterans proliferated, among them a group called the Brown Shirts. Their leader was an ex-soldier, political newcomer, and riveting speaker named Adolf Hitler (1889–1945), a favorite among antigovernment crowds. In the wake of the Ruhr occupation of 1923, Hitler and German military leader Erich Ludendorff launched a coup from a beer hall in Munich. Government troops suppressed the Beer Hall Putsch; Hitler spent less than a year in jail, and Ludendorff was acquitted. To conservative judges, former aristocrats, and most of the prewar bureaucrats who still staffed the government, such men were national heroes.

In France and Britain, parties of the right had less effect than elsewhere because representative institutions were better established and the upper classes were not plotting to restore an authoritarian monarchy. In France, politicians from the conservative right and moderate left successively formed coalitions and rallied general support to rebuild war-torn regions and to force Germany to pay for the reconstruction. Hoping to stimulate population growth after the country's devastating loss of life, the French parliament made distributing birth-control information illegal and abortion a severely punished crime.

Britain encountered postwar boom and bust and continuing conflict in Ireland. Ramsay MacDonald, elected the first Labour prime minister, in 1924, represented the political strength of workers. Like other postwar British leaders, he had to face the fact that although Britain had the largest world empire, many of its industries were obsolete or in poor condition. A showdown came in the ailing coal industry, where prices fell and wages plummeted once the Ruhr mines reopened and began to compete with Britain again. On May 3, 1926, workers launched a nine-day general strike against wage cuts and dangerous conditions in the mines. The strike prompted unprecedented middle-class resistance. University students, homemakers, and businessmen shut down the strike by driving trains, working on docks, and replacing workers in other jobs. Citizens from many walks of life revived the wartime spirit to defeat those who appeared to them to be attacking the national economy.

In Ireland, the British government's continuing failure to allow home rule provoked bloody confrontations. In January 1919, republican leaders declared Ireland's independence from Britain and created a separate parliament. The British government refused to recognize the parliament and sent in the Black and Tans, a volunteer army of demobilized soldiers named for the color of their uniforms. Terror reigned in Ireland, as both the pro-independence forces and the Black and Tans waged guerrilla warfare, taking hostages, blowing up buildings, and even shooting into crowds at soccer matches. By 1921, public outcry forced the British to negotiate a treaty. It reversed the Irish declaration of independence and made the Irish Free State a self-governing dominion owing allegiance to the British crown. Northern Ireland, a group of six northern counties referred to as Ulster and containing a majority of Protestants, gained a separate status: it became self-governing but still had representation in the British Parliament. The settlement left bitter discontent; violence soon erupted again.

The Irish Free State and Ulster, 1921

War changed everything in the colonies, too. Colonized peoples who had fought in the war expected more rights and even independence. Indeed, European politicians and military recruiters had actually promised them the vote and other reforms in exchange for their support. These peoples' political activism, now boosted by increasing education, trade, and experience with the West, mostly met with a brutal response. British forces massacred protesters at Amritsar in India in 1919 and put down revolts against the mandate system in Egypt and Iran in the early 1920s. The Dutch jailed political leaders in Indonesia; the French punished Indochinese nationalists. For many Western governments, maintaining empires abroad was crucial to ensuring democracy at home, for any hint of declining national prestige fed antidemocratic forces.

Despite such resistance, the 1920s marked the high tide of imperialism. Britain and France, enjoying new access to Germany's colonies in Africa and the territories of the fallen Ottoman Empire in the Middle East, were at the height of their global power. No matter how battered they were by the war, all the imperial powers took advantage of the growing profitability that enterprise around the world could bring. Middle Eastern and Indonesian oil increasingly heated homes and fueled the growing numbers of automobiles, airplanes, trucks, ships, and buses. Products such as chocolate and tropical fruit became regular items in Westerners' diets, and some businessmen built fortunes by selling these products from the colonies.

Reconstructing the Economy

The war had weakened European economies and allowed newcomers and rivals—Japan, India, the United States, Australia, and Canada—to flourish in their place. At the same time, the war had forced European manufacturing to become more efficient and had expanded the demand for automotive and air transport, electrical products, and synthetic goods. The prewar pattern of mergers and cartels continued after 1918, giving rise to gigantic food-processing firms such as Nestlé in Switzerland and petroleum enterprises such as Royal Dutch Shell. Owners of these large manufacturing conglomerates wielded more financial and political power than entire small countries. By the late 1920s, Europe had overcome the wild economic swings of the immediate postwar years and was enjoying renewed economic prosperity.

Some European businesspeople recognized that the United States had become the trendsetter in economic modernization. Many made pilgrimages to the Ford Motor Company's Detroit assembly line, which by 1929 produced a Ford automobile every ten seconds. Increased productivity, founder Henry Ford pointed out, resulted in a lower cost of living and increased purchasing power for workers. Whereas France, Germany, and Britain combined had fewer than two million cars, some seventeen million cars were on U.S. streets in 1925, reinforcing Ford's point.

Scientific management also aimed to raise productivity. American efficiency expert Frederick Taylor developed methods to streamline workers' tasks and movements for maximum productivity. European industrialists adopted Taylor's methods during the war and after, but they were also influenced by European psychologists who emphasized the mental aspects of productivity and the need to balance work and leisure activities. In theory, increased productivity not only produced prosperity for all but also helped unite workers and management in a common purpose, avoiding Russian-style worker revolution. For many workers, however, the emphasis on efficiency seemed inhumane; in some workplaces, the restrictions on time and motion were so severe that workers were allowed to use the bathroom only on a fixed schedule. "When I left the factory, it followed me," wrote one worker. "In my dreams I was a machine."

The managerial sector in industry had expanded during the war and continued to do so thereafter. Workers' initiative became devalued; managers alone were seen as creative and innovative. Managers reorganized work procedures and classified workers' skills. They categorized work that required less skill as "female jobs" that deserved lower wages, thus adapting the old segmentation of the labor market to the new working conditions. With male workers' jobs increasingly threatened by laborsaving machines, unions usually agreed with management to hold down women's wages to keep women from competing with men for high-paying jobs. Like the managerial sector, union bureaucracy had ballooned during World War I to help monitor labor's part in the war. Union bureaucrats became specialists: negotiators, membership organizers, educators and propagandists, and political liaisons.

Playing a key role in political life, they could mobilize masses of people, as they demonstrated when they blocked coups against the Weimar government in the 1920s and organized the general strike in Great Britain in 1926.

Restoring Society

Postwar society met the returning millions of brutalized, incapacitated, and shell-shocked veterans with combined joy and apprehension. Civilian concerns were often valid. Tens of thousands of German, central European, and Italian soldiers refused to disband; some British veterans vandalized university classrooms and assaulted women workers. Many veterans harbored hostility toward civilians, some of whom had protested against wartime conditions instead of patriotically enduring them. The world to which the veterans returned differed from the one they had left. The war had blurred some class distinctions, giving rise to the belief that life would be fairer. Massive battlefield casualties had made it possible for commoners to become officers, suggesting greater postwar openness. British author Rudyard Kipling, whose son had been killed on the battlefield, was among those who influenced the decision that the mass graves of British soldiers killed in the war, whether rich or poor, would be marked as individual ones by identical, evenly spaced crosses in military cemeteries. Wealth, he maintained, should not allow some to "proclaim their grief above other people's grief" when all had died for the same cause.

In contrast to their expectations, however, returning veterans often had no jobs open to them, and some found that their wives and sweethearts had abandoned them. Veterans faced other changes: middle-class women did their own housework, because former servants could earn more money in factories, and greater numbers of middle-class women worked outside the home. Women of all classes cut their hair short, wore sleeker clothes, and had money of their own because of war work. Patriotic when war erupted, civilians sometimes felt estranged from returning warriors, who had inflicted so much death and had lived daily with filth, rats, and decaying animal and human flesh. Women who had served at the front had seen the soldiers' experiences firsthand and could sympathize with them. But many suffragists in Britain, for instance, who had fought for greater equality in men's and women's lives before the war now reembraced separate spheres, so fearful were they of returning veterans.

Governments tried to improve civilian life to reintegrate men into society and to reduce the appeal of communism. Politicians believed in the calming power of family life and supported social programs such as veterans' pensions, benefits for out-of-work men, and housing for veterans. The new housing—"homes for heroes," as politicians called the program—was an improvement over nineteenth-century working-class tenements. In Vienna, Frankfurt, Berlin, and Stockholm, modern housing projects provided common laundries, day-care centers, and rooms for socializing. They featured gardens, terraces, and balconies to provide a soothing,

Le Corbusier's Paris of the Future
While the war profoundly disillusioned many in the West, peace aroused utopian hopes for a better future. For modern architects like Swiss-born Le Corbusier, the "future city" and the "radiant city" would organize space, and thus life, for ordinary people. Horizontal windows, roof gardens, and plain facades were hallmarks of this new design—a dramatic break with the ornate prewar building styles. (Fondation Le Corbusier/© 2010 Artists Rights Society [ARS], NY/ADAGP, Paris/FLC.)

country atmosphere. Inside they boasted modern kitchens, indoor plumbing, central heating, and electricity.

Despite government efforts to restore family life, the war had dissolved many middle-class conventions, among them attempts to keep unmarried young men and women apart. Freer relationships and more open discussions of sex characterized the 1920s. Middle-class youths of both sexes visited jazz clubs and attended movies together. Revealing bathing suits, short skirts, and body-hugging clothing emphasized women's sexuality, seeming to invite men and women to join together and replenish the postwar population. In the long run, though, the context for sexuality remained marriage. British scientist Marie Stopes published the best seller *Married Love* in 1918, and the wildly successful *Ideal Marriage: Its Physiology and Technique* by Dutch author Theodor van de Velde appeared in 1927. Both described sex in glowing terms and offered precise information about birth control and sexual physiology. Changing ideas about sex were not limited to the middle and upper classes. One Viennese reformer described working-class marriage as "an erotic-comradely relationship of equals" rather than the economic partnership of past centuries. The flapper, a sexually liberated working woman, surpassed the dedicated housewife as representing the ordinary woman. Meanwhile, British writer D. H. Lawrence and American author Ernest Hemingway glorified men's sexual vigor in, respectively,

The Flapper
This modern working woman smoking her cigarette stood for all that had changed—or was said to have changed—in the postwar world. Women worked and had money of their own, were out in public, could vote in many countries, and were liberated from old restrictions on their sexual and other behavior. (Getty Images.)

Women in Love (1920) and *The Sun Also Rises* (1926). Mass culture's focus on heterosexuality encouraged the return to traditional social norms after the gender disorder of the prewar and war years.

As images of men and women changed, people paid more attention to bodily improvement. The increasing use of toothbrushes and toothpaste, safety and electric razors, and deodorants reflected new standards of personal hygiene and grooming. A multibillion-dollar cosmetics industry sprang up almost overnight. Women went to beauty parlors regularly to have their short hair cut, set, dyed, conditioned, straightened, or curled. They also tweezed their eyebrows, applied makeup, and even submitted to cosmetic surgery. Ordinary women "painted" their faces as formerly only prostitutes had done and competed in beauty contests that judged physical appearance. Instead of wanting to look plump and prosperous, people aimed to become thin and tanned, often through exercise and sports. Consumers' new focus on personal health coincided with industry's need for a physically fit workforce.

As prosperity returned late in the 1920s, people bought more consumer goods. Middle- and upper-class families snapped up sleek modern furniture, washing machines, and vacuum cleaners. Other modern conveniences such as electric irons and gas stoves appeared in better-off working-class households. Installment buying, popularized from the 1920s on, helped finance these purchases. Housework became more mechanized, and family intimacy increasingly depended on machines of mass communication, such as radios and phonographs, and even on automobiles. These new products not only transformed private life but also brought unforeseen changes in the public world of culture and mass politics.

> REVIEW   What were the major social and economic problems facing postwar Europe, and how did leaders address them?

Mass Culture and the Rise of Modern Dictators

Wartime propaganda had aimed to unite all classes against a common enemy. In the 1920s, new technology made the process of bringing diverse groups together in a single mass culture easier. The tools of mass culture—primarily radio, films, and newspapers—expanded their influence in the 1920s. Whereas some intellectuals urged elites to form an experimental avant-garde that refused to cater to "the drab mass of society," others wanted to use modern media and art to reach out to and even control the masses. The media had the potential for creating an informed citizenry and thus enhancing democracy. At the same time, it allowed authoritarian rulers and dictators such as Benito Mussolini, Joseph Stalin, and Adolf Hitler to shape political thought and behavior and to control citizens far more than earlier rulers had been able to do.

Culture for the Masses

The media had received a big boost from the war. Bulletins from the battlefront had stimulated the public's craving for news and real-life stories, and sales of nonfiction books soared. After years of deprivation, people were driven to achieve material success, and they devoured books that told them how to gain it. Henry Ford's biography, telling his story of upward mobility and technological accomplishment, became a best seller in Germany. With postwar readers pursuing practical knowledge, institutes and night schools became popular, and school systems promoted reading in geography, science, and history. Phonographs, radio, and movies also widened the scope of national culture.

In the 1920s, filmmaking changed from an experimental medium to a thriving international business in which large corporations set up theater chains and marketed films worldwide. Specialization emerged, with directors, producers, marketers, photographers, film editors, and many others subdividing the process. A "star" system turned film personalities into celebrities, promoted by professional publicity and living like royalty. Films of literary classics and political events developed people's sense of a common heritage and were often financed by governments. Bolshevik leaders backed the inventive work of director Sergei Eisenstein, whose films *Potemkin* (1925) and *Ten Days That Shook the World* (1927–1928) presented a Bolshevik view of history to Russian and international audiences.

Films incorporated familiar elements from everyday life. The piano accompani-ment of silent films derived from music halls; comic characters and slapstick humor were borrowed from street or burlesque shows and from trends in postwar living. The popular comedies of the 1920s made the flapper more visible to the masses and poked fun at men's and women's inept attempts at marriage and emotional intimacy. Films played to postwar fantasies and fears. In Germany, the influential hit *The Cabinet of Doctor Caligari* (1919) depicted frightening events in an insane asylum as horrifying symbols of state power. Popular detective and cowboy films portrayed heroes who could restore wholeness to the disordered world of murder, crime, and injustice. The plight of gangsters appealed to veterans, who had seen the cheap value of life in the modern world. Charlie Chaplin, an English comedian, actor, and producer, created the character of the Little Tramp, who won interna-tional popularity as the defeated hero and the anonymous modern man, trying to preserve his dignity in a mechanized world. Films featured characters from around the world and were set in faraway deserts or mountain ranges; newsreels showed international sporting events such as boxing and cricket.

Like film, radio evolved from an experimental medium to an instrument of mass culture during the 1920s (see "Taking Measure"). Developed from Guglielmo

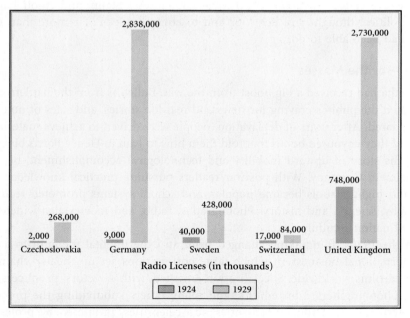

Taking Measure The Growth of Radio, 1924–1929
Radio technology, like the earlier development of printing, advanced the cultural and political unity of nation-states. Radio spread most rapidly in industrially and commercially developed societies. Governments taxed radios and, at first, provided the programming. Because of this centralized control and the paperwork it created, historians can track and compare the growth of radio in Europe and much of the rest of the world.

Marconi's wireless technology, radio broadcasts in the first half of the 1920s were heard by mass audiences in public halls (much like movie theaters) and featured orchestras and songs followed by audience discussion. The radio quickly became an affordable consumer item, and public concerts and lectures could then penetrate the individual's private living space. Disabled veterans loved radio because it allowed them to participate in public events and keep up to date, but by the 1930s radio also became downright menacing, allowing authoritarian politicians to reach the masses wherever they might be—even alone at home.

Cultural Debates over the Future

Cultural leaders in the 1920s either were obsessed with the horrendous wartime experience or, like the modernists before the war, held high hopes of creating a fresh utopian future that would have little relation to the past. Those haunted by the war produced bleak or violent visions—a common feature of postwar German art. Käthe Kollwitz, whose son died in the war, portrayed in her woodcuts bereaved parents, starving children, and other heart-wrenching, antiwar images. Others thought that Europeans needed to search for answers in far-off cultures. Seeing Europe as morally bankrupt, many turned to the spiritual richness of Asian philosophies and religions. An "Asiatic fever" seemed to grip intellectuals and artists, including English writer Virginia Woolf, who drew on ideas of reincarnation in her novel *Orlando* (1928), and Russian filmmaker Sergei Eisenstein, who modeled his new technique of juxtaposing shots (montage) on Japanese calligraphy.

Other artists used satire and contempt to express postwar rage at civilization's wartime failure. George Grosz, stunned by the war's carnage, joined Dada, an artistic and literary movement that had emerged during the war. Dadaists produced works marked by nonsense and shrieking expressions of alienation. Grosz's paintings and cartoons of maimed soldiers and brutally murdered women reflected his emotional wounds and his desire "to bellow back." In the postwar years, the modernist practice of shocking audiences intensified. Portrayals of sleazy everyday life flourished in cabarets and theaters in the 1920s and confirmed veterans' visions of civilian decadence. The art world itself became a battlefield, especially in defeated Germany, where art mirrored the Weimar Republic's contentious politics. Popular writers such as Ernst Jünger glorified life in the trenches and called for the militarization of society to restore order. Erich Maria Remarque cried out for an end to war in his controversial novel *All Quiet on the Western Front* (1928). This international best seller depicted the life shared by enemies on the battlefield, thus aiming to overcome the national hatred aroused by wartime propaganda.

Poets reflected on postwar conditions in more general terms, using styles that rejected the comforting rhymes or accessible metaphors of earlier verse. T. S. Eliot, an American-born poet who had studied Buddhism and other Asian thought and who for a time worked as a banker in Britain, portrayed postwar life as petty and futile in *The Waste Land* (1922) and "The Hollow Men" (1925). The Irish nationalist

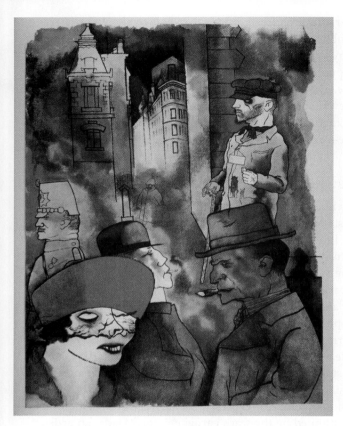

George Grosz, *Twilight* (1922)
This painting is part of Grosz's series of postwar art called Ecce Homo (Behold the Man), named after a book by Friedrich Nietzsche. The "man" to behold was the veteran, opportunistically called a "hero" by postwar politicians to get veterans' votes but in fact living a grim existence, as Grosz saw it. Surrounded by prosperous businessmen, fashionable women, and strutting military officers, the veteran was pushed to the background, gray and lonely amid the colorful peacetime society. (Bildarchiv Preussischer Kulturbesitz/Art Resource, NY/© Estate of George Grosz/Licensed by VAGA, New York, NY.)

poet William Butler Yeats joined Eliot in mourning the replacement of traditional society, with its religious and moral convictions, with a new, superficial generation dancing to jazz and engaging in promiscuous sex. Yeats's "Sailing to Byzantium" (1928) starts this way:

> That is no country for old men. The young
> In one another's arms, birds in the trees
> —Those dying generations

Both poets had an uneasy relationship with modern values and at times advocated authoritarianism rather than democracy.

The postwar arts produced many a utopian fantasy turned upside down; dystopias of life in postrevolutionary, traumatized Europe flourished. In the bizarre stories of Franz Kafka, an employee of a large insurance company in Prague, the world is a vast, impersonal machine. His novels *The Trial* (1925) and *The Castle* (1926) show the hopelessness of individuals caught in the cogs of society's relentlessly turning gears. His theme seemed to capture for civilian life the helplessness that soldiers had felt at the front. As an old social order collapsed in the face of political and technological innovation, other writers depicted the complex, sometimes nightmarish inner life of individuals.

The Irish writer James Joyce and the English writer Virginia Woolf portrayed this interior self built on memories and sensations, many of them from the war. Joyce's *Ulysses* (1922) and Woolf's *Mrs. Dalloway* (1925) illuminate the fast-moving inner lives of their characters in the course of a single day. In one of the most celebrated passages in *Ulysses,* a long interior monologue traces a woman's lifetime of erotic and emotional sensations. The technique of using a character's thoughts to propel a story was called stream of consciousness. For Woolf the war had dissolved the solid society on which absorbing stories and fascinating characters once depended. Her characters experience fragmented conversations, momentary sensations, and incomplete relationships. The character Orlando in Woolf's novel of the same name lives hundreds of years and in the course of his long life is eventually reborn as a woman.

There was another side to the postwar story—one based not on the interior thoughts of a traumatized society but on the bright promises of technology. Before the war, avant-garde artists had celebrated the new, the futuristic, the utopian. After the war, like Jules Amar crafting prostheses for shattered limbs, they were optimistic that technology could make an entire society whole. The aim of art, observed one of them, "is not to decorate our life but to organize it." German architects and artists influenced by the Bauhaus, a school of design whose name suggested a craft association, or *Bauhütte,* created streamlined office buildings and designed functional furniture, utensils, and decorative objects, many of them inspired by forms from "untainted" East Asia and Africa. Russian artists, temporarily caught up in the Communist experiment, optimistically wrote novels about cement factories and created ballets about steel.

Artists fascinated by technology and machinery were drawn to the most modern of all countries, the United States. Hollywood films, glossy advertisements, and the bustling metropolis of New York tempted careworn Europeans. They loved films and stories about the Wild West or the carefree "modern American girl." They were especially attracted to jazz, the improvisational music emanating from Harlem. Performers such as Josephine Baker and Louis Armstrong became international sensations when they toured Europe's capitals. Like jazz, the New York skyscrapers pointed to the future, not to the grim wartime past.

The Communist Utopia

Communism also promised a shining future and a modern, technological culture. As the Bolsheviks met powerful resistance, however, they became more ruthless and authoritarian. In the early 1920s, peasant bands called Green Armies revolted against the Bolshevik policy of war communism that confiscated their crops and animals. Industrial production stood at only 13 percent of prewar levels, shortages of housing affected the entire population, and millions of refugees clogged the cities and roamed the countryside. In the early spring of 1921, workers in Petrograd and sailors at the nearby naval base at Kronstadt revolted. They protested their short rations and the privileged standard of living their Bolshevik supervisors enjoyed. They called for "soviets without Communists"—that is, a worker state without elite leaders.

The Bolsheviks had many of the rebels shot, but the Kronstadt revolt pushed Lenin to institute reforms. His New Economic Policy (NEP) returned parts of the economy to the free market—a temporary retreat to capitalist methods that allowed peasants to sell their grain freely and others to trade consumer goods. Although the state still controlled large industries and banking, the NEP encouraged people to produce, sell, and even, in the words of one official, "get rich." As a result, more consumer goods and more abundant food soon became available. Although many people remained impoverished, some peasants and merchants prospered. The rise of these wealthy "NEPmen," who bought and furnished splendid homes, broke with the Marxist promise of a classless utopia.

Further protests erupted within the Communists' ranks. At the 1921 party congress, a group called the Worker Opposition objected to the party's takeover of economic control from workers' organizations and pointed out that the NEP was an agrarian program, not a proletarian one for workers. Lenin suppressed the Worker Opposition and set up procedures for purging party dissidents—a policy that would become a deadly feature of Communist rule. Bolshevik leaders also worked to make the Communist revolution a cultural reality in people's daily lives and thinking. Party leaders invaded the countryside, setting up classes in a variety of political and social subjects, and volunteers struggled to increase the literacy rate, which had been only 40 percent on the eve of World War I. To facilitate social equality between men and women, which was part of the Marxist vision of the future, the state made birth control, abortion, and divorce readily available. The commissar for public welfare, Aleksandra Kollontai, promoted birth-control education, day-care programs for children of working parents, and equality between women and men.

The bureaucracy swelled to bring modern culture to every corner of life, and *hygiene* and *efficiency* became watchwords, as they were in the rest of Europe. Agencies such as the Zhenotdel (Women's Bureau) sought to teach women about their rights under communism and about sanitary housekeeping. Efficiency experts aimed to replace tsarist backwardness with technological modernity based on American techniques. The short-lived government agency Proletkult tried to develop proletarian culture through undertakings such as workers' universities and a workers' theater. Russian artists experimented with blending high art and technology in mass culture. Poet Vladimir Mayakovsky wrote verse praising his Communist passport and essays promoting brushing one's teeth, while composers punctuated their music with the sound of train or factory whistles.

As with war communism, many resisted the reshaping of everyday life and culture. As Zhenotdel workers moved into the countryside, for example, they attempted to teach women to behave as men's equals. Peasant families, still strongly patriarchal, resisted. In Islamic regions of central Asia, incorporated from the old Russian Empire into the new Communist one, Bolsheviks urged Muslim women to remove their veils and change their way of life, but fervent Muslims often attacked both Zhenotdel workers and women who followed their advice.

El Lissitzky, *Beat the Whites with the Red Wedge* (1919)
Russian artist El Lissitzky traveled Europe to bring news of Communist experimentation in all areas of life, including the arts. In particular, Lissitzky, like other avant-garde artists, was taken with the new physics, reflected in the use of geometric forms. Abstract art was also political. In this 1919 painting, the "red" wedge uses the force described in the laws of physics to defeat the greater counterrevolutionary power of the "whites." (David King Collection, London. © 2010 Artists Rights Society [ARS], NY/VG Bild-Kunst, Bonn.)

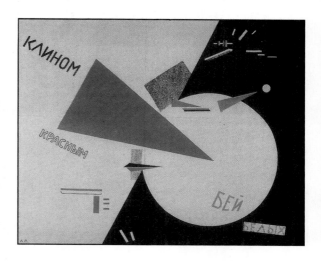

Lenin suffered a debilitating stroke in the spring of 1922. Amid ongoing cultural experimentation and factional fighting, the architect of the Bolshevik Revolution died in January 1924. The party congress declared the day of his death a permanent holiday, changed the name of Petrograd to Leningrad, and elevated the deceased leader to a secular god. After Lenin's death, no one was allowed to criticize anything associated with his name, a situation that opened the way for abuses of power by later Communist leaders.

Joseph Stalin (1879–1953), who served in the powerful position of general secretary of the Communist Party, was the chief mourner at Lenin's funeral, using the occasion to hand out good jobs and other patronage. He advertised his role in joining Russian and non-Russian regions into the Union of Soviet Socialist Republics (USSR) in 1923 as an example of his leadership skills, though he had used his dealings with thousands of local party officials to distribute favors in exchange for their support. Already concerned with Stalin's growing influence and ruthlessness, Lenin in his last will and testament had asked that "the comrades find a way to remove Stalin." Stalin, however, discredited his chief rival, Leon Trotsky, and prevented Lenin's will from being publicized. Simultaneously, Stalin organized the Lenin cult, which included the public display of Lenin's embalmed corpse (still on view today). Bringing in several hundred thousand new party members who owed their positions in government and industry to him, Stalin had achieved virtually complete control of the USSR by 1929.

Fascism on the March in Italy

In Italy, the war remained alive in the rise to power of Benito Mussolini (1883–1945), who, like the Bolsheviks, promised an efficient utopia. Italians raged when the Allies at Paris had refused to honor the territorial promises of the Treaty of London.

Mussolini and the Black Shirts
For movements like Fascism in Italy, the best society was one controlled by militarized politicians who killed their critics and political opponents. Fascism saw parliamentary democracies as effeminate and doomed in the modern world, which would need dictators and obedient warriors to make it strong, efficient, and machinelike. Thus, in the name of promoting state power, Mussolini gained adherents both within and outside of Italy. (Farabolafoto.)

Peasants and workers protested their economic plight, made worse by the slump of the early 1920s. Since the late nineteenth century, many Europeans had come to blame parliaments for their troubles, so Italians were responsive when Mussolini, a socialist journalist who turned politically to the right, built a personal army (the Black Shirts) of veterans and the unemployed to overturn parliamentary government. In 1922, his supporters, known as the Fascists, started the **march on Rome**, forcing the king to make the dynamic Mussolini prime minister.

The Fascist movement grew because of poverty and wounded national pride. The Black Shirts attracted many young men who felt cheated of glory by the Allies, as well as veterans who missed the vigor of military life in the Great War. The fasces, an ancient Roman symbol depicting a bundle of sticks wrapped around an ax with the blade exposed, served as the movement's emblem; it represented both unity and force to Mussolini's supporters. Unlike Marxism, Fascism scoffed at coherent ideology. "Fascism is not a church," Mussolini announced upon taking power in 1922. "It is more like a training ground." Fascism was defined by deeds, including its promotion of male violence and its attacks on the "antinationalist" socialist movement and parliamentary rule.

Mussolini secured his power by criminalizing any criticism of the state and by using violence against opponents in parliament. Fascist bands wrecked socialist offices, attacked striking workers, used the tactic of forcing castor oil (which causes diarrhea) down the throats of socialists, and even murdered political opponents. Yet this brutality and the sight of the Black Shirts marching through the streets like disciplined soldiers signaled to many Italians that their country was orderly and modern. Large landowners and businessmen approved Fascist attacks on strikers and supported the movement financially. Their generous funding allowed Mussolini to build a large staff by hiring the unemployed and thus advance the belief that the Fascists could rescue the economy when no one else could.

Like a wartime leader, Mussolini used mass propaganda to build support for a kind of military campaign to remake Italy. Peasant men huddled around radios to hear him call for a "battle of wheat" to enhance farm productivity. Peasant women, responding to his praise of maternal duty, adored him for appearing to value womanhood. In the cities, the government launched avant-garde architecture projects and used public relations promoters to advertise its achievements. The modern city became a stage set for Fascist spectacles, as broad avenues were built for Fascist parades, captured by newsreel cameras and broadcast by radio. Mussolini claimed that he made the trains run on time, and this triumph of modern technology raised people's hopes that he could restore order—even if it was military order.

Mussolini added a strong dose of traditional values and prejudices to his rule. Although he was an atheist, he recognized the power of Catholicism in Italian life. In 1929, the Lateran Agreement between the Italian government and the church made the Vatican an independent state under papal sovereignty. The government recognized the Catholic church's right to determine marriage and family policy and supported its role in education. In return, the church ended its criticism of Fascist tactics. Mussolini also introduced a "corporate" state that denied individual political rights in favor of duty to the state, as in wartime. Corporatist decrees in 1926 outlawed labor unions, replacing them with organized groups or corporations of employers, workers, and professionals to settle grievances and determine conditions of work. Mussolini drew praise from business leaders when he announced cuts in women's wages, and later he won the approval of civil servants, lawyers, and professors by banning women from those professions. Mussolini did not want women out of the workforce altogether but aimed to confine them to low-paying jobs as part of his scheme for reinvigorating men.

Mussolini's admirers were numerous across the West and included Adolf Hitler, who throughout the 1920s had been building a paramilitary group of storm troopers and a political organization called the National Socialist German Workers' Party, or Nazis.

During his brief stint in jail for the Beer Hall Putsch in 1923, Hitler wrote *Mein Kampf* (*My Struggle,* 1925), which expressed both his vicious anti-Semitism and his political psychology for manipulating the masses. Hitler was fascinated by the details of Mussolini's success: the dramatic march on Rome, Mussolini's legal accession to power, and his triumph over all opposition. Although Hitler was welding the Nazi Party into a strong political instrument, the Weimar parliamentary government was actually working well as the decade neared its end.

REVIEW   How did the postwar cultural atmosphere encourage both beneficial innovations and the trend toward dictatorship?

Conclusion

The year 1929 was to prove just as fateful as 1914 had been. In 1914, an orgy of death had begun, causing tens of millions of casualties, the destruction of major dynasties, and the collapse of aristocratic classes. For four years, war promoted military technology, fierce nationalism, and the control of everyday life by a bureaucracy. While dynasties fell at the war's end, the centralization of power increased the scope of the nation-state. The Peace of Paris treaties of 1919–1920 left Germans bitterly resentful, while in eastern and central Europe the intense mingling of ethnicities, religions, and languages in the new states created by the treaties failed to guarantee a peaceful future. Massive migrations provoked additional chaos as some new nations expelled minority groups.

War furthered the development of mass society. It leveled social classes on the battlefield and in the graveyard, standardized political thinking through wartime propaganda, and extended many political rights to women to reward their wartime effort. Production techniques, improved during wartime, were used in peacetime for manufacturing consumer goods. Technological innovations, such as the prostheses built by Jules Amar, air transport, and films and radio, became available to more people. Modernity in the arts intensified, probing the nightmarish war that continued to haunt the population.

The war had so militarized politics that by the end of the 1920s, strongmen had come to power in Hungary, Poland, Romania, the Soviet Union, and Italy, with Adolf Hitler waiting in the wings in Germany. Many Westerners were impressed

Mapping the West Europe and the World, 1929
This map reflects the partitions and nations that came into being as a result of war and revolution, while it obscures the increasing movement toward throwing off colonial rule. The year 1929 was the true high point of empire: the drive for overseas empire would diminish thereafter, except in Italy, which still craved colonies, and in Japan, which continued searching for land and resources to fuel its rapid growth. Observe the League of Nations membership also depicted in the map. What common bonds, if any, united these nations?

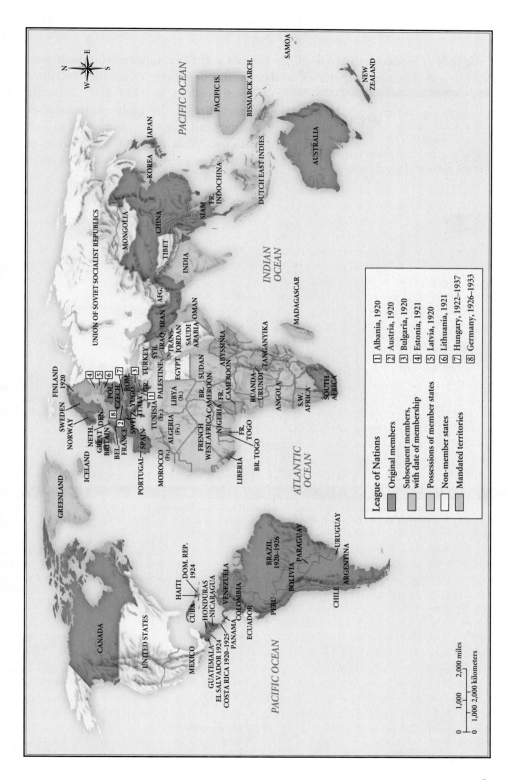

PACIFIC OCEAN

PACIFIC IS.

SAMOA

BISMARCK ARCH.

NEW ZEALAND

AUSTRALIA

JAPAN

KOREA

CHINA

MONGOLIA

TIBET

INDIA

SIAM

FR. INDOCHINA

DUTCH EAST INDIES

INDIAN OCEAN

MADAGASCAR

UNION OF SOVIET SOCIALIST REPUBLICS

AFG.

IRAN

IRAQ

SYR.

TURKEY

GR.

PALESTINE

TRANS-JORDAN

SAUDI ARABIA

OMAN

EGYPT

SUDAN

ABYSSINIA

TANGANYIKA

RUANDA-URUNDI

ANGOLA

S.W. AFRICA

SOUTH AFRICA

CAMEROON

BR. SUDAN

LIBYA (It.)

TUNISIA (Fr.)

ALGERIA (Fr.)

MOROCCO (Fr.)

NIGERIA

FR. TOGO

BR. TOGO

LIBERIA

FRENCH WEST AFRICA

FR. CAMEROON

FINLAND 1920

SWEDEN

NORWAY

ICELAND

GREENLAND

NETH.

GREAT BRITAIN

DEN.

BEL.

FRANCE

SWITZ.

SPAIN

PORTUGAL

ITALY

POL.

CZECH

ROM.

YUGO.

[4] [5] [6] [7]
[2] [8] [3]
[1]

ATLANTIC OCEAN

CANADA

UNITED STATES

MEXICO

GUATEMALA 1924

EL SALVADOR 1924

COSTA RICA 1920–1925

PANAMA

HONDURAS

NICARAGUA

CUBA

HAITI

DOM. REP. 1924

VENEZUELA

COLOMBIA

ECUADOR

PERU

BRAZIL 1920–1926

BOLIVIA

PARAGUAY

URUGUAY

ARGENTINA

CHILE

PACIFIC OCEAN

League of Nations

■ Original members

■ Subsequent members, with date of membership

■ Possessions of member states

□ Non-member states

■ Mandated territories

|1| Albania, 1920
|2| Austria, 1920
|3| Bulgaria, 1920
|4| Estonia, 1921
|5| Latvia, 1920
|6| Lithuania, 1921
|7| Hungary, 1922–1937
|8| Germany, 1926–1933

0   1,000   2,000 miles

0 1,000 2,000 kilometers

by the tough, modern efficiency of the Fascists and Communists, who made parliaments and citizen rule seem out-of-date, even effeminate. When the U.S. stock market crashed in 1929 and economic disaster circled the globe, authoritarian solutions and militarism continued to look appealing. What followed was a series of catastrophes even more devastating than World War I.

CHAPTER REVIEW QUESTIONS

1. How was postwar mass politics shaped by the experience of World War I?
2. What social changes from World War I carried over into the postwar years and why?

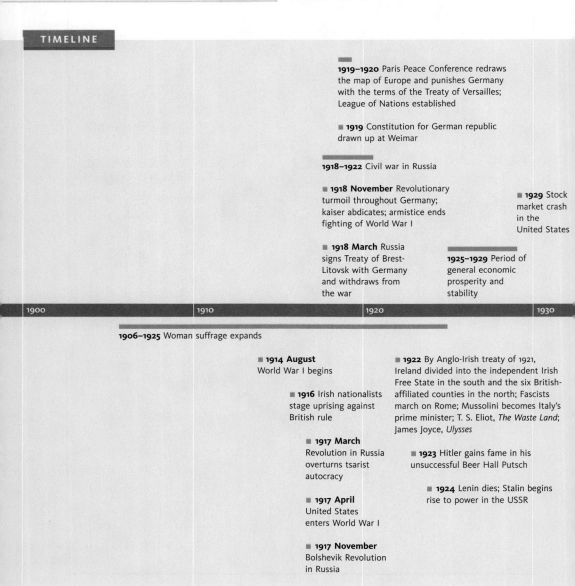

TIMELINE

1919–1920 Paris Peace Conference redraws the map of Europe and punishes Germany with the terms of the Treaty of Versailles; League of Nations established

1919 Constitution for German republic drawn up at Weimar

1918–1922 Civil war in Russia

1918 November Revolutionary turmoil throughout Germany; kaiser abdicates; armistice ends fighting of World War I

1918 March Russia signs Treaty of Brest-Litovsk with Germany and withdraws from the war

1929 Stock market crash in the United States

1925–1929 Period of general economic prosperity and stability

| 1900 | 1910 | 1920 | 1930 |

1906–1925 Woman suffrage expands

1914 August World War I begins

1916 Irish nationalists stage uprising against British rule

1917 March Revolution in Russia overturns tsarist autocracy

1917 April United States enters World War I

1917 November Bolshevik Revolution in Russia

1922 By Anglo-Irish treaty of 1921, Ireland divided into the independent Irish Free State in the south and the six British-affiliated counties in the north; Fascists march on Rome; Mussolini becomes Italy's prime minister; T. S. Eliot, *The Waste Land*; James Joyce, *Ulysses*

1923 Hitler gains fame in his unsuccessful Beer Hall Putsch

1924 Lenin dies; Stalin begins rise to power in the USSR

For practice quizzes and other study tools, see the Online Study Guide at
bedfordstmartins.com/huntconcise.

For primary-source material from this period, see Chapter 25 of
Sources of THE MAKING OF THE WEST, Third Edition.

Suggested References

The most recent histories of the Great War consider its military, technological, psychic, social, and economic aspects. This vision of the war as a phenomenon occurring both on and off the battlefield characterizes the newest scholarship. Histories of the war's end show deprivation, ongoing mass slaughter, the eruption of revolutions, and the complexities of peacemaking.

Barry, John. *The Great Influenza: The Epic Story of the Greatest Plague in History.* 2004.

Hanna, Martha. *Your Death Would Be Mine: Paul and Marie Pireaud in the Great War.* 2006.

Healy, Maureen. *Vienna and the Fall of the Habsburg Empire: Total War and Everyday Life in World War I.* 2004.

Holquist, Peter. *Making War, Forging Revolution: Russia's Continuum of Crisis, 1914–1921.* 2002.

Horne, John, ed. *State, Society, and Mobilization in Europe during the First World War.* 2002.

Kent, Susan Kingsley. *Aftershocks: The Politics of Trauma in Britain, 1918–1931.* 2009.

Liulevicius, Vejas Gabriel. *War Land on the Eastern Front: Culture, National Identity and German Occupation in World War I.* 2000.

Makaman, Douglas, and Michael Mays, eds. *World War I and the Cultures of Modernity.* 2000.

Marks, Sally. *The Ebbing of European Ascendancy: An International History of the World.* 2002.

Northrup, Douglas. *Veiled Empire: Gender and Power in Stalinist Central Asia.* 2004.

Panchasi, Roxanne. "Reconstructions: Prosthetics and the Rehabilitation of the Male Body in World War I." *Differences.* 1995.

Robb, George. *British Culture and the First World War.* 2002.

Roshwald, Aviel. *Ethnic Nationalism and the Fall of Empires: Central Europe, Russia and the Middle East, 1914–1923.* 2001.

Scales, Rebecca. "Radio Broadcasting, Disabled Veterans, and Politics of National Recovery in Interwar France." *French Historical Studies.* 2008.

Weitz, Eric D. *Weimar Germany: Promise and Tragedy.* 2007.

World War I Documents Archive: http://www.lib.byu.edu/%7Erdh/wwi

An Age of Catastrophes

WHEN ETTY HILLESUM MOVED TO AMSTERDAM from the Dutch provinces in 1932 to attend law school, an economic depression gripped the world. A resourceful young woman, Hillesum pieced together a living as a house-keeper and part-time language teacher. The pressures and pleasures of everyday life blinded her, however, to Adolf Hitler's spectacular rise to power in Germany, even when he demonized her fellow Jews as responsible for the economic slump. In 1939, the outbreak of World War II awakened her to reality. The German conquest of the Netherlands in 1940 led to the persecution of Dutch Jews and brought Hillesum to this shattering thought, noted in her diary: "What they are after is our total destruction." The Nazis started relocating Jews to camps in Germany and Poland. Hillesum went to work for Amsterdam's Jewish Council, which was forced to organize the transport of Jews to the east. Changing from self-absorbed student to heroine, she did what she could to help other Jews and began carefully recording the deportation. When she was taken prisoner and deported in turn, she smuggled out letters from the transit camps, describing the brutal treatment and inhumane conditions. "I wish I could live for a long time so that one day I may know how to explain it," she wrote. Etty Hillesum never got her wish; she died at Auschwitz in November 1943.

Nazis on Parade

By the time Adolf Hitler came to power in 1933, Germany was mired in the global economic depression. Hated by Communists, Nazis, and conservatives alike, the German republic had few supporters. To Germans still reeling from their defeat in World War I, the Nazis looked as though they would restore national power by defeat-ing enemies both within and beyond Germany's borders. Hitler took his cue from Benito Mussolini by presenting showy parades such as this one and by promising an end to democracy and tolerance. **For more help analyzing this image, see the visual activity for this chapter in the Online Study Guide at** bedfordstmartins.com/huntconcise. *(Time Life Pictures/Getty Images.)*

The economic recovery of the late 1920s came to a crashing halt with the collapse of the U.S. stock market in 1929. The financial col-lapse in the United States became part of the worldwide Great Depression. Economic distress intensified social grievances. In Europe, people turned to military-style strongmen for solutions to their problems. Among these dictators was Adolf Hitler, who called on the German masses to restore the national glory that had been damaged by defeat in World War I. He urged them to scorn democratic rights and root out those he considered to be inferior, including Jews, Slavs, and Gypsies. Authoritarian and militaristic regimes also took hold in Portugal, Spain, Poland, Hungary, Japan, China, and countries of Latin America, crushing representative institutions. In the Soviet Union, Joseph Stalin justified the killing of millions of people as being necessary for the USSR's industrialization and the survival of communism. For millions of hard-pressed people in the difficult 1930s, dictatorship had great appeal.

Elected leaders in the democracies reacted cautiously to both economic depression and the dictators' aggressive acts. In an age of mass media, leaders following democratic procedures appeared timid, while dictators dressed in uniforms looked bold and decisive. Only the German invasion of Poland in 1939 finally pushed the democracies to respond, as World War II erupted in Europe. By the end of 1941, the war had spread across the globe, with the United States, Great Britain, and the Soviet Union allied in combat against Germany, Italy, and Japan. Tens of millions of people would perish in this war because both technology and ideology had become even more deadly than they had been just two decades earlier. More than half of those killed were civilians, among them Etty Hillesum, whose only crime was being Jewish.

CHAPTER FOCUS QUESTION What were the main economic, social, and political challenges of the years 1929–1945, and how did governments and individuals respond to them?

The Great Depression

The U.S. stock market crash of 1929 and economic developments around the world triggered the Great Depression of the 1930s. Rural and urban folk alike suffered as tens of millions lost their jobs. The whole world felt the depression's impact: commerce and investment in industry fell off, social order and gender roles were upset, and the birthrate sank. From peasants in Asia to industrial workers in Germany and the United States, the Great Depression shattered the lives of millions.

Economic Disaster Strikes

In the 1920s, U.S. corporations and banks as well as millions of individual Americans had optimistically invested their money in the stock market or, more often, borrowed money to invest. Confident that prices would always rise, they used easy credit to buy shares in popular new companies based on electric, automotive, and other new technologies with full confidence in ever-rising stock prices. By the end of the decade, the Federal Reserve Bank—the nation's central bank, which controlled financial policy—tried to slow speculation by limiting credit availability. To meet the new restrictions on credit, brokers had to demand that their clients immediately repay the money they had borrowed to buy stocks. When millions of shares of stocks were sold to raise the necessary cash, the market collapsed. Between early October and mid-November 1929, the value of businesses listed on U.S. stock exchanges dropped from $87 billion to $30 billion. For individuals and for the economy as a whole, it was the beginning of catastrophe.

The crash helped bring on a global depression because the United States, a leading international creditor, had financed the economic growth of the previous five years. Suddenly lacking credit, U.S. financiers cut back on loans and called in debts, undermining businesses at home and abroad. Europe faced a decline in consumer buying, overproduction, and competition from low-cost U.S. and Japanese goods, which further slowed the European economy, including the new factories of eastern Europe.

The Great Depression hurt all sectors of the world economy, and government actions made the situation worse. Governments instituted budget cuts and high tariffs against foreign goods to restart their economies, but these policies further reduced individual spending and dampened trade. By 1933, almost six million German workers, about one-third of the workforce, were unemployed, and many other Germans were underemployed. Even in France, which had a more self-sufficient economy based on small businesses, firms began to fail, and by the mid-1930s more than 800,000 French people had lost their jobs.

Agricultural prices had been declining for several years because of technological innovation and abundant harvests around the world. Now creditors confiscated farms and equipment. With incomes declining, millions of small farmers had no money to buy the chemical

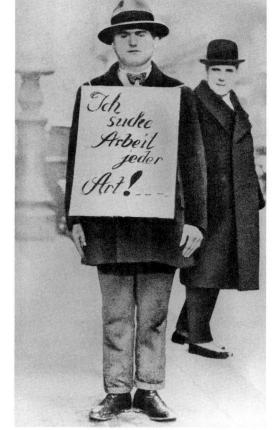

Unemployed in Germany (1932)
"I'm looking for work of any kind," this respectably dressed unemployed man announces on his sign. Germans were among those hardest hit by the Great Depression, and when demagogues pointed to such sights as evidence that democracy didn't work, it helped pull down the rule of republics based on constitutions, representative government, and guaranteed rights.
(ullstein bild/The Granger Collection, NY.)

fertilizers and motorized machinery they needed to remain competitive, and they too went under. Eastern and southern European peasants, who had pressed for the redistribution of land after World War I, could not afford to operate their newly acquired farms. In Poland, many of the 700,000 new landowners fell into debt trying to improve their farms. Eastern European governments often ignored the farmers' plight as they poured available funds into industrialization—a policy that increased tensions in rural society.

Social Effects of the Depression

The depression had complex effects on society. First, life was not uniformly bleak in the 1930s. Despite the slump, modernization continued. Bordering English slums, one traveler in the mid-1930s noticed, were "filling stations and factories that look like exhibition buildings, giant cinemas and dance halls and cafés, bungalows with tiny garages, cocktail bars, Woolworth's [and] swimming pools." Municipal and national governments continued road construction and sanitation projects. Running water, electricity, and sewage pipes were installed in many homes for the first time. New factories manufactured synthetic fabrics, electrical products such as stoves, and automobiles—all of them in demand. With government assistance, eastern European industry developed: Romanian industrial production, for example, increased by 55 percent between 1929 and 1939.

Second, the majority of Europeans and Americans had jobs throughout the 1930s, and people with steady employment benefited from a drastic drop in prices. Service workers, managers, and business leaders often prospered. In towns with heavy industry, however, sometimes more than half the population was out of work. In Britain in the mid-1930s, close to 20 percent of the population lacked adequate food, clothing, or housing. In a 1932 school assignment, a German youth wrote, "My father has been out of work for two and a half years. He thinks that I'll never find a job." Despite the prosperity of many people, the Great Depression spread fear beyond the unemployed.

Economic catastrophe upset gender relations and weakened social ties. Women often found low-paying jobs doing laundry and cleaning houses, while unemployed men sometimes stayed home all day. Men who stayed home sometimes took over the housekeeping chores but often felt that this "women's work" chipped away at their masculinity. As many women became breadwinners, though at low wages, men could be seen standing on street corners begging—a change in gender roles that fed discontent. Young men in cities faced severe unemployment. With nothing to do but loiter in parks, they became ripe for movements like Nazism. As the number of farmworkers decreased, rural men faced the erosion of patriarchal authority, once central to the organization of labor and to decisions about distributing property to offspring. Demagogues everywhere attacked parliamentary politicians for their failure to stop the collapse of traditional values, clearing the way for Nazi and fascist politicians who promised to restore male dignity.

Politicians from all parties also attacked the low birthrate, which despite a brief postwar upturn, had steadily declined. The reason was clear: in difficult economic times, people chose to have fewer children. In addition, compulsory education and more years of required schooling, enforced more strictly after World War I, reduced the income children earned for poorer families, resulting in increased costs for each additional child. Family planning centers opened, receiving many clients, and knowledge of birth control spread to the working and lower middle classes, who continued the half-century-long trend of cutting family size.

Many politicians used the population "crisis" to arouse fear of national decline and to gain votes by igniting racism. "Superior" peoples were selfishly failing to breed, they charged, and "inferior" peoples were poised to take their place. This racism took a violent form in eastern Europe, where the rural population was growing because of increased life expectancies despite the declining birthrates. As financial hardships increased, eastern European peasant political parties blamed Jewish bankers for farm foreclosures and Jewish civil servants (of whom there were actually very few) for new taxes and inadequate relief programs. Thus, population issues along with economic misery produced discord, especially in the form of ethnic hatred and anti-Semitism, opening the way for dictators who promised that eliminating Jews and other undesirables would restore individual and national prosperity.

Global Dimensions of the Crash

The effects of the depression extended beyond the West, spreading discontent in European empires. World War I and postwar investment had produced economic growth, a rising population, and explosive urbanization in Asia, Africa, and Latin America. Japan in particular had become a formidable economic rival between 1920 and 1940. The depression, however, cut the demand for copper, tin, and other raw materials and for the finished products made in urban factories worldwide. Rising agricultural productivity drove down the prices of foodstuffs like rice and coffee—a disaster for people who had been forced to grow a single cash crop. Just as in Europe, however, the economic picture was uneven. For instance, established industrial sectors of the Indian economy such as textiles gained strength, with India achieving virtual independence from British cloth imports.

Economic distress fueled anger, and anger led to action. Colonial farmers withheld produce like cocoa from imperial trade, and colonial workers went on strike to protest wage cuts imposed by imperial landlords. The colonial governments' response to the depression added to ordinary people's grievances. They insisted that all taxes and loans be paid and manipulated currency rates in favor of the mother country so that those taxes were even higher than before. As a result, the millions of African and Asian colonial veterans of World War I were more than ever determined to be free from colonial rule.

In India anger toward the British boiled over. Millions of working people, including hundreds of thousands of veterans, joined with upper-class Indians who had organized to gain rights from Britain in the late nineteenth century. Mohandas Gandhi (1869–1948; called Mahatma, or "great-souled") emerged as the charismatic leader for Indian independence. Trained in England as a Western-style lawyer, Gandhi preached Hindu self-denial, rejecting elaborate British manners and ceremonies. He wore simple clothing made of thread he had spun himself and advocated **civil disobedience**—intentionally but peacefully breaking the law—a tactic he claimed to have taken from British suffragists and from the teachings of spiritual leaders such as Jesus and Buddha. Boycotting British-made goods and disobeying British laws, he aimed to end Indians' respect toward the British. The British jailed Gandhi repeatedly and tried to split the independence movement by encouraging the rival Muslim League and promoting Hindu-Muslim conflict. Instead, Indian commitment to independence grew.

The end of the Ottoman Empire following World War I led to efforts to build nations in the Middle East. Mustafa Kemal (1881–1938), known as Atatürk (first among Turks), led the Turks to found the independent republic of Turkey in 1923 and to craft a capitalist economy. Kemal moved the national capital from Constantinople to Ankara in 1923 and officially changed the ancient Greek *Constantinople* to the Turkish *Istanbul* in 1930. In an effort to Westernize Turkish culture and the new Turkish state, Kemal mandated Western dress for men and women, introduced

A Historic Act of Civil Disobedience
Mohandas Gandhi used nonviolent resistance to challenge British rule. Because of the British government's monopoly on salt, Indians were prohibited from gathering this natural product, and every Indian family had to pay a tax on salt. In 1930, Gandhi led his supporters on a two-hundred-mile march to India's salt flats, on the coast, to protest the hated salt tax and to extract salt from seawater. Gandhi was arrested and jailed, but his followers continued their march to the sea.
(© Bettmann/Corbis.)

the Latin alphabet, and abolished polygamy. In 1936, women received the vote and became eligible to serve in the Turkish parliament. Like Atatürk, nationalist leaders in Persia and Egypt sought to loosen the financial and political grip of Europeans on their countries.

France made few concessions in its colonies. Like all imperial powers during the depression, it depended increasingly on the profits it could make from its colonies. Thus, French trade with them increased as trade with Europe lagged. France also depended on the colonies for sheer numbers of people, and the rising colonial population boosted French morale. One official estimated what colonial population numbers could mean for national security: "One hundred and ten million strong, France can stand up to Germany." Like other Western-educated anti-colonial leaders, Ho Chi Minh, founder of the Indochinese Communist Party, protested this subjection, but in 1930 the French crushed a peasant uprising he led. Needing their empires, Britain and France strengthened their military positions around the world. As a result, totalitarian forces went largely unchecked in Europe during the 1930s.

> **REVIEW** How did the Great Depression affect society and politics?

Totalitarian Triumph

Representative government collapsed in many countries under the weight of social and economic crisis. After 1929, Italy's Benito Mussolini, the Soviet Union's Joseph Stalin, and Germany's Adolf Hitler were able to mobilize vast support for their regimes. Many admired Mussolini and Hitler for the discipline they brought to social and economic life. Desperate for economic relief, citizens supported political violence as key to restoring well-being. The common use of violence has led some scholars to apply the term **totalitarianism** to the Fascist, Communist, and Nazi regimes of the 1930s. The term refers to highly centralized systems of government that attempt to control society and ensure conformity through a single party and police terror. Born during World War I and gaining strength in its aftermath, these regimes broke with the liberal principles of the rule of law and basic rights and came to wage war on their own citizens.

The Rise of Stalinism

In the 1930s, Joseph Stalin led the remarkable transformation of the USSR from a rural society into an industrial power. Stalin ended Lenin's New Economic Policy (NEP) and in 1929 laid out the first of several **five-year plans** for industrializing the country. The first plan outlined a program for massive increases in the output of coal, steel, and industrial goods. Without an end to economic backwardness, Stalin warned, "the advanced countries . . . will crush us." He thus established central economic planning—a policy used on both sides in World War I and increasingly favored by bureaucrats around the world. Between 1928 and 1940, the number of

Soviet workers in industry, construction, and transportation grew from 4.6 million to 12.6 million, and factory output soared. Stalin's first five-year plan helped make the USSR a leading industrial nation.

A new elite of bureaucrats put the plans into operation. Mostly party officials and technical experts, these managers dominated Soviet workers by limiting their ability to change jobs or move from place to place. Despite these limitations, skilled workers benefited substantially from the redistribution of privileges that accompanied industrialism and central planning. Compared with people working the land, both managers and industrial workers had better housing and higher wages. Communist officials enjoyed additional rewards, such as country homes and luxurious vacations.

Unskilled workers enjoyed no such benefits. Newcomers from the countryside were herded into barracks-like dwellings, even tents, and subjected to dangerous factory conditions. Despite the hardships, many took pride in their new skills: "We mastered this profession—completely new to us—with great pleasure," a female lathe operator recalled. More often, workers fresh from the countryside lacked the technical knowledge to accomplish the goals of the five-year plans. Because meeting these goals had top priority as a measure of progress toward the Communist utopia, official lying about productivity became part of the economic system. The attempt to turn an illiterate peasant society into an advanced industrial economy in a single decade brought intense suffering. Hardship was tolerated because Soviet workers believed that in the process of achieving a Communist society, as one worker put it, "man himself is being rebuilt."

In country and city alike, politics influenced work. Stalin demanded output from industry and more grain from peasants, both to feed the urban workforce and to provide exports to finance industrialization. Peasants resisted government demands by cutting production or withholding produce from the market, prompting Stalin to demand a "liquidation of the kulaks." *Kulak,* which means "fist," was a negative term for prosperous peasants, but in practice it applied to almost anyone. Party workers searched villages, forcing residents to identify the kulaks among them. Propagandists stirred up hatred. One Russian remembered believing that kulaks were "bloodsuckers, cattle, swine, loathsome, repulsive: they had no souls; they stank." Denounced as "enemies of the state," whole families and even entire villages were robbed of their possessions and left to starve, or even murdered outright. Confiscated kulak land formed the basis of the new collective farm, or kolkhoz, where the remaining peasants were to create a Communist agricultural system of cooperative farming using shared machinery.

Economic disaster followed collectivization and rapid industrialization, producing violent **purges**, because success in work life was defined as central to communism. Failures were common because factory workers and party officials were too inexperienced with advanced industrialization to meet quotas. The experiment with collectivization, combined with the murder of farmers, resulted in a drop in the grain harvest from 83 million tons in 1930 to 67 million in 1934. Soviet citizens starved. Blaming all failures on "wreckers" deliberately plotting against communism, Stalin instituted purges—state violence in the form of widespread arrests, imprisonment in labor camps, and executions. These purges touched nearly all segments of society, beginning with engineers who were condemned for causing low productivity. Starting in 1936, the government charged prominent Bolshevik leaders with conspiring to overthrow Soviet rule in a series of "show trials"—trials based on trumped-up charges, phony evidence, and coerced confessions. Some of the top leaders accepted their fate, seeing the purges—a "great and bold political idea," one of the accused wrote—as good for the future of communism. Tortured and forced to confess in court, most of those found guilty were shot.

The spirit of purge swept through society. One woman poet described the scene: "Great concert and lecture halls were turned into public confessionals. . . . People did penance for [everything]. . . . Beating their breasts, the 'guilty' would lament that they had 'shown political short-sightedness' and 'lack of vigilance' . . . and were full of 'rotten liberalism.'" In 1937 and 1938, military leaders were arrested and executed without public trials; some ranks were entirely wiped out. Simultaneously, the government centralized and vastly expanded the number of prison camps stretching several thousand miles from Moscow to Siberia. Called the Gulag—an acronym for the administrative arm of the camps founded under Lenin—the system held millions of prisoners under deadly conditions. Prisoners aided the economy by doing every kind of work, from digging canals to building apartment buildings. Some one million Gulag prisoners died annually as a result of insufficient food and housing and twelve- to sixteen-hour workdays of crushing physical labor. Regular beatings and murders contributed to the harsh conditions of Gulag life, becoming another aspect of totalitarian violence.

The 1930s also marked an end to toleration in Soviet social life, as social and sexual freedom began to disappear. As in the rest of Europe, the birthrate in the USSR declined rapidly in the 1930s. The Soviet Union needed to replace the millions of people lost since 1914, motivating Stalin to restrict access to birth-control information and abortion. More lavish wedding ceremonies came back into fashion, divorces became difficult to obtain, and the state made homosexuality a crime. The Bolsheviks had once scorned the family as a "bourgeois" institution; now propaganda referred to the family as a "school for socialism." At the same time, women in rural areas made gains in literacy and received improved health care. As the purges continued, positions in the lower ranks of the party were opened to women, and more women were accepted into the professions. However, women, particularly those in the industrial workforce, faced increased stress. After putting in a long workday, they had to wait in long lines to obtain scarce consumer goods and perform all household and child-care tasks.

Avant-garde experimentation in the arts ended under Stalin. He called artists and writers "engineers of the soul" and, recognizing their influence, controlled their

N. J. Altman, *Anna Akhmatova*
This modernist painting portrays the poet Anna Akhmatova (1889–1966) in 1914, when she was a centerpiece of literary salon life in Russia. In the 1930s and 1940s, Akhmatova refused to follow the optimistic socialist realist style and instead gave poetic voice to Soviet suffering, recording in her verse ordinary people's endurance of purges and warfare. As she encouraged people to resist the Nazis during World War II, Stalin allowed her to revive Russian patriotism instead of promoting socialist international- ism. (© State Russian Museum, St. Petersburg, Russia/The Bridgeman Art Library. Art © Estate of N. J. Altman/RAO, Moscow/VAGA, New York, NY.)

output through the Union of Soviet Writers. The union not only assigned housing, office space, equipment, and secretarial help but also determined the types of books authors could write. In return, the "comrade artist" adhered to the official style of "socialist realism," derived from the 1920s focus on the common worker as a type of social hero. Although some artists and writers went underground, secretly creat- ing works that are still coming to light, many others found ways to adjust to the state's demands. Sergei Prokofiev, for example, composed music for the delightful *Peter and the Wolf* and for Sergei Eisenstein's 1938 film *Alexander Nevsky,* a work that flatteringly compared Stalin with the towering medieval rulers of the Russian people. Aided by adaptable artists, workers, and bureaucrats, Stalin stood trium- phant as the 1930s drew to a close. He was, as two different workers put it, "our beloved Leader" and "a god on earth."

Hitler's Rise to Power

A different but no less violent system emerged when Adolf Hitler put an end to democracy in Germany. Since the early 1920s, he had ranted that the German people should crush the fragile Weimar Republic and had spread a message of anti-Semitism and the rebirth of the German "race." When the Great Depression struck Germany in 1929, his Nazi Party began to pass its rivals in elections. Film and press mogul Alfred Hugenberg's newspapers helped, constantly slamming the Weimar government and blaming it for the disastrous economy and the loss of German pride after World War I. Nazi supporters attacked young Communist groups agitating on behalf of the new Soviet experiment. Hugenberg's newspapers always reported such incidents as the work of Communist thugs who had assaulted blameless Nazis, thus building sympathy for the Nazis among the middle classes.

Parliamentary government in Germany practically ground to a halt in the face of economic crisis. The Reichstag failed to approve emergency plans to improve the economy. As a result of its inaction, sympathetic media coverage, and its own street tactics, the Nazi Party, which had received only slightly more than 2 percent of the vote in the Reichstag elections of 1928, won almost 20 percent in 1930 and more than doubled its representation in 1932. Members of every age group and class supported Hitler, but he especially attracted young people. In 1930, 70 percent of Nazi Party members were under forty. Full of idealism, the young had faith that a better world was possible if Hitler took control. The largest number of supporters came from the industrial working class, but many white-collar workers and members of the lower middle class also joined the party in percentages out of proportion with their numbers in the population. The inflation that had wiped out their savings had left them especially bitter and open to Hitler's rhetoric, even if he did seem rough around the edges.

Hitler used modern propaganda techniques to build his following. Nazi Party members passed out thousands of recordings of Hitler's speeches and other Nazi mementos to German citizens. Teenagers painted their fingernails with swastikas, and soldiers flashed metal match covers with Nazi insignia. Nazi rallies were masterful displays in which Hitler captivated the crowds, who saw him as their strong, superior *Führer,* or leader. Frenzied and inspirational, he seemed neither a calculating politician nor a wooden bureaucrat but a "creative element," as one poet put it. In reality, however, Hitler viewed the masses with contempt. In *Mein Kampf,* he discussed how to deal with them:

> The receptivity of the great masses is very limited, their intelligence is small. In consequence of these facts, all effective propaganda must be limited to a very few points and must harp on those in slogans until the last member of the public understands what you want him to understand.

Hitler's media techniques were so successful that they continue to influence political campaigns today, particularly in the use of sound bites and simple, often hate-filled and threatening messages.

In the 1932 elections, both the Nazis and Communists did very well, making the leader of one of those parties the logical choice as chancellor. Influential conservative politicians loathed the Communists for their opposition to private property and favored Hitler as someone they could manipulate. When Hitler was invited to become chancellor in January 1933, he accepted.

Toys Depicting Nazis
As a totalitarian ideology, Nazism permeated everyday life. Nazi insignia decorated clothing, dishes, cigarette lighters, and even toys. Men and women became husbands and wives in accordance with Nazi rules and enrolled their children in Nazi clubs and organizations. Nazi songs, Nazi parades and festivals, and Nazi radio filled Germans' leisure time. (Imperial War Museum, London.)

The Nazification of German Politics

Millions of Germans celebrated Hitler's ascent to power. One recalled that upon hearing of Hitler's selection as chancellor, "my father went down to the cellar and brought up our best bottles of wine . . . and my mother wept for joy." Tens of thousands of Hitler's paramilitary supporters, called storm troopers (SA or Stürmabteilung), paraded through the streets with blazing torches. Instead of being easy to control, however, Hitler took command brutally, closing down representative government with an ugly show of force.

Within a month of his taking power, the Nazi state was in place. When the Reichstag building was gutted by fire in February 1933, Nazis used the fire as an excuse for suspending civil rights, imposing censorship of the press, and prohibiting meetings of other political parties. Indeed, Hitler had always claimed to hate democracy and differing political opinions. "Our opponents complain that we National Socialists, and I in particular, are intolerant," he declared. "They are right, we are intolerant! I have set myself one task, namely to sweep those parties out of Germany."

The storm troopers' violence became a way of life, silencing democratic politicians. At the end of March, intimidated Reichstag delegates let pass the **Enabling Act**, which suspended the constitution for four years and allowed Nazi laws to take effect without parliamentary approval. Solid middle-class Germans approved the Enabling Act as a way to advance the creation of a *Volksgemeinschaft* (people's community) of like-minded, racially pure Germans—"Aryans" in Nazi terms. Heinrich Himmler headed the elite SS (Schutzstaffel), an organization that protected Hitler, and he commanded the political police system. The Gestapo, a political police force organized by Hermann Goering, enforced complete obedience to Nazism. These organizations had vast powers to arrest, execute, or imprison people in concentration camps, the first of which opened at Dachau near Munich in March 1933. The Nazis filled it and later camps with socialists, homosexuals, Jews, and others said to interfere with the Volksgemeinschaft. One Nazi leader proclaimed:

> [National socialism] does not believe that one soul is equal to another, one man equal to another. It does not believe in rights as such. It aims to create the German man of strength, its task is to protect the German people, and all . . . must be subordinate to this goal.

Hitler deliberately blurred authority in the government and the Nazi Party so that confusion and bitter competition reigned. He then settled disputes that arose among them, often with violence. When Ernst Roehm, leader of the SA and Hitler's longtime collaborator, called for a "second revolution" to end the business and military elites' influence on top Nazis, Hitler ordered Roehm's assassination. The bloody Night of the Long Knives (June 30, 1934), during which hundreds of SA leaders and innocent civilians were killed, enhanced Hitler's support among conservatives. They saw that he would deal ruthlessly with those favoring a leveling of social privilege. Nazism's terrorist politics served as the foundation of Hitler's Third Reich—a German empire he described as succeeding the empires of Charlemagne and William II.

Like violence, new economic and social programs, especially those putting people back to work, were crucial to the survival of Hitler's regime. Economic revival built popular support, strengthened military industries, and provided the basis for German expansion. The Nazi government pursued **pump priming**—stimulating the economy through government spending on tanks and airplanes and on the Autobahn, the German highway system. Unemployment declined from a peak of almost 6 million in 1932 to 1.6 million by 1936. As labor shortages appeared in some areas, the government drafted single women into forced service as farmworkers and domestics. The Nazi Party closed down labor unions, and government managers determined work procedures and set pay levels, rating women's jobs lower than men's regardless of the level of skill required. Imitating Stalin, Hitler announced a four-year plan in 1936 with the secret aim of preparing Germany for war by 1940. His programs produced large deficits, but he was already planning to conquer and loot neighboring countries to recover the costs.

The Nazi government set policies to control everyday life, including gender roles. In June 1933, a bill took effect that encouraged Aryans to marry and have children. The bill provided for loans to Aryan newlyweds, but only to those couples in which the wife left the workforce. The loans were forgiven on the birth of a couple's fourth child. The ideal woman gave up her job, gave birth to many children, and surrendered her will to that of her husband, allowing him to feel powerful despite military defeat and economic depression. A good wife "joyfully sacrifices and fulfills her fate," one Nazi leader explained.

The government also controlled culture, destroying the rich creativity of the Weimar years. Although 70 percent of households had "people's radios" by 1938, programs were severely censored. In May 1933, a huge book-burning ceremony rid libraries of works by Jews, socialists, homosexuals, and modernist writers. Modern art in museums and private collections was destroyed or confiscated. In the Hitler Youth organization, which boys and girls over age ten were required to join, children learned to report to Nazi authorities those adults they suspected of disloyalty to the government, even their own parents. Germans boasted that they could leave their bicycles outdoors at night without fear of the bicycles being stolen, but their world was filled with informers—some 100,000 of whom were on the Nazi payroll. In general, the improved economy led many to believe that Hitler was working an economic miracle while restoring both national pride and the harmonious community of an imaginary past. For hundreds of thousands if not millions of Germans, however, Nazi rule brought anything but harmony and community.

Nazi Racism

Hitler attacked many ethnic and social groups, but he propelled the nineteenth-century politics of anti-Semitism to new and frightening heights. The Nazis defined Jews as an inferior "race" dangerous to the superior Aryan or Germanic "race" and responsible for most of Germany's problems, including its defeat in World War I and the economic depression. In the rhetoric of Nazism, Jews were "vermin," "abscesses," "parasites," and "Bolsheviks," whom the Germans would have to eliminate to create a true Volksgemeinschaft. By defining the Jews as evil financiers and businessmen and as working-class Bolsheviks, Hitler fashioned an enemy for many segments of the German population to hate.

Nazis insisted that terms such as *Aryan* and *Jewish* (a religious category) were scientific racial classifications that could be determined by physical characteristics such as the shape of one's nose. In 1935, the government enacted the **Nuremberg Laws**, which deprived Jews of citizenship and prohibited marriage between Jews and other Germans. Abortions and birth-control information were easily available to outcast groups, including Jews, Gypsies, Slavs, and mentally or physically disabled people. In the name of improving the Aryan race, German doctors helped organize the T4 project, which used carbon monoxide poisoning and other means to kill 200,000 elderly and disabled people—in the late 1930s. Killing people with disabilities was necessary, the Nazis argued, to eliminate those whose "inferiority" endangered Aryans. These murders prepared the way for the even larger mass exterminations in the future.

Jews were forced into slave labor, evicted from their apartments, and prevented from buying most clothing and food. In 1938, a Jewish teenager, reacting to such harassment of his parents, killed a German official. In retaliation, on the night of November 9–10, Nazis attacked some two hundred synagogues, smashed windows of Jewish-owned stores, ransacked apartments of known or suspected Jews, and threw more than twenty thousand Jews into prisons and concentration camps. That event became known as Kristallnacht, the "Night of Broken Glass." Faced with this relentless persecution, more than half of Germany's 500,000 Jews fled the country before the outbreak of World War II in 1939. Their enormous emigration fees helped finance Germany's economic recovery; their neighbors and individual Nazis used anti-Semitism to justify taking the personal possessions and jobs they left behind.

> **REVIEW**   What role did violence play in the Soviet and Nazi regimes?

Democracies on the Defensive

Nazism, communism, and fascism offered bold new approaches to modern politics. These ideologies maintained that democracy wasted precious time in building consensus and that additionally it was effeminate. Totalitarian leaders' energetic, military style of mobilizing the masses made the democratic values of the United States, France, and Great Britain appear feeble—a sign that these societies were on the decline in the struggle for survival. The appeal of totalitarianism put democracies on the defensive as they aimed to uphold individual rights and the rule of law while restoring economic well-being.

Confronting the Economic Crisis

As the depression wore on through the 1930s, some governments experimented with ways to solve social and economic crises while preserving democracy. In the early days of the slump, U.S. president Herbert Hoover opposed direct federal help to the unemployed and even ordered the army to use tanks to break up a march of unemployed World War I veterans in Washington, D.C. With unemployment close to fifteen million, Franklin Delano Roosevelt (1882–1945), the wealthy, patrician governor of New York, defeated Hoover in the presidential election of 1932 on the promise of relief and recovery. Roosevelt pushed through a torrent of legislation known collectively as the New Deal: relief for businesses, price supports for hard-pressed farmers, and public works programs for unemployed youths. The Social Security Act of 1935 set up a fund to which employers and employees contributed. It provided retirement benefits for workers, unemployment insurance, and payments to dependent mothers, their children, and people with disabilities.

Roosevelt's New Deal advanced the trend toward the **welfare state**—that is, a government that guarantees a certain level of economic well-being for individuals and businesses—that was taking shape across the West. The New Deal angered some businesspeople and wealthy Americans, who saw it as socialist, but Roosevelt maintained widespread support. Like other successful politicians of the 1930s, he was an expert at using the mass media, especially in his "fireside chats," broadcast by radio to the American people. Unlike Mussolini and Hitler, Roosevelt used the media to make speeches that promoted rather than attacked faith in democratic

Fireside Chat with FDR
President Franklin Delano Roosevelt was a master of words, uttering many memorable phrases that inspired Americans during the depression and World War II. Here he addresses the nation on August 23, 1938, over a radio hookup while his wife, Eleanor (left), and his mother, Sarah, observe. Although Roosevelt was disabled by polio, wore leg braces, and could not walk unassisted, the press never showed or mentioned his impairment, even on the rare occasions when he used crutches or a wheelchair in public. (Hulton Archive/Getty Images.)

rights and popular government. The participation of First Lady Eleanor Roosevelt contrasted sharply with the antiwoman ideology of the fascists, and the Roosevelts insisted that justice and human rights not be surrendered in difficult times. "We Americans of today . . . are characters in the living book of democracy," President Roosevelt told a group of teenagers in 1939. "But we are also its author." Even so, lynching of blacks and other racial violence continued to cause enormous suffering in the United States during the Roosevelt administration, and the economy did not recover fully. The president, however, was able to keep Americans' faith in democracy strong.

Sweden also developed a coherent program for solving economic and population problems, assigning government a central role in promoting social welfare and economic democracy. Sweden instituted central planning in the 1930s and devalued the currency to make Swedish exports more attractive on the international market. Thanks to pump-priming programs, Swedish productivity rose 20 percent between 1929 and 1935, a time when other democracies were still experiencing an economic decline.

Sweden addressed the population problem with government programs but without racist and antidemocratic coercion. Alva Myrdal, a leading member of parliament, believed that boosting the birthrate depended on both the economy and individual well-being. Acting on Myrdal's advice to promote "voluntary parenthood," the government started a loan program for married couples in 1937 and introduced prenatal care, free childbirth in a hospital, a food relief program, and subsidized housing for large families. By the end of the decade, almost 50 percent of all Swedish mothers received government aid. Long a concern of feminists and other social reformers, support of families became an important task of the modern state, which took on increasing responsibility for citizen welfare in hard times.

The most powerful democracy, the United States, had withdrawn from world leadership by refusing to participate in the League of Nations, leaving Britain and France with greater responsibility for maintaining international peace than their postwar resources could sustain. When the Great Depression hit, British prime minister Ramsay MacDonald faced a drop in government income. Although he was the leader of the Labour Party, he reduced payments to the unemployed, and Parliament denied unemployment insurance to women even though they had contributed to the unemployment fund. To protect jobs, the government imposed huge protective tariffs on imported goods, but that only discouraged a revival of international trade. Finally, in 1933, with the economy continuing to worsen, the government undertook massive programs of slum clearance, new housing construction, and health insurance for the needy. Previously, British leaders had seen pump priming of the economy as untested and thus resorted to it only when all else had failed.

Depression struck later in France than elsewhere, but the country endured a decade of public strife in the 1930s due to severe postwar demoralization and stagnant population growth. Deputies with opposing views on the economic crisis frequently came to blows in the Chamber of Deputies, and administrations were voted in and out with dizzying speed. Parisians took to the streets to protest the government's belt-tightening policies, and Nazi-style paramilitary groups flourished, attracting the unemployed, students, and veterans to the cause of ending representative government. In February 1934, these paramilitary groups joined Communists and other outraged citizens in starting riots around the parliament building. "Let's string up the deputies," chanted the crowd. "And if we can't string them up, let's beat in their faces, let's reduce them to a pulp." Hundreds of demonstrators were wounded or killed, but the antirepublican right lacked both substantial support outside Paris and a charismatic leader like Hitler or Mussolini.

Shocked into action by fascist violence, French liberals, socialists, and Communists established an antifascist coalition known as the Popular Front. Until that time, such a merging of groups had been impossible in democratic countries because Stalin directed Communist parties across Europe not to cooperate with other parties. As fascism spread throughout Europe, however, Stalin reversed course and allowed Communists to join such efforts to protect democracy. For just over a year in 1936–1937 and again briefly in 1938, the French Popular Front led the government, with the socialist leader Léon Blum as premier. Like the American New Dealers and the Swedish reformers, the French Popular Front instituted social welfare programs, including family subsidies and welfare benefits. Blum appointed women to his government (though women in France still were not allowed to vote). In June 1936, the government guaranteed workers a two-week paid vacation, a forty-hour workweek, and the right to bargain collectively. Working people would long remember Blum as the man who improved their living standards and provided them with the right to vacations.

During its brief life, the Popular Front offered the masses a youthful but democratic political culture. "In 1936 everyone was twenty years old," one man recalled, evoking the atmosphere of idealism. To express their opposition to fascism, citizens celebrated democratic holidays like Bastille Day with new enthusiasm. Not everyone liked the Popular Front, however. Powerful business leaders sent their money out of the country, leaving France financially strapped. "Better Hitler Than Blum" was the slogan of the upper classes. Blum's government fell when it lost crucial support from pro–Popular Front voters for refusing to aid the fight against fascism in Spain. Because of antiwar sentiment, France, like Britain, kept its military budgets small and refused to engage in military confrontations, even to help the cause of democratic government in Spain. The collapse of the antifascist Popular Front showed the difficulties that democratic societies had in the face of economic crisis and militaristic nationalism.

Fledgling democracies in central Europe, hit hard by the depression, also fought the twin struggle for economic survival and representative government, but less successfully. In 1932, Engelbert Dollfuss came to power in Austria, dismissing the parliament and ruling briefly as a dictator. Despite his authoritarian views, Dollfuss would not submit to the Nazis, who assassinated him in 1934. In Hungary, where outrage over the Peace of Paris remained intense, a crippled economy allowed right-wing general Gyula Gömbös to take over in 1932. Gömbös reoriented his country's foreign policy toward Mussolini and Hitler. He stirred up anti-Semitism and ethnic hatreds and left behind considerable pro-Nazi feeling after his death in 1936. President Tomas Masaryk worked to maintain a democratic Czechoslovakia, but the Slovaks, who were both poorer and less educated than the urbanized Czechs, built the strong Slovak Fascist Party, while the Communists also attacked democratic government there. In many of the new states created by the Peace of Paris, the appeal of fascism and communism flourished during the Great Depression.

Cultural Visions in Hard Times

Responding to the crisis of economic hard times and political menace, cultural leaders produced art that captured the spirit of everyday struggle. Some sympathized with the situations of factory workers, homemakers, and shopgirls straining to support themselves or their families. Others identified more with the ever-growing numbers of the unemployed and destitute. Artists portrayed the inhuman regimented side of modern life. In 1931, French director René Clair's film À nous la liberté (Give Us

Liberty) related the routine of prison life to working on a factory assembly line. In the film *Modern Times* (1936), the Little Tramp character created by Charlie Chaplin is a factory worker who has been so influenced by his monotonous job that he assumes anything he sees, even a coworker's body, needs mechanical adjustment.

Media sympathy poured out to other victims of the crisis, with women portrayed alternately as the cause and the cure for society's problems. *The Blue Angel* (1930), a German film starring Marlene Dietrich, contrasted a vital and seductive modern woman with an impractical, bumbling professor, showing how mixed-up gender roles could destroy a man—and ultimately civilization. Such films worked to strengthen fascist claims. In comedies and musicals, by comparison, heroines behaved bravely, pulling their men out of the depths of despair and setting things right again. In films such as *Keep Smiling* (1938), the British comedienne Gracie Fields portrayed spunky working-class women who remained cheerful despite hard times.

To drive home their antifascist, pacifist, or pro-worker beliefs, writers created realistic studies of human misery and the threat of war, which haunted life in the 1930s. British writer George Orwell described his experiences among the poor of Paris and London, wrote investigative pieces about the unemployed in the north

Gracie Fields Keeps Smiling
Like Roosevelt and many cultural leaders during the Great Depression, British film stars such as Gracie Fields, shown here in the hit film *Shipyard Sally* (1939), urged viewers to be courageous and maintain their self-respect as workers and citizens despite hard times. This was in stark contrast to fascist advocacy of conquest, war, and violence toward neighbors at home and abroad. (20th Century Fox/The Kobal Collection.)

of England, and published an account of atrocities committed by both sides during the Spanish Civil War (1936–1939). German writer Thomas Mann, a Christian, was so outraged by Hitler's rise to power that he went into voluntary exile. Mann's series of novels based on the Old Testament hero Joseph convey the struggle between humane values and barbarism. The fourth volume, *Joseph the Provider* (1944), praises Joseph's welfare state, in which the granaries are full and the rich pay taxes so the poor might live decent lives. In *Three Guineas* (1938), English writer Virginia Woolf directly attacked militarism, poverty, and the oppression of women, claiming they were interconnected parts of a single, devastating set of values undermining Europe in the 1930s.

While writers renewed moral concerns, scientists in research institutes and universities continued to point out limits to human understanding—limits that seemed at odds with the megalomaniacal pronouncements of dictators. Astronomer Edwin Hubble in California determined in the early 1930s that the universe was an expanding entity and thus an unpredictably changing one. Czech mathematician Kurt Gödel maintained that all mathematical systems contain some propositions that are undecidable. German physicist Werner Heisenberg developed the uncertainty, or indeterminacy, principle. Scientific observation of atomic behavior, according to this theory, itself disturbs the atom, thereby making precise formulations impossible. Even scientists, Heisenberg asserted, had to settle for statistical probability. Probability and limits to understanding were not concepts that dictators welcomed, and even people in democracies had a difficult time reconciling these new ideas with science's reputation for certainty.

Religious leaders helped foster a spirit of resistance to dictatorship among the faithful. Swiss theologian Karl Barth encouraged rebellion against the Nazis, teaching that religious people had to take seriously biblical calls for resistance to oppression. In his 1931 address to the world on social issues, Pope Pius XI condemned the failure of modern societies to provide their citizens with a decent, moral life. To critics, the proclamation seemed to endorse the heavy-handed intervention of the fascists. In Germany, nonetheless, Catholics frequently opposed Hitler, and religious commitment inspired many other individuals to contest the rising tide of fascism.

REVIEW How did the democracies work to maintain their values while facing the twin challenges of economic depression and the rise of fascism?

The Road to Global War

The economic crash intensified competition among the major powers and made external colonies more important than ever. Hitler, Mussolini, and Japan's military leaders believed that their nations deserved to rule far larger territories. At first, statesmen in Britain and France hoped that sanctions imposed by the League of Nations would stop aggression. Others, still traumatized by memories of World War I, wanted to turn a blind eye to German, Italian, and Japanese expansionism and to the fascist attack on the Spanish republic. The unchecked brutality of these states in the 1930s led to another, more deadly war.

A Surge in Global Imperialism

The surging global imperialism of the 1930s ultimately led to a thoroughly global war. The British, French, and other European powers increased their grip on the colonies, while in Palestine European Jews continued to arrive and claim the area from local people, especially as Hitler enacted his harsh anti-Jewish policies. Also troubled economically, Japan, Germany, and Italy increased the competition for land and wealth in areas both close at hand and far away.

The Road to World War II	
1929	Global depression begins with the U.S. stock market crash
1931	Japan invades Manchuria
1933	Hitler comes to power in Germany
1935	Italy invades Ethiopia
1936	Civil war breaks out in Spain; Hitler remilitarizes the Rhineland
1937	Japan invades China
1938	Germany annexes Austria; European leaders meet in Munich to negotiate with Hitler
1939	Germany seizes Czechoslovakia; Hitler and Stalin sign a nonaggression pact; Germany invades Poland; Britain and France declare war on Germany

Japan, which had once borrowed from European institutions to become modern and powerful, now decided to chase Europeans out of Asia. Japan's military and business leaders wanted to control more of Asia and saw China, the Soviet Union, and the Western powers as obstacles to the empire's prosperity and the fulfillment of its destiny. Japan suffered from a weak monarchy in the person of Hirohito, just twenty-five years old when he became emperor in 1926, leading military and other groups to seek control of the government. Nationalists encouraged these leaders to pursue military success for Japan as the key to pulling agriculture and small business out of the depths of economic depression. A belief in racial superiority linked Japan with Germany and Italy in the 1930s, laying the groundwork for a global alliance.

The Japanese army swung into action in 1931, when Japanese officers blew up a train in the Chinese province of Manchuria, where Japanese businesses had invested heavily. Making the incident look like a Chinese plot, the army used the explosion as an excuse to invade Manchuria, set up a puppet government, and push farther into China. The Japanese public agreed with journalistic calls for aggressive expansion, and from 1931 on, Japan continued to attack China, angering the United States, on which Japan depended for natural resources and markets. Advocating Asian conquest as part of Japan's "divine mission," the military extended its influence in the government. By 1936–1937, Japan was spending 47 percent of its budget on arms.

The situation in East Asia affected international politics. The League of Nations condemned the invasion of Manchuria, but it imposed no sanctions on Japan to back up its condemnation. Yet, the league's condemnation outraged Japanese citizens and goaded the government to ally with Hitler and Mussolini. In 1937, Japan attacked China again, justifying its offensive as the first step toward liberating the region from Western imperialism. Hundreds of thousands of Chinese were massacred in the Rape of Nanjing—an atrocity so named because of the brutality toward girls and women and other acts of torture perpetrated by the Japanese. President Roosevelt immediately announced a U.S. embargo on the exportation of airplane parts to Japan and later drastically cut the flow of crucial raw materials that supplied Japanese industry. Nonetheless, the Western powers, including the Soviet Union, did not effectively resist Japan's territorial expansion in Asia and the Pacific.

Like Japanese leaders, Mussolini and Hitler called their countries "have-nots" and demanded land and resources more in line with those of the other imperial powers. Mussolini threatened "permanent conflict" to expand Italy's borders, and Hitler's agenda included breaking free from the Versailles treaty's military restrictions on Germany and gaining *Lebensraum*—"living space" in which superior Aryans could thrive. This space would be taken from the "inferior" Slavic peoples and Bolsheviks, who would be moved to Siberia or serve as slaves. Both dictators portrayed themselves as peace-loving men who resorted to extreme measures only to benefit their countries and humanity. Their anticommunism appealed to statesmen across Europe, and Hitler's anti-Semitism found widespread support as well.

Both leaders moved to plunder other countries boldly and openly. In the autumn of 1933, Germany withdrew from the League of Nations. In 1935, Hitler loudly

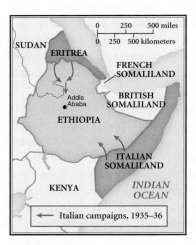

The Ethiopian War, 1935–1936

rejected the clauses of the Treaty of Versailles that limited German military strength as he reintroduced military conscription and started openly rearming. (Germany had been rearming in secret for years.) Mussolini chose 1935 to invade Ethiopia, one of the few African states not overwhelmed by European imperialism. He wanted to demonstrate his regime's youth and vigor and to raise Italy's standing in the world. "The Roman legionnaires are again on the march," one soldier exulted. The poorly equipped Ethiopians resisted, but their capital, Addis Ababa, fell in the spring of 1936. The League of Nations voted sanctions against Italy; Britain and France, however, opposed an embargo on oil, thus keeping the sanctions from being effective while also suggesting a lack of resolve to fight aggression.

In March 1936, Hitler, profiting from world attention on Italy's attack on Ethiopia, defiantly sent his troops into the Rhineland (bordering France), which was supposed to be a permanently demilitarized zone. The inhabitants greeted the Germans with wild enthusiasm, and the French, whose security was most endangered by this action, protested to the League of Nations instead of occupying the region. The British simply accepted the remilitarization. Hitler and Mussolini thus appeared as powerful military heroes, creating, in Mussolini's muscular phrase, the "Rome-Berlin Axis." Next to them, the politicians of France and Great Britain looked timid and weak.

The Spanish Civil War, 1936–1939

Spain seemed to be headed toward democracy in the early 1930s. In 1931, Spanish republicans overthrew the monarchy and the dictatorship that ruled in its name. For centuries the Spanish state had backed the rule of large landowners and the Catholic clergy over the countryside. With cities like Barcelona and Bilbao industrializing, these ruling elites kept the impoverished peasantry in their grip, making Spain a country of economic extremes. Urban groups reacted enthusiastically to the end of the dictatorship and began debating the course of change, with Communists, social-ists, anarchists, constitutionalists, and other groups all disagreeing on how to create a democratic nation. Democratic groups so battled one another that the republic had a hard time putting in place a political program that would gain it support in the countryside. Instead of building popular loyalty and reducing the strength of the political right through land redistribution, republicans failed to mount a unified effort against their reactionary opponents. In 1936, pro-republican groups temporar-ily banded together in the Popular Front coalition to win elections and prevent the republic from collapsing under the weight of growing monarchist opposition.

In response to the Popular Front victory, the forces of the right drew closer together, using their considerable wealth to undermine the government. In 1936, a group of army officers staged an uprising against the republican government in Madrid (Map 21.1). The rebel officers soon found a determined leader, General Francisco Franco (1892–1975), and an alliance of monarchists, landowners, the clergy, and the fascist Falange Party soon gained support from fascists in other parts of Europe. Spain became a training ground for World War II. Hitler and

Map 21.1 The Spanish Civil War, 1936–1939
Pro-republican and antirepublican forces fought one another to determine whether Spain would be a democracy or an authoritarian state. Germany and Italy sent opponents of the Spanish republic military assistance, notably airplanes to experiment with bombing civilians, while volunteers from around the world arrived to fight for the republic. Defeating these ill-organized groups, General Francisco Franco insti-tuted a pro-fascist government that sent many people to jail and into exile.

Mussolini sent military personnel to support Franco, gaining an opportunity to test new weapons and to practice the terror bombing of civilians. In 1937, low-flying German planes attacked the Spanish town of Guernica on market day, mowing down civilians in the streets. This useless slaughter inspired Pablo Picasso's memorial mural to the dead, *Guernica* (1937), in which the intense suffering is starkly displayed in monochromatic grays and whites.

The Spanish republic appealed everywhere for assistance, but only the Soviet Union answered. In 1938, as the Spanish government's position weakened, Stalin withdrew his support. Britain and France showed their war-wariness by refusing to provide crucial aid. Instead, a few thousand volunteers from a variety of countries—including students, journalists, and artists—remained to fight for the republic. These volunteers believed that with Mussolini and Hitler on a rampage in Europe, "Spain was the place to stop fascism." The conflict was bitter and bloody, with atrocities committed on both sides, but the splinter groups and citizen armies with which the Spanish republic defended itself could not hold. Franco's troops, bolstered decisively by aid from Hitler and Mussolini, defeated the republicans in 1939, strengthening the cause of military authoritarianism in Europe. Tens of thousands fled, while many others found themselves jailed or killed by Franco's new pro-fascist government.

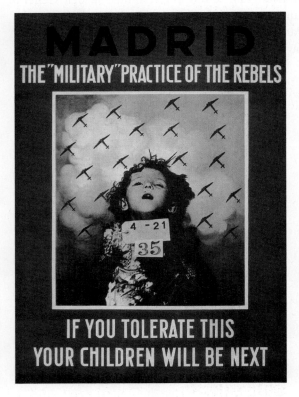

The Spanish Republic Appeals for Aid
The government of the Spanish republic sent out modern advertising and propaganda to attract support from the democracies, especially Great Britain and France. Antiwar sentiment remained high among the British and French, however, and despite the horrifying and deliberate bombing of civilians by Franco's German allies, aid for the republic failed to arrive. (Imperial War Museum, London.)

Hitler's Conquest of Central Europe, 1938–1939

The next step toward World War II was Germany's annexation of Austria in 1938 (Map 21.2). Many Austrians had actually wished for such a merger, or *Anschluss,* after the Paris peace settlement had stripped them of their empire, and Hitler himself had been born in Austria. So Hitler's troops easily entered Austria, and the enthusiasm of Nazi sympathizers made the Anschluss appear to reflect the Wilsonian

Map 21.2 The Growth of Nazi Germany, 1933–1939
German expansion was rapid and surprising, as Hitler's forces and Nazi diplomacy brought about the annexation of the new states of central and eastern Europe. Though committed to defending the sovereignty of these states through the League of Nations, French and British diplomats were more interested in satisfying Hitler because they believed that doing so would prevent his claiming even more of Europe. They were mistaken, and Hitler proceeded to take the human and material resources of adjacent countries to support the Third Reich. **For more help analyzing this map, see the map activity for this chapter in the Online Study Guide at** bedfordstmartins.com/huntconcise.

idea of self-determination. The annexation began the so-called unification of Aryan peoples into one greater German nation, and Hitler's seizure of Austrian gold supplies marked the next step in taking over central and eastern Europe. Austria was declared a German province, and Nazi thugs ruled once cosmopolitan Vienna. An observer later commented on the scene: "University professors were obliged to scrub the streets with their naked hands, pious white-bearded Jews were dragged into the synagogue by hooting youths and forced to do knee-exercises and to shout 'Heil Hitler' in chorus." The Nazis gained additional support in Austria by solving the stubborn problem of unemployment. Factories sprang up overnight, mostly to fuel rearmament, and new "Hitler housing" became available to workers. German policies eliminated some of the psychological pain Austrians had suffered when their empire had been reduced to a small country after World War I.

With Austria firmly in his grasp, Hitler turned next to Czechoslovakia and its rich resources. Conquering this democracy looked more difficult, however, because Czechoslovakia had a large army, strong border defenses, and efficient armament factories, and most Czech citizens were prepared to fight for their country. The Nazi propaganda machine swung into action, accusing Czechoslovakia of persecuting its German minority. By October 1, 1938, Hitler warned, Czechoslovakia would have to grant autonomy (tantamount to Nazi rule) to the German-populated border region, the Sudetenland, or face German invasion.

Hitler gambled correctly that the other Western powers would not interfere. As the October deadline approached, British prime minister Neville Chamberlain, French premier Edouard Daladier, and Mussolini met with Hitler in Munich and agreed not to oppose Germany's claim to the Sudetenland. The Czechs themselves had no say in the matter. The strategy of preventing a war by making concessions for grievances (in this case, the alleged affront to Germans in the Peace of Paris) was called **appeasement**. At the time, these concessions were widely seen as positive, and the Munich Pact among Germany, Great Britain, France, and Italy prompted Chamberlain to announce that he had secured "peace in our time." Having portrayed himself as a man of peace, Hitler waited until March 1939 to invade Czechoslovakia. Britain and France responded by promising military support to Poland, Romania, Greece, and Turkey in case of Nazi invasion. In May 1939, Hitler and Mussolini countered this agreement by signing a pledge of offensive and defensive support called the Pact of Steel.

Some historians have sharply criticized the Munich Pact because it bought Hitler time to build his army and seemed to give him the green light for further aggression. They believe that a confrontation might have stopped Hitler and that even if war had resulted, the democracies would have triumphed at less cost than they later did. According to this view, each military move by Germany, Italy, and Japan should have been met with stiff opposition, and the Soviet Union should have been made a partner in this resistance. Others counter that appeasement gave France and Britain precious time to beef up their own armies, which the Munich crisis prompted them to do.

Stalin, excluded from the Munich deliberations, saw that the democracies were not going to fight to protect eastern Europe. He took action. To the astonishment of people in the West, on August 23, 1939, Germany and the USSR signed a nonaggression agreement. The **Nazi-Soviet Pact** provided that if one country became involved in war, the other country would remain neutral. Moreover, the two dictators secretly agreed to divide Poland and the Baltic states—Latvia, Estonia, and Lithuania—at some future date. The Nazi-Soviet Pact ensured that if war came, the democracies would be fighting a Germany with no fear of attack on its eastern borders. The pact also benefited the USSR. Despite Hitler's ambition to wipe Bolshevism from the face of the earth, the pact allowed Stalin time to rebuild his officer corps, which had been destroyed in the purges. Believing that Great Britain and perhaps even France would continue not to resist him, Hitler moved to enlarge his empire further and aimed his forces at Poland.

> **REVIEW** How did the aggression of Japan, Germany, and Italy create the conditions for global war?

World War II, 1939–1945

World War II officially began when Germany launched an all-out attack on Poland on September 1, 1939. In contrast to 1914, no jubilation in Berlin accompanied the invasion; when Britain and France declared war two days later, the mood in their capitals was similarly grim. Although Japan, Italy, and the United States did not join the battle immediately, their eventual participation spread the fighting throughout the world. By the time World War II ended in 1945, millions were starving, entire countries lay in ruins, and unparalleled atrocities, including technological genocide, had killed six million Jews and six million Slavs, Gypsies, homosexuals, and other civilian enemies of fascism.

The German Onslaught

German forces quickly defeated the ill-equipped Polish troops by launching an overpowering **Blitzkrieg** (lightning war). The Germans concentrated airplanes, tanks, and motorized infantry to encircle Polish defenders and capture the capital, Warsaw, with blinding speed. Allowing the German army to conserve supplies, Blitzkrieg assured Germans at home that the human costs of gaining Lebensraum would be low. On September 17, 1939, Soviet forces invaded Poland from the east. By the end of the month, the Polish army was in shambles, and the victors had divided Poland according to the Nazi-Soviet Pact. Within the Reich, Hitler sold the war as one of self-defense, especially from what German propagandists called the "warlike menace" of world Jewry.

Hitler ordered an attack on France in November 1939, but his generals, who feared that Germany was ill prepared for total war, were able to postpone the offensive until the spring of 1940. In April 1940, Blitzkrieg crushed Denmark and Norway; the

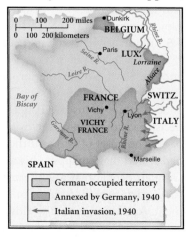

The Division of France, 1940

battles of Belgium, the Netherlands, and France followed in May and June. On June 5, Mussolini, eyeing future spoils for Italy, invaded France from the southeast. The French and their British allies could not withstand the German onslaught. Trapped on the beaches of Dunkirk in northern France, 370,000 British and French soldiers were rescued in a heroic effort by an improvised fleet of naval ships, fishing boats, and pleasure craft. A dejected French government surrendered on June 22, 1940, leaving Germany to rule the northern half of France, including Paris. In the south, known as Vichy France after the spa town where the government sat, Germany allowed the reactionary and aged World War I hero Henri Philippe Pétain to govern. Stalin used the diversion in western Europe to annex the Baltic states.

Britain now stood alone. Blaming Germany's rapid victories on Chamberlain's policy of appeasement, British voters swept him out of office and replaced him as prime minister with Winston Churchill (1874–1965), an early advocate of resistance to Hitler. After Hitler ordered the bombardment of Britain in the summer of 1940, Churchill rallied the nation by radio—now in more than nine million British homes—to protect the ideals of liberty with their "blood, toil, tears, and sweat." In the battle of Britain, or Blitz as the British called it, the German air force (Luftwaffe) bombed public buildings, monuments, weapons depots, and factories. Using the wealth of its colonies, Britain poured resources into antiaircraft weapons, a highly successful code-breaking group called Ultra, and the development of radar. At year's end, the British air industry was outproducing the Germans by 50 percent.

By the fall of 1940, German air losses forced Hitler to abandon his plan for a naval invasion of Britain. By forcing Hungary, Romania, and Bulgaria to join the Axis powers, Germany gained access to more food and oil. Hitler then made his fatal decision to attack the Soviet Union—the "center of judeobolshevism," as he called it. In June 1941, the German army crossed the Soviet border, breaking the Nazi-Soviet Pact, while Hitler promised to "raze Moscow and Leningrad to the ground." Three million German and other troops quickly penetrated Soviet lines along a two-thousand-mile front, and by July the German army had rolled to within two hundred miles of Moscow, eventually reaching its suburbs. Using a strategy of rapid encirclement, the Germans killed, captured, and wounded more than half the 4.5 million Soviet soldiers defending the border.

Amid this rapid success, Hitler blundered. Considering himself a military genius and the Slavic people inferior, he proposed attacking Leningrad, the Baltic states, and the Ukraine simultaneously, a plan that went against his generals' recommendation to concentrate on Moscow. Hitler's grand scheme cost precious time without achieving a decisive victory, and driven by Stalin and local party members, the Soviet people fought back. The onset of winter turned Nazi soldiers into frostbitten wretches because Hitler had feared that equipping his army for the harsh Russian winter would suggest to the German people that a long campaign lay in store, as in fact it did. Germany's poorly supplied armies succumbed to the weather, disease, and ultimately a shortage of equipment. As the war spread worldwide, Germany continued to have an inflated sense of its own power even though the Russian campaign suggested the limits of that power.

The War Expands: The Pacific and Beyond

With the outbreak of war in Europe, Japan took territories in the British Empire, bullied the Dutch in Indonesia, and invaded French Indochina to procure raw materials for its industrial and military expansion. The militarist Japanese government decided to settle matters with the United States, which was trying to block Japan's expansion, and launched an all-out attack on Pearl Harbor in Hawaii on December 7, 1941. After bombing Pearl Harbor, Japanese planes decimated a fleet of U.S. airplanes in the Philippines. Roosevelt immediately summoned Congress to declare war on Japan. By the spring of 1942, the Japanese had conquered Guam, the Philippines, Malaya, Burma, Indonesia, Singapore, and much of the southwestern Pacific. Like Hitler's early conquests, these victories strengthened the Japanese military's confidence. "The era of democracy is finished," the foreign minister announced.

Within days of Pearl Harbor, Germany joined its Japanese ally and declared war on the United States—an enemy, Hitler proclaimed, that was "half Judaized and the other half Negrified." Mussolini followed suit. The United States was not prepared for a long struggle, partly because isolationist sentiment remained strong. Its armed forces numbered only 1.6 million, and no plan existed for producing the necessary guns, tanks, and airplanes. In addition, the United States and the Soviet Union did not trust each other. Despite these obstacles to cooperation, Hitler's four enemies came together in the Grand Alliance of Great Britain, the Free French (a government in exile in London led by General Charles de Gaulle), the Soviet Union, and the United States. The Grand Alliance formed a larger coalition with twenty other countries, which became known as the Allies. Given the urgency of war and the partners' competing interests, the Allies had much internal strife to overcome in their struggle against the Axis powers (Germany, Italy, and Japan). Yet in the long run, the Allies had distinct advantages: their vast potential for war in terms of manpower and resources and their experience in waging war on many continents. Meeting frequently, the Allied leaders worked hard to wage an effective war, while the Axis rulers paid less attention to cooperation and to the material realities of waging total war.

The War against Civilians

Far more civilians than soldiers died in World War II. The Axis powers and Allies alike bombed cities simply to destroy civilians' will to resist—a tactic that seemed to backfire by inspiring defiance rather than surrender. Two such Allied attacks were the firebombing of Dresden and Tokyo, which killed tens of thousands of civilians, though Axis attacks were far more widespread. As the German army swept through eastern Europe, it slaughtered Jews, Communists, Slavs, and others whom the Nazis deemed "racial inferiors" and enemies. In Poland, the SS murdered hundreds of thousands of Polish citizens or relocated them to forced labor camps, with confiscated Polish land and homes being given to "racially pure" Aryans from Germany and other central European countries. Literate people in conquered areas were the most vulnerable, because Hitler, like Stalin, saw them as leading members of the people he wanted to destroy. Because many in the German army initially rebelled at killing innocent civilians simply because they could read, special Gestapo forces took charge of herding their victims into woods and ravines, or even against town walls, where they would be shot en masse. The Japanese did the same in China, Southeast Asia, and the islands of the Pacific. The number of casualties in China alone has been estimated at thirty million, with untold millions murdered elsewhere.

The Nazis focused on the extermination of the Jews, herding them first into urban ghettos with minimal provisions. Around captured Soviet towns, Jews were usually shot in pits, some of which they had been forced to dig themselves. After shedding their clothes and putting them in orderly piles for later Nazi use, ten thousand or more at a time were killed, often with the help of anti-Semitic villagers. In Jedwabne, Poland, some eight hundred citizens on their own initiative beat and burned their Jewish neighbors to death and took their property—evidence that the **Holocaust** was not simply a Nazi program. At this time, however, the "Final Solution"—the Nazis' evil plan to exterminate all of Europe's Jews—was not yet fully under way.

Life in the Warsaw Ghetto
The occupying Nazis resettled Warsaw's Jews into a minuscule area of the city in order, the Germans explained, to bring "moral purification" and to keep Germans from being infected by these "carriers of the bacteria of epidemics." Surviving on extremely small amounts of food and fuel, Warsaw's Jews died daily on the streets. Corpses were a common sight for the average citizen—young or old. (ullstein bild/The Granger Collection, NY.)

A more organized, technological system for rounding up Jews and transporting them to extermination sites had taken shape by the fall of 1941. Hitler had long predicted "the destruction of the Jewish race in Europe," so although no order written by Hitler exists, his responsibility for it is clear. He discussed the Final Solution's progress, issued oral directives for it, and made violent anti-Semitism a basis for Nazism from the beginning. Efficient scientists, doctors, lawyers, and government workers also made the Holocaust work. Six camps in Poland were developed specifically for the purpose of mass murder, although some, like Auschwitz-Birkenau, served as both extermination and labor camps (Map 21.3). Using techniques developed in the T4 project in the late 1930s, the camp at Chelmno first gassed Christian Poles and Soviet prisoners of war. Specially designed crematoria for the mass burning of corpses started functioning in 1943. By then, Auschwitz had the capacity to burn 1.7 million bodies per year. About 60 percent of new arrivals—particularly children, women, and the elderly—were selected for immediate murder in the gas chambers; the other 40 percent labored until, utterly used up, they too were gassed.

Victims from all over Europe were sent to the extermination camps. In the ghettos of various European cities, councils of Jewish leaders, such as the one in Amsterdam where Etty Hillesum worked, were ordered to decide on those to be "resettled in the east." For weakened, poorly armed ghetto inhabitants, open resistance meant certain death. When Jews rose up against their Nazi captors in Warsaw in 1943, they were mercilessly butchered. The Nazis also took pains to cloak their true purposes in the extermination camps. Bands played to greet incoming trainloads of victims; some new arrivals were given postcards with reassuring messages to mail home. Those not

Map 21.3 Concentration Camps and Extermination Sites in Europe This map shows the major extermination sites and concentration camps in Europe, but the entire continent was dotted with thousands of lesser camps to which the Nazis' victims were transported. Some of these lesser camps were merely way stations on the path to ultimate extermination. In focusing on the major camps, historians often lose sight of the other deportation and extermination centers that blanketed Europe.

chosen for immediate murder had their heads shaved, were disinfected, and were given prison garments. So began life in "a living hell," as one survivor wrote.

The camps were scenes of the struggle for life in the face of torture and death. Overworked inmates were extremely undernourished, usually receiving less than five hundred calories per day. This left them vulnerable to typhus and other diseases that swept through the camps. Prisoners sometimes went mad, as did many of the guards. In the name of advancing "racial science," doctors performed unbelievably cruel experiments with no anesthesia on pregnant women, twins, and others. Despite the harsh conditions, some people maintained their spirit: prisoners forged new friendships, and women in particular observed religious holidays and celebrated birthdays—all of which helped in the struggle for survival. Thanks to those sharing a bread ration and doing him favors, wrote the Auschwitz survivor Primo Levi, "I managed not to forget that I myself was a man." Yet part of the horror of the Holocaust was how systematically and efficiently mass murder was carried out. Ordinary, supposedly civilized people committed this vast genocidal crime, whose planned, bureaucratic organization still shocks and outrages the world.

Societies at War

Even more than World War I, World War II depended on industrial productivity aimed totally toward war and mass killings. The Axis countries remained at a disadvantage throughout the war, for the Allies simply outproduced them. Even while Germany occupied the Soviet industrial heartland and besieged many of its cities, the USSR increased its production of weapons. Both Japan and Germany made the most of their lower capacity, especially in the use of the Blitzkrieg. Hitler had to avoid imposing wartime austerity because he had come to power promising to end economic suffering, not increase it. The use of millions of slave laborers and foreign resources from occupied areas helped, but both Japan's and Germany's belief in their racial superiority worked against them by preventing them from accurately estimating the capabilities of the enemies they held in contempt.

The Allied governments were overwhelmingly successful in mobilizing civilians, especially women. In the Axis countries, where government policy particularly exalted motherhood and kept women out of good jobs, officials realized too late that women were desperately needed in the workforce. They could not change their propaganda effectively enough to convince women to take the low-paid work offered them. In contrast, Soviet women constituted more than half the workforce by war's end, and 800,000 volunteered for the military, even serving as pilots. As the Germans invaded the USSR, Soviet citizens moved entire factories eastward. In a dramatic about-face, the government encouraged devotion to the Russian Orthodox church as a way of inspiring patriotism.

Even more than in World War I, civilians were bombarded with huge amounts of propaganda when they went to the movies or listened to the radio. People were glued to their radios for war news, but much of it was tightly controlled. The totalitarian powers often withheld news of defeats and high casualty numbers to keep civilian support. Wartime films depicted aviation heroes and infantrymen as well as the working women and wives left behind. Government agencies monitored filmmaking and allocated supplies only to approved films.

Between 1939 and 1945, governments organized many aspects of everyday life—a necessity because resources such as food had to be shifted away from civilians toward soldiers and military needs. In most countries, it was simply taken for granted that civilians would not receive what they needed to survive in good health. A high number of Soviet children and old people were among the one million residents who starved to death during the German siege of Leningrad. Government agencies regulated the production and distribution of clothing and household products, all of which were rationed and generally of low quality. They gave hints for preparing meals without meat, sugar, fat, and other staples and urged women and children to embrace deprivation so that fighting men could have more. With governments standardizing items such as food, clothing, and entertainment, World War II furthered the development of a mass society in which people lived and thought in similar ways.

On both sides, propaganda and government policies promoted racial thinking. Since the early 1930s, the German government had published ugly caricatures of Jews, Slavs, and Gypsies. Similarly, Allied propaganda during the war depicted Germans as perverts and "Japs" as insectlike fanatics. The U.S. government forced citizens of Japanese origin into internment camps. In the Soviet Union, Muslims and minority ethnic groups were uprooted and relocated away from the front lines as potential Nazi collaborators. Both sides drew colonized peoples into the war through forced labor and conscription into their armies. Some two million Indians served the Allied cause, as did several hundred thousand Africans. As the Japanese swept through the Pacific and parts of East Asia, they too conscripted men into their army.

From Resistance to Allied Victory

Resistance to fascism and Nazi control began early in the war. General Charles de Gaulle directed the Free French government and its forces from England. The Free French were a mixed organization of troops of colonized Asians and Africans, French troops who had been evacuated from Dunkirk, and volunteers from Axis-occupied countries. Less well known than the Free French were Communist-dominated groups of resisters throughout occupied Europe, some of whom gathered information to aid a planned Allied landing on the French coast. Rural partisans in many countries not only plotted assassinations of traitors and German officers but also bombed bridges, rail lines, and military facilities in German-occupied areas. The Polish resistance worked tirelessly against the Nazis, as did individuals such as Swedish diplomat Raoul Wallenberg, whose dealings with Nazi officials saved thousands of Hungarian Jews.

People fought back through everyday activities. Homemakers circulated newsletters urging demonstrations at prisons where civilians were detained. In central Europe, hikers smuggled Jews and others through dangerous mountain passes.

Danish villagers created vast escape networks, while women resisters used stereo-types to good advantage, often carrying weapons to assassination sites in the correct belief that the Nazis were not likely to suspect or search them. They also seduced and murdered enemy officers. Other actions subtly undermined the demands of fascist leaders. "Naturally the Germans didn't think that a woman could have carried a bomb," explained one Italian resister, "so this became the woman's task." Resistance kept alive the liberal ideal of individual political action in the face of tyranny.

Both subtle and dramatically visible resistance took place in fascist countries. Couples in Germany and Italy limited family size in defiance of pro-birth policies. German teenagers danced the forbidden American jitterbug, thus disobeying the Nazis and forcing the use of scarce manpower to police their groups. More spectacu-larly, in July 1944 a group of German military officers, fearing their country's military humiliation, tried but failed to assassinate Hitler—one of several such attempts. Some ask whether the assassination attempt came too late in the war to count as true resis-tance. However, some five million Germans alone, and millions more people of other nationalities, lost their lives in the last nine months of the war. Had Hitler died even as late as the summer of 1944, the relief to humanity would have been considerable.

Amid civilian resistance, Allied forces turned the frontline war against the Axis powers beginning in mid-1942 at the battle of Stalingrad (Map 21.4)—a battle to gain access to Soviet oil. Months of ferocious fighting ended when the Soviet army captured the ninety thousand German survivors in February 1943. Allied victories in North Africa in 1942, where British code-breaking capabilities foiled German general Erwin Rommel's innovative tactics, were followed in July 1943 by an Allied landing in Sicily, provoking a German invasion and takeover of Italy's war effort. A slow, bitter fight for the Italian peninsula lasted until April 1945, when Allied forces finally triumphed. After Italy's liberation, partisans shot Mussolini and his mistress and hung their dead bodies for public display.

The victory at Stalingrad marked the beginning of the Soviet drive westward, dur-ing which the Soviets bore the brunt of the Nazi war machine. From the air, Britain and the United States bombed German cities, aiming to destroy war industries and demoralize citizens. But it was an invasion from the west that Stalin wanted from his allies. Finally, on June 6, 1944, the combined Allied forces under the command of U.S. general Dwight Eisenhower landed on the heavily fortified beaches of Normandy and then fought their way through the German-held territory of western France. In late July, Allied forces broke through German defenses and a month later helped liberate Paris. The Soviets meanwhile captured the Baltic states and entered Poland, pausing

Map 21.4 World War II in Europe and North Africa
The Axis and Allied powers waged war in Europe and Africa, inflicting massive loss of life on civilians and armies alike and widespread destruction of property, including the infrastructure—factories, equipment, and agriculture—needed to wage total war. The war affected the entire European con-tinent, as well as areas of Africa colonized by or allied with the major powers. Ultimately, the Allies crushed the Axis powers by squeezing them from the east, west, and south.

The Siege of Leningrad
In the face of the Nazi invasion in 1941, Soviet citizens reacted heroically, moving entire factories to the interior of the country and building fortifications. Nowhere was their resolve so tested as in Leningrad (now St. Petersburg). For more than two years, the German army besieged the city, causing the deaths of hundreds of thousands of people. Before the Allied landing at Normandy in 1944, the people of the USSR bore the brunt of Nazi military might in Hitler's attempt to defeat what he called "judeobolshevism." (Sovfoto/Eastfoto.)

for desperately needed supplies from behind their lines. The Germans took advantage of the pause to put down an uprising of the Polish resistance in 1944, which gave the Soviets a freer hand in eastern Europe after the war. Facing more than twice as many troops as on the western front, the Soviet army took Bulgaria and Romania and then faced fierce German fighting in Hungary during the winter of 1944–1945. British, Canadian, U.S., and other Allied forces simultaneously fought their way eastward to join the Soviets in squeezing the Third Reich to its final defeat.

As the Allies advanced, Hitler maintained that the German people were proving themselves unworthy of his greatness and deserved to perish in a bloody downfall. He thus refused all negotiations that might have spared them further death and destruction from the relentless bombing. As the Soviet army took Berlin, Hitler and his wife, Eva Braun, committed suicide. Although many German soldiers remained loyal to the Third Reich, Germany finally surrendered on May 8, 1945.

The Allies had followed a "Europe first" strategy in conducting the war. They had nonetheless pursued the Japanese in the Pacific without pause (Map 21.5). In 1940 and 1941, Japan had ousted the Europeans from many colonial holdings in Asia,

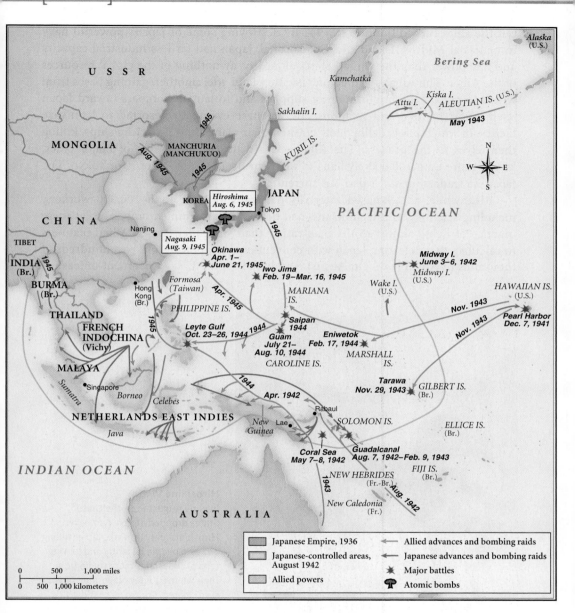

Map 21.5 World War II in the Pacific

As in Europe, the early days of World War II gave the advantage to the Axis powers in the Pacific, as Japan took the offensive in conquering islands and parts of Asia, many of them colonies of Allied states. Britain countered by mobilizing a vast Indian army. After the disastrous losses at Pearl Harbor and in the Philippines, the Allies gradually gained the upper hand by conducting costly assaults, island by island. The Japanese strategy of fighting to the last person instead of surrendering when a loss was in sight was one factor in the decision to drop the atomic bombs in August 1945.

but the allies turned the tide in 1942 by destroying some of Japan's powerful navy in battles at Midway Island and Guadalcanal. Japan had far less industrial capacity and manpower than the United States alone, to say nothing of the global resources of the Allies. The Allies stormed one Pacific island after another, gaining bases from which to cut off the importation of supplies and to launch bombers toward Japan itself. Short of men and weapons, the Japanese eventually resorted to kamikaze tactics, in which pilots deliberately crashed their planes into American ships, killing themselves in the process. The Allies stepped up their bombing of major cities, killing more than 100,000 civilians in their spring 1945 firebombing of Tokyo. The Japanese leadership still ruled out surrender.

Meanwhile, a U.S.-based international team of more than 100,000 workers, including scientists and technicians, had developed an atomic bomb. The Japanese practice of dying almost to the man rather than surrender caused Allied planners to calculate that defeating Japan with conventional weapons might cost hundreds of thousands of Allied lives. On August 6 and 9, 1945, the U.S. government unleashed

Hiroshima Victim
In early August 1945, the United States dropped atomic bombs on Hiroshima and Nagasaki, Japan, killing 140,000 people instantly and leaving tens of thousands more to die from their wounds. A few days later, Japan surrendered. Controversy still swirls around the decision to drop the bombs. People who see it as a racist act point out that no atomic weapons were dropped on Germany. People who see it as a justified act of warfare point out that Japan's no-surrender policy increased the likelihood of countless more casualties. (Tokyo/Fuji/ Sumiko Kurita/Gamma.)

its new atomic weapon on Hiroshima and Nagasaki, respectively, killing 140,000 people instantly; tens of thousands later died from burns, wounds, and other afflictions. Hard-liners in the Japanese military still wanted to continue the war, but on August 14, 1945, Japan surrendered.

An Uneasy Postwar Settlement

Throughout the war, Allied leaders had met not only to plan strategy but also to resolve postwar issues. Unlike after World War I, however, there was neither a celebrated peace conference nor a definitive, formal agreement among all the Allies about the final terms for peace. Yet peace and recovery were more important than ever: Europe lay in ruins, and tens of millions were starving. Because the victorious Allies distrusted one another in varying degrees, with the United States and Soviet Union moving toward another war, the future looked grim.

Wartime agreements among members of the Grand Alliance about the future reflected their differences and became the subject of intense postwar debate. In 1941, Roosevelt and Churchill crafted the Atlantic Charter, which condemned aggression and supported collective security and the right of all peoples to choose their governments. Not only did the Allies support these ideals, but so did colonized peoples to whom, Churchill had said, the charter was not meant to apply. In October 1944, Churchill and Stalin agreed on the postwar distribution of territories. The Soviet Union would control Romania and Bulgaria, Britain would control Greece, and they would oversee Hungary and Yugoslavia together. These agreements went against Roosevelt's faith in collective security, self-determination, and open doors in trade. In February 1945, the "Big Three"—Roosevelt, Churchill, and Stalin—met in the Crimean town of Yalta. Roosevelt advocated for the formation of the United Nations to replace the League of Nations as a global peace mechanism, and he supported future Soviet influence in Korea, Manchuria, Sakhalin Island, and the Kuril Islands. The last meeting of the Allied leaders, with Harry Truman replacing Roosevelt, who had died in April, took place in Potsdam, Germany, in the summer of 1945. At Potsdam, they agreed to give the Soviets control of eastern Poland, to give a large stretch of eastern Germany to Poland, and to finalize a temporary four-way occupation of Germany, set out at Yalta, that would include France as one of the supervising powers.

The Great Depression had inflicted global suffering, while World War II had left an estimated 100 million people dead worldwide, more than 50 million refugees without homes, and one of the most abominable moral legacies in human history. Forced into armies or labor camps for war production, colonial peoples in Asia and Africa were in full rebellion or close to it. For a second time in three decades, they had seen their imperial masters killing one another, slaughtered by the very technology that was supposed to show European superiority. Deference to Europe was virtually finished, with independence only a matter of time.

The war weakened and even destroyed standards of decency and truth. Demo-cratic Europe had given in to continuous wartime values, and it was this Europe that George Orwell captured in his novel *1984* (1949). Orwell had worked for Britain's wartime Ministry of Information (called the Ministry of Truth in the novel), where he made up phony news for wartime audiences. Truth hardly mattered: *battle fatigue* substituted for *insanity,* and *liberating* a country could mean invading it and mur-dering its civilians. Poor food, ragged clothing, and careworn people walking grimy streets—all characterized both wartime London and Orwell's fictional state, Oceania. Millions cheered the end of Nazi evil in 1945, but Orwell saw the war as killing prosperity, deadening creativity, and bringing big government into everyday life. For Orwell, bureaucratic domination depended on continuing conflict, and fresh conflict was indeed brewing even before the war ended. As the Allied powers com-peted for territory, a new struggle called the cold war was beginning.

REVIEW   What were the major events and consequences of World War II?

Conclusion

The Great Depression, which brought fear, hunger, and joblessness to millions, created a setting in which dictators thrived because they promised to restore prosperity by destroying democracy and representative government. Desperate people believed the promises of dynamic new leaders—Mussolini, Stalin, and Hitler—and often forgave the brutality of their regimes. In the USSR, Stalin's pro-gram of rapid industrialization was an amazing achievement, but it cost the lives of millions. With the democracies preoccupied with economic recovery while preserving the rule of law and still haunted by memories of World War I, Hitler and Mussolini menaced Europe unchallenged. At the same time, Japan began a program of conquest aimed at ending Western domination. The coalition of Allies that finally formed to stop the Axis powers of Germany, Italy, and Japan was an uneasy alliance among Britain, Free France, the Soviet Union, and the United States. World War II ended European domination. Its economies were shattered, its colonies were on the verge of independence, and its peoples were starving and homeless.

The costs of a bloody war—one waged against civilians as well as armies—taught these powers different lessons. The United States, Britain, and France were convinced that a minimum of citizen well-being was necessary to prevent a return of fascism. The devastation of the USSR's population and resources made Stalin increasingly obsessed with national security and compensation for the damage inflicted by Germany. Britain and France faced the end of their imperial might, underscoring Orwell's insight that the war had utterly transformed society. The

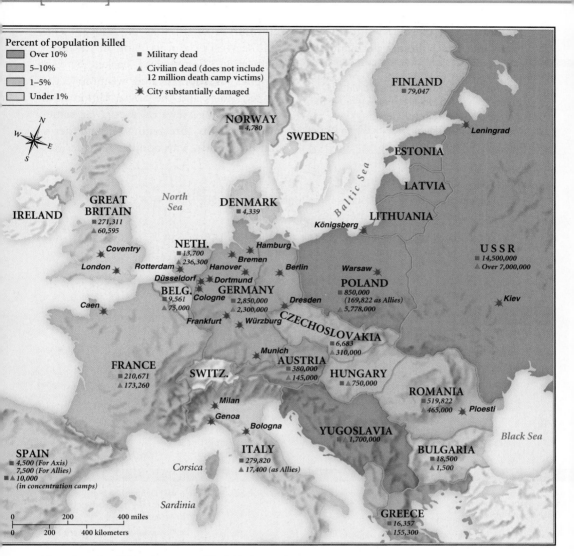

Percent of population killed

- Over 10%
- 5–10%
- 1–5%
- Under 1%

- ■ Military dead
- ▲ Civilian dead (does not include 12 million death camp victims)
- ✳ City substantially damaged

FINLAND ■ 79,047

NORWAY ■ 4,780

SWEDEN

Leningrad

ESTONIA

LATVIA

Baltic Sea

North Sea

DENMARK ■ 4,339

LITHUANIA

Königsberg

USSR ■ 14,500,000 ▲ Over 7,000,000

IRELAND

GREAT BRITAIN ■ 271,311 ▲ 60,595

Coventry

London ✳

NETH. ■ 13,700 ▲ 236,300

Hamburg ✳

Bremen ✳

Rotterdam ✳ Hanover ✳

Berlin ✳

Warsaw ✳

POLAND ■ 850,000 (169,822 as Allies) ▲ 5,778,000

Kiev ✳

Düsseldorf ✳ ✳Dortmund

BELG. ■ 9,561 ▲ 75,000

Cologne ✳

GERMANY ■ 2,850,000 ▲ 2,300,000

Dresden ✳

Caen ✳

Frankfurt ✳ ✳ Würzburg

CZECHOSLOVAKIA ■ 6,683 ▲ 310,000

Munich ✳

AUSTRIA ■ 380,000 ▲ 145,000

HUNGARY ■▲ 750,000

FRANCE ■ 210,671 ▲ 173,260

SWITZ.

ROMANIA ■ 519,822 ▲ 465,000 ✳ Ploesti

Milan ✳

Genoa ✳

Bologna ✳

YUGOSLAVIA ■▲ 1,700,000

Black Sea

SPAIN ■ 4,500 (For Axis) 7,500 (For Allies) ■▲ 10,000 (in concentration camps)

Corsica

ITALY ■ 279,820 ▲ 17,400 (as Allies)

BULGARIA ■ 18,500 ▲ 1,500

Sardinia

GREECE ■ 16,357 ▲ 155,300

0   200   400 miles
0   200   400 kilometers

Mapping the West   Europe at War's End, 1945
All of Europe was severely shocked during the age of catastrophes, and wartime damage left scars that would last for decades. Major German cities were bombed to bits. The Soviet Union suffered an unimaginable toll of perhaps as many as forty-five million deaths due to the war alone. In addition to the vast civilian and military losses shown on this map, historians estimate that no less than twelve million people were murdered in the Nazi death camps. Everything from politics to family life needed rebuilding.

militarization of society and the deliberate murder of millions of innocent citizens like Etty Hillesum permanently injured the West's claim to being an advanced civilization. Nonetheless, backed by vast supplies of sophisticated weaponry, the United States and the Soviet Union used their opposing views on a postwar settlement to justify threatening one another—and the world—with another horrific war.

CHAPTER REVIEW QUESTIONS
1. Compare fascist ideas about the individual with the idea of individual rights that drove the American and French revolutions.
2. What are the major differences between World War I and World War II?

For practice quizzes and other study tools, see the Online Study Guide at bedfordstmartins.com/huntconcise.

For primary-source material from this period, see Chapter 26 of *Sources of THE MAKING OF THE WEST*, Third Edition.

TIMELINE

- **1930s** Sweden constructs a welfare state

- **1930** Nationalist ruler Mustafa Kemal changes the name of Turkey's capital from Constantinople to Istanbul; French crush a peasant uprising in Indochina; Marlene Dietrich stars in *The Blue Angel*

- **1940** France falls to the German army; British air force fends off German attacks in the battle of Britain

- **1939** Germany invades Poland; World War II begins; Spanish Civil War ends

- **1938** Nazi attacks on Jews in Kristallnacht; Virginia Woolf, *Three Guineas*

- **1945** Germany surrenders; United States drops atomic bombs on Hiroshima and Nagasaki; World War II ends

| 1929 | 1933 | 1937 | 1941 | 1945 |

1920s–1930s Movement for Indian Independence

- **1929** U.S. stock market crashes; global depression begins; Soviet leaders launch a war against the kulaks

- **1933** Hitler comes to power in Germany

- **1935** Nazis enact the Nuremberg Laws, denying rights to Jews in Germany

- **1936** Stalin starts purges of top Communist Party officials and later military leaders in show trials; Spanish Civil War begins

- **1941** Germany invades the USSR; Japan attacks Pearl Harbor; United States enters the war

1941–1945 Holocaust

1942–1943 Siege of Stalingrad

- **1944** Allied forces land at Normandy

Suggested References

The vicious dictators Stalin, Hitler, and Mussolini and the intricacies of World War II are among the most popular subjects for historians and readers alike. Recent historical works have moved beyond this fascination to investigate their mobilization of art and the mass media and to consider the public's engagement with both totalitarian regimes and democracies.

Alvarez, Luis. *The Power of the Zoot: Youth Culture and Resistance during World War II.* 2008.

Balderston, Theo, ed. *The World Economy and National Economies in the Interwar Slump.* 2003.

Ben-Ghiat, Ruth. *Fascist Modernities: Italy, 1922–1945.* 2001.

Burleigh, Michael. *The Third Reich: A New History.* 2000.

Chickering, Roger, et al., eds. *A World at Total War: Global Conflict and the Politics of Destruction, 1937–1945.* 2005.

*Dawidowicz, Lucy S., ed. *A Holocaust Reader.* 1976.

Fenner, Angelica, and Eric D. Weitz. *Fascism and Neofascism: Critical Writings on the Radical Right in Europe.* 2004.

Fink, Carole. *Defending the Rights of Others: The Great Powers, the Jews, and International Minority Protection, 1878–1938.* 2004.

Helstosky, Carol. *Garlic and Oil: The Politics of Food in Italy.* 2004.

Maas, Ad, and Hans Hooimaijers, eds. *Scientific Research in World War II: What Scientists Did in the War.* 2009.

Pennington, Reina, and John Erickson. *Wings, Women, and War: Soviet Airwomen in World War II.* 2004.

Petrone, Karen. *Life Has Become More Joyous, Comrades: Celebrations in the Time of Stalin.* 2000.

Rose, Sonya O. *Which People's War: National Identity and Citizenship, 1939–1945.* 2003.

Siegel, Mona L. *The Moral Disarmament of France: Education, Pacifism, and Patriotism, 1914–1940.* 2004.

South Asia and Gandhi: http://www.columbia.edu/cu/libraries/indiv/area/sarai

U.S. Holocaust Museum: http://www.ushmm.org

Weinberg, Gerhard. *A World at Arms: A Global History of World War II.* 2005.

A LOVE CAUGHT IN THE FIRE OF REVOLUTIO

Turbulent were the times and fiery was the love story of Zhivago, his wife... and the passionate, tender Lara.

METRO-GOLDWYN-MAYER presents A CARLO PONTI PRODUCTION

DAVID LEAN'S FILM OF BORIS PASTERNAKS

DOCTOR ZHIVAGO

STARRING

GERALDINE CHAPLIN · JULIE CHRISTIE · TOM COURTENAY
ALEC GUINNESS · SIOBHAN McKENNA · RALPH RICHARDSON
OMAR SHARIF (AS ZHIVAGO) ROD STEIGER · RITA TUSHINGHAM

WINNIN 6 ACADEM AWARD

SCREEN PLAY BY ROBERT BOLT · DIRECTED BY DAVID LEAN   IN PANAVISION® AND METROCOLOR   MGM

The Cold War and the Remaking of Europe

1945–1960s

L ATE IN 1945, WITH THE USSR still reeling from the devastation of World War II, Soviet poet Boris Pasternak set out on a new project—*Doctor Zhivago,* a novel about a thoughtful medical man caught up in the Russian Revolution. Like others in the USSR, Pasternak expected the postwar era to bring about, as he put it, "a great renewal of Russian life," ending the violence and famine of the past three decades. He struggled on with his epic work even as **cold war** tensions between the United States and the USSR began. In 1953, Stalin's sudden death raised Pasternak's hopes that a more tolerant political climate would allow his masterwork to receive a warm reception. Those hopes were dashed, however, when the Soviets forbade the book's publication.

Doctor Zhivago
As soon as Boris Pasternak's forbidden novel *Doctor Zhivago* was published in Italy in 1957, Hollywood's MGM studio went after the rights for the film. Finally completed in 1965, the movie was a cold war blockbuster—an epic of life and love in postrevolutionary Russia. The story is more or less summarized in this advertising poster: two incredibly attractive people fall in love and are torn apart by the crushing Bolshevik system. *(MGM/The Kobal Collection.)*

A determined Pasternak bypassed Soviet authorities and published *Doctor Zhivago* in 1957 in Italy—now an anti-Soviet ally of the United States in the cold war. The book became a best seller, showing its readers that the Russian Revolution was far from perfect and so angering the Soviet establishment that Stalin's successor, Nikita Khrushchev, forced Pasternak to decline the Nobel Prize for Literature awarded him in 1958. But if the Soviets tried to suppress *Doctor Zhivago* for cold war reasons and frightened people into denouncing its author, it was the cold war that allowed *Doctor Zhivago* to live on. Soon after the novel appeared, the famed Hollywood studio MGM bought the rights to the book and turned it into a blockbuster film (1965), seen by tens of millions of people. By that time, however, Pasternak was dead—a broken victim of cold war persecutions that continued long after the tragic years of World War II had ended.

As the cold war opened, people in Europe, Japan, and much of East and Southeast Asia were starving and homeless. Evidence of genocide and other inhumanity was everywhere, and nuclear annihilation menaced the world. The old international order was gone, replaced by the rivalry of the United States and the Soviet Union for control of a shattered Europe. The nuclear arsenals of the two superpowers grew massively in the 1950s, but they were enemies who did not fight outright. Thus their terrifying rivalry was called the cold war. The cold war divided the West and led to political persecution in many areas, even the wealthy and secure United States.

At the same time, the defeat of Nazism inspired cautious optimism like Pasternak's. A heroic effort had defeated fascism, and that defeat raised hopes that a new age would begin. Atomic science promised advances in medicine, and nuclear energy was seen as a replacement for coal and oil. The creation of the **United Nations (UN)** suggested the beginning of real international cooperation. Around the globe, colonial peoples won independence from European masters, while in the United States the civil rights movement grew in strength. The welfare state expanded, and by the end of the 1950s economic rebirth had made much of Europe more prosperous than ever before. An "economic miracle" had occurred.

The postwar period was one of redefinition, as the experience of total war transformed both society and the international order. Gone was the definition of a West composed of Europe and its cultural relatives such as the United States and an East comprising Asian countries such as India, China, and Japan. During the cold war, the word *West* came to stand for the United States and its allies in western Europe, while *East* meant the Soviet Union and its bloc of satellites in eastern Europe. Still another terminology arose in the 1950s, one that divided the globe into the first world, or capitalist bloc of countries; the second world, or socialist bloc; and the **third world**, or countries emerging from imperial domination. This last term initially aimed to compare those rising nations to the Third Estate—the rising citizens of the French Revolution—but it is now considered an insult. As the world's people redefined themselves, the superpowers took the world to the brink of nuclear disaster when the United States discovered Soviet missile sites on the island of Cuba. From the dropping of atomic bombs on Japan in 1945 to the **Cuban missile crisis** of 1962, fear and personal anguish like that of Pasternak gripped much of the world, even in the midst of prosperity and Europe's rebirth.

CHAPTER FOCUS QUESTION   How did the cold war shape the politics, economy, social life, and culture of post–World War II Europe?

World Politics Transformed

World War II ended Europe's global leadership. Many countries lay in ruins by the summer of 1945, and conditions would deteriorate before they got better. Continuing turmoil destroyed the lives of millions in eastern and central Europe. In contrast, the United States, whose territory was virtually untouched in the war, emerged as the world's sole economic giant, and the Soviet Union, despite suffering immense destruction, was an impressive military power. Occupying Europe as part of the victorious alliance against Nazism and fascism, the two superpowers used Germany—at the heart of the continent—to divide Europe in two. By the late 1940s, the USSR had imposed Communist rule throughout most of eastern Europe, and western Europeans found themselves at least partially controlled by the very U.S. economic power that helped them rebuild, especially because the United States maintained air bases and nuclear weapons on their soil. The new age of bipolar world politics made Europe its testing ground.

Chaos in Europe

In contrast to the often stationary trench warfare of World War I, armies in World War II had fought a war of movement on the ground and in the air. Massive air strikes had leveled thousands of square miles of territory, whole cities were clogged with rubble, and homeless survivors wandered the streets. On the Rhine River, almost no bridge remained standing; in the Soviet Union, seventy thousand villages and more than a thousand cities lay in shambles. Everywhere people were suffering. In the Netherlands, the severity of Nazi occupation left the Dutch population close to death, relieved only by a U.S. airlift of supplies. Allied troops in Germany were often the only source of food. "To see the children fighting for food," one British soldier noted, "was like watching animals being fed in a zoo." There was social disorder, even chaos, at the war's end but no mass uprisings as after World War I. Until the late 1940s, people were too exhausted by the struggle for bare survival to protest.

The tens of millions of refugees and homeless people suffered the most, as they wandered a continent where resources were slim and the dangers of assault and robbery great. An estimated thirty million Europeans, many of German ethnicity, were forced from Poland, Czechoslovakia, and Hungary (Map 22.1). Often refugees fled to western Europe, making it one of the world's most densely populated regions. Others ultimately found homes in countries that experienced little or no war damage, such as Denmark, Sweden, Canada, and Australia. The USSR lobbied hard for the return of several million Soviet prisoners of war, only to execute many of the returnees for being "contaminated" by Western ideas.

Survivors of the concentration camps also discovered that their suffering had not ended with Germany's defeat. Many returned home diseased and disoriented, while others had no home to return to, as property had been confiscated and entire communities destroyed. Anti-Semitism—official policy under the Nazis—lingered in popular attitudes. In the summer of 1946, a vicious crowd in Kielce, Poland, attacked 250 returning Jewish survivors, killing at least 40. The use of violence as a way to maintain the wealth and upward mobility gained from fascist anti-Semitism was common throughout eastern Europe. Meanwhile, some officials across the continent even denied that unprecedented atrocities had been committed and refused Jews any help. Survivors hoped to escape to Palestine, where Zionists had been settling for half a century. Many European countries seemed simply to have lost their moral bearings.

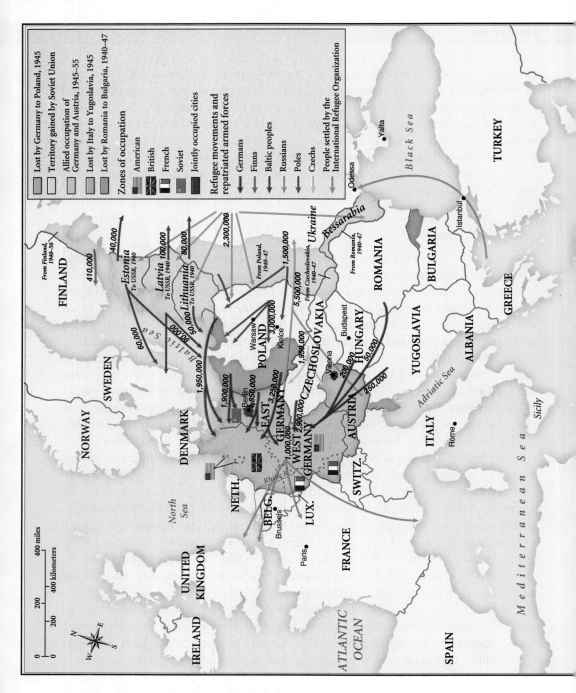

Map 22.1 The Impact of World War II on Europe
European governments, many of them struggling to provide food and other necessities for their populations, found themselves responsible for hundreds of thousands, if not millions, of refugees. At the same time, millions of prisoners of war, servicemen, and slave laborers were returned to the Soviet Union, many of them by force. This situation unfolded amid political instability and even violence.

New Superpowers: The United States and the Soviet Union

Only two powerful countries were left in 1945: the United States and the Soviet Union. The United States was now the richest country in the world. Its industrial output had increased by a remarkable 15 percent annually between 1940 and 1944. By 1947, it controlled almost two-thirds of the world's gold bullion and more than half of the world's commercial shipping. Continued spending on industrial and military research added to its prosperity, boosting the confident mood that now swept the country. In contrast to the post–World War I policy of isolationism, Americans embraced global leadership. Many had learned about the world while tracking the war's progress; hundreds of thousands of soldiers, government officials, and relief workers had had direct experience of Europe, Africa, and Asia.

The Soviets also emerged from the war with a well-justified sense of accomplishment. Despite horrendous losses, they had resisted the most massive onslaught ever launched against a nation. Instead of being outcasts as they had been after World War I, the Soviets expected respect and influence on the world stage, and many Europeans and Americans gratefully acknowledged their leadership in Hitler's defeat. Ordinary Soviet citizens believed that their wartime sacrifices, especially the loss of as many as forty-five million lives, would lead to improvements in everyday conditions. Rumors spread among the peasants that the collective farms would be divided and returned to them as individual property now that the war had been won. "Life will become pleasant," one writer prophesied. "There will be much coming and going, and a lot of contacts with the West." Boris Pasternak was among those who expected an end to decades of hardship and repression.

Stalin took a different view and moved ruthlessly to reassert control. In 1946, his new five-year plan increased production goals and mandated harsher collectivization of agriculture. For him, rapid recovery meant more work, not less, and more order, not greater freedom. Stalin turned his attention to the low birthrate, a result of wartime male casualties and women's long working days, which discouraged them from adding child care to their already heavy responsibilities. He introduced an intense propaganda campaign emphasizing that women should hold down jobs and also fulfill their "true nature" by producing many children. A crackdown on freedom took place, and a new round of purges began. Jews were especially targeted, and in 1953 the government announced that doctors—most of them Jews—had long been assassinating Soviet leaders and murdering newborns and patients in hospitals. Hysteria gripped the nation, as people feared for their lives. "I am a simple worker and not an anti-Semite," one Moscow resident wrote, "but I say . . . it's time to clean these people out." This atmosphere of fear fed the cold war.

Origins of the Cold War

The cold war between the United States and the Soviet Union, which began immediately after World War II, would afflict the world for more than four decades. No peace conference or treaties officially ended the war to document what went

The Cold War, to 1962

1945–1949	USSR establishes satellite states in eastern Europe
1947	Truman Doctrine announces U.S. commitment to contain communism; U.S. Marshall Plan provides massive aid to rebuild Europe
1948–1949	Soviet troops blockade Berlin; United States airlifts provisions to Berliners
1949	Western democracies form the North Atlantic Treaty Organization (NATO); Soviet bloc establishes the Council for Mutual Economic Assistance (COMECON); USSR tests its first nuclear weapon
1950–1953	Korean War
1950–1954	U.S. senator Joseph McCarthy leads the hunt for American Communists
1953	Stalin dies
1955	USSR and eastern-bloc countries form a military alliance called the Warsaw Pact
1956	Khrushchev denounces Stalin in the "secret speech" to a Communist Party congress; Hungarians revolt unsuccessfully against Soviet domination
1959	Castro comes to power in Cuba
1961	Berlin Wall begun
1962	Cuban missile crisis

wrong. As a result, the origins of the cold war remain a matter of debate, with historians faulting both sides for starting the dangerous rivalry. Some point to consistent U.S., British, and French hostility toward the Soviets, which began as far back as the Bolshevik Revolution of 1917 and continued through the depression. Others stress Stalin's aggressive policies, notably the Nazi-Soviet Pact in 1939 and Stalin's seizure of Polish territory and the Baltic states when World War II broke out. In this view, the Western countries naturally feared unlimited Soviet expansionism.

Suspicions ran deep among the Allied leaders during World War II. Stalin believed that Churchill and Roosevelt were deliberately letting the USSR bear the brunt of Hitler's rampage across the continent as part of their anti-Communist policy. He rightly viewed Churchill in particular as interested mainly in preserving Britain's imperial power, no matter what the cost in Soviet lives. At the time, some Americans believed that dropping the atomic bombs on Japan would frighten the Soviets and discourage them from making any more landgrabs. In addition, the new U.S. president, Harry Truman, cut off aid to the Soviets as the last gun was fired, fueling Stalin's belief that the United States was aiming for his country's utter collapse. Seeing a threat to his west, Stalin judged that the USSR needed a permanent "buffer zone" of European states loyal to it. Across the Atlantic, Truman saw the Soviet occupation of eastern Europe as the beginning of a series of Communist takeovers around the world. Members of the U.S. State Department increased U.S. fears by describing Stalin as a neurotic Asian tyrant thirsting for world domination.

The cold war thus became a series of moves and countermoves by two very different countries that jointly occupied the rich but devastated European heartland. In line with the view of its geopolitical needs, the USSR repressed democratic coalition governments of liberals, socialists, Communists, and peasant parties in central and eastern Europe between 1945 and 1949. It imposed Communist rule almost immediately in Bulgaria and Romania. In Romania, Stalin cited citizen violence in 1945 as the excuse for removing all non-Communists from government. In Poland, the Communists rigged the elections in 1945 and 1946 to create the illusion of popular support for communism. Nevertheless, between 1945 and 1947 the Communists there had to share power with the popular Peasant Party, which had a large following of rural workers and peasant landowners.

The United States now put its new interventionist spirit to work, promoting American influence. It acknowledged the USSR's authority in Soviet-occupied areas of central and eastern Europe but worried that Communist power would spread to western Europe, where memories of Communist leadership in the resistance to fascism gave it a powerful appeal. In Greece, for example, the Communists had enough of a following to threaten the right-wing monarchy the British had installed in 1944. In March 1947, Truman reacted to this threat by announcing what quickly became known as the **Truman Doctrine**—the use of economic and military aid to block communism. The president asked the U.S. Congress for $400 million in military aid for Greece and Turkey, where the Communists were also exerting pressure. Fearing that Americans would resist backing nondemocratic Greece, Congress would agree to the program only if, as one congressman put it, Truman would "scare the hell out of the country." Truman thus publicized an expensive aid program as necessary to prevent Soviet conquest of the world. The show of American support convinced the Communists to back off, and in 1949 the Greek rebels declared a cease-fire.

In 1947, the United States also devised the **Marshall Plan**, a program of massive economic aid to alleviate the daily hardships that were making communism attractive to Europeans. "The seeds of totalitarian regimes are nurtured by misery and want," Truman warned. Named after Secretary of State George C. Marshall, who announced the plan, the program's direct aid would immediately improve everyday life, while its loans and financial credits would restart international trade. The government claimed that the Marshall Plan was not directed "against any country or doctrine but against hunger, poverty, desperation, and chaos." By the early 1950s, the United States had sent Europe more than $12 billion in food, equipment, and services, reducing the appeal of communism in the countries of western Europe that received the aid.

Stalin saw the Marshall Plan as a U.S. political trick because the devastated USSR had nothing similar to offer. He thus clamped down even harder on eastern and central European governments, preventing them from responding to the U.S. offer of assistance and eliminating the last remnants of democracy in Hungary and Poland. In the autumn of 1947, a purge of non-Communist officials began in Czechoslovakia. By June 1948, Czechoslovakia's socialist president, Edvard Beneš, had resigned and been replaced by a Communist figurehead. The Czech people accepted the change so passively that Communist leaders said the takeover was "like cutting butter with a knife."

The only exception to the Soviet sweep in eastern Europe was Yugoslavia, ruled by the Communist leader known as Tito (Josip Broz). During the war, Tito had led the powerful anti-Nazi Yugoslav "partisans." After the war, he drew on support from Serbs, Croats, and Muslims to mount a Communist revolution in 1948. His revolution, however, was explicitly meant to avoid Soviet influence. "We study and take as an example the Soviet system," Tito remarked, "but we are developing social-

ism in our country in somewhat different forms." Stalin was furious at Tito's independence. None-theless, Yugoslavia emerged from its revolution as a culturally diverse federation of six republics and two independent provinces within Serbia. Tito's break with Stalin intensified the purges in the USSR, because the Soviet government could point to Tito as a vivid example of the treachery supposedly at work in the heart of the Communist world. Tito used his forceful personality and strong organization to hold diverse groups of south Slavs together until his death in 1980.

Yugoslavia after the Revolution, 1948

The Division of Germany

The superpowers' struggle for control of Germany took the cold war to a menacing level. The agreements reached at the Yalta and Potsdam conferences in 1945 divided Germany into four occupied zones, each of which was controlled by one of the four principal victors in World War II—the United States, the Soviet Union, Britain, and France (Map 22.2). However, the superpowers disagreed on how to treat Germany. First, many in the United States had come to believe that there was something wrong with the German character—a fatal flaw that had resulted in two world wars and the Holocaust. After the war, U.S. occupation forces undertook a reprogramming of German attitudes by censoring all media in the U.S. zone to ensure that they did not perpetuate fascist values. In contrast, Stalin believed that Nazism was merely an extreme form of capitalism. His solution was to confiscate the estates of wealthy Germans and redistribute them to ordinary people and Communist supporters.

A second disagreement, concerning the economy, led to Germany's partition. According to the American plan for coordinating the German economy, surplus produce from the Soviet-occupied areas would feed urban populations in the western zones; in turn, industrial goods would be sent to the USSR. The Soviets upset this plan. Following the Allied agreement that the USSR would receive reparations from German resources, the Soviets simply seized German equipment and shipped it to the Soviet Union. They transported skilled German workers, engineers, and scientists to the USSR to work as forced laborers. The Soviets also manipulated the currency in their zone, enabling the USSR to buy German goods at unfairly low prices.

In response, in 1948 the Western Allies merged their individual zones into one West German state, escalating cold war tensions. Instead of limiting Germany's power, as the wartime agreements called for, the United States also began an eco-nomic buildup of the western zone under the Marshall Plan. By 1948, notions of

Map 22.2 Divided Germany and the Berlin Airlift, 1946–1949
Berlin, controlled by the United States, Great Britain, France, and the Soviet Union, was deep in the Soviet zone of occupation and became a major point of contention among the former Allies. When the USSR blockaded the western half of the city, the United States responded with a massive airlift. To stop movement between the two zones, the USSR built a wall in 1961 and used troops to patrol it.

a permanently weakened Germany ended, and the United States enlisted many former Nazi officials as spies and bureaucrats to pursue the cold war.

On July 24, 1948, Stalin retaliated by blockading Germany's capital, Berlin. Like Germany as a whole, the city—located more than one hundred miles inside the Soviet zone and thus cut off from western territory—had been divided into four occupation zones. Expecting the United States and its allies to give up Berlin, the Soviets declared that the city was now part of their zone of occupation and refused to allow western vehicles from outside their bloc to travel through the Soviet zone to reach it. The United States responded decisively, flying in millions of tons of provisions to Berliners. During the winter of 1948–1949, the Berlin airlift—"Operation Vittles," as U.S. pilots called it—even funneled in coal to warm some two million isolated citizens. Given the limited number of planes involved, pilots kept the engines running so that they could turn around quickly and thus ensure the delivery of enough provisions. The Soviets ended their blockade in May 1949, but cold war rhetoric made the divided capital a symbol of the capitalist-communist divide—of good versus evil.

The creation of competing institutions, military alliances, and entirely new nations added to cold war tensions. A few months after the establishment of the West German state, the USSR created an East German state. In 1949, the United States, Canada, and their allies in western Europe and Scandinavia formed the **North Atlantic Treaty Organization (NATO)**, which provided a unified military force for its member countries (Map 22.3). In 1955, after the United States forced France and Britain to invite West Germany to join NATO, the Soviet Union retaliated by establishing with its satellite countries the military organization commonly called

Map 22.3 European NATO Members and the Warsaw Pact in the 1950s
The two superpowers intensified their rivalry by creating large military alliances: NATO, formed in 1949, and the Warsaw Pact, formed in 1955 after NATO invited West Germany to join. The United States and Canada also were NATO members. International politics revolved around these two alliances, which faced off in the heart of Europe. Military planners on both sides devised war games to plan strategies for fighting a massive war in central Europe over control of Germany. **For more help analyzing this map, see the map activity for this chapter in the Online Study Guide at** bedfordstmartins.com/huntconcise.

the **Warsaw Pact.** By that time, both the United States and the USSR had accelerated the buildup of arms. The Soviets had exploded their own atomic bomb in 1949, and both nations had then tested increasingly powerful nuclear weapons. These two massive regional alliances, armed to the teeth, backed cold war politics with military muscle, definitively outstripping the individual might of the European powers.

REVIEW   What major events led to and widened the cold war?

Political and Economic Recovery in Europe

The cold war served as a backdrop to the remarkable recovery that took place in Europe. The first two items on the political agenda were the eradication of the Nazi past and the creation of peacetime governments. While western Europe revived its democratic political structures, its individualistic culture, and its productive capabilities, eastern Europe was far less prosperous and far more repressive under the Stalinism of the postwar period. Even to the east, however, the conditions of everyday life improved as peasant societies were forced to modernize and as basic consumer goods became available. By the 1960s, people across the continent were enjoying a higher standard of living than ever before. Governments took increasing responsibility for the health and well-being of citizens, making the cold war era also the age of the welfare state.

Dealing with the Nazi Past

In May 1945, Europeans lived under a complex system in which local resistance leaders, Allied armies of occupation, international relief workers, and the remnants of bureaucracies—among them Nazi sympathizers—competed for authority. The goals of feeding civilians, dealing with millions of refugees, and purging Nazis all needed attention. Governments in exile returned to claim their rightful share of power, but they often ran up against occupying armies that covered much of the continent and were a law unto themselves. The Soviets were especially feared for inflicting rape and robbery—abuses they justified by pointing to tens of millions of Soviet deaths at the hands of the Nazis. The desire for revenge against the Nazis hardened with the discovery of the death camps' skeletal survivors and the remains of the millions murdered there. Civilians released pent-up rage by themselves punishing collaborators for occupation crimes. In France, villagers often shaved the heads of women suspected of associating with Germans and made some of them parade naked through the streets. Members of the resistance executed tens of thousands of Nazi officers and collaborators on the spot.

The Punishment of Collaborators
Women in France who had romantic involvements with German occupiers were called "horizontal" collaborators to suggest that they were traitorous prostitutes. After the war, they were often forced to parade through cities and towns enduring verbal and other abuse with their heads shaved and sometimes stripped of their clothing. The public shaming of these women served as the basis for the film *Hiroshima Mon Amour*, which gripped audiences in the late 1950s. (© Robert Capa/Magnum Photos Inc.)

Allied representatives undertook what they claimed to be a more systematic "denazification" that ranged from forcing German civilians to view the death camps to prosecuting major Axis leaders, most notably at the Nuremberg trials, held in the fall of 1945. Although international law lacked a precedent for defining genocide as a crime, the judges at Nuremberg found sufficient evidence from the Nazis' own records to impose death sentences on half of the twenty-four defendants, among them Hitler's closest associates, and to send the rest to prison. The Nuremberg trials introduced today's notion of prosecuting crimes against humanity.

Allied prosecution of Axis leaders was hardly thorough or evenhanded. Some of the leaders most responsible for war crimes simply disappeared and were not pursued, leaving many citizens skeptical about Allied intentions. As women in Germany faced violence at the hands of occupying troops, endured starvation, and were forced to do the rough manual labor of clearing rubble in bombed-out cities, Germans came to believe that they themselves were the main victims of the war. They interpreted the trials of Nazis as simple payback rather than honest punishment of the guilty. Distrust mounted when Allied officials hired former high-ranking Nazis and Fascists in the service of the cold war. Soon the new West German government proclaimed that the war's real casualties were the German prisoners of war still being held in Soviet camps.

Rebirth of the West

Following the immediate postwar chaos, Europe's revival accelerated in the 1950s. In western Europe, reform-minded civilian governments reflected the broad membership of the resistance movements to the Nazis. They conspicuously emphasized democratic values to show their rejection of the totalitarian regimes that had earlier attracted so many Europeans. Rebuilding devastated towns and cities spurred recovery, while bold projects for economic cooperation produced a brisk trade in consumer goods in western Europe by the late 1950s. Memories of the war remained vivid, but prosperity restored confidence.

Resistance leaders made the first claim on political offices in post-fascist western Europe. In France, the leader of the Free French, General Charles de Gaulle, governed briefly as chief of state. In 1946, the French approved a constitution that established the Fourth Republic and finally granted the vote to women. De Gaulle wanted a more conservative political system with a strong executive, and failing to get that, he soon resigned in favor of leftist and centrist parties. Meanwhile, Italy replaced its constitutional monarchy with a full parliamentary system that also allowed women the vote. As in France, a resistance-based government initially took control. Then, in late 1945, socialist and labor politicians were replaced by a coalition headed by the conservative Christian Democrats, descended from the traditional Catholic centrist parties of the prewar period. Other countries likewise saw the growing influence of Christian parties because of their participation in the resistance.

Many voters in western Europe also favored the Communist Party. Symbol of the common citizen, the Soviet soldier was a hero to many western Europeans outside occupied Germany. People also remembered the common man's struggle in the depression of the 1930s. Thus, in Britain, despite the wartime successes of Winston Churchill's Conservative Party leadership, the Labour Party of Clement Attlee won elections because it seemed more likely to fulfill promises to share prosperity fairly across the classes through expanded social welfare programs. The extreme difficulties of the immediate postwar years added to the appeal of politicians who appeared to represent the millions of ordinary people who had suffered, fought, and worked so hard during the war.

In West Germany, however, with the Communist takeovers going on directly to the east, communism and the left in general had little appeal. In 1949, centrist politicians helped govern the new state, the German Federal Republic, whose constitution aimed to prevent the reemergence of a dictator and to guarantee individual rights. West Germany's first chancellor was the seventy-three-year-old Catholic anti-Communist Konrad Adenauer, who allied himself with the economist Ludwig Erhard. Erhard stabilized the postwar German currency so that people would have enough confidence in its soundness to begin normal trade and other economic activity. Successfully guiding Germany away from both fascism and communism, the economist and the politician restored the representative government that Hitler had destroyed.

Paradoxically, given its leadership in the fight against fascism, the United States was a country in which individual freedom and democracy were imperiled after the war. As the cold war intensified in 1947 and 1948, the media and several politicians fanned a growing fear that American Communists were working as secret domestic spies in support of the Soviet Union. As during the Soviet purges, people of all occupations, including government workers, film stars, and union leaders, were called before congressional panels to testify against friends or to admit having held Communist thoughts or sympathies.

Two events in 1949—the Soviet Union's successful test of an atomic bomb and the Communist revolution in China—soon brought to the fore Joseph McCarthy, a U.S. senator from Wisconsin who was unknown outside his state. To make a name for himself and to tap into the nervous public mood, McCarthy warned of a great Communist conspiracy to overthrow the United States. The atmosphere was electric with confusion, for only five years before, the mass media had run glowing stories about Stalin and the Soviet system. During the war, Americans were told to think of Stalin as a friendly "Uncle Joe." By 1952, however, millions of Americans had been investigated, imprisoned, or fired from their jobs. McCarthy had books such as Thomas Paine's *Common Sense,* written in the eighteenth century to support the American Revolution, removed from government shelves, and he personally oversaw book burnings. Although the Senate finally voted to censure McCarthy in the winter of 1954, the assault on freedom had been devastating, and anticommunism had come to dominate political life.

Given the wartime destruction, the economic rebirth of western Europe was even more surprising than the revival of democracy. In the first months after the war, the job of rebuilding often involved menial physical labor that mobilized entire populations. Initially governments directed labor and capital into rebuilding infrastructure—transportation, communications, and industrial capacity—and away from producing consumer goods. In the midst of growing discontent over the lack of basic necessities, however, the Marshall Plan boosted recovery with American dollars; food became more plentiful; and demand for automobiles, washing machines, and vacuum cleaners drove economic growth. Increased production wiped out most unemployment.

The postwar recovery also featured the adaptation of wartime technology to consumer industry. Civilian travel expanded as nations organized their own airline industries based on improved airplane technology. Developed to relieve wartime shortages, synthetics such as nylon now became part of peacetime civilian life. Factories churned out a vast assortment of plastic products, ranging from pipes to rainwear. In the climate of cold war, military needs also remained high; governments ordered bombs, fighter planes, tanks, and missiles and sponsored military research. The outbreak of the Korean War in 1950 increased U.S. orders for manufactured goods to wage that war, further sustaining economic growth in Europe. Ultimately, the cold war prevented a repeat of the 1920s, when reduced military spending threw people out of their jobs and the resulting financial insecurity fed the growth of fascism.

Large and small states alike developed and redeveloped modern economies in short order. In the twelve principal countries of western Europe, the annual rate of economic growth had been 1.3 percent per inhabitant between 1870 and 1913. Those countries almost tripled that rate between 1950 and 1973, attaining an annual per capita growth rate of 3.8 percent. Among the larger powers, West Germany surprisingly became the economic leader by the 1960s. The smaller Scandinavian countries also achieved a notable recovery. Sweden succeeded in the development of automobile, truck, and shipbuilding industries. Finland modernized its industry in order to pay the reparations demanded by the Soviet Union for resisting its invasion. It also modernized its agricultural sector, which in turn forced the surplus farm population to seek factory work. Scandinavian women joined the workforce in record numbers, which also boosted economic growth and expanded prosperity. The thirty years after World War II were a golden age of European economic growth (see "Taking Measure," page 883).

The creation of the Common Market, which evolved over time to become the European Union, was the final ingredient in the postwar recovery. In 1951, Italy, France, Germany, Belgium, Luxembourg, and the Netherlands took a major step toward cooperation when they formed the European Coal and Steel Community (ECSC), an organization to manage the joint production of basic resources. Importantly, it arranged for West Germany's abundant output of coal and steel to benefit all of western Europe. According to the ECSC's principal architect, Robert Schuman,

Taking Measure **World Manufacturing Output, 1950–1970**
During the "long boom" from the 1950s through the early 1970s, the world experienced increased industrial output, better agricultural production, and rising consumerism. This era of prosperity resulted from both the demand generated by the need to rebuild Europe and the adaptation of war technology to peacetime uses. The General Agreement on Trade and Tariffs (GATT) was also implemented after the war, lowering tariffs and thus advancing trade.

this economic cooperation would make another war "materially impossible." Simply put, the bonds of common production and trade would keep France and Germany from another cataclysmic conflict.

The success of the ECSC led to a momentous step. In 1957, the six ECSC members signed the Treaty of Rome, which provided for a more general trading partnership called the **European Economic Community (EEC)**, known popularly as the Common Market. The EEC reduced tariffs among the six partners and developed common trade policies. It brought under one cooperative economic umbrella more than 200 million consumers and would eventually add several hundred million more. According to one of its founders, the EEC aimed to "prevent the race of nationalism, which is the true curse of the modern world." Increased cooperation produced great economic rewards for the six members, whose rates of economic growth soared. Britain pointedly refused to join the partnership at first, since membership would have required surrendering certain imperial trading rights among its Commonwealth partners such as Canada and Australia. Since 1945, British statesmen had shunned the developing continental trading bloc because, as one of them put it, participation would make Britain "just another European country." Even without Britain, the rising prosperity of a new western Europe joined in the Common Market was striking.

Economic planning and coordination by specialists (as developed during wartime) shaped the Common Market. Called technocrats, specialists working for the Common Market were to base decisions on expertise rather than on the demands of any one nation. The aim was to reduce the potential for irrationality and violence in politics, both domestic and international. Administered by a commission in Brussels, Belgium, the Common Market transcended the borders of the nation-state and thus exceeded the power of elected officials. Some critics insisted (and some still insist today) that expert planning would diminish democracy by transferring power from legislatures to a powerful transnational bureaucracy. Defenders were just as insistent that planning and cooperation would be the surest tools of prosperity and lasting peace.

The Welfare State: Common Ground East and West

On both sides of the cold war, governments channeled new resources into state-financed programs such as pensions, disability insurance, and national health care. These social programs became known as the welfare state, indicating that states were no longer interested solely in maintaining order and building their power. Veterans' pensions were primary, but the welfare state extended beyond those who had fought in the war. Because the European population had declined during the war, almost all countries now desperately wanted to boost the birthrate and thus gave couples direct financial aid for having children. Imitating the sweeping Swedish programs of the 1930s, nations expanded or created family allowances and programs for pregnant women and new mothers. The French gave larger family allowances for each birth after the first; for many French families, this allowance provided as much as a third of the household income.

Some welfare-state policies had a strong bias against women. Britain's maternity benefits and child allowances provided little coverage for working women. The West German government passed strict legislation that forced employers to give women maternity leave, in effect discouraging them from hiring women at all. It also cut or eliminated benefits to married women. West Germans bragged about removing women from the workforce, claiming that this distinguished democratic practices from Communist ones. The refusal to build day-care centers or to allow stores to remain open in the evening so that working women could buy food for their families led West Germany to have among the lowest rates of female employment of any industrial country and the highest rate of female poverty in old age.

By contrast, in eastern Europe and the Soviet Union, where wartime loss of life had been enormous, women worked nearly full-time and usually outnumbered men in the workforce. As in many western European countries, however, child-care programs, family allowances, and maternity benefits were designed to encourage pregnancies by working women. A national health program provided medical

The Welfare State in Action, 1947
The Danish *crèche*, or day-care center, here shows the welfare state in action. Government programs to maintain the well-being of citizens became almost universally available in Europe, Canada, and (to a lesser extent) the United States. Children were seen as particularly important given the loss of life in the war. Governments encouraged couples to have more children through up-to-date health care systems, day-care centers, and generous family allowances. (Getty Images.)

services, as in most countries to the west, but the hardships of everyday life undermined the drive to increase population. The scarcity of consumer goods, the housing shortages, and the lack of household conveniences discouraged working women in Communist countries from having large families no matter what the government wanted. Because women bore the sole burden of domestic duties under such conditions on top of their paying jobs, they rarely wanted more children. As a result, the birthrate in the eastern bloc stagnated.

Across Europe, welfare-state programs aimed to improve people's health. State-funded health care systems covered medical needs in most industrial nations except the United States. The combination of better material conditions and state provision of health care dramatically extended life expectancies and lowered rates of infant mortality. Contributing to the overall progress, the number of doctors and dentists more than doubled between the end of World War I and 1950, and vaccines greatly reduced the death toll from diseases such as tuberculosis, diphtheria, measles, and polio. In England, schoolchildren stood on the average an inch taller than children the same age had a decade earlier.

State initiatives in other areas played a role in raising the standard of living. A growing network of government-built atomic power plants brought more thorough electrification of eastern Europe and the Soviet Union. Governments legislated more leisure time for workers. Beginning in 1955, Italian workers received twenty-eight paid holidays annually; in Sweden, workers received twenty-nine vacation days, a number that grew in the 1960s. Housing shortages brought on by three decades of economic depression and destructive war meant that postwar Europeans often lived with three generations sharing one or two rooms. To rebuild, governments sponsored a postwar housing boom. New suburbs and even entire cities formed around the edges of major urban areas in both the East and West. Many buildings went up slapdash, and although some cities were said to scar the environment, they dramatically improved living conditions for postwar refugees, workers, and immigrants.

Recovery in the East

To create a Soviet bloc according to Stalin's vision, Communists revived the harsh methods that had transformed peasant economies earlier in the century. In Hungary, for example, Communists reapportioned all estates over twelve hundred acres. Having gained support of the poorer peasants through this redistribution, Communists later took away their prized lands and pushed them into cooperative farming. Only in Poland did a substantial number of private farms remain. The process of collectivization was brutal, and rural people later looked back on the 1950s as dreadful. But some among those in the countryside felt that their lives and their children's lives had improved. "Before we peasants were dirty and poor, we worked like dogs. . . . Was that a good life? No sir, it wasn't. . . . I was a miserable sharecropper and my son is an engineer," said one Romanian peasant. Despite modernization, government investment in agriculture was never high enough to produce the bumper crops of western Europe, and even the USSR depended on produce from the small plots that enterprising farmers cultivated on the side.

Stalin prodded the Communist economies to match U.S. productivity. The Soviet Union formed regional organizations like those in the West, instituting the Council for Mutual Economic Assistance (COMECON) in 1949 to coordinate economic relations among the satellite countries and Moscow. The terms of COMECON actually worked against development of the satellite states, however, for the USSR was allowed to buy goods from these states at bargain prices and to sell products to them at exorbitant ones. Nonetheless, these formerly peasant states became oriented toward technology and bureaucratically directed industrial economies, thus creating opportunities for new careers. Tired of the struggles on the land, rural people moved to cities, where they received better education, health care, and ultimately jobs, albeit at the price of repression. The Roman Catholic church, which often protested the imposition of communism, was subdued as much as possible or infiltrated by government agents. Communists discriminated against agrarian elites, intellectuals, and other members of the middle class or imprisoned them. Political prisoners in East German camps did hard labor in uranium and other dangerous mines.

Culture, along with science, was a building block of Stalinism in the satellite countries. State-instituted programs aimed to build loyalty to the modernizing regime, and thus citizens found themselves obliged to attend adult education classes, women's groups, and public ceremonies. An intense program of Russification and de-Christianization forced students in eastern Europe to read histories of the war that ignored their own countries' resistance and gave the Red Army sole credit for fighting the Nazis. Rigid censorship resulted in what one staunchly socialist writer in the USSR characterized as "a dreary torrent of colorless, mediocre literature." Stalin also purged prominent wartime leaders to ensure conformity. Marshal Zhukov, a popular leader of the Soviet armed forces, was shipped to a distant command, while Anna Akhmatova, the great poet whose widely admired writing had emphasized perseverance during the war, was confined to a crowded hospital room because she refused to glorify Stalin in her postwar poetry.

In March 1953, amid growing repression, Stalin died, and it soon became clear that the old ways would not hold. Political prisoners in the labor camps rebelled, leading to the release of more than a million people from the Gulag. At the other end of the social order, many Soviet officials, despite enjoying luxury goods and plentiful food, had come to distrust Stalinism and now favored change. As protests took place across the Soviet bloc, governments stepped up the production of consumer goods—a policy called "goulash communism" after the Hungarian stew, because it provided more food for ordinary people. The future remained uncertain, however.

In 1955, Nikita Khrushchev (1894–1971), an illiterate coal miner before the revolution, became the undisputed leader of the Soviet Union, but he did so without

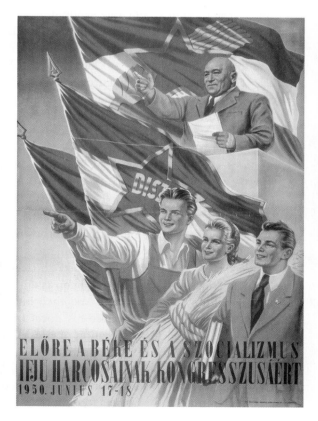

Re-creating Hungarian Youth
"Forward for the Congress of the Young Fighters of Peace and Socialism," exhorts this poster informing Hungarian youth about a conference to be held in June 1950. After World War II, people across Europe focused on the well-being of young people, and regimes in the Soviet sphere took steps to provide education in communism. Youth groups like those in the early Stalinist USSR served this end, and vivid posters in the Soviet realist style carried inspirational messages. **For more help analyzing this image, see the visual activity for this chapter in the Online Study Guide at** bedfordstmartins.com/huntconcise. (Magyar Nemzeti Múzeum, Budapest [Hungarian National Museum].)

executing his rivals. Khrushchev listened to popular complaints about conditions in both city and countryside and then made the surprising move of openly attacking Stalin. At a party congress in 1956, Khrushchev denounced the "cult of personality" Stalin had built about himself and announced that Stalinism did not equal communism. Khrushchev thus cagily attributed problems with communism to a single individual. The "secret speech"—it was not published in the USSR but became widely known—was a bombshell. People experienced, in the words of one writer, "a holiday of the soul." Debates broke out in public, and books championing the ordinary worker against the party bureaucracy appeared. The climate of relative tolerance for free speech was called "the thaw."

Protest erupted once more in the summer of 1956 when discontented Polish railroad workers struck for better wages. Popular support for their cause brought about policies providing new resources for ordinary people's needs. Inspired by the Polish example and angry at living under communism, Hungarians rebelled against forced collectivization in October 1956. As in Poland, economic issues and reports of Stalin's crimes sparked violence against the entire Communist system. Tens of thousands of protesters filled the streets of Budapest and succeeded in returning a popular hero, Imre Nagy, to power. When Nagy announced that Hungary might leave the Warsaw Pact, however, Soviet troops moved in, killing tens of thousands and causing hundreds of thousands more to flee to the West. Nagy was hanged. Crushing the Hungarian Revolution vividly displayed the limits to the thaw. Despite a rhetoric of democracy, the United States refused to intervene in Hungary, choosing not to risk World War III by challenging the Soviet sphere of influence.

The failure of eastern European uprisings overshadowed significant changes following Stalin's death. While defeating his rivals, Khrushchev ended the Stalinist purges and reformed the courts, which came to function according to procedures instead of staging show trials. The gates of the Gulag opened further, and the secret police lost many of its arbitrary powers. "It has become more interesting to visit and see people," Boris Pasternak said of the changes. "It has become easier to work." In 1957 the Soviets successfully launched the first artificial earth satellite, *Sputnik*, and in 1961 they put the first cosmonaut, Yuri Gagarin, in orbit around the earth. The Soviets' edge in space technology shocked the Western bloc and motivated the United States to create the National Aeronautics and Space Administration (NASA). For Soviets, such successes indicated that the USSR had achieved Stalin's goal of modernization and might inch closer to freedom.

Khrushchev, however, was inconsistent, showing himself open to changes in Soviet culture at one moment and then bullying honest writers at another. After condemning Pasternak because his novel *Doctor Zhivago* (1957) valued the individual, he allowed the publication of Aleksandr Solzhenitsyn's *One Day in the Life of Ivan Denisovitch* in 1961. This chilling account of life in the Gulag was useful in confirming Stalin's crimes. Under the thaw, Khrushchev made several trips to the West and was more widely seen by the public than Stalin had been. More confident and more affluent, the Soviets took steps to reduce their diplomacy's paranoid style and to expand communism's appeal in the new nations emerging from colonialism.

Despite the USSR's more relaxed posture, the cold war advanced, and the superpowers moved the world nearer to the nuclear brink.

> **REVIEW** What factors drove economic recovery in western Europe? In eastern Europe?

Decolonization in a Cold War Climate

After World War II, activists in colonized regions used the postwar chaos in Europe and other parts of the world to achieve their long-held goal of liberation. At the war's end, the colonial powers brutally repressed nationalist groups, often with the help of the Japanese and U.S. armies, and attempted to reimpose their control. As in World War I, colonized peoples had been on the front lines defending the West, and they had witnessed the full barbarism of Western warfare. Like African American soldiers in the U.S. army, they experienced discrimination even while saving the West, and when they returned home, they did not receive the equal rights promised them. Moreover, successive wars had allowed local industries to develop outside the West, while industry in the imperial homelands fell into decline. As a result of the war, people in Asia, Africa, and the Middle East, often led by individuals steeped in Western values and experienced in war and its technology, sped toward independence.

The path to achieving independence—a process called **decolonization**—was paved with difficulties. In Africa, a continent whose peoples spoke several thousand languages and dialects, the European creation of convenient administrative units such as Nigeria and Rhodesia cut across ethnic lines and undermined local cultures. Religion played a divisive role in independence movements. In India, Hindus, Muslims, and Sikhs battled one another even though they shared the goal of eliminating British rule. In the Middle East and North Africa, pan-Arab and pan-Islamic movements—that is, those wanting to bring together all Arabs or all Muslims—might seem to have been unifying forces. Yet many Muslims were not Arab, many Arabs were not Muslim, and Islam itself encompassed competing beliefs and sects. Religious, ethnic, and cultural differences—many of them invented or promoted by the colonizers to divide and rule—worked against political unity. Despite these complications, various peoples in what was coming to be called the third world were able to overthrow imperialism, while the United States and the Soviet Union rushed to gain their support in the cold war.

The End of Empire in Asia

At the end of World War II, leaders in Asia succeeded in mobilizing mass discontent to drive out foreign rulers. Declining from an imperial power to a small island nation, Britain was the biggest loser. In 1947, it parted with India, whose independence it had promised in the 1930s. During World War II, some two million Indian men were mobilized to fight for the Allies in the Middle East and Asia, and India's domestic industries became important suppliers of war goods. Also during the war, Indian business leaders bought out local British entrepreneurs short of cash. Once the war ended, armed with economic might and military experience, Indians began to confront the British in strikes and other protests.

Britain quickly faced reality. So great was the mistrust the British had sown between the Indian National Congress and the Muslim League, however, that Britain decreed that two countries should emerge from the old colony. In 1947, India was created for Hindus, and Pakistan (itself later subdivided into two parts) was established for Muslims. During the independence year, tensions exploded between these two religious groups. The Sikhs, who felt totally ignored in the settlement, also contributed to the violence. Hundreds of thousands were massacred in the great shift of populations between India and Pakistan. In 1948, a radical Hindu assassinated Gandhi, who though a Hindu himself had continued to champion reconciliation among all the groups. Elsewhere, as some half a billion Asians gained their independence, Britain's sole notable colony was Hong Kong.

In 1949, after a lengthy civil war, a Communist victory in China brought into power a government led by Mao Zedong (1893–1976) that was no longer the plaything of the colonial powers. The new People's Republic of China under communism emphasized above all the welfare of the peasantry, rather than the industrial proletariat, and was thus distinct from Marxism and Stalinism. At the same time, backed by Stalin, Mao instituted reforms such as civil equality for women but also imposed Soviet-style collectivization, industrialization, and repression.

The Korean War, 1950–1953

The United States and the Soviet Union were deeply interested in East Asia—the United States because of the region's economic importance and the USSR because of its shared borders. The victory of the Chinese Communists spurred both superpowers to increase their involvement in Asian politics, where they faced off first in Korea, which had been split at the thirty-eighth parallel after World War II. In 1950, North Korea, with the support of the Soviet Union, invaded U.S.-backed South Korea, whose agents had been stirring up tensions with raids across the border. The United States maneuvered the United Nations into approving a "police action" against North Korea, and UN forces quickly drove well into North Korean territory, where they were met by the Chinese army. After two and a half years of a horribly destructive stalemate, the opposing sides finally agreed to a settlement in 1953: Korea would remain split at its prewar border, the thirty-eighth parallel. As a result of the Korean War, the United States increased its military spending from $10.9 billion in 1948 to almost $60 billion in 1953. The expansion of the cold war to Asia prompted the creation of an Asian counterpart to NATO—the Southeast Asia Treaty Organization (SEATO), established in 1954. Another important effect of the Korean War was the rapid reindustrialization of Japan to provide the United States with supplies.

The cold war then spread to Indochina, where nationalists had struggled against the postwar revival of French imperialism. Their leader, the European-educated Ho Chi Minh (1890–1969), built a powerful organization, the Viet Minh, to fight colonial rule. He advocated the redistribution of land held by big landowners, especially in the rich agricultural area in southern Indochina, where some six thousand owners possessed more than 60 percent of the land. Viet Minh peasant guerrillas ultimately defeated the technologically advanced French army, which was receiving aid from the United States, in the bloody battle of Dien Bien Phu in 1954. Later that year, the Geneva Conference carved out an independent Laos and divided Vietnam into North and South, each free from French control. The Communist-backed Viet Minh ruled in the north, while the United States supported an unpopular regime in the south, leaving the call for an independent Vietnamese nation basically unsettled.

Indochina, 1954

The Struggle for Identity in the Middle East

Independence struggles in the Middle East highlighted the world's growing need for oil and showed the ability of small countries to maneuver between the superpowers. As in other regions dominated by the West, Middle Eastern peoples resisted attempts to reimpose imperial control after 1945. Weakened by the war, British oil companies wanted to tighten their grip on profits, as the value of this energy source soared. But British leaders arrogantly behaved as if they were still dominant, leading Middle Eastern states to increase their economic and political clout by renegotiating higher payments for drilling rights from Western companies.

The legacy of the Holocaust complicated the Middle Eastern political scene. Western commitment to securing a Jewish nation in the Middle East stirred Arab determination not to be pushed out of their homeland. When World War II broke out, 600,000 Jewish settlers and twice as many Arabs lived tensely in British-controlled Palestine. In 1947, an exhausted Britain turned the area over to the United Nations, which in the aftermath of the Holocaust voted to partition Palestine into an Arab region and a Jewish one (Map 22.4). Conflicting claims, however, led to a war in which

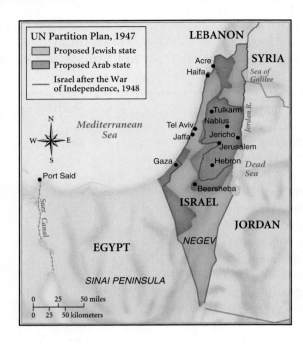

UN Partition Plan, 1947
☐ Proposed Jewish state
☐ Proposed Arab state
— Israel after the War of Independence, 1948

LEBANON
SYRIA
Acre
Haifa
Sea of Galilee
Mediterranean Sea
Tulkarm
Tel Aviv
Nablus
Jaffa
Jericho
Jerusalem
Gaza
Hebron
Dead Sea
Port Said
Beersheba
ISRAEL
JORDAN
NEGEV
EGYPT
SINAI PENINSULA
Suez Canal
Jordan R.

0   25   50 miles
0   25   50 kilometers

Map 22.4 The Partition of Palestine and the Creation of Israel, 1947–1948
The creation of the Jewish state of Israel in 1948 against a backdrop of ongoing wars among Jews and indigenous Arab peoples made the Middle East a powder keg. The struggle to secure resources and establish the borders of viable nation-states was at the heart of these bitter contests threatening to pull the superpowers into a third world war.

Jewish military forces prevailed. On May 14, 1948, the state of Israel came into being. "The dream had come true," Golda Meir, the future prime minister of Israel, observed, but "too late to save those who had perished in the Holocaust." Israel opened its gates to immigrants, whose ambition for land pressured their Arab neighbors.

One of those neighbors, Egypt, had gained its independence from Britain at the end of the war. Britain, however, retained its dominance in shipping to Asia through its control of the Suez Canal, which was owned by a British-run company. In 1952, Colonel Gamal Abdel Nasser became Egypt's president on a platform of economic modernization and true national independence—meaning Egyptian control of the canal. In July 1956, Nasser nationalized the canal. "I am speaking in the name of every Egyptian Arab," he remarked in his speech explaining the takeover, "and in the name of all those who believe in liberty and are ready to defend it." Nasser became a hero to Arabs, especially when Britain, Israel, and France attacked Egypt while the Hungarian revolt was in full swing. The British branded Nasser another Hitler and hoped that the Hungarian revolt would distract the superpowers. But the United States, fearing that Egypt would turn to the USSR, made the British back down. Nasser's triumph inspired confidence that colonized peoples around the world could force the imperial powers to surrender not just political but economic power.

New Nations in Africa

In sub-Saharan Africa, nationalist leaders roused their people to challenge Europe's increasing demands for resources and labor, which resulted in poverty for most African peoples. "The European Merchant is my shepherd, and I am in want," went one African version of the Twenty-third Psalm. Many Africans flocked to shanty-towns in cities during World War II, where they kept themselves alive doing menial labor for whites and scavenging. At the war's end, as veterans returned home, protests mounted. Kwame Nkrumah (1909–1972) led the inhabitants of the British-controlled West African Gold Coast in Gandhian-style passive resistance, finally driving the British to withdraw and bringing the state of Ghana into being in 1957. Nigeria, the most populous African colony, achieved independence from Britain in 1960, and many other African states also became free (Map 22.5).

Where the population was mostly black, independence came less violently than in mixed-race territory with large settler populations. The east coast of Africa, as well as

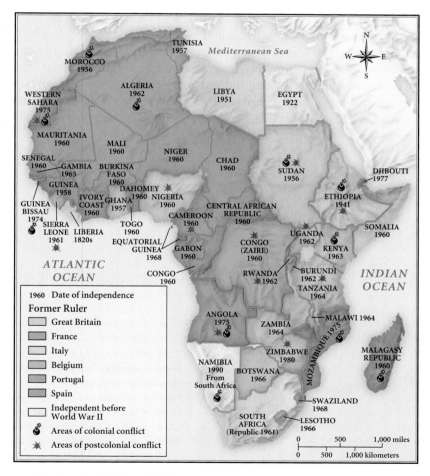

Map 22.5 The Decolonization of Africa, 1951–1990
The liberation of Africa from European rule was an uneven process, sometimes occurring peacefully and at other times demanding armed struggle to drive out European settlers, governments, and armies. After liberation, the difficult process of nation building—forming governments, educating children, providing social services, and the like—began. Creating national unity also proved challenging, except in places where the struggle against colonialism had already brought people together.

southern and central areas, had numerous European settlers, who violently resisted independence movements. In British East Africa, where white settlers ruled in splendor and blacks lacked both land and economic opportunity, violence erupted in the 1950s. African men formed rebel groups collectively called the Land Freedom Army, nicknamed the Mau Mau. With women serving as provisioners, messengers, and weapon stealers, Mau Mau bands, composed mostly of war veterans from the Kikuyu ethnic group, tried to recover land from whites. In 1963, Kenya gained formal independence, but only after the British had put hundreds of thousands of Kikuyus in concentration camps, called the "British Gulag" by those tortured there, and murdered tens of thousands more.

France granted independence with relatively little bloodshed to territories such as Tunisia, Morocco, and West Africa, where there were fewer white settlers. In Algeria, however, which had one million settlers of European descent, the French fought bitterly to keep control. At the end of World War II, the French army massacred tens of thousands of Algerian nationalists seeking independence. The liberation group resurfaced with new intensity in 1954 as the Front for National Liberation (FNL). The French dug in, sending more than 400,000 troops to Algeria. Neither side fought according to the accepted rules of warfare. The French savagely tortured Algerian Arabs; Algerian women, shielded by gender stereotypes, planted bombs in European cafés and carried weapons to assassination sites. The FNL, far less powerful than France, took its case to the court of world opinion. Reports of the

Jomo Kenyatta, First President of the New Kenyan Nation
Educated in England, Kenyatta wrote *Facing Mount Kenya,* a work that explained his native Kikuyu culture to Westerners. After a costly struggle during which he was imprisoned by the British, Kenyatta became president (1964–1978) of the new republic of Kenya. He stifled political debate by outlawing opposition parties. His one-party government brought social calm, which made Kenya a good place for Western investment. (© Bettmann/Corbis.)

French army's barbarous practices against Algeria's Muslim population prompted protests in Paris and around the globe.

France's Fourth Republic collapsed over Algeria, and Charles de Gaulle returned to power in 1958. While promising an end to the Algerian nightmare, he demanded the creation of a new republican government in France (the Fifth Republic), one with a strong president who chose the prime minister and could exercise emergency power. As de Gaulle's plans to decolonize Algeria unfolded, the French military, which had staked its prestige on keeping Algeria, launched a campaign of terrorism within metropolitan France. By 1962, de Gaulle had negotiated independence with the Algerian nationalists, and hundreds of thousands of *pieds noirs*—"black feet," as the French condescendingly called Europeans in Algeria—along with their Arab supporters, fled to France.

Violent resistance to the return of colonial rule also ended the Dutch and Belgian empires, and as newly independent nations emerged in Asia, Africa, and the Middle East, structures arose to promote international security and worldwide deliberations that included representation from the new states. Foremost among these was the United Nations, which convened for the first time in 1945. One notable change ensured the UN a greater chance of success than the League of Nations: both the United States and the Soviet Union were active members from the outset. The UN's charter outlined a collective global authority that would resolve conflicts and provide military protection if any members were threatened by aggression. In 1955, the Indonesian president Sukarno, who had succeeded in wrenching Indonesian independence from the Dutch, sponsored the Bandung Conference of nonaligned nations to set a common policy for achieving modernization and facing the superpowers. Both UN deliberations and meetings of emerging nations such as the Bandung Conference began raising major global issues such as human rights and inequities between countries of the north, which had prospered through colonial plunder, and those of the south, which had been plundered.

Newcomers Arrive in Europe

Amid the uncertainties of wars of liberation and independence, people from the former colonies began migrating to Europe—a reversal of the nineteenth-century trend of migration out of Europe. The first non-European newcomers came from Britain's Caribbean possessions right after the war. Next, labor shortages in northern Europe drove governments to negotiate with southern European countries for temporary workers. The German situation was especially serious because in 1950, the working-age population (people between the ages of fifteen and sixty-four) was composed of 15.5 million men and 18 million women. In an ideological climate that wanted women out of the workforce, the government desperately needed immigrant labor. After southern European reserves proved insufficient, Germany and France turned to North African and then to sub-Saharan countries in the 1960s. Countries in the Soviet bloc took in refugees from war-torn Southeast Asia. By the late 1970s, clandestine workers from Africa and Asia began entering countries such as Italy that had formerly exported labor. Scandinavia received immigrants from around the world, who flocked there because of reportedly greater opportunity and social programs to integrate newcomers. By the 1980s, some 8 percent of the European population was foreign-born, compared with 6 percent in the United States.

According to negotiated agreements, immigrant workers would have only temporary resident status and then return to their homeland. Initially, these workers were housed in barracks-like dormitories, and few Europeans paid any attention to the quality of their lives. Instead of settling into wider communities, they kept to themselves. Temporary workers made economic sense: virtually none of the welfare-state benefits applied to them, because their menial work was often off the books. "As they are young," one French business publication explained, "the immigrants often pay more in taxes than they receive in allowances." Most immigrants did jobs that people in the West avoided: they collected garbage, built roads, and cleaned homes. Although men predominated among immigrant workers, women performed undesirable jobs for even less pay.

The First "New" Europeans (1949)
Many immigrants from around the world came to Europe after World War II in search of economic well-being. Some of the first people to arrive in the late 1940s were from the Caribbean (like the men in the photograph looking for work in Britain) and from South Asia. Expanding welfare states hired some of them to do menial work in hospitals, clinics, and construction, no matter what their qualifications. But when race riots erupted and immigration continued to increase in the 1950s, the British House of Commons began debating the rights of these new Europeans. While governments and businesses in western Europe needed new laborers to rebuild after the war, some Europeans questioned whether they—or their wives and children—should be allowed to become citizens. (© Hulton Deutsch Collection/Corbis.)

Immigrants saw Europe as a land of relatively good government, wealth, and opportunity, and they appreciated the decent living conditions. As one Chinese immigrant to Spain put it, "If you want to be a millionaire, you must go to Singapore; if you want to be rich, you must go to Germany; but if you want good weather and an easy life, go to Spain." As empires collapsed, the composition of the European population became more diverse in terms of race, religion, and ethnicity. Whether in Europe or the United States, many of these newcomers eventually became citizens, and their children achieved good positions in government, business, education, and the professions.

REVIEW What were the results of decolonization?

Daily Life and Culture in the Shadow of Nuclear War

Both World War II and the cold war shaped postwar leisure and political culture. People engaged in heated debates over who had been responsible for Nazism, the subject of ethnic and racial justice, and the merits of the two superpowers. During this period of intense self-scrutiny, Europeans discussed the Americanization that seemed to accompany the influx of U.S. dollars, consumer goods, and cultural media. Were they becoming too materialistic like the Americans or too intolerant like the Soviets? As Europeans examined their war-filled past and their renewed prosperity, the cold war menaced hopes for peace and stability. In October 1962, the world held its breath while the leaders of the Soviet Union and the United States nearly provoked a nuclear conflagration over the issue of missiles on the island of Cuba. In hindsight, the existence of an extreme nuclear threat in an age of unprecedented prosperity seems utterly bewildering, but for those who lived with the threat of global annihilation, the dangers were all too real.

Restoring "Western" Values

After the inhumanity of Nazism, cultural currents in Europe and the United States reemphasized universal values and spiritual renewal. Some saw the churches as central to the restoration of values through an active commitment to "re-Christianizing" not only the West but the world. Responding to what he saw as a crisis in faith, Pope John XXIII (r. 1958–1963) in 1962 convened the Second Vatican Council, known as **Vatican II**. The Council modernized the liturgy, democratized many church procedures, and during the last session in 1965 renounced church doctrine that condemned the Jewish people as guilty of killing Jesus. Vatican II promoted ecumenism—cooperation among the world's faiths—and outreach to the world, which differed from the church's old spirit of missionary crusading on behalf of empire.

Despite religious reform, the trend toward a more secular culture continued. In the early postwar years, people in the U.S. bloc emphasized the triumph of "Western" civilization and "Western" values over fascism, and they characterized the war as one "to defend civilization [from] a conspiracy against man." This definition of the West often emphasized the heritage of Greece and Rome and the rise of national governments in Britain, France, and western Europe as these societies struggled against "barbaric" forces, be they nomadic tribes, Nazi armies, Communist agents, or national liberation movements in Asia and Africa. University courses in Western civilization flourished after the war to reaffirm those values.

Readers around the world snapped up memoirs of the death camps and tales of resistance to fascism. Rescued from the Third Reich in 1940, Nelly Sachs won the Nobel Prize for Literature in 1966 for her poetry about the Holocaust. Anne Frank's *Diary of a Young Girl* (1947), the moving record of a teenager hidden with her family in an Amsterdam house, showed the survival of Western values in the face of Nazi persecution. Amid the menacing evils of Nazism, Anne wrote that she never stopped believing that "people are really good at heart." Governments erected permanent plaques at spots where resisters had been killed, and organizations of resisters publicly commemorated their role in winning the war, hiding the fact of widespread collaboration in the mythical story of resistance.

By the end of the 1940s, **existentialism** was all the rage among the cultural elites and students in universities. This philosophy explored the meaning of human existence in a world where evil flourished. Two of its leaders, Albert Camus and Jean-Paul Sartre, had written for the resistance during the war, and in its aftermath they raised the question of "being," given what they perceived as the absence of God and the breakdown of morality during the war. Their answer was that being, or existing, was not the automatic process of either God's creation or humans' birth into the natural world. One was not born with spiritual goodness in the image of a creator, but instead one created an "authentic" existence through action and choice. Camus's novels, such as *The Stranger* (1942) and *The Plague* (1947), explored the responsibility of humans living under an evil and corrupt political order. Sartre's writings emphasized political activism and resistance under totalitarianism. Even though they never faced the enormous problems of making choices while living under fascism, young people in the 1950s found existentialism gripping and made it the most fashionable philosophy of the day.

In 1949, Simone de Beauvoir, Sartre's lifelong companion, published the twentieth century's most important work on the condition of women, *The Second Sex*. Beauvoir believed that most women had failed to take the kind of action necessary to lead authentic lives. Instead they lived in the world of biological necessity, devoting themselves exclusively to reproduction and motherhood. Failing to create an authentic self through action and accomplishment, they had become its opposite—an object, or "Other." Moreover, instead of struggling to define themselves and assert their freedom, women passively accepted their lives as defined by men. Beauvoir's classic book was a smash hit, in large part because people thought Sartre had written it. Both writers became celebrities, as the media spread the new commitment to humane values.

People of color in Africa and Asia contributed new theories of humanity by exploring topics of liberation and racial difference. During the 1950s, Frantz Fanon, a black psychiatrist from the French colony of Martinique, began analyzing liberation movements.

He wrote that the mental functioning of the colonized person was "traumatized" by the brutal imposition of an outside culture. Ruled by guns, the colonized person knew only violence and would thus naturally decolonize by means of violence. Translated into many languages, Fanon's *Black Skin, White Masks* (1952) and *The Wretched of the Earth* (1961) posed the question of how to decolonize one's culture and mind.

Simultaneous with decolonization, the commitment of such long-standing organizations as the National Association for the Advancement of Colored People (NAACP, founded 1909) to the cause of civil rights intensified in the 1950s. African Americans had fought in the war to defeat the Nazi idea of white racial superiority; as civilians, they now hoped to advance their ideals in the United States. With its ruling in *Brown v. Board of Education* (1954), the U.S. Supreme Court declared that segregated education violated the U.S. Constitution. On December 1, 1955, in Montgomery, Alabama, Rosa Parks, a part-time secretary for the local branch of the NAACP, boarded a bus and took the first available seat in the so-called colored section toward the back. When a white man found himself without a seat, the driver screamed at Parks, "Nigger, move back." By refusing to give up her seat at that moment, Parks violated discriminatory and often brutal southern laws affecting African Americans. She confronted that system through the studied practice of civil disobedience. Her action led to her arrest, followed by a community-wide boycott of public transportation by African Americans.

Civil rights groups boycotted discriminatory businesses and registered black voters disenfranchised by local regulations. Talented leaders emerged, foremost among them the great orator Martin Luther King Jr. (1929–1968), a young Baptist pastor originally from Georgia, whose speeches roused activists to nonviolent resistance and "soulforce"—Gandhi's *satyagraha,* or "holding to truth"—to counter aggression. The postwar culture of nonviolence would shape the civil rights movement for a few years, until the influence of Fanon and other anti-colonial activists turned it toward more violent measures.

Consumerism and Shifting Gender Norms

Government spending on European reconstruction and welfare helped prevent the kind of upheaval that had followed World War I. A rising birthrate and bustling youth culture boosted consumer spending, which in turn created jobs for veterans. Nonetheless, the war affected men's roles and sense of themselves. Young men who had missed World War II adopted the rough, violent style of soldiers, and roaming gangs posed as tough military types. While Soviet youths admired aviator aces, elsewhere groups such as the "teddy boys" in England (named after their Edwardian style of dress) and the *gamberros* (hooligans) in Spain took their cues from rock-and-roll music and films.

The leader of rock and roll was the American singer Elvis Presley. Sporting slicked-back hair and an aviator-style jacket, Presley bucked his hips and sang sexual lyrics to screaming and devoted fans. Rock-and-roll concerts and movies fired up young people across Europe, including in the Soviet bloc, where teens demanded the production of blue jeans and leather jackets. In a German nightclub late in the 1950s, members of a British rock group called the Quarrymen performed, yelling at and fighting with one another as part of their show. They would soon become known as the Beatles. Rebellious young American film stars like James Dean in *Rebel without a Cause* (1955) and Marlon Brando in *The Wild One* (1953) created the beginnings of a conspicuous postwar youth culture, in which the ideal was to be a bad boy.

The rebellious masculine style appeared also in literature, such as James Watson's autobiography, *The Double Helix* (1968), explaining how he and Francis Crick had discovered the structure of the gene by stealing other people's findings. German novelist Heinrich Böll, who decades later admitted to having been a Nazi soldier, protested that West Germany's postwar goal of respectability had allowed the people who had produced Nazism to become prominent once again. In Böll's novel *The Clown* (1963), a young middle-class hero leaves home and takes up life as a vagabond clown, mocking his audiences with clever pantomimes about the folly of their lives. He winds up begging in a railroad station, not a breadwinner but a bum. American "Beat" poets similarly rejected traditional ideals of the upright male breadwinner and family man.

Both high and low culture revealed that two horrendous world wars had weakened the Enlightenment view of men as rational, responsible achievers. The 1953 inaugural issue of the American magazine *Playboy,* and the hundreds of magazines that came

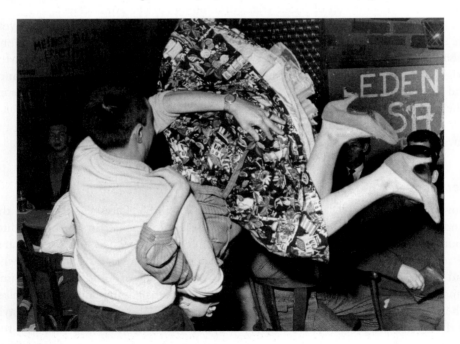

Rock and Roll
Rock and roll, born in the 1950s, spread around the world with unprecedented energy and speed. Teenage girls wore the voluminous skirts that the "new look" had made fashionable, and young men sported hairdos like Elvis Presley's. East and West, teens thronged, and even rioted, to attend rock concerts and would continue to do so despite public criticism and even police action against them. (ullstein bild/The Granger Collection, NY.)

to imitate it, ushered in a new and startling male identity. This new media presented modern man as sexually aggressive and independent of dull domestic life—just as he had been in the war. Breadwinning for a family destroyed a man's freedom and sense of self, this new male culture claimed. The definition of men's liberty came to include not just political rights but also sexual freedom outside of marriage.

In contrast, Western society promoted a postwar model for women that differed from their wartime roles. Rather than being seen as valued workers and heads of families in the absence of their men, postwar women were to symbolize the return to normalcy by leading a domestic and submissive life at home. Late in the 1940s, the fashion house of Christian Dior launched a clothing style called the "new look." It featured a pinched waist, tightly fitting bodice, and voluminous skirt. This restoration of the nineteenth-century female silhouette called for a renewal of older gender roles. Women's magazines publicized the new look and urged women to give up ambitions for themselves. Even in the hard-pressed Soviet Union, domesticity flourished: recipes for homemade face creams passed from woman to woman, and beauty parlors did a brisk business. In the West, household products such as refrigerators and washing machines raised standards for housekeeping by giving women the means to be "perfect" housewives.

However, new-look propaganda did not mesh with reality or even with all social norms. Dressmaking fabric was still being rationed in the late 1940s, and well into the next decade women could not always get enough to make voluminous skirts. In Europe, where people had barely enough to eat, the underwear needed for new-look contours simply did not exist, although the semistarved look was, for many, easy enough to achieve. In Spain, women were said to perform their role best by being religious and concerned with the spiritual well-being of their families. Spanish advertising, however, promoted physical beauty available through the consumption of cosmetics and clothing. European women continued to work outside the home after the war; indeed, mature women and mothers were working more than ever before—especially in the Soviet bloc. A major change was occurring, as the female workforce gradually became populated by wives and mothers who would hold jobs all their lives despite being bombarded with images of nineteenth-century femininity.

The advertising business helped create these cultural messages and promoted the widespread consumerism that accompanied recovery. Guided by marketing experts, western Europeans imitated Americans by driving some forty million motorized vehicles, including motorbikes, cars, buses, and trucks. They drank Coca-Cola and used American detergents, toothpaste, and soap. The number of radios in homes grew steadily, and radio remained the most influential medium throughout the 1950s, even as television loomed on the horizon. Only in the 1960s did television become an important consumer item for most Europeans.

The Culture of Cold War

Films, books, and other media added both criticism and support to the culture of cold war. Books such as George Orwell's *1984* (1949) were claimed by ideologues on both sides to support their beliefs. Ray Bradbury's popular *Fahrenheit 451* (1953), whose title indicates the temperature at which books would burn, condemned the cold war for restricting intellectual freedom. In the USSR, official writers churned out spy stories, and espionage novels topped best-seller lists in the West. *Casino Royale* (1953), by the British author Ian Fleming, introduced James Bond, who tested his wit and physical skill against Communist and other political villains. Soviet pilots would not take off when the work of Yulian Simyonov, the Russian counterpart of Ian Fleming, was playing on radio or television. Reports of Soviet- and U.S.-bloc characters—fictional or real—facing one another down became part of everyday life.

High and low culture alike contributed to the cold war climate. While many Europeans admired American innovation, the Communist Party in France led a successful campaign to ban Coca-Cola for a time in the 1950s. Soviet magazines carried fashion photos praised for their "decency" in contrast to the highly sexualized garments for women in the West. Both sides tried to win the cold war by pouring vast sums of money into high culture, although the United States did it by secretly channeling government money into foundations to award fellowships to designated artists or promote favorable journalism around the world. As leadership of the art world passed to the United States, art became part of the cold war. Abstract expressionism, practiced by American artists such as Jackson Pollock, produced nonrepresentational works by dripping, spattering, and pouring paint. Abstract expressionists spoke of the importance of the artist's self-discovery. "If I stretch my arms next to the rest of myself and wonder where my fingers are, that is all the space I need as a painter," commented one of them on his relationship with his canvas. Said to prove Western freedom, such painters were given shows in Europe and awarded commissions at the secret direction of the U.S. Central Intelligence Agency (CIA).

The USSR openly promoted an official Communist culture. When a show of abstract art opened in the Soviet Union, Khrushchev yelled at the exhibition itself that it was "dog shit." Pro-Soviet critics focused on workers and the oppressed races in the United States. In Italy, the neorealist technique was developed by filmmakers such as Vittorio De Sica in *The Bicycle Thief* (1948). Such works challenged Hollywood-style sets and costumes by using ordinary characters living in devastated, impoverished cities. They criticized both middle-class prosperity and fascist pretense. "We are in rags? Let's show everyone our rags," said one Italian director. Many of these left-leaning directors associated support for the suffering masses with the Communist cause, while on the pro-American side, the film *Doctor Zhivago* became a hit celebrating individualism and condemning the Communist way of life. Seen or unseen, the cold war entered cultural life.

The Atomic Brink

Radio was at the center of the cold war. As superpower rivalry heated up, radio's propaganda function remained strong, as it had in wartime. During the late 1940s and early 1950s, the Voice of America broadcast in thirty-eight languages from one hundred transmitters to provide an alternative source of news for people in eastern Europe.

Barbara Hepworth, *Single Form* (1961–1964)
Like others in the West, British sculptor Barbara Hepworth was strangely buoyed by the end of World War II, hoping that it meant the dawn of a new age. Full of renewed energy, Hepworth believed that art should follow pure forms, which some called "primitive," as a way of expressing enduring values. Her twenty-one-foot abstract sculpture *Single Form,* shown here as a plaster cast, was installed at the United Nations building in New York to commemorate the life of her friend Dag Hammarskjöld, who served as secretary-general of the United Nations from 1953 to 1961. (Photo Morgan-Wells, London/© Bowness, Hepworth Estate.)

The Soviet counterpart broadcast in Russian around the clock but initially spent much of its wattage jamming U.S. programming. Russian programs stressed a uniform Communist culture and values; the United States, by contrast, emphasized diverse programming and featured debate about current affairs. U.S. radio aimed to contrast the dictatorial nature of Communist society with America's commitment to choice and free speech. The public also heard reports of a nuclear buildup, while at school children rehearsed for nuclear war. At home families built bomb shelters in their backyards.

It was in this upsetting climate of cold war that John Fitzgerald Kennedy (1917–1963) became U.S. president in 1960. Kennedy represented American affluence and youth and also the nation's commitment to cold war. Kennedy's media advisers recognized how perfect a match their articulate, good-looking president was for the power of television. A war hero and early fan of the fictional cold war spy James Bond, Kennedy escalated the cold war. Some of this escalation occurred over the nearby island of Cuba, where in 1959 Fidel Castro had come to power after overthrowing a corrupt dictatorship. After being rejected by the United States, Castro allied his new government with the USSR. In the spring of 1961, Kennedy, assured of success by the CIA, launched an invasion of Cuba at the Bay of Pigs to overthrow Castro. The invasion failed miserably and humiliated the United States.

Cold war tensions increased. In the summer of 1961, the East German government directed workers to stack bales of barbed wire across miles of the city's east-west border as the beginning of the Berlin Wall. The divided city had served as an escape route by which some three million people had fled to the West. Kennedy responded by calling for increased defense spending. In October 1962, tensions came to a head in the Cuban missile crisis, when the CIA reported the installation of silos to house Soviet missiles in Cuba. Kennedy acted forcefully, ordering a naval blockade of ships headed for Cuba and demanding removal of the installations. For several days, the world stood on the brink of nuclear disaster. Then, between October 25 and 27, Khrushchev and Kennedy negotiated an end to the crisis. Kennedy spent the remainder of his short life working to improve nuclear diplomacy; Khrushchev did the same. In the summer of 1963, less than a year after the shock of the Cuban missile crisis, the United States and the Soviet Union signed a test-ban treaty outlawing the explosion of nuclear weapons in the atmosphere and the seas. Allowing the superpowers to back away from the brink, the treaty held out hope that the cold war and its culture would give way to something better.

REVIEW   How did the cold war affect everyday culture and social life?

Conclusion

Nikita Khrushchev was ousted in 1964 for his erratic policies and for appearing to back down in the Cuban missile crisis. In his forced retirement, he expressed regret at his brutal treatment of Boris Pasternak. "We shouldn't have banned [*Doctor Zhivago*]," he said. "There's nothing anti-Soviet in it." But the postwar decades were bleak diplomatically. The two superpowers—the Soviet Union and the United States—each controlling atomic arsenals, overshadowed the old European powers and engaged in a menacing cold war, complete with the threat of nuclear annihilation. The cold war saturated everyday life, giving birth to bomb shelters, spies, and

Mapping the West The Cold War World, c. 1960
Superpower rivalry resulted in the division of much of the industrial world into cold war alliances. The United States and the Soviet Union also vied for the allegiance of the newly decolonized countries of Asia and Africa by providing military, economic, and technological assistance. Wars such as those in Vietnam and Korea were also products of the cold war. How might this map be said to convey the idea of a first, second, and third world?

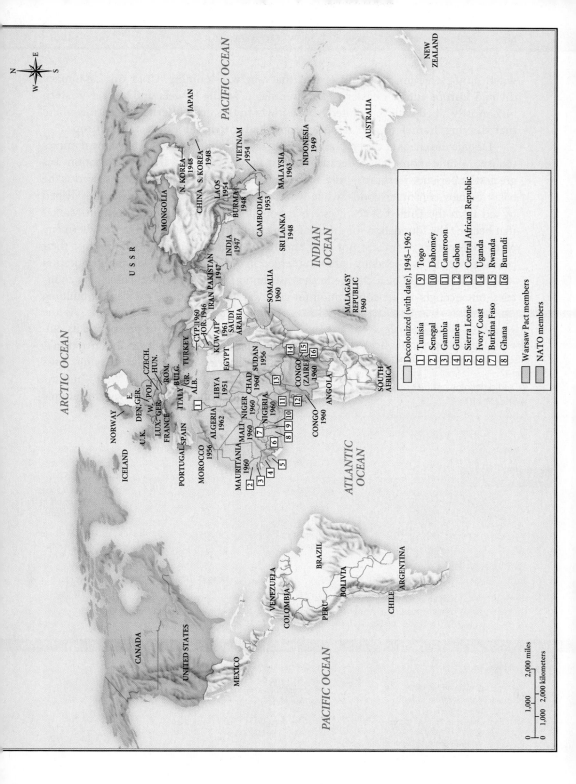

ARCTIC OCEAN

PACIFIC OCEAN

PACIFIC OCEAN

ATLANTIC OCEAN

INDIAN OCEAN

NEW ZEALAND

AUSTRALIA

JAPAN

N. KOREA 1948
S. KOREA 1948
CHINA 1949
VIETNAM 1954
LAOS 1954
BURMA 1948
CAMBODIA 1953
MALAYSIA 1963
INDONESIA 1949

MONGOLIA

USSR

INDIA 1947
PAKISTAN 1947
IRAN 1946
SRI LANKA 1948

SOMALIA 1960

MALAGASY REPUBLIC 1960

SOUTH AFRICA

ANGOLA

CONGO 1960

CONGO (ZAIRE) 1960

SUDAN 1956

CHAD 1960

NIGER 1960

NIGERIA 1960

MALI 1960

MAURITANIA 1960

ALGERIA 1962

MOROCCO 1956

LIBYA 1951

EGYPT

SAUDI ARABIA

KUWAIT 1961

JOR. 1946

CYP. 1960

TURKEY

GR.

ALB.

BULG.

ROM.

ITALY

HUN.

CZECH.

W. GER.

POL.

LUX.

FRANCE

E. GER.

DEN.

U.K.

NORWAY

ICELAND

PORTUGAL

SPAIN

CANADA

UNITED STATES

MEXICO

VENEZUELA

COLOMBIA

PERU

BOLIVIA

BRAZIL

CHILE

ARGENTINA

1 Tunisia
2 Senegal
3 Gambia
4 Guinea
5 Sierra Leone
6 Ivory Coast
7 Burkina Faso
8 Ghana
9 Togo
10 Dahomey
11 Cameroon
12 Gabon
13 Central African Republic
14 Uganda
15 Rwanda
16 Burundi

Decolonized (with date), 1945–1962

Warsaw Pact members

NATO members

1 3 4 5 6 7 8 9 10 11 12 13 14 15 16 2

0   1,000   2,000 miles
0   1,000   2,000 kilometers

witch hunts, creating a culture of fear that war was looming. Cold war diplomacy divided Europe into an eastern bloc dominated by the Soviets and a freer western bloc mostly allied with the United States. It was in this grim international atmosphere that starving, homeless, and refugee people had to rebuild a devastated Europe.

Despite the chaos at the end of 1945, both halves of Europe recovered almost miraculously in little more than a decade. Eastern Europe, where wartime devastation was greatest, experienced less prosperity. In western Europe wartime technology served as the basis for new consumer goods, while welfare-state programs improved health. Helped by aid from the United States, western Europe formed a successful Common Market that became the foundation for greater European unity. As a result of the war, Germany recovered as two countries, not one, and the weakened European powers lost their colonies. Newly independent nations emerged in Asia and Africa, leaving in question whether there would be a change in the distribution of global power. These new countries, often caught in the competition for cold war allies, faced the problem of building political and economic institutions. As the West as a whole grew in prosperity, its cultural life focused paradoxically on rethinking Western values while enjoying mass consumerism. Above all, the West—and the rest of the world—had to survive the atomic rivalry of the superpowers.

CHAPTER REVIEW QUESTIONS
1. How did the political climate after World War II differ from the political climate after World War I?
2. Why did decolonization occur so soon after World War II?

TIMELINE

- **1962** United States and USSR face off in the Cuban missile crisis
- **1953** Stalin dies; Korean War ends; first issue of *Playboy*
- **1961** East German workers begin to construct the Berlin Wall
- **1950** Korean War begins
- **1958** Fifth Republic begins in France
- **1949** Mao Zedong leads Communist revolution in China; Western allies establish NATO; Simone de Beauvoir, *The Second Sex*
- **1957** Boris Pasternak, *Doctor Zhivago*; USSR launches *Sputnik*; European Economic Community formed

1945	1950	1955	1960	1965

- **1945** Cold war begins
- **1947** India and Pakistan win independence from Britain; U.S. president Harry Truman announces the Truman Doctrine
- **1948** State of Israel established
- **1954** *Brown v. Board of Education* prohibits segregated schools in the United States; Vietnamese forces defeat the French at Dien Bien Phu
- **1955** Soviet Union establishes the Warsaw Pact
- **1956** Egyptian leader General Gamal Abdel Nasser nationalizes the Suez Canal; uprising in Hungary against the USSR

For practice quizzes and other study tools, see the Online Study Guide at
bedfordstmartins.com/huntconcise.

For primary-source material from this period, see Chapter 27 of
Sources of The Making of the West, Third Edition.

Suggested References

In the past decades, the opening of Soviet archives and careful research in U.S.
records have allowed for more informed views of the diplomacy and politics of the
cold war. The Cold War Files Web site, supported by the Woodrow Wilson Center
and George Washington University, contains biographies of the main players, documents, and miscellaneous details of cold war events.

Cold War Files: Interpreting History through Documents: http://coldwarfiles.org

Crowley, David, and Susan E. Reid, eds. *Socialist Spaces: Sites of Everyday Life in the Eastern Bloc.* 2002.

Frommer, Benjamin. *National Cleansing: Retribution against Nazi Collaborators in Postwar Czechoslovakia.* 2005.

Gaddis, John. *The Cold War: A New History.* 2006.

Grossman, Atina. *Jews, Germans, and Allies: Close Encounters in Occupied Germany, 1945–1949.* 2007.

Herzog, Dagmar. *Sex after Fascism: Memory and Morality in Twentieth-Century Germany.* 2005.

Jobs, Richard I. *Riding the New Wave: Youth and the Rejuvenation of France after World War II.* 2007.

Judt, Tony. *Postwar: A History of Europe since 1945.* 2006.

Milward, Alan S. *The United Kingdom and the Economic Community.* 2002.

Moeller, Robert. *War Stories: The Search for a Usable Past in the Federal Republic of Germany.* 2001.

Naimark, Norman, and Leonid Gbianshii, eds. *The Establishment of Communist Regimes in Eastern Europe.* 1997.

Poiger, Uta. *Jazz, Rock, and Rebels: Cold War Politics and American Culture in a Divided Germany.* 2000.

Shepard, Todd. *The Invention of Decolonization: The Algerian War and the Remaking of France.* 2006.

Spector, Ronald H. *In the Ruins of Empire: The Japanese Surrender and the Battle for Postwar Asia.* 2007.

Statler, Kathryn, and Andrew Johns, eds. *The Eisenhower Administration, the Third World, and the Globalization of the Cold War.* 2006.

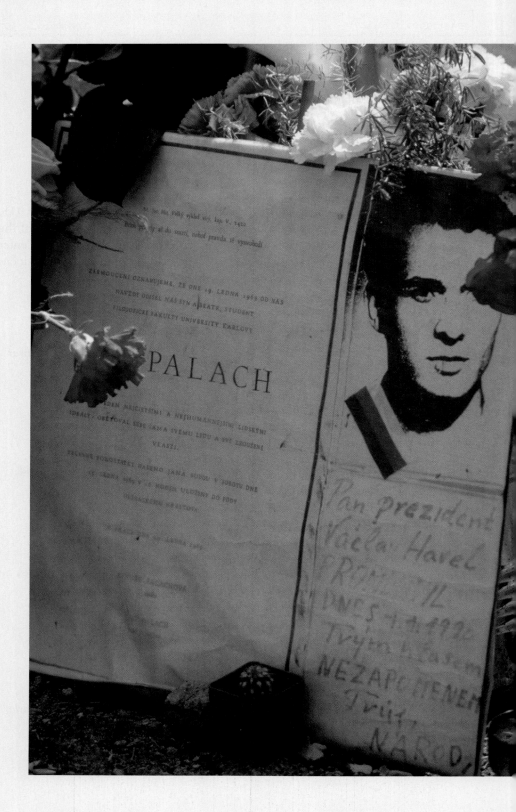

Postindustrial Society and the End of the Cold War Order

1965–1989

I N JANUARY 1969, JAN PALACH, a twenty-one-year-old philosophy student, drove to a main square in Prague, doused his body with gasoline, and set himself ablaze. Before that, he had put aside his coat with a message in it demanding an end to Communist repression in Czechoslovakia. It promised more such suicides unless the government lifted state censorship. The manifesto was signed "Torch No. 1." Palach's suicide stunned his nation. Black flags hung from windows, and close to a million people flocked to his funeral. In the next months, more Czech youth followed Palach's grim example and became torches for freedom.

Shrine to Jan Palach

Jan Palach was a martyr to the cause of an independent Czechoslovakia, free to pursue a non-Soviet destiny. His self-immolation on behalf of that cause in 1969 roused the nation. As makeshift shrines sprang up and multiplied throughout the 1970s and 1980s, they served as common rallying points that ultimately contributed to the overthrow of Communist rule. Václav Havel, the future president of a liberated Czechoslovakia, was arrested early in the momentous year of 1989 for commemorating Palach's sacrifice at the shrine. In light of so many other deaths in the Soviet bloc, why did Palach's death become so powerful a force? (© Marc Garanger/Corbis.)

Before his self-immolation, Jan Palach was an ordinary, well-educated citizen of an increasingly technological society. Having recovered from World War II, the West shifted from a manufacturing economy based on heavy industry to a service economy that depended on technical knowledge in fields such as engineering, health care, and finance. This new service economy has been labeled "postindustrial." To staff it, institutions of higher education sprang up at a dizzying rate and attracted more students than ever before. Young men like Palach—along with women, minorities, and many other activists in the 1960s and 1970s—struck out against war and cold war, inequality and repression, and even against knowledge and technology. From Czechoslovakia to the United States and around the world, protesters warned that postindustrial nations in general and the superpowers in particular were becoming technological monsters. Before long, countries in both the Soviet and U.S. blocs were close to political revolution.

The challenge posed by young reformers came at a bad time for the superpowers and other leading European states. An agonizing war in Vietnam weakened the United States, and China confronted the Soviet Union on its borders. In a dramatic turn of events, the oil-producing states of the Middle East formed a cartel and reduced the flow of oil to the leading industrial nations in the 1970s. The resulting price increases helped bring on a recession, threatening the postindustrial economy. Extremists turned to **terrorism** to achieve their goals, and there was no guarantee that the superpowers—despite their wealth and military might—would emerge victorious in this age of increasingly global competition. As the USSR experienced economic decay, a reform-minded leader, Mikhail Gorbachev, directed his nation to change course. It was too late: in 1989, the Soviet bloc collapsed, helped by countless acts of protest, not the least of them the individual heroism of Jan Palach and his fellow human torches.

CHAPTER FOCUS QUESTION   How did technological, economic, and social change contribute to increased activism, and what were the political results of that activism?

The Revolution in Technology

The protests of the 1960s and after took place in the midst of astonishing technological advances. These advances steadily boosted prosperity and changed daily life in the West, where people awoke to instantaneous radio and television news, worked with computers, and used revolutionary contraceptives to control reproduction. Satellites orbiting the earth relayed telephone signals and collected military intelligence. Smaller gadgets—electric popcorn poppers, portable radios and tape players, automatic garage door openers—made life more pleasant. The reliance of humans on machines led one philosopher to insist that people were no longer self-sufficient individuals but rather cyborgs—humans who needed machines for ordinary life processes.

The Information Age: Television and Computers

Information technology brought about change in the postindustrial period just as innovations in textile making and the spread of railroads had in the nineteenth century. This technology's ability to transmit knowledge, culture, and political information globally appeared even more revolutionary. In the first half of the twentieth century, mass journalism, radio, and films had created a more uniform society based on shared information and images. In the last third of the century, television, computers, and telecommunications made information even more accessible and standardized. Once remote villages were linked to urban capitals on the other side of the world thanks to videocassettes, satellite television, and telecommunications.

Between the mid-1950s and the mid-1970s, Europeans followed Americans in rapidly adopting television as a major entertainment and communications medium. In 1954, just 1 percent of French households had a television; by 1974, almost 80 percent did. With the average viewer tuning in about four and a half hours a day, the audience for newspapers and theater declined. "We devote more . . . hours per year to television than [to] any other single artifact," one sociologist commented in 1969. As with radio, European governments funded television broadcasting with tax dollars and controlled TV programming to avoid what they perceived as the substandard fare offered by American commercial TV. The French launched popular programs featuring philosophers and other writers; others broadcast drama, ballet, concerts, variety shows, and news. The welfare state, in Europe at least, thereby gained more power to shape daily life.

The emergence of communications satellites and video recorders in the 1960s brought competition to state-sponsored television. Worldwide audiences enjoyed broadcasts from around the globe as satellite technology allowed for the transmission of sports broadcasts and other programming. Feature films on videotape became readily available to television stations (although not yet to individuals) and competed with made-for-television movies and other programs. The competition increased in 1969 when the Sony Corporation introduced the first affordable color videocassette recorder to the consumer market. Critics complained that although TV provided more information than had ever been available before, the resulting shared culture represented the lowest common denominator.

East and West, television exercised a powerful political and cultural influence. Even in a rural area of the Soviet Union, more than 70 percent of the inhabitants watched television regularly in the late 1970s. Educational programming united the far-flung population of the USSR by broadcasting shows designed to advance Soviet culture. At the same time, with travel impossible or forbidden to many, shows about foreign lands were among the most popular. Heads of state could usually bump regular programming. In the 1960s, French president Charles de Gaulle addressed his fellow citizens frequently, employing the grandiose gestures of an imperial ruler to stir patriotism. As electoral success in western Europe increasingly depended on cultivating an appealing media image, politicians needed media experts as much as they did policy experts.

Just as revolutionary as television, the computer reshaped work in science, defense, and industry. Computers had evolved dramatically since the first electronic ones, among them the Colossus, which the British used in 1943 to decode Nazi military and diplomatic messages. After the war, computing machines shrank from the size of a gymnasium in the 1940s to that of an attaché case in the mid-1980s. They also became far less expensive and fantastically more powerful, thanks to the development of increasingly sophisticated digital electronic circuitry implanted on tiny silicon chips. Within a few decades, the computer could perform hundreds of millions of operations per second, and the price of the integrated circuit at the heart of computer technology would fall to less than a dollar.

Computers changed the pace and patterns of work not only by speeding up but also by performing many operations that workers had once done themselves. In garment making, for example, experienced workers no longer painstakingly figured out how to arrange patterns on cloth for maximum economy. Instead, a computer determined the best positioning of pattern pieces, and trained workers, usually women, followed the machine's directions. Soon, like outworkers in the eighteenth century, people could work for industries at home, connected to a central mainframe. In 1981 the French phone company launched a public Internet server, the

Minitel—a forerunner of the World Wide Web—through which individuals could make reservations, perform stock transactions, and gain information.

Whereas during the Industrial Revolution mechanical power replaced human energy, the computer technology of the information revolution added to brainpower. Many believed that computers would profoundly expand mental life, providing, in the words of one scientist, "boundless opportunities . . . to resolve the puzzles of cosmology, of life, and of the society of man." Others argued that computers programmed people, reducing human initiative and ability to solve problems. Such predictions are still untested even today, because the information revolution continues to unfold.

The Space Age

The Soviet launch of the *Sputnik* satellite in 1957 marked the start of the space race with the United States. The competition led to increasingly complex spaceflights that tested humans' ability to survive the process of space exploration, including weightlessness. Astronauts walked in space, endured weeks (and later months) in orbit, fixed satellites, and carried out experiments for the military and private industry. In addition, a series of unmanned rockets filled the earth's gravitational sphere with weather, television, intelligence, and other communications satellites. In July 1969, a worldwide television audience watched as U.S. astronauts Neil Armstrong and Edwin "Buzz" Aldrin walked on the moon's surface—the climactic moment in the space race.

Valentina Tereshkova, Russian Cosmonaut
People sent into space were heroes, representing modern values of courage, strength, and well-honed skills. Insofar as the space age was part of the cold war race for superpower superiority, the USSR held the lead during the first decade. The Soviets trained both women and men, and the 1963 flight of Valentina Tereshkova, the first woman in space, supported Soviet claims of gender equality in contrast to the all-male superstar image of the early U.S. space program. (Hulton Archive/Getty Images.)

The space race also influenced culture. Astronauts and cosmonauts were perhaps the era's most admired heroes: Yuri Gagarin, John Glenn, and Valentina Tereshkova—the first woman in space—topped the list. Children's toys and games centered increasingly on space. Films such as *2001: A Space Odyssey* (1968) portrayed space explorers answering questions about life that were formerly the domain of church leaders. Polish author Stanislaw Lem's popular novel *Solaris* (1971), later made into a film, described space age individuals engaged in personal quests for meaning and drew readers and viewers into futuristic fantasy.

The space age grew out of cold war concerns and relied on advances in the same rocket technology that powered missiles. At the same time, the space age depended on global cooperation. From the 1960s on, U.S. spaceflights often involved the participation of other countries. In 1965, an international consortium headed by the United States launched the first commercial communications satellite, *Intelsat I,* and by the 1970s some 150 countries worked together at more than four hundred stations worldwide to maintain global satellite communications. Although half of all satellites were used for spying, the rest made international communication possible and transnational cooperation a necessity.

Pure science flourished amid the space race. Astronomers used mineral samples from the moon to calculate the age of the solar system with unprecedented precision. Unmanned spacecraft provided data on cosmic radiation, magnetic fields, and infrared sources. Although the media touted the human conquerors of space, breakthroughs in space exploration and astronomy also depended on technology, including the radio telescope, which depicted space by receiving, measuring, and calculating nonvisible rays. These findings reinforced the so-called big bang theory of the origins of the universe, first outlined in the 1930s by American astronomer Edwin Hubble and given crucial support in the 1950s by the discovery of a low level of radiation permeating the universe in all directions. The big bang theory proposes that the universe began with the explosion of superdense, superhot matter some ten billion to twenty billion years ago.

Revolutions in Biology, Reproductive Technology, and Sexual Behavior

A revolution in the life sciences brought about dramatic new health benefits and ultimately changed reproduction itself. In 1952, scientists Francis Crick, an Englishman, and James Watson, an American, discovered the structure of **DNA**, the material in a cell's chromosomes that carries hereditary information. They showed how the double helix of the DNA molecule splits to form the basis of each new cell. This genetic material, biologists concluded, provides a chemical pattern for an individual organism's life. Beginning in the 1960s, genetics and the new field of molecular biology progressed rapidly. Growing understanding of nucleic acids and proteins advanced knowledge about viruses and bacteria that effectively ended the ravages of polio, tetanus, syphilis, tuberculosis, and such dangerous childhood diseases as mumps and measles in the West.

Scientists used their understanding of DNA to alter the makeup of plants and to bypass natural animal reproduction in a process called cloning—obtaining the cells of an organism and dividing or reproducing them in an exact copy in a laboratory. In 1997, one group of British researchers successfully produced a cloned sheep named Dolly, though she suffered an array of disabilities and died six years later. Cloning raised questions of whether scientists should interfere with so basic and essential a process as reproduction. The possibility of genetically altering species and even creating new ones (for instance, to control agricultural pests) led to concern about how such actions would affect the balance of nature. In 1967, Dr. Christiaan Barnard of South Africa performed the first successful heart transplant, and U.S. doctors later developed an artificial heart. As major breakthroughs like these occurred, commentators asked whether the enormous cost of new medical technology to save a few people would be better spent on helping the many who lacked even basic health care.

Technology also influenced the most intimate areas of human relations—sexuality and procreation. Matching family size to agricultural productivity no longer shaped sexual behavior in the industrialized and urbanized West. With reliable birth-control devices more readily available, young people began having sexual relations earlier, with less risk of pregnancy. These trends accelerated in the 1960s when the birth-control

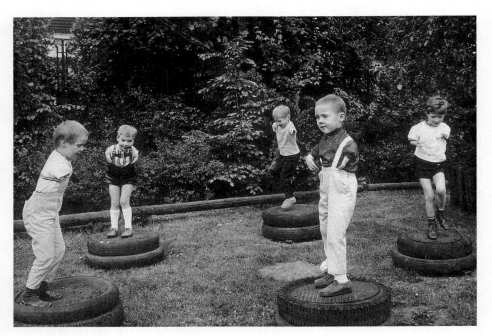

Thalidomide Children
In the last third of the twentieth century, increasingly destructive side effects of powerful medicines became apparent. Women who took the sedative thalidomide while pregnant gave birth to children with severe disabilities. The race to profit from scientific and technological developments sometimes ignored human well-being, and the public condemned companies selling untested products. When children affected by thalidomide became adults, they were among those who launched the disability rights movement. **For more help analyzing this image, see the visual activity for this chapter in the Online Study Guide at** bedfordstmartins.com/huntconcise. (Deutsche Presse Agentur.)

pill, first tested on women in developing areas, came on the market. Millions also sought out voluntary surgical sterilization through tubal ligations and vasectomies. New techniques brought abortion, traditionally performed by amateurs, into the hands of medical professionals, making it a safe procedure for the first time.

Childbirth and conception were similarly transformed. Whereas only a small minority of Western births took place in hospitals in 1920, more than 90 percent did by 1970. Obstetricians now performed much of the work midwives had once done. As pregnancy and birth became a medical process, new procedures and equipment made it possible to monitor women and fetuses throughout pregnancy, labor, and delivery. In 1978, the first "test-tube baby," Louise Brown, was born to an English couple. She had been conceived when her mother's eggs were fertilized with her father's sperm in a laboratory dish and then implanted in her mother's uterus—a complex process called **in vitro fertilization**. If a woman could not carry a child to term, the laboratory-fertilized embryo could be implanted in the uterus of a surrogate, or substitute, mother. Researchers even began working on an artificial womb to allow for reproduction entirely outside the body—from storage bank to artificial embryonic environment.

> REVIEW   What were the technological and scientific advances of the 1960s and 1970s, and how did they change human life and society?

Postindustrial Society and Culture

Soaring investments in science and the spread of technology put Western countries on what has been called a postindustrial course. Instead of being centered on manufacturing and heavy industry, the postindustrial economy emphasized the distribution of services such as health care and education. The service sector was the leading force in the economy, and this meant that intellectual work, not industrial or manufacturing work, was central to creating jobs and profits. Moreover, all parts of society and industry interlocked, forming a system constantly in need of complex analysis, as in the nuclear industry. These characteristics of postindustrial society would carry over from the 1960s and 1970s into the next century.

A major development of the postindustrial era was the **multinational corporation**. Multinationals produced goods and services for a global market and conducted business worldwide, but unlike older kinds of international firms, they established major factories in countries other than their home bases. For example, of the five hundred largest businesses in the United States in 1970, more than one hundred did over a quarter of their business abroad, with IBM operating in more than one hundred countries. Although U.S.-based corporations led the way, European and Japanese multinationals like Volkswagen, Shell, Nestlé, and Sony also had a broad global reach.

Some multinationals had bigger revenues than entire nations. In the first years after World War II, multinationals preferred European employees, who constituted a highly educated labor pool and had well-developed consumer habits. Then, beginning in the 1960s, multinationals moved more of their operations to formerly colonized states to reduce labor costs and avoid taxes. Although these companies provided jobs in developing areas, profits usually enriched foreign stockholders and thus looked to some like imperialism in a new form.

Many firms believed that they could stay competitive only by expanding, merging with other companies, or becoming partners with government in doing business. In France, for example, a massive glass conglomerate merged with a metallurgical company to form a new group specializing in all phases of construction—a wise move given the postwar building boom. Firms also increased their investment in research and cooperated internationally to produce major new products. The British-French supersonic aircraft Concorde, which, beginning with its first flight in 1976, flew from London to New York in less than four hours, was one result. Another venture was the Airbus, a more practical series of passenger jets inaugurated in 1972 by a consortium of European firms. Both projects grew from the strong relationship among government, business, and science as well as from the international cooperation in manufacturing among members of the Common Market. Such relationships allowed for successful competition in the global business world.

The New Worker

In the early years of industry, workers often labored to exhaustion and lived in poor conditions. This scenario changed fundamentally in postwar Europe with the reduction of the blue-collar workforce, the growth of offshore manufacturing, and increased automation of industrial work. Manufacturing was simply cleaner and less dangerous than before. Within firms, the relationship of workers to bosses shifted as management started grouping workers into teams that set their own production quotas, organized and assigned tasks, and competed with other teams to produce more. As workers took on responsibilities once assigned to managers, union membership declined.

In both the U.S. and Soviet blocs, a new kind of working class of white-collar service personnel emerged. Its rise undermined economic distinctions based on the way one worked, for those who performed service work were not necessarily better paid than blue-collar workers. The ranks of service workers swelled with researchers, health care and medical workers, technicians, planners, and government staff. As the emphasis on service work grew, entire categories of employees such as flight attendants spent a good part of their time serving the psychological well-being of customers. The consumer economy provided more jobs in restaurants and personal health, fitness and grooming, and hotels and tourism. By 1969, the percentage of service-sector employees had passed that of manufacturing workers in several industrialized countries: 61.1 percent versus 33.7 percent in the United States and 48.8 percent versus 41.1 percent in Sweden.

Postindustrial work life differed somewhat in the Soviet bloc, where the percentage of farmers remained higher than in western Europe. A huge difference between professional occupations and those involving physical work also remained in socialist countries because of declining investment in advanced machinery and cleaner work processes. Men in both blocs generally earned higher pay and had better jobs than women. Somewhere between 80 and 95 percent of women in socialist countries worked, mostly under difficult conditions.

Farming changed as well, consolidating and becoming more scientific. Small landowners sold family plots to agribusinesses—that is, vast holdings devoted to commercial rather than peasant farming. Governments, farmers' cooperatives, and planning agencies influenced the decision making of the individual farmer; they set production quotas and handled an array of marketing transactions. Genetic research that yielded pest-resistant seeds and the skyrocketing use of pesticides, fertilizers, and machinery contributed to growth. Between 1965 and 1979, the number of tractors in Germany more than tripled from 384,000 to 1,340,000.

Planners played a crucial role in transforming agriculture. For example, in the 1970s French farmer Fernande Pelletier made a living on her hundred-acre farm in southwestern France in the new setting of international agribusiness. Advised by a government expert, Pelletier produced whatever foods might sell competitively in the Common Market. On expert advice, she switched from lamb and veal to foie gras and walnuts, and she joined with other farmers in her region to buy heavy machinery and sell her products. Agricultural prosperity required as much managerial effort and up-to-date information as did success in other sectors.

The Boom in Education and Research

Education and research were key to running postindustrial society and were the means by which nations maintained their economic and military might. Common sense, hard work, and creative intuition had launched the earliest successes of the Industrial Revolution. By the late twentieth century, success in business or government required a wide variety of expertise and ever-growing staffs of researchers—"the accumulation of knowledge, not of wealth," as one official put it.

Investment in research fueled military and industrial leadership. The United States funneled more than 20 percent of its gross national product into research in the 1960s, attracting many of Europe's leading intellectuals and technicians to the United States in a so-called brain drain. Complex systems—for example, nuclear power generation with its many components, from scientific conceptualization to plant construction to the publicly supervised disposal of radioactive waste—required intricate coordination and professional oversight. Scientists and bureaucrats often made more crucial decisions than did elected politicians in the realm of space programs, weapons development, and economic policy. Here, East-West differences became important: Soviet-bloc nations were less successful at linking their considerable achievements in science to actual applications because of bureaucratic red tape. In the 1960s, some 40 percent of Soviet-bloc scientific findings became obsolete before the government approved them for application to technology. An invisible backsliding from superpower effectiveness and leadership had begun in the USSR—much of it due to the lack of systems coordination and cooperation.

The centrality of sophisticated knowledge to success in postindustrial society led to unprecedented growth in education, especially universities and scientific institutes. The number of university students in Sweden rose by about 580 percent and in West Germany by 250 percent between 1950 and 1969. Great Britain established a network of technical universities to encourage the practical research that traditional elite universities often scorned. France set up administrative schools for future high-level experts in administration. The scientific establishment in the Soviet Union grew so rapidly that the number of its advanced researchers surpassed the number in the United States by the late 1970s. Meanwhile, institutions of higher learning added courses in business management, information technology, and systems analysis designed to build a new pool of postindustrial workers.

Changing Family Life and the Generation Gap

Just as education changed dramatically to meet the needs of postindustrial society, family roles and the relationship between parents and children shifted from what they had been a century earlier. Households became more varied, with many headed by a single parent, by remarried parents merging two sets of unrelated children, by unmarried couples cohabiting, or by traditionally married parents who had few or no children. Households of same-sex partners also became more common. At the end of the 1970s, the marriage rate in the West had fallen by 30 percent from its 1960s level, and the divorce rate continued to climb. After almost two decades of the baby boom, the birthrate dropped significantly. On average, a Belgian woman, for example, bore 2.6 children in 1960 but only 1.8 by the end of the 1970s. In the Soviet bloc, the birthrate was even lower. Although the birthrate fell, the percentage of children born outside of marriage soared.

Daily life within the family also changed. Technological consumer items filled the home, with radio and television often forming the basis of the household's common life. Appliances became more affordable and more widespread, reducing (in theory) the time women had to devote to household work and raising standards of cleanliness. More women worked outside the home during these years to pay for the longer economic dependence of children, but working mothers still did the housework and provided child care almost entirely themselves.

Whereas the early modern family organized labor, taught craft skills, and monitored reproductive behavior, the modern family seemed to have a primarily psychological mission, giving emotional nurturance to their children, who acquired their intellectual skills in school. Parents turned to psychologists, social workers, and other experts for advice on rearing children. Television and other media also offered advice on and models of how to deal with life in postindustrial society.

Postindustrial society transformed teenagers' lives most dramatically. A century earlier, teens had been full-time wage earners; now, in the new knowledge-based society, most were students, often financially dependent on their parents into their twenties. Despite teenagers' longer financial childhood, sexual activity began at an ever younger age, and people talked more openly about sex, prompting the Western media to announce the arrival of a "sexual revolution" where young people were concerned.

Youths simultaneously gained new roles as consumers. Seeing baby boomers as a multibillion-dollar market, advertisers and industrialists wooed them with consumer items associated with rock music—records, portable radios, stereos. Rock music celebrated youthful rebellion against adult culture in biting and often explicitly sexual lyrics. Sex roles for the young did not change, however. Despite the popularity of a few individual women rockers, promoters focused on men, whom they depicted as heroic, surrounded by worshipping female "groupies." The new models for youths, such as the Beatles, were themselves the products of savvy mass marketing to a mass youth audience. "What's your message for American teenagers?" the Beatles were asked. "Buy some more Beatles records," they responded. The mixture of high-tech music, pop-star marketing, and the youthful hysteria of fans contributed to a sense that there was a unique youth culture separating the young from their parents—the so-called generation gap.

Art, Ideas, and Religion in a Technocratic Society

Cultural trends developed alongside the march of consumer society and technology. A new style in the visual arts was called **pop art**. It featured images from everyday life and employed the glossy techniques of what these artists called admass, or mass advertising. Robert Rauschenberg, a leading U.S. practitioner, made collages from comic strips, magazine clippings, and fabric to fulfill his vision that "a picture is more like the real world when it's made out of the real world." The movement became a financial success by the early 1960s, boosted by such maverick American artists as Andy Warhol, who lampooned modern commercialism. Through images of actress Marilyn Monroe and former U.S. first lady Jacqueline Kennedy,

The Rolling Stones, 1976
The Rolling Stones were more energetic, sexual, and flamboyant than the earlier British rock sensation, the Beatles. Astute marketing experts for big record companies helped such rock groups target youth successfully. What exactly was the appeal of the Beatles, the Rolling Stones, and other celebrated rock stars who followed in their wake? (Getty Images.)

Warhol showed, for example, how the female body was used to sell products in the 1960s and 1970s. He depicted Campbell's soup cans as they appeared in advertisements and sold these works as elite artistic creations.

Swedish-born artist Claes Oldenburg portrayed the grotesque aspects of ordinary consumer products in *Giant Hamburger with Pickle Attached* (1962) and *Lipstick Ascending on Caterpillar Tractor* (1967). Capturing this mocking world of art, German artist Sigmar Polke did cartoon-like drawings of products and of those who craved them. Others practicing this "high art" picked up not merely commercial goods, but actually "low" objects such as scraps of metal, cigarette butts, dirt, and even excrement. Swiss sculptor Jean Tinguely used rusted parts of old machines—the "junk" of industrial society—to make fountains that could move. His partner Niki de Saint-Phalle then decorated them with huge, gaudy figures—many of them inspired by the folk traditions of the Caribbean and Africa. Their colorful, mobile fountains adorned main squares in Stockholm, Paris, and other cities.

American composer John Cage worked in a similar vein when he added sounds produced by everyday items such as combs, pieces of wood, and radio noise to his musical scores. Buddhist influence led Cage to include silence in his music and to compose by randomly tossing coins and then choosing notes by the corresponding

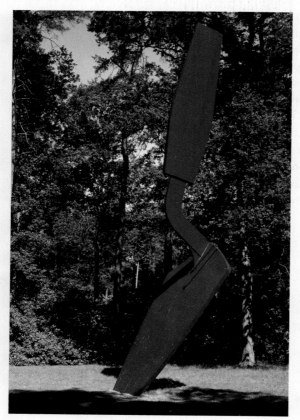

numbers in the ancient Chinese *I Ching* (*Book of Changes*). These developments continued the trend away from melody in classical music that had begun with modernism. Other composers, called minimalists, simplified music by featuring repetition and sustained notes instead of producing the romantic melodies of nineteenth-century symphonies

Claes Oldenburg, *Trowel* (1971)
Claes Oldenburg captured the playful mood of pop art when he began duplicating ordinary objects such as vacuum cleaners, telephones, and even raisin bread on a larger-than-life scale. Pop art seemed to make a mockery of consumerism and everyday life, but museums and wealthy collectors snapped it up, eventually making celebrities of the artists and paying tens of millions of dollars for their work. (Nicolas Sapieha/Art Resource, NY.)

and piano music. Arvo Pärt, the famed Estonian composer, wrote minimalist pieces in the 1970s using only three or four notes in total; he called this style starvation music to underscore the lack of both freedom and goods in the Soviet bloc.

German composer Karlheinz Stockhausen introduced electronic music in classical compositions in 1953; Cage also used it soon after. Influenced by his own travels, Stockhausen continued the modern style of fully exploring non-Western musical patterns in such 1970s pieces as *Ceylon*. Even though this music echoed familiar electronic sounds, many listeners hated what seemed to them unpleasant noise. Yet improved recording technology and mass marketing brought music of all varieties to a wider home audience than ever before.

The social sciences reached the peak of their influence during these decades, often because of the increasing use of statistical models and predictions made possible by new technology. Social scientists produced detailed studies that claimed to demonstrate rules for understanding behavior with great certainty. Anthropology was among the most exciting of the social sciences, for it brought to young university students information about societies that seemed untouched by modern technology and industry. Colorful ethnographic films revealed different lifestyles and seemingly exotic practices. While studying people who came to be called "the other," young students had their sense of freedom reinforced by the vision of going back to nature. Whatever their discipline, social scientists announced that, like technicians and engineers, their specialized methods and factual knowledge were key to both managing complex postindustrial societies and setting policy for developing nations.

At the same time, the social sciences undermined Enlightenment beliefs that individuals had true freedom. French anthropologist Claude Lévi-Strauss developed a theory called structuralism, which insisted that all societies function within controlling structures—kinship and exchange, for example. By challenging existentialism's claim that humans could create a free existence, structuralism shook the social sciences' faith in the triumph of rationality. Lévi-Strauss's book *The Savage Mind* (1966) also demonstrated that people outside the West, even though they did not use Western scientific methods, had their own extremely effective systems of problem solving. In the 1960s and 1970s, the findings of social scientists echoed concerns that technology and highly managed bureaucratic systems were creating a society where people lacked freedom and individuality.

Religious leaders and the faithful responded to the changing times in a variety of ways. Pope Paul VI opposed artificial birth control while simultaneously becoming the first pontiff to put the global vision of Vatican II into action by visiting Africa, Asia, and South America. In some places, religious fervor at the grass roots surged in the face of scientific advances and the threat of nuclear annihilation. Growing numbers of U.S. Protestants joined sects that stressed the literal truth of the Bible and denied the validity of past scientific discoveries such as the age of the universe and the evolution of species. In western Europe, however, Christian churchgoing remained at a low level. In the 1970s, for example, only 10 percent of the British population went to religious services—about the same number that attended live soccer matches.

Most striking was the changing composition of the Western religious public. The immigration of people from former colonies and other parts of the world increased the strength of non-Christian religions such as Islam and varieties of Hinduism. Mosques, Buddhist temples, and shrines to other creeds appeared in cities and towns. New religious values sometimes mixed tensely with Western culture.

REVIEW How did Western society change in the postindustrial age?

Protesting Cold War Conditions

The United States and the Soviet Union reached new heights of power in the 1960s, but trouble was brewing for the superpowers. By 1965, the six nations of the Common Market had replaced the United States as the leader in worldwide trade, and they often acted in their own self-interest, not in the interest of the superpowers. In 1973, Britain joined the Common Market, followed by Ireland and Denmark, boosting the market's exports to almost three times those of the United States. The USSR faced competition, too. Communist China, along with countries in eastern Europe, contested Soviet leadership, and many decolonizing regions refused to ally with either of the superpowers. The struggle for Indochinese independence continued, and by the mid-1960s the United States waged a devastating war in Vietnam to block a Communist-led independence movement there. At the end of the 1970s, the USSR became involved in an equally devastating war in Afghanistan. Rising citizen discontent and dramatic acts of protest like that of Jan Palach presented another serious challenge to the cold war order. From the 1960s until 1989, people rose up against the consequences of technological development, the lack of fundamental rights, and the potential for nuclear holocaust.

Cracks in the Cold War Order

Across the social and political spectrum, there were calls to soften the effects of the cold war in this age of unprecedented progress and technological change. In the Soviet Union, the new middle class of bureaucrats and managers demanded a better standard of living and a reduction in the cold war tensions that made everyday life so menacing. Voters in western European countries elected politicians who promoted an increasing array of social programs designed to guarantee the economic democracy of the welfare state. A significant minority shifted their votes away from the centrist Christian Democratic coalitions that supported U.S. political goals.

The German and French governments both made visible changes in policy, which unsettled the cold war status quo. In Germany, Social Democratic politicians pushed to reallocate funds from defense spending to domestic programs. Willy Brandt, the Socialist mayor of West Berlin, became foreign minister in 1966 and worked to improve relations with Communist East Germany in order to open up trade. This anti–cold war policy, known as **Ostpolitik**, gave West German business leaders what they wanted: "the depoliticization of Germany's foreign trade," as one industrialist put it, and an opening of consumerism in the Soviet bloc. West German trade with eastern Europe grew rapidly, but it left the relatively poorer countries of the Soviet bloc burdened with a mounting debt—some $45 billion annually by 1970. Nevertheless, commerce began building a bridge across the U.S.-Soviet cold war divide.

To break the cold war stranglehold on international politics, French president Charles de Gaulle poured huge sums into French nuclear development, withdrew French forces from NATO, and signed trade treaties with the Soviet bloc. Communist China and France also grew closer. However, de Gaulle protected France's good relations with West Germany to prevent further encroachments from the Soviet bloc. At home, de Gaulle's government sponsored the construction of modern housing and ordered the exterior cleaning of all Parisian buildings—a massive project taking years—to wipe away more than a century of industrial grime and to highlight community, not cold war, values. With his haughty and stubborn pursuit of French grandeur, de Gaulle offered an alternative to submissively obeying the superpowers.

Brandt's Ostpolitik and de Gaulle's independence had their echoes in Soviet-bloc reforms. After the ouster of Soviet premier Nikita Khrushchev in 1964, the new leadership of Leonid Brezhnev (1909–1982) and Alexei Kosygin (1904–1980) initially continued attempts at reform, encouraging plant managers to turn a profit, allowing the production of televisions and household appliances and the construction of cheap housing to lessen the discontent of an increasingly educated and informed citizenry. The government also allowed more cultural and scientific meetings with Westerners. The Soviet satellite countries in eastern Europe took the opportunity presented by Moscow's relaxed posture. For example, Hungarian leader János Kádár introduced elements of a market system into the national economy by encouraging small businesses and trade to develop outside the Communist-controlled state network.

In the arts, Soviet-bloc writers continued for a time to break the hold of socialist realism on the arts and reduce their praise for the Soviet past. Dissident artists' paintings rejected the brightly colored scenes of socialist realism and instead depicted Soviet citizens as worn and tired in grays and other drab colors. Ukrainian poet Yevgeny Yevtushenko pointed out Soviet involvement in the Holocaust in *Babi Yar* (1961), a passionate protest against the slaughter of tens of thousands of Jews near Kiev during World War II. Challenging the celebratory nature of Communist literature, East Berlin writer Christa Wolf showed a couple tragically divided by the Berlin Wall in her novel *Divided Heaven* (1965). Repression of artistic thought returned later in the 1960s and 1970s, however, as the Soviet government took to bulldozing outdoor art shows, thereby forcing artists to hold secret exhibitions in their apartments. For their part, writers relied on samizdat culture, a key form of dissident activity in which novels and essays were written out by hand and passed from reader to reader, thus building a foundation for the successful resistance of the 1980s.

Other issues challenged U.S. leadership of the free world during the cold war. The assassination of President John F. Kennedy in November 1963 shocked the

Leonid Sokov, *Project to Construct Glasses for Every Soviet Person* (1976)
In the cold war era, the Soviets persecuted those who produced abstract or critical art. Dissident artists were adept, however, at incorporating Soviet icons into works critical of the regime. They might, for instance, include Lenin's portrait, but with citizens turning their backs on it instead of being inspired by it. In this sculpture, Leonid Sokov created a Communist version of rose-colored glasses. His work paralleled that of pop artists in the West, who mocked the array of consumer items that filled people's lives.
(Jane Voorhees Zimmerli Art Museum, Rutgers, The State University of New Jersey, The Norton and Nancy Dodge Collection of Nonconformist Art from the Soviet Union 1991.0873/07809. Photograph by Jack Abraham.)

nation and the world, but it did not stop the rising demands for civil rights for African Americans and other minorities. White segregationists murdered and brutalized those attempting to integrate lunch counters or simply march on behalf of freedom. In response to white violence, Kennedy had introduced civil rights legislation and forced the desegregation of schools and universities. Lyndon B. Johnson, Kennedy's successor, steered the Civil Rights Act through Congress in 1964. This legislation forbade segregation in public facilities and created the Equal Employment Opportunity Commission (EEOC) to fight job discrimination based on "race, color, national origin, religion, and sex." Modeling himself on his hero Franklin Roosevelt, Johnson envisioned what he called the Great Society, which would arise from programs such as Project Head Start for disadvantaged preschool children and the Job Corps for training youth. Black novelist Ralph Ellison called Johnson "the greatest American president for the poor and the Negroes."

Still, the cold war did not go away, and the United States became increasingly embroiled in Vietnam (Map 23.1). After the Geneva Conference in 1954, which divided Vietnam into North and South, the United States escalated its support for the corrupt leaders of non-Communist South Vietnam. North Vietnam, China, and the Soviet Union backed the rebel Vietcong, or South Vietnamese Communists.

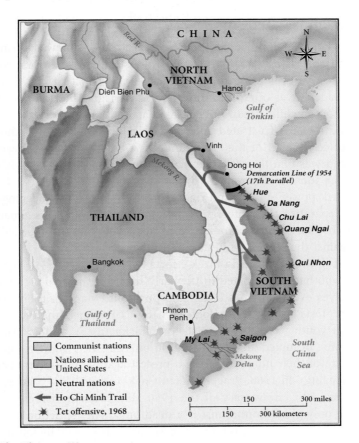

Map 23.1 The Vietnam War, 1954–1975
The local peoples of Southeast Asia had long resisted incursions by their neighbors. They also resisted French rule beginning at the end of the nineteenth century and never more fiercely than in the war that liberated them after World War II. Ill prepared by comparison with the French, the Vietnamese nonetheless triumphed in the battle of Dien Bien Phu in 1954. But the Americans soon became involved, trying to stem what they saw as the tide of Communist influence behind the Vietnamese liberation movement. The ensuing war in Vietnam in the 1960s and 1970s spread into neighboring countries, making the region the scene of vast destruction. **For more help analyzing this map, see the map activity for this chapter in the Online Study Guide at** bedfordstmartins .com/huntconcise.

By the end of 1967, the United States had nearly half a million soldiers in South Vietnam, yet the strength of the Vietcong seemed to grow daily. Despite suffering massive bombing, the insurgents, who had struggled against colonialism for decades, rejected a negotiated peace even as Johnson's advisers regularly appeared on television, telling Americans that the United States was winning the war. Faced with mounting casualties and growing antiwar sentiment, President Johnson announced in March 1968 that he would not run for reelection.

The Outbreak of Civic Activism

In the midst of cold war conflict and technological advance, a new activism emerged. Prosperity and the rising benefits of a postindustrial, service-oriented economy helped make people ever more eager for peace and justice. The U.S. civil rights movement broadened, as other minorities joined African Americans in demanding fair treatment. Meanwhile, urban riots erupted across the United States in 1965 and subsequent summers as frustrated and angry black activists turned their struggle into a militant celebration of their race under the banner "Black is beautiful." The issue they faced was one they felt they had in common with decolonizing people: how to shape an identity different from that of their white oppressors. Some urged a push for "black power" to demand rights forcefully instead of "begging" for them nonviolently. Separatism, not integration, became the goal of others. Small cadres of militants like the Black Panthers took up arms, believing that they needed to protect themselves against the violent whites around them.

As a result of the new turn in black efforts for change, white American university students who had participated in the early stages of the civil rights movement found themselves excluded from leadership positions. Many of them soon joined the swelling protests against technological change, consumerism, and the Vietnam War. European youth were also feverish for reform. In the mid-1960s, university students in Rome occupied an administration building after right-wing opponents assassinated one of their number during a protest against the university's 200-to-1 student-teacher ratio. In 1966, Prague students held carnival-like processions, commemorated the tenth anniversary of the 1956 Hungarian uprisings, and took to chanting "The only good Communist is a dead one." The "situationists" in France called on students to wake up from the slumber of mass society by jolting individuals into action with shocking graffiti and street theater.

Throughout the 1960s, students criticized the traditional university curriculum and showed off their own countercultural values. They questioned how studying Plato or Dante would help them after graduation. "How to Train Stuffed Geese" was French students' satirical version of the teaching methods they experienced in the classroom. "No professors over forty" and "Don't trust anyone over thirty" were powerful slogans of the day. Long hair, communal living, and scorn for personal cleanliness announced students' rejection of middle-class values. Widespread use of the pill made abstinence unnecessary as a method of birth control, and open promiscuity brought the sexual revolution into public view. Marijuana use became common among students, and amphetamines, hallucinogens, and barbiturates added to the drug culture, which had its own rituals, music, and gathering places. Sneered at by students, big business nonetheless made billions of dollars by selling blue jeans, dolls dressed as "hippies," natural foods, and drugs to students and by packaging and managing the rock stars of the counterculture.

Women's activism erupted across the political spectrum. Working for reproductive rights, women in France helped end the ban on birth control in 1965. American journalist Betty Friedan, author of the international best seller *The Feminine Mystique* (1963), attracted middle-class women by pointing to the stagnating talents of many housewives. Friedan helped organize the National Organization for Women (NOW) in 1966 "to bring women into full participation in the mainstream of American society now." NOW advocated equal pay and a variety of other legal and economic reforms. In Sweden, women lobbied to make tasks both at home and in the workplace less gender segregated, and a few Soviet women began speaking out against their low-paid and unpaid work, which kept the USSR running.

Women engaged in the civil rights and student movements soon realized that many protest organizations devalued women just as society at large did. Male activists adopted the leather-jacketed machismo style of their film and rock heroes, and women in the movements were often judged by the status of their activist lovers. "A woman was to 'inspire' her man," African American activist Angela Davis complained, adding that women seeking equality were accused of wanting "to rob [male activists] of their manhood." West German women students tossed tomatoes at male protest leaders to dispute male domination of the movement and standards set by men for ladylike behavior.

Women also took to the streets on behalf of issues such as abortion rights and the decriminalization of gay and lesbian sexuality. Many rebelled against social conventions in their attire, language, and attitudes and spoke openly about taboo subjects such as their sexual feelings and illegal abortions. This brand of feminist activity was meant to shock polite society, and it did. Many women of color, however, broke with feminist solidarity and spoke out against the "double jeopardy" of being "black and female." Concrete change followed: in Catholic Italy, for example, feminists won the right to

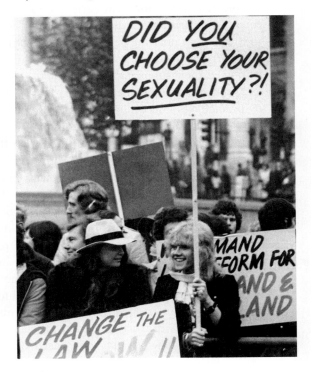

Gay Activists in London, 1974
The reformist spirit of the 1960s and 1970s changed the focus of homosexuals' activism. Instead of concentrating mostly on legal protection from criminal prosecution, gays and lesbians began affirming a special and positive identity. As other groups that had endured discrimination began making similar affirmations, "identity politics" was born. Critics charged that traditional universal values were sufficient and that homosexuals and others constituted special-interest groups. Gays, women, and ethnic and racial minorities countercharged that in practice the universal values first put forth in the Enlightenment seemed to apply only to a privileged few. (© Hulton-Deutsch Collection/ Corbis.)

divorce, to gain access to birth-control information, and to obtain legal abortions. Throughout the 1970s and beyond, thousands of women's groups continued to demand equal pay, job opportunities, and protection from rape, incest, and battering.

1968: Year of Crisis

Protest and calls for reform boiled over in 1968. In January, on the first day of Tet, the Vietnamese New Year, the Vietcong and the North Vietnamese attacked more than one hundred South Vietnamese towns and American bases, inflicting heavy casualties. The Tet offensive caused many people in the United States and the rest of the West to conclude that the war might be unwinnable and fueled the antiwar movement around the world. Rising war protest intersected with African American anguish and rage when, on April 4, 1968, a white racist assassinated Martin Luther King Jr. More than a hundred cities in the United States exploded in strife. "Burn, baby, burn," chanted rioters who, rejecting King's message of nonviolent resistance, destroyed the grim inner cities around them. On campuses, bitter clashes over the intertwined issues of war, technology, racism, and sexism closed down classes.

Similar student unrest erupted around the world, most dramatically in France. In January, students at Nanterre, outside of Paris, went on strike, invading administration offices to protest what they saw as a second-rate education. They called themselves a proletariat—an exploited working class—and, rejecting the Soviet brand of communism, considered themselves part of "a new left." When students at the prestigious Sorbonne in Paris also took to the streets in protest, police assaulted them. The Parisian middle classes reacted with unexpected if temporary sympathy to the student uprising because of their own resentment of bureaucracy. They were also horrified at seeing police beating middle-class students and even passersby who expressed their support.

French workers joined in the protest. Some nine million went on strike, occupying factories and calling not only for higher wages but also for participation in everyday decision making. The combined revolt looked as if it might explode into another French Revolution, so unified were the expressions of political opposition. Charles de Gaulle sent tanks into Paris and in June announced a raise for workers, while businesses offered them more involvement in decision making. Many citizens, having grown tired of the street violence, the destruction of private property, and the breakdown of services (for example, the garbage had not been collected for weeks), began to sympathize with the government instead of the students. Although demonstrations continued throughout June, the revolutionary moment had passed.

By contrast, the 1968 revolt in Prague began within the Czechoslovak Communist Party itself. At a party congress in the fall of 1967, Alexander Dubček, head of the Slovak branch of the party, had called for more social and political openness. Attacked as an inferior Slovak by the Communist leadership, Dubček nonetheless struck a chord with frustrated party officials and intellectuals. Czechoslovaks began to dream of a new society—one based on "socialism with a human face." Party delegates elevated Dubček to the top position, where he quickly changed the Communist style of government by ending censorship, instituting the secret ballot for party elections, and allowing competing political groups to form. "Look!" one little girl in the street remarked as the new government took power. "Everyone's smiling today." The Prague Spring had begun—"an orgy of free expression," one Czech journalist called it. People bought uncensored publications, packed uncensored theater productions, and engaged in almost nonstop political debate.

Dubček faced the enormous problem of negotiating policies acceptable to the USSR, the party bureaucracy, and reform-minded citizens. His government handed down reforms with warnings about maintaining "discipline" and showing "wise behavior." Fearing change, the Polish, East German, and Soviet regimes threatened the reform government daily. When Dubček failed to attend a meeting of Warsaw Pact leaders, Soviet threats became more intense, until finally, in August 1968, Soviet tanks rolled into Prague in a massive show of force. Citizens tried to halt the return to Communist orthodoxy through sabotage. They painted graffiti on the tanks and removed street signs to confuse invading troops. Merchants refused to sell

Invasion Puts Down Prague Spring
When the Soviet Union and other Warsaw Pact members cracked down on the Prague Spring, they met determined citizen resistance. People refused assistance of any kind to the invaders and personally talked to them about the Czech cause. Despite the repression, protests small and large continued until the final fall of Communist rule two decades later. (© Bettmann/Corbis.)

food and other goods to Soviet troops. These actions did not stop the determined Soviet leadership, which removed reformers from power. Jan Palach and other university students immolated themselves the following January, but the moment of reform-minded change passed here, too.

Protest in 1968 challenged the political direction of individual nations, but little turned out the way reformers hoped, as governments worked to end criticism of the cold war status quo. In November 1968, the Soviets announced the Brezhnev Doctrine, which stated that reform movements, a "common problem" of all socialist countries, would be stamped out. As the hard-liner Brezhnev clamped down on critics, dissident morale ebbed. "The shock of our tanks crushing the Prague Spring . . . convinced us that the Soviet colossus was invincible," explained one pessimistic Soviet liberal. Other voices persisted, however. In 1974, Brezhnev expelled author Aleksandr Solzhenitsyn from the USSR after the publication of the first volume of *The Gulag Archipelago* (1973–1976) in the U.S. bloc. Composed from firsthand reports and other sources, Solzhenitsyn's story of the Gulag documented the brutal conditions endured by Soviet prisoners under Stalin. More than any other single work, *The Gulag Archipelago* disillusioned loyal Communists around the world.

The USSR also persecuted ordinary citizens who did not have Solzhenitsyn's international reputation. Soviet psychologists, working with the government, certified the "mental illness" of dissidents, who often wound up as virtual prisoners in mental institutions. In a revival of tsarist Russia's anti-Semitism, Jews faced educational restrictions (especially in university admissions), severe job discrimination, and a constant assault on their religious practices. Soviet officials commonly charged that Jews were "unreliable, they think only of emigrating. . . . It's madness to give them an education, because it's state money wasted." Ironically, dissidents blamed Jews for the Bolshevik Revolution and terror under Stalin. As attacks intensified in the 1970s, Soviet Jews sought to emigrate to Israel or the United States, often unsuccessfully.

The brain drain of eastern European intellectuals increased. Celebrated composer Gyorgy Ligeti had left Hungary in 1956, after which his work was celebrated in concert halls and in such classic films as *2001: A Space Odyssey*. From exile in Paris, Czech writer Milan Kundera enthralled audiences with *The Book of Laughter and Forgetting* (1979) and *The Unbearable Lightness of Being* (1984). His novels chronicled his own descent from enthusiasm for communism to a despair characterized by bitter humor. Kundera claimed that Communist regimes depended on making people forget by, for instance, erasing fallen leaders from history books. Individuals often tried to forget the grim reality of Communist rule by engaging in excessive sexual activity. Like the escapees from fascism in the 1930s, these newcomers to the West—from noted intellectuals to skilled craftspeople and dancers—enriched the culture of the countries that welcomed them.

In the United States the reaction against activists was different, though the impulse to restore order was strong there, too. Elected in 1968, the conservative

President Richard Nixon promised to bring peace to Southeast Asia, but in 1970 he ordered U.S. troops to invade Cambodia, the site of North Vietnamese bases. Campuses erupted again in protest, and on May 4 the National Guard killed four students and wounded eleven others at a demonstration at Kent State University in Ohio. Nixon called the victims "bums," and a growing reaction against the counter-culture made many Americans agree with him. Despite signing agreements to end hostilities in 1973, the United States and North Vietnam continued fighting until 1975, when a North Vietnamese offensive defeated South Vietnam and its U.S. ally and forcibly reunified the country. The United States reeled from the defeat, hav-ing suffered the loss of thousands of young lives, turbulence at home, vast military costs, and a weakening of its reputation around the world. Yet a strong current of public opinion turned against antiwar activists, born of the belief that they—not the war, government corruption, or the huge war debt—had brought down the United States. Both superpowers were being tested, almost to the limits, creat-ing a climate of uncertainty not only about politics but also about the future of postindustrial prosperity.

> **REVIEW**   What were the main issues for protesters in the 1960s, and how did governments address them?

The Testing of Superpower Domination and the End of the Cold War

The 1970s brought a lessening of cold war tensions called détente, during which both superpowers limited the nuclear arms race in the face of instability at home. Despite this relaxation in the cold war, internal corruption, open terrorism, compe-tition from the oil-producing states, and continuing attempts to control the world beyond their borders threw the superpowers and their allies off balance, allowing reform-minded politicians to come to power. The two most famous innovators were Margaret Thatcher in Britain and Mikhail Gorbachev in the USSR, who introduced drastic new policies in the 1980s to keep their economies moving forward. But in the Soviet bloc, postindustrial prosperity was simply unattainable under the old system, and in 1989, astonishingly, that system collapsed.

A Changing Balance of World Power

In the midst of turmoil at home and the draining war in Vietnam, Henry Kissinger, Nixon's secretary of state and a believer—like Otto von Bismarck—in Realpolitik, decided to take advantage of the ongoing USSR-China rivalry and arranged for Nixon to visit China in 1972. The visit linked, if only tentatively, two very dif-ferent great nations that both faced problems at home. Within China, the meet-ing helped stop the brutality and excesses of Mao's Cultural Revolution, during which Mao had incited students to decimate schools, destroy property, and injure and even kill "class enemies." The visit also helped advance the careers of Chinese pragmatists interested in technology, trade, and relations with the West who laid the groundwork for China's boom later in the century. At the same time, the diplomatic success of the visit sped up the process of détente between the United States and the Soviet Union. Fearful of the Chinese diplomatic advantage and similarly confronted by popular protest, the Soviets approached the U.S. bloc. In 1972, the superpowers signed the first Strategic Arms Limitation Treaty (SALT I), which set a cap on the number of antiballistic missiles each country could have. In 1975, in the Helsinki accords on human rights, the western bloc officially acknowledged Soviet territorial gains in World War II in exchange for the Soviet bloc's guarantee of basic human rights.

Despite these diplomatic successes, the war in Vietnam left the United States billions of dollars in debt to other countries. The international currency system collapsed under the weight of this imbalance. In the face of the resulting global economic chaos, the Common Market countries united to force the United States to relinquish its single-handed direction of Western economic strategy. Another blow to U.S. leadership followed when it was revealed that Nixon's office had worked to undermine free elections by authorizing the burglary and wiretapping of the Democratic Party headquarters in Washington's Watergate building during the 1972 election campaign. The Watergate scandal forced Nixon to resign in disgrace in the summer of 1974—the first U.S. president ever to do so. That its own leader would work to undermine democracy further weakened U.S. superpower status in the 1960s and 1970s.

Amid the instability in the United States, the Middle East's oil-producing nations dealt Western dominance yet another blow. In two wars in 1967 and 1973, U.S.-backed Israeli forces defeated Arab troops and seized Gaza and the Sinai peninsula from Egypt, the Golan Heights from Syria, and the West Bank from Jordan. Having failed militarily, the Arab nations decided to use economic force, striking at the West's weakest point—its dependence on Middle Eastern oil for its industries and postindustrial lifestyle. Arab nations in the **Organization of Petroleum Exporting Countries (OPEC)**, a relatively loose consortium before the 1973 Israeli war with Egypt, combined to quadruple the price of their oil and imposed an embargo, cutting off all exports of oil to the United States and its allies because they backed Israel. For the first time since imperialism's heyday, the producers of raw materials, not the industrial powers, controlled the flow of commodities and set prices to their own advantage (Figure 23.1). The West was now mired in an oil crisis.

Israel after the Six-Day War, 1967

Figure 23.1 Fluctuating Oil Prices, 1955–1985
Colonization allowed the Western imperial powers to obtain raw materials at advantageous prices or even without paying at all. Even with decolonization, European and American firms were often so firmly entrenched in the newly independent economies that they were able to set the terms of trade. OPEC's oil embargo and price hikes of the 1970s were signs of change, which included the exercise of decolonized countries' control over their own resources. Not only did OPEC's action lead to a decade-long economic downturn, but it also caused some European governments to improve public transportation, encourage the production of fuel-efficient cars, and enact policies that led individual consumers to cut back on their use of oil.

Throughout the 1970s, oil-dependent Westerners watched in astonishment as OPEC upset the balance of economic power and helped provoke a recession in the West. The oil embargo and price hike not only caused inflation to soar but also caused unemployment to rise by more than 50 percent in Europe and the United States. By the end of 1973, the inflation rate had jumped to over 8 percent in West Germany, 12 percent in France, and 20 percent in Portugal. Eastern-bloc countries, dependent on Soviet oil, fared little better because the West could no longer afford their products and the Soviets boosted the price of their own oil. Skyrocketing interest rates discouraged both industrial investment and consumer buying. With prices, unemployment, and interest rates all rising—an unusual combination of economic conditions dubbed **stagflation**—western Europe drastically cut back on its oil dependence by undertaking conservation, enhancing public transportation, and raising the price of gasoline to encourage the development of fuel-efficient cars.

The U.S. bloc had farther to fall. In the late 1970s, students, clerics, shopkeepers, and unemployed men in Iran began a religious agitation that brought to power the Islamic religious leader Ayatollah Ruhollah Khomeini. Using audiocassettes to spread his message, he called for a transformation of the country into a truly Islamic society, which meant the renunciation of the Western ways advocated by the American-backed shah, who as a result was overthrown. In the autumn of 1979, revolutionary supporters of Khomeini took hostages at the American embassy in Teheran. The United States was essentially paralyzed in the face of Islamic militancy, further OPEC price hikes, and a downwardly spiraling economy.

The Western Bloc Meets Challenges with Reform

As the 1980s opened, the first agenda item for non-Communist governments in the West was to put their economic houses in order. On top of the economic challenge

Nationalist Movements of the 1970s

was the growing threat of terrorism—that is, coordinated and targeted political violence by opposition groups at home and abroad. In the 1970s, terrorist bands of young people in Europe responded to the suppression of activism and the worsening economic conditions with kidnappings, bank robberies, bombings, and assassinations. Eager to bring down the Social Democratic coalition that had led West Germany throughout the 1970s, the Red Army Faction assassinated prominent businessmen, judges, and other public officials. Italy's Red Brigades kidnapped and then murdered the head of the dominant Christian Democrats in 1978. Advocates of independence for the Basque nation in northern Spain assassinated Spanish politicians and police officers.

In the 1970s, Catholics in Northern Ireland pitted themselves against the dominant Protestants to protest job discrimination and a lack of civil rights. Demonstrators urged union with the Irish Republic, and with protests escalating, the British government sent in troops. On January 30, 1972, which became known as Bloody Sunday, British troops fired on demonstrators and killed thirteen, setting off a cycle of violence that left five hundred dead in 1972 alone. Protestants, fearful of losing their dominant position, combated a determined Irish Republican Army (IRA), which carried out bombings and assassinations to achieve the union of the two Irelands and an end to the oppression of Catholics.

Terrorists failed in their goal of overturning the existing democracies, and battered as it was, parliamentary government scored a few important successes in the 1970s. Spain and Portugal, suffering under dictatorship since the 1930s, regained their freedom and became more prosperous. The death of Spain's Francisco Franco in 1975 ended more than three decades of dictatorial rule. Franco's handpicked successor, King Juan Carlos, surprisingly steered his nation toward a Western-style constitutional monarchy, facing down threatened military coups. Portugal and Greece also ousted right-wing dictators, thus paving the way for their integration into western Europe and for economic growth. Despite these democratic advances, the economies of the West still appeared to be troubled.

More than anyone else, Margaret Thatcher, the leader of Britain's Conservative Party and prime minister from 1979 to 1990, reshaped the West's political and economic ideas to meet the crisis. Believing that only a resurgence of private enterprise could revive the declining British economy, Thatcher lashed out at union leaders, Labour Party politicians, and people who received welfare-state benefits as enemies of British prosperity. Her anti–welfare-state policies struck a revolutionary chord, and she called herself "a nineteenth-century liberal," in reference to the economic individualism of that age. In her view, businesspeople were the key members of society. She characterized immigrants, whose low wages contributed greatly to corporate profits, as inferior. Under Thatcher, even workers blamed labor leaders or newcomers for Britain's troubles.

The policies of "Thatcherism" were based on monetarist, or supply-side, economic theory. According to monetarist theory, inflation results when government pumps money into the economy at a rate higher than a nation's economic growth rate. Thus, government should keep a tight rein on the money supply to keep prices from rising rapidly. Supply-side economists maintain that the economy as a whole flourishes when businesses grow and their prosperity "trickles down" throughout society. To implement such theories, the British government cut income taxes on the wealthy to spur new investment and increased sales taxes to compensate for the

Margaret Thatcher at a Conservative Party Conference, 1983
As British prime minister for more than a decade (1979–1990), Margaret Thatcher profoundly influenced the course of modern government by rolling back the welfare state. Thatcher was convinced—and convinced others—that the welfare state did not advance society and its citizens but made them lazy by rewarding people with handouts. Her tenure in office encouraged other leaders, from Ronald Reagan to Helmut Kohl, to make similar cuts in social programs. (© Bettmann/Corbis.)

lost revenue. The result was an increased burden on working people, who bore the brunt of the higher sales taxes. Thatcher also sold publicly owned businesses and utilities such as British Airways, refused to prop up "outmoded" industries such as coal mining, and slashed education and health programs. As Thatcher's package of economic policies spread through the West and the world, it came to be known as **neoliberalism**. The quality of universities, public transportation, highways, and hospitals deteriorated; leading scholars and scientists left the country in a new brain drain; and social unity fragmented, as blacks and Asians rioted in major cities. Although Britain had embraced welfare-state programs in the postwar period, now it was pioneering a change in course.

In the United States, President Ronald Reagan, who took office in 1981, followed a similar road to combat the economic crisis there. Dividing citizens into the good and the bad, Reagan vowed to promote the values of the "moral majority," which included a commitment to Bible-based religion, a dedication to work, and unquestioned patriotism. Those who disagreed were labeled immoral, spendthrift "liberals"—a confusing use of the word that Thatcher adopted to describe her "small government" approach. Reagan blasted "liberals" when he introduced "Reaganomics"—his program of large income-tax cuts for the wealthy combined with massive reductions in federal spending for student loans, school lunch programs, and mass transit, because these "welfare" programs only encouraged "bad" Americans to be "lazy." Like Thatcher, Reagan believed that cutting programs and cutting taxes for the wealthy would lead to investment and thus help the economy.

In foreign policy, Reagan warned of the menacing Soviet Union—the "evil empire," as he called it—and rolled back détente. He demanded huge military budgets for programs such as the Strategic Defense Initiative (SDI), known popularly as Star Wars, a costly plan to put lasers in space to defend the United States against a nuclear attack. The combination of tax cuts and military expansion had pushed the U.S. federal budget deficit to $200 billion by 1986. As in Britain, inflation was brought under control, and American prosperity returned.

Other Western leaders also limited welfare-state benefits in the face of stagflation, though without the socially divisive rhetoric of Thatcher and Reagan. West German leader Helmut Kohl, who took power in 1982, reduced welfare spending, froze government wages, and cut corporate taxes. By 1984, the inflation rate was only 2 percent, and West Germany had acquired a 10 percent share of world trade. Unlike Thatcher, Kohl did not encourage class and racial hatreds. The politics of divisiveness was particularly unwise in Germany, where terrorism on the left and on the right continued. Moreover, the legacy of Nazism loomed menacingly. When an unemployed German youth said of immigrant Turkish workers, "Let's gas 'em," the revival of Nazi language appalled many in Germany's middle class.

By 1981 stagflation had put more than 1.5 million people out of work in France, but the French took a different political path to deal with the economic slump. The French elected a socialist president, François Mitterrand, who national-ized the banks and certain industries and increased social spending to stimulate the economy—the opposite of Thatcherism. New public buildings like museums and libraries arose along with new subway lines and improved public transport. When conservative Jacques Chirac succeeded Mitterrand in 1995, he adopted neo-liberal policies. As unemployment remained high, divisive politics strengthened: the politically racist National Front Party, for example, consistently won 10 percent and sometimes more of the popular vote with promises to deport African and Middle Eastern immigrants so that whites could remain dominant economically and politically.

At the same time, smaller European states without heavy defense commitments began to thrive, some of them by slashing welfare programs. Spain joined the Com-mon Market in 1986 and used Common Market investment and tourist dollars to help rebuild its neglected infrastructure. In Ireland, new investment in education for high-tech jobs combined with low wages attracted much new business to the country in the 1990s. Austria prospered, too, in part by reducing government pen-sions and aid to businesses. Austrian chancellor Franz Vranitsky summed up the new focus of government: "In Austria, the shelter that the state has given to almost everyone—employee as well as entrepreneur—has led . . . a lot of people [to] think not only what they can do to solve a problem but what the state can do. . . . This needs to change." The century-long growth of the welfare state slowed by the 1990s as new economic theories took hold.

Almost alone, Sweden maintained a full array of social programs, including a wide choice of subsidized housing for immigrants. Such programs were expensive: the tax rate on income over $46,000 was 80 percent. Although the Swedes reduced their costly dependence on foreign oil by cutting consumption in half between 1976 and 1986, their welfare state came to seem extreme as Sweden's overall prosperity dropped. As elsewhere, immigrants were cast as a major threat to the country. "How long will it be before our Swedish children will have to turn their faces toward Mecca?" asked one politician in 1993.

The Collapse of Communism in the Soviet Bloc

Beginning in 1985, reform came to the Soviet Union as well. In that year, a new leader, Mikhail Gorbachev, unexpectedly opened an era of change. The son of peasants, Gorbachev had risen through the party ranks as an agricultural spe-cialist and had traveled abroad to gain a firsthand glimpse of life in the West. At home, he saw the results of economic stagnation in the USSR. As in much of the Soviet bloc, ordinary people decided not to have children. The country was forced to import massive amounts of grain because 20 to 30 percent of the grain that was produced in the USSR rotted before it could be harvested or shipped to market, so great was the inefficiency of the state-directed economy. A massive and privi-leged party bureaucracy feared innovation and failed to achieve socialism's stated goal of a decent standard of living for working people. Alcoholism was rampant. To match American military growth, the Soviet Union diverted 15 to 20 percent of its gross national product (more than double the U.S. proportion) to armaments, further crippling the economy's chances of raising living standards. As these problems grew, a new generation came of age that had no memory of World War II or of Stalin's purges. "They believe in nothing," a mother said of Soviet youth in 1984.

Gorbachev quickly proposed several programs to improve the desperately inadequate Soviet system. A crucial economic reform, **perestroika** (restructuring), aimed to improve productivity, increase the rate of capital investment, encourage the use of up-to-date technology, and gradually introduce market features such as profits. The complement to economic change was the policy of **glasnost** (usually translated as "openness" or "publicity"), which called for allowing "wide, prompt, and frank information" and for giving Soviet citizens new measures of free speech. When officials complained that glasnost threatened their status, Gorbachev replaced more than a third of the Communist Party's leadership. The pressing need for glasnost became most evident after the Chernobyl catastrophe in 1986, when a nuclear reactor exploded and spewed radioactive dust into the atmosphere. Bureaucratic

Mikhail and Raisa Gorbachev
Mikhail Gorbachev and his wife, Raisa, gave a fresh look to Soviet politics. They traveled, made friends abroad, and were fashionable and modern. While the Gorbachevs became part of Western celebrity culture, average citizens back home saw their privileged lifestyle as the continuation of the Communist government's disregard for ordinary people. (© Peter Turnley/Corbis.)

cover-ups delayed the release of information about the accident, with lethal consequences for people living near the plant.

After Chernobyl, even the Communist Party and Marxism-Leninism were opened to public criticism. Party meetings suddenly included complaints about the highest leaders, and television shows adopted the outspoken methods of American investigative reporting: one program showed, for instance, the plight of Leningrad's homeless children—an admission of communism's failings. Instead of publishing made-up letters praising the great Soviet state, newspapers were flooded with real ones complaining of shortages and abuse. One outraged "mother of two" protested that the cost-cutting policy of reusing syringes in hospitals was a source of AIDS—a disease that had begun to spread rapidly around the world. "Why should little kids have to pay for the criminal actions of our Ministry of Health?" she asked. Factions arose: in the fall of 1987, Gorbachev ally Boris Yeltsin quit the governing Politburo after criticizing perestroika as inadequate. Yeltsin's political daring, which in the past might have brought harassment or prison, inspired others to oppose Communist rule, and by the spring of 1989, in a remarkably free balloting in Moscow's local elections, not a single Communist was chosen.

Gorbachev also scaled back missile production, and in early 1989, the year that ended the Soviet system and the cold war, he withdrew his country's forces from the debilitating war in Afghanistan. Meanwhile, Gorbachev's reforms in the USSR started spiraling out of his control, as dissent rose across the Soviet bloc. Already in 1980, Poles had reacted furiously to government-increased food prices by going on strike and forming an independent union, **Solidarity**, led by electrician Lech Walesa and crane operator Anna Walentynowicz of the Gdańsk shipyards. The organization soon attracted much of the adult population, including a million members of the Communist Party. They paraded through the streets, waving Polish flags and carrying giant portraits of the Virgin Mary and Pope John Paul II, a Polish native. Tens of thousands of women marched in the streets crying "We're hungry!" and protesting working conditions. The police and the army, with Soviet support, imposed a military government under General Wojciech Jaruzelski and in the winter of 1981 outlawed Solidarity. Solidarity remained alive as a force both inside and outside of Poland, as poets read dissident verse to overflow crowds, and university professors lectured to Solidarity members on such forbidden topics as Polish resistance during World War II.

Ongoing activism in Poland set the stage for the unexpected downfall of communism in 1989, but first came a surprising attack on the Communist state in China. Inspired by Gorbachev's visit to China's capital, Beijing, in the spring of 1989, thousands of students massed in the city's Tiananmen Square, the world's largest public square, to demand democracy. They used telex machines to rush their messages to the international community, and they effectively conveyed their goals through the cameras that Western television trained on them. China's aged Communist leaders, while pushing economic modernization, refused to consider the introduction of democracy. As workers began joining the pro-democracy forces, the government crushed the movement and executed as many as a thousand rebels.

The protests in Tiananmen Square were galvanizing. In June 1989, the Polish government, weakened by its own bungling of the economy and lacking Soviet support for further repression, held free parliamentary elections. Solidarity candidates won overwhelmingly, and in early 1990 Walesa became president, hastening Poland's transition to a market economy. Gorbachev openly reversed the Brezhnev Doctrine in the Polish case, refusing to interfere in the political course of another nation. When it became clear that the Soviet Union would not intervene in Poland, the fall of communism repeated itself across the Soviet bloc.

Communism collapsed first in Poland and next in Hungary in part because of those countries' early introduction of free-market measures. In Hungary, which had experimented with "market socialism" since the 1960s, officials slowly realized that political democracy had to accompany economic freedom. Citizens were protesting against ecologically unsound projects like the construction of a new dam, and they encouraged boycotts of Communist holidays. A multiparty system emerged by 1989, which, along with the popular demands for political freedom, led the Hungarian parliament to change the name of the country from the People's Republic of Hungary to simply the Republic of Hungary. People across the country tore down Soviet and Communist symbols, while free elections for parliament took place in the spring of 1990.

The most potent symbol of a divided Europe—the Berlin Wall—stood in the midst of a divided Germany. East Germans had attempted to escape over the wall for more than two decades, and since the early 1980s dissidents had held peace vigils in cities across East Germany. In the summer of 1989, crowds of East Germans flocked to the borders in hopes of escaping the crumbling Soviet bloc, and hundreds of thousands of protesters rallied throughout the fall against the regime. Satellite television brought them visions of postindustrial prosperity and of free and open public debate in West Germany. The crowds intensified in November, when Gorbachev, taken as a hero by many, visited East Germany. On November 9, guards allowed free passage through the wall to West Berlin, turning the protest into a festive holiday: as they strolled freely in the streets, East Berliners saw firsthand the goods available in a successful postindustrial society. The Communist party of East Germany finally collapsed with the elections in March 1990, while East and West Germans released years of frustration by assaulting the Berlin Wall with sledgehammers. The government finished the destruction in the fall of 1990.

In Czechoslovakia, which after 1968 had been firmly restored to Soviet-style rule, people watched the progress of glasnost expectantly. Persecuted, dissidents had maintained their critique of Communist rule, such as the accusation that Marxism-Leninism made people materialistic and indifferent to public life. In 1977, intellectuals and workers, including playwright Václav Havel, signed Charter 77, a public

Reunited Berliners Welcome the New Year
On New Year's Eve, 1989, Berliners and supporters from around the world celebrated the fall of the Berlin Wall and the prospect of a new Germany. The exuberant crowd tore the Communist seal from the flag and then hoisted the flag above the Brandenburg Gate as fireworks added to the intense emotion of the moment. The difficult transition to a reunified Germany, which included disposing of the remnants of communism, lay in the future. (ullstein bild-Boening.)

protest against the regime that resulted in the arrest of its signers. In the mid-1980s, watching Gorbachev on television calling for free speech, ordinary people took to the streets on behalf of democracy. The turning point came in November 1989 when Alexander Dubček, leader of the Prague Spring of 1968, addressed the crowds in Prague's Wenceslas Square to call for the ouster of Stalinists from the government after police had beaten student demonstrators. Almost immediately, the Communist leadership resigned. Capping the country's "velvet revolution," as it became known for its lack of bloodshed, the formerly Communist-dominated parliament elevated the dissident Havel to the presidency.

The world's attention now fastened on an unfolding political drama in Romania. From the mid-1960s on, Nicolae Ceauşescu had ruled as the harshest dictator in Communist Europe since Stalin. In the name of modernization, he destroyed whole villages; to build up the population, he outlawed contraceptives and abortion, a restriction that led to the abandonment of tens of thousands of children. He preached the virtues of a very slim body so that he could cut rations and use the savings on his pet projects, such as buying up private castles and building himself an enormous palace in Bucharest. To this end, he tore down entire neighborhoods and dozens of historical buildings, and he crushed opponents of the gaudy project so that it seemed to have unanimous support. Yet in early December 1989, an opposition movement rose up; workers demonstrated against the dictatorial government, and the army turned on Ceauşescu loyalists. On Christmas Day, viewers watched on television as the dictator and his wife were tried by a military court and then executed. For many, the death of Ceauşescu meant that the very worst of communism was over.

REVIEW   What factors led to the collapse of communism in the Soviet bloc?

Conclusion

The fall of the Berlin Wall in 1989 symbolized the end of the cold war, even though the USSR still stood as a Communist power. The collapse of communism in the Soviet satellites was an utter surprise, for U.S.-bloc analysts had erroneously reported throughout the 1980s that the Soviet empire was in dangerously robust health. But no one should have been unaware of dissent or economic discontent. Since the 1960s, rebellious youths, ethnic and racial minorities, and women had condemned conditions across the West, along with criticizing the threat posed by the cold war. By the early 1980s, wars in Vietnam and Afghanistan, protests against deprivation in the Soviet bloc, the power of oil-producing states, and the growing political force of Islam had cost the superpowers their resources and reputations. Margaret Thatcher in Britain, Ronald Reagan in the United States, and Mikhail Gorbachev in the Soviet Union tried with varying degrees of success to put their postindustrial and cold war houses in order. The first two succeeded, while Gorbachev's policies of glasnost and perestroika—aimed at political and economic improvements—brought on collapse.

Glasnost and perestroika were supposed to bring about the high levels of postindustrial prosperity enjoyed outside the Soviet bloc. Across the West an unprecedented technological development had transformed businesses, the exploration of space, and the functioning of government. Technological advances also had had an enormous impact on everyday life. Work changed, as society reached a postindustrial stage in which the service sector predominated. New patterns of family life, new relationships among the generations, and revised standards of sexual behavior also characterized these years. But it was only in the United States, western Europe, and a few other Western-allied countries that the consumer benefits of postindustrialization reached ordinary people. A thoroughgoing consumer, service, and high-tech society demanded levels of efficiency, coordination, and cooperation that had not been reached in the Soviet bloc.

Mapping the West The Collapse of Communism in Europe, 1989–1990
The overthrow of Communist governments in the Soviet bloc occurred with surprising rapidity. The transformation began in Poland when Polish voters tossed out Communist Party leaders in June 1989 and then accelerated in September when thousands of East Germans fled to Hungary, Poland, and Czechoslovakia. Between October 1989 and March 1990, Communist regimes were replaced in Czechoslovakia, Bulgaria, Romania, and East Germany. Within three years, the Baltic states would declare their independence, the USSR itself would be dissolved, and the breakup of Yugoslavia would lead to war in the Balkans.

Many complained, nonetheless, about the dramatic changes resulting from postindustrial development. The protesters of the late 1960s addressed postindustrial society's stubborn problems: concentrations of bureaucratic and industrial power, social inequality, and environmental degradation. In the Soviet sphere, these protests were continuous but were little heeded until the collapse of Soviet domination of eastern Europe in 1989. Soon communism would be overturned in the USSR itself. However, the downfall of communism opened an era of painful adjustment, impoverishment, and even violence. Ending the cold war also hastened the process of globalization.

CHAPTER REVIEW QUESTIONS

1. How was the industrial society of the late nineteenth century different from the postindustrial society of the late twentieth century?

2. Why were there so many protests, acts of terrorism, and uprisings across the West between 1960 and 1990?

For practice quizzes and other study tools, see the Online Study Guide at bedfordstmartins.com/huntconcise.

For primary-source material from this period, see Chapter 28 of *Sources of THE MAKING OF THE WEST,* Third Edition.

TIMELINE

■ **1973** North Vietnam and the United States sign peace agreements, but fighting continues until 1975; OPEC raises oil prices and imposes an oil embargo on the West

■ **1967** South Africa's Dr. Christiaan Barnard performs the first successful human heart transplant

■ **1966** West German foreign minister Willy Brandt develops Ostpolitik, a policy designed to bridge tensions between the two Germanys

■ **1972** SALT I results in an antiballistic missile treaty between the United States and the Soviet Union

1962	1966	1970	1974

1962–1965 Vatican II reforms Catholic ritual and dogma

■ **1963** Betty Friedan, *The Feminine Mystique*

■ **1968** Revolution in Czechoslovakia against communism; student uprisings throughout Europe and the United States

■ **1969** U.S. astronauts walk on the moon

1973–1976 Aleksandr Solzhenitsyn, *The Gulag Archipelago*

Suggested References

Wartime technological development had profound consequences for the peacetime lives of individuals and for society. Technology created a postindustrial workplace, changing work and social life. The strains of an interlocked technological society along with citizen activism ultimately brought down the Soviet empire.

Bauer, Martin W., and George Gaskell, eds. *Biotechnology: The Making of a Global Controversy.* 2002.

Chaplin, Tamara. *Turning On the Mind: French Philosophers on Television.* 2007.

Dahl, Henne Marlene, and Tine Rask Eriksen, eds. *Dilemmas of Care in the Nordic Welfare State: Continuity and Change.* 2005.

Fink, Carole, et al. *1968: The World Transformed.* 1998.

*Freedman, Estelle B. *The Essential Feminist Reader,* 2007.

Green parties worldwide: http://www.greens.org

Harvey, Brian. *Europe's Space Program: To Ariane and Beyond.* 2003.

Kenney, Padraic. *Carnival of Revolution: Central Europe, 1989.* 2002.

Kotkin, Steven. *Armageddon Averted: Soviet Collapse, 1970–2000.* 2008.

Martin Luther King Jr. Papers Project at Stanford University: http://mlk-kpp01.stanford.edu/

Natalicchi, Giorgio. *Wiring Europe: Reshaping the European Telecommunications Regime.* 2001.

Ouimet, Matthew J. *The Rise and Fall of the Brezhnev Doctrine in Soviet Foreign Policy.* 2003.

Reiton, Earl A. *The Thatcher Revolution: Margaret Thatcher, John Major, Tony Blair, and the Transformation of Modern Britain.* 2002.

Siani-Davies, Peter. *The Romanian Revolution of December 1989.* 2005.

Suri, Jeremy. *Power and Protest: Global Revolution and the Rise of Détente.* 2003.

Varon, Jeremy. *Bringing the War Home: The Weather Underground, the Red Army Faction, and Revolutionary Violence in the Sixties and Seventies.* 2004.

Williams, Walter L., and Yolanda Retter. *Gay and Lesbian Rights in the United States: A Documentary History.* 2003.

■ **1981** Ronald Reagan becomes U.S. president

■ **Early 1980s** AIDS epidemic strikes the West

■ **1980** Independent trade union, Solidarity, organizes resistance to Polish communism; Prime Minister Margaret Thatcher begins dismantling the welfare state in Britain

■ **1989** Chinese students revolt in Tiananmen Square, and the government suppresses them; Communist governments ousted in eastern Europe; fall of the Berlin Wall

1978	1982	1986	1990

■ **1978** First test-tube baby born, in England

■ **1978–1979** Islamic revolution in Iran; hostages taken at the U.S. embassy in Teheran

■ **1985** Mikhail Gorbachev comes to power in the USSR

■ **1986** Explosion at a Soviet nuclear plant in Chernobyl

The New Globalism

1989 to the Present

THERESE IS A CONGOLESE IMMIGRANT TO PARIS, who arrived there in the late 1970s with the help of a brother who worked for an airline. Therese had been well known in Africa as the teenage girlfriend of pop singer Bozi Boziana, who wrote a hit song about her. But Congo's political troubles made her search for safety in Paris. Once there, Therese remained famous among African immigrants because she ran *nganda,* or informal bars. Like Therese, the immigrants who frequent her nganda are often Congolese and other Africans who have settled in Paris, many of them illegally. They flock to her nganda because they like her stylish dress, the African food she cooks, the African music she plays, and the African products she sells. Many of Therese's small bars and eateries have flourished, only to be closed down by landlords who want more of her handsome profits. Despite such obstacles, Therese keeps business going by moving her faithful clientele around her Paris neighborhood from basement to shop front to spare room. Therese is a new global citizen, working networks back home for supplies, constantly on the move because she lives on the edges of the law, and always striving to make a good living for herself and her family.

Global Citizens
The world's migrants at the turn of the twenty-first century sought safety, education, or jobs in the West's manufacturing and service occupations. Like these young immigrants from Senegal who are sharing a meal at a café in Paris, they also appreciated Western amenities. Children of immigrants were sometimes disillusioned, however, not wanting the life of extreme sacrifice that their parents had lived. Their frustrations at not being accepted as full citizens occasionally erupted into protest and even violence. *(© Directphoto .org/Alamy.)*

Therese's experience is just one example of the ease with which people in the post–cold war world crossed national boundaries while maintaining important ties around the globe. The end of the cold war rivalry between the superpowers and their allies paved the way for this more closely connected world. In the 1990s, globalization advanced with the dramatic collapse of communism in Yugoslavia and then the breakup of the Soviet Union itself. The world was no longer divided in two by the heavily guarded borders of the cold war, allowing nations and individuals more opportunity to trade and interact freely. The Common Market transformed itself into the **European Union (EU)**, which from 2004 on admitted many states from the former Soviet bloc. The telecommunications systems put in place beginning in the 1960s advanced globalization, binding peoples and cultures together in an ever more complicated social and economic web.

The global age brought vast national and international migration of tens of millions of people; an expanding global marketplace; and rapid cultural exchange of popular music, books, films, and television shows. On the negative side, greater globalization also brought widespread epidemic diseases, environmental deterioration, genocide, and terrorism. Nations in the West faced competition from the rising economic power of Japan, China, India, and Latin America. As millions of workers found new jobs in an interlinked economy, they discovered that the global age was one of opportunity and also insecurity.

While the end of superpower rivalry made global exchange easier, it also resulted in the dominance of a single power, the United States, in world affairs. As the United States exercised global power through warfare, however, the West itself seemed to fragment. European states started to resist the United States, although far less dramatically than the Soviet satellites had pulled away from the USSR. The economic power of Asian, Middle Eastern, and other countries and the cultural might of Islam created new centers of influence. Some observers predicted a huge "clash of civilizations" based on the differences between Western civilization and cultures beyond the West. Others saw a different clash—one between a Europe reborn after decades of disastrous wars as a peace-seeking group of nations defying an imperial United States, which, like Europe in the nineteenth century, increasingly waged war around the world. According to both of these models, globalization, instead of bringing connections and understanding, seemed to be a harmful development.

For historians, understanding the recent past is a challenge. Every day since 1989 receives instantaneous reporting because of global communication technology. Unlike journalists, historians do not choose from this mass the most sensational story of the moment. Rather, they are interested in judging which items from the unfiltered mass of information are actually true and, of these, which will be important in the long run. Historians want to identify social, cultural, and political events that are uniquely important or generally significant for people's everyday lives, and they need time to collect facts from more than one national source of news. They make the most reliable evaluations when phenomena are no longer "news"—that is, after a good period of time has shown their staying power and influence.

When we first started writing this book, we held our breath in the face of rapidly changing events and judged that the fall of communism and the increasing interconnectedness of the world's peoples and cultures were the challenges not only of the moment but also of history. In the second edition, we persisted in that judgment, even though the fall of communism and coming of globalism had brought greater perils than we had seen only five or six years earlier. Other forces, such as the Internet, escaped our notice altogether. Today, almost a decade after we made our first selections of important trends, we judge the gradual unification of the European continent as potentially momentous. We also see the forces of terrorism and a global economic crisis as possible events with historical staying power. As an experiment in history, you might note the important events of the months in which you take this course, put your list away for several years or more, and then see if they—along with the events discussed in this chapter— stand the test of time.

> **CHAPTER FOCUS QUESTION**   How has globalization been both a unifying and a divisive influence in the West in the twenty-first century?

Soviet Collapse Releases Global Forces

Following the fall of communism in eastern Europe and the fall of the Berlin Wall in 1989, rejection of communism spread in the early 1990s, turning events in unpredictable and often violent directions. Yugoslavia and then the Soviet Union itself fell apart, as nationality groups in both countries began to demand political and cultural autonomy. The USSR had held together more than one hundred ethnic groups, and the five republics of Soviet Central Asia were home to fifty million Muslims. Successive governments had attempted to instill Russian and Soviet culture and thus hold together this vast multicultural empire. The policy failed to build any heartfelt allegiance, leading to a swift collapse of the USSR. In Yugoslavia, Communist rulers had also enforced unity among religious and ethnic groups, and intermarriage among them occurred regularly. During the unstable years of the 1990s, however, ambitious politicians seeking to build a following whipped up ethnic hatreds. Throughout the decade, it was unclear whether peaceful, democratic nations would emerge. Amid this uncertainty, future control of the massive Soviet arsenal of nuclear weapons posed an even more dangerous threat.

The Breakup of Yugoslavia

Ethnic nationalism shaped the post-Communist future in Yugoslavia. Tensions erupted there in 1990 when Serb Communist Slobodan Milosevic became president of Serbia and began to promote Serb control of the entire Yugoslav federation as a replacement for communism. Other ethnic groups resisted Milosevic's militant pro-Serb nationalism and called for secession. "Slovenians . . . have one more reason to say they are in favor of independence," warned one of them in the face of mounting Serb pressure to take control of the other small republics that made up Yugoslavia. In the summer of 1991, two of these republics, Slovenia and Croatia, seceded, but Croatia soon lost almost a quarter of its territory when the Serb-dominated Yugoslav army, eager to enforce Serb supremacy, invaded (Map 24.1). A devastating civil war broke out in Bosnia-Herzegovina when that republic's Muslim majority tried to create a multicultural and multiethnic state. With the military support of Milosevic's government, Bosnian Serbs formed a guerrilla army and gained the upper hand.

Map 24.1 The Former Yugoslavia, c. 2000
After a decade of destructive civil war, United Nations forces and UN-brokered agreements attempted to protect the civilians of the former Yugoslavia from the brutal consequences of post-Communist rule. Ambitious politicians, most notably Slobodan Milosevic, used the twentieth-century Western strategy of fostering ethnic and religious hatreds as a powerful tool to build support for themselves while making those favoring peace look softhearted and unfit to rule. What issues of national identity does the breakup of Yugoslavia indicate? Have these changed since the nineteenth century?

Violence was inflicted on neighbors in parts of the former Yugoslavia with the aim of creating "ethnically pure" states in a region where ethnic mixture was in fact the norm. Serbs under Milosevic's leadership pursued a policy they called **ethnic cleansing**—that is, genocide—against the other ethnicities and religions. They raped women to leave them pregnant with Serb babies as a form of conquest. In 1995 Croatian forces massacred Serbs who had helped seize land from Croatia. That same year, the Serbs retaliated by slaughtering eight thousand men and boys in the town of Srebrenica, where the commander of the Serb forces ordered them to "kill the lot." Military units on all sides destroyed libraries and museums, architectural treasures like the Mostar Bridge, and cities rich with history such as Dubrovnik.

Ethnic cleansing thus involved eliminating both actual people and all traces of their complex past. Many in the West explained this violence as part of "age-old" blood feuds typical of a backward, almost "Asian" society in the Balkans. Others saw the use of genocide to achieve national power as a modern political practice employed by several politicians, including Adolf Hitler.

As with German, Italian, and Japanese aggression in the 1930s, no one stepped in to stop the violence in the former Yugoslavia. Peacekeepers were put in place, but they turned their backs on such atrocities as the Srebrenica massacre. Late in the 1990s, Serb forces moved to attack Muslims of Albanian ethnicity living in the Yugoslav province of Kosovo. From 1997 to 1999, crowds of Albanian Kosovars fled their homes as Serb militias and the Yugoslav army slaughtered the civilian population. NATO pilots bombed the region in an attempt to drive back the army and Serb militias. UN peacekeeping forces arrived to enforce an interethnic truce, but people throughout the world felt that this intervention came far too late to protect human rights and human lives. Alongside the decimated republics of Bosnia and Croatia, a new regime emerged in Serbia, and Milosevic was turned over to the International Court of Justice, or World Court, in the Netherlands to be tried for crimes against humanity. In 2003, Milosevic loyalists assassinated the new Serb president. Across a fragmenting eastern Europe, racial, ethnic, and religious hostilities were animated to shape political agendas.

The Soviet Union Comes Apart

At the beginning of January 1992, amid deteriorating conditions and the threat of violence, the Soviet Union itself collapsed. Perestroika had failed to restore the Soviet economy; people faced soaring prices, the threat of unemployment, and an even greater scarcity of goods than in the past. Although Mikhail Gorbachev announced late in 1990 that there was "no alternative to the transition to the market [economy]," his plan offered too little, too late. In 1991, the Russian parliament elected Boris Yeltsin as president of the Russian Republic over a Communist candidate. Yeltsin's election was the last straw for a group of eight antireform hard-liners, including the powerful head of the Soviet secret police, or KGB, who attempted a coup to overthrow the Soviet government. As coup leaders held Gorbachev under house arrest, Yeltsin defiantly stood atop a tank outside the Russian parliament building and called for mass resistance. Residents of Moscow and Leningrad filled the streets, and army units defected to protect Yeltsin's headquarters. People used fax machines and computers to coordinate opposition and send messages to the rest of the world. Citizen action defeated the coup and prevented a return to the Communist past.

After the failed coup, the Soviet Union disintegrated. People tore down statues of Soviet heroes; Yeltsin outlawed the Communist Party newspaper, *Pravda*. At the end of August 1991, the Soviet parliament suspended operations of the Communist Party itself. The Baltic states of Estonia, Latvia, and Lithuania declared their independence in September; other republics followed their lead. Bloody ethnic conflicts erupted in the disintegrating Soviet world. In the Soviet republic of Tajikistan, native Tajiks rioted against Armenians living there; in Azerbaijan, Azeris and Armenians clashed over contested territory; and in the Baltic states, anti-Semitism revived as a political tool. The USSR formally dissolved on January 1, 1992. Twelve of the fifteen former Soviet republics banded together in the Russian-dominated Commonwealth of Independent States, or CIS (Map 24.2).

Weakened by the coup attempt, Gorbachev abandoned politics. Yeltsin stepped in and accelerated the change to a market economy, introducing new problems as he did so. Plagued by corruption, the Russian economy entered an ever-deepening crisis. Yeltsin's political allies bought up national resources cheaply, stripped them of their value, and sent billions of dollars out of the country. By 1999, Yeltsin's own family appeared to be deeply implicated in stealing the wealth once seen as belonging to all the people. Managers, military officers, and bureaucrats took whatever goods they could lay their hands on, including weaponry, and sold it. In an attempt to consolidate support, Yeltsin launched destructive military action against the resource-rich Russian province of Chechnya, which wanted independence. Organized criminals interfered in the distribution of goods and services and assassinated businesspeople, legislators, and anyone who criticized them. As the Russian parliament pursued an investigation into the business dealings of Yeltsin, his family, and his allies, he resigned on December 31, 1999, and appointed Vladimir Putin as interim president.

Putin was a little-known member of Russia's new security force, which had evolved from the old KGB. In the presidential election of 2000, Putin surprised everyone when the electorate voted him in. Though associated with the Yeltsin family corruption, he initially stressed legality. "Democracy," he announced, "is the dictatorship of law." With a solid victory, Putin drove from power the major figures in both the regional and central governments, usually the henchmen of the robber barons. Faced with a desperate economic situation, Putin proclaimed the need to restore "strong government" and end the influence of a "handful of billionaires with only egotistical concerns." Putin's popularity rose even higher when the government arrested the billionaire head of Yukos Oil, one of Russia's largest oil companies, in 2003. The pillaging of the country—the source of ordinary citizens' suffering—was finally being punished. According to critics, however, Putin was merely transferring Russia's natural resources and other assets to his allies, while extending the vicious and destructive war in Chechnya to crush the independence movement.

Toward a Market Economy

Developing a free market and republican government brought misery to Russia and the rest of eastern Europe. The conditions of everyday life grew increasingly dire as salaries went unpaid, food remained in short supply, and essential services deteriorated. In 1994, inflation soared at a rate of 14 percent a month in Russia, while industrial production dropped by 15 percent. People took drastic steps to stay alive. Hotel lobbies became clogged with prostitutes because women were the first people fired as the economy slumped. Unpaid soldiers sold their services to

Map 24.2 Countries of the Former Soviet Union, c. 2000

The breakup of the Soviet Union in the 1990s was one of the extraordinary events of the twentieth century. As nation-states dissolved, regional alliances such as the Commonwealth of Independent States and European Union were necessary to meet the political and economic challenges of the global age with coordinated action. As the map shows, Russia remained a Goliath even after Soviet satellite countries declared their independence and dominated the politics and economy of the region. **For more help analyzing this map, see the map activity for this chapter in the Online Study Guide at** bedfordstmartins.com/huntconcise.

the Russian Mafia. Ordinary citizens stood on the sidewalks of major cities selling their household possessions. "Anything and everything is for sale," one critic noted at the time. Simultaneously, a pent-up demand for items never before available was unleashed. An enormous underground economy existed in goods such as imported automobiles stolen from people in other countries.

There were, of course, many pluses. People with enough money were able to travel freely for the first time, and the media were initially more open than ever before in Russian history. Some workers, many of them young and highly educated, profited from technology and business contacts. However, their frequent emigration to more prosperous parts of the world further drained Russia's human resources. At the same time, as the different republics of the former Soviet Union became independent, many of the hundreds of thousands of Russians whose families had decades earlier been sent there by the state as colonizers returned as refugees, putting greater demands on the chaotic Russian economy. The undoing of communism was thus more complicated and painful than anyone had imagined it would be.

For many in the former Soviet bloc, the first priority was getting economies running again—but on new terms. Replacing a government-controlled economy with a market one could not happen automatically but would require government planning. Given the growing misery, however, many opposed the introduction of

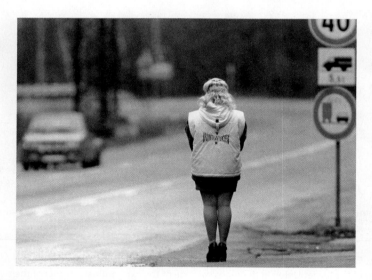

Czech Prostitute on German Border

The collapse of communism and the Soviet Union created financial disaster, particularly for women, who represented more than two-thirds of all the unemployed. Communists advocated the belief that all people, regardless of gender, should work and that they should be paid equally. While this equality never worked in practice, it did provide jobs so that women could support themselves and their children. Under the free-market system, however, women were eliminated from good jobs and paid less. Many resorted to prostitution, which often took place on borders with more prosperous countries such as Germany, as shown here. (Getty Images.)

new market-oriented measures. With collective farms up for sale, most farmers faced landlessness and starvation. The countries that experienced the most success were those in which administrators had previously introduced some ingredients of free trade, such as allowing farmers to sell their produce on the open market or encouraging independent entrepreneurs or even government factories to conduct international trade. Hungary and Poland thus emerged from the transition with less strain because both had favored market elements early on and had hired advisers to speed the transformation of the economy. These countries set up business schools and other institutions to foster trade and successfully attracted foreign capital, thus anchoring them in the world economy.

Elsewhere, however, the transition happened differently. The former Soviet Union itself, in the words of one critic, became simply one vast "kleptocracy" in the 1990s as the country's resources—theoretically the property of all the people—were stolen for personal gain. One Polish adviser noted that democracy and a successful transition to a free market went hand in hand, for unless the people were effectively represented in the government and institutionally powerful enough to prevent it, former officials would simply operate as criminals. This was especially true given the inheritance of the Soviet system of corruption, tax evasion, and off-the-books dealing. In addition to corruption, the long-standing practice of shielding the economy from global developments prevented industry from benefiting from technological change. Because plants and personnel were hopelessly out-of-date, even worthless, the introduction of competition and free trade meant closing factories and firing all the workers.

A final element in post-Soviet economic difficulties stemmed from a brain drain that struck the region. The economic chaos that followed the fall of communism set off a rush of migration from eastern Europe to western Europe, often involving those with marketable skills. Emigrants left for several reasons, including the lack of jobs, the upsurge of ethnic hatreds, and the availability of higher salaries for well-educated workers in other countries. "I knew in my heart that communism would collapse," said one ex-dissident, commenting sadly on the departure of young people from his country, "but it never crossed my mind that the future would look like this." Escaping anti-Semitism also played a role. Post-Communist politicians used the rallying cry of hatred of Jews to build a following, just as Hitler and many others had done so effectively during troubled times in the past. Banditry and violence inflicted by organized crime added to the disadvantages of remaining in eastern Europe.

The everyday advantages of living in western Europe included clean drinking water, better housing, better roads, personal safety, and at least a minimal level of social services. Although western Europe was now on a firm neoliberal course of cutting welfare-state spending, most benefits had disappeared entirely in the former Communist countries. Pensions for veterans and retired workers were rarely paid, and even when they were, they were often worthless given the countries' soaring inflation. Day-care centers, kindergartens, and homes for the elderly closed their doors, and hospitals and health care deteriorated. In these circumstances, the benefits of citizenship in western European countries were a powerful attraction.

International Politics and the New Russia

Although Gorbachev had pulled the Soviet Union out of its disastrous war with Afghanistan, his successors opened another war to prevent the secession of oil-rich Chechnya and to provide a nationalist rallying cry to shore up domestic support for the administration. For decades, Chechens had been integrated into the Soviet bureaucracy and military, but in the fall of 1991, the National Congress of the Chechen People took over the government of the region from the USSR, moving toward the same kind of independence sought by the Baltic nations and other former Soviet republics. In June 1992, Chechen rebels got control of massive numbers of Russian weapons, including airplanes, tanks, and some forty thousand automatic weapons and machine guns.

In December 1994, the Russian government sealed the Chechen borders and invaded. A high Russian official defended the war as crucial to bolstering Yeltsin's position: "We now need a small victorious war. . . . We must raise the President's rating." Despite the Russian population's opposition to the war,

Terrorist Attack on a Moscow Bus, 1996
Terrorism became more widespread from the 1970s on, taking many forms and espousing many causes. Terrorists for the most part engineered attacks on random citizens to increase the loss of life. Post-Soviet Russia experienced such attacks at the hands of various groups, among them breakaway Chechens, whose independence Russia violently resisted. Large-scale bombings also occurred in the Paris subway, on London streets, and on Spanish trains, causing these countries to cover public wastebaskets and to exhort people to be vigilant about parcels in streets, public buildings, and train and subway stations. Terrorists used the wartime strategy of targeting civilians during peacetime. (© Ivo Lorenc/Sygma/Corbis.)

Chechnya's capital city of Grozny was pounded to bits. Casualties mounted not only among Chechen civilians but among Russians, too. In 2002, Chechen loyalists took hundreds of hostages in a Moscow theater; Chechen suicide bombers blew up airplanes, buses, and apartment buildings. Putin pursued the Chechen war into the twenty-first century, reducing the international reputation of the post-Communist government.

Putin also expanded Russian influence in Ukraine, Belarus, India, and China by taking advantage of the politics of energy. Russia had the commodities—especially oil and gas—needed to sustain the fantastic growth of emerging industries around the world. Its natural resources made Russia a major player in the global economy even after a dramatic recession struck the world in 2008. Achieving democratic values remained a more elusive goal. Putin's critics were mercilessly assassinated, newspapers and radios were closed down, and a general distrust of politics grew.

> **REVIEW** What were the major issues facing the former Communist world in the 1990s and early 2000s?

The Nation-State in a Global Age

Although the end of the Soviet system fractured one large regional economy, it gave a boost to European unification. In the 1990s and early 2000s, the European Community was healthy in comparison to other regions of the world that were plagued with civil wars and violence. The union's economic success provoked the formation of other transnational institutions, including the North American Free Trade Agreement (NAFTA), which established a free-trade zone composed of the United States, Canada, and Mexico. As new forms of world governance and large regional blocs took shape in the 1990s, traditional Western nation-states and capital cities began to look and function differently.

Europe Looks beyond the Nation-State

From the 1990s on, Europeans worked to strengthen their shared institutions beyond those of the traditional nation-state, first by expanding the range of their common efforts. In 1992, the twelve countries of the Common Market ended national distinctions in certain business activities and border controls, effectively closing down identity checks at their common borders. Citizens of the member countries carried a uniform burgundy-colored passport, and governments, whether municipal or national, had to treat all member nations' businesses the same. In 1994, by the terms of the **Maastricht Treaty**, the European Community became the European Union, and in 1999 a common currency, the **euro**, came into being, first for transactions among financial institutions and then in 2002 for general use by the public. Some countries—most notably Britain—refused to adopt the euro, but otherwise common policies governed everything from pollution controls on automobiles to health warnings on cigarette packages. The EU parliament convened regularly in Strasbourg, France, and an EU central bank came into being to set interest rates and economic policy for the countries using the euro.

The EU was seen as key to a peaceful Europe. "People with the same money don't go to war with one another," said a French nuclear scientist about the introduction of the euro. In 2002 and 2003, Greece pushed for its traditional enemy Turkey to be admitted to the EU, despite the resistance of some who argued that a predominantly Muslim country could never fit in with the Christian traditions of EU members. Both Greece and Turkey stood to benefit by having their disputes adjudicated by the EU, principally because they would be able to cut those parts of their defense budgets used for weapons against each other. Like the rivalry between Germany and France, that between Turkey and Greece, it was hoped, would dissolve if both were bound by the strong economic and political ties of the EU. As of 2009, however, Turkey was still awaiting acceptance of its application.

Eastern European nations clamored to join the EU, working hard to meet not only the EU's budgetary requirements but also those pertaining to human rights and social policy. They saw the benefits of EU membership demonstrated in such countries as Greece, long considered the poor relative of the other EU states. Greece joined the European Community in 1981; its per capita gross domestic product was 64 percent of the European average in 1985. During the 1990s, however, Greek leaders and the EU made a real effort to bring the country closer to EU norms. By the early twenty-first century, thanks to advice from the EU and an infusion of funds, Greece had reached 80 percent of the EU per capita gross domestic product.

In 2004, the EU admitted ten new members—Estonia, Latvia, Lithuania, Poland, the Czech Republic, Slovakia, Hungary, Slovenia, Malta, and Cyprus—and in 2007 it welcomed Romania and Bulgaria (Map 24.3). Just before Poland's admission to the EU, its standard of living was 39 percent of EU standards, up from 33 percent in 1995. The Czech Republic and Hungary were at 55 and 50 percent, respectively. In all three cases, these figures masked differences between the ailing countryside and thriving cities. Citizens in eastern Europe were not always happy at the prospect of joining the EU. One retiree foresaw the cost of beer going up and said, "If I wanted to join anything in the West, I would have defected." Still others felt that having just established an independent national identity, they should not allow themselves to be swallowed up once again. People in older member states were having second thoughts, too. In the spring of 2005, a majority of voters in France and the Netherlands defeated a newly drafted constitution that would have strengthened EU ties. Commentators explained the rejection as stemming from popular anger at the EU bureaucracy's failure to consult ordinary people in its decision making.

Although still weak by comparison with most of western Europe, economic life in eastern Europe picked up considerably early in the twenty-first century. In contrast to the first bleak years of massive layoffs, soaring inflation, and unpaid salaries, purchasing power in Poland, Slovenia, and Estonia was some 40 percent higher in 2002 than in 1989. Outsourcing by international companies began to

Map 24.3 The European Union in 2009
The European Union appeared to increase the economic health of its members despite the rocky start of its common currency, the euro. The EU helped end the traditional competition among its members and facilitated trade and worker migration by providing common passports and business laws, and open borders. But many critics worried about a loss of cultural distinctiveness among peoples because of the EU, and those in the more prosperous countries came to fear that the global crisis that began in 2008 would make them financially responsible for the weak economies of eastern Europe.

flourish across the region, increasing opportunities for those with language and technical skills, and more people enjoyed consumer items such as freezers, computers, and portable telephones. The shopping malls that were built mostly around the capital cities testified to the urban nature of the benefits of the new economy. Eastern Europe was seen as a great new market consisting of 100 million customers for superstores like the Swedish furniture giant IKEA or the electronics firm Electroworld. "When Electroworld opened in Budapest [April 2002], it provoked a riot. Two hundred thousand people crowded to get in the doors," reported one observer. Critics worried that eastern Europeans had fallen prey to uncontrolled materialism and frenzied shopping, a Western disease they called "consumania."

Prague Supermarket, 2002
For people living in former eastern-bloc countries, daily life in the post-Communist world was one of extremes. Within several years, entrepreneurs opened supermarkets filled with more goods than most people had ever seen before, like the different irons available to this Prague shopper. Along with the unprecedented array of goods, the collapse of communism brought new dangers, such as bombings of public transportation and economic instability for those who did not benefit from the uneasy transition to capitalism. (Getty Images.)

Consumers themselves, however, learned to read labels and to use the superstores, where prices were lower. Proudly, many believed that they had left Communist poverty behind.

Globalizing Cities and Fragmenting Nations

After the collapse of communism, the West changed still further. It both fragmented into more nation-states than it had had fifty years earlier and developed new features—most notably the globalization of major cities. These were cities whose institutions and values were global rather than regional or national. They contained stock markets, legal firms, insurance companies, financial service organizations, and other enterprises that operated across national borders and were linked to similar enterprises in other global cities. Within these cities, high-level decision makers set global economic policy and enacted global business. The high-powered and high-priced nature of such global business operations made life in global cities extremely costly, driving middle managers and engineers to lower-priced living quarters in the suburbs that nonetheless provided good schools and other benefits for well-educated white-collar workers. Crowded into the slums of global cities and poorer suburbs were the lowest-paid service providers—the maintenance, domestic, and other workers whose menial labor was essential around the clock to attend to the needs and comfort of those at the top.

Global cities often had the best transportation and telecommunication facilities and thus became centers of migration for highly skilled and more modest workers alike. Paris, London, and New York were global spaces where workers maintained direct and constant contact with people around the world. Global cities drew criticism for their concentrated wealth, seen to be taken at the expense of poorer people in southern countries, and for their lack of patriotic focus on national causes. They contained huge diasporas of prosperous migrants, such as the estimated ninety thousand Japanese in England in the mid-1990s who staffed Japan's thriving global businesses. Because these migrants did not aim to become citizens, they made no economic or political claims on the adopted country and were thus sometimes called invisible migrants. As a result, global cities were said to produce a "deterritorialization of identities," meaning that many city dwellers lacked both a national and a local sense of themselves.

Ironically, as globalization took hold economically and culturally, there were more nations in Europe in 2000 than there had been in 1945 (Map 24.4). Belief in ethnic distinctiveness caused individual nation-states to break up. Despite two centuries aimed at unification of the Slavs, for example, in the 1990s and early 2000s, Slavs separated into their own states. In 1993, Czechoslovakia split into the Czech Republic and Slovakia. Yugoslavia came apart into several states, and Russia fought to keep Chechnya from breaking away as had many other states of the former Soviet Union.

Activists launched movements for regional independence in France, Italy, and Spain. Some Bretons and Corsicans demanded their freedom from France; Belgians threatened to split the country in two; northern Italians created an independence movement; and Basque nationalists in northern Spain assassinated tourists, police, and other public servants in an effort to gain autonomy. Although in 2005 the Basque nationalists publicly renounced terrorism, the violence did not stop. As cities globalized and nations fragmented, new combinations of local, national, and global identities took shape. Nganda manager Therese enjoyed her neighborhood in Paris, her identity as an immigrant to France, and continuing contact with friends and family in Congo. Nonetheless, these developments plus the overall expansion of the EU called into question the future of the nation-state.

Global Organizations

Supranational organizations, some of them regulating international finance and trade but others addressing social problems, had been in place for decades but became more active and powerful with globalization. Sponsored by large numbers of individual nations, the **World Bank**, International Monetary Fund, and World Trade Organization, for example, dealt with the terms of trade among countries and the economic well-being of individual peoples. Raising money from national governments, the

Map 24.4 Eastern Europe in the 1990s
In the 1990s, the countries of eastern Europe tried to forge their own destinies free from the direction of either Russia or the United States. The transition was far from easy. Old states like Czechoslovakia fragmented, and many state borders were contested. Turning definitively from Russia, the leadership of these countries began to look to western Europe, most of them eventually opting for membership in the European Union even though everyone relied on Russia's oil and natural gas. Compare this map with the sharp divisions between eastern and western Europe shown in Map 22.3 (page 878). What were the most significant changes to the region in the post–cold war era?

International Monetary Fund made loans to developing countries but only on the condition that they restructure their economies according to neoliberal principles. Other supranational organizations were charitable foundations, research institutes, or service organizations acting independently of government, many of them based in Europe and the United States. They were called **nongovernmental organizations (NGOs)**. Because some—the Rockefeller, Ford, and Open Society foundations, for example—had so much money, these NGOs often had considerable international power. After the fall of the Soviet bloc, NGOs used their resources to shape economic and social policy and the course of political reform. Some charitable and activist NGOs, like the French-based Doctors without Borders, raised money through global contributions and used it to provide medical care in places such as the war-torn former Yugoslavia. Like the EU, the larger NGOs were sometimes criticized for exercising their power with little regard for democratic processes or citizens' own preferences.

In the 1990s, there was a growing movement to attack globalization itself. In 1998, Bernard Cassen of France founded the Association for the Benefit of Citizens (ATTAC, after its French name). The organization, which soon had adherents in forty countries, stood against the control of globalization by financial institutions and held well-attended conferences to find new directions for countries suffering from global development. A globally known activist, French farmer José Bové, protested the opening of McDonald's restaurants in France and destroyed genetically modified seeds. "The only regret I have now," Bové claimed at his trial in 2003, "is that I didn't destroy more of it." Bové went to jail for his protests, but he remained a hero to antiglobalism activists, who saw him as a simple champion of, in his own words, "good food" and an enemy of standardization.

> **REVIEW** What trends suggest that the nation-state was a declining institution at the beginning of the twenty-first century?

Global Challenges and Discontents

The rising tide of globalization brought as many challenges as opportunities. First, the health of the world's people and their environment came under a multipronged attack from nuclear disaster, acid rain, and surging population. Second, economic prosperity and physical safety continued to elude great masses of people, especially in the southern half of the globe. Third, as suprastate organizations developed, transnational allegiances and religious and ethnic movements also competed for power and influence. Growing wealth in Latin America, Asia, and the Middle East gave leaders in these regions the confidence to state that it was time for the West to surrender some of its power.

Pollution and Environmental Activism

By the early twenty-first century, many people had become aware of the dangers of industrial growth—once seen as an unqualified blessing—to the environment. In the aftermath of the 1986 nuclear explosion at Chernobyl, levels of radioactivity rose for hundreds of miles in all directions. By the 1990s cancer rates in the region were soaring, particularly among children, and thousands were perishing slowly from the effects of radiation poisoning. Fossil fuel pollutants, such as those from natural gas, coal, and oil, mixed with atmospheric moisture to produce acid rain, a poisonous brew that destroyed forests and inflicted ailments such as chronic bronchial disease on people. In less industrial areas, clearing the world's rain forests depleted the global oxygen supply and threatened the biological diversity of the planet. By the late 1980s, scientists determined that the use of chlorofluorocarbons (CFCs), chemicals found in aerosol and refrigeration products, had blown a hole in the earth's ozone layer, the part of the blanket of atmospheric gases that prevents harmful ultraviolet rays from reaching the planet. Simultaneously, automobile and industrial emissions of chemicals were adding to that thermal blanket. The result was **global warming**, an increase in the temperature of the earth's lower atmosphere. Changes in temperature and dramatic weather cycles of drought or drenching rain indicated that a "greenhouse effect" might be permanently warming the earth. Already in the 1990s, the Arctic pack ice was breaking up, allowing Finland to ship oil along the once-iced-over route in 2002. Scientists predicted dire consequences: the rate of global melting, which had more than doubled since 1988, would raise sea levels by more than ten inches by 2100, flooding coastal areas, disturbing fragile ecosystems, and harming freshwater supplies.

Activism protesting unchecked industrial growth now became an effective political force. An escapee from Nazi Germany, E. F. "Fritz" Schumacher, produced one of the bibles of the environmental movement, *Small Is Beautiful* (1973), which spelled out how technology and industrialization actually threatened the earth and its inhabitants. Behind him stood the legacy of American environmentalist Rachel Carson, author of *Silent Spring* (1962), a powerful critique that advocated the immediate rescue of rivers, forests, and the soil from the ravages of factories and chemical farming. In 1979, the Green Party was founded in West Germany, and Green Party candidates across Europe came to force other politicians to voice their concern for the environment. As the horrific effects of unchecked pollution in eastern Europe became known, protests mounted and solutions began to unfold.

Inspired by Green Party ideas, Europeans attacked environmental problems on the local and global levels. Some European cities such as Frankfurt developed car-free zones, and Venice operated completely without automobiles because of the threat they posed to the city's very existence. In Paris, whenever automobile emissions reached dangerous levels, cars were banned from city streets until the emission levels dropped. The Smart car, a very small car using less fuel than larger cars, became a fashionable way to reduce dependence on fossil fuels. Cities also developed bicycle lanes on major city streets. Parts of Europe developed wind power to such an extent that 20 percent of some countries' electricity was generated by wind. Many cities in the West began to recycle waste materials.

These were success stories, involving changing habits in some of the most industrialized countries of the world. By 1999, some eighty-four countries, including EU members, had signed the Kyoto Protocol, an international treaty whose signatories agreed to reduce their pollution levels to specified targets. The Kyoto emissions reductions finally went into effect in February 2005, but with the world's leading polluter at the time—the United States—still refusing to join the effort. In 2009, however, Barack Obama became the first African American president on a

Smart Cars in Europe
The havoc caused by the oil crisis of the 1970s spurred many European states to encourage the development of alternative sources of energy and transportation. By the twenty-first century, the landscape was dotted not only with windmills but also with tiny, fuel-efficient automobiles like the Smart car shown here. European governments also heavily taxed gasoline, with the result that it cost at least twice as much as in the United States, thus further encouraging people to buy the Smart car rather than an SUV—a far rarer sight in Europe than in the United States. (© David Cooper/Toronto Star/ZUMA/Corbis.)

platform that included a commitment to environmental responsibility, turning back the sense that the West was fragmenting over environmental issues.

Population, Health, and Disease

The issue of population was as difficult in the early twenty-first century as it had been in the 1930s. Nations with less-developed economies struggled with the pressing problem of surging populations, while Europe experienced negative population growth (more deaths than births) after 1995. The less industrially developed countries accounted for 98 percent of worldwide population growth, in part because the spread of Western medicine enabled people there to live much longer than before. By late 1999, the earth's population had reached six billion and was expected to double by 2045 (see "Taking Measure," page 966). Yet because many European countries were not replacing their populations, they were facing problems related to an aging citizenry and a shortage of younger people. In fact, Europe as a region had the lowest fertility rate in the world. The fertility rate in Italy and Spain was only 1.3 children per woman of reproductive age, far below the replacement level of 2.1 needed to maintain a steady population. Some forecasters predicted that this low rate meant that the population of Europe would fall from 725 million to 600 million by 2050.

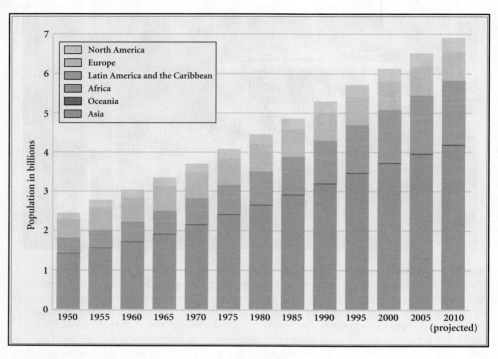

Taking Measure World Population Growth, 1950–2010
In the twenty-first century, a major question is whether the global environment can sustain billions
of people indefinitely. In the early modern period, local communities had lived according to unwrit-
ten rules that balanced population size with the productive capacities of individual farming regions.
Centuries later, the same need for balance had reached global proportions. As fertility dropped around
the planet because of contraception, population continued to grow because of improved health.

One consequence of this decline would be fewer workers paying into the social
security system to fund retirees' pensions.

Population problems were especially urgent in former Soviet-bloc countries,
where life expectancy was declining at a catastrophic rate from a peak of seventy
years for Russian men in the mid-1970s to fifty-one years at the beginning of the
twenty-first century. Heart disease and cancer were the leading causes of male
death, and these stark death rates were generally attributed to increased drinking
(one in seven men in Russia was an alcoholic), smoking, drug use, poor diet, and
general stress. Meanwhile, fertility rates were also declining: the lowest levels of
fertility in 2003 were in the Czech Republic and Ukraine with a rate of 1.1 children, and children in eastern Europe lived on average twelve years less than their
counterparts in western Europe. Between 1992 and 2002, the Russian population
declined from 149 million to 144 million, with predictions that it would fall below
100 million by 2050.

Good health was spread unevenly around the world. Western medicine brought better health to many in the less-developed world through the increased use of vaccines and drugs for diseases such as malaria and smallpox. However, half of all Africans lacked basic public health facilities and safe drinking water. Drought and poverty, along with the corruption of politicians in some cases, spread famine in Sudan, Somalia, Ethiopia, and elsewhere. Around the world, the poor and the unemployed suffered more chronic illnesses than those who were better-off, but they received less care. Whereas in many parts of the world people still died from malnutrition and infectious diseases, in the West noncontagious diseases—heart and autoimmune diseases, stroke, cancer, and depression—were more deadly. The distribution of health services—heart transplants for the wealthy versus preventive health care for a wider range of people—became a hotly debated issue in the general argument about whether technological solutions could remedy global problems.

Disease, like population and technology, operated on a global terrain. In the early 1980s, both Western values and Western technological expertise were challenged by the spread of acquired immunodeficiency syndrome (AIDS). An incurable, highly virulent killer that effectively shuts down the body's immune system, AIDS initially afflicted heterosexuals in central Africa. The disease later turned up in Haitian immigrants to the United States and in homosexual men worldwide. Within a decade, AIDS became a global epidemic. The disease spread especially quickly and widely among the heterosexual populations of Africa and Asia, passed mainly by men to and through women, but in 2009 the U.S. capital, Washington, D.C., had a rate of infection as high as that in Africa. By the late 1990s, no cure had yet been discovered, although protease-inhibiting drugs helped alleviate the symptoms. The mounting death toll made some equate AIDS with the Black Death. Treatment was often not provided to poor people living in places such as sub-Saharan Africa and the slums of Asian cities, but efforts were under way to provide more lifesaving drugs to these people. In addition to the AIDS epidemic, the deadly Ebola virus and dozens of other viruses smoldered while others, such as severe acute respiratory syndrome (SARS), avian flu, and swine flu, traveled the world even as health professionals worked to contain them. Diseases as much as environmental dangers underscored the interconnectedness of the world's peoples.

North versus South?

During the 1980s and 1990s, world leaders tried to address the growing divide between the earth's northern and southern regions. Other than Australians and New Zealanders, southern peoples generally had lower living standards and poorer health than northerners. Recently emerging from colonial rule and economic exploitation by northerners, citizens in the southern regions could not yet count on their new governments to provide welfare-state services or education. Funding for such programs generally came from northern countries, with international organizations such as the World Bank and the International Monetary Fund providing loans for economic development. However, the conditions of those loans, such as cutting government spending for education and health care, led to criticism that ordinary citizens gained no real benefit from them. Some early-twenty-first-century leaders advocated that wealthy countries simply give southern countries the money they needed as reparation for centuries of imperial plunder.

Southern regions experienced various barriers to economic development. Latin American nations grappled with government corruption, multibillion-dollar debts, widespread crime, and grinding poverty, although some countries—prominent among them Brazil—began to strengthen their economies by marketing their oil and other natural resources more effectively. Africa suffered from drought, famine, and civil war. In countries such as Rwanda, Somalia, and Sudan, military rule and ethnic or religious antagonism encouraged under imperialism produced conflict and genocide in the 1990s and early 2000s. Millions perished; others were left starving and homeless due to "kleptocracies" that stole resources, including aid provided by charitable groups. Although some African countries began turning away from military dictatorship and toward constitutional government, economic advance was uneven on the continent, and in the twenty-first century the scourge of AIDS and other unchecked diseases added to the weight of Africa's problems.

Islam Meets the West

North-South antagonisms became evident in the rise of militant Islam, which often flourished where democracy and prosperity for the masses were missing. The Iranian hostage crisis (1979–1981) showed religion, nationalism, and anti-Western sentiment commanding the world's attention. The charismatic leaders of the 1980s and 1990s—Iran's Ayatollah Ruhollah Khomeini; Libya's Muammar Qaddafi; Iraq's Saddam Hussein; and Osama bin Laden, leader of the al-Qaeda transnational terrorist organization—variously promoted a pan-Arabic or pan-Islamic world order that gathered increasing support. Khomeini's program—"Neither East, nor West, only the Islamic Republic"—had wide appeal. Renouncing the Westernization that had flourished under the shah, Khomeini's regime in Iran required women once again to cover their bodies almost totally in special clothing and eliminated a range of their former rights. Aided by the prosperity that oil had brought, Islamic revolutionaries believed that a strict theocracy would restore the pride and Islamic identity that imperialism had stripped from Middle Eastern men. Khomeini built widespread support among Shi'ite Muslims by proclaiming the ascendancy of the Shi'ite clergy. Although the Shi'ites were numerous, they had long been discriminated against by Sunni Muslims.

Islamic leaders did not achieve their unifying goals (Map 24.5). Instead, war plagued the region. In 1980, Saddam Hussein, fearing a rebellion from Shi'ites in Iraq, attacked Iran, hoping to channel Shi'ite discontent into a patriotic crusade against non-Arab Iranians. The United States provided Iraq with massive aid in the struggle against Iran, but after eight years of combat and extensive loss of life

Map 24.5 The Middle East in the Twenty-first Century

Tensions among states in the Middle East, especially the ongoing conflict between the Palestinians and Israelis and animosities between Shi'ites and Sunnis, became more complicated from the 1990s on. The situation grew more uncertain in 2003 when a U.S.- and British-led invasion of Iraq deteriorated into escalating violence among competing religious and ethnic groups in the country. Additionally, for thirty-four days in the summer of 2006, Israel bombed Lebanon, including its capital city and refugee camps, with fire returned by Hezbollah and Hamas forces in the region. This violence was followed in 2009 by Israel's shelling and invading of Gaza at the end of a cease-fire and new Palestinian rocket attacks.

on both sides, the war ended in a stalemate. At about the same time, the Soviet Union became embroiled in a war against Islam in Afghanistan when the Soviets supported a coup by a Communist faction against the government in 1979. Tens of thousands of Soviets fought in Afghanistan, using the most advanced missiles and artillery to combat a powerful group of Muslim resisters. The United States, China, Saudi Arabia, and Pakistan provided weapons to this resistance movement, some of whose members united to become the Taliban—a militant Islamic political group. The war in Afghanistan so drained the USSR that it withdrew its troops in 1989. In the late 1990s, the Taliban took over the government of Afghanistan and imposed a regime that, among other things, forbade girls to attend school and women to leave their homes without a male escort.

The Middle East remained in turmoil, as Saddam Hussein tested the post–cold war waters by invading Kuwait in 1990 in hopes of annexing the oil-rich country to debt-ridden Iraq. A UN coalition, led by the United States, quickly stopped the invasion and defeated the Iraqi army, but discontent mounted in the region. Conflict between the Israelis and the Palestinians continued. In the late 1990s, as Israeli settlers began seizing Palestinian land, Palestinian suicide bombers began murdering Israeli civilians. The Israeli government retaliated with missiles, machine guns, and tanks, often killing Palestinian civilians in turn. In 2006, the Israelis, responding to the political militia Hezbollah's kidnapping of Israeli sol- diers, attacked Lebanon, destroying infrastructure, sending missiles into its capi- tal city of Beirut, and killing hundreds of civilians. In 2009, Israel's invasion and bombing of Gaza had the same results. Beginning in the 1980s and continuing into the 2000s, terrorists from the Middle East and North Africa planted bombs in many European cities, blew airplanes out of the sky, and bombed the Paris subway system. These attacks, causing widespread destruction and loss of life, were said to be punishment for the West's support of Israel and the repressive regimes in other Middle Eastern countries.

On September 11, 2001, the ongoing terrorism in Europe and around the world finally caught the full attention of the United States. In an unprecedented act, Muslim militants hijacked four commercial airplanes in the United States and flew two of them into the World Trade Center in New York City and one into the Pentagon in Virginia. The fourth plane, en route to the U.S. Capitol, crashed in Pennsylvania when passengers forced the hijackers to lose control of the aircraft. The hijackers, most of whom were from Saudi Arabia, had been inspired by the wealthy radical leader Osama bin Laden, who sought to end the presence of U.S. forces in Saudi Arabia. They had trained in bin Laden's terrorist camps in Afghanistan and learned to pilot planes in the United States. The loss of more than three thousand lives led the United States to declare a "war against terrorism." The administration of U.S. president George W. Bush forged a multinational coalition, which included the vital cooperation of Islamic countries such as Pakistan, with the main goal of driving the ruling Taliban out of Afghanistan and capturing bin Laden. After some initial

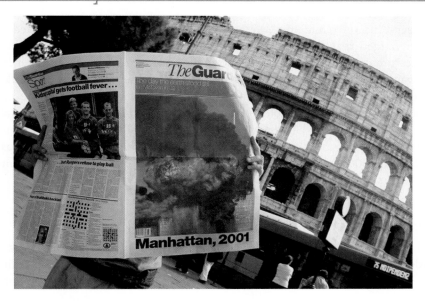

Europeans React to 9/11 Terror
On September 11, 2001, terrorists killed thousands of people from dozens of countries in air-plane attacks on the World Trade Center in New York and the Pentagon outside Washington, D.C. Throughout the world, people expressed their shock and sorrow, and many, like this British tourist in Rome, remained glued to the news. Terrorism, which had plagued Europeans for several decades, easily traveled the world in these days of more open borders, economic globalization, and cultural exchange, finally reaching the sole superpower left after the collapse of the Soviet Union. **For more help analyzing this image, see the visual activity for this chapter in the Online Study Guide at** bedfordstmartins.com/huntconcise**.** (© Pizzoli Alberto/Sygma/Corbis.)

coalition success in Afghanistan, by 2009 the Taliban was reestablishing its authority there, and bin Laden was still at large.

At first, the September 11 attacks and other lethal bombings around the world promoted global cooperation. European countries rounded up terrorists and conducted the first successful trials of them in the spring of 2003. Ultimately, however, the West became divided when the United States claimed that Saddam Hussein was concealing weapons of mass destruction in Iraq and suggested ties between Saddam and bin Laden's terrorist group. Great Britain, Spain, and Poland were among the countries that joined the United States in invading Iraq in March 2003, but other powerful European states, including Germany, Russia, and France, refused. Many people in the United States were furious at this refusal, and some engaged in a round of "French bashing," even promoting the renaming of French fries to "freedom fries." U.S. war fever mounted with the suggestion that Syria and Iran should also be invaded, while many in the rest of the world condemned what seemed a sudden American thirst for blood. Europeans in general, including the British public, accused the United States of becoming a world military dictatorship in order to preserve its only remaining value—wasteful consumerism. The United States counphercharged that the Europeans were too selfishly enjoying their democracy and creature comforts to help fund the military defense of freedom under attack. The Spanish withdrew from the U.S. occupation of Iraq after terrorists linked to al-Qaeda bombed four Madrid commuter trains on March 11, 2004. The British, too, reeled when terrorists exploded bombs in three subway cars and a bus in central London in July 2005. As the war in Iraq approached its seventh year, there was a sense that the West was coming apart, yet some felt that Obama's election as U.S. president in 2008 would lead to a quicker end to the conflict, given his campaign promise to set a timetable for troop withdrawals.

World Economies on the Rise

Amid the violence, incredible industrial and technological development took place outside the West. Just as economic change in the early modern period had redirected European affairs from the Mediterranean to the Atlantic, so explosive productivity from Japan to Singapore in the 1980s and 1990s spread economic power from the Atlantic region to the Pacific. In 1982, the Asian Pacific nations accounted for 16.4 per-

Tigers of the Pacific Rim, c. 1995

cent of global gross domestic product, a figure that had doubled since the 1960s. By 1989, East Asia's share of world production had grown to more than 25 percent as that of the West had declined. By 2006, China alone was achieving economic growth rates of over 10 percent per year, while Japan had developed the world's second-largest national economy (after the United States). By 2009, China had edged out Germany for third place.

South Korea, Taiwan, Singapore, and Hong Kong were popularly called **Pacific tigers** for the ferocity of their growth in the 1980s and 1990s. By the 1990s, China, pursuing a policy of economic modernization and market orientation, had joined the surge in productivity. Japan, however, led the initial charge of Asian economies, with investment in high-tech consumer industries driving the Japanese economy. For example, in 1982 Japan had thirty-two thousand industrial robots in operation, western Europe had only nine thousand, and the United States had seven thousand. In 1989, the Japanese government and private businesses invested $549 billion to modernize Japan's industrial capacity, a full $36 billion more than U.S. public and private investment. Such spending paid off substantially, as buyers around the world snapped up automobiles, televisions, videocassette recorders, and computers from Japanese or other Asian Pacific companies. As the United States poured vast sums into its military budgets and a series of wars, Asian and Middle Eastern governments purchased U.S. government bonds, thus financing America's ballooning national debt. Forty years after its total defeat in World War II, Japan was bankrolling its former conqueror.

Despite rising national prosperity, individual workers, particularly those outside Japan, often paid dearly for this newly created wealth. For example, industrial safety standards in China were abominable, leading to horrendous mining and other disasters. Women in South Korea, Taiwan, and Central America labored in sweatshops to produce clothing for such U.S.-based companies as JCPenney and Calvin Klein. Using the lure of a low-paid and docile female workforce, governments were able to attract electronics and other industries. However, educational standards for these women did rise, along with access to birth control and other medical care.

Other emerging economies in the Southern Hemisphere continued to increase their share of the world's gross domestic product during the 1980s and 1990s, and some achieved political gains as well. In South Africa, native peoples began winning the struggle for political rights when, in 1990, the moderate government of F. W. de Klerk released political leader Nelson Mandela, imprisoned for almost three decades because of his antiapartheid activism. In free elections in 1994, Mandela was elected president. South Africa, Russia, Brazil, Iran, Saudi Arabia, Nigeria, and Chile all profited from the global need for vast quantities of raw materials such as oil and ores. India made strides in education, women's rights, and local cooperation (calming bitter rivalries), but the assassinations of prime ministers raised the question of whether India would continue to have the strong leadership necessary to attract investment and thus continue to modernize. After the brief rule of a Hindu nationalist government that often blocked development, India's economy took off in the early twenty-first century, taking business away from Western firms and making global acquisitions that gave it, for example, the world's largest steel industry. Although Western multinationals faced more competition, they also profited from increasing prosperity worldwide, which allowed more people to buy their products.

There was a downside to global development. Beginning in 1997, when speculators brought down the Thai baht, and continuing with the collapse of the ruble in 1998 and the bursting of the technology bubble in the early 2000s, the global economy suffered a series of shocks. Then in 2008, the real estate bubble burst in the United States, setting in motion a financial crisis of enormous proportions. For several years, lenders had been making home mortgages available to consumers on easy terms in the United States, which had helped prop up the economy. Financiers then distributed this U.S. debt around the world to those who hoped to make handsome profits based on rate increases written into the mortgage contracts. When people were unable to make their monthly mortgage payments and pay their ballooning credit card debt, credit became unavailable both to ordinary people and to banks and industry. A credit collapse followed, just as it had in the stock market crash of 1929. Beginning

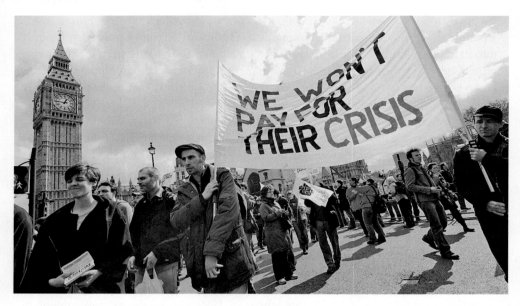

Protesting the Global Economic Crisis, London, 2009
In the spring of 2009, citizens and activists from around the world converged on London to confront the Group of Twenty, or G-20, established to bring together the leaders of the world's twenty largest economies. These demonstrators protested the use of their tax dollars to prop up banks whose officers had brought the global economy to a virtual halt through their manipulations of finance worldwide in order to boost their profits. Protesters demanded that more humane values govern the world, even as some of them rioted and destroyed property. (© Andy Rain/epa/Corbis.)

in the United States, banks and industries became insolvent and governments around the world tried to prop them up with billions of dollars. Unemployment rose, as businesses and consumers alike stopped purchasing goods. The globalization of economic crises was another of the perils faced by the world's population.

> **REVIEW**   What were the most important challenges facing the West in the new millennium?

Global Culture and Society in the Twenty-first Century

At the beginning of the twenty-first century, increased migration and growing global communication led many to ask what would become of national cultures and Western civilization. Would the world become a uniform mass, with everyone wearing the same kind of clothing, eating the same kind of food, and watching the same films (perhaps on their cell phones)? Some critics predicted a clash of civilizations, in which antagonistic religions and cultures would lead to a global holocaust. Others asked whether the West would collapse as the United States wore itself out waging war while much of Europe turned away.

Migration, the spread of disease, global climate change, the information revolution, and the global sharing of culture argued against the cultural purity of any group, Western or otherwise. "Civilizations," Indian economist and Nobel Prize winner Amartya Sen wrote after the terrorist attacks of September 11, "are hard to partition . . . given the diversities within each society as well as the linkages among different countries and cultures." Through migration and communication, Western society changed even more rapidly in the 1980s and 1990s than it had hundreds of years earlier when it had come into intense contact with the rest of the globe. Culture transcended national boundaries, as East, West, North, and South became saturated with one another's products and customs. Some observers labeled the new century an era of denationalization—meaning that national cultures as well as national boundaries were becoming less distinct.

Redefining the West: The Impact of Global Migration

The global movement of people was massive in the last third of the twentieth century and into the twenty-first century. Uneven economic development, political persecution, and warfare (which claimed more than 100 million victims after 1945) sent tens of millions in search of opportunity and safety. By 2001, France had some 6 million Muslims within its borders, and Europe as a whole had between 35 million and 50 million. Other parts of the world also had millions of migrants from other

Headscarf Controversy in Germany
Western countries have long debated the relationship between religion and the nation-state. In particular, that debate targeted the need for religiously neutral education in order to develop citizens with undivided national loyalties. In an age of global migration, the issue of religion in the schools resurfaced, this time focusing on the headscarves worn by many Muslim women. Although in 2003 Germany upheld the right of the teacher Fereshta Ludin, pictured here, to wear the headscarf while teaching on the grounds of religious freedom, it simultaneously asserted the right of children to a religiously neutral education. (Michael Latz/ddp Berlin.)

cultures. The oil-producing nations of the Middle East employed countless foreign workers, who generally constituted one-third of the labor force. Violence in Africa sent Rwandans, Congolese, and others to South Africa, as its government became dominated by blacks. War in Afghanistan increased the number of refugees to Iran to nearly two million in 1995, while successive attacks on Iraq by the West sent millions more fleeing. By 2000, there were some 120 million migrants worldwide, many of them headed to the West.

Migrants often earned desperately needed income for family members who remained in their native countries, and in some cases they propped up the economies of entire nations. In countries as different as Yugoslavia (before its breakup), Egypt, Spain, Mexico, and Pakistan, money sent home from abroad constituted up to 60 percent of the national income. Sometimes migration was coerced; for example, many eastern European and Asian prostitutes were held in international sex rings that controlled their passports, wages, and lives. Others came to the West voluntarily, seeking opportunity and a better life. "I do not want to go back to China," said one woman restaurant owner in Hungary in the 1990s. "Some of my relatives there also have restaurants. . . . They have to have good relations with officials, . . . and sometimes they have to bribe somebody. . . . I would not be happy living like that." Like the illegal Congolese café proprietor Therese, whose story opens this chapter, many lived on the margins of the law, supporting networks of family and maintaining global economic ties from a new base in the West.

Foreign workers were often scapegoats for native peoples suffering from economic woes such as unemployment caused by downsizing. On the eve of EU enlargement in 2004, the highly respected weekly magazine *The Economist* included an article titled "The Coming Hordes," which warned of Britain's being overrun by Roma (Gypsies) from eastern Europe. Political parties with racist programs sprang to life in Europe, aided by celebrities. The Moscow rock band Corroded Metals campaigned for anti-immigrant candidates with hate-filled songs and chants in English of "Kill, kill, kill, kill the bloody foreigners" running in the background. Even citizens of immigrant descent often had a difficult time being accepted. In Austria, France, the Netherlands, Sweden, and many other Western countries, thriving anti-immigrant and white supremacist politicians challenged centrist parties. In Austria and the Netherlands, anti-immigration candidates were elected to head the government. Nonetheless, because employers sought out illegal immigrants for the low wages they could be paid, the West remained a place of opportunity.

Global Networks and the Economy

Like migration, rapid technological change also weakened traditional political, cultural, and economic borders. In 1969, the U.S. Department of Defense developed a computer network to carry communications in case of nuclear war. This system and others like it in universities, government, and business grew over the next decades into an unregulated system of more than ten thousand networks globally. These came to be known as the Internet—shorthand for *internetworking*. By 1995, users in more than 137 countries were connected to the Internet, creating new "communities" based on business needs, shared cultural interests, or other factors that went beyond the borders of a particular nation-state. An online global marketplace gradually emerged, offering goods and services ranging from books and discount airfares to advanced weaponry and organ transplants. While enthusiasts claimed that the Internet could promote world democracy, critics charged that this new communications technology favored elites and disadvantaged those without computer skills.

By 2000, as postindustrial skills spread, the Internet brought service jobs to countries that had heretofore suffered unemployment and real poverty. One of the first countries to recognize the possibilities of computing and help-desk services was Ireland, which pushed computer literacy to attract business. In 2003, U.S. firms spent $8.3 billion on outsourcing to Ireland and $7.7 billion on outsourcing to India. The Internet allowed for jobs to be apportioned anywhere. Moroccans did help-desk work for French or Spanish speakers, and in the twenty-first century Estonia, Hungary, the Czech Republic, and the Philippines were rebuilding their economies successfully by providing call-center and other business services. The Internet allowed service industries to globalize just as the manufacturing sector had done much earlier through multinational corporations.

Globalization of the economy affected the West in complex ways. Those who worked in outsourcing enterprises were more likely than those in domestic firms to participate in the global consumer economy, much of it for Western goods. Benefiting from the booming global economy of the 1990s, the Irish and eastern Europeans used their new disposable income to purchase items such as luxury automobiles, CD players, and personal computers that would have been far beyond their means a

Call Center in Bangalore, India
Modern communications have permitted the outsourcing not just of manufacturing jobs, which began after World War II, but also of service jobs to places like eastern Europe, Africa, and South Asia. These workers in southern India, who are answering a customer service hotline, are bilingual or polylingual, enabling them to service customers in Europe and the United States. What are the advantages and disadvantages of a division of labor that operates internationally?
(© Jagadeesh/Reuters/Corbis.)

decade earlier. Non-Westerners may have taken jobs from the West, but they often sent funds back. A twenty-one-year-old Indian woman, working for a service provider in Bangalore under the English name Sharon, used her salary to buy Western consumer items, such as a cell phone from the Finnish company Nokia. "As a teenager I wished for so many things," she said. "Now I'm my own Santa Claus." Ordinary Western workers often discovered that this global revolution threatened their jobs. In Germany, where taxes for social security and other welfare-state financing accounted for 42 percent of payroll costs in 2003, the attraction of countries with lower costs was strong. Globalization redistributed jobs across the West and reworked economic networks, and it also contributed to the global economic crisis beginning in 2008.

A Global Culture?

As far back as the first millennium of human history, culture has crossed political boundaries. In the ancient world, Greek philosophers and traders knew of distant Asian religious beliefs, while in the eighteenth and nineteenth centuries, Western scholars immersed themselves in Asian languages. By the early 1990s, tourism had become the largest single industry in Britain and in many other Western countries, promoting cultural exchange. Chinese students in Tiananmen Square in 1989 testified to the power of the West in the world's imagination when in the name of freedom they rallied around a model of the Statue of Liberty (which itself was a gift from France to the United States). In Japan, businesspeople wore Western-style clothing and watched soccer, baseball, and other Western sports using English terms, while Europeans and Americans ate sushi, wore flip-flops, and carried umbrellas—all imports from beyond the West.

Innovations in communications integrated cultures and made the earth seem a much smaller place, though possibly one with a Western flavor. Videotapes and satellite-beamed telecasts transported American television shows to Hong Kong and Japanese movies to Europe and North America. American rock music sold briskly in Russia and elsewhere in the former Soviet bloc. When more than 100,000 Czechoslovakian rock fans, including President Václav Havel, attended a Rolling Stones concert in Prague in 1990, it was clear that despite half a century of supposedly insular Communist culture, Czechs and Slovaks had tuned in to the larger world. Young black immigrants forged transnational culture when they created hip-hop and other pop music styles by combining elements of Africa, the Caribbean, Afro-America, and Europe. Athletes like the Brazilian soccer player Ronaldo, the American golfer Tiger Woods, and the Japanese baseball star Ichiro Suzuki became better known to countless people than their own national leaders were. Film entrepreneurs marketed such international blockbusters as the Chinese *Crouching Tiger, Hidden Dragon* (2000). With their messages conveyed around the world, even today's moral leaders—Nobel Peace Prize winners Nelson Mandela, former president of South Africa; the Dalai Lama, spiritual leader of Tibet; and Aung San Suu Kyi, opposition leader in Myanmar (Burma)—are global figures.

As it had done for centuries, the West continued to devour material from other cultures—whether Hong Kong films, African textiles, Indian music, or Latin American pop culture. One of the most important influences in the West came from what was called the "boom" in Latin American literature. Latin American authors developed a style known as magical realism that melded everyday events with Latin American history and geography, while also incorporating elements of myth, magic, and religion. The novels of Colombian-born Nobel Prize winner Gabriel García Márquez were translated into dozens of languages. His lush fantasies, including *One Hundred Years of Solitude* (1967), *Love in the Time of Cholera* (1988), and many later works, portray people of titanic ambitions and passions who endure war and all manner of personal trials. García Márquez narrated the tradition of dictators in Latin America, but he also paid close attention to the effects of global business. *One Hundred Years of Solitude,* for example, closes with the machine-gunning in 1928 of thousands of workers for the American United Fruit company because they asked for one day off per week, breaks to use the toilet, and other improvements in their working conditions. Wherever they lived, readers snapped up the book, which sold thirty million copies worldwide. García Márquez's work inspired a host of other outstanding novels in the magical realism tradition, including Laura Esquivel's *Like Water for Chocolate* (1989). In the 1990s, the work was translated into two dozen languages and became a hit film because of its setting in a Mexican kitchen during the revolution of 1910, where cooking, sexuality, and brutality are intertwined. The Latin American "boom" continued into the early twenty-first century, with innumerable authors in the West adopting aspects of García Márquez's style.

Magical realism influenced a range of Western writers, including those migrating to Europe. Some described how the experience of Western culture felt to the transnational person. British-born Zadie Smith, daughter of a Jamaican mother, became a prizewinning author with her novel *White Teeth* (2000), which describes postimperial Britain through the lives of often bizarre and larger-than-life characters from many ethnic backgrounds. Odd science fiction technology, deep emotional wounds, and weird but hilarious situations guide a plot full of heartbreak. Equally drawn to aspects of the magical realist style, Indian-born Salman Rushdie published the novel *The Satanic Verses* (1988), which outraged Muslims around the world because it appeared to blaspheme the Prophet, Muhammad. From Iran, Ayatollah Khomeini issued a fatwa promising both a monetary reward and salvation in the afterlife to anyone who would assassinate the writer. Rushdie's Norwegian publisher was shot, and his Italian and Japanese translators were murdered, but in a display of Western cultural unity, international leaders took bold steps to protect Rushdie until the threat to his life was lifted a decade later.

The mainstream literary world became fraught with conflict as groups outside the accepted circles engaged in artistic production. From within the West, novelist Toni Morrison became, in 1993, the first African American woman to win the Nobel Prize for Literature. In works such as *Beloved* (1987), *Jazz* (1992), and *A Mercy* (2008), Morrison describes the nightmares, daily experiences, achievements, and dreams of those who were brought as slaves to the United States and their descendants. But some parents objected to the inclusion of Morrison's work in school curricula alongside Shakespeare and other white authors. Critics charged that unlike Shakespeare's universal Western truth, the writing of African Americans, native Americans, and

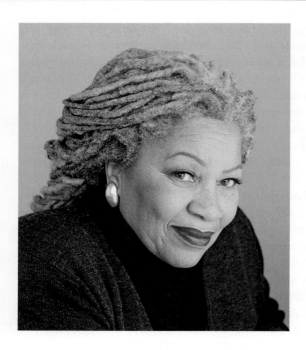

Toni Morrison
The first African American woman to receive the Nobel Prize for Literature, Toni Morrison has used her literary talent to depict the condition of blacks under slavery and after emancipation into contemporary times. Morrison also has published essays on social, racial, and gender issues in the United States. (© Deborah Feingold/Corbis.)

women represented only propaganda, not great literature. In both the United States and Europe, politicians on the right saw the presence of multiculturalism as a sign of deterioration similar to that brought about by immigration.

In the former Soviet bloc, artists and writers faced unique challenges. After the Soviet Union collapsed, classical writers like Mikhail Bulgakov (1891–1940), famous in the West for his novel *The Master and Margarita* (published posthumously in 1966–1967), became known in their homeland. At the same time, the collapse put literary dissidents out of business; having helped bring down the Soviet regime, they had lost their subject matter—the critique of a tyrannical system. State-sponsored authors, suddenly without jobs, had to sell their products on the free market in countries where economic conditions were so harsh that books were an unaffordable luxury. Eastern-bloc writers who formerly found both critical and financial success in the West seemed less heroic—and less talented—in the post-Soviet world. The work of Czech writer Milan Kundera, for example, lost its luster. It had been, according to one critic, merely about Western publishers' hype—that is, not literature but merely a "line of business." To make matters worse, there was no idea of what the post-Communist arts should be, sending artists in the former Soviet bloc scurrying for solutions.

Talented fresh voices rang out, too. Andrei Makine, an expatriate Russian author, became popular worldwide for his poignant yet disturbing novels of the collapse of communism, many of them showing the attraction of western European culture and the continuing impact of World War II and the Gulag on the imaginations of eastern-bloc people, including teenagers and older people. Both *Dreams of My*

Russian Summers (1995) and *Once Upon the River Love* (1994) describe young people bred to fantasize about the wealth, sexiness, and material goods of western Europe and America. Victor Pelevin wrote more satirically and bitingly in works such as *The Life of Insects* (1993), in which insect-humans buzz around Russia trying to discover who they are in the post-Soviet world. Pelevin, a Buddhist and former engineer, mocked politicians and the almost sacred Soviet space program, depicting it as a media sham, run from the depths of the Moscow subway system, in which hundreds of cosmonaut-celebrities are killed to prevent the truth from getting out. For him, "any politician is a TV program, and this doesn't change from one government to another." One simply judged politicians by their haircuts, ties, and other aspects of personal style, as he showed in his novel *Homo Zapiens* (2002), in which politicians are all "virtual"—that is, produced by technical effects and scriptwriters.

In music and the other arts, much energy in the former Soviet bloc was spent on recovering and absorbing all the underground works that had been hidden since 1917. The situation was utterly astonishing as the works of dozens of first-rate composers, for example, emerged. They had written their classical works in private for fear that these pieces might contain phrasings, sounds, and rhythms that would be labeled treasonous. Meanwhile, they had often earned a living writing for films, as did Giya Kancheli, who wrote immensely popular music for more than forty films but was in addition a gifted composer of classical music. Other composers simply became known to a wider world. Alfred Schnittke (1934–1998) produced dozens of operas, symphonies, chamber music pieces, concertos, and other works that were extremely sad, punctuated with anger in loud bursts of dissonance, and set in a somber bass register.

The political and economic power of the United States gave its culture an edge for many of these years. U.S. success in "marketing" culture, along with the legacy of British imperialism, helped make English the dominant international language by the end of the twentieth century. Such English words as *stop, shopping, parking, okay, weekend,* and *rock* infiltrated dozens of non-English vocabularies. English became one of the official languages of the European Union; across Europe it served as the main language of higher education, science, and tourism. In the 1960s, French president Charles de Gaulle, fearing the corruption of the French language, banned such new words as *computer* in government documents, and succeeding administrations followed his lead; this did not stop the influx of English into scientific, diplomatic, and daily life, however. In another sign of the cultural divide, the EU's parliament and national cultural ministries regulated the amount of American programming on television and in cinemas.

Nevertheless, American influence in films was dominant. Films such as *Titanic* (1997) and *The Matrix Reloaded* (2003) earned hundreds of millions of dollars from global audiences. Simultaneously, the United States itself welcomed films from around the world, including the Mexican *Y Tu Mamá También* (2001) and the Italian *Life Is Beautiful* (1997). "Bollywood" films—happy, lavish films from the Indian movie industry—had a huge following in the West, even influencing the plots of some American productions, and by the twenty-first century Bollywood had surpassed Hollywood in sales and viewers. The fastest-growing medium in the United States in the twenty-first century was Spanish-language television, just one more indication that even in the United States, culture was based on mixture and global exchange.

Some have called the global culture of the late twentieth and early twenty-first centuries **postmodernism**, defined in part as intense stylistic mixing in the arts without a central unifying theme or elite set of standards guiding them. Striking examples of postmodern art abounded in Western society, including the AT&T building (now known as the Sony Building) in New York City, which looks sleek and modern. Its entryway, however, is a Roman arch, and its cloud-piercing top suggests eighteenth-century Chippendale furniture. Postmodern buildings drew from cultural styles that spanned millennia and continents without valuing one style above others. The Guggenheim Museum in Bilbao, Spain, designed by American architect Frank Gehry and considered bizarre by classical or even "modern" standards, includes forms, materials, and perspectives that, according to the rules of earlier decades, do not belong together. Architects from around the world, working in a variety of hybrid styles, completed the postunification rebuilding of Berlin. One crowning achievement was the rebuilding of the Reichstag, whose traditional facade was given a modern dome of glass and steel. To add to the changing reality, all of these postmodern buildings could be visited virtually on the World Wide Web.

Some intellectuals defined postmodernism in political terms, as part of the decline of the eighteenth-century Enlightenment ideals of human rights, individualism, and personal freedom, which were seen as "modern." This political postmodernism included the decline of the Western nation-state. A structure like the Bilbao Guggenheim was simply an international tourist attraction rather than an institution reflecting Spanish traditions or Spain's national values. To commentators, it represented consumption, global technology, mass communications, and international migration rather than citizenship, nationalism, and rights. These qualities made it a rootless structure, unlike the Louvre in Paris, for example, which was built by the French monarchy to serve its own purposes. Critics saw the Bilbao Guggenheim as drifting, more like the nomadic businesswoman Therese, who moved between nations and cultures with no set identity. Cities and nations alike were losing their function as places providing social roots, personal identity, or human rights. For postmodernists of a political bent, computers had replaced the autonomous, free self, and transnational bureaucracies had made representative government obsolete.

The issues raised by postmodernism—whether in architecture, political thought, or the popular media—focused on the basic ingredients of Western identity as it had been defined over the past two hundred years. Postmodernism was part of the rethinking and questioning that accompanied globalization. Such critical thinking—whatever its tentative conclusions may be—is today, as in the past, a key ingredient in the making of the West.

REVIEW What social and cultural questions has globalization raised?

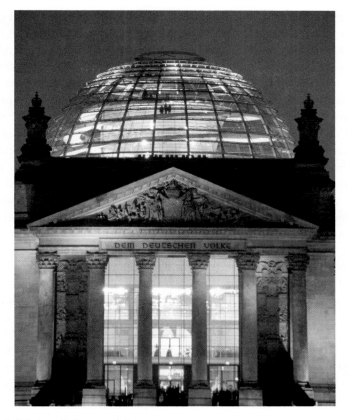

The German Reichstag: Reborn and Green
Nothing better symbolizes the end of the postwar era and the new millennium than the restoration of the Reichstag, the parliament building in Berlin. Like other manifestations of postmodernism, the restoration—designed by a British architect—preserves the old facade, while adding a new glass dome, complete with solar panels that make the building energy independent. As visitors walk around the dome, they can watch their elected representatives deliberating below. (© Svenja-Foto/zefa/Corbis.)

Conclusion: The Making of the West Continues .

Postmodernism has not fully eclipsed Enlightenment values in the global age. Its critics point to the looming problems of contemporary life—population explosion, scarce resources, North-South inequities, global pollution, ethnic hatreds, global terrorism, and world economic crises—and find the exercise of humane values and rational thought more important than ever. Postmodernists and other philosophers counter that attempts at rational decision making fall short because of the issue of "unintended consequences"—that is, one cannot know in advance the consequences of an act. Who would have predicted, for example, the scale of human misery and rising criminality initially resulting from the fall of the Soviet empire? Reformers rationally seeking improved conditions by bringing down Soviet and Yugoslav communism unleashed bloodshed, sickness, and even genocide. Yet events from South Africa and Northern Ireland, for example, indicated that certain long-feuding groups could rationally put aside decades of bloodshed and work toward peace.

The consequences of such global change and increasing globalization are still being determined. While the Internet and migration suggest that people often relate positively to one another worldwide, militants from Saudi Arabia, Egypt, Indonesia, the Philippines, North Africa, Britain, and elsewhere have unleashed unprecedented terrorism on the world in an attempt to push back global forces. Even as globalization has raised standards of living and education in many parts of the world, in other areas—such as poorer regions of Africa and Asia—people face disease and the dramatic social and economic deterioration associated with the global age. Rational results of planning and inexplicable consequences coexist in the present world.

Western traditions of democracy, human rights, and economic equality have much to offer. Given that these were initially intended for a limited number of people—white men in powerful Western nations—debates about their value and defects are found everywhere in today's world even as many aim to achieve them. The nation-state, which protected those values for the privileged and denied them to many others, is another legacy of the West that must be rethought in an age of transnationalism. Migrants, for example, demand the dignity of citizenship, and nations often resist these demands—even though governments welcome migrants' work and tax dollars. Yet it is often supranational organizations rather than the nation-state that advocate for worldwide prosperity and human values. At the same time, the West faces questions of its own unity and cultural identity—an identity that more than ever includes people from Asia, Africa, and the Americas—areas far from Europe, the traditional center of the West. Non-Westerners of all kinds have challenged, criticized, refashioned, and made enormous contributions to Western culture; they have also served the West's citizens as slaves, servants, and menial workers. One of the greatest challenges to the West and the world in this global millennium is to determine how diverse peoples and cultures can live together on terms that are fair for everyone. In other words, how can the tradition of rights and humane values continue to advance along with globalization?

A final challenge to the West involves the inventive human spirit. Over the past five hundred years, the West has benefited from its scientific and technological advances. Longevity and improved material well-being have spread to many places. In the past

Mapping the West The World in the New Millennium

By the twenty-first century, the Internet had transformed communications and economic organizations into an interconnected global network. People in the northern half of the globe had greater access to this network in 2010 than did people in the southern half, and for the most part they enjoyed greater wealth than they had a century earlier. Despite globalization, including global economic crises, historians still find local and national conditions of political, social, and economic life important in telling the full story of peoples and cultures.

The World's Wealth

Income bands
High
Middle
Low
No data available

Internet Use by Percent
of Country Population
76–100%
51–75%
26–50%
0–25%
No data available

0   1,000   2,000 miles

0   1,000   2,000 kilometers

century, communications and information technology have brought people closer to one another than ever before. Simultaneously, through the use of technology, the period from the last century to the present one is the bloodiest era in human history— one during which the use of technology threatens the future of the earth as a home for the human race. War, genocide, terrorism, and environmental deterioration are among technology's hallmarks, posing perhaps the greatest challenge to the West and to the world. The making of the West has been a constantly inventive undertaking, but also a deadly one. The question is, how will the West and the world manage both the promises and challenges of technology to protect the creativity of the human race in the years ahead?

CHAPTER REVIEW QUESTIONS
1. How did global connections at the beginning of the twenty-first century differ from global connections at the start of the twentieth century?
2. How did the Western nation-state of the early twenty-first century differ from the Western nation-state at the opening of the twentieth century?

For practice quizzes and other study tools, see the Online Study Guide at bedfordstmartins.com/huntconcise.

For primary-source material from this period, see Chapter 29 of *Sources of THE MAKING OF THE WEST*, Third Edition.

TIMELINE

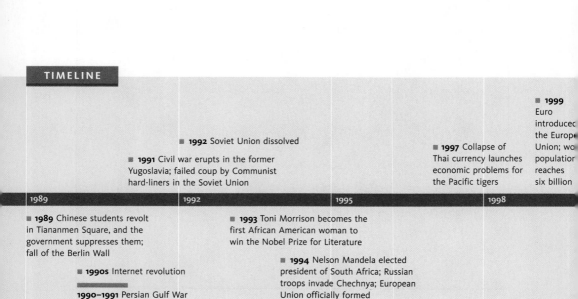

■ **1999** Euro introduced the Europe Union; wo population reaches six billion

■ **1992** Soviet Union dissolved

■ **1991** Civil war erupts in the former Yugoslavia; failed coup by Communist hard-liners in the Soviet Union

■ **1997** Collapse of Thai currency launches economic problems for the Pacific tigers

1989   1992   1995   1998

■ **1989** Chinese students revolt in Tiananmen Square, and the government suppresses them; fall of the Berlin Wall

■ **1993** Toni Morrison becomes the first African American woman to win the Nobel Prize for Literature

■ **1990s** Internet revolution

■ **1994** Nelson Mandela elected president of South Africa; Russian troops invade Chechnya; European Union officially formed

1990–1991 Persian Gulf War

Suggested References

Historians see the challenges since 1989 as enormously diverse, ranging from conditions in the environment to issues of leadership in international affairs to the safety of the world's citizens in a global age. Many of these books investigate the challenges, benefits, and costs of globalization, while the European Union's Web site offers information on pending EU membership and on policies across the spectrum of its activity.

Baldwin, Peter. *Disease and Democracy: The Industrialized World Faces AIDS.* 2005.

Bass, Gary J. *Freedom's Battle: The Origins of Humanitarian Intervention.* 2008.

Benson, Leslie. *Yugoslavia: A Concise History.* 2004.

Bess, Michael. *The Light-Green Society: Economic and Technological Modernity in France.* 2003.

European Union: http://europa.eu.int

Goldman, Marshall. *The Piratization of Russia: Russian Reform Goes Awry.* 2003.

Hoerder, Dirk. *Cultures in Contact: World Migrations in the 2nd Millennium.* 2002.

Humphrey, Caroline. *The Unmaking of Soviet Life: Everyday Economies after Socialism.* 2002.

Kenney, Padraic. *The Burdens of Freedom: Eastern Europe since 1989.* 2006.

MacGaffey, Janet, et al. *Congo-Paris: Transnational Traders on the Margins of the Law.* 2000.

Osumare, Halifu. *The Africanist Aesthetic in Global Hip-Hop: Power Moves.* 2007

Rashid, Ahmed. *Jihad: The Rise of Militant Islam in Central Asia.* 2002.

Ried, T. R. *The United States of Europe: The New Superpower and the End of American Supremacy.* 2005.

Rives, Janet, and Mahmood Yousefi. *Economic Dimensions of Gender Inequality: A Global Perspective.* 1997.

Rosefielde, Steven. *Russia in the 21st Century: The Prodigal Superpower.* 2006.

Sinno, Abdulkader H., ed. *Muslims in Western Politics.* 2008.

United Nations population data: http://www.unfpa.org/swp/swpmain.htm

2009 Barack Obama inaugurated as president of the United States

2003 United States–led coalition invades Iraq; West divides on this policy; European Union draft constitution rejected by France and the Netherlands

2008 Global economic crisis begins

| 2001 | 2004 | 2007 | 2010 |

2000 Vladimir Putin becomes president of Russia

2001 Terrorist attack on the United States; United States declares "war against terrorism"

2004 Ten additional countries join the European Union; terrorist bombings on Madrid trains

2005 Terrorist bombings in central London

Glossary of Key Terms

This glossary of key terms contains definitions of words and ideas that are central to your understanding of the material covered in this textbook. Each term in the glossary is in **boldface** in the text when it is first defined. We have also included the page number on which the full discussion of the term appears so that you can easily locate the complete explanation to strengthen your historical vocabulary.

For words not defined here, two additional resources may be useful: the index, which will direct you to many more topics discussed in the text, and a good dictionary.

Abbasids (272): The caliphal dynasty that came to power in 750. The Abbasids built their capital at Baghdad, where they exercised considerable power over the entire Islamic world until the late ninth century.

absolutism (481): A system of government in which the ruler claimed sole and uncontestable power.

agora (57): The central market square of a Greek city-state; a popular place to gather for conversation.

agricultural revolution (532): Increasingly aggressive attitudes toward investment in and management of land that increased production of food in the 1700s; this revolution developed first in England and then spread to the continent.

Anabaptists (435): Sixteenth-century religious dissenters who believed that humans have free will and that people must knowingly select the Christian faith through rebaptism as adults. They advocated radical separation from society; though originally pacifist, some chose violent paths to religious renewal.

anarchism (715): The belief that people should not have government; it was popular among peasants and workers in the last half of the nineteenth century and the first decades of the twentieth.

apocalypticism (29): A religious belief about the end of the world; literally, "uncovering the future."

apostate (207): Literally, "renegade from the faith"; the emperor Julian (r. 361–363), who rejected Christianity and tried to restore traditional religion as the state religion, was given the nickname "the Apostate."

apostolic succession (185): The principle by which Christian bishops traced their authority back to Jesus's Apostles.

appeasement (850): The strategy of preventing a war by making concessions for grievances.

Arianism (210): The Christian doctrine named after Arius, who argued that Jesus was "begotten" by God and did not have an identical nature with his Father.

art nouveau (757): A successful style in the arts, household and fashion design, and graphics that featured flowing, sinuous lines that contrasted with the mechanical influence of the early twentieth century. It borrowed many of its motifs from Asian and African art and was internationally popular.

asceticism (213): The practice of self-denial of pleasure (from the Greek *askesis*, "training"), as in the lives of monks; a doctrine for Christians emphasized by Augustine.

atheists (565): People who do not believe in the existence of God.

Atlantic system (522): The triangular pattern of trade established in the 1700s that bound together western Europe, Africa, and the Americas. Europeans sold slaves from western Africa and bought commodities such as coffee and sugar that were produced by the new colonial plantations in North and South America and the Caribbean.

auctoritas (158): Literally, "moral authority"; the authority derived from respect on which the Roman princeps' power rested.

Augustus (158): The title meaning "divinely favored" that Rome's Senate granted Octavian and that became shorthand for "Roman imperial ruler."

ban (298): The rights to collect taxes, hear court cases, levy fines, and muster men for defense. It was largely understood as a complex of royal rights, but around 1000, local rulers as well as kings began exercising the ban as well.

baroque (469): An artistic style of the seventeenth century that featured curves, exaggerated lighting, intense emotions, release from restraint, and even a kind of artistic sensationalism; like mannerism, it departed from the Renaissance emphasis on harmonious design, unity, and clarity.

Black Death (393): The term historians give to the plague that swept through Europe in 1346–1353.

Blitzkrieg (851): Literally, "lightning war"; a strategy for the conduct of war in which motorized firepower quickly and over-whelmingly attacks the enemy, leaving it in a state of shock and awe and unable to resist psychologically or militarily.

buccaneers (529): Pirates of the Caribbean who governed themselves and preyed on international shipping.

bureaucracy (486): A network of state officials carrying out orders according to a regular and routine line of authority.

Byzantine Empire (198): Historians' name for the eastern Roman Empire from about 500 to 1453, derived from Byzantium, the original name of Constantinople.

Capetian dynasty (303): A long-lasting dynasty of French kings taking their name from Hugh Capet (r. 987–996).

Carolingian (283): The Frankish dynasty that ruled a western European empire from 751 to the late 800s; its greatest vigor was in the time of Charlemagne (r. 768–814) and Louis the Pious (r. 814–840).

castellan (298): A person who controlled a castle. After around 1000, these castles were the seats of local power in France.

Chartism (675): The movement of supporters of the People's Charter (drawn up in Britain in 1838), which demanded universal man-hood suffrage, vote by secret ballot, equal electoral districts, annual elections, and the elimination of property qualifications for and the payment of stipends to members of Parliament. Chartism attracted many working-class adherents.

cholera (647): An epidemic, usually fatal disease that appeared in the 1830s in Europe; it is caused by a waterborne bacterium that induces violent vomiting and diarrhea and leaves the skin blue, eyes sunken and dull, and hands and feet ice cold.

Christ (179): Greek for "anointed one" (the corresponding English word is *Messiah*); in apocalyptic religious thinking, the agent of God sent to conquer the forces of evil.

city-state (8): A state consisting of an urban center exercising political and economic control over the countryside around it.

Civil Code (627): The French legal code formulated by Napoleon in 1804 (hence also called the Napoleonic Code); it ensured equal treatment under the law to all classes of men and guaranteed religious liberty but curtailed many of the rights of women.

civil disobedience (830): Deliberately but peacefully breaking the law, a tactic used by Mohandas Gandhi in India and earlier by British suffragists to protest oppression and obtain political change.

civilization (3): A way of life that includes political states based on cities with dense populations, large buildings constructed for communal activities, diverse economies, a sense of local identity, and some knowledge of writing.

classicism (511): A style of painting and architecture that reflected the ideals of the art of antiquity; in classicism, geometric shapes, order, and harmony of lines took precedence over the sensuous, exuberant, and emotional forms of the baroque.

cold war (869): The rivalry between the United States and the Soviet Union following World War II that led to massive growth in nuclear weapons on both sides.

Colosseum (171): Rome's giant amphitheater for gladiatorial shows and other spectacles.

commercial revolution (312): The economic transformation of Europe, especially western Europe, from rural to urban and from gift-based to cash-based.

communes (316): Sworn associations of citizens who formed a legal corporate body. Communes were the normal institution of self-government in many medieval towns.

communists (655): Those socialists who advocated the abolition of private property in favor of communal, collective ownership. The term was invented in 1840 but was mainly used after 1870.

conservatism (652): A political doctrine that emerged after 1815 and rejected much of the Enlightenment and the French Revolution, preferring monarchies over republics, tradition over revolution, and established religion over Enlightenment skepticism.

constitutionalism (482): A system of government in which rulers had to share power with parliaments made up of elected representatives.

consumer revolution (530): The rapid increase in consumption of new staples produced in the Atlantic system as well as of other items of daily life, such as mirrors, that were previously unavailable or beyond the reach of ordinary people.

Continental System (631): The system inaugurated by Napoleon's order in 1806 that France and its satellites boycott British goods; after some early successes in blocking British trade, the system was undermined by smuggling.

Corn Laws (653): Tariffs on grain in Great Britain that benefited landowners by preventing the import of cheap foreign grain; after agitation by the Anti–Corn Law League, the tariffs were repealed by the British government in 1846.

Cuban missile crisis (870): The confrontation in 1962 between the United States and the USSR over Soviet installation of missile sites off the American coast; both John F. Kennedy and Nikita Khrushchev backed down from using nuclear weapons to resolve the situation.

cuneiform (11): The earliest form of writing, invented in Mesopotamia and formed with wedge-shaped characters.

curials (203): The social elite in the Roman Empire's towns who were responsible for collecting taxes for the imperial government and paying for any shortfalls themselves.

debasement of coinage (189): Putting less silver in a coin without changing its face value; practiced during the third-century crisis in Rome, which contributed to inflation.

de-Christianization (616): The campaign of extremist republicans against organized churches; militants forced priests to give up their vocations and marry, sold off the buildings of the Catholic church, and set up festivals of reason to compete with Catholicism.

Declaration of the Rights of Man and of the Citizen (606): The preamble to the French constitution drafted in August 1789; it established the sovereignty of the nation and the equality of rights of citizens and granted freedom of religion, freedom of the press, equality of taxation, and equality before the law.

decolonization (889): The process—both violent and peaceful—by which colonies gained their independence from the imperial powers after World War II.

deists (565): Those who believe in God but who give God no active role in human affairs. Deists of the Enlightenment believed that a benevolent, all-knowing God had designed the universe and set it in motion but no longer intervened in the functioning of the universe. A deist might belong to no particular church (Catholic or Protestant).

Delian League (52): The naval alliance headed by Athens after the Persian Wars, and the basis of the Athenian Empire.

DNA (913): The genetic material that forms the basis of each cell; the discovery of its structure in 1952 revolutionized genetics, molecular biology, and other scientific and medical fields.

domesticity (649): The set of beliefs, prevailing in the early to mid-nineteenth century, purporting that women should live their lives within the domestic sphere and devote themselves to their families and the home.

dominate (198): Roman rule from Diocletian (r. 284–305) onward; a blatantly authoritarian style of rule; derived from dominus ("master"; "lord") and contrasted with principate (156).

Dual Alliance (771): A defensive alliance forged by German chancellor Otto von Bismarck between Germany and Austria-Hungary in 1879 as part of his system of alliances to prevent or limit war; after Italy joined in 1882, it was called the Triple Alliance.

dualism (90): The concept that spiritual being and physical being are separate.

dual monarchy (697): A shared power arrangement between the Habsburg Empire and Hungary after the Prussian defeat of the Austrian Empire in 1867.

Edict of Milan (204): Constantine and Licinius's proclamation of religious toleration that also expressed their favoring of Christianity.

empire (5): A political unit in which one or more formerly independent territories or peoples are ruled by a single sovereign power.

Enabling Act (836): The legislation passed in 1933 suspending constitutional government for four years in order to meet the crisis in the German economy.

enlightened despots (581): A political term that refers to rulers who tried to promote reform without giving up their own supreme political power; the best examples were Catherine the Great of Russia, Frederick the Great of Prussia, and Joseph II of Austria. Also called enlightened absolutists.

Enlightenment (522): The eighteenth-century intellectual movement whose proponents believed that human beings could apply a critical, reasoning spirit to every problem. Based on a popularization of scientific discoveries, the movement often challenged religious and secular authorities.

Entente Cordiale (771): An alliance between Britain and France that began with an agreement in 1904 to honor colonial holdings.

Epicureanism (109): The philosophy initiated by Epicurus of Athens to help people achieve pleasure (meaning an "absence of disturbance") in their lives.

epigrams (105): Short poems covering a variety of themes, especially love, and a favorite genre of Hellenistic women poets.

Estates General (601): A body of deputies from the three estates, or orders, of France; the clergy (First Estate), the nobility (Second Estate), and everyone else (Third Estate); disputes about procedures of voting in this body in 1789 opened the way to the French Revolution.

ethnic cleansing (950): The mass murder—or genocide—of people of different ethnicities.

euro (957): The common currency accepted by twelve of the fifteen members of the European Union. It went into effect gradually, becoming the denominator of business transfers in 1999 and entering public circulation in 2002.

European Economic Community (EEC or Common Market) (883): A consortium of six European countries established to promote free trade and economic cooperation among its members. Since its founding in 1957, it has expanded its membership and also its sphere of activity.

European Union (EU) (948): Formerly the European Economic Community (EEC, or Common Market), and then the European Community; instituted in 1994 by the terms of the 1992 Maastricht Treaty. Its members have political ties through the European parliament as well as common economic, legal, and business mechanisms; as of 2007, it consists of twenty-seven member countries.

existentialism (898): A philosophy prominent after World War II that stressed the importance of action in the creation of an authentic self.

Fascism (780): A doctrine advocated by Benito Mussolini that glorified the state over the people and their individual or civil rights. Beginning in the 1920s, Fascism was politically grounded in an instinctual male violence and opposed to the so-called antinationalist socialist movement and parliamentary rule.

fealty (296): The promise of faithfulness that a vassal made to his lord.

First Consul (623): The most important of the three consuls established by the French Constitution of 1799; the title, given to Napoleon Bonaparte, was taken from the ancient Roman republic.

First Triumvirate (149): The coalition formed in 60 B.C.E. by Gnaeus Pompey, Licinius Crassus, and Julius Caesar (the word *triumvirate* means "a group of three").

five-year plans (831): Centralized programs for long-range economic development first used by Joseph Stalin and copied by Adolf Hitler; these plans set production priorities and gave production targets for individual industries and agriculture.

Fourteen Points (791): A proposal by U.S. president Woodrow Wilson for peace during World War I. The Fourteen Points called for a peace based on settlement rather than on victory or a definitive conquest and thus helped bring about the surrender of the Central Powers.

Freemasons (575): Members of Masonic lodges, which were based on the rituals of stonemasons' guilds and provided a place where nobles and middle-class professionals (and even some artisans) shared interest in the Enlightenment and reform; lodges drew up constitutions and voted in elections. The movement began in Great Britain and spread eastward across Europe.

friars (347): "Brothers" of the mendicant orders, such as the Franciscans and Dominicans.

Fronde (483): A series of revolts in France, 1648–1653, that challenged the authority of young Louis XIV and his minister Mazarin.

gift economy (258): System of give-and-take that determined most seventh- and eighth-century economic transactions; kings and other powerful people amassed large treasuries and foodstuffs that they distributed at will to mark their power, boost their prestige, and demonstrate their generosity.

glasnost (938): Literally, "openness" or "publicity"; a policy instituted in the 1980s by Soviet premier Mikhail Gorbachev calling for greater openness in speech and in thinking, which translated to the reduction of censorship in publishing, radio, television, and other media.

global warming (964): An increase in the temperature of the earth's lower atmosphere resulting from a buildup of chemical emissions, causing a greenhouse effect.

Glorious Revolution (504): The events when the English Parliament deposed King James II in 1688 and replaced him with William, prince of Orange, and James's daughter Mary.

Golden Horde (364): The name for the Mongol Empire in Russia.

Gothic (383): A style of architecture characterized by pointed arches, ribbed vaults, and large stained-glass windows.

Great Fear (603): The term used by historians to describe the rural panic of 1789; fears of an aristocratic plot to pay beggars and vagrants to burn crops or barns sometimes turned into peasant attacks on aristocrats or on seigneurial records of peasants' dues.

Great Persecution (204): The violent program initiated by Diocletian in 303 to make Christians convert to traditional religion or risk confiscation of their property and even death.

Great Schism (319, 393): The term *Great Schism* refers to two different periods in the history of the Christian church. The first, in 1054, refers to the separation of the Latin Catholic church and the Greek Orthodox church; the second, to the period from 1378 to 1417, when the church had two and sometimes three popes.

Gregorian reform (319): The movement for church reform—including clerical celibacy and an end to lay investiture—associated with Pope Gregory VII.

guilds (315): Religious, economic, and trade associations. They regulated, protected, and policed their memberships, setting up standards for professional practices.

Hanseatic League (377): A league of northern European cities formed in the fourteenth century to protect their mutual interests in trade and defense.

Hasidim (572): A religious group within Judaism whose members pray in a highly emotional fashion; founded by the Ba'al Shem Tov in the 1740s and 1750s, and especially important in Poland-Lithuania. (The word is Hebrew for "most pious.")

Haussmannization (707): The process of urban renewal followed by many governments after the middle of the nineteenth century and named after its primary practitioner, Georges-Eugène Haussmann.

heliocentrism (472): The view articulated by Polish clergyman Nicolaus Copernicus that the earth and planets revolve around the sun; Galileo Galilei was condemned by the Catholic church for supporting this view.

Hellenistic (86): An adjective meaning "Greek-like" that is today used as a chronological term for the period 323 to 30 B.C.E.

hero cults (61): Religious rituals that people performed at the tombs of extraordinarily famous local men and women to ask for predictions about the future and protection in everyday life.

hierarchy (4): Social system that ranks certain people as more important and more dominant than others; the earliest evidence of social differentiation comes from the Paleolithic period.

Holocaust (854): A term used after World War II to name the mass murder of European Jews by the Nazis.

hubris (75): The Greek term for excessive arrogance, especially when an overconfident human being goes against the will of the gods.

Huguenots (451): The name given to Calvinists in France after 1560; its linguistic origin remains uncertain.

humanism (415): A literary and intellectual movement that arose in the early fifteenth century to valorize the writings of Greco-Roman antiquity; it was so named because its practitioners studied and supported the liberal arts, or humanities.

humanitas (142): Cicero's ideal of "humaneness," meaning generous and honest treatment of others based on natural law.

Hundred Years' War (393): The long war between England and France, 1337–1453; it produced numerous social upheavals yet left both states more powerful than before.

iconoclasm (252): Literally, "icon breaking"; the destruction of icons, or images of holy people (e.g., Christ, Mary, the saints). Byzantine emperors banned icons from 726 to 787; a modified ban was revived in 815 and lasted until 843.

ideology (640): A coherent set of beliefs (conservatism, liberalism, socialism, etc.) about the way the social and political order should be organized and changed; the word was coined during the French Revolution.

imperialism (669): European dominance of the non-West through economic exploitation and political rule (as distinct from the word *colonialism,* which usually implied establishment of settler colonies, often with slavery as the labor system).

impressionism (719): A mid- to late-nineteenth-century artistic style that captured the sensation of light in images, derived from Japanese influences and from an opposition to the realism of photographs.

indulgences (436): In Roman Catholic doctrine, a remission of sin earned by performing certain religious tasks to lessen time in purgatory after death. By the fourteenth century they could be purchased. The Catholic clergy's practice of selling indulgences came under fire during the Reformation.

industrialization (640): The process of economic transformation that began in Great Britain in the 1770s and 1780s; its most striking features were the introduction of steam engines to power machinery and the concentration of those machines in factories that mass-produced cloth from cotton grown in the British colonies.

Inquisition (354): The court of inquiry permanently set up by the church in 1233; its purpose was to ferret out and punish heretics.

Investiture Conflict (320): The conflict between Pope Gregory VII and Henry IV over the right of laymen and even anointed kings to appoint bishops and install them in their offices.

in vitro fertilization (915): A process developed in the 1970s by which eggs are fertilized by sperm outside the human body and then implanted in a woman's uterus.

Jacobin Club (608): The first and most influential of the political clubs formed during the French Revolution; the Paris Jacobin Club inspired the formation of a national network of Jacobin clubs whose members dominated the revolutionary government during the period known as the Terror.

Koine (111): The "common" or "shared" form of the Greek language that became the international language in the Hellenistic period.

ladder of offices (133): The series of Roman elective government offices from quaestor to consul.

laissez-faire (567): An economic doctrine developed by Adam Smith based on his reading of the French physiocrats who advocated freeing the economy from government intervention and control. (The term is French for "leave alone.")

law of universal gravitation (474): Newton's law uniting celestial and terrestrial mechanics held that every body in the universe exerts over every other body an attractive force directly proportional to the product of their masses and inversely proportional to the square of the distance between them.

League of Nations (799): The international organization set up following World War I to maintain peace by arbitrating disputes and promoting collective security.

liberalism (652): An economic and political doctrine that emphasized free trade and the constitutional guarantees of individual rights such as freedom of speech and religion; liberals were favorable to the Enlightenment but critical of the violence of the French Revolution.

Maastricht Treaty (957): The agreement among the members of the European Community to have a closer alliance, including the use of common passports and eventually the development of a common currency; by the terms of this treaty, the European Community became the European Union (EU) in 1994.

madrasa (283): A school located within or attached to a mosque.

mannerism (469): A late-sixteenth-century style of painting in which a distorted perspective created bizarre and theatrical effects that contrasted with the precise, harmonious lines of Renaissance painting.

manors (289): Great estates consisting (normally) of arable fields, vineyards, meadows, and woodlands, ordinarily owned by a lord (which could as easily be a monastery or a church as a layperson) and cultivated by serfs.

march on Rome (818): The threat by Benito Mussolini and his followers in 1922 to take over the Italian government in a military convergence on Rome; the march forced King Victor Emmanuel II to make Mussolini prime minister.

Marshall Plan (875): A post–World War II program funded by the United States to get Europe back on its feet economically and thereby reduce the appeal of communism. It played an important role in the rebirth of European prosperity in the 1950s.

martyr (184): Greek for "witness," designating someone who dies for his or her religious beliefs.

Marxism (715): A body of thought about the organization of production, social inequality, and the processes of revolutionary change as devised by the philosopher and economist Karl Marx.

materialism (109): The philosophical doctrine that only things made of matter truly exist and thus denies the existence of the soul or any nonmaterial phenomena.

Meiji Restoration (715): A change in the Japanese government in 1867 that reinstalled the emperor as legitimate ruler in place of the military leader, or shogun.

mercantilism (487): The doctrine that governments must intervene to increase national wealth by whatever means possible.

Merovingian dynasty (261): The dynasty that ruled as kings of the Franks from about 485 to 751.

mestizos (528): People born to Spanish fathers and native American mothers.

metaphysics (90): Ideas about the ultimate nature of reality beyond the reach of human senses.

Methodism (572): A religious movement founded by John Wesley that broke away from the Anglican church in Great Britain and insisted on strict self-discipline and a "methodical" approach to religious study and observance. Wesley emphasized an intense personal experience of salvation and a life of thrift, abstinence, and hard work.

metics (65): Foreigners granted permanent residency permits in Greek city-states in return for obligations to pay taxes and do military service.

mir (688): A Russian farm community fortified by the emancipation of the serfs in 1861 that provided for holding the land in common and regulating the movements of any individual by the group. The mir hindered the free movement of labor and individual agricultural enterprise, including modernization.

Mitteleuropa (772): Literally, "central Europe," but used by influential military leaders in Germany before World War I to refer to land in both central and eastern Europe that they hoped to acquire. This territory ultimately became a war aim in World War I and for Hitler thereafter.

modernism (753): Changes in the arts at the end of the nineteenth century that featured a break with realism in art and literature and with lyricism in music.

modernity (730): The accelerated pace of life, the rise of mass politics, the spread of industrial production, and the decline of a rural social order that were visible in the West from the late nineteenth century onward.

monotheism (21): The belief in only one god, as in Judaism, Christianity, and Islam.

mos maiorum (120): Literally, "the way of the ancestors"; the set of Roman traditional values.

multinational corporation (915): A business that operates in many foreign countries by sending large segments of its manufacturing, finance, sales, and other business components abroad.

mystery cult (61): Sets of prayers, hymns, ritual purification, sacrifices, and other forms of worship undertaken to gain divine protection; each cult was connected to a particular divinity and centered on initiation into secret knowledge about the divine and human worlds.

nationalism (656): A political doctrine that holds that all peoples derive their identities from their nations and should have states to express their common language and shared cultural traditions.

natural selection (723): Theory developed by Charles Darwin that life developed from lower forms through a primal battle for survival and through the sexual selection of mates.

Nazi-Soviet Pact (851): The agreement reached in 1939 by Germany and the Soviet Union in which both agreed not to attack the other in case of war. The agreement secretly divided up territory that would later be conquered.

neoliberalism (936): A theory promoted by Margaret Thatcher, Britain's prime minister from 1979 to 1990, and those who followed her calling for a return to liberal principles of the nineteenth century, including the reduction of welfare-state programs and the cutting of taxes for wealthy people in order to promote economic growth.

Neoplatonism (187): The spiritual philosophy developed by Plotinus (c. 205–270) that was based on Plato's ideas and was very influential among Christian intellectuals.

new woman (745): A woman of the turn of the twentieth century, often from the middle class, who dressed practically, moved about freely, lived apart from her family, and supported herself.

nongovernmental organizations (NGOs) (962): Charitable foundations and activist groups such as Doctors without Borders that often work internationally on political, economic, and relief issues; also, organizations such as the Rockefeller, Ford, and Open Society Foundations that shape economic and social policy and the course of political reform.

North Atlantic Treaty Organization (NATO) (877): The security alliance formed in 1949 to provide a unified military force for the United States, Canada, and their allies

in western Europe and Scandinavia. The corresponding alliance of the Soviet Union and its allies was known as the Warsaw Pact.

Nuremberg Laws (838): Legislation in 1935 that deprived Jewish Germans of their citizenship and imposed many other hardships on them.

opium (669): An addictive drug derived from the heads of poppy plants; it was imported to Europe from the Ottoman Empire and India, available in various forms, and often used by ordinary people until restricted by governments after the 1860s.

Organization of Petroleum Exporting Countries (OPEC) (932): A consortium that regulated the supply and export of oil and that acted with more unanimity after the United States supported Israel against the Arabs in the wars of the late 1960s and early 1970s.

Ostpolitik (922): A policy initiated by Willy Brandt in the late 1960s in which West Germany sought better economic relations with the Communist countries of eastern Europe.

ostracism (55): Athenian democracy's annual procedure to block tyranny by sending a citizen into exile for ten years by a vote of six thousand citizens in the assembly.

Pacific tigers (972): Countries of East Asia so named because of their massive economic growth, much of it from the 1970s and 1980s on; foremost among these were Japan and China.

Pan-Slavism (698): A movement in the nineteenth century that called for the unity of all Slavs across national and regional boundaries.

parlements (483): High courts in France (the term comes from the French *parler*, "to speak"). Each region had its parlement; the parlements could not propose laws, but they could review laws presented by the king and refuse to register them (the king could also insist on their registration).

patria potestas (122): Literally, "father's power"; the legal right of a father in ancient Rome to own the property of his children and slaves and to control their lives.

patriarchy (9): Social system in which men exert control over political, social, and economic life.

patron-client system (122): The interlocking network of mutual obligations between Roman patrons (social superiors) and clients (social inferiors).

Pax Romana (156): The period of "Roman peace" under the principate in the first and second centuries C.E.

Peace of God (300): A movement begun by bishops in the south of France first to limit the violence done to property and later (with the Truce of God) to limit fighting between warriors.

Peace of Paris (799): The series of peace treaties that provided the settlement of World War I. These treaties were resented, especially by Germany and Hungary, as well as by states of the Middle East in which England and France took over the government.

perestroika (938): Literally, "restructuring"; an economic policy instituted in the 1980s by Soviet premier Mikhail Gorbachev calling for the introduction of market mechanisms and the achievement of greater efficiency in manufacturing, agriculture, and services.

philosophes (562): Public intellectuals of the Enlightenment who wrote on subjects ranging from current affairs to art criticism with the goal of furthering reform in society. (The word in French means "philosophers.")

physiocrats (587): French economists who advocated deregulation of the grain trade and a more equitable tax system to encourage agricultural productivity.

Pietism (540): A Protestant revivalist movement that emphasized deeply emotional individual religious experience.

plantations (522): Large tracts of land producing staple crops such as sugar, coffee, and tobacco; farmed by slave labor; and owned by a colonial settler who emigrated from western Europe.

plebiscites (133): Laws passed by the Plebeian Assembly in the Roman republic.

polis (34): The Greek term for an independent city-state based on citizenship.

politiques (453): Political advisers during the French Wars of Religion who argued that compromise in matters of religion—limited toleration for the Calvinists—would strengthen the monarchy.

polyphony (382): Music that consists of two or more melodies performed simultaneously.

polytheism (10): The worship of multiple gods.

pop art (919): A style in the visual arts that mimicked advertising and consumerism and that used ordinary objects in paintings and other compositions.

positivism (718): A theory, developed in the mid-nineteenth century, stating that the study of facts would generate accurate, or "positive," laws of society; these laws could, in turn, help formulate policy and legislation.

postmodernism (982): A term applied in the late twentieth century to both an intense stylistic mixture in the arts and a critique of Enlightenment and scientific beliefs in rationality and the possibility for precise knowledge.

praetorian guard (160): The group of soldiers stationed in Rome under the emperor's control; first formed by Augustus.

predestination (442): John Calvin's doctrine that God preordained salvation or damnation for each person before creation; those chosen for salvation were considered the "elect."

principate (156): The political system invented by Augustus as a disguised monarchy with the *princeps* ("first man") as emperor.

proletarians (134): In the Roman republic, the mass of people so poor that males were not eligible to serve in the army.

Protestants (435): Members of the Christian branch that formed when Martin Luther and his followers broke from the Catholic church in 1517; the name was first used in 1529 in an imperial diet by German princes who protested Emperor Charles V's edict to repress religious dissent.

Provisional Government (792): The initial government to take control in Russia after the overthrow of the Romanov empire in 1917. The government was composed of aristocrats and members of the middle class, often deputies in the Duma—the assembly created after the Revolution of 1905.

psychoanalysis (729): Sigmund Freud's theory of human mental processes and his method for treating their malfunctioning.

pump priming (837): An economic policy used by governments to stimulate the economy through public works programs and other infusions to public funds.

purges (832): The series of attacks instituted by Joseph Stalin on citizens of the USSR in the 1930s and later. The victims were accused of being "wreckers," or saboteurs of communism, while the public grew hysterical and pliable because of its fear.

Puritans (444): Strict Calvinists who opposed all vestiges of Catholic ritual in the Church of England.

radical democracy (52): The ancient Athenian system of democracy, established in the 460s and 450s B.C.E., that extended direct political power and participation in the court system to the mass of adult male citizens.

raison d'état (462): French for "reason of state." The political doctrine, first proposed by Cardinal Richelieu of France, that held that the state's interests should prevail over those of religion; Richelieu, for example, allied with the Lutheran king of Sweden even though he himself was a leading official of the Catholic church.

rationalism (42): The philosophic idea that people must justify their claims by logic and reason.

realism (684): An art style that arose in the mid-nineteenth century and was dedicated to depicting society realistically without romantic or idealistic overtones.

Realpolitik (683): Policies associated initially with nation building that are said to be based on hardheaded realities rather than the romantic notions of earlier nationalists. The term has come to mean any policy based on considerations of power alone.

reconquista (319): The Christian conquest of Spain.

redistributive economy (10): A system in which state officials control the production and distribution of goods.

rococo (538): A style of painting that emphasized irregularity and asymmetry, as well as movement and curvature, but on a smaller, more intimate scale than the baroque.

Romanesque (343): The term for the art and architecture in western Europe during the period before around 1150, characterized by monumentality and solidity enhanced by sculpture and painting.

Romanization (175): The spread of Roman law and culture in the provinces of the Roman Empire.

Roman republic (122): A system of government based on shared political decision making and the election of male officials by assemblies organized by social hierarchy; the republic lasted from 509 to 287 B.C.E.

romanticism (571): An artistic movement of the early nineteenth century that glorified nature, emotion, genius, and imagination.

ruler cults (112): Cults that involved worship of a Hellenistic ruler as a savior god.

Russification (690): A program for the integration of Russia's many nationality groups involving the forced acquisition of Russian language and the practice of Russian orthodoxy as well as the settlement of ethnic Russians among other nationality groups.

salons (564): Informal gatherings, usually sponsored by middle-class or aristocratic women, that provided a forum for new ideas and an opportunity to establish new intellectual contacts among supporters of the Enlightenment; works that could not be published officially were read aloud. (The word in French means "living rooms.")

sans-culottes (608): French for "without breeches"; the name given to politically active men from the lower classes. They worked with their hands and wore the long trousers of workingmen rather than the knee breeches of the upper classes.

Sasanid Empire (243): The empire of the Sasanid dynasty of Persia, which lasted from 224 until its conquest by Islamic armies from 637 to 661.

scholasticism (379): The body of theological and philosophical thought of the scholastics, the scholars of the medieval universities.

scientific method (472): A combination of experimental observation and mathematical deduction to determine the laws of nature; it became the secular standard of truth and as such challenged the hold of both the churches and popular beliefs.

Second International (760): A transnational organization of workers established in 1889, mostly committed to Marxian socialism.

serfs (297): Semi-free peasants. Serfs could not legally leave the land they tilled; they owed labor services and either produce or money to their lords. Yet they were not slaves: they had the right to marry, to keep part of their produce, and to remain on the land.

simony (318): Derived from the name of Simon Magus, a magician in the New Testament who offers St. Peter money to have the power to confer the Holy Spirit (Acts 8:9–24), the term came to mean the giving of gifts or money for church offices.

social contract (482): The doctrine found in the writings of Hobbes and Locke that all political authority derives not from divine right but from an implicit contract between citizens and their rulers.

Socratic method (71): Socrates' method of conversation, in which he asked probing questions to make his listeners examine their most cherished assumptions before drawing conclusions.

Solidarity (939): An outlawed Polish labor union of the 1980s that contested Communist Party programs and eventually succeeded in ousting the party from the Polish government.

Sophists (60): Competitive intellectuals and teachers who offered a new form of education and new philosophical and religious ideas beginning about 450 B.C.E.

soviets (792): Councils of workers and soldiers first formed in Russia during the Revolution of 1905; they took shape to represent the people in the early days of the 1917 Russian Revolution. These groups saw themselves as a more legitimate political force than the Provisional Government.

stagflation (933): The combination of a stagnant economy and soaring inflation; a period of stagflation occurred in the West in the 1970s as a result of the OPEC embargo on oil.

Stoicism (110): The most influential Hellenistic philosophy, which taught the goal of living a virtuous life in harmony with nature.

struggle of the orders (132): Turmoil between elite Roman families (patricians) and the rest of Rome's population (plebeians) that centered on social and economic issues and resulted in greater sharing of political power between 509 and 287 B.C.E.

subjectivism (69): The belief, especially associated with the Sophist Protagoras, that there is no absolute reality behind and independent of appearances.

successor kings (99): Alexander's commanders (Antigonus, Seleucus, and Ptolemy) who took over portions of his empire to create personal monarchies after his death.

summa (342): A scholastic treatise that characteristically took up a topic and explored it exhaustively, resulting in a "summary" of all opinions and their resolution.

symposia (singular: symposium) (65): Drinking parties for Greek men with entertainment ranging from philosophical conversation to hired female companions.

temperance movement (649): A movement in the United States and Europe begun in the early nineteenth century to discourage consumption of alcohol.

Terror (611): The emergency government established under the direction of the Committee of Public Safety during the French Revolution; the government aimed to establish a republic of virtue, but to do so it arrested hundreds of thousands of political suspects and executed thousands of ordinary people.

terrorism (910): Coordinated and targeted political violence by opposition groups.

tetrarchy (200): Literally, "rule by four"; devised by Diocletian to put into practice his principle of subdivision of power in ruling the Roman Empire.

Thermidorian Reaction (620): The violent backlash against the rule of Robespierre that began with his arrest and execution; most of the instruments of the Terror were dismantled, and supporters of the Jacobins were harassed or even murdered.

third world (870): A term devised after World War II to designate those countries outside either the capitalist world of the U.S. bloc or the socialist world of the Soviet bloc—most of them emerging from imperial domination.

tithe (297): A tax, taken by the church, equivalent to one-tenth of the parishioner's annual income.

totalitarianism (831): Highly centralized systems of government that attempt to control society in its most private details and ensure conformity through police terror and single-party rule.

total war (780): A war built on full mobilization of soldiers, civilians, and the technological capacities of the nations involved. The term also refers to a highly destructive war and one that is both a physical war and a war for ideas and ideologies.

Treaty of Verdun (288): The treaty that, in 843, split the Carolingian Empire into three parts; its borders roughly outline modern western European states.

Truman Doctrine (875): The U.S. policy to limit communism after World War II by countering political crises with economic and military aid.

Umayyad caliphate (244): The successors of Muhammad who traced their ancestry to Umayyah, a member of Muhammad's tribe. The dynasty lasted from 661 to 750.

ummah (240): The community of believers in Islam.

United Nations (UN) (870): An organization for collective security and deliberation set up as World War II closed; it replaced the ineffective League of Nations and has proved active in resolving international conflicts both through negotiation and by the use of force.

vassals (294): Free warriors who pledged homage and fealty to a lord, thereby creating a bond that implied mutual obligations, among them to fight for one another.

Vatican II (897): A Catholic Council held between 1962 and 1965 to modernize some aspects of church teachings (such as condemnation of Jews), update the liturgy, and promote cooperation among the faiths (i.e., ecumenism).

Warsaw Pact (878): Military alliance established in 1955 by the Soviet Union with its satellite countries in response to West Germany's admission to the North Atlantic Treaty Organization.

Weimar Republic (797): The parliamentary republic established in 1919 in Germany to replace the imperial form of government.

welfare state (839): A system comprising state-sponsored programs for citizens, including veterans' pensions, social security, health care, family allowances, and disability insurance. Most highly developed after World War II, the welfare state intervened in society to bring economic democracy (to supplement political democracy) by setting a minimum standard of well-being.

wergild (224): Under Frankish law, money or goods a murderer had to pay as compensation for his crime; most went to the victim's kin, but the king received about one-third.

Westernization (546): The effort, especially in Peter the Great's Russia, to make society and social customs resemble counterparts in western Europe, especially France, Britain, and the Dutch Republic.

World Bank (961): An international institution of credit created in the 1940s. With the globalization of finances and of national economies from the 1980s on, it became increasingly powerful.

Zionism (768): A movement that began in the late nineteenth century among European Jews to found a Jewish state.

Index

A note about the index:
Names of individuals appear in boldface.
Letters following pages refer to:
(i)   illustrations, including photographs and artifacts
(f)   figures, including charts and graphs
(m) maps
(n)   footnotes